Primary Mathematics Today
New metric edition

Primary Mathematics Today

New metric edition

Elizabeth Williams and Hilary Shuard

Longman

LONGMAN GROUP LIMITED
London
*Associated companies, branches and representatives
throughout the world*

© Longman Group 1970, 1976

First published 1970
New edition 1976

Cased Edition
ISBN 0 582 18042 2

Limp Edition
ISBN 0 582 18043 0

Printed in Hong Kong by
Sheck Wah Tong Printing Press Ltd.

Preface

In recent years, many writing teams have attempted to cover wide ranges of work in modern school mathematics: we have had various series of books from such teams, covering the age range 11–18, together with teachers' guides following work through year by year and topic by topic; we have also had teachers' guides on modern methods in mathematics teaching and some class texts for the age range 5–13. However, very few individual authors, or pairs of authors in collaboration, have attempted the formidable task of covering a wide age range in this way. It is certainly not a task to be set about lightly. Miss Shuard and Mrs Williams are to be congratulated on having tackled it so successfully.

Under one cover we have here a text which brings together, for each stage of development in primary and middle school, both general guidance for the teacher and detailed indications of how to approach the appropriate individual topic in the classroom. If any lecturer, or student in a college of education, or practising teacher in a classroom, is in any doubt about the implications of modernising mathematical work at this level in schools, here is a book to settle his doubts. As such, it deserves to become a standard work for all who are concerned to teach mathematics to younger children. It combines in a comprehensive fashion a thoughtfulness about child development with a thorough knowledge of the mathematics needed in this development, together with clear evidence of the authors' knowledge of practical classroom activity in the subject.

W. H. COCKCROFT

University of Hull

Contents

Note on the Structure of the Book

The table below classifies the chapters according to the main themes to which they contribute. The teacher may find it helpful to follow a particular theme, such as the development of the number system, through later chapters. In the early part of the book, odd-numbered chapters often emphasize children's activities, and are immediately followed by chapters which bring out the mathematical structure underlying the activities. Later, children's activities and the ideas on which they are based are so closely interwoven that a separation would be artificial.

Theme	Chapters
Children's early mathematical development	1, 2
Children's activities using number	3, 7, 9, 13, 16, 25, 31
The development of the number system	4, 8, 10, 18, 20, 26, 32, 35, 38
The growth of notation and representation	17, 29, 30
Children's ideas of space	11, 19, 21, 34, 37, 39
The development of spatial concepts	12, 22, 36
Children's experience of quantity and its measurement	5, 15, 23, 24, 27
The development of the idea of measurement	6, 14, 33
The use of mechanisms	28
The unity of mathematical structure	40

Introduction

The intention of this book is to present a survey of primary school mathematics in the light of the important changes in mathematics and its teaching which are now taking place. The major influences making for change came from very different sources but each has a part to play in shaping a fuller and more coherent programme of mathematical education. The book is not in the first instance a text-book of mathematics for teachers. It is rather a study of primary children learning mathematics in these newer ways. We try to show how children can, with the help of a sympathetic and encouraging teacher, take part in this more meaningful programme. Some mathematical ideas which may be new to many teachers are, however, fully explained alongside the sections of the book where we describe activities through which they can be presented to children.

New thinking is affecting every aspect of mathematical education. Deeper insight into children's ways of learning is modifying our conception of the means by which the development of their thinking can be stimulated and guided. The art of teaching mathematics is being transformed into the art of devising situations in which a child will wish to probe, to organize things and ideas in his world, and to notice and make connections between them. During his explorations he will shape his perceptions into clear thoughts; these he will be able to display in pictures, diagrams and symbols which will be memorable to himself and meaningful to others. This is the start of mathematical thinking.

Throughout this book it is assumed that each new mathematical idea must develop in a child's mind through his own activities, handling objects, comparing measurements or shapes, reflecting on the results of his experiments and communicating them to others. Much of children's mathematical work will be a co-operative effort. A group of children will often explore freely, with the teacher's guidance, a situation which interests them. If the new understanding and new knowledge thus gained are to become part of a child's mathematical equipment, it is important that he should eventually see them in relation to other mathematical ideas, and so build an organized mental structure. Systematization without a basis of ideas springing from experience has been a feature of much mathematical education in the past. Experience which children never build into an inter-related body of ideas would be an equally unfortunate development. In this book we try to show how children's mathematical explorations can form a foundation for coherent mathematical thinking.

A highly influential factor in the development of primary mathematics has been the introduction of structural materials and apparatus especially designed to enable children to see by means of their own experimenting how a number system is built up, how operations can be carried out on numbers, and what relationships can be discovered among certain sets of numbers. The mathematical significance of such material and its wide variety of analogies with number is examined, and set within a wide range of mathematical experiences.

With these changes in the methods of learning available to children, there has come also a difference in the mathematical work they actually do. Instead of being called upon to practise memorized arithmetical skills for most of the time devoted to mathematics, children in many schools write descriptions of what they have discovered and record the results of their own investigations. They are thus developing a wide mathematical vocabulary. The great extension of the use of many kinds of graph is a consequence of this endeavour to record observations and to search for connections between them. A graph may often reveal hitherto unsuspected relationships and patterns.

Technological changes, bringing the calculating machine and the computer into extensive use, have induced a change in the aim of mathematics teaching. We no longer need the skill to perform very complicated calculations; a machine can do these better than a man. There is now a demand for people who can analyse a problem and devise the means of solving it, setting out a programme for its solution which can be fed into a machine. The *understanding* of numerical operations is now the capacity required of a human mind which has an arithmetical machine to command. The actual calculations may be carried out by a machine but the person in charge must decide what operations are needed for the solution of a problem and then issue instructions to the machine. A desk calculating machine gives a first introduction to mechanical computation, and has considerable educational value in a primary school; it can illustrate the notation and structure of the number system and make possible a modern approach to mathematics in which ideas are more important than the mechanical carrying out of processes.

The change which presents the greatest difficulty to teachers at present is the enlargement of the content of mathematics in the primary school. Some of the material now being introduced into primary schools has previously been taught at the secondary stage, for example the properties of similar shapes, and this is familiar to many primary teachers although its presentation to younger children is necessarily different. But some ideas now being introduced are entirely new to school mathematics. A similar development can be seen in the teaching of science; both subjects have grown and changed tremendously in the last hundred years. The universities must take their students to the borders of knowledge where research begins and therefore they exert pressure on

1

secondary schools to send up students prepared for contemporary university courses. New schemes of secondary mathematics, such as the School Mathematics Project and the Midlands Mathematical Experiment, have been greatly influenced by developments in mathematicians' understanding of the structure of mathematics. These reforms might have been carried through without any corresponding changes in primary schools but for one important fact. Some of the new ideas with which mathematicians work are so fundamental and so simple that children can use them with understanding in their first approaches to shape and number. Moreover they understand mathematics better when these ideas are used from the beginning. Changes do not then have to be made in the children's approach at a later stage, when it is necessary for them to think in terms of modern concepts.

The new ideas which a teacher needs to understand are few in number and are easy to grasp in terms of our everyday experience. The basic concept springs from a child's ability to recognize and pick out things which are alike or different. When he has made a collection of things which have some common property, such as colour, size, position or purpose, he has had a first experience of the basic concept of a *set*. It will be seen that it is derived from the child's capacity to *classify*. Before children learn to count they will meet the notion of *correspondence* when they handle sets of things. For example, if they have a set of spoons and a set of forks it may happen that to each fork there corresponds a spoon and vice versa. The two sets have the same number. Number *operations* are studied very carefully in a modern programme, both to see the effects of an operation, such as addition, on the numbers to which it is applied and also to discover the conditions under which it can work. Another aspect of the new material is the study of movement and change. The idea of *invariance*, that is, of a property which is not altered when certain changes are made, is of great importance; for instance, the fact that pouring water from one container to another of different shape does not alter the quantity of water lies at the basis of the measurement of quantity. Movement is further investigated in order to study the changes or *transformations* which certain movements bring about in lines and shapes.

The government's decision to replace traditional scales of measurement by the metric system has hardly influenced the schools as yet. Children now in primary schools will find that both systems are in everyday use when they enter the adult world. We therefore recommend an early introduction to centimetres, grams, etc. alongside the feet, inches, pounds, ounces and so on, which will continue to be used at home and in shopping for some years to come. *Written* calculations with traditional units are ceasing to have any practical value. We therefore stress the difference between a number system founded on ten, or some other base, and the British system of measures with its variety of links between one unit and another, as in our use of yards,

feet and inches. The fact that the decimal coinage and the metric system have the same pattern as the tens notation for number is brought out clearly.

The book begins with a child's first experiences of objects and events, and traces the growth of mathematical ideas in the light of the findings of research workers like Piaget who have studied the development of children's thinking. Properties of space become familiar to children at an early age; recognition of shape, relative position and size precedes awareness of number. The experience of handling objects and using them constructively yields mental patterns which are necessary to the mental activity of thinking. A child needs to find means of representing such properties as order, correspondence and ratio if he is to develop the mental imagery on which mathematical growth depends. This representation may be in symbols or number sentences, or by means of tabulations or diagrams, or it may be in words. A child is forming continually, deliberately or spontaneously, images of the objects of his thought. These images are a necessary part of the understanding of abstract ideas. It is a remarkable fact that our number system is very clearly represented by points on a line; operations on numbers can be matched by operations on lengths marked on a line. The use of such a *number line* is fully developed in this book.

The plan of the book is based on the stages of development of children's thinking from their early intuitions to the capacity for handling abstract ideas which is becoming evident at the end of the primary school. The lines of growth are followed through in three fields: spatial properties, number and the measurement of quantity. Although these three aspects are usually treated in separate chapters in Parts 1, 2 and 3 of the book, their interconnections are constantly stressed so that the unity of mathematics is not lost. For example, spatial apparatus is used to stimulate understanding of shape, size and number. Another link is found in studying movement which is fundamental to operations with numbers, to measuring, and to changes of shape and position. For older juniors, the three aspects have become so closely interwoven that they are often treated as a unity, for instance in the handling of such topics as graphs, ratio and approximations, in Parts 4 and 5 of the book.

Not all children can be expected to cover all the subject-matter that is suggested. The age of transfer from primary to secondary schools is very varied and time may be available for some children to follow a fuller programme. In any case the abler children need the challenge that some of the more difficult topics offer. Mathematics is a growing body of knowledge which is used extensively and powerfully in the contemporary world. The patterns and structures which are its concern are essential to scientists, engineers and spacecraft designers. Children want to find out about ideas which they can see are important; we should encourage them to use their curiosity and inventiveness to the full.

It is hoped that this book will be helpful to students in a College of Education as well as to experienced teachers. Only a minority of primary teachers have had special mathematical training; the language and the ideas presented here have therefore been kept as simple as possible. Over-simplification, however, would carry the risk that major mathematical points would be missed or distorted. We are encouraged by the persistence and imaginative adaptability of teachers who have worked with us, and who have played a considerable part in the development of the ideas in this book, to believe that very many teachers will be prepared to find a new light and fresh enjoyment in a renewed study of mathematics.

Authors' note on new metric edition

Recent developments in school mathematics programmes and changes in currency and measuring units have made necessary a substantial revision of the original book published in 1970.

In Britain the government's decision to ask for plans for the general adoption of the metric system to be ready by 1975 has brought about a steady rise in the number of enterprises which have changed to metric units. Children are becoming accustomed to seeing prices and quantities written in decimal form. Although halves and quarters and a few other simple fractions are likely to continue in use, computation with fractions is now rarely needed. This means a radical change in the order of learning how to express and to manipulate parts of a unit. Decimal forms are now common in the environment and will appear naturally in situations demanding calculation, replacing the traditional fractions. Adapting to this change has required a complete replanning of the order and the mode of introducing decimal and fractional forms. Many teachers who have successfully encouraged children's logical thinking through their new programmes of classification, comparison, ordering and similar ideas are ready to give fuller consideration to mathematical structure; this structure is stressed in Chapters 4, 14, 25, 35, and 40 which are more generally concerned with relations and operations.

This new edition has enabled us to include numerous extensions and modifications of the text and various improvements to the diagrams, usually intended to give greater clarity. It is our hope that primary school teachers, whether in infants', junior, first or middle schools, will find that this book gives them a confident command of the mathematics it presents and a good stock of realistic suggestions for planning children's effective learning.

Part I
First Discoveries

1 The Child's First Discoveries

Early experiences

A child is born into a world of space and time. Events take place in succession, often with a pattern of repetition and routine. People and objects come and go, move and change. Experiences appear to come in isolation, as sensations provoking a physical or emotional response; e.g. a child may *see* a bright light, *hear* a tone of voice, or *feel* the touch of his own body. There is little that is obviously mathematical in such experiences but gradually repetition of a sensation brings recognition of the thing repeated, for instance the sight of a feeding cup, or the sound of his mother's footsteps. Change, particularly movement, draws attention to the changing object and stimulates awareness of it. For example, the shape of a feeding cup becomes obviously known, and if it is removed the baby follows its movement with his eyes. An unfamiliar object, say a cat, is noticed just because it moves, whereas unmoving objects form an undifferentiated background. During the five years before he starts school a child has a vast range of experiences building up familiarity with a great variety of things and the ways in which they change. These he sorts out and relates to one another, organizing them in his mind. All children have pre-school experiences of this kind and it is out of this body of natural early mathematical activity that the future learning of mathematics must grow.

Permanence

Although a child begins early to recognize things, he does not at first realize that they are still in existence when he does not see them. For instance, if a toy is hidden, he behaves in the early stages as though it had disappeared for ever. In time, through putting things in certain places and finding them again, watching a thing disappear and reappear, or enclosing a toy inside a box, he learns that things continue to exist when out of sight. This awareness of *conservation*, as it is called, is essential if he is to realize that a set will still have as many things

in it when he rearranges it, or that he will have the same amount of biscuit if he breaks it into two or more parts. We deal with this notion of constancy again in later chapters when we consider counting and measuring.

Recognition of likenesses and differences

The sorting or classifying of experiences depends on recognizing similarities and differences. This is seen clearly in a child's awareness of shape. He identifies a shape in a very general way, not perceiving minor differences, but he rejects a shape that is substantially different in its general outline. This recognition, though *global,* is definite. A child under two years of age will firmly reject a substitute for his favourite Teddy or his own spoon or bowl. An adult has similar experience of forming a general impression without registering detail. For instance, in driving through a strange town he may receive a series of unanalysed impressions. On a second visit he has a sense of 'having been here before', yet without recognizing particular features. With repeated visits more detail is observed and changes from previous observations will be noticed. A young child first notices large obvious differences such as the general outlines of shape, whether a box is open or closed, whether there are any holes or big dents in a surface, or if one dog is considerably larger than another. With more experience he perceives finer differences and more detailed likenesses. It is through handling an object and discovering what he or others can do with it that he comes to notice some of its properties. When he has a variety of things to handle he begins to discriminate between some that are very similar and to recognize certain ways in which they differ: whether they are round or have corners; whether they are big or small, near or far away and so on. Some of the shapes he distinguishes are shown in Figure 1:1.

Differences of shape, size and position become familiar and are more precisely distinguished. Thus we can see

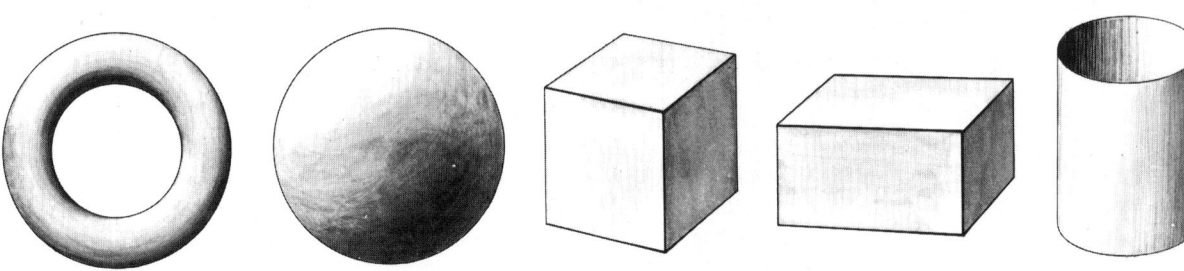

Figure 1:1

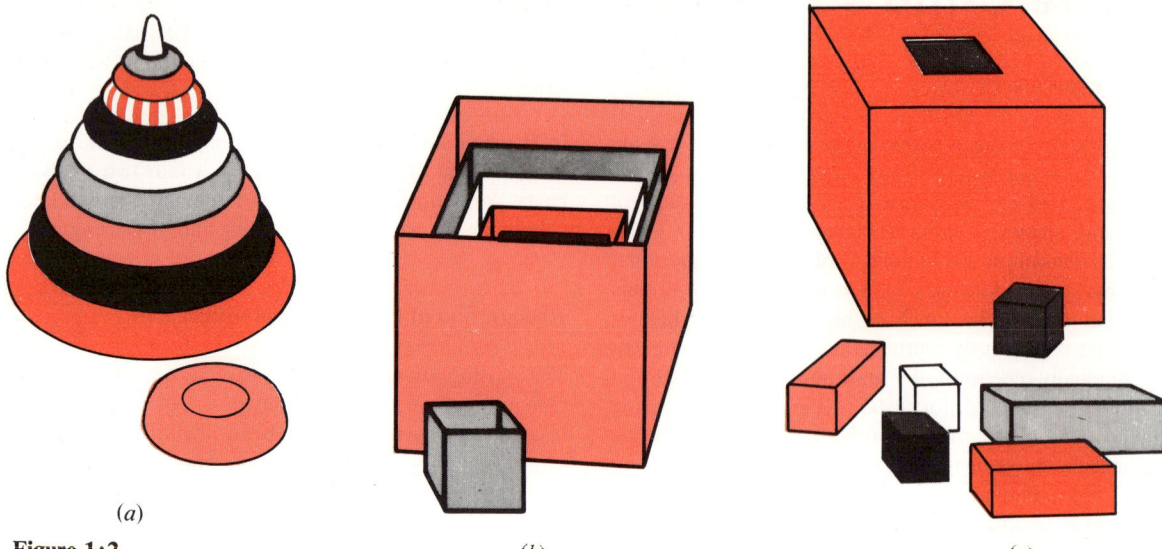

(a)

(b)

(c)

Figure 1:2

that a child's awareness of mathematical properties comes from three types of experience:

i) repetition of experiences of the *same* object or event
ii) the contrast between two *different* things or events
iii) his own *manipulation* of things or his *observation* of their behaviour.

The influence of play

A child's voluntary activities are most clearly seen in his play. At first his actions are purely exploratory and manipulative; he is discovering what is around him and what he can do with the things he discovers, including his own limbs. It is chiefly through movement, sight and touch that his discoveries come to him at this period, known as the stage of *sensori-motor* perception. A wide range of toys, differing in colour, size and shape, and providing opportunities for a variety of movements and arrangements, proves invaluable from an early age. Three different types of mathematical toy are shown above to illustrate the kind of shape and the forms of activity which will give important mathematical ideas over a period of several years.

First the *shapes* are distinguished. If an adult selects a ring, or a cube or a box from these three toys a child of a year or so will choose a ring, a cube or a box to match the toy which the adult has chosen. Later, he will try to reconstruct a toy such as (*a*) or (*b*) but fails because he cannot yet discriminate between the sizes of the rings or boxes. Before two years of age he can put a ring on the mushroom stalk (*a*), a small box into the larger open box (*b*) and a cube into the slot in the top of box (*c*).

But only by chance will he choose the right *sizes* to put *two* rings on the mushroom or *two* boxes into the large one. Further possibilities of experiment with these toys are discussed on page 97.

Realistic toys such as animals, cotton reels, beakers, miniature cars, are a valuable source of mathematical perceptions but it is significant that children enjoy toys like those in Figure 1:2 which are constructed entirely on a mathematical pattern. Play with such materials shows that children spontaneously take to the sorting and matching which the toys stimulate. All through the primary school children need to experiment with both kinds of things: the realistic in which mathematics can be discovered, and the structural which make mathematical relations easy to see.

Bodily movements are an equally important source of perceptions. Stretching, turning, balancing, climbing and clapping give notions of position, distance, direction and rhythm, all of which will be developed at a later stage.

The influence of environment

Toys are given to a child not only for enjoyment but also to provide activities which increase his understanding of things about him. But the incidents of daily life are at least equally stimulating to his growing awareness of how one thing or person is related to another and particularly to himself. The variety in what goes on around a child is immense; his own actions are nearly as diverse. He can put a spoon in his cup, see over the table, or find that a shoe is too small to go on his foot. He can turn a handle, he wants more to drink, and so on. He watches the movements of his mother, of a car, of the wheel on a machine and

8

sees how to fit a lid on to a tin. It is from these experiences with actual things and people that mathematical ideas are developed. In due time an abstract mathematical idea will be distilled from some of them, e.g. the idea of roundness or of one thing fitting on to another. This idea will itself become so real a part of mental life that in its turn it will be related to other ideas and so give rise to new abstractions. This foundation of practical experience is essential to a coherent growth of mathematical insights and is needed as a basis for each extension into a new field of mathematical thinking.

Reactions to environment

When a new experience comes to a child he tends to relate it to previous experiences of a similar kind. He recognizes some elements which are alike and proceeds often to identify the new thing completely with the old. Thus a child who has only known a dog among animals, will assume that a new kind of animal is also a dog though it may be a cat or a deer. This may mean that some aspect of the new object or event is distorted by his mind to make it fit into his previous idea. For example, a child who has a doll which can lie in a toy cot will expect that a much larger doll will do the same thing. It is from watching such actions that we can see which ideas have already formed in the child's mind. When he meets a discrepancy with what he already knows a child may simply ignore it, putting the new thing aside or pretending that in fact it did behave as he expected. In such a case he learns nothing new and does not extend the range of his ideas. Alternatively he may experiment and compare, and thus realize that in some respects there is a difference between the new experience and the old; thus his observation enlarges his field of understanding. For example, the child whose doll is too long for the cot may try first one doll and then the other and be led to a comparison of lengths. When he accommodates his actions and thinking to the new experience he changes his own pattern of behaviour and modifies his earlier concept.

Perception and the development of language

Many things are recognized or differentiated by a young child before any language is used to name or describe them. As a child begins to rely more on perception of things around him so great a number of impressions come to him that he needs to be able to represent them in some way. Just as language develops through the need to talk about the categories of things that are important in everyday life, e.g. drink, bed, dog, man, car, so mathematical language is required to describe the experiences of shape, pattern and relationship that a child finds in his active play and observation. His vocabulary soon includes such words as *more, hole, under, round, flat, out, tall, sharp, fast, gone, throw.* Most of these refer to shape, size, position or movement. The use of these words in conversation with others helps a child to form an idea of a range of objects or situations to which a word applies and to recognize the common elements that belong to them. Words are also an aid in distinguishing the qualities that belong to some objects and not to others. For example, 'car' is at first used for any vehicle or model that has a general shape of bonnet, body and wheels. Later 'lorry' names a special type within the notion of 'car'. As discrimination grows 'tractor', 'fire engine' etc. are named from their shapes.

Words also help to make relationships clear, e.g. 'inside', 'belongs to', 'more', 'some', 'all'. As experience increases the words are used more precisely and show the greater discrimination which a child is using. It can be seen that this recognition of special subdivisions within a whole category is the starting point for the partitioning of collections of things which leads to the operations of adding and subtracting (*see page* 75). At every stage of mathematical education we find that new discoveries demand the development of a language that gives the neatest expression to the relations and operations that are being considered. The way is then open for further discoveries through the use of the ideas expressed in language.

Representation

Language is not the only way in which experiences are represented. Play becomes representational while continuing also to include purely manipulative activities. For example, boxes will serve as garages for toy cars. A child acts out, with whatever materials are available, events that have interested him in his surroundings and reveals in so doing what it is that has impressed him. He will also represent an interesting object by another which is at hand and has some property that makes it a suitable symbol; e.g. he will use a rod as a train. In these procedures the child is calling upon mental patterns that he has already formed, and is developing them further through his actions. The pattern and form of events and things are taking shape in his mind, as his ability to use representative objects shows. As examples we can quote the child who plays at pouring out spoonfuls of medicine to give to her dolls, matching a spoonful to the dolls in turn; or a child may float a piece of wood for a ship recognizing that wood floats on water. In each case an awareness of a mathematical relationship is shown in the particular representation but it is clearly without precision. Further attempts at representation either in play or in drawing, or it may be in imitation, may reveal to the child the shortcomings of the representation and lead to the realization of details and relations that had previously escaped notice. For instance, he may observe that trucks must be fastened together if they are to be pulled. Moreover, the manipulation of symbolic objects, their combination or separation, may be possible when the original objects are too large or inaccessible, as in the case of a child who acts or draws an aeroplane landing. The growth in understanding that comes from devising a way of representing a thing or a situation will be seen in later chapters both in regard to number and to spatial properties. To the teacher a study of a child's spontaneous representations reveals the mental structures that he has already formed, the properties of which he is aware and those that have so far not been fully realized. Piaget[1] notes the difficulty a child has in drawing a house or a tree on the side of a hill and shows that at 5 or 6 years of age they will be drawn perpendicular to the slope as in Figure 1:3 instead of vertically. This representation shows that the idea of vertical and horizontal has not yet been established (*see page* 267).

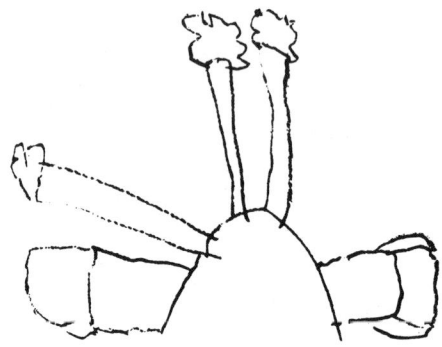

Figure 1:3

Early spatial concepts

In the early stages a child has no interest in *How much?*, or *How many?* Questions of quantity and number do not enter into his play. '*Big*' is used only to distinguish one object from a '*little*' one. He may miss a *particular* toy but he does not notice if one *unnamed* one, say a brick or car, is missing from several of the same kind. We see that a child's first discoveries of a mathematical kind are concerned with space. Notions of quantity and number develop later. Even in his growing awareness of spatial properties such as shape and position he ignores the metric properties of Euclidean space, i.e. those that include some idea of measurement, for instance straight lines, lengths, angles, equalities. These have no place in his thinking though he may move in a straight line to go to his mother or push a truck along a straight path. For example, in making a fenced yard for his miniature animals he may make opposite edges neither equal nor straight. Children notice what are called *topological* properties first, i.e. those not involving

[1] Piaget, J. *The Child's Conception of Space,* page 382.

measurement but concerned with such things as the general outline of a shape, whether it is open or closed or has one or more holes in it, the nearness of one thing to another, the position of a thing between two others. Thus, though distance has little meaning for them, they understand what is meant by '*next to*' and '*between*'. These trends can be observed in a child's interest in fitting or pushing things into holes, in his arrangements of his toys, and in his own position relative to members of his family. From these first simple relationships will develop the number and spatial concepts which are fundamental to mathematics.

The prelude to number

The value of the early experience of handling a variety of things and playing with them freely is that a child builds up a large number of mental pictures and stores up memories of patterns of actions. These he can recall and use for identification of similar objects. Recognition comes from his recall of touch, sound or movement, and their association with a mental picture of the thing itself. From a wealth of such activities there gradually emerges a notion of a whole *class* of things which are alike in some way and can be distinguished from all others. It starts with recognizing that there is *another* thing like the first, and then *another*, and *another,* and so on. This is the beginning of true classification and the idea of a *set* or recognizable collection of things.

Another idea, which develops later, is that of an *order* or *sequence*. This may be an order of events, such as putting on one's clothes, or an order of size as in placing dolls or cars in order of size, the largest first. It is important to notice that this making of a sequence begins (as in the making of a set) by taking only two things at first and selecting the 'big one' and placing the 'small one' next to it. Another one of the set is then taken and placed where it will fit in size, first if it is the biggest, last if it is the smallest, or between the other two if it is smaller than one and bigger than the other.[2] It can be seen that this is a complicated judgement to make and few children can deal with more than three things in this way before school age.[3] Yet most children will have now developed a clear idea of two—two shoes, two children, two biscuits—and will be able to relate two things in a variety of ways: smaller, nearer, under, etc. But the general idea of a number has yet to be reached.

These two ideas of *set* and *sequence* are fundamental to the understanding of number, time, measurement and many

[2] Cf. the story of the three bears.

[3] Cf. the ordering of sizes possible with the toys shown in Figure 1:2 (*a*) and (*b*). This can be done by children in a practical experimental way with the rings or cubes.

other important mathematical concepts. They may be compared with the two types of pattern found in music and analysed only at a much later age:

 i) a chord as a set of notes played together,
ii) a tune as a sequence of notes, and a rhythm as a sequence of time intervals.

The practical experiences of likenesses, differences, regularities and relationships, from which these two basic ideas of a set and a sequence develop, are necessary for their proper growth. At 5 years of age children still need many such experiences. For those whose play activities have hitherto been restricted a considerable range of manipulative and representative forms of play have to be provided. Before such an abstract and complex idea as number can be formed in a child's mind he needs to have carried out with concrete materials these operations of sorting, separating, combining and ordering, out of which a number sequence grows.

2 The Growth of Thinking: Patterns in the Mind

The dawn of thinking

Mathematics is concerned with structures and operations, i.e. with mental images and the ways in which they can be manipulated in the mind. In other words, mathematics depends upon thinking.

The new-born child does not think; he responds to certain physical sensations with a physical response. Thinking comes with the development of his body, experiences of movement, and the growing activity of the brain in recording and organizing impressions. These impressions may be the result of impacts from outside or of the baby's own movements. As soon as he can move and see he begins to come to terms with his environment. He has to develop awareness of the different kinds of order and relatedness which will help him to recognize, forecast and control both his own actions and the behaviour of things around him. There are three mathematical fields of experience, each having its own characteristic kinds of relationships, which children must become familiar with: the experience of *space*, the experience of *number*, and the experience of *quantity*. These are not entirely separate. Numbers are used in a world of space and can tell us about some of its properties. Certain shapes can be so organized that they illustrate the ways in which numbers are related. Figure 2:1 shows two ways of putting 4 cubes together, and the arrangement of 9 triangular tiles in rows holding 1, 3, 5 tiles.

Without number we cannot measure quantity since we must count the measuring units. Yet comparisons of quantity lead to a deeper understanding of numbers as well as revealing some unnoticed properties of space. For instance, measuring a length will show that whole numbers cannot give us a sufficiently exact answer, and we have to think about fractions. Measuring the lengths of the two diagonals of a rectangle suggests that the diagonals must be equal (Figure 2:2).

Mathematical thinking develops through active experience in all three fields. Action and experience necessarily precede thinking. As Piaget says,[1] 'Thought can only

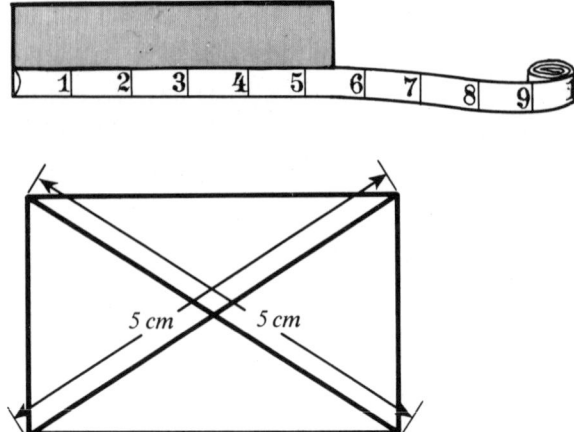

Figure 2:2

replace action on the basis of the data which action itself provides.'

During this century psychologists have made extensive studies of the development of thought in children. In particular Piaget and the investigators who work with him at his research institute in Geneva have spent many years in trying to trace the gradual growth of ideas about numbers, quantity and space, and in studying the ways in which children's thinking changes as they grow older. Children do not think like adults until adolescence. The complex processes of thought are acquired gradually, developing from the extremely simple forms found in the young infant. What the psychologists have observed is of the greatest importance to teachers in planning the experiences they will offer to children. It is these experiences of making discoveries through his own actions and

[1] Piaget, J. *The Child's Conception of Space*, page 453.

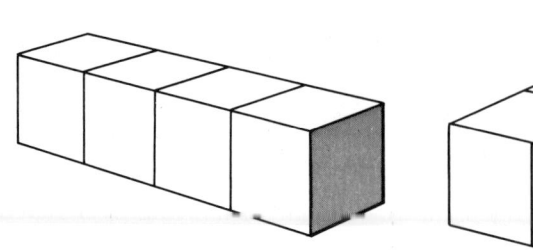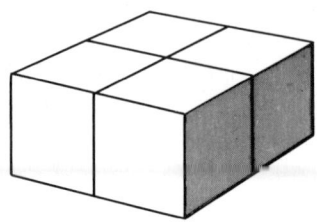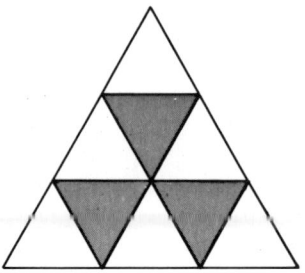

Figure 2:1

12

attempting to express what he has discovered which enable a child to *think* mathematics instead of merely carrying out operations mechanically and without real understanding. Moreover, familiarity with the characteristic growth of children's thinking helps a teacher to identify the stage which an individual child has reached. Many of the experiments and observations undertaken and analysed by the Geneva School have been repeated in this country and checked by alternative methods. Not all Piaget's findings have been confirmed but a considerable number have been verified and a general pattern of development seems to have been established.

Stages of growth

The following stages of growth have been distinguished, though some writers number them differently.

(1) The *period of sensori-motor intelligence,* from birth to $1\frac{1}{2}/2$ years: when sensations and actions are the important things in a child's experience and the means through which he learns.
(2) The *period of preparation for and organization of concrete operations*
    (*a*) from $1\frac{1}{2}/2$ years to 4 years: the stage when *representation* becomes possible in the form of language, imaginative play and drawing
    (*b*) from 4 years to 7/8 years: the period of *intuitive thinking* when judgements about size, shape, relationships, etc., are based on a child's experiences and his interpretations of his experiences, and are made without reasoning

(*c*) from 7/8 years to 11/12 years: the stage when *logical operations* can be carried out *with concrete materials* or in a particular situation.
(3) The *period of formal operations,* from 11/12 years: logical operations can now be carried out in the mind without the aid of concrete materials.

These stages are well-marked but the ages differ among children. Their rate of development depends in part on innate ability but there is strong evidence that it is influenced considerably by the kind and range of exploratory and constructional activities that have been open to a child. The transition from one stage to the next is not sudden. A child will show on occasion during stage 1 some of the characteristic thinking of stage 2, and during stage 2 he will sometimes operate at the level of stage 1. Regression to an earlier way of thinking may take place at any age in the face of a completely novel situation or a very difficult problem. We will now examine each of these stages in more detail.

Stage 1. The period of sensori-motor intelligence

In this stage a child passes from experiencing actions and sensations as unrelated episodes to the co-ordination of the images he receives and the systematization of his actions. He first discovers that things continue to exist even when he cannot see them (*see page* 7). This means that he has a mental picture and not merely the direct visual image of an object in front of him. The establishment of a mental picture of a thing not seen is the prerequisite of thinking. The awareness that things still

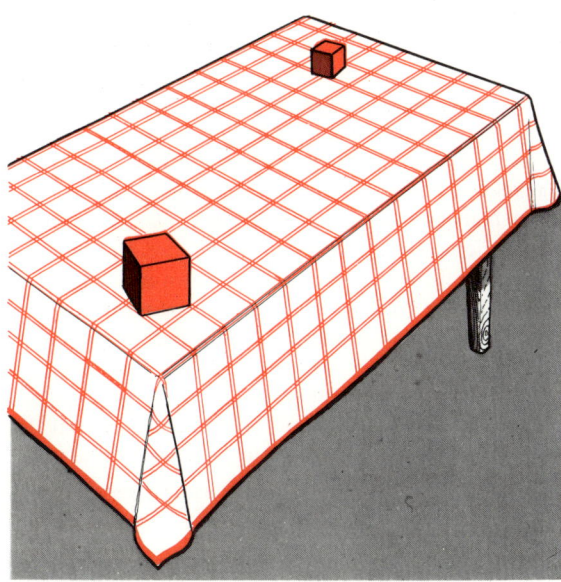

Figure 2:3

Figure 2:4

exist when they are out of sight is then extended. An object may be moved nearer to a child or farther away, or turned in another direction. The object looks different but he now recognizes that it is the same object although its *apparent* size and its *apparent* shape have changed with the shift of position.

The examination of Figures 2:3 and 2:4 will show how skilled is this recognition of sameness. It seems to develop through handling, say, the brick in Figure 2:3 and seeing the different presentations of its shape as the hands turn it about. This variety of shapes gives rise to a composite mental picture and from this the brick in any position will be *perceived*, i.e. recognized as a brick when any *particular* visual image of it is presented. Similarly *movement* of an object, or of a child relative to the object, will produce awareness of the constancy of the object in spite of its apparent change of size or shape.

It will be noticed that the things which the child is learning to recognize in different positions are all seen in relation to himself. Although he moves objects about he does not yet relate them in his mind to one another. They remain independent of one another in his thinking.

The systematizing of actions which takes place during this period is particularly important because the organization of simple movements is the foundation of the mental structures which will develop in subsequent stages. For example, a child learns to *reverse an action,* such as picking up and putting down, and this is a preliminary to going back in thought, as when a child sees that $3 + 2 = 5$ implies that $5 - 2 = 3$. He also carries out a *chain of actions* leading to a satisfactory result; for instance, he sees a toy on a chair, crawls across the floor and reaches up to take it. This is the forerunner to following out a chain of thought to reach a new understanding or to work out a plan. The two procedures of reversing and forming a chain can then be combined and the whole sequence of actions can be reversed.

Towards the end of this period children begin to make experiments with things. For example, they put one brick on another to see whether it will balance to make a tower. This foreshadows with concrete material the experiment in the mind which an adult carries out when faced with a difficult situation; he *thinks out* or pictures to himself what would happen if he took a certain line of action. He may imagine two or more possible courses of action, visualizing their results, and then selecting the one which will lead to success. As Piaget says, 'A logic of action precedes a logic of thought.'

This dependence of the development of thinking on patterns of action continues throughout Stages 1 and 2. New types of thinking require new action patterns as a necessary preliminary.

Stage 2(a). The development of representation

In Stage 2(a) the power of representation emerges. This is probably the most powerful instrument of mathematical thinking, as we shall see when we consider the part played by symbols in later periods. Speech provides the first symbols which come to stand for the composite pictures and the patterns of action which have been developed in the mind during Stage 1. A child can use word symbols to state briefly

i) a pattern of *action,* e.g. he will *fetch* the toy
ii) a *collection* of things, e.g. *all* the balls
iii) a *connection* between two things, such as a toy *in* the basket.

He can then combine these symbols to represent a complex series of actions; he will say that he will *fetch all* the balls and put them *in* the basket. The use of words greatly increases the range of mental activity which a child can carry out. He is no longer limited to mental pictures as the tools of his thinking.

During this period imaginative play expresses a child's feelings and enables him to represent and act out experiences which have been important for him. Given a set of bricks, for example the gay and varied shapes included in Poleidoblocs,[2] or a supply of boxes, tins and rings, he will make shapes which for *him* represent a house, a bed, an aeroplane, a bridge, or people. Through symbolizing the actual things in this way he extends his power to understand how they behave and how he can influence them. This kind of play reveals that a child is still looking at things in reference to himself, noticing what they mean to *him* and what *he* can do with them.

Drawings can be equally fruitful both in showing us what a child has really observed and in stimulating him to further insights. The representations are not photographic but represent what the child has perceived. They correspond in their structure to the mental pictures he has formed. They show clearly how egocentric are his impressions and how limited is his awareness of the connections between the things themselves. For example, in drawings of a man, a child at $3\frac{1}{2}$ years may show a head and a body not connected by a neck, two arms which may be joined to head or body and two legs vaguely attached to the body. A hat will be drawn *above* the head but not *on* the head because the child has not yet seen the relationship of fitting the hat to part of the head (Figure 2:5).

His ideas about many situations are similarly unrelated. For instance, he will hold two contradictory ideas at the same time, believing that a quantity is larger than another in one position and smaller if the position is changed

[2] Designed by Dr Margaret Lowenfeld.

Figure 2:5

(*see page* 52). He is unable as yet to relate two ideas together either to see that they are not contradictory or to produce from them a new idea.

Representation in speech or drawing permits communication with others and conversation helps children to discover the contradictions and lack of accuracy in their drawings and descriptions (*see page* 10). This is, therefore, a period of considerable growth towards relating mental structure to actual forms and relationships.

Stage 2(b). The period of intuitive thinking

The stage from 4 years to 7/8 years is of particular interest to teachers because for many children it covers the first two or three years at school. In this period children's thinking is dominated by their *perceptions,* i.e. by the *interpretations* they give to their experiences of seeing,

hearing, touching, moving, etc. These may be mistaken. As the proverb says, appearances are deceptive, and a child may be the more deceived because he tends to identify what he sees with similar but not identical things seen before. It is not possible to reverse a perception as one can an action because it depends on earlier experiences as well as on the visual image one is actually seeing. A door standing ajar is seen as such in a flash and a very young child will say 'door' because the visual picture before him fits into his complex set of images of the objects to which the name *door* is given. He has not reached this recognition by any *sequence* of actions or thinking which could now be reversed. In order to be further developed a percept must be co-ordinated with another percept; it may then be corrected for inaccuracies.

A child may wrongly say that the beads in Figure 2:6(a) are more than those in 2:6(b), which are grouped together

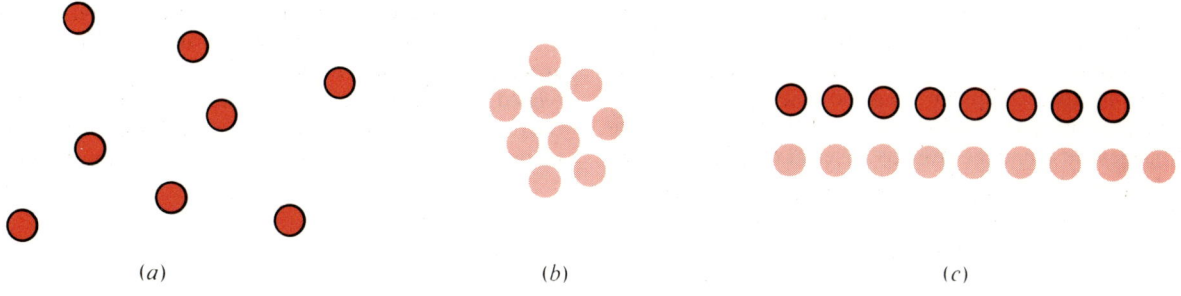

(*a*)   (*b*)   (*c*)

Figure 2:6

more closely. If he then sets them out so that each bead in (b) is opposite one bead from (a) he will see whether one of the sets has more beads than the other (Figure 2:6(c)). Children perform such co-ordinations during this period but since perception is not reversible, thinking that depends on perceptions can still be erratic or inconsistent; it can be contradicted by a new perception which is not fully co-ordinated with it. For example, a child at this stage will agree that two squares, one red and one blue, are equal because one fits on the other. The blue one is then cut in half as in Figure 2:7(B). A green square is then treated in the same way and its two halves placed end to end as in Figure 2:7(C). The child will agree that the two halves in (B) are equal to (A). He agrees that the square which made (C) was equal to (A). But he will say that (C) is bigger than (B). Apparently he is judging only by length and has not taken into account the change in width. Expressed in symbols he agrees that $(A) = (B)$ and $(A) = (C)$ but he does not recognize that $(C) = (B)$. He *perceives* that $(C) > (B)$, *mistakenly*.

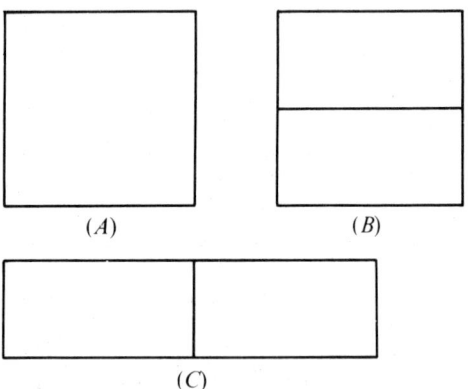

(A)   (B)

(C)

Figure 2:7

Thinking which is based on perceptions and not on reasoning is said to be *intuitive*. Since perceptions are mental structures produced by sensations, past as well as present, it is clear that intuitive thinking about a thing or a situation takes place only when there is a direct contact with the object of thought. For instance, towards the end of this period a child will suddenly 'see' intuitively that the square and the 'diamond' in Figure 2:8 are identical shapes, one of which has been rotated.

Such an intuitive judgement, based as it is on past actions and perhaps on head movements made by the child at the time, comes often in a flash. Reasons for the judgement cannot be given by the child but clearly he has built up correspondences, matching sides and corners in an imagined movement. The revelation of the identity of the two shapes is entirely convincing. This kind of intuitive thinking, stimulated by rich experiences of manipulating things, continues through the years and applies to increasingly complex situations. It is indeed an essential

16

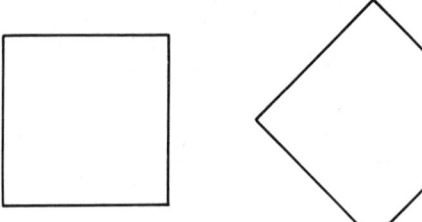

Figure 2:8

feature of creative mathematics. Fostered throughout the Primary years it will strengthen and bring inventiveness to the learning of mathematics at the Secondary stage.

Stage 2(c). The period of concrete operations

This is the stage when logical operations can be carried out with concrete materials. A child can now begin to think logically provided his thinking is guided by contact with real things and actual situations. By the age of 7 or 8 his experiences should have been wide enough for his view of the world to be less self-centred; he can now discover and consider relationships between things without reference to his own viewpoint. His thinking will therefore have a much wider range and his conclusions will be more general and also more precise. We say that it is a period of *logical operations* with concrete materials; we must consider what we mean by *operations* in this sense and what the word *logical* implies here.

We have seen that mathematics has two aspects: it is concerned with patterns or structures which can be pictured in the mind; it is also concerned with *operations*,[3] i.e. with the mental manipulation of these mental pictures. The mental images are created by many experiences of things, observing them, handling them, constructing imaginatively with them. Such images are of many kinds: a variety of shapes and constructions, symbols, sequences, symbolic statements. Figure 2:9 shows but a few examples of mental images which a child may have, though they may fluctuate and be vaguer than these diagrams suggest.

Activities of many kinds, such as moving bricks and toy cars to make constructions, giving one plate of a set to each of a collection of dolls, cutting squares into triangles, filling a square cavity with small cubes, are the forerunners to carrying out similar actions entirely 'in the imagination', as we say. The mental pictures of the different objects are related to one another or moved about in the mind and the results of such mental movements are seen as mental pictures. These activities of the mind, developed from

---

[3] An operation also has a structure and can become a mental image and an object of thought.

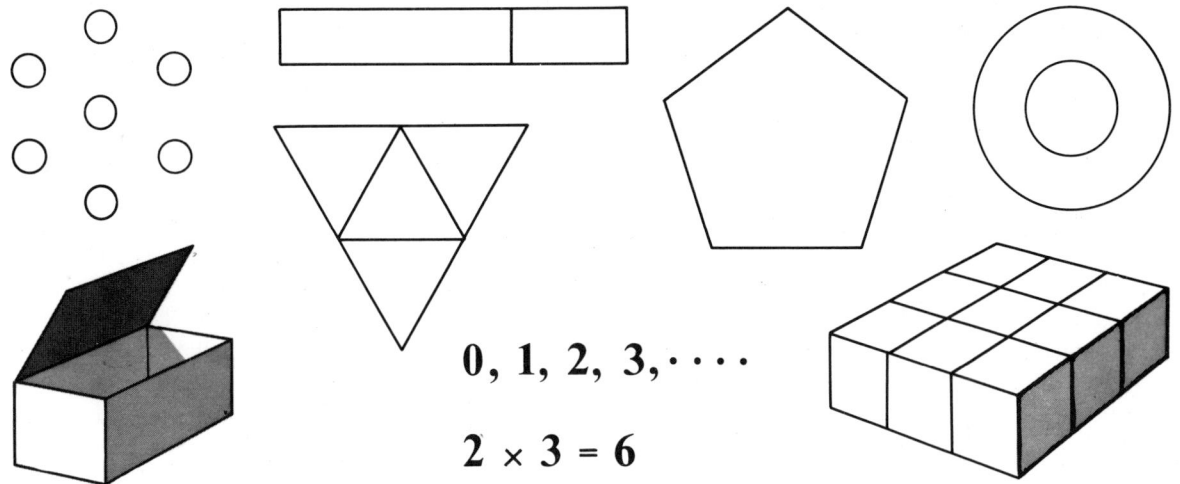

Figure 2:9

$$0, 1, 2, 3, \cdots$$

$$2 \times 3 = 6$$

actual observations and handling of physical objects, are called *operations*. Piaget speaks of operations as internalized actions, a phrase which reminds us that these mental activities can take place when the objects involved are no longer present and the physical actions on which they are based are past. In fact the actions may not be consciously recalled. For example, a child who knows that he has five toy cars is promised two more. He has a mental picture, probably vague, of his five cars; he pictures the two more, puts them mentally with the five, visualizes the new collection and makes the count of seven (or counts on two beyond five). The result is expressed as, 'I shall have seven cars.' The important characteristic of mental operations is their fluidity. In his mind a child can go back to the five cars he actually has; he can mentally remove the extra two and return to his starting point (*see page* 88). He can mentally take to pieces the building he has made and build a different shape in his mind; this, too, he can undo. This feature of operations, that they can be mentally undone by the thinker so that he goes back to his starting point, is called *reversibility*. Piaget says, An operation may be defined as an action which can return to its starting point, and which can be integrated with other actions also possessing this feature of reversibility.[4] An example will show how a sequence of actions, each reversible, leads to a sequence of mental operations. A child has a collection of small cubes. He begins to build with them using the notion of twos. First he makes a rod or cuboid of two of them; he puts two such cuboids together and has a square-shaped layer; another such layer is placed on this one and he now has a cube. Each action can be reversed, and the entire sequence can finally be

[4] Piaget, J. *The Child's Conception of Space,* page 39.

reversed; the child will then have the separate cubes he started with.

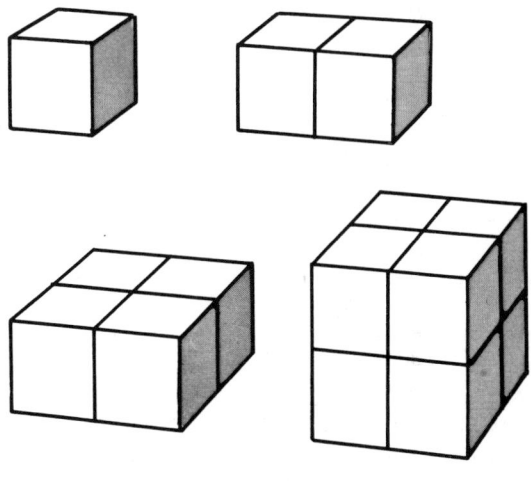

Figure 2:10

After such experience the child can create the whole procedure in his mind and use his knowledge of counting to match the number of cubes he has used to each shape in turn, forming mentally the number sequence 1, 2, 4, 8. The important factor here is the practical experience which made possible the mental imagery both of shapes and of the actions.

During the period of concrete operations children master a variety of operations, some of them quite complex. These grow from three simple operations which are fundamental to the process of counting and underlie all mathematical thinking. The sources of these three

17

operations are the following patterns of action:

i) *classification*. Through recognizing the likeness of one thing to another and distinguishing it as different from other things, a child can form a collection or *class* of things that are alike, say cars, farm animals or cups. He can sort out his model farm animals into separate classes: pigs, horses, cows. He is *not* thinking of *how many* of each class he possesses but only of where any particular animal belongs;

ii) forming *one-to-one correspondences*. This is the operation of matching each of one kind of thing to each thing of another kind, e.g. one packet of crayons to each child at a table, or one 'cup of tea' to each doll. From these matchings he sees the *relationships* 'more than', or 'less than', or 'the same as' ('just as many as');

iii) *seriation* or forming sequences. For example, dolls are arranged in order of height, jugs according to how much they hold, boxes in order of mass. This means that a child is using the *relationship* of more or less for the purpose of putting an object into its proper place in a sequence.

These elementary patterns of action give rise to mental operations. A child becomes able to sort out in his mind things that he can image, say steam engines from diesel engines; he can match in his mind the number of spoons to the number of people expected; he can arrange in order the steps he must take to make a paper boat, and so on. He is relating things in his mind and the relationship is the connection he has perceived between certain things. He will now be able to recognize this relationship and use it in his thinking, e.g. matching forks to spoons without reference to the people for whom they are required. From these basic operations of classifying, matching and ordering more complex operations are evolved and more complicated relationships are perceived.

The simplest operation which creates more complex relationships is that of putting together or adding. We use the word addition usually to mean putting two numbers or two lengths etc. together. It has a broader meaning which we use here; it signifies putting together two classes, or two sequences, or two relations and so on, without necessarily involving the numbers or sizes of the things concerned. We will give examples to illustrate this development in a child's powers.

Classification. A girl sorts out all the dolls' coats she has; she also sorts out all the dolls' hats. She combines them into one class called the dolls' outdoor clothes. This may be written as coats + hats ↔ outdoor clothes, or in symbols

$$C + H \leftrightarrow O$$

A boy has a collection of toy animals in a box; he sorts them into sheep, horses and cows. He has another collection in a basket; these animals he sorts into sheep, goats and pigs. He decides to put the two classifications together. The four classes of horses, cows, goats and pigs still remain, but the two collections of sheep can be put into *one class*

(sheep, horses and cows) with (sheep, goats and pigs)
↔(sheep, horses, cows, goats and pigs)

If we write in symbols what has happened to the sheep it is

class S + class $S \leftrightarrow$ class S

This is not a statement about the numbers in each class but states only that two classes of the same class form one class. Through these experiences of combining the classes into which things can be sorted a child gradually builds up more general ideas of classes and will be able to think of *all* the domesticated animals, *all* the wild animals, and finally of *all* the animals in the world. Such a general awareness is shown when a child sees that squares and oblong rectangles make up the whole class of rectangles (Figure 2:11).

Correspondences also can be combined. Each doll can be given a cup; a saucer can be placed under each cup. Then a child can see that each doll has been given a saucer and he can use this kind of matching in his thinking.

We have seen that *seriation* depends on using the relation 'bigger' (or smaller) to connect each successive pair of things in a sequence. Such *relations* can also be added. If one tin is taller than another, and the second tin is taller than a third, then the child putting the two relations together, will be able to say that the first tin is taller than the third (Figure 2:12).

Two *sequences* can be matched. For example, if toy cars are to be put in garages of different sizes so that the biggest car goes into the biggest garage and so on, in stages 2(*a*) and 2(*b*) a child may carry this out by trial and error. At stage 2(*c*) (*see pages* 16–17) he can make two

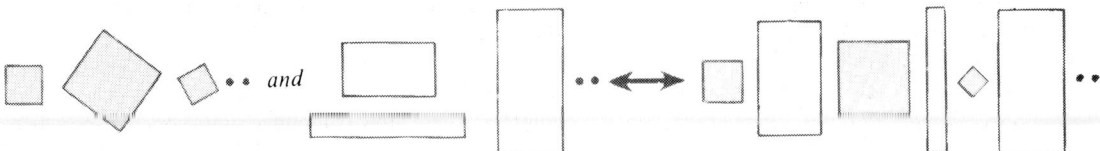

Figure 2:11

18

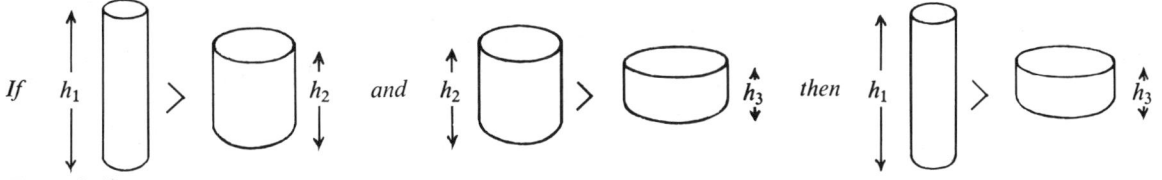

$$\text{If} \quad h_1 \quad > \quad h_2 \quad \text{and} \quad h_2 \quad > \quad h_3 \quad \text{then} \quad h_1 \quad > \quad h_3$$

Figure 2:12

sequences arranged according to size in his mind and fit the smallest car to the smallest garage and so in order up to the largest car in the largest garage. This he can do without actual experiment.

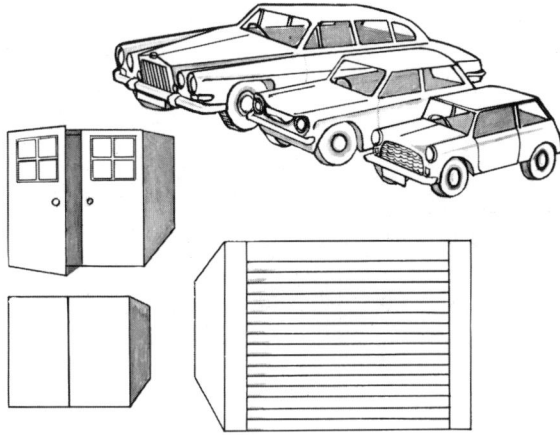

Figure 2:13

Similarly he will be able to select suitable cylinders to represent chimneys on models of houses in a sequence of sizes.

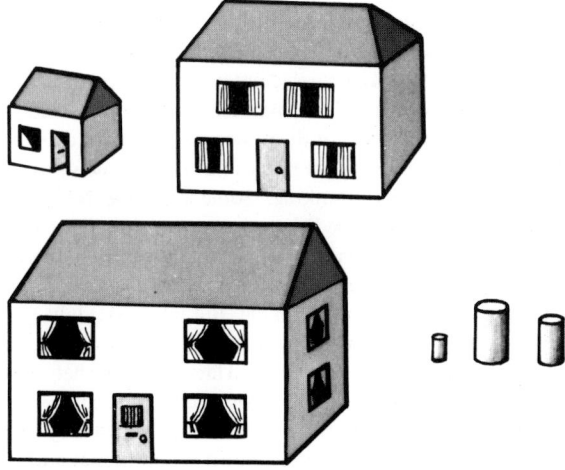

Figure 2:14

In Chapter 5 we shall see how important this matching of sequences is in dealing with changes which take place in successive intervals of time.

Two sequences of the same kind can be put together by dovetailing to make a new sequence, as in the discs shown in Figure 2:15.

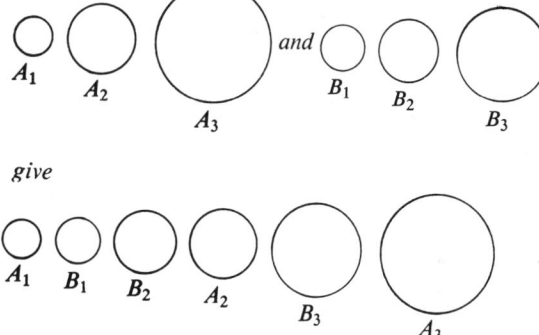

give

Figure 2:15

Similarly the sequence of odd numbers and the sequence of even numbers can be combined to give the sequence of whole numbers.

$(1, 3, 5, 7\ldots)$ and $(2, 4, 6, 8\ldots) \rightarrow (1, 2, 3, 4, 5, 6, 7, 8\ldots)$
In this instance the reverse operation, i.e.
$(1, 2, 3, 4, 5, 6, 7, 8\ldots) \rightarrow (1, 3, 5, 7\ldots)$ and $(2, 4, 6, 8\ldots)$

is likely to be discovered first.

A more complex operation arises when two *different* relations have to be taken into account at the same time. For instance if two glass jars differ in height and also in diameter their capacity can only be compared if both factors are considered. At the stage we are considering, a child cannot yet calculate the volumes but he can make an estimated comparison by thinking about the two kinds of measurement, height and diameter.

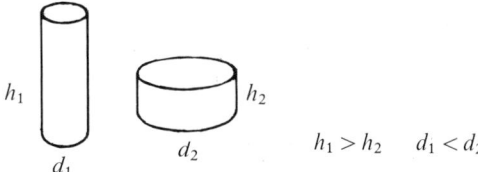

$h_1 > h_2 \quad d_1 < d_2$

The capacities might be equal

Figure 2:16

19

If two rectangles are to be compared with regard to their surfaces (areas) both length and breadth must be considered.

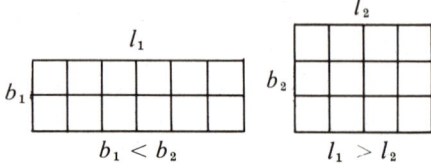

Figure 2:17

The two relations are said to be *multiplied*. In the case of the rectangle we can see that multiplication of the numbers of units in the length and breadth would in fact give the areas, but by multiplication of relations we mean the wider procedure in which we consider two relations at the same time, whatever kind of connection there may be between them.

An experience in which two relations have to be considered simultaneously is the common one of finding the way home after a journey on a strange road. Two changes are involved. What was behind on the way out is now in front; what was on the right is now on the left. If children who have recently come to a school are asked to draw a plan of the journey home, the difficulties they have in making the changes from their images of the journey to school are quite apparent. Estimations of directions and the positions of landmarks may all be faulty. In the period from 7 to 11 years of age considerable development in dealing with the relations involved can be seen.

An operation which is similar in kind to the one just discussed is that of classifying according to two different qualities, say shape and colour, or age and height. A collection of beads is classified first for shape, round or square.

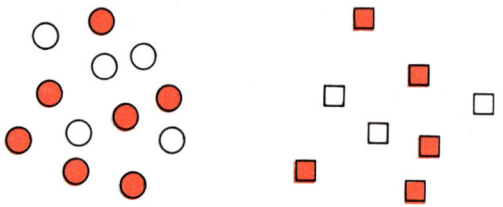

Figure 2:18

In each pile some are red and some are white. They are now sorted according to colour putting red above and white below. A pattern at once emerges in which all the round and all the square are separated and also all the white and all the red are separated. There are now four classes:

red and round;	red and square;
white and round;	white and square.

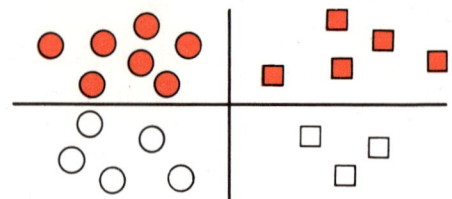

Figure 2:19

They have been formed from two classes different in colour and two classes different in shape. If there had been three different colours and two different shapes the result of carrying out both classifications would have been six classes as Figure 2:20 shows.

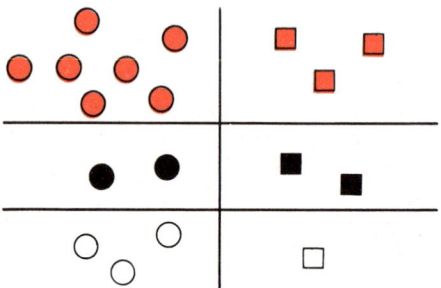

Figure 2:20

It is easy to see why this procedure is called the multiplication of classes but it must be remembered that it is the resulting *kinds of classes* that are thought about here rather than the *numbers* produced. Experience of such classifications and attempts to work out the resulting patterns mentally is an interesting and valuable task.

The operations we have been describing were referred to as *logical* operations carried out with concrete material; we said that we would discuss the word *logical* as used here. Logic is the study of the principles of human reasoning. Logical operations are part of this system and so obey the rules of logical thinking. Some of these rules are discussed in Chapter 4. When we apply 'logical' to this stage of children's thinking we mean that the mental operations that they are able to carry out at Stage 2(c) have some of the structures of adult thinking. But whereas adults are able to think and reason without the use of physical aids, or indeed without reference to physical facts, children between 7/8 and 11/12 years require a basis of concrete experience for their mental operations. The reasoning which they can then carry through is in sharp contrast to intuitional judgements. The best justification that a child can give for an intuitional judgement is that, 'you can *see* that it is so'. In reasoning, on the other hand, the operations of comparing, matching, etc., will be carefully used to show the truth of a judgement. At the stage of intuitive thinking, a child will

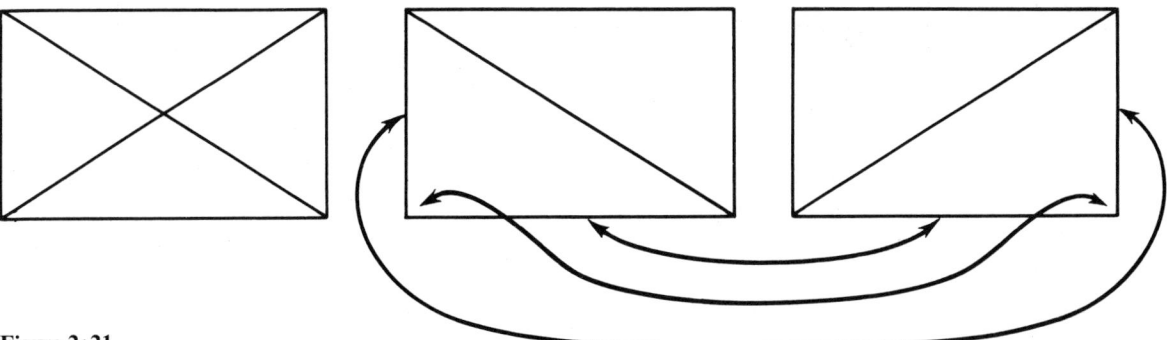

Figure 2:21

say that the diagonals of a rectangle are equal because they *look* equal; later, he will mentally match the sides and angles of the two diagonal triangles in the rectangle to *reason* that they are equal (Figure 2:21).

Operations of the complex character which children from 7 to 11 years carry out are much easier for children who have plenty of opportunities for the constructive play which is characteristic of this age. The requirements of many constructions oblige a child to take a number of factors into account and thus encourage the kind of logical thinking that is necessary in all aspects of mathematics. Towards the end of this period many of the concepts formed should have become sufficiently clear and meaningful for a child to think effectively without contact with actual material and to carry out steps of thinking entirely in terms of concepts, where these have been firmly established.

Stage 3. The period of formal operations

From the age of 11/12 years thinking can take place without reference to actual objects or to events in the real world. It is now possible, and often pleasurable, for young people to invent some hypothesis and work out logical consequences. The construction of logical systems is the method of advanced mathematics and has proved valuable in providing structures which scientists can use. For most pupils in secondary schools logical reasoning will be con-cerned with the world of number, space, quantity and time, and for such thinking they will need the sure foundation of active manipulation and concrete operations already outlined.

Fostering the growth of thinking

In this chapter we have tried to trace the growth of a child's power to think mathematically and to carry out the operations which are the fundamental ways of dealing with the numerical, quantitative and spatial properties of the things and events he encounters. The study of his growth is important to the teacher because his chief purpose in teaching mathematics to children must be to foster in them the understanding of relationships and the capacity for sound thinking which a scientific and technological environment requires. To help each child to develop his natural gift for such mental activity a teacher must be able to recognize at any time the kind of thinking that a child's work reveals. Only then can the next steps be planned to encourage further growth. Our knowledge of the stages through which children's thinking passes should convince us of the necessity of allowing them ample opportunities for experimenting and constructing with a wide range of objects and materials, for making their own judgements, for expressing their findings in their own ways, and for thinking through for themselves the way to new discoveries and the solution to problems.

3 The Beginning of Counting

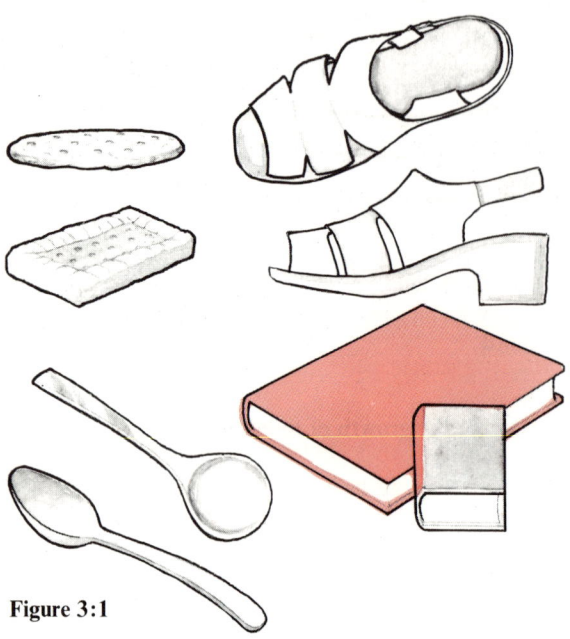

Figure 3:1

Experiences preliminary to counting

A child begins to be aware of number as a feature of things in his surroundings through two kinds of experience: he finds that there are *many* objects of the same kind, though he does not yet know *how many*; he also begins to recognize the presence of *two* things, for example two shoes, two spoons, two biscuits (Figure 3:1). The first kind of experience depends on his recognition of the likeness of such things as balls or cars or children and on his capacity to distinguish them from other kinds of things, i.e. on his power of classification. The second type of experience appears to be a recognition of the pattern made by two like things, i.e. of the existence of 'one and another'. We must consider how these two simple forms of recognition lead to the ability to count the objects that he can handle or see, and later to recognize the patterns and structures of a system of numbers.

Classes and sets

By the time a child starts school he has a large stock of nouns in his vocabulary that show that he has recognized many classes of things that he uses, sees or plays with at home or out of doors. He may have played at shops, an airfield, or a farm, and deliberately sorted and arranged things of the same kind together. Nevertheless, he may not yet have spontaneously classified a box of bricks into different shapes or colours; he may not have noticed the different kinds of leaves on plants or the various shapes of tins. Experience of classifying toys, materials, and the collections of interesting things that children and teacher bring to school will be valuable both in stimulating the child's observation and in giving him the basis on which the notion of number will be built. From the earliest days he

Figure 3:2

Figure 3:3

should meet the word *set* used to mean a collection of any kind of thing that he can recognize as belonging to the set and to which he could add another of the same kind (if one exists), e.g. a set of shells, a set of toy elephants, the set of acorns or berries brought by the class, the set of empty milkbottles, or a set of packets to put in the class shop, and so on (Figure 3:2). There is no thought of *counting* yet, but 'more', 'a few', 'a lot' will be used in discussing the various sets. More important is the awareness of the connection between the members of a set, the common property which makes it possible to decide whether another object belongs to the set or not. All members are related to one another in the possession of this *'likeness'*. Those objects that are *'not like'* the members in this respect are *outside* the set.

Some of the children's imaginative and constructional activities will strengthen their familiarity with the idea of sets and give them the pleasure of putting sets of things together to make, say, a large picture of a village or farm, or a gay and satisfying pattern of coloured shapes. If a class works in small groups, each group can make a set of a particular animal, building or shape, and then decide where to place their contributions to the scheme the class is carrying out. It is important that children should have

this experience of combining sets into a whole as well as finding various sets within a large collection (Figure 3:3).

Comparison of sets

Comparison of collections is the next step towards counting. The companionship of other children in the class and a child's awareness of those sitting near him making different things, or having more of some things than he has, will lead naturally to comparison. He needs to know how to check whether another child's set has more or fewer things in it than his own, or whether he has enough pencils for the children at his table or in his group. He begins to match the two sets, one thing from the first to one thing from the second. This he will do by placing them side by side or close together in some way. The teacher can make similar matchings on the blackboard, drawing simple pictures of things brought by two different sets of children, recording the things in two rows or two columns.

In Figure 3:4 we notice that size and shape do not matter but the things in the picture are recognizably shells. One set contains shells that are alike in belonging to Mary. The other set, quite distinct from Mary's set, contains shells

Peter's set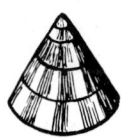

Mary's set

Figure 3:4

that are alike in belonging to Peter. The class can now *see* that Mary's set has more shells and some of the children may say that it has *one* more than Peter's set.

To ensure that the members of the two sets are placed in positions where the one-to-one matching can be seen, it is useful to have squared paper 5-cm or 2-cm squares[1] on which pictures or drawings or name-cards of objects can be arranged in rows or columns starting from a common base. For example, children can record the children whose birthdays fall during this month or will fall next month. Each child places his name-card in the appropriate squares in the correct column.

Figure 3:5

Or the class may record the children whose names begin with letters B and M.

B	Bruce	Brenda	Brian	Barry	
M	Mark	Mandy	Mary	Martin	Moira

Figure 3:6

Another type of comparison comes from sorting tins brought by the children for their shop, say into rounded tins and square tins. Each child can draw or cut out the shape of one tin and fix the picture on a square in the appropriate row.

When these records have been made, the children then say whether one set contains 'more than', 'less than' or 'as many as' the other set. The relationship of one set to the

Figure 3:7

other has been discovered.

The first numbers

It will be noticed that the use of the word 'one' has been assumed. At this stage it means a single thing and is not yet part of a count. The active life of the classroom will soon lead any children who have not recognized *two* before to become aware of two things and to discriminate between one and two quite consistently. Statements about the differences between sets should now be freely made and if matching shows the difference in number to be *one* or *two* a sentence should record it in the children's own simple language. Games, rhymes, matching pairs of things, labelling pictures of sets of two things, folding and cutting shapes into halves to make two pieces, finding sets of two to match a given set, all these activities will help to make the names 'one', 'two' and the symbols 1, 2, for these two numbers familiar.

Comparison of several sets: ordering

The comparison of sets of things without counting is now extended to include several collections. For example, different groups of children in the class can each choose something which they could find in the garden or playground. They are asked to bring in a few. They may bring leaves, berries, twigs, flowers. These are recorded after discussion by putting pictures on squared paper as in Figure 3:8.

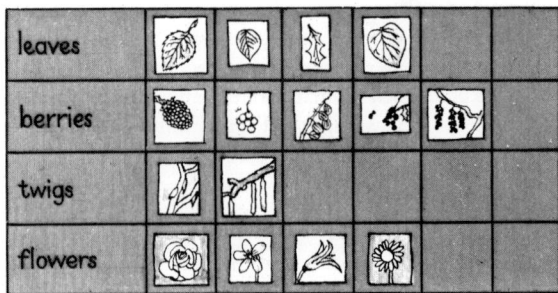

Figure 3:8

The children find that the berries make the set with most things in it, the twigs the set with fewest things. Between them are the sets of leaves and of flowers. The set of

[1] If suitable squared paper cannot be bought a square of paper with 32-cm sides can easily be successively folded to give 4-cm or 2-cm squares.

flowers has just as many in it as the set of leaves; they can be matched exactly. There is one more in the set of berries than in the set of leaves. There are two twigs, there are two more flowers than twigs.

Given a heap of mixed shapes, either three-dimensional solid shapes (such as Poleidoblocs) or flat tiles (discs, squares, triangles, etc.), a child can sort and make sets of things of the same shape. He can match the sets either by placing them side by side, one-to-one, or by arranging them on squared paper. He can say which shape makes the set with most things in it, which set has the fewest, and whether any sets match exactly. It is now a short step to putting the sets in order. Small sets such as those shown in Figure 3:9 are easily ordered.

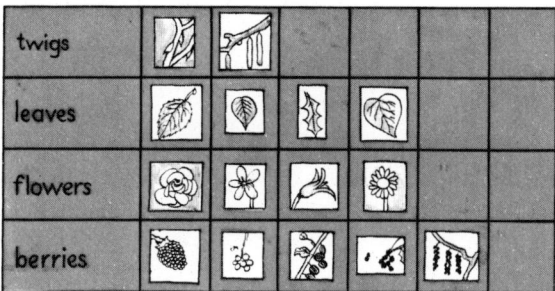

Figure 3:9

The differences between the sets can now be clearly seen. Leaves and flowers are obviously matching sets.

An abacus with four or five rods, open at the top, can also be used for sorting and ordering, using beads of different colours or shapes. Figure 3:10 shows the random order, and then the ordering on another abacus according to which set has most, fewer, etc.

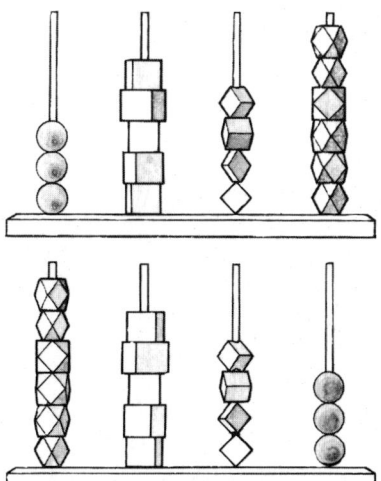

Figure 3:10

Later on a child will use beads to *represent* objects of some other kind, toys perhaps, matching a bead to each toy.

The empty set

As children sort a mixture of things into two or more sets they can put them into separate boxes labelled with a suitable picture or word. Some of these classifications can be recorded by the children in drawings; each set can then be enclosed in a ring to show that all the objects in it were put into the same box. See Figure 3:11 for a classification of shapes.

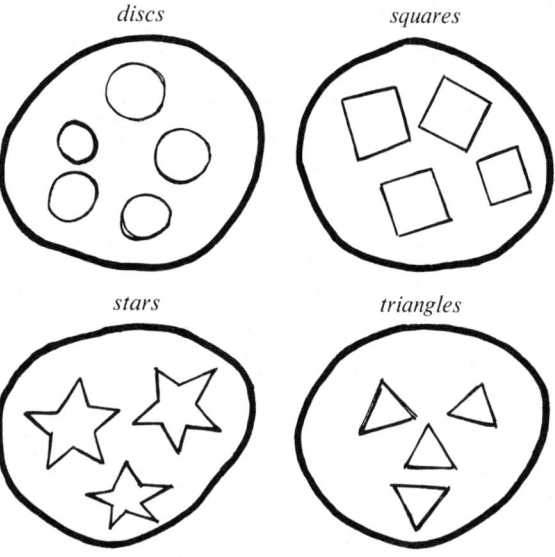

Figure 3:11

The sets can then be matched and ordered. If there are four different kinds of things in a large collection and a small haphazard handful is drawn from it, sorting this handful will sometimes show that one of the four kinds is entirely absent. Of the four boxes into which the separate sets were to be put one box is empty. The word *'empty'* and the phrase *'none at all'* should be used in talking about this situation (Figure 3:12).

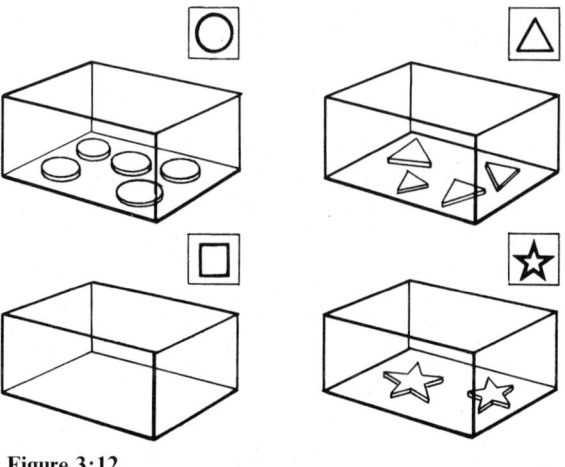

Figure 3:12

25

The box for the squares is empty; it has no squares in it at all. If the sets are ordered as before the set of squares will be the smallest; it has none at all. An empty ring is a good symbol for the number of things in *'the empty set'*[2] and the children will find it easy after these experiments to write 0 for zero when they want to state the number of things in an empty set.

Making sets

So far, many of the sets which the children have made have been the result of classifying although they have also handled sets of mixed objects during some activities. They can also *make* sets of mixed objects provided that they can say how the collection was made or what each set contains. For example, a child could make in clay a pig, a cow, a horse and a sheep to be 'the animals on my toy farm'; or he might use various tins and boxes and bricks and cotton reels to make an engine; the objects are not alike but he can say 'these are the things I used for my engine'. In these instances he can define the set although he did not begin with a classification. To show that he is thinking of these objects together he can put a ring, or curly brackets round their pictures, and if he can write their names he can put curly brackets (or braces) round them, as in Figure 3:13.

{ *horse, pig, sheep, cow* }

Figure 3:13

Enclosure in curly brackets is the conventional symbol for a set but it is for the teacher to choose whether she will introduce it now or later. Children could continue to put a ring round the objects in a set for some time to come.

Much experience of making and matching sets is needed. Examples can be taken from the life of the classroom. The names of children absent each day are written on a blackboard. Today's list is compared with yesterday's; are there more, fewer, or just as many as yesterday? Children match

---

milkbottles or plates to the children at one table. A set of spoons is matched to a set of bottles, shown in a picture, as in Figure 3:14. Pictures of sets can be widely used now as material for questions, stories and discussions.

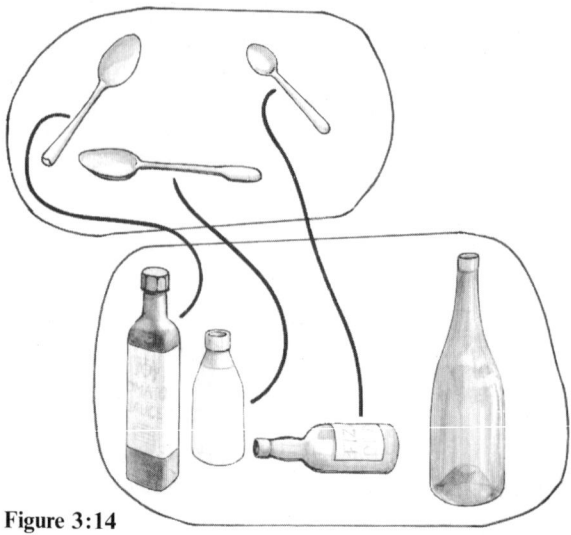

Figure 3:14

Matching sets

It will be seen that the matching of sets leads to the idea of number. When two sets can be matched exactly, each member of one set being matched by one member of the other, and no member being left unmatched, the two sets, however different their members, are said to have the same *number*. Any other set which can be matched exactly to them also has the same number. Any set of *two* things matches any other set of *two* things, and children who now know the look of two things will pick out matching sets of two things at sight. Similarly any set of *three* things matches any other set containing three members. Practice in matching such sets will build up the notion of the number three (Figure 3:15).

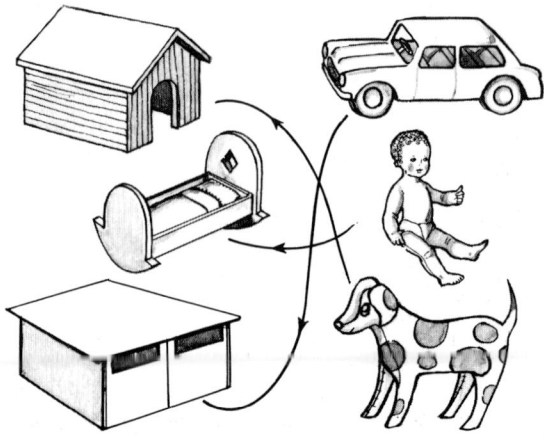

Figure 3:15

---

[2] See Chapter 8 for further discussion of the empty set.

From a number of picture sets a child can pick out the sets that match exactly. We have a special symbol for matching, or *equivalence*; it is a double-headed arrow: 'set $A \leftrightarrow$ set B' says 'set A matches set B'. In Figure 3:16 set A is not equivalent to set B or to set C, but set $B \leftrightarrow$ set C.

Figure 3:16

We do not use the equal sign for sets except when the two sets have exactly the same *members*; e.g. {dog, cat, pig} and {cat, pig, dog}. The equal sign is used for the *numbers* of members of equivalent sets, so that we can say that the *number* of set B equals the *number* of set C when set $B \leftrightarrow$ set C. Children will not need to use this statement of equality of *numbers* until the notion of number has become well established.

The idea of inclusion

Although children can clearly see that one set has more members than another and can sort and separate one class of things from a mixed collection, they do not easily recognize one special kind as *part* of the whole. To help them to form this concept they need practical experience. Among the mixed toy-farm animals in a meadow they can sort the sheep and put them all together in the middle. A fence can be put round them as shown in Figure 3:17.

Figure 3:17

The idea of *inclusion* is important for understanding both numbers and measuring. It is dealt with more fully in later chapters. Here it is sufficient to notice that a child finds it difficult to answer the question 'Are there more animals (of all kinds) than there are sheep?', but he sees that there are other animals as well as sheep and is therefore beginning to see that sheep form part of the whole set of animals and that animals *include* sheep. Various activities and discussions are required to build up this part-whole or inclusion idea. For example, the family includes the children; the children include 'me', 'my brother', 'my sister'. Poleidoblocs contain a set of pointed shapes (pyramids and cones) which can be placed together among the rest. When a child begins to recognize numbers greater than two he must come to realize that a set of three things includes a set of two things, a set of four things includes a set of three things·and also includes a set of two things; for example, Figure 3:18 shows the sets of two things which are included in set A.

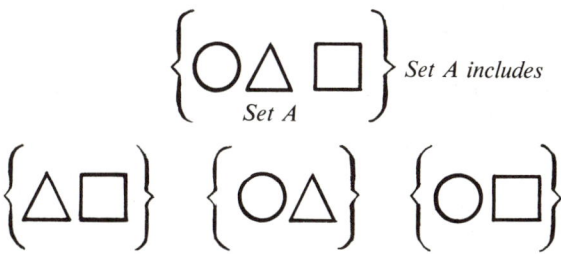

Figure 3:18

Discovering three

Through continued handling of sets with more or fewer members, a child is growing more aware of the number property of sets, and he will soon be ready to count. Meanwhile he will almost certainly have learned to recognize the look of three things, realizing that three is one more than two. The visual patterns which a set of three things can make are basically of only two kinds, either a row or a triangle (Figure 3:19).

Figure 3:19

These patterns show three as one and one and one, and also as two and one (or one and two). The three of a family, 'me' and 'Mum' and 'Dad', is a basic grouping and there will be many occasions for matching it with other sets of three. The patterns made by three are easily recognized and recalled and therefore children quickly learn the number name, *three*, and the numeral, *3*. They will use them for all the sets of three things they encounter. A child can now name the order of sets of one, two and three members and the sequence becomes very familiar; it may even suggest to a child that it could be followed farther (Figure 3:20).

Figure 3:20

Experimenting with a set of coloured rods such as Cuisenaire or Colour Factor may lead to an ordering of the rods according to their length (*see page 38*). This emphasizes a sequence which increases by equal steps. Before the number names from one to ten are taught it is well to establish the equivalence of the two-rod to two unit cubes; a set of three cubes can be replaced by the three-rod. Thereafter the sequence may be carried farther, when the child is ready.

Discovering four

Four is easily recognized when a set of four things is in view. Its patterns are simple (Figure 3:21).

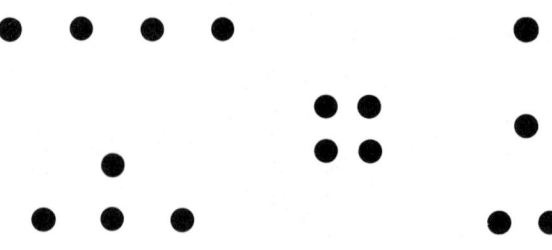

Figure 3:21

These patterns are seen as

i) one and one and one and one
ii) three and one (or one and three)
iii) two and two
iv) one and one and two (or two and one and one).

Shapes made with rods, sticks and strips will also illustrate these patterns.

Sets of one, two, three and four members can now be put in order and matched with their numbers, the names and numerals being attached. Any four objects in a set can now be matched with the four number symbols in whatever order we choose to select them (Figure 3:22).

A child frequently meets 'four': four children at a table, 'Mum' and 'Dad' and 'me' and 'my sister', a square made by four equal rods. There are plenty of opportunities for using four both practically and in imaginative play.

Matching number names to sets: ordinal numbers first to fourth

The order of the first four number names is learned quickly and it is the matching of these names in order to each of four things in turn which probably constitutes a child's first true count. As he counts, touching or moving each thing as he says 'one, two, three, four', he is using the idea of order, matching the order of the number names to the order in which he touches the things. If four children are asked to come to the teacher, the order in which they come may lead to using the ordinal numbers *first, second, third,*

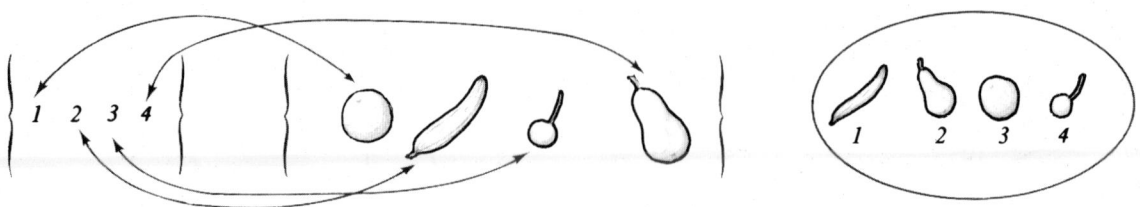

Figure 3:22

fourth, linking each to the name of a child. If children at a table are asked to see who can do something very quickly, the ordinal numbers, first, second, etc. will be used as they hurry to finish. At this point they can also learn another ordinal number, *last.* The way in which the counting (cardinal) numbers and the ordering (ordinal) numbers become connected in a child's mind is discussed on pages 67 to 69. At the present stage the children's experience of them is entirely practical. They are learning through this experience the vocabulary of counting and ordering the small sets in which they can recognize the number of members on sight.

Learning the sequence of number names

The social situations in a classroom provide children with many reasons for counting small numbers and also matching larger sets. Some interesting experiences occur when they compare the capacities of jars and jugs by recording cupfuls, or compare the heights of two growing plants seen against squared paper. Such opportunities should be fully used. As is pointed out in Chapter 5, comparisons of quantity extend the notion of number beyond that attached to a set of separate objects. Both kinds of experience should be available to children at this stage. Children appreciate not only the practical use of counting; they also enjoy the patterns and rhythms which reflect the structures of numbers and their sequences.

The number names up to twenty will be learned by most children before they have understood the meaning of a number such as nine or seventeen. The reciting of the *sequence* one, two, three, . . . , nineteen, twenty can establish the pattern of sound-names which will presently need to be used. It is a valuable acquisition so long as the teacher does not assume that because a child can repeat the names he knows how to use the numbers. The time spent in handling uncounted sets and the first four counting sets gives a foundation of confident understanding which makes for continued interest and rapid learning in later years. It ensures that symbols are always introduced to describe something that a child has made or discovered. These symbols have a meaning and can therefore be used to describe similar situations or to make new discoveries.

4 Classification, Sets and the Beginning of Structure

Types of classification

Through his sorting and other activities a young child is building up mental patterns which are fundamental both for mathematics and for the logical thinking which he will develop later. Piaget believes[1] that children's thinking, by the stage of concrete operations, has itself a logical and mathematical structure which becomes more complex in successive stages of development.

If a teacher understands the type of mental structure which a child is capable of constructing at a particular stage in his development, he may be able to provide experience which will enable the child to develop more rapidly or more easily. It is not yet known how far experience planned by the teacher can influence the development of mental structures, nor whether it is necessarily desirable to attempt to force the development. But the parallel study of mathematical structure and of the development of thinking in children must illuminate the teaching of mathematics. If a child has not reached a stage when he can handle the logical structure of a topic in mathematics he will not be able to understand it, or to learn it other than by rote. The teacher will find that the three strands:

  i) the structure of mathematics,
  ii) the analysis of logical thinking,
  iii) the psychology of children's mental development,

all throw light on one another, and on the variety of experiences which children need in their mathematics learning.

In Chapter 1 we gave an outline of the stages of children's mental development in the light of the investigations of Piaget and others. We now try to relate that mental development to some of the logical and mathematical structures which the young child is building up. We also begin to develop a language and a symbolism which can be used to describe these structures.

As he plays with different materials, experiments with his surroundings, sorts through his toys, talks to his family, and begins to notice similarities and differences, a young child is gradually forming in his mind two interrelated systems of classification. One is non-numerical. This will be used to establish patterns and relationships among the objects in his world and provide a framework for the logical thinking which he will later develop. The second will lead to numerical experiences.

When a child sorts through a box of materials and separates out the buttons from the other things in it, he is setting up the (non-numerical) classification of the *class of buttons*. Buttons have certain properties in common which distinguish them from everything else in the world. As a child learns to name things correctly and to apply the names with greater discrimination, so his system of classification becomes more organized. The word 'motor car' implies the existence of the *class of motor cars*, but the child will then distinguish the *class of lorries*, the *class of buses*, and the *class of milk vans* from the class of motor cars, so giving the classification a finer structure.

The question 'How many?' is not a question which a child will ask about this general class of motor cars. The only sensible question is 'Is this a car?'; that is, 'Does this particular object belong to the class of motor cars?'

But alongside the developing power of classification comes the idea that some classes or sets[2] contain more or fewer things than others (*see page* 38). The class of dogs cannot be compared numerically with the class of cats, because it is not a *practical* possibility to count all the cats and dogs in the world, although *theoretically* they form a limited set which could be counted. All that a child can do is to decide whether an animal belongs, say, to the class of dogs or the class of cats; but the set of cups on the table can be compared numerically with the set of saucers on the table. When we form the general concept of the class of dogs, we take no account of any characteristic of the animals other than their quality of being dogs. But the objects in the set of cups on the table can be distinguished from one another by their position, or by the order in which they are pointed to or thought of, and so the set of cups can be compared quantitatively with other sets.

When we *count,* the members of a set must be put into an order by the very act of counting, but when we *classify,* the members of the class need not be ordered in any way.

When a child first uses the idea, a *set* is a collection of *things*. In everyday language he has many names for sets:

a flock of sheep	a pair of gloves
a class of children[3]	a train set or a tea-set

[2] We shall, as far as possible, use the word *class* for a general classification, and *set* when the members are regarded as distinguishable and the set can be compared numerically with other sets.

[3] It is unfortunate the word 'class' is used for a limited set of children who are taught together, when *the class of children* is the general classification for all human beings under a certain age.

[1] See, for instance, Piaget, J. *Logic and Psychology.*

but when he talks in school about sets of things, he will use the word 'set' more and more as the mathematical name for a collection. A set may have many or few members. The set consisting of the staff of a one-teacher school has a single member; the set consisting of all the cars on the roads of the world at the present moment has very many members; and the set consisting of all the points which go to make up a line has infinitely many members.

When defining a set, it is necessary that such a clear description of it be given that the question 'Does any particular object belong to the set?' can always be answered with an unequivocal yes or no. 'The set of boys' needs an upper age limit for complete definition, but the set consisting of 'all the boys in this school' leaves no doubt, for the registers can be consulted.

A set can usually be defined in one of two ways, either by making a list of its members,[4] or by giving some property by which those members can be distinguished.[5] The set, all of whose members have the property of belonging to a particular school, can equally well be defined by giving a list of their names. The set whose members are the odd numbers less than 10 can equally well be described as the set whose members are 1, 3, 5, 7, 9.

As children grow older they extend their idea of a set. At first, the members of a set must have a common quality.[6] A young child will count 4 cups on the table, but does not yet realize that he can count a set of things which are not alike, and it is only later that he will count a set consisting of a cup, a saucer and two knives as a set of 4 objects. The members of a set need have no inherent common property; all that is necessary is that they should be separated in thought from everything else in the world. An understanding of this point is needed for the understanding of addition, for when a child combines two sets, such as a set of red bricks and a set of blue bricks, he can only add if he can see the red and the blue bricks together as one total set which can be counted.

Children also extend their idea of a set by realizing that the members of a set need not necessarily be *things*.

By the end of their junior school years many children can hold in their minds the ideas of such sets as

the set of multiples of 2
the set of prime numbers
the set of shapes which a child could draw.

All of these are abstract, unlimited sets. The members of a set may themselves be sets. Each class of a school is a set of children, and a head teacher will sometimes think of his school as a set of classes. The conscious organization of sets into hierarchies in this way is a somewhat sophisticated mental development, but it is inherent in the structure of our number system. A ten is a set of ones; a hundred is a set of tens; and a thousand is a set of hundreds.

It seems likely that the handling of structural apparatus such as the Dienes Multibase Arithmetic Blocks (*see page* 160), where a 'hundred' can be changed for ten 'tens' or for a hundred 'ones', may help children in the hierarchical organization of sets. For some time, however, children using the apparatus appear to keep in mind only two adjacent types of unit at the same time, changing 'ones' for 'rods' (*see page* 159), and then to focus on another adjacent pair and change 'rods' for 'layers'. The understanding that a thousand is at the same time ten hundreds, a hundred tens and a thousand ones comes fairly late.

It now becomes clear that a set is not the same as its members. A choir is not the same as the individual members of the choir. They have become a unity and can be thought of as a single body. A set of ten things, the object which teachers call 'a ten', is different from ten isolated things. It is because the separate objects can be held in the mind as a unity that they are said to have the structure of a set.

The relationship between a set and its members is very well illustrated by the type of structural apparatus known as Unifix (*see page* 70), which consists of interlocking plastic cubes. A child who makes a set of cubes does not have to hold in mind that the cubes form a set, but can physically lock those cubes together into a unity (Figure 4:1) or break the set apart into its elements, thus symbolizing the relationship between the set and the members from which it is composed.

[4] Definition *by extension*.

[5] Definition *by intension*. Inhelder and Piaget, in *The Early Growth of Logic in the Child*, describe some difficulties which young children encounter in relating these two methods of classification.

[6] That is, the set is part of a *class*.

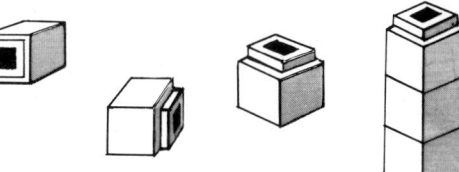

Figure 4:1

Subsets and the inclusion relation

Diagrams can often help the visualization of relationships between sets (*see plate 5*). Figure 4:2 shows the method which a class used to show the relationships between various *subsets* of itself, the girls, the children wearing dark jerseys, and those wearing black wellingtons.[7]

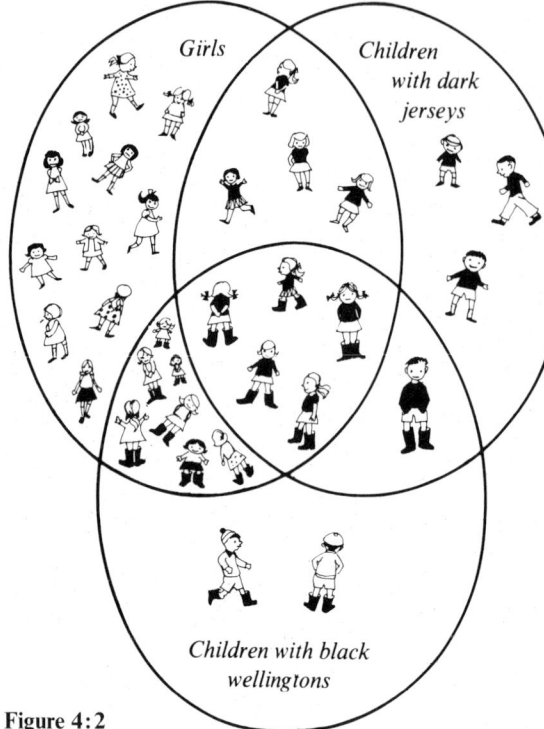

Figure 4:2

At first, children will need to draw or symbolize the members of a set within the 'fence' which separates the things which belong to the set from those which do not, but later they will come to see the space inside the fence as a symbol for the set, containing as many or as few members as necessary. Diagrams of this second type are called *Venn diagrams*. Figure 4:3 shows the relationship between a set of children and a subset of them who stay to school dinner.

When any set is defined, the words 'the set of' will always be needed, and it simplifies the writing to use a symbol for the words 'the set of'. The usual symbol is a pair of curly brackets { }, and

$$C = \text{the set of children in Class I}$$
is abbreviated $C = \{\text{children in Class I}\}$

The brackets show that we have in mind the *set of children*, rather than the individual children. The other set shown in Figure 4:3 can be written

$$D = \{\text{children in Class I who stay to school dinner}\}$$

---

[7] Another way in which classification into subsets can be recorded is shown in Figures 3:7 and 3:8.

32

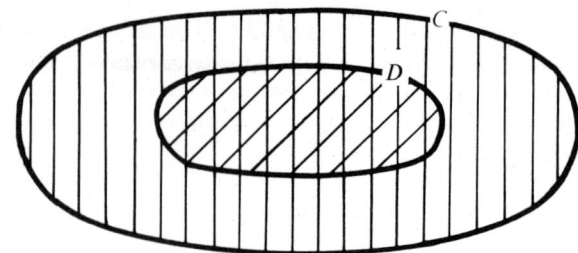

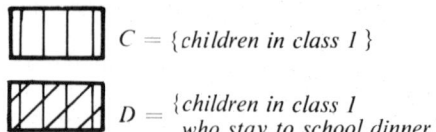

$C = \{children\ in\ class\ 1\}$

$D = \{children\ in\ class\ 1\ who\ stay\ to\ school\ dinner\}$

Figure 4:3

It is clear from the diagram that set D is contained in set C; this relationship will be written $D \subseteq C$, where the symbol $\subseteq$ means 'is contained in'.

To define the relationship more generally, we say that set A *is contained* or *included in* set B if every member of set A is also a member of set B (Figure 4:4). A is also called a *subset* of B.

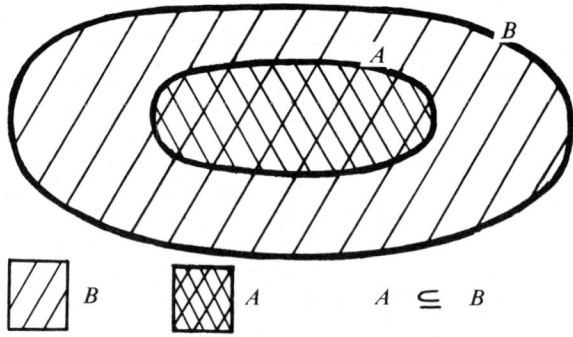

B A $A \subseteq B$

Figure 4:4

When a child eats some of his sweets, the set of sweets he eats is a subset of the set of sweets he had. If

$$E = \{\text{sweets which John has eaten today}\}$$
and $S = \{\text{sweets which John originally had}\}$,

then $E \subseteq S$. Of course, John may have eaten all his sweets, but even in that case $E \subseteq S$, as every sweet which John ate is one which he had. But it is now also true that $S \subseteq E$, as every sweet which John had is one he ate. Then the two sets have exactly the same members, and are equal to each other: $S = E$ if $S \subseteq E$ and $E \subseteq S$.

This relation between two sets, that one set is contained or included in the other one, is of fundamental importance. A child's set of yellow bricks is contained in his set of bricks of various colours, and the set of children at his working table is contained in the set of children in his class. It is only as he begins to understand the relation of inclusion that he can begin to construct a coherent mental structure for his world. He can now understand and think with relations such as

i) all sheep are animals, but there are animals which are not sheep;
ii) a set of 2 things can be included in a set of 5 things, which leads to $5 = 2+3$;
iii) all squares are rectangles, but not all rectangles are squares.

It is only a short step from the understanding of these ideas to the construction of a logical train of thought which he might, but will probably not, put in such words as 'I should like to sleep in a tent'; 'the scout troop sleeps in tents when it goes camping; therefore I want to join the Scout troop'. This train of thought, with its relations of inclusion, is symbolized by the Venn diagram of Figure 4:5.

Figure 4:5

Piaget sees in the mastery of the inclusion relation between sets an essential difference between the pre-operational stage of intuitive thinking and the concrete-operational stage of thinking. The child at the concrete-operational stage can hold in his mind completely the relation between a set and its subsets, and can think reversibly about the relationship, whereas at the previous stage when he fixed his attention on a subset he lost contact with the whole set which included it.

The following situation, which illustrates this difficulty, is equivalent to an experiment described by Piaget.[8] Children were shown a collection of brightly-coloured green sweets, most of which were wrapped in transparent cellophane, but a few were unwrapped. The conversation given is typical of a child of five or six who is at the stage of intuitive thinking:

> What colour are the wrapped sweets?—*Green*—What colour are the unwrapped sweets?—*Green*—Are there more green sweets or more wrapped sweets?—*More wrapped*—But aren't these green too? (pointing to the unwrapped sweets)—*Oh yes*—Well then, are there more green sweets or more wrapped sweets?—*More wrapped sweets.*

[8] Piaget, J. *The Child's Conception of Number.*

This child is not yet able to move backwards and forwards in thought between the set of green sweets and its subset of wrapped sweets. When he thinks of the wrapped sweets the only other set he can see at the same time is the set of those which are not wrapped, so it is this set which he compares with the set of wrapped sweets.

A child who has reached the stage of concrete operations reacts to the same situation with complete comprehension, knowing without doubt that there are more green sweets because the unwrapped ones are green too.

The evidence available suggests that six-year-old children who have been specifically encouraged at school to sort things into sets and to look for relationships between sets appear to be rather more advanced and more confident in their understanding of this and similar situations than those whose mathematical work has been more traditional in character.

Partitioning a set

A particularly important example of the formation of subsets occurs when a set or class is broken up into non-overlapping subsets. The class of children is made up of the class of boys and the class of girls, and these have no members in common. We say that these subclasses form a *partition* of the class of children. The set of books in the classroom library can be partitioned into fiction and non-fiction, but the classes of fiction and picture books do not partition the set of books; they may have some members in common. A partition is a separation of a set into non-overlapping subsets in such a way that every member of the original set belongs to just one of the subsets. In the previous section, the set of sweets was partitioned in two different ways, into wrapped sweets and unwrapped sweets, and into green sweets and non-green sweets. The child could not cope with these two partitionings at the same time.

The logical multiplication of classes, and the intersection of sets

As a child becomes more skilled in making sets from the things around him, he begins to think of the property defining a set first, and then to collect all the objects belonging to that set. He soon begins to do this in more than one way, and to hold two different qualities in mind at the same time, so forming the class of things which belong to *both* of two classes. He can think, when sorting beads, of a class of black beads, or he may sort according to shape and obtain a class of round beads. The logical multiplication of these classes gives the class of round black beads. This process of logical multiplication gives rise to several classes. If the beads are either black or white, and either round or square, the process of holding in mind

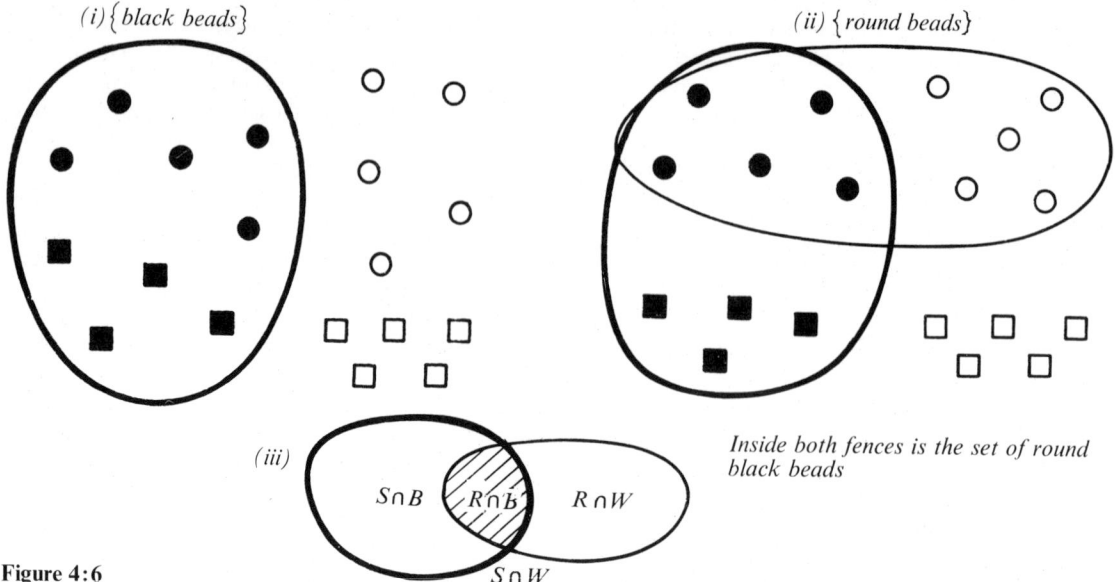

(i) {black beads}

(ii) {round beads}

Inside both fences is the set of round black beads

(iii)

$S \cap B$ $R \cap B$ $R \cap W$

$S \cap W$

Figure 4:6

both colour and shape at the same time gives rise to four classes: round black beads, round white beads, square black beads and square white beads.

A child who is sorting a limited set of beads may find the device of drawing a fence around those beads which belong to the same set helpful (Figure 4:6).

The set of beads which belongs to *both* the black set and the round set is called the *intersection* of the black set and the round set. The symbol ∩ is often used for intersection so that the intersection of the black and round sets may be written $R \cap B$ (Figure 4:7).[9]

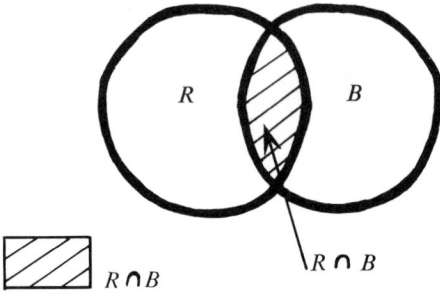

$R \cap B$

$R \cap B$

Figure 4:7

For Piaget, reasoning consists in the ability to handle such relationships as these, and he says:

'Just as arithmetical, algebraic or geometrical reasoning consists of combining objects (numbers, signs or figures) by means of the operations of arithmetic, algebra or spatial construction, so in the case of classi-

fication, reasoning consists of combining objects by means of operations on classes (logical addition and multiplication, etc.), and in this grouping of objects and classes in hierarchical systems, or separating them one from another.'[10]

Attribute Blocks such as those of Z. P. Dienes have been designed to give much experience of the intersection of sets and other operations on sets thus leading children towards an understanding of logical relations. Dienes' blocks have the four attributes of shape, colour, size and thickness, and can be put into sets by using any combination of these properties. A child can form the set of large blocks and the set of square blocks, and the intersection is the set of large square blocks. Each block has a name, such as the large thick red square block, describing its four characteristics, and many games can be devised which enable children to manipulate combinations of the basic sets into which the blocks fall. For instance, in the 'one-difference game' a train of blocks is built in which each block must differ in exactly one attribute from its neighbours (Figure 4:8). There are 48 blocks in all, each one of which represents the intersection of four basic sets. Thus

$$\begin{Bmatrix} \text{large thick red} \\ \text{triangular block} \end{Bmatrix} = \begin{Bmatrix} \text{large} \\ \text{blocks} \end{Bmatrix} \cap \begin{Bmatrix} \text{thick} \\ \text{blocks} \end{Bmatrix}$$
$$\cap \begin{Bmatrix} \text{red} \\ \text{blocks} \end{Bmatrix} \cap \begin{Bmatrix} \text{triangular} \\ \text{blocks} \end{Bmatrix}$$

Other apparatus can also be used to give similar experiences, and the children themselves can form sets with properties such as

staying to dinner
having a pet

[9] 'Intersection' is of course merely another name for logical product. The words 'union' and 'intersection' are commonly used by mathematicians, who find it convenient to use terms which do not carry the arithmetical associations from which the words 'sum' and 'product' cannot be divorced.

[10] Piaget, J. *The Child's Conception of Number*, page 180.

34

The 'one-difference game'

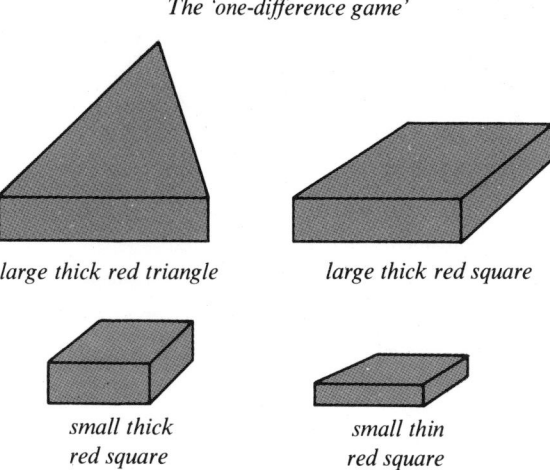

large thick red triangle   *large thick red square*

*small thick
red square*   *small thin
red square*

Figure 4:8

having brothers, sisters, both, or neither
wearing a red jersey, a blue jersey, or neither of these.

The logical addition of classes, and the union of sets

Another operation with which children come to terms at the stage of concrete operations is that of the *logical addition* of classes. If two different classes are combined the result is a new *kind* of class. This method of combination is *logical addition*. For example the class of animals added to the class of *plants* forms the class of *living things*. This is a statement about the *classes* without reference to the *numbers* in the classes. This logical addition is a mental operation on the classes, not on the things themselves. It is also *reversible*; that is, the class of living things with the class of plants excluded is the class of animals. The operation also depends on an understanding of the idea of inclusion, for both the class of animals and the class of plants are included in the class of living things.

Logical addition of classes is independent of number, and is a reversible mental operation which follows earlier experience of classifying sets of objects in this way. For example, the set of triangular Attribute Blocks can be partitioned into the three subsets of red triangular blocks, blue triangular blocks and yellow triangular blocks, and these can be recombined into the complete set of triangular blocks.

In this case, the subsets do not overlap, but the operation of combining subsets can be performed even if the subsets have some members in common. The operation of combining two sets in this way is called forming the *union of the sets*. For instance, within a school, there will be some children who have cats at home, and some who have dogs.

Let $C = \{$children who have cats$\}$
and $D = \{$children who have dogs$\}$

Then the *union of set C and set D* is

{children who have cats or dogs at home}

This set is written $C \cup D$, and is illustrated by the Venn diagram shown in Figure 4:9.

In general, the union of two sets A and B is the set whose members are members *either* of *A or B* or *both*.

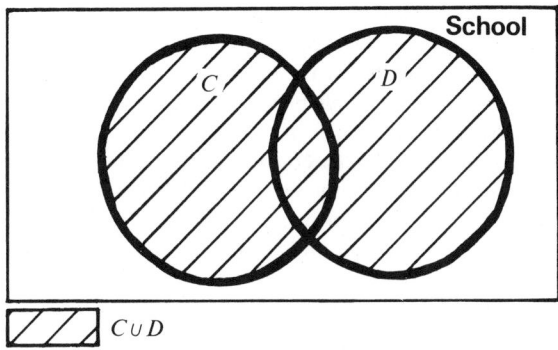

Figure 4:9

The operation of forming the union of two sets is clearly only another way of stating the operation of the logical addition of classes, and is closely related to the arithmetical operation of adding numbers. It is, however, a more general idea than that of adding numbers. No counting is involved: the actual *sets* are combined rather than the *numbers* of things in them, and indeed the number of things in the union may very well be less than the sum of the numbers of things in the original sets. For instance, some children may have both cats and dogs. If 15 children have cats and 7 have dogs, the number with cats or dogs may be 22, but it may very well be less. If 4 children have both cats and dogs, there will only be 18 in the set of those who have cats or dogs at home.

This type of overlapping classification occurs frequently. The set of children in a class may be divided into three sets:

 $B = \{$children with brothers$\}$
 $S = \{$children with sisters$\}$
 $N = \{$children without brothers or sisters$\}$

The relations between those sets are shown in Figure 4:10, and children seem able to handle this classification with

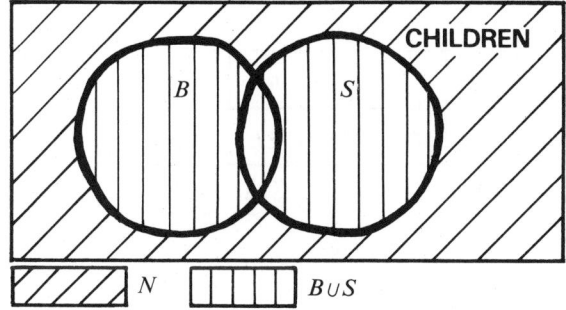

Figure 4:10 $B \cup S = \{$*children with brothers or sisters*$\}$

35

confidence at the concrete-operational stage and to realize that the simple addition of numbers is inappropriate to it.

Relations between sets

As children become familiar with classification into sets, they see that often the members of two sets are related together. For example, the fact that some children have dogs as pets, some have cats, and some have jerbils, makes a linking process possible between the set of children and the set of animals (Figure 4:11). David has a dog and a cat, Elizabeth has a jerbil, Peter has a cat, and nobody has an elephant. The arrows linking the members of the sets all stand for *has as a pet*. Such a set of links is called a *relation* between the two sets. Children will find very many relations between the sets they make. The set of children is

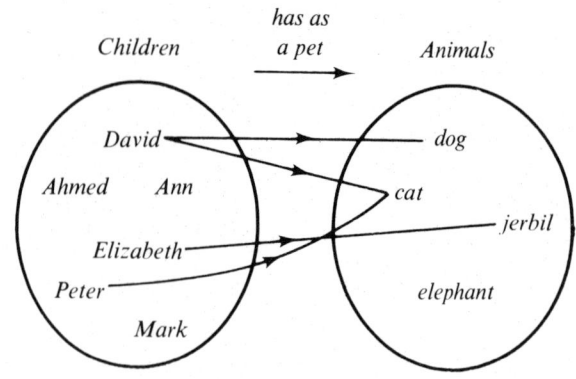

Figure 4:11

related to the set of months in which they have their birthdays, and to the set of colours of their jerseys, and to

(i)

Books — has been read by → Children

Dr. Doolittle
Railway Children
Paddington
Iron Man
Mary Plain

Ahmed
Mary
John
Liz
Dave
Peter
Mike

(ii)

		Ahmed		
		Mary		
Liz		John		
Dave		Liz		Mary
Ahmed		Dave		Mike
Peter	Liz	Peter	John	Liz
John	Mary	Mike	Liz	Dave
Dr. Doolittle	Railway Children	Paddington	Iron Man	Mary Plain

(iii)

	Dr. Doolittle	Railway Children	Paddington	Iron Man	Mary Plain			
Ahmed	■		■					
Mary		■	■		■			
John	■		■	■				
Liz	■	■	■	■	■			
Dave	■				■			
Peter	■		■					
Mike			■		■			

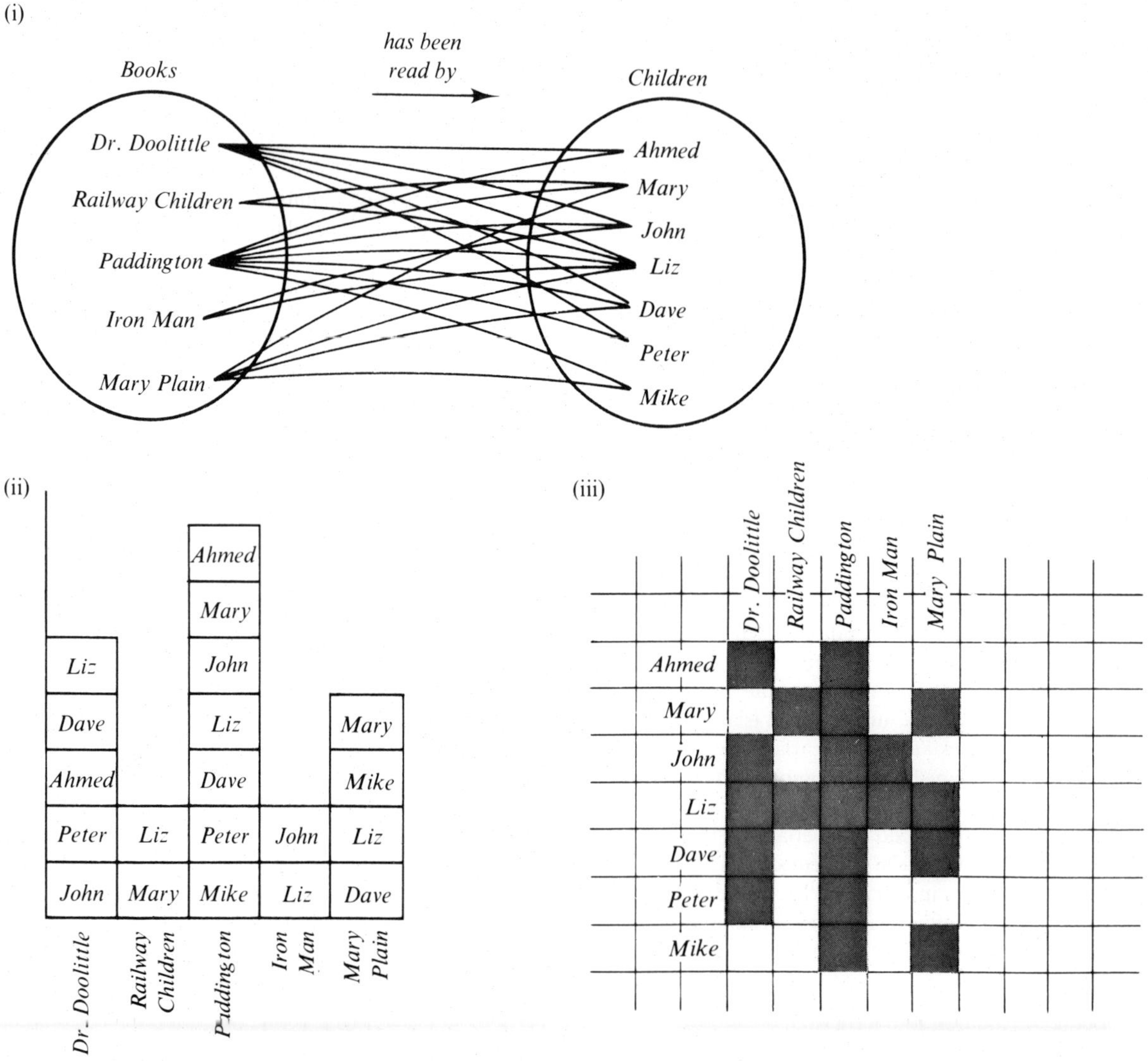

Figure 4:12

36

the set of foods they may have at teatime, and to many other sets. The set of books in the classroom is related to the set of children by the relation 'has been read by', or to the set of numbers by the relation 'the number of pages in . . . is . . .'. Children should be encouraged to find such relations between sets, and to record them in some of the ways shown in Figure 4:12.

Much work in mathematics depends on the study of relations between sets; counting, in particular, is concerned with a very simple relation between sets, that of *one-one correspondence*. This is discussed on pages 38 and 39.

Relations between the members of a single set

The set of children at a table can record their relation to various other sets such as the set of books, but they can also think of themselves as related to each other. For example, they can make a record of the children whom they sit next to. This can be shown in a number of ways (Figure 4:13).

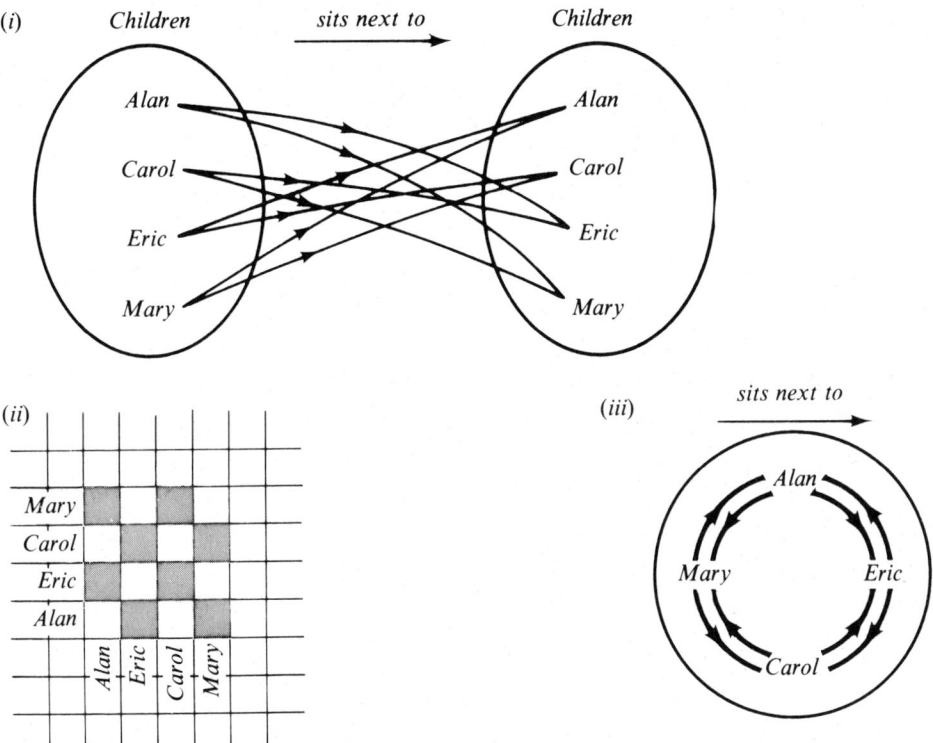

Figure 4:13

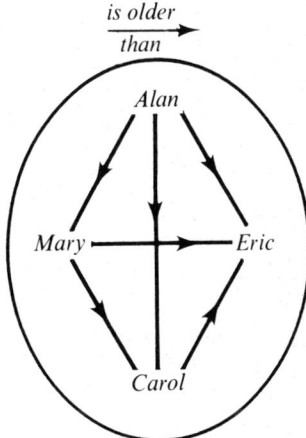

Figure 4:14

The last diagram, in which the set is only shown once, and each member is linked to those members related to it, is probably the clearest. The relation 'is older than' is rather more complicated than 'sits next to', for if Alan is older than Carol, and Carol is older than Eric, then also Alan is older than Eric (Figure 4:14).

In order to find this statement obvious, a child needs to hold the two facts in mind at the same time, and must recognize intuitively that the transitive[11] relation holds. We shall not expect him to be able to do this until the stage of concrete operations, when he will be able to handle with confidence, using concrete materials, combinations of relations such as these.

[11] See page 435.

The logical addition and multiplication of relations

As he moves into the concrete-operational stage of thought, we see that a child not only learns, with concrete materials, to handle logical operations on the combination of classes, but also begins to use very similar logical operations on the *relations* between objects belonging to a class. Some further examples of the logical addition and multiplication of relations are now given.

i) *Logical addition of relations*
   A relation which children recognize at a very early age is that of 'bigger than' or 'smaller than'. As we have seen (*see page* 8), they use it to arrange things in a sequence, each thing bigger (or smaller) than that which precedes it. A child who has made a 'staircase' from bricks or rods of different lengths, such as those found in the Cuisenaire or Stern apparatus (*see plate 1a*), so that each rod in the staircase is longer than the one before it, will eventually be able mentally to combine all the relations which he can see between neighbouring rods. He will then know, without direct comparison,

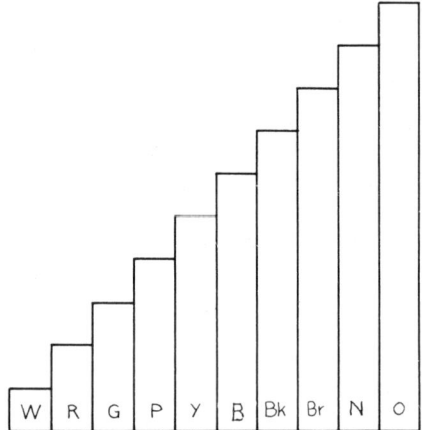

| W | R | G | P | Y | B | Bk | Br | N | O |

Figure 4:15

that because the orange rod is longer than the navy blue rod and the navy blue rod is longer than the brown rod, that it follows that the orange rod is longer than the brown rod, and so on all the way down the staircase. In symbols, if > is used to mean 'is longer than' then the child knows that

if $O > N$ and $N > Br$,   then $O > Br$.

At this stage he is able to *add logically* all the relations between pairs of neighbouring rods.

   Similarly, a series of several blocks of different weights may now be arranged in order of increasing weight by putting pairs of them in the opposite pans of a balance to find which of the pair is heavier.

ii) *Logical multiplication of relations*
   If two *different* relations have to be taken into account

at the same time they are said to be multiplied. At the pre-operational stage a child is unable to hold in mind more than one relation at a time, so that he is unable to compare, for instance, the capacities of two jugs which differ in width as well as in height. He may indeed think that if the water is poured out of one container into a narrower container (Figure 4:16), so that the water level becomes higher, there is now more water. At a later stage he is able to take into account at the same time both the greater height and the smaller base, and so to recognize that the volume is unaltered by the change in its shape. This grasp of the *logical multiplication of relations* is a characteristic of the concrete-operational stage of thinking.

Figure 4:16

One-one correspondence: the emergence of number

Alongside the development of the structure of classes, sets and relations, the idea of number is growing in a young child's mind. Logically, he must first be able to isolate a set of objects in his mind as an unchanging whole, which is unaffected by any rearrangement of them, before he can understand the property of a set which we call *number*. In practice, the development of the idea of number seems to proceed alongside the development of classification, and to be based both on classification, and on two relations involving sets. These are *one-one correspondences* between the members of two sets, and the *seriation*, or putting into a serial order, of the members of a set.

   Children can set up a one-one correspondence between the members of two sets before they can count. A child who lays a table for a meal will do so without counting by putting a spoon in front of each chair, and so setting up a one-one correspondence between the set of chairs and the set of spoons. He may be able to give out pencils to his class, and say that there are not enough, long before he can count the children in the class. He has tried to set up a one-one correspondence between the set of children and the set of pencils. The knowledge that two sets have the same number of things in them is more fundamental than knowing what that number is. Two sets *contain the same number of things* or *have the same number* if their members can be put in one-one correspondence with each other. In the same way, *'more'* and *'fewer'* are fundamental ideas which do not involve counting.

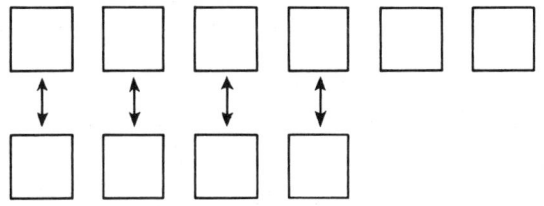

Figure 4:17

The sets of bricks in Figure 4:17 cannot be put into one-one correspondence. A child who cannot yet count how many there are in each set can decide that the upper set has *more* and the lower set *fewer*.

For a child at the stage of intuitive thinking, appearances can interfere with the achievement of one-one correspondence. A game involving the matching of eggs and egg-cups, given by Piaget,[12] shows a stage at which the correspondence between two sets is global and intuitive, rather than one-one. The egg-cups are arranged in a row and the child is asked to take enough eggs for the egg-cups, and to put each egg in front of its cup. These same eggs are then moved closer together, so that they make a shorter line, and the child is asked if there are now enough eggs for the egg-cups. A young child, aged 4 or 5, at the stage of intuitive thinking, will often judge the eggs on overall appearance, not realizing the importance of the one-one correspondence he has made between eggs and cups, and will say that there are not now enough eggs.

At the next stage, a child has completely grasped that mere changes of position do not alter the number of things in a set, and, with the one-one correspondence in mind, has no doubt that the eggs still match the cups.

When a child begins to count, he must learn to say the names of the first members of the number sequence in the correct order. This is not counting, in any real sense of the word, but it gives him a permanent, invariable set of sounds which can be put in one-one correspondence with any set of things he wishes to count. He goes along his set of bricks, pointing to each one in turn and saying a number name as he points. He is actually physically setting up a one-one correspondence between the bricks and the sounds at the beginning of the number sequence.

The unending sequence of number names is always available for the setting up of a one-one correspondence, but only the beginning of the sequence is ever used in any actual counting operation. As the number names are always used in the same order, the last one which has been named can then be used to describe the whole set of things. So a child says 'four bricks' to describe the fact that he has set up a one-one correspondence between the set of bricks and the set of words 'one, two, three, four'.

A young child sometimes fails to count correctly because he does not yet understand the importance of an exact one-one correspondence, and is merely imitating an activity which he has seen. He says a number word while making a vague movement with his hand, without making the sound correspond with any object, or else he passes over an object without saying a number word.

Seriation

The process of counting or pointing to the objects in a set demands the operation of *seriation* or *ordering* of the set. The objects must be pointed to one after the other, that is, in an order. This seriation, which involves the logical addition of relations, is well understood at the concrete-operational stage. The following are some examples of seriations which children at this stage will handle.

i) A set of children may draw round their feet and cut out the resulting footprints. They can now arrange several of these cut-outs on a graph in order of length, and each child will be able to relate the size of his feet to those of the other children (Figure 4:19).

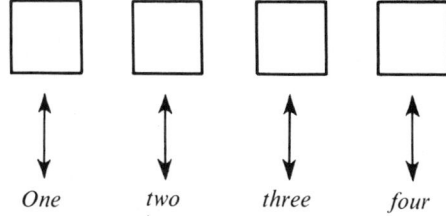

One   two   three   four

Figure 4:18

[12] Piaget, J. *The Child's Conception of Number*, Chapter III.

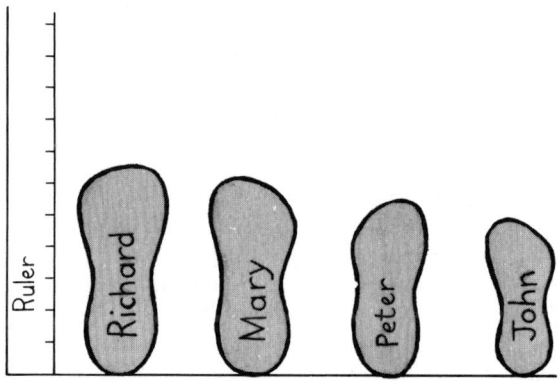

Figure 4:19

ii) When children play a game such as skittles and each player has several turns, each child may record his score at each turn by colouring a row of squares on a graph to represent the number he has scored (Figure 4:20). After each turn the children will know who is first, who is second, and so on, by comparing the lengths of their coloured rows, although these are not arranged in order of increasing size.

Figure 4:20

iii) A record is kept, and a block graph made from the growth in length each week of a young animal, a kitten or hamster, for example. A child at this stage understands the matching of the sequences of weeks and lengths, and can make deductions from the graph.

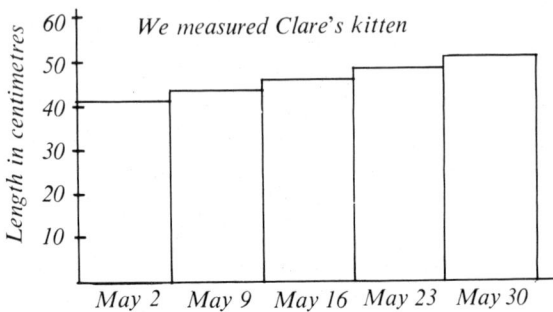

Figure 4:21

In these examples, a correct ordering is inherent in the material which the child is using. But when he counts a set, any ordering will do. He may count the set in either of the ways shown in Figure 4:22, or in several other ways, and the one one correspondence with the set of number names always stops at the same word. This realization, too, can only come from experience and experiment with the rearrangement of sets.

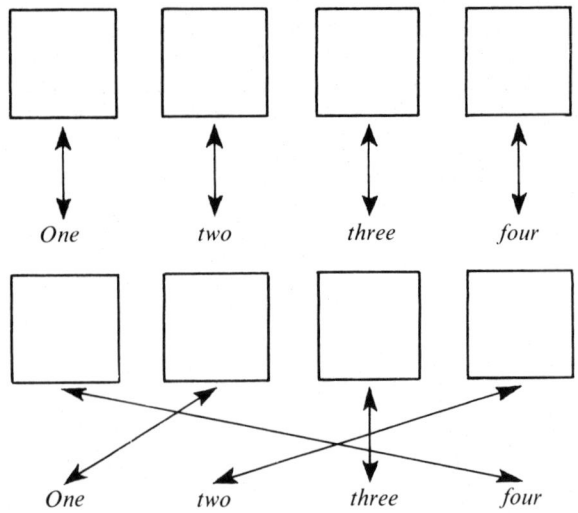

Figure 4:22

The grouping structure of operations

We have tried to show how, as a child's understanding increases, he becomes able to perform mentally certain operations on classes or sets, and on relations, out of which develops an understanding of numbers and operations on them. The structure and behaviour of operations on numbers is the subject-matter of a large part of mathematics, and we shall see later[13] how close is the parallel between the mathematical structure of numbers and the thought-structure which is within a child's capacity when he handles real things at the concrete-operational stage. The following five properties are involved in the thought-structure of logical operations which Piaget calls a *grouping*, and which he suggests are characteristic of a child's thinking at the stage of concrete operations.

i) *Composition.* Two mental operations such as classification or relation can be combined, compounded or taken account of at the same time by a process such as logical addition. In the set of living things, $A \cup P = L$ (*see page* 35).

ii) *Reversibility.* Combinations are reversible. $A \cup P = L$, for example, can be reversed into L *without* P *is* A.

iii) *An operation can be cancelled by its opposite.* If a set of red beads is united with a set of blue beads, this operation can be cancelled by removing the red beads. Symbolically if B is the class of blue beads and R the class of red beads, the effect of the two operations is shown by $(B \cup R)$ *without* R *is* B.

iv) *The associative law.* The result of combining three classifications does not depend on the order in which the combination is made. For instance, the result of

[13] Chapter 40.

the classification of triangular blocks into red, blue and yellow blocks does not depend on whether the red blocks or the yellow blocks are picked out first. Symbolically

$$R \cup (B \cup Y) = (R \cup B) \cup Y$$

v) *Special identities.*[14] The combination of an operation such as classification with itself adds nothing new to the situation.

The class of boys $\cup$ the class of boys = the class of boys,

$$B \cup B = B[15]$$

Logical structure and mathematical structure do not develop separately in a child's mind, for the two structures are very closely related. His developing ability to count a set and to arrive at the same number every time helps a child to understand the invariant properties of a set or class, and to become aware of its constancy in spite of changes in its appearance. On the other hand, it is only when he understands the invariance of a set that he can count meaningfully, for only a collection which remains constant in number during the counting can be counted.

Needless to say, a child is unaware of the structure which thought possesses and of the mathematical patterns towards which he is struggling. Hence, a source of difficulty for the teacher is that the child does not know what mental structures are missing when he cannot understand something. It is only by a careful analysis of the thought-process which leads to the development of a mathematical idea that a teacher can provide a progression of suitable experiences through which a child will grow mathematically and will be able to handle mentally more complicated structures.

If the framework of mathematical ideas a child develops at this stage is sufficiently coherent and well-understood in concrete situations, he will then more easily be able, at a later stage, to organize his abstract thinking, and to build up a logical structure of abstract mathematical ideas on the basis of this concrete experience.

[14] For the mathematical use of the word 'identity', which is employed here, see page 170.

[15] This behaviour of logical systems is to be contrasted with the behaviour of numbers in a similar situation. For numbers, $3+3=6$, but for classes, $B \cup B = B$. Differences are beginning to arise between the structure of numbers and the structure of logical operations.

5 Discovering Quantity

The idea of quantity

As we have seen in Chapter 1, young children do not spontaneously ask 'How many?' or 'How much?' The idea of quantity grows slowly from the first comparisons of *more* or *less* to an understanding of both counting and measuring. There are two kinds of comparisons of quantities: the first concerns sets of separate things; the second involves objects which have some continuous property, such as length, surface, or mass, in regard to which they may differ. Comparing two *sets* of distinct things leads to matching and *counting* and so to a number system.
Comparing *lengths* or *masses* of objects begins with some physical action such as putting one beside the other or balancing them in the hands or on a bar. It then develops into the complicated process we know as *measuring*; by this we mean finding some unit and using it to enable us *to attach a number to any quantity*. We shall first consider the kinds of experience which foster the ability to deal with quantity in these two ways.

Contrast and comparison

A child's first interest in size (of any kind) arises through contrast: big or little, soon or long time, fast or slow (of movement), a little or a lot. Sorting at this stage means putting all 'big' shapes into one box or pile and putting all the 'little' ones into another. This activity covers many of the things (cars, animals, balls, sticks) with which children play in their first days at school. Such contrasts of size appear in their stories: the great big giant, the tiny little mouse. When a child comes to school he will need many experiences which will stimulate him to take the next step, i.e. to make judgements about a difference between two things which he will describe in words such as smaller, quicker, more, heavier. He is now comparing two quantities, and seeing a relationship between them.

The actions of bringing two things together, pouring from one container into another, cutting up a shape to see whether it will cover another, will give him the certainty that the quantities are not altered by these movements; he makes his comparisons with confidence (Figure 5:1).

Pairs of coloured sticks, rods, nails, ribbons, etc. can be sorted into longer and shorter; the differences between them will be seen with greater discrimination as experience grows. Two shoes, two children, toy cars, dolls, can be placed side by side; their silhouettes can be cut to size and the appropriate label (taller, shorter, longer) attached. Squares or discs can be compared, the smaller square or disc being placed on the larger. Jugs and beakers can be tested to see which holds more, or less, by pouring water or fine grain from one to the other. The children should check that if one holds more the other holds less, and vice versa. In Figure 5:2 pictures (*a*) and (*b*) show the experiment of filling the beaker from the larger jug; pictures (*c*) and (*d*) show the partial filling of the jug from the full beaker.

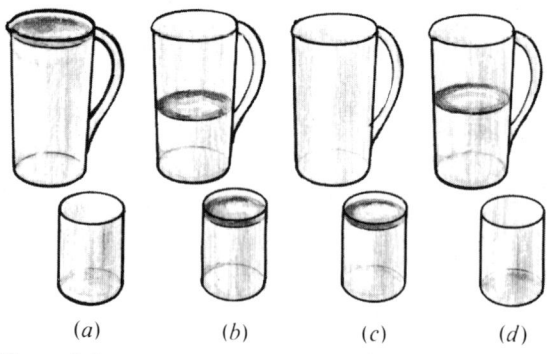

(*a*)   (*b*)   (*c*)   (*d*)

Figure 5:2

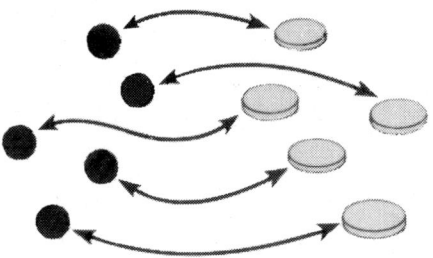

Matching two sets

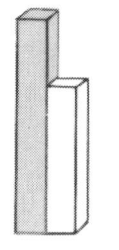

Comparing two rods

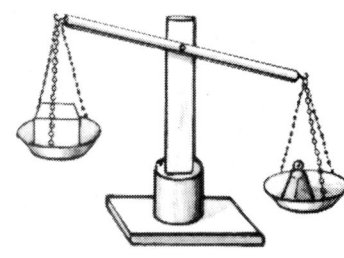

Comparing two masses

Figure 5:1

Birthdays give an opportunity for learning 'older' and 'younger' by talking about the child who is 'six today' and another whose birthday has still to come.

A balance bar and a see-saw introduce 'lighter' and 'heavier' when comparing the weights of two children, two sets of conkers, two pet animals, and so on.

All such discoveries through comparing need to be recorded, for example by placing all the longer ones of the couples in a particular box, or by putting an appropriate word or letter on the objects, or by putting drawings or pictures into blanks in given sentence such as the following:

The (blue) rod is longer than the (red) rod
The (flat) tin is heavier than the (tall) tin
(Mary) is older than (Paul)

The opposite sentences should also be written; e.g.

The (red) rod is shorter than the (blue) rod.

Activity of these kinds does more than prepare a child for the idea of measurement; it also makes him more aware of the physical properties of the objects and shapes which he handles. He begins to notice that a doll, for example, has *height* and is not merely *big*. It is a problem to know how to compare two such heights since there is no line along an edge which could be placed beside a corresponding edge. Weight can be felt when a child lifts a heavy thing and lets it pull his hand down. Capacity is seen to be an important property of a cup or bottle but to be independent of shape. It is essential for a child to know about these physical properties since they decide how the objects possessing them can be used. The act of measuring them serves only to help us to use them efficiently. Without a thorough understanding of the properties, measuring degenerates into working with numbers without knowing the meaning or purpose of what is being done. The importance of the pre-measuring stage cannot be over-stressed.

Matching and ordering quantities

During this period of *qualitative* comparison of such properties as length, capacity or mass, the comparison of sets will be taking place along the lines suggested in Chapter 3. The idea of *number* will be gradually emerging from the processes of matching and ordering sets. The idea of *length* begins to develop when objects are found which can be matched when placed alongside. For example, two or more rods can be fitted against a longer rod, or two bricks can fill the gap left by one brick of larger size (Figure 5:3). The *equivalence* of lengths is being established: an essential preliminary to measuring with ruler or tape measure.

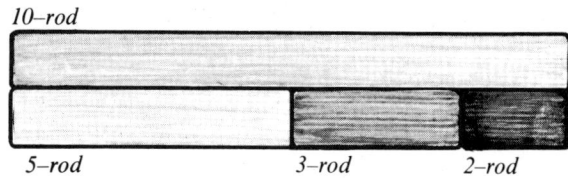

10–rod

5–rod   *3–rod*   *2–rod*

Figure 5:3

The next step is to place several lengths in order to form a *sequence*. A few children can be placed in a row and the class invited to put them in order, the tallest (or shortest) first. Silhouettes of a larger number of children can be drawn and the silhouettes placed in order of height. This brings out the necessity of placing all the feet of the silhouettes on the same 'ground' line so that the tops show the true heights. Sets of rods, pieces of braid, packets, tins, etc. can be placed in order, making a kind of staircase. The 'steps' from one to the next can be discussed. 'Are there any very big steps?' (Figure 5:4).

Figure 5:4

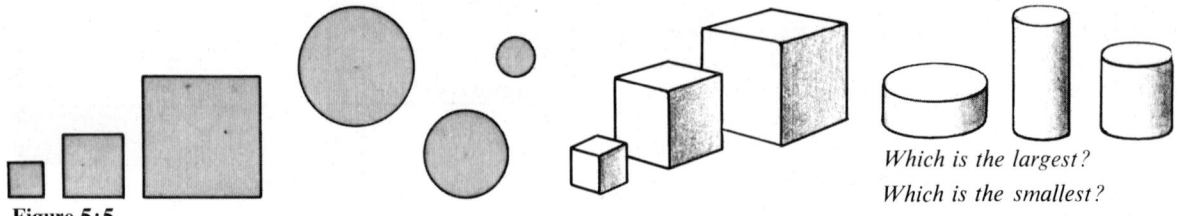

Which is the largest?
Which is the smallest?

Figure 5:5

When children are handling solid shapes they will see differences of *surface* as well as of length. For instance, they will have square tiles and discs of varying sizes. These are most easily ordered by placing one upon another. Such objects as cubes and cylinders cannot be reliably compared at this stage unless they are of the same shape, that is unless all their dimensions are in proportion; this is because many children of this age cannot yet take into account two differences, such as height and diameter, at the same time when one must be considered as compensating for the other; for example the height of one cylinder may be greater than the other but its diameter less. This means that notions of *area* and *volume* cannot be thought about in any general way (Figure 5:5).

Capacities are troublesome to order by comparing two quantities at a time but a first step in using a strip for recording can be taken. If a transparent vessel has a strip pasted to its side, a child can mark on it the level of water poured from various containers in turn and thus obtain the order of their capacities. A letter or colour symbol will have to be given to each vessel at this stage.

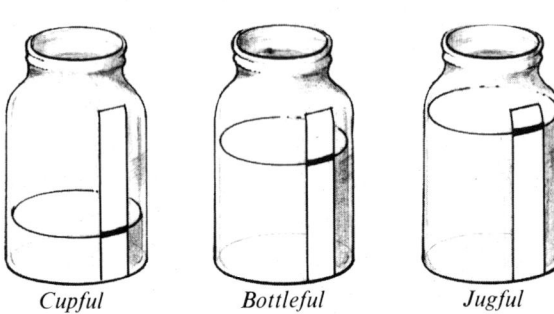

Cupful   *Bottleful*   *Jugful*

Figure 5:6

The ordering of *masses* is much more difficult than forming a sequence of sets, lengths or capacities, because we cannot measure mass directly but must relate it to force. In particular, for young children we connect it with the pull of *gravity*, that is, with *weight*. Even quite young children today are likely to have heard of weightlessness during a journey to the moon and to have seen pictures of weightless objects floating in a spacecraft. But they know that the *mass* of the sugar (or other material) is unchanged. It will sweeten just as many cups of tea as when it was on the ground.

To understand that the 'heaviness' of an object is due to a pull, children need experiences of the effect of pulls and pushes. Strong springs, securely fastened to a post or beam, will give opportunities for children to feel for themselves the pull needed to stretch the spring (or the push to compress it). They can compare the pulls of two children by the stretches they cause in the spring. If they compare the sensation of the strong downward pull of a heavy mass in one hand with the weak pull of a light mass in the other hand, they will experience the same difference as that shown by the stretches each mass will cause when connected to a spring. The mass that feels heavier stretches the spring further than the other. The stretch caused by each mass can be recorded on a strip of paper placed behind the spring (Figure 5:7). The stretches caused by several masses could be shown on the strip. Thus the *order* of the masses, from lightest to heaviest, would be represented on the diagram.

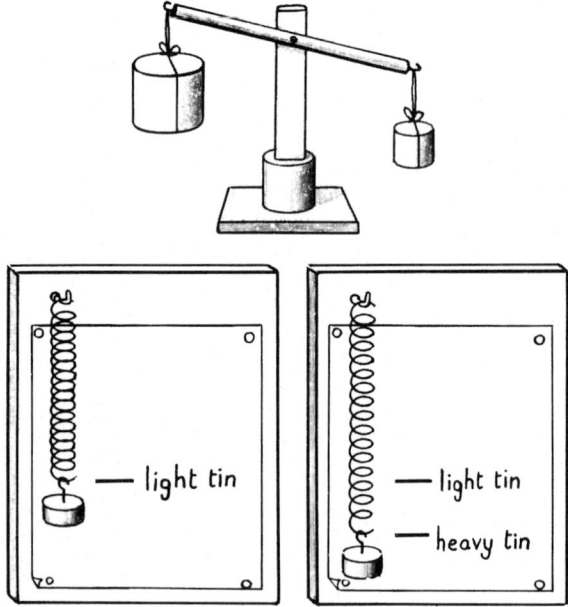

— light tin

— light tin

— heavy tin

Figure 5:7

Alternatively two masses can be compared by placing them on a balance bar (Figure 5:7). The heavier mass pulls the bar down on the side where it is hung. But such a bar can show the difference between only *two* masses at a time. To arrange three masses in sequence using a balance bar is a very instructive experience since the third mass must be compared with both of the others before its position can be decided. The result can cause a young child some surprise if the size of the objects gives no clue, a small heavy object and a large light one having been included.

In the early stages the ordering of *time* is in effect a sequence of events. 'First we must put away our bricks then we drink our milk and then we can go out to play.' Such sequences can be recorded in simple flow charts made with pictures and sentences. Cards can be used, each card containing a sentence which a child can match to a picture. The cards are then put in sequence as in Figure 5:8.

Figure 5:8

The time measurer, the clock, has moving hands and the sequence can be seen in the different positions of the hands. This marking of the time of an event by the pattern of the hands is important because it is the first step towards the reckoning of the passing of time by the *rotation* of the hands. The use of a clock whose hands can be moved to show a sequence of happenings in which the children are interested is a valuable aid.

Money is another very abstract idea. Its use for the exchange of goods can be begun by letting children use one kind of coin for the purchase of things at the class shop. This will be closely related to the beginnings of counting.

Discovering units of measure

The ability to count depends not only on matching the members of a set to the sequence of number names. As we have seen it also involves realizing that the natural numbers increase by unit steps, i.e. two is one more than one, three is one more than two, etc. A similar idea must develop with regard to length, mass and other quantities. It must be possible to think of unit increases. Unit cubes can be placed against a rod, or a series of rods; unit squares can be put alongside strips. A staircase can be formed in which each step is one unit; a number sequence emerges. Simple counts can be made and statements written about the lengths: e.g. 'the rod is as long as five cubes'. This is the first time that a number has been attached to a length and clearly the ability to do this must depend on a child's progress with counting. Yet even if this counting of units is correctly done there is no guarantee that the child has really grasped that he is finding a measure of length. Much of his matching of rods and cubes is taken by teachers as an aid to understanding *numbers*. Although a child is using his intuitive judgement of lengths in relating numbers through such apparatus, he may not see that the units he uses tell him something about the length of a particular rod. Nevertheless, he has used the procedure of repeating a unit along a length and this is an essential element in the repetition of a unit in measuring.

Just as any length could be compared with any chosen unit of length, so cotton reels or a similar set of equal masses can be used to balance a mass, such as a toy car. Or a strip of paper, placed beside a spring, can be graduated to show the stretch caused by 1, 2, 3, ... cotton reels. The toy car can then be hung on the spring and its pull measured by the stretch, shown perhaps as between the 3-reel and the 4-reel marks.

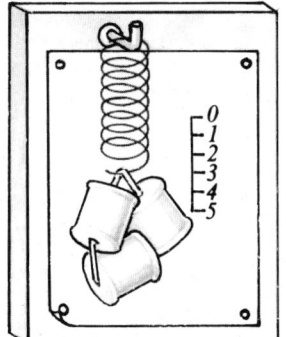 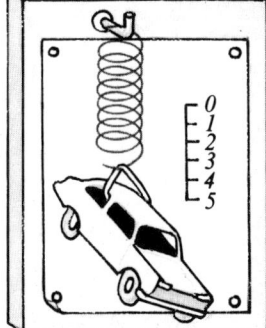

Figure 5:9

In all these comparisons and sequences it has been possible to put the objects into a direct physical relationship either in position or through balancing, etc. A simple count of equivalents or an intuitive judgement is all that has been attempted. True measuring in its fullest sense does not develop until a child can compare or order quantities which cannot be brought together.

John's Tower

Pat's Tower

Pats Tower

Handspan measuring

Figure 5:10

He found that one child will notice the positions of the tops of the objects relative to his own body, not taking account of whether the feet are on the same level; another will try to keep his hand at the level of the top of the first object while he walks to the second one. Some children will measure in handspans, or use a convenient stick, and so will iterate a unit of their own choice along the objects to be compared. Others will take a long stick or string and mark the ends of the two things; this reveals that the child is thinking of the lengths or heights as parts of, or nested within, the total length of his stick or string—an important idea in connection with a graduated measurer. The crucial feature of this experience is that a child must find a go-between, something which can be applied to each object in turn. This opens the way to the general use of a unit of measure, which at this stage will be a matter of personal choice.

When a child has chosen a unit, e.g. a rod, the length of his foot, or the width of his palm, he must repeat the movement of placing it against the object, knowing that the unit is not changed by being moved. To compare the two objects he must now be able to count the number of 'placings' he has made. Once more number and measuring go hand in hand. If the numbers he wants for his measures are within his range he can record them in writing. An alternative recording, and one of great value, is to show the measure on a line of paper. If large-square graph paper is used (2-cm or 5-cm) it provides vertical and horizontal guide lines. The height of the snowman, say, can be shown by stepping off the correct number of chosen units up one of the vertical lines; the other snowman can be shown beside him and their comparison discussed. The outline of the snowmen will usually be drawn in, too. The lengths of the two trains could be drawn in the same way along horizontal lines. Suitable captions will be supplied by the children.

Finding a go-between

If two groups of children build snowmen or make long trains from junk material they may be eager to know which snowman is *taller* or which train is *longer*. But the objects cannot be moved. How can they be compared? Direct comparison is impossible. The children should be left to experiment with ways of making a comparison. Piaget has studied children's reactions to this problem.[1]

[1] Piaget, J. *The Child's Conception of Geometry,* Chapter II.

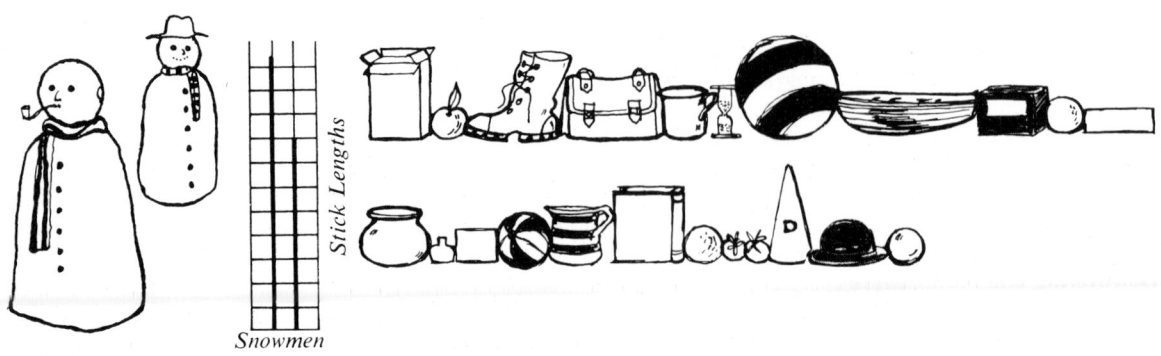

Stick Lengths

Snowmen

Figure 5:11

Units of capacity are usually the teaspoonfuls or cupfuls of the familiar environment. The comparison of a set of containers will usually be through a count of the units as so many teaspoonfuls, etc. These, too, can be recorded on squared paper. For each spoonful a spoon is drawn in a square along a row or up a column. The various containers can then be seen in terms of their capacity (Figure 5:12).

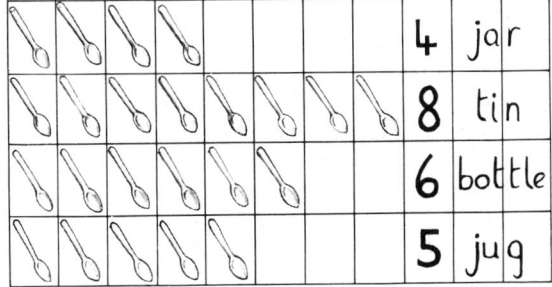

Figure 5:12

It is less easy for children to find in the classroom things that can be used as units of mass. Film spools, screws, conkers may be suggested and children soon show that they recognize which of these have a standardized mass and therefore make good units to use with a balance or for graduating a spring scale. A count will be recorded for comparison as before, and a chart on squared paper can also be drawn using picture symbols for the units.

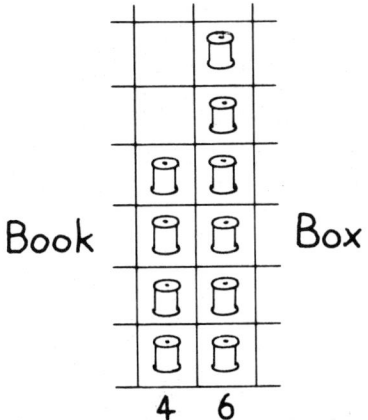

Mass in cotton reels

Figure 5:13

As many occasions as possible should be found for children to use this new skill of comparing quantities through the measuring unit, encouraging them first to *guess* which of the set is largest and so on. Such estimating leads a child to *think* about the lengths, the feel of the weights, the look of the liquid in the jars, etc. and he realizes what quality it is that he is trying to assess. He will look at both top and bottom of a tower, running his eye up and down; he will not be misled into judging weights by look, nor will he forget to take both width and height into account when comparing surface or volume.

One reason for measuring is that size may change with time. The hamster grows heavier, the plant grows taller: we must measure and record today so that we can compare tomorrow. Recording these changes in size on graph paper is the beginning of a scientific study of growth. In fact many of the observations of things on the science or nature table can include measures which may be recorded.

Graduation and approximate measures

The use of a strip of paper for recording capacities or the stretch of a spring can be most valuably extended at this stage by *graduating* the strip. Once the unit of capacity has been decided upon, a strip can be marked as one spoonful after another is poured into the container. This produces a fairly short 'number line' on which future measures can be read. It can also be used for finding any required quantity, such as three teaspoonfuls of sugar for making a cake in a class project.

A height strip can be used to record the heights of the children, at first without graduation but merely showing where on the vertical strip each child's head reaches. Usually a good many of the class are near to average height and this crowds the marking about the average point. This will not matter if each child's name is attached to a string and fastened a little way from the strip. This recording will tell us about the children in this class if we can see the markings but no child will be able to *tell* his mother how tall he is nor compare his height with that of a cousin in Canada. Even if the strip is then graduated using, say, the length of a stick, it will not do all we want. But children live among people who use standard measures and they hear about centimetres; some child is almost certain to suggest a 'proper' centimetre measure. Most children of this age will be familiar with the Cuisenaire number apparatus or similar material based on a 1-centimetre unit. The rods may have been used informally for measuring, taking the edge of the cube or one of the rods as a unit. Now they learn that the edge of the cube is 1 centimetre long and the rods measure 2, 3, 4, . . . , 10 centimetres. A long strip can be graduated in centimetres and then used for measuring the children's heights, etc. This will give occasion for counting up to and beyond 100, so extending the range of numbers the children understand.

The use of a graduated strip, whether for capacity or for length, in improvised or standard units, brings home to children very sharply that the end of the measured quantity is rarely exactly on a mark. The bowl holds *about* 5 cupfuls, or *nearly* 6 cupfuls, or a *little over* 4 cupfuls. This result is, of course, inevitable when we are dealing with a

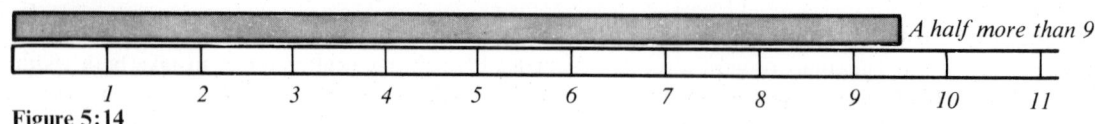

A half more than 9

1   2   3   4   5   6   7   8   9   10   11

Figure 5:14

continuous quantity. Since a child grows in height continuously, he must sometimes find that the top of his head is between two of the fixed marks on the strip. In any case the children see how hard it is to measure accurately and they will be content to give measurement as nearly as possible.

If graduated strips are widely used, e.g. by having one on the edge of a table and one horizontally along a wall, the class will use them freely and talk about what they find. In an effort to state a measure more exactly some child will probably use a *half* to describe the point which seems to be no nearer to 9, say, than to 10. He may say 'a half more than 9' and we should accept this with pleasure and mention it to the other children. See Figure 5:14.

clever child may hit on the method of splitting a kilo of 'sugar' into equal shares in the two scale-pans. This shows a considerable understanding of a half, for he knows that each half has the same mass. Every opportunity should be taken of letting the children work out such new ideas about quantity and number.

Because of the difficulty of giving a measure of mass precisely, it is useful to state it in a slightly different form from the 'nearly' or 'a little more than' which is a sensible way of describing a length. For mass, which we measure on a balance by finding when the units we are putting on the scale are too many or too few, it is more helpful to say that the weight is *between* 6 hectos and 7 hectos, or whatever the nearest two numbers may be; 6 hectos is too light, 7 hectos is too heavy.

Weighing out in conventional units

The metric units of mass are not very convenient for young children with only a limited range of counting. The gram is much too small for them to handle, even if their weighing apparatus were accurate enough to show a difference of 1 gram. On the other hand, the kilogram is too large for most of the objects a young child can handle. The 100-gram mass is the best unit at this stage, treated and counted as 1 unit without connecting it with the kilogram or the gram. So far it has not been given a popular name but children could call it a hecto, short for hectogram, its metric name which is not used in the International Standard but is available for informal usage.[2] In these early experiences some standard masses should be at hand for children to choose the one suitable for a particular measuring task: kilogram, $\frac{1}{2}$-kilogram, 100-gram and perhaps 10-gram and 20-gram. These standard masses will be used separately and will not be linked until later, unless a child spontaneously experiments and discovers the link between the two of them. It is much easier for children at this stage to weigh out a required mass, than to find the mass of a parcel. Both kinds of experience are necessary but accurate weighing belongs to a later stage. For shop play we weigh out sweets in packets of 1, 2, 3, . . . hectos (100 grams), and fruit, etc., in $\frac{1}{2}$-kilos or in hectos, as in real shops. If no $\frac{1}{2}$-kilo mass is available a

6 is too light

7 is too heavy

Figure 5:15

[2] The use of the notation 100-gram for a unit may be used by children before counting to 100 has been mastered. It can be accepted in the same way as 10p for a tenpenny coin or 100 pence for a pound.

48

Conventional units of length

The centimetre has already been introduced to children as a convenient unit for their heights. When outdoor lengths are measured a child will often use the length of his foot or a footstep. His footstep may vary but his foot provides a fairly stable unit. It has one disadvantage, however. Other children in his class cannot use it; their feet are not usually the same length. Consequently they attach a different number to the same quantity. This will inevitably lead to the proposal to use a ruler or a standard unit. Useful as personal and primitive measuring units may be, our children live in a world which constantly uses and talks about measures in a variety of standardized units. We must expect them to know some of these and to want to use them. The essential thing is that they should actually use them at school and learn to know what it is they measure and when it is sensible to use one kind of unit rather than another. Nevertheless, a kind of Robinson Crusoe skill in measuring without sophisticated tools is appreciated.

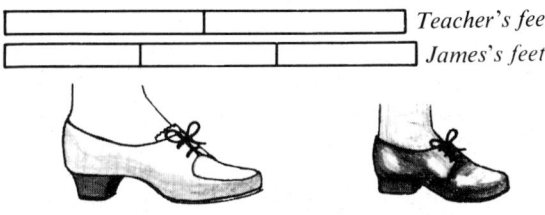
Teacher's feet
James's feet

Figure 5:16

If children are provided with 10-cm rods and metre strings they will be able to choose for themselves an interesting range of measuring both inside the school and in the playground. Their findings should be recorded and then discussed and checked with another group. It is all too easy to let children measure in a haphazard and unfruitful way. They become bored and see no purpose in what they are doing. It is much better to have some plan, project or question in mind to which measuring will make a contribution. Perhaps this is where the ingenuity and understanding of the teacher are most needed.

Distance—an abstract property

There are two kinds of length which a child finds difficult to measure: both are in a way invisible. The first is the distance between two unconnected objects; the second is the height of a solid object such as a pyramid.

There is a physical edge to a floor and a line of mortar across a wall but there may be no line between one tree and another, or between the starting-point of a jump and its finishing point. A child has many experiences of holes and gaps and knows that they differ in size, but no line is there to be measured. It is interesting that a child can walk

directly towards his mother and can visualize the line between them. He can picture the line between two trees, but how can he *measure* it? He must find a go-between. A rod or stick is difficult to iterate in a straight line. A stretched rope is the answer, and it will probably be suggested by children who have already invented ways of comparing inaccessible lengths. Once a rope has been stretched between two points a child sees that he now has a straight line that he can measure with a metre rod or metre string (Figure 5:17).

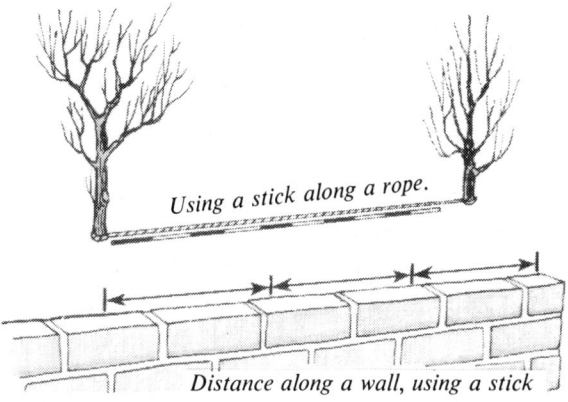
Using a stick along a rope.

Distance along a wall, using a stick

Figure 5:17

The height of a cone or pyramid is seen by a child as a property which differs between one cone and a taller one. But how can he say *how* tall it is? One experience which can help him is experimenting with bridges. A set of rods or of various shapes such as Poleidoblocs, will enable him to build bridges of different heights. These heights can be measured if the supports are upright rods. Then he can find out whether a certain cone will pass under his bridge. Is it too tall? Or is there a gap above it as it is pushed through? Probably he can make a bridge which it will just pass through, or one which is too tall and one which is too low. He will then be able to make some statement about the height of the cone and perhaps even to estimate how high it is.

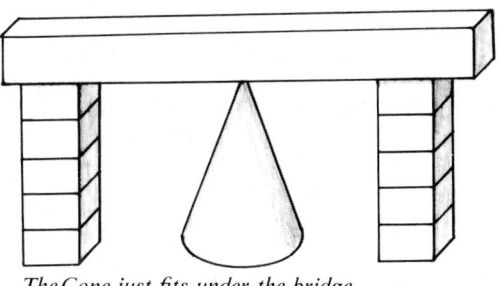
The Cone just fits under the bridge.
It is as high as 5 cubes.
Figure 5:18

49

Units of capacity

Informal units of capacity are easy to find: cupfuls, jugfuls, spoonfuls, etc. A group of children can agree to adopt a certain jug as the one they will use as a unit for a variety of comparisons. In the past a pint was a very familiar unit for measuring milk, drinks and seeds. The metric measure, the litre, is too large for many household purposes and the ½-litre is likely to be more frequently used. Fortunately large quantities of water are used in buckets and watering cans, and a litre jug can be used to find how much some vessels of this kind hold, estimating a ½-litre when necessary.

Spoonfuls are used for smaller quantities for such things as salt, vinegar, medicines. But spoons show wide variations in the amount they hold. In cooking and in hospital play, children may suggest the 'medicine spoon' as the standard. The fact that the capacity of the official spoon is 5 millilitres will have no significance at this stage but it will have importance later on when children discover that 1 millilitre has the same volume as 1 cubic centimetre. Meantime children can play with the medicine spoon and use it realistically to graduate bottles or jars and compare the quantities of interesting substances that different vessels contain.

Measuring time

Time, like space, is a condition of our existence and our bodies have a number of time patterns built into them. Rhythm is recognized as the repeat pattern of time and to measure time we must make use of this repetition. The invisible flow of time is a difficult concept for a young child but he experiences the basic rhythms of day and night, hunger and feeding, breathing and heartbeat. He also gets to know the rhythms imposed by our routines of school and family. The clock-face shows him some patterns made by the hands which match these routine events. But he has yet to learn how we measure the passage of time, i.e. *duration*. He can see the hands of the clock moving from one hour to the next and begins to associate this movement with the passing from the time of one event to the time of another. The graduation of the clock-face becomes very familiar and we should associate this with his learning of the number twelve and with his experiments with discs and paper circles. The sequence of the hours is then established, but it is the passing of the minutes which will give him the more precise idea of measuring time and for this we require an acquaintance with numbers up to sixty. Before this is acquired we can use the knowledge he has gained of halves and quarters through measuring length and mass, and folding circles. The telling of time and simple questions about 'How long until?' or 'What will the clock say in half an hour?' can be dealt with if a clock-face can be used. This indicates that children should

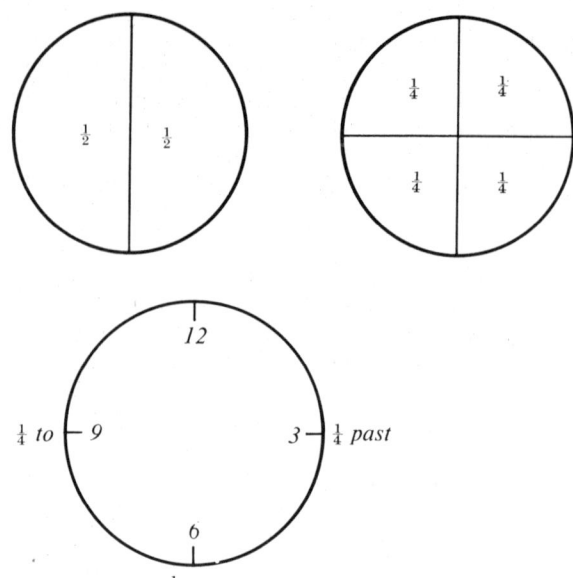

Figure 5:19

use actual rotations to enable them to find answers to these questions. They can later count the minutes, stressing the fives and the tens.

One of the rhythms that we find in everyday life is of special importance for the measuring of time; this is the pendulum. Some children may have seen it swinging in a clock. The teacher can easily set up two or three simple pendulums with strings of different lengths which the children can set in motion and observe. They will find that one is slower or faster than another, and will be able to discover that the longer pendulum swings more slowly and the shorter one swings faster (Figure 5:20).

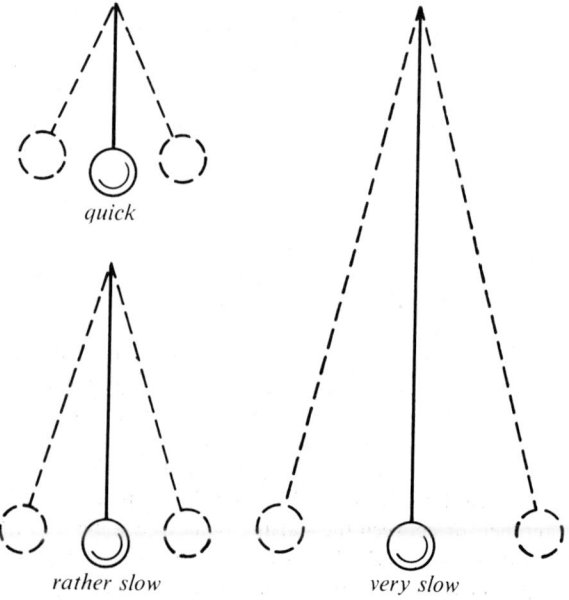

Figure 5:20

50

The next step is to time some of the children's activities by the number of swings of one of the pendulums. The use of a seconds pendulum can follow when minutes and seconds are studied later on.

Money

To a child money has no connection with measuring. It is used only for buying and he pays in coins for what he wants, giving the number of coins he is asked for, two pence, four pence, etc. The idea of money as measuring the exchange value of goods will be beyond him for a long time to come. He knows only that a price is attached to goods and he must know what coins to offer. This means that we must treat money differently from the properties of length, mass, etc., which have been discussed earlier in this chapter. Instead of choosing a unit to give us a measure of length by repeating it along a line, we must accept that a number of different coins are already familiar to the children and they must learn the relationships between these standard coins. In length, capacity, mass, etc., we prefer to let the children discover a unit and how it can be used, deferring the use of more than one unit in a single measurement. In money, however, we must take the units as given, and find out how many of one coin are equivalent to another; then a child must learn to match available coins to price.

It is quite obvious that there is a very close connection between the learning of the numbers from one upwards and the handling of coins. The activities at the class shop, which can be controlled by the prices on the goods and the coins made available to the children, must relate to the child's ability to deal with number. For example, the five-penny piece which is exchanged for five pennies *represents* a set of five pennies and can be used instead of five pennies at the shop. Practice in using these equivalents, both at a 'change counter' and in shopping, will greatly help the study of ten. The use of our written ways of showing money belongs to the next stage.

Summary

In this chapter we have shown how the idea of quantity grows from experiences of the properties of real things and ways of comparing them. Equivalence of a number of small quantities to a larger one must be realized. The need for a unit as an intermediary arises when direct comparison is impossible. Placing quantities in sequence according to size leads on to the repetition or iteration of the unit. This is parallel to the use of the number line to represent the sequence of numbers. The continuity of a quantity such as length or capacity means that a precise count of a whole number of units is not generally possible and thus approximate measures and fractional parts have to be used to give a sensible measure. Money is in a different position from the continuous properties we measure and it is well to link it with sets and number. It will be seen that the early stages of learning about measuring are confined to dealing with the growth of understanding through direct experiences with very small numbers. Recording is through diagrams or simple descriptions.

6 The Foundations of Measuring

The importance of measuring

A technological society depends for its efficient running on highly accurate measuring of a wide range of quantities, such as voltages, wind-speeds, fall-out, and so on. New discoveries and inventions add new kinds of measuring to the list and often lead to new types of measuring units.

Measuring can be considered as an extension of the use of number from counting to stating the quantity contained in a continuous whole. Separate objects can be counted and the number of the set of them tells us how many members it contains. Blood counts and Geiger counters remind us of the importance of such counting for science and human welfare. But some things are continuous, with no discernible subdivisions; time, for instance, which flows without ceasing (though there is a pattern of days and of seasons); a piece of string (though it has an end and a beginning); the mass of a bag of flour. For practical life we must match events to time, decide whether the string is long enough for our purposes, or the quantity of flour sufficient for a recipe. Comparison, fitting, or matching is sometimes necessary and this demands that we should find a way of assessing a quantity without resorting to experimenting with the actual objects.

The difference between numbers and measures

The distinction between numbers and measures can be clearly seen. Number is a concept which has been set free from the nature or the arrangement of the objects in a particular set. The idea of number develops as the common property of matching sets. The structure of a number such as 12, and number operations such as addition and multiplication are independent of time and place. They do not change however we vary the nature or arrangement of the sets they refer to. We can use them through our mental imagery without in fact relating them to any objects at all. For example, we can think of 12 as $5+7$ and change this to $5+5+2$ by the simple process of using what we know about 7. On the other hand measures always refer to properties encountered in real situations, whether in the length of an actual path or the pressure of a particular tyre, etc. We find that numbers provide the means for making useful comparisons of such properties, but also that the problems which occur in measuring broaden our conception of the number system, for instance in regard to fractions, ratio and approximations.

Intuitive assessment of quantity

The primitive way of assessing a quantity is based on a visual or manipulative estimate, comparing one whole thing with another or with an image recalled from past experience. Such estimates can become remarkably accurate after many repetitions; but people also develop techniques to help them and these techniques throw light on the way in which the procedures of measuring have grown up. A man who wishes to estimate a long distance will compare it mentally with a distance that he recalls, such as the length of a cricket pitch or a familiar path. He may have grown used to carrying 20 kg and will estimate a heavier mass by its feel in comparison with the remembered sensation of carrying a 20-kg mass. In other words he mentally divides the whole length or mass into parts. Measuring a continuous property depends on this awareness of a whole and its parts.

When a child needs to compare sizes he also makes a judgement 'by eye'. At first he makes a direct comparison of two things both within view. Piaget has shown that this intuitive judgement is the earliest step towards measuring. The child has no previous experience on which to base a *mental* comparison. But his intuitive assessment is often faulty. Differences in the position of two equal rods may cause him to think that one is longer than the other.

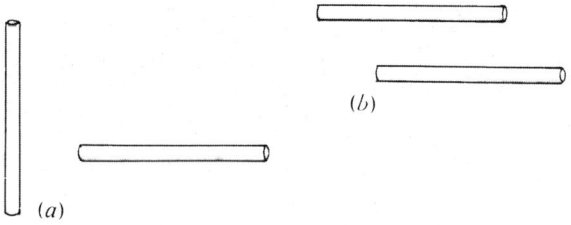

Figure 6:1

At this stage the child is not thinking in terms of parts. In Figure 6:1(*b*) he does not equate the projecting part of one rod to the projecting part of the other. Nevertheless, the child knows that the lengths will not be altered by a change of position and he places the rods side by side. He can then say whether one rod is longer, shorter, or the same length as the other. Similarly if two rectangles are placed in the different positions shown in Figure 6:2 children will differ in their opinions about the relative sizes of the two resulting shapes. Yet they can reach a judgement by placing one pair of rectangles on the other. In both cases the comparison depends on intuition, and experience is needed before the next step can be taken, and the equality of the pairs recognized without experimenting. When this stage is reached it is possible for a child to devise means of comparing the properties of two objects which are not both present to view.

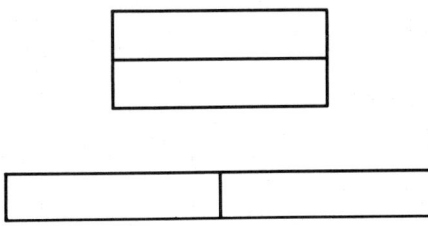

Figure 6:2

The first use of a go-between

When two objects cannot be directly compared some inventiveness is required to make it possible to say whether or not they are equal with regard to some property. Piaget has shown that when children are asked to say which of two lengths is longer when they cannot see them at the same time, they find it simpler to use an object longer than either and to mark the respective lengths upon it. This is significant because it shows that a child is still thinking in terms of wholes. It also suggests that the marking of heights, lengths or water levels on a strip has meaning at this stage for children. This first attempt to compare lengths along a line opens the way to the building up of a succession of equal lengths which will produce a graduated strip and lead to the idea of counting the parts. Once such counting can be carried out it becomes possible to state a measure as a number of units.

The relationship of a whole to its parts

The number which is the measure of a continuous quantity (say a length), must come from the equal parts into which it can be partitioned. The whole must be seen as the sum of such parts. Various experiences give rise to awareness of this equivalence. First, smaller quantities are put together so that their sum matches the whole length, mass or capacity. These parts are not necessarily all equal at first but the combination of equal parts will bring special interest. The repetition of the same quantity produces a pattern or rhythm which is noticeable and leads to a count.

Before this count can be made the equality must be established. In the case of a length this can be done by placing one part against each of the others. In effect this is stepping off one part against the others. It can now be seen that two lengths can be compared by repeating, or iterating, the same part or unit against each length and counting the number of parts or units required for equivalence (Figure 6:3).

In attempting to compare the capacities of two containers the recognition of a unit which can be repeated and counted arises very naturally. It is a common experience to put a succession of cupfuls, spoonfuls or jugfuls into a larger vessel, a bottle or a bucket, in order to fill it. The fixing of a strip on which the successive levels can be marked stimulates the impulse to count the intervals.

The establishment of the equality of small masses which together balance a larger mass is much more difficult. It is possible to check each mass against a chosen one and to discard those that do not balance. It is more likely that children will assume the equality of such things as conkers that look alike in size and will be content with counting them. But it is valuable to let them make a number of bags or boxes that will balance one another when the required amount of filling is put into them. A child can then weigh out quantities of different materials which will have the same mass. Using a spring or a piece of elastic to show the stretch which a mass produces has the advantage that equal masses produce the same extension and thus a graduation can be made. The counts on this strip will match what has already been done for length and capacity; a repetition of a unit can be seen along a line and the steps can be counted. It will be noticed that the use of a graduated strip reinforces the idea of the number line which has already been used in counting.

The nesting of quantities

The process of repeating a unit and making a count produces a pattern which consists of a starting point and a sequence of equal intervals. This can be seen as a nesting of successive lengths that begin at the same starting point and have end-points which come ever nearer to the end of the length to be measured (Figure 6:4).

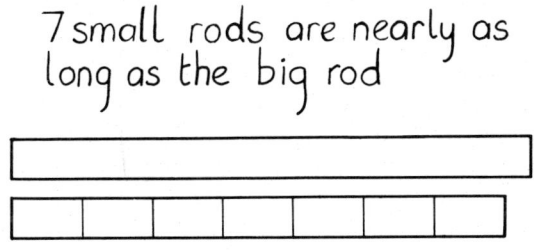

Figure 6:3

Figure 6:4

53

This pattern is similar to the one made by a count of separate objects. In Figure 6:5 the first object counted is named as one. In counting units of a continuous quantity the *first step* from the starting point is counted as one. It is easy, therefore, to give the starting point the label 0 and the name *zero*.

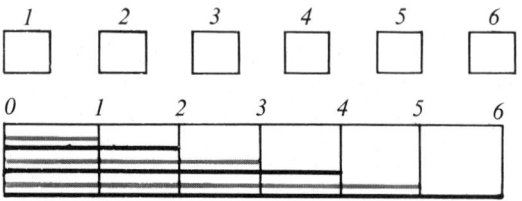

Figure 6:5

When a graduated strip such as a ruler or tape-measure is placed against a length, the nesting process shows how measuring may entail fitting the required length *between* two lengths marked on the scale. In Figure 6:6 the length to be measured lies between the length of measure 5 and the length of measure 6. The length may be stated as *'nearly 6 units'* or *'a little more than* 5 units'. The three lengths have the same starting point and the mind can think back to this starting point and realize that length is a continuous quantity. The end-points of the three lines show the between-ness of the length that has been measured.

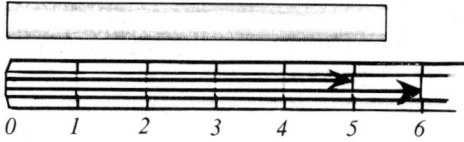

Figure 6:6

The need for a smaller unit

The fact that a chosen unit will rarely appear to fit a required length is clearly seen when a short rod is iterated along some edge or rod which has been selected at random. When the unit has been stepped as many times as possible along the edge a small piece remains which the unit does not fit. To complete the equivalence it may be necessary to fill the end space with single cubes. (See Figure 6:7). The length can then be stated as two rods and three cubes, say. This foreshadows the later use of two-unit measuring.

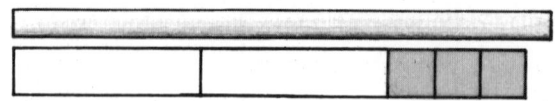

Figure 6:7

It is possible that even the additional cubes do not give an exact apparent equivalence and the extra piece may be described in a different way. A child may say that it looks like a half of the rod. He is now using the rod only and is on the way to expressing the measure as a ratio, such as $3\frac{1}{2}$ times the rod (Figure 6:8). But at this stage, he is comparing the extra piece with the rod intuitively; he may also be able to use the fractions $\frac{1}{4}$ and $\frac{1}{3}$ to express what he sees.

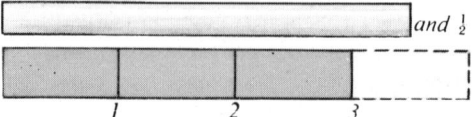

Figure 6:8

At this point it is important for the teacher to realize that measuring is never truly exact. It depends on the use of the human eye in reading the marking on a scale, and on the accuracy of the measuring instrument. If there seems to be a precise correspondence between the end-point of a length and a graduation on a scale it can be examined through a magnifying lens and a discrepancy may at once be obvious as shown in Figure 6:9. Children should be encouraged to recognize that their measuring can only be as near as they can make it and to look for ways of making it nearer to the actual quantity.

Measuring and aspects of division

The experiences of measuring described in the last paragraph give a practical basis to two ways of regarding division. When a child steps off a unit length along a line he is answering the question, 'How many of this short length will be equal to the long one?'; he may be asking, 'How many of the two-rods will match the ten-rod?' In terms of number this is $10 \div 2$, but as in all questions concerned with measuring the answer must be given in practical

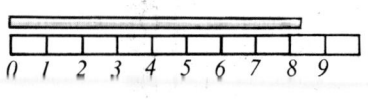

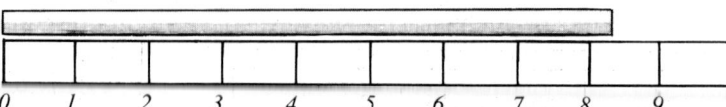

Figure 6:9

54

terms. It must state '5 two-rods match the ten-rod'.

The use of a fraction to compare the extra piece with the measuring unit shows a first approach to the division of a quantity by 2, 3, or 4. The child recognizes both the *number* of equal parts which make the whole unit, and the length which is *one part* of the unit.

It can be seen that the process of measuring, based as it is on the recognition of parts and wholes, gives fundamental activities which prepare the way for the related ideas of division and fractions.

Measuring curved paths and boundaries

Intuitive estimates of length begin with comparisons of objects in which length is an obvious and interesting property, objects which have straight edges against which straight rods or a stretched string can be placed. But if children compare some of the dimensions of their own bodies they will be faced with measuring closed curves such as the distance round the chest, wrist or head. Some of the shapes they handle, particularly cylindrical jars and tins, are circular in cross-section. Some of the paths or drives in the school grounds may be curved. Piaget has demonstrated that young children do not recognize that a zigzag arrangement of sticks has the same length as the sticks placed end to end (Figure 6:10). Nor are they convinced that a curved string is just as long as the string stretched straight, provided it is not elastic. Considerable experience of handling string, braid, plastic wire, etc. is needed so that children feel the invariance of the length as the shape is changed.

When this has been established, the use of string (and later of a tape-measure) to decide which is the longer of two paths or boundaries can be fully understood. When children can count unit measures in measuring straight edges, strings on which lengths of curves have been marked can be placed against a graduated strip and the lengths stated in whatever units have been adopted. It helps understanding if the marked strings can be compared directly or their lengths drawn side by side on the floor or blackboard.

A trundle wheel (click wheel or way-wiser) may have been used in free play, but it is now possible for a child to run it along a path of any shape and to count the clicks which mark the revolutions (Figure 6:11). A rough com-

Figure 6:11

parison of the lengths of two paths can thus be found and recorded. This is an instance of the repetition of the counting unit, in this case the circumference of the wheel; but the successive units *cannot be seen* though they *may be heard* as each click is made.

Measuring the empty distance between two objects

A child's own bodily movements create distances which he may wish to measure. Not only does he use the length of his foot or the breadth of his palm as a handy measuring unit, he may also use his handspan or the length of his normal stride. These latter are empty distances but he is able to measure them on suitable measuring strips. Such experience makes it easy for him to suggest using a stretched string or a rigid rod to bridge the gap between two positions, say of posts or trees or children. The string or rod is then measured. Measuring the width of a road or the distance of a child from a wall cannot yet be handled mathematically, but an intuitive procedure, guessing the

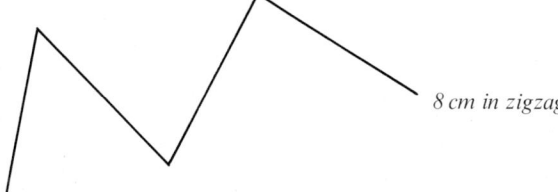

8 cm in zigzag

8 cm in a straight line

Figure 6:10

position of the guide rope, can satisfy children at this stage if it looks right. Figure 6:12 illustrates the procedures.

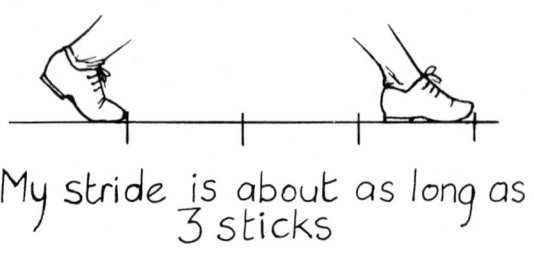

My stride is about as long as 3 sticks

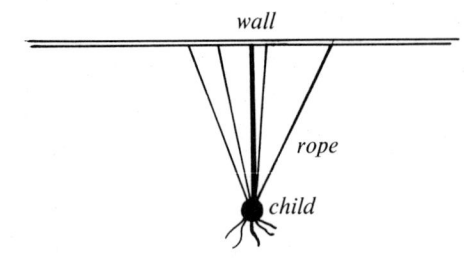

Figure 6:12

The introduction of standard measuring units

The sole advantage of standard units is that they are in common use and have general recognition. They therefore enable us to communicate measurements to others in different times and places. Most children will know the names of such units in daily use as metre, gram, litre, but they may not have realized the quantity which each of them names. Since a unit must be selected for convenient measuring in any particular situation, children should become familiar with the size of each unit as they begin to use it. They need to use and to be given opportunities of choosing, a 10-cm rod or a metre-stick, a 100-gram mass or a kilogram, according to the task in hand. But at this first introduction to conventional units they should use one unit only for a particular measurement and state it as a whole number, perhaps making use of a half or a quarter for the extra piece.

Bodily measurements such as the stride, foot or wrist can now be translated into standard units. A group of children can compare their individual measurements. Various classroom and playground measurements may also be found and sent to another class or school for comparison, thus showing the special purpose of standardized units.

At this stage we can expect children to accept freely the separate units of length, capacity and mass as measures of continuous properties with which they have become familiar. The need to relate the different units which are used for length (or mass or capacity) will not arise until a

56

child wants to state a measure more precisely. However, it is possible that a tape-measure which shows both metres and decimetres will be seen, and an informal statement of a length as, say, one metre and three decimetres will be made spontaneously. Such a development corresponds to the experience of putting a ten-rod and a three-rod (or three cubes) on end to show the number 13, i.e. to the use of a counting set of ten. This is the second stage in the representation of number (Figure 6:13).

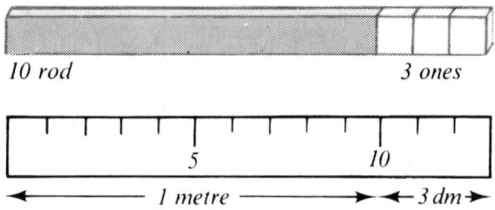

Figure 6:13

Time and the clock-face

The measurement of time does not actually occur until a child realizes that intervals of time separate events. If his mother goes out he may have to wait for her return. A lesson may last from one reading on the clock to another which he recognizes. At this stage he focuses his attention on the movements of the hands and the changes in the patterns they make. He sees the minute hand moving through equal distances along the graduated rim of the clock-face. The tip of the hand is marking the equal intervals of time represented by these distances. The units are not yet identified as 5-minute intervals. Each is simply the time taken for the tip of the minute hand to move from one numeral to the next. He comes to realize that this interval is 5 minutes though he cannot yet reckon in fives or recognize the number of minutes past the hour that any particular position records. For the moment he names the position of the hand by the numeral nearest to its tip.

The movement of the hour hand is too slow for young children to observe but they see that it has moved when it points to the next numeral. They can therefore recognize the marking of hour intervals by the small hand and can say, for example, that it is just 10 o'clock, nearly or just after 10 o'clock. It can be seen in Figure 6:14 that the process of iterating a unit and counting the number of units from a particular starting point is now being carried out round a circle instead of along a line. It is a peculiarity of the clock-face that the starting point is labelled 12. This can be explained to the children as midday (noon) or midnight. It is the end of one rotation round the clock and the beginning of another. It marks zero as well as twelve.

Figure 6:14

Telling the time precisely involves the use of two units, hours and minutes. These standardized units have to be accepted by a child as those that we all use. Before he can deal with two units together he will be able to identify the position of the minute hand at the beginning of an hour, and to see that it has returned to this position at the end of an hour, when the small hand again points to a numeral. He thus has two measures of an hour: the complete revolution of the minute hand and the passage of the hour hand from one numeral to the next. This may be his first encounter with the equivalence of measures in two different units. He will meet similar equivalences when he matches metres to cm, kg to grams, and so on. This relationship is of considerable importance and it is worth while to encourage children to watch how the hands of a clock move in a pattern.

The measurement of time is the one basic non-metric system. This is partly due to the very ancient tradition of using sixths and twelfths because these were the parts of a circle which were easiest to find, and partly to the ancient belief that there were 360 days in a year. Not many forms of computation are involved in our daily use of time but we need to remember that calculating in hours and minutes is very different from the standard decimal computations with other systems of units of measurement. Children will need help in acquiring the necessary number skills in dealing with timetables and calculating intervals between two points of time.

An informal approach to area

A child's early judgements of the relative size of objects are global and, as we have seen earlier, are subject to error because he cannot take into account the different dimensions: length, breadth or diameter, and height. Yet in comparing shapes drawn on the flat he is able to take a first step towards recognizing the quantity of surface in rectangular shapes. First he compares similar shapes such as squares or circles by placing one upon another. He then finds that some shapes can be covered by repeating a small shape over the whole surface. For example, he can cover a square with suitable smaller squares, and can count how many he has used, though he cannot cover a circle with smaller circles.

Children can also fold a square into four small squares and realize the equivalence of the four squares to the original larger one. If they are given squared paper and invited to draw patterns on it they will make interesting shapes consisting of a countable number of squares. On the other hand a child can take a certain number of square tiles and make a variety of shapes with them. As he realizes that they all cover the same amount of surface he can state the number of squares in each of the equivalent shapes (Figure 6:15).

Play with cubes and cuboids will produce surface patterns which show the arrangement of equal rows of squares covering a rectangle. This may be discussed and recorded but a more precise treatment is best deferred until multiplication emerges from the study of equivalent sets and the rectangular arrays in which their members may be placed (Figure 6:16).

Operations with measures

When children can show that two rods placed end to end match a single rod, or can say which of two rods is the

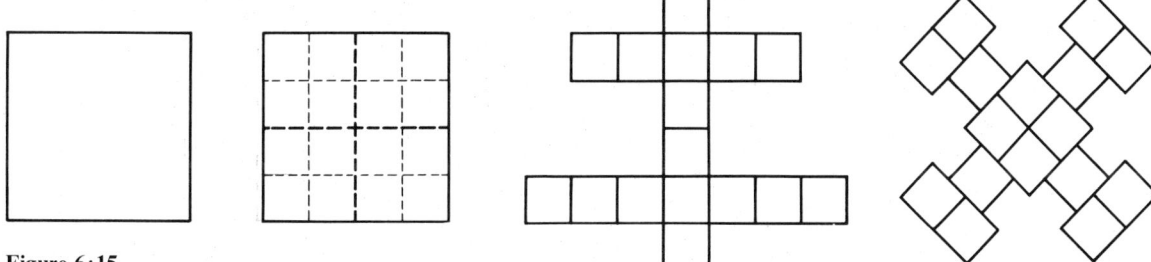

Figure 6:15

57

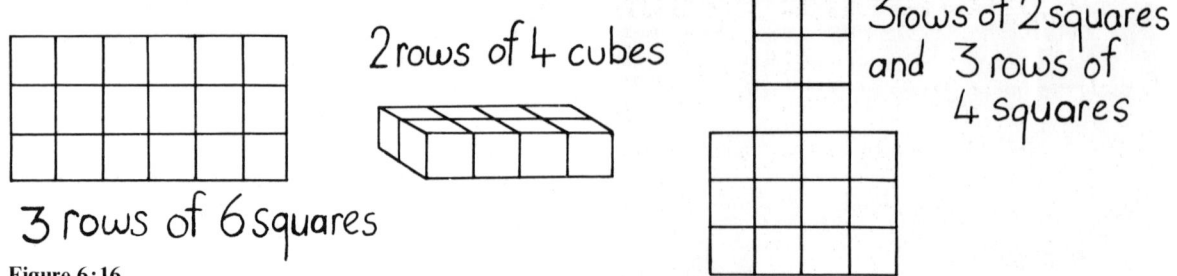

3 rows of 6 squares

2 rows of 4 cubes

3 rows of 2 squares
and 3 rows of
4 squares

Figure 6:16

longer, they are on the threshold of addition and sub-traction of lengths. Similarly the iteration of a unit length along a line represents a combination or addition of lengths. But a child may carry out these actions, and use words about them such as 'longer' and 'shorter', and yet not have developed a clear idea of the property of length. He may still be thinking in terms of objects and actions, and may not have formed the concepts and mental images which enable him to think of lengths as quantities to which he has attached numbers that can be added or subtracted and thus tell him total lengths or differences of length. The importance to a child of carrying out the actual measuring of lengths, capacities or masses is that he is building up abstract ideas both of the properties and of the ways in which the quantities can be measured. When these ideas are established the addition operation will have meaning.

Some children will actually discover addition by measur-ing on from a certain length to find a total. For example, they will measure one part of a path and then another to find how far they have moved altogether. Such experience makes possible the first statement of addition of length, e.g.

5 metres and 3 metres = 8 metres altogether

The development of operations with measures and its importance for a fuller understanding of number is dis-cussed in Chapter 13.

Understanding money

The concept of money as a measure of value comes slowly, but the idea of a pennyworth will arise in class shopping. 'How much is it worth?' may also be asked of stamps, etc. The exchange value of coins also carries a hint of equivalence of value. But these ideas are at a very simple level and should be left to grow with experience of prices and costs. Yet it is important for the *teacher* to be clear about what children must come to know about the social function of money.

The counting sets required for changing different coins, for example pence and five-penny pieces, give wide and useful experience of numbers. Money should be thought of in this context rather than in relation to the continuous quantities with which this chapter has been concerned.

7 Counting and Recording

Learning to count

The first necessary steps towards understanding numbers have been taken when a child can compare and order sets. Those sets that match, each element of one to an element of the other, have this property in common, that of matching. We say they have the same number. If two sets do not match exactly, one set has more things in it than the other. In this case the child who has learned the first few numbers will be able to say *how many more* if the difference is within his limited number knowledge, even though he may not yet be able to count the number of things in the sets (Figure 7:1).

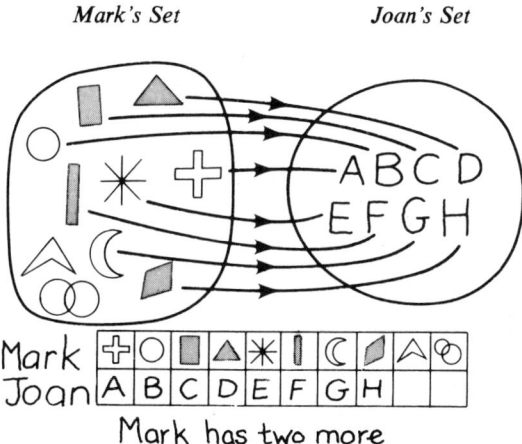

Mark's Set   *Joan's Set*

Mark has two more

Figure 7:1

Several sets can be placed in order of number without counting, if they are compared two at a time. The larger of each pair is placed to the right. A third can be greater than the first and less than the second one considered. It will be placed *between* the other two. In this way a sequence of sets is made, as shown in Figure 7:2.

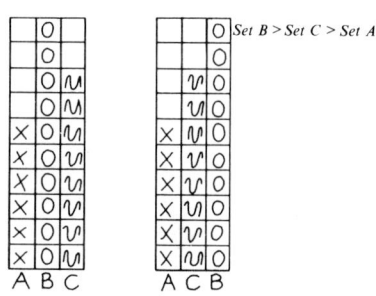

Figure 7:2

Already, as we have seen in Chapter 3, a child who has learned the numbers one to four can identify sets having those numbers. By ordering sets, some with more than four members, and forming a sequence of sets he can extend his number knowledge. He knows and can say the sequence of number names to twenty or beyond. Now he has to increase his range of experience with sets of objects or their pictures so that he can match the correct number name to sets with five or more members.

Numbers from five to ten

i) *Four and one more*. The basic property of the counting numbers is that each of them is one more than the number which precedes it. This fact has already been brought out for the numbers one to four. There are several kinds of experience which will show that putting one more object to a set gives a set which has the next number. A set of four things given one more becomes five: one, two, three, four, five.

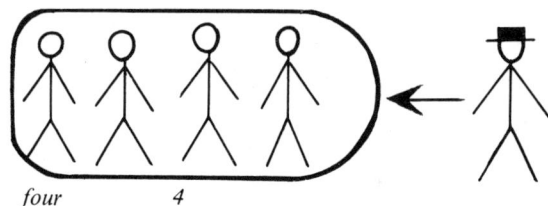

four   4

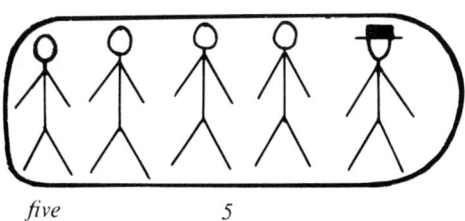

five   5

Figure 7:3

We write the number names, or place a card with the correct symbol under the new set. We name the number 'five' and write both the word and the symbol, 5. See Figure 7:3.

[1] The symbol > means here that one set has more things in it than the other.

ii) *Learning about five.* A set of Cuisenaire or similar rods can be used to make a staircase. One unit cube can be placed above each rod in turn and will thus make a height equal to the next rod. One to four are known; we associate the number five with the next rod. Four and one more is five. We take the five-rod and place unit cubes above it, counting one, two, three, four, five (Figure 7:4). Again we write the number name and its symbol, 'five' and 5.

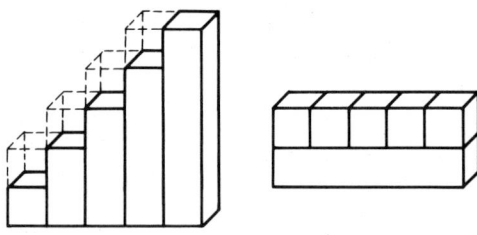

Figure 7:4

The number five should now be found in as many activities as possible. Children should think of things that come in fives, making collections with five members and illustrating with pictures: fingers on a hand, petals on some flowers, pence in a fivepence, corners of a square pyramid, panes of glass in some windows, families of five, etc. Given pictures of two, three or four things, children can put more pictures to make sets of five things, e.g. {trumpet, soldier, drum} becomes {trumpet, whistle, soldier, drum, doll}. The recognition of fives in pictures, buying five things at 1 penny each in the class shop (and counting five pennies to pay for them), home play for a family of five (including stories about the family and its needs), letting children take five strides to see who goes farthest, all these are but examples of the activities which a teacher can provide. Clapping rhythms in fives helps to bring out the patterns of the ones, twos, or threes which make up sequences of five. 1..2..345 or 12..345 or 12..34..5 are examples of such partitions.

These patterns are seen even more clearly if children are given five shapes, such as discs, squares, stars, etc., in two or more colours and asked to make patterns. They can draw what they have made and write what they can see (Figure 7:5).

Counting backwards as a set of things is dismantled, 5, 4, 3, 2, 1, helps to establish the sequence in the mind, relating each number to the preceding one. Some children, having heard a count-down, may continue to zero. If so, the teacher should accept it and match it to the fact that after dismantling or putting away we are left with nothing at all. The name zero and the symbol 0 for the number of the empty set can be used on any such occasion when they would mean something to the class.

The ordinal aspect of five must be taught as an extension of first, second, third, fourth, which we dealt with in Chapter 3. If children are arranged in fives for games, races or other activities, they can be called or recorded in order and the *fifth* one identified. This account of learning about five has been given in some detail to show how the ideas of set, sequence, partitioning and order all find a place. The numbers from six to nine will need similar treatment.

iii) *Numbers six to nine.* The names of numbers six to nine and their symbols will present no difficulty but it has to be remembered that a set with more than five members cannot be recognized on sight without counting. It is thus most important that such sets should be recognized in various patterns. The special characteristics of these numbers should be discovered by children through their own experiments.

The difficulty of recognizing the number of a set which has more than five members is met by special features in some types of abacus still in use today. A Russian abacus frequently seen in the shops and offices has the 5th and 6th beads on each column coloured differently from the other beads. This arrangement makes it easy to identify 7, 8 and 9, as can be seen in Figure 7:6.

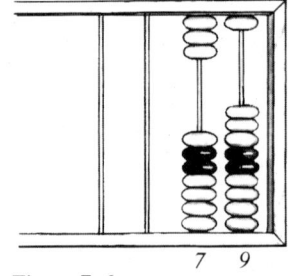

7   9

Figure 7:6

Figure 7:5

3 black
2 white
I have 5

The Japanese *soroban* has a separate bead to represent five, so that six is shown by the five-bead and one unit bead (Figure 7:7). This reminds us of the Roman use of *vi* for six and *vii* for seven.

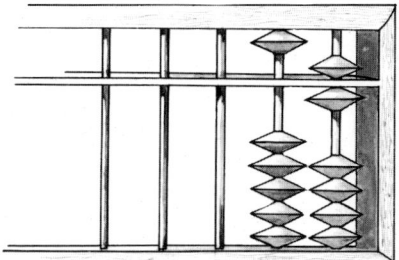

Figure 7:7

A set of *six* things makes some interesting patterns and its subsets become very apparent (Figure 7:8).

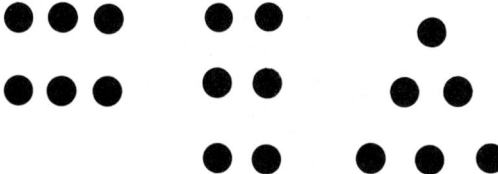

Figure 7:8

The children can write what these patterns show, using symbols:

$6 = 3+3$ $6 = 2+2+2$ $6 = 1+2+3$

It must be emphasized that at this stage we are thinking about the *numbers*, the sets they refer to, the ways of partitioning a set, and the patterns a set can make. We are not yet dealing with the *operations* of adding or subtracting numbers; we are comparing, arranging or fitting *things* as a preliminary to operations with *numbers*. We use the symbols to describe what we have discovered about the numbers through such activities.

A six-rod will demonstrate similar patterns to those shown in Figure 7:8. A square tray like that provided in Stern apparatus allows the six to be matched by pairs of rods or any other combinations of rods. Each matching can be recorded, e.g. $2+2+1+1 = 6$. In play with shapes six appears in the number of faces of the familiar cubes and dice; a six-pointed star can be made from two triangles; six triangles fit together to make a hexagon; some children will be having their sixth birthday at about this time (Figure 7:9). Six pennies can be exchanged for 1 fivepence + 1 penny.

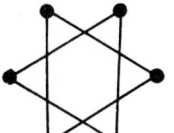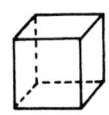

Figure 7:9

Seven is remembered as the number of days in the week. The names of the days can be written as a set and another set of seven written to match: perhaps the names of the children who are to fill in the weather chart for each day.

Monday   John
Tuesday   Pam
Wednesday   Jean
Thursday   Paul
Friday   Lucy
Saturday   Alan
Sunday   Tony

Seven also makes pleasing patterns such as those shown in Figure 7:10.

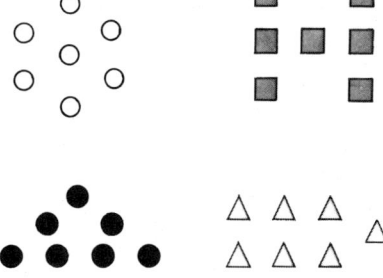

Figure 7:10

The important fact about *eight* is that it is four and four. Like six, a set of eight things makes two equal rows. This property can also be seen in the shape made by two squares as in Figure 7:11. It may be compared with the triangles in Figure 7:9.

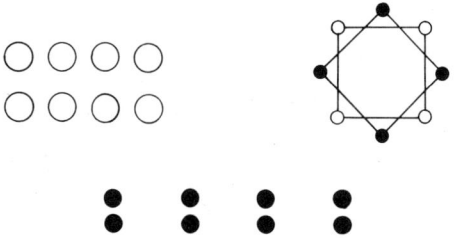

Figure 7:11

61

Nine reminds us of six because a set of nine things also makes rows of three. As there are three rows of three they can be arranged as a square. This should be the basic pattern of nine though it will later be known as one less than ten, when the staircase using ten rods is counted down (Figure 7:12).

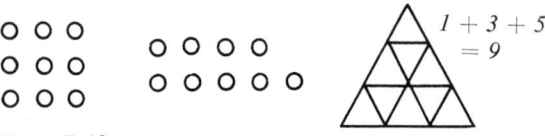

Figure 7:12

iv) The *number ten* can be learned at first without reference to the reasons for the special way of writing it. It is represented by the tallest of the set of Cuisenaire or Stern rods and thus has a special place in a child's experience. Ten discs make two rows of five and can also be arranged as a triangle with rows of 1, 2, 3, 4 discs as Figure 7:13 shows.

Figure 7:13

Ten quickly becomes familiar through its constant use in money and measuring.

Recording

Before the notation for numbers greater than ten is studied and the special properties of such numbers are discovered, a great deal of counting and recording should be encouraged, with emphasis on numbers up to ten. Children will count and record beyond ten, perhaps up to a hundred, but without knowing the structure of the tens and ones shown in the numerals.

The open abacus is a useful means of keeping a daily record, or the individual scores of a team. Cards at the foot of a column will show the numbers. Comparisons between the various scores are easily made and thus differences between pairs of numbers become known (*see page* 82).

Daily records of things the children bring or talk about, and counts of things in the classroom, can be listed in numeral form and represented on squared paper. We have seen how comparisons can be made on such a recording without counting the sets. Now the squares show *how many* things in each set and the *numbers* can be written on lines which serve as axes of reference (Figure 7:14).

On Wednesday no extra bottles were needed. We wrote this as O.

Figure 7:14

Individual children will keep such records, say of tractors seen, and will show the numbers both as numerals and on a chart. Simple sentences can be written beside the chart.

'I saw seven tractors.' 'David saw nine.' 'David saw two more.'

Attention has been drawn to the numbers whose sets can make two equal rows: 4, 6, 8, 10. They can also be seen as making pairs. Shoes, children, or coloured pencils can be paired. As we count them each number is two more than the one before it (Figure 7:15).

2   4   6   8   10

Figure 7:15

These numbers can be shown on squared paper and the steps will be seen to be twos. Going *downstairs* two at a time gives us 10, 8, 6, 4, 2, and then? We see that zero is the starting number. The numeral 0 should be well known now both as the symbol for the number of the empty set and as the beginning from which we measure.

Ten as the counting set

We have remarked that sets having the numbers six to ten are difficult to distinguish at a glance. Sets with numbers greater than ten are even more difficult to distinguish. This is why they are organized into tens. Ten is used as a counting set. When we have one more than ten we keep the one and the ten separated and write one ten and one unit, or say simply 'a ten and a one'. Now we can see why eleven is written '11', it means 1 ten and 1 one. The numbers to twenty can be counted now as 1 ten and two, 12; 1 ten and three, 13; and so on, up to 2 tens, twenty.

Besides the usual experiences of putting things together as a packet (or bundle) of *ten* and the extra *ones* when making a count, children will be helped by the use of structured apparatus in which ten is the largest number represented by a rod. Then when the combination of two rods exceeds the length of the ten-rod the extra length required can be made up with unit cubes or a short rod to represent them.

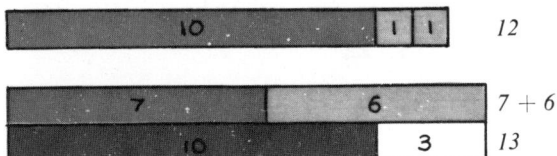

Figure 7:16

On page 78 more detail is given about the use of such apparatus in building up the addition pairs which are equivalent to each of the numbers from eleven to twenty, with particular reference to the Stern twenty-tray. Here we are chiefly concerned to see how the notation develops an understanding of the structure which the rods disclose.

Most children will not be content to stop at writing 20. They can *say* the number names well beyond twenty and they may well wish to represent them in rods or bundles as well as to use the symbols. It will be noticed that a child can now give meaning to the zeros which occur in writing 10, 20, 30, etc. These numbers can be shown in *tens* without any extra *ones*.

Numbers eleven to twenty

The numbers from ten to twenty are particularly important because they provide the pattern for operations with tens and units in the higher decades. If the combinations and partitions of sets with these numbers are well known, formal work with larger numbers will develop smoothly. Moreover, the organization of a set into counting sets and ones is parallel to the use of two kinds of coin, e.g. tenpences and pence, or metric measures such as decimetres and centimetres.

Children need the experience of representing a count of 13 things in several ways, e.g. in a grouping of ten and 3 ones, as a ten-rod and a three-rod, and on a graph as a block of ten squares and three squares.

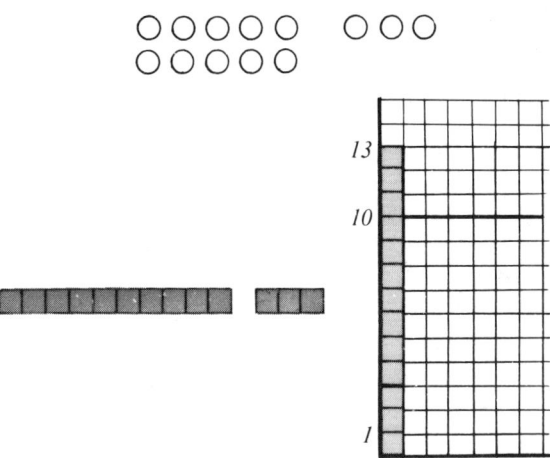

Figure 7:17

The abacus is now used differently. In place of recording various counts on the different rods, we arrange ones on the right-hand rod and let the beads on the next rod represent the counting sets of ten. Clearly this must follow the experience of arranging a number in sets of ten and recognizing that these sets must be counted so that the number can be written in symbols or shown on the abacus (Figure 7:18).

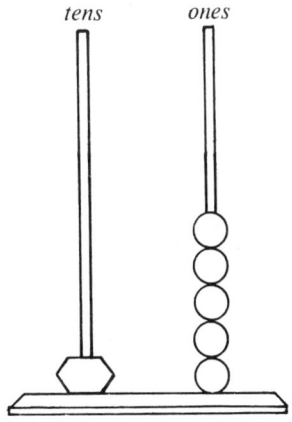

Figure 7:18

63

The activities and explorations suggested for the numbers one to ten must now be extended to these larger numbers so that their special properties become equally well known. We will now look at some of these properties and patterns.

Eleven is not a very interesting number until its multiples are studied. Its behaviour depends chiefly on the way we write it as 1 ten and 1 one. Written in the base of eight as 1 eight and 3 ones it loses even this unique property. Nor does eleven yield any particularly pleasing patterns. A few possibilities are shown in Figure 7:19.

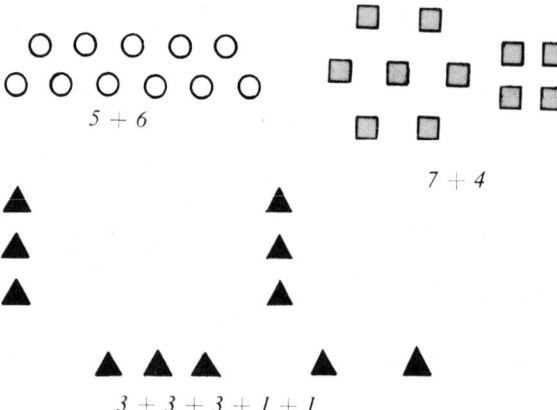

5 + 6

7 + 4

3 + 3 + 3 + 1 + 1

Figure 7:19

Twelve has many attractive and useful features. A set of twelve things will make two rows and so twelve continues the list of numbers that can be counted in twos. A set of twelve things can also be arranged in threes, fours and sixes as can be seen in Figure 7:20.

These arrangements can also be shown in shapes made with strips or milk-straws (Figure 7:21).

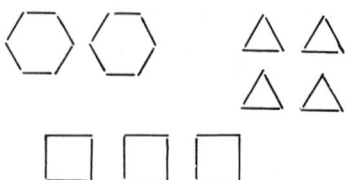

Figure 7:21

The clock gives interesting experiences of 12, particularly if children fold paper circles to make their own clock faces. Some of the unequal partitions of a set of twelve things are shown in Figure 7:22. All such partitions should be found by children, using as many situations as possible.

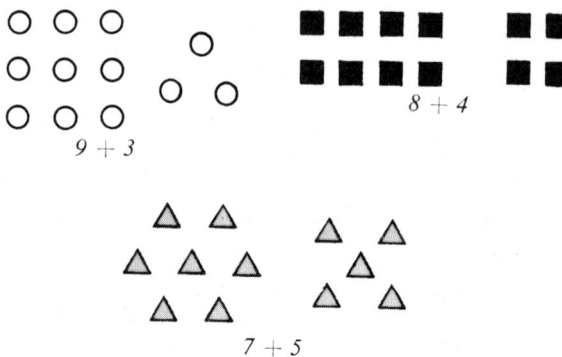

9 + 3

8 + 4

7 + 5

Figure 7:22

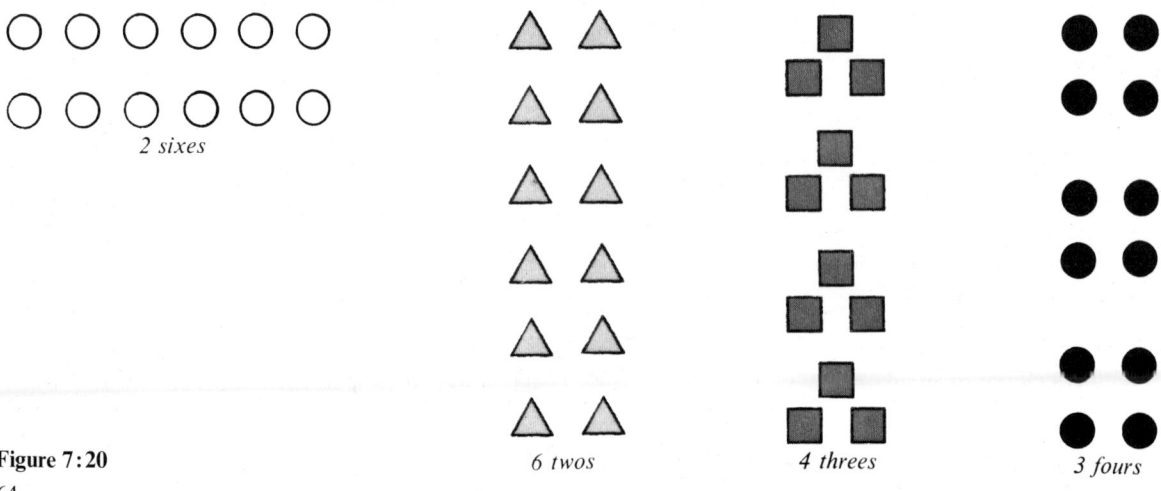

2 sixes

6 twos

4 threes

3 fours

Figure 7:20

64

Thirteen has a bad reputation among the superstitious. In fact a set of thirteen things cannot make equal rows of any kind and thus 13 is less useful than its neighbour, 12, or even 14. But it can be arranged in some interesting patterns; e.g. it can make two squares by a partition into four and nine. Also, since it splits into six and seven it can make a six-pointed star (Figure 7:23).

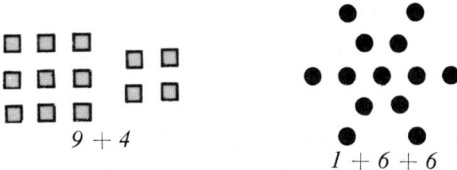

Figure 7:23

Each of the numbers 14, 16, 18, 20 will correspond to sets with 2 equal rows; sets of 15 and 18 make three equal rows. Sets of 17 and 19 do not make equal rows but 17 can be arranged in a pattern of squares and 19 extends the star made with 13. A set of fifteen makes a larger triangle of the kind made by ten (Figure 7:24).

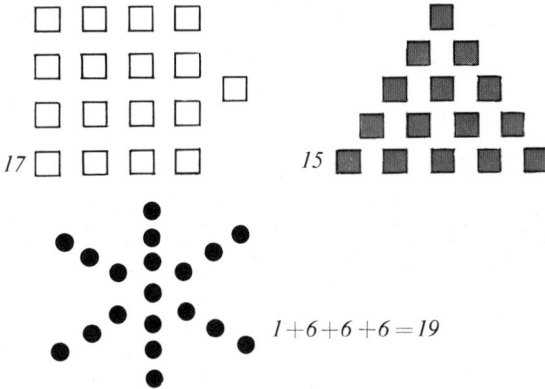

Figure 7:24

Given freedom to invent, children will produce a great variety of number patterns, describing them in words and writing something about them in symbols.

Recording number sequences

As well as recording on squared paper the many counts of sets which give numbers from ten to twenty, a child can now represent the sequence of numbers he has found which will correspond to two equal rows: 2, 4, 6, ..., 16, 18, 20. They can be drawn on $\frac{1}{2}$-cm squared paper and will make a long staircase (Figure 7:25).

The numbers which correspond to rows of threes can be similarly represented. The squares may, of course, contain pictures of objects or may be suitably coloured.

Children can read the graphs of 2-row and 3-row numbers both up and down and can discuss the patterns made by the tops of the columns, the tens, and the individual rows or rods which have their own colours.

It is important that familiarity with the numbers to twenty should be built up not only through the counting of sets of objects, the use of rods and expression on squared paper, as outlined in this chapter. Counting in units of measure, handspans, spoonfuls, footstrips, etc. should go on at the same time, on lines suggested in Chapter 5. Frequent handling of 1-penny and 10-penny coins will further strengthen understanding. It is in these experiences with numbers between 10 and 20 that the foundation of the decimal notation is laid.

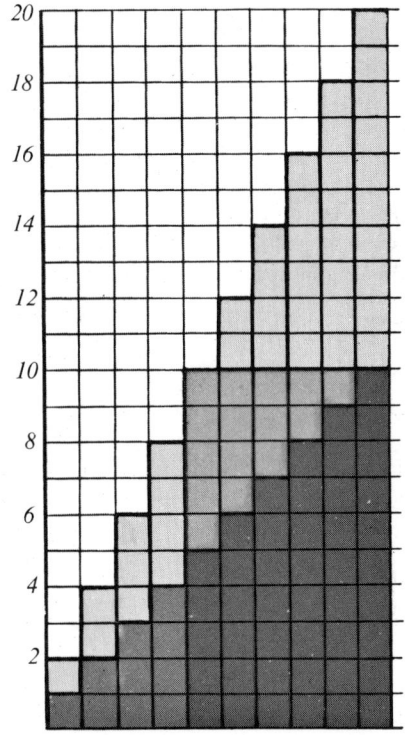

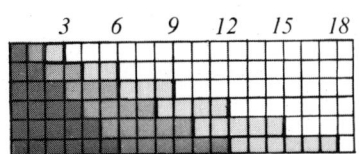

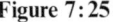

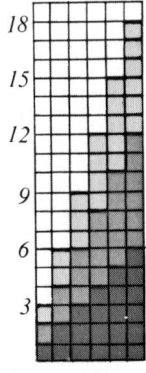

Figure 7:25

8 The Structure of Number: Early Stages

From concrete to abstract number

In Chapter 4 we saw how a child forms an idea of number from the ideas of a set of things and of the seriation of that set into an order so that its members can be put into one-one correspondence with the beginning of the sequence of number names. At this stage, number is a very concrete experience to a child. He uses the word 'three' to describe a set which he has put into one-one correspondence with the set of sounds 'one, two, three'. So 'three' is a descriptive word, an adjective which always describes a set of things. But as he grows older, he must take a further very large step, and detach numbers from the particular sets to which they are attached, arriving at a generalization.[1] Out of 'three bricks' and 'three apples' must grow the general idea of 'three'. From experiences of counting sets of things such as those shown in Figure 8:1, children will come not only to understand 7 apples and 7 animals, but also the number 7. The number 7 becomes detached from apples and animals, and becomes a thing-in-itself, apart from its concrete illustrations. In fact, a number such as 7 changes its function from an adjective to a noun.

Figure 8:1

What is the noun 'seven'? Has it an independent existence, apart from the examples of seven things with which we surround children? Or is it more like such abstract nouns as 'love' and 'truth', which must be explained by examples and stories, rather than by direct definition? Much mathematical thought is built on the basis of the numbers 'one, two, three, four, ...', but can 'seven' be defined other than by saying 'here is a set of seven things'? Children can only come to understand the natural numbers

through concrete examples of sets of things, but a teacher may wish to examine the nature of the abstraction which children may eventually reach.

It is only within the last eighty years that the definition of number and the foundations of arithmetic have been put on a firm theoretical footing. A method of defining the natural numbers in the abstract, which was given by Bertrand Russell, is interesting because it parallels very closely the stages a child passes through in his developing understanding of number.[2]

Russell takes as his starting point the idea that two sets 'have the same number' if they can be put into one-one correspondence (*see page* 18). This makes it possible to classify all the sets of things that there are or could be. We imagine a collection of boxes into which sets are to be put. All sets which 'have the same number', that is, which can be put into one-one correspondence with one another, go into the same box. For instance, there is a box into which are put all sets which can be put into one-one correspondence with the sound 'one'. In another box is a collection of sets which can be put into one-one correspondence with the set of sounds 'one, two'; in another box a collection of sets which can be put into one-one correspondence with the set of sounds 'one, two, three', and so on.[3] Then corresponding to each box there is a class of sets, and Russell defines the *number* of a set to be *the class of all sets which can be put in one-one correspondence with it*. Two is the class of all pairs, *three* the class of all trios, *four* the class of all quartets, and so on. As Russell says:

> '... there is no doubt about the class of couples: it is indubitable and not difficult to define, whereas the number 2, in any other sense, is a metaphysical entity about which we can never feel sure that it exists, or that we have tracked it down.'

This construction of a class of sets is often seen in infant classrooms, where the teacher uses a row of boxes, each labelled with a number, into which the children put sets. Any couple of things is put into the box labelled 'two', so that children are learning to distinguish couples from other sets; that is, they are forming the idea *of the class of couples,* and are attaching the label 'two' to it. Similarly,

---

[1] This is the first of many generalizations which go into the formation of an adult concept of number.

[2] The most readable account of this which Russell has given is to be found in his *Introduction to Mathematical Philosophy.*

[3] It is helpful to imagine each set of three things being contained in a bag. All these bags can be put into the box labelled three. By this device the identity of each set of three things is not lost.

the children put any trio they find into the box labelled 'three', and so the idea of the class of sets which have 'threeness' in common is built up. A number is a class of sets which have 'twoness' or 'threeness' or some similar property in common.

It is therefore important that a distinction should be made between the abstract number *three* and any *set of three things*. This distinction is often made in writing, when a set is distinguished by a pair of curly brackets { }, by putting the letter *n* in front of the brackets to denote the *number of the set*. For example, the number of the set of letters of the alphabet is 26, and so we write

$$n\{A, B, C, \ldots, X, Y, Z\} = 26.$$

The set itself is not equal to 26; it is the *number* of things in the set which is 26.

The empty set and the number zero

When he first forms sets and begins to operate with them, a child will always be using sets which he has physically made, that is, sets which have some members. But not all sets have members. The set of children in the next room may be empty. When all a child's money is spent, the set of his pennies is empty. He may have an empty set of pennies even when he has some money. The state of 'not having any . . .' always corresponds to the empty set. The empty set is always an abstraction; a child has to conceive of the possibility of having a set of objects of some type, and then notice that he has not in fact got any of these objects. It seems unlikely that, while a set remains to a child only a physical collection of things, he will be able to understand the possibility of an empty set.

The *number* corresponding to the empty set is *zero*. Using the Russell definition of number, zero is the *class of empty sets*. For a child, therefore, zero must make its appearance in connection with what might be there, but is not. He has 1 cat and 3 hamsters, but 0 goldfish. When he uses structural apparatus, he may have 3 red rods, but 0 white rods. He had 5 sweets, but he has eaten them all; he now has 0 sweets.

It is logically necessary to distinguish between the *empty set* and the *number zero*, which is the number of the empty set. Zero bears the same relation to the empty set as the number 10 does to the set of a child's toes. The mathematical sign for the empty set is 0, and can be used in contexts in which the number is quite inappropriate. The intersection of the class of boys and the class of girls is empty. Symbolically, $B \cap G = 0$. This statement is a statement not about numbers, but about sets.

At the stage of concrete operations it seems likely that children often use the number zero to indicate the absence of any numbers of things, rather than as a number. It is therefore not a number to them in the same sense that 1, 2, 3, . . . are numbers. It also has oddities of behaviour,

such as the fact that $3 \times 0 = 0$, which seems to set it apart from the other numbers. It is important, however, for the later development of the number system, that children should come to think of zero as a number, rather than as a symbol for the absence of number. The use of number in measuring, where 0 symbolizes the starting point of the ruler, and in graphical work[4] may help to set zero among the other numbers, and so, in particular, to smooth the introduction of positive and negative directed numbers at a later stage.

Cardinal and ordinal numbers

We have described the genesis in children's thought of the set of numbers

$$\{0, 1, 2, 3, \ldots\},$$

and we turn now to another aspect of these numbers with which young children have some difficulty at the pre-operational stage. The emphasis, so far, has been on the fact that number is derived from sets of things; that, for instance, all sets of three things can be put in one-one correspondence, and that 'threeness' is common to all such sets. This aspect of number is known as *cardinal number*, and the number three to which it gives rise is the *cardinal number three*, in contrast to another aspect of the number, which leads to the development of the *ordinal number*.

An emphasis on seriation (*see page* 39), or putting things in order, gives rise to the ordinal numbers. The order may be order of size, among a child's toys or bricks, order of age among his brothers and sisters, or order of time among the habitually recurring events of his day.

When he seriates and counts along a row of toy cars, a child is not only setting up a one-one correspondence with the set of number names, but he is also naming each car by its position in the row. Number two is the *second* in the row, number three the *third*, and so on. When he says 'three', he is not necessarily thinking of the set of three cars he has counted, but rather that this car is third in the row. He is concerned with the *ordinal number three* or the third position, rather than with the cardinal number three, or the set of three things.

Figure 8:2

[4] See, for instance, page 143.

For the ordinal aspect of number to be present, the things counted must be seen in order. The important feature of a date such as the fourth of January is that it comes after the first, second and third of January, and before the fifth, sixth and later days of the month. The cardinal idea of the set of four days up to and including the 4th January remains in the background.

When one consults page 42 of a book, the numbers are used to show the order of the pages. If the book is opened at page 38, it is too early in the sequence of pages; if at page 45, it is too late. The set of pages 1–42 is a subsidiary idea. But when a child says, 'I have read 42 pages of this book', the cardinal idea of the set of pages which he has read is uppermost in his mind, and the ordinal idea that he is on the forty-second page is subsidiary.

For a full appreciation of number, both cardinal and ordinal aspects must be present, but in the early stages of a child's learning they may develop separately, and only come together after considerable experience, as Piaget has shown in some of the experiments which he describes in *The Child's Conception of Number*. Two of his experiments are of particular interest in this context.

In the first experiment,[5] a child is given a set of ten dolls of increasing height. Sets of ten walking sticks of increasing length and ten balls of increasing size are also available. The child is asked to match the dolls and the sticks, or the dolls and the balls, so that each doll can easily find its own stick or ball. This causes considerable difficulty to young children (*see page 26*), but children who are old enough to be able to make the correspondence arrange the dolls and balls in parallel rows of increasing size, so that the one-one correspondence between each doll and its ball is clear. Then the experimenter displaces the balls slightly, so that they are no longer opposite the corresponding dolls, and asks the child to find the ball belong-

ing to a particular doll. The mistakes which some children make in answering this question throw light on the difficulty of coordinating cardinal and ordinal numbers.

One child,[6] for instance, when asked for the ball corresponding to doll number 6, persisted in choosing ball number 5, and when asked why, counted dolls 1 to 5, that is the set of dolls in front of doll 6, and then balls 1 to 5, and pointed to the last ball he had counted, that is to ball 5. Other children made very similar mistakes. A child who was asked for the ball corresponding to doll 5 said, 'There are four in front,' and so pointed to ball 4 (Figure 8:3). He had seen the cardinal number 4, the set of four dolls in front of the fifth, but he confused this when counting the balls with the ordinal number 4, and so pointed to the fourth ball.

A child who understood the situation completely pointed correctly to the fifth ball and said 'I looked to see if there were four' (that is, four in front). To reach complete understanding of the relationship between cardinal and ordinal numbers a child has to realize, as he counts a row of things, that when he says 'five' he is pointing to the fifth (ordinal) object, and that in doing so he has now counted as a set whose cardinal number is 5 (Figure 8:4).

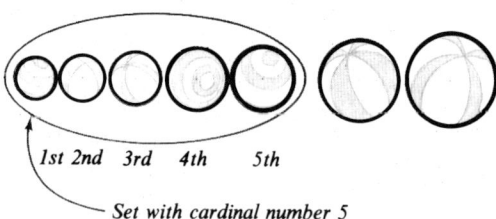

1st 2nd   3rd   4th   5th

Set with cardinal number 5

Figure 8:4

[5] Piaget, J. *The Child's Conception of Number,* Chapter V.

[6] Op. cit., page 110.

Figure 8:3

The relations between cardinal and ordinal numbers are brought out further by Piaget's next experiment, which also throws light on the concepts involved in the use of structural number apparatus. The experimenter gives a child ten strips of cardboard (Figure 8:5), of which the second (*B*) is twice the length of the first (*A*), the next (*C*) three times the length of *A*, and so on. The child puts the cards in order of length and is asked how many cards like *A* could be made from *B*, how many cards like *A* could be made from *C*, and so on. When he has answered correctly for each successive card, a card such as *F* is taken at random, the staircase remaining in position, and the child is asked how many units it represents. A child who has completely grasped the connection between cardinal and ordinal number will realize at once that the card in the sixth position must be six units long, and so will count along the staircase to find that *F* is the sixth card, and answer that it is six units long. A child who does not yet understand this connection between position and cardinal number will use card *A* with which to measure card *F*, and will find that he needs to use card *A* six times to cover card *F*. Both the earlier and the later of these stages are found among children aged 5 and 6.

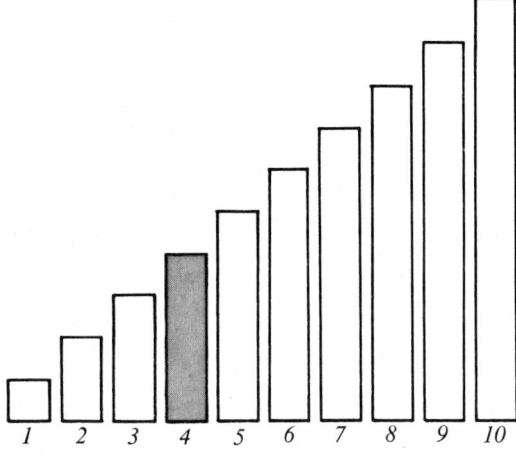

Figure 8:6

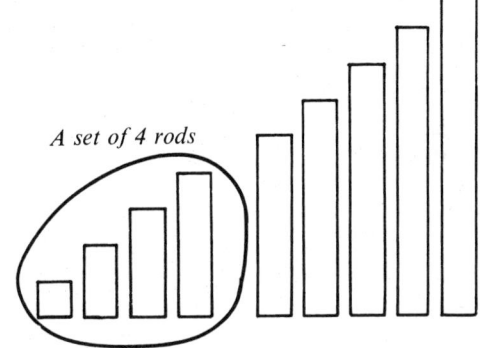

A set of 4 rods

Figure 8:7

senting numbers, he may simply be counting how many rods there are (Figure 8:7), and so using the *cardinal number four* in another sense.

When a child has used structural apparatus, which usually depends on the representation of numbers by lengths, for some time, the different senses in which he uses a word such as 'four' come together in his mind, so that he uses that sense of the number word which is appropriate in any situation.

Different types of structural apparatus

The principle of using length to represent number is seen in almost all the types of structural number apparatus which are intended to help children to clarify their early ideas of number. A convenient object, which is usually a cube, but may be a cuboid, disc or other shape, is chosen to represent *one unit*. Numbers greater than one are represented by repetition, so that three is represented by a set of three units, usually placed end to end so that the length of the resulting block is three times the length of the original unit. Figure 8:8 shows the shape of the unit in some of the common types of structural apparatus.

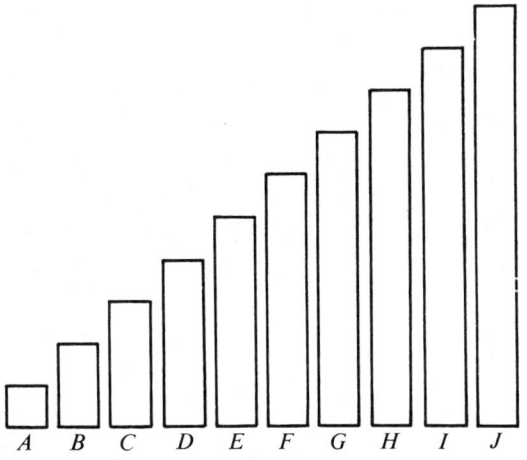

A   B   C   D   E   F   G   H   I   J

Figure 8:5

In setting up a staircase of strips or rods and counting along it (Figure 8:6) a child may use a number word such as 'four' in several different ways:
   i) he is pointing to the fourth rod, and so is using the *ordinal number four*;
   ii) he is pointing to a rod which could be broken up into four unit rods, and so is using the rod as a *representation of the cardinal number four*;
   iii) he is pointing to a rod which is four times as long as the first rod, so that the number four indicates a *ratio*, a relationship between lengths;
   iv) if he does not think of the rods themselves as repre-

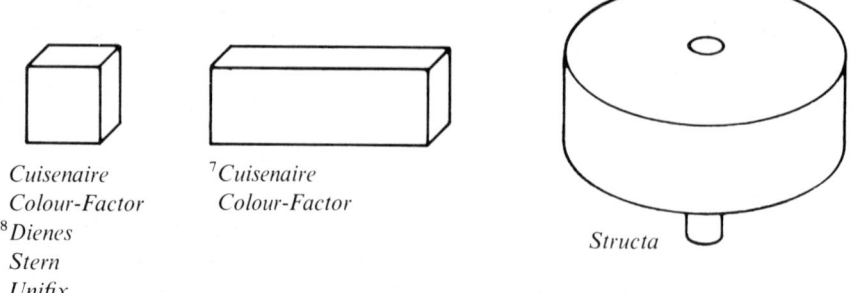

Cuisenaire
Colour-Factor

[7]Cuisenaire
Colour-Factor

[8]Dienes
Stern
Unifix

Structa

Figure 8:8

In most types of apparatus indivisible pieces are supplied to represent two units, three units, and so on, but the plastic Unifix cubes lock together as do the Structa cylinders so that a child can make his own rod or cylinder of three units, handle it as a whole, and break it down into sets of three constituent units. Figure 8:9 shows representations of three using some types of structural apparatus.

The rods representing two units, three units, and so on, in the Stern apparatus are marked in unit divisions, so that a child using a three-rod can count and can see that the three-rod is built up from three unit cubes. In the Cuisenaire and Colour-Factor apparatus, on the other hand, divisions are not marked on the longer rods, but rods of different lengths are systematically dyed in different colours, in order that they may easily be distinguished. Here the emphasis is on length, and so on the *ratio* aspect of number, rather than on breaking a rod down into units. The dark-green Cuisenaire rod is six times the length of the white rod, and a child has to measure it with white rods to verify that this is so. Often he will take the white rod to represent one unit, and then the dark-green rod, six times its length, represents six. But the red rod may equally well be taken to represent one unit. The red rod is twice the length of the white rod, and so

the dark-green rod is three times the red rod. If the red rod represents one, the dark-green rod will represent three.

The absence of divisions on the Cuisenaire and Colour-Factor rods makes them more flexible in use, as soon as a child understands that he is comparing lengths when he gives each rod a number name. If the white rod which is first in the staircase represents one, the subset of the staircase consisting of the red, crimson, dark-green, brown and orange rods represents two, four, six, eight and ten (Figure 8:10). But if the red rod represents one unit, the second staircase will be 1, 2, 3, 4, 5, and the original staircase will be $\frac{1}{2}$, 1, $1\frac{1}{2}$, 2, $2\frac{1}{2}$, 3, $3\frac{1}{2}$, 4, $4\frac{1}{2}$, 5 (Figure 8:11). It is a comparative, or ratio, idea of number which is developing here.

Many other staircases are of course possible, using

[7] This rod is not the smallest provided. This point is discussed further below.

[8] The Dienes Multibase Arithmetic Blocks are included in this classification, as this apparatus rests upon the same principle as other types of structural apparatus. It is not, however, intended for the first stages of number work, but to develop understanding of the notational system. The Dienes apparatus is discussed in Chapter 13.

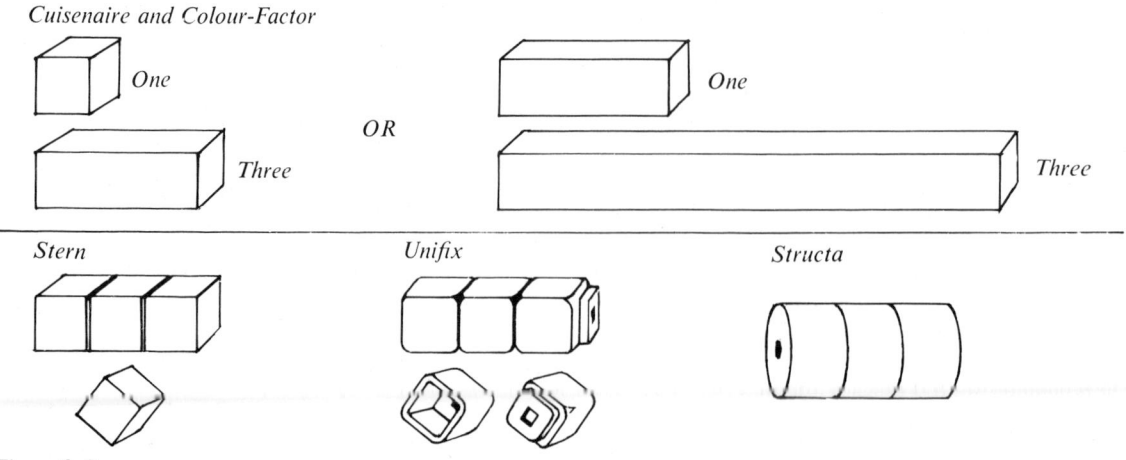

Cuisenaire and Colour-Factor

One

One

OR

Three

Three

Stern

Unifix

Structa

Figure 8:9

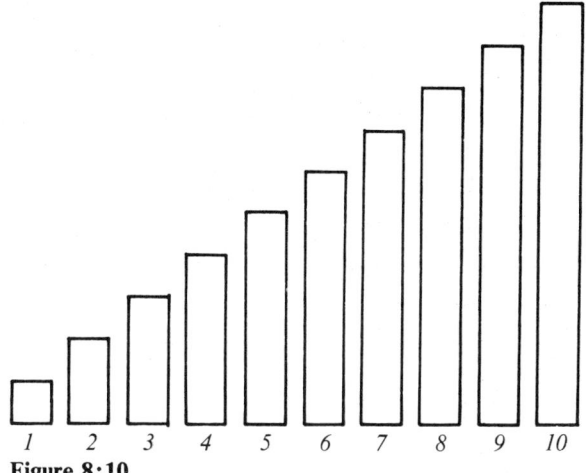

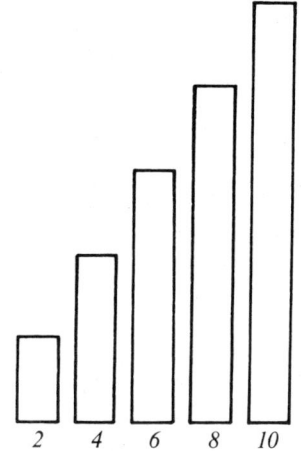

Figure 8:10

different rods to represent the unit, and so introducing the representation of different fractions, e.g. $\frac{2}{3}$, $\frac{3}{5}$.

The use of the lengths of rods to represent numbers also introduces another important representation of numbers, the *number line*. When a child makes a staircase and compares the lengths of the rods which go up in equal steps, he can make a record of what he has done in a different way as well as drawing the staircase. Figure 8:12 shows how a strip of card can be graduated by marking how far each rod reaches along the card. As the child does this, he is building up a ruler by a process very similar to that he can use in graduating a measuring jar (*see page* 44). He is also taking a first step towards a fundamental mental picture, the number line, in which each number is represented by a length measured from a starting point or zero. Figure 8:13 shows part of two more number lines, built up from Cuisenaire rods, using first the red rod, and then the orange rod to represent one unit. The teacher will see that all these illustrations are only diagrams of the same number line drawn to different scales, and that the number line has an abstract universal character which is independent of the unit of measurement.

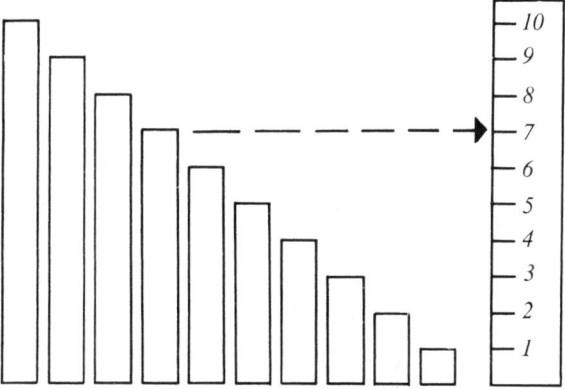

Figure 8:12

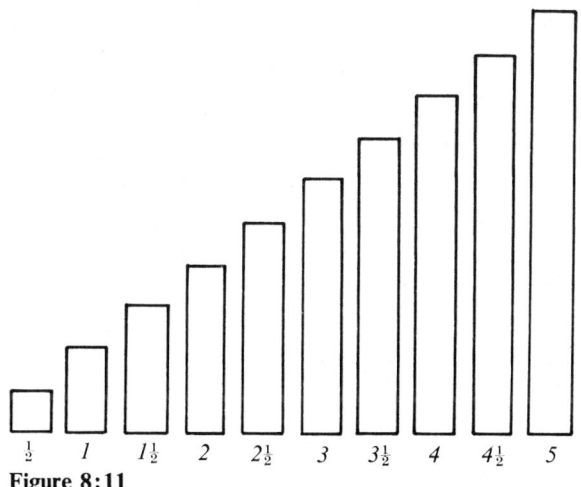

Figure 8:11

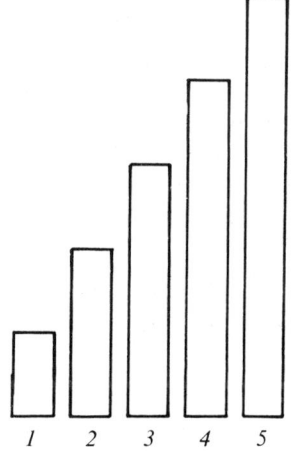

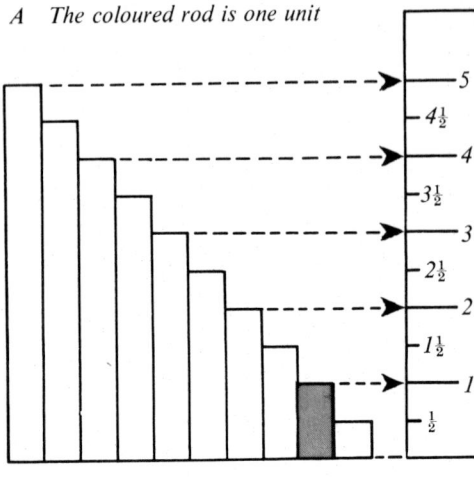

A   *The coloured rod is one unit*

B   *The coloured rod is one unit*

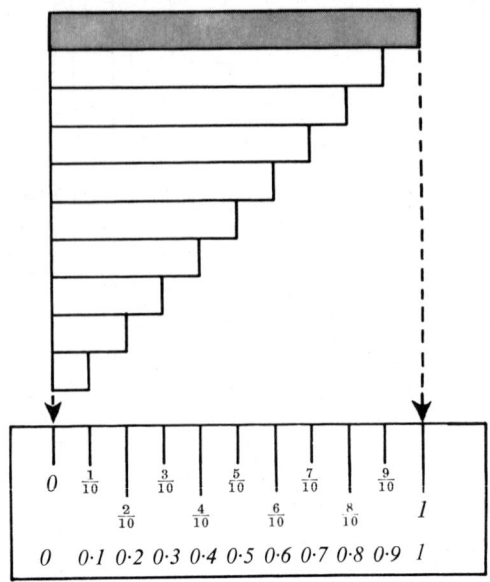

Figure 8:13

The economy of mathematical language

It will be seen from the analysis of the idea of number in Chapter 4 and this chapter that a mathematical word such as 'three' is used with a variety of different, but closely inter-related, meanings in different contexts. This variety of meaning is a very useful feature of mathematical language. A full appreciation of 'three' involves understanding of its cardinal and ordinal senses, and of the relationships between them, appreciation of the use of 'three' as a ratio, and further extensions of the use of the word as in the contrast between $(+3)$ and (-3), which a child will gradually acquire as his understanding of mathematical structure develops. Some of these extensions will be discussed in later chapters. It is helpful for most purposes to use the same word 'three' in all these contexts, as the behaviour of all the different 'threes' is so similar that, when numbers are manipulated, it hardly matters which 'three' we are dealing with. It is most important, however, that children should become aware of as many aspects of number as possible, by meeting numbers in many different situations, as a full appreciation of 'three' only comes when all the senses in which the idea and the word are used are integrated into one whole. When a child reaches this stage, the ideas of 'a third object', 'a set of three things', 'three times as much', and other ideas

which he has attached to the word 'three' are all equally available, and he can move from one to another and choose the one which is most appropriate to any situation.

It is a temptation in the teaching of mathematics to withhold from children some aspects of a concept in the hope of simplifying the idea. This urge to simplify is nearly always mistaken, for children build up concepts by the mental reconciliation and unification of a variety of examples where the concept occurs in situations and in things which they have handled. Simplification too easily becomes over-simplification; if, for instance, a child only meets situations which emphasize cardinal number to the exclusion of the ratio aspect of number, he can only form a concept of number which may be so limited that it is impossible for him to understand mathematical developments he will meet with later.

The concepts formed at one stage are the building-bricks for the next storey in the tower of a child's mathematical growth. If he has not had the opportunity to form satisfactory concepts he may be unable to take the next step, or indeed to take a step which may be required several years later, so that his mathematical growth is permanently stunted. It is therefore particularly important that children should have a rich variety of mathematical experiences at the stage when early concepts of number and of space are being formed.

Part II
Concrete Operations

9 Addition and Subtraction

The discovery of addition

While children are finding the patterns they can make with sets of things, they are partitioning these sets into smaller subsets.[1] They will make statements about the numbers of things in the subsets, and these statements can be recorded in addition form (Figure 9:1). In this way the idea of addition arises from splitting up or partitioning a set into subsets.

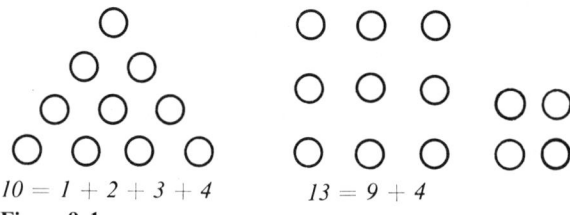

$$10 = 1 + 2 + 3 + 4 \qquad 13 = 9 + 4$$

Figure 9:1

The reverse of this process is that of starting with two separate sets and combining them to make a total set, as

[1] See Chapter 4.

Combining two sets to make a total set

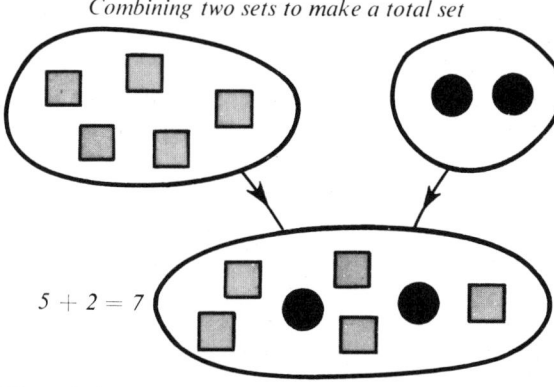

$5 + 2 = 7$

Figure 9:2

in Figure 9:2. The number content of this situation will be written $5+2=7$.

Children need to have experience both of partitioning a set into subsets, and of combining two sets which they have made separately into a total set, and of making number statements in both situations. At first, splitting up a set of seven bricks into two subsets of five bricks and two bricks is a very different action from combining a set of five bricks and a set of two bricks. After some experience, these two actions come together in a child's mind, and he realizes that $7 = 5+2$ and $5+2 = 7$ are two statements about the same situation. The actions have become internalized and reversible (*see page 17*); an *operation* has emerged.

Any addition statement such as $5+2=7$ occurs in a great variety of situations, and can be recorded in several ways. Not only will a child combine sets; he will put the 5-rod and the 2-rod of structural apparatus end to end; he will put 5 spoonfuls of water into a graduated bottle and then another 2 spoonfuls, and find that the water reached the 7-spoonful mark; he will put out the money that he needs to buy something costing 5 pence and something costing 2 pence, and see that he has 7 pence altogether; and so on. Recording on squared paper is often useful, and both horizontal and vertical recording of addition should be used (Figure 9:3).

Another distinction which a child may make is that between the actions of adding $5+2$ and $2+5$. The action of adding 2 bricks to 5 which are already on the table is

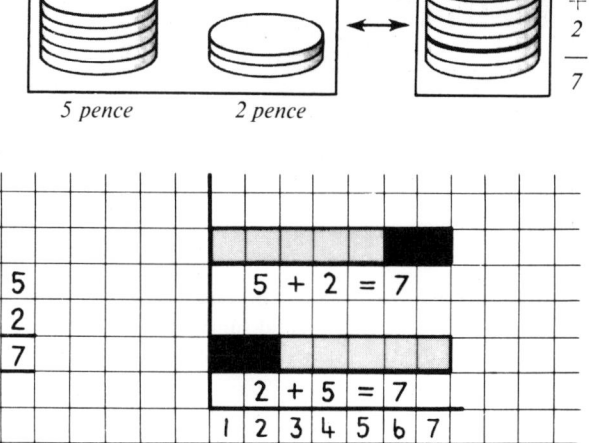

5 pence   *2 pence*

Figure 9:3

75

very different from the action of adding 5 bricks to 2 which are on the table. The results of these two actions are, however, the same, so that when the action has become mental the child will write either $5+2$ or $2+5$ for either operation. The order in which the operation is performed has lost its importance, and he now moves freely between the two forms.[2]

The teacher will probably notice three stages in a child's development as he makes and puts together sets of five things and two things.

i) At first he counts out a set of five bricks and a set of two bricks. Then he puts these sets together and counts all the bricks again.
ii) A little later he can hold in his mind the idea of the set of five bricks which he has counted while he makes a set of two bricks. He therefore only needs to count on from five, and counts the two bricks as 'six, seven'.
iii) After more experience he *remembers* that a set of five things and a set of two things always makes a set of seven things, so he no longer needs to count.

It is important that children should reach the third stage, and should be able to use with understanding and confidence all the addition facts which they will need in later work.

Children will be helped to understand and remember number facts if they use some type of structural apparatus. They quickly come to associate those combinations of rods which together make up a particular longer one.

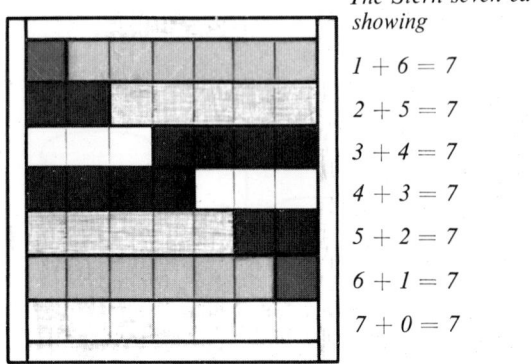

The Stern seven-case showing

$1 + 6 = 7$
$2 + 5 = 7$
$3 + 4 = 7$
$4 + 3 = 7$
$5 + 2 = 7$
$6 + 1 = 7$
$7 + 0 = 7$

Figure 9:4

It is also easy for children to verify with structural apparatus that $5+2 = 2+5$, and similar facts. The Stern number case clearly shows this commutative law for addition.

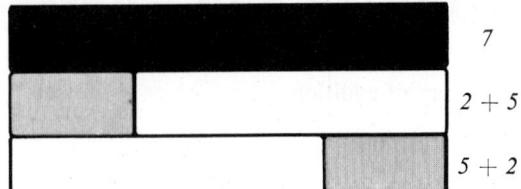

7

$2 + 5$

$5 + 2$

Figure 9:5

More addition situations

A child has to abstract the mathematical operation of addition from all the situations of forming the union of two disjoint sets which he meets.[3] He must also find out that the same numerical relationships turn up when he combines two quantities, or two sums of money. At this stage, he will need much experience of situations like the following:

i) He finds that he can balance a bar of chocolate against 5 ten-gram masses, and a bag of sweets against 4 ten-gram masses. He puts them on the scales together and finds he needs 9 ten-gram masses to balance them.
ii) He puts two rods, one measuring 5 centimetres, and the other measuring 4 centimetres, end to end and finds that they fit alongside a rod of length 9 centimetres.
iii) He buys at the shop a pencil for 2 pence, and some sweets for 3 pence. He has to pay 5 pence altogether.

$$2 \text{ pence} + 3 \text{ pence} = 5 \text{ pence}$$

The teacher will be able to provide children with many experiences using measures whose numerical content is equivalent to that found in the combination of sets. For her own satisfaction, the teacher may also ponder on situations where the addition of numbers is inappropriate, such as:

i) mixing a jug of water whose temperature is 20° with a jug of water whose temperature is 30° does not give a temperature of 50°.
ii) playing, on the piano, the second note of a scale together with the third note does not give the fifth note.

From a variety of experiences, children come to learn the different situations in which quantities can be added, and so to abstract the idea of addition from its various concrete embodiments.

It should be emphasized that experience of addition, and discovery of the addition facts, in a variety of different practical situations is more valuable to children than constant repetition of sums on paper, for only through practical experience can children understand what addition means.

---

[2] Addition has become commutative (*see page* 88).

[3] *Disjoint* sets are sets which have no members in common.

Further steps in addition

Through the variety of their practical experience children become very much at home with the smaller numbers, so that a child knows immediately that a toy car has two front wheels and two back wheels, making four wheels in all, or that if he has tenpence to spend and spends fourpence, he will be left with sixpence. This complete familiarity with numbers up to ten will be helped by the use of structural apparatus. Building walls with Cuisenaire rods, or filling in the Stern number cases, gives a great deal of practice in the analysis of each number up to ten (Figure 9:6).

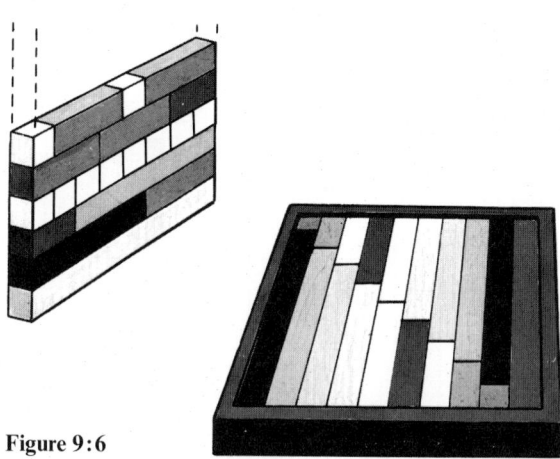

Figure 9:6

The analysis of a number can also be recorded, in a more permanent form, on squared paper, using coloured squares or strips of gummed paper (Figure 9:7).

It is important that the detailed knowledge of numbers which is obtained by analysing them should not stop at ten, but should gradually be built up during the early school years so that children are very familiar with the numbers up to twenty. This will help them to use numbers easily as they grow older.

We shall see how useful knowledge of the numbers from 11 to 20 is in further addition and in subtraction (*see page 124*). Let us consider 15. A child must first see it as made up of 10 and 5. Here again structural apparatus, whose longest rod is the ten-rod, is useful, for a child is driven to make 15 in two parts, as 10 and 5. But he can also make 15 in various other ways, sometimes using two rods, sometimes more. Some of the possibilities are shown in Figure 9:8. These are of two sorts:

i) those which include a ten in one of the numbers:

$$13 + 2 = 15,$$

ii) those which do not show a ten, such as

$$8 + 7 = 15.$$

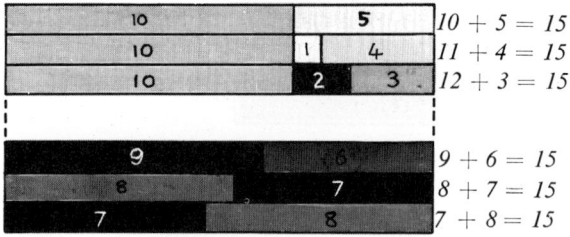

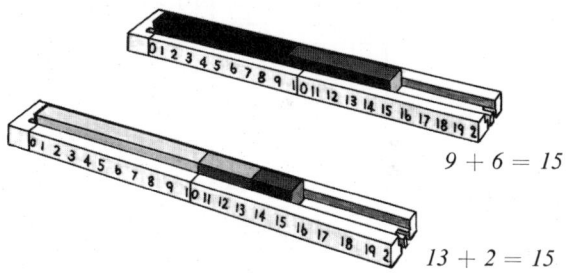

Figure 9:8

Two ways of recording the analysis of 5

1	+	4	=	5
2	+	3	=	5
3	+	2	=	5
4	+	1	=	5
5	+	0	=	5

	1	2	3	4	5
+	4	+3	+2	+1	+0
	5	5	5	5	5

Figure 9:7

The structure of both types of addition fact should be known by the time children come to do more complicated addition and subtraction.

Use of the twenty-tray of the Stern apparatus or similar work on graph paper or with other structural apparatus enables children to see the repetition of the pattern of the numbers 1 to 10 in the pattern of the numbers 11 to 20. A graph can be continued to show the further repetition of the pattern in higher decades.

The Stern twenty tray

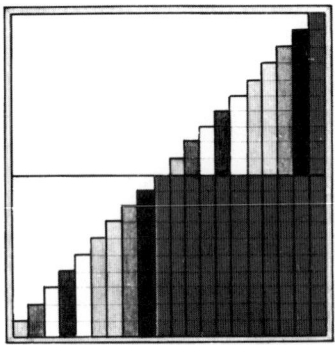

How numbers grow

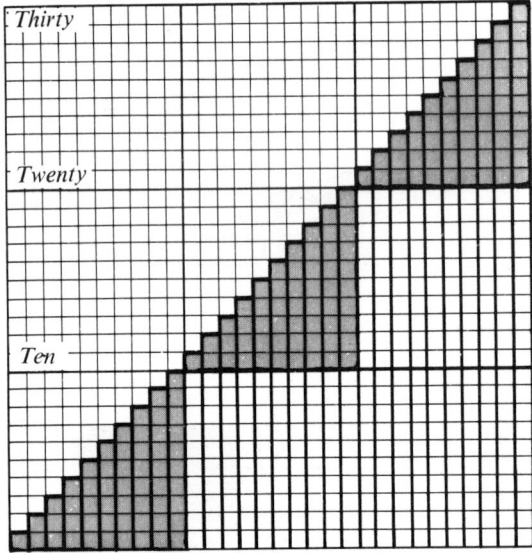

Figure 9:9

The Stern number-track is another useful device for emphasizing the building of tens. Children very easily see how pushing in a ten, and then another ten, at the beginning of the track converts $3+2 = 5$ into $13+2 = 15$, $23+2 = 25$ and so on (Figure 9:10).

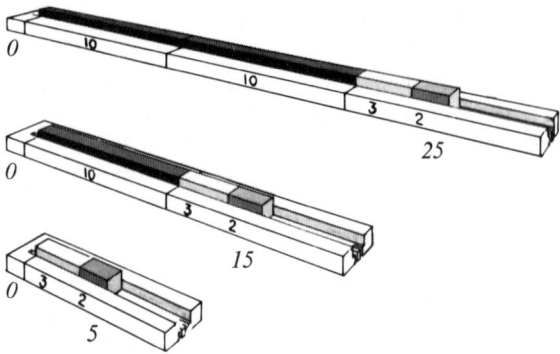

Figure 9:10

Graphical expression on 1-cm or $\frac{1}{2}$-cm squared paper is visually impressive (Figure 9:11).

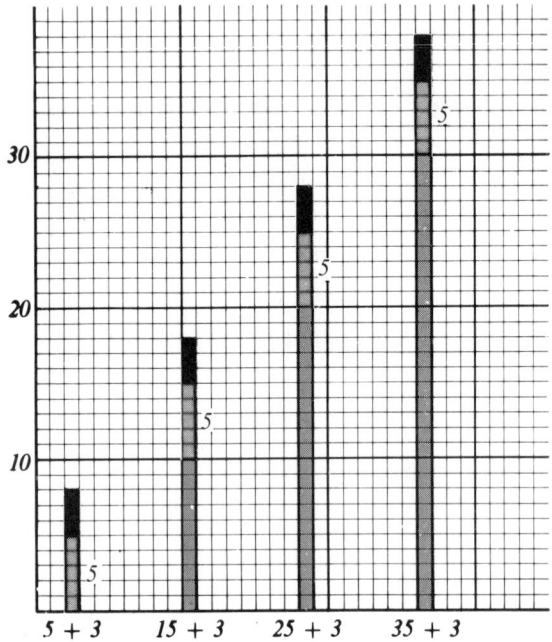

Figure 9:11

The teacher will see that this process of 'moving up ten' forms the basis for all higher decade addition; a child will, however, only be able to make full use of this if he knows at sight the sum of any two single digit numbers; that is, if he can immediately and automatically regroup $8+7$ as $10+5$ or fifteen.[4] The use of structural apparatus helps this regrouping (Figure 9:12) and the process of 'moving up ten' can be extended to cover such facts as $18+7$, $28+7$,

---

[4] In order to be able to subtract with confidence, he will need to regroup 15 as $8+7$ (*see page 85*).

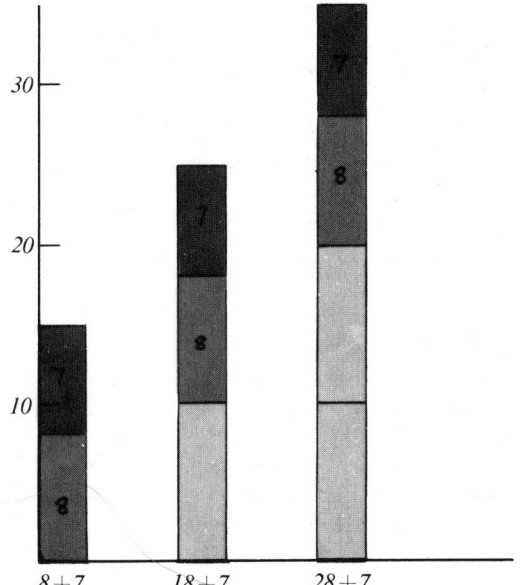

Figure 9:12

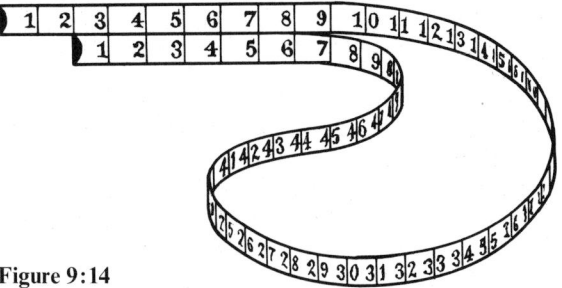

Figure 9:14

The language of addition

Children abstract the idea of addition from a great variety of real experience (*see page* 75). If they talk about these experiences, as they should, they will talk about each one in the everyday language appropriate to it. Examples of such language are:

 i) 'The chocolate and the sweets *together balance* 90 *grams*.'
 ii) 'I *spent* 6 pence *altogether*.'
 iii) 'The box *measures* 22 cm *all the way round*.'
 iv) 'When I put another litre of water in the saucepan, *it comes up to* the 3-litre mark.'

It is important that different situations should be described in the language appropriate to each one, but as children realize that the numbers occurring in each situation are combined in the same way, they begin to need signs and language, not only for the numbers, but for the ways in which they are combined. The process of abstraction is helped by the fact that the + and = signs are used in all the contexts in which, for instance, the combination of 5 and 3 is found to be 8. It will also help children if they use the same neutral words, which are not tied to any particular context, when they read the signs. Suitable neutral words for '+' and '=' are 'plus' and 'equals'.

'Five and three *makes* eight' is not a good way of reading

$$5+3=8,$$

as a child will soon have to learn that

$$5-3=2$$

is read as 'five take away three *leaves* two'. It is confusing if the sign = is read differently in the two sentences. The

and so on. This stage is often left out in children's discovery of number, so that children who know that $8+7=15$ often do not see that $38+7$ is related to it, and so count laboriously 7 onwards from 38.

Another piece of apparatus which is useful in the discovery of the behaviour of numbers greater than ten is a slide-rule made from two tape-measures. It is convenient to have one of these fixed to the wall, or to a table, the other being movable (Figure 9:13). A child who wishes to examine $8+7$, $18+7$, $28+7$ and so on measures 7 centimetres on from the 8 centimetre mark, the 18 centimetre mark and so on. If a tape-measure has markings on both sides, the two ends of it can be used in the same way (Figure 9:14).

The slide-rule can also be used to add any two numbers whose sum is less than the length of the tape-measure, although further understanding of this addition will await understanding of the system of notation (*see page* 120). The tape-measure slide-rule is also extremely useful for subtraction (*see page* 83).

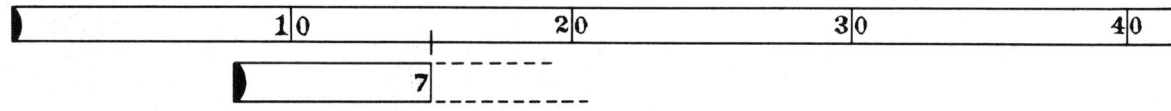

Figure 9:13

more contexts a mathematical word can be used in, the more it helps to direct attention to the mathematical abstraction rather than to the particular context. 'Equals' is a good word, because $5+3$ equals 8, and $5-3$ equals 2; 'makes' and 'leaves' are less good, because they only apply to addition and subtraction, respectively.

'Add' would be a good reading of the sign '+' if it were not grammatically incorrect. Mathematics is a language, and, like English, is written in sentences, each with its verb. The verb in the sentence $5+3 = 8$ is 'equals', so it is bad mathematical style also to read '+' as a verb. The word 'plus', which is a conjunction, does not suffer from this disadvantage. Children acquire their mathematical style, as they do their English style, from the language which they hear, speak, read and write. It is important that mathematical language should be carefully and accurately used from the beginning, and that children should avoid slang usages in mathematics which they will later have to alter.

Transformations

When children have made a staircase with structural apparatus, they often add a unit rod to each step of the staircase. This operation transforms the 'one to ten' staircase into a 'two to eleven' staircase. Similarly, the addition of a 2-rod to each step transforms the set of numbers

$$\{1, 2, 3, \ldots, 10\}$$

into the set of numbers

$$\{3, 4, 5, \ldots, 12\}$$

and the addition of a 10-rod transforms the set

$$\{1, 2, 3, \ldots, 10\}$$

into the set

$$\{11, 12, 13, \ldots, 20\}$$

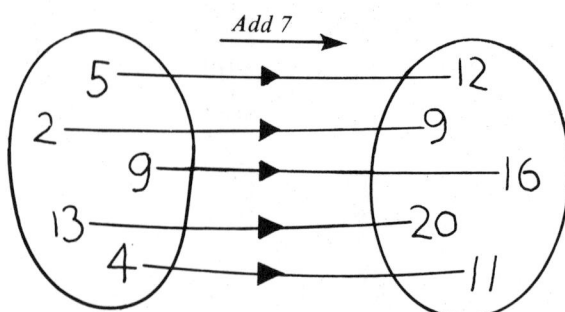

Figure 9:16

We can think of the operation of *adding one*, or *adding seven*, or adding any other number, as an operation which transforms the whole set of numbers. A child may like to show his skill at adding seven by taking a set of numbers at random and performing the *transformation* 'add 7' on the whole set (Figure 9:16).

A more systematic way of showing this transformation is to draw part of the 'number track' or *number line* twice, and to show what happens to each number on it if 7 is added (Figure 9:17).

Transformations are also called *mappings,* as each member of a set of numbers is *mapped on to* a member of another set of numbers. A transformation can be illustrated by a relation diagram such as Figure 9:16 or 9:17, or by a graph (Figure 9:18). We see that transformations are relations in which only one arrow leaves each member of the set which is transformed.

(Figure 9:15).

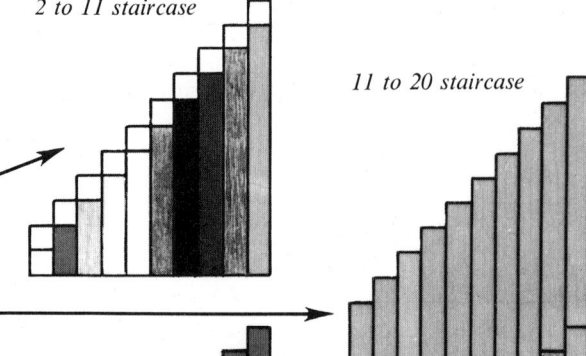

Figure 9:15

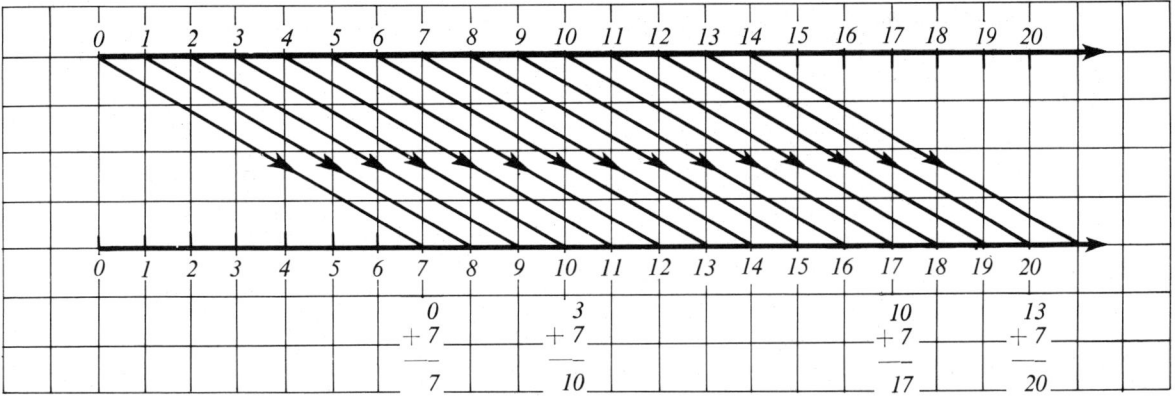

Figure 9:17

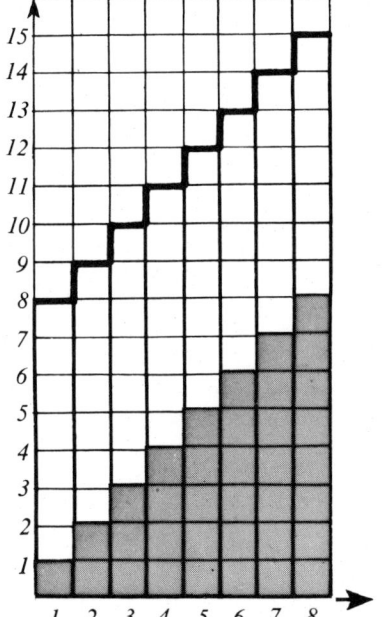

Figure 9:18

Subtraction and its relation to addition

When a child first meets the idea of subtraction, it does not seem to him to be related to addition. He has lost something; he has eaten some of his sweets or has drunk some of his milk. He had fivepence, but he has spent fourpence, and only one penny is left. The fourpence has permanently and irreversibly gone. Sweets which have been eaten have gone for ever. But if a child is to deal mathematically with subtraction situations, this process must become reversible. Before he spends his money, he must be encouraged to look at the 4 pence which he will spend, together with the remaining 1 penny, and see that they make 5 pence. He must also be able to separate his 5 sweets into 3 to be eaten and 2 to be kept, so that he can

see that he is dealing with another example of addition.

Subtraction is only fully understood when it is seen as an aspect of addition. Figure 9:19 shows that 3 sweets out of 5 have been eaten, and illustrates the parallel experience using structural apparatus. The partitioning of a set of 5 things into two subsets is exactly the same whether it is described by

$$3+2 = 5 \quad \text{or} \quad 2+3 = 5$$
$$\text{or } 5-3 = 2 \quad \text{or} \quad 5-2 = 3$$

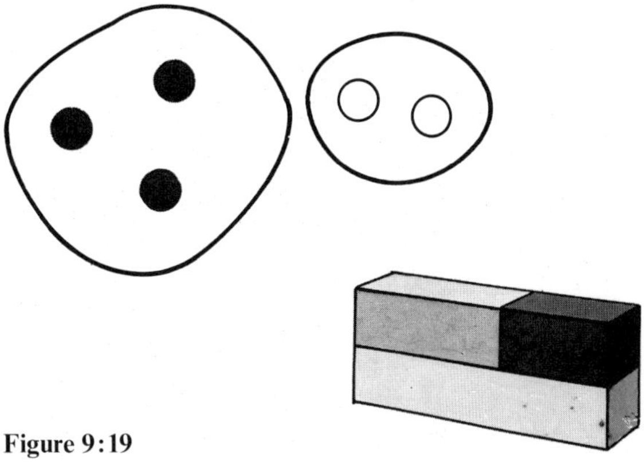

Figure 9:19

The physical process of 'taking away' follows the partitioning of the set into its subsets. Children can use the numerical knowledge which they already possess to carry out subtraction if they see its relation to addition, and so they should be encouraged to think of subtraction as a regrouping of a number: '5−2 = 3 because 2+3 = 5'. The use of structural apparatus, and the discovery of number patterns (see Chapter 7) is helpful here. Each of the diagrams illustrating addition in this chapter also illustrates two related subtractions. For instance, Figure 9:10 shows

$$\left.\begin{array}{l} 3+2 = 5 \\ 13+2 = 15 \\ 23+2 = 25 \end{array}\right\} \quad \text{and} \quad \left\{\begin{array}{ll} 5-\ 3 = 2, & 5-2 = 3 \\ 15-13 = 2, & 15-2 = 13 \\ 25-23 = 2, & 25-2 = 23 \end{array}\right.$$

81

The language of subtraction

The language of the practical situations in which children use the idea of subtraction is even more varied than for addition. Some examples follow, with illustrations emphasizing the fact that in each case a set is partitioned into two subsets.

i) The children play skittles. A ball *knocks down* 3 of the 9 skittles. Only 6 are *left* standing.

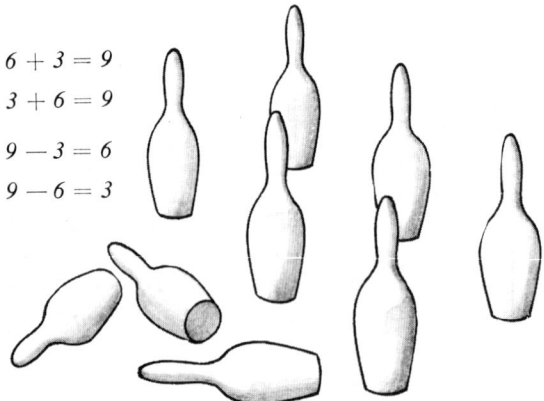

$6 + 3 = 9$

$3 + 6 = 9$

$9 - 3 = 6$

$9 - 6 = 3$

Figure 9:20

ii) Peter buys a pencil *costing* 8 pence. He has 2 pence *change* from a tenpenny piece.

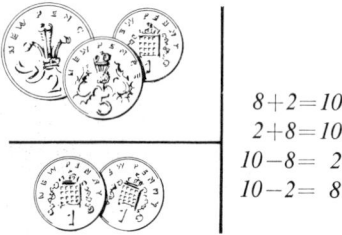

$8+2=10$
$2+8=10$
$10-8= 2$
$10-2= 8$

Figure 9:21

iii) Sally has 9 pence. Simon has 4 pence. He has 5 pence *less than* Sally.

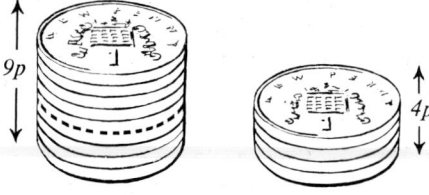

9p

4p

Figure 9:22

82

iv) Robert has 7 marbles. Peter has 4 marbles. Robert has 3 marbles *more* than Peter.

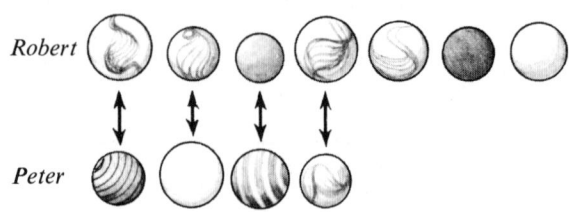

Robert

Peter

Figure 9:23

v) Alan has 8 dominoes. Robert has 5 dominoes. If he takes 3 *more*, they will have *the same* number.

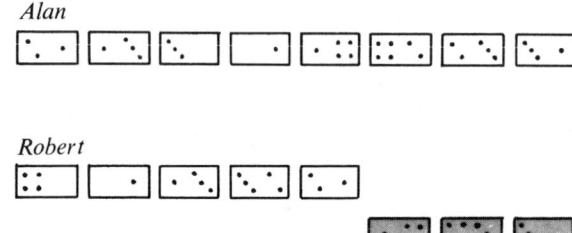

Alan

Robert

Figure 9:24

Children need varied experience to see that in all these situations the idea of splitting a set into subsets is present. In each situation there is a dominant idea:

i) *taking away*, as in 'John has 5 sweets; he eats 2; how many are left?' or

ii) *inverse* or *complementary addition*, as in, 'What must be added to 2 to make 5?' or

iii) *comparison*, as in, 'How much more is 5 than 2?'

The teacher must provide a sufficient variety of experiences for children to realize that the numerical content of all the types (i), (ii) and (iii) is the same, and for them to abstract the idea of subtraction, $5-2 = 3$, from all three situations. Graphical work can provide a starting point for many *comparisons* (Figure 9:25) and the teacher can take the opportunity of letting the children describe the comparisons in a variety of ways.

Shopping, the numbers of children absent, the number of children who do not drink milk, and various events in the classroom, will provide opportunities for *taking away* and *inverse addition*.

When it embodies so many experiences, how is the sentence '$5-2 = 3$' to be read? It should be read as a sentence, so that the most acceptable form of words which is detached from a particular context is 'five *minus* two equals three'. A child should also see and hear $5-2$ as 'What must be added to 2 to make 5?' This link between

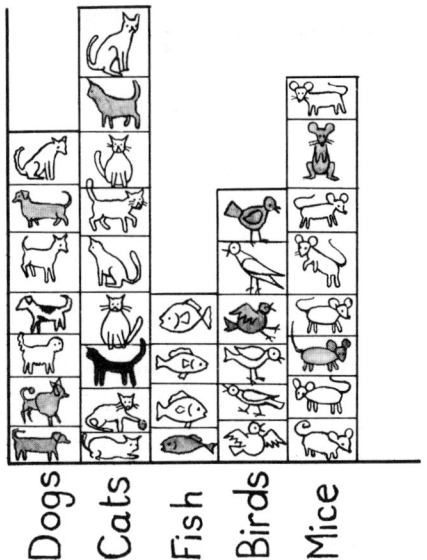

Dogs Cats Fish Birds Mice

Figure 9:25

subtraction and addition is all-important and should be emphasized continually.

Even at this early stage, the teacher should bear in mind the fact that a child's conception of addition and sub-traction will change and develop as he grows older. He will have to make 'inverse addition' the central idea in his concept of subtraction before he can, later on, make sense of 2−5 (*see pages* 337–341). It is not possible to take 5 things from 2 things, and so a concept of subtraction as 'taking away' will be inadequate to meet this new situation. Too much use of the words 'take away', and too great a concentration on 'taking away' situations in subtraction, may hinder or prevent the development of thought which makes understanding of negative numbers possible. The reading of 5−2 as '5 minus 2' is greatly to be preferred, and so is a treatment of subtraction which stresses both the variety of circumstances in which it occurs, and the fact that subtraction is basically inverse addition.

More about subtraction: the slide rule

The tape-measure slide-rule can be used for subtraction as well as for addition. It will probably be used in two main ways. A child who wants to find a number 3 less than 11 will count back 3 from the 11-unit mark. This starts to build up a concept of subtraction which will be more

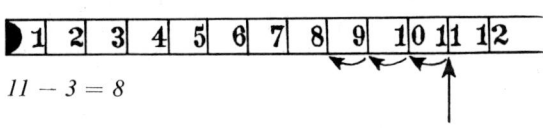

11 − 3 = 8

Figure 9:26

useful later,[5] and will also enable him to subtract accurately using any numbers within the range of the tape-measure. If the numbers involved are large, children will find it more convenient to measure backwards, using another tape-measure or the back of the same tape, instead of counting backwards. At the same time as, or just before, the *tens system of notation* is explored,[6] children may gain useful

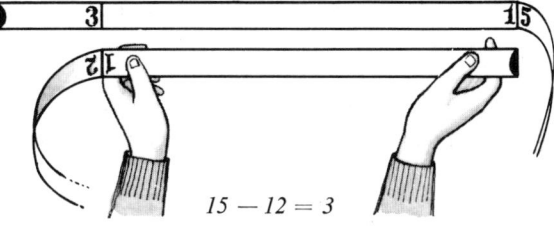

15 − 12 = 3

Figure 9:27

experience by using the tape-measure slide-rule to find the results of such related additions and subtractions as

$$2+10 =$$
$$2+20 = \quad \text{and} \quad 12+10 =$$
$$2+30 = \quad \text{and} \quad 12+20 = \quad \text{and} \quad 22+10 =$$

and so on; and in reverse

$$52-10 =$$
$$52-20 = \quad \text{and} \quad 42-10 =$$
$$52-30 = \quad \text{and} \quad 42-20 = \quad \text{and} \quad 32-10 =$$

and so on. Children should be encouraged to look for pattern in this type of work, and to invent their own patterns. Repeated addition and subtraction of numbers other than 10 on the slide-rule can be used to give multi-plication and division experience (*see page* 143), and to lead towards the use of the desk calculating machine (*see page* 166).

The slide-rule can also be used as an aid when sub-traction is thought of as inverse addition. A child who wants to know 16−9 may think of it as, '9 plus what equals 16?' He will then count or measure onwards from the 9-unit mark of the tape-measure until he reaches the 16-unit mark. This use of the slide-rule is exactly parallel to the use of structural apparatus for 16−9, when a child places a 9-rod alongside rods making up 16, and then finds which rod fills the gap.

It is advisable to use both the tape-measure slide-rule and structural apparatus, for each has its advantages. Through repeated use of structural apparatus children

[5] It is necessary for the understanding of directed numbers (*see page* 337).

[6] See Chapter 13.

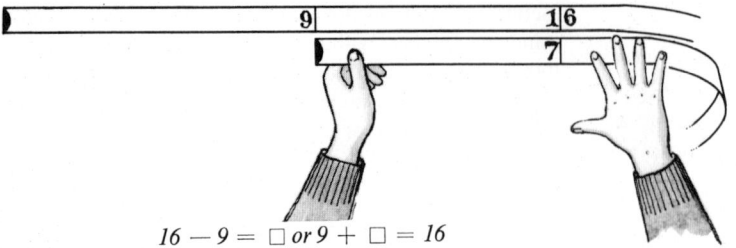

$$16 - 9 = \square \; or \; 9 + \square = 16$$

Figure 9:28

come to remember which rods fit together, and so to remember the addition facts and to associate addition and subtraction with one another. The slide-rule, on the other hand, associates addition and subtraction with movement in a way which will be important for later developments.[7] A child who counts or measures onward or back along the tape-measure moves his finger or his eye forward or backward along the number line, whereas when he uses structural apparatus he estimates what length will fill a gap, without taking account of the direction in which that length is measured.

The use of the tape-measure slide-rule for measuring backwards in subtraction will also help children to see that they can make *subtraction transformations* as well as addition transformations of sets of numbers. Figure 9:29 illustrates the transformation 'subtract 7'.

Children will discover that they cannot apply this transformation to the complete set of numbers. Figure 9:29 illustrates this difficulty very clearly, showing the attempt to subtract 7 from every member of the set {1, 2, 3, . . . , 14, 15}. A child may suggest at this point that more numbers could be put in to show units below the starting point. Even if this idea does not appear, the graph focuses attention on a problem which is solved later by the introduction of directed numbers.[8]

[7] See the sections on vectors and directed numbers, pages 90 and 334.

[8] See Chapter 35.

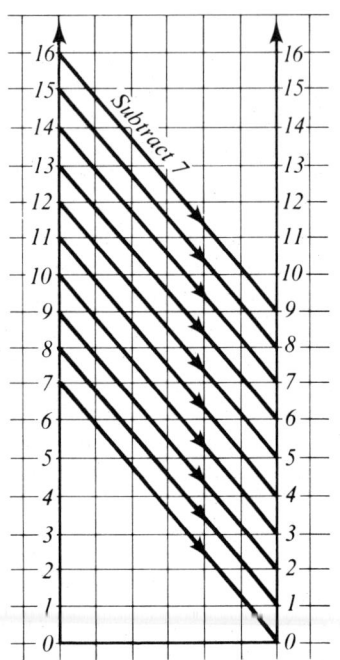

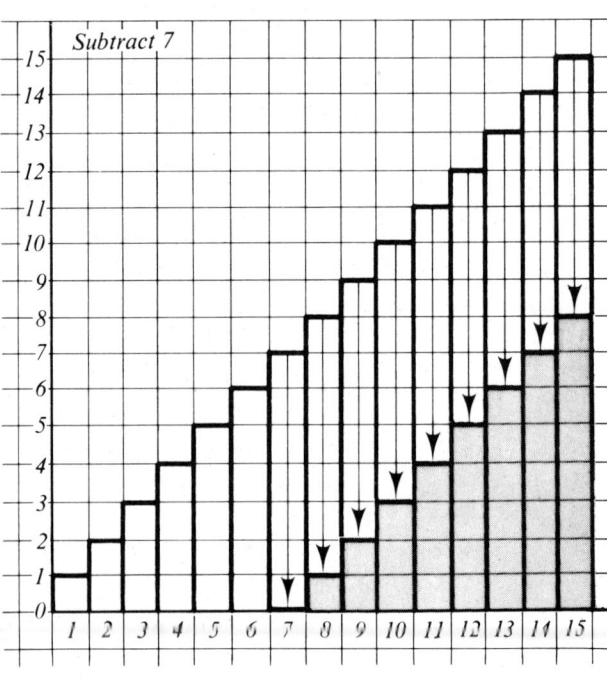

Figure 9:29

Alongside children's discovery of the meaning of subtraction, and of its relation to addition, their familiarity with the numbers up to 20 will be developing. The regrouping of 15 as $8+7$ will be most important in dealing with a subtraction like $35-17$. Whether such regroupings are basically matters of addition or subtraction does not matter. They have a variety of uses, and children at this stage, in their practical activities, should constantly be meeting such situations as the following, which involve regrouping.

i) The same distance is measured with rods and with a tape-measure, involving the regrouping of 19 centimetres as 10 centimetres and 9 cm.

ii) Two things each costing 9 pence are bought together. The cost is regrouped so that a child can pay with a tenpenny piece and eight pennies.

iii) The shopkeeper giving change regroups the money paid to him, literally or in the imagination, into two parts. He often uses a 'counting on' method in doing this (*see page* 82).

Addition and subtraction which involve numbers greater than 20, sums of money involving more than ten pence, and similar quantities, demand understanding of our system of notation, and will be discussed in Chapter 13. Familiarity with, and regrouping of, numbers up to 20 is a necessary preliminary to this.

10 The Natural Numbers, Movement and Vectors

The natural numbers

In previous chapters we have seen how children acquire their first knowledge of numbers, and how they begin to combine these numbers by the operations of addition and subtraction. The numbers which the children are using are only a limited selection from a much wider range of numbers used in mathematics. The fractions and the positive and negative directed numbers have not yet been used systematically, although children will have begun to use halves and quarters in their measuring; these kinds of numbers are like the whole numbers in some ways but unlike them in other ways.

We shall need to distinguish the set of numbers $\{0, 1, 2, 3, \ldots\}$ from the other types of number which appear in later work. The set of numbers $\{0, 1, 2, 3, \ldots\}$ is called the set of *natural numbers*.[1] We shall use the letter N to stand for the set of natural numbers, so that

$$N = \{0, 1, 2, 3, \ldots\}$$

The set N has no end, and there is no largest, or last, natural number. None of $\frac{1}{2}, (-4), 0\cdot3333\ldots$, is a natural number. The natural numbers are those numbers which arise only from counting, combining and partitioning sets of things. At the stage which we are discussing, a child will only have a very hazy idea of the existence of numbers such as $\frac{1}{2}$, which are not natural numbers, and his thought is unlikely to have developed to a stage when he could think of (-4) as a number.

The natural numbers are the building blocks from which a large part of mathematics is constructed. But the construction of mathematics starts, not with numbers in isolation, but with combinations of numbers, the patterns which numbers make when they combine, and the laws which these operations obey. In the last chapter we saw how children begin to combine numbers and to build up the operations of addition and subtraction. We now look at some mathematical features of the operations of adding and subtracting the natural numbers.

Closure

Although we have only discussed children's discovery of two operations on natural numbers, addition and sub-

traction, these operations will lead them to multiplication and division, and it will be useful when discussing the mathematical structure of operations on numbers to take examples from multiplication and division as well as from addition and subtraction.

The first point which we notice about the four operations on numbers, addition, subtraction, multiplication and division, is that the numbers with which we operate have always been (so far) chosen from the set of natural numbers, but the resulting number may or may not be a natural number. Consider the numbers resulting from applying the four operations of arithmetic to 3 and 7:

i) $3 + 7$ is a natural number;
ii) $3 - 7$ is not a natural number, although $7 - 3$ is;
iii) 3×7 is a natural number;
iv) neither $3 \div 7$ nor $7 \div 3$ is a natural number.

Children who know only the natural numbers will express this by saying that they can do $3 + 7$, $7 - 3$ and 3×7, but they cannot do $3 - 7$ (to them it does not make sense), nor can they divide 3 by 7, nor 7 by 3 without leaving a remainder.

We have brought out a property which is true for addition and multiplication, but not true for subtraction and division. The result of adding or multiplying any two natural numbers is *always* a natural number. But, if we are given any pair of natural numbers, such as 3 and 7, it is not always possible to subtract them or divide them *in that order* and obtain a natural number. We describe this situation by saying that *the set of natural numbers is closed for addition* and is *closed for multiplication,* but *the set of natural numbers is not closed for subtraction or for division*.

+	0	1	2	3	4	5	.
0	0	1	2	3	4	5	.
1	1	2	3	4	5	6	.
2	2	3	4	5	6	7	.
3	3	4	5	6	7	8	.
4	4	5	6	7	8	9	.
5	5	6	7	8	9	10	.
.	.	.	.	.	.	.	.

Figure 10:1

[1] Some authors use natural numbers as a name for the set $\{1, 2, 3, \ldots\}$ excluding 0, but we shall prefer to include 0, so that the set of natural numbers is the set of numbers used in a child's first experiences of counting, adding and subtracting.

The set of natural numbers is incomplete for subtraction. Any addition of natural numbers can be done, but only some subtractions have natural numbers as answers. We can visualize the construction of a complete addition table for the natural numbers (Figure 10:1). The reader will notice that this table is symmetrical about its leading diagonal (Figure 10:2). The table for any commutative operation (*see page* 88) possesses this symmetry.

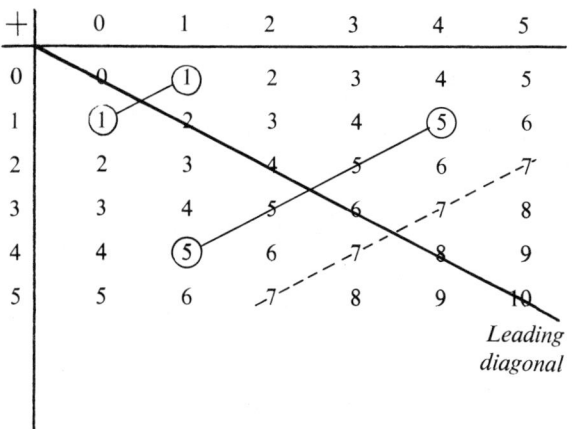

Figure 10:2

This table is arranged so that the result of the addition $3+4$ is read from the *row* marked 3 (the first number) and the *column marked* 4 (the second number). The order in which the table is read is shown in Figure 10:3. This order

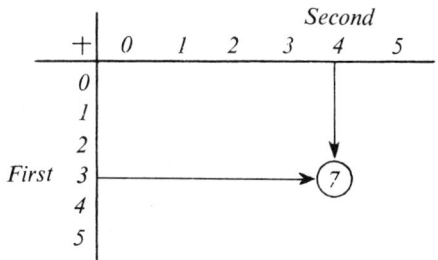

Figure 10:3

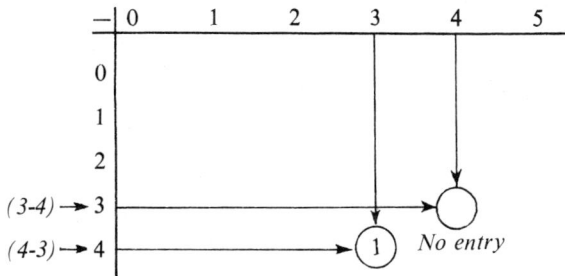

Figure 10:4

−	0	1	2	3	4	5
0	0					
1	1	0				
2	2	1	0			
3	3	2	1	0		
4	4	3	2	1	0	
5	5	4	3	2	1	0
·	·	·	·	·	·	·

Figure 10:5

becomes important if we construct a natural number subtraction table. There is no entry for $3-4$, as this is not a natural number, but $4-3=1$ has an entry (Figure 10:4). The beginning of the subtraction table is shown in Figure 10:5, blank spaces being left when a subtraction is not possible in the set of natural numbers.

There are some stages in children's development when the property of closure limits the freedom of their work. A child who can only deal with numbers in tens and ones, that is the set of numbers $\{0, 1, 2, \ldots 99\}$, cannot yet tackle the sum $98+99$. The answer is out of his range; his set of numbers $\{0, 1, 2, \ldots 99\}$ is not closed for addition. This fact gives a motive for the extension of his number system; more than 9 tens will turn up at some time in his experience, so he is led to discover a new, extended system of numbers, the set $\{0, 1, 2, 3, \ldots 999\}$; and eventually he extends his set of numbers until he can add any pair of numbers belonging to the infinite set of natural numbers $N = \{0, 1, 2, 3, \ldots\}$, which is closed for addition.

Sets of numbers which are not closed for some arithmetical operation often give a motive for the discovery of new mathematical systems. The set of natural numbers is inadequate; it is a frustrating limitation that not every subtraction is possible. Can a new set of numbers be constructed in which every subtraction has an answer? In the search for answers to such questions as this, mathematics grows and adapts itself to changing situations. As children grow older, they need help in finding the limitations of their mathematics, and in seeing the need for new extensions and discoveries. The problem of finding a set of numbers which is closed for subtraction reappears in this book, and is finally answered in Chapter 32.

Digression on language

The definition given on page 86 of the *closure* of a set of numbers for an operation, illustrates a feature of mathematical language which may not be obvious at first sight. The technical words of mathematics are not always new words, invented for the purpose, but words which have a common everyday use. When a word like 'closed' is taken into mathematics, it is given a precise meaning which is not quite the same as its everyday one; the everyday meaning, however, reminds us of the mathematical meaning. 'Closed for addition' is a sensible description of a set of numbers such that we never get outside them by the operation of addition. It is as if the numbers were in a room with a closed door. But the set of natural numbers is not closed for subtraction; the door is open for the construction of new numbers which will make $3-7$ possible.

This way of inventing technical words helps the memory, but we must remember that mathematical words, whether or not they are used in everyday language, have a precise, clear, exact meaning. As children gain mathematical experience, they must be helped to learn the language of mathematics by building up a vocabulary of mathematical words which they will use to describe their mathematical ideas. Words such as 'minus', 'rectangle' and 'cuboid' are not too difficult for young children if these words precisely express real mathematical experience. 'Aeroplane' is a difficult word, but it is meaningfully used by small children because they see aeroplanes and play with model aeroplanes. In the same way, children use mathematical words correctly and meaningfully if these words express what they have handled and understood.

The commutative law

A feature of the addition of natural numbers is that the order in which the operation is performed makes no difference to the answer. This feature is more interesting when it is absent than when it is present. In the subtraction of natural numbers, the order of subtraction makes a good deal of difference; $7-3=4$, but $3-7$ has no answer in the set of natural numbers, and even if we work in the set of the positive and negative integers (*see page* 341), where $3-7=-4$, it is certainly not true that $3-7$ is equal to $7-3$.

The order of the numbers in subtraction is vital, but the order of the numbers in addition is immaterial. It is much more convenient to perform an operation when order does not matter, and when the numbers can be arranged in whatever order suits us best; that is when the order of the numbers can be interchanged, or *commuted*, without making any difference to the result. The operation of addition is *commutative*, and for any pair of numbers a and b,

$$a+b=b+a,$$

but the operation of subtraction is not commutative, and in general

$$b-a \neq a-b.$$

Multiplication is commutative, so that for instance $3 \times 4 = 4 \times 3$; but division is not commutative, and $3 \div 4 \neq 4 \div 3$.

We often automatically use the commutative property of addition. When calculating $3+22$ mentally it is usual to change the order, and starting with 22, add 3 to it, so replacing $3+22$ by $22+3$. When we add up a bill, we usually check the result by adding in the opposite direction, in the certainty that addition is commutative. Some mistakes which children make in subtraction are due to a failure to understand that subtraction is not commutative. A child who writes

$$\begin{array}{r} 34 \\ -15 \\ \hline 21 \\ \hline \end{array}$$

that is, a child who when he cannot subtract 5 from 4 subtracts 4 from 5 instead, has not had enough real experience of concrete subtraction. He can only make this mistake if he thinks of subtraction as a process to be performed on paper; he will never make it if he sees subtraction as a real situation which is very obviously not commutative.

We shall discuss more examples of commutative and non-commutative operations as the work proceeds, and we shall notice how much children use the commutative law in calculation, and how much it contributes to their understanding, in particular, of the operation of multiplication (*see page* 145).

Addition and subtraction

So far in this chapter we have treated addition and subtraction as if they were two unrelated operations. This was possible while we discussed closure and commutativity, which are properties belonging to an operation on a set of numbers. Both addition and subtraction are operations and can be used to illustrate these properties; but we must not lose sight of the close connection between addition and subtraction.

In Chapter 9 we said that 'subtraction is only fully understood when it is seen as an aspect of addition' (*see page* 81). The statement $8-5=3$ is another aspect of $5+3=8$, and '$8-5$' can equally well be thought of as 'take 5 away from 8' or 'What must be added to 5 to give 8?' Subtraction is inverse addition in the sense that we are asked to find the missing number in an addition sum.

We shall use an empty box to represent a missing number. This is convenient for children, because they can write the missing number in the box. We see that $8-5=\square$ is another way of writing $5+\square=8$, and a child will use his knowledge of the addition fact $5+3=8$ to fill the box in $8-5=\square$. Until he has seen this connection between addition and subtraction, he will either have to use apparatus to 'take away 5 from 8', or he will count back 5 from 8. The use of structural apparatus will help him to realize in how many different ways the language of mathematics describes the same situation (Figure 10:6) so that he can move freely between the descriptions, and form a unified concept of addition and subtraction.

The same arrangement of rods answers all these questions

$5 + 3 = \square$	$3 + 5 = \square$
$\square = 5 + 3$	$\square = 3 + 5$
$5 + \square = 8$	$\square + 3 = 8$
$8 - 5 = \square$	$8 - 3 = \square$

Figure 10:6

Sentences in the language of mathematics

By this stage, children are using the language of number freely, and are writing sentences in mathematical language to express their discoveries.

$5 + 3 = 8$ is a simple mathematical sentence, consisting of a subject (five plus three), a verb (is equal to) and a complement (eight). It is also a *true* sentence. If a child makes a mistake and writes $5 + 3 = 7$, he has still written a mathematical sentence, but this sentence is *false*. A sentence such as $5 + \square = 8$ is neither true nor false until it is completed by writing a number in the space. It is an *open sentence,* and as we ask children to complete it by filling in a number which will make the sentence into a true statement. An *open sentence* is a sentence which has some number or numbers in it missing, so that we cannot decide whether it is true or false. All the statements in Figure 10:6 are open sentences. They become true or false statements when the child writes a number in the space.

Some open sentences can be truthfully completed in more than one way. The sentence $\square \times 0 = 0$ is true whatever number is written in the blank space. We say that the *truth set* or *solution set* of the open sentence $\square \times 0 = 0$ is the set of all numbers, because, for example

$$2 \times 0 = 0, \quad 3 \times 0 = 0, \quad 5\tfrac{1}{2} \times 0 = 0, \quad (-2) \times 0 = 0$$

and so on. Some open sentences can never be completed truthfully. It is not possible to put a number in the blank space of the open sentence $\square \times 0 = 1$ which will make the sentence into a true statement. The solution set of this open sentence is the empty set, which has no members (*see page* 25). The empty box serves as a *place-holder* in an open sentence. It holds open the space, which can be filled by any number. We always try to fill the space so

as to convert the open sentence into a true sentence.

As children get older, they will find it more convenient to write a letter instead of the empty box as a place-holder in an open sentence. The sentence $5 + \square = 8$ becomes the sentence $5 + x = 8$. Instead of $5 + \boxed{3} = 8$ to make the open sentence into a true statement, a child will now write

$$5 + x = 8$$
$$\Rightarrow x = 3$$

The sign $\Rightarrow$ shows that the second statement follows from the first. It is usually read 'if (1st statement), then (2nd statement). The above sentence is read: If $5 + x = 8$, then $x = 3$. Thus the child has written down the value of x which makes the open sentence $5 + x = 8$ into a true sentence.

Open sentences such as $n \times 0 = 0$, which are true for any value of the place-holder, are called *identities*. Another important identity is the commutative law of addition

$$a + b = b + a$$

This is a true sentence whatever numbers are substituted for the place-holders a and b.[2] Children become convinced of the truth of identities by seeing that they work in a large number of particular cases, and that they cannot find cases in which the identity is not true.[3] If the teacher wishes children to think about the commutative law explicitly rather than to accept it intuitively, filling in values of the place-holders which make a series of open sentences such as the following into true statements may be helpful.

$$\square + 1 = 1 + 3, \qquad \square + 5 = 5 + 8$$
$$2 + 4 = 4 + \square, \qquad 6 + \square = \square + 6$$
$$\square + 0 = 0 + \square, \qquad \square + 2 = \triangle + \square\,[4]$$
$$\square + \triangle = \triangle + \square$$

Some of these sentences can be made into true sentences in one way; other are identities, which can be completed in a variety of ways.

We can now express the statements made on page 88 in a different way. Children do not have an adequate conception of subtraction until they realize that open sentences such as

$$8 - 5 = x \quad \text{and} \quad 5 + x = 8$$

---

[2] The same number must be substituted for a letter whenever it occurs in the open sentence. If we substitute $a = 3$ and $b = 4$ in this sentence the sentence will read $3 + 4 = 4 + 3$.

[3] As a warning, the teacher might consider the open sentence, 'If x is a natural number, $x^2 - x + 41$ is a prime number' (*see page* 317). This is a true sentence if $x = 0, 1, 2, 3, \ldots, 40$, but is false when $x = 41$.

[4] When more than one place-holder occurs in an open sentence, different shaped boxes have been used.

are equivalent; that is, that they are two different ways of saying the same thing, and that they are satisfied by the same value of x. During much of their primary education, children's understanding of this relationship will be intuitive and informal rather than precise and formalized, and most children will only formalize it in later years. The teacher should, however, help children to find the relation between addition and subtraction from the beginning.

Three-number addition and the associative law for addition

Children's shopping activities, their increasing skill at measuring and their greater facility in the use of numbers will lead them to situations where they wish to add three or more numbers together, e.g. to find the distance all the way round a triangle.

At the stage at which apparatus is used for addition, adding three numbers is not much more complicated than adding two numbers. However, as a child progresses to being able to add mentally and to hold a number in mind while he adds another number to it, we find that addition of three numbers uses the same skills which have been learned in adding two numbers, together with an extra skill. For example, consider $6+9+7$. The child knows that $6+9 = 15$, and he then has to deal with $15+7$. He can do this mentally with ease if he realizes that he knows that $5+7 = 12$, and that $15+7$ is ten more than $5+7$. In fact he needs to be able to split up the 15 into $10+5$, and then regroup $(10+5)+7$ into $10+(5+7)$, so that he can use his knowledge of $5+7$. He then regroups $5+7$ into $10+2$, and finally combines the tens:

$$15+7 = (10+5)+7$$
$$= 10+(5+7)$$
$$= 10+(10+2)$$
$$= (10+10)+2$$
$$= 22$$

In practice, the thought-process is much briefer than this, and the child just focuses his attention on $5+7$, and then adds one ten. Similarly, he adds 35 and 7 by performing $5+7$, and then adds 1 ten to the 3 tens to obtain 42.

We see that all three-number addition depends on the regrouping of the numbers to make the addition easier. The fact that such regrouping is possible is known as *the associative law for addition*. This states that for any numbers a, b and c,

$$(a+b)+c = a+(b+c)$$

We see another example of the associative law at work in the thought-process of a child who prefers to add 15 and 7 by regrouping the 7 and using 20 as an intermediate resting place:

$$15+7 = 15+(5+2)$$
$$= (15+5)+2$$
$$= 20+2$$
$$= 22$$

A child who does not understand the regrouping implied by the associative law, and so cannot make use of his previous knowledge of addition, can only add 15 and 7 by counting 7 on from 15. It is fairly common to find children who know that $5+7 = 12$, but have not yet seen how to make use of this knowledge when they need to do $15+7$ or $35+7$, and so they count on laboriously.

The teacher will realize how much use he makes of the associative law for addition to regroup the numbers as he adds up a column of figures. Figure 10:7 shows the thought-process in adding down a column of figures, although in practice this is much abbreviated. The numbers in heavy type show where the associative law is used.

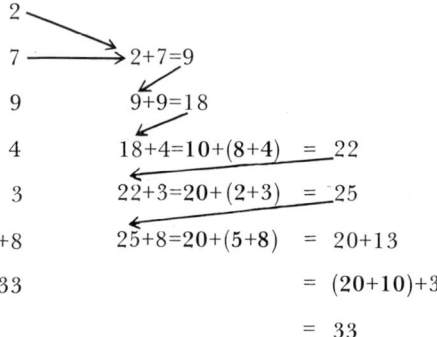

Figure 10:7

We shall see later that an associative law is also true for multiplication (*see page* 167), and that considerable use is made of it in long multiplication.

Vectors

In the early experiences of addition children meet two very different situations: sometimes the arrangement of the things which are added is unimportant; sometimes the arrangement is vital. Five things and three things together make eight things however the things are arranged, but if a child uses structural apparatus for addition he must put the rods end to end; no other arrangement will do (Figure 10:8). If a child uses the tape-measure slide-rule to find $5+3$, he must measure *onwards* three units from the 5 units mark (Figure 10:9). Lengths are only added when they are placed *end to end*. In these situations addition is associated with movement onward in the same direction.

We very often associate a measurement with a direction. When a child measures a corridor with a rod, he moves his rod on and on along the corridor, moving along the

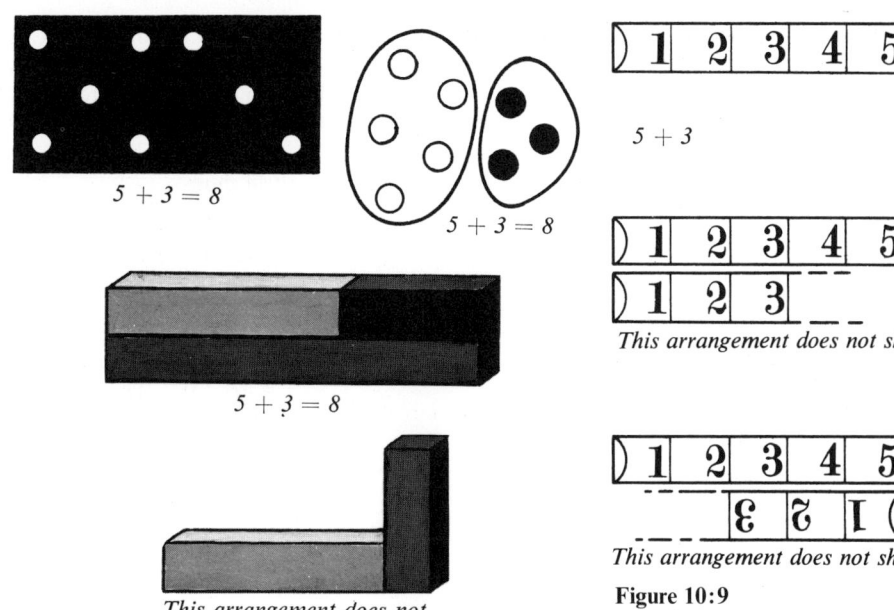

$5 + 3 = 8$

$5 + 3 = 8$

$5 + 3 = 8$

This arrangement does not show a child that $5 + 3 = 8$

Figure 10:8

$5 + 3$

This arrangement does not show $5 + 3$

This arrangement does not show $5 + 3$

Figure 10:9

corridor in a particular direction as he goes. If he is to measure the length accurately, he must keep moving in the same direction.

A child who goes 10 metres North from the school door will arrive at a different spot from a child who goes 10 metres East from the same place. The direction of the movement is as important as the distance. When adding with structural apparatus, and placing a second rod end-on to a first, the rods must be in the same direction. The direction is as important as the length of the rods.

Mathematics is full of examples of lengths which are measured in particular directions. These quantities are instances of *vectors*.[5] A movement of 6 units to the right along the tape-measure is a vector, and is a different vector from the one which represents a movement of 6 units to the left. A child measuring the playground travels along a different vector if he paces 50 metres to the East from the vector he would cover if he paced 50 metres to the North. When a child adds with the tape-measure he is adding vectors. Figure 10:10 shows the addition of a vector 6 centimetres to the right to a vector 3 centimetres to the right and to a vector 12 centimetres to the right.

The statement $\vec{3} + \vec{6} = \vec{9}$ conveys the idea: 'A movement of 3 units to the right *followed* by a movement of 6 units to the right *has the same effect as a single movement* of 9 units to the right.' The addition sign stands for the

[5] Later, the word *vector* will also be used to describe other quantities, such as *force* and *velocity*, which have direction as well as magnitude but which are not distances.

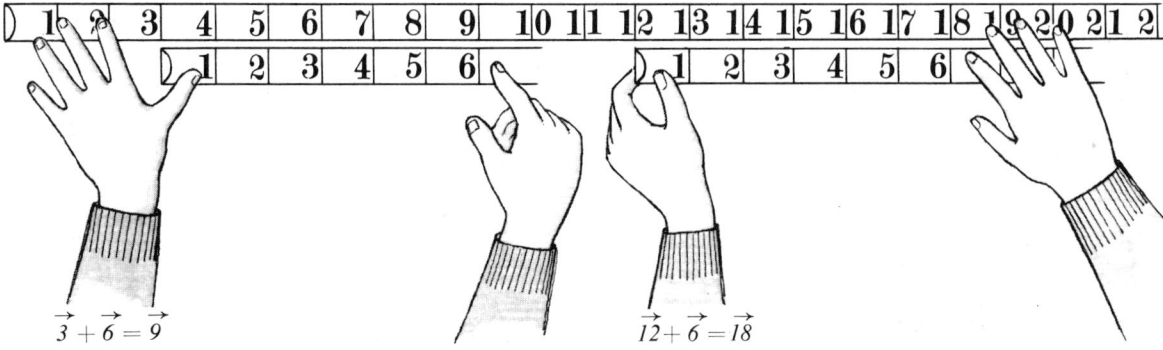

$\vec{3} + \vec{6} = \vec{9}$

$\vec{12} + \vec{6} = \vec{18}$

Figure 10:10

operation of combining two vectors by placing them end-on (Figure 10:11).

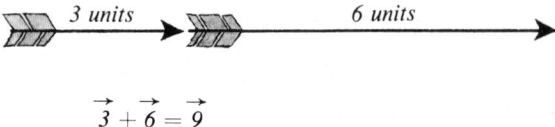

$$\vec{3} + \vec{6} = \vec{9}$$

Figure 10:11

Vectors can be combined even if their directions are not the same. Figure 10:12 shows a child's walk home. He went 30 metres along the road from the bus stop, and then 40 metres along the path home. He could go home in a straight line across the field. The movement in a straight line across the field is the *sum* of the two movements of 30 metres East and 40 metres North.

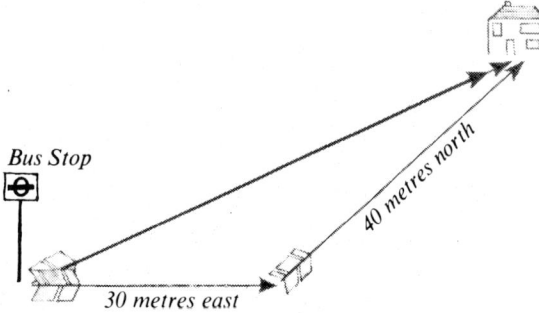

Figure 10:12

We write

(30 metres East) + (40 metres North)

As was the case for the addition of vectors in the same direction, the plus sign means 'one vector *followed by* the other vector'. If we draw to scale a plan of the journey home (Figure 10:13) and measure the length and direction of the short cut on it, we find that

(30 metres East) + (40 metres North)
$$= (50 \text{ metres N37}^\circ \text{E})$$

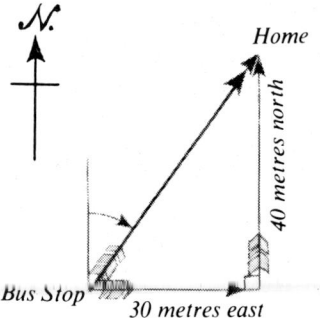

Figure 10:13

92

The sum of two vectors often has to be found by scale drawing.[6] This is not necessary when the two vectors happen to be in the same direction (or opposite directions).

On the tape-measure we can add vectors in opposite directions.

Both diagrams in Figure 10:14 show

(a movement of 9 centimetres to the right) followed by
(a movement of 3 centimetres to the left)
= (a single movement of 6 centimetres to the right).

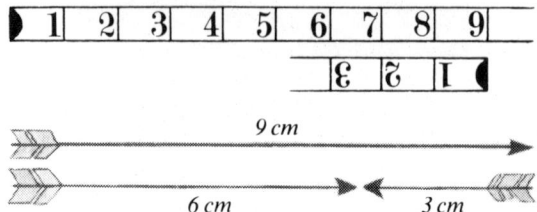

Figure 10:14

(9 centimetres to the right) + (3 centimetres to the left)
$$= (6 \text{ centimetres to the right}).$$

Here two vectors in opposite directions along the same line have been added. The subtraction of vectors will not be discussed until Chapter 35, but the reader should compare Figure 10:14 with Figure 9:27.

It is important to distinguish clearly between the sum of two vectors and the addition of two distances. If $\overrightarrow{AB}$ and $\overrightarrow{BC}$ are two vectors of lengths 10 units and 7 units in given directions, $\overrightarrow{AC}$ is their sum. If the vectors are in the same direction (Figure 10:15(a)) $\overrightarrow{AC}$ is of length 17 units in the same direction. When $\overrightarrow{AC}$ and $\overrightarrow{BC}$ are in the directions shown in Figure 10:15(b) their sum is $\overrightarrow{AC}$, of length 14 units in the direction shown. The single movement $\overrightarrow{AC}$ is equivalent to the two movements of $\overrightarrow{AB}$ followed by $\overrightarrow{BC}$

(*a*)

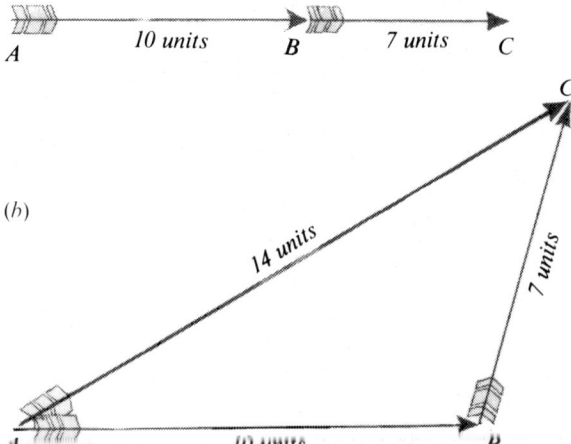

(*b*)

Figure 10:15

[6] Or trigonometry.

and we write $\overrightarrow{AB}+\overrightarrow{BC}=\overrightarrow{AC}$ = (14 units along AC). But if a man walked from A to B and then from B to C he would have travelled the distance $AB+BC$, which is 17 units. Quantities such as this which take account of magnitude only and ignore direction are called *scalars*. We can thus make the statement about scalars

$$AB+BC = 17 \text{ units,}$$

but $\overrightarrow{AB}+\overrightarrow{BC}$ = 14 units along AC.[7]

The laws of operations for vectors

A vector of length 3 units in a direction moving from West to East is certainly very different from the natural number 3, which has no direction. But we constantly use the addition of vectors as a model for the addition of natural numbers, both on the tape-measure and in structural apparatus, so there must be a very close resemblance between the structure of addition of natural numbers and of vectors. This resemblance enables us to substitute one for the other, and to use the tape-measure as a model when a child wishes to find the total number in the class of 17 boys and 14 girls, although the numbers in this example certainly do not have a direction. In this section we shall pick out a resemblance and a difference in structure between vectors and natural numbers. Other properties of vectors will be discussed later.

The addition of natural numbers is commutative (*see* page 88); the order of addition does not matter. For vectors, the commutative law is also true. A movement of 6 units to the right followed by a movement of 3 units to the right is a different action from a movement of 3 units to the right followed by a movement of 6 units to the right (Figure 10:16).

(6 units to the right)+(3 units to the right)

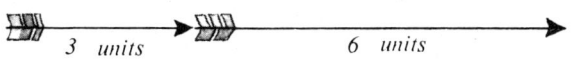

(3 units to the right)+(6 units to the right)

Figure 10:16

The result is the same, but the actions are different. If the order of addition in Figures 10:12 and 10:13 is

[7] Vectors are often written with an arrow $\overrightarrow{AB}$. They are printed in bold type **AB** or **a**.

reversed, the situation is altered. Figure 10:17 shows what happens if the child does

(40 metres North)+(30 metres East)

Again, the result is the same, but the situation is different from that of Figure 10:13.

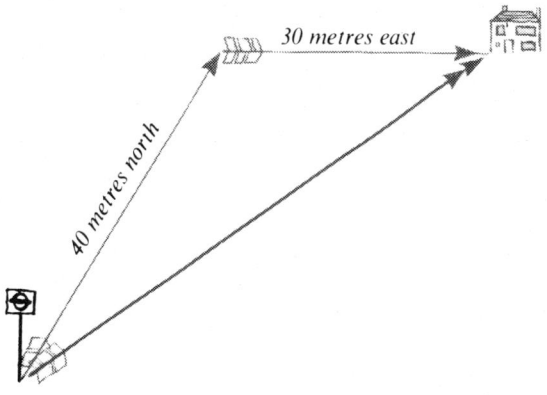

Figure 10:17

The addition of vectors is commutative; for any pair of vectors **a** and **b**,

$$\mathbf{a}+\mathbf{b} = \mathbf{b}+\mathbf{a}$$

Figure 10:18 shows the commutative law for addition of vectors in a more general situation, where **a** and **b** are neither in the same direction nor at right angles.

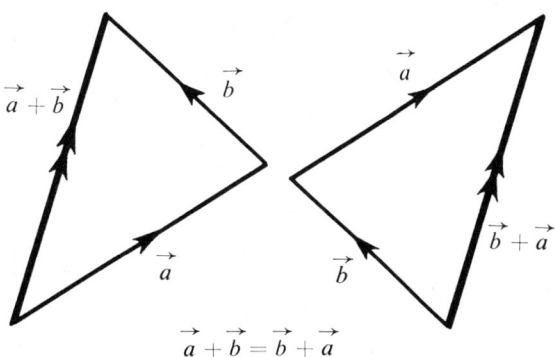

Figure 10:18

The equality of the sums **a**+**b** and **b**+**a** in Figure 10:18 is more easily seen if the vectors are arranged as in Figure 10:19. Since the vectors we are using are movements in a certain direction, the same vector can be used in many different positions. If the teacher asks his class to move 3 paces forward, each child will move over the same vector of (3 paces forward) *from where he is*. If now each child moves 4 paces to the right, he will be

(3 paces forward)+(4 paces to the right)

from his own starting point. Both children in Figure 10:10 are adding a vector of (6 centimetres to the right) to another vector, although the starting points of their vectors are different. Children automatically accept this situation when working with tape-measures or structural apparatus, but it may look rather odd in Figure 10:18 or Figure 10:19 when the same vector is drawn starting from different places. If a vector is thought of as a movement this difficulty, however, will disappear. Children do, in fact, race one another from corner to opposite corner of a rectangular marking on the playground along different edges, and the equivalence of the vectors they travel is obvious to them.

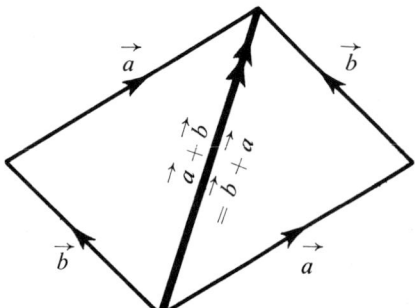

Figure 10:19

The arithmetic of vectors resembles the addition of natural numbers in that both additions are commutative. We shall find other likenesses between the two arithmetics later, but we shall first discuss a most important difference. Every vector has an *opposite*. If a child has moved over the vector (3 paces forward) and the teacher wants him to go back to where he was, he can be asked to move over the vector (3 paces back). The *opposite* of (3 paces forward) is (3 paces back). The opposite of any vector $\vec{a}$ is *the vector which undoes the effect* of the movement $\vec{a}$. The opposite of a vector is often called the *negative of the vector*, and is written $(-\vec{a})$ (Figure 10:21).

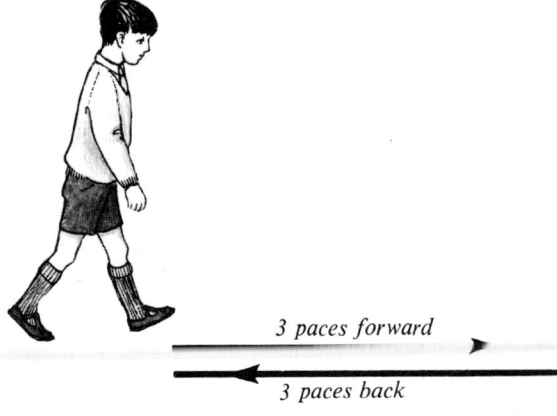

Figure 10:20

94

If we move over the vector $\vec{a}$, and then over the vector $(-\vec{a})$, we are back where we started. In symbols

$$\vec{a}+(-\vec{a}) = 0$$

This statement says nothing about *negative numbers*. It only says

(movement $\vec{a}$ followed by (the opposite of $\vec{a}$)
$\qquad\qquad$ = ('movement' of standing still)

The '+' sign here is the sign for addition of vectors, not the sign for addition of natural numbers; the '−' sign in $(-\vec{a})$ is the sign for the opposite of a vector, not the sign for the subtraction of natural numbers. It would no doubt be better in some ways to have two different signs to stand for the 'plus' in

$$3+5 = 8$$

which is addition of natural numbers, and in

(3 paces to the right) + (5 paces to the left)
$\qquad$ = (2 paces to the left),

which is addition of vectors, but these two operations are alike in so many ways that no confusion usually arises in making the same sign do for both.

We have used the symbol **0** for the vector of (not moving at all). This vector is called the *zero vector* or *null vector*, and behaves very like the zero of the natural numbers. We can now state mathematically a major difference between natural numbers and vectors. Every vector has an opposite, but with the single exception of zero no natural number has an opposite. We cannot fill in with a natural number the blank space in the sentence

$$3+\square = 0;$$

there is no natural number which added to 3 gives 0, and so 3 has no opposite natural number. But we can fill in the blank space in the vector equation

(3 paces to the right) + $\square$ = **0**,

so the vector has an opposite. For any natural number a which we start with (apart from the exception $a = 0$) we cannot find a natural number x which makes the sentence $a+x = 0$ true; but for any vector $\vec{a}$ with which we start, we can *always* find a vector $\vec{x}$ which makes the sentence $\vec{a}+\vec{x} = \mathbf{0}$ true.

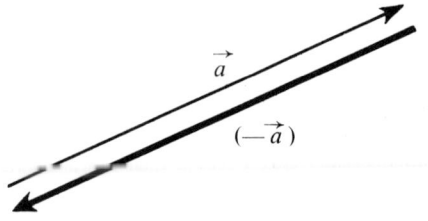

Figure 10:21

As we progress in mathematics, we shall find the limitation that the natural numbers do not have opposites more and more inconvenient; vectors and those numbers which have opposites will be used more and more. We shall see that children are often unable to understand directed numbers because their idea of number is limited to the natural numbers and the counting of sets of things, and does not include vectors and the idea of movement.

11 Learning About Space

Pre-measuring activities and first uses of measurement

Why we learn about space

The study of the properties of space has several important purposes:

i) It is intended to build up in the mind of a child, in the course of the primary years, a picture of the spatial structure in which we live, i.e. the universe with the heavenly bodies and the earth seen in relation to one another, and so create some awareness of their relative movements. He must also know the shape of our earth and the properties of its surface which have enabled man to build roads and navigate ships and aircraft, and represent on maps their positions and routes.

ii) It is equally important for children to know that both living and non-living bodies have characteristic shapes and structures; there are many wonderful examples, such as the bones in the wing of a bird, a spider's web, a snow crystal.

Figure 11:1

    Man makes complicated structures and mechanisms using similar shapes and forms; these the children can observe and model.

iii) Through his own inventiveness a child will learn to appreciate the patterns and forms which men have used for decoration and enjoyment.

iv) Different kinds of manipulations of shapes involve some operations which are common to all kinds of mathematical activity: sorting, combining, partitioning, matching, ordering and the fundamental types of movement.

    Practical experience of spatial relationships is one of the foundations on which other mathematical relationships and operations can be built.

The starting-point for primary school work

When a child first comes to school he has had many experiences which have given him some of the basic concepts of space which are related to shape, position and size. He knows that an object remains the same even when a change of position alters its apparent shape and size; but he may not identify the representation of a shape drawn in two different positions.

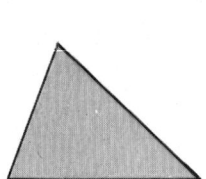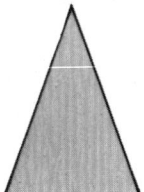

Figure 11:2

    He sees shapes in relation to his own position and cannot imagine what they will look like to an observer in a different position (*see page* 14). Certain differences of shape and size can be distinguished but his discrimination is still very limited and he cannot combine different kinds of relationship or easily fit objects into their place in a sequence. Nor can he measure (*see page* 43). He has developed language and simple representative drawing, but he judges by his perception and does not yet analyse shapes according to the number of their sides or the forms of their corners.

Spatial 'play'

Given the new play materials that a school provides, children usually begin spontaneously with simple manipulative play to discover what they can do with the things, or they may start with representational play if the things suggest something which interests them. This free play, dependent on the children's own curiosity or impulse, is of great value and should not be curtailed too soon. When fresh material is introduced later on, a period of free experiment with it should normally be allowed to give a child his own insight into some of its properties. Representational play, in which geometrical shapes may represent a garage, a person, an aircraft or a bed, depends very much on likenesses of outline and shape; the representation of a *situation* such as lorries and cars on

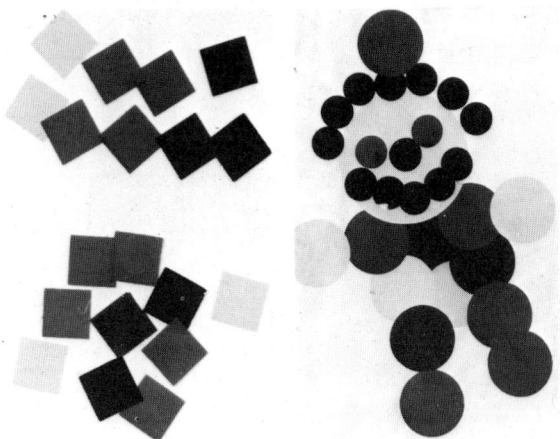

Figure 11:3

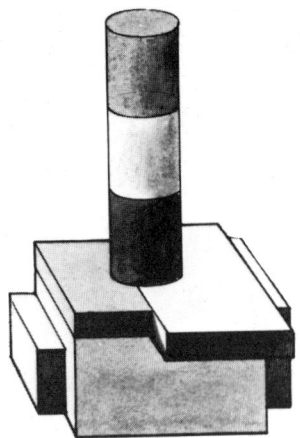

Figure 11:4

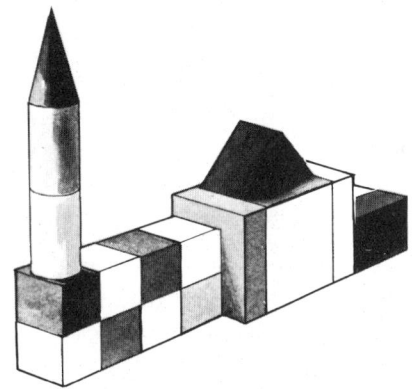

Figure 11:6

a road, or dolls at a tea-party, will bring out relative positions, independent of their relations to the child himself. Some toys, such as mosaics and boards with coloured pegs, will stimulate a child immediately to make repetitive patterns, often foreshadowing counting in ones, twos, threes, etc. (*see page* 143). Sometimes such pattern-making shows the child's awareness of shapes such as squares, rectangles, triangles (Figures 11:3 and 11:4).

Constructional play is often seen at the age of five, and a child will set out to build a bridge from simple unit shapes and make a stable structure out of them. Or he may build similarly 'my Daddy's office' using a variety of shapes to make a recognizable structure. This power to visualize a construction and select materials to carry it out will grow considerably during the first two years at school and is obviously a means of developing mental pictures to guide a child's purposeful actions.

Free play can be followed by controlled activity with the teacher suggesting ways in which the materials can be used, or setting some constructional goal before the children. For instance, 'Can you make this pattern?' (Figure 11:5),

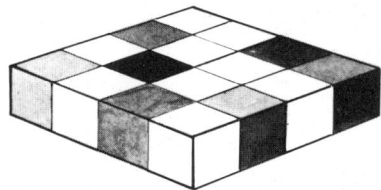

Figure 11:5

Or, 'Can you build a church?' Various forms would be produced but one like Figure 11:6 might appear if the children had the pyramid and the triangular prism or wedge to represent the tower and the roof.

Spatial materials and their uses

A. THREE-DIMENSIONAL OBJECTS

It will be noticed that the materials referred to in the preceding section are all three-dimensional things like those we handle or see in ordinary life. Children sort, match, fit, combine and compare them in the same way as they do the sets of objects which lead to number operations. The significance of three-dimensional material lies in its realism but it also has the advantage of leading a child to consider more than one feature at a time. Not only length but breadth and height also must be taken into account; not one face (*see page* 176) but several faces must look right. Thus the child is learning to synthesize two or more properties as he fits these shapes together.

The materials to be provided are of two kinds: (1) everyday things in which shape and size are significant and (2) mathematical shapes which have constructional interest in themselves and can also be used for representational building (*see page* 70).

Figure 11:7

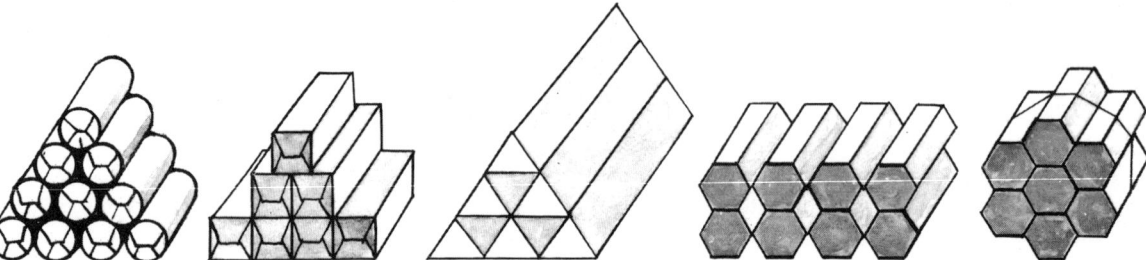

Figure 11:8

(1) *Everyday materials*. Collections of packets for a sweet-shop or a grocer's shop give a wonderful variety of shapes as shown in Figure 11:7.

The properties of these shapes become known through packing them in boxes or arranging a counter display.

Children often use such packets imaginatively to make an engine, aircraft, lorry, a block of flats in the town, or a church or barn in the village (Figure 11:9).

pouring a quantity of water or sand into different containers (some transparent) and thus discovering that the same quantity may occupy different shapes. These activities precede measurement and prepare for more precise experiments in later years (*see page* 48).

Piling packets, or fitting them into boxes in rows and/or layers, gives patterns which illustrate the operations of addition and multiplication, as can be seen in Figures 11:8 and 11:10.

Figure 11:9

Packets of different sizes but of the same shape can be put in order and if filled with small beans or other light small things can also be compared for mass on a simple balance (*see page* 42). Comparing two packets is easy but it is difficult at this age to arrange several in order of mass.

Comparison of the contents of packets of different shapes, some of which are the same size, leads to judgements of *more, less*, or the *same* and will lead on to

Figure 11:10

(2) *Mathematically structured shapes*. Mathematical shapes in wood or plastic are now available in shapes and sizes designed to show a good range of mathematical properties, and children can use them freely to produce representational constructions. The coloured Poleidoblocs

98

designed by Dr Margaret Lowenfeld have proved very attractive and stimulating to children. The shapes, colours, precision and weight all contribute to children's satisfaction in using them (Figure 11:11).

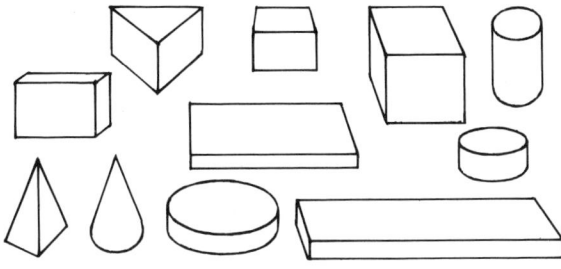

Figure 11:11

The cubes and cuboids, their halves and quarters, the cylinders and cones stir the children to make quite complex structures representing what they see around them; for example, Figure 11:12 shows the production of a child of five (*see also plate 2*).

Figure 11:12

Poleidoblocs include the same shape in different sizes and this leads to pattern-making which illustrates number relations in terms of lengths, surface areas or volumes, but without the child feeling at first the need to measure. Fitting shapes alongside one another gives a comparison of length; putting one block upon another gives a comparison of the areas of their top surfaces; reassembling the different partitions of a cube shows equality of volume in different shapes.

When a child has fitted together such shapes as are shown in Figure 11:13, he may say:

i) two blue rods are as long as one green rod;
ii) three blue tiles just cover one yellow tile;
iii) these two halves of a cube are different shapes but each of them is half a cube.

He should, of course, express these discoveries in his own way. It must be emphasized once more that free imaginative representation must precede the controlled activities which lead to the precise comparisons contained in these statements. The selection of the block (or set of blocks) which is neither too big nor too little but just fits is the necessary preliminary to the procedure of measuring to discover the required size.

Another aspect of fitting which is important mathematically, though it is often neglected, is the making of a hole, cavity or nest into which a certain shape will fit, or alternatively finding the shape (or shapes) needed to fill a given enclosure. In Figure 11:14, the same four rods enclose three different holes.

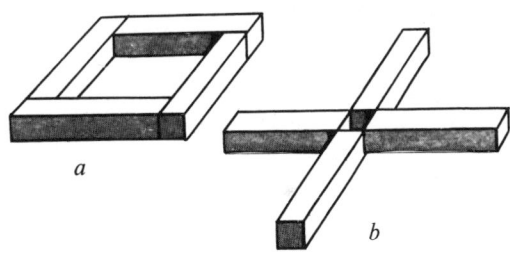

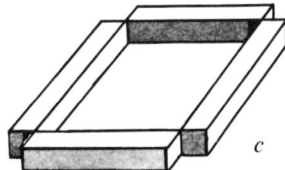

Figure 11:14

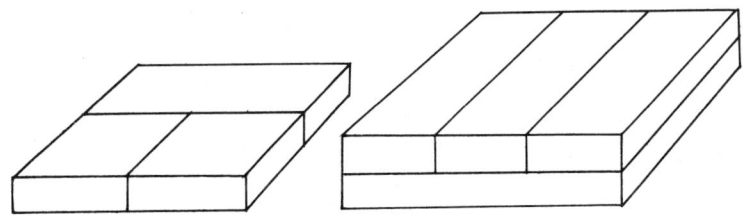

Figure 11:13

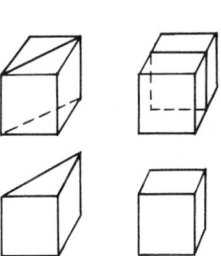

 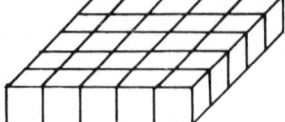 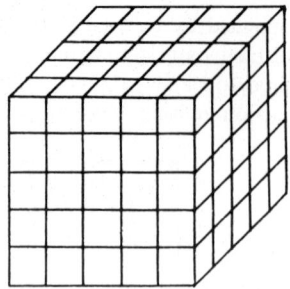

Figure 11:15

A significant feature of three-dimensional shapes which has only been generally realized in recent years is that they can provide a good model or analogue of our number system. Structured apparatus, such as that provided by Cuisenaire, Dienes, Stern, and others, which is commonly used to enable children to understand number notation and number operations, depends on the way in which cubes and cuboids can be combined. If they all have the same square cross-section they can be placed end to end to form new cuboids. Five cubes placed side by side form a cuboid or rod whose length is five times that of the cube. If we now make a number system based on five instead of ten we see how the cubes will represent it (Figure 11:15).

Now that a large cube has been formed we can continue, making 5 large cubes into one large long cuboid or rod, and 5 of the large rods into one large flat cuboid, and so on without limit. It can be seen that if ten had been chosen as the base number for counting, the shapes made would have been equivalent to 10, 100, 1000, 10,000, etc., cubes, and so would represent the place values of the figures in our decimal number system. This spatial structure is a memorable way of visualizing a number notation based on powers of a chosen number, say, 10^1, 10^2, 10^3, 10^4, 10^5, ... It can be built by children in free play before its number significance is realized through counting (*see also chapter 8*).

An experience which often surprises children at this stage is that the same quantity of material can take different shapes which appear to be unequal. So strongly are they influenced by perception that they will say that they *are* unequal. For instance they may take a lump of dough, clay, Plasticine or wet sand and roll it into a long thin sausage; they then change its shape and make a short thick sausage. Some children will think the long one bigger, others that the thick one is bigger (Figure 11:16).

Only repeated experience and an awareness that length and thickness are both involved will enable a child to be certain that the quantity does not change when the shape is altered. Obviously the children should have a good many activities of this kind, e.g. making a ball of clay, and changing it to a flat disc, a ring, a cube, a cone, etc.

B. TWO-DIMENSIONAL MATERIALS

Three-dimensional shapes have a particular importance because they correspond to the objects of daily experience. Two-dimensional shapes are either flat patterns as seen on walls or floors, for example, or are representative drawings. It is therefore wise to give ample opportunities for experimenting with solid forms at an early stage, but a child's familiarity with pictures in books and his growing pleasure in his own drawing as a means of expression make two-dimensional materials suitable and significant. They have the added advantage that patterns and structures made from them can often be easily drawn by the children or pasted on paper and thus a record of achievements can be made.

Coloured cardboard or plastic tiles in a variety of shapes provide the means for imaginative play. Just as cylinders, cones and pyramids are attractive to children so are circles, semicircles, triangles and rectangles (*see also page 101*) stimulating to the imagination. The square with its useful symmetries is as important as the cube and will be extensively used. Decorative patterns will be made as well as representations of ships, planes, animals, human figures, etc. The results of such play with tiles are transient but its value lies in the comparative ease with which children can handle the tiles, if they are made of strong card or a non-slip plastic, thus growing familiar with their shapes. The tiles should have several sizes in each shape, say 2-cm, 4-cm and 5-cm sides or diameters, so that fitting and repetition give coherent forms. Triangles provided should include the equilateral triangle and the diagonal halves of squares and rectangles. (Figure 11:17.)

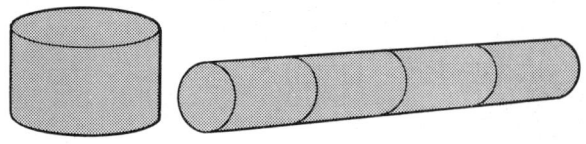

Figure 11:16

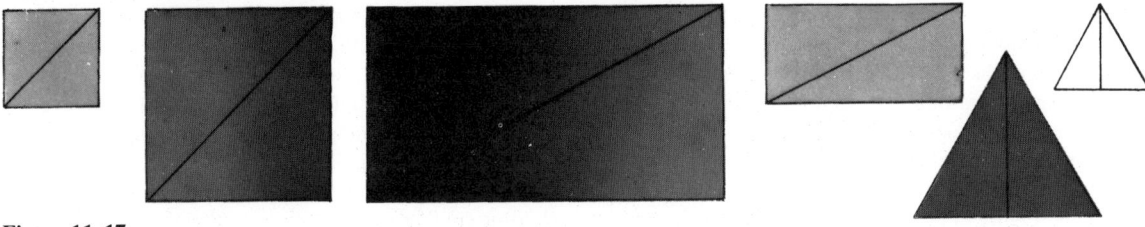

Figure 11:17

Circles and semicircles should have diameters corresponding to the sides of the straight-edged shapes.

As dexterity grows children can use gummed coloured paper shapes and stick them on to paper so that all the class can see the designs produced by individuals (*see plates 3 and 4*). Trial efforts using flannelgraph or plastic sheets are a useful preparation for the more permanent stick-on task. If templates are provided children can cut out fairly accurately geometrical shapes like those in Figure 11:18 which are usefully related in size.

The next stage requires more skill. Children can cut out shapes they would like to use to make a class frieze. The whole class will be concerned with placing the shapes to make a 'good' pattern but each child has to think out the way to cut the shape he wants. The shapes need not be confined to those familiar through using tiles, though the tiles could be used as templates; children can also cut quite freely. In the latter case they often show great originality, cutting out stars, spirals, crescents, etc., about which they will learn more in the future.

Since several identical shapes are usually included in a set given to children, some patterns may give number experience. A simple pattern made from only two different shapes, say squares and triangles, may lead to writing a number sentence about it (Figure 11:19). Or if two or more colours of the same shape are used a number statement can be made (Figure 11:20).

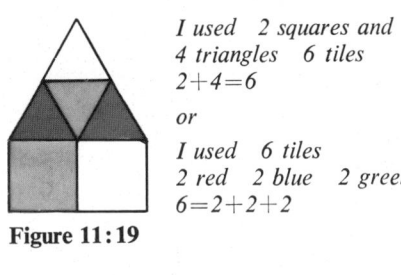

*I used   2 squares and
4 triangles   6 tiles
2+4=6*

or

*I used   6 tiles
2 red   2 blue   2 green
6=2+2+2*

Figure 11:19

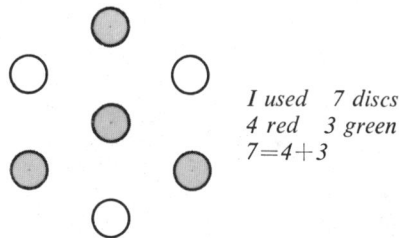

*I used   7 discs
4 red   3 green
7=4+3*

Figure 11:20

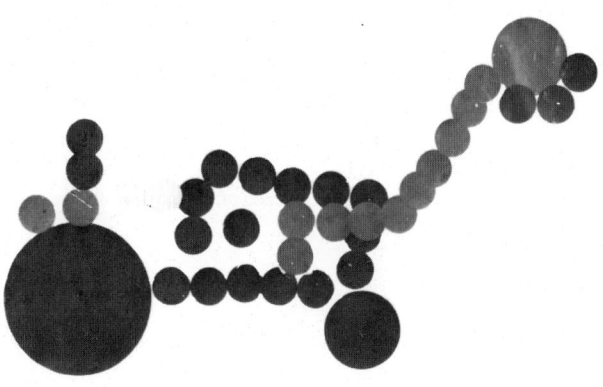

Figure 11:18

101

When the children can cut fairly competently they can fold paper shapes into halves, colour the halves differently and cut them out. When different folds are used the halves may have different shapes and the children's own actions in making the halves will help to convince them that these differently shaped halves of the same thing are equal in size. Figure 11:21(a) shows two shapes of a half-square. Figure 11:21(b) shows three shapes of a half-rectangle.[1] The diagonal halves do not *fold* on to one another so that a child may not think they are halves. He needs to *cut* them out and then fit one on to another.

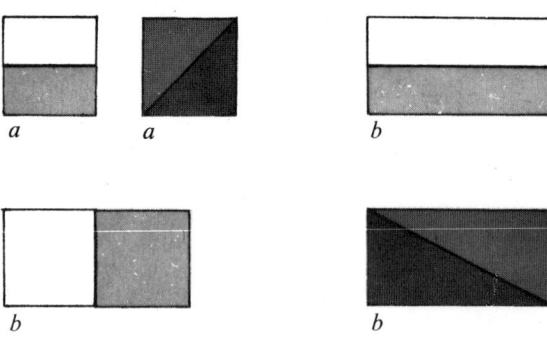

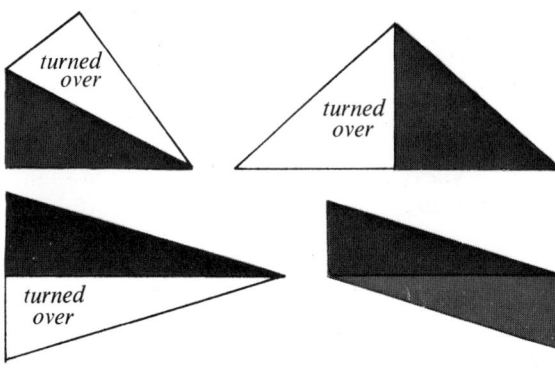

Figure 11:21

It will be seen in Figure 11:22 that the diagonal halves of the rectangle can be recombined in several ways.

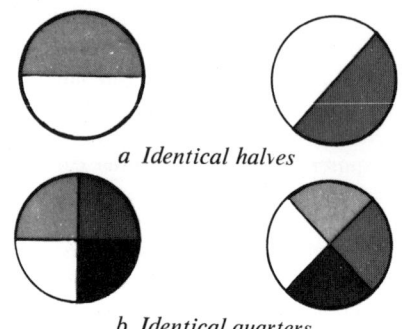

Figure 11:22

[1] Children should also have experience of rectangles of other shapes, say 3 cm by 9 cm.

Older children can experiment to see how many shapes they can make from these two halves. For younger children they afford the opportunity of making a greater variety of patterns. They may notice that the square is a special kind of rectangle and produces only one other shape from its triangular halves.

Halves of circles have a special property. When children cut them out they discover that they have the same shape wherever the fold is made. For these experiments each child needs two or three circles of the same size. He can make them by drawing round a suitable round tin lid and cutting out. Plain filter papers as used in science are cheap. The shapes made from these can be coloured and pasted into a book. Coloured gummed circles are obtainable but they are more expensive. Folding half-circles

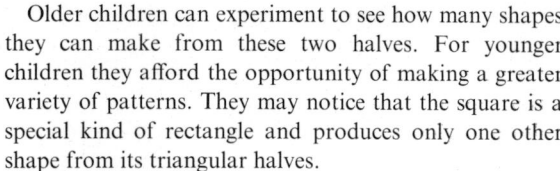

a Identical halves

b Identical quarters

Figure 11:23

again into halves will give 4 pieces or quarters. The notation $\frac{1}{2}$ and $\frac{1}{4}$ is easy to learn; we use $\frac{1}{2}$ when we have cut a shape into *two* equal pieces and $\frac{1}{4}$ when we have cut it into *four* equal pieces. The children will notice that all quarters of circles are the same shape and if any four of them, cut from the same sized circle, are fitted together they can only make a circle. Perhaps some

11:23(b) shows that the pattern on the right is the same as the one on the left, but turned round, and they may start a discussion on the rotation of wheels.

Experiments and puzzles with two-dimensional shapes are a good challenge to inventiveness at about 7 years of age. Some examples can be seen below.

Give a child 10 cut-outs of an equilateral triangle. How many different shapes can he make using all of them or some of them? Figure 11:24 shows *some* possible shapes.

3

4

6
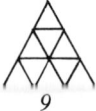
9
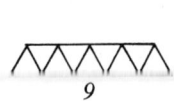
9

10

Figure 11:24

A child may have as many of the shapes shown in Figure 11:25 as he chooses: Can he fill the large square in more than one way?

Figure 11:25

Figure 11:26 shows how a child fitted small squares on to a larger square.

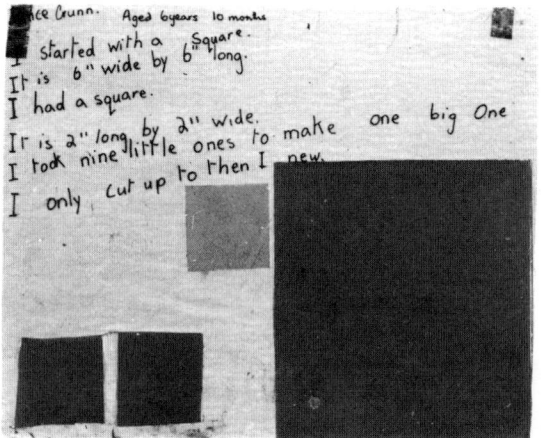

ce Crunn.   Aged 6years 10 months

Started with a Square.
It is 6" wide by 6" long.
I had a square.
It is 2" long by 2" wide.   one big One
I took nine little ones to make
I only cut up to then I new.

Figure 11:26

The growth of mathematical language

The activities discussed so far in this chapter involve shapes and operations which are generally new to the children. The new concepts which are being acquired must be expressed in some way so that they may be clear in the children's minds and available for use in new thinking. We know that at this age children have a good range of spoken language in which to express their actions, observations and ideas but they have yet to acquire the skills of reading and writing. They have some capacity in drawing of a representational kind though it is independent of measurement and without the accuracy that analysis could give. How then can children register and record the mathematics that they are learning?

Mathematics has three main types of language. It uses the words of common speech and adds to them special words to denote the things it is talking about, the relationships between them and the operations which are performed in mathematics. Children have to learn this special vocabulary and it is important that they should begin to do so as soon as they meet mathematical forms and carry out simple operations. Thus we should expect children to use the names of shapes correctly as soon as they can recognize and manipulate them. Triangle, circle, cylinder are no more difficult than aeroplane and radio; if they have as much meaning for a child he will learn them as readily. The written form of such words will constantly be seen and they will form part of the reading vocabulary acquired during the early years.

Before a child can read or write (as well as afterwards) he will talk about what he has been making or discovering and this expression will often be the teacher's main guide to his range of understanding. Group and class discussions are of the highest importance at the early stages and some of the class talks on daily events and the exhibits on a nature or science table should include references to shape and pattern as well as number. As soon as possible children should be encouraged to write, say, a caption to a diagram or a simple description of what they have done. Both writing and spelling will improve with practice.[2]

The second form of mathematical language is the use of diagrams, and in these early years this is a most convincing way of expressing the relationships which children perceive. In this chapter we suggest diagrams of many kinds, made from blocks, tiles or paper cut-outs. Children begin to draw diagrams, too, but while their drawing skill is limited, using squared paper (1-cm or $\frac{1}{2}$-cm for individual use) will help them to draw what they have seen. Accurate drawing on plain paper has to wait until drawing a straight line and measuring have been mastered. Meanwhile, free representative drawing has a valuable place.

The mathematical language which is most abstract is the use of symbols: 3, 29, $+$, $=$, etc. Because it is abstract, symbolic language normally begins later than the other two forms and is used to express briefly what has already been said in everyday speech and possibly also shown in a diagram.[3] The introduction of a symbol should obviously be made when the idea which it represents is already in the child's mind. For instance, after using tiles of rectangular shape he finds other things— door, blackboard, box, book—which have similar shapes, and he learns the name 'rectangle' and perhaps notices its 'square corners'.

The spatial activities described in this chapter lead to all three forms of expression, including the symbols for numbers and operations, but the one that we emphasize here is the correct use of spatial terms.

[2] See the errors in the child's work shown in Figure 11:26.

[3] See Figure 11:19.

Horizontal and Vertical

As we have seen, children's exploration of space depends to a great extent on their powers of movement and their observations. They stand and move in an *upright* position normally; usually they see things *balanced* on a *level* base and with a *vertical* axis. Shapes come to be recognized most easily in the position in which they are most frequently seen; if the position is different a child will often think he sees a different shape.[4] The cube cut diagonally in half provides a good illustration. The 'roof' position is not identified as a half-cube by a young child until manipulative experience makes it clear. See Figure 11:27.

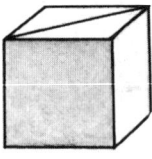

Figure 11:27

The notion of *upright* develops from children building brick towers, making fences or trees from twigs, or telephone poles in a model of a street. *Level* is an idea which grows more slowly. Watching a ball or marble rolling down a desk or path leads to a discussion and a model road can be made with slopes as well as level stretches. A simple levelling device is a bottle of water with a small airbubble; alternatively a cheap spirit level can be provided. It may also be possible for the class to see a builder's level being used in making a wall. Children can now test surfaces inside the school and outside in the playground, as well as in their own constructions, to see whether they are level in any direction.

A plumb bob for testing the upright position is easily made by tying a small heavy bead to a piece of string. Experiments will show that a ball dropped at the top of the line falls down along the line of the string. Older children will learn the words *vertical* and *horizontal*. The making of a simple balance bar, hung on a string loop at the point which allows the bar to rest in the level position, gives useful illustrations of vertical, horizontal, and different slopes. Tin lids supported by strings from the bar enable simple comparisons of weights to be made. See Figure 11:28.

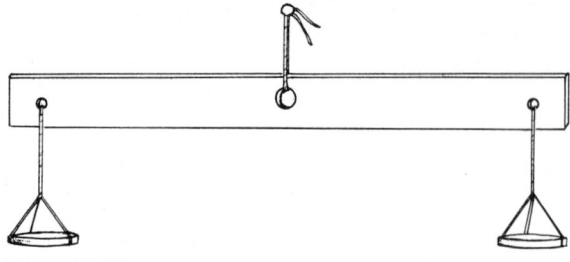

Figure 11:28

Symmetry: folding

Balancing leads on to finding shapes that *look* balanced; a glass, a spoon, a chair, an animal, etc. Two halves look alike. Making shapes that balance is a fascinating game that has plenty of variety and yet leads to a practical appreciation of one of the most important concepts of mathematics—the idea of symmetry. Here are some suggestions:

i) A blob of mixed paint or ink can be put next to a fold on a piece of paper. If it is then pressed down firmly along the fold and opened out, the result is surprising and often beautiful (Figure 11:29).

Figure 11:29

ii) A piece of paper is folded in half and a pattern torn or cut out along the edges. The result is opened out. The children will produce some amusing or pretty designs (Figure 11:30).

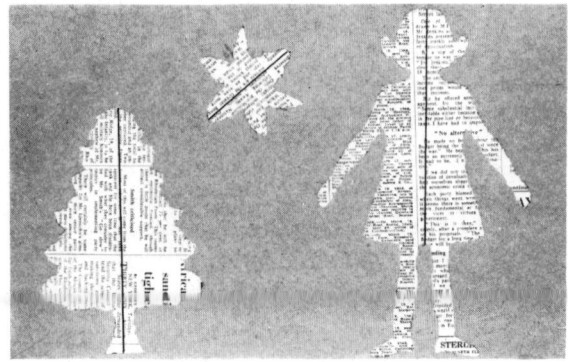

[4] See Figure 2:4 and Figure 11:2.

104

Figure 11:30

iii) Using a folded piece of squared paper, half of a given shape is copied. The squares can be counted to give accuracy. The other half is obtained by pricking through. This method brings out clearly that in a symmetrical shape each point on one side is matched by a point on the other side which is the same distance from the fold (Figure 11:31).

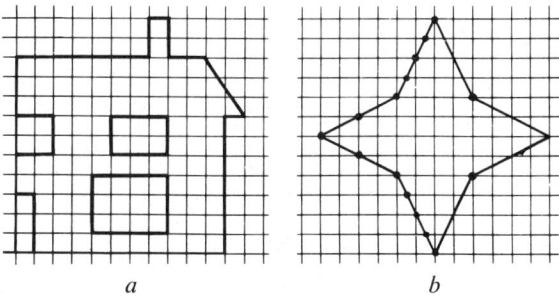

a   b

Figure 11:31

Up to the age of about seven children do not distinguish left from right with any certainty. This is understandable because it depends on the point of view of the observer which of two points is seen as left and which as right (Figure 11:32).

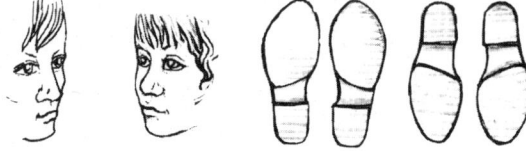

Figure 11:32

Making symmetrical shapes helps children to know left from right. Shoes and gloves and double swing doors have this symmetrical relationship and one of the pair must be distinguished as left. Turning a pair of shoes upside down makes it difficult for a child to identify which is his left one.

Folding a sheet into quarters introduces symmetry about two axes, and children can make interesting patterns by tearing or cutting round the edge and cutting out holes.

Figure 11:33

It can be seen that Figure 11:31(b) also has symmetry about two other axes, and this pattern could have been made by folding the paper into eighths. As children's dexterity grows they will invent ways of making very attractive paper mats using four-fold symmetry.

It is now possible to look again at squares, rectangles, circles, etc. and see which of them can be folded to make two halves which fit (*see page* 102). Any shape can be folded but the two parts are not, of course, usually the same shape. But even the most irregular flat shape, a leaf or a jagged piece of paper, can be folded flat so that the fold is a straight line. Stiff paper folded in this way makes a good edge for ruling a straight line. A further fold, keeping the parts of the first fold together, will make a square corner or right angle. Notice the irregularity of the paper used in Figure 11:34; this makes the right angle stand out clearly. A circle folded in this way is a neat alternative to the jagged paper.

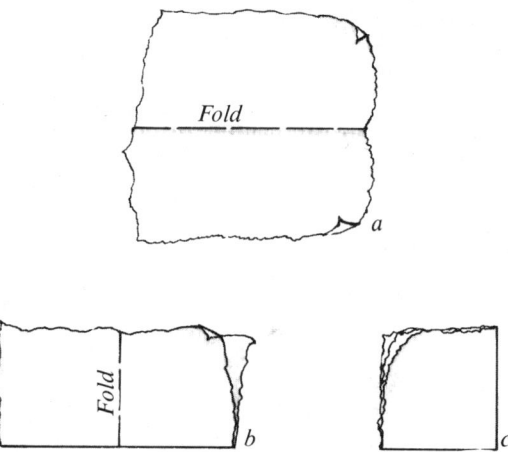

Figure 11:34

If the paper is unfolded the creases show the fitting together of four right angles (Figure 11:35). A right angle made in this way will serve as a home-made set square, and a child can use it to check right angles which occur in the classroom, and in particular to discover the way in

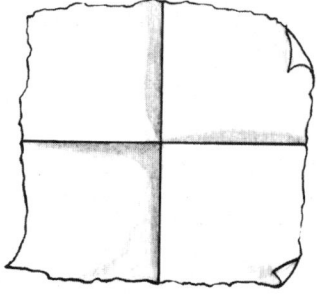

Figure 11:35

which three right angles fit together at the corner of a room. See Figures 11:36 and 11:37.

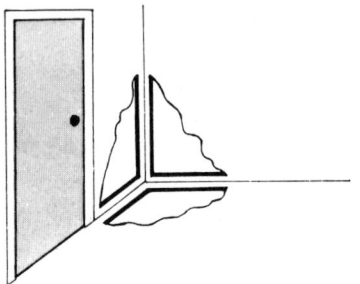

Figure 11:36

Figure 11:37

He will also find (Figure 11:37) that if he opens a book which is standing upright on a table, in one position three right angles fit together, but that the book will also stand with its parts farther open than a right angle, or less far open than a right angle. He may also check that a pencil is vertical when it stands upright on a horizontal table if his set square fits against it *in any position.*

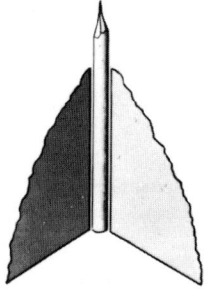 

Figure 11:38

Two arrangements such as those shown in Figure 11:38 can also be produced with a pile of pence.

The set square has many practical uses. Put against a plumb bob it can be used to test a horizontal. It is also needed in drawing squares and rectangles. The first rectangles which children can draw accurately are on squared paper where the right angles are already drawn.

106

Particular lengths can be drawn accurately by counting squares. A first box can be made in this way; a child draws a rectangle on squared paper and draws equal squares in each corner. He cuts along one side of each of these squares and folds up along the dotted lines shown in Figure 11:39. He then folds the squares round and sticks them to the sides of the box.

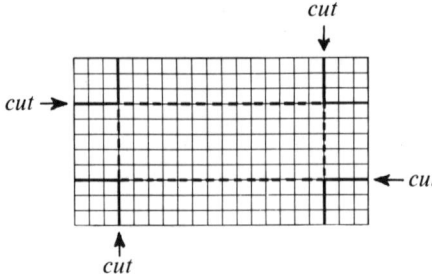

Figure 11:39

If a box made in this way can first be shown to the children and then opened out to show how it was made, the children can invent their own way of making a similar box. They can then experiment with making a box with a lid. The same construction will enable them to make a counter or stall for a shop or the body of a truck.

When children have learned to measure and to draw straight lines with a ruler (at 7 or 8 years of age) they can draw a rectangle on plain paper or card. They can now use their set squares to make the corners the right shape.

Translation: repeated patterns

There is another movement which is fundamental in mathematics and is also common in the experience of children. It is motion in a straight line without any change of direction. A child sees this every day on the roads and in his own actions. One way in which he can develop this idea in the early years is through making patterns. He has already seen how to make a good pattern by *reflection* or folding; he can now see that repeating a shape along a line produces an interesting pattern too. For example the rhombus (or diamond), circle, spiral can all be effectively used in simple repeats (Figure 11:40).

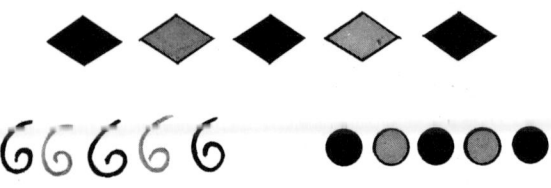

Figure 11:40

Colour may disguise the repeat but it adds interest.

A combination of two shapes can form a unit and this unit can be *translated horizontally*, or the movement could be vertical instead of horizontal (Figure 11:41), or in a sloping direction.

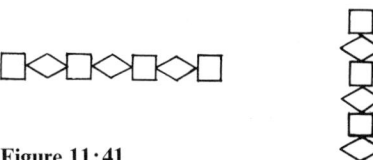

Figure 11:41

A further variation is to reflect a shape and then to translate the new shape (Figure 11:42).

Figure 11:42

Making border patterns using these ideas can give rise to some very pleasing designs.

Rotation: a different kind of movement

The movements of the hands of a clock, the turning of wheels and the child's own power of turning round give him a good idea of what *rotation* means. As we have seen in earlier sections he cannot always recognize the results of a rotation. He has to have experience of watching things turn, to notice the results, and to discover that we can measure how much rotation has taken place. When a child learns to tell the time he is in fact using a whole revolution of the minute hand to measure 1 hour, half a revolution to measure half an hour, and so on (Figure 11:43).

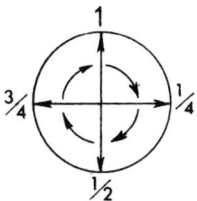

Figure 11:43

He should also watch and draw on the ground the shadow cast by a stick on a sunny day hour by hour and notice how the shadow has turned during each hour. This will lead him to find the North-South line and to make a compass card to show the four main points, and later to add NE, SE, SW, NW (Figure 11:44).

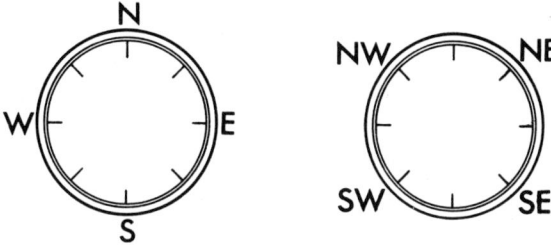

Figure 11:44

A compass with a simple compass card will show children how the needle swings and how the compass must be turned until North lies along the needle when it comes to rest. They can express the turning as a quarter, three eighths, three quarters, etc. of a revolution. This measure of rotation is developed further in the work on fractions in Chapters 19 and 20.

Rotation can also be used to make more complex patterns. The familiar square can be rotated through a quarter of a revolution and the 'diamond' appears. Shapes cut out in card can be rotated about a pin through their central point and the new shapes drawn (Figure 11:45).

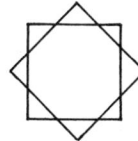 

Figure 11:45

The shapes can be drawn side by side to form a unit for translation and so produce a new type of border pattern (Figure 11:46). They can also be drawn round the rim of a disc and so reveal the appearance of the shape in different orientations (*see plate* 4).

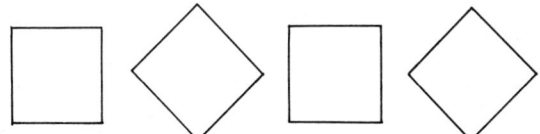

Figure 11:46

It can be seen that the great range of spatial experiences which this chapter suggests will give a child by the time he is about 8 years of age a much greater familiarity with mathematical ideas than he can obtain from number alone and at the same time it will deepen his grasp of numbers and of operations on them.

12 The Growth of Spatial Concepts

Shapes and movements

Space only has meaning when it contains objects which we can see in relation to one another, or can observe in motion, as they *change their position* relative to ourselves or to one another.

Two aspects of space interest a child from early days:

i) Shapes and their properties. Two questions guide children's investigations in this field. What can be made with shapes of particular kinds and how can a certain shape be made?

ii) Movements. These may either change the position of an object or alter the structure of the object itself.

Shapes and their properties

In Chapters 1 and 11 we have considered a variety of activities which help children to become aware of many shapes and some of their important properties. Now we try to clarify and summarize the ideas that a teacher can find revealed in the way children handle shapes. When a teacher sees the emergence of new concepts he can help to make them more precise if his own understanding is clear.

One of the earliest characteristics which a child discerns in a shape is whether it is *open* or *closed*. This is an important property of a topological kind, that is, a property which is independent of shape and length. Examples are given in Figure 12:1. A child will want to know, 'Can the cow get out of the field, or the fly out of the bottle, or the boy out of the maze?'

Solid or *hollow*. This seems an easy idea. A solid cube or cylinder is easily distinguished from a hollow one by the difference in weight, if they are made of the same materials, but it is difficult for a child to think about the solid shape which forms a cup. Nor can he easily visualize the region within the boundary surfaces of a body like a cone, and think, for instance, of the height of the vertex above the base. Experience of filling open vessels and weighing their contents hastens the growth of the idea of solidity and of the region within a surface. Immersing bodies in water also gives opportunities for comparison. A solid cube, a closed hollow cube and an open hollow cube all of the same size can be immersed in turn and the effects observed. Without such experiences a child cannot develop early the concept of a measurable volume for a solid shape as well as for an open container.

It is also stimulating for pupils to make model cuboids or square pyramids in different ways. A solid version can be modelled in clay or Plasticine, a hollow model can be made from a paper net, and a third variation could be carried out with milk straws, which thus show a skeleton of the shape through which the whole of the interior can be seen.

The various parts of the surface of a three-dimensional object may be either *flat* or *curved*. This decides how objects can be fitted one against another. Flat surfaces can be placed together without any gaps. Most curved surfaces cannot be placed in this way. Yet some curved surfaces can be stacked one inside another. Figure 12:2 shows the difference.

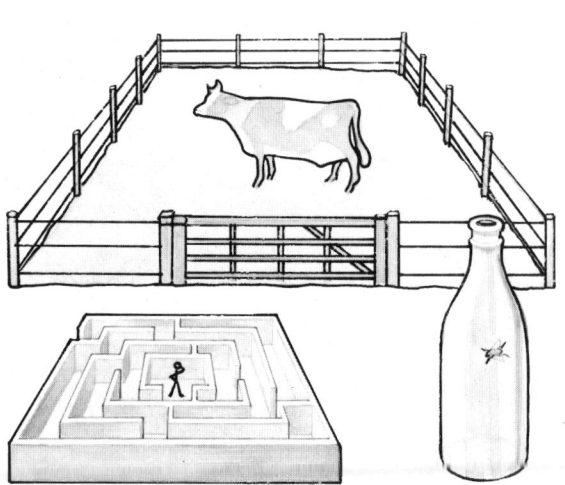

Figure 12:1

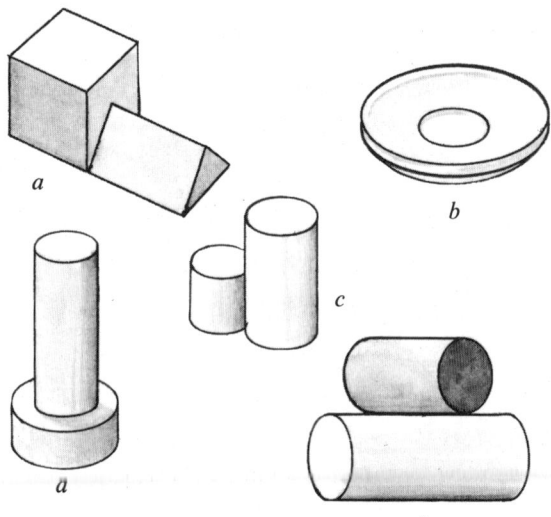

Figure 12:2

108

The straight edge of a ruler will lie anywhere along a flat surface. It will not lie along most curved surfaces, for instance the surface of a sphere, wherever it is placed; but there are some shapes, such as cylinders and cones, on which it is possible to place a ruler to lie along the curved surface in certain positions only (Figure 12:2(c)).

A flat portion of a surface, such as the circular end of a cylinder or a square which is part of the surface of a cube, is known as a *face*.

A face of a three-dimensional shape can be extended in the imagination in any direction; it can then be seen to be part of a plane: later on a child will realize that the points of the face are a subset of the set of points in the plane.

Concave or *convex*. This notion is closely linked with the experience of being inside or outside, but the two ideas must be distinguished. The word *inside* used precisely means within the region enclosed by lines or surfaces. *Outside* means lying beyond the boundary of the region. *Concave* describes a property of a line or surface when it is viewed from a particular standpoint. To the observer a concave line or surface appears as part of a boundary surface which curves towards him so that he feels himself to be inside it. The word *convex* describes the boundary as seen from the other side so that it curves away from the observer. It must be stressed that the words concave and convex apply to open as well as to closed figures. A cup illustrates well the concave property when we look at its interior and the convex property when we view its exterior. These properties can be observed and recorded by children when they make various shapes in clay or Plasticine or bend paper to make mobiles.

Among the most fascinating experiences of concavity and convexity are those of the sand castle and jelly mould type, where a concave surface is filled with moist or plastic material which will set sufficiently to retain its shape when turned out. The concave mould and the convex cast can be compared. A great variety of impressions in Plasticine or wax can be made by children and casts produced from them; leaves, fruits and embossed designs can be used. Two halves of a solid form can be impressed separately, the shapes compared for symmetry, and the two casts subsequently joined to show the whole object, e.g. a puppet head.

The reflections in concave or convex mirrors are fascinating, as are distortions seen in the reflections on the two sides of a brightly polished spoon. A hollow rubber ball with a hole pierced in it can be deformed to make part of its surface concave. Concave surfaces are used as reflectors in torches and electric fires. A radio telescope is a good example of the many uses of concave surfaces in modern science and industry. Children can find many others.

The hills and valleys and lakes of a model landscape or island can be seen as convex and concave surfaces. Some interesting questions about measuring depths and heights may arise and lead to enterprising experiments.

To an observer a convex surface seems to fall away from the nearest point whereas the concave surface appears to close in. There are some surfaces which are neither wholly convex nor wholly concave. A pass between two mountains is broadly of this type. It is known as a saddle-back pass because the riding saddle used on horses is of the same shape. Viewed along the length of the horse it is seen to rise towards both the head and the tail. It is concave in this direction. Viewed across the horse it is seen to drop on both sides to the flanks. In this direction it is convex. This is a complex situation which will appeal to many children.

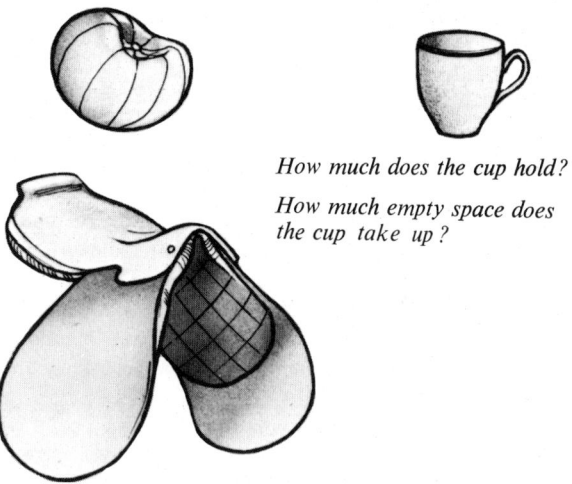

How much does the cup hold?

How much empty space does the cup take up?

Figure 12:3

Faces, edges and vertices

Children handle many shapes whose edges they recognize as straight or curved. Cups and saucers have *curved edges*; bricks, boxes and packets of cuboid shapes have *straight edges*. Balls have *no edges*; many shapes which could be made from a ball of Plasticine have no edges. The *torus* or shape of a tyre inner-tube has a hole through the middle and has no edges. Shapes can be devised which have some straight and some curved edges (Figure 12:4).

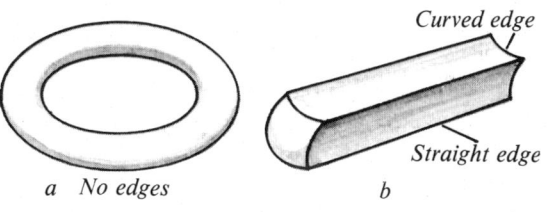

Curved edge

Straight edge

a   No edges   *b*

Figure 12:4

Edges are formed where two faces of a three-dimensional shape meet. Thus an edge is the set of points common to both faces. If we think of a face as a set of points, an edge is the intersection of the two sets of points which constitute the two faces. The net of a triangular pyramid shows the edges of the base as the straight lines made by folding. The other edges are made when two of the triangular faces are joined (Figure 12:5).

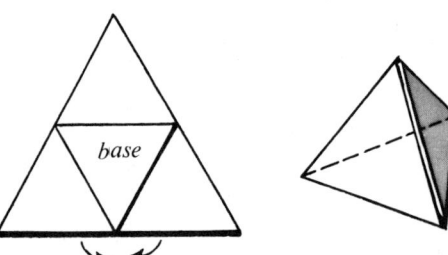

Figure 12:5

It will be seen that each edge is a side of the two faces that intersect. We speak of *edges* of a three-dimensional shape but use *sides* for the lines which enclose a two-dimensional shape. The correct use of these words, for instance the *sides* of a rectangle but the *edges* of a cuboid, makes it easier for children to describe accurately the shapes they make or use.

The importance of edges is brought out when children attempt to make three-dimensional shapes with strips, rods or milk-straws. They quickly find the necessity of giving firmness or rigidity to their constructions by the use of rods additional to those used for the edges. The triangular *pyramid* is *rigid* when made with rods as edges but the triangular *prism* can be *deformed* unless some diagonal rods are inserted in the rectangular faces. See Figure 12:6.

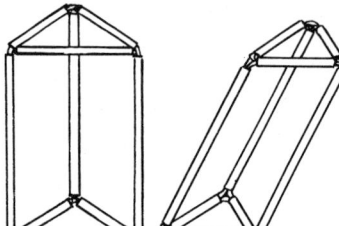

Figure 12:6

Children associate the *corners* of everyday objects, such as tables and boxes, with *points* and this is mathematically correct. Two lines which cross have a point in common, the intersection of the two sets of points which constitute the lines. Thus two sides of a flat shape will meet in a point. But the corner of a three-dimensional shape cannot be made with fewer than three faces; this means that three edges at least meet at the corner or *vertex*. Children can

examine the vertices of pyramids, cubes, etc., and notice the different shapes of the corners.

The idea of an angle begins to form when the corner of a face or of any two-dimensional shape is noticed. At this stage a child discriminates between such corners only as right (square), blunt or sharp angles (Figure 12:7). A clearer idea of angle develops with experience of rotation. Chapter 21 carries the study of angles further.

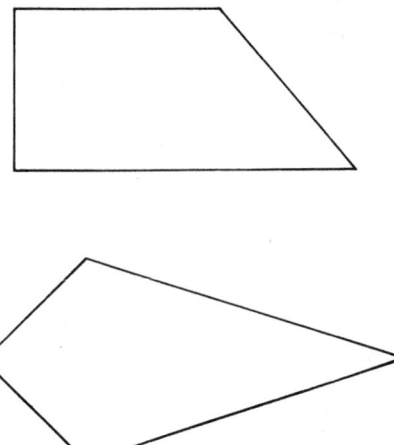

Figure 12:7

When a plane figure is made on a nail- or peg-board the vertices define the shape. Suppose that 5 points are chosen as vertices. An elastic band can be placed round every pair of nails or pegs, as shown in Figure 12:8. Five of these bands enclose a region, but another 5 form a star-shaped figure inside it. How many bands pass round each nail? We see that 4 line segments (lines of limited length) begin at each vertex. Each of the 5 vertices is the end-point of 4 line segments, but of course each line segment has 2 end-points. The number of segments is therefore $(5 \times 4) \div 2$, i.e. 10. Other figures made in this way can be studied and a rule for the number of lines discovered.

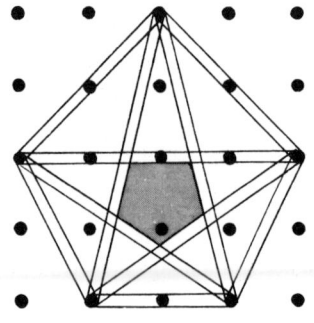

Figure 12:8

110

This is a good example of the way in which a spatial structure and the number relationship embodied in it illustrate a more general mathematical pattern. It can be compared with the process of finding how many pairs of children could be formed from a set of five children. Each child could have any one of four partners. This makes 5 times 4 pairs, i.e. 20 pairs. But if Ann has Betty for a partner the same pair is formed as when Betty has Ann for a partner. The number of pairs is therefore half of 20, i.e. 10. Figure 12:9 shows the possible pairs and the identity of such pairs as (Ann and Betty) and (Betty and Ann).

	A	B	C	D	E
Ann		AB	AC	AD	AE
Betty	BA		BC	BD	BE
Carol	CA	CB		CD	CE
Dora	DA	DB	DC		DE
Enid	EA	EB	EC	ED	

Figure 12:9

Symmetrical and regular shapes

The property of balance in a shape, with the right and the left identical except for position, is one which gives aesthetic pleasure and is thus easily recognized and remembered. As discrimination grows, many details of the shape are seen to be equal in size. Intuition gives awareness of properties which in less pleasing shapes might remain unnoticed; for example, the equality of the angles at the base of an isosceles triangle is noticed. A symmetrical configuration naturally leads to the idea of halves; an axis of symmetry of a polygon frequently divides a side into halves (Figure 12:10). See pages 115–117 for a fuller discussion of symmetry.

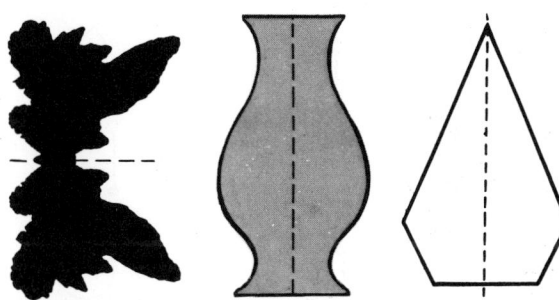

Figure 12:10

A regular two-dimensional figure has all its sides equal, and its angles equal. This means that every corner is exactly like every other corner. This involves symmetry about more than one axis. The triangle is a special case because if its sides are equal its angles are also equal. In other shapes equal sides can be accompanied by unequal angles, as Figure 12:11 shows. As can be seen, the equilateral triangle is a regular figure and has three axes of symmetry.

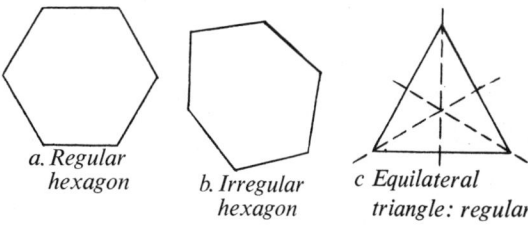

a. Regular hexagon   *b. Irregular hexagon*   *c Equilateral triangle: regular*

Figure 12:11

Movements

In the last paragraphs we have been considering shapes in themselves without regard to any changes which might take place. We now turn to a dynamic study and examine the effects of movements. Children explore space spontaneously through the natural movements of their bodies, particularly of their limbs. There are three main types of movement:
  i) a jabbing or pointing movement
  ii) movement to and fro or up and down
  iii) moving round and round, with head, hand or the whole body.

These movements can be seen in a child's early attempts at drawing and writing (Figure 12:12).

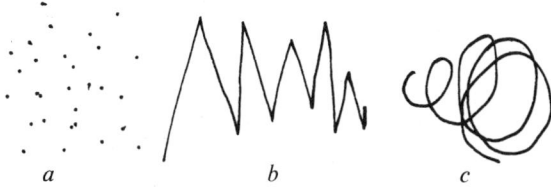

a   *b*   *c*

Figure 12:12

A child makes similar movements in his play with toys and materials. The observation of vehicles, machines, living creatures and other natural objects shows the same types of motion. Through these experiences children become aware of certain spatial relationships.

(1) Pointing, taking aim, interpreting an arrow sign all indicate a straight line in a particular direction and also indicate the point to which the line leads. The abstract idea

of a line is thus forming in the mind of a child, since in these instances the line from the observer to the object is not drawn or marked. A point begins to be understood as marking a position. Further experience of movement will bring clearer understanding of the relationship between points and lines. For example, copying a shape by pricking through a succession of points, or pegging out a path, will bring out the idea that a line or path is a set of points (Figure 12:13).

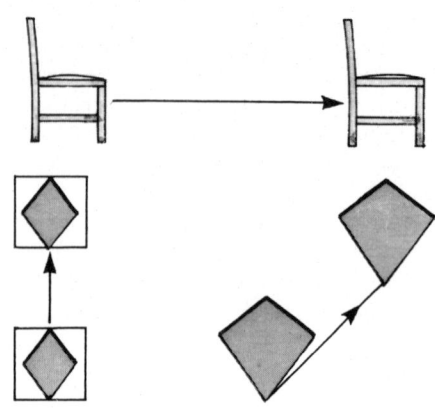

Figure 12:14

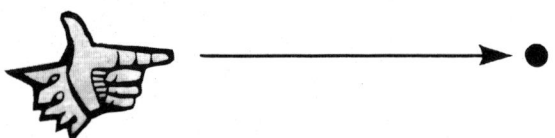

Figure 12:13

(2) Moving a body may change its apparent size or shape. It is important to discover which properties change and which remain invariant when the position of the body is altered. The movement to-and-fro or up-and-down takes place in a straight line, as when an engine moves along a straight track or a lift goes up and comes down. The shape and size of the object are easily seen not to change during such movements. Nor does any turning take place. The *site* of the object is simply moved along a straight line. Such a movement is defined as a *translation*. It will be noticed that the motion could be continued along the line without limit. It can also be seen in Figure 12:14 that the edges of the shape remain parallel to their original positions.

(3) Turning, or moving round and round, is probably the earliest arm movement which an infant makes. He sees human beings and animals turn round and he becomes accustomed to different views of the same object. As we saw in Chapter 2 a young child soon recognizes that the various views belong to the same object. Nevertheless, a child may not see that the *shape* of the thing is not itself changed by this turning movement or *rotation*. In fact the inherent shape is invariant but the orientation or lie may be changed by a particular rotation. Turning takes place about a fixed point, as in the movement of the hands of a clock. This turning movement could be reversed and the shape brought back to its original position. The shape can be turned about a fixed point in itself. It may be fixed by a pin and then given a spin. In Figure 12:15 various shapes are given a succession of turns and their new positions drawn out separately. The arrows help to indicate the amount of turning.

Rotation is a very important movement, not only in the turning movement of wheels but also in various forms of measuring dial (for time, pressure, electricity, etc.). As we shall see in Chapter 40 it helps us to understand certain numerical and algebraic structures. Translation along a line illustrates the basic operations of addition and subtraction of numbers (*see pages* 75–85); such a movement may be continued *without limit* in either direction and

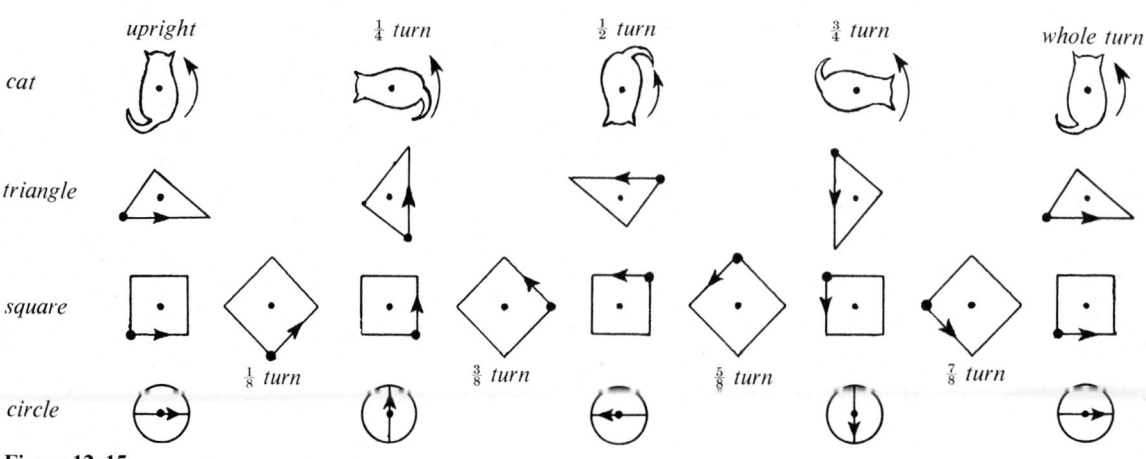

Figure 12:15

needs negative as well as positive numbers for its description; the movement of rotation, as on a clock-face, gives rise to a *finite* number system limited to the numbers placed on the dial (Figure 12:16). When a second revolution is carried out the numbers are repeated, and so on for succeeding revolutions; the number readings are the same.

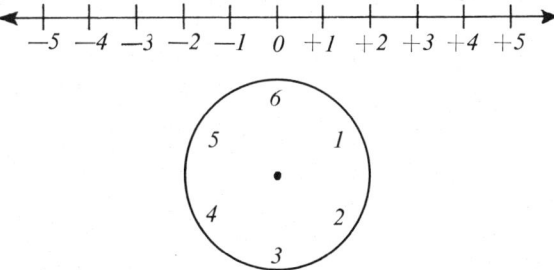

Figure 12:16

Children can learn about rotations through experimenting with a pendulum, using a trundle wheel, and marking out circles. They can graduate their own compass card or a clock-face. With some help, they may be able to make a model with a dial to measure the compression of a spring when various weights are placed in a scale pan resting upon it.

(4) In addition to the movements which a child can make with his own limbs there are other operations on shapes which change them in significant ways. *Reflection* is one which a child understands readily because he can actually produce a reflected image of a shape by a simple fold. Alternatively he can see the reflected image in a mirror. The important property of reflection is that it produces a shape which, though corresponding closely with the original, has a substantial difference: an irregular figure in a plane has a reflected image which cannot be made to fit on to the original by a movement in the plane, such as a translation or a rotation or any combination of these two movements. For example, to obtain the reflected shape shown in Figure 12:17(*a*), one might rotate the figure about the axis of reflection, but this movement would carry it out of the plane.

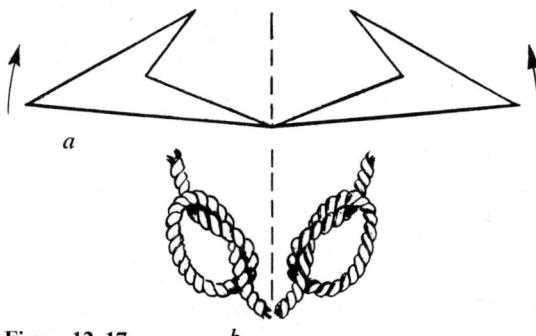

Figure 12:17

a

b

In three dimensions a mirror image is familiar in the right-hand left-hand pairing of gloves, shoes, houses, etc. These forms cannot be fitted into the same site by any translation or rotation. The right-hand glove can be made to look like a left-hand glove only by turning it inside out. This fact of real space is remarkable enough for a child to be allowed to discover it for himself (Figure 12:18).

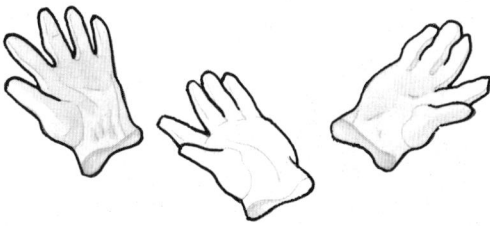

Figure 12:18

(5) *Stretch* or *enlargement*. When a picture is projected on to a screen or a blown-up balloon is blown up still further, the shape remains the same but the *size* is *increased*. This movement outwards from a centre is thus different in its effects from the movements already studied. A set of points sited in space could also be moved so that the distances between any pair of points were increased in the same ratio. The shape of the set remains the same. The movement which enlarges distances could be reversed. Any given shape can be made smaller, all lengths being *reduced* in the same ratio. This kind of movement is clearly the basis of scale drawing and map reading (Figure 12:19).

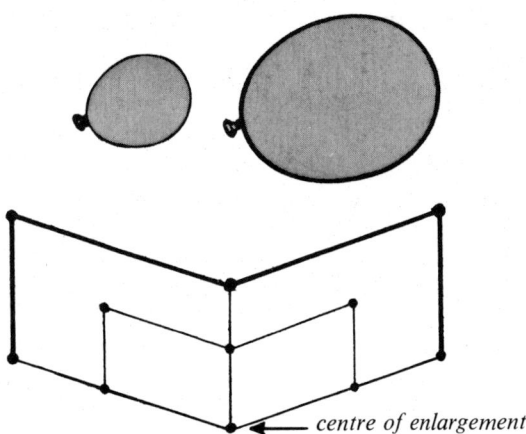

centre of enlargement

Figure 12:19

(6) *Shear*. Children sometimes notice that books or a set of cuboid rods arranged in a pile may be moved, so that each book or rod projects a certain distance beyond the one below it and yet the pile does not collapse. The base of the pile and its height remain the same. If a thick packet

of paper is treated in the same way a change in the face of the pile can easily be seen: the rectangle has become a parallelogram. The amount of surface area has not altered because clearly the face still consists of the thicknesses of the sheets of paper. The study of this movement is most suitably undertaken when the area of rectangular shapes has been understood and the question of finding the area of other shapes has been raised. The position of each sheet has been changed, and this has altered the shape of the face, but the area has not been changed (Figure 12:20).

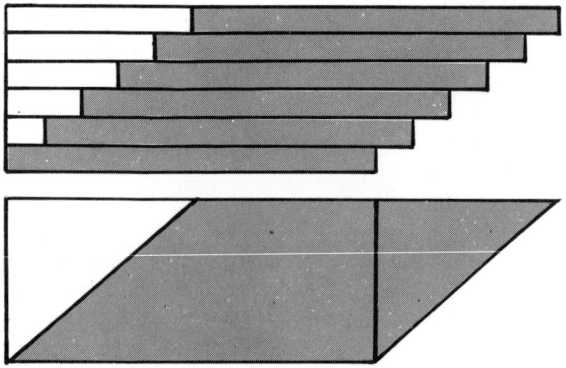

Figure 12:20

Transformations: translation and rotation

A mathematician studying the effects of movements on sets of points or shapes describes the procedures by which new points are found as *transformations*. An original point is transformed or mapped into another point by some rule which is applied to the whole set. Each point of the *transform* is called the *image point* of the original point. In the process of transformation some properties of the set of points will be changed; others remain unaltered, i.e. they are invariant. We will now examine the transformations that are related to the movements described in the preceding paragraphs.

Translation. To carry out this transformation, which shows the effect of a movement of sliding without turning, each point of the set must be transformed into a point a certain distance away in a given direction. We now have

two sets of points, the original set and the image set created by the transformation. In Figure 12:21 we see, for instance, two crescents, the original and its transform. Shape and size are invariant. The appearance of the shapes is the same; measurement of lengths such as sides, diagonals, perimeters will confirm that these are unchanged. The new shape could be fitted into the site of the original; when this is true the two figures are said to be *congruent*. Corresponding angles are equal and when children can measure angles they can check this equality. The orientation of the shape is also unaltered. Any line remains parallel to its original position. These invariants can be seen in the illustrations of Figure 12:21.

In Chapter 9 the use of a tape-measure slide-rule was shown to involve movements which give an addition or subtraction transformation of a set of *numbers*. In this situation the numbers are represented on a number line by points. If the numbers are to be transformed by the addition of 3, each of the points representing them will be translated 3 units to the right. The image points represent the transformed numbers (Figure 12:22).

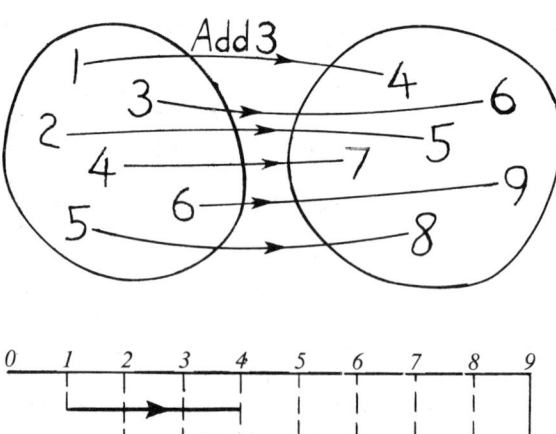

Figure 12:22

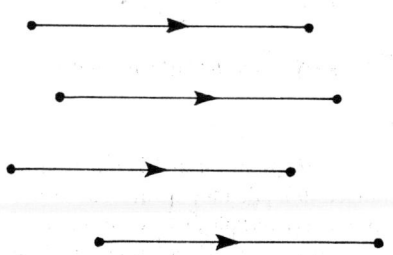
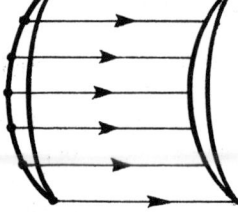
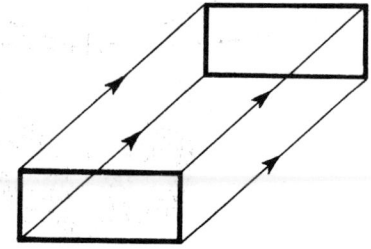

Figure 12:21

Later on, when children have learned to name the position of a point by its co-ordinates, they will see how to describe a translation of a point by the change in its co-ordinates. For example, in Figure 12:23 the point (1,3) is translated 2 units parallel to the *x*-axis. Its new co-ordinates are (3,3). The point (2,4) is translated 1 unit parallel to the *y*-axis; its new co-ordinates are (2,5). A point may receive two translations, one parallel to the *x*-axis, the other parallel to the *y*-axis. The effect will be to change both co-ordinates and obtain an image point which could have been found by a single translation, as shown in Figure 12:23. Point (1,3) is transformed into (3,4) by performing *both* translations.

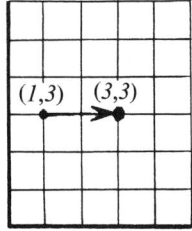
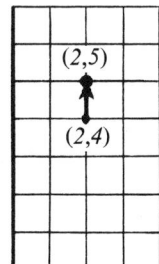

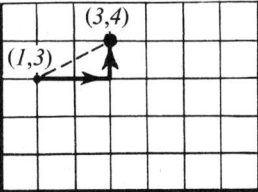

Figure 12:23

These translations can be expressed by formulae. If a point (x, y) is translated *a* units parallel to the *x*-axis its transform is $(x+a, y)$; if it is next translated *b* units parallel to the *y*-axis its new transform will be

$$(x+a, y+b)$$

Although only the brightest children are likely to be able to discover such a formula while still at the primary school, it is helpful for a teacher to be aware of this possibility. The use of an arrow to show a transformation is the accepted notation. We write

$$(x, y) \rightarrow (x+a, y+b)$$

Rotation. A set of points or a shape can be transformed by matching each point in the given set with one that could be reached by turning. There must be a fixed point as the centre of rotation and the amount of turning must be the same for each pair of corresponding points. This amount can be expressed as a fraction of a whole turn or revolution; later it will be stated as an angle measured in degrees.

We can imagine a rod 3 units long being rotated about one end, O, and can think about the other endpoint. If the rotation is one eighth of a turn the image of the end-point will stay the same distance from O but it will move into a different position; there is an angle between the lines joining O to the original point and to its image, an angle which is one eighth of a turn. The position of the image of the point relative to the original position of the rod can be stated as (d, θ) where *d* is the distance of the point from O and θ is the angle of rotation. Figure 12:24 shows the image points for several rotations. Their positions could be given as $(3, \frac{1}{8}$ revolution), $(3, \frac{1}{4}$ revolution), $(3, \frac{1}{2}$ revolution) where the angle is stated as a fraction of a turn. It will be noticed that under rotation only the angle changes. Measures of length and angle, used to define a position are called *polar co-ordinates*. They are particularly convenient for points related by rotation.

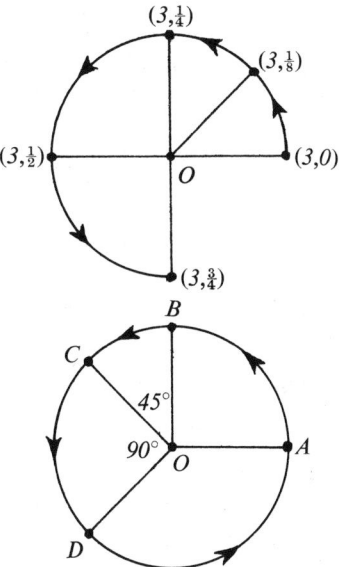

Figure 12:24

Point *A* in Figure 12:24 shows the result of a *complete* turn when the point is in the original position; the image of *A* under this rotation is *itself*. Succeeding complete rotations will produce the same image points as the first one. This property of rotations raises some interesting questions about the successive transformations of shapes under rotation.

Figure 12:25 shows an equilateral triangle *ABC* with its corners marked so that we can distinguish them. The shaded triangle *PQR* represents the hole left by the triangle when it was cut out. *ABC* would fit into *PQR* in its original position with *A* upon *P*. If triangle *ABC* is rotated when will it again be in a position to fit into *PQR*? After one third of a turn *B* would lie on *P* if the triangle were fitted

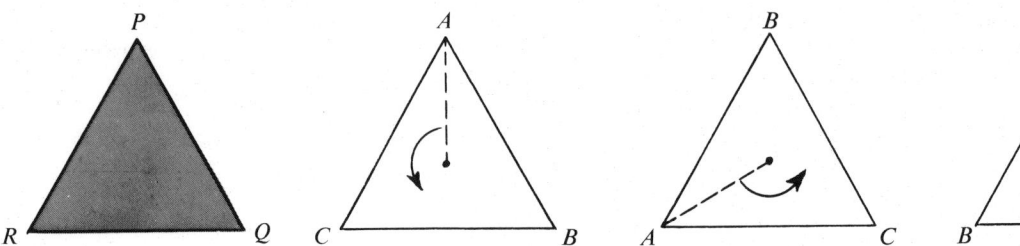

Figure 12:25

into the hole. It can be seen that a further rotation of one third would bring C on to P. If the triangle is rotated another third of a turn it will lie in its original position with A on P.

There are thus three different positions in which the image will fit into the hole, i.e. after one-third or two-thirds of a turn or a whole turn. These are called the rotational symmetry operations of the triangle. Children can experiment with a number of plane shapes to discover their angles of rotational symmetry; suitable shapes are a square, hexagon, circle, rectangle, kite, parallelogram. For a circle any rotation will do; for a kite, only a complete turn.

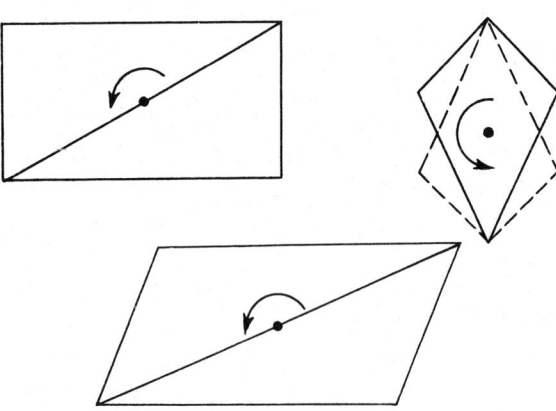

Figure 12:26

To summarize, we see that under rotation there is a point of the plane which remains unchanged; the distance of any point from the centre of rotation is also invariant;

lengths and angles of a figure are unchanged but the *position* of a point is changed and the *orientation* of a figure changes. A complete turn always fits the image onto the original.

Reflection

This is the transformation which most clearly shows a rule for finding the position of a transformed point. When a plane figure is reflected by folding a piece of paper about a line in its plane, the fold represents the axis of the reflection. After the fold has been made a prick can be made through any point of the original and will mark the corresponding point which lies beneath it. On opening out the paper the pairs of corresponding points are seen to lie on a line *perpendicular* to the axis, on *opposite sides* of it and at *equal distances* from the axis. A point *on* the axis will transform into itself. In Figure 12:27(a) the points A and E belong to both the original and the transform.

Figure 12:27(b) shows a series of reflections of the letter p about equidistant parallel axes. The transforms are all either like the original or are its mirror image.

In Figure 12:27(c) the point labelled R_0 and the set of points making up this form of p have been reflected in the y-axis. The image of R_0 is R_1. We next reflect this reflection in the x-axis, so that the image of R_1 is R_2. If this image is compared with the original, it will be seen that it could have been obtained by rotation about O. Thus the two reflections have the same effect as one rotation through half a turn. If R_2 is now reflected in the y-axis, R_3 is obtained. This is related to R_1 by rotation in the same way that R_2 is related to R_0. The reflection of R_3 in the x-axis

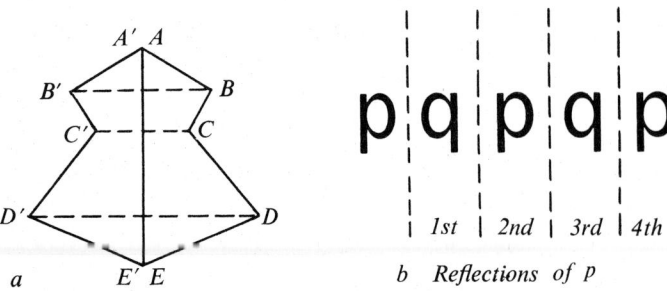

a

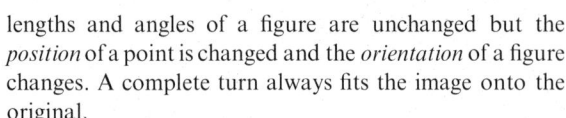

b   Reflections of p

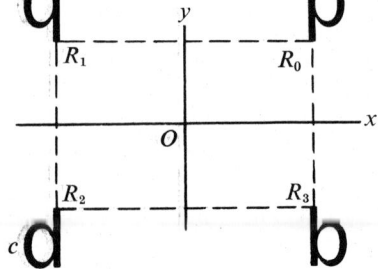

c

Figure 12:27

116

then finally brings us back to R_0. The position of these four points suggests the use of a special sign to represent a distance to the *left* of the vertical axis, or *below* the horizontal axis. If R_0 is two units from one of these axes, then $^+2$ could represent the distance to the right (or above) and $^-2$ the distance to the left (or below). Enterprising children may invent their own special signs in place of the conventional $+$ and $-$.

The symmetry created by a reflection is a valuable tool for discovering properties of shapes, for instance the properties of rectangles. Recognizing symmetry in a mirror image can lead to new insights (Figure 12:28).

Figure 12:28

There is another kind of pattern which children see in the shapes of some flowers, in pictures of snow crystals, or in some decorative designs. The pattern has parts which are of the same shape and size as one another and are arranged round a centre. Figure 12:29 shows some examples of this arrangement.

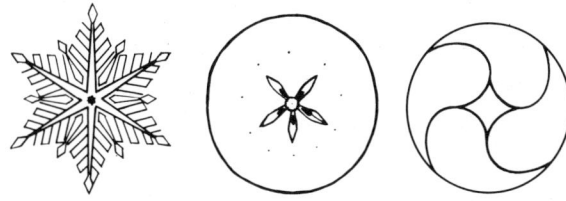

Figure 12:29

It can be seen that the whole shape could be rotated about a centre and after a certain fraction of a complete turn the shape would fit on to its original position. In a five-petalled flower a turn of $\frac{1}{5}$, $\frac{2}{5}$, $\frac{3}{5}$, $\frac{4}{5}$ or a complete revolution would bring the shape to a position where it would fit into its original place. For the three-legged shape $\frac{1}{3}$, $\frac{2}{3}$, or a complete revolution would be required (Figure 12:30). This form of symmetry is called *rotational* or *cyclic* symmetry.

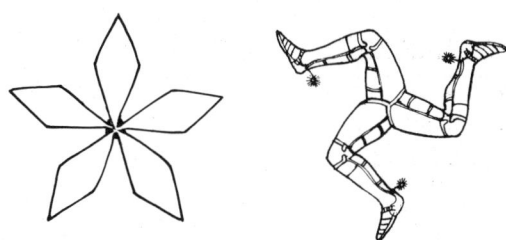

Figure 12:30

A special case of rotational symmetry is seen in those shapes which require half a complete turn to bring them to a position that fits on to the original. The letter S, a parallelogram and such an irregular shape as that shown in Figure 12:31(*c*) illustrate this type of symmetry.

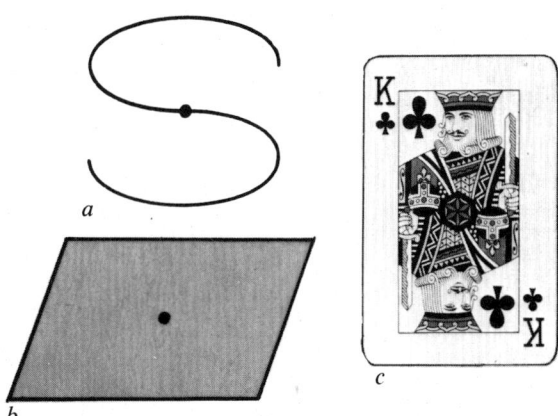

Figure 12:31

Each of these shapes could be given a half-turn about a point marked in the diagram and would then fit into the same position as it originally occupied. Symmetry of this type is known as *half-turn symmetry*.

In three dimensions solids can be reflected in a plane. The perpendicular distances of corresponding points from the plane are equal. Distances, angles, shape and size are all preserved. A change occurs in the reversal of the directions of line segments perpendicular to the plane of symmetry.

Enlargement

To effect this transformation a centre of enlargement must be chosen. Distances from this centre to all points of the given set of points are increased in a fixed ratio say, two to one. Experiment will show that the position of the centre will make no difference to the shape and size of the transform but it will affect its position.

117

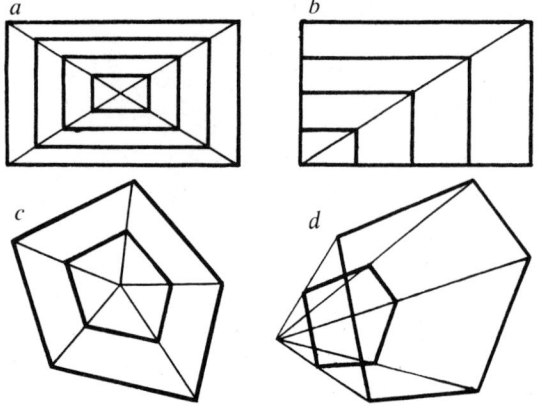

Figure 12:32

Shape is invariant under enlargement but lengths such as sides and diagonals are increased in a constant ratio. We may ask what is the effect of this transformation on the area of a two-dimensional shape or on the volume of a three-dimensional shape. These questions are discussed in Chapter 24.

If a shape is to be enlarged in a certain ratio it is possible, of course, to calculate the lengths of the sides of an enlargement and then to construct it in any position we choose. In this chapter, however, we have described the way in which an enlargement can be produced by transforming each point of the original by movement. No calculation is necessary because when the enlarged length corresponding to one original side is known, all other lengths can be found from such a mapping as is shown in Figure 12:33. Work on maps which show a known real distance brings home very clearly the underlying principle of ratio in a more general way than do numerical exercises.

Shear

This is the most difficult transformation which primary pupils can profitably study and it is best left to the later years. But teachers need to know how it produces changes in shape without affecting areas.

Equal rods, such as the ten-rods of Cuisenaire, can be placed one upon another to show a rectangular face. Each rod is then made to slide so that it projects a given distance, say a units, beyond the one below it. The face of the rods has now changed so that the ends lie on a parallelogram (*see page* 114). In this transformation each point has been translated horizontally through a distance proportional to its height above the base. If a point 1 unit above the base is translated a units to the right, a point 2 units above the base will move $2a$ units to the right. The general rule is that a point b units above the base will move $b \times a$ units horizontally. The length of the base and the height of the face are invariant. If the rods become very thin strips, like the edges of very fine paper, the face is seen to change from a rectangle to a parallelogram when sheared. For any value of a, and so for any parallelogram made in this way from a given rectangle, the area of the parallelogram is the same as that of the rectangle (Figure 12:34).

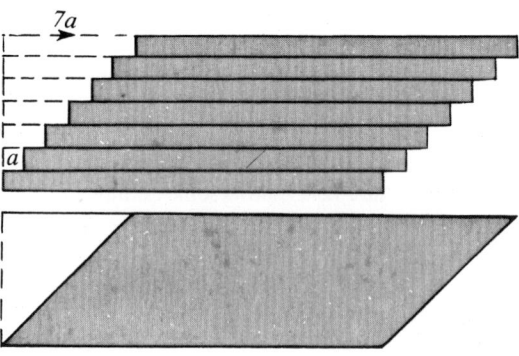

Figure 12:34

A nail-board can show this transformation. A rubber band is placed so as to enclose a rectangle. Another band is put round the ends of the base line and about two points

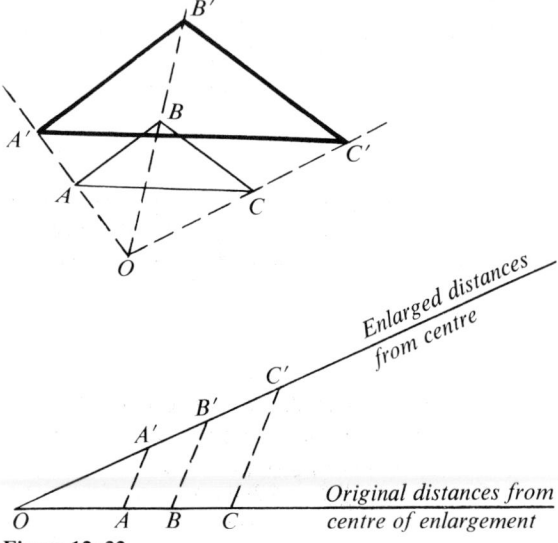

Figure 12:33

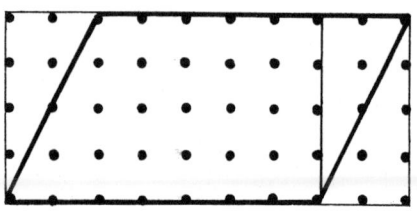

Figure 12:35

at equal distances to the right of the other vertices. It will enclose the parallelogram which is the image of the rectangle under shearing (Figure 12:35).

This property is brought out clearly if shearing is contrasted with the effect of deforming a rectangular framework made of two pairs of equal Meccano strips, bolted at their ends. If the framework is deformed into a parallelogram the lengths of the sides remain unaltered but the area of the enclosed region is changed.

The situation shown in shearing is important because it makes clear that area (and volume in three dimensions) can remain unaltered even when length and angle are changed.

Static and dynamic properties

The investigation of space outlined in this chapter includes both the study of shapes when they are static and their properties can be observed and recorded, and also the effects of movement. This dynamic treatment is of practical value today. When it is handled mathematically in a more abstract way as a study of transformations we can recognize that spatial forms can be handled in ways which are similar to those which we use for numbers. Invariance, sets, one-one correspondence and number operations all find a place in spatial work.

13 The Mastery of Decimal Notation

The beginnings of number notation

Large numbers were needed by men as soon as they began to live in communities. When famines came, food had to be stored, listed and shared. Big buildings required planning; lengths had to be decided and the amount of necessary material estimated. Herds of cattle had to be counted to avoid disputes about ownership. For many such purposes records of the numbers involved had to be kept. Some method had to be devised for writing numbers in a concise way. The first way of recording was to make a stroke for each object involved. As soon as large numbers had to be written, dealing with the long row of strokes became intolerably clumsy. For numbers from one to five the pattern of the strokes could easily be recognised and these numbers were given names. The next important step, taken by various peoples at different periods, was to group the strokes and record the groupings. If the number of groupings was small they could count the groupings using the number names they already had.

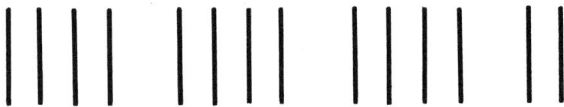

These strokes would be counted as 3 sets of 4 and 2 strokes.

Figure 13:1

Various groupings were used by different peoples; e.g. five, ten, twenty, sixty, but ten has become the established counting set and the number we call twenty-three is generally organized into two sets of ten and three single things. A name and a symbol were devised for the counting set; for example the Romans, counting in tens, wrote twenty-three as XXIII. The number shown in Figure 13:1 could be more economically written in some such way as

where each grouping of four has been formed into a concise symbol.

To make a second grouping was now an easy step forward. A hundred was a grouping of ten tens. Then a thousand was used for ten hundreds and so on. Even when the number of times each counting set was used was written as a symbol, e.g. 3 tens, to write a large number

as 3 thousands 7 hundreds 2 tens and 3 ones was clumsy. Abbreviations for the names shortened the writing but a new idea was needed before our modern system came into being. This idea, which opened the way to new understanding of numbers, was that the *names* of the groupings should be dropped entirely. A code was adopted by which the *position* of the figures should tell which groupings they referred to. Thus 4723 could be read at sight as four thousand seven hundred and twenty three because it was known that groupings increase in size with each move to the left from the ones. A single new sign only was required, a symbol to put into a place that turned out to be empty when the groupings were made. Hence the invention of 0 for use as a placeholder, as in writing 806, where 8 is seen to occupy the hundreds place because a zero has been written in the tens place.[1]

Children's first introduction to number notation

In earlier chapters we have shown how children come to understand and use the accepted notation for the smaller numbers that occur in their experience. They pass through stages which are similar to those outlined above for man's invention of a system that enables any number to be written concisely. Very few additional symbols have had to be invented to express the other kinds of numbers, such as fractions, negative numbers, and irrational numbers, by which the natural numbers have been supplemented to form the whole system of real numbers (*see pages* 400–402). The importance of children's thorough understanding of their first steps in number notation is evident if they are to follow easily the later developments.

At first children record and compare sets, as did early man, without counting. They use beads, pictures, cubes, squares, and may even use strokes as their forefathers did. Names and symbols for the small and easily recognized numbers are soon learned. The sequence of number names to one hundred and beyond may be familiar before the written forms are known. But as soon as numbers greater than ten need to be written the first introduction to the structure of our notation has to be made. The important operation of grouping must be undertaken and the idea of recording the number of equivalent counting sets made by the grouping has to emerge. The use of a rod to represent a counting set helps a child in this recording. For instance, as he

---

[1] A fuller account of the historical development of number notations is given in Chapter 17.

groups cubes in fives he can replace each set of five by a five-rod. Sets of ten will be replaced by ten-rods. It is common practice to introduce tens early to children. Frequently no other counting set is experienced by a child. For example, the number twenty-nine is known to him in only two ways: as the number which occurs after twenty-eight when the number names are recited in order, and also as the number which is equivalent to two tens and nine ones. Because we use ten as the counting set successively throughout our number system from tens to millions and beyond, it is important that the structure of numbers in terms of tens and ones should be well understood. Nevertheless, number notations based on other counting sets have their uses and children should have opportunities of organizing numbers by means of groupings other than in tens. The experience of using a variety of bases or counting sets for number notation helps a child to generalize the formation or structure which is common to all the resulting systems.

Groupings should be carried out with actual objects. For example, children may take twenty-five rods or matchsticks and make as many *triangles* as possible from them. They are then grouping in threes. (Figure 13:2.) They can write 25 = 8 threes and 1 one.

If they make squares instead they will be able to write, as in Figure 13:3. 25 = 6 fours and 1 one.

If they pack the sticks in sets of five they will write 25 = 5 fives and 0 ones (Figure 13:4).

Putting each pair of fives together a child makes groupings of ten and writes 25 = 2 tens and 5 ones. At this point the way of writing twenty-five takes on new meaning: the 2 and the 5 are explained.

Cubes and rods of the Cuisenaire, Colour Factor or Dienes types can show similar number structures. Given a set of 17 unit cubes and a handful of five-rods a child can match a five-rod to each set of 5 cubes as in Figure 13:5. He writes 17 = 3 fives and 2 ones.

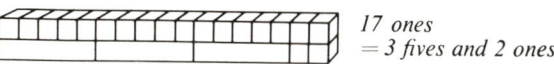

17 ones
= 3 fives and 2 ones

Figure 13:5

Given six-rods or eight-rods he obtains two new groupings for 17 as shown in Figure 13:6.

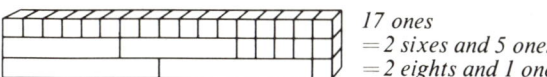

17 ones
= 2 sixes and 5 ones
= 2 eights and 1 one

Figure 13:6

With ten-rods he obtains the pattern that matches the notation 17 as shown in Figure 13:7.

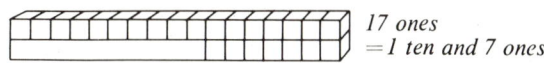

17 ones
= 1 ten and 7 ones

Figure 13:7

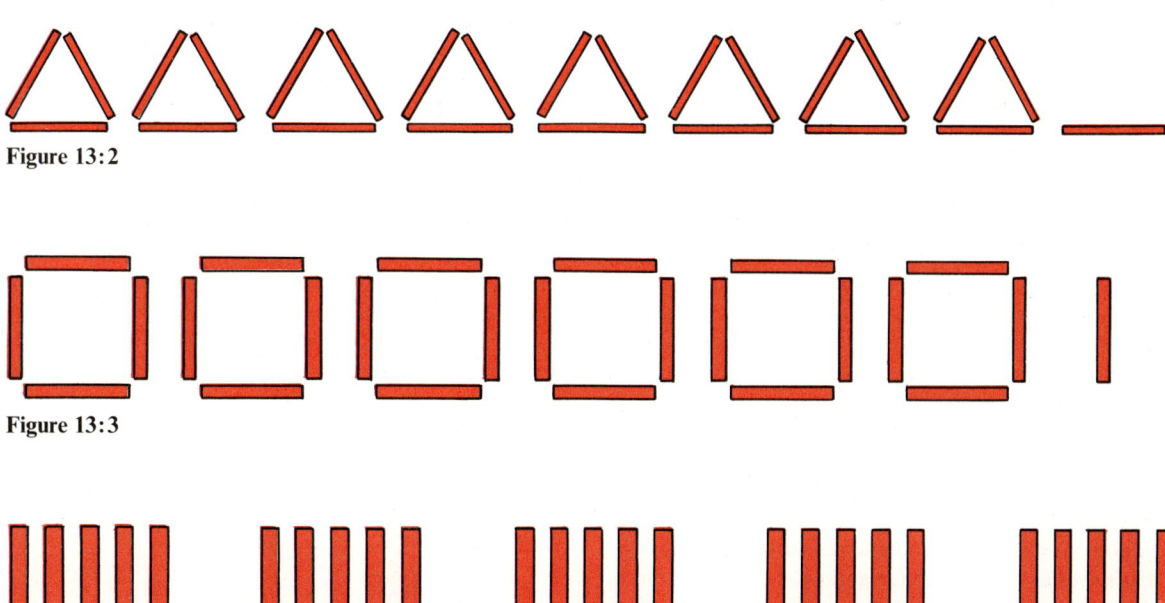

Figure 13:2

Figure 13:3

Figure 13:4

121

Such constructions make children familiar with the number patterns they will find in multiplication and division. Here the emphasis is on the practical experience of grouping. The manipulation of cubes and rods has the further advantage that it shows how such a grouping can be continued. Children quickly discover that 3 three-rods placed side by side form a square. Given 17 unit cubes and some three-rods they can replace the 17 cubes with 1 square layer, 2 three-rods and 2 unit cubes. (Figure 13:8.)

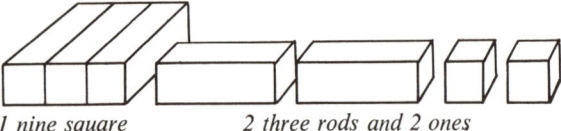

1 nine square   *2 three rods and 2 ones*

Figure 13:8

The square trays included in the Stern apparatus provide for varied experiences of this kind, using squares which have 2, 3, 4, . . . , 10 units along an edge.

16 cubes or 4 rods fill one square

Figure 13:9

At this stage no formal work is developed beyond recording the squares, rods and unit cubes that have been used. But it can be seen that basically the children are learning the structure that they will use when they write 100s and 10s and ones in such a number as 322.

When we write 28 the 2 tells us how many tens and 8 tells how many ones together make twenty-eight. A child will know at once that 2 ten-rods and 8 unit cubes represents 28. In Chapter 32 we show how number systems using counting sets other than ten, say five, six or eight, as in Figures 13:5 and 13:6, can be written so that the number of fives, sixes or eights and their squares, cubes, etc., can be read at sight.[1] In the present chapter we are suggesting only the *practical* experience of grouping in such sets so that children fully understand the procedure of grouping and do not think of tens and ones as providing the only means of organizing a number.

So far we have made no attempt to develop the idea that the *order* of writing the figures has any importance, although we have consistently written the number of

counting sets on the left of the number of ones. Up to the age of seven many children reverse this order sometimes, writing 82 instead of 28 when they mean 2 ten-rods and 8 cubes. From their point of view there is no reason why they should not work from right to left in placing the rods to match the equivalent number of cubes, as in Figure 13:10.

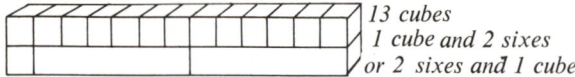

13 cubes
1 cube and 2 sixes
or 2 sixes and 1 cube

Figure 13:10

The teacher's consistent use of a left to right movement will help the children to develop the same habit. But the introduction of some form of abacus is the occasion for deliberately establishing the reading and writing of numbers from left to right, the largest grouping always being placed on the left and the ones on the extreme right.

The abacus

The abacus has already been suggested in Chapter 2 as a useful way of recording sets so that they may easily be compared. For this purpose the beads placed on any column have the same value; each represents *one* member of a set. Figure 13:11 shows five sets.

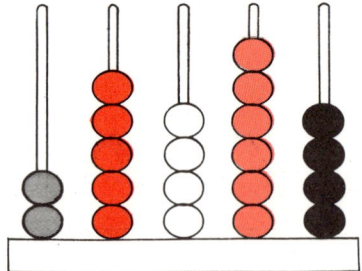

Figure 13:11

In Chapter 7 a two-column abacus was used to illustrate the structure of the numbers from ten to twenty. In this case the left-hand column records the number of ten-rods or sets of ten things that can be found when a given number, say seventeen or twenty, is organized in a grouping of ten.

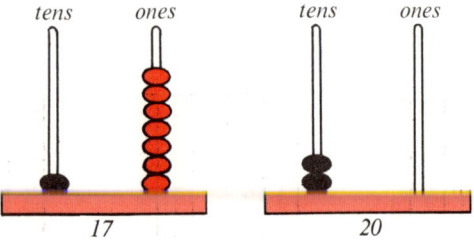

tens   ones   *tens   ones*

17   *20*

Figure 13:12

---

[1] Grouping in this way is an essential foundation for multiplying, since the children are counting, say, 3 fives as 15 and vice versa.

The value of each bead on the left-hand column is ten. The right-hand column still represents ones. Notice the empty column in the representation of twenty in Figure 13:12. At first each column should be labelled. Beads of a different colour on each rod help a child to remember the difference in value of the beads but this distinction should shortly be dropped so that the *position* of the beads is emphasized. Extensive use of the two-column abacus should now be made to record counts and to translate into written form numbers up to 99. Many different counts which are of interest to children should be made: children present in class, pencils, coins, distances measured in metres, windows or doors in the school, the numbers of various shapes in a room, the number of balls in a box, cars in a car park, berries on a branch, and so on. Children show their count on an abacus and then write the number in symbols. The abacus may in fact be drawn on paper and rings or squares used for the count. Grooves in a sand-tray with pebbles as counters serve equally well and remind us that such an abacus was in use two thousand and more years ago. The purpose of this work is to establish written notation on a firm basis before learning to add and subtract *formally* with two columns of figures. Decimal currency helps children in dealing with a counting set of ten. A ten-penny piece can replace ten pennies, and a pound note is equivalent to ten tenpenny pieces.

Measures expressed in two units

Practical work with two measuring units of different value, e.g. ten-rods and unit cubes, or kilos and hectos, provides a variety of experience in grouping. The many activities suggested in Chapter 15 give rise to recording in two-unit form the results of measuring length, capacity, mass, time, etc., as well as the value in tenpences and pence of sets of coins. In many instances only two distinct units are necessary, and familiarity with two-unit procedures should be well established before a third measuring unit is introduced. For example, metres and decimetres are used together for measuring a path, decimetres and centimetres are sufficient for shorter lengths.

As children work with pairs of units in these different fields, writing their experiences with coins, tape-measures, clock-faces or litre jugs, they can be led to see that the operations they are carrying out are of the same kind as those they perform on tens and ones. When they record a height in centimetres only, or a mass in grams only, they express the number in tens and ones, e.g. 47 cm; to convert the measure to a pair of units they read 47 as 4 tens and 7 ones and 47 cm as 4 dm and 7 cm. A measuring strip can be made to show both forms of stating the length. So long as children confine their working to two measuring units the parallel between this work and the use of tens and ones is clear. It is a great advantage if

practical work with measures, and the statements and calculations that record it, can be developed alongside activities with numbers written in tens and ones. This stage is a very important one for understanding the procedures needed to carry through addition, subtraction, multiplication and division of large numbers when two different values, (such as ten and one), must be given to the figures used in writing the numbers. If sufficient time is allowed for the range of practical activities which should be the basis of learning the patterns of these operations involving 2-figure numbers, the extension to 3-figure and 4-figure numbers will be mastered later without difficulty.

Written procedures with two-unit numbers and measures

When a child can think of numbers and measures without needing actual objects to guide his thinking, he is ready to learn to carry out with written symbols the operations of addition and subtraction with which he is already familiar through combining and comparing sets or measures. Such operations with numbers greater than ten demand an effective understanding of the notation we use. If the recording of counts of sets in tens and ones has been done as suggested earlier in this chapter children will have little difficulty in carrying out additions and subtractions in which there has to be a carry-over from ones to tens or vice-versa.

If a number greater than nine is written in two columns labelled *tens* and *ones* a child is reminded of the value of the figure in the left-hand column. When he labels the columns of a measure in such units as metres and dm he has no reminder of the equivalence of 10 dm to 1 metre. It is helpful to label the columns as in Figure 13:13 when using two measuring units.

		10's			
tens	ones	m	dm	litres	tenths
3	6	3	6	3	6
+2	7	+2	7	+2	7
1	3	1	3	1	3
5	0	5	0	5	0
6	3	6	3	6	3

Figure 13:13

The close link between subtraction and addition which was stressed in Chapter 9 can now be continued and will help children to understand what must be done in subtraction when the *ones* figure of the number *to be subtracted* (subtrahend) is larger than the *ones* figure of the number it is to be taken from. Addition is learned first. Then addition and subtraction can be carried out side by side, the full working being set out as in Figure 13:14.

Addition			Subtraction, the inverse of addition				
tens	ones		tens	ones		tens	ones
2	8		3	5		2	15
+	7		−	7		−	7
1	5					2	8
2	0						
3	5						

Figure 13:14

The regrouping, a word which recalls the grouping of ten ones into one ten, can be illustrated by structural apparatus. (Figure 13:15.) The correspondences between Figure 13:15(a) and 13:15(c) stand out clearly.

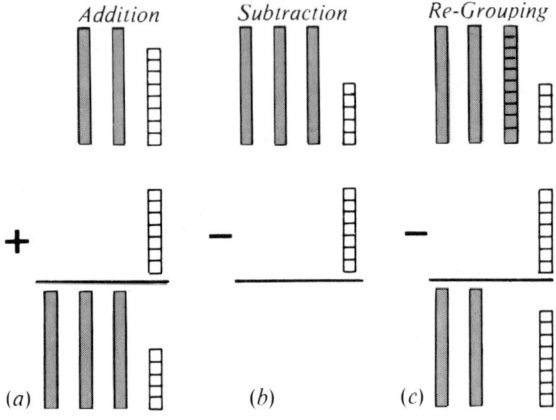

Figure 13:15

Notice that the addition operation reminds a child of what he should already know about the number 15, viz. that $15 = 8+7$, a fact he should link with $15-7 = 8$.

The idea of regrouping can be reinforced by writing it in full as in Figure 13:14 until children can carry it out in their minds. They may still use an abbreviated reminder for a time if the teacher sees that they need it.

It will be seen that regrouping is similar to the method of subtraction called *decomposition* but it uses a more fundamental idea. It assumes that such relationships as $15-7 = 8$ are remembered without requiring that the ten shall be *decomposed* into ten ones. The linking of subtraction with addition also makes the regrouping arrangements suitable to the method known as *complementary addition* in which, instead of saying, '7 from 15', we say '7 and what number make 15?' Children are used to writing this as $7+\square = 15$, and they should know at once the number required to make this a true statement (*see page* 88).

If the method of subtraction known as *equal additions* is used, a different idea is introduced, i.e. a ten is added to each

124

of the numbers whose difference is to be found. The writing pattern is illustrated in Figure 13:16.

tens	ones			tens	ones
3	5			3	15
− 1	7	*(a) is rewritten as in (b)*		− 2	7
(a)				*(b)*	

Figure 13:16

It should be noticed that in adding a ten to each number, 5 in the ones column of the larger number becomes 15, and the 1 in the tens column of the subtrahend becomes 2. This method is more difficult than regrouping because a ten is introduced from outside; the numbers which are actually subtracted are not those which were given. The procedure is thus somewhat artificial and is based on convenience rather than developed from a situation which leads to subtraction.

In subtraction involving two measuring units connected by a counting set other than ten the same principle of regrouping can be used: e.g. finding the interval between two times stated in hours and minutes (Figure 13:17).

hours	min		hours	min		hours	min
9	15		8	60+15		8	75
− 7	30		− 7	30		− 7	30
						1	45

Figure 13:17

The second grouping: square layers

Many counting experiences will lead children beyond one hundred; e.g. the number of steps a child takes to cross the playground, the number of acorns in a class collection, the number of visitors who attend a school concert (and the chairs to be placed for them). The written numerals which represent such large numbers must be understood as expressing successive groupings into tens. This can be made clear by the rhythm of the count, each complete ten being stressed, . . . *ten* . . . *twenty* . . . *thirty* . . . *one hundred*. The acorns can be counted in tens, put into boxes or plastic bags and these tens assembled into hundreds; the number is then written so that each digit has its meaning, e.g. 2 sets of 100, 7 bags of 10 and 5 acorns: 275. When a child steps across the playground, markers can be placed at the end of each set of 10 steps and a larger marker put at the end of 100 steps, and so on. Children enjoy exercising their skill in these large counts and will extend a numbered strip beyond 100 units until it reaches along a whole wall

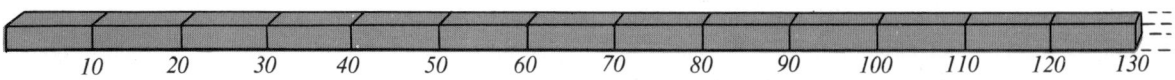

Figure 13:18

or even round a room.

All the available ten-rods in apparatus of the Cuisenaire type can be placed end to end and a count made of the equivalent cubes. (Figure 13:18.)

If the children have already made square layers of 3 three-rods, 4 four-rods, etc. (*described on page* 100), they will know that 10 of the ten-rods will make a square layer which is equivalent to 100 cubes. The square becomes the shape associated with *any* second grouping using the same counting set as the first grouping. The structure of a three-digit number can then be represented by square layers, rods and unit cubes, whatever counting set is used (Figure 13:19).

It will be noticed that no new principle is required in carrying out written calculations with numbers greater than 99. The step to adding and subtracting numbers between 100 and 1000 should be made easily after the counting and recording activities that we have suggested.

Two successive groupings of sevens

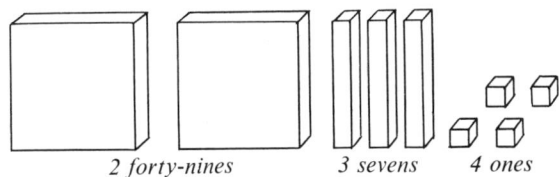

2 forty-nines   *3 sevens*   *4 ones*

Two successive groupings of tens

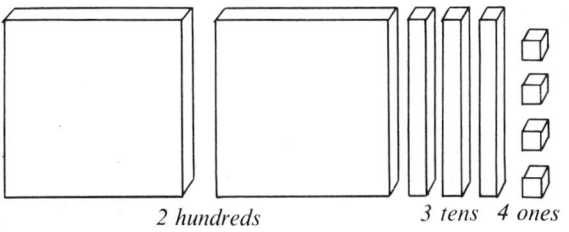

2 hundreds   *3 tens* *4 ones*

Figure 13:19

Decimal coinage: hundreds

In the British decimal currency there is one main unit, the pound. This is equivalent to 100 pence. An intermediate coin represents 10 of these pence. Thus it is possible to symbolize the decimal notation for numbers from 1 to 100s by coins representing pennies or tenpences, and notes each worth 100 pence or £1. Sums of money which contain other intermediate coins worth five pence or twopence can be written in three columns labelled £, 10p, p, as shown in Figure 13:20. This illustrates the meaning of the decimal form stated in pounds.

In columns			As a decimal	In pence
£	10p	p		
2	3	8	£2·38	238p
5	0	7	£5·07	507p
1	9	0	£1·90	190p

Figure 13:20

Extension to larger numbers

When children use structural apparatus and diagrams to represent the ones, tens and hundreds that they write in columns, they become aware of the relation between the values represented by neighbouring columns. For example, they come to realize that a 3 in the tens place is worth ten times a 3 in the ones column, and conversely a 3 in the ones column is worth one-tenth of a 3 in the tens column. A ten is 10 times a one, and is also one-tenth of a hundred. (Figure 13:21.)

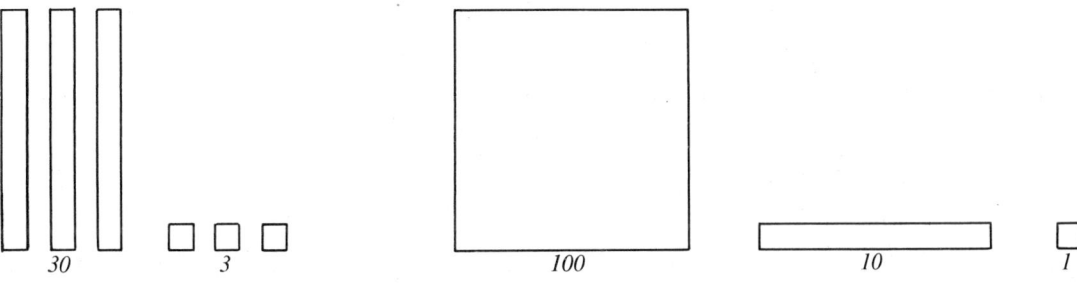

30   *3*   *100*   *10*   *1*

Figure 13:21

125

As a child looks at the columns to the left of the ones column he sees that each has a value *ten times* that of the column on its *right*. If, however, he begins at the left-hand column, say the hundreds, and moves to the right, the value of any column is one-tenth of that of the column to its *left*; a ten is one-tenth of a hundred and a one is one-tenth of a ten.

The way is now open to further grouping without limit. In general children do not master this concept of an unending process of grouping until they are about 9 years of age. It has to be built up by extending the notation through thousands to millions and then evoking awareness that counting in millions can be carried forward indefinitely. The realization that counting can never reach an end is a startling and memorable experience for most children. Our vast number structure can hardly have much meaning for a child unless he encounters some of the very large numbers necessary for recording air journeys, astronomical distances, population figures, etc., and can relate them to his own experiences of crowds and large collections. Nevertheless, children are fascinated by numbers so large that they are difficult to imagine, and they will sometimes undertake prodigious counts. One class of 9 to 10-year-old children used $\frac{1}{10}$-inch squared paper to make a count beyond 10 000. One $\frac{1}{10}$-inch square represented 1 unit, so that a row of ten 1-inch squares represented 1 000. Ten rows represented 10 000. Repeating this large square to make a row of ten made 100 000 and so they continued. Another class of this age spent their spare time for several weeks in a determined effort to count out, in successive groupings of ten, a million barley corns. At the end of this task they certainly understood our tens notation.

The first use of decimal fractions

Experience of the notation used in a decimal currency prepares children for the extension of number notation to the *right* of the units column. The ten to one relationship of £1 to a tenpence and of a tenpence to a penny leads children to recognize that a penny is a tenth of 1 tenpence and a tenpence is a tenth of £1. The columns in which money is written can now be described as pounds, tenths and hundredths, because 100 pence make £1 (Figure 13:22).

£	10p	p		£	tenths	hundredths	
2	3	8		2	3	8	£2·38

Figure 13:22

The point separates the pounds from the tenpences and thus comes between pounds and tenths of a pound. This is the fundamental step in realising the *general* use of the point showing which is the *ones* column and which figure shows *tenths*.

When a child begins to need to measure lengths with an accuracy greater than to the nearest unit he will use a sub-unit for the piece smaller than 1 unit. Now he should be introduced to *tenths* of a unit in place of a named sub-unit. For instance, instead of recording a length as 2 metres 7 decimetres he can *say* two and seven tenths metres and *write* $2\frac{7}{10}$m, or he can *write* 2·7m and *say* two point seven metres.

It is desirable, if possible, to introduce the metric system alongside the decimal system of notation, in order to provide experience of a set of measuring units in which the principal unit (the metre in the measurement of length) is subdivided into tenths and hundredths. The use of a metre ruler for measurement will lead children to know that one metre is equivalent to 10 decimetres or to 100 centimetres. A child should know that he can describe his height in a variety of ways, of which the following are examples:

$$
\begin{aligned}
\text{1 metre 2 decimetres 4 centimetres} \\
= \text{12 decimetres 4 centimetres} \\
= \text{124 centimetres}
\end{aligned}
$$

The use of fractions and decimals gives further expressions, such as:

$$
\begin{aligned}
\text{12 dm 4 cm} &= 12\tfrac{4}{10}\,\text{dm} \\
&= 12\text{·}4\,\text{dm} \\
&= \text{1 m 2 dm 4 cm} \\
&= 1\,\text{m} + \tfrac{2}{10}\,\text{m} + \tfrac{4}{100}\,\text{m} \\
&= 1\tfrac{24}{100}\,\text{m}
\end{aligned}
$$

The usual way of giving this height as 1·24 m will lead to the introduction of the second decimal place, the hundredths place (Figure 13:23).

The extension of decimal fractions beyond hundredths is likely to occur on account of the 1000 to 1 relationship between the standard metric units which gives in reverse the 1 to 1000 relationship. For example:

1 km = 1000 m	1 m = 1 thousandth of 1 km
	= 0·001 km
1 litre = 1000 ml	1 ml = 1 thousandth of 1 litre
	= 0·001 litre
1 kg = 1000 g	1g = 1 thousandth of 1 kg
	= 0·001 kg.

The millimetre and the gram are too small for a single unit to have much practical value but a medicine spoon holds 5 ml, which can be written as 0·005 litres, and a standard litre measure has minor markings in 50 ml. The mass of the contents of a tin of meat is given on the outside,

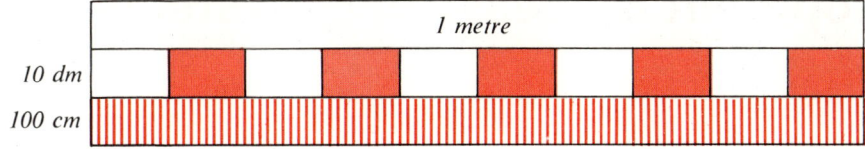

Figure 13:23

correct to 1 gram or 0·001 kg. Millimetres are not very practical for children's use, but they will be found marked on rulers and tape measures and as a ruling on cm/mm graph paper. They serve to give a greater accuracy in graphs and scale drawings where decimal fractions are commonly used. From the notational standpoint they have some importance in suggesting that further extensions of the decimal fraction system could be made.

14 The Development of Measuring Systems

The choice of units

When children begin to measure quantities which interest them—mass, capacity, length, for instance—they use a unit which seems suited to the object they are concerned with. It may be an improvised unit such as a piece of string, a marble, an empty tin, but it is chosen because it seems likely to produce a fairly small number when it is compared with the quantity to be measured. The history of measures shows how through the centuries a people would agree on the units they would use for particular ranges of objects, such as gallons that a milkpan would hold, yards for the distance across a plot of land. There was no thought of inventing a whole *system* of units of length or mass. In order to measure the length of a track, the size of a brick, the amount of ploughing done in a day, the weight of a bag of corn or of a silver coin, a special unit was required in each case. So unconnected units such as the mile, inch, yard, pint, gallon, furlong, stone, ounce continued in use for many years. For ordinary folk in their daily activities these separate measures were adequate but for the merchant or the builder recording and accounting such units demanded numerical skill. Numbers had been organized into a system of tens at an early stage and this system had to be used for each separate unit of measurement without the possibility of converting one unit into another. There was also the problem of ensuring that *each* separate unit was kept at a standard quantity since it was not related to another unit as our measures are today. Few attempts were made to create new systems of measurement until the end of the eighteenth century, when the metric system was devised. Until then systematizing consisted of standardizing existing units and relating them by the nearest whole number to the ratio which tradition had developed. Consequently we find the prime numbers 2, 3, 5, 7, 11 all occurring as factors in our traditional tables of measure.

Linking units

The system of the British measures of length illustrates well the complicated history of the different units. Parts of the human body were natural choices for measuring units: the inch as the width of the thumb (or the length of the top joint), the foot from the heel to the toe, the yard as the girth of a man (or the distance from the nose to the tip of the outstretched arm). The now rarely used cubit and fathom were respectively the length from the elbow to the finger tip and the width of the outstretched arms. Such measures varied from one individual to another and any connection between them was an approximate

128

ratio as it chanced to occur in nature. Neither the length of a particular unit nor the ratio of one unit to another was at first fixed by statute but gradually it became necessary to safeguard traders by having a legal standard for a unit and a compulsory system of equivalences. The approximate equivalences of 12 thumb-joints to one foot-length became a fixed artificial relation and both inch and foot were prescribed fractions of the standard yard. Thus the 12 and the 3 which were among the first ratios of units of length learned by our children sprang from the proportions of two parts of the human body.

Twelve has a long history from before Roman times; it has the advantage of having 2, 3, 4 and 6 as factors and the Romans found its properties so useful that they had a special column for twelfths on their abacus. The still surviving use of the dozen and the gross demonstrates its usefulness. But with the adoption of metric measures in industry and commerce and the general use of decimal currency this special familiarity with twelve will decline.

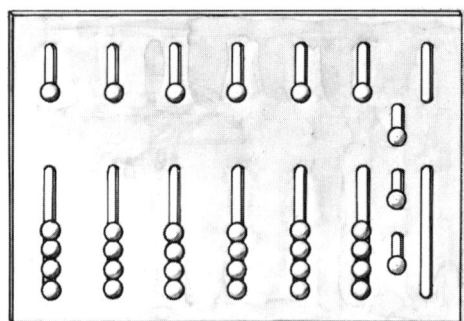

A Roman abacus showing places for twelfths on the right

Figure 14:1

Some of our units of length derived from the need to measure the amount of work done. The furlong was the length that an animal could draw a plough before resting. This is the unit on which our mile was based. The *rod* (pole or perch) is thought to have been the yoke pole used in Anglo-Saxon times for the four pairs of oxen used in ploughing. The rod was also the basis of land measuring and was originally quite distinct from the yard used for cloth. When yards and rods were linked to fit into a complete length-measuring *system,* the inconvenient $5\frac{1}{2}$ yards appeared as the equivalent of a rod. Children will be interested to know that it is through the use of the rod that eleven appeared as a factor in the number of yards in a chain, a furlong and a mile, i.e. 22, 220 and 1760 yards respectively.

The mile was built on the furlong and we see that the $\frac{1}{4}$-mile, $\frac{1}{2}$-mile and mile were obtained from the furlong by successive doubling, a pattern which is seen frequently in other measures.

The *chain* is a particularly interesting unit. It is derived from the measuring rope which was used in Egypt and other ancient cultures, and may be known to children in their own measuring. A chain was equal to 4 rods and to one-tenth of a furlong. It has another link with tens; since the seventeenth century it has been used by surveyors as a measuring chain divided into 100 links. This means that work with these two units, chains and links, follows the pattern of hundreds, tens and units, with 1 chain used as the name for 100 links. A Gunter chain, which is literally made up of 100 links, is a useful piece of equipment for older classes. See Figure 14:2. The measurement of land

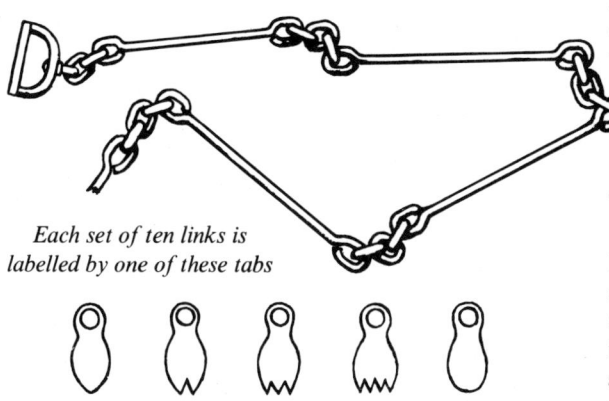

Each set of ten links is labelled by one of these tabs

Figure 14:2

area also uses the chain. The acre is equal to the area of a rectangle 10 chains long and 1 chain wide. Although the chain does not occur frequently in the daily usage of many people the chain of 22 yards is well known as the length of a cricket pitch. These various interests, mathematical and others, make it worth while to include the modern chain of 20 metres in the school programme.

The influence of ten

Calculations are considerably eased when one unit is equivalent to ten smaller units, or a multiple or a power of ten of a smaller unit. The practically minded Romans made their mile equal to 1000 paces[1]. Measurements could easily be recorded in their decimal notation with its symbols for a thousand (M), a hundred (C) and ten (X).

[1] The Roman pace was about one and a half metres long, the same as a Scout pace today.

Ten occurs as a factor of sixty in relating minutes and seconds to hours. This goes back to the Babylonians and their interest in astronomy. The apparent movement of the sun across the sky and the rotation which we observe in the stars in the night sky led to the use of the circle as the image of these movements. The six arose because it is easy to divide a circle into six parts by drawing the inscribed hexagon. The further division by ten gave the rotation 60 parts which matched the counting set of 60 which was the Babylonian number base. It was natural to link 60 with the number of days in the year which was thought to be 360 by the Babylonians. Although we now have discarded 360 as the number of days in a year we keep it as the number of degrees in a complete revolution and we still use 60 seconds to the minute and 60 minutes to the hour.

These are all separate and unsystematic uses of ten in linking units of measure. No measuring system based exclusively on ten came into use until the metric system was adopted in France in 1795.

The introduction of a metric system

In that great period of scientific initiatives in Europe, the seventeenth century, it was proposed in England to adopt a set of measuring units which would be convenient to use for practical purposes, would have world-wide validity, and would be likely to produce numerical results of recognizable accuracy. It is not surprising that the unit of *length* was considered to be basic, because not only is it extensively used, but also it can be measured directly (when accessible) by placing the unit repeatedly along the actual length. Various suggestions were made for a new unit of length from which successive powers of ten could be derived to serve as larger units. These ideas came to nothing until, over a hundred years later, at the time of the Revolution, France devised and adopted the metric system which was to become the recognized system for scientific use throughout the world. It was built on the basis of the metre, then defined as one-forty-millionth of the length of the meridian through Paris and now recognized as 1 650 763·73 wavelengths of the light emitted by the orange-red spectrum line of the gas krypton–86, measured in a vacuum. Each other unit was linked with the next larger in the ratio 1 to 10.

It is remarkable that not all the most highly developed nations have yet adopted the metric units for general public use. Where it has been established, the simplification of the arithmetic required by the ordinary citizen has had welcome repercussions on the computations taught in primary schools. The decrease in the time spent on skill in calculating has meant that more time can be given to teaching important mathematical ideas.

Halving and doubling

Alongside the tendency to use tens when larger quantities had to be measured, there persisted the primitive method of halving or doubling units to make counting easier. In fact some systems show complete dependence on these two basic procedures. The measure of capacity as used in daily life is one good example, with its gallons, $\frac{1}{2}$-gallons, quarts, pints and $\frac{1}{2}$-pints.

The 'weights' traditionally provided with the common kitchen scales give an outstanding example of repeated halving. In addition to 4-lb and 2-lb weights there were single weights of 1-lb, $\frac{1}{2}$-lb, $\frac{1}{4}$-lb, 2-oz, 1-oz, $\frac{1}{2}$-oz and $\frac{1}{4}$-oz. This means that they gave a run of eight successive halvings, and can be compared with the binary scale sequence: 1, 2, 4, 8, 16, 32, 64, 128, 256, which shows successive doublings. Similarly, the 7 days of the week depend on halving the 28 days of the moon's cycle, to give a fortnight, and halving those 14 days to give a week. In this case the seven seems inevitable.

It is interesting to compare the weighing units from 1 oz upwards, obtained by repeated doubling, with the traditional units made in Ghana for weighing their main product, gold. These increase by *equal steps* of approximately $\frac{1}{2}$-oz starting at 1 oz and continuing to $8\frac{1}{2}$ oz at least. A large number of weights is required because combinations are not provided for. This contrasts with the binary system of weighing where numbers of ounces can be expressed as the sum of a few of the binary weights supplied. For example, no special weight is needed for 3 oz because it is the sum of 2 oz and 1 oz. As can be seen in Figure 14:3 the form of the Ghanaian weight is significant and their manufacture one of the most pleasing of traditional crafts. There was no desire to economise in

their number. Indeed the variety of form is immense, there being several figures to each weight. They are made of brass and are therefore reliable in use, but they also have a cultural meaning: each piece represents either a familiar activity or a commonly used proverb. (Figure 14:3.)

The tendency to use tens and twos in systems of measures is interesting in view of the modern use of the denary and binary scales. Our number system is decimal and like many other countries we now use a decimal system of measures. At the same time digital computers are working on a binary scale. It is clearly an advantage to children if they have ample experience of seeing the value of both these modern usages, and have a practical foundation for the more abstract consideration of number notation.

The development of fractions

When a small unit is iterated to measure a quantity the resulting number may be large. The small units can then be grouped to form a larger one, e.g. 100 cm to make one metre, 1000 grams to make one kg. But the formation of a second unit may arise in another way. A piece less than a unit may remain to be included in the total measure. This piece may look like half a unit and may be so called: half a litre, half a km, etc. With experience, $\frac{1}{4}$ and $\frac{3}{4}$ become recognizable too. The possibility of splitting a unit into a number of parts other than two or four is realized (though it may be difficult to carry out), and thirds, eighths, fifths and twelfths come into use. Where children have a tape or ruler graduated in small parts they will readily use them, saying how many parts there are, say, to 1 cm and how many are required to make up the quantity

Figure 14:3

they are measuring, e.g. 3 tenths of a cm. They have two ideas in mind: that one unit is equal to a certain number of equal parts, and that the number of these parts required for the measuring must be counted and given a name. Thus the two-number notation for fractions is built up, e.g. three quarters of a litre using the numbers three and four; $\frac{7}{10}$ in using 10 and 7.

It should be noted that certain parts of some units have been given special names, for instance hundredths of a metre are called centimetres, but no special names are given in other cases, such as quarters of a litre or a kilogram. But the concept is the same and the same operations of addition, subtraction, etc., may be carried out. For example, 1 tenth plus 2 tenths is equal to 3 tenths and it will be realized that 8 eighths of a metre make one whole metre. It is through these measuring situations that a true understanding of fractions develops. The fractional way of writing the relationship of equivalence of units strengthens this development. For example, the statement 1 cm = 10 mm should be matched with the statement 1 mm = $\frac{1}{10}$ of 1 cm.

The two-number structure of fractions

The naming of a part as $\frac{1}{3}$, $\frac{1}{8}$, etc., is straightforward. These aliquot fractions[2] were well-known to the Egyptians, but of all the other possible fractions only $\frac{2}{3}$ was actually used by them. Such a fraction as $\frac{3}{5}$ had to be rewritten as $\frac{1}{2} + \frac{1}{10}$ before they could calculate with it.

For the Greeks a fraction such as $\frac{3}{5}$ was seen as the ratio of 3 to 5, and they had a clear idea that a fraction involved a *pair* of numbers, even when, as in the case of $\frac{1}{8}$, one of the pair is 1. This concept of a fraction as a pair of numbers with a ratio will develop as a child has experience of scale in drawings and maps. For the moment he sees only a comparison of quantities, principally the comparison of one part to the whole, e.g. $\frac{1}{4}$ litre to 1 litre. But he will also realize the relation of fractional parts of the same kind to one another, for example the relation of $\frac{1}{4}$ to $\frac{3}{4}$ and of $\frac{1}{10}$ to $\frac{3}{10}$.

When children tabulate the equivalences of quantities expressed in different units, e.g. cm and metres, they will see that the *number* of cm is 100 *times* the corresponding *number* of metres, and also that the number of metres is $\frac{1}{100}$ of the number of cm. This is an approach to the idea of ratio which will grow more precise later on when children draw graphs of the equivalences.

The equivalence of fractional parts, e.g. $\frac{1}{2}$, $\frac{2}{4}$, $\frac{4}{8}$, is seen very clearly in measuring activities. It is the *same quantity* which is expressed as 1 half, or 2 quarters, or 4 eighths, and the relation between the two numbers which express

the fraction appears as the result of partitioning each part. For instance *each half* has been partitioned into 4 equal parts to give 4/8; hence the *4* corresponds to *1 half* and the *8* to *2 halves*.

Decimal systems

(i) *Place value* All the measuring systems that we call metric are decimal systems of the same pattern as the length system although they measure different properties such as mass and volume. Each has a basic unit (metre, gram, litre) with larger and smaller units derived from it by successively using the factor 10 or 1-tenth. Although these units are named from the basic unit by a prefix which tells the relation of the derived to the basic unit, e.g. kilometre, hectometre, dekametre, metre, decimetre, centimetre, millimetre, very few of these are in common use. Yet they show the tens pattern which is found in the denary notation for numbers.

numbers	1000	100	10	1	$\frac{1}{10}$	$\frac{1}{100}$	$\frac{1}{1000}$
metres	kilo	hecto	deka	metre	deci	centi	milli

We can therefore identify the unit to which any digit in a number of metres relates. For instance, 2137·485 m means the sum of 2 km 1 hm 3 dam 7 m 4 dm 8 cm 5 mm. It is easy too to write this length in km as 2·137485 since the relation of one unit to the next is unchanged. In fact it is usual to write a metric quantity in terms of one unit, using a decimal fraction for any part less than the unit. For this purpose the units of the Système International are commonly used, that is, the kilometre, the metre and the millimetre and the corresponding units of mass and volume, e.g. 27·36 gram, 305 ml (millilitre). It will be noticed that the recognized units (the basic unit and the kilo- and milli-units) are linked by a factor of 1000 which is a convenient bond but too large for young children to handle.

To achieve a confident handling of metric measurements children have to build up through experience a familiarity with units and tenths, then with hundredths and tenths, and finally with the range from thousands to thousandths of the basic unit; with this there must be the capacity to convert readily from one unit to another by adjusting the position of the decimal point. They will begin by using units and tenths to record measurements actually made, and will discover the value of the standard decimal notation when they need to add and subtract in order to solve problems involving other measurements.

(ii) *Tenths and hundredths* So long as grams or centimetres are taught in isolation the special tens structure of the metric system is not apparent. We have seen in Chapters 6 and 13 that children begin measuring with one unit and state the result to the nearest unit, *about 9 cupfuls*, *nearly 3 handspans*, *between 3 and 4 hectos*. In

[2] *Aliquot fractions* are fractions whose numerator is 1.

an effort to be more precise they may use a smaller unit and state the result in the two units: 4 ten-rods and 3 cubes; and, later, 4 decimetres and 3 centimetres using the convenient units for domestic measuring. Even abbreviated to 4 dm 3 cm this is still a little clumsy. Since a child is familiar with the use of a point in stating money in the form £2·58 it is simple to adopt 4·3 dm as a clearer statement and to realize that the 3 after the point is the number of centimetres beyond the 4 dm. Addition of lengths is now exactly as for the natural numbers except for the point needed to identify the unit. It is also important for a child to be able to write the length as 43 cm so that he can add the length if necessary to other lengths measured in centimetres.

The question of when to introduce a decimal point to show tenths next to ones is a matter for the teacher's discretion. In practice teachers often find that this symbol is easier for a child than the fractional form, provided that its use is begun in practical situations and well before a full treatment of decimal notation is begun. Similar work with metre sticks and decimetre rods, with kilos and hectos and with litres and graduations in tenths will make the common structure (unit and tenths) clear. Although the decimal fractions are confined to tenths at this stage the number skills required will be in the range of 3- and 4-digit numbers. For example a trundle wheel graduated to show metres and decimetres may well be used for lengths in excess of 10 metres.

The extension to the second decimal place is particularly simple because the children will know the notation for pounds and pence so well. The tenpenny piece is $\frac{1}{10}$ of £1 and the penny is $\frac{1}{10}$ of a tenpence and so, since this makes 100 pence in the £, a penny is $\frac{1}{100}$ of £1. The decimal fractions of £1 will be thought of as tenpences and pence for the tenths and hundredths places.

When the metre and the centimetre are used together the same 100 link can be seen as occurs in decimal currencies. The relation between pounds and pence should strengthen the understanding of the hundreds and hundredths used in the number system and metric measures.

Actual measuring, using a tape measure or metre rod graduated in centimetres, will make many interesting discoveries possible in the classroom and outdoors. Total lengths, perimeters, comparisons of heights, lengths of jumps, comparisons of shapes and sizes will readily be proposed and carried out; checking by calculation, and checking computations by alternative methods or orders of operation will ensure careful mathematical thinking. During this stage the usual practice of writing a 0 in the units place if the measurement is less than 1 unit should be well established.

(iii) *Thousandths and main units* When the thousandths place is introduced it is well to stress its importance in using the international standard units of measuring which are linked by the 1000 to one relationship. For instance

$$1000 \, mm = 1 \, m \qquad 1000 \, m = 1 \, km$$
$$1000 \, mg = 1 \, g \qquad 1000 \, g = 1 \, kg$$

For heavy loads there is an additional unit of mass

$$1 \, tonne = 1000 \, kg$$

Also $1000 \, ml = 1 \, litre$

Most of these units can be used by the children in the classroom or outdoors, but the milligram is too small for handling, though it can be seen on the labels of medicine bottles. The millilitre is likely to be seen only in graduations of 50 ml or 100 ml until its connection with the cubic centimetre is made in the fuller study of volume (see Chapter 24). A kilometre may be set out on the ground and used for timing various rates of walking, running, etc. A tonne will become familiar from observing lorry loads, registered masses, etc. The most vivid presentation of a thousandth part of a unit is probably the metre-length tape measure marked and numbered to show 100 centimetres, with the multiples of ten in bolder figures, and graduated in millimetres throughout. The equivalence of 1 metre, 10 decimetres, 100 centimetres, 1000 millimetres is clearly shown and 1 mm is seen to be 1 thousandth of 1 metre.

The emphasis on international units will demand a good mastery of decimal notation. Zero will be needed frequently to ensure the correct placing of the digits when the measuring unit is changed. For instance, $7 \, m = 0 \cdot 007 \, km$. The 1000 to 1 relationship will be seen to have special meaning later when the volume of solids is studied.

(iv) *Graph paper* Since graph paper is ruled in metric units of length it is useful in many ways when children are able to draw and measure in cm and mm units. In the first uses of squared paper the unit is unimportant and a variety of units will have been encountered. As measurement becomes important children will realize that the paper they use for recording patterns made with Cuisenaire rods has in fact centimetre squares. But other rulings, 5-cm and 2-cm, are useful and provide occasions for valuable comparisons. A cheap quality of 1-cm squared paper is obtainable and is very generally used for finding perimeters and other lengths in shapes drawn or placed upon it. It can also provide strips for measuring fixed objects and furnishings. Scale models can also be made from squared paper nets and measurements can be compared and recorded. When the graph paper is ruled in tenths as well as units it can offer more varied experiences; graduating strips to measure the stretch of a spring; enlarging a shape in the ratio 10 to 1, etc. The most useful ruling for primary school children is probably 2 cm/2 mm, in which 2 cm is the unit and 2 mm is 0·1; an instructive situation for children at this stage.

Graduation on strips and discs

A characteristic of modern measuring is the mechanization which enables many different properties to be expressed in numbers and read on a scale or a dial. Making and using graduated strips for measuring capacity and mass are recommended in Chapters 5 and 15. The construction of such strips will help children to study the use of graduation in thermometers, steelyards, speedometers, pressure gauges, etc., and so to learn how wide a range of properties are quantified today and to recognize the units in which they are measured.

The graduated strip has the obvious defect that it becomes inconveniently long if a quantity varies from a very small to a very large measure, as in recording time in a 24-hour day when accuracy to a minute is needed. The trundle wheel is an example of a device which economizes space. The revolving wheel measures a distance in small units, metres and centimetres, and each whole rotation is marked by a click which can be counted. The measuring scale is limited to the circumference of the wheel but the distance measured can be extended indefinitely. The clock-face shows a similar dual count, one hand recording the minutes and the other showing the number of revolutions made by the minute hand, i.e. the hours. Two revolutions are usually needed to show the full 24-hour clock, since few clocks are yet graduated to show 24 hours. Now that time-tables are based on a 24-hour day it is well to let children see the hours from 13 to 24 on an outer rim of a classroom clock. The economy of space and the ease of reading a dial have led to variety of other uses which children can discover and record.

Another device is to have a system of wheels which record the digits of the measuring number. As the geared wheels turn, the number seen through a window changes. The apparatus is similar to the operation of a simple calculating machine. An example familiar to many children is the odometer on a car or bicycle. On this there is often a place for tenths of a kilometre and this may be a child's first encounter with a mechanism recording tenths by putting them to the right of the ones.

Future developments

In this chapter we have outlined the remarkable growth of measuring and its dependence on number: the development of the one influences the understanding of the other. We shall examine the means of making more accurate and more complex measurements in Chapters 23 and 24. For penetration into the physical nature of the universe ever smaller units of length and mass are required. For the exploration of space by new types of craft and telescope greater units of length are necessary. Such units will be related on the one hand to physical entities which appear to be constant, such as the speed of light, or the wavelength of a particular type of light. On the other hand they will be based on very large numbers such as thousands of millions. They will therefore stimulate the growth of a number system which can express large numbers very concisely. We return to the development of number notation in Chapter 17.

15 The Use of Measures

Measuring as an aid to understanding

Measuring activities lead young children to informal combining and comparing of quantities such as lengths, capacities and masses. Simple statements can be made to describe the results of these activities. When children are learning about the addition and subtraction of numbers up to 100 or beyond, the practical tasks of measuring give them situations in which adding and subtracting are seen to be operations of wide usefulness, and thus fuller understanding results. As a child's scientific curiosity about the physical world grows, he finds an increasing need to investigate through measuring and the recording of measures. Daily or weekly measuring of the length or mass of a growing plant or animal can lead to a discussion about the actual increase during each interval. Subtraction provides the means of measuring the increases; a record can be made and studied. After some weeks the records made week by week can be converted by addition into fortnightly records. If graphs are drawn for the two recordings, weekly and fortnightly, their shapes can be compared. See Figure 15:1. Many of the most interesting instances of what can be learned from a set of measurements will arise in this way from recording a set of observations. A close link with scientific and geographical inquiries is as important as maintaining a connection between concrete procedures with quantities and the abstract operations with numbers.

When a child is using a single unit for his measurements, e.g. handspans, metres or litres, he finds that many of the resulting numbers are greater than ten. Consequently when he wishes to add these larger quantities he will require the same number operations as when he is dealing with sets of objects. Not only will he write the result of measuring a *single quantity*, he will also describe the procedure of putting two or more lengths, masses, etc., together and will state the *total measure*. Similarly he will find and state the difference between two such quantities. In these experiences he is realizing the nature of the *operation* he is using, addition or subtraction, and is thus forming clearer concepts of them. Moreover, the same pairs of numbers repeatedly occur and children grow more familiar with the results of adding or subtracting numbers greater than ten.

The addition of quantities

Two quantities, say two masses, can be added in the sense that a single quantity can be found which will match, balance or produce the same effect as the two separate quantities taken together. Children have already added lengths by placing rods end to end. They have used a tape-measure as a slide-rule for adding and subtracting numbers. This has implied the addition and subtraction of lengths. Now they are ready to add *measured lengths*, using the numbers that measuring has provided. The statements that can be made about the quantities are exactly similar to number statements.

For two collections of shells $24 + 13 = 37$
For two lengths $24\,\text{cm} + 13\,\text{cm} = 37\,\text{cm}$

So long as measurements are expressed in a single unit the

weekly observations

week	1	2	3	4	5	6	7	8	9	10	11
height	7	8	10	12	15	19	22	24	26	27	28

weekly increases

end of week	1	2	3	4	5	6	7	8	9	10
increase	1	2	2	3	4	3	2	2	1	1

fortnightly increases

end of fortnight	1	2	3	4	5
increase	3	5	7	4	2

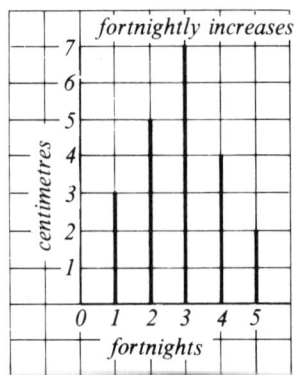

Figure 15:1

134

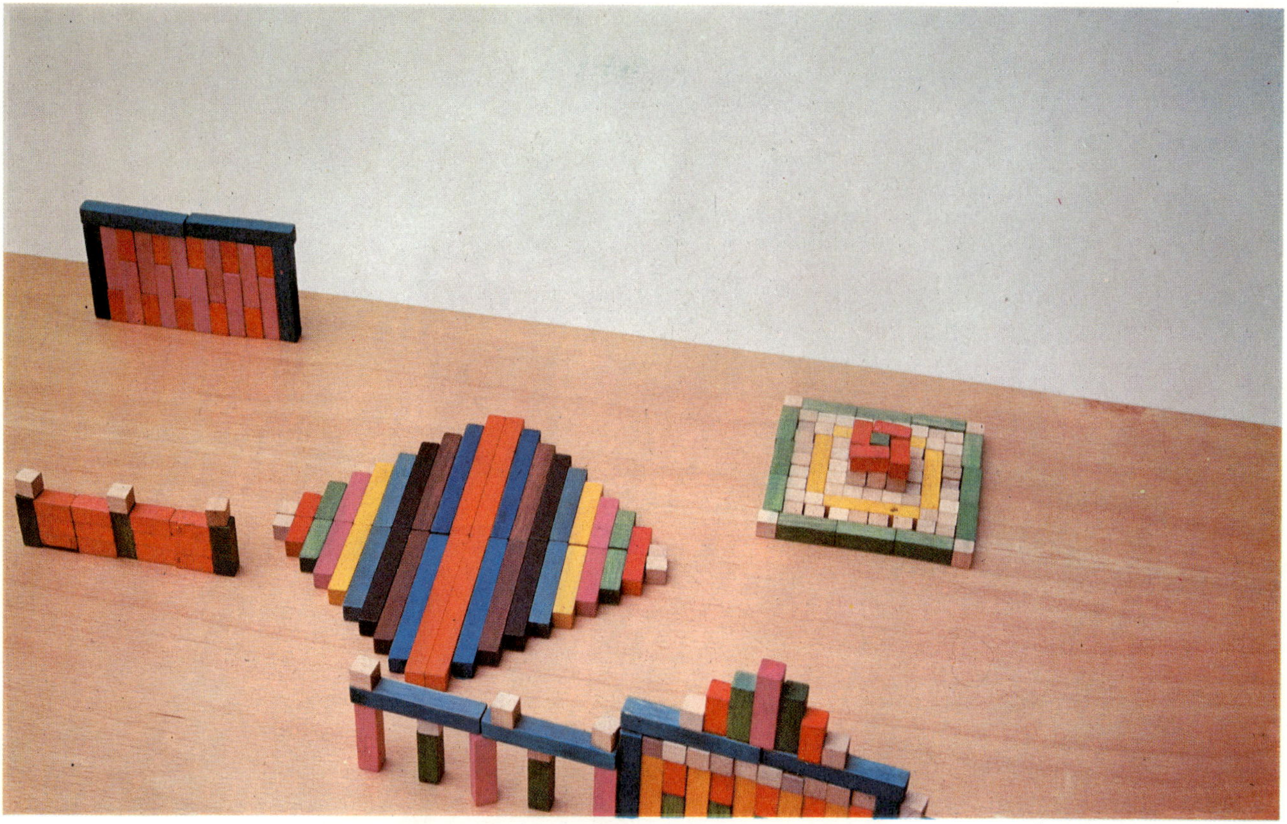

plate 1a: Cuisenaire rods

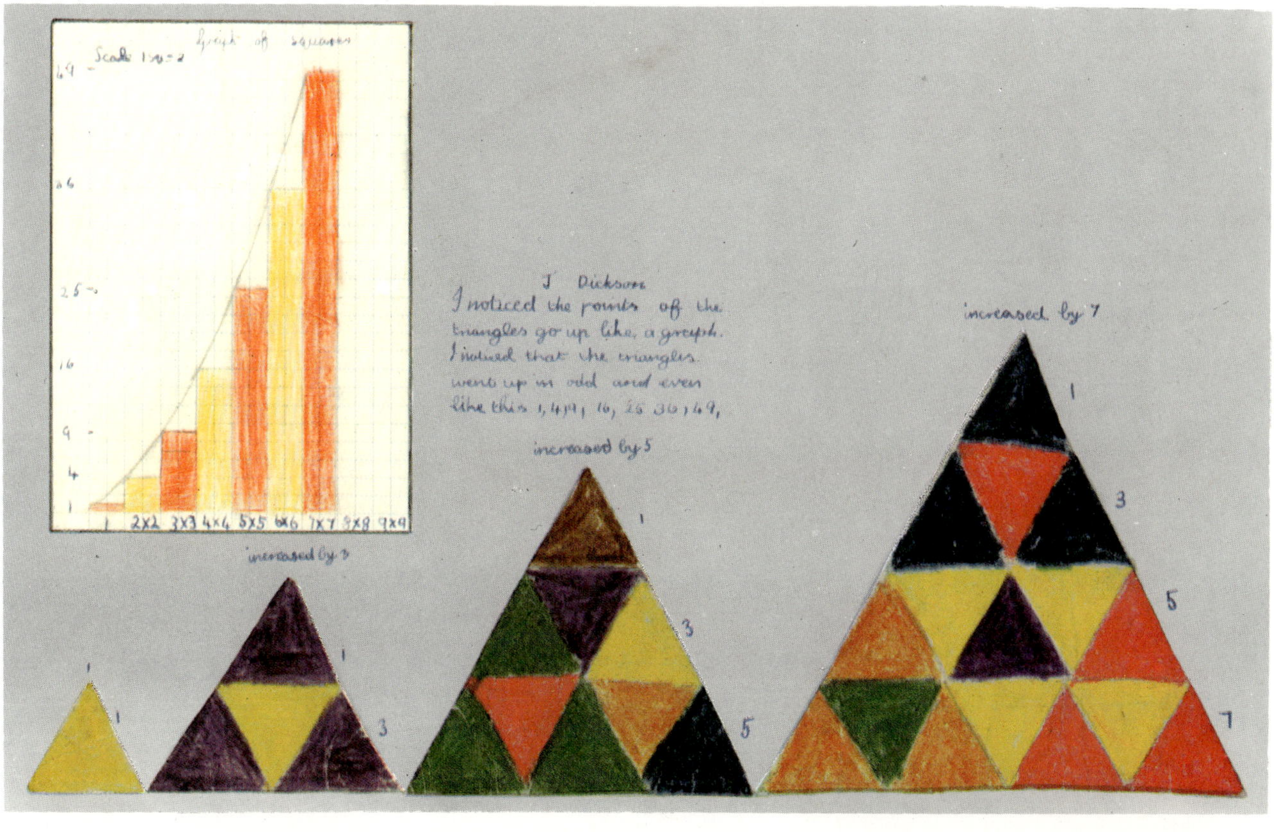
J Dickson
I noticed the points of the
triangles go up like a graph.
I noticed that the triangles
went up in odd and even
like this 1, 4, 9, 16, 25 36, 49,
increased by 3
increased by 5
increased by 7
49
36
25
16
9
4
1
1 2x2 3x3 4x4 5x5 6x6 7x7 8x8 9x9

plate 1b: Sequence of triangles

plate 2: *Child's model using all the pieces of Poleidoblocs G*

this is a garden
With a tree.
They are made of
rectangles. It has 4
windows and a
garage.

I have circles
use

the mand is on the tractor

plate 3: Children's patterns

JILL Keenon

Aged 6 years. 2 months

I have made a

plate for my mummy

There are eight yellow 8

circles.

I have nine red triangles 9

There is one orange 1

plate 4: A child's pattern

diamond.

similarity of the two statements is very clear. The addition of lengths and the addition of numbers can profitably be learnt side by side because the same structure can be seen in both; numbers and lengths combine in the same way, obeying the same rules. For example, a change of order does not affect the result of adding in either case; both additions are commutative.

$$29 + 18 = 18 + 29$$
$$29\,\text{cm} + 18\,\text{cm} = 18\,\text{cm} + 29\,\text{cm}$$

The addition of lengths

Every opportunity that classroom or outdoor activities can provide should be taken to let children find total lengths in any particular unit, choosing the one most suited to the length to be measured. The following examples of measuring show three different situations.

i) 'A toy lorry is 16 cm long; a trailer is 13 cm long. Use a tape-measure to find how long they are when placed end to end. Write what you find.'

$$16\,\text{cm} + 13\,\text{cm} = 29\,\text{cm}$$

Together they are 29 cm long. (Figure 15:2.)

Figure 15:2

ii) If two tables were to be placed side by side how long would the length be altogether? If the tables are placed together in fact the total can be found by measuring; but this is an addition situation and if we work the addition sum we can say how long they will be without moving them (Figure 15:3).

The first table measures	96 cm
The second table measures	93 cm
Together they measure	189 cm

This result would be confirmed if the tables were actually moved, of course.

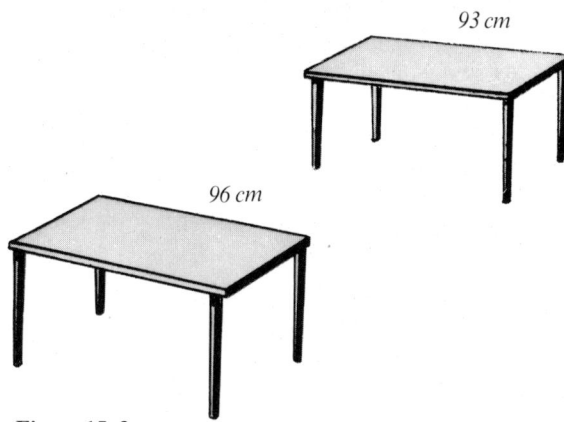

Figure 15:3

iii) Two bookshelves are fixed one above the other. The top one is 44 cm long and the bottom one is 78 cm long. What length of bookshelf is there altogether? We cannot put these shelves side by side but we can add their lengths (Figure 15:4).

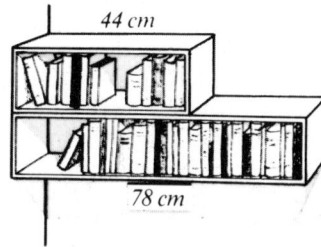

Figure 15:4

This can be checked practically in several ways. A 150-cm measuring-tape or a 10-cm strip marked in cm can be used to mark first 78 cm and then 44 cm beyond it along a line, or the two lengths can be marked off in succession along a graduated strip.

An example of addition of measures in *metres* occurs when a cupboard prevents the continuous measurement of the length of a wall (Figure 15:5).

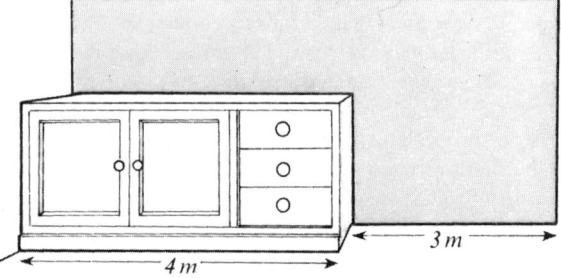

Figure 15:5

The width of the cupboard, say 4 m, must be added to the length of the accessible part of the wall:

$$4\,\text{m} + 3\,\text{m} = 7\,\text{m}$$

135

Addition of lengths in *metres* also arises when children wish to know the length of a path which consists of several parts, one of which is curved. A tape can be used to measure the straight sections and a trundle wheel gives the length of the curve. In the example shown in Figure 15:6

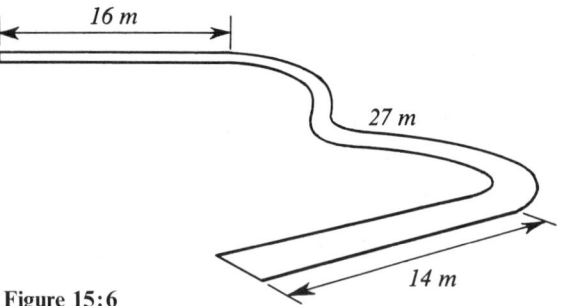

Figure 15:6

the children will probably add 16 and 27 first and then add 14 to 43. They can learn to add the three numbers in a column as soon as they can carry the sum of two single-digit numbers in their heads. In this case they must *remember* 11 and add 6 to it, or remember 13 and add 4 to it, without any written help. The ability to retain a number in mind and use it in an operation should have been achieved through such previous experiences as combining several sets, placing several rods end to end, and adding more than two *small* quantities, e.g. 5 cm + 4 cm + 7 cm. The addition of the lengths shown in Figure 15:6 cannot easily be checked by measuring on the ground, though a trundle wheel will serve. It is possible to check the numerical work on a number line or track, but this involves using a scale, one unit of the track representing 1 metre.

The value of checking

It must be noted that checking an arithmetical operation by measuring or vice versa does not mean that the one operation can *prove* that the other is correct. We know that measuring is liable to error and in any case that it is never *exact*. The value of finding a solution to a problem, such as finding a total length, by two different methods is to provide two results which can be compared. If they do not agree the discrepancy must be investigated. Has there been an error in addition, or a mistake in measuring? The error can be discovered and put right. If the two results *do* agree there is a very good chance that they are right but, of course, there is a possibility that there has been a mistake in both operations.

The procedure of checking a calculation by a practical method is important in another way; it recalls the actual situation which gave rise to the number operation, addition for example; it may also show the detailed steps which

are taken in a complex calculation, such as adding tens and ones. For instance, in example (iii) in the preceding section, 44 must be marked along a number line starting from the 78 mark. This may be carried out by merely reading off the final number on the line, 122. A child, however, may count 10, 20, 30, 40, 44, along the line, reading on from 78: 88, 98, 108, 118, 122; or he may count 4, 14, 24, 34, 44 along the line, reading 82, 92, 102, 112, 122 (Figure 15:7).

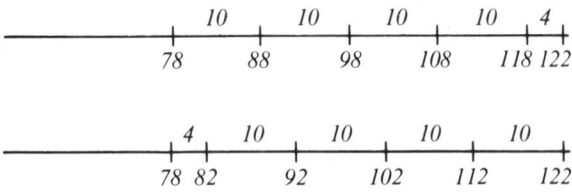

Figure 15:7

Each of these procedures gives meaning to the formalized sum. A child who is flexible enough to use *either* of these counting methods well understands the structure of tens and ones. It is the second method, of course, which matches the usual written procedure of adding the ones column before the tens.

When practical measuring is carried out first, the calculation which follows is a way of ensuring that on another occasion a child would know that he could find a total length without the need to measure.

Perimeters

The lengths of boundaries, walls and fences provide many occasions when measuring discloses some of the properties of important shapes, particularly of rectangles, including squares. Finding the perimeter of the classroom, of a games pitch or a garden bed will lead the children to see the equality of the opposite sides of a rectangle and to use this property to save some of the measuring. It will also show them that when two sides are equal the length of one can be doubled to give the total. Thus an introduction to multiplying quantities occurs. Sketches of the measured shapes can be drawn and the lengths shown on them. If the sketches are drawn on squared paper children will often devise simple scales for themselves.

Measuring the boundaries of interesting two-dimensional shapes, such as triangles, hexagons, stars of various kinds, extends the knowledge of forms in common use. Children will compare different shapes which have equal perimeters and also shapes which differ only in size. The triangle and the hexagon shown in Figure 15:8 are easily drawn on isometric (triangular grid) paper. They will be found to have equal perimeters.

Figure 15:8

Three-dimensional shapes made with milk-straws or plastic wire show their form through their edges only. These can be measured and the total length found. Cubes, cuboids and pyramids, etc. can be compared (Figure 15:9).

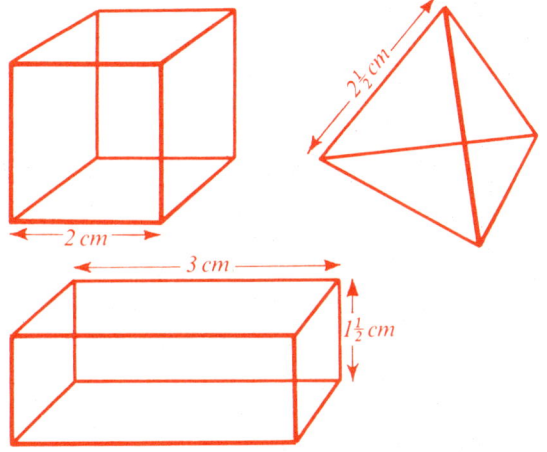

Figure 15:9

The kites in Figure 15:10 have the same shape but the sides of the larger are twice as long as those of the smaller. What can be said about their perimeters? Shapes of this kind are best cut out in thick card. If the sides sometimes have an odd $\frac{1}{2}$-cm in their lengths the children will discover for themselves how to add or double the half. Alternatively they can measure with a strip marked in $\frac{1}{2}$-cm and change to whole cm by counting in twos.

Figure 15:10

Decimal calculations and measurements

Measuring in a single unit may involve very large numbers, as in stating the distance along a road in metres. It may also produce fractional results which are not easy to compare, e.g. $\frac{1}{4}$ m and $\frac{3}{10}$ m. Yet children will usually want their measuring to give them results accurate enough to be informative yet simple enough for them to use in calculations. The use of two units such as metres and decimetres seems to meet the needs. A tape measure marked in decimetres and centimetres, or in centimetres only, may introduce the idea of using tenths and hundredths of a metre just as tenths and hundredths of £1 are used in money calculations. The notation of a decimal point to indicate the units figure is quickly adopted.

Much of the early work on the addition of lengths will be adequately carried out with two places of decimals in the measurements. This stage cannot last long in view of the accepted practice of using International (SI) Units (linked by the 1000 to 1 ratio) and decimal fractions of those units, e.g. 3·742 metres for a length correct to 1 mm. The International Units for length, kilometre, metre and millimetre, will all have a useful role in the investigations children undertake to discover the spatial properties that are constantly used in the movements and constructions in their immediate surroundings. Grams and kilograms are in evidence in the masses marked on packages and in the measurements quoted in various sports. Milligrams are so small that they are best deferred until they are required in science. But 'tonnes' (1000 kilograms) can be seen on the sides of lorries indicating their maximum loads and on container crates. Litres and millilitres are the only units of capacity that children will notice at this stage.

Decimal fractions in measuring

The star in Figure 15:11 is based on a pentagon. The long point has sides twice as long as those of the shorter sides. Children may find the perimeter of the star, and how much tinsel would be needed to go round a star which has sides twice as long.

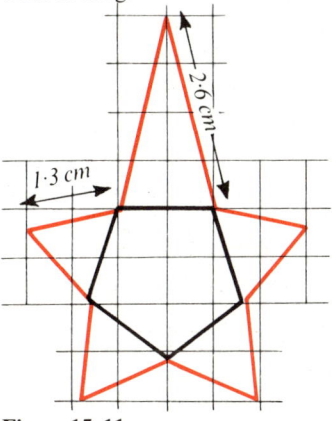

Figure 15:11

137

Children can compare the lengths of the boundaries of the different rectangular faces to be found in a set of varied blocks, e.g. in the G Poleidoblocs (*see Plate 2*). They can find which of the faces are squares. They may also discover that the perimeter of a square is four times the length of the side.

The cylinder with its curved edges is of special interest. A cylinder's circumference can be measured by placing a tape-measure tightly round each edge but it is also valuable to make a cylinder from a rectangle of stiff paper and to realize that the length of the rectangle gives the length of the curved edge, allowing, of course, for any overlap needed to stick the other edges of the rectangle. The diameter of the cylinder can also be found reliably enough by taking the greatest distance across its circular face as shown by moving a ruler over the surface. (Figure 15:12.)

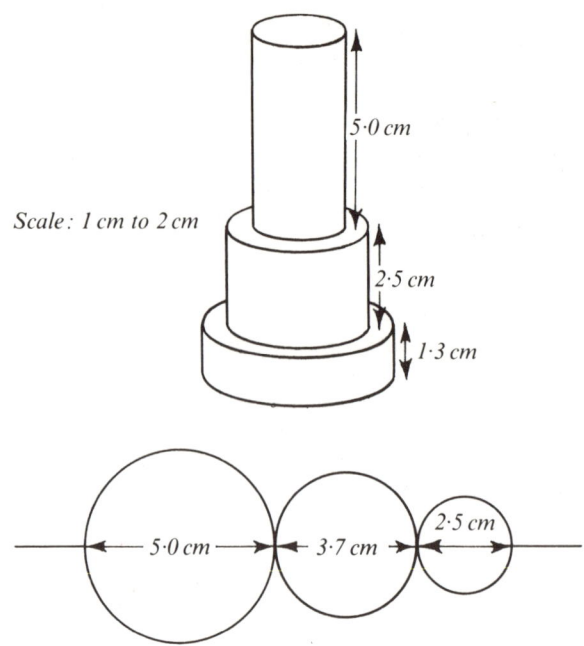

Scale: 1 cm to 2 cm

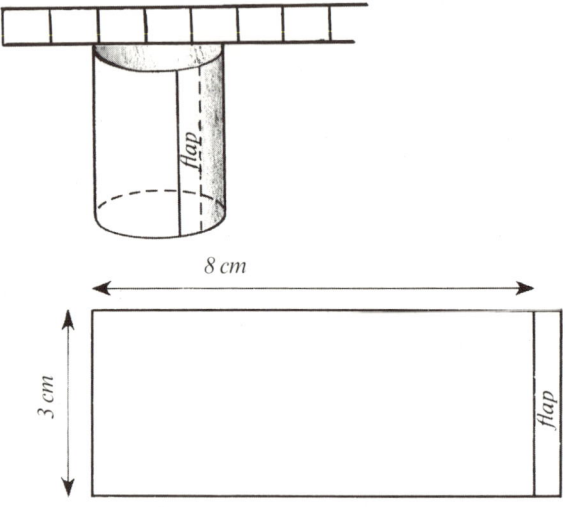

Figure 15:12

A comparison of the three cylinders included in Poleidoblocs G gives interesting results. Their diameters and heights can be compared. Do they increase in the same way? If they are placed in a line or in a tower will the length of the line or the height of the tower be greater? Half-units will occur again here (Figure 15:13).

Figure 15:13

The first four quadrilaterals shown in Figure 15:14 will be found to have equal boundaries. This figure also shows what happens to the perimeter of a rectangle when a square is cut out from it. Many similar inquiries can be devised by the pupils.

Measuring distance

In the previous paragraphs all the lengths to be measured (except the diameters of the cylinders) were along lines or edges which permitted a ruler or tape to be placed alongside. Where a distance from one object to another or the distance across a space has to be measured a child must visualize the line and iterate his unit along it. If a rope will not stretch across the whole distance he must measure in sections, ensuring that the sections are in a straight line. This introduces a new property of the straight line: we *look* in straight lines; the line of sighting is straight. We can therefore mark a straight line by placing children so that

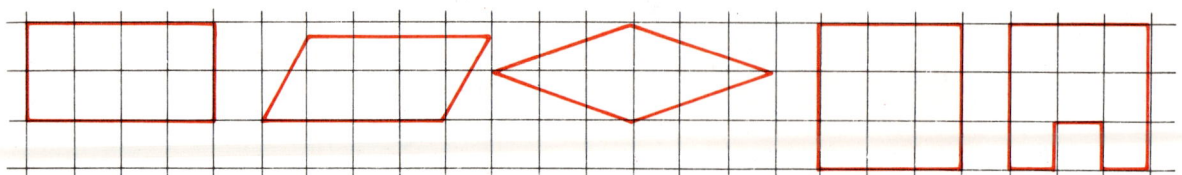

Figure 15:14

138

an observer sees one behind another. Or we can place upright sticks so that they are covered when sighted. To measure the diagonal distance across part of the playground it may be necessary to have two or three sections marked in this way, at distances which are short enough for the rope to stretch across the section (Figure 15:15).

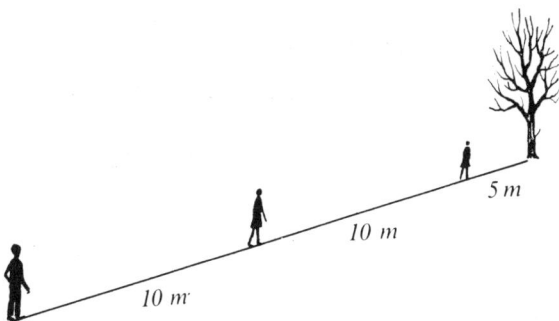

Figure 15:15

The line of sight can now be used to find the shortest distance between two points of interest or to mark out a distance, say 25 m, for a race. In the latter case a subtraction situation arises, since the 10-m rope will only measure up to 20 m; to reach 25 m a further 5 m must be measured. We now consider other ways in which the operation of subtracting lengths may occur.

The subtraction of lengths

In the last paragraph we saw that to complete a distance of 25 m we must ask, 'how many metres beyond 20 m will give 25 m?' Symbolically we write:

$$20 + \square = 25$$

The number 5 is needed for the box. We must mark 5 m beyond 20 m. This can be written

$$25\,m - 20\,m = 5\,m$$

Comparison of the distances that two children can hop in a given time, or the lengths of two walls, will entail the questions, 'How much longer?' and 'How much shorter?' If a measuring-tape is used the subtraction operation is recognized because a tape has already been used for the subtraction of numbers.

One wall is 23·4 m wide; the other is 16·8 m wide.

$$23\cdot4\,m - 16\cdot8\,m = 6\cdot6\,m$$

This statement *says* what the measuring-tape *shows*. We write, 'The first wall is 6·6 m longer than the other wall.'

In some kinds of model-making which children undertake, a certain length of material may be required. From a strip 24 cm long a piece 15 cm long is wanted. How much will be left? Will this piece fit a 6-cm edge?

$$24\,cm - 15\,cm = 9\,cm$$

The 9-cm length is too long to fit the 6-cm edge exactly

$$9\,cm - 6\,cm = 3\,cm$$

There will be 3 cm left.

It is noteworthy that in these practical activities the necessity to decide *which* is longer and therefore which number can be subtracted from the other becomes obvious.

Measuring heights

Comparison and addition of heights. Children are familiar at this stage with the method of finding their own heights by standing against a vertical strip, using a sliding horizontal rod or a book to mark the tops of their heads. They can now compare heights and find how much one is taller than another by the operation of subtraction. Differences of reach can also be found when children stand on tiptoe and touch the highest possible point. They can stand on a chair or table and find by addition their highest reach from that vantage point. A weighted string will show the vertical line along which to measure (Figure 15:16). The line will be graduated usually in metres and centimetres. The measurements can be written in metres and decimals.

Figure 15:16

A more difficult problem is to find how high a pile of boxes will be. The height of each box can be measured and added. But how can the answer be checked if the height is beyond the children's reach? After experiment they may hit upon the idea of using a stick to reach the top. They can then measure from the top of the stick to the point where it is held and add this length to the height of the point above the ground, say 1·6 m + 0·9 m.

The same device can be used to find the height of the classroom. A long rod or slat of wood can have a plumb bob attached; the rod is held so that the plumb line hangs parallel to the edge of the slat. Alternatively a large set square of stiff paper can be used. One edge from the right-angled corner must be placed along a known horizontal such as the top or bottom edge of the blackboard. The other edge will show where the slat must be held. Now the distance from the ceiling to the blackboard edge must be added to the height of this edge above the floor. See Figure 15:17.

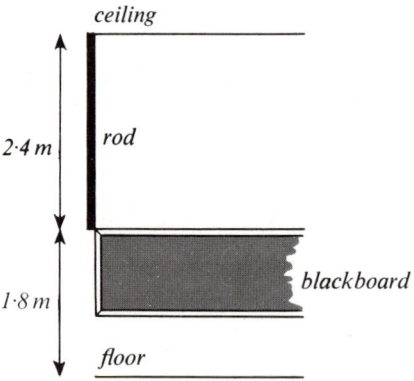

Figure 15:17

The height of two cones or two plants can be compared if a technique similar to that of finding a child's height is used. A set square slides down a vertical wall or stake until one edge just touches the top of the cone or plant. The two heights can be marked on the same line and the subtraction checked. In these instances heights have been found when there is no visible line to measure (Figure 15:18).

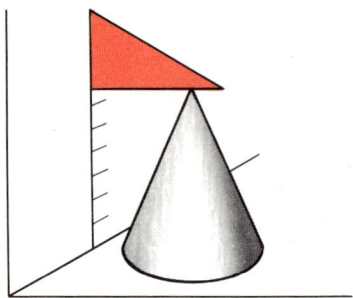

Figure 15:18

These investigations provide opportunities of handling metres and centimetres together and also of the decimal notation for expressing a length in metres and a decimal fraction.

Position in a room; distances from a wall. When two children wish to know which of them is nearer to a wall they must decide how to measure their distances. They may experiment with a rope to find the distance of each child from his nearest point on the wall. With guidance they may place a large set square so that its right-angled corner fits between the taut measuring-rope and the wall. Where the

140

taut rope lies from the child to the wall is the shortest or perpendicular distance, and shows the proper line to measure. If at the outset a child estimates which child is nearer, and by how much, his estimate can now be checked. In the classroom the distances of two children from the

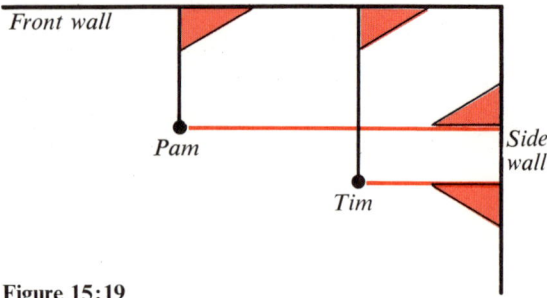

Figure 15:19

front can be found, and also their distances from a side wall. Pam may be nearer the front but Tim may be nearer the side. A first hint of two co-ordinates for fixing position may thus be given (Figure 15:19).

Addition and subtraction of masses

The need to combine and compare masses occurs much less frequently in a child's experience than operations with length. Making up a parcel or finding the mass of a basket of shopping may arise from the class post office or shop. For example, the tins in the shop may be labelled 480 g, 440 g, 250 g, though if they are empty a child who handles them will not experience the masses. They can have sand put in until their masses match the labels. Addition gives the total mass which can then be checked by weighing. A kilogram can be used for 1000 g and the checking count of the masses then goes thus:

grams	Masses in balance pan
	1 kg
480	100 g
440	50 g
250	20 g
1170	1 kg 170 g

The total mass is 1·170 kg.

It will be seen that children use trial and error at first in finding the actual masses to balance the scales rather than working systematically through the combinations of weights. It is much easier to use a spring balance and watch the pointer move to 480, 920, 1170 as the tins are put on the scale-pan one by one.

Parcels of books may be made up and weighed to find the total, or the difference, of their masses, or the number required to make up to a specified mass.

The mass in kilograms of pairs of children can be compared for the purpose of getting reasonably balanced partners for games. Scientific observations will also involve comparison, e.g. of the masses of equal cubes of different materials such as wood, plastic, brass.

Today labels often state mass in grams, especially on many tins of food. The numbers often run to hundreds. It therefore seems that grams should be introduced when hundreds are being learned. The use of thousands will accompany using grams and kilograms together. The investigation of the loads carried by lorries and railway trucks will involve tonnes (1000 kg = 1 tonne) and further calculations with thousands.

Temperature

Weather reports make children familiar with temperatures and the presence of a thermometer in the classroom may suggest recording the temperature at certain times in the day. The existence of the two scales, Celsius and Fahrenheit, may present some difficulty but children will use only the Celsius scale in school, reading degrees Celsius on the graduated strip. An outdoor thermometer provides much greater variation than one in the classroom and records of its readings can be linked with weather observations. Changes in temperature and differences between outdoor and indoor recordings can be found. If water is studied as a topic in science, the temperatures at which water boils and freezes should be read on the Celsius scale.

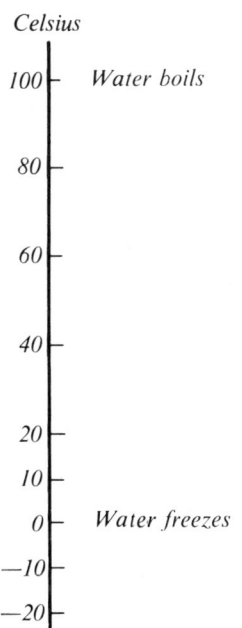

Figure 15:20

The indirect measurement of temperature through the expansion of a column of liquid is a good example of the use of a graduated strip. It is very impressive that our rather vague sensations of cold and heat can be converted into marks on a number line which give us remarkably exact and important information. An outdoor thermometer will sometimes fall below freezing point during the winter. The readings −1, −2, −3, etc., on the Celsius scale will have the obvious meaning of being *below* freezing point. The use of negative numbers in this simple sense of 'below a level named as zero' may well have been introduced before children are made aware of it on a thermometer.

Capacity

The numbers involved in using two units of capacity are the familiar 10's, 100's, 1000's used in graduating a litre in millilitres. There are only a few occasions when computations are needed with litres and millilitres but some comparison of the capacities of different containers is useful. Combinations of fluids may occur in cooking and gardening projects. Medicines to be taken in water are prescribed in millilitres. Concentrations of fruit juice can be diluted to taste and the recipe written in millilitres and litres.

Time

A child sees hours and minutes marked on a clock-face and hears the names frequently at home and at school. As he learns to tell the time he will use some of the sets of five shown on the clock: 5, 10, 20, or 25 past the hour; but the rhythm is broken by the quarter past, half past and quarter to the hour. The minutes reappear with 25 to and 20 to the hour, but these do not build up to the 60 minutes of a whole hour. Before a child can add or subtract intervals of time he must be able to give the time in hours and minutes, i.e. in time-table form. By adding fives he can build the sequence 5, 10, 15, 20, . . . , 50, 55, 60 round the clock and practise converting from ordinary to timetable ways of stating the time and vice versa. Addition and subtraction of time are needed only for discovering the end or the beginning or the duration of an interval, as in cooking or travelling, or for combining or comparing two intervals. The use of a kitchen pinger to record an interval combines well with a clock to show the result of adding and can check a calculation. For example, a cake needs 25 minutes to cook. The time is now ten to eleven, i.e. 10.50. Set the pinger at 25 minutes. Add 25 minutes to 10 hours 50 minutes. In place of a formal sum a child will almost certainly say, '10 minutes and it will be 11 o'clock; 15 minutes still to go.' The cake will be ready at 11.15 or a quarter past 11. The pinger will in fact check this when it rings at 11.15 on the clock (Figure 15:21).

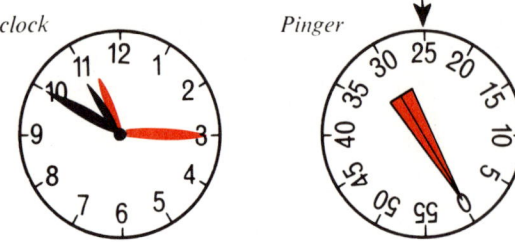

Figure 15:21

The activities of a class will include races, competitions and journeys which call for a great deal of totalling and comparing of times; these may well involve hours as well as minutes.

Formal subtraction will sometimes be needed to find the time of a long journey but this is best postponed until the 24-hour clock is introduced to the children. Practice in reading and stating times on a 24-hour clock will arise in studying time-tables for buses, trains and aeroplanes.

Further developments through measuring

It is apparent that the occurrence of equal quantities, as in the sides of a square, the masses of standardized packets or the certified contents of some bottles, opens the door to multiplication. The tabulation of equivalences of units, e.g.

containers	1	2	3	4	5…
litres		8	16	24	32	40…

is also an iteration which leads to multiplication. Experiences of this kind are useful in developing the concept of multiplication of numbers. In the concrete situation of adding equal quantities, say 5 metres + 5 metres + 5 metres, and re-writing it as 3×5 metres, we see clearly the distinction between the kind of answers which must be given when we ask, 'How many pieces of 5 metre length can be cut from a strip 15 metres long?' and, 'What is the length of each strip when a strip 15 metres long is cut into 3 equal pieces?' These questions suggest the kind of activities that children need before multiplication and division can be treated in an abstract way. Certainly they need many such experiences before they are able to select multiplication as the operation required to solve an entirely new kind of problem.

As we have seen, fractional parts appear in measuring; the use of $\frac{1}{2}, \frac{1}{4}, \frac{1}{10}$, in connection with lengths, masses, times, etc., builds up a knowledge of the ways in which some of these fractions are related. Even more important is the growth in understanding of the decimal notation for fractions and the consequent grasp of the usefulness of place value notation in stating quantities to a required degree of accuracy. See Chapters 13 and 32.

16 Multiplication and Division

Iteration of the counting set

As children use a small counting set in making counts of things around them, they quickly acquire skill in counting in twos, threes and other numbers. Some things, such as eyes, gloves or feet will naturally be counted in pairs, counting 'two, four, six, eight , . . .'. The wheels of toy cars will be counted 'four, eight, twelve, . . .'. When children have grouped sticks into triangles to make counting sets of three (*see page* 121), they will count again the total number of sticks, using the count 'three, six, nine, . . .'. From such experiences the idea of adding equal numbers, or of multiplication, develops.

A conventional way of recording such facts as they are discovered is to tabulate them:

Triangles	1	2	3	4 . . .
Sticks	3	6	9	12 . . .

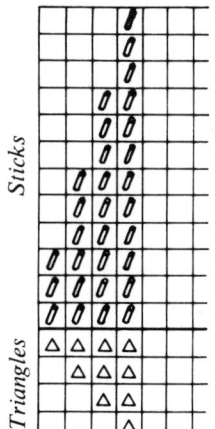

Figure 16:1

The facts can also be shown in a picture graph on squared paper. A very simple arrangement is shown in Figure 16:2. Above the line, each in one square, are arranged the sticks, and below the lines the equivalent number of triangles.

Figure 16:2

Children who are used to recording counts on squared paper will find this a natural arrangement, and it is one which develops very easily, as the children grow older, into a conventional conversion graph. In order to show this

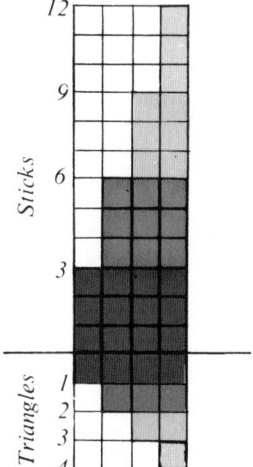

Figure 16:3

development Figures 16:3 to 16:6 show the same graph constructed at four stages in the development of children's graphical work.

In Figure 16:3 the sticks and triangles used in the first graph are replaced by squares of coloured paper, making a block or bar graph. In Figure 16:4, the number of triangles is no longer shown by blocks, but is written along the horizontal axis.

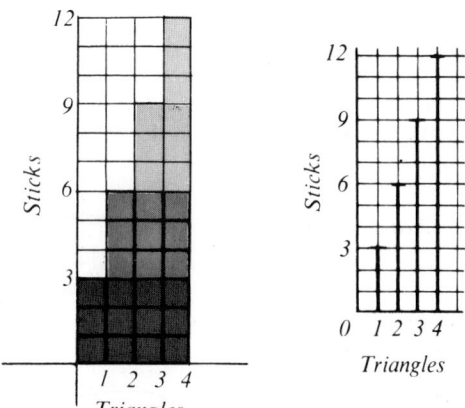

Figure 16:4   **Figure 16:5**

In Figure 16:5 the blocks of the bar graphs are replaced by lines (the lines of the graph paper have been used). At this stage the additional fact that 0 triangles have 0 sides has been shown on the graph.

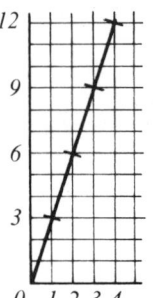

Figure 16:6

In Figure 16:6 only the highest points of the vertical lines are marked, and these are joined by a line. The line is an aid to visibility and can also be used for interpolation. The graph has also become an abstract graph of threes, instead of a representation of triangles and from it can be read such information as

$$1\tfrac{1}{2} \text{ threes} = 4\tfrac{1}{2}$$

which has no meaning in terms of triangles and sides.

From the time children begin to count in twos and threes, they will record their counts in writing as well as in graphs or pictures. A count of Wellington boots in the classroom on a wet day might be recorded as in Figure 16:7.

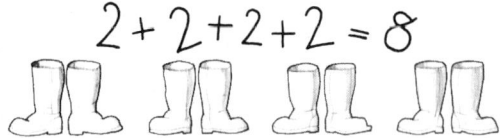

Figure 16:7

A table of twos can be built up from this (Figure 16:8). At first, children read $2+2+2+2$ as 'four twos', and learn that another way of writing it is 4×2. The meaning of the multiplication sign is extended later (*see page* 146).

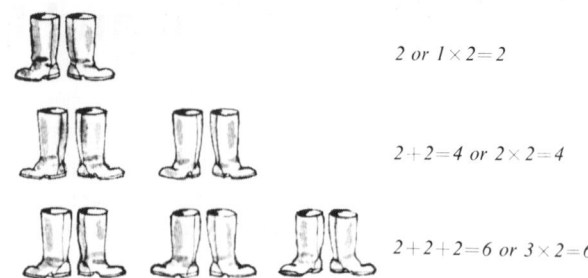

2 or $1 \times 2 = 2$

$2+2=4$ or $2 \times 2 = 4$

$2+2+2=6$ or $3 \times 2 = 6$

Figure 16:8

Children can build up other multiplication tables by using equal groupings of things which they can find. An example is shown in Figure 16:9.

Five is the number of fingers on a hand, and seven the number of days in a week. Ten is the number of pence in a tenpenny piece, and is the base of our notational system. It is this last property which makes the table of tens both the easiest and the most important of the multiplication tables. Figure 16:10 shows the beginning of the table of tens laid out using structural apparatus and a tape-measure.

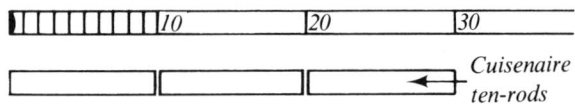

Cuisenaire ten-rods

Figure 16:10

1 car has 4 wheels

2 cars have 8 wheels

3 cars have 12 wheels

Figure 16:9

When children are learning to tell the time, they count minutes round the clock in fives, and so build up the table of fives (Figure 16:11). They can also learn the 'gate' method of recording counts, which is useful in such

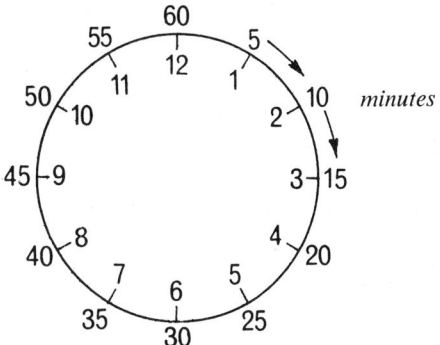

Figure 16:11

activities as making a traffic census. Every time a car goes by a mark is made, but a long row of marks is confusing to count.

The largest number of things which can easily be recognized without counting is 4, so the fifth mark is made across the first four

and a new 'gate' is then started. The number 18 would be represented by

This gives further practice in counting in fives.

The commutative law for multiplication

When a child writes 3×4, he may arrange the three fours as three rows of four things, or if he uses structural apparatus he may make a rectangular block from the rods. A rectangular block of the same size and shape can be made from four threes (Figure 16:12).

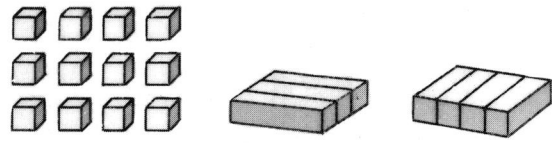

Figure 16:12

From this arrangement it can be seen that four threes are equal to three fours.

The fact that the order of a multiplication does not matter, that $3 \times 4 = 4 \times 3$, and in general that $a \times b = b \times a$, becomes so familiar to us by constant use that it is difficult to remember how surprising it can be at first. This law is known as the *commutative law for multiplication*. For any two numbers a and b,

$$a \times b = b \times a.$$

Children need a good deal of experience of the commutative law for multiplication if it is to become part of their mathematical equipment; it is very necessary that they should be able to use it spontaneously. At first, 3×4 means $4+4+4$, and 4×3 means $3+3+3+3$. The two situations look very different, and when illustrated in a concrete way, the illustrations of them are very different (Figure 16:13).

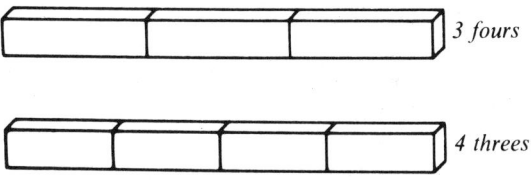

3 fours

4 threes

Figure 16:13

The rectangular crate of milk bottles provides a convenient classroom illustration where

5 rows of 6 bottles = 6 rows of 5 bottles.

Figure 16:14

During the first few school years children are abstracting the concept of number from many concrete situations involving numbers of things and they also begin to abstract the concept of multiplication of numbers from varied experiences of counting equal groupings of things. If they are given enough suitable concrete experiences like those suggested above, in which they can arrange equivalent sets in two different ways, they will abstract from these experiences the fact that the order of the numbers which are multiplied together does not matter. When he has reached this stage, a child who counts the milkbottles in the crate can think of the number of bottles as 5 multiplied by 6, irrespective of whether he has counted 5 rows of 6 or 6 rows of 5. Then the commutative law for multiplication has become meaningful, and he can write 5×6 for either 5 sixes or 6 fives.

'Three times as much . . .'

In many of its uses the idea of multiplication has a slightly different emphasis from that stressed in the previous sections. This emphasis is found in the words 'three times as much' or 'multiplied by three'. This is the aspect of multiplication which is used in working out the cost of 3 metres of cloth, in enlarging a plan to 3 times its original (linear) dimensions, or in adapting a recipe for 3 times the number of people. In each of these examples, every quantity is increased so that it becomes 3 times the original size, and every number becomes three times the original number. A relation diagram shows clearly the 'three times as much' aspect of multiplication by three.

Each length on the upper number line of Figure 16:15 is increased on the lower number line to three times its original length.

The three times table

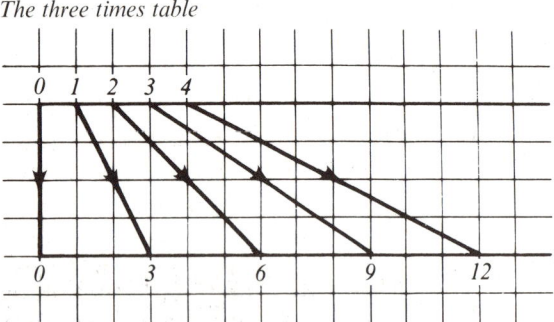

Figure 16:15

The multiplication table which is needed for this operation has a different appearance from the table of threes which the children have built up earlier. Figure 16:16 shows the *table of threes* and the *table of 'three times as much'* together, arranged as bar graphs.

By the commutative law, the two tables in Figure 16:16 are equivalent to one another and can be used interchangeably, but only when a child has reached an understanding of the commutative law can he move freely from one to the other. A child who has built up his concept of multiplication through a sufficient variety of experiences will eventually use 3×4 as an expression of all the interchangeable ideas:

   i) three fours,
   ii) four threes,
   iii) three times [as much as][1] four,
   iv) four times [as much as] three,

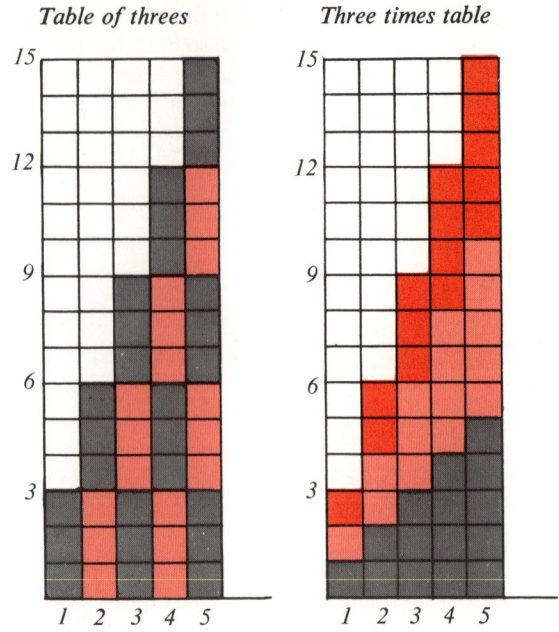

Figure 16:16

   v) three multiplied by four (that is, three increased to four times its size),
   vi) four multiplied by three.

The multiplication tables and their patterns

The basic multiplication facts are much more valuable when known separately, rather than only as parts of a table. After much use a child should know each fact as well as he knows the addition bonds, so that the mention of any two of the three numbers 7, 8 and 56 in a multiplication situation will immediately call to mind the remaining one, just as in addition situations the three numbers 7, 8 and 15 are indissolubly linked together.

Using multiplication operations in such contexts as the shop, and in weighing and measuring, will provide some of the practice in multiplication which children need in order to remember the facts. Several other activities such as graphical work and the search for pattern in the tables will be suggested in this section. All these activities help to fix the multiplication facts in the memory, to make them more meaningful, and so cut down the burden of rote learning.

By using the commutative law for multiplication, the number of multiplication facts which must be known for future use in the multiplication and division of larger numbers is reduced to 45. These are shown in Figure 16:17, and only the facts in the lower right-hand part of this

[1] The words in square brackets are often left unsaid, but are implicit in 'three times four'.

146

1×1

2×1 2×2

3×1 3×2 3×3

4×1 4×2 4×3 4×4

5×1 5×2 5×3 5×4 5×5

6×1 6×2 6×3 6×4 6×5 6×6

7×1 7×2 7×3 7×4 7×5 7×6 7×7

8×1 8×2 8×3 8×4 8×5 8×6 8×7 8×8

9×1 9×2 9×3 9×4 9×5 9×6 9×7 9×8 9×9

Figure 16:17

table are likely to be troublesome to the memory. When children make the conventional multiplication square (Figure 16:18), they should notice its symmetry about the leading diagonal as an expression of the commutative law, and should notice that the square numbers (*see page* 321) lie on the leading diagonal. Other patterns in the numbers will be suggested later, and it is an interesting activity for children to find, and explain, as many patterns as possible in the square. Underlining every even number or every multiple of 3 in the square will provoke discussion. Figures 16:19 and 16:20 show the patterns made by colouring multiples of 3 and 4.

1	**2**	3	**4**	5	**6**	7	**8**	9	**10**
2	**4**	**6**	**8**	**10**	**12**	**14**	**16**	**18**	**20**
3	**6**	9	**12**	15	**18**	21	**24**	27	**30**
4	**8**	**12**	**16**	**20**	**24**	**28**	**32**	**36**	**40**
5	**10**	15	**20**	25	**30**	35	**40**	45	**50**
6	**12**	**18**	**24**	**30**	**36**	**42**	**48**	**54**	**60**
7	**14**	21	**28**	35	**42**	49	**56**	63	**70**
8	**16**	**24**	**32**	**40**	**48**	**56**	**64**	**72**	**80**
9	**18**	27	**36**	45	**54**	63	**72**	81	**90**
10	**20**	**30**	**40**	**50**	**60**	**70**	**80**	**90**	**100**

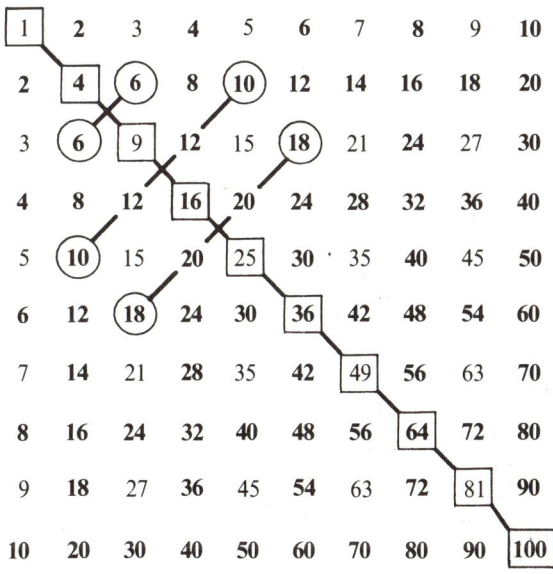

Figure 16:18

Multiples of 3

1	2	3	4	5	6	7	8	9	10	11	12
2	4	6	8	10	12	14	16	18	20	22	24
3	6	9	12	15	18	21	24	27	30	33	36
4	8	12	16	20	24	28	32	36	40	44	48
5	10	15	20	25	30	35	40	45	50	55	60
6	12	18	24	30	36	42	48	54	60	66	72
7	14	21	28	35	42	49	56	63	70	77	84
8	16	24	32	40	48	56	64	72	80	88	96
9	18	27	36	45	54	63	72	81	90	99	108
10	20	30	40	50	60	70	80	90	100	110	120
11	22	33	44	55	66	77	88	99	110	121	132
12	24	36	48	60	72	84	96	108	120	132	144

Figure 16:19

Multiples of 4

1	2	3	4	5	6	7	8	9	10	11	12
2	4	6	8	10	12	14	16	18	20	22	24
3	6	9	12	15	18	21	24	27	30	33	36
4	8	12	16	20	24	28	32	36	40	44	48
5	10	15	20	25	30	35	40	45	50	55	60
6	12	18	24	30	36	42	48	54	60	66	72
7	14	21	28	35	42	49	56	63	70	77	84
8	16	24	32	40	48	56	64	72	80	88	96
9	18	27	36	45	54	63	72	81	90	99	108
10	20	30	40	50	60	70	80	90	100	110	120
11	22	33	44	55	66	77	88	99	110	121	132
12	24	36	48	60	72	84	96	108	120	132	144

Figure 16:20

The table of 10 is intimately linked with the place-value system, and an *understanding* of it is vital. The table of ten appears more impressive when written in symbols than are the words corresponding to the figures.

$1 \times 10 = 10$ one ten is shown by 1 in the tens column

$2 \times 10 = 20$ two tens are shown by 2 in the tens column

$3 \times 10 = 30$ three tens are shown by 3 in the tens column

. . . .

$10 \times 1 = 10$ ten ones are shown by 1 in the tens column

$10 \times 2 = 20$ ten twos are shown by 2 in the tens column

$10 \times 3 = 30$ ten threes are shown by 3 in the tens column

. . . .

Children enjoy searching for patterns in all the tables, and once a pattern has been found it helps them to remember the table. A useful piece of apparatus for showing multiplication patterns visually is paper marked in a grid of 100 squares, each square with sides about 1 cm long. The squares can either be blank or numbered from 1 to 100. This can be used in different ways at different stages. Children can colour successive blocks of 2 squares, 3 squares, etc., in different colours. Counting such equivalent sets leads to multiplication, and also produces attractive patterns. Later on every second square, every third square, etc., on the numbered grid can be coloured, familiarizing the children with the numbers in each table, and associating the tables with visual patterns, a few of which are shown in Figure 16:21.

Older children, by superimposing the patterns of different tables upon one another, can begin to study factors, multiples and prime numbers.

As well as spatial patterns such as these, children enjoy finding patterns among the digits of the numbers in the tables. An obvious example is that in the table of nines the tens digit *increases* by one and the units digit *decreases* by one on each line of the table. Consideration of the reason for this may lead older children to feel a need for algebraic symbolism, to examine similar patterns in other bases, and to learn the old device of 'casting out nines' as a check on arithmetical calculations.

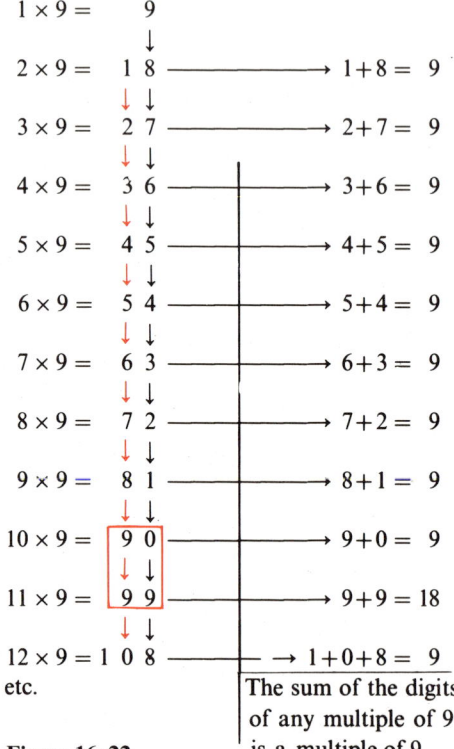

Figure 16:22

The sum of the digits of any multiple of 9 is a multiple of 9

Table of threes

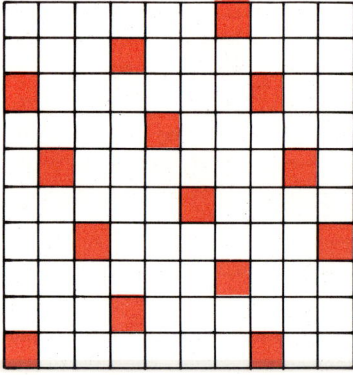

Table of sevens

1	2	3	4	5	6	7	8	9	10
11	12	13	14	15	16	17	18	19	20
21	22	23	24	25	26	27	28	29	30
31	32	33	34	35	36	37	38	39	40
41	42	43	44	45	46	47	48	49	50
51	52	53	54	55	56	57	58	59	60
61	62	63	64	65	66	67	68	69	70
71	72	73	74	75	76	77	78	79	80
81	82	83	84	85	86	87	88	89	90
91	92	93	94	95	96	97	98	99	100

Table of eights

Figure 16:21

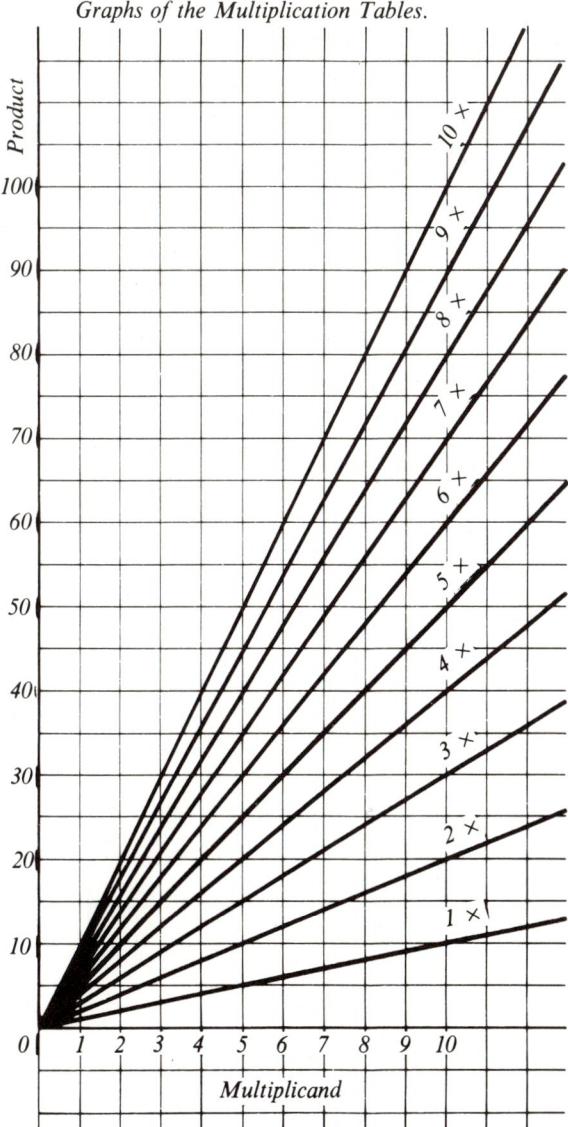

Graphs of the Multiplication Tables.

Figure 16:23

Children may also plot all the multiplication tables which they are using on the same graph for comparison (Figure 16:23).[2]

As they draw this graph, children are gaining experience which will lead to the development of concepts such as that a straight line graph shows steady growth, and that more rapid growth is shown by a steeper graph.[3]

---

[2] It may be advisable to reduce the scale on the vertical axis, for if this is not done a piece of graph paper whose height is at least 10 times its width will be needed. As a wall-chart, this gives a real impression of the rates of growth.

[3] This will lead on to the gradient of a line, the tangent of an angle, and the ideas of differential calculus at the Secondary stage.

Discussion of graphs which would occupy the area of Figure 16:23 below the 'one times table', and of interpolation (*see page* 304) on the graph, will lead to the multiplication of decimal fractions. The graph can also be used to answer such questions as, 'How many 8's in 96?'.

Multiplication facts involving zero are shown in Figure 16:23, as each of the graphs passes through the origin. These facts call for special mention, as children often make mistakes such as $5 \times 0 = 5$ which are due to failure to visualize the situation. A child who knows that 5×0 means $0 + 0 + 0 + 0 + 0$ will not make this mistake, and a graph of the 'table of 0's' is sufficiently startling to fix it in the memory (Figure 16:24).

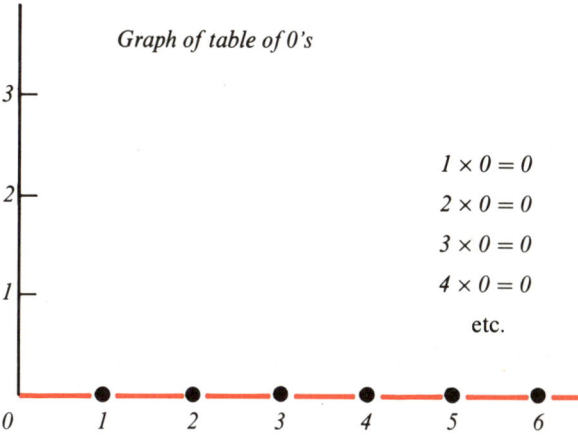

Graph of table of 0's

$1 \times 0 = 0$

$2 \times 0 = 0$

$3 \times 0 = 0$

$4 \times 0 = 0$

etc.

The graph is shown by the heavy coloured line.

Figure 16:24

Other pictorial representations of multiplication

Children who have seen the effect of such a transformation as 'add 3' on a set of numbers (*see page* 80) will also think of multiplication by a fixed number as a transformation which can act on any set of numbers. The transformation 'multiply by 4' transforms the set of numbers $\{1, 2, 3, \ldots, 10\}$ into the set $\{4, 8, 12, \ldots, 40\}$. Each multiplication table states the result of applying a multiplication transformation to the set $\{1, 2, 3, \ldots, 10\}$. Figure 16:25 illustrates two of these transformations.

Such transformations can be illustrated more clearly by number lines. Figure 16:26 shows a relation diagram of the transformation 'multiply by 4'. For an addition transformation, the lines joining each point of the number line to its image are parallel (*see page* 81); for a multiplication transformation, these lines are not parallel, but radiate from a point. The diagram shows very clearly the result of multiplying *any length* on the number line by 4.

149

(a) *The transformation '× 4'*

Multiply by 4
→

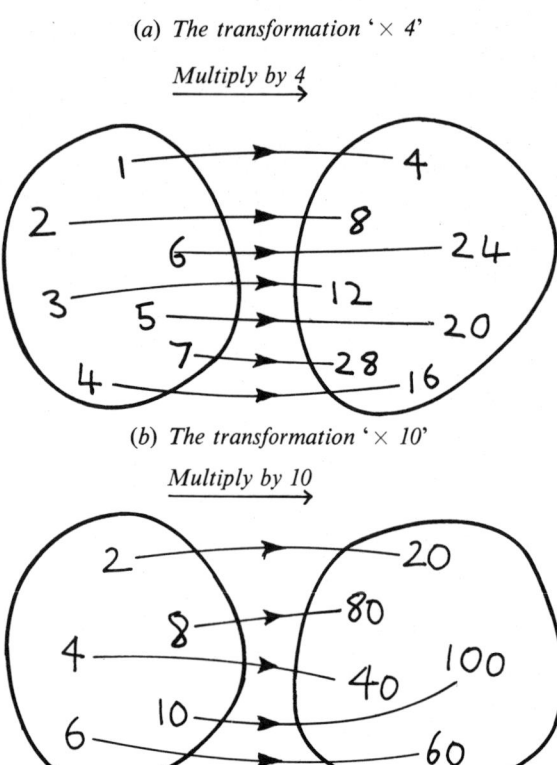

(b) *The transformation '× 10'*

Multiply by 10
→

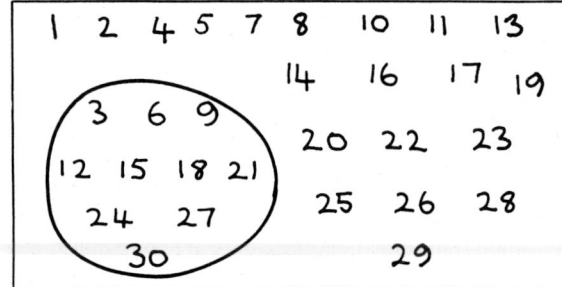

Figure 16:25

For example, we see that a line of length 6 units, enlarged to 4 times its length, becomes 24 units long. Also, although 10 does not belong to the set of whole number multiples of 4,

$$10 = 2\tfrac{1}{2} \times 4$$

Children may also use a set of cards, each one bearing a number, for instance up to 30, to sort out the sets of multiples of 2, 3, etc., and will illustrate their results in Venn diagrams as in Figures 16:27 and 16:28.

Multiples of 3

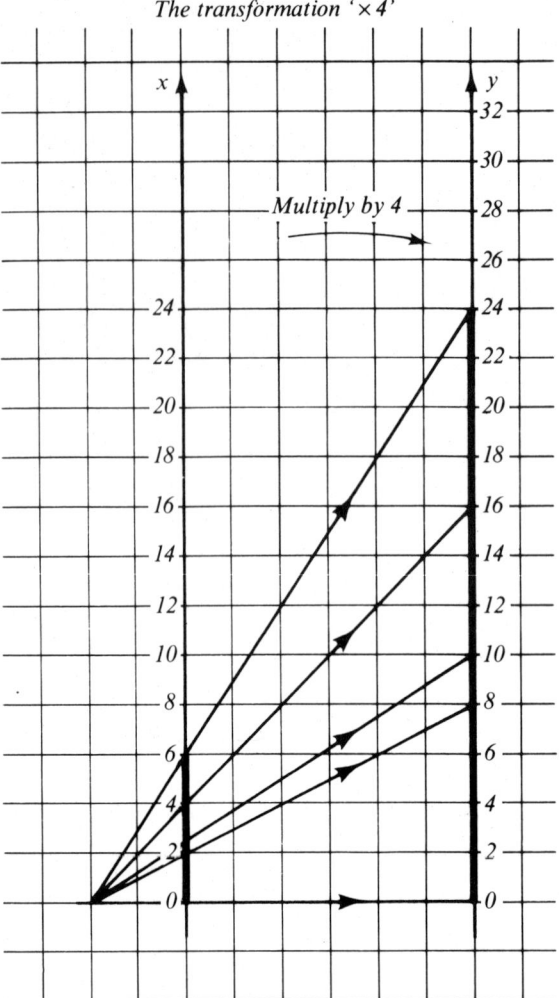

The transformation '×4'

Figure 16:26

Multiples of 2 and of 3

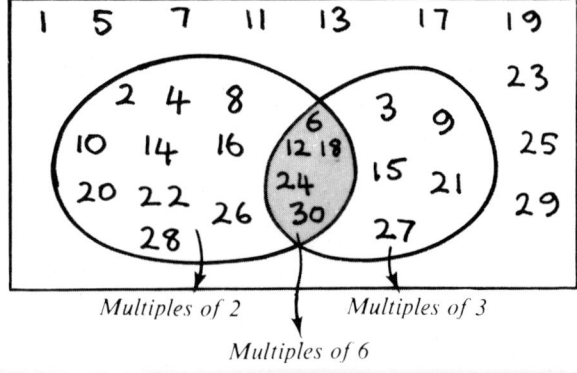

Figure 16:27

Figure 16:28

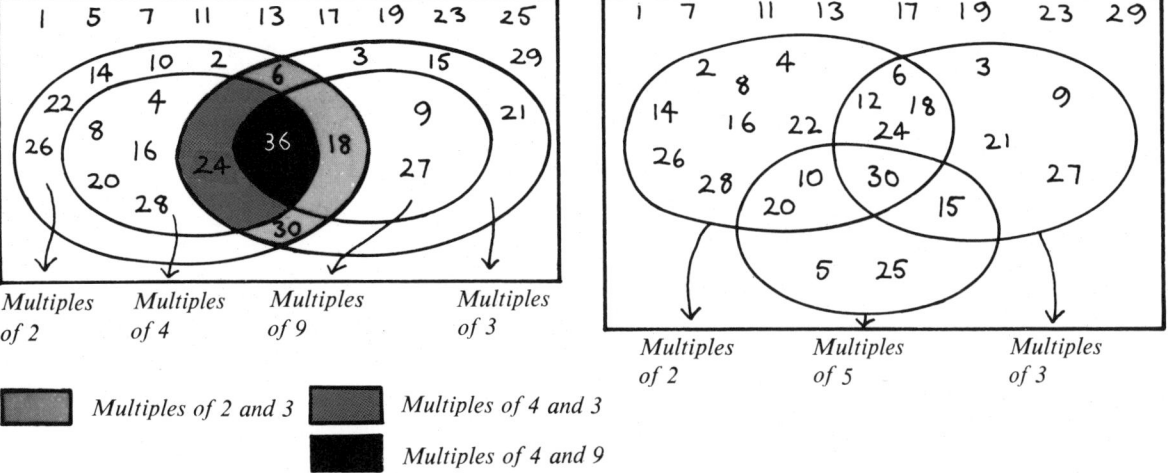

(a) Multiples of 2, 3, 4 and 9   (b) Multiples of 2, 3 and 5

Multiples of 2 and 3   Multiples of 4 and 3

Multiples of 4 and 9

Figure 16:29

They will find that numbers which are multiples of both 2 and 3 are in fact multiples of 6, and this will lead on to later work on factors. As children become older and more able to handle complicated classifications, they may extend their Venn diagrams to illustrate classifications such as those shown in Figure 16:29.

The beginning of division

Division is the inverse operation of multiplication, and is related to it in the same way that subtraction, the inverse operation of addition, is related to addition. Children, however, first use the idea of division at a very early stage, long before the concept of multiplication has become at all precise. A child uses two fundamentally different types of division, the first of which occurs when he shares out sweets with his friends, and the second when he tries to find out how many twopenny bars of chocolate he can buy with a tenpenny piece.

The first type of division, *sharing* or *partition,* is mathematically less simple, but children usually use it earlier, as no counting is needed at first. Sweets can be shared, or cards dealt out, without the child knowing either how many sweets there are, or how many children they are to be shared between. All he has to do is to go round and round the set of children, giving one sweet to each child until there are no more sweets, or until there are not enough for another round. This is a mathematical experience of sharing, but it does not become numerical until the child knows that there are 12 sweets and 4 children, so that any mishaps in the sharing can be checked by each child seeing that he has 3 sweets.

In sharing, the *number in the total set* (12 sweets) to be shared is known, and the *number of subsets* into which it is to

be shared is known (there are 4 children). The unknown quantity is the *number in each share.* Sharing is mathematically a rather advanced operation, as a child cannot predict the size of a share until he can answer the question, 'Four times what equals twelve?', and this demands considerable familiarity with the numbers. Of course he can *do* the sharing much earlier, and should have the experience of sharing things out and recording his results.

To look further at the mathematical difficulty of sharing, we shall use structural apparatus to solve the sharing problem, 'Divide 20 centimetres of string into 4 equal parts.' Structural apparatus is certainly not ideal for this problem; it is much easier with a piece of string, which can be folded into four equal parts. But a child equipped with structural apparatus will put out 20, and then has to find four equal rods which together make the 20. Unless he knows that four fives equal 20, he can only use his estimate of length, and trial and error, to guide him in the choice of five-rods (Figure 16:30).

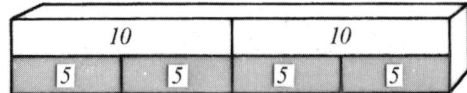

Figure 16:30

The other aspect of division, *grouping* or *quotition,* is mathematically rather simpler, but seems at first to children to be completely unrelated to the operation of sharing. *Grouping* is splitting up a set into counting sets of known number. How many twopenny bars of chocolate can be bought with a tenpenny piece? How many triangles can be made with 12 sticks? How many 2-centimetre-wide strips of paper can be cut from a 12-centimetre-wide piece? The child groups his set of 10 pennies into subsets each containing 2 pennies or he makes triangles with his sticks

151

Sharing

12 petals

3 flowers.
How many petals
on each flower?

Grouping

12 petals

4 petals on each
flower.
How many flowers?

Figure 16:31

and sees that he has 4 of them. He measures 2 centimetres on his piece of paper and cuts off a strip, and then another and another until there is nothing left. In grouping, the *size of the total set* is known, and the *size of each part* or subset is known. The unknown quantity is the *number of subsets*.

Grouping problems are more easily solved by the use of structural apparatus than are sharing problems. The problem of finding how many twopenny bars of chocolate can be bought with 10 pence, or of finding how many 2's there are in 10, is solved by putting two-rods end to end to make up 10, and counting how many rods were used. The child knows which rod to choose, and has to find how many he needs to make 10.

To sum up, a *sharing* problem is of the type

divide 12 into 4 equal parts,

whereas a *grouping* problem is of the type

how many 4's are there in 12?

(See Figure 16:31)

The relation between sharing and grouping

It is usual to give the name of *division* to both sharing and grouping problems, and to represent both situations by the same symbols $\frac{12}{4}$ or $12 \div 4$, but when children first use division ideas these should always be set in a practical situation so that an appropriate method can be used—a sharing method for a sharing problem, or a grouping method for a grouping problem. A child's power over division increases when he begins to understand the connection between sharing and grouping, and to connect both operations with other operations on numbers.

Grouping he may think of as repeated subtraction. He wants to find how many fours there are in 12, so he takes four away from 12, and then takes away another four and another four until he cannot go any farther.

$$12 - 4 - 4 - 4 = 0$$

152

He sees that he has taken away 3 fours, so there are 3 fours in 12. Division is often performed on desk calculating machines by this method (*see page* 169). Alternatively, a child may think of grouping as the inverse of repeated addition. He wants to find out how many fours there are in 12, so he builds up in fours until he reaches 12. Figure 16:32 shows this done with structural apparatus. A desk calculating machine can also be used to build up in this way (*see page* 170), and to perform division by counting how many times the divisor must be added on to make the dividend.

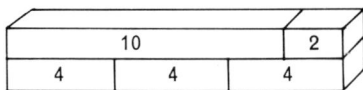

Figure 16:32

Division is also inverse multiplication. In the example of figure 16:32 we supply the missing number in the multiplication, 'What number of fours is equal to twelve?' or

$$\boxed{n} \times 4 = 12$$

Sharing, however, presents a different arrangement. 'Divide a set of 12 things into 4 equal parts' requires the choice of 4 sub-sets with the same number of members which together give 12, or finding the missing number in the multiplication, 'Four times what number is equal to twelve?' or

$$4 \times \boxed{n} = 12$$

Both types of division are inverse of multiplication; that is, multiplications in which the product is known and one of its factors is missing. Exactly similarly, subtraction is inverse addition, in which the sum is known and one of the parts is missing. The subtraction of 4 from 12 requires the finding of the missing number in

$$4 + \boxed{n} = 12$$

The division of 12 by 4 requires the finding of the missing

number in either

$$4 \times \boxed{n} = 12 \quad \text{(sharing)}$$

or

$$\boxed{n} \times 4 = 12 \quad \text{(grouping)}.$$

There are two different division arrangements because the missing number may be either the multiplier or the multiplicand, the number of sets or the number of each set. In concrete situations these two numbers have clearly differentiated functions and are not interchangeable. So at the concrete stage grouping and sharing are very different to children, and must be distinguished.

This complication does not arise in subtraction, as the order of the two numbers n and 4 in $n+4 = 12$ is unimportant to a child. He knows that addition is commutative long before he knows that multiplication is commutative, for concrete situations involving multiplication are not symmetrical.

When the commutativity of multiplication is understood, it becomes clear that there must be a close connection between sharing and grouping, since $4 \times n = n \times 4$, so that a solution of $4 \times n = 12$ is also a solution of $n \times 4 = 12$. Grouping is also the method usually chosen for the division of large numbers. The division $324 \div 9$ is usually worked by finding how many nines there are in 324 (grouping), rather than by dividing 324 into 9 equal parts (sharing). Even if 324 is the number of children to be shared between, and taught by, 9 teachers in a school, the method of calculation used by many adults seems to be based on the grouping method of finding how many 9's there are in 324.

We shall now examine the connection between concrete situations involving sharing and those involving grouping. Suppose that 12 cards are to be dealt out to 4 children. This is the sharing process of dividing into 4 equal parts, but if the dealing is done one round at a time it becomes a grouping process. For the first round of dealing a set of 4 cards is used, and one of them is given to each child.

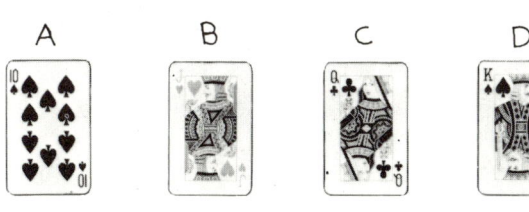

Figure 16:33

In the next round another set of 4 cards is used, and so on until the cards are exhausted. Each child receives one card from each set of four cards. The problem of dividing 12 cards into 4 equivalent sets has been replaced by the problem of dividing 12 cards into sets containing 4 cards. The sharing has been replaced by a two-stage process:

i) grouping in sets of 4, and then
ii) sharing each set of 4, one card to each child.

Figure 16:34

This method can be used for any sharing problem, and children often use it spontaneously. If the teacher watches a child sharing bricks between himself and a friend, he will find that the child will often take a brick in each hand, forming a set of 2 bricks, and then put one of these bricks in each pile. Most children, however, need to have this

Figure 16:35

153

24 ÷	1	2	3	4	5	6	7	8	9
Quotient	24	12	8	6		4		3	

natural process made explicit to them, so that they realize that sharing and grouping are interchangeable as far as the *numbers* are concerned.

Inverse multiplication

If division is to become a meaningful rather than a mechanical process, children must pass through the three stages of:

i) using grouping and sharing as two different operations and solving problems by the use of concrete apparatus,
ii) relating sharing to grouping,
iii) using their knowledge of multiplication to deal with both types of division by the same numerical procedure.

At the last stage the long descriptions which were necessary in order to express sharing and grouping situations can be replaced by the abstract 'divide 12 by 4'. *Divide* is a general, neutral word which is not tied to either sharing or grouping; it is appropriately used at the stage at which it no longer matters to a child whether he is sharing or grouping. He is now performing the operation inverse to multiplication, and is performing that operation with abstract numbers. 'Divide 12 by 4' corresponds to either

i) 'how many 4's equal 12?' or
ii) '4 times what number equals 12?',
    and the answer is '3, because 3 multiplied by 4 = 12'.

Some division activities

As children move into the final stage of seeing division as inverse multiplication it may be helpful to describe some of the multiplication activities suggested on page 149 in the language of division. Figure 16:36 shows the use of the graph of multiplication tables to find 96 ÷ 8.

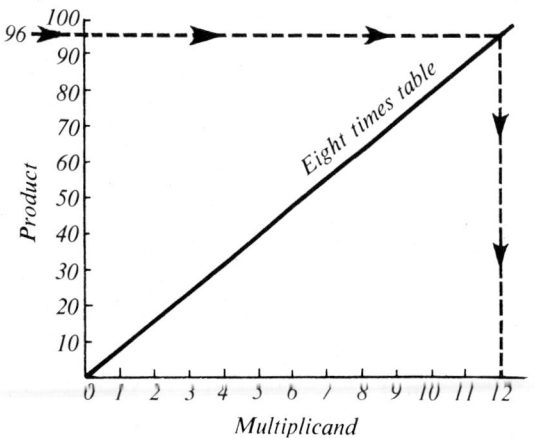

Figure 16:36

154

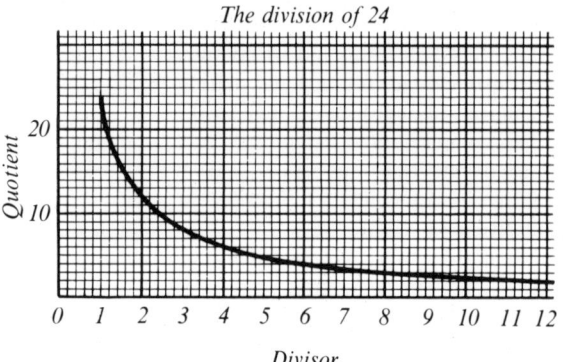

The division of 24

Figure 16:37

Older children may like to take a number such as 24, which has many factors, and draw a graph of the results of dividing it by 1, 2, 3, 4, ... (Figure 16:37).

The discussion of the spaces left blank in this table, and putting in values of the divisor greater than 24 or less than 1, can help children to understand such facts as

$$24 \div 5 = 4 \cdot 8$$

and

$$24 \div 0 \cdot 5 = 48$$

This graph is also a useful example of a curved graph. Some points on the same graph (which is a rectangular hyperbola (*see page* 306)) can also be obtained by marking all the positions of the number 24 in the multiplication table of Figure 16:18 (see Figure 16:38). The equivalence of Figures 16:37 and 16:38 can be discussed.

Older children should also investigate divisions involving 0, and may realize not only that

$0 \div 2 = 0$, since the solution of $\boxed{n} \times 2 = 0$ is $n = 0$,
$0 \div 5 = 0$, since the solution of $\boxed{n} \times 5 = 0$ is $n = 0$,

and so on, but that

$2 \div 0$ has no answer, since $\boxed{n} \times 0 = 2$ has no solutions

and that

$0 \div 0$ may be any number,

since the equation $\boxed{n} \times 0 = 0$ has every number as a solution.

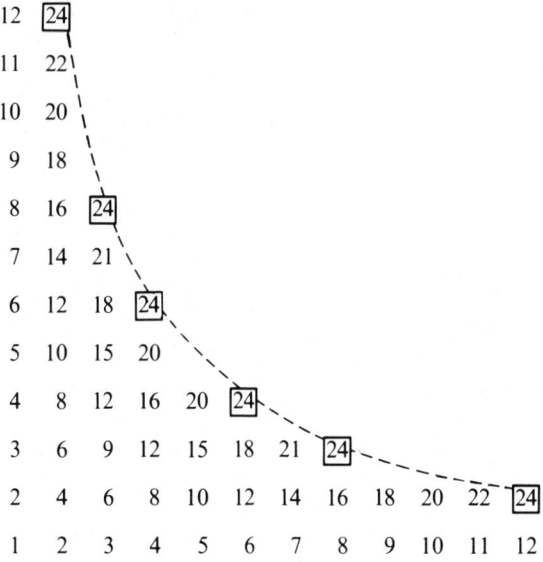

12	24										
11	22										
10	20										
9	18										
8	16	24									
7	14	21									
6	12	18	24								
5	10	15	20								
4	8	12	16	20	24						
3	6	9	12	15	18	21	24				
2	4	6	8	10	12	14	16	18	20	22	24
1	2	3	4	5	6	7	8	9	10	11	12

Figure 16:38

The language of division

Some very odd forms of wording are occasionally used in the hope of making multiplication and division clear to children. The words which can be heard on some children's lips: 'You times it by 3' are objectionable, but the reading of 12 ÷ 3 as 'share 12 by 3' is not much better. 'Share 12 between 3 people' and 'divide 12 by 3' are both correct, but the hybrid will have to be unlearnt later, and is not needed, although the word 'share' must be used in sharing situations.

The very common reading of 8)72 as 'eights into 72' is not clear, and could be replaced by, 'How many eights are there in 72?', or 'one-eighth of 72', either of which is a correct interpretation of the symbols 72 ÷ 8. It is a great advantage if the wording used for the arithmetical processes which become habits is not only mathematically correct, but also illuminates and reveals the thought-processes contained in the mechanical operations.

17 The Development of Number Systems

Early ways of writing numbers

Most children in English-speaking countries have met numbers written in Roman figures. They see them on some clock-faces, on old tombstones, and at the head of chapters in some books. The difference between these numerals and those that have come down to us from the Hindus via the Arabs strikes a child at once. He notices that familiar letters are used in place of figures and these letters may be repeated. He sees that strokes or ones appear at the right of the letters, e.g. LXXIII. These Roman numerals tell us a great deal about how our modern system of notation developed.

The use of a simple sign such as a stroke, or the shape made by pressing the end of a pointed stick into a clay tablet, was very common in early civilizations for recording a count. The Egyptians used strokes for the numbers from one to nine, grouping them to make them more easily recognizable, as in Figure 17:1.

Four   *Seven*   *Nine*

Figure 17:1

The Babylonians used a similar method in wedge-shaped or cuneiform markings (Figure 17:2).

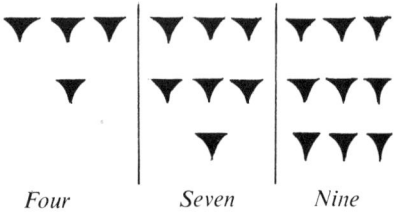

Four   *Seven*   *Nine*

Figure 17:2

Children may record a set similarly, or they may use beads, cubes or sticks as 'counters'. A one-one correspondence is thus made between things (the members of a set) and the strokes or other symbols used. Since there are as many separate symbols as there are things no economy has been made and no true counting may yet have taken place.

Grouping objects and animals was a common experience of primitive man and he soon gave names to the smaller groupings. A great step forward came when he recorded groupings as well as separate objects which are too few to make a grouping. Different cultures have used different groupings but most of them devised a special

symbol for a grouping and recorded the number of the groupings of a particular size by repeating the symbol, just as they repeated strokes to write the smaller numbers (Figure 17:3).

Roman Symbols	**III**	**XX**	**XXXII**
Arabic Symbols	*3*	*20*	*32*

Figure 17:3

Because finger-counting is so convenient, grouping in tens developed in many countries and has replaced the groupings in fives, twelves, twenties and sixties which have appeared in some ancient civilizations. We know a great deal about the early use of numbers grouped in tens from the Ahmes papyrus, a remarkable survival from Egypt of about 1700 B.C. Much of the papyrus is in the British Museum where a facsimile is exhibited (Figure 17:4).

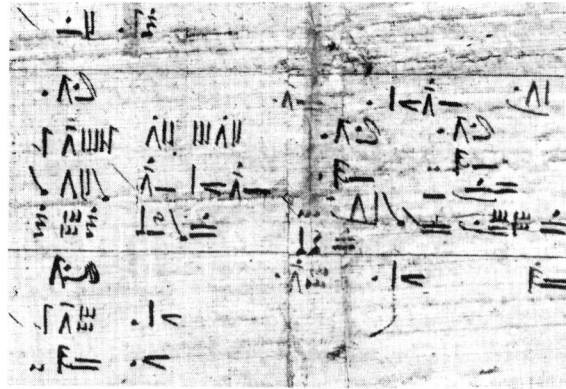

Figure 17:4

Many of the calculations recorded in the papyrus concern rationing during famines. This reminds us of the famines in the story of Joseph in the Bible. Joseph lived in Egypt during the era of the Ahmes papyrus and when he organized the storage of part of the harvests during the good years the Egyptian priests were able to work out fair shares for people and cattle in the lean years. The papyrus shows the calculations that were carried out, the ways in which addition and subtraction were performed and the ingenious device for multiplying that was invented to overcome the limitations of the Egyptian number notation. We consider this notation now in some detail as an example of the way that a number system can help or hinder the development of understanding and skill in using numbers.

Egyptian numerals

For a grouping of ten the Egyptians used the symbol . Thus fifty-three would appear as $\cap\cap\cap\ \cap\cap\ |||$.

The next grouping, ten tens or a hundred, was written $\mathcal{9}$. Eight hundred and fifty-three would be written

$$\begin{matrix}\mathcal{9}\mathcal{9}\mathcal{9}\\\mathcal{9}\mathcal{9}\mathcal{9}\\\mathcal{9}\mathcal{9}\end{matrix}\quad\begin{matrix}\cap\cap\cap\\\cap\cap\end{matrix}\quad |||$$

Symbols for one thousand, ten thousand, etc., were also invented and were used in the same repetitive way. No particular order was laid down for writing the symbols; tens could be placed either to the right or left of the units. But addition and subtraction are so much easier when like groupings are placed in the same column that the habit of writing the symbols in order of the size of the grouping, beginning with the largest on the left, became established. The use of a counting tray or abacus stabilized this order. The parallel between the Egyptian notation and the experience with structured apparatus and the abacus which a modern child is offered can be seen in Figure 17:5 which represents the number three hundred and forty two.

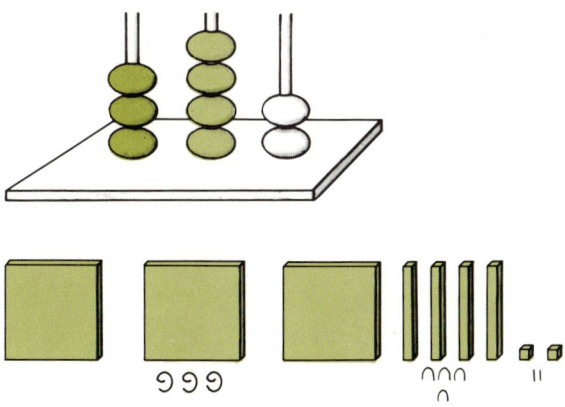

Figure 17:5

It seems to us a very short step from this stage to the form of numeral we use today, 342, but in fact it was many centuries before our system became general in Europe.

Addition in Egyptian numerals was cumbersome in appearance but the thought involved in the process was similar to our own, as can be seen in Figure 17:6.

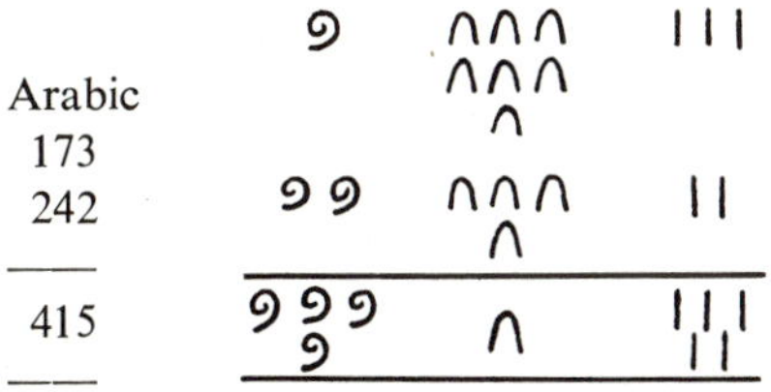

Arabic			
173	$\mathcal{9}$	$\cap\cap\cap$ $\cap\cap\cap$ $\cap$	$|||$
242	$\mathcal{9}\mathcal{9}$	$\cap\cap\cap$ $\cap$	$||$
415	$\mathcal{9}\mathcal{9}\mathcal{9}$ $\mathcal{9}$	$\cap$	$|||$ $||$

Figure 17:6

Multiplication in such a system involves so many symbols that it would be difficult to memorize the products. For an example, see Figure 17:7.

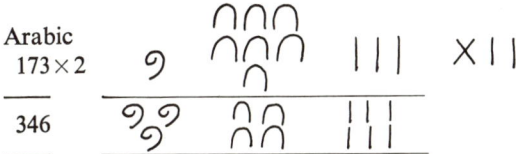

Arabic				
173×2	$\mathcal{9}$	$\begin{matrix}\cap\cap\cap\\\cap\cap\cap\\\cap\end{matrix}$	$|||$	$\times\ |\ |$
346	$\mathcal{9}\mathcal{9}$ $\mathcal{9}$	$\cap\cap$ $\cap\cap$	$|||$ $|||$	

Figure 17:7

Multiplication by a number greater than two could be performed by continuing to add the multiplicand. To multiply by eleven or more in this way is a tedious proceeding. Instead the Egyptians used a system of successive doubling which is similar to the modern use of the binary scale in computers. In Figure 17:8 we show the way in which seventeen × thirteen was carried out in the Egyptian system; Arabic notation is used to make the process easier to follow. The successive products are found by continuously adding the last product; e.g. 34 is added to 34 to obtain 68.

$$17 = 1 \times 17$$
$$34 = 2 \times 17 \qquad \text{Now } 13 = 8+4+1 \qquad 136$$
$$68 = 4 \times 17 \qquad \text{Therefore} \qquad\qquad 68$$
$$136 = 8 \times 17 \qquad 13 \times 17 = 136+68+17 \qquad \underline{17}$$
$$\overline{221} = 13 \times 17$$

Figure 17:8

With so cumbersome a notation it is not surprising that fractions were not understood except for the manipulation of simple aliquot forms such as $\frac{1}{4}$, $\frac{1}{8}$. Decimal fractions could not develop without a new advance towards the idea of place value.

Roman numerals

Basically, the Romans, like the Egyptians, counted in powers of ten.

$$X = 10$$
$$C = 10 \times 10$$
$$M = 10 \times 10 \times 10$$

They also recorded groupings by repeating symbols:

231 (Arabic) = CCXXXI (Roman)

But a special feature of the Roman notation is a symbol for the five of each grouping, a half-way point to the next main grouping.

$$V = 5$$
$$L = 50$$
$$D = 500$$

This is reminiscent of counting on the fingers of one hand. It has the important advantage of making numerals easier to recognize. LXXVI is a neat way to write 76 compared with the Egyptian

∩∩∩ |||
∩∩∩ |||
∩

But the Roman system had the great disadvantage that it was based on alternating groupings, by five and by two. Out of such a notation it would be difficult to evolve a system like the Arabic in which the *position* of a figure is sufficient to tell us its value. However, the Romans made one notable advance; they used position to show whether a number was to be added to or taken from the next higher grouping when writing or reading a number. For example,

VI means V+I, i.e. 6   IV means V−I, i.e. 4
LX means L+X, i.e. 60   XL means L−X, i.e. 40

This is a first step towards making a code based on the relative position of the digits.

The Arabic system

The numerals 1 to 9 which we use today are thought to have originated in India about 2000 years ago, though their form has changed a good deal with the passing of the centuries. The Hindus used one of these signs to write the *number* of any grouping in place of repeating its symbol; thus 2674 would be written 2 thousands 6 hundreds 7 tens and 4, using of course the Hindu names. Even if the names were abbreviated this was still a lengthy numeral to write but names were necessary until an unknown scholar in India thought of using a symbol to show that none of any particular grouping occurred. This idea of emptiness or nothingness still fascinates children and we now tend to let them use a symbol for it at 5 or 6 years of age to represent the emptiness of a plate or bowl.

The round zero is a very suitable symbol for the number of the empty set. Its importance for notation is obvious: with it the count of every set can be given a symbol using only the numerals 0 to 9. The pattern of beads on an abacus, where every rod or groove corresponds to a grouping, can always be expressed as a numeral where the digits match the beads on each column, even on an empty column. The groupings need no written names because

there is a digit, beginning with the ones digit on the right, for each grouping (Figure 17:9).

In Figure 17:9, 6 is the number of tens; the zero shows that there are *no* hundreds; therefore the 3 must count thousands.

Since the columns can be extended as far as we please to the left we can write a number as large as we wish using only the ten symbols 0, 1, 2, . . . , 9. Because the *position* of any grouping is known, the algorithms or written forms of

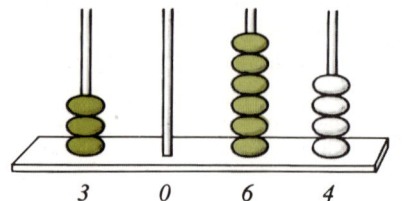

3   0   6   4

Figure 17:9

computations can be neatly arranged in columns without labels. The simplifications which resulted from the general adoption of this system in Europe in the sixteenth century were of tremendous benefit to the expanding trade of the Renaissance period. Further developments have been stimulated by the demands of commerce and science. The very large numbers required in astronomy or social statistics and the very small numbers used in modern physics have given rise to yet more concise means of symbolizing numbers and operations. Some of these extensions are well within the grasp of Primary School children (*see page* 341).

Symbols for fractions

We have seen that the Egyptians found fractions difficult to handle. The idea of a part was familiar. It was frequently thought of in relation to measures as being a smaller unit. For example, one-sixtieth part of an hour was called a *minute* or small part. A sixtieth part of a minute was called a *second* part of an hour. Given a name such as minute or second these parts could be expressed in whole numbers and calculations could be carried out in well-known ways. Difficulty arose when multiplication involving fractions

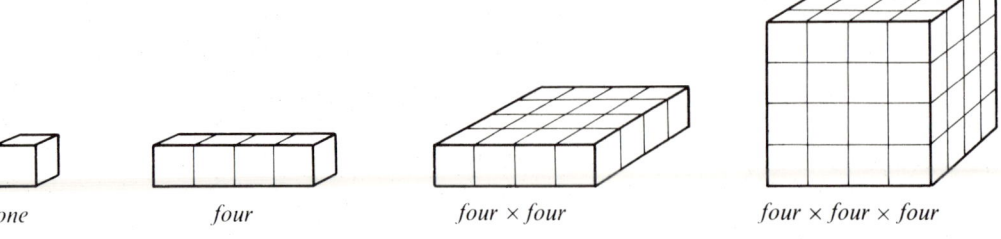

one   four   four × four   four × four × four

Figure 17:10

158

was required, as in finding the area of a rectangle with dimensions involving fractions. This problem led to new notations. Symbols were needed which would make the computations easier both to carry out and to understand. The standard way of writing fractions is by means of a pair of numbers separated by a horizontal line. An alternative arrangement is the use of the solidus or sloping line as in 4/5 for four-fifths; printers prefer this because it does not break the run of the type. The vertical arrangement is used in schools because it is easier to distinguish the name of each part, the *denominator*, from the number of the parts, the *numerator*. This is useful because fractions must frequently be transformed so that their denominators are identical, so that they are all expressed in parts of the same size. This notation can then allow operations to be carried out in terms of whole numbers.

The decimal notation for fractions

Even this simple notation is too unwieldy to commend itself to those who must deal with fractional parts of small size or those who need to know precisely the degree of accuracy of the numbers they have computed. It is astonishing that it took mankind so long to extend the Arabic notation downwards so that successive columns, moving to the right, would show not only tens and ones but also tenths, hundredths, etc., each having a place value one-tenth of that to the left. Only one symbol was required to make this system intelligible: a sign to show which is the units figure. There is still diversity about this symbol. France, U.S.A. and Great Britain each print their own; the French use a comma, the Americans a point on the line. The British usually print a point above the line.

Any fraction can be expressed as the sum of decimal fractions, tenths, hundredths, etc., by continuously dividing numerator by denominator, for example

$$\tfrac{5}{8} = 0.625 \quad \text{by division.}$$

Notice the zero in the units place, serving to draw attention to the decimal point. Decimal fractions share the advantage of decimal integers in that they can be arranged in columns for addition, etc. Moreover, we can write them to the degree of accuracy that we need, stopping at the second, third, or nth decimal place. Clearly we can extend decimal fractions as far as we please since there is no end

to the places we can move to the right. This brings out the value of the place-value system: we can write fairly concisely as large or as small a number as we choose to think about. Félix, in *The Modern Aspect of Mathematics* quotes Lebesgue, 'Our teaching does not yet fully use this historic achievement, perhaps the most important in the history of the sciences, the invention of decimal notation.' A smaller unit is always ready when it is needed, a tenth of the last unit. The system of subdivision into smaller units is based on the *ten* in exactly the same way as the notational system for whole numbers. It has the further advantage that in this era of mechanical and electronic computation a machine carries out exactly the same computations (except for the position of the decimal point) in performing the additions

$$123 + 276 \quad \text{and} \quad 1.23 + 2.76$$

or in obtaining

$$473 \times 42 \quad \text{and} \quad 47300 \times 0.42$$

In those sections devoted to number we shall use decimal notation fully as children will find it being used in trade and technology.

Notation in various bases

The purpose of notation is to give a neat way of representing numbers so that we can carry them in the mind as well as write them on paper. We can see how a number is organized, what structures it contains, how it is related to other numbers, and what will be the effect upon it of operations we can carry out mentally. The decimal notation enables us to do these things very well. But it is possible to increase a child's understanding and skills if we enrich the *symbolic* representation by spatial images resulting from handling suitable shapes. We can use discs, round beads, cylinders, etc. to illustrate groupings but the shape that gives the closest parallel to a place-value notation is the cube. Because its faces are all squares of the same size we can fit a cube to other cubes in three directions. We need not confine our groupings to tens. In Figure 17:10 we group cubes in fours.

The *shapes* are the same if we group in sevens, twelves or tens.

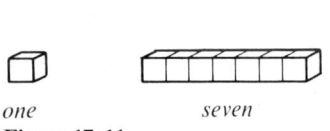

one   *seven*

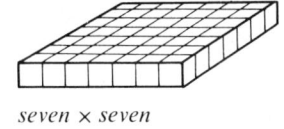

seven × seven

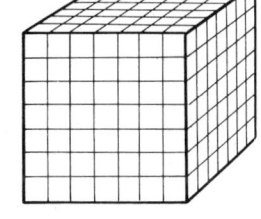

seven × seven × seven

Figure 17:11

159

We see that four × four × four small cubes make a large cube. So do seven × seven × seven (Figure 17:11). We can now group these larger cubes and obtain long rods to represent four × four × four × four, and so on. The groupings are now producing the same shapes as before, and children can build up to a huge cube that represents four × four × four × four × four × four, or seven × seven × seven × seven × seven. If they group in tens they can produce the million cube. Now they could go on grouping for ever in the imagination.

A large number of small cubes can be organized into groupings of threes, fours, etc. For example, a handful of seventy cubes can be organized into three-rods, then into three × three layers, and then into three × three × three cubes. This gives

2 large cubes	3 × 3 × 3	fifty-four
1 square layer	3 × 3	nine
2 rods	3	six
1 cube	1	one

We can write this in columns

(3 × 3 × 3)	(3 × 3)	3	1
2	1	2	1

More shortly it can be written without labels using place value only but naming the counting set or *base*.

2121 (base three)

Children can also set out with appropriate cubes a representation of a number given in any base. These activities will lead to discussion of the number of symbols needed to write numbers in different bases and they will find that for base three they need only 0, 1 and 2. They enjoy inventing their own symbols, e.g. 0, /, ∟.

The Dienes Multibase Arithmetic Blocks consist of unit cubes and rods, square layers and large cubes produced in blocks marked to show the equivalent small cubes. These are convenient for children to handle. A counting set of four unit cubes can be exchanged for a four-rod, and four of these rods for a four × four layer, and so on. The material includes bases two, three, four, five, six and ten. Large as the blocks seem when working in base six or base ten, it is important for children to experience the organizing of a number into each of these bases. They will then realize that a number of unit cubes can be put together in ways which illustrate a notation based on *any* counting set. The cubes provide an analogue for the place-value notation because the organization of the cubes is parallel to the number grouping.

The process of building up from unit cubes to larger and larger units can be paralleled by a process of breaking down into smaller units. If we take a large cube as a unit (Figure 17:12), it can be broken down into say seven square layers, each one of which is made up of seven rods, each one of which is made up of seven small cubes, each one of

which is made up of seven small square layers, each one of which. . . .

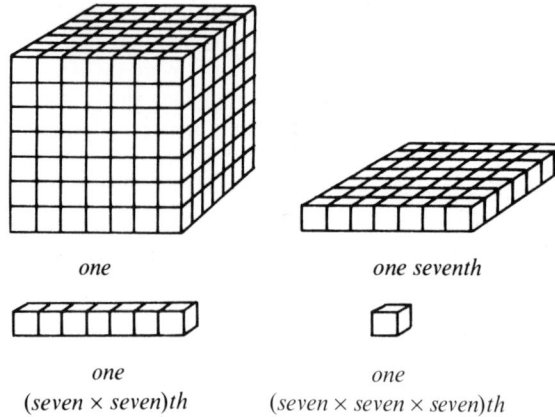

one

one seventh

one
(seven × seven)th

one
(seven × seven × seven)th

Figure 17:12

Thus the positional system of notation in base seven could easily be extended downwards to accommodate fractions of a unit as well as whole numbers of units.

Figure 17:13 shows this extension of the positional notation in base seven.

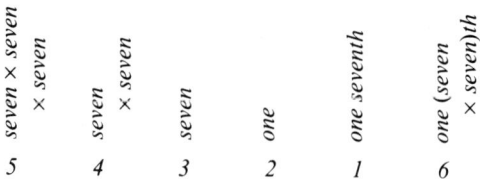

seven × seven × seven	seven × seven	seven	one	one seventh	one (seven × seven)th
5	4	3	2	1	6

Figure 17:13

The number shown is

5 seven × seven × sevens
4 seven × sevens
3 sevens
2 ones
1 seventh
6 (seven × seven)ths.

Children will become much more familiar with this positional notation in base ten than in any other base, and they should realize that a piece of any size in the Multibase Arithmetic Blocks can be used to represent one unit, and the other pieces take their value from this. The pieces shown in Figure 17:14 might represent either:

i) 1 one, 3 tenths, 2 hundredths, 4 thousandths; that is 1·324, if the large cube represents one; or
ii) 1 ten, 3 ones, 2 tenths, 4 hundredths; that is 13·24, if the square layer represents one; or
iii) 1 thousand, 3 hundreds, 2 tens, 4 ones; that is 1324, if the small cube represents one.
Other values are also possible.

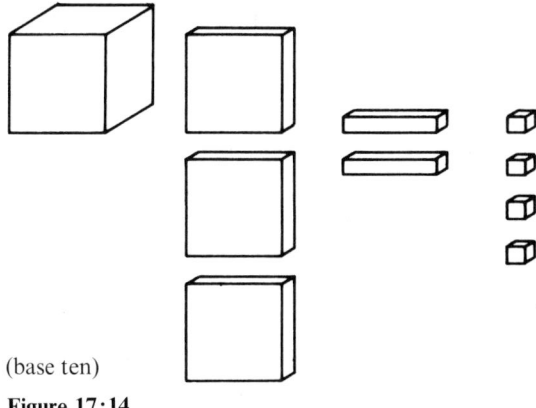

(base ten)

Figure 17:14

The index notation

We have seen that in base seven a number can be illustrated with unit cubes as follows:

$$1 \text{ rod} = 7 \text{ ones}$$
$$1 \text{ square layer} = 7 \text{ rods} = 7 \times 7 \text{ ones}$$
$$1 \text{ cube} = 7 \text{ square layers} = 7 \times 7 \text{ rods}$$
$$= 7 \times 7 \times 7 \text{ ones}.$$

A similar pattern occurs in any base. For instance, if base five is used:

$$1 \text{ rod} = 5 \text{ ones}$$
$$1 \text{ square layer} = 5 \text{ rods} = 5 \times 5 \text{ ones}$$
$$1 \text{ cube} = 5 \text{ square layers} = 5 \times 5 \text{ rods}$$
$$= 5 \times 5 \times 5 \text{ ones}.$$

It is convenient to abbreviate 5×5 as 5^2 (five squared) and $5 \times 5 \times 5$ as 5^3 (five cubed), so that in base five:

$$1 \text{ rod} = 5 \text{ ones} \quad 1 \text{ square layer} = 5^2 \text{ ones}$$
$$1 \text{ cube} = 5^3 \text{ ones}$$

The words 'rod', 'square layer' and 'cube' which we have used for the larger groupings of units will be replaced by:

$$\text{base} \equiv \text{rod}$$
$$\text{square (of base)} \equiv \text{square layer}$$
$$\text{cube (of base)} \equiv \text{cube}$$

which reflect their mathematical structure more fully.

We now consider numbers of units greater than the cube of the base. The notation is easily extended to accommodate such large numbers. In base five, whenever five pieces of the same size occur, they are grouped together to form a piece of the next size. This process is illustrated in Figure 17:15. When five pieces whose size is the cube of the base (5^3) occur, they are grouped together to form a piece which bears the same relation to the 'cube' as does the 'rod' to the unit. Children may call this piece a 'big rod', and similarly call the next piece a 'big layer' and the next a 'big cube'. The 'big cube', like the 'cube' and the unit, is cubical in shape, and so can be used as the starting point of further building in 'rods', 'layers' and 'cubes'. This process can clearly be continued indefinitely, so that any number, however large, can be written in base five, or similarly in any other base. It is natural to extend the notation used earlier to describe the larger pieces. In base five, Figure 17:15 shows that:

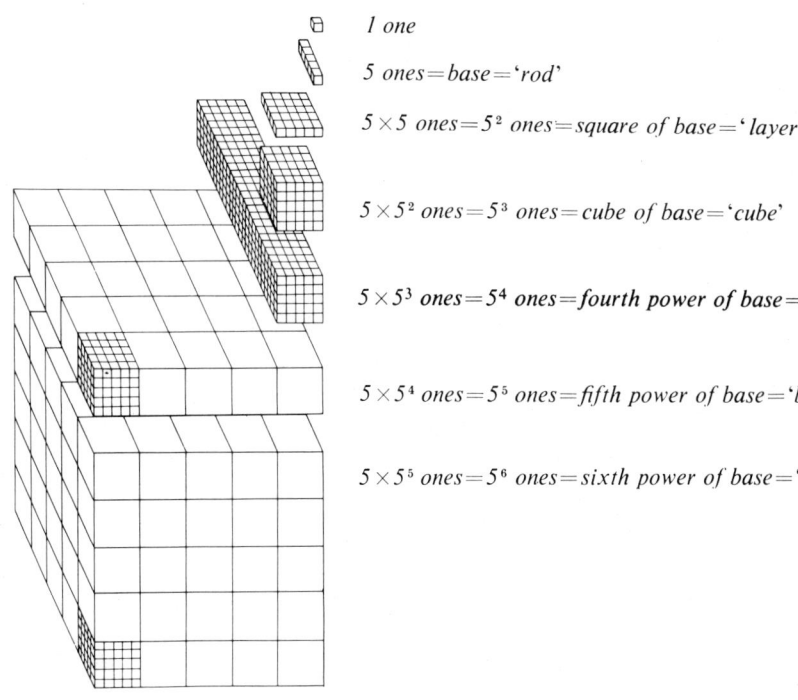

1 one

5 ones = base = 'rod'

5×5 ones = 5^2 ones = square of base = 'layer'

5×5^2 ones = 5^3 ones = cube of base = 'cube'

5×5^3 ones = 5^4 ones = fourth power of base = 'big rod'

5×5^4 ones = 5^5 ones = fifth power of base = 'big layer'

5×5^5 ones = 5^6 ones = sixth power of base = 'big cube'

Figure 17:15

Base:
1 rod = 5 ones

Square of base:
1 layer = 5 rods = 5×5 ones = 5^2 ones

Cube of base:
1 cube = 5 layers = 5×5 rods = $5 \times 5 \times 5$ ones
= 5^3 ones

Fourth power of base:
1 big rod = 5 cubes = 5×5 layers
= $5 \times 5 \times 5$ rods
= $5 \times 5 \times 5 \times 5$ ones = 5^4 ones

Fifth power of base:
1 big layer = 5 big rods = 5×5 cubes
= $5 \times 5 \times 5$ layers = $5 \times 5 \times 5 \times 5$ rods
= $5 \times 5 \times 5 \times 5 \times 5$ ones = 5^5 ones

and so on.

A symbol such as 5^6, 5 *raised to the sixth power*, indicates that six factors, each equal to 5, are multiplied together; that is

$$5^6 = 5 \times 5 \times 5 \times 5 \times 5 \times 5$$
6 factors

Similarly, 5 (or any other number) can be raised to any power, the *index* showing the power to which the base has been raised.

The columns in which children write numbers when they use the Dienes apparatus:

Big rods *Cubes* *Square* *Rods* *Units*
            layers

can appropriately be labelled:

Fourth *Cubes* *Squares* *Bases* *Ones*
powers

The number *1 111 111* (base ten)

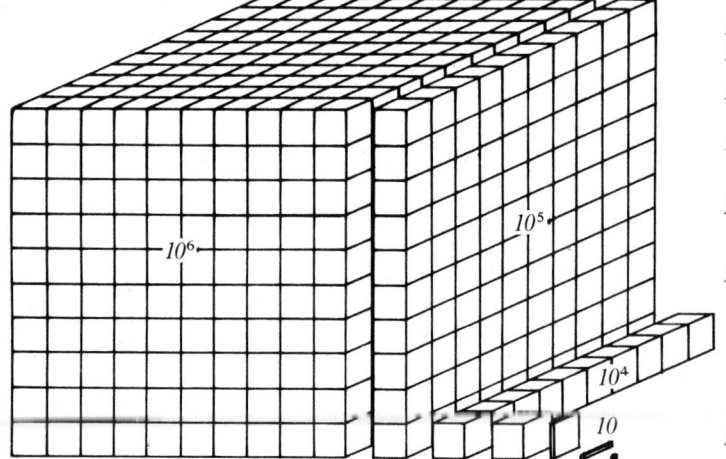

Figure 17:16
162

or in base five:

5^4 5^3 5^2 5 1

The number 43 232 (base five) is made up of

$$(4 \times 5^4) + (3 \times 5^3) + (2 \times 5^2) + (3 \times 5) + (2 \times 1)$$

The same notation applies in any base, and it is important that children should understand the relationships which are implicit in the building up of base ten. Figure 17:16 illustrates notation in base ten.
The number 3 456 789 (base ten) is made up of

$$(3 \times 10^6) + (4 \times 10^5) + (5 \times 10^4) + (6 \times 10^3)$$
$$+ (7 \times 10^2) + (8 \times 10) + (9 \times 1)$$

Further relations within the system of notation which children need to recognize are of the following type:

1 thousand = 10 hundreds = 100 tens   = 1000 ones
$10^3 = 10 \times (10^2)$ = 100×10 = 1000×1
= $(10^2) \times 10 = (10^3) \times 1$

and

1 million = 10 hundred-thousands
= 100 ten-thousands = 1000 thousands
or $10^6 = 10 \times (10^5)$
= $100 \times (10^4)$ = $1000 \times (10^3)$
= $10^2 \times 10^4$ = $10^3 \times 10^3$, etc.

They will come to know the index form for any power of ten:

$10^2 =$ 100
$10^3 =$ 1 000
$10^4 =$ 10 000
$10^5 =$ 100 000
$10^6 =$ 1 000 000
$10^{12} =$ 1 000 000 000 000

1 one
10 ones = 1 ten

100 ones = 10^2 ones = 1 hundred

1 000 ones = 10^3 ones = 1 thousand

10 000 ones = 10^4 ones = 1 ten-thousand

100 000 ones = 10^5 ones = 1 hundred-thousand

1 000 000 ones = 10^6 ones = 1 million

This table may be extended to include smaller as well as larger numbers. Clearly $10^1 = 10$ is sensible, and the pattern is completed by $10^0 = 1$. We notice that an increase of 1 in the index has the effect of multiplying the number by ten, and a decrease of 1 in the index has the effect of dividing the number by ten. The pattern now is:

$10^0 =$ ⠀⠀1
$10^1 =$ ⠀⠀⠀10
$10^2 =$ ⠀⠀100
$10^3 =$ ⠀1 000
$10^4 = 10 000$ and so on,

and the headings of the columns in the decimal system of notation:

Ten-thousands⠀Thousands⠀Hundreds⠀Tens⠀Units

may be written:

10^4⠀⠀⠀⠀⠀10^3⠀⠀⠀⠀⠀10^2⠀⠀⠀⠀10^1⠀⠀10^0

Notation on the abacus

Numbers written in any base can be shown on an abacus. The columns should be labelled in the base notation, as in Figure 17:17, but may also show the decimal form of the number. Children can choose a number to show on the abacus with a selected base and then translate it into decimal notation. They can also use the abacus to record the results of their organizing of cubes, as shown on page 122. This will encourage further discussion of the symbols needed to write what is seen on the abacus. It is very important *not* to use the base-ten words at this stage but to speak a number such as 312 (base four) in the way we give a telephone number: three-one-two (base four). It

would be quite wrong, of course, to say three hundred and twelve, even if the words 'base four' were added.

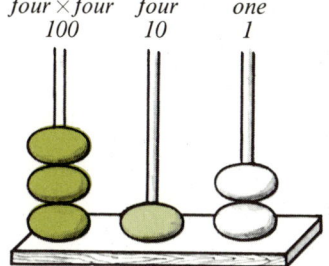

four × four⠀⠀*four*⠀⠀⠀⠀⠀*one*
⠀⠀*100*⠀⠀⠀⠀⠀*10*⠀⠀⠀⠀⠀⠀*1*

Figure 17:17

The emergence of the place-value concept

From the variety of forms in which children experience our number system—the cubes and rods, recordings of sums of money and measuring, graphs, the abacus and symbols for numerals—there develops a capacity to read and write numbers with a confident recognition of their meaning. Behind the symbols children recognize the number itself and can look critically at a number sentence and say whether it is sensible or true. They will be ready to adopt new notations and to understand their scope and usefulness.

Our number notation and the measures in daily use are so closely bound up with our history that new meaning is given to them if their origins are known. There is considerable value in letting children read for themselves about the inventions that have gone to the making of our number system. Some good books on the history of numbers are now available for class libraries.

18 The Calculating Machine and the Laws of Arithmetic

Multiplication of larger numbers

As children become familiar with the idea of multiplication, the size of the numbers which they can use increases and gradually they learn the multiplication tables so that eventually they know the result of any multiplication up to 9 × 9. The method of building up multiplication by continued addition whenever the result is not known is, however, inadequate for larger numbers, and must be supplemented by methods which make use of the positional notation for writing numbers. The use of any type of structural apparatus will encourage a child to discover such methods for himself.

A child who uses Cuisenaire rods to obtain the answer to 3 × 14 (three fourteens) may put out a fourteen made up of 10+4, followed by another fourteen and another fourteen, or he may prefer to put out 3 tens and 3 fours (Figure 18:1).

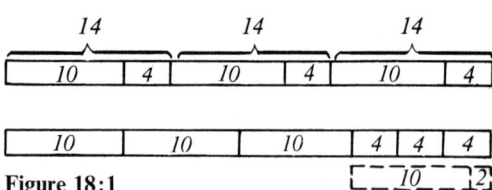

Figure 18:1

The result is the same by either method, but the second method is the more convenient for future calculation on paper. When this experience is recorded on paper as

$$\begin{array}{r} 14 \\ \times\ 3 \\ \hline 42 \\ 1 \\ \end{array}$$

and when it is thought out in such words as

'3 times 4 equals 12,
1 ten and 2 *ones*
3 times 1 ten equals 3 tens,
3 tens plus 1 ten equals *4 tens*'

the words used correspond exactly to the arrangement which the child constructed in Figure 18:1.

Similarly, a child who uses the Dienes Multibase Arithmetic Blocks or similar apparatus to multiply

1 cube   3 square layers   1 rod   2 ones   (base four)

by 2 will put out the apparatus shown in Figure 18:2, and

will gather together first all the ones, then all the rods, then all the square layers, then all the cubes, and will record his work, thinking first of the multiplication of the ones by 2, then of the multiplication of the rods by 2, and so on. This

2 × 1312 (base four)

Figure 18:2

	Cubes	Square Layers	Rods	Ones	
	1	3	1	2	(base four)
×				2	
	3	2	3	0	
	1		1		

thought-process and the method of working based on it persist unchanged as the use of apparatus is discarded, and form the foundation for all multiplication of larger numbers.

The distributive law

The mathematical law which expresses the idea used above is the *distributive law*.[1] The multiplication 3 × 14, or 3 × (10+4), can be replaced by (3 × 10) + (3 × 4). In fact,

$$3 \times (10+4) = (3 \times 10) + (3 \times 4)$$

Similarly,

$$3 \times (1 \text{ metre 4 centimetres})$$
$$= 3 \times (1 \text{ metre}) + 3 \times (4 \text{ centimetres}).$$

In general, the distributive law states that, for any numbers a, b and c,

$$a \times (b+c) = (a \times b) + (a \times c)$$

---

[1] The name 'distributive law' expresses the fact that multiplication is 'distributed out' over addition.

164

This law can also be illustrated by building a rectangular layer like the one shown in Figure 18:3. This rectangle consists of either

i) *a* rows of (*b*+*c*) bricks, that is *a* × (*b*+*c*) bricks, or
ii) *a* rows of *b* bricks together with *a* rows of *c* bricks, giving (*a* × *b*) + (*a* × *c*) bricks in all, so that

$$a \times (b+c) = (a \times b) + (a \times c)$$

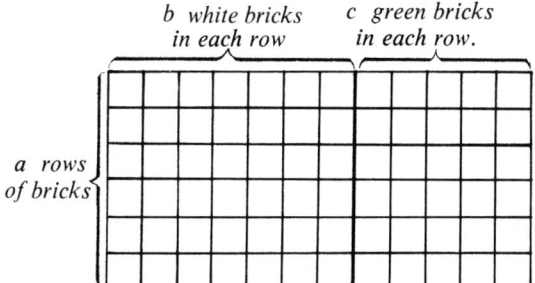

Figure 18:3

Children find little difficulty in using the distributive law when multiplying. It is much more obviously true than is the commutative law for multiplication. Dienes quotes the case of a child who, having been provided with concrete apparatus from which she could generalize the distributive law, said, '3 times F and 3 times S is 3 times F and S. That seems so obvious.'

Multiplication by the base

The next step in understanding multiplication when numbers are written in a particular base is the realization of what happens when a number is multiplied by the base number. Children need to understand that for instance,

$$10 \times 24 = 240 \text{ (base ten)}$$

and,

$$10 \times 2 \text{ pence} = 2 \text{ tenpences.}$$

Similarly,

$$100 \times 2 \text{ pence} = £2$$

and

$$100 \times 2 \text{ centimetres} = 2 \text{ metres.}$$

This behaviour is surprising, and children often regard it as a curious coincidence, without understanding, but it forms the basis of long multiplication, so that it is important that the point should be understood. The following practical experiences may be helpful.

i) Multiplication of 3 ones by 10 (base ten) (Figure 18:4).

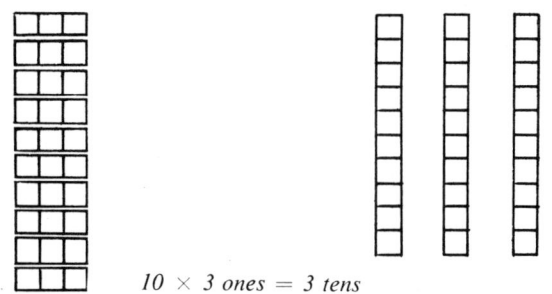

$$10 \times 3 \text{ ones} = 3 \text{ tens}$$

Figure 18:4

ii) A slight change of emphasis in an earlier multiplication graph may be helpful (Figure 18:5).

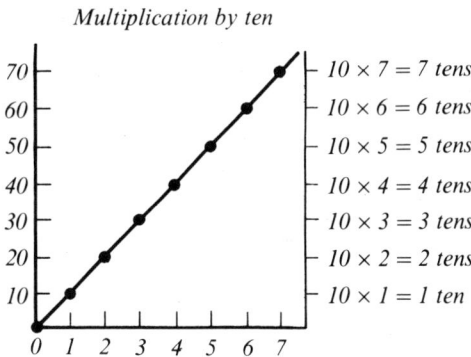

Multiplication by ten

$$10 \times 7 = 7 \text{ tens}$$
$$10 \times 6 = 6 \text{ tens}$$
$$10 \times 5 = 5 \text{ tens}$$
$$10 \times 4 = 4 \text{ tens}$$
$$10 \times 3 = 3 \text{ tens}$$
$$10 \times 2 = 2 \text{ tens}$$
$$10 \times 1 = 1 \text{ ten}$$

Figure 18:5

iii) Multiplication of larger numbers by the base shows that

$$10 \times 3 \text{ tens} = 30 \text{ tens}$$
$$= 3 \text{ hundreds,}$$

or

$$10 \times 30 \quad = 300$$

iv) Similarly,

$$10 \times 30 \text{ centimetres} = 10 \times 3 \text{ ten-centimetre rods}$$
$$= 30 \text{ ten-centimetre rods}$$
$$= 3 \text{ metres,}$$

and

$$10 \times 3 \text{ tenpenny pieces} = £3$$

The principle which children must grasp here is that multiplication (within a notational system) by the base has the effect of moving each digit of the number multiplied one column to the left. Since the practical examples found at this stage are all in base ten, the examples below are of multiplication by ten.

$$\begin{array}{cc} £ & p \\ & 20 \times 10 \\ \hline 2 & 00 \end{array} \quad \text{or} \quad \begin{array}{c} £ \\ 0 . 20 \times 10 \\ \hline 2 . 00 \end{array}$$

$$\begin{array}{cc} m & cm \\ & 23 \times 10 \\ \hline 2 & 30 \end{array} \quad \text{or} \quad \begin{array}{c} m \\ 0 . 23 \times 10 \\ \hline 2 . 30 \end{array}$$

Similarly, multiplication by the square of the base moves the digits two places to the left.

$$\begin{array}{cc} £ & p \\ & 2 \times 100 \\ \hline 2 & 00 \end{array} \quad \text{or} \quad \begin{array}{c} £ \\ 0 . 02 \times 100 \\ \hline 2 . 00 \end{array}$$

$$\begin{array}{cc} m & cm \\ & 23 \times 100 \\ \hline 23 & 00 \end{array} \quad \text{or} \quad \begin{array}{c} m \\ 0 . 23 \times 100 \\ \hline 23 . 00 \end{array}$$

Children will come to understand this principle by practical experience of concrete multiplication by the base number, but the principle used must become abstract, and the digits be moved automatically before the idea can be used as a basis for long multiplication.

If a desk calculating machine is available it can very well be used at this point to help children understand multiplication by the base and long multiplication. The use of a desk calculating machine is therefore now described, and it will be used as an illustration in the discussion of long multiplication and division.

The desk calculating machine

The various hand-operated desk calculating machines on the market all have a similar structure; a typical machine is shown in Figure 18:6.

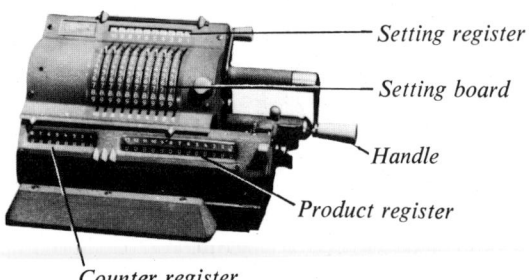

— Setting register

— Setting board

— Handle

— Product register

Counter register

Figure 18:6

166

Numbers are fed into the machine by moving the levers on the *setting board* (in some machines by pressing keys), and appear in the *setting register*. A turn of the handle in the clockwise direction transfers the number in the setting register to the spaces directly below it in the *product register*, adding this number to any number which is already present in the product register. The *counter register* records how many times the handle has been turned. A turn of the handle in the anticlockwise direction *subtracts* the number in the setting register from that in the product register. The product and counter registers are mounted on a *carriage* similar to a typewriter carriage which can be moved to left or right. There are levers which will clear any register of its contents.

Desk calculating machines are basically mechanical devices for the rapid performance of addition and subtraction in the base of ten, and are therefore well suited to showing children the structure of multiplication as repeated addition, and division as repeated subtraction. Most of these machines are of extremely sturdy construction and will withstand continued handling by children, for whom they hold a great fascination. Children must be told that only one lever may be moved at a time, but may then safely be allowed to discover the operation of the machine for themselves.

Among the early discoveries is likely to be how to build a multiplication table. A number, such as 4, is placed in the setting register. A turn of the handle transfers it to the (empty) product register. Another turn of the handle adds the 4 which is still in the setting register to the 4 in the product register, another turn adds another 4, and so on (Figure 18:7). The counter register shows how many fours

		Setting register
Set 4 in the		0 0 0 0 0 0 0 4
setting register.	0 0 0 0 0 0	0 0 0 0 0 0 0 0 0 0
	Counter register	Product register
		0 0 0 0 0 0 0 4
Turn handle once clockwise.	0 0 0 0 0 1	0 0 0 0 0 0 0 0 0 4
		0 0 0 0 0 0 0 4
Turn handle a second time clockwise.	0 0 0 0 0 2	0 0 0 0 0 0 0 0 0 8
		0 0 0 0 0 0 0 4
Turn handle a ninth time clockwise.	0 0 0 0 0 9	0 0 0 0 0 0 0 3 6

Figure 18:7

have been added. Children should be encouraged to build up multiplication tables for large numbers in this way, and to notice the behaviour of the digits whenever a number is multiplied by ten, which is the base number of the machine (Figure 18:8).

10×1486

Set 1486 in the
setting register.

| 0 0 0 0 0 1 4 8 6 |
| 0 0 0 0 0 0 | 0 0 0 0 0 0 0 0 0 0 0 |

After nine clockwise
turns

| 0 0 0 0 0 1 4 8 6 |
| 0 0 0 0 0 9 | 0 0 0 0 0 0 0 1 3 3 7 4 |

After a tenth
clockwise turn.

| 0 0 0 0 0 1 4 8 6 |
| 0 0 0 0 1 0 | 0 0 0 0 0 0 0 1 4 8 6 0 |

Figure 18:8

When children have discovered that multiplication of a number by *ten* moves all the digits of the number one place to the left, the next stage is the realization that ten turns of the handle are unnecessary for multiplication by ten. All that is needed is to move the carriage, which holds the product register, one place to the right, '*into the tens position*', and turn the handle once (Figure 18:9).

10×1486

Set 1486 in the
setting register.

| 0 0 0 0 0 1 4 8 6 |
| 0 0 0 0 0 0 | 0 0 0 0 0 0 0 0 0 0 0 |

Move carriage to
tens position

| 0 0 0 0 0 1 4 8 6 |
| 0 0 0 0 0 0 | 0 0 0 0 0 0 0 0 0 0 0 |

Turn handle
once clockwise.

| 0 0 0 0 0 1 4 8 6 |
| 0 0 0 0 1 0 | 0 0 0 0 0 0 0 1 4 8 6 0 |

Figure 18:9

Multiplication by 100 can be achieved by moving the carriage two places to the right '*into the hundreds position*', and turning the handle once, and so on.

In order to understand long multiplication, children must first understand the property that multiplication by the base moves the digits of a number one place to the left, multiplication by the square of the base moves the digits two places to the left, and so on. The use of a calculating machine alone will not produce complete understanding of this property, but it will help to fix it securely in children's minds.

The desk calculating machine can also be used to show short-cut multiplication by 20, 30, 40, . . . (base ten). The carriage is moved into the tens position, performing multiplication by ten, and the handle is turned 2, 3, 4, . . . times (Figure 18:10).

The mathematical law upon which the process of multiplying by a multiple of the base rests is seen when the 30 in

30×1486 *(base ten)*

Set 1486 in the
setting register.

| 0 0 0 0 0 0 1 4 8 6 |
| 0 0 0 0 0 0 | 0 0 0 0 0 0 0 0 0 0 0 0 |

Move carriage
to tens position

| 0 0 0 0 0 0 1 4 8 6 |
| 0 0 0 0 0 0 | 0 0 0 0 0 0 0 0 0 0 0 0 |

Turn handle
three times
clockwise

| 0 0 0 0 0 0 1 4 8 6 |
| 0 0 0 0 3 0 | 0 0 0 0 0 0 0 0 4 4 5 8 0 |

Figure 18:10

30×1486 is written as 3×10. Then

$$30 \times 1486$$
$$= (3 \times 10) \times 1486$$
$$= 3 \times (10 \times 1486),$$

where the brackets show that multiplication by 10 is performed first, and the result is then multiplied by 3. In general, if a, b and c are any numbers,

$$(a \times b) \times c = a \times (b \times c)$$

This law, the *associative law for multiplication*, in effect states that if three numbers are to be multiplied together, the order in which the multiplication is performed may be varied according to convenience. The associative law for multiplication will be seen to correspond extremely closely to the associative law for addition (*see page* 90).

$$(a+b)+c = a+(b+c)$$

which plays an important part in simplifying the addition of large numbers.

A further illustration of the truth of the associative law for multiplication may be obtained from the building of a cuboid out of cubical bricks (Figure 18:11). The floor contains a rows of b bricks, or $(a \times b)$ bricks, and so the

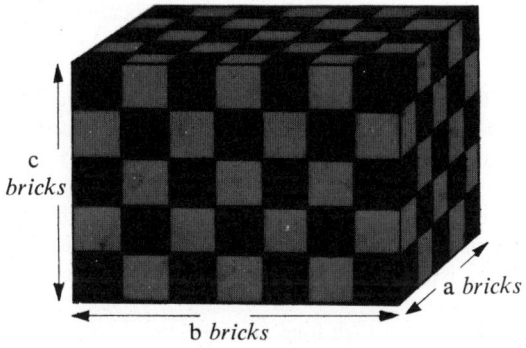

c
bricks

a bricks

b bricks

Figure 18:11

cuboid, which has c layers of bricks, contains $(a \times b) \times c$ bricks. Alternatively, the front wall has $(b \times c)$ bricks in it and the cuboid is a layers thick, so that

$$a \times (b \times c) = (a \times b) \times c$$

Children do not easily connect this experience of the associative law for multiplication with its use in the multiplication of a number by a multiple of the base unless the link between the experiences is made clear. The evaluation of triple multiplications such as

$$(8 \times 9) \times 7 = 72 \times 7$$
$$= 504$$

and

$$8 \times (9 \times 7) = 8 \times 63$$
$$= 504$$

may help to make the link clearer.

Although an associative law is true for both addition and multiplication, it is not true for subtraction or division. For instance,

$$60 \div (6 \div 2) = 60 \div 3 = 20,$$
but $\quad (60 \div 6) \div 2 = 10 \div 2 = 5,$
so that $\; 60 \div (6 \div 2) \neq (60 \div 6) \div 2$

Long multiplication:
a second form of the distributive law

The final stage in long multiplication is reached when a child realizes that if he wishes to multiply for instance 476 by 23 (base ten), he can do so in three steps, by multiplying 476 by 20 and multiplying 476 by 3 and adding the results together. This construction is implicit in the very first stages of multiplication. When a young child puts out apparatus to find 3×8 he will often put the eights out one at a time, and when he has put out two eights he knows he needs another one; that is, he knows that

$$3 \times 8 = (2 \times 8) + (1 \times 8)$$

Exactly the same law is used in long multiplication;

$$23 \times 476 = (20 \times 476) + (3 \times 476);$$

and children who have understood the previous stages find little difficulty in grasping this, either with structural apparatus, an abacus, a desk calculating machine (Figure 18:12), or in calculation on paper. When calculating on paper or with a calculating machine it is of course immaterial whether the multiplication by 20 or by 3 is done first, but it is perhaps advisable for children to form a habit and stick to it.

The law upon which long multiplication is based is a second form of the *distributive law*. The statement:

168

$$23 \times 476 \quad (base\ ten)$$

Set 476 in the setting register.

Multiply by 3.

Move carriage into tens position.
Multiply by 20 and add in result.

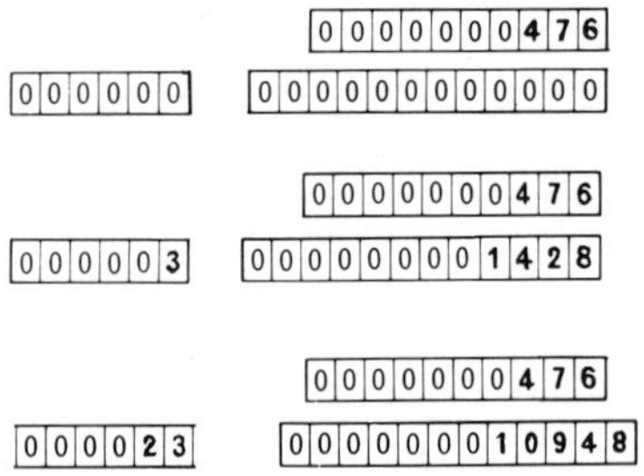

Figure 18:12

$$23 \times 476 = (20 \times 476) + (3 \times 476)$$

is a special case of:

$$(a+b) \times c = (a \times c) + (b \times c)$$

This distributive law is noticeably similar to that given on page 164.

$$a \times (b+c) = (a \times b) + (a \times c)$$

In one case the multiplier is split up, and in the other case the multiplicand. It is possible that the two distributive laws may appear to children to be different, as the multiplier (in the example the number of times 476 is to be repeated) plays a very different part at the concrete stage from the multiplicand 476, which is set out in concrete form. However, as the commutative law for multiplication (*see page* 145) is assimilated, and as children's ideas of number become more abstract, the two distributive laws become completely interchangeable.

The teacher should notice how often the distributive laws are used in such a multiplication as:

$$
\begin{array}{r}
76 \\
\times \quad 29 \\
\hline
1520 \\
684 \\
\hline
2204 \\
\end{array}
$$

the steps of which are more easily analysed when it is written in equation form:

$$29 \times 76 = (20 \times 76) + (9 \times 76) \quad \text{(distributive law)}$$
$$= 2 \times (10 \times 76) + (9 \times 76) \quad \text{(associative law)}$$
$$= \quad (2 \times 760) \quad + \quad (9 \times 76)$$

$$= (2 \times 700) + (2 \times 60) + (9 \times 70) + (9 \times 6)$$
$$\text{(distributive law)}$$

In such a calculation as this, if a child is using a calculating machine, he should be encouraged to find a labour-saving method. Treating 29×76 as $(30 \times 76) - (1 \times 76)$, which uses a distributive law for multiplication over subtraction

$$(a-b) \times c = (a \times c) - (b \times c),$$

involves only four turns of the calculating-machine handle, instead of the eleven turns which are needed to carry out $(20 \times 76) + (9 \times 76)$.

Division on the calculating machine

When the handle of a desk calculating machine is turned in an *anti-clockwise* direction, the number shown in the setting register is subtracted from that shown in the product register. Repeated turns of the handle repeat this subtraction, thus performing division as repeated subtraction. The technique of performing a simple division is shown in Figure 18:13.

This method of performing division by *repeated subtraction* contrasts with that used by the human calculator who, equipped with a knowledge of the multiplication tables, prefers to say that, '$73 \div 9 = 8$ remainder 1, because $8 \times 9 = 72$', thus performing *inverse multiplication*.

73 ÷ 9 (base ten)

Transfer 73 to product register from setting register. Clear setting register and counter register.

`0 0 0 0 0 0 0 0 0 0`
`0 0 0 0 0 0` `0 0 0 0 0 0 0 0 0 0 7 3`

Set 9 in setting register.

`0 0 0 0 0 0 0 0 0 9`
`0 0 0 0 0 0` `0 0 0 0 0 0 0 0 0 0 7 3`

*Turn handle repeatedly anticlockwise. (**When** bell rings handle has been turned too far. Turn back one revolution).*

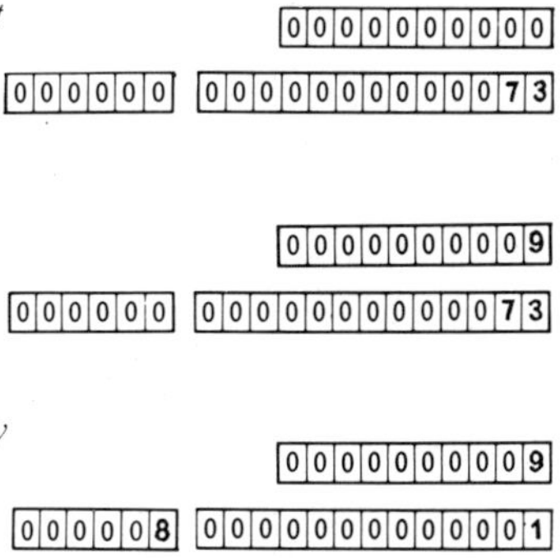

`0 0 0 0 0 0 0 0 0 9`
`0 0 0 0 0 8` `0 0 0 0 0 0 0 0 0 0 0 1`

73—9—9—9—9—9—9—9—9= 1
Hence 73 ÷ 9 = 8 remainder 1

Figure 18:13

Children will very soon discover the connection between the two methods of division if they are encouraged to use the machine to subtract, for instance, 4 from 48; they will find that zero remains when 4 has been subtracted 12 times.

A more labour-saving method of performing division than repeated subtraction becomes necessary when 284 has to be divided by 4. Such problems are usually encountered at a fairly early stage, and because they are outside the range of the multiplication tables which a child knows, they lead to the development of the methods of long and short division.

Division outside the range of the multiplication tables

The division method used for

$$84 \div 4 = 21$$

is based upon a distributive law

$$(80+4) \div 4 = (80 \div 4) + (4 \div 4) = 20+1,$$

and the division

$$96 \div 4 = 24$$

is based upon

$$(80+16) \div 4 = (80 \div 4) + (16 \div 4) = 20+4.$$

These are special cases of a *distributive law for division*[2]

$$(a+b) \div c = (a \div c) + (b \div c).$$

For the understanding of two-step division it is therefore necessary for a child to know some multiplication facts, and hence some division facts, which lie outside the range of the multiplication tables, such as $20 \times 4 = 80$ and so $80 \div 4 = 20$. These additional multiplication facts are easily found by a child who understands multiplication by a multiple of the base (*see page* 165), so that he can use his knowledge of the table of fours to give him such additional facts as

$10 \times 4 = \quad 40$	$100 \times 4 = \quad 400$	$1000 \times 4 = \quad 4000$
$20 \times 4 = \quad 80$	$200 \times 4 = \quad 800$	$2000 \times 4 = \quad 8000$
$30 \times 4 = 120$	$300 \times 4 = 1200$	$3000 \times 4 = 12000$
etc.	etc.	etc.

Equipped with this knowledge, the traditional 'long division' arrangement of

```
    1326
4)5304
    4
   ─
   13
   12
   ──
   10
    8
   ──
   24
   24
   ──
    0
```

is seen to be an abbreviation of an arrangement which

---

[2] It should be noticed that while for the distribution of multiplication over addition there are two distributive laws:

$$(a+b) \times c = (a \times c) + (b \times c)$$
and $a \times (b+c) = (a \times b) + (a \times c),$

only one distributive law

$$(a+b) \div c = (a \div c) + (b \div c)$$

is true for division, and that

$$a \div (b+c) \neq (a \div b) + (a \div c)$$

since division is not commutative.

records the thought-process of inverse multiplication:

5304 ÷ 4 (base ten)

Transfer 5304 to product register from setting register. Clear setting register and counter register.

Set 4 in setting register in thousands position.

Turn handle anticlockwise (Repeat until bell rings. Turn back once.)

Move carriage one place to left (4 now in hundreds position.) Turn handle repeatedly anticlockwise.

Move carriage one place to left and repeat.

5304 ÷ 4 = 1326

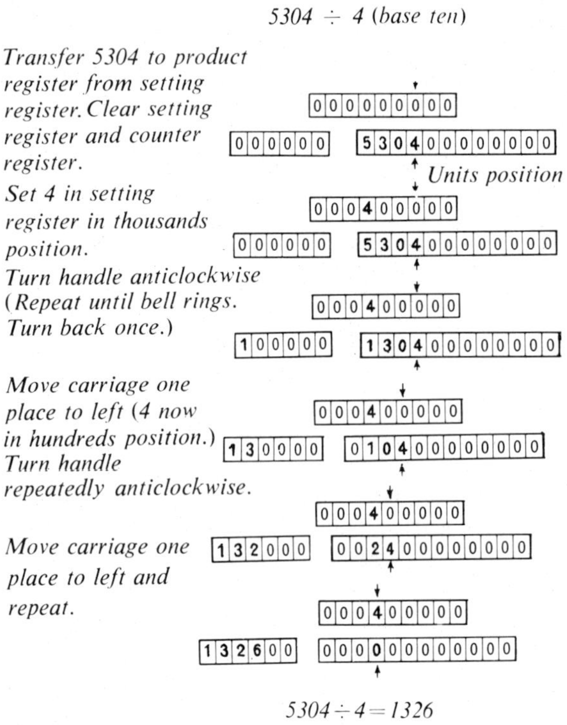

Figure 18:14

```
     1326
 4)5304
     4000      1000 × 4 = 4000
     ————
     1304
     1200       300 × 4 = 1200
     ————
      104
       80        20 × 4 =   80
      ———
       24
       24         6 × 4 =   24
       ——
        0
```

The corresponding arrangement on the calculating machine, using repeated subtraction instead of inverse multiplication is shown in Figure 18:14.

The method of long division can of course be used whether the corresponding multiplication table is known or not, but when the multiplication table is not known, children who are not using a calculating machine will need help at first in choosing the correct 'trial divisor'.

When carrying out divisions in which the multiplication table is known, children should eventually replace the 'long division' arrangement by 'short division', in which almost all the working is done mentally.

```
   1 3 2 6
4)5¹3¹0²4
```

Because multiplication can be performed so quickly on the calculating machine, and any mistake is immediately erased by turning the handle in the opposite direction, an alternative method of performing division is available. To divide 5304 by 4, that multiple of 4 which is nearest to 5304 is built up on the machine. The number 4 is set on the setting register, and the calculation proceeds as follows:

$$1000 \times 4 = 4000$$
$$2000 \times 4 = 8000 \quad \text{(too large)}$$
$$1300 \times 4 = 5200$$
$$1400 \times 4 = 5600 \quad \text{(too large)}$$
$$1320 \times 4 = 5280$$
$$1330 \times 4 = 5320 \quad \text{(too large)}$$
$$1326 \times 4 = 5304$$

This method of division will only be performed successfully when a child really understands the ordering of the numbers in order of magnitude, but it is then a quick and reliable method, and is a true inverse multiplication.

Peculiar numbers: 0 and 1

In Chapter 16 we discussed the odd behaviour of 0 in multiplication and division (see pages 149 and 154). To summarize this behaviour, for every number n

i) $n \times 0 = 0$
   Rewriting this statement as a division statement,
ii) $0 \div n = 0$, but
iii) $n \div 0$ has no value if $n \neq 0$, since there is no number which multiplied by 0 gives a non-zero answer;
iv) $0 \div 0$ may have any value, since any number multiplied by 0 gives 0.

The number 1 also has interesting multiplication properties. It is the only number which does not alter the value of any number by which it is multiplied. That is, for any number n,

$$n \times 1 = 1 \times n = n$$

In this respect, the behaviour of 1 in multiplication exactly parallels the behaviour of 0 in addition. Zero is the only number which does not change the value of any number to which it is added. That is, for any number n,

$$n + 0 = 0 + n = n$$

A number which behaves in this way is called an *identity*. The *identity for addition* is 0, since

$$n + 0 = 0 + n = n \quad \text{for all } n$$

The *identity for multiplication* is 1, since

$$n \times 1 = 1 \times n = n \quad \text{for all } n.$$

Some laws of arithmetic for the natural numbers

We have now seen that the operations of addition, subtraction, multiplication and division in the arithmetic of natural numbers are based upon the repeated application of certain laws of behaviour which are true of all the natural numbers. As these laws are fundamental, not only for elementary arithmetic, but for all further study of numbers, we conclude this chapter by summarizing the laws which addition and multiplication of natural numbers obey.

ADDITION

1 *Closure*. The set of natural numbers is closed for addition (*see page* 86).

2 *The commutative law*

$$a+b = b+a$$

(*see page* 88).

3 *The associative law*

$$(a+b)+c = a+(b+c)$$

(*see page* 90).

MULTIPLICATION

1 *Closure*. The set of natural numbers is closed for multiplication (*see page* 86).

2 *The commutative law*

$$a \times b = b \times a$$

(*see page* 145).

3 *The associative law*

$$(a \times b) \times c = a \times (b \times c)$$

(*see page* 167).

4   *The distributive laws*

$$a \times (b+c) = (a \times b) + (a \times c) \quad (\textit{see page } 164)$$
$$(a+b) \times c = (a \times c) + (b \times c) \quad (\textit{see page } 168)$$

5 *The identity*
0 is the identity for addition

$$n+0 = 0+n = n$$

(*see page* 170).

5 *The identity*
1 is the identity for multiplication

$$n \times 1 = 1 \times n = n$$

(*see page* 170).

6 *Subtraction*
Subtraction is the inverse operation of addition.

$$\boxed{x} = a-b$$

means

$$\boxed{x}+b = a$$

(*see page* 88).

6 *Division*
Division is the inverse operation of multiplication.

$$\boxed{x} = a \div b$$

means

$$\boxed{x} \times b = a$$

(*see page* 154).

In later chapters, as the set of numbers used in mathematics is extended from the natural numbers to include numbers of other types, we shall see that the above laws are retained and used, but that more extensive number systems also obey laws which are not true for the natural numbers.

Part III
Extending Ideas of Number and Space

19 The Representation of Space

Building up spatial ideas

Children show a keen interest in the spatial properties of their world. From the earliest years they notice and respond to shapes and patterns. Given opportunities of seeing pictures they quickly recognize what they are intended to represent. As we saw in Chapter 1, a child's mental life includes representing his experiences in a variety of forms. These representations may be expressed in words or symbols but they often take shape as models or drawings of things that have interested him.

In the early primary school years, children begin to take special notice of distances along roads, the slopes of hills, the shapes of aeroplanes or pylons, machines such as excavators or bicycles, and the many constructions that are so effective a part of modern life. They become familiar with new words, like orbit, gradient, and with symbols like those in Figure 19:1.

Figure 19:1

Underlying the phenomena and objects he observes a child comes to recognize structures which he tries to represent in his mind. Gradually he builds up an 'ideal space', a body of images and ideas which are somewhat loosely connected but yet serve as the mental space in which he thinks of himself as living, and within which objects are situated and movements take place. In this age of satellites and spacecraft most adults have had the experience of enlarging their own idea of space. In the child's urge to express his experiences and the relationships that he has perceived he tries to show on paper some of the shapes and movements that have struck him as significant. His drawings show at the outset (and still in imaginative drawing later on) that he is not attempting an exact copy of what he has seen but is trying to represent those features that he has particularly noticed. At about the age of 8 children have acquired a wider range of perception and greater skill of hand. They can now measure and can use instruments with more control and thus can produce fairly accurate and informative representations on paper (*see plate* 6). In turn these drawings become registered in the mind and provide the means for further thought and inquiry.

Representation in models and drawings

Three types of drawing or modelling can be distinguished in children's work.

i) A child draws quite spontaneously in response to an inner urge. The spatial relations which he shows at first are not at all precise: things are shown in the right relative positions, between or beyond, inside or outside; and their sizes are correctly related, i.e. they are bigger or smaller, but proportions are not maintained nor are objects usually shown in perspective. Gradually children acquire the capacity to draw things of such a size that distance can be inferred and of such a shape that their true shape is conveyed. But the growth is slow and the ability to show perspective is not usually seen until 9 years of age when a system of co-ordinated relations is beginning to form. Children vary considerably in their rate of development in this matter. A class of untutored African children about 7 years of age, when given crayons for the first time and told to draw what they liked, produced several pictures of a round hut with the base shown as an ellipse. Others drew a flat triangle for a hut.

ii) Long before perspective is mastered, children make drawings or models which are meant to be a record rather than a picture. A purpose directs such a representation. The child may be drawing types of aircraft or of costume, a house or a bicycle. These will have certain spatial features deliberately embodied but they will be diagrammatic and not in perspective. Figure 19:2 shows a 6-year-old child's drawing of a swimming bath.

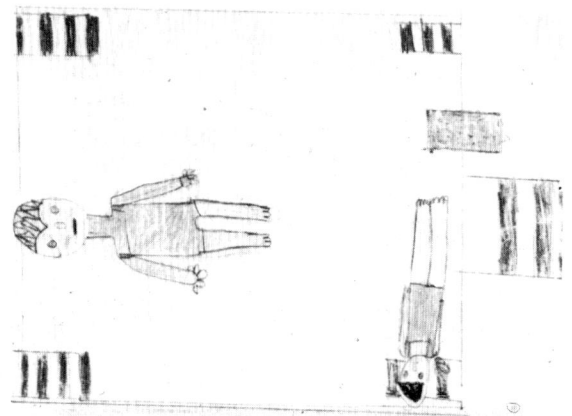

Figure 19:2

175

iii) In the third stage fairly exact copies are modelled or drawn and may actually be reproduced to scale. Experience of scale models of cars and aircraft as toys or in shop-window displays stimulate thinking about scale. The widespread use of road maps and street plans may enable a child to learn to read a map at an early age, long before he understands how it is constructed. He can put himself 'on the map' so to speak and visualize walking or driving along a road. From this point he can begin to draw a map for himself.

The desire for accuracy

Making miniature figures and objects is a very ancient art in human history and a child given plastic material will make realistic dolls, animals, lorries, etc. Yet these are not constructed with any reference to their measurements. Similarly, in early civilizations, a design or emblem was varied in size to fit the space it was to occupy. A child will also fit parts of the right size to the drawing of a given object, e.g. a door to a house; but in each case without measuring. The question we have to ask is, 'For what reasons does a child begin to seek for *accuracy* in his representations?'

As Piaget says, 'Children reconstruct their own movements or changes of position by drawing their own conceptions of the spatial field . . . as they grow in maturity the latter become increasingly co-ordinated.' When a scene or object is seen with this unity of relationships a child is ready to think about an *exact* reproduction. But why should he wish to do so? He experiences a growing dissatisfaction with drawings or models which *do not look right*. He wants to make things which are *exact enough to work*; therefore they must be structurally right and their parts must fit. To quote Piaget again, he will seek for accuracy when he wishes or 'is asked to make a construction which he recognizes sooner or later as one which demands a degree of precision that only measuring can guarantee.' He knows that for a good model the measurements must 'match' those of the original.

There are other pressures: a child wishes to communicate what he has discovered, to share it and perhaps to obtain co-operation; he also wants to convince himself that he has really mastered a problem or skill; hence the need to make a map, diagram or model. These are the motives which a teacher will use to encourage a child to develop his capacity for useful representations.

First ideas of scale

Making an accurate model or drawing requires the co-ordination of the measurements of the original with those of the model to be constructed. A child must therefore have reached the stage when he can hold in mind these

various lengths and the shapes they make. He must see the way in which the parts of the original are related to one another so that he can co-ordinate the matching parts in the model. Such a complex system of co-ordination is not easily achieved and cannot be expected before about 8 years of age. The capacity to see the relationships in increasingly complex situations develops over a period of years, making it necessary to plan courses in the representation of space for university students of engineering, architecture, etc., as well as for pupils in Junior and Secondary schools.

The way in which an attempt at representation assists children to take account of several properties of a shape at the same time was well illustrated by a small group of boys, 8 to 9 years old, who were trying to shape the roof of a Butter Cross for a class model of a medieval village. The picture from which they were working showed the roof as a square pyramid. The boys inferred that four triangles would be needed. They knew that the bases of the triangles would be horizontal when placed in position and that an edge was shared by two triangles. They therefore placed two triangles side by side, the two bases being equal and in the same straight line. A third triangle was drawn to match the second, as in Figure 19:3. At this stage the shape looked to the boys as though it would produce the correct roof.

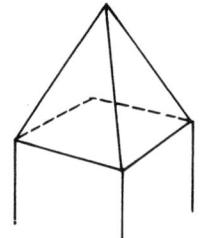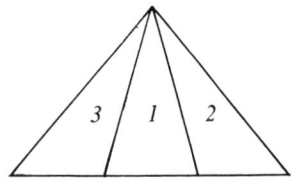

Figure 19:3

But where should they put the fourth triangle? As soon as it was drawn next to triangle 3 the discrepancy was obvious. The edges clearly would not fit. Lively discussion and renewed observation produced the realization that the triangles must all be of the same shape as well as having equal bases. Folding would then give a square base and would enable matching edges of triangles 2 and 4 to be fitted together. (Figure 19:4.)

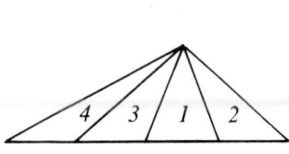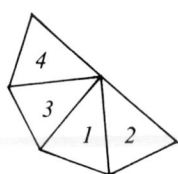

Figure 19:4

If an accurate model or drawing is to be made smaller than the original a child must realize that a short length can represent a longer one. It need not be a measured length but it must always be used for the same length of the original. Any rod or straight stick could provide the unit length. If the original has two pieces of fencing, the model must have two pieces but made from the chosen unit, as shown in Figure 19:5. This quickly leads to problems in the number relations involved.

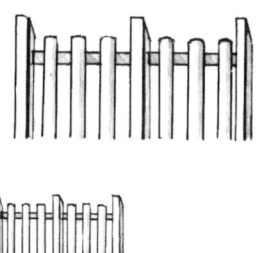

Figure 19:5

If the sticks which make the fence are smaller in the model than in the real one, how does the child know *how close* to place the sticks to make the fence look right? Children who have done much practical measuring will soon suggest some numerical relations, e.g. an 8-cm stick to represent a 16-m pole, and thus develop the idea of scale. It is essential for a child to recognize now that there is a constant relation between the lengths of corresponding sides, edges, diagonals, boundaries, etc., in the real object and in its representation. He may express the relation in various ways as we shall see on page 371, but to understand it he must have plenty of experience of handling sets of similar shapes of different size in situations where lengths need to be compared, e.g. in fitting pyramids on to prisms, or a cone into a cylinder to make a raingauge, or in projecting a drawing on to a screen. (Figure 19:6.)

In this way the early recognition of a real object seen in a picture (of which a child under two is capable) is converted into the ability to see the precise connection between two similar shapes, including an object and its model, and a site and its plan.

The first maps

A map is generally understood to mean the representation on a flat piece of paper of some part of the earth's surface. Since the earth is roughly a sphere, making a map is a very skilled mathematical feat. For a young child, not yet aware of the earth's shape, the beginning of map-making can most easily be undertaken through an attempt to record the path of a walk he has actually taken. On such a journey children receive a large number of visual impressions, a few clear and memorable, most of them vague pictures not easily recalled but recognized when the path is traversed again. The clear impressions will be of buildings or other sights which have a particular interest for children, a toyshop, a railway bridge, a garage, a bus-stop. Some other places will be linked with these special places which serve as landmarks or points of reference for the children. The whole path may not be sufficiently connected to be open to recall; only separate sections related to the landmarks will show co-ordination.

At this stage a group of children about 6 years old will draw a sketch-map of their route through their village, or along a road, showing certain bends and turnings and pictures of landmarks, all in the right order but not accurately placed. Figure 19:7 shows an example.

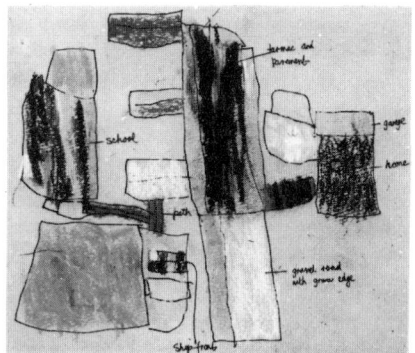

Figure 19:7 *A 6-year-old's map of the way to school*

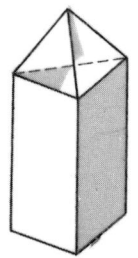  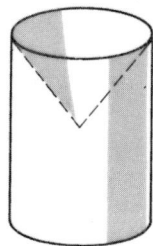  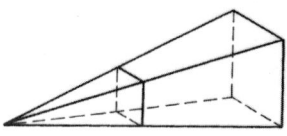

Figure 19:6

Many buildings will be omitted because they have not been truly *seen*; the child has not registered mentally what was received by sight. Between the neighbourhoods of the landmarks there will be such vagueness that even the distances cannot be estimated.

Measuring, of course, has not yet developed sufficiently to be of use. Later on, a child will be able to picture himself walking along the entire path, if it is not too long or complicated, and may even be able to give reliable instructions for a journey to school or to a bus station. The various neighbourhoods about the landmarks have become co-ordinated. With a measuring-tape or marked rope a group of children can measure distances along the road, and between turnings, and fix the position of landmarks by finding the distance from one to another. Some of the larger buildings can have their frontages measured. Notebooks should be available for the children to describe or sketch the measurements made. After the walk a 'map' of the road can be made from these measurements, the map lengths being related in an approximate way to the actual lengths by comparisons of more or less. If a length is chosen to represent the total distance, the lengths of the various sections will be gauged as parts of the whole. But at this stage it is possible that some children will suggest a simple scale such as 1 cm to 10 metres and will draw to the nearest cm or $\frac{1}{2}$ cm. If so, full use should be made of such a good opportunity. See Figure 19:8.

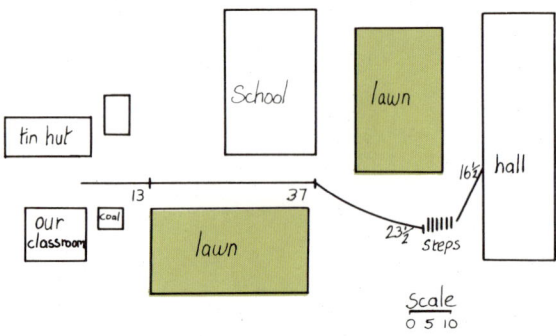

Figure 19:8

This kind of map, involving only drawing a line and marking the features seen along its length, is the easiest for a child because he can see himself as the central figure walking along the line. Various parts of the walk in which he has been interested become linked together and the whole walk is a co-ordinated structure which the map can illustrate to the child. This helps him to see the structure from an outside point of view, independent of his own actions.

The map of a region

A second type of map which children will want to draw is

more difficult because it must be based on a number of different perceptions. It is the map of a region, say a wall or floor, or an outdoor site. To make a map of this kind the child must be able to see it from outside; it cannot be simply a picture of his own movements, much as he will be helped by personal exploration. He must be aware of its shape, the nature of its boundaries, and the lengths of its bounding sides. It will help him if he has sketched the shape as he visualizes it and checked this by a comparison with the original.

The simplest example to start with is a map of a wall which he can see and whose shape he can recognize. On such a map he can place windows or door or blackboard in correct position. It is easy to draw this map on squared paper where the right angles are given and the side of a square can represent a particular actual length, e.g. 30 cm, or 3 dm (3 ten-rods).

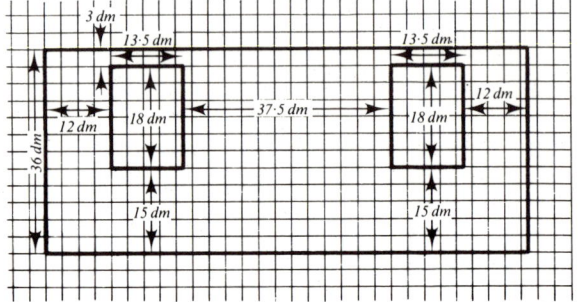

Figure 19:9

This drawing follows naturally from the measuring activities suggested in Chapter 15. It will be noticed that fixing the position of a window requires two measurements (in addition to the dimensions of the window), the distance of an edge from the end of the wall and the height of the lower edge above the floor. This is the beginning of the use of co-ordinates, where two measurements are used to fix the position of a point. (Figure 19:9.)

More difficult for a child to visualize is a horizontal region such as the floor of the classroom or part of the playground. He must picture this as seen from above, a skill which comes more easily to a child who has looked down on a site from a hill or a window, or has seen the ground from an aeroplane or looked at aerial photographs. Without such experiences he can imagine the view from above if he has explored the region and attempted to sketch it, inserting the measurements he has made. If objects are to be shown on this map in their true positions a child must be able to co-ordinate relations not only in a line, as in the map of a walk, but in two directions: before or behind, and left or right. The effort to show his own seat in the classroom or the spot in the playground where the class has placed a windvane will thus lead again to the use of co-ordinates, that is of two measured distances. (Figure 19:10.) The possible use of an angle as one of the measures is discussed in Chapter 21.

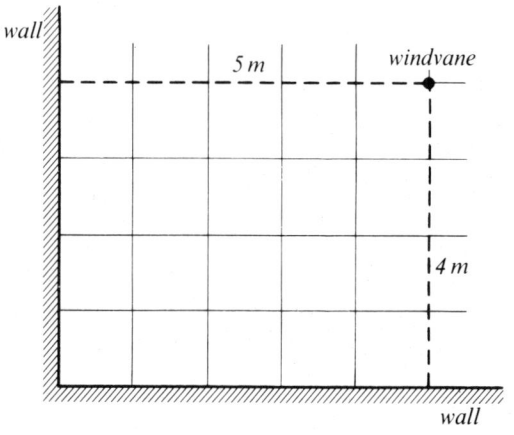

Plan of part of playground

wall

5 m   windvane

|4 m

wall

Scale:
Side of square to 1 m

Figure 19:10

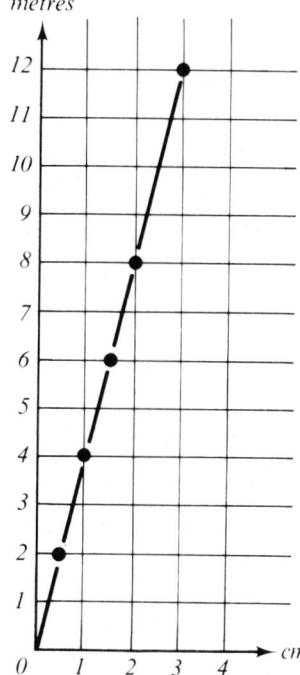

Graph to show scale 1 cm to 4 m

metres

cm

Figure 19:12

Development of scale

The informal uses of scale so far discussed have been based on the idea that one length can represent another and larger length. The selected representative length may be chosen arbitrarily and without considering its measurement. One of the Cuisenaire rods could be used, or the side of a square on squared paper, without reference to its measured length, 4 cm, 2 cm, or $1\frac{1}{2}$ cm. A small conventional unit could be chosen, such as 1 cm, to represent a larger unit, say 1 metre. But scale is not fully understood until it is seen as the ratio of a representative length to the corresponding actual length. This is brought out fully when sets of similar shapes are studied in Chapter 36. At the present stage, when maps are being drawn, the correspondence between scale length and actual length can be emphasized by tabulating the two sets of corresponding measurements. For example, a scale of 1 cm to 4 m may be shown as in Figure 19:11.

A graph could be drawn to enable scale length to be read when the actual length is known and vice versa (see Figure 19:12).

Questions about the actual reduction in size can be considered. This gives the true ratio of *actual length* to *scale length* (or vice versa); for instance, in the example shown the ratio of scale length to actual length is 1 to 400. The study of a map with scale of 1 cm to 1 km leads to numbers which a child finds surprisingly large.[1]

The other approach to the idea of the ratio of representative length to true length is through drawings of patterns and shapes reduced in size. Occasion for such drawings will be found among the stars, polygons and lattices described in Chapter 21. Copies will be made $\frac{1}{2}$ size, $\frac{1}{4}$ size and so on to fit the available space. Dimensions must be compared; the use of squared paper brings out the relationship (see Figure 19:21). Rulings in 5 cm, 2 cm,

[1] See Chapter 36, page 375.

Scale 1 cm to 4 m

Scale length in cm	1	2	3	4	$\frac{1}{2}$	$\frac{1}{4}$	$1\frac{1}{2}$	$1\frac{1}{4}$
Actual length in m	4	8	12	16	2	1	6	5

Figure 19:11

1 cm and $\frac{1}{2}$ cm squares are obtainable; a shape drawn on one ruling can readily be reproduced, enlarged or reduced, on another ruling. Comparisons of length can easily be made. In these cases the *representative fraction* can be used to state the scale. For instance, a pattern reduced from 5 cm squared paper to 1 cm squared paper would be reproduced on a scale whose representative fraction is $\frac{1}{5}$.

Growth of the use of fractions

It is customary to base the introduction of fractions on the partitioning of a shape, usually a rectangle, triangle or circle. This is discussed in Chapter 25. It is a valuable method because the equality of the parts which make the whole and the equivalence of different forms of the same fraction are so easily seen. The partitioning of a set into subsets is also splitting up of a whole into parts which may be equivalent. But a set has an integral number of elements; therefore a fraction of an integer is formed. A set of 12 cups can be arranged as 4 subsets of 3 cups. Similarly $\frac{1}{4}$ of 1 metre is $\frac{1}{4}$ of 100 cm, i.e. 25 cm. A much wider range of experience with fractions is provided by the practical situations in which measuring and representation are required. As soon as measurements are stated in fractions of a unit, say $\frac{1}{2}$ cm or $\frac{1}{4}$ metre, the operations of adding or subtracting can be carried out not by a rule which has been taught, but by using a tape or ruler to show the sum or difference required. Thus the result of adding the numbers $2\frac{1}{4}$ and $3\frac{5}{8}$ may be shown on a strip graduated in eighths of a unit to be $6\frac{3}{8}$. See Figure 19:13.

When fractions are used in scale drawings multiplication and division can be treated similarly. For example, if 1 cm represents $\frac{1}{2}$ metre, then $\frac{1}{2}$ cm can be seen to show $\frac{1}{2}$ of $\frac{1}{2}$ of a metre or $\frac{1}{4}$ metre. If $\frac{1}{2}$ cm represents 1 km then the question 'What does a length of $3\frac{1}{2}$ cm show?' is thought of as 'How many halves in $3\frac{1}{2}$?' and leads at once to the answer 7: $3\frac{1}{2}$ cm represents 7 km.

This basic practical work is the opportunity for children to use the written forms with understanding. We are concerned here with the *language* of fractions. Formal procedures for manipulating them come later. When a ratio is used to state the relation between a scale length and the actual length, the idea of a fraction is dominant. If a drawing is reduced to $\frac{3}{4}$ of the original dimensions, a tabulation of matching lengths will involve finding $\frac{3}{4}$ of each original measurement in decimal form. It will be

noticed that the decimal forms must be stated to the degree of accuracy required for drawing the graph. In the tabulation for the graph in Figure 19:14 the lengths are given correct to 1 decimal place.

Actual length in cm	6	3	2	1	4	5	10
Scale length in m	4·5	2·3	1·5	0·8	3·0	3·8	7·5

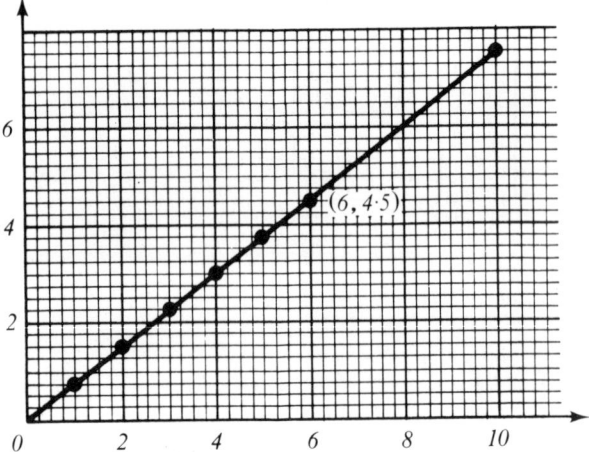

Graph to show reduction in lengths in ratio 3:4

Figure 19:14

The use of drawing instruments

Children appreciate the tools they learn to use from 7 to about 9 years of age for the increased skill and exactness they allow. But these tools are also important for the understanding to which their use can lead. The instruments may serve two purposes: they may be measuring tools, and/or instruments for use in some constructive task. For example, a ruler enables one to draw straight lines, taking the place of the less reliable fold in a sheet of paper; but if it is graduated it can be used for measuring a straight length. We will consider each instrument in turn.

(1) *The ruler.* Probably most children think of a ruler first as an instrument for measuring. They take its straightness for granted; they can use printed lines on a page when they wish to draw straight lines. They will be measuring in centimetres before they learn to hold a ruler firmly enough to draw a straight line on plain paper.

A ruler marked in centimetres is a model of part of the

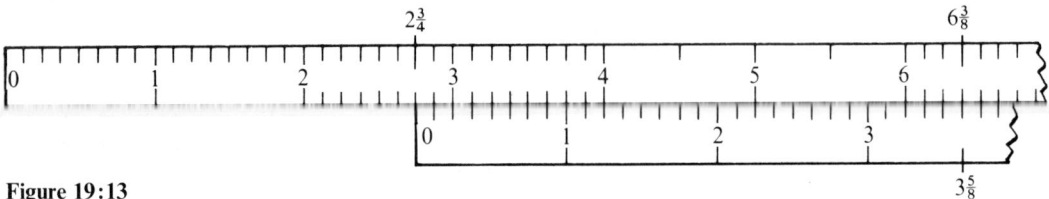

Figure 19:13

number line. A child will have used it to show addition and subtraction of whole numbers by translations along it. If it is also graduated in fractions his idea of numbers will be enlarged to include fractional numbers which can be added and subtracted in the same way as integers along the ruler. The study of the number line in a more systematic manner will follow later. Meanwhile a ruler marked in various fractions will be needed for scale drawings and will demand two skills. It can be used to measure a given length; it can also be used to mark a required scale length along a line. For example the ruler can be used to measure the width of the blackboard; on the corresponding scale drawing it will show where, on the line representing the edge of the board, the end of the board must be marked. The first skill is fairly well mastered by 7 years of age, but the second demands more precision and standards must be adjusted to the age of the child. As always, the child will be encouraged to make his measures as accurate as possible; they can never be absolute (Figure 19:15).

Measuring the blackboard

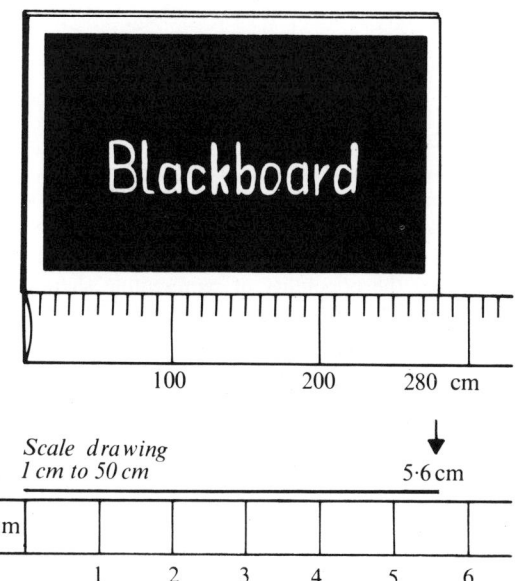

Figure 19:15

(2) *Compasses*. The set of points which constitute a circle is often drawn on the ground by children using a piece of string and chalk or a stick. Cotton or a strip of cardboard may be used for a smaller circle on paper, or a disc may be used as a template. But none of these methods gives as much accuracy or variety in drawing interesting patterns based on the circle as a pair of compasses. To children of 8 or 9 the invention and colouring of such patterns gives great pleasure; it also shows them many surprising relations between the centres and radii of circles of different sizes used in combination. As well as helping children to invent patterns, compasses have a practical function in some scale

drawings. With compasses a child can mark a length of 5·4 cm along a line with considerable accuracy, fixing the length of the radius carefully on his ruler (Figure 19:16). Drawing an equilateral triangle is a good example of what a child can now do.

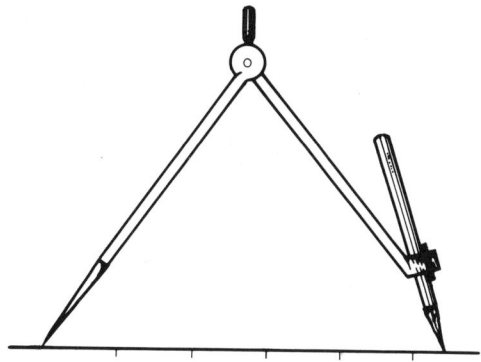

Figure 19:16

(3) *The protractor*. The clock-face with a hand marking out the rotations is usually a child's first informal protractor. At a later stage, folding a disc into 24 parts will give angles at intervals of 15°.[2] This is sufficiently exact for many of the representative drawings children wish to make at this level. Moreover, they can copy *any* angle by making a fold to match it in a disc, or half-disc. See Figure 19:17.

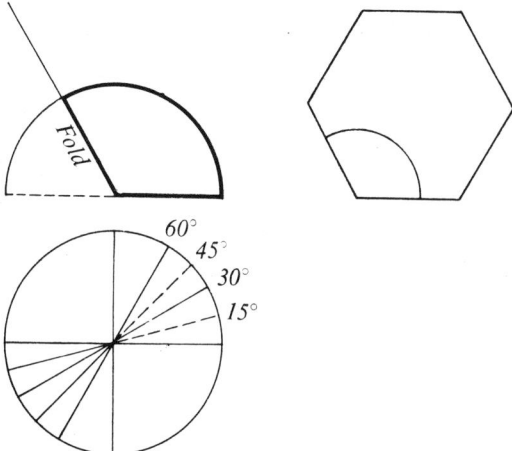

Figure 19:17

[2] See Chapter 21 and Figure 21:42 for a method of folding $\frac{1}{3}$ of a circle to give an angle of 120°.

181

Nevertheless, using a properly made tool like a plastic protractor will help a child to produce an accurate representation when the time comes for him to fix the position of a tree or other object by its directions from two points of observation (Figure 19:18).

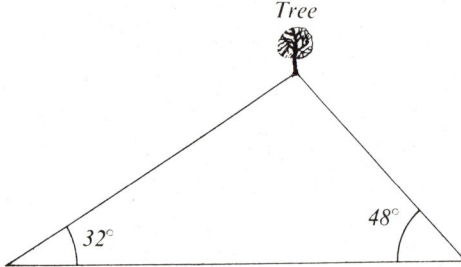

Figure 19:18

(4) *The set square.* Children first used a set square in the form of a folded paper 'corner' or right angle, such as a paper circle folded symmetrically into four parts.[3] They can use it to see whether angles are equal to, or more or less than a right angle. It can also serve to make a right angle for the corner of a square or rectangle when needed for the plan of a room, etc. The conventional instrument of wood or metal can be used constructively (though a home-made version, a half-square cut diagonally from stout card, would serve) to draw parallel lines by translating the set square along a line (Figure 19:19). This may be useful when putting parallel roads on a map, or in drawing a lattice of parallelograms. In general this kind of use belongs to the upper end of the primary school.

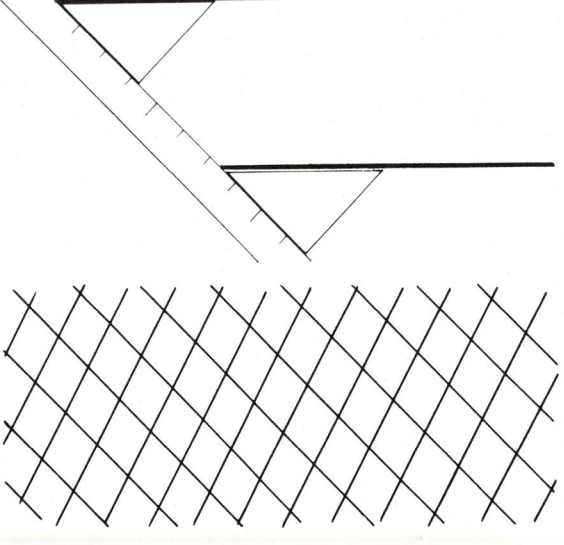

Figure 19:19

[3] See Chapter 11, page 105.

Drawing shapes and patterns

During the exploratory activities which lead to map and plan making children will notice many shapes in buildings, such as towers, windows, doorways and roofs, as well as in bridges, vehicles and machinery. Some of the shapes are regular in form and frequently used, e.g. cylinders, triangles, cuboids, parallelograms. These can be recorded in drawings; their properties can be studied, and if the shape is appropriate it can be embodied in a pattern. Less common shapes will be found, as in many church windows; they can be experimentally reproduced and similar shapes devised (Figure 19:20).

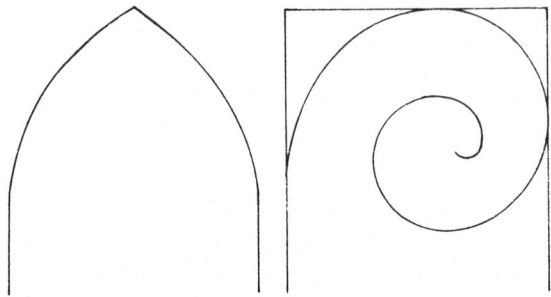

Figure 19:20

The important aspect of these experiences for children at this stage is that they develop growing awareness of the dependence of form on properties of lengths and angles. Hence comes the possibility of representing shapes accurately in models or plans through the correspondences of shapes, lines and points between the original and its representation. Drawing on squared paper brings out such relations well because an all-over square pattern can be seen in terms of squares, lines or points, as Figure 19:21 shows. The different relations are emphasized by the kind of representation selected.

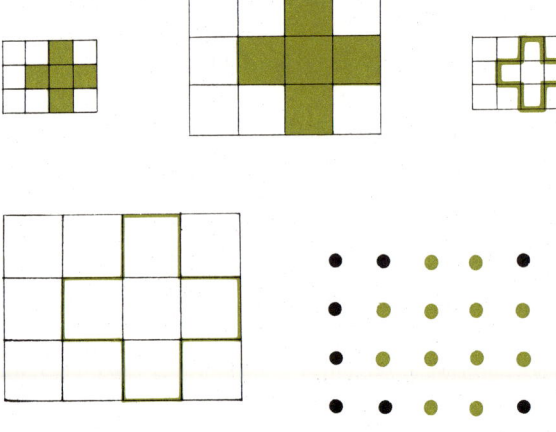

Figure 19:21

20 Numbers between the Natural Numbers

The number line

Many of the physical representations of number which children use at the concrete-operational stage of thinking use lengths as models for numbers. Among the more important representations of numbers are

  i) the ruler or the tape-measure,
 ii) types of structural apparatus such as Cuisenaire or Stern, and
iii) the labelling of an axis of a graph with numbers.

As a child grows older, his idea of how numbers are represented on a ruler changes, and the type of ruler which he can handle changes to match his evolving ideas. Length is becoming a *continuous quantity,* rather than a number of separate units.

The distinction between the measurement of continuous quantities and the counting of discontinuous individual units is a very important one. Whole numbers of units can never be good enough for the measurement of continuous quantities such as length, mass, time or volume. A child may balance a book by putting it in one pan of a balance and putting a number of individual ten-gram masses in the other pan. Unless he has been most extraordinarily lucky in his book, or unless his balance is very insensitive, he will find that, for instance, 150 grams do not tip the scale, but 160 grams send it down heavily. The difference of 10 grams between successive masses is too great. The same is true of length, time, capacity, area, volume, temperature, air-pressure, and all the other continuous quantities which we attempt to measure. The difference between successive units, however small they may be, is always too large for total accuracy, so that completely accurate measurement must always be impossible.

Eventually, through much experience of measuring and of graduating their own measures, children visualize a continuously increasing scale of length, mass or capacity, containing some isolated landmarks which represent the units. The ruler, the kitchen scales, and the graduated measuring jug all show units as isolated landmarks on a continuous scale of measurement (Figure 20:1).

As a result of these experiences a number comes to correspond in a child's mind not only to a set of things, but also to a measurement, and so to a *point on a number line.* The one-unit marks on a ruler have come to represent numbers.

The same development in the representation of numbers is shown in a change in children's graphical work. The earliest graphs are always picture or block graphs, in which a number is represented by a number of unit blocks which can be counted (Figure 20:2(a)); but block graphs are later supplemented by line graphs such as Figure 20:2(b), in which numbers are represented by equally spaced points on the axes.

In such line graphs as Figure 20:2(b), *interpolation* becomes possible. A child who has used the graph to find how many twos there are in 16 may then try to use it to find out how many twos there are in 17, arriving at a point on the horizontal axis half-way between that which represents 8 and that which represents 9 (Figure 20:3). Interpolation is not possible on a block graph; there is nothing between the block which represents 8 and that which represents 9.

(a) *Graph to show number of balls which each class has.*

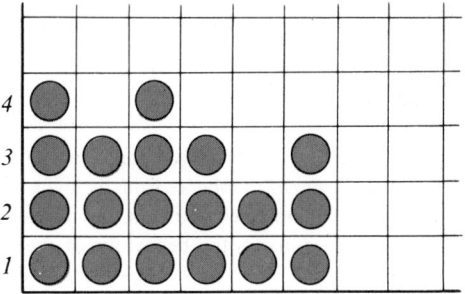

(b) *Graph of multiples of 2.*

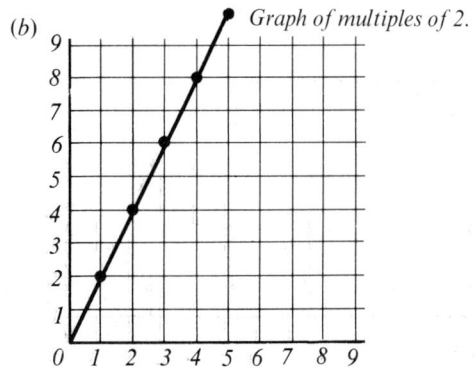

Figure 20:1

Figure 20:2

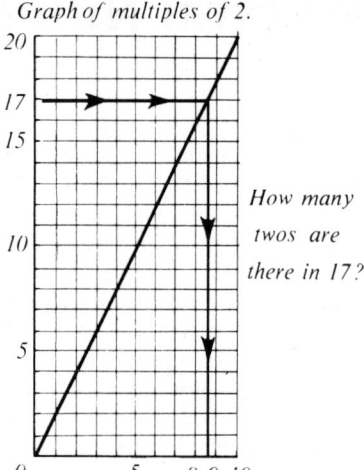

Graph of multiples of 2.

How many twos are there in 17?

Figure 20:3

In such ways the representation of the natural numbers by equally spaced points on a number line takes shape, and with it comes the realization that there are other numbers as well as the natural numbers, and that these other numbers also will correspond to points on the number line.

The number line shown in Figure 20:4 begins to be seen as *representing* a continuously increasing range of numbers, among which is a sequence of equally spaced landmarks, corresponding to the natural numbers. Between these can be placed other numbers, the fractions.

Isomorphism

In what sense can the equally spaced points on the number line be said to *represent* numbers? Equally spaced points on a line are not themselves numbers, but the structure of points on a line mirrors the behaviour of the natural numbers in some of their most important properties,

provided that we think of the line as extending without limit in one direction.

The first such property is that both the natural numbers and the spaced points on a line have an *order*. Each natural number except 0 has unique *neighbours*; 4 has 3 on one side of it and 5 on the other side.[2] Corresponding to this property of natural numbers, each spaced point on the line except for the starting point of the half-line also has a neighbouring spaced point on each side of it. After any natural number, however large it may be, there is always a *next* natural number; to the right of any point of the line, however far from the starting point of the half-line it may be, there is always a *next* spaced point. These two properties enable the *one-to-one correspondence* shown in Figure 20:5 to be set up between the set of natural numbers and the set of spaced points, so that neighbouring natural numbers always correspond to neighbouring points, and the larger of two numbers always corresponds to the right-hand member of a pair of points.

The one-to-one correspondence which has been set up also mirrors the structure of the addition and subtraction of natural numbers by a structure of addition and subtraction on the number line. The structure of addition and subtraction of vector lengths in the same direction along a line is identical with the structure of addition and subtraction for natural numbers derived from sets of things.

(5 cm to the right) + (3 cm to the right)
= (8 cm to the right)
For numbers $5 + 3 = 8$

When subtraction is seen as inverse addition, the correspondence would be:

(5 cm to the right) + ☐
= (8 cm to the right)
For numbers $5 + ☐ = 8$

The correspondence is exact: in the first equation, the

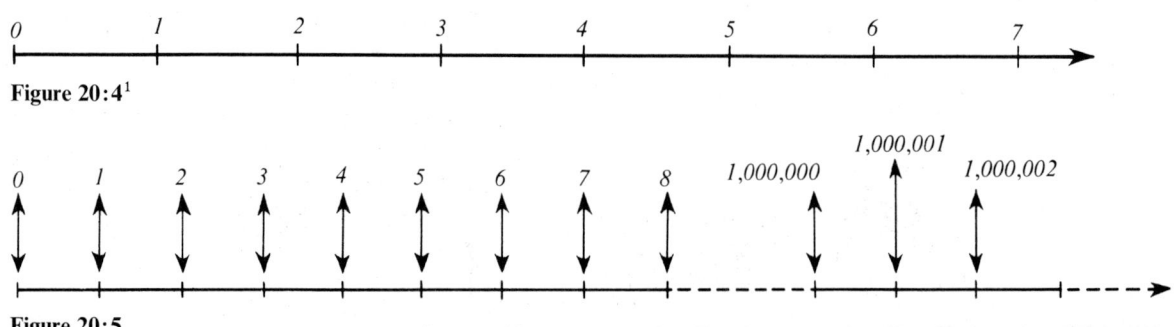

Figure 20:4[1]

Figure 20:5

[1] This 'line' is in fact a *half-line* or *ray*, starting from the point 0 and extending without limit in one direction.

[2] 0 has only one neighbour, the number 1.

184

vector *3 centimetres to the right* fills the empty space, and in the second equation the corresponding number 3 fills the empty space. The structure of the addition and subtraction of vectors measured along the number line is identical with the structure of addition and subtraction of natural numbers.

There are some addition and subtraction structures which do not behave in the same way as these. On the clock, for instance, 5 hours after 8 o'clock the time is 1 o'clock. Symbolically

$$8 + 5 = 1$$

But in the arithmetic of natural numbers,

$$8 + 5 = 13$$

so that it is not possible to set up a one-to-one correspondence between clock numbers and natural numbers which preserves the structure of addition (*see page* 437).

Because the structures of the natural numbers and of lengths on a line are identical, either can be used as an image or model of the other, and children often make this transference. A child replaces one structure by the other when he uses a tape-measure or structural apparatus[3] to find the answer to

15 marbles + 17 marbles,

or when he counts on his fingers to find the answer to

7 centimetres + 6 centimetres.

Two structures which behave in exactly the same way so that the results of operations such as additions and subtractions correspond are said to be *isomorphic*.[4] Isomorphic structures are used in mathematics whenever a real situation is replaced by a model like structural apparatus, or by a mental model like the natural numbers. The addition and subtraction of natural numbers is isomorphic with the addition and subtraction of lengths, or masses, or the rods of structural apparatus, but there are other structures, such as the addition of hours on the clock, with which the addition of natural numbers is not isomorphic. It would be foolish to pretend that a two-rod of structural apparatus *is* the number 2, or that placing a two-rod end to end with a three-rod *is* the addition of the abstract natural numbers 2 and 3, but the two structures are isomorphic, so that the concrete structure can be used as a very satisfactory model of the abstract one, or indeed of other concrete structures, like

2 kilograms + 3 kilograms

---

[3] Since structural apparatus uses length as a model of number, its structure is the same as that of the tape-measure.

[4] *Noun*: isomorphism. From Greek ισος (isos) equal, and μορφε (morphe) form, structure, as in *isosceles* (equal sides) and *morphology* (the science of form).

Thus children develop the idea that the number line, or its concrete embodiments the tape-measure and the axis of a graph, are models whose structure is isomorphic with the structure of the natural numbers. Of course children do not consciously formulate the isomorphism, but it is certainly present.

Zero on the number line

As the idea of the number line develops in a child's mind, zero takes a more satisfactory place among the

(*a*)   *Number of children wearing jerseys*

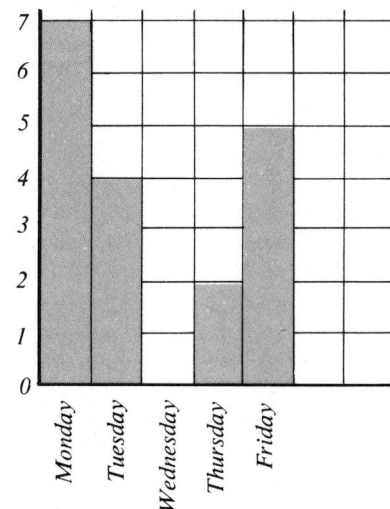

(*b*)   *Graph of two times table*

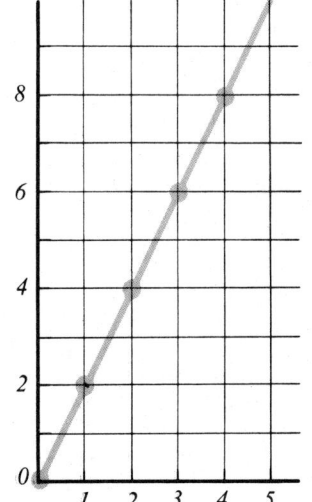

$$2 \times 0 = 0$$
$$2 \times 1 = 2$$
$$2 \times 2 = 4$$
$$2 \times 3 = 6$$
etc.

Figure 20:6

185

numbers than it has hitherto held. Measurement forwards and backwards with a tape-measure gives such results as

$$(7\,\text{cm}) - (7\,\text{cm}) = (0\,\text{cm}),$$

and so 0 becomes the label for the starting point of the number line, and is a number like other numbers (which are also labels for points on the number line) rather than a symbol for the absence of number, which it may previously have been. The same change in the status of zero is seen in graphical work. In the graph of the number of children wearing jerseys, shown in Figure 20:6(*a*), zero is a symbol which to the child may stand for the absence of any children wearing jerseys, but it is also the label of the starting point of the number line. When the child has reached the stage shown in Figure 20:6(*b*), $2 \times 0 = 0$ has taken its place alongside $2 \times 1 = 2$ and $2 \times 2 = 4$, and zero has become a number which is symbolized on the number line in the same way that other numbers are symbolized.

The appearance of fractions

The two structures of equally spaced points on the number line and of the natural numbers are isomorphic, but the number line has some additional features which do not mirror the structure of the natural numbers. Two of these features point the way towards extensions of the number system from natural numbers to new types of number.

i) The set of natural numbers extends without limit to give larger and larger natural numbers, which are represented by points at an increasing distance from the starting point of the number line. But a line can be extended in both directions. The usual idea of a line is not of the half-line with a starting point:

but of a line which can be produced in either direction:

This property of a line suggests the extension of the number system to the positive and negative directed numbers, which usually come into a child's experience at a fairly late stage. They will be discussed in Chapter 32.[5]

ii) There is no natural number between, for instance, 3 and 4, but there are many points on the number line between the point which represents 3 and that which represents 4. Filling in some of these spaces on the number line corresponds to the introduction of fractions into the number system.

Ways in which children gain their early experience of fractions have been discussed in Chapter 19, and will be developed further in Chapter 25. Here we shall be concerned with some aspects of the concept of a fraction, with the interlocking of these aspects, and with setting fractions in their places on the number line.

Parts of a divisible unit

Some units can be divided into parts, some cannot. We never halve a child, a dog, a balloon or a glass marble, but a cake, a metre, a litre or an hour can be divided into parts of any size. The units of continuous quantities such as length or mass or time can always be divided into parts, but discontinuous separate units such as people or things usually cannot. In their work in folding and cutting shapes into parts and in weighing, measuring liquids, measuring lengths and telling the time, children gain experience of units which can be divided into parts, and learn the names and the symbols for the simpler fractions of a unit, such as the half, quarter and third. They also learn that, if the names of the fractions are to be used correctly, the unit must be divided, not merely into a number of parts, but into a number of *equal* parts (Figure 20:7). At first, the equality of the parts will be checked by folding or cutting and fitting them over one another, or, in the case of masses, by balancing them against one another, or for volumes, by seeing that they reach the same level in equal measuring jars. After some experience of making fractions of different things, and of recording the fractions which they have made, children come to realize that when a fraction such as $\frac{3}{4}$ is named, the bottom number or *denominator* of the fraction shows or denominates the number of equal parts into which the unit has been divided, and the top number or *numerator* shows the number of those parts which are being considered. In the fraction $\frac{3}{4}$, a unit has been divided into 4 equal parts, and 3 of these parts are being considered (Figure 20:8). When decimal notation is used, the number of parts into which the unit is divided is not written, but children need to know that 0·7 shows that the unit is divided into 10 equal parts, and that 7 of them are considered.

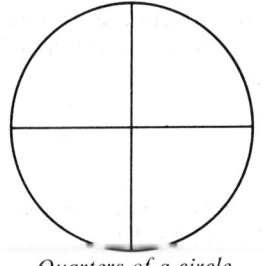 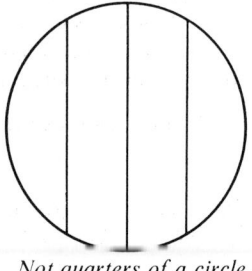

Quarters of a circle.   *Not quarters of a circle.*

Figure 20:7

[5] This order of presentation is arbitrary, and it seems natural for children to meet directed numbers at an earlier stage than they usually do at present.

Some concrete embodiments of $\frac{3}{4}$ and 0·7

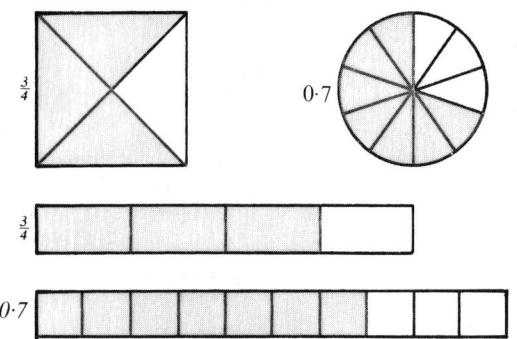

Figure 20:8

It is also important that children should realize that $\frac{3}{4}$ is always three quarters of *some unit* or *whole*, and that $\frac{3}{4}$ will appear in many different forms according to the unit to which it is referred. A fraction only exists in relation to its unit. The shaded area in Figure 20:9, taken by itself consists of 3 squares. If the shaded area is related to the square (*b*) as unit, it is $\frac{3}{4}$ of square (*b*), but if it is related to the rectangle (*c*) as unit, the shaded area is $\frac{1}{2}$ of rectangle (*c*). Similarly, a decimal fraction has many concrete embodiments in relation to different units. Thus, 0·7 may be represented by 7 decimetres in relation to a metre, or by 7 centimetres in relation to a decimetre, or by 7 tenpenny pieces in relation to a £1 note.

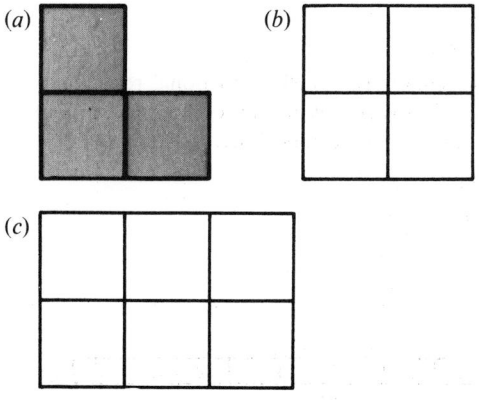

Figure 20:9

The unit is a fraction of itself: it may be visualized as 4 quarters of itself, or 10 tenths of itself. A quantity which is larger than the unit may also be described as a fraction of the unit. In Figure 20:10 each rod is a fraction of the

unit rod, although one of the rods is longer than the unit rod.

There are two numbers essential to describing any fraction, the numerator and the denominator. In order to know the value of a fraction like $\frac{3}{4}$, we need to know that it is built up from 3 and 4; that is, the fraction is built up by using the *ordered pair* of whole numbers 3 and 4, by using the first number as numerator and the second as denominator. The pair of whole numbers used to build a fraction is *ordered*, as the fraction $\frac{4}{3}$ built from 4 and 3 is different from the fraction $\frac{3}{4}$ built from 3 and 4. In later mathematics, this aspect of a fraction as an *ordered pair* of integers or whole numbers becomes increasingly important. New types of numbers are often built up from ordered pairs of numbers of a type already known.

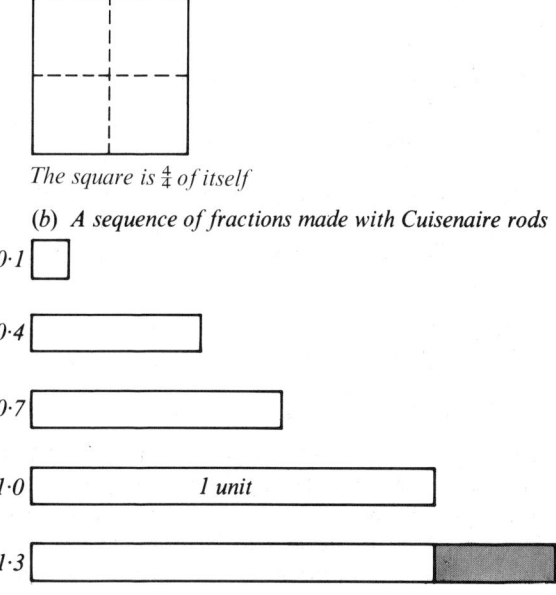

(a) The unit

The square is $\frac{4}{4}$ of itself

(b) A sequence of fractions made with Cuisenaire rods

Figure 20:10

When we use decimal notation, the second number of the pair, or the denominator of the fraction, has to be supplied from our knowledge of the number system. For example, 0·7 is the same number as $\frac{7}{10}$, and so is built up from the ordered pair of integers 7 and 10. Similarly, 1·7 is 17 tenths, and is built up from the ordered pair (17, 10). The decimal fraction 0·23 is 23 hundredths, and so is built up from (23, 100).

Fractions, multiplication and division

Representations of $\frac{1}{3}$ as part of some unit, using structural apparatus, are closely related to the arrangements of rods which children make when they use structural apparatus to

187

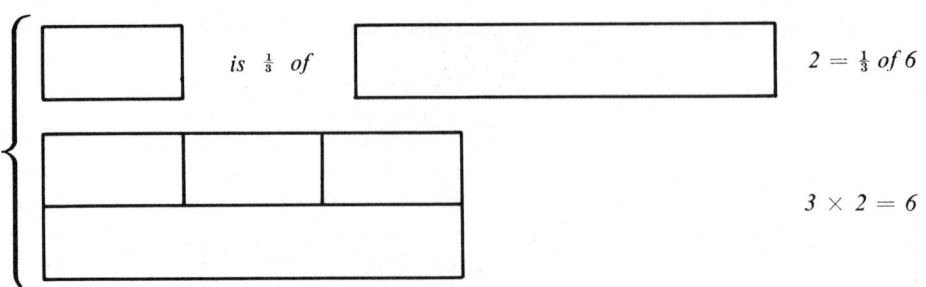

$$2 = \tfrac{1}{3} \text{ of } 6$$

$$3 \times 2 = 6$$

Figure 20:11

multiply natural numbers. If a child needs to discover $\tfrac{1}{3}$ of 6, he will have to find which rod repeated 3 times makes up 6 (Figure 20:11), so building a multiplication situation.

The operation of *finding a third of* a number is the inverse of the operation of *finding three times* as much as a number; that is, it is the inverse of multiplying by 3. The statement

$$\tfrac{1}{3} \text{ of } 6 = 2$$

is equivalent to

$$3 \times 2 = 6$$

and another way of putting, 'Find $\tfrac{1}{3}$ of 6' is 'Find the number n such that $3 \times \boxed{n} = 6$.' We said earlier that the operation inverse to multiplication was division, and we rewrote

$$3 \times \boxed{n} = 6$$

as

$$\boxed{n} = 6 \div 3$$

But the operation of dividing a quantity into 3 equal parts and the operation of finding $\tfrac{1}{3}$ of that quantity are clearly only different descriptions of the same process.[6] The graph of 'three times as much' shown in Figure 20:12 could equally well be described by saying that the grey columns are $\tfrac{1}{3}$ *of* the outline columns,[7] or that the outline columns have been *divided by 3* to produce the grey columns. Children should use the language of fractions and decimals alongside the language of division from the first to describe the relationship between a part and its whole or unit. Any of the relationships shown in Figure 20:12 can be described, and children should be accustomed to describing it, in three ways. For instance:

$$3 \times 5 = 15$$
$$\tfrac{1}{3} \text{ of } 15 = 5$$
$$15 \div 3 = 5$$

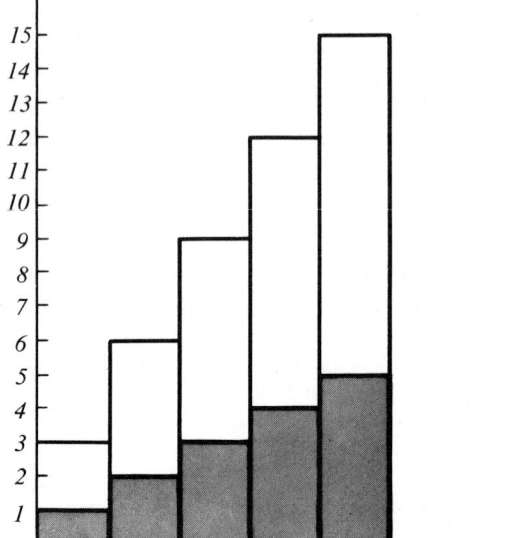

Each outline column is 3 times the grey column
Each grey column is $\tfrac{1}{3}$ of the outline column.
Each outline column is divided by 3 to produce the grey column.

Figure 20:12

Decimal representations as well as fractional representations should be used when they are appropriate, as in Figure 20:13 where the situation can be described by any of

$$10 \times 2 = 20$$
$$0 \cdot 1 \text{ of } 20 = 2$$
$$20 \div 10 = 2$$

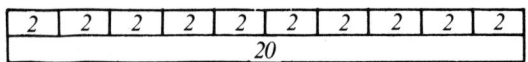

Figure 20:13

As children's experience widens, they will find that the fractional method of describing the relationship between two quantities can be used in situations where a multi-

[6] The aspect of division used here is 'sharing' (*see page* 151).

[7] Cf. page 146.

plication or division relationship cannot so easily be used. The relation between the shaded area and the whole rectangle in Figure 20:14 cannot be expressed directly by a single multiplication or division statement.

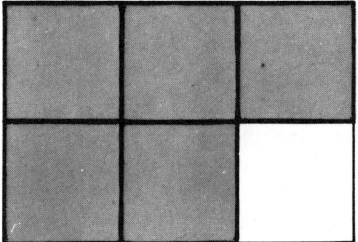

Figure 20:14

But fractions can be used to express this relation in two ways:

i) the shaded area $= \frac{5}{6}$ of the rectangle, or
ii) the rectangle $= \frac{6}{5}$ of the shaded area.

The second statement is obtained by thinking of the shaded area, which consists of 5 squares, as the *unit*, and expressing the relationship of the rectangle consisting of 6 squares to the unit of 5 squares.

The division of a unit into a number of equal parts can always be expressed in terms of a fraction whose numerator is 1. 'Divide by 6' and 'take $\frac{1}{6}$ of' mean the same. If this were the only idea which a fraction could express, the fraction notation would have very little advantage over the division notation, but 'take $\frac{5}{6}$ of' is a considerable extension of this idea, and it can only be expressed conveniently by using fractional language.[8]

Fractions as ratios

We have seen that a fraction expresses a relationship, or *ratio*, between two quantities. The fraction $\frac{5}{6}$ represents any of the relationships shown in Figure 20:15, and many others as well.

[8] The ancient Egyptians could only work in terms of fractions whose numerators were 1. They wrote, for example, $\frac{4}{5}$ as $\frac{1}{2} + \frac{1}{4} + \frac{1}{20}$.

$\frac{5}{6}$ *is the relation between:*

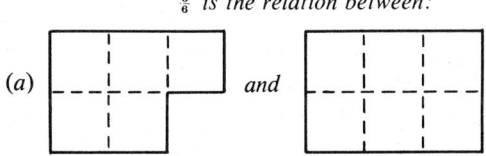

Figure 20:15

Figure 20:16

This *ratio* aspect of the fraction concept deserves more attention than it often receives. Children, for instance, often see $\frac{3}{4}$ kg of sugar as three separate packets or units, each of which weighs a quarter of a kg, without thinking of the relationship of $\frac{3}{4}$ kg to 1 kg, or of 3 packets to 4 packets. Understanding that the ratio or relationship of lengths is the same in each of the four pairs of rods shown in Figure 20:16 needs considerable insight, which often does not develop until fairly late.

This is possibly because children are asked so often to make comparisons between quantities in terms of the *difference* between them, rather than in terms of their *ratio*. Both methods of comparison are valid and useful in different circumstances. Two sets of comparisons between the crimson and dark-green Cuisenaire rods are shown in Figure 20:17, those based on the ideas of sum and difference, and those based on the ideas of fraction and ratio.

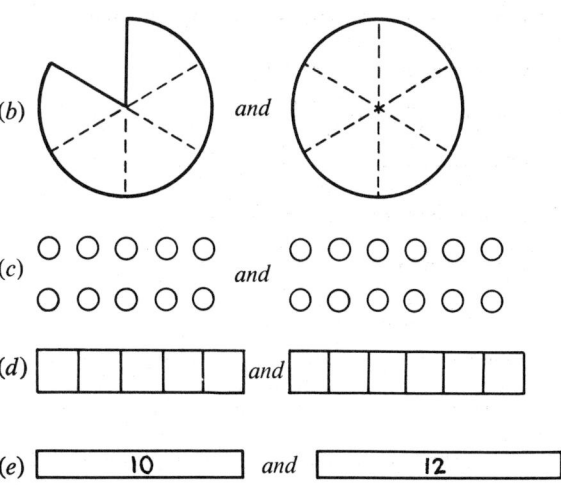

189

Comparison of length based on

difference	ratio
	For these rods:
$6 - 4 = 2$	*crimson rod* $= \frac{2}{3}$ *of (dark green rod)*
$4 + 2 = 6$	*dark-green rod* $= \frac{3}{2}$ *of (crimson rod)*
	crimson rod : dark-green rod $= 2 : 3$
	$\dfrac{crimson\ rod}{dark\text{-}green\ rod} = \dfrac{2}{3}$
	dark-green rod : crimson rod $= 3 : 2$
	$\dfrac{dark\text{-}green\ rod}{crimson\ rod} = \dfrac{3}{2}$

Figure 20:17[9]

Fractions on the number line

As children make and examine fractions, they will begin to compare the relative sizes of fractions *of the same unit*. Clearly

$$\tfrac{1}{2} > \tfrac{1}{3} > \tfrac{1}{4} > \tfrac{1}{5} > \ldots$$

since in each case the same unit has been cut into 2 equal parts, 3 equal parts, 4 equal parts, 5 equal parts, ... so that at each step the size of the parts decreases. Figure 20:18 shows two illustrations of this property, the unit being a circle in (*a*), and the length of a line in (*b*).

Children need to become consciously aware of the fact that, for instance, $\tfrac{1}{3} > \tfrac{1}{4}$, since they already know very thoroughly that $4 > 3$, and hence often seem to expect, when they have written down the two fractions that $\tfrac{1}{4}$ will be greater than $\tfrac{1}{3}$, and that they will be able to perform

[9]The sign : indicates ratio. This statement reads, 'the ratio of the dark-green to the crimson rod is equal to the ratio of the number 2 to the number 3'. The sentence $\dfrac{crimson\ rod}{dark\text{-}green\ rod} = \dfrac{2}{3}$ is an alternative way of writing the same statement, and expresses the ratio in a fractional form.

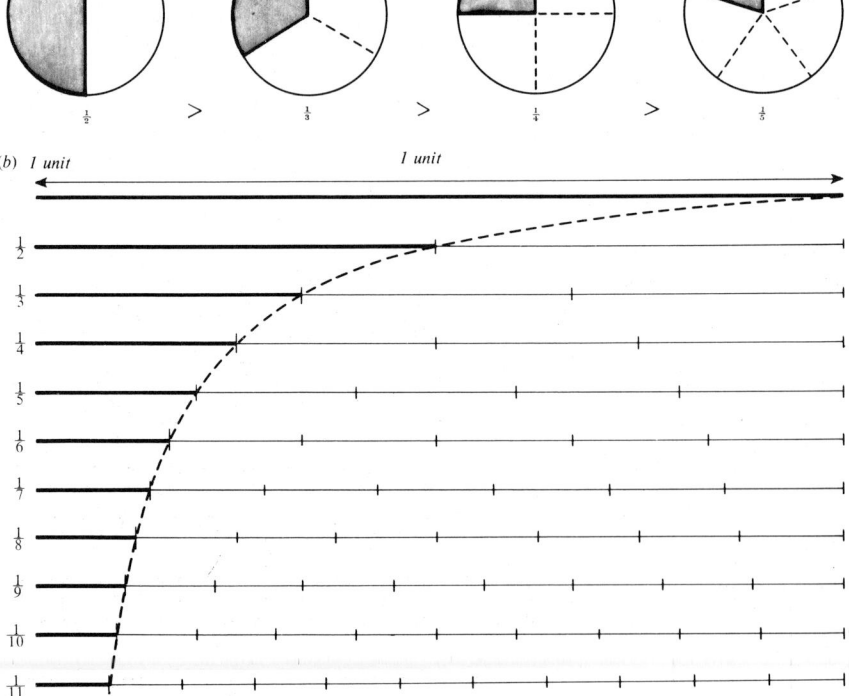

Figure 20:18

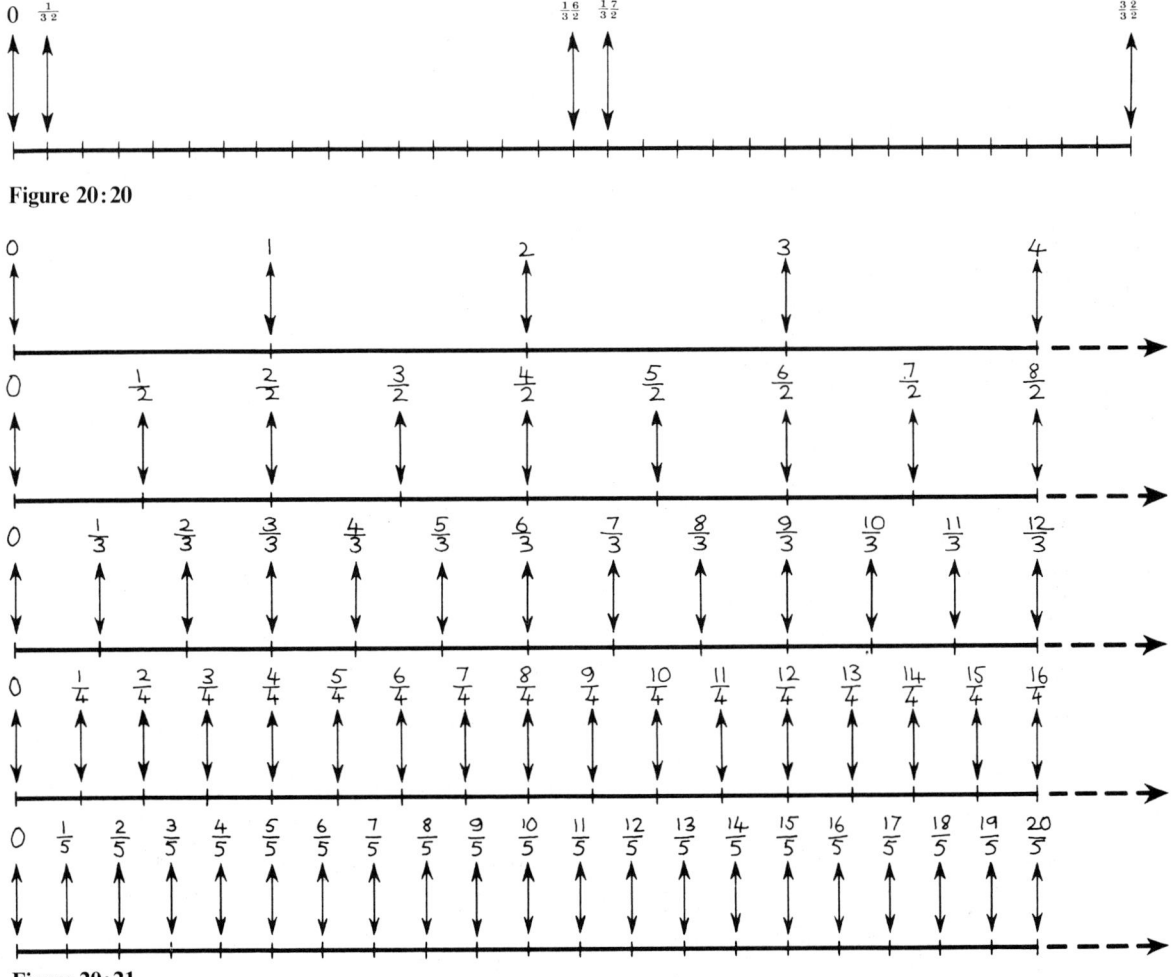

Figure 20:19[10]

such an operation as $\frac{1}{4} - \frac{1}{3}$. Frequent reference to a real situation prevents misunderstandings of this sort.

We can further illustrate the relative sizes of different fractions by superimposing the separate lines of Figure 20:18(b), forming a diagram which we have begun to build up in Figure 20:19.

The diagram sets up a one-to-one correspondence between the set of fractions between 0 and 1 inclusive and a set of points on a segment[11] of unit length. Every possible fraction between 0 and 1 can be made to correspond to a point of the segment. To obtain the point corresponding for instance to the fraction $\frac{17}{32}$, the unit line is divided into 32 equal parts, and the end-points of these divisions are put into one-to-one correspondence with the fractions

$$\tfrac{1}{32}, \tfrac{2}{32}, \tfrac{3}{32}, \ldots \tfrac{16}{32}, \tfrac{17}{32}, \ldots \tfrac{32}{32} \ (=1). \text{ (Figure 20:20.)}$$

This segment can be regarded as that part of the number line consisting of the points corresponding to the numbers 0 and 1, and the points between them. If the same process is applied to the whole of the number line, not only those fractions between 0 and 1, but all fractions can be put into correspondence with points of the number line. In Figure 20:21 this process is shown for part of the number line.

Figure 20:20

Figure 20:21

[10] It is of course impossible to show, in any physical diagram, more than a small selection of the fractions between 0 and 1.

[11] A *segment of the line* is part of a line consisting of two *end-points* and every point of the line *between* the end-points.

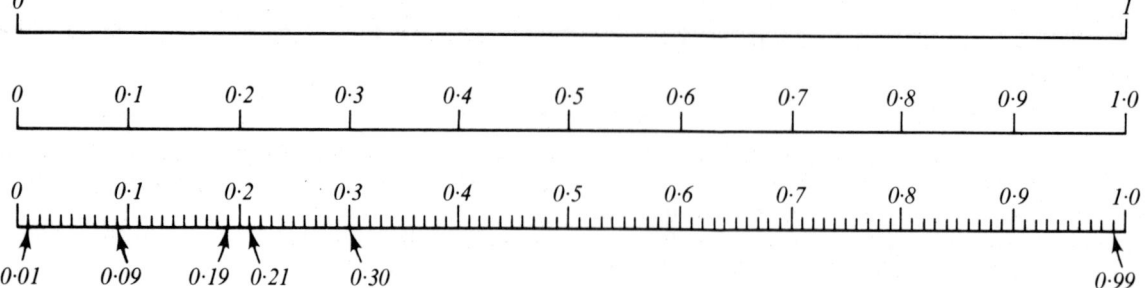

Figure 20:22

For convenience, the points corresponding to halves, thirds, quarters... are shown on separate lines, but it is then possible to visualize all these lines on top of one another to form a complete number line. On this line, *any* fraction will correspond to a definite point on the line.

The point of the number line which is made to correspond to the fraction $\frac{1}{2}$ in the second line of Figure 20:21 also corresponds to the fraction $\frac{2}{4}$, the fraction $\frac{3}{6}$ and so on. But $\frac{1}{2} = \frac{2}{4} = \frac{3}{6} = \frac{4}{8} = \ldots$, and $\frac{1}{2}, \frac{2}{4}, \frac{3}{6}, \ldots$ are different names for the same fraction or ratio. Hence every possible fraction has a unique point on the number line corresponding to it.

The decimal system of notation gives another important illustration of the principle that smaller and smaller subdivisions of a unit of the number line correspond to fractions (Figure 20:22).

The unit is first divided into ten equal parts, so that the points of division represent $0.1, 0.2, \ldots, 0.9$. Each of these parts is divided again into ten equal parts, and the points of division correspond, for instance, to 0.21, $0.22, \ldots, 0.29$. This process can, of course, be repeated indefinitely.

The number line has become very much more tightly packed with numbers since, in our earliest description of it, only points corresponding to the natural numbers had any meaning. Now there is a point on the number line corresponding to each one of the *doubly infinite array* of numbers:

1	2	3	4	5	6	.	.	.
$\frac{1}{2}$	$\frac{2}{2}$	$\frac{3}{2}$	$\frac{4}{2}$	$\frac{5}{2}$	$\frac{6}{2}$	.	.	.
$\frac{1}{3}$	$\frac{2}{3}$	$\frac{3}{3}$	$\frac{4}{3}$	$\frac{5}{3}$	$\frac{6}{3}$	.	.	.
$\frac{1}{4}$	$\frac{2}{4}$	$\frac{3}{4}$	$\frac{4}{4}$	$\frac{5}{4}$	$\frac{6}{4}$	.	.	.
.	.	.	.	.	.	.	.	.
.	.	.	.	.	.	.	.	.
.	.	.	.	.	.	.	.	.

That the number line is packed with fractions is implicit in a child's mind when he tries to interpolate in such a graph as Figure 20:23 in order to find a number whose square is 29 (*see page* 386). If he has drawn the graph on a fairly small scale he will probably give his result as approximately 5.4; if the scale of his graph is larger he may be able to estimate 5.38. At this stage a child is prepared to think of the same unit as divided up into 10, or 8, or any other convenient number of equal parts. He has implicitly reached a correspondence between the set of all possible fractions and a set of points on the number line, although this correspondence may not be explicitly expressed until the secondary stage.[12]

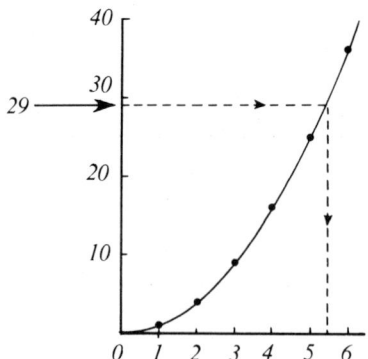

Figure 20:23

A part of several units

We now discuss another aspect of the concept of a fraction, which must be integrated with the aspects previously described if children are to have a full appreciation of fractions. The fraction $\frac{2}{3}$ has been presented as:

i) 2 out of 3 equal parts of some unit, and
ii) the ratio or relationship between 2 units and 3 units.

---

[12] It will be noticed that the correspondence has been described as being between *all possible* fractions and *a set of* points on the number line, not *all possible points* on the number line. This leads to a further generalization of the idea of number. See Chapter 40.

The fraction $\frac{2}{3}$ is also the result of dividing *two units* by 3, that is, of taking $\frac{1}{3}$ of 2 units. Figure 20:24 shows, on a number line, $\frac{1}{3}$ of 2 units and $\frac{2}{3}$ of 1 unit. The reason for the equality of the results is not very easily seen from this diagram, but a rearrangement of the units will make the reason clear. In order to obtain $\frac{1}{3}$ of 2 units, a simple method is to find $\frac{1}{3}$ of *each* unit and combine the results. If 2 cakes are to be shared between 3 people it is usually simplest to give each person $\frac{1}{3}$ of each

cake. Figure 20:25 illustrates this, and also shows the application of the same idea to the length shown in Figure 20:24.

The process of finding $\frac{1}{3}$ of 2 units can be symbolized by $2 \div 3$ in the same way as the process of finding $\frac{1}{3}$ of 6 units can be symbolized as $6 \div 3$. When 6 is to be divided by 3, if the units can be broken up the operation can be performed by dividing each of the 6 units into 3 equal parts, and then re-combining the 6 thirds of a unit to make 2 complete units (Figure 20:26).

It is clear that all the following phrases are equivalent, and that the same operation has been described in several ways:

$$6 \div 3 = \tfrac{1}{3} \text{ of } 6 = 6 \text{ thirds} = \tfrac{6}{3} = 2$$

Similarly, from Figure 20:25:

$$2 \div 3 = \tfrac{1}{3} \text{ of } 2 = 2 \text{ thirds} = \tfrac{2}{3}$$

In general, the fraction $\dfrac{m}{n}$ can be visualized as the result of dividing m units into n equal parts, or as one nth of m units.

$$\frac{m}{n} = \frac{1}{n} \text{ of } m = m \div n$$

Eventually, all these inter-related aspects of the fraction concept will come together in a child's mind, so that he will be able to think of such a fraction as $\frac{4}{5}$ as any of:

i) four *fifths of 1 unit,*
ii) one fifth of *4 units,*
iii) the ratio of *4 units* to *5 units,*

and he will be able to move easily between these interpretations, and to use the one which is appropriate in any circumstances.[13]

[13] In this paragraph, the division sign has been used in the sense of 'sharing': $2 \div 3$ means, 'divide 2 units into 3 equal parts.' The application of the 'grouping' aspect of division to $2 \div 3$ is discussed in Chapter 26.

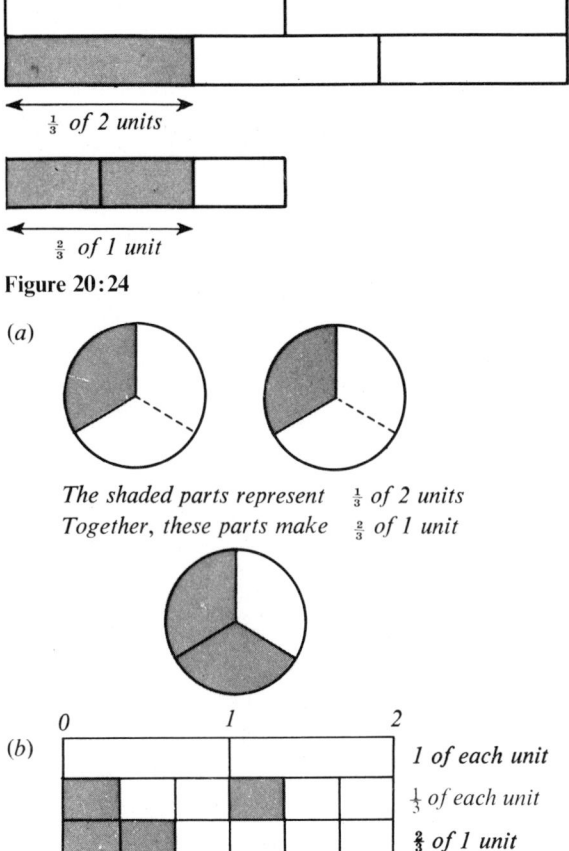

$\frac{1}{3}$ *of 2 units*

$\frac{2}{3}$ *of 1 unit*

Figure 20:24

(*a*)

The shaded parts represent $\frac{1}{3}$ *of 2 units*
Together, these parts make $\frac{2}{3}$ *of 1 unit*

0   1   2

(*b*)

1 of each unit
$\frac{1}{3}$ *of each unit*
$\frac{2}{3}$ *of 1 unit*

Figure 20:25

$$6 \div 3 = \tfrac{1}{3} \text{ of } 6 = 6 \text{ thirds} = \tfrac{6}{3} = 2$$

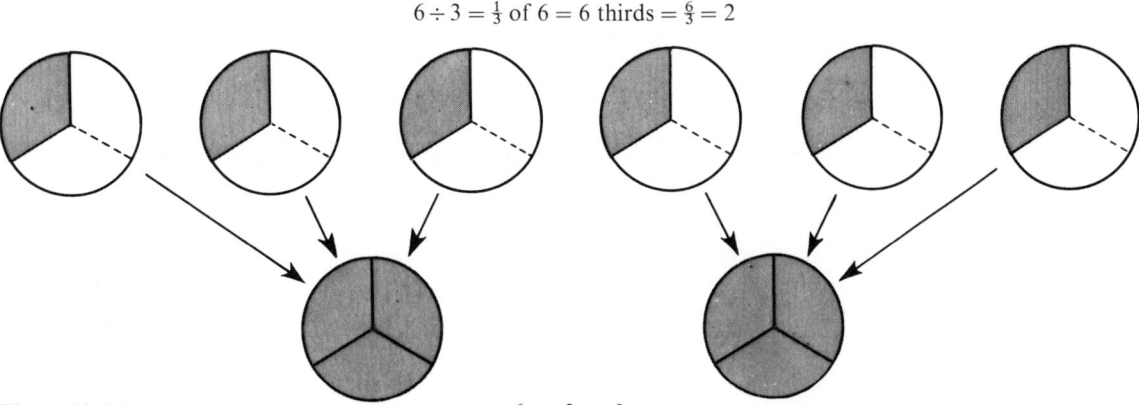

Figure 20:26 $6 \div 3 = 2$

In all the interpretations of $\frac{4}{5}$, the numbers 4 and 5 appear, in that order, but in a slightly different context in each interpretation. As a child grows older he ceases to rely on a particular interpretation, and so he will begin to think of the fraction $\frac{4}{5}$ as the ordered pair of numbers (4, 5), which obey certain rules of behaviour; he no longer has to return to one of the interpretations of the fraction. This stage will probably not, however, be reached until fairly late in the Secondary school, and it is essential at the Primary stage that a child should have many concrete embodiments of fractions and decimals at his disposal, from which he will later make the abstraction.

21 Plane Shapes and the Idea of an Angle

Patterns of bricks and tiles

Builders make brick walls by fitting together large numbers of equal geometrical solids in the shape of bricks; bathroom walls are often covered with equal square tiles; many floors are covered with parquet, or equal rectangular wooden blocks. The study of shapes which can be fitted together to build a wall, or to cover a floor, can be a useful source of geometrical experience.

A suitable experience for young children is making a pattern with flat square tiles of different colours. Basically, the only possible regular repeating patterns are those in Figures 21:1, 21:2 and 21:3, if the multitude of different ways of colouring such patterns is ignored. In this chapter we shall look only at the shapes which make patterns, and so we shall ignore variations produced by different colouring, but children will want to colour and decorate the patterns they make, and will learn much by doing so.

If rectangular tiles are used instead of square ones, a greater variety of patterns is possible. Those shown in Figures 21:4 to 21:7 can be made out of equal rectangles of any size and shape, but the pattern shown in Figure 21:8 can only be made when the rectangle has been obtained by cutting a square into equal parts.

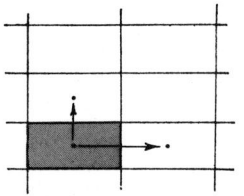

Figure 21:4   Figure 21:5

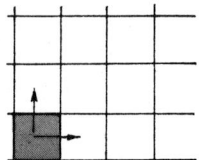

Figure 21:1

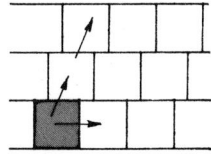

Figure 21:2

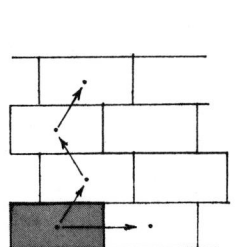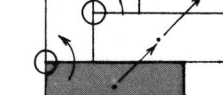

Figure 21:6   Figure 21:7

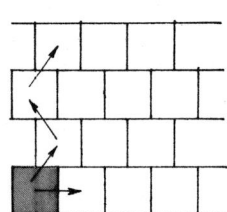

Figure 21:3

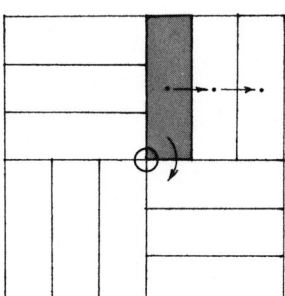

Figure 21:8

In all these patterns, the arrows show the movements from a tile to the next one. Each tile is derived from the shaded one by translation or rotation (*see page* 114). A particular example of Figures 21:5 and 21:6, in which each row of bricks is displaced half the length of a brick, is commonly found in those brick walls which are only the thickness of one layer of bricks, and is shown in Figure 21:9. Brick-layers call it *stretching bond*.

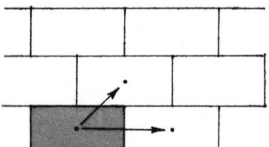

Figure 21:9

Children may find other rectangular patterns in parquet floors, and may also notice in buildings two common brick patterns known as *Flemish bond* (Figure 21:10) and *English bond* (Figure 21:11) in which bricks are placed both as 'headers' (end on) and 'stretchers' (lengthways). Viewed as patterns these are coverings of the plane using rectangles of two shapes, instead of rectangles of one shape only.

Collecting the different repeating patterns used for covering plane surfaces in walls, floors, patchwork quilts and wallpaper patterns is a valuable activity; it leads to a child making drawings and models of the patterns and inventing his own repeating patterns.

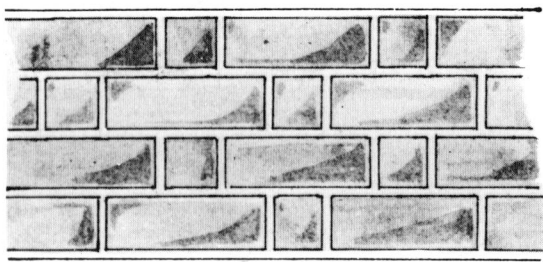

Flemish bond

Figure 21:10

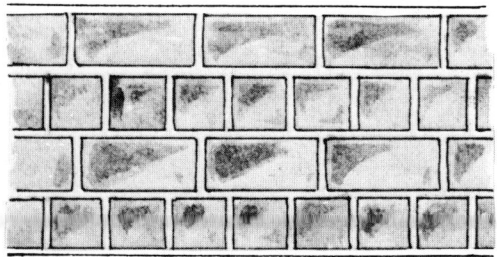

English bond

Figure 21:11

All these patterns of bricks and tiles are examples of covering a plane using rectangles of one or more shapes. Tiles in the shape of polygons other than rectangles or squares can also be used to cover a plane. When the plane is covered completely so that no gaps are left between the tiles, the pattern is called a *tessellation*.[1] The tiles are the *faces* of the tessellation, and the points where two or more corners of the tiles meet are *vertices* of the tessellation.

An interesting problem for a child is making tessellations using shapes which are not rectangular. He may be successful, as he will be if he uses regular hexagons and produces a honeycomb pattern (Figure 21:12), but he will be unsuccessful if he uses regular dodecagons such as pre-decimal threepenny bits (Figure 21:13).

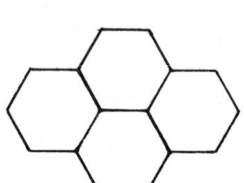

Figure 21:12   **Figure 21:13**

He can only succeed if the angles of the tiles which meet together at the vertex of the tessellation completely fill the space around that vertex. When we look at the tessellations of squares and rectangles, the tessellation is successful in each case because any vertex has the space around it completely filled either with four right angles (Figure 21:14) or with two right angles, which make up a straight angle, together with another straight angle (Figure 21:15).

There are two important properties of right angles: two right angles together make a straight angle; four right angles together completely fill the space around a point.

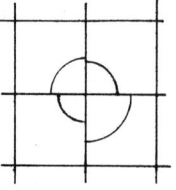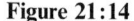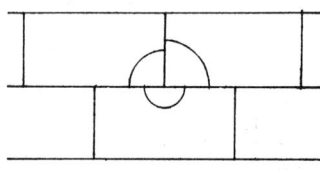

Figure 21:14   **Figure 21:15**

[1] In a Roman tessellated pavement the tiles were usually more or less square, but were set in cement with gaps between them.

The idea of an angle

Through his work in collecting and making geometrical shapes and patterns, a child grasps the concept of an angle, and he comes to realize the importance of right angles, and the existence of other angles which are wider open or less wide open than right angles.

Two different types of experience of angles need to come together and to combine in a child's mind, for him to have a thorough understanding of the concept of angle.

The first set of experiences is static. An angle is the shape of a corner. It may be sharp or blunt, or right angled. It can be compared with a right angle by seeing whether a set square will fit into it or not (Figure 21:16).

Figure 21:16

Much more fruitful than the static conception of an angle is the dynamic conception of the measure of an angle. If a book is gradually opened, its pages make a growing angle with each other (Figure 21:17).

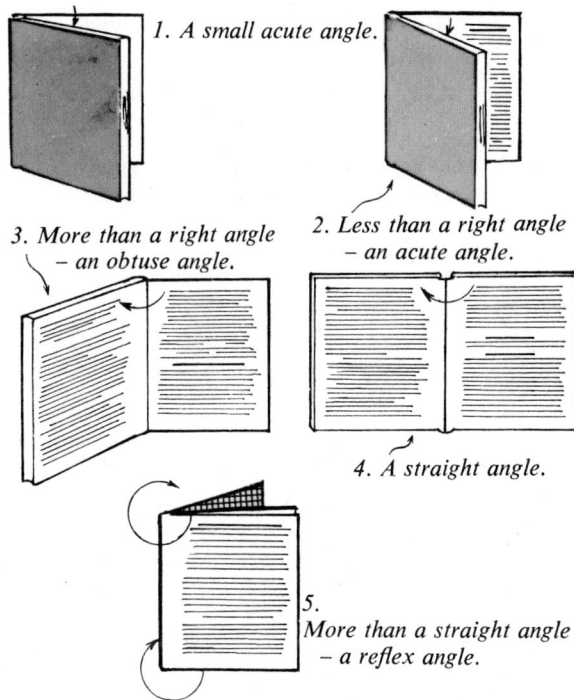

1. A small acute angle.

2. Less than a right angle – an acute angle.

3. More than a right angle – an obtuse angle.

4. A straight angle.

5. More than a straight angle – a reflex angle.

Figure 21:17

The growth of an angle when one of its arms is rotated may also be seen by bolting two Meccano strips together, or by letting a child turn round, pointing in the direction in which he is facing. (Figure 21:18).

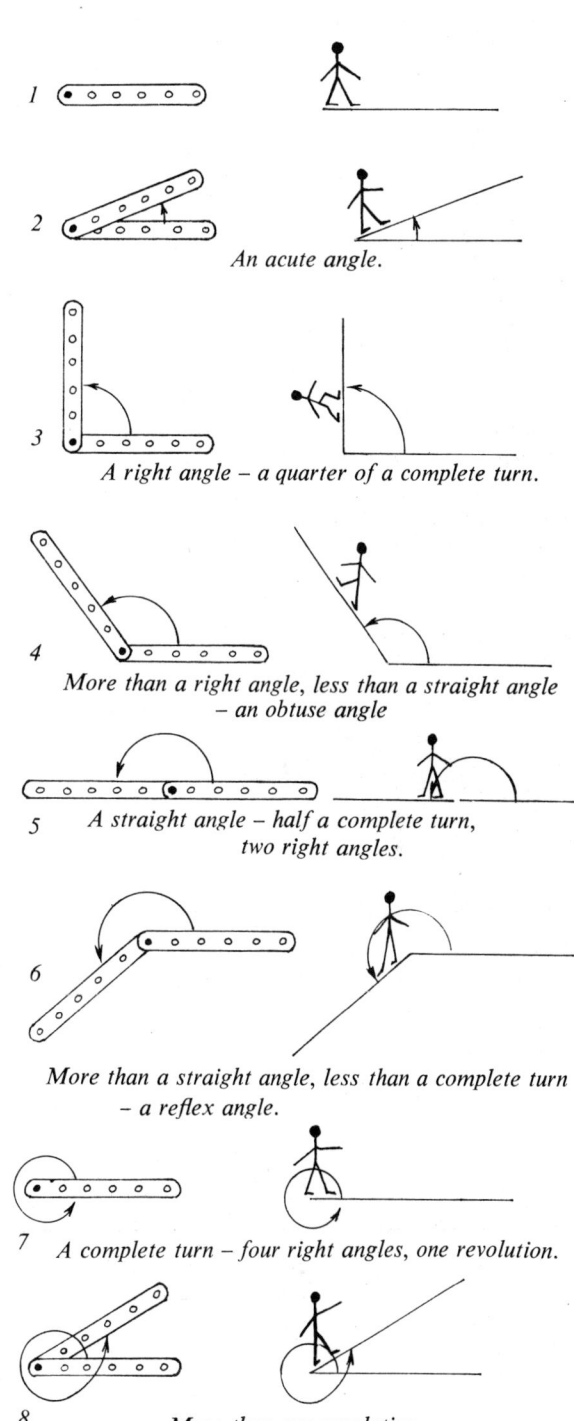

1

2 An acute angle.

3 A right angle – a quarter of a complete turn.

4 More than a right angle, less than a straight angle – an obtuse angle

5 A straight angle – half a complete turn, two right angles.

6 More than a straight angle, less than a complete turn – a reflex angle.

7 A complete turn – four right angles, one revolution.

8 More than one revolution.

Figure 21:18

197

There is no limit to the size of an angle when it is thought of as a measure of rotation. Between mid-day and midnight the minute hand of a clock turns through an angle of 12 revolutions, whereas the hour hand turns through an angle of 1 revolution. Between 3 o'clock and 6 o'clock the minute hand of the clock turns through 3 revolutions, while the hour hand turns through $\frac{1}{4}$ of a revolution (Figure 21:19).

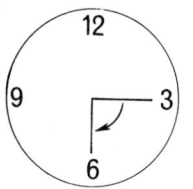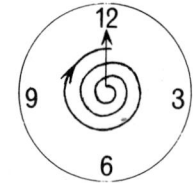

Figure 21:19

It is important that the static and dynamic conceptions of angle should fuse in a child's mind, so that when he looks at a shape like the one in Figure 21:20 he realizes that the measure of the angle at A is a measure of how far open its arms are, or by how much the line AB would

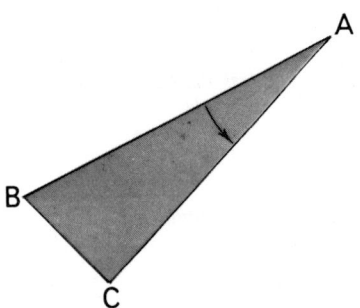

Figure 21:20

have to rotate in order for it to lie along AC. It then becomes clear that the natural measures of angle are the right angle, the straight angle, and the revolution, and that these measures are conected by the relationships:

$$1 \text{ right angle} = \tfrac{1}{2} \text{ straight angle}$$
$$= \tfrac{1}{4} \text{ revolution,}$$
$$1 \text{ straight angle} = 2 \text{ right angles}$$
$$= \tfrac{1}{2} \text{ revolution,}$$
$$1 \text{ revolution} = 4 \text{ right angles}$$
$$= 2 \text{ straight angles.}$$

More plane tessellations

As a child tries to make tessellations with other shapes, he will find that he is using some angles which are easily described in terms of right angles or complete revolutions and their parts, and others which are not.

Children who have used an isosceles right-angled triangle as a tile in tessellations may decide to make new tiles by combining several of the original ones. Among the polygons which can be produced from these triangles is a hexagon made from six triangles (Figure 21:21).

This hexagon, whose angles are equal either to $1\frac{1}{2}$ right angles or 1 right angle, gives an interesting tessellation of non-regular hexagons. A useful link between geometrical and numerical aspects of the work is formed by checking that the sum of the angles at a vertex of the tessellation is one revolution. The angles in Figure 21:21 marked with a circular arc each measure $(\frac{1}{4} + \frac{1}{8})$ revolution, or $\frac{3}{8}$ revolution. Therefore,

the sum of angles at $A = \frac{3}{8} + \frac{3}{8} + \frac{1}{4}$ revolution
$$= 1 \text{ revolution}$$

Simpler fractional work can be obtained by expressing the angles in terms of right angles or straight angles.

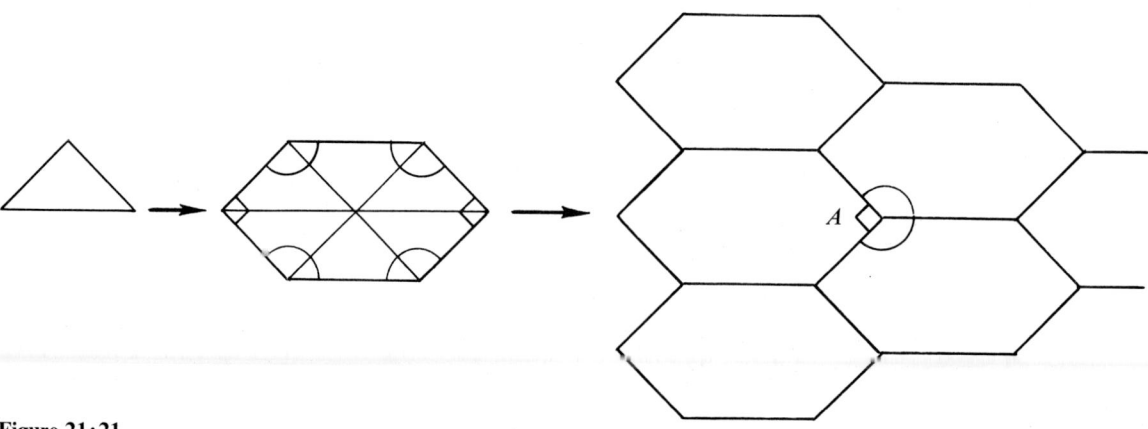

Figure 21:21
198

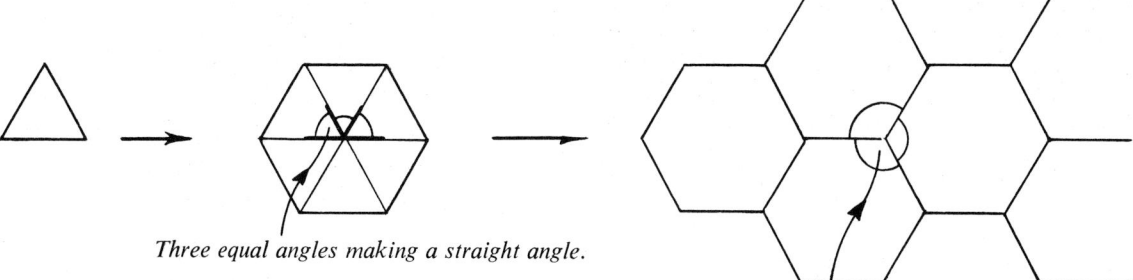

Three equal angles making a straight angle.

Three equal angles making a revolution.

Figure 21:22

Children will also discover that a *regular* hexagon can be made out of six *equilateral triangles* (Figure 21:22). By looking at the way equilateral triangles fit into a regular hexagon, they will find that the angles of an equilateral triangle are each $\frac{1}{3}$ of 2 right angles, or $\frac{2}{3}$ of a right angle, and that the angles of the regular hexagon are twice this size, that is $1\frac{1}{3}$ right angles, or are $\frac{1}{3}$ of a complete revolution, which is $\frac{1}{3}$ of 4 right angles.

Tessellations can also be made by using a triangle of any shape as a tile. So that children can recognize its different positions in their patterns, the triangle used should have sides which are of clearly different lengths, and none of its angles should be a right angle. Children will discover such patterns as those in Figures 21:23, 21:24 and 21:25.

In the study of these patterns, it becomes very inconvenient to use the right angle as the unit of measure for

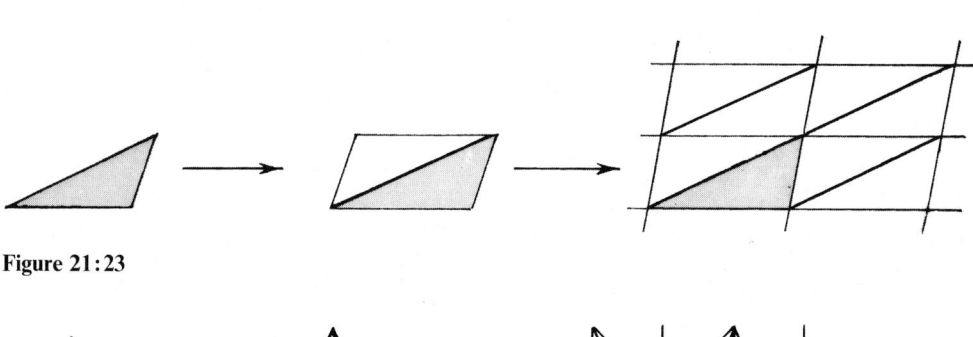

Figure 21:23

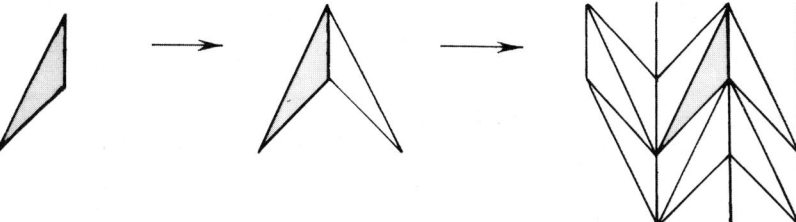

Figure 21:24

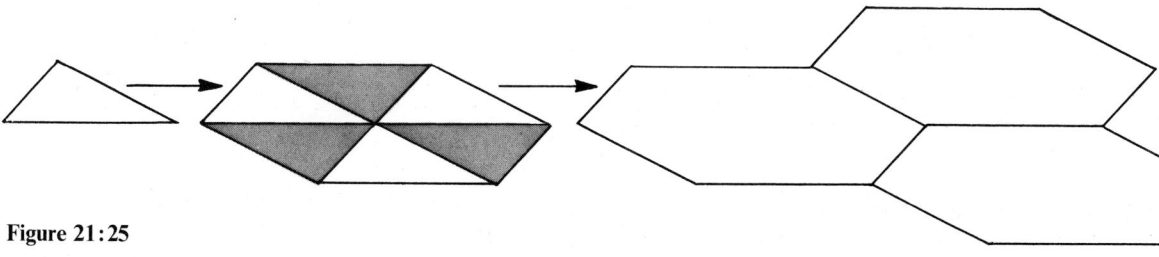

Figure 21:25

199

angles. At this stage, therefore, it is necessary to introduce a smaller unit of measure. The *degree* is a ninetieth part of a right angle. When they have been introduced to degrees, children will then easily use a protractor to measure angles in the triangles they have made, and will appreciate that:

a straight angle = 2 right angles = 180°

and

a complete revolution = 4 right angles = 360°.

It is, however, unnecessary for a protractor to be used when a teacher wishes the children to find out that the sum of the angles of any triangle is a straight angle. The hexagon shown in Figure 21:25 is made from six equal triangles which can be of any selected shape. In Figure 21:26 the angles of the top three triangles which are equal to one another are marked.

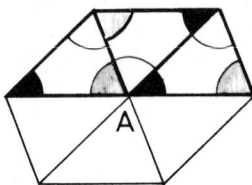

Figure 21:26

It will be seen that the three angles which together make up the straight angle at *A* are the three angles of the basic triangle. The same arrangement of three angles which together make a straight angle can also be found in the tessallations of Figures 21:23 and 21:24. Other ways of showing that the sum of the angles of any triangle is a straight angle are shown in Figures 21:27 and 21:28, where the angles of a paper triangle are torn off or folded together to make the straight angle.[2]

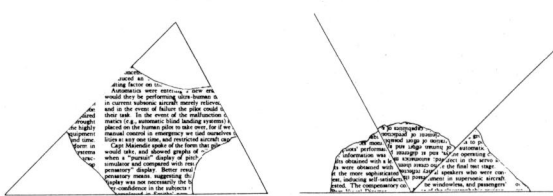

Figure 21:27

A child should have no difficulty now in finding several ways of showing that the sum of the angles of any

[2] Each of the unshaded triangles in Figure 21:28 has been reflected in its 'fold line' to give its new position. See page 116.

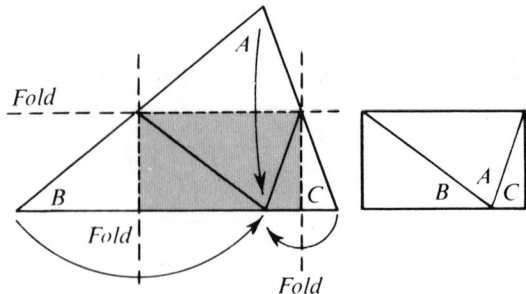

Figure 21:28

quadrilateral is a complete revolution, by making a tessellation (Figure 21:29), by tearing off the angles (Figure 21:30), or by cutting up the quadrilateral into two triangles (Figure 21:31).

Some children will wish to explore further, and find the sum of the angles of polygons with five, six or more sides.

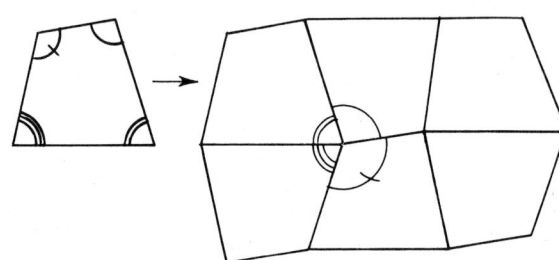

Figure 21:29

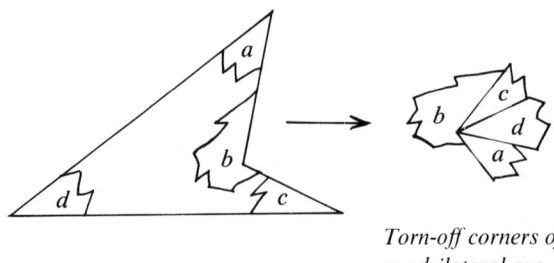

Torn-off corners of quadrilateral are rearranged as shown.

Figure 21:30

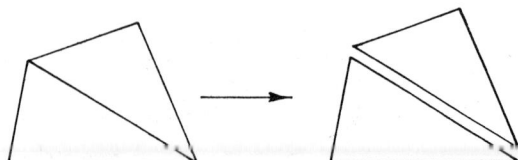

The quadrilateral is cut into two triangles.

Figure 21:31

They will discover that only in a few particular cases can tessellations be made with such polygons.

The last method of finding the sum of two angles of a polygon, that of dividing the polygon up into triangles, is the most convenient, and is mathematically the most important method, because it works for a polygon with any number of sides. The results may be tabulated and a graph drawn (Figure 21:32).

Number of sides in polygon	3	4	5	6
Number of triangles		1	2	3	4
Sum of angles (in straight angles)		1	2	3	4

Children can add another line to the table, to show the sum of the angles in degrees.

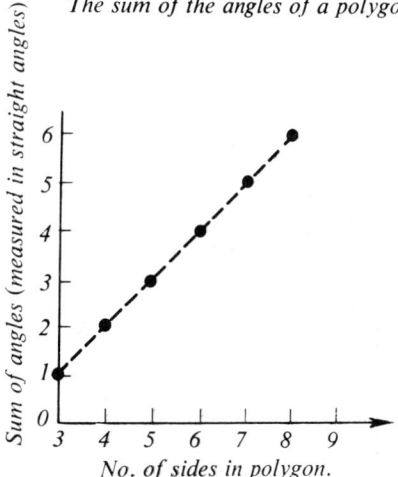

Figure 21:32

The vertical axis of the graph in Figure 21:32 might also be labelled in degrees. The points of the graph have been joined with a dotted line only, to help the eye, since no meaning can be attached to the idea of a polygon with, say, $3\frac{1}{2}$ sides.

Regular polygons

A *regular polygon* is a polygon in which all the sides are of equal length, and all the angles are equal to one another. Both these conditions are necessary. A child might try making a polygon with, say, six equal sides out of Meccano strips, and examining how the angles can be altered. He might also make a polygon with six equal angles, each of 120°, and see that the sides are not necessarily equal.

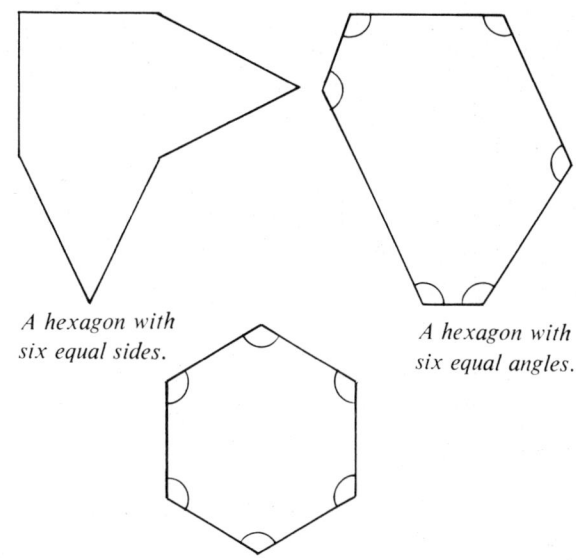

A hexagon with six equal sides.

A hexagon with six equal angles.

A hexagon with six equal sides and six equal angles.

Figure 21:33

From his previous experience, he should know by now at least three regular polygons:

NAME	NUMBER OF SIDES	MEASURE OF EACH ANGLE
Equilateral triangle	3	60°
Square	4	90°
Regular hexagon	6	120°

Other common regular polygons are the regular octagon (8 sides) which appears in the tessellation of Figure 21:34, but which cannot be used alone to make a tessellation, and the regular dodecagon (12 sides).

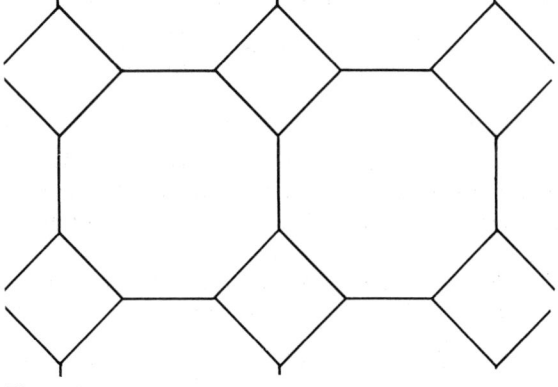

Figure 21:34

It can be seen from Figure 21:34 that each angle of the regular octagon is $1\frac{1}{2}$ right angles, or 135°. The table of regular polygons now takes the form:

The angles of a regular polygon[3]

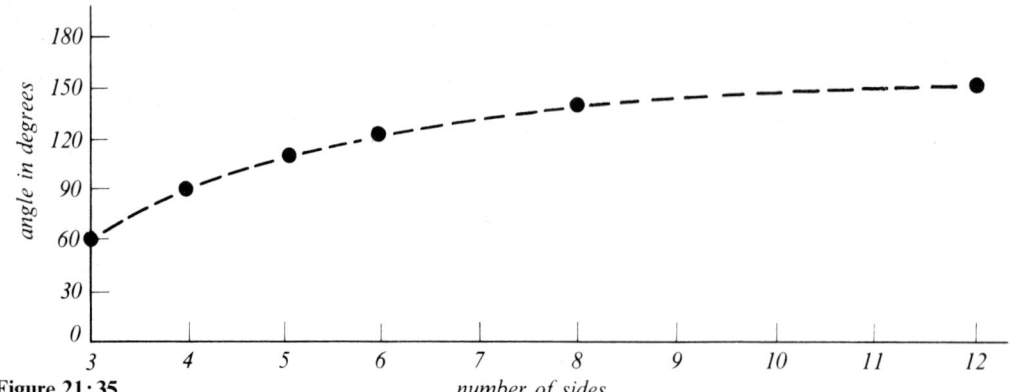

Figure 21:35

NAME	NUMBER OF SIDES	MEASURE OF EACH ANGLE
Equilateral triangle	3	60°
Square	4	90°
Regular *penta*gon[4]	5	
Regular *hexa*gon	6	120°
Regular *hepta*gon	7	
Regular *octa*gon	8	135°
Regular *nona*gon[5]	9	
Regular *deca*gon	10	
Regular *hendeca*gon	11	
Regular *dodeca*gon	12	

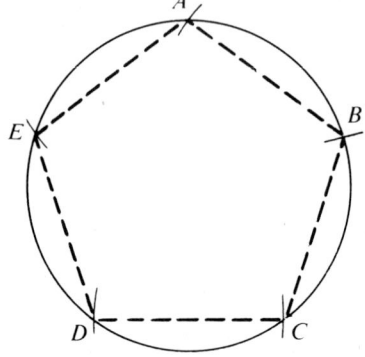

The incomplete information provided by this table gives rise to an interesting graph (which is not a straight line) (Figure 21:35). The missing angles may be filled in by reference to the table of Figure 21:32. For instance,

$$\text{sum of angles of any pentagon} = 3 \text{ straight angles}$$
$$= 3 \times 180°$$
$$= 540°$$

In a regular pentagon all these angles are equal, so

$$\text{each angle of a regular pentagon} = 540° \div 5$$
$$= 108°$$

A simple way to make a regular pentagon is to make five equally spaced marks on the circumference of a circle, and join them up (Figure 21:36). To do this, we must make

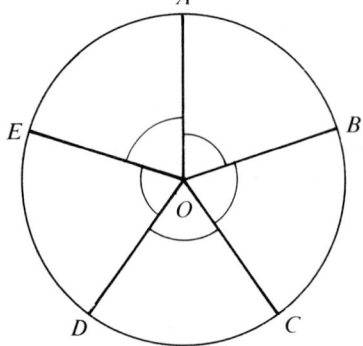

Figure 21:36

each angle at the centre(AÔB, BÔC, ...) $\frac{1}{5}$ of a complete revolution. That is,

$$\text{AÔB} = 360° \div 5$$
$$= 72°$$

When a child knows how to use a protractor, he can construct any regular polygon within a circle in this way.

In the next section we shall describe some methods of making regular polygons which do not involve the measurement of angles.

---

[3] The shape of this graph should be compared with the shape of the graph of aliquot fractions (*see page* 190). The equation of the graph is $y = 180\left(1 - \dfrac{2}{x}\right)$.

[4] The names of the polygons could be compared with the Greek names of the numerals from 1 to 12.

[5] Or *enneagon*.

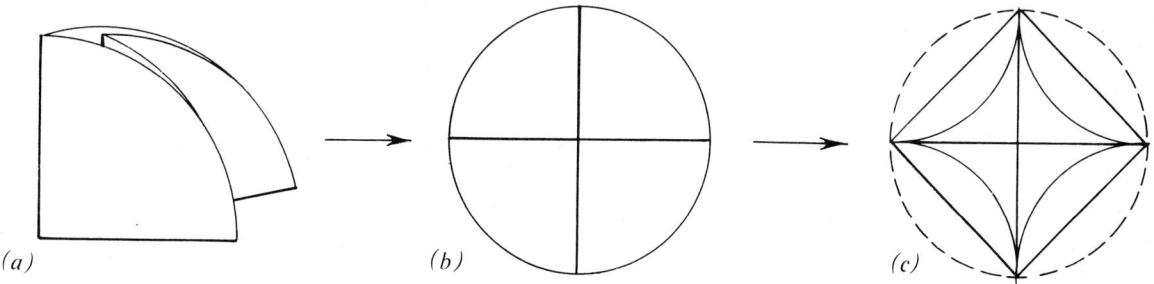

Figure 21:37

Folding and knotting regular polygons

Filter paper is very suitable for making regular polygons; it provides a cheap source of paper circles of a convenient size. The centre of a piece of filter paper can be found by folding it in quarters. It is then simple to fold the paper to make a square (Figure 21:37) or a regular octagon (Figure 21:38). Regular 16-gons, 32-gons, etc., could be made in the same way.

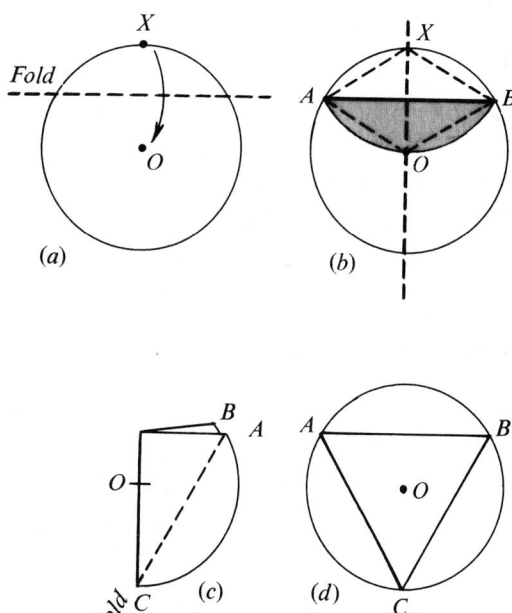

Figure 21:40 [6]

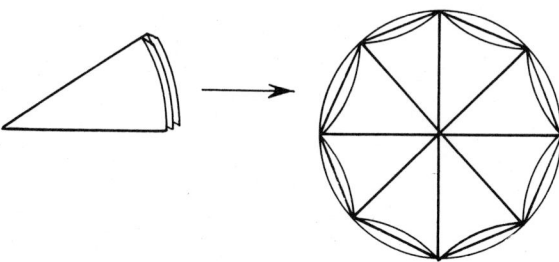

Figure 21:38

Other regular polygons can be based on the equilateral triangle. This is very easily constructed with ruler and compasses (Figure 21:39) or it can be folded out of a paper circle by folding a point on the edge of the paper to the centre of the circle (Figure 21:40).

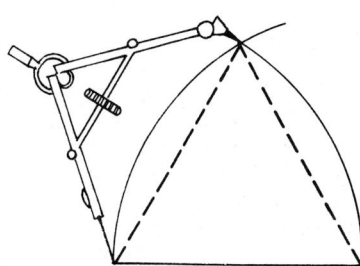

Figure 21:39

A regular hexagon is made up of six equilateral triangles within a circle, and so can be constructed by using compasses to step the radius of a circle six times round the circumference (Figure 21:41), or by refolding the circle from which an equilateral triangle has been folded (Figure 21:42). A regular dodecagon may be made similarly by refolding a regular hexagon.

[6] In diagram (b) AX and XB fold down on to AO and OB, and so are equal in length to the radius of the circle. Therefore, triangles AOX and XOB are equilateral, and $AOB = 120°$.

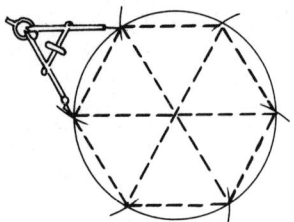

Figure 21:41

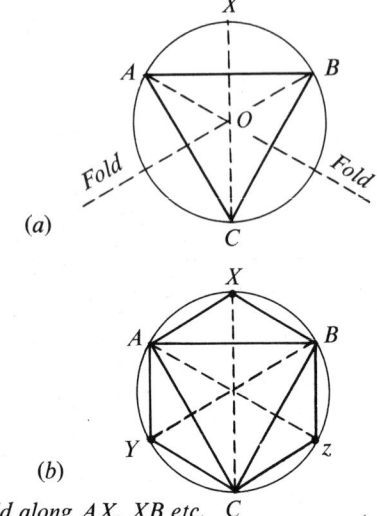

(a)

(b)

Fold along AX, XB etc.

Figure 21:42

The vertices of the regular pentagon *ABCDE* can then be marked on paper and the pentagon cut out for use as a template. Similarly, a regular nonagon could be approximated by removing three of the twelve triangles formed in making a regular dodecagon, and sticking the resulting figure together in the form of a pyramid whose base is an approximately regular nonagon.

A regular pentagon may also be made by making a single knot in a long strip of paper. When the knot is pulled up and flattened, it takes the shape of a regular pentagon (Figure 21:44).

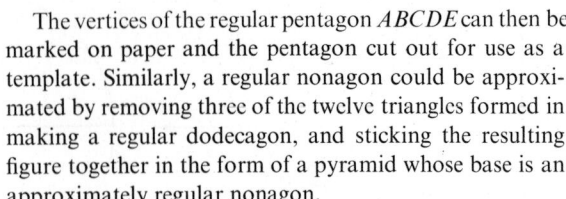

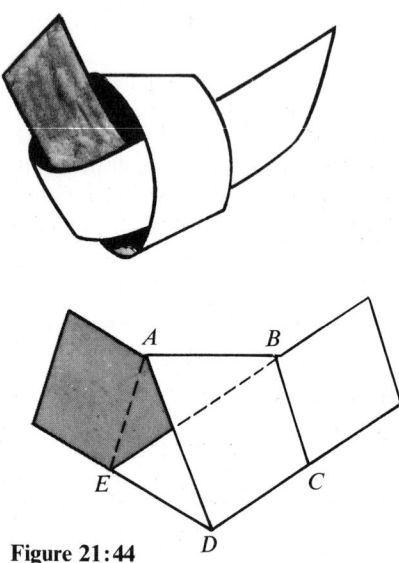

Figure 21:44

Other regular polygons are more difficult to make by folding, but approximations to them, which may be sufficiently accurate for children to use, can be made by cutting up the regular polygons which have already been folded. If the regular hexagon *ABCDEF* (Figure 21:43) is cut along *AO*, and stuck together with triangle *AOB* covering triangle *FOA*, it will take the shape of a pyramid with an approximately regular pentagon as its base.

If a child draws all the diagonals of a regular pentagon, a five-pointed star, a *pentagram,* appears. This has a smaller regular pentagon in it, which has another pentagram in it. A child could go on for ever making smaller and smaller pentagrams.

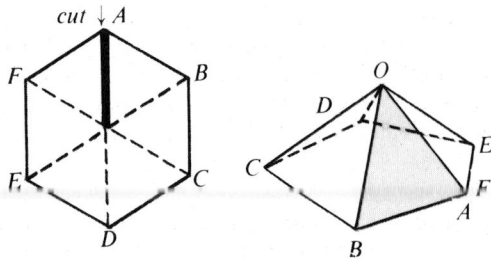

Figure 21:43

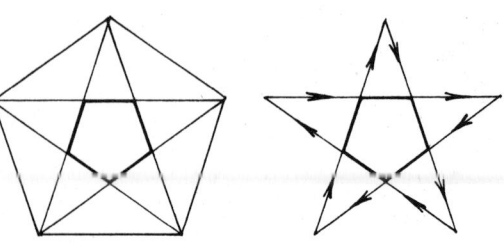

Figure 21:45

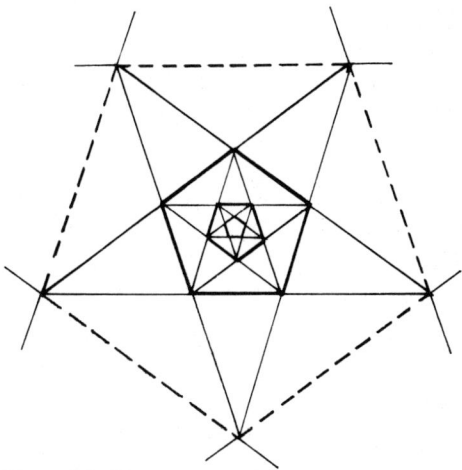

Figure 21:46

Similarly he could go on making larger and larger pentagons without limit by producing the sides of the pentagon until they meet and make another pentagram (Figure 21:46).

The pentagram is very like a regular pentagon in many ways; it can be drawn without lifting the pencil from the paper, and has five equal sides and five equal angles. It can be called a 'stellated' regular pentagon.

Children may examine the possibility of obtaining other stellated regular polygons, by producing the sides of regular polygons. (Figures 21:46 and 21:47.) Suitable questions for investigation include:

i) Can the stellated polygon be drawn without lifting the pencil from the paper?
ii) If so, how many times has the pencil encircled the centre of the polygon?
iii) Can an equilateral triangle be stellated?
iv) Can a square be stellated?

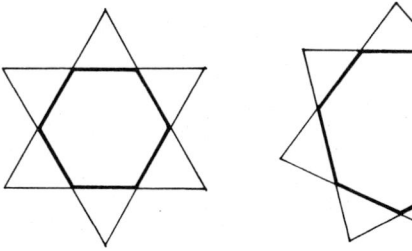

Figure 21:47

A few more tessellations

It is now clear that the only *regular* polygons which can be used *alone* for tessellations are equilateral triangles, squares and regular hexagons. This is so because two conditions are necessary for a tessellation to be possible:

i) the sum of the angles of the polygons which surround any vertex of a tessellation is 360°, because the space around a vertex must be filled.
ii) at least 3 polygons meet at each vertex.
The only possibilities are:
6 equilateral triangles meeting at each vertex,
4 squares meeting at each vertex,
3 regular hexagons meeting at each vertex.

These possibilities are all shown in Figure 21:48, together with an attempt to make a tessellation with regular pentagons. This is impossible, since each angle of a regular pentagon is 108°.

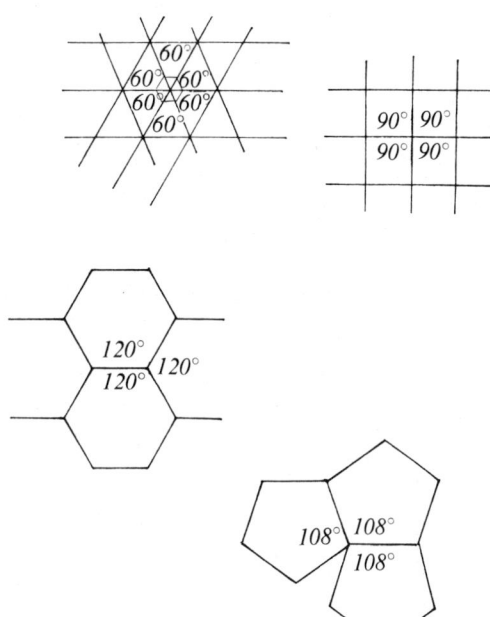

Figure 21:48

No regular polygon with more than six sides can be used *alone* to make a tessellation, for the graph of Figure 21:34 shows that the measure of each angle of a regular polygon increases as the number of sides increases. Three regular hexagons meeting at a vertex give an angle sum of 360°, so three regular polygons with more than six sides would give an angle sum of more that 360°. This makes tessellation impossible (Figure 21:49).

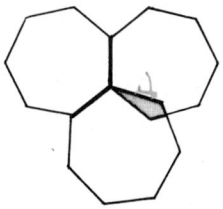

Three regular heptagons meeting at a vertex (with overlapping)
Figure 21:49

We conclude this chapter with an example of a tessellation which uses more than one regular polygon, and two which use irregular polygons. (Figure 21:50.) Further examples will be found in Cundy and Rollett's *Mathematical Models*.

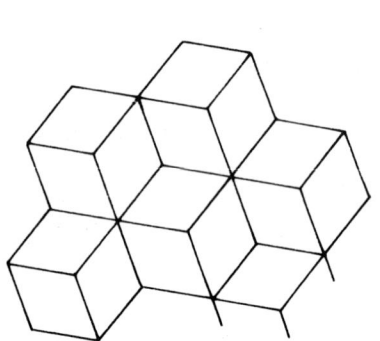 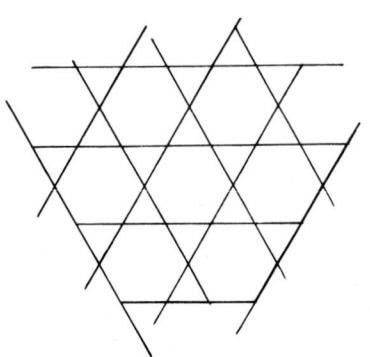 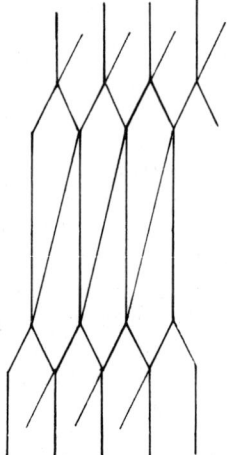

Figure 21:50

22 Three-Dimensional Shapes

Introduction: polyhedra

In Chapter 11 we have seen how children discover that their world is made up of solids of different shapes and sizes, and how they begin to classify solids into sets which have similarities of shape and give these solids names.

Among the important subsets of the sets of solids is the set of those solids which are bounded by plane surfaces only. These solids are called *polyhedra*. Children will find and make a varied collection of polyhedra, which occur in cartons, packets and in the shapes of buildings. Some are shown in Figure 22:1.

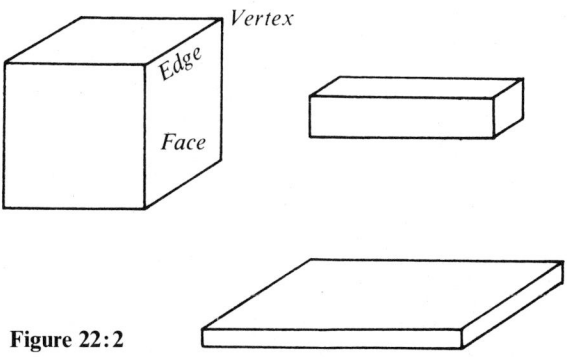

Figure 22:2

Another set of polyhedra of which children will find many examples are those with a top and a bottom face which are parallel equal polygons, and all the other faces are rectangles. These polyhedra are *prisms*. A hexagonal pencil is a prism. So are two of the solids in Figure 22:1; more prisms are shown in Figure 22:3.

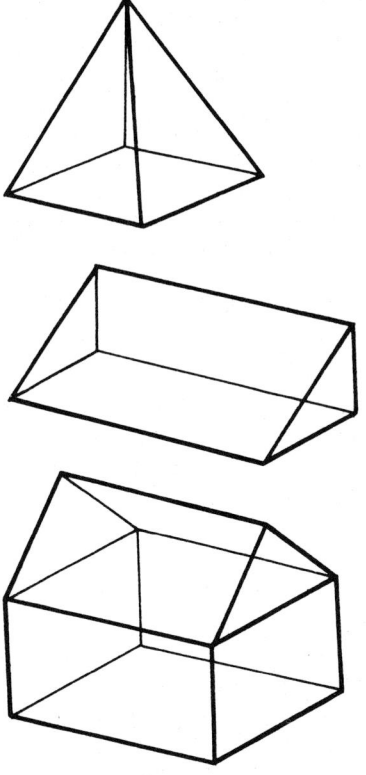

Figure 22:1

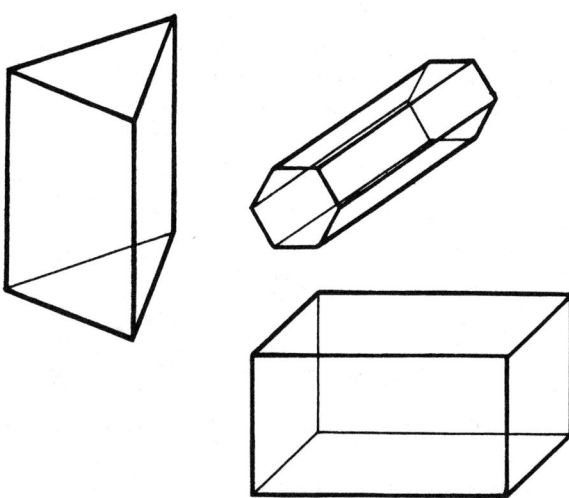

Figure 22:3

An attempt to sort polyhedra into sets will probably lead first to the classification and naming of *cubes* and *cuboids* (Figure 22:2). As children talk about polyhedra, they will need words to describe the different parts of the shape. Each plane surface on the boundary of a polyhedron is a *face*; two faces meet in a straight line, an *edge*; and a number of edges meet at each corner, or *vertex*, of the solid. A cube has six faces, each of which is a square, twelve edges and eight vertices. The six faces of a cuboid may be either oblong rectangles or squares.

Many sweet packets are prisms of various shapes, so are garden sheds and swimming baths. Prisms are named according to the shape of their bases, as, for instance, the triangular prism and hexagonal prism shown in Figure 22:3. Pyramids are also named according to the shape of their bases. Figure 22:1 shows a square pyramid, and the shape obtained by carefully sharpening a hexagonal pencil with a penknife is a hexagonal pyramid (Figure 22:4). There are also many polyhedra like the sweet packet in Figure 22:4, which cannot be classified as cuboids, prisms or pyramids. All polyhedra can, however, be named according to the total number of their faces. The ending *-hedron* is combined with the Greek word for the number of faces. The solids in Figure 22:4 are a heptahedron and an octahedron.

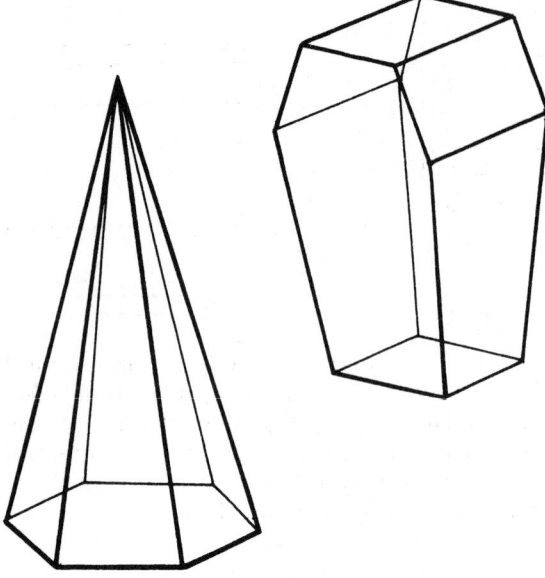

Figure 22:4

As children find examples of polyhedra, it is useful for them to keep a list of the names of each one, together with the numbers of faces, edges and vertices.

Name	Number of faces	Number of edges	Number of vertices
cube	6	12	8
square pyramid	5	8	5

Even at an early stage, children should be encouraged to look for patterns in this list. The pattern will be discussed later, when more examples have been found. Making models of polyhedra from their *nets* is another useful activity. If a child cannot see at once how to arrange the net of a solid, it is often helpful to allow him to cut along the edges of a cardboard model until he can open it out flat. This can usually be done in several ways.[1] Both the nets shown in Figure 22:5 can be made up into the same square pyramid.

Two different nets of a square pyramid

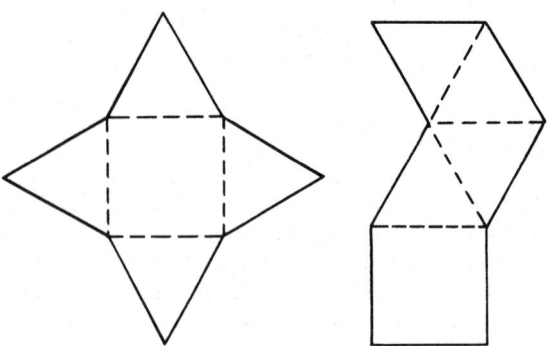

Figure 22:5[2]

In making polyhedra from their nets, a child will notice that the edges of two faces which are to be joined together must be the same length, and he will also begin to notice the angles of the polygons which meet at a vertex of the polyhedron.

In Figure 22:6, a polyhedron has been cut away until just one vertex, and the faces which surround that vertex, remain. A cut along one edge will now allow the figure to be opened out flat. The sum of the angles which surround the vertex must therefore be less than one revolution.[3] The

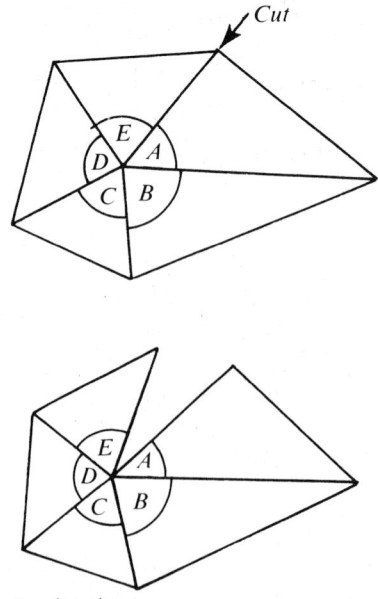

$$\hat{A} + \hat{B} + \hat{C} + \hat{D} + \hat{E} \quad < 360°$$

Figure 22:6

[2] If the triangles are equilateral (which they need not be) the second version of the net shows part of a tessellation of equilateral triangles.

[3] This may not be true if the solid angle at the vertex is not convex.

[1] If each face of the model is made separately, and all the edges are joined with Sellotape, a child can cut freely along any edge, and can stick the model together again for later use.

smaller the sum of the plane angles which meet at the vertex, the more 'pointed' the vertex will be. We can also see that at least three faces must meet at a vertex of the solid.

The regular solids

There are some polyhedra whose faces are all equal regular polygons. For instance, all the faces of a cube are equal squares. It would seem natural to call such polyhedra *regular solids*, but only some of them are regular. In two dimensions, a regular polygon must have equal angles as well as equal sides. In three dimensions, for a polygon to be regular, not only must all the faces be equal regular polygons, but *the solid angles at each vertex must also be exactly the same shape.*

For example, Figure 22:7 shows a triangular pyramid, each of whose faces is an equilateral triangle. Whichever face it stands on, it looks exactly the same. The solid angles at all the vertices are the same shape. It is a *regular tetrahedron.*

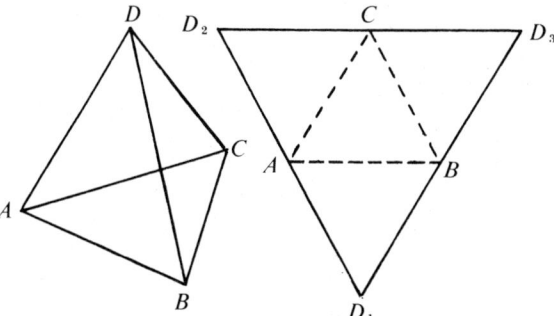

Figure 22:7

If two regular tetrahedra are stuck together, we get the solid, shown in Figure 22:8, which has six faces, each one an equilateral triangle, but it is not a regular polyhedron. Three equilateral triangles meet at vertices D and E, but at vertices A, B and C, four equilateral triangles meet. The solid angles at A, B and C are not the same shape as those at D and E.

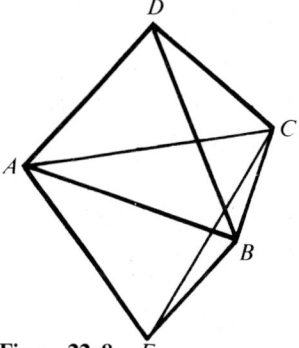

Figure 22:8

So we see that a regular polyhedron is a solid with:

i) each face a regular polygon,
ii) all the faces congruent,
iii) the same number of faces meeting at each vertex.

The cube is another example of a regular solid. We now consider whether there are any more regular solids. The algebraic demonstration which follows is intended for the teacher rather than for children, but it prepares the way for the geometrical work which follows and will lead children to discover more regular solids.

Let us try to build a regular solid, each of whose faces is a regular polygon with p sides (Figure 22:9). The sum of the angles of this polygon is $(p-2)$ straight angles, so that each angle of the polygon is $\left(\dfrac{p-2}{p}\right)$ straight angles.

Suppose that n polygons meet at each vertex. Then the sum of the angles at a vertex is

$$\left(\frac{p-2}{p}\right) \times n \text{ straight angles.}$$

But this must be less than a complete revolution or two straight angles.

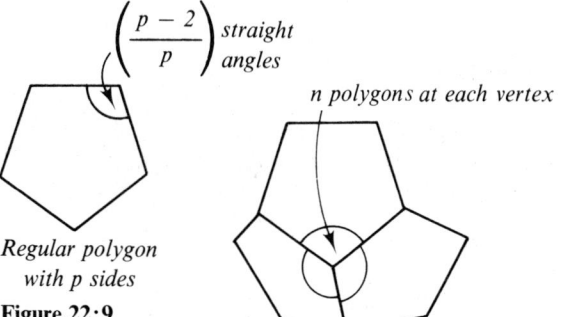

Figure 22:9

Hence $\left(\dfrac{p-2}{p}\right) \times n < 2$,

so that $(p-2) \times n < 2p$.

Now every polygon has three or more sides, so $p \geqslant 3$; and three or more polygons meet at each vertex of the solid, so $n \geqslant 3$. We try various possible values in the inequality.

If $p = 3$, $n < 6$; so n may be 3, 4 or 5.
If $p = 4$, $2n < 8$; so n can only be 3.
If $p = 5$, $3n < 10$; so n can only be 3.
If $p = 6$, $4n < 12$; there are no possible values of n.

It is useless to try values of p greater than 6, for we know that even a plane tessellation cannot be made out of polygons with more than six sides. So there is no possibility of using these polygons for the net of a solid. There are therefore only five possibilities which we can try.

i) $p = 3$, $n = 3$. Each face is an equilateral triangle, and three faces meet at each vertex. We have already met this solid, the *regular tetrahedron* (Figure 22:7). It should be noticed that its net can be cut out from a tessellation of equilateral triangles.

ii) $p = 3$, $n = 4$. Each face is an equilateral triangle, and four faces meet at each vertex. The solid, which has eight faces, and its net are shown in Figure 22:10. It is the *regular octahedron*, and can be thought of as two square pyramids stuck together by their bases. Children should turn it round to see that it looks exactly the same from any angle.[4]

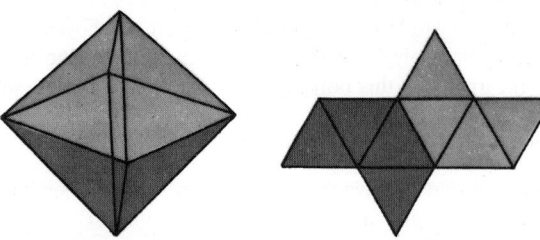

Figure 22:10

iii) $p = 3$, $n = 5$. Five equilateral triangles meet at each vertex. The solid, the *regular icosahedron*,[5] has twenty faces, and is shown in Figure 22:11.

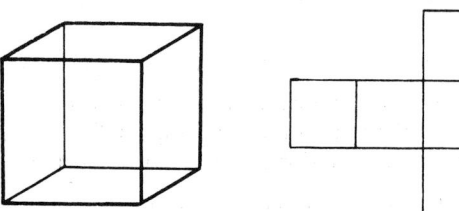

Figure 22:11

iv) $p = 4$, $n = 3$. Each face of the solid is a square; three faces meet at each vertex. The solid is the *cube*.[6]

Figure 22:12

v) $p = 5$, $n = 3$. Each face is a regular pentagon; three faces meet at each vertex. The solid, the *regular dodecahedron*, has twelve faces. It is most easily made as two bowl-shaped parts, which are easily fitted together.

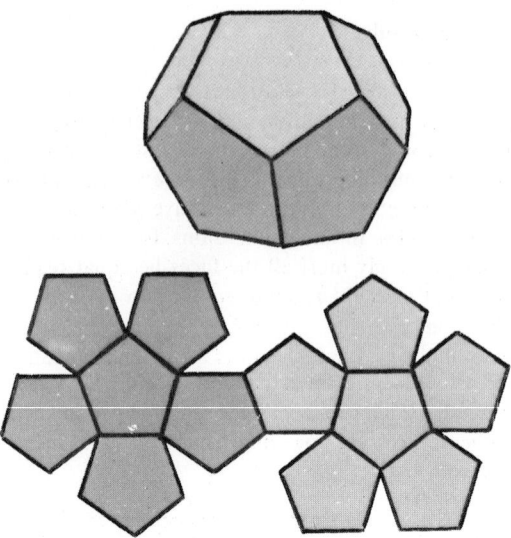

Figure 22:13

Alternatively, the nets of the two halves of a dodecahedron can be made separately of strong card, arranged one above the other as in Figure 22:14, and laced together with a strong elastic band. If the folds have been scored through, the elastic will pull the model into the shape of a regular dodecahedron, held together by the band round its equator.

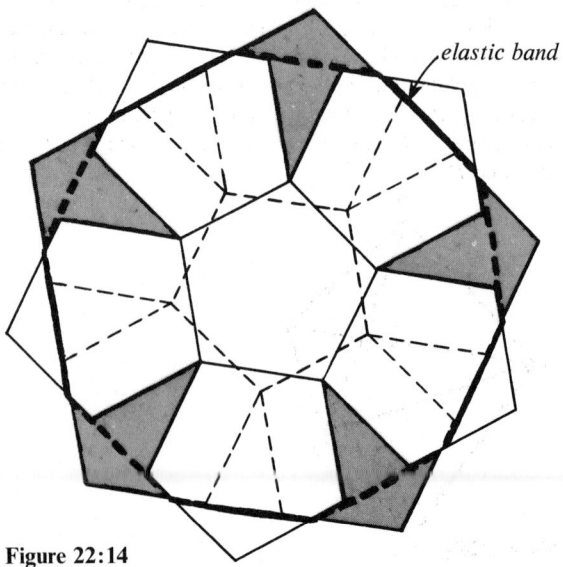

elastic band

Figure 22:14

---

[4] Again, the net is part of the tessellation of equilateral triangles; several other arrangements of the net are possible.

[5] Greek ἔικοσι (eikosi) twenty.

[6] The net is part of the tessellation of squares.

210

If the model-maker wishes to assemble his models by sticking together flaps which can be hidden inside the model, rather than by using Sellotape on the outside, it is enough to put flaps on alternate edges of the net, as shown on the net of a cuboid in Figure 22:15.

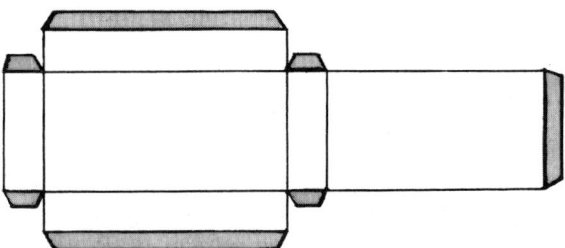

Figure 22:15

Figure 22:16

The five regular solids are known as the Platonic solids. They were all known to the Greeks, and Plato associated the tetrahedron, octahedron, cube and icosahedron with the four elements of fire, air, earth and water, and saw the dodecahedron as a symbol of the universe as a whole. While we no longer associate ourselves with such mystical symbolism in mathematics, we can still feel a shock of surprise at the fact that, although in two dimensions it is possible to construct regular polygons with any number of sides, in three dimensions there are only five different regular solids.

It is possible to make four more regular solids, the Kepler-Poinsot polyhedra, if the solid angle at each vertex is not required to be convex, or if the faces of the solid are allowed to be pentagrams (Figure 22:16). Details of the construction of these most beautiful star polyhedra will be found in Cundy and Rollett's *Mathematical Models*. The easiest to make is the great stellated dodecahedron. The

others are likely to be beyond the technical skill of most primary school children.

Children's experimental discovery of the five regular solids

Children can be led to discover the five Platonic regular solids by cutting up the three regular tessellations. If the faces of a solid are to be regular polygons which occur in a tessellation, the part of the net surrounding a vertex can be made by cutting out a part of the tessellation.

From the tessellation of equilateral triangles, a solid angle can be made by cutting away one of the six triangles which surround a vertex, and joining the remaining five triangles into a pyramid (Figure 22:17). Similarly, four or three triangles at a vertex of the tessellation can be used to make a solid angle.

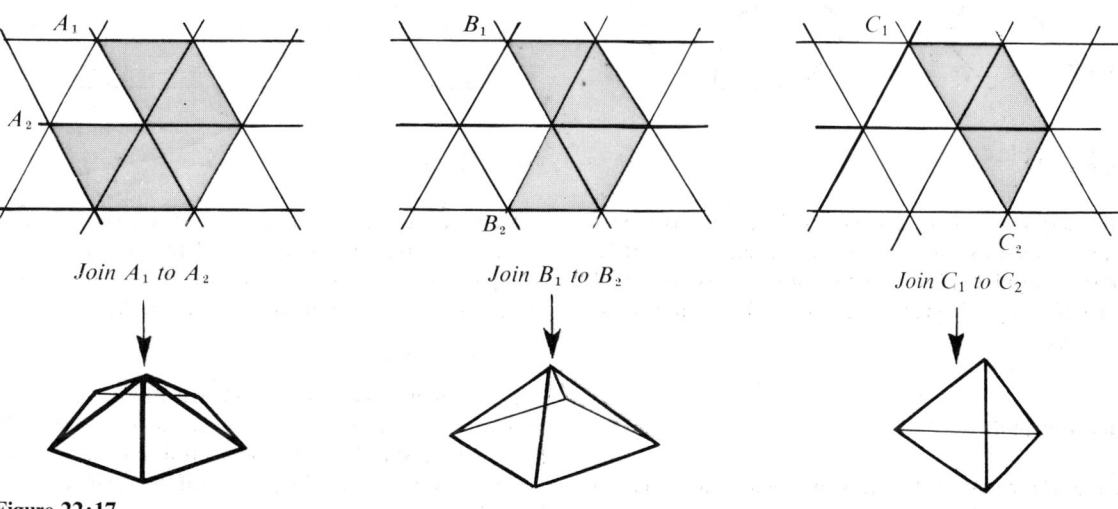

Join A_1 to A_2   *Join B_1 to B_2*   *Join C_1 to C_2*

Figure 22:17

211

Children may prefer to make a regular hexagon by folding a circle and then to cut out one or more triangles from the hexagon, producing a solid angle whose faces are equilateral triangles.

A solid angle can then be stuck to other equal solid angles until a regular solid is built up. Children will then see that only three regular solids, the regular tetrahedron, octahedron and icosahedron can be made from equilateral triangles.

In the same way, cutting up the tessellation of squares gives a cube (Figure 22:18).

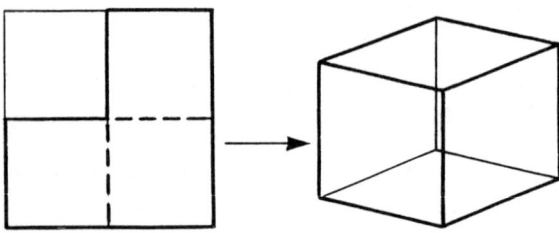

Figure 22:18

Children will see that a solid angle cannot be made from the tessellation of regular hexagons, as three hexagons completely fill the angle of 360° at a vertex, leaving no space for cutting out.

A child who has tried to make a tessellation of regular pentagons will see that he can make a solid angle which has regular pentagons as faces. This leads to the regular dodecahedron (Figure 22:19).

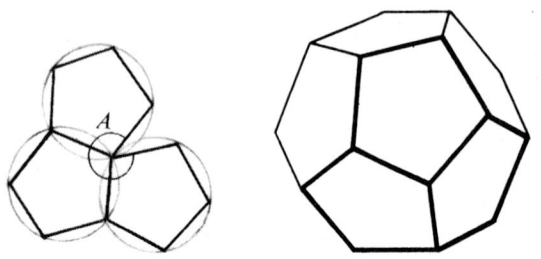

Figure 22:19

It is easy to see that a regular solid cannot have faces with more than six sides, because a tessellation cannot be made with regular polygons with more than six sides, and the net of a polyhedron must leave space for cutting out at any vertex.

Euler's formula

A child who has kept the list of polyhedra suggested on page 208, with the numbers of their faces, edges and

212

vertices, may search for a pattern in the table. The arrangement of the table shown below may help him.

Name	Number of faces (F)	Number of vertices (V)	Number of edges (E)
Square pyramid	5	5	8
Hexagonal prism	8	12	18
Regular solids			
Regular tetrahedron	4	4	6
Cube	6	8	12
Regular octahedron	8	6	12
Regular dodecahedron	12	20	30
Regular icosahedron	20	12	30

He will notice that the number of edges is always greater than the number of faces or vertices, and pairing the regular solids may suggest that $F + V$ is important. A graph of E against $(F + V)$ (Figure 22:20) will confirm this for all the solids on his list, not only the regular solids.

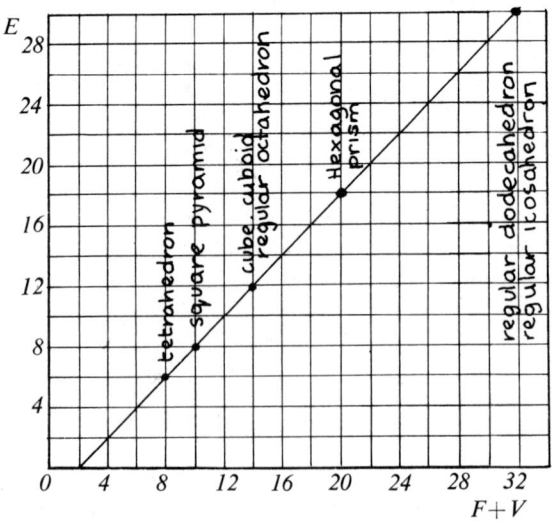

Figure 22:20

A curious feature of this graph is that each point of it will usually correspond to several different solids. For each solid, the sum of the number of faces and vertices is two more than the number of edges. Symbolically,

$$F + V = E + 2$$

This formula was proved by Leonard Euler in 1735. A primary school child will be content to notice that the formula is satisfied by every polyhedron he knows, but the teacher may be interested in a proof of the formula, which is similar to that given by Euler.

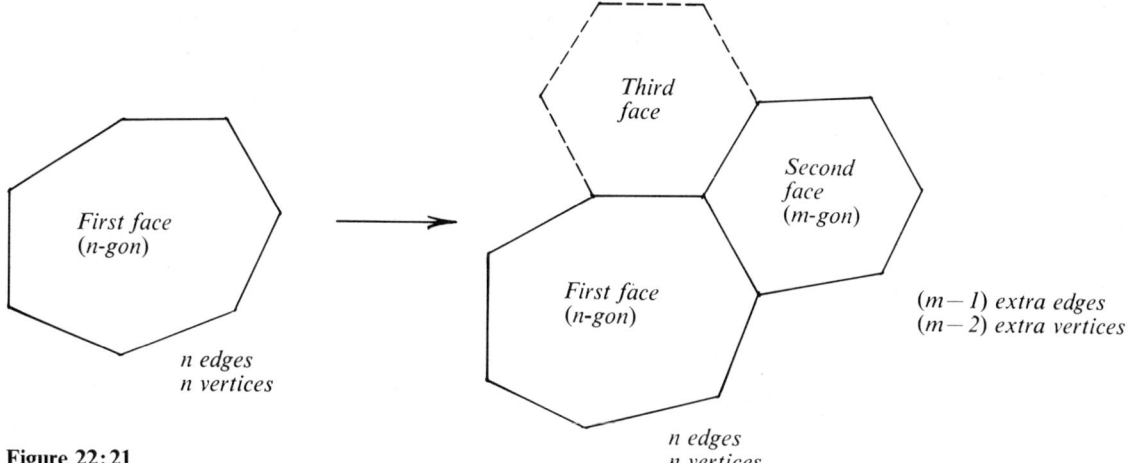

Figure 22:21

Imagine that we build up a polyhedron by adding one face to it at a time, and notice how the number

$$N = F + V - E$$

changes as each successive face is added to the polyhedron. Suppose that the first face is a polygon with n sides (and n vertices). At this stage $F = 1$, $V = n$, $E = n$, and $N = F + V - E = 1$.

Now add another face, a polygon with m sides. It will be built on to one edge of the first face, so it has one edge and two vertices in common with the first face. So one face, $(m-1)$ edges, and $(m-2)$ vertices have been added. For the two faces together,

$$F = 2, \quad V = n + m - 2, \quad E = n + m - 1,$$
and
$$N = F + V - E$$
$$= 2 + (n + m - 2) - (n + m - 1)$$
$$= 1$$

It looks likely that N remains equal to one as we add more and more faces. This is so, as we can show that adding another face at any stage does not change the value of N, provided it does not complete the polyhedron. As time goes on, it will be necessary to add polygons which have more than one edge in common with what has already been built (Figure 22:21). Suppose that at some stage, when the part already built has f faces, v vertices, and e edges, we add a polygon with p sides, which has k consecutive edges in common with the part already built. It will have $(k+1)$ vertices in common with the part already built, so, at this stage,

$$F = f + 1, \quad V = v + p - (k+1), \quad E = e + p - k,$$
and
$$N = F + V - E$$
$$= (f + 1) + (v + p - k - 1) - (e + p - k)$$
$$= f + v - e.$$

So adding another face does not change N. At the beginning $N = 1$, so each time a face is added without closing the polyhedron,[7] N stays equal to one.

When the last face is added to close the polyhedron, the number of faces is increased by one without adding any more vertices or edges. This increases $N = F + V - E$ by one, so for the completed polyhedron

$$N = F + V - E = 2,$$
or
$$F + V = E + 2$$

This formula is true whether the polyhedron is regular or not. The only restriction is that it must be possible to build it up by adding faces which only have *consecutive* edges in common with what has already been built. All polyhedra which a child is likely to meet at this stage satisfy this requirement.

Rigidity of polygons and polyhedra

Children can make polygons and tessellations by using Meccano strips to make the edges of the polygons. The fact that they will find it difficult to tighten up nuts and bolts sufficiently to prevent the strips from moving will lead them to study *rigidity*. They will quickly find that any triangle is rigid, but that any other polygon can be deformed and made to alter its shape in various ways. Squares will turn into rhombuses, and rectangles into parallelograms (Figure 22:22). But if a quadrilateral is made with both pairs of opposite sides equal, however it is pushed about, the opposite sides will always stay *parallel*, so that although the shape of the polygon changes, it always remains a parallelogram.

[7] The reader should find the reason for this proviso.

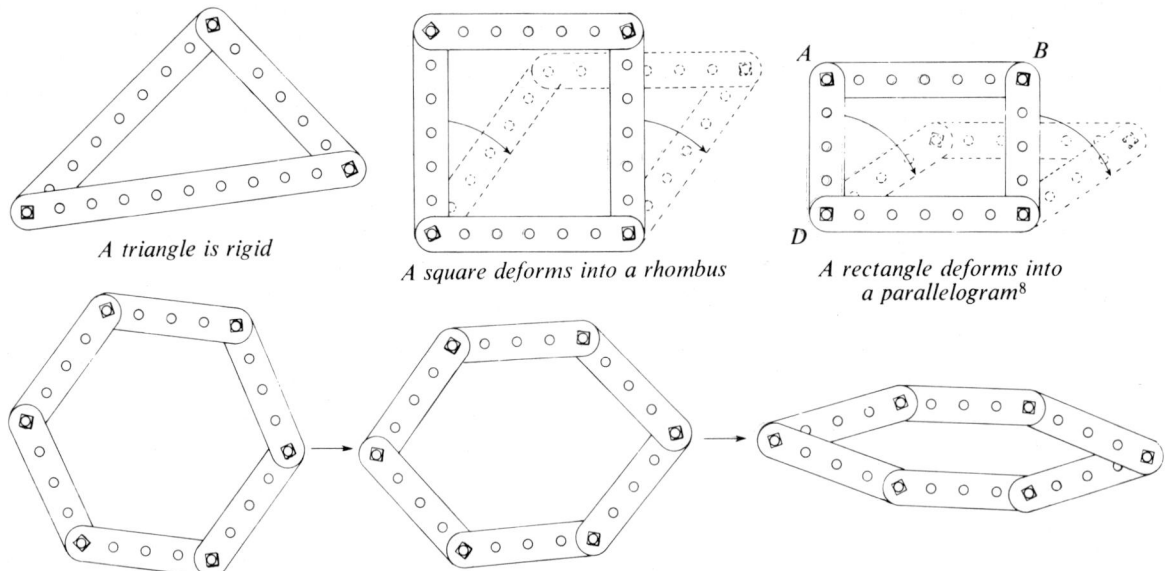

A triangle is rigid

A square deforms into a rhombus

A rectangle deforms into a parallelogram[8]

Collapse of a regular hexagon

Figure 22:22

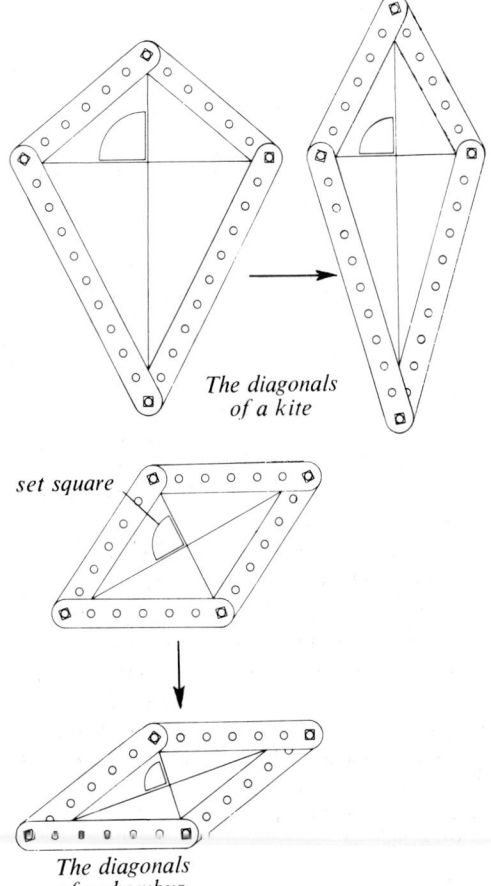

The diagonals of a kite

set square

The diagonals of a rhombus

Figure 22:23

Children can discover a good deal about the diagonals of polygons if they use shirring elastic to make the diagonals of the Meccano models,[9] and watch what happens as they change the shape of a model (Figure 22:23).

[8] We notice that *AD* and *BC* have been rotated about *D* and *C* respectively, whereas *AB* has been translated parallel to itself.

[9] This can be knotted round the bolts.

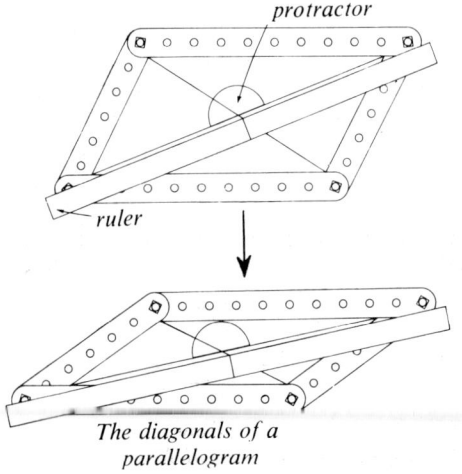

protractor

ruler

The diagonals of a parallelogram

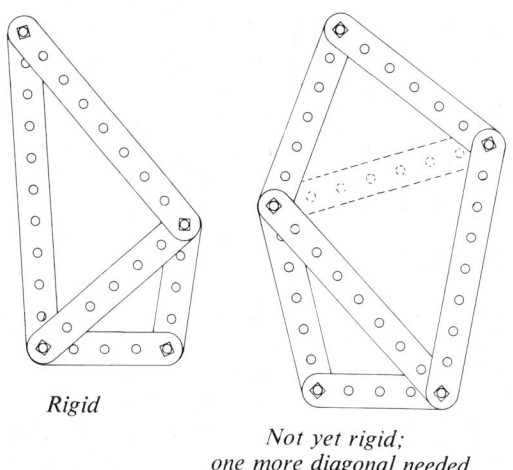

Rigid

Not yet rigid;
one more diagonal needed

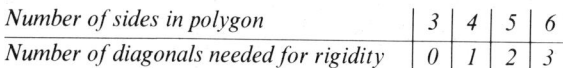

Number of sides in polygon		3	4	5	6
Number of diagonals needed for rigidity		0	1	2	3

Figure 22:24

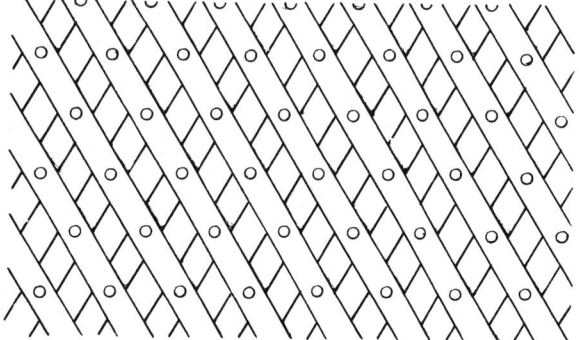

Children may also discover how many rigid diagonals made of Meccano they need to put in before a polygon is rigid.[10] This experiment lends itself to graphical treatment, and should be compared with Figure 21:32.

Children will soon see that the triangle is the only rigid polygon, and that other polygons can be made rigid by struts which make them into triangles. They will be able to collect many examples of this fact in use in five-barred gates, electricity pylons, bridges and roofing girders. (Figure 22:25.)

Tessellations made from Meccano strips are certainly not rigid unless they are made of triangles. An interesting application of this fact is found in lattice-work fencing panels, which stretch to make variable lengths of fence

(Figure 22:26).[11] A parallelogram lattice, made on this principle from Meccano strips, can be used to enable

Figure 22:26

[10] The total number of diagonals which can be put in also makes an interesting graph.

[11] Nailing the lattice to a cross-piece makes it rigid, because the cross-piece produces triangles.

Figure 22:25

children to discover all the well-known angle properties of parallel lines (Figure 22:27). As the shape of the lattice changes, angles A, B and C change in shape, but remain equal to one another.

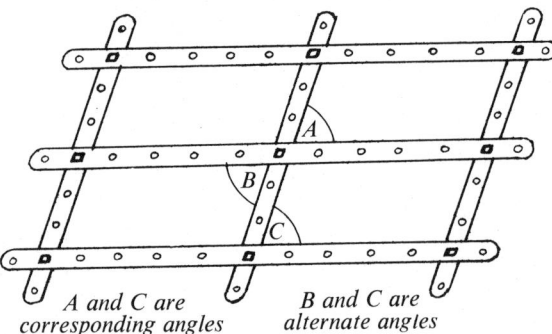

A and C are corresponding angles   *B and C are alternate angles*

Figure 22:27

In order for children to be able to examine the problem of building rigid shapes in three dimensions, they must be able to use joints which can move in any direction. Meccano will not make such joints, but milk straws can be used for the edges of solids which are made by threading cotton through the straws and tying them. More permanent models can be made with plastic drinking straws and shirring elastic.

Children will find that triangles and tetrahedra are rigid figures in three dimensions, but that the number of struts needed to make a plane polygon rigid in two dimensions is insufficient in three dimensions (Figure 22:28(b)). Many examples of the use of a tetrahedron to make a rigid framework will be found in pylons. Children may also like to examine the number of ropes needed to steady a flagpole, or the corner of a cricket net, and to consider in what ways these situations differ (Figure 22:29).

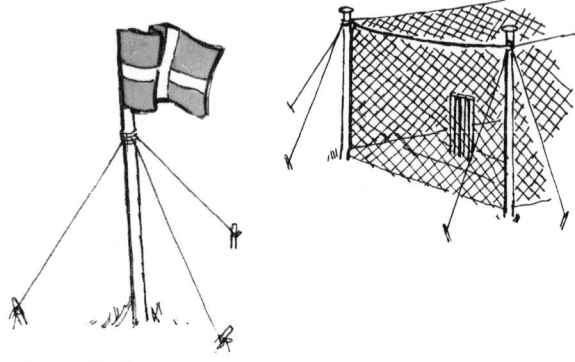

Figure 22:29

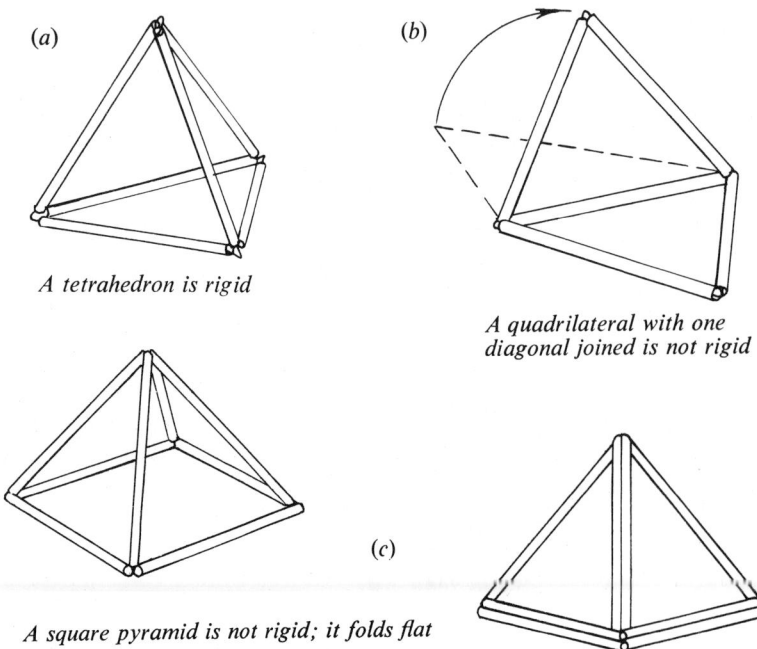

(a) *A tetrahedron is rigid*

(b) *A quadrilateral with one diagonal joined is not rigid*

(c) *A square pyramid is not rigid; it folds flat*

Figure 22:28

216

A cube made from milk-straws is quite astonishingly deformable (Figure 22:30) and children may enjoy experimenting to see how few struts will make it rigid.

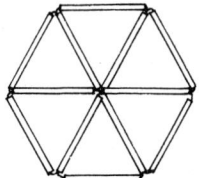

This is one shape made from a collapsed cube.

Figure 22:30

More rigid models can be made with straws; a firmer joint is made by pushing a short piece of pipe-cleaner into the ends of two straws. This method has the disadvantage that it conceals the problem of rigidity by cutting down the freedom of movement in the joint (Figure 22:31).

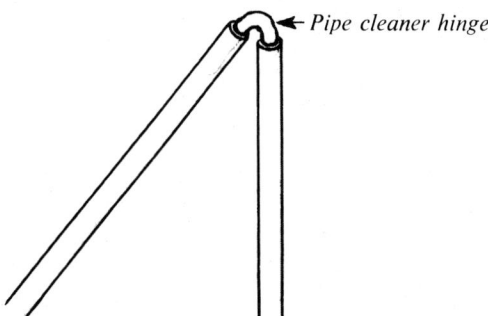

← *Pipe cleaner hinge*

Figure 22:31

23 Measuring Area

Early experiences of surfaces

By 8 or 9 years of age children have become familiar with flat or plane surfaces as opposed to those that bulge or are indented. Mounds and dips are seen in the country-side or in road excavations; a saucer right way up looks different from one placed upside down. A smooth plane surface is horizontal when things on it do not roll or slide of their own accord; if a ball placed on a surface does not roll, the surface is horizontal. A vertical surface may suggest balance or stability. If it is sloping it may offer a good slide or look like an unstable tower, the face of a roof or the partly open lid of a box. But none of these examples of surface, flat or curved, appear to raise the question of *how much* surface there is.

Experience of cutting up paper shapes and reassembling the parts to make a new shape leads a child to realize that the *size* of the shape, i.e. the amount of surface, does not vary with a rearrangement of its parts. For example, a unit square centimetre may take up a variety of forms. (Figure 23:1.)

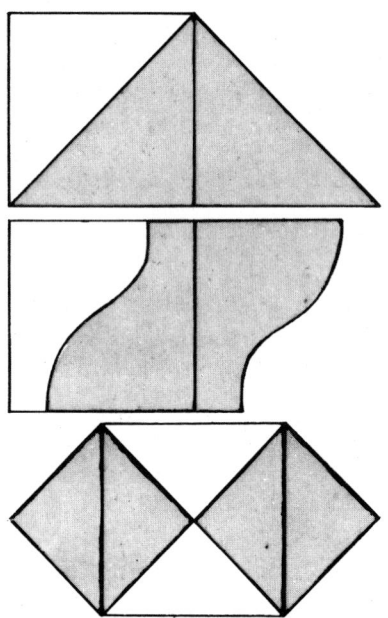

Figure 23:1

A set of similar shapes, such as rectangles, circles, triangles, will probably have been compared for size using an intuitive judgement, or by placing one upon another, to test whether they fit or one is larger than the other. Several such shapes have probably been put in order of size. Folding and cutting have shown that two equal parts

of a shape can be made to fit one on another; thus each is a half of the whole surface. But suppose they cannot be made to fit and each projects in some places over the other; can we tell whether they have the same amount of surface? Can we detect whether a round biscuit is the same size as a rectangular one (ignoring their thickness)? (Figure 23:2.)

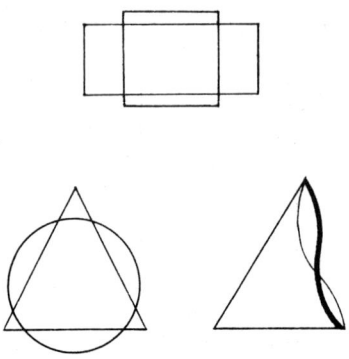

Figure 23:2

The surfaces of three-dimensional objects have been interesting hitherto chiefly for their shapes or the properties of their faces. For example, cubes, pyramids and cones have exhibited squares, triangles or parts of circles in their surfaces. Such objects have been made by folding and joining plane shapes. Clearly some forms, the sphere for instance, cannot be produced from a plane surface; yet such objects have a surface and obviously a large ball has more surface than a smaller one. The human body shows similar differences: a tall, broad-shouldered man has much more skin surface than a short, slight man. A child can be given opportunities of inventing ways of comparing such surfaces and can experiment with simple rectangular shapes in the playground. At 8 or 9 years of age children often compare length and breadth or perimeter and show no awareness of the quantity of *surface*.

Covering a surface

One of the most formative experiences that will direct children's thinking about the measure of a surface is making all-over patterns. Covering a plane surface with repetitions of a particular shape may readily lead to the question, 'How *many* such shapes were needed?' Using

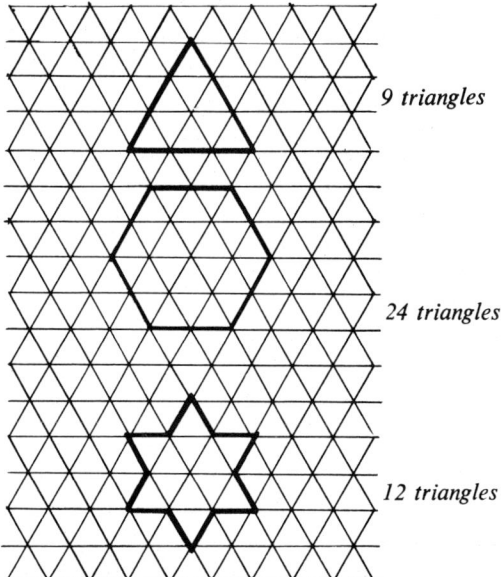

9 triangles

24 triangles

12 triangles

Figure 23:3

triangles, parallelograms, rectangles or hexagons to cover two or more surfaces may lead to the idea that the *number* of one particular shape required to cover a surface enables us to compare it with another surface. There will be a correspondence between the numbers of the unit shapes and the respective sizes of the two surfaces. In fact a way of measuring surface will have been discovered. Isometric ruling on paper, as used in Figure 23:3 permits the easy comparison of shapes drawn on it because the triangles are already there to be counted.

A lattice of parallelograms allows a comparison to be made between the regions enclosed by pairs of parallel lines by counting the number of parallelograms of unit size enclosed. In Figure 23:4, parallelogram *A* contains 6 unit parallelograms and figure *B* contains 8 units.

Some valuable experience of quantities of surface can be found from the shapes made by elastic bands stretched round nails on a nail-board. In the region enclosed by the band there are no lines to show smaller shapes. A unit for comparing the surfaces of two enclosures must be devised. The placing of the nails suggests a square but as will be seen in Figure 23:5 whole squares do not cover some

of the shapes that can be made. Half a square will be recognized readily from symmetry and this half-unit will often occur.

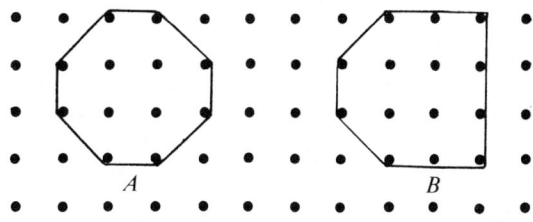

Figure 23:5

The amount of surface or *area* in shape *A* is 5 squares and 4 half-squares, the area of shape *B* is 7 squares and 2 half-squares. Thus shape *A* contains 7 square units and shape *B* contains 8 square units.

In Figure 23:6 a more complicated problem involves the recognition that the triangular part is half of *two* of the squares. The advantage of using a square as a unit is seen to lie in its symmetry and in the ease of counting in rows.

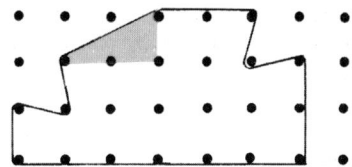

Figure 23:6

Children can find other patterns of tiles and floor coverings that enable them to make counts in order to compare the size of two surfaces. For example, parquet flooring consists of a rectangular tessellation and a count can be made of the basic rectangles which have been used for a particular surface.

The surface of a wall can be stated in terms of brick-faces, including the mortar with the brick. Since a brick

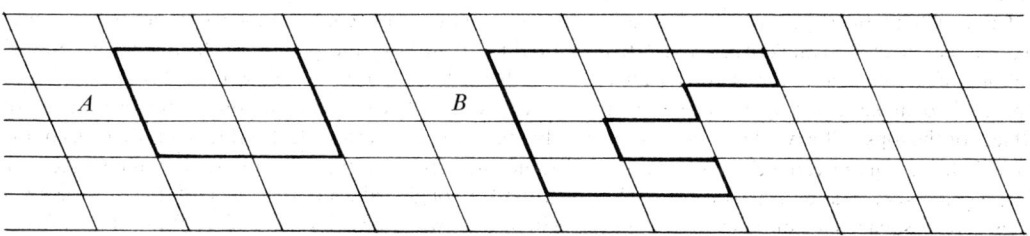

Figure 23:4

is half as wide as it is long the various types of bond (see Chapter 21) give counts of 'bricks' and 'half-bricks'. Figure 23:7 shows rectangular pieces of wall in stretcher bond and Flemish bond. The patterns of whole bricks and half-bricks are different and so the counts made in finding the areas of the pieces of wall will be different.

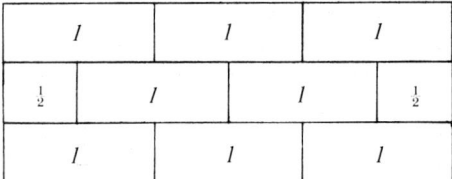

Stretcher bond

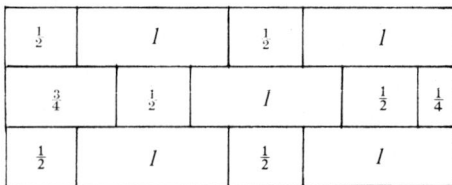

Flemish bond

Figure 23:7

In similar ways the areas of floors, ceilings and windows can be found in terms of tiles, block-faces, panes, etc., and their halves or quarters.

Standard units of area

When the principle of measuring surface by counting unit shapes has been established the standard units can be taught, though it frequently happens that children who have used graph paper of various rulings extensively will themselves suggest a square centimetre as a unit. The fractions of a square cm which can be seen on $\frac{1}{2}$-cm squared paper will be used spontaneously.

The square metre can be built up from the square cm and actual squares of this size should be cut out by the pupils, given a stiff backing, and used by groups of children to form a variety of shapes of specified area. For example, several shapes made by 12 square units could be marked on the floor or playground, using the square unit as a template. The variability of shape for a stated area is thus established and the tendency to think of area as related only to the surface of a rectangle is avoided. If twelve 1-cm cubes are used to make a variety of single layer shapes the surfaces of the tops will have the same area.

It will be noted that a square can be named by the length of a side, e.g. a $1\frac{1}{2}$-cm square or a 1-m square. Its area is stated as $\frac{1}{4}$ of a square cm, or 1 square m and written as $\frac{1}{4}$ cm^2 or 1 m^2.

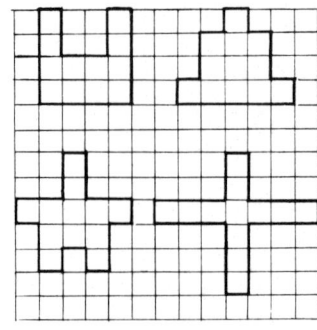

Shapes made from 12 square centimetres

Figure 23:8

The area of irregular shapes

Irregular shapes with right-angled corners have probably been encountered in the course of covering floors or parts of walls. Other shapes, with curved boundaries or unequal angles, will occur, for example in leaves, stars, or a lake on a map. To find the area of such a shape we must endeavour to use one of the standard units and make an approximate count. The outline of the shape can be drawn on squared paper or a sheet of transparent squared paper can be placed over the shape. Children can then carry out the count using one of two rules: in each case first count all the whole squares and then *either* (a) count as whole units the pieces that appear to be equal to or more than half of a whole square and ignore the pieces that are less, *or* (b) collect pairs or sets of pieces which together are about equal to a whole square. The total of unit squares obtained by either method usually gives a reasonably good approximation to the area (Figure 23:9).

(a) $\frac{1}{2}$ square or more counted as 1 (b) pieces parallel to make 1

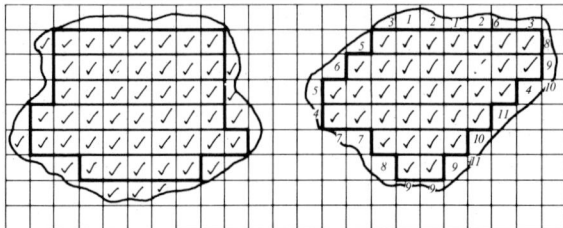

Figure 23:9

It is well to stress counting the whole squares in rows, marking them and the pieces which are being counted e.g. $9+8+9+9+10+7+3$. (Figure 23:9.)

The study of leaf surfaces, comparing two leaves of different shape or the total leaf surfaces on two twigs of the same length, is interesting (Figure 23:10). It is possible, too, to find a rough value for the area of the surface of a child by drawing the silhouettes of the four aspects, front, back and the two sides.

Figure 23:10

The area of a rectangle

Children will usually have discovered by this time how easy it is to find the area of a rectangle when it contains a whole number of rows each consisting of a whole number of squares. The product of the number of units in the length and the number in the breadth recalls early work on making patterns with rods or strips to show what multiplication means. Now children realize that this product states the area in terms of a square unit.

In general, however, rectangles do not have sides which are an exact number of measuring units in length. Yet they have a quantity of surface and it must be possible to find a way of measuring it.

A series of diagrams will build up an understanding of the way to calculate the area of rectangles with fractional or decimal measurements. First a rectangle with sides $\frac{1}{2}$ unit and $\frac{1}{3}$ unit could be drawn in the corner of a unit square. Other rectangles of the same size can be drawn to fill the square. It is seen at once that six of these rectangles fill the square. So the area of one of the

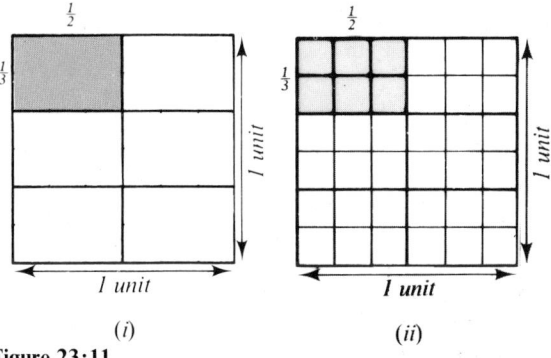

Figure 23:11

rectangles $\frac{1}{2}$ by $\frac{1}{3}$ is $\frac{1}{6}$ of the unit square (Figure 23:11(i)). It is easier for a child to use squared paper for this diagram, choosing a unit length such that 6 small squares fit along the unit side. The child can now readily mark $\frac{1}{2}$ and $\frac{1}{3}$ along the unit sides. The diagram can be completed as before and the result checked by counting the small squares. (Figure 23:11(ii).)

The rectangle $\frac{1}{2}$ by $\frac{1}{3}$ contains 6 small squares.
The unit square contains 36 small squares.
The rectangle is $\frac{1}{6}$ of the unit square.

Measurements of the sides of rectangles will usually be made in metric units with decimal notation for any parts of a unit. A unit square could now be drawn on squared paper so that 10 small squares lie along one edge. There are 10 rows of 10 squares in the unit square. If a rectangle 0·5 units long and 0·2 units wide is drawn in a corner of the square it can be seen that 5×2 such rectangles can fill the square.

10 rectangles fill the square.
1 rectangle is $\frac{1}{10}$ of the square or 0·1 of the square.

This is the result we get if we *multiply* 0·5 by 0·2, remembering that 0·5 is a half (Figure 23:12).

We can also check by counting the small squares. The rectangle 0·5 by 0·2 contains 10 small squares. The unit square contains 100 small squares. So the rectangle is $\frac{1}{10}$ of the unit square. We can also say that it is $\frac{10}{100}$ of the unit, of course, or 0·10.

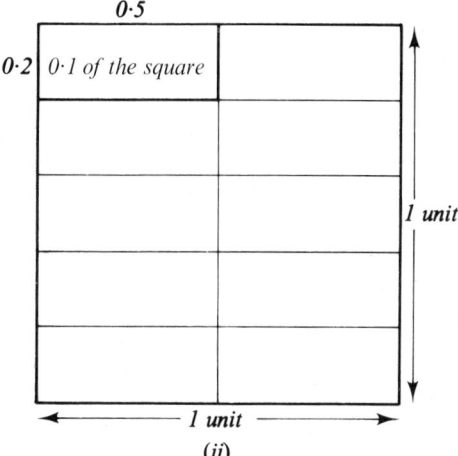

Figure 23:12

Finally we have to look at mixed numbers as the measurements of the sides of a rectangle. A diagram can illustrate the process of finding the area of a rectangle where the sides are measured in the standard unit, the metre; e.g. a rectangle 2·5 m by 1·4 m. This rectangle can be drawn to scale on squared paper. The parts of the rectangle shown in Figure 23:13 are such that their areas can immediately be found.

221

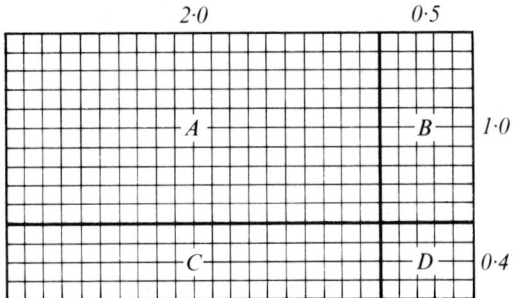

Figure 23:13

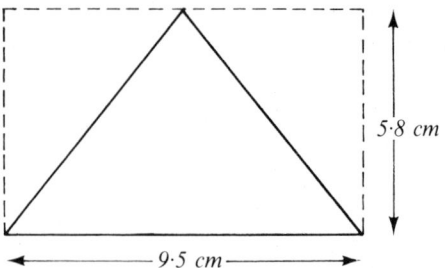

Figure 23:14

A has area $2 \cdot 0 \times 1 \cdot 0 \, \text{m}^2 = 2 \cdot 0 \, \text{m}^2$
B has area $0 \cdot 5 \times 1 \cdot 0 \, \text{m}^2 = 0 \cdot 5 \, \text{m}^2$
C has area $2 \cdot 0 \times 0 \cdot 4 \, \text{m}^2 = 0 \cdot 8 \, \text{m}^2$
D has area $0 \cdot 5 \times 0 \cdot 4 \, \text{m}^2 = 0 \cdot 2 \, \text{m}^2$

Area of whole rectangle is $(2 \cdot 5 \times 1 \cdot 0) + (2 \cdot 5 \times 0 \cdot 4) \, \text{m}^2$
or $2 \cdot 5 \times 1 \cdot 4 \, \text{m}^2$

which by addition of the four parts is $3 \cdot 5 \, \text{m}^2$.

It can be seen that this identification of the parts and their area is the foundation on which the formal multiplication procedure is based.

Children may discover that some of the larger rectangles that they are familiar with, such as a games pitch, a building site, a cornfield, are measured in hectares. They recognize the prefix *hecto* as meaning 100 from its use in *hectogram*. They will find it easier to remember that 1 hectare is the area of a square with a 100-metre side.

1 hectare $= 10,000 \, \text{m}^2$

These larger areas are usually stated in hectares and a decimal, and can be calculated in the same way as the other rectangles dealt with in this section; the area will first be found in metre squares and then converted to hectares.

Area and the multiplication of decimals

Techniques for the multiplication of decimals do not become important to children until they wish to find the areas of shapes which they have measured. For instance, if a child wishes to find the area of a triangle such as that in Figure 23:14, which he has made as part of the end of a model house, he may realize that the triangle has half the area of the enclosing rectangle, but the rectangle does not have very convenient measurements. Certainly the measurements could all be changed into millimetres, so that he finds the area of a rectangle 95 millimetres by 58 millimetres. But a square millimetre is not a very convenient unit of area, and it is more sensible to find the area in square centimetres, particularly if the original model has been built on a scale which 1 centimetre represents 1 metre, so that 1 square centimetre represents 1 square metre.

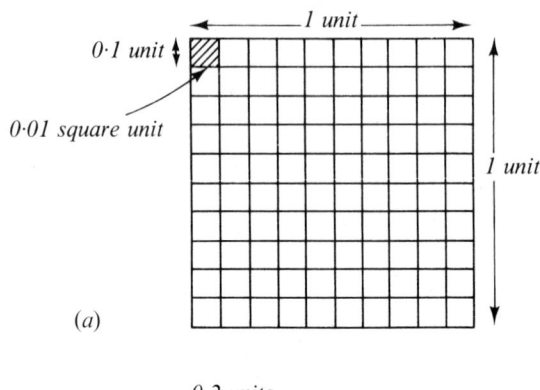

(a)

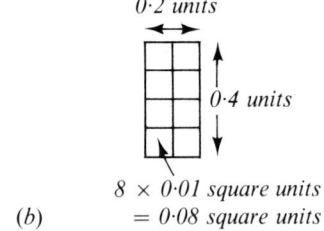

(b) $8 \times 0 \cdot 01$ square units
= $0 \cdot 08$ square units

Figure 23:15

The key to an understanding of area in decimal units is an appreciation of the fact that the area of a square 1 tenth of a unit by 1 tenth of a unit is 1 hundredth of a square unit. This is shown in Figure 23:15(*a*) where it can be seen that 100 small squares, each measuring $0 \cdot 1$ unit by $0 \cdot 1$ unit, fit into the unit square. We have already seen that

1 tenth of 1 tenth = 1 hundredth

or

$0 \cdot 1 \times 0 \cdot 1 = 0 \cdot 01$,

so that in this case, multiplication of the number of units in the length of a rectangle by the number of units in its breadth gives the number of square units in its area. Similarly, the area of a rectangle measuring $0 \cdot 2$ units by $0 \cdot 4$ units is made up of 8 small squares, each of which is 1 hundredth of a square unit (Figure 23:15(*b*)).

Similarly, the child who is finding the area of the triangle in Figure 23:14 will find it convenient to perform his calculation in the following way:

area of triangle

$= \frac{1}{2}$ (area of rectangle)

$= \frac{1}{2}$ $(9\cdot5 \times 5\cdot8$ square cm$)$

$= \frac{1}{2} \times 55\cdot1$ square cm

$= 27\cdot55$ square cm

$5\cdot8 \times$	$9\cdot5$
5	47·5
0·8	7·60
	55·10

Further important uses of decimal calculation will be found when volume is studied, in work on circles which involves taking an approximation to π such as $3\cdot14$, and in the scientific calculations of the secondary school, where slide rules are becoming widely used as aids to calculation.

Areas of shapes related to rectangles

(1) A *square*, as a special kind of rectangle, in which the length and breadth are equal, has a peculiar interest. It provides the standard units for measuring area. The numbers which connect these units, $100\,dm^2$ to $1\,m^2$ and the square on $2\,dm$ as $4\,dm^2$, recall the numbers found in the diagonal line of the table of multiples. This suggests looking at the other numbers on the diagonal and connecting them with the areas of squares: 4, 16, 25, 36, etc. Placing these squares at a common vertex we see how rapidly the area increases with the side of the square. (Figure 23:16.) If the squares are drawn on squared paper, the strip shaped like a rotated L which must be added to one square to form the next in the sequence can be stated in unit squares. This gives the sequence

$1+3 = 4$
$4+5 = 9$
$9+7 = 16$
$16+9 = 25$
$25+11 = 36$
$36+13 = 49$
$\ldots$

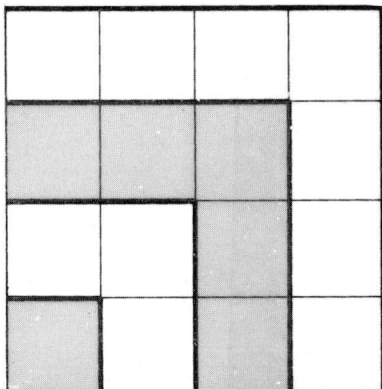

Figure 23:16

The pupils will identify the numbers represented by the strips, 3, 5, 7, ... as the sequence of odd numbers. The areas of the squares can then be graphed from the tabulation:

Side of square in cm	1	2	3	4	5...
Area in square cm	1	4	9	16	25...

The areas of some squares with fractional or decimal sides can then be read from the graph. (Figure 23:17.)

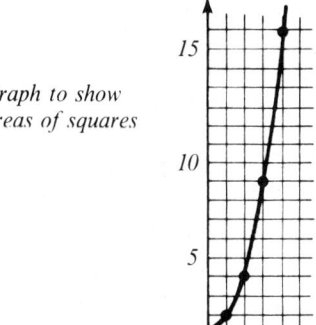

Graph to show areas of squares

Figure 23:17

(2) A *triangle* may be one of several types. The one most closely related to the rectangle is the right-angled triangle which is the diagonal half of a rectangle. If such a triangle is rotated about the middle point of its longest side through half a revolution the new and the old positions form a rectangle. Clearly the area of each triangle is half that of the rectangle. Thus every right-angled triangle has a surface area which is half that of the rectangle whose sides are the same as those that enclose the right angle in the triangle (Figure 23:18).

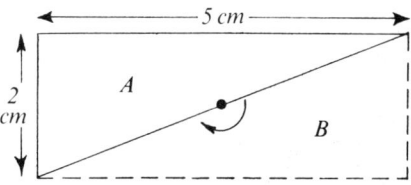

Figure 23:18

Area of triangle $A = \frac{1}{2}(5 \times 2)\,cm^2$
$= 5\,cm^2$

The triangle with two equal sides has symmetrical halves and is easy to convert into a rectangle by replacing one half and rotating it until the two halves together form a rectangle one of whose sides is half the base of the triangle and the other side is the fold line or altitude (Figure 23:19). This can lead to the formula:

Area of a right-angled triangle $= \frac{1}{2}$ base $\times$ height

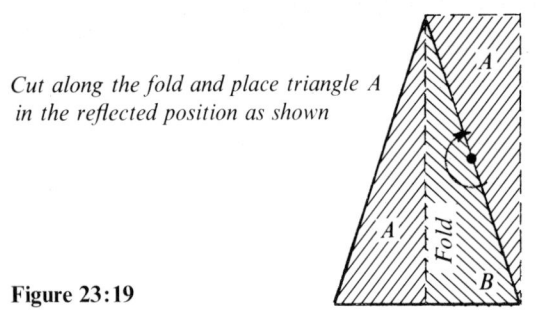

Cut along the fold and place triangle A in the reflected position as shown

Figure 23:19

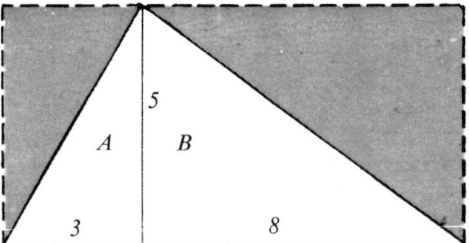

Figure 23:20

From this special case it is easy to move to the general rule which gives the area of any triangle through finding related rectangles.

Any triangle, whatever its shape may be, can be made into two right-angled triangles with a common side. If a scalene triangle, that is, one with unequal sides, is cut out in paper, one of its sides can be folded upon itself so that the fold passes through a vertex. The pupils are familiar with this folding as one which produces a right angle. When the triangle is opened out it is found that the fold is the dividing line between two right-angled triangles each of which is half a rectangle. In fact the two rectangles together form a larger rectangle, and the pattern of areas illustrates neatly the operation of the distributive law for multiplication over addition. In Figure 23:20 the original triangle has a side 11 units long which is divided by an altitude of 5 units into two parts, 3 and 8 units long. The use of the two right-angled triangles, *A* and *B*, enables us to find the area of the given triangle as follows:

$$\text{Area of triangle } A \text{ in square units} = \tfrac{1}{2} \times 5 \times 3$$
$$= \tfrac{1}{2} \times 15 = 7\tfrac{1}{2}$$
$$\text{Area of triangle } B \text{ in square units} = \tfrac{1}{2} \times 5 \times 8$$
$$= \tfrac{1}{2} \times 40 = 20$$
$$\text{Area of whole triangle} = 27\tfrac{1}{2} \text{ sq. units}$$

It is not difficult for children to see that the calculation could be shortened by first adding the two parts of the base and multiplying the sum, 11, by $\tfrac{1}{2} \times 5$, giving $\tfrac{55}{2}$ or $27\tfrac{1}{2}$. This is in fact the use of the distributive law

$$(\tfrac{1}{2} \times 5 \times 3) + (\tfrac{1}{2} \times 5 \times 8) = (\tfrac{1}{2} \times 5)(3 + 8)$$

Once more we have reached the method of finding the area

224

of a triangle by multiplying half the base by the height (or the base by half the height).

The practical method may give place to *drawing* the fold, using a set square, but at this stage, though children can work from a construction like that in Figure 23:20, it is unusual for them to understand the formula for the area of a triangle without actually drawing the related rectangle. If they are given calculations to carry out by rule of thumb from a formula they derive little, if any, benefit.

(3) A *parallelogram* can be obtained from a rectangle by a movement known as a shear. (See Chapter 12, page 118). The base of the rectangle is not moved but each 'layer' is

Figure 23:21

moved to the right (or left) parallel to the base for a given distance beyond the 'layer' below it. A pile of paper or thin pamphlets illustrates the transformation and makes it clear that the amount of surface on a vertical face is unchanged by the transformation. This can be checked by cutting off a triangle from one end of the rectangle and placing it to fit on the other end (Figure 23:21). The shape is now a parallelogram but the area is the same as that of the rectangle. The children can then be given a parallelogram and be left to invent a way of finding a rectangle to which it is equivalent in area.

Two possibilities are shown in Figure 23:22. The more general arrangement, Figure 23:22(*b*), is seen in the translation of any piece made by a line drawn at right angles to the base. When the equivalent rectangle has been found a child will measure its height and find the area of the parallelogram. The interest here lies more in the *method* of finding the area of such a shape than in the practical value of the exercise.

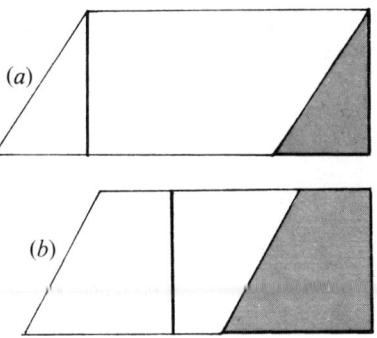

Figure 23:22

Areas of shapes related to triangles

In Chapter 21 the regular polygons were studied and these interesting shapes were found to be made up of a number of like triangles, five of one kind for a pentagon, eight of another kind for the octagon and so on. A group of able pupils could now draw several of these polygons in circles with the same radius and work out ways of finding the area of one triangle of the pentagon, say, and then of the

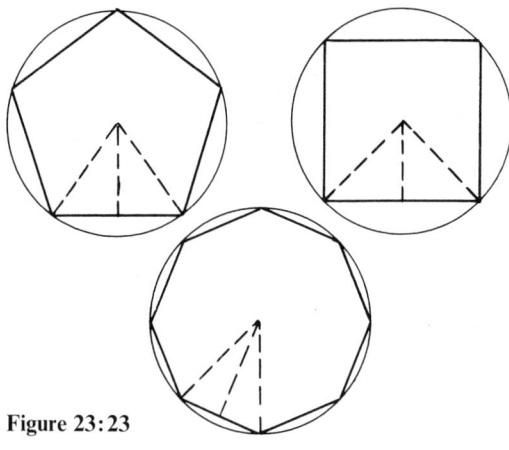

Figure 23:23

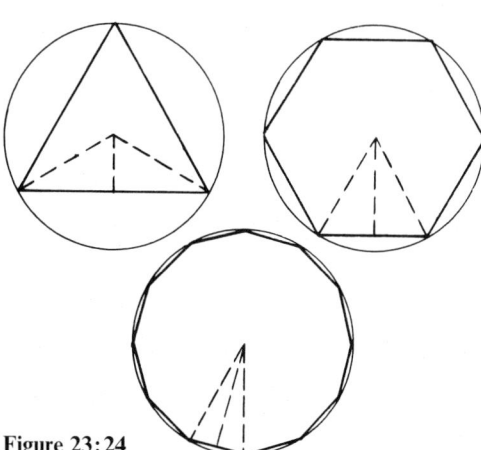

Figure 23:24

whole polygon. A square and an octagon drawn in equal circles can be compared with regard to the area. A sequence of triangle, hexagon and dodecagon can also be related (Figure 23:23).

Problems of this kind where differences are small provide good opportunities for using small units, taking measurements to the nearest $\frac{1}{4}$ unit or $\frac{1}{10}$ cm. The fractional work on pages 221–223 will have made children aware that the square on $\frac{1}{4}$ unit is $\frac{1}{16}$ square unit and that a $\frac{1}{10}$-cm square has an area of $\frac{1}{100}$ square cm. For convenience in using such small fractions the radius of the circle should be not less than 5 cm.

The usefulness of the multiplication of decimals is apparent in finding areas where tenths of a unit are used in the lengths.

Children may notice that as the number of sides increases a polygon occupies more of the space inside a circle (Figure 23:24). They may well then attempt to find the area of the circle itself by counting squares.

Surfaces of three-dimensional shapes

(1) The *cube* and its six square faces are well-known to children but it sometimes surprises them to find that a 2-cm cube is composed of eight 1-cm cubes whereas it takes twenty-four 1-cm squares to cover its surface. The surface area of a sequence of cubes, 1-cm, 2-cm, 3-cm, etc., can be tabulated and the graph compared with that of the areas of squares on page 223. An interesting inquiry is to find the

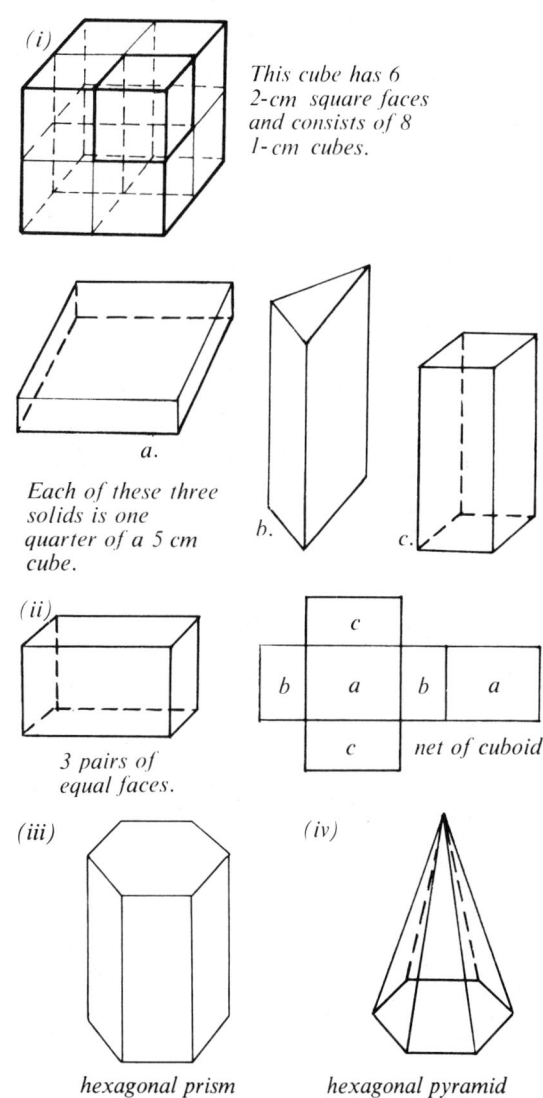

(i) This cube has 6 2-cm square faces and consists of 8 1-cm cubes.

a.

Each of these three solids is one quarter of a 5 cm cube.

b.

c.

(ii) 3 pairs of equal faces.

c

b | *a* | *b* | *a*

c

net of cuboid

(iii) hexagonal prism

(iv) hexagonal pyramid

Figure 23:25

surface area of various shapes made by cutting a cube in half. Poleidoblocs include several different-shaped quarters of a 5-cm cube and the areas of their surfaces can be compared.

(2) The surface area of a *cuboid* has a practical value since this shape is so often used for boxes and rooms. The recognition of congruent faces makes computation easier and may lead to a simple formula. If the net of a box is drawn the method of finding the area is made clearer. The use of square centimetres in finding the surface area of Cuisenaire rods is particularly convenient.

(3) *Prisms* on a triangular, hexagonal or octagonal base give areas of surface which lead up to that of the cylinder.

(4) Covering a *pyramid* may occur in making a spire for a model church, or in making decorative shapes. The importance of the triangle is emphasized. The increasing number of triangles in a sequence of triangular, square, hexagonal and octagonal pyramids bears a relation to the total surface area and may point the way to investigating the cone (Figure 23:25).

Summary

In this chapter we have considered the ways of finding the quantity of a plane surface and the units that can be used to measure it. If the region is enclosed within a shape bounded by straight lines it has been shown that sub-divisions of the region make it possible to compute the total area in terms of a unit square. Where the boundary is irregular or curved, the device of making an approximate count of squares was adopted.

We have seen that area depends on two properties which may be found in a shape: the number of strips required to cover it and the number of unit shapes that a strip contains. In the case of a rectangular shape the strips are of equal length and so these two properties are the length and breadth of the rectangle. The need to take two properties into account when considering areas is a complication which makes new demands on a child's thinking, and he must have considerable experience of practical investigations before he can understand the nature of area.

24 Volume, Weight and Density

The internal volume of hollow shapes

Measuring the contents of hollow containers such as cups, bottles, hollow cubes and cuboids, by using water or sand or rice, is an easy procedure. These substances can be poured from the container to be measured into a container graduated to show standard measures such as litres or spoonfuls. Fluids can take any shape and thus the units required for measuring capacity do not refer to lengths. For instance a litre jug need not be of a specified shape. It may not have a uniform cross-section. If the cross-section varies the intervals between graduation marks on the jug will not be equal. The graduation line will not have the regular intervals of a number line. For accurate reading of a graduation it is best to have a container such as a cylinder or a rectangular vessel which will give regular intervals when graduated to show decimal parts (Figure 24:1). Children will find that many of the packages that they use or see in shops are either cylindrical or rectangular.

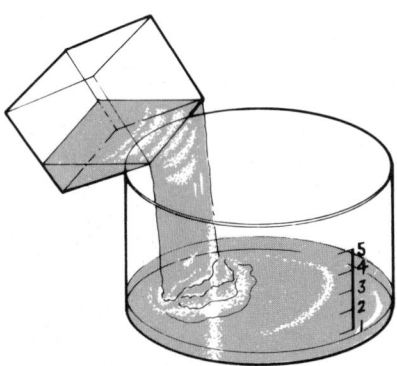

Figure 24:1

Of the two forms it is the cuboid which is most commonly used because it gives dense packing. A collection of such rectangular packets will enable children to discover that two packets may differ in length, breadth and height yet have the same capacity. It would be convenient if we could relate the measurements of the packets to their volume and thus avoid the necessity to measure the capacity. We could calculate the volume if we knew just how the volume depends on the measurements of the cuboid. With the experience of finding a unit for measuring area behind him, a child may well recall the use of the square unit and suggest the unit cube for measuring volume.

The next step is to make a unit cube and use it. The 1-cm cube is too small for children to make and manipulate precisely. A 2-cm cube is possible but a 5-cm cube can be stronger; 5-cm graph paper is useful in drawing the net of the cube. Figure 24:2 shows how the cube can be

strengthened by folding the extra squares back to reinforce the faces of the cube.

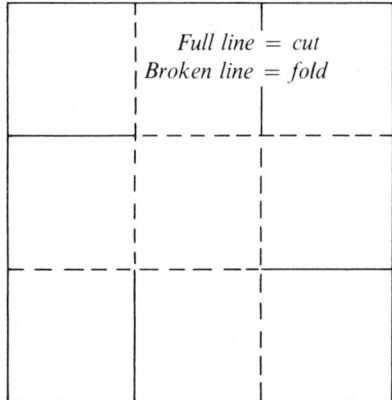

Full line = cut
Broken line = fold

Figure 24:2

The unit cube can be used to graduate a cylinder or cuboid which will serve to measure the internal volume of many containers in terms of the adopted unit cube.

The next step must be to link centimetre cubes to the litre. Children can make a strong 10-cm cube which will hold light cereal or plastic grains. When the cube has been filled its contents can be poured into a litre measure and the children will see that the 10-cm cube holds a litre. A 10-cm cube can be filled from eight of the 5-cm cubes already made but the important question now is: 'How many 1-cm cubes are needed to hold a litre?'

Building with unit cubes

So far we have been considering the volume of the contents of a container but the idea of volume is wider than capacity. It means the space occupied by a *solid* body as well as the space *inside* a *hollow* body. It is easy to use fluids to measure internal volume. It is more difficult to find units with which to measure the volume of any solid body. Which shapes fit together well so that we can count how many small ones are equivalent to a larger one? Children who are familiar with the cubes and rods of number apparatus will supply the answer. Cubes fit together to makes rows, layers and cuboids or cubes. See page 158 The centimetre cubes of the Cuisenaire apparatus can be used to make cuboids whose edges can be stated in centimetres and the volume found by counting the number of 1-cm cubes in each row, in each layer and in the whole cuboid.

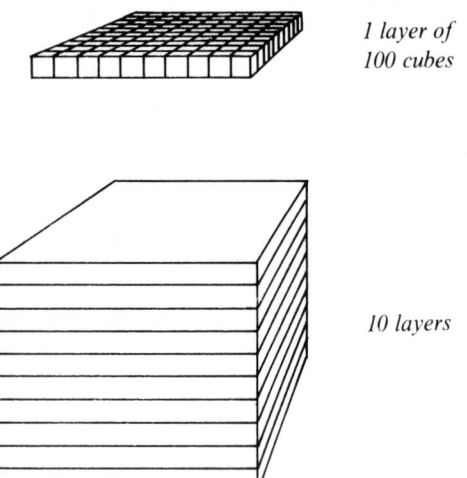

1 layer of 100 cubes

10 layers

Figure 24:3

The number of 1-cm cubes in the 10-cm cube already made can now be counted by building up such a cube in solid form with the 10-rods of Cuisenaire material. When children have found that 1000 cm-cubes are equal in volume to 1 litre they can recall the millilitre and realize that 1 millilitre and 1 cm³ have the same volume. Shapes which have a regular form may now be studied to discover the dependence of their volume on the lengths of their edges, altitudes, and so on. Thus ways of *calculating* the volume of some of the simpler shapes will evolve. The first step is to experiment with forms that can be made from a set of unit cubes so that counting cubes may show equality of volume in objects of different shape. Models of modern architectural forms give excellent examples of solids whose volumes can easily be found and pupils can make interesting designs. If it is possible to acquire some architect's models these will give a variety of forms to investigate. Some recording should be made of the numbers of units in the rows and layers used in any particular construction. Wooden unit cubes are useful in this type of modelling and can be bought cheaply in bags of 100. Each of the models in Figure 24:4 contains 48 cubes.

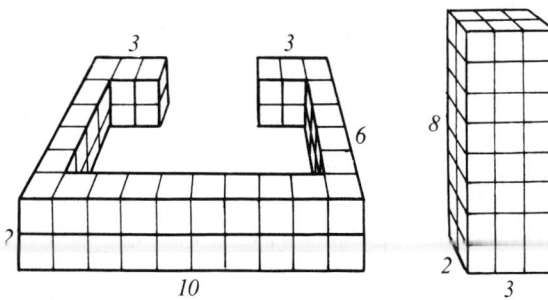

Figure 24:4

Volumes of rectangular blocks

The way is now clear for finding the volume of any cuboid by counting the unit cubes it contains. After experience of finding the area of a rectangle by multiplying the numbers of units in its length and breadth, children will readily see that multiplying the numbers of units in the length, breadth and height together will give the number of units of volume in a cuboid. The volume of a variety of interesting packets, boxes, etc., can now be found; that is, the amount of space they occupy on a shelf or in a carton. An important aspect of being able to deal with volumes is that many types of goods such as wood, gravel, etc., are sold or distributed in cubic metres. The size of a metre cube often surprises children. A class of seven-year-olds set up a cubic metre in the corner of their classroom with the aid of a vertical metre rod and metre-square sheets of paper. As many children as possible crowded, crouching, into the cube. They were astonished to find that there was room for 14 children. It is interesting too, for children to measure the space under a table, and similarly to find how many children can be accommodated within it.

Another development is to find the internal and the external volume of a box or tank made from fairly thick material. This makes use of both the total space occupied by the object and its internal capacity. It also shows the volume of the actual material used in making the object. The question of whether a lid is included appears in such problems. It is essential that a real situation should be presented to children for investigation so that verbal ambiguities do not occur and the lengths to be used are measured by the pupils. A description of the procedure followed and a statement of what has been found show the lines of thought which the children have followed.

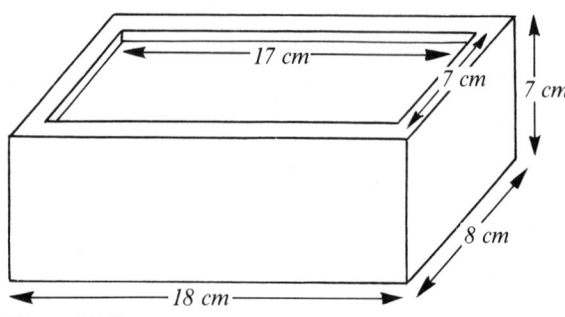

Figure 24:5

The immersion of solids in water

Experiment will show that some substances sink and others float. Through experience children become skilled in guessing whether a solid piece of material will float or not. First we study the effect of immersing objects that sink, such as stone, a lump of lead or a piece of plasticine.

The level of the water rises and, if the container is of a suitable size so that the rise in water level is noticeable, pupils can mark the levels on a strip and compare these levels with their own previously estimated order of size of the objects immersed.

Obviously the solids take up some of the space that was occupied by water. The question arises: what happens when the objects are taken back into the air? They still occupy space and must displace air when they are moved, as we notice when a draught of air is created by a moving object. Children may ask how much space a particular object occupies.

Previous experiences of measuring capacity in cubic centimetres should now tie up with experiments in immersing objects in water. A vessel graduated to show cubic centimetres can be used to record the volume in cubic centimetres which corresponds to the rise in the water level when a particular solid is immersed. Interesting objects whose volume has importance should be chosen for measuring, the pupils themselves producing things whose size they would like to compare, like heavy balls or tins (Figure 24:6).

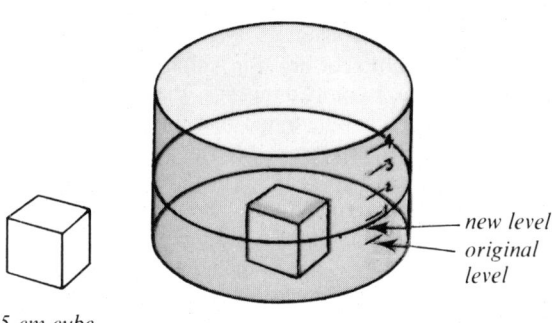

5-cm cube

Figure 24:6

Volumes of shapes used for packing

Cubes and cuboids are well-known for their property of packing closely together in a cuboid container. Half-cubes also possess this property because they can be combined into cubes. If a diagonal cut is made the cube yields two identical triangular prisms whose volumes we can find because each is half that of the cube. It will be noticed

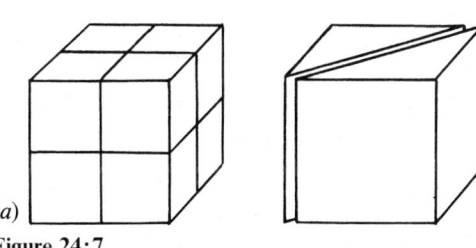

(a)

Figure 24:7

that the prism has a right-angled triangle for its base whose area is half that of the square face of the cube. The height of the prism is the same as that of the cube. It follows that to find the volume of such a prism we can multiply the area of its base by its height. (Figure 24:7(a).)

A cuboid could be halved in the same way and produce triangular prisms with base half the rectangular base of the cuboid. Again we multiply area of the base by the height to find the volume of the prism. (Figure 24:7(b).)

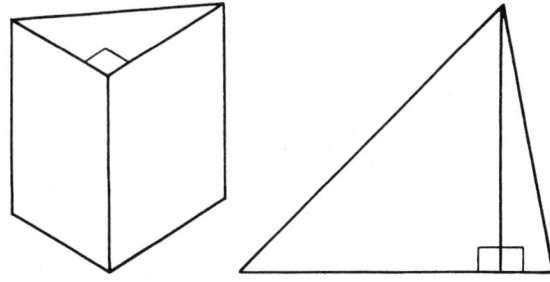

Figure 24:8

The base of this prism is a right-angled triangle. It has already been found that *any* triangle can be divided into two right-angled triangles and this fact has been used to find the area of a triangle. We can use such a prism as that in Figure 24:8 to find the volume of *any* triangular prism.

The triangular prism which is most used in packaging is the one whose base is an equilateral triangle. The containers used for Toblerone chocolate demonstrate that as the rectangular faces are all congruent the prisms can be packed into cartons with great speed, as shown in Figure 24:9. The volume of one such prism can be found, for

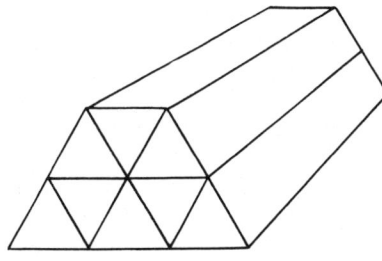

Figure 24:9

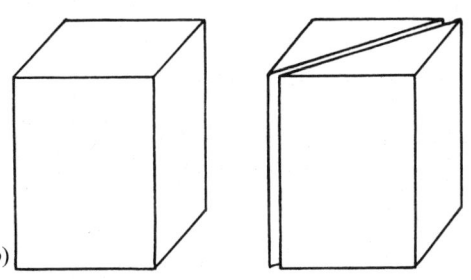

(b)

if the prism is cut through an axis of symmetry of the triangular face, two prisms will be produced each on a base which is a right-angled triangle half the area of the base of the original prism.

Another three-dimensional shape which can be used to fill a space is a hexagonal prism (Figure 24:10). This is also used for packing some kinds of sweets. Since it is composed of six prisms on an equilateral triangle as base its volume can easily be found from the work of the last paragraph. Pupils can experiment with triangular and hexagonal prisms and discover these methods for themselves. They depend very largely on the area properties discussed in Chapter 23. Some pupils will go on to find the volumes of other types of prism and may be able to state a general rule such as, 'To find the volume of a prism multiply the area of the base by the height'.

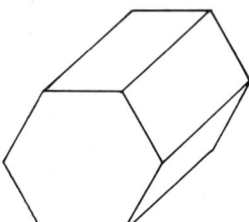

Figure 24:10

Many of the shapes in Poleidoblocs can now be studied and their volumes found and compared. Cylinders, cones and pyramids will probably lie beyond children's skill in calculation at this stage but some members of the class may propose using the method of immersion for these solids. Since wood floats in water, they will have to face the problem of making the solids sink. See page 232.

Cuisenaire rods and approximately the Dienes Multibase Arithmetic Blocks are based on the centimetre. The cube found in both sets can profitably be used as a unit to find the volumes of all the other cubes and cuboids. On this foundation of experience with metric units of volume pupils could find in cubic centimetres the internal volume of some tins which have the weight of their contents stated in grams on the labels. They could compare the volumes of equal masses of different substances.

Relation of surface area to volume

The comparison of the surface area of a 2-cm cube (24 sq. cm) and the number of unit cubes which composed it was mentioned on page 225. We can now take a series of cubes with edges 1 cm, 2 cm, 3 cm, 4 cm, ... and find the surface area and the volume of each, tabulating the results.

Edge of cube in cm	Surface area in cm^2	Volume in cm^3	Ratio of number of units of area to units of volume
1	6	1	6:1
2	24	8	3:1
3	54	27	2:1
4	96	64	1·5:1
5	150	125	6:5
			or 1·2:1

The rates at which surface area and volume grow can be seen and graphs of the two sets of numbers can be drawn. But the most interesting feature of the table is the changing relation of surface to volume. The decrease in the ratio of the units of surface area to the units of volume is striking and is important for living creatures. It means that smaller organisms have a larger area of skin in relation to volume. For small warm-blooded creatures this involves a greater loss of heat than for larger creatures. A baby loses heat more rapidly than a full-grown person in the same conditions. Consequently a baby needs more heat-producing food than an adult to maintain its body temperature. Similarly a mouse needs more food, in proportion to its size, than an elephant.

If the set of ratios of areas to volumes of the cubes tabulated above is plotted against the corresponding lengths of edges it will be found that the points lie on a curve which can be recognized as having the same shape as the one drawn in Chapter 16, page 154. The product of corresponding pairs of numbers is constant. It can be verified from the table that the product is 6. Pupils may wish to find additional points to show the shape of the curve more clearly (Figure 24:11).

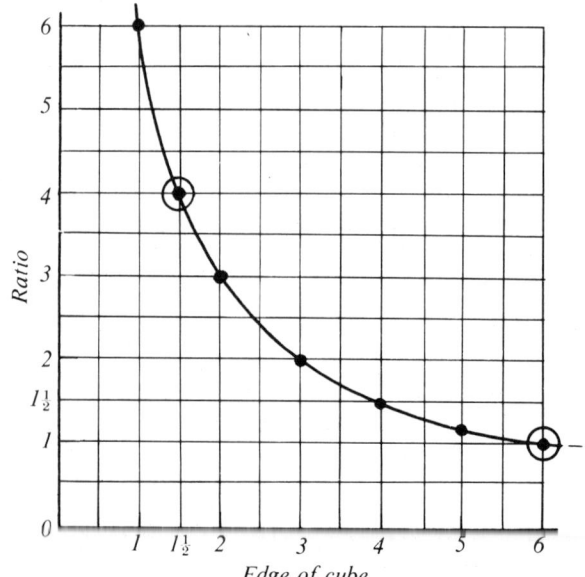

Figure 24:11

Any set of similar solids will show this characteristic relationship and pupils can find corresponding sets of ratios for cuboids and possibly other shapes. The growth of crystals illustrates the principle well since crystals maintain their shape as they grow.

In Chapter 24, page 228, a variety of shapes was made with the same volume. It is now interesting to compare the volumes of cuboids with the same surface area. Which shape has the greatest volume for a given area of surface? This is a task suited only to the abler pupils. They can make different cuboids with same amount of surface if they first choose the base and then discover what the height must be to give the required surface.

If a 5-cm cube is taken as the first cuboid every other cuboid must have 150 cm² of surface. When we make a cuboid with 150 cm² of surface on a base 6 cm by 4 cm, we first notice that the base and the top together have an area of 48 cm² leaving 102 cm² for the four side faces. But the perimeter of the base is $2 \times (6+4)$ cm, i.e. 20 cm.

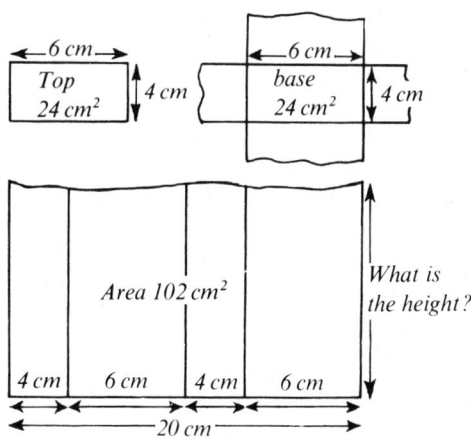

Figure 24:12

If the area is to be 102 cm² the height of the cuboid must be $(102 \div 20)$ cm, i.e. 5·1 cm. This should be checked. The base of the cuboid is 6 cm by 4 cm.

$$\text{Its surface area} = (2 \times 6 \times 4) + (2 \times 5 \cdot 1 \times 6)$$
$$+ (2 \times 5 \cdot 1 \times 4) \text{ cm}^2$$
$$= 48 + 61 \cdot 2 + 40 \cdot 8 \text{ cm}^2$$
$$= 150 \text{ cm}^2$$
$$\text{Its volume} = 6 \times 4 \times 5 \cdot 1 \text{ cm}^3$$
$$= 122 \cdot 4 \text{ cm}^3$$

This calculation is quite complicated and should be carried out in relation to the actual model being made. Figure 24:12 shows two stages in the process of making a paper model.

The following table shows the dimensions and volumes of several possible cuboids and indicates that the cube has the greatest volume for a given surface area.

Dimensions of base (in any given unit)	Height (in same units)	Volume (in cubic units)
2 by 2	2	8
2 by 1	$3\frac{1}{3}$	$6\frac{2}{3}$
3 by 1	$2\frac{1}{4}$	$6\frac{3}{4}$
4 by 1	$1\frac{3}{5}$	$6\frac{2}{5}$
2 by 3	$1\frac{1}{5}$	$7\frac{1}{5}$
2 by 4	$\frac{2}{3}$	$5\frac{1}{3}$

The relation of mass to volume

We now consider the relationship between two quite different properties possessed by objects: mass and volume, which are measured in unrelated units. When surface and volume are compared each is measured in terms of a unit based on a length. If this unit of length is one centimetre then the unit of area is 1 square cm and the unit of volume 1 cubic cm. Although the properties being compared are different in kind we can usefully think of the *ratio* of the *number* of units involved in an area (or volume) to the *number* of units of length because of the interdependence of the units concerned. In comparing such different properties as mass and volume it is best to think of the relation as a *rate*, stating the mass of a specified volume, e.g. grams per cubic centimetre. This rate, mass per unit of volume, is known as the *density* of a substance and is usually studied as part of the science programme. The mathematical aspects should be integrated with this programme.

First we must show that for any particular substance mass increases regularly as volume increases. Weighing 1 cm³, 2 cm³, 3 cm³, . . . of a substance we find that mass is doubled, trebled, etc. Any cubic cm of the same substance will therefore have the same mass. Hence if we weigh a volume of 7 cm³ we can divide the mass by 7 to find the mass per cu. cm. Archimedes used this principle in his brilliant solution of the problem: Was the king's new crown made of pure gold or had some silver been introduced into it? He made a crown in pure gold and of the same mass as the one in question. If both crowns were of the same substance they should have the same volume. But how could their volumes be measured? His famous discovery was that immersing the crowns in water would cause the water level to rise the same amount if the volumes were equal. In the event the original crown displaced more water, and so its volume was greater. It therefore contained a substance lighter than gold, producing more volume for an equal mass. Hence the suspicion that the crown contained some silver was confirmed.

In finding the volumes of various objects pupils will have realized again that large objects may be light to handle and small things heavy. If the objects are solid the differences must be due to the substances of which they are made. To investigate this it is necessary to consider objects of the same size but of different materials. A set of 2-cm cubes made from brass, wood, cheese, Plasticine, etc., may be available. For example, a 2-cm cube of brass weighs 60 g approximately, cheese 14 g, wood 7 g. In cases where 1 cm³ of the substance is not available the volume of the piece used must be found. The mass divided by the number of cm³ gives the mass per cm³. For instance, a strip of brass 20 cm by 2·5 cm by 1·3 cm weighs 490 g. The volume of the cuboid is 65 cm³. The mass per cm³ is 7·5 g.

When the substance has an irregular shape its volume must be found by the immersion method described on page 229.

Fluids and granular substances or powders have usually to be weighed in a container. This presents the problem of finding the weight of the contents alone. Children should be able to *find* a method of doing this. The container is first weighed empty and then filled with the substance; subtraction gives the mass of the contents. But we need the mass of *1 cm³* of the liquid. We must therefore either have a measured volume to start with or we must find the volume in the container.

The following examples could be worked out in an ordinary classroom. A small tin of mustard powder is sold full and labelled as containing 113 g of mustard.

The full tin weighs 169 g
Thus the empty tin weighs 56 g
Filled with water it weighs 271 g
The water must weigh 215 g

The tin has an internal volume of 216 cm³. Therefore we can state the weight per cm³ of

mustard as $113 \div 216 = 0·5$ g approx.
water as $215 \div 216 = 1·0$ g approx.

Since a gram is the mass of 1 cubic centimetre of water the density of water is stated as 1 gram per cm³. It is therefore easy to compare the density of any substance with that of water.

Flotation

So far we have experimented with objects which sink when placed in water or whose shape enabled us to calculate their volume. Is it possible to find the density of a body of irregular shape which floats? For example, finding the density of a piece of cork is a problem which demands inventiveness from children.

The question is whether a floating body can be made to sink so that we can find its volume by displacement. Experiments with a variety of materials which float, such as wood, plastics and paraffin wax will help. The flotation of hollow bodies and the children's own ability to float in

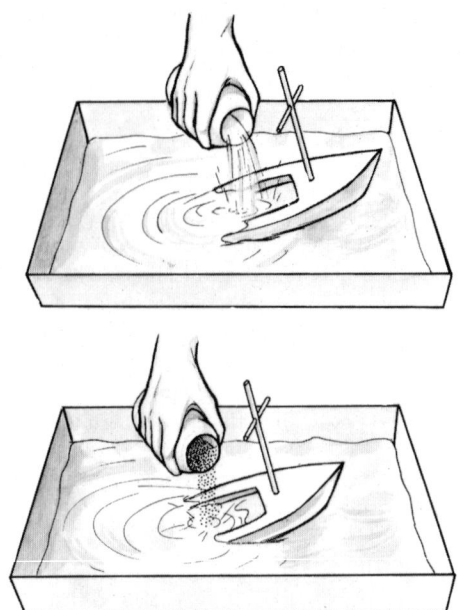

Figure 24:13

water will provoke discussion, as will the position in which a piece of ice floats. When a light object is placed so that it floats in the water in a small tank, the level of the water rises. The mass of the floating object can be compared with the mass of the water which has risen above the original level. The mass of the water displaced may be found by using a displacement can or by an improvised method. It will be found that the mass of water displaced equals the mass of the object. A study of ships and small model boats, observing the variations in their water line according to their load or cargo, will make the principle clear. When a light hollow vessel is floating and water is slowly poured into it the moment will come when it will sink. The levels of the water inside and outside the boat should be noted when it is on the point of sinking. The water that was added should be weighed. Instead of water, sand can be put in and the same procedure followed. The level of the sand at the point of sinking is not the same as that of the water. But the mass should be compared.

Now that a floating hollow body has been made to sink and the equality of mass between the water displaced and the body submerged established, the pupils can consider the problem of finding the volume of *solid* bodies which are *lighter* than water. All that is required is that the body shall have added to it something heavy enough to bring about the sinking. A piece of paraffin wax can be attached, by thin cotton, to a piece of metal. If the volume of the metal is known it can be subtracted from the total volume as recorded by the rise in the water level. The mass of the wax must then be divided by its volume to give its density. The pupils are now in a position to compile a list of the densities of some substances which are lighter than water and of some that are heavier.

Conclusion

The work of this chapter has been concerned with measuring important properties of solid bodies, their volumes, masses and densities. The experiments suggested should lead to a fundamental grasp of these properties and their relationships with one another. The range of shapes for which volume can be calculated at this stage is limited, but the procedure of immersion may lead the more enterprising pupils to investigate the volumes of pyramids, cones, cylinders and spheres.

25 Some Operations on Fractions and Decimals

Children's informal experience of fractions

Early on in children's mathematical work, concrete examples of fractions appear almost as often as concrete examples of natural numbers. On many occasions the language of halves, quarters and thirds will be needed, and children should be encouraged to use these terms whenever possible. In the early years in school children should have handled many concrete examples of fractions of shapes, numbers, lengths, masses, volumes and times. The following examples show some ways in which the language of fractions can be used alongside that of multiplication and division.

i) Two 500 millilitre jugs fill a litre jug. The smaller jug holds *half* a litre.

ii) Five 200 gram masses balance a kilogram. A 200 gram mass is *one-fifth* of a kilogram.

iii) In 15 minutes the minute hand of a clock makes a *quarter* of a turn. Four quarter-turns make a complete turn. Four times 15 minutes is an hour; 15 minutes is a *quarter* of an hour.

iv) Using Cuisenaire rods, five red rods are equivalent to an orange rod. The red rod is *one-fifth* of the length of the orange rod.

v) A bar of chocolate can be broken into eight equal pieces. Each piece is *one-eighth* of the bar.

When children fold or cut a square of paper into four equal parts, each part is a *quarter* of the square. They may become interested in exploring the number of different ways in which they can make quarters of a square. Figure 25:1 shows some possibilities, and the variety of these possibilities may be contrasted with the single simple method of dividing a circle into quarters.

If fractional language is used consistently in such situations as these, and if children are encouraged to discuss and record their work, a number of ideas about fractions take shape informally in their minds. These ideas may need clarification later, but they grow out of this informal experience, and meaningful later work with fractions depends on them.

The first of these ideas is that a whole or unit has been divided into a number of *equal* parts. This may need stressing, as children sometimes hear outside school the word 'half' being used merely for a part of a whole, rather than for one of two equal parts. Children also become aware that, in concrete terms, the unit may be anything which can be divided up: a shape, a length, a mass, a time, or a set of things; so they use fractions naturally in some situations and not in others. They cannot talk about a quarter of a child in the same way that they can talk about

234

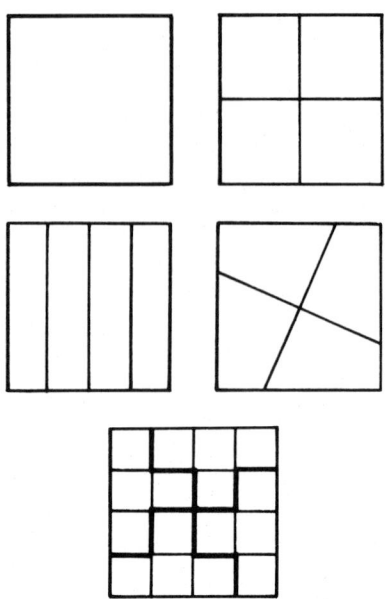

Figure 25:1

a quarter of a cake, although they can see the relationship between a set of two children and a set of eight children, and say that there are a quarter as many children in the first set.

It may happen that these informal experiences make children familiar with $\frac{1}{2}$, $\frac{1}{4}$ and $\frac{1}{10}$ of a unit, but not with $\frac{2}{3}$, $\frac{2}{4}$ or $\frac{3}{4}$ of a unit. When children, for instance, fold a square into quarters they should therefore be encouraged to look at and use not just one quarter of the square, but to fit together two of the quarters or three of the quarters, and to notice that when one quarter of the square has been cut out, three quarters are left. Children will also come across the expression 'three-quarters of an hour', and should notice that two quarter-hours make half an hour.

Equivalence

As soon as they begin to use sub-units freely, children notice that two quarters of any unit are the same as one half of that unit. This provides the first example of *equivalence* between fractions; that is, of the idea that the same part of a unit can be described in many different ways. Children need much experience of equivalence in different situations and with fractions of varied units if they are to grasp this idea. Shape provides one convenient illustration, for circles, squares and rectangles can easily be divided into halves, quarters and eighths. Figure 25:2 shows some illustrations of equivalences among fractions of different unit shapes which are divided into halves,

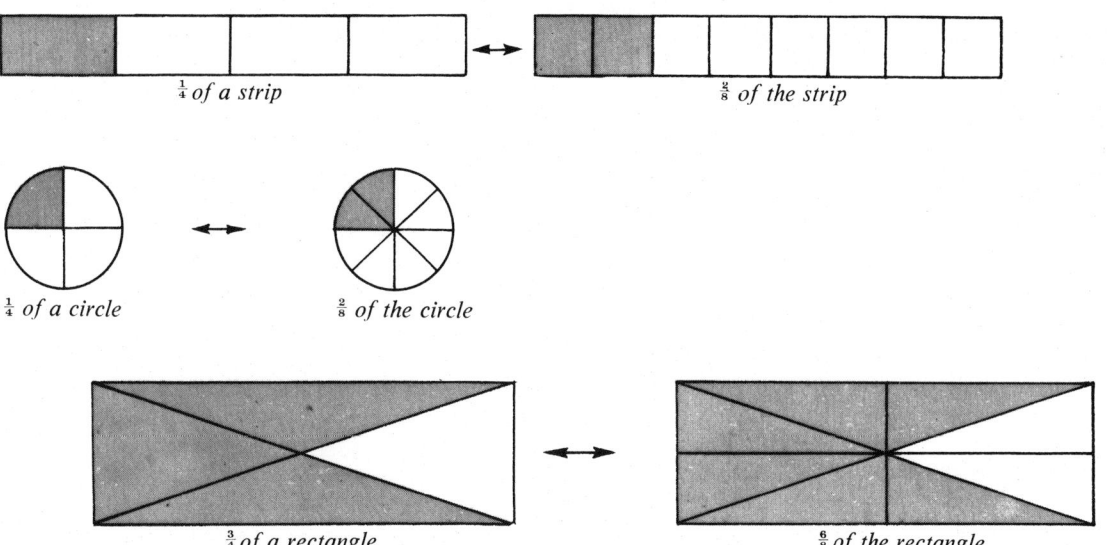

¼ of a strip ↔ 2/8 of the strip

¼ of a circle ↔ 2/8 of the circle

¾ of a rectangle ↔ 6/8 of the rectangle

Figure 25:2

quarters and eighths. A more sophisticated example than the others shows that the quarters ▷ and ▽ of the rectangle are not the same shape, although each quarter is made up of two eighths ◺ which are the same shape. Children may at first refuse to accept that the parts are quarters, since they cannot be fitted over one another without further cutting up. In fact, the quarters which are being formed in this and other examples are quarters of the *area* of the rectangle. When fractions of plane shapes are made, it is this area property which is used. When equivalences between fractions are found, children can keep a list of them. Measuring units, particularly the metre, and units of money give further important examples, e.g.

$$0 \cdot 5 \text{ metre} = \tfrac{5}{10} \text{ metre} = \tfrac{1}{2} \text{ metre},$$

leading to the number statement,

$$0 \cdot 5 = \tfrac{5}{10} = \tfrac{1}{2},$$

and

$$25 \text{ pence} = £\tfrac{1}{4},$$

leading to

$$0 \cdot 25 = \tfrac{1}{4}$$

As a result of their practical experience, children will quickly build up the following sets of equivalent fractions:

$$\tfrac{1}{2} = \tfrac{2}{4} = \tfrac{4}{8} = \tfrac{5}{10} = 0 \cdot 5$$
$$\tfrac{1}{4} = \tfrac{2}{8} = \tfrac{25}{100} = 0 \cdot 25$$
$$\tfrac{3}{4} = \tfrac{6}{8} = \tfrac{75}{100} = 0 \cdot 75$$
$$\tfrac{1}{5} = \tfrac{2}{10} = 0 \cdot 2$$

and a few others. More complicated sets of equivalent fractions can remain for detailed study at a later stage.

Extending decimal notation

Children will not at this stage need to use decimal fractions smaller than one-thousandth, but the teacher should realize that the notational system which uses *place value* enables numbers, however large or small, to be written briefly, using only a small number of symbols. We there-

2 thousands 5 hundreds 7 tens 6 ones 9 tenths 4 hundredths 3 thousandths

Thousands	Hundreds	Tens	Ones	Tenths	Hundredths	Thousandths
2	5	7	6	9	4	3

10 thousandths = 1 hundredth

10 hundredths = 1 tenth

10 tenths = 1 one

10 ones = 1 ten

10 tens = 1 hundred

10 hundreds = 1 thousand

Figure 25:3

235

fore now extend the place-value system of notation (base ten) so that it can be used to write smaller and smaller fractions of a unit.

The extension of place-value notation to include fractions of a unit is immediately clear to the adult reader who is already completely familiar with the place-value notation for natural numbers. Children may, however, first meet the decimal system of notation for fractions before they have a complete grasp of notation for natural numbers; the gradual and practical introduction of decimals, which make use of the place-value system, can do much to help children to understand notation, and so to strengthen their grasp of the number system.

Decimal and fractional notation

Children who are using both decimal and fractional notations for parts of a unit will wish to be able to move easily between the two notations. In simple cases this presents no problems. For instance, 0·9 is 9 tenths, and so can also be written as $\frac{9}{10}$. Many conversions from decimal to fractional notation depend, however, on the use of equivalence. Thus,

$$0\cdot4 = \tfrac{4}{10},$$

but $\frac{4}{10}$ can easily be recognized in the equivalent form $\frac{2}{5}$. Similarly,

$$0\cdot24 = 2 \text{ tenths } 4 \text{ hundredths},$$

and

$$2 \text{ tenths} = 20 \text{ hundredths},$$

so that

$$0\cdot24 = 24 \text{ hundredths}$$
$$= \tfrac{24}{100}$$
$$= \tfrac{6}{25}$$

This last step is not easy for a child to see. It depends on a detailed knowledge of equivalence between fractions, which should not be expected until later. Thus it is advisable for a child who has started a piece of recording using decimal notation to stay within that notation rather than try to change to fractional notation. This is particularly desirable because calculations involving addition and subtraction are far easier in decimal than in fractional notation.

Addition and subtraction of decimals

If a child knows how to add and subtract whole numbers, and particularly how to find the total of a bill in pounds and pence, and how to give change from a sum of money, no new problems arise in decimal calculations. For instance, the sum of £1 27 pence and £2 35 pence can be

236

recorded either as

£	tenpences	pence
1	2	7
+2	3	5
	1	2
3	5	
3	6	2

or as

$$
\begin{array}{r}
£1 . 27 \\
+ \;\; 2 . 35 \\
\hline
3 . 62
\end{array}
$$

The principle that pence must be added to pence, tenpences to tenpences and pounds to pounds, becomes the principle that hundredths are added to hundredths, tenths are added to tenths, ones are added to ones, and so on. Of course, ten hundredths are changed to one tenth in exactly the same way that ten pence are changed to one tenpence.

Subtraction follows exactly the same principle. If 37 centimetres of ribbon are cut from 1 metre 50 centimetres, the calculation of the remaining length can be recorded either as

m	dm	cm
1	5	0
−	3	7

and regrouped as

m	dm	cm
1	4	10
−	3	7
1	1	3

or recorded as

$$
\begin{array}{r}
\text{m} \\
1 \cdot 50 \\
-0 \cdot 37 \\
\hline
1 \cdot 13
\end{array}
$$

By this time, since column headings are no longer used, children should be encouraged to perform the regrouping mentally. We see that all addition and subtraction is based on the same principle of working with each sub-unit in turn, and changing to the next sub-unit when necessary.

Activities like making boxes, model building and so on, provide older children with many opportunities for measuring in centimetres and millimetres, and making decimal calculations. The four walls of a model building may be made from a continuous strip of card, whose length must be found and measured out. Placing a door in the centre of a wall will give rise to more calculations using decimal measurements. Figure 25:4 shows a few of the calculations used in building a model of a village church.

We see also in this calculation that multiplying a decimal by a whole number presents no problems.

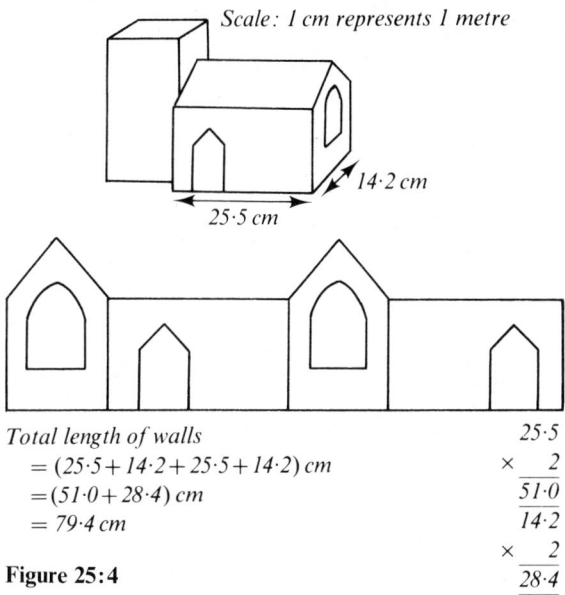

Scale: 1 cm represents 1 metre

14·2 cm

25·5 cm

Total length of walls
= (25·5 + 14·2 + 25·5 + 14·2) cm
= (51·0 + 28·4) cm
= 79·4 cm

$$\begin{array}{r} 25·5 \\ \times\ \ 2 \\ \hline 51·0 \\ 14·2 \\ \times\ \ 2 \\ \hline 28·4 \end{array}$$

Figure 25:4

Fractions of numbers

We have seen that a fraction is a part of some divisible unit; but in most of the illustrations the unit has been a quantity such as a metre, or a shape such as a rectangle whose area can be divided into parts. That is, the unit which is subdivided is a measurable quantity to which a number can be attached, such as a number of units of area. The number may be attached to this divisible unit in various ways; we can talk about $\frac{1}{4}$ of *one* metre or $\frac{1}{4}$ of 100 centimetres. Thus, $\frac{1}{4}$ of 100 begins to be meaningful. A set of things can also have a number attached to it, the *number of things in the set*. Children will say that a set of 4 bricks contains *half as many* as a set of 8 bricks. Hence $\frac{1}{2}$ of 8 is equal to 4. Similarly, the set of 8 children in the class wearing brown shoes contains a *quarter as many* as the set of 32 children in the class; $\frac{1}{4}$ of 32 is equal to 8. By generalization from many such situations, a fraction of a *number* takes on meaning for children, so that they will understand and be able to find $\frac{1}{2}$ of 8 and $\frac{1}{4}$ of 32. They will have had much experience of this sort previously, but may only have expressed it in the language of division, as $8 \div 2$, $32 \div 4$ and so on. It is desirable, however, that the fractional wording 'one quarter of 32' should be used alongside '32 divided by 4' when children find situations which involve division.

The idea of a fraction may occur in building up larger sets from smaller ones as well as in the comparison of two sets and the partitioning of a set into subsets. A child may build a tower from 2 red bricks, 3 blue bricks and 3 green bricks. When he has reached the concrete-operational

stage of thinking and can see that the set of red bricks (R) is contained in the set of bricks (B) which he has used, (i.e. $R \subseteq B$), the next step is to see that the number of the set of red bricks is a quarter of the number of the complete set of bricks (Figure 25:5). He may express this as $n\{R\} = \frac{1}{4}$ of $n\{B\}$, or, using the numbers of the sets, as $2 = \frac{1}{4}$ of 8.

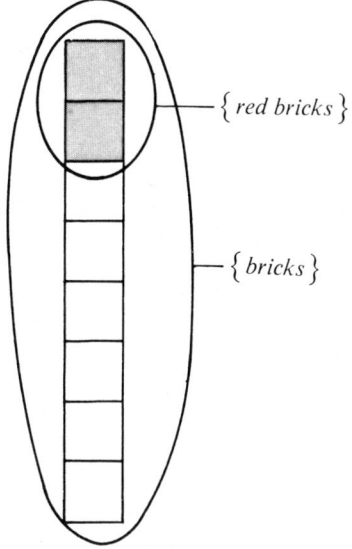

{ red bricks }

{ bricks }

Figure 25:5

Later, these experiences will be extended to the finding of fractions such as $\frac{3}{4}$ of 24,[1] and the more systematic study of such a fraction as $\frac{3}{4}$. Figure 25:6 shows this in terms of structural apparatus, and then by a graph.

This graph makes interpolation possible, and children will find that $\frac{3}{4}$ of 10 = $7\frac{1}{2}$. This can be verified in terms of length by folding a piece of paper 10 cm long, or by folding up the first 10 cm of a tape-measure.

The similarity between this graph and the multiplication graphs of Chapter 16 is easily seen. Figure 25:7 shows several such graphs drawn on the same axes, and forms a useful preliminary to the linking of 'a fraction of' with multiplication.

---

[1] This brings out the idea that $\frac{3}{4}$ of 24 is 3 times ($\frac{1}{4}$ of 24), or that $\frac{3}{4} = 3 \times \frac{1}{4}$.

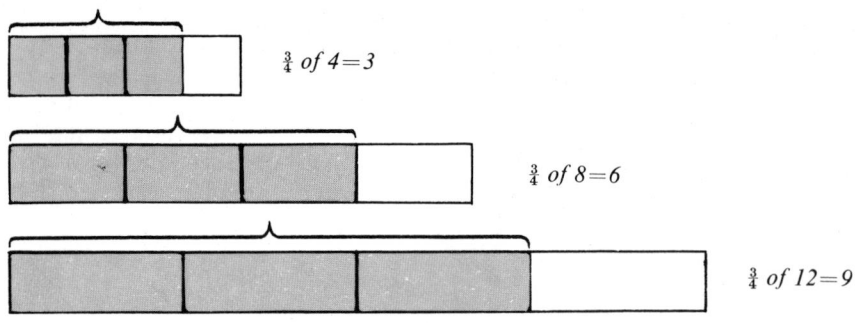

$\frac{3}{4}$ of $4=3$

$\frac{3}{4}$ of $8=6$

$\frac{3}{4}$ of $12=9$

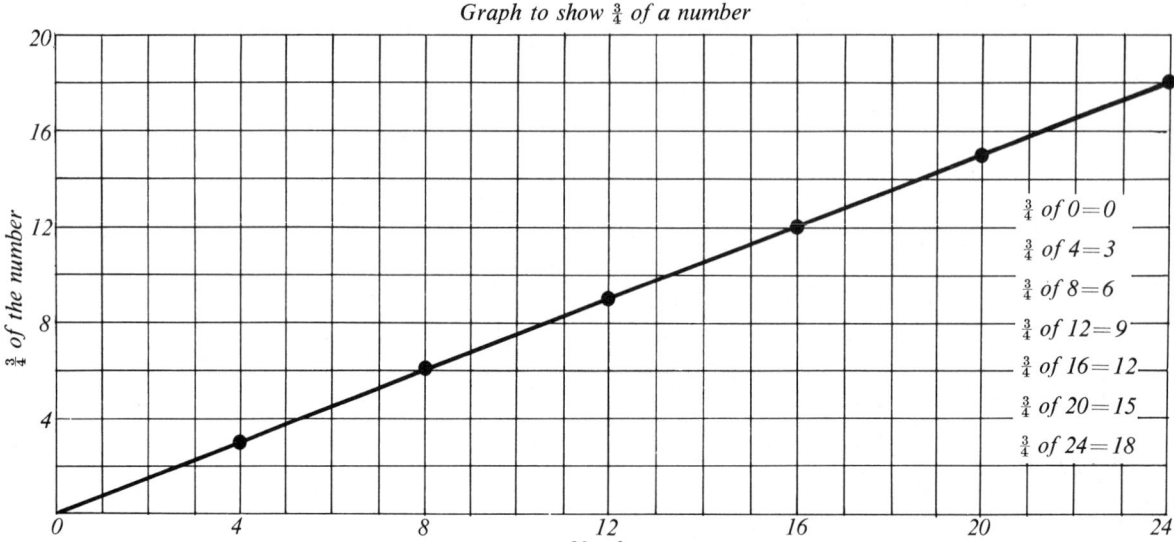

Graph to show $\frac{3}{4}$ of a number

$\frac{3}{4}$ of the number

Number

$\frac{3}{4}$ of $0=0$
$\frac{3}{4}$ of $4=3$
$\frac{3}{4}$ of $8=6$
$\frac{3}{4}$ of $12=9$
$\frac{3}{4}$ of $16=12$
$\frac{3}{4}$ of $20=15$
$\frac{3}{4}$ of $24=18$

Figure 25:6

Graph to show fractions of numbers

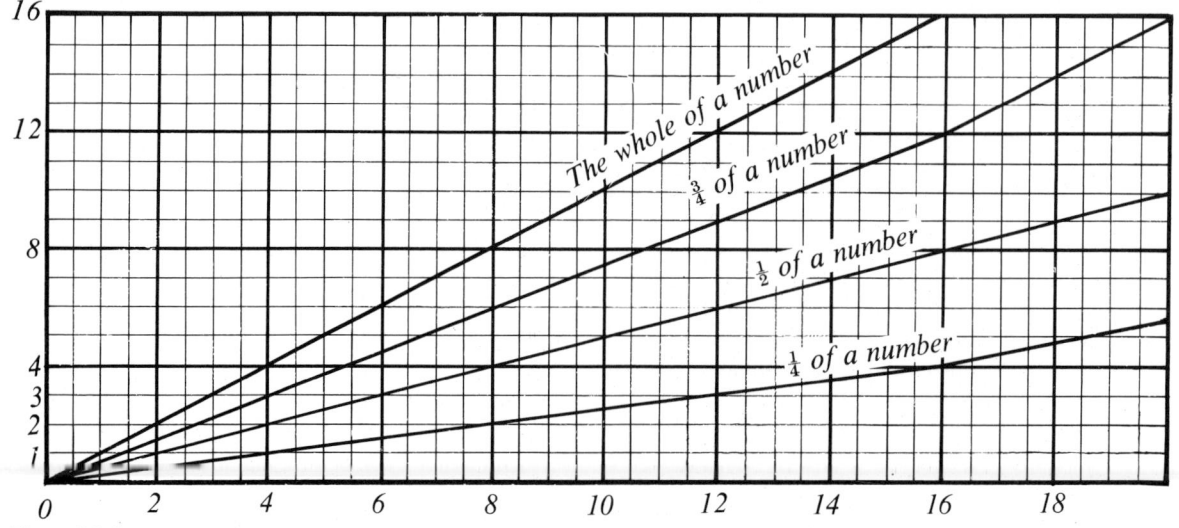

The whole of a number

$\frac{3}{4}$ of a number

$\frac{1}{2}$ of a number

$\frac{1}{4}$ of a number

Figure 25:7

238

Addition and subtraction of fractions

We now turn to other discoveries which children make very early in their exploration of fractions. From their concrete experiences children not only discover equivalences between fractions, but also find ways in which fractions of quantities can be put together, compared and taken apart, which will lead them to addition and subtraction, multiplication and division of fractional numbers.

The exploration of shapes also gives many instances of the ways in which parts of a unit area combine to make the unit, or to make other fractions of the unit. The simple folding of a unit square into quarters shown in Figure 25:8 illustrates not only the equivalence $\frac{1}{2} = \frac{2}{4}$, but also a great variety of other facts, such as the following, which children can find for themselves.

$$\frac{1}{2} + \frac{1}{2} = 1 \qquad 1 - \frac{1}{2} = \frac{1}{2}$$
$$\frac{1}{4} + \frac{3}{4} = 1 \qquad 1 - \frac{3}{4} = \frac{1}{4} \qquad 1 - \frac{1}{4} = \frac{3}{4}$$
$$\frac{1}{4} + \frac{1}{2} = \frac{3}{4} \qquad \frac{3}{4} - \frac{1}{2} = \frac{1}{4} \qquad \frac{3}{4} - \frac{1}{4} = \frac{1}{2}$$
$$\frac{1}{4} + \frac{1}{4} = \frac{1}{2} \qquad \frac{1}{2} - \frac{1}{4} = \frac{1}{4}$$

$$\frac{1}{4} + \frac{1}{4} = 2 \times \frac{1}{4} = \frac{1}{2} \qquad \frac{1}{2} \div 2 = \frac{1}{4}$$
$$\frac{1}{4} + \frac{1}{4} + \frac{1}{4} = 3 \times \frac{1}{4} = \frac{3}{4} \qquad \frac{3}{4} \div 3 = \frac{1}{4}$$
$$\frac{1}{4} + \frac{1}{4} + \frac{1}{4} + \frac{1}{4} = 4 \times \frac{1}{4} = 1 \qquad \frac{1}{2} \text{ of } \frac{1}{2} = \frac{1}{4}$$
$$\frac{1}{3} \text{ of } \frac{3}{4} = \frac{1}{4}$$

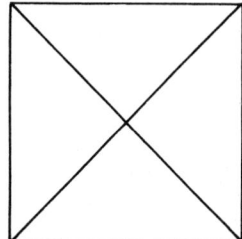

Figure 25:8

The last two sets of facts will be discussed later, but are included here to show what can be found. All these combinations are illustrated whenever a piece of paper is folded into quarters, and children may be encouraged to see how many mathematical facts they can find in a simple and familiar situation such as this. Some children will tackle such a problem systematically, and dividing a circle (a cake or pie) into 6 equal parts (Figure 25:9) may produce

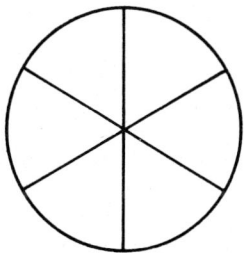

Figure 25:9

such an orderly list of additions and subtractions as the following, together with multiplication and division statements.

$$\frac{1}{6} + \frac{5}{6} = 1 \qquad 1 - \frac{5}{6} = \frac{1}{6} \qquad 1 - \frac{1}{6} = \frac{5}{6}$$
$$\frac{2}{6} + \frac{4}{6} = 1 \qquad 1 - \frac{4}{6} = \frac{2}{6} \qquad 1 - \frac{2}{6} = \frac{4}{6}$$
$$\frac{3}{6} + \frac{3}{6} = 1 \qquad 1 - \frac{3}{6} = \frac{3}{6}$$
$$\frac{4}{6} + \frac{2}{6} = 1 \qquad 1 - \frac{2}{6} = \frac{4}{6} \qquad 1 - \frac{4}{6} = \frac{2}{6}$$
$$\frac{5}{6} + \frac{1}{6} = 1 \qquad 1 - \frac{1}{6} = \frac{5}{6} \qquad 1 - \frac{5}{6} = \frac{1}{6}$$
$$\frac{1}{6} + \frac{4}{6} = \frac{5}{6} \qquad \frac{5}{6} - \frac{4}{6} = \frac{1}{6} \qquad \frac{5}{6} - \frac{1}{6} = \frac{4}{6}$$
$$\text{etc.}$$
$$\frac{1}{6} + \frac{3}{6} = \frac{4}{6} \quad \text{etc.}$$

Children at an early stage of generalization and insight into structure are less systematic, often putting two haphazardly chosen pieces together, and comparing them purely empirically with the unit. A free situation such as this, in which a child is able to make his own problems, will reveal a good deal about the development of his thinking.

Among the most interesting statements which are produced in this way are those, such as $\frac{3}{4} + \frac{1}{8} = \frac{7}{8}$ and $\frac{2}{3} - \frac{1}{6} = \frac{1}{2}$, where the denominators of the fractions are not the same; that is, where the unit has not been divided into the same number of parts each time. The statement $\frac{3}{4} + \frac{1}{8} = \frac{7}{8}$ is only another way of putting $\frac{6}{8} + \frac{1}{8} = \frac{7}{8}$ (Figure 25:10), and a child soon realizes that in order to see the relationship between $\frac{3}{4}$ and $\frac{1}{8}$ he must think of $\frac{3}{4}$ as $\frac{6}{8}$; that is, he must replace $\frac{3}{4}$ by an equivalent fraction which he can handle more easily in a given situation. The fractions $\frac{3}{4}$ and $\frac{1}{8}$ cannot immediately be added, as they are measured in terms of different sub-units; $\frac{3}{4}$ must be replaced by $\frac{6}{8}$. Now both fractions are measured in eighths, and so they can be added. Even the very simple $1 - \frac{1}{3}$ involves thinking of 1 as $\frac{3}{3}$, so that it can be compared with $\frac{1}{3}$.

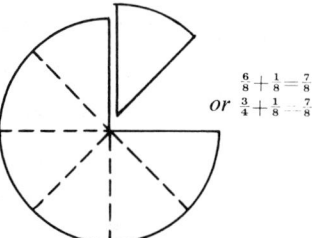

$$\text{or} \quad \begin{array}{c} \frac{6}{8} + \frac{1}{8} = \frac{7}{8} \\ \frac{3}{4} + \frac{1}{8} = \frac{7}{8} \end{array}$$

Figure 25:10

If children are encouraged to make their own problems in addition and subtraction, and to solve them practically, they will find that they are using two principles.

(1) Only fractions which are measured in terms of the same sub-unit can be added or subtracted immediately; in fact a child very rarely needs to use any form of apparatus for $\frac{2}{6} + \frac{3}{6}$ or for $\frac{7}{8} - \frac{2}{8}$.

(2) If the fractions which he wishes to add or subtract are not measured in terms of the same sub-unit, a child can

replace them by equivalent fractions which are measured in the same sub-unit. Then the writing of

$$\tfrac{3}{4}+\tfrac{1}{8}=\tfrac{6}{8}+\tfrac{1}{8} \quad \text{or} \quad 1-\tfrac{2}{5}=\tfrac{5}{5}-\tfrac{2}{5}$$
$$=\tfrac{7}{8} \qquad\qquad\qquad =\tfrac{3}{5}$$

is a record of an action which the child has performed either physically or mentally.

Finding $\tfrac{1}{6}+\tfrac{1}{4}$ is more difficult for a child than $\tfrac{1}{8}+\tfrac{1}{4}$, because one fraction is not an immediate subdivision of the other. Here, both quarters and sixths must be replaced by twelfths, obtaining

$$\tfrac{1}{6}+\tfrac{1}{4}=\tfrac{2}{12}+\tfrac{3}{12}$$
$$=\tfrac{5}{12}$$

Problems of this type very rarely occur in practical situations, and a child will not wish to tackle them until he can generalize enough to ask, 'Can *any* two fractions be added together?' By then he will understand equivalence sufficiently to search for suitable equivalent fractions by which to replace $\tfrac{1}{6}$ and $\tfrac{1}{4}$, until he finds a pair which he can add because they are measured in the same sub-unit.

It is not recommended that rules for the addition and subtraction of fractions, such as methods of finding a common denominator, should be given at this stage. For practical purposes children will work with decimal fractions, and a further systematization of equivalence of fractions is only given here so that the teacher may have a more complete picture of the fraction notation.

More about equivalent fractions

The notion that there is more than one way of writing the same number, that $\tfrac{1}{2}$, $\tfrac{2}{4}$, $\tfrac{5}{10}$ and so on, all represent the same fraction of a unit, is an idea which is very similar to that of writing the same natural number using different bases. From examination of the sets of equivalent fractions which have been built up, there will eventually emerge the generalization that two fractions are *equivalent*, or have the same value, when the numerator and denominator of one fraction are the same multiples of the numerator and denominator of the other. The fraction $\tfrac{15}{24}$ is equivalent to $\tfrac{5}{8}$, and the numerical relationship between the two expressions is $15 = 3 \times 5$, $24 = 3 \times 8$. Numerator and denominator have both been multiplied by 3. The sets of equivalences

$$\frac{3}{4}=\frac{6}{8}=\frac{9}{12}=\frac{12}{16}=\frac{15}{20}=\cdots$$

can be written as

$$\frac{3}{4}=\frac{2\times3}{2\times4}=\frac{3\times3}{3\times4}=\frac{4\times3}{4\times4}=\frac{5\times3}{5\times4}=\cdots$$

It must be emphasized that this result is not an arbitrary rule, but a generalization from a number of real experiences, and that when children need to use equivalent

240

fractions, they must be given experiences from which they can make this generalization.

A tabulation of equivalences such as that in Figure 25:11 may be built up as a result of practical experiences, and

$\tfrac{1}{2}$	$\tfrac{2}{4}$	$\tfrac{3}{6}$	$\tfrac{4}{8}$	$\tfrac{5}{10}$	.	$\tfrac{50}{100}$	.
$\tfrac{1}{3}$	$\tfrac{2}{6}$	$\tfrac{3}{9}$	$\tfrac{4}{12}$	$\tfrac{5}{15}$	.	.	.
$\tfrac{2}{3}$	$\tfrac{4}{6}$	$\tfrac{6}{9}$	$\tfrac{8}{12}$	$\tfrac{10}{15}$	.	.	.
$\tfrac{1}{4}$	$\tfrac{2}{8}$	$\tfrac{3}{12}$	$\tfrac{4}{16}$	$\tfrac{5}{20}$	.	$\tfrac{25}{100}$	.
$\tfrac{3}{4}$	$\tfrac{6}{8}$	$\tfrac{9}{12}$	$\tfrac{12}{16}$	$\tfrac{15}{20}$	.	$\tfrac{75}{100}$	.
$\tfrac{1}{5}$	$\tfrac{2}{10}$	$\tfrac{3}{15}$	$\tfrac{4}{20}$	$\tfrac{5}{25}$	.	$\tfrac{20}{100}$	.
$\tfrac{2}{5}$	$\tfrac{4}{10}$	$\tfrac{6}{15}$	$\tfrac{8}{20}$	$\tfrac{10}{25}$	.	$\tfrac{40}{100}$	.
$\tfrac{3}{5}$	$\tfrac{6}{10}$	$\tfrac{9}{15}$	$\tfrac{12}{20}$	$\tfrac{15}{25}$	.	$\tfrac{60}{100}$	.

Figure 25:11

some children will be able to generalize from this table, and to make a statement such as 'You get an equivalent fraction by multiplying the numerator and denominator of any fraction by the same number.' The next step is to express algebraically the generalization which has been arrived at in words. This is a more difficult process, not to be expected until the Secondary school stage. The algebraic method of stating the generalization, as

$$\frac{m}{n}=\frac{p\times m}{p\times n},$$

will then be found very satisfactory, as it is less cumbersome than words. Figure 25:12 illustrates this generalization. Here the *area* of a rectangle is used to represent the unit rather than using a length.

When the idea of equivalence has become fully operational a child will know that the process of replacing a fraction by an equivalent one is reversible, so that he not only knows that $\tfrac{3}{4}$ is equal to $\tfrac{9}{12}$, but that $\tfrac{9}{12}$ can be replaced by the simpler equivalent fraction $\tfrac{3}{4}$. Thus he can obtain an equivalent fraction by dividing the numerator and denominator by the same number.

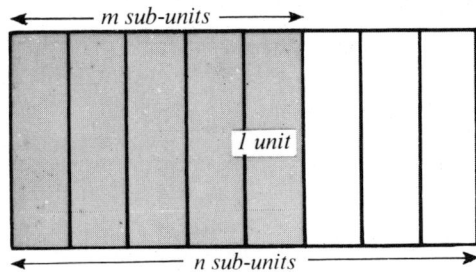

m sub-units

1 unit

n sub-units

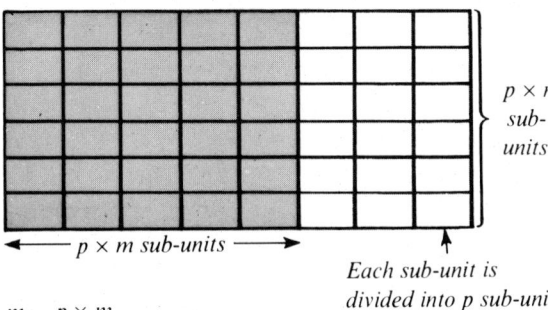

$p \times n$ sub-units

$p \times m$ sub-units

Each sub-unit is divided into p sub-units

$$\frac{m}{n} = \frac{p \times m}{p \times n}$$

Figure 25:12

The division aspect of fractions and decimals

We have used the language of fractions and decimals to describe many experiences which a child will also describe in other ways. He says 'one third of 6' as an alternative to '6 divided by three' and a further aspect of the idea of a fraction is based on the interchangeability of the language of fractions and of division.

In Figure 25:13 the construction of a graph of quarters of numbers is described in two ways. Children can use this graph to find such further facts as $\frac{1}{4}$ of 9 or $9 \div 4 = 2\frac{1}{4}$. When natural numbers only are used, and the units remain indivisible, the only way of dealing with $9 \div 4$ is to divide eight of the nine units by four, leaving an indivisible remainder of one unit; but when fractions are used the one remaining unit is no longer indivisible, and now $9 \div 4 = 2\frac{1}{4}$. Writing this in terms of improper fractions, $9 \div 4 = \frac{9}{4}$. We see that all the following expressions are equal:

$$\tfrac{1}{4} \text{ of } 9 = 9 \div 4 = 9 \times \tfrac{1}{4} = \tfrac{9}{4} = 2\tfrac{1}{4}$$

It is necessary for later understanding that among the ideas of $\frac{9}{4}$ which children form, there should not only be

i) 9 quarters of one unit, but also
ii) 9 units divided by 4, or one-quarter of 9 units.

It is particularly important that children should understand how this relationship applies to tenths, so that they think of 0·3 not only as

i) 3 tenths of one unit, but also
ii) 3 units divided by 10, or one tenth of 3 units.

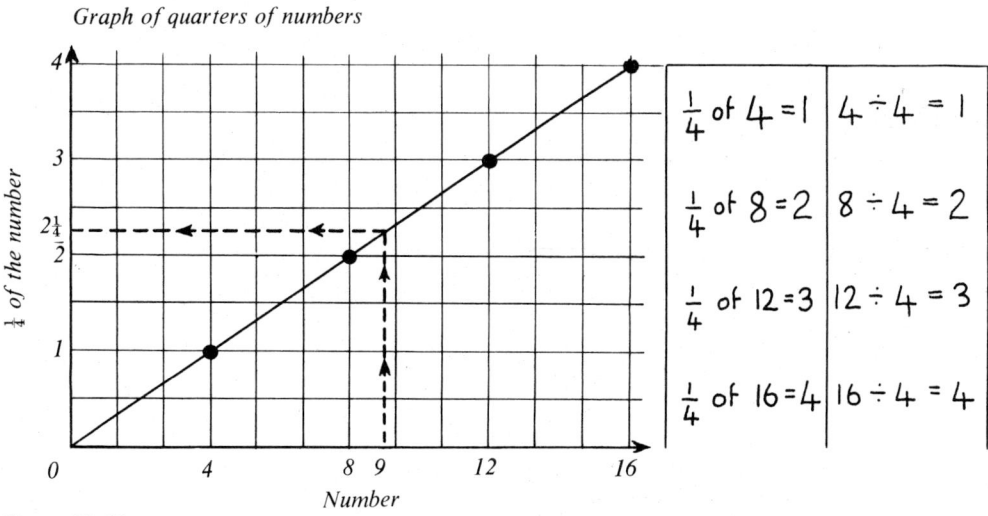

Graph of quarters of numbers

$\frac{1}{4}$ of 4 = 1	4 ÷ 4 = 1
$\frac{1}{4}$ of 8 = 2	8 ÷ 4 = 2
$\frac{1}{4}$ of 12 = 3	12 ÷ 4 = 3
$\frac{1}{4}$ of 16 = 4	16 ÷ 4 = 4

Figure 25:13

241

$$9 \div 4$$

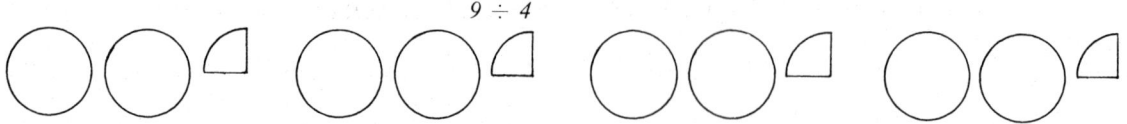

Figure 25:14

Various division experiences, on the lines of those suggested below, can help to build up these ideas.

(1) Divisible units such as cakes are shared between a number of people. In Figure 25:14, 9 cakes are shared between 4 people.

(2) In Figure 25:15, 3 units have been divided by 10, using base ten blocks with the large cube as unit. The diagram also shows the division of 3 units by 100, and by 1000.

The pattern which arises from these divisions by 10, 100, and 1000 is of great importance:

$$3 \div 10 = 0 \cdot 3 \quad \text{(3 tenths)}$$
$$3 \div 100 = 0 \cdot 03 \quad \text{(3 hundredths)}$$
$$3 \div 1000 = 0 \cdot 003 \quad \text{(3 thousandths)}$$

It will eventually be seen as an extension of the pattern of multiplication by the base:

$$3 \times 10 = 30 \quad \text{(3 tens)}$$
$$3 \times 100 = 300 \quad \text{(3 hundreds)}$$
$$3 \times 1000 = 3000 \quad \text{(3 thousands)}$$

and will form the basis for the multiplication of decimal numbers.

A division such as $9 \div 4$, which has been discussed in the context of fractions, can also be carried out within the decimal system, for any remaining units can always be changed into sub-units, as the following example shows.

$$9 \text{ units} \div 4 = 2 \text{ units} + (1 \text{ unit} \div 4)$$
$$= 2 \text{ units} + (10 \text{ tenths} \div 4)$$
$$= 2 \text{ units} + 2 \text{ tenths} + (2 \text{ tenths} \div 4)$$
$$= 2 \text{ units} + 2 \text{ tenths} + (20 \text{ hundredths} \div 4)$$
$$= 2 \text{ units} + 2 \text{ tenths} + 5 \text{ hundredths}$$
$$= 2 \cdot 25$$

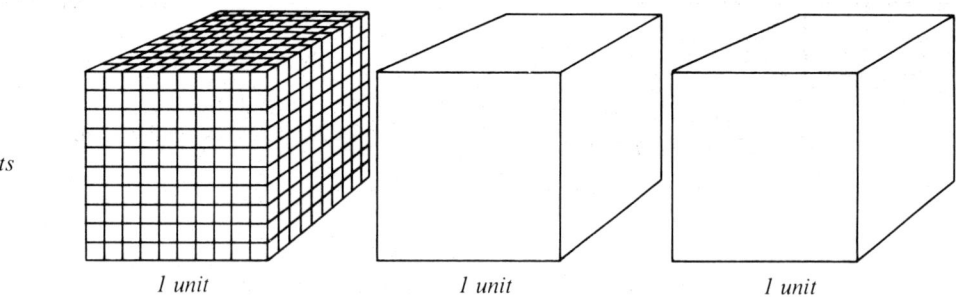

3 units

1 unit   *1 unit*   *1 unit*

1 tenth of 3 units

1 tenth   *1 tenth*   *1 tenth*

1 hundredth of 3 units

1 hundredth   *1 hundredth*   *1 hundredth*

1 thousandth of 3 units   *1 thousandth*   *1 thousandth*   *1 thousandth*

$$3 \div 10 = 3 \text{ tenths} = 0 \cdot 3 = \tfrac{3}{10}$$
$$3 \div 100 = 3 \text{ hundredths} = 0 \cdot 03 = \tfrac{3}{100}$$
$$3 \div 100 = 3 \text{ thousandths} = 0 \cdot 003 = \tfrac{3}{1000}$$

Figure 25:15

This process is illustrated in Figure 25:16. and the working is conventionally abbreviated to

$$\begin{array}{r} 2 \cdot 25 \\ 4\overline{)9 \cdot 00} \\ 8 \\ \overline{10} \\ 8 \\ \overline{20} \\ 20 \\ \overline{} \end{array} \quad \text{or} \quad \begin{array}{r} 2 \cdot 25 \\ 4\overline{)9 \cdot 00} \end{array}$$

The ability to perform any division within the decimal system makes it possible for any fraction to be expressed in decimal form. For instance, in a very simple case, $\frac{1}{4} = 1$ unit $\div 4$, so we have,

$\frac{1}{4} = 1$ unit $\div 4$
  $= 10$ tenths $\div 4$
  $= 2$ tenths $+ (2$ tenths $\div 4)$
  $= 2$ tenths $+ (20$ hundredths $\div 4)$
  $= 2$ tenths $+ 5$ hundredths
  $= 0 \cdot 25$

or by a conventional division process,

$\frac{1}{4} = 1$ unit $\div 4$ $\qquad \begin{array}{r} 0 \cdot 25 \\ 4\overline{)1 \cdot 00} \end{array}$
  $= 0 \cdot 25$

When a remainder occurs in the hundredths place, further decimal places are needed:

$$\begin{array}{r} 0 \cdot 375 \\ 8\overline{)3 \cdot 00} \\ 24 \\ \overline{60} \\ 56 \\ \overline{40} \\ 40 \\ \overline{} \end{array}$$

$\frac{3}{8} = 3$ units $\div 8$
  $= 30$ tenths $\div 8$
  $= 3$ tenths $+ (6$ tenths $\div 8)$
  $= 3$ tenths $+ (60$ hundredths $\div 8)$
  $= 3$ tenths $+ 7$ hundredths $+ (4$ hundredths $\div 8)$
  $= 3$ tenths $+ 7$ hundredths $+ (40$ thousandths $\div 8)$
  $= 3$ tenths $+ 7$ hundredths $+ 5$ thousandths
  $= 0 \cdot 375$

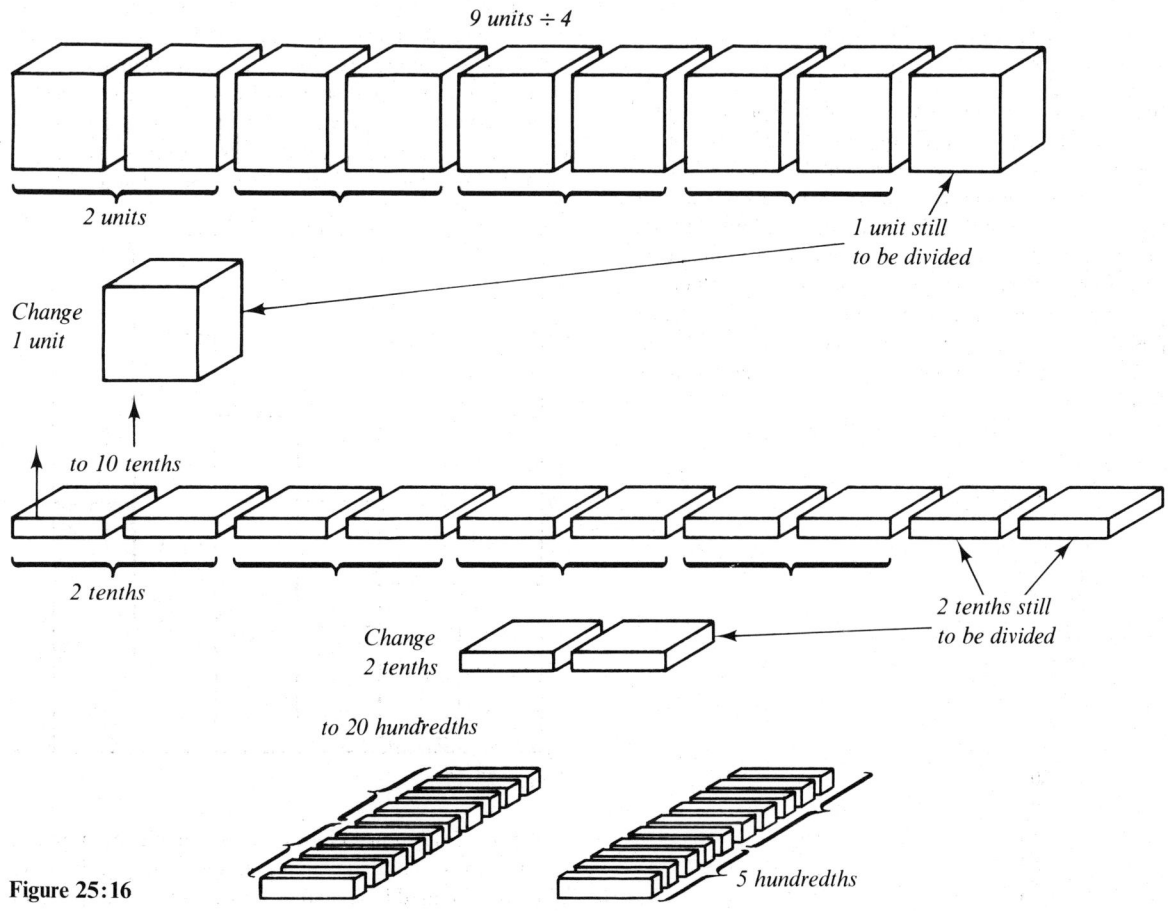

Figure 25:16

Recurring decimals

Children will realize that remainders may continue to occur:

$\frac{1}{3}$ = 1 unit ÷ 3
  = 10 tenths ÷ 3
  = 3 tenths + (1 tenth ÷ 3)
  = 3 tenths + (10 hundredths ÷ 3)
  = 3 tenths + 3 hundredths + (1 hundredth ÷ 3), etc.
  = 0·333 . . .

For practical measuring, only the second place of decimals is likely to occur, unless the unit is very large, and 0·33 is a good enough approximation to $\frac{1}{3}$ for many purposes.

However, it is important for children to realize that 0·33 is only an approximation to $\frac{1}{3}$, and that in fact

$$3 \times 0·33 = 0·99$$

When the division $1 \div 3$ is performed, there always is a remainder at any stage, so that if we stop the division after any number of decimal places, we only have an approximation to $\frac{1}{3}$, and the decimal form of $\frac{1}{3}$ is a *recurring decimal*.

Many fractions, in their decimal forms, are recurring decimals. For instance,

$\frac{1}{9} = 0·1111 \ldots \qquad = 0·\dot{1}$,
$\frac{1}{7} = 0·1428571428 \ldots = 0·\dot{1}4285\dot{7}$,
$\frac{1}{11} = 0·09090 \ldots \qquad = 0·\dot{0}\dot{9}$

In writing a recurring decimal, a dot is placed over the recurring digit, or if a cycle of digits recurs, over the first and last digits of the cycle or *period*. Children may verify that the length of the recurring period is always less than the denominator of the fraction. No more digits can occur in the period since, when division by a number n is performed, only $(n-1)$ different non-zero remainders are possible. For instance, when we evaluate $1 \div 7$, the only possible remainders at any step of the division are 0, 1, 2, 3, 4, 5, 6. If 0 occurs as a remainder, the decimal terminates. If not, it recurs.

```
      0·1428571
  7)1·0
      7
      30
      28
      20
      14
      60
      56
      40
      35
      50
      49
      10
       7
       3
```

In this case, all the possible non-zero remainders occur, and the period of the recurring decimal is 6 digits.

It can also be verified that the decimal equivalent of a fraction only terminates if the denominator of the fraction has 2 or 5 or both 2 and 5 (possibly repeated) as its only factors. For example

$$\frac{1}{4} = \frac{1}{2 \times 2} = 0·25,$$

$$\frac{1}{50} = \frac{1}{2 \times 5 \times 5} = 0·02$$

$$\frac{1}{125} = \frac{1}{5 \times 5 \times 5} = 0·008$$

Fractions as ratios

A further aspect of the concept of a fraction is that a fraction expresses a relationship, or *ratio*, between two numbers or quantities. This idea may be more difficult for children to grasp than some of the other ideas involved in the understanding of fractions. Ratio is, however, a concept which appears very often in later mathematical work, and one which is often not understood because of inadequate preparation at the Primary school stage. Experience which leads to the idea of ratio and its link with fractions is certainly within the grasp of Primary school children; indeed, the idea of a ratio is present in much of their work on multiplication, on fractions and in scale-drawing. In these topics the language of ratio gives a new emphasis to familiar subject-matter. (See Chapter 20.)

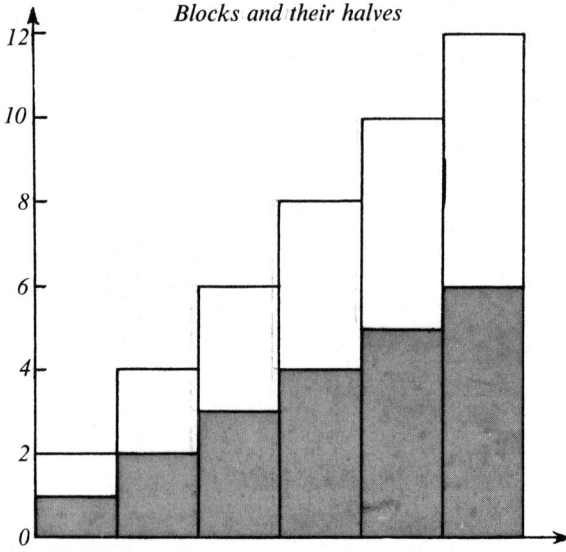

Figure 25:17

Figure 25:17 shows a block graph of halves of numbers. Such graphs and their corresponding line graphs have already been used in several ways. From the ratio point of

244

view, the aspect to be emphasized is that the height of each shaded block bears the same relation to the height of its corresponding outline block; its height is always half that of the outline block. Hence the relation of a shaded block to its outline block is always expressed by the ratio 1:2, and the ratio of an outline block to its shaded block is 2:1. But, for instance, the last pair of blocks shown on the graph are of heights 6 units and 12 units, so that here the ratio is 6:12. The ratio 6:12 is equivalent to the ratio 1:2. This is more conveniently written in fractional form as $\frac{6}{12} = \frac{1}{2}$. Each column of the graph is a different embodiment of the ratio 1:2, and successive columns of the graph illustrate the equivalent ratios or fractions

$$\frac{1}{2} = \frac{2}{4} = \frac{3}{6} = \frac{4}{8} = \frac{5}{10} = \frac{6}{12}$$

A scale model car may be related to the actual car by the fact that each measurement of the model is $\frac{1}{72}$ of the corresponding measurement of the car. A photograph and its enlargement, or a map and the piece of country of which it is a map, are other examples of constant ratio.

Figure 25:18 shows parts of two maps of the same area. Each length on the larger map is $2\frac{1}{2}$ times the corresponding length on the smaller-scale map.[2] Each length on the smaller map is $\frac{2}{5}$ of the corresponding length on the larger-scale map. Every pair of corresponding distances, such as ab and AB, or bc and BC, or the distances representing the same road on the two maps, is an embodiment of the fraction, or ratio, $\frac{2}{5}$. This may be shown on a graph which represents the fraction $\frac{2}{5}$ (Figure 25:19). The longer of each pair of corresponding lines is plotted horizontally, and the shorter one vertically, so that each vertical line is $\frac{2}{5}$ of its corresponding horizontal line. It is not necessary to measure the distances on the two maps. They can be transferred directly to the graph by using a piece of cotton.

---

[2] The ratio of lengths in the two maps is only approximately 5:2, as the scales of the maps are in fact 1:63 360 and 1:25 000.

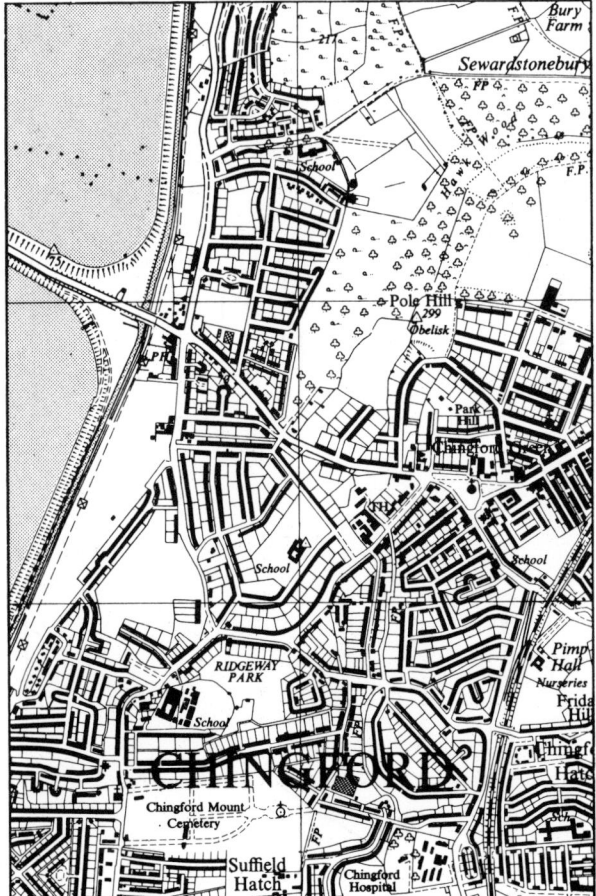

Figure 25:18

This graph could be described either as a graph of the fraction or ratio $\frac{2}{5}$, or as a graph which shows $\frac{2}{5}$ of different lengths. After their earlier experience of multiplication graphs, and of graphs showing fractions of numbers, children will expect it to be a straight-line graph.

If a graph obtained in this way by plotting corresponding distances on two maps is not a straight line, the ratio of these distances is not constant, and one map is a distortion of the other. It is possible to test whether two toys of different sizes or two models of the same thing are similar in shape, by drawing a graph of their corresponding measurements (Figure 25:20).

A set of several similar geometrical shapes can also be used to give a set of examples of the same ratio. If children make five-pointed stars of different sizes, for instance, they may show the distance across each star and the distance between the points of the star on a graph (Figure 25:21).

In all these activities, children are developing the habit of looking for a relationship or ratio between two quantities, and of seeing the same ratio expressed in many forms; the ratio of 3 cm to 4 cm is the same as the ratio of 6 cm to 8 cm, or of 9 cm to 12 cm, and all these representations of the same ratio can be expressed by the set of equivalent fractions $\frac{3}{4} = \frac{6}{8} = \frac{9}{12} = \cdots$.

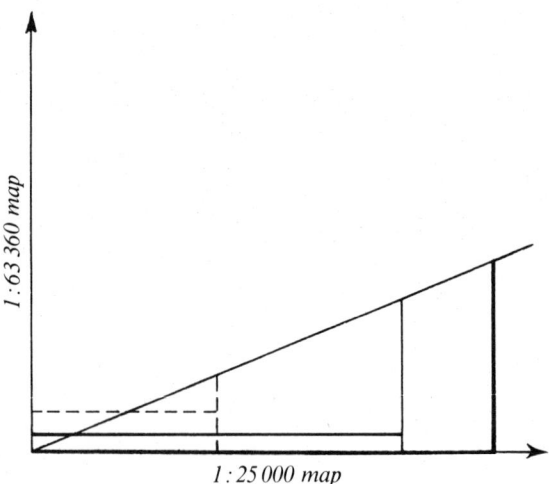

Figure 25:19

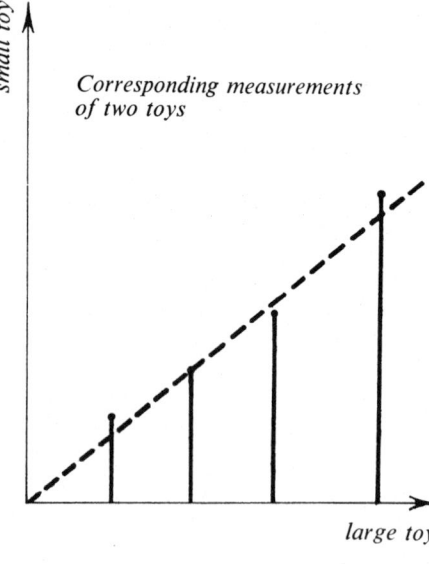

Figure 25:20

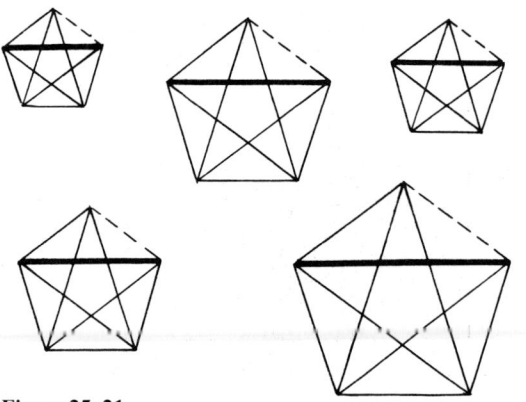

Figure 25:21

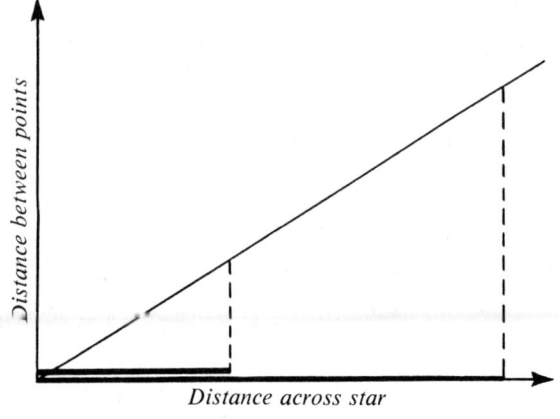

26 Operations on Fractions and Decimals: Multiplication and Division

Extending the idea of multiplication

The multiplication of natural numbers is based on repeated addition of the same number. This idea extends very easily to fractions, and just as children learn to record $5+5+5+5$ more briefly as 4×5, they will find it natural to write $4 \times \frac{1}{3}$ instead of $\frac{1}{3}+\frac{1}{3}+\frac{1}{3}+\frac{1}{3}$, and $4 \times 0 \cdot 2$ instead of $0 \cdot 2 + 0 \cdot 2 + 0 \cdot 2 + 0 \cdot 2$. Thus we have the idea that repeated addition of fractions is symbolized by the multiplication sign. This is a very natural extension of the previous idea of multiplication. The calculation is carried out in exactly the same way as similar calculations for whole numbers.

$$4 \times \tfrac{1}{3} = 4 \text{ thirds}$$
$$= 1\tfrac{1}{3}$$

$$4 \times 0 \cdot 2 = 4 \times (2 \text{ tenths})$$
$$= 8 \text{ tenths}$$
$$= 0 \cdot 8$$

Children will come to realize that exactly as they can build up tables of multiples of 2, 3, 4,..., they can also build up tables of multiplies of $\frac{1}{2}$, $\frac{1}{3}$, $\frac{2}{3}$ and they will represent these tables by graphs and relation diagrams. Similarly using decimal notation, tables of multiples of $0 \cdot 1$, $0 \cdot 2$, $0 \cdot 25$, etc. will be graphed. Figure 26:1 shows graphs of multiples of some of the simpler fractions together with multiples of natural numbers. In Figure 26:2 we show a relation diagram for multiples of $0 \cdot 75$.

In this example, 2 is mapped onto $1 \cdot 5$, since $2 \times 0 \cdot 75 = 1 \cdot 5$. Similarly 3 is mapped onto $2 \cdot 25$, since $3 \times 0 \cdot 75 = 2 \cdot 25$, and so on. In this way, children learn to think of $3 \times 0 \cdot 75$ as an abbreviation for the repeated addition $0 \cdot 75 + 0 \cdot 75 + 0 \cdot 75$. How are they to think of $0 \cdot 75 \times 3$, and where does a need for the writing of $0 \cdot 75 \times 3$ and similar multiplications occur? The idea of repeated addition of threes cannot be used when considering $0 \cdot 75 \times 3$ in the way it was for 4×3, since there is not now a whole number of threes to be added together. But we not only think of 4×3 as 'four threes', but also as '*four times as much as* 3', and this interpretation helps in the consideration of $0 \cdot 75 \times 3$.

The reverse of a child's statement, 'John has *twice as much* pocket money as I have' is 'I have only *half as much* pocket money as John.' If the child has 10 pence, he will think of John as having 2×10 pence, or 20 pence. Since '*twice as much*...' is symbolized by $2 \times ...$, it is natural to think of $\frac{1}{2} \times ...$ as meaning '*half as much*...'. Starting with John's 20 pence, the other child's money would then be described as $\frac{1}{2} \times 20$ pence. Similarly, '$\frac{3}{4}$ *as much as* 3' will be written as $\frac{3}{4} \times 3$ and '3 *times as much as* $\frac{3}{4}$' can be

A graph of multiples

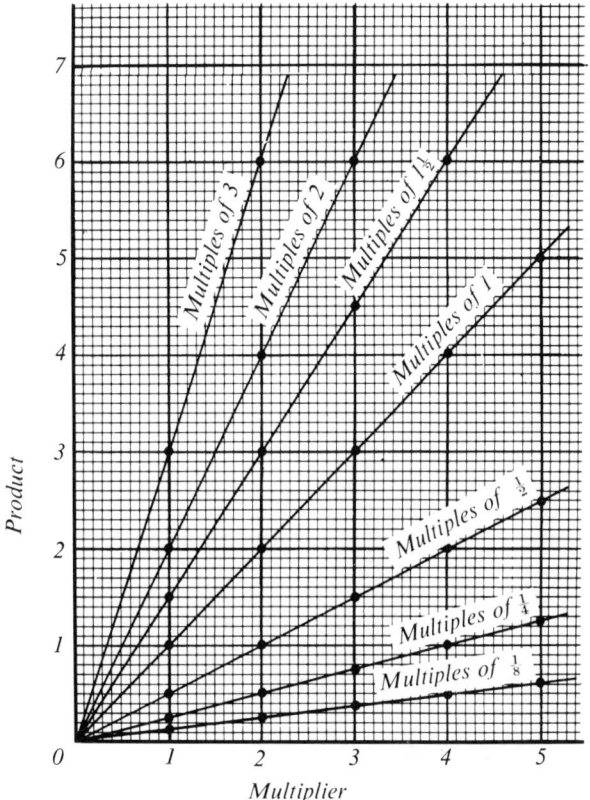

Figure 26:1

The relation $x \rightarrow x \times 0 \cdot 75$

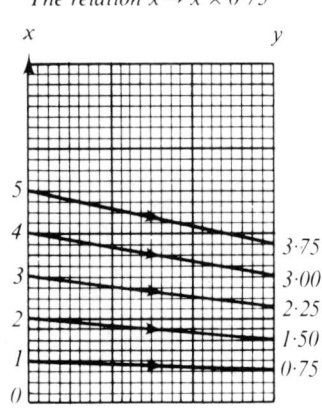

Figure 26:2

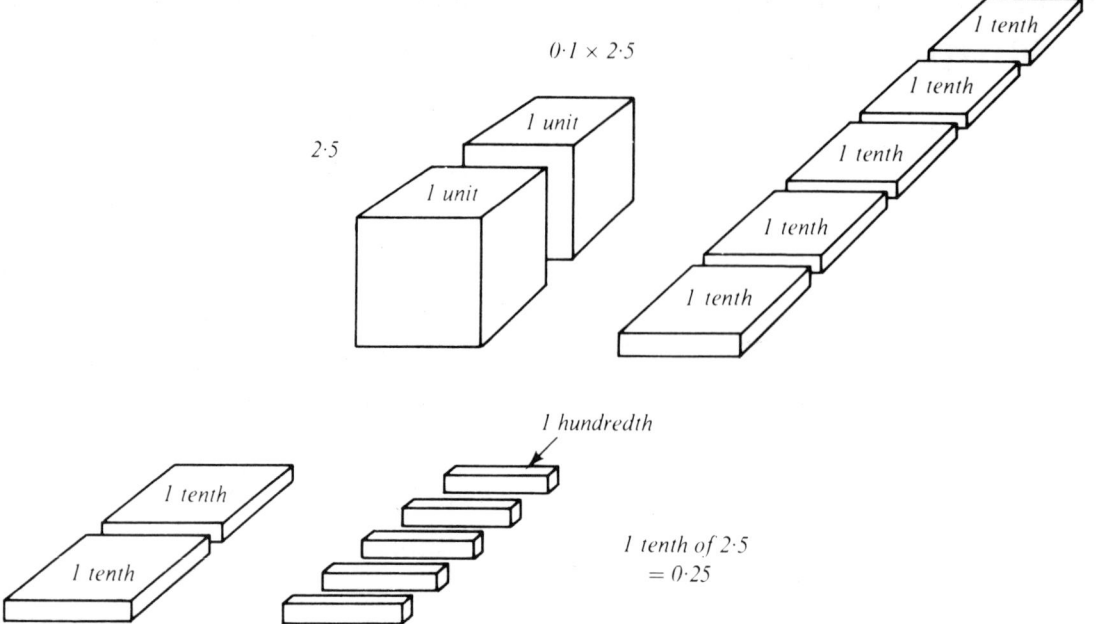

$0 \cdot 1 \times 2 \cdot 5$

$2 \cdot 5$

1 unit

1 unit

1 tenth

1 tenth

1 tenth

1 tenth

1 tenth

1 hundredth

1 tenth

1 tenth

1 tenth of 2·5
= 0·25

Figure 26:3

written $3 \times \frac{3}{4}$. The words '...*times as much as*...' are always symbolized by a multiplication sign; when the number of times may be fractional this is usually abbreviated to 'as much as'.

Hence the statement '$\frac{1}{2}$ as much as 6' is written $\frac{1}{2} \times 6$. This idea is also very closely related to the idea of '$\frac{1}{2}$ *of* 6', and similarly, '$\frac{1}{10}$ as much of 3' conveys the same idea as '$\frac{1}{10}$ of 3'. The wording '$\frac{1}{10}$ of 3' is simpler and clearer, so it is often convenient to read $\frac{1}{10} \times 3$ as '$\frac{1}{10}$ of 3'. We thus have a number of equivalent forms:

$$\frac{1}{10} \times 3 = \frac{1}{10} \text{ as much as } 3$$
$$= \frac{1}{10} \text{ of } 3$$
$$= 3 \div 10$$
$$= 3 \text{ tenths}$$

which can be written 0·3 or $\frac{3}{10}$.

$0 \cdot 1 \times$

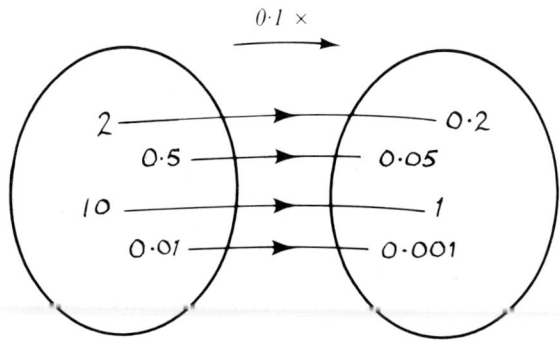

Figure 26:4
248

Multiplication of Decimals

We can now apply this idea of the meaning of multiplication to fractional numbers when they are written in decimal form. A very simple example is $0 \cdot 1 \times 2 \cdot 5$. This means 1 tenth of 2·5. At first, a child may need to represent this by blocks, as shown in Figure 26:3.

He will soon realize that
  1 tenth of 2 units is 2 tenths
and
  1 tenth of 5 tenths is 5 hundredths, and will record what
  he has done as $0 \cdot 1 \times 2 \cdot 5$
                    $\overline{0 \cdot 25}$

It is not helpful in this recording to arrange the numbers 0·1 and 2·5 with their units digits under one another. A child needs rather to observe the effect of multiplication by 0·1 on each digit of 2·5, noting that 2 units have become 2 tenths, and 5 tenths have become 5 hundreths. The relation diagram of Figure 26:4 may help to make this transformation explicit.

The same principle is seen at work in all the examples of Figure 26:5. We observe that multiplication by

  ...0·01, 0·1, 1, 10, 100,...

has the effect of moving the digits of a decimal number, as follows:

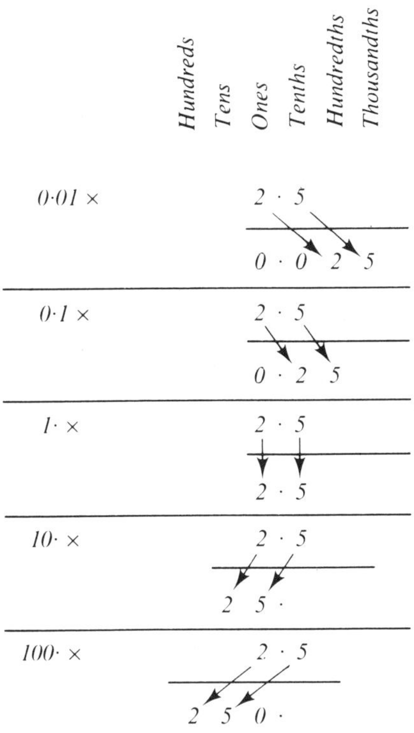

| | Hundreds | Tens | Ones | Tenths | Hundredths | Thousandths |

$0.01 \times$

$0.1 \times$

$1. \times$

$10. \times$

$100. \times$

Figure 26:5

$0.01 \times$ digits move 2 places to right
$0.1 \ \times$ digits move 1 place to right
$1. \ \ \times$ digits move 0 places
$10. \ \times$ digits move 1 place to left
$100. \times$ digits move 2 places to left.

This property, together with the associative law for multiplication, enables us to multiply decimal numbers easily by other decimals. For instance

$$0.2 \times 2.5 = (2 \times 0.1) \times 2.5$$
$$= 2 \times (0.1 \times 2.5) \text{ by the associative law}$$
$$= 2 \times 0.25$$
$$= 0.50$$

In practice, this calculation is recorded as

$$\frac{0.2 \times 2.5}{0.50}$$

the digits being moved one place to the right and multiplication by 2 carried out in one step.

It now becomes very easy to perform such a multiplication as 1.2×2.5.

$1.2 \times$	2.5
$1.0 \times$	2.5
$0.2 \times$	0.50
	3.00

The calculation is broken up into stages using the distributive law

$$(a \times b) \times c = (a \times c) + (b \times c)$$

in exactly the same way that the long multiplication of whole numbers is broken up (see page 168). The conventional arrangement is an abbreviation of

$$1.2 \times 2.5 = (1.0 + 0.2) \times 2.5$$
$$= (1.0 \times 2.5) + (0.2 \times 2.5)$$
$$= 2.50 + 0.50$$
$$= 3.00$$

The desk calculating machine and multiplication of decimals

The provision of decimal point markers on the desk calculating machine enables the machine to be used as easily for calculations using decimals as for those in whole numbers. The fact that aids to computation such as desk calculating machines and computers can accept decimal numbers as easily as whole numbers has given a considerable impetus to the change to decimal coinage and metric measures, and has encouraged the replacement of methods of calculation which use fractions by methods which use decimals. Children should be encouraged to take advantage of this simplification, and to choose decimal methods when possible.

Decimal pointer markers are provided on all three registers of the desk calculating machine, and have to be set by hand. There is also an arrow on the frame of the machine above the counter register, which indicates how many places the carriage has been moved from its starting position, and has the important function of indicating which digit in the counter register is increased by 1 when the handle is turned. When performing a decimal multiplication, room must be allowed for movements of the carriage of the machine which corresponds to moving digits when multiplying by 0.1, etc. Figure 26:6 shows

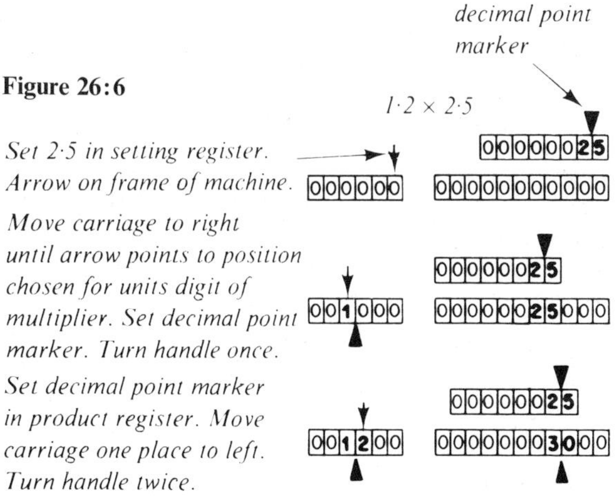

Figure 26:6

1.2×2.5

Set 2·5 in setting register.
Arrow on frame of machine.

Move carriage to right until arrow points to position chosen for units digit of multiplier. Set decimal point marker. Turn handle once.

Set decimal point marker in product register. Move carriage one place to left. Turn handle twice.

249

how the multiplication 1.2×2.5 is carried out on the machine.

After some experiment, children will find the decimal point markers can be set in advance, by noticing that the number of decimal places needed in the product registers is the sum of the numbers of decimal places shown in the setting and counter registers (Figure 26:7).

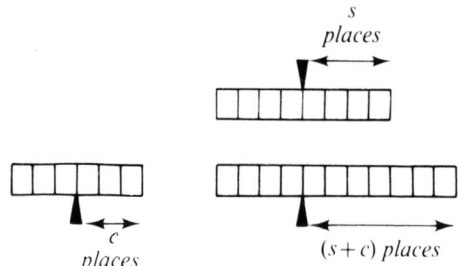

Figure 26:7

The reason for this is easily seen if we examine the multiplication of a number such as 0.1234 by 0.001.

$$0.001 \times 0.1234$$
$$\overline{0.0001234}$$

The digit in the fourth decimal place of 0.1234 is moved 3 places to the right into the seventh decimal place. The same principle can be seen to apply to any other example.

Experienced users of a calculating machine often set the decimal point markers into fixed positions before starting to calculate, giving say 4 decimal places in both the setting and counter registers, and 8 decimal places in the product register. This technique is shown in Figure 26:8.

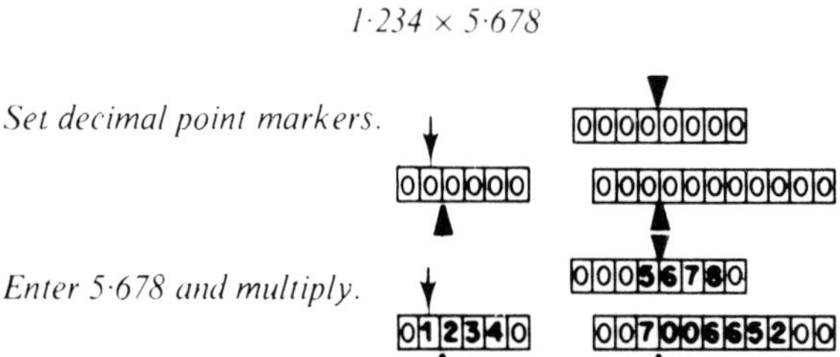

$$1.234 \times 5.678$$

Set decimal point markers.

Enter 5·678 and multiply.

Figure 26:8

This technique of placing the decimal point is that used in the method of multiplying decimals as if they were whole numbers, and then placing the decimal point in the product by obtaining the sum of the numbers of decimal places in the numbers multiplied, as shown in Figure 26:9.

250

3 *dec. pl.*   2 *dec. pl.*

$$\overbrace{0.012} \times \overbrace{5.17}$$
$$= 0.06204$$
$$\underbrace{\quad}_{5 \; dec. \; pl.}$$

```
        517
         12
       5170
       1034
       6204
```

Figure 26:9

Children often eventually learn this method of placing the decimal point in a product, as it is useful and reliable in later work, but they should not use it until they have appreciated why it works.

Fractions of a fraction and the multiplication of fractions

At a later stage, when theoretical work with fractions becomes more important, it is necessary to be able to multiply together any two fractional numbers, whether they are written in decimal or fractional notation. We then need to find such products as $\frac{1}{3} \times \frac{2}{5}$, and to generalize to $\frac{a}{b} \times \frac{c}{d}$. These results are deduced from facts such as

$$\tfrac{2}{3} \times \tfrac{1}{5} = \tfrac{1}{3} \text{ of } \tfrac{2}{5}$$

This can be found practically by drawing or folding, but children at the primary school age find it difficult to abstract the idea of a fraction of a fraction, although they very often make fractions of a fraction in the course of their work.

When a child folds a semicircle in two, he makes half of the semicircle, or a quarter of the whole circle (Figure 25:10). When he opens out the folds he relates his new subdivision to the original unit. Whenever a child subdivides a fraction of a unit by folding it again, he makes a fraction of a fraction of the original unit. The subdivision of a circle into twelve equal parts (Figure 26:10) contains many examples of fractions of a fraction.

Children should be encouraged to look for such relationships, but they may find difficulty in expressing them, although the relationship is implicit in the folding.

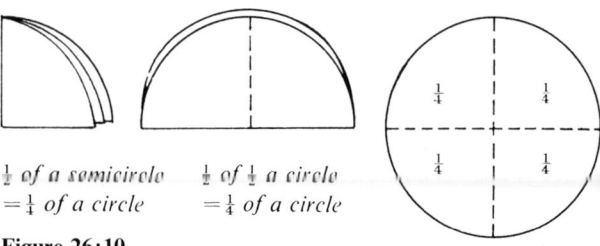

$\frac{1}{2}$ *of a semicircle* $\frac{1}{2}$ *of* $\frac{1}{2}$ *a circle*
$= \frac{1}{4}$ *of a circle* $= \frac{1}{4}$ *of a circle*

Figure 26:10

The difficulty lies in the double role played by the shape obtained at the first fold: it is first of all a fraction of the original unit, and then the unit of the fraction produced by the second fold (Figure 26:11).

The child has to bear both relationships in mind at the same time. We have seen that this logical multiplication of relations is only achieved at the concrete-operational stage of thinking. A child must be able to move backwards and forwards easily in thought between a unit and its part if he is to relate $\frac{1}{2}$ of a quarter to $\frac{1}{8}$ of the original unit.

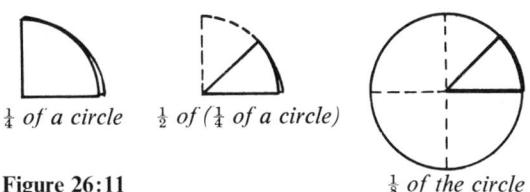

$\frac{1}{4}$ *of a circle* $\frac{1}{2}$ *of ($\frac{1}{4}$ of a circle)*

Figure 26:11 $\frac{1}{8}$ *of the circle*

However, the teacher will be able, in Figure 26:12, to relate the heavily shaded area to the original rectangle and to see that

$$\tfrac{1}{3} \times \tfrac{2}{5} = \tfrac{1}{3} \text{ of } \tfrac{2}{5}$$
$$= \tfrac{2}{15}$$

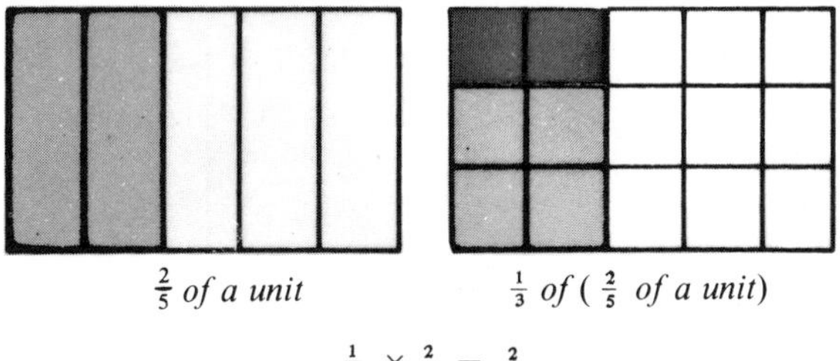

$\frac{2}{5}$ *of a unit* $\frac{1}{3}$ *of ($\frac{2}{5}$ of a unit)*

$$\tfrac{1}{3} \times \tfrac{2}{5} = \tfrac{2}{15}$$

Figure 26:12

In general we find that

$$\frac{a}{b} \times \frac{c}{d} = \frac{a}{b} \text{ of } \frac{c}{d} = \frac{a \times c}{b \times d}$$

This is illustrated in Figure 26:13, where we see that $\frac{1}{b}$ of $\left(\frac{1}{d} \text{ of a unit}\right)$ divides the unit into $b \times d$ parts, so

that $\left(\frac{1}{b} \text{ of } \frac{c}{d}\right)$ is $\frac{c}{b \times d}$ of a unit. Then $\left(\frac{a}{b} \text{ of } \frac{c}{d}\right)$ is a times as

much as $\left(\frac{1}{b} \text{ of } \frac{c}{d}\right)$, or $\frac{a \times c}{b \times d}$ of a unit.

It is an interesting fact that it is always possible to recover the unit from any fraction, such as $\frac{2}{3}$, by taking the correct fraction of it. In fact $\frac{3}{2} \times \frac{2}{3} = 1$ (Figure 26:14). The fraction $\frac{3}{2}$ is called the *reciprocal* of $\frac{2}{3}$.

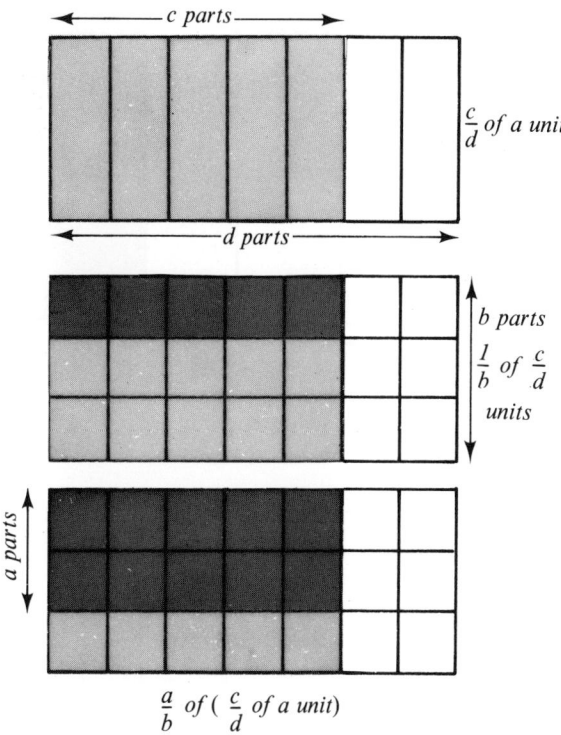

← c parts →

$\frac{c}{d}$ *of a unit*

← d parts →

b parts

$\frac{1}{b}$ *of* $\frac{c}{d}$ *units*

a parts

$\frac{a}{b}$ *of ($\frac{c}{d}$ of a unit)*

The unit is divided into b × d parts of which a × c are shaded

$$\frac{a}{b} \times \frac{c}{d} = \frac{a}{b} \text{ of } \frac{c}{d} = \frac{a \times c}{b \times d}$$

Figure 26:13

Similarly, $\frac{2}{3} \times \frac{3}{2} = \frac{2}{3}$ of $\frac{3}{2} = 1$ (Figure 26:15) and $\frac{2}{3}$ is the reciprocal of $\frac{3}{2}$. In general, $\frac{a}{b} \times \frac{b}{a} = \frac{b}{a} \times \frac{a}{b} = 1$, and $\frac{a}{b}$ is the reciprocal of $\frac{b}{a}$. This fact is much used in the theoretical study of the structure of operations on fractions.

The commutative law for the multiplication of fractions

When children first multiply natural numbers, it does not occur to them that multiplication is commutative. To them, 3×4 means $4+4+4$, and 4×3 means $3+3+3+3$; a child does not at first see any reason why the different operations yield the same result. But as his experience widens, he comes to understand and take for granted the fact that the result of a multiplication does not depend on the order in which the numbers are handled. That is, he accepts the fact that the multiplication of natural numbers is commutative.

We have begun to see that the multiplication of fractions is also commutative; this fact does not, however, follow

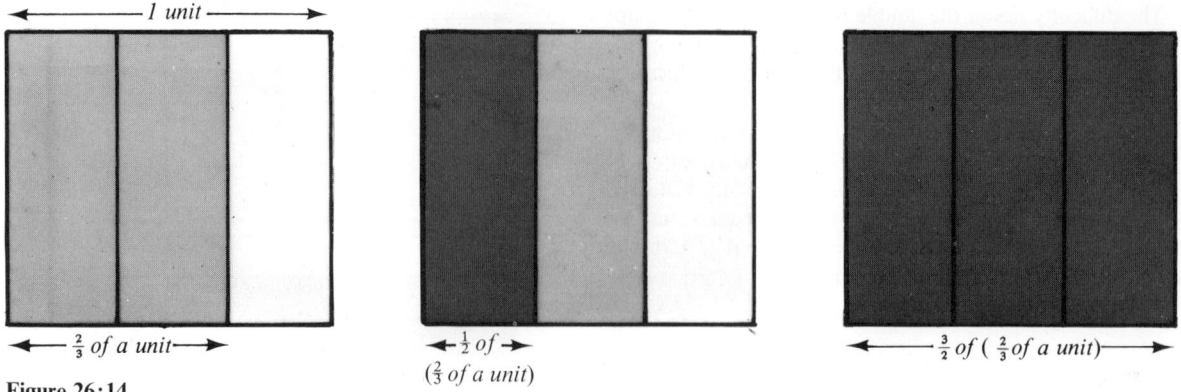

$\frac{2}{3}$ of a unit

$\frac{1}{2}$ of ($\frac{2}{3}$ of a unit)

$\frac{3}{2}$ of ($\frac{2}{3}$ of a unit)

Figure 26:14

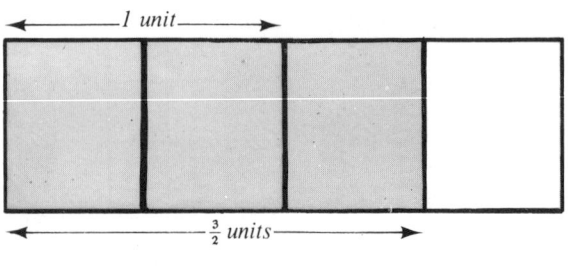

$\frac{3}{2}$ units

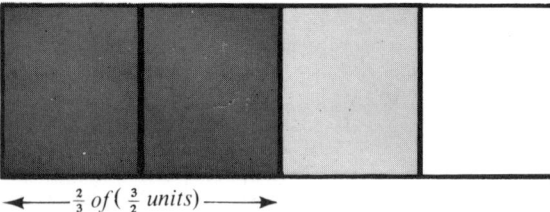

$\frac{2}{3}$ of ($\frac{3}{2}$ units)

$$\frac{2}{3} \times \frac{3}{2} = \frac{2}{3} \text{ of } \frac{3}{2} = 1$$

Figure 26:15[1]

simply because the multiplication of natural numbers is commutative.

When a child first uses one of the operations which he will eventually think of as multiplication of fractions, he is finding a *fraction of a fraction*. Finding $\frac{1}{2}$ of $\frac{3}{4}$ is an entirely different problem from finding $\frac{3}{4}$ of $\frac{1}{2}$. Finding 1 tenth of a hundredth is not the same as finding 1 hundredth of 1 tenth. This is exactly parallel to the situation encountered with whole numbers, when ten hundreds do not look like a hundred tens. It is surprising that the results of the two operations are the same, and it is only after some experience of doing both operations that children will expect the results always to be the same.

Figure 26:16 illustrates the equality of $\frac{1}{4}$ of $\frac{1}{2}$ and $\frac{1}{2}$ of $\frac{1}{4}$. The numbers of children in different sets could also be used to illustrate this relation. A variety of concrete situations in different circumstances should be used.

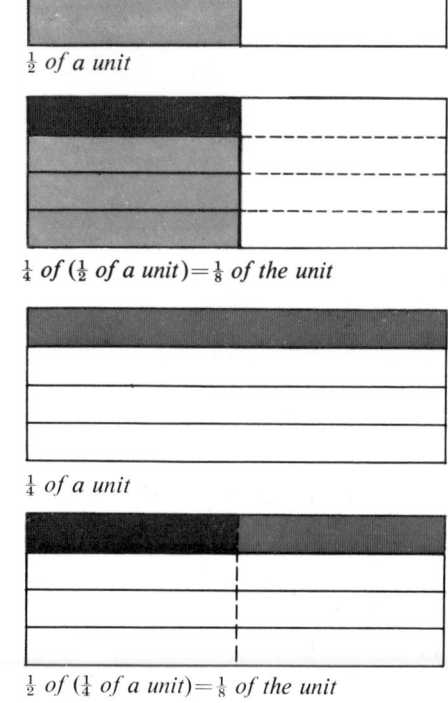

$\frac{1}{2}$ of a unit

$\frac{1}{4}$ of ($\frac{1}{2}$ of a unit)$=\frac{1}{8}$ of the unit

$\frac{1}{4}$ of a unit

$\frac{1}{2}$ of ($\frac{1}{4}$ of a unit)$=\frac{1}{8}$ of the unit

Figure 26:16

---

[1] In these illustrations it is convenient to make the second subdivision of the unit area in the same direction as the first, as the lines needed are already there.

252

Figure 26:17 shows the equality of $\left(\dfrac{a}{b} \times \dfrac{c}{d}\right)$ and $\left(\dfrac{c}{d} \times \dfrac{a}{b}\right)$ In this case the area of a rectangle has been chosen as unit.[2]

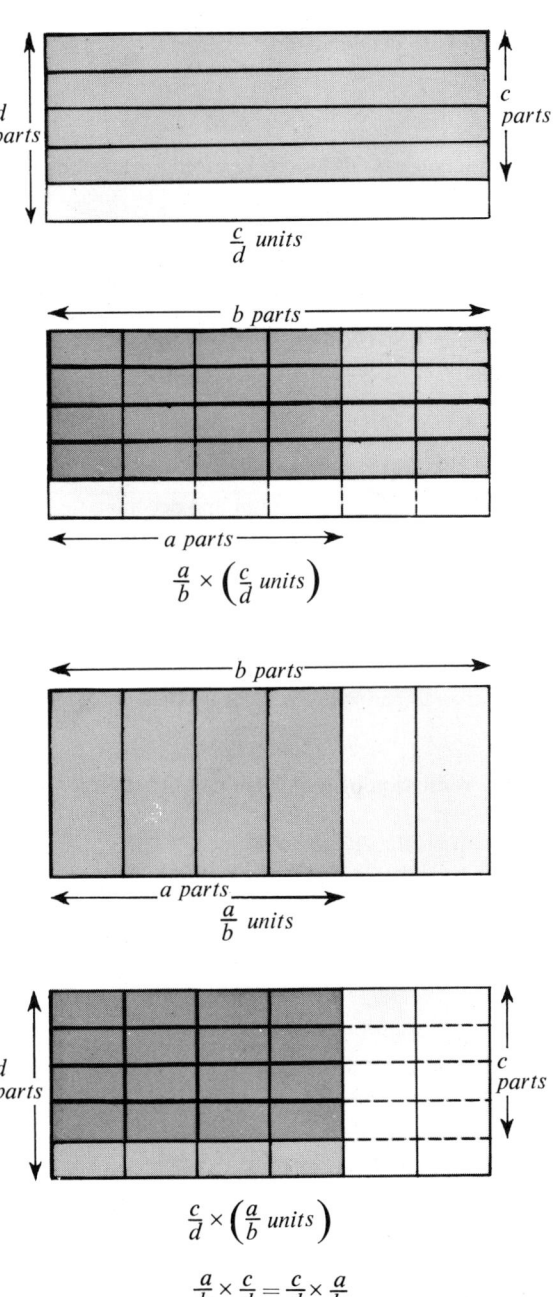

$$\frac{a}{b} \times \frac{c}{d} = \frac{c}{d} \times \frac{a}{b}$$

Figure 26:17

[2] The diagram shows the case in which both $\dfrac{a}{b}$ and $\dfrac{c}{d}$ are fractions less than 1. Similar diagrams can be constructed to illustrate the cases in which one or both fractions are greater than 1.

The operation of multiplying two fractions hence satisfies the *commutative law for multiplication of fractions*:

$$\frac{a}{b} \times \frac{c}{d} = \frac{c}{d} \times \frac{a}{b}$$

The fractions may of course be written in decimal form, so that for instance

$$1 \cdot 2 \times 3 \cdot 5 = 3 \cdot 5 \times 1 \cdot 2$$

With understanding of the commutative law of multiplication comes the unification in a child's mind of two separate processes, the multiplication of natural numbers and the multiplication of fractions, making one united whole—the multiplication of numbers.[3] It is now clear that among the multiples of a number such as 4 there are not only 2×4, 3×4, 4×4, and so on, but fractional multiples such as $\frac{1}{3} \times 4$ and $2 \cdot 3 \times 4$, and that there exists an indefinite number of such fractional multiples (Figure 26:18). It is also plain that not only whole numbers have

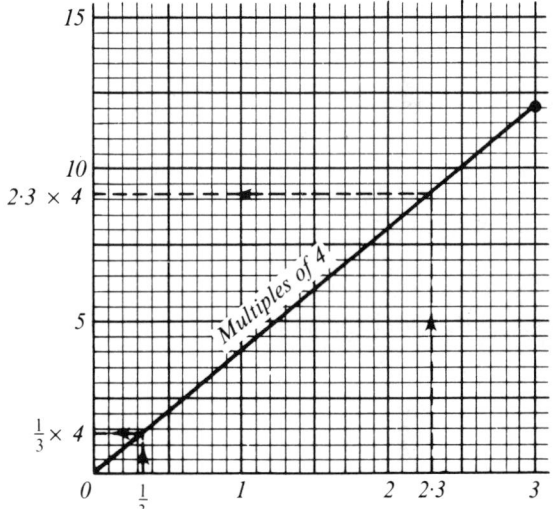

Figure 26:18

multiples. The multiples of 2, 3, 4, ... which a child has known for some time are only a few specimens among the set of multiples of all numbers, which include multiples of $\frac{1}{2}$, 0·6, 4·3 and so on. These multiples may be whole number multiples, such as $2 \times 4 \cdot 3$, or they may be fractional multiples, $1 \cdot 7 \times 4 \cdot 3$ or $\frac{1}{2} \times 4 \cdot 3$ (Figure 26:19).

[3] The 'numbers' used here are the *signless rational numbers*.

253

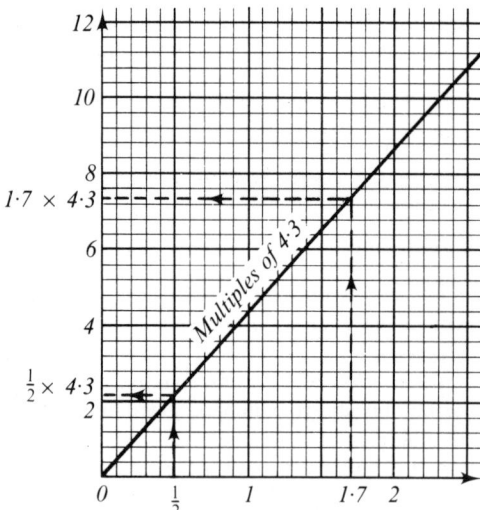

Figure 26:19

Just as a child can replace 4×3 by 3×4 if he wishes, using the commutative law for multiplication, so also he can now replace 0.7×6 by 6×0.7 or 4.3×1.7 by 1.7×4.3, using the commutative law for multiplication, if he finds one operation more convenient than the other. At this stage, also, the reading of $\frac{3}{4} \times \frac{1}{3}$ as '$\frac{3}{4}$ multiplied by $\frac{1}{3}$' becomes natural, for no longer is the order of the factors of any importance.

Equivalence and the multiplication of fractions

The level of understanding of the multiplication of fractions which will eventually be reached is that at which a child will find $1\frac{2}{3} \times \frac{3}{4}$ or ($\frac{5}{3}$ of $\frac{3}{4}$) by saying that thirds of quarters are twelfths, and so 5 thirds of 3 quarters are equal to 15 twelfths. That is,

$$1\frac{2}{3} \times \frac{3}{4} = \frac{5}{3} \text{ of } \frac{3}{4}$$
$$= \frac{15}{12}$$

This is not the simplest form of the result, and should be replaced by the simpler equivalent fraction $\frac{5}{4}$, or $1\frac{1}{4}$, numerator and denominator having been divided by 3. This method is simple and straightforward, but it often requires the handling of large numbers in the calculation. We now examine what happens to the numerator and denominator during the operation of multiplication.

$$1\frac{2}{3} \times \frac{3}{4} = \frac{5}{3} \text{ of } \frac{3}{4} \qquad \ldots \text{(i)}$$
$$= \frac{15}{12}$$
$$= \frac{5}{4} \qquad \ldots \text{(ii)}$$
$$= 1\frac{1}{4}$$

Between lines (i) and (ii), in the numerator 5 has been multiplied by 3 and then divided by 3, and in the denominator 4 has been multiplied by 3 and then divided

254

by 3. This repeated labour can be avoided once a child is able to hold in his mind and manipulate mentally the following two facts:

(1) the numerator of the product of two fractions is obtained by multiplying numerators, and the denominator by multiplying denominators;

$$\frac{a}{b} \times \frac{c}{d} = \frac{a \times c}{b \times d}$$

(2) a fraction can always be replaced by an equivalent fraction (which has the same value) by dividing the numerator and denominator by the same number.

The working will be less laborious if the second of these steps is performed (if possible) as early in the operation as it can be. It is possible to perform the second step first because $(a \times b) \div c = (a \div c) \times b$. The working now becomes

$$1\frac{2}{3} \times \frac{3}{4} = \frac{5}{3} \times \frac{3}{4}$$
$$= \frac{5 \times 3}{3 \times 4}$$
$$= \frac{5}{4} \text{ dividing numerator and denominator by 3}$$
$$= 1\frac{1}{4}$$

It should not be expected that children can understand this sophisticated process in the primary school. Although the method of multiplying fractions is very easy to perform, it is much better for children to defer it to the secondary school than to perform it without understanding.

The introduction of the division of fractions

A child meets the division of a fraction into a number of equal parts, that is, the division of a fraction by a whole number, very early in his exploration of fractions, and he will soon be able to describe the number content of what he has done in folding up the semi-circle of Figure 26:20 into 4 equal parts as

$$\frac{1}{2} \div 4 = \frac{1}{8}$$

or perhaps

$$\frac{1}{4} \text{ of } \frac{1}{2} = \frac{1}{8}$$

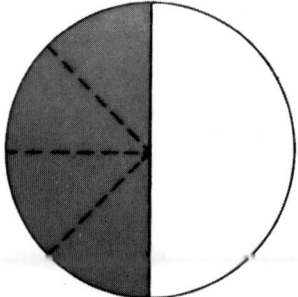

Figure 26:20

where the area of the complete circle has been taken as unit. He will later add to these descriptions the third expression $\frac{1}{4} \times \frac{1}{2} = \frac{1}{8}$.

The inverse operation of putting the 4 small pieces together again to make the semicircle can be described numerically by

$$4 \times \frac{1}{8} = \frac{1}{2}$$

We thus see that the operation inverse to finding 4 *times a fraction* can be written in either of the ways

i) the fraction is divided by 4; $\frac{1}{2} \div 4 = \frac{1}{8}$
ii) $\frac{1}{4}$ *of* the fraction is found; $\frac{1}{4}$ of $\frac{1}{2} = \frac{1}{8}$.

The first of these expressions is very familiar from the division of natural numbers. The operation inverse to multiplying a natural number by 4 is dividing by 4; $4 \times 3 = 12$ can be inverted to $12 \div 4 = 3$. One of the images with which this operation of division is often coupled in a child's mind is that of dividing into equal parts (Figure 26:21).

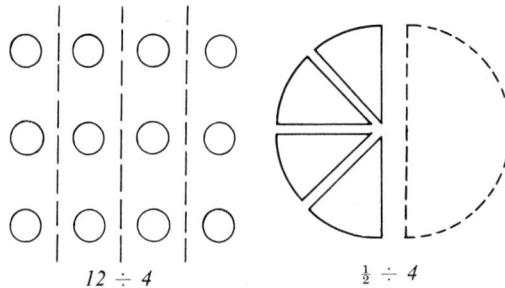

$12 \div 4$ $\frac{1}{2} \div 4$
(12 divided into 4 equal parts) *($\frac{1}{2}$ divided into 4 equal parts)*

Figure 26:21

The mental picture of division as *sharing* is insufficient to enable children to understand any division involving fractions other than the division of a fraction by a whole number. A child using this image can understand $\frac{1}{2} \div 4$, but can make nothing of $4 \div \frac{1}{2}$ or $4 \div 0\cdot1$. He can divide $\frac{1}{2}$ into 4 equal parts, but it is meaningless to imagine dividing 4 into '$\frac{1}{2}$ an equal part' or '1 tenth of an equal part'. If the symbols $4 \div \frac{1}{2}$ are not to remain meaningless, they must take on a meaning derived from some other situation than that of 'sharing'.

We have already seen that the idea of 'sharing' only corresponds to some of the situations in which the division of natural numbers is used, and that it must be supplemented by, and assimilated with, the idea of 'grouping'. 'How many fours are there in 12 units?' is the *grouping* idea corresponding to $12 \div 4$. It is possible and natural to ask similar questions involving fractions, such as, 'How many quarters of a unit are there in 12 units?' This should by analogy, be described by $12 \div \frac{1}{4}$. Similarly we can ask 'how many tenths of a unit are there in 12 units?' and symbolize the question by $12 \div 0\cdot1$.

A child has many experiences which lead him to this idea of division by a fraction, two of which are listed below:

i) The question, 'How many halfpennies in tenpence?' leads to $10 \div \frac{1}{2} = 20$.
ii) 'How many $1\cdot5$ cm lengths of ribbon can be cut from 15 cm?' gives $15 \div 1\cdot5 = 10$. This is exactly parallel to the recording of 'How many 3 cm lengths can be cut from 15 cm?' by using $15 \div 3 = 5$.

(i) How many $1\frac{1}{2}$ cm lengths in 6 cm?

$$3 \div 1\frac{1}{2} = 4 \quad or \quad 3 \div 1\cdot5 = 4$$

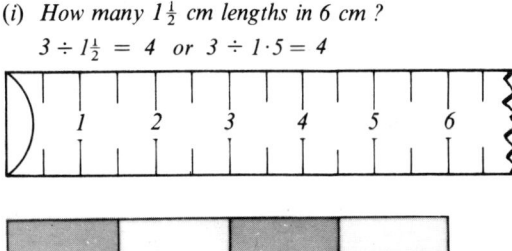

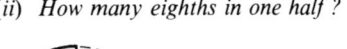

(ii) How many eighths in one half?

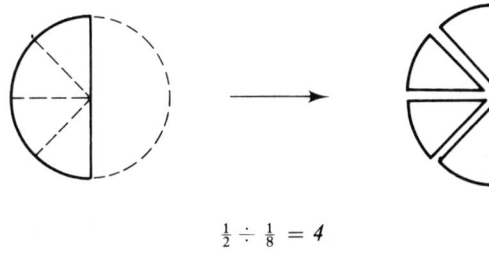

$$\frac{1}{2} \div \frac{1}{8} = 4$$

Figure 26:22

Children should be encouraged to see the possibility of grouping in equal sub-units each of which contains a fraction of a unit, as well as grouping in equal sub-units each of which contains a whole number of units. Figure 26:22 shows some possibilities.

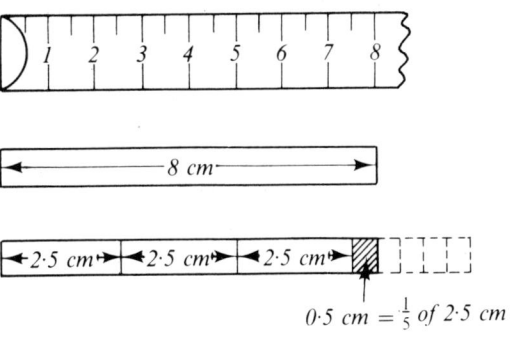

$0\cdot5$ cm $= \frac{1}{5}$ of $2\cdot5$ cm

$3\cdot2$ pieces can be cut

Figure 26:23

In all the examples shown so far the result of the grouping has been an exact whole number of sub-units.

This is not necessarily the case. The question, 'How many 2·5 cm pieces of ribbon can be cut from an 8 cm piece?' yields the answer '3 complete pieces, with some ribbon left over.' The length of ribbon left over, which is (8 − 7·5) cm, or 0·5 cm, is in fact $\frac{1}{5}$ of the next piece, or 0·2 of the next piece. So the number of pieces which can be cut is 3·2 (Figure 26:23). The situation can be described as 8 ÷ 2·5 = 3·2.

Division of decimals and the calculating machine

We now examine how the calculation of 8 ÷ 2·5 is performed on the desk calculating machine, since this throws further light on the remainder of 0·5 which is left at the first step of the division. First, 8·0 is set into the product register in a suitable position (Figure 26:24) and 2·5 placed over it in the setting register with the decimal points in a vertical line. The arrow on the frame of the machine indicates the place of the units digit in the quotient. The handle is turned 3 times subtractively, so that 3 × 2·5 is subtracted from 8, leaving 0·5. On paper this can be recorded as:

$$\begin{array}{r} 3· \\ 2·5)\overline{8·0} \\ 7·5 \quad\longleftarrow\quad 3\times 2·5 = 7·5 \\ \overline{0·5} \end{array}$$

Since 0·5 is less than 2·5, no further whole number multiples of 2·5 can be subtracted. However, it is possible to subtract some *tenths* of 2·5 from 0·5, since

1 tenth of 2·5 = 0·25
2 tenths of 2·5 = 0·50

$$8 \div 2·5$$

Set 8·0 with 2·5 above it. Arrow shows units digit of quotient. Set decimal point marker in setting register.

Turn handle 3 times subtractively.

Move carriage one place to left.

Complete division.

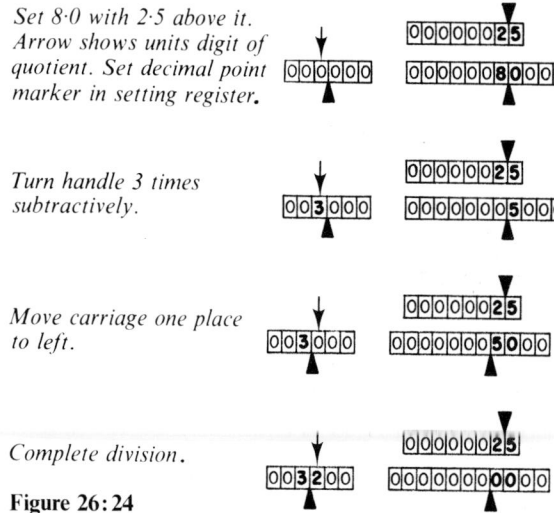

Figure 26:24

256

This subtraction of tenths of 2·5, or multiples of 0·25, is achieved on the calculating machine by moving the carriage one place to the left, which is equivalent to moving the setting register one place to the right before subtracting. On paper the calculation now takes the form

$$\begin{array}{r} 3·2 \\ 2·5)\overline{8·0} \\ 7·5 \quad\longleftarrow\quad 3\times 2·5 = 7·5 \\ \overline{0·50} \\ 0·50 \quad\longleftarrow\quad 0·2 \times 2·5 = 0·50 \end{array}$$

The result can of course be checked by noting that 2·5 × 3·2 = 8·00.

If remainders continue to occur, the process can be repeated for as many figures as are needed, or until a zero remainder occurs, as shown in the following example.

$$\begin{array}{r} 0·136 \\ 2·5)\overline{0·34} \\ 0·25 \quad\longleftarrow\quad 0·1 \times 2·5 = 0·25 \\ \overline{0·090} \\ 0·075 \quad\longleftarrow\quad 0·03 \times 2·5 = 0·075 \\ \overline{0·0150} \\ 0·0150 \quad\longleftarrow\quad 0·006 \times 2·5 = 0·0150 \end{array}$$

It will be noticed that on the calculating machine, the decimal point markers are automatically set, in the process illustrated in Figure 26:24, in such a way that the number of decimal places in the product register is the sum of the numbers of decimal places in the other two registers. Hence there is never any difficulty, when working on the machine in determining the position of the decimal point in the quotient. However, when working on paper, children often find difficulty in positioning the decimal point when the divisor is not a whole number, as in 0·34 ÷ 2·5. On the other hand, difficulty is not found in dividing a decimal by a whole number. For instance, the positioning of the decimal point in the quotient of 0·075 ÷ 25 is natural, as the working below shows.

$$\begin{array}{r} 0·003 \\ 25)\overline{0·075} \\ 75 \end{array}$$

Since 3   × 25 = 75
0·3   × 25 = 7·5
0·03   × 25 = 0·75
0·003   × 25 = 0·075

The correct value of the digit 3 in the quotient is automatically obtained by placing it in the thousandths position above the thousandths digit of 0·075. This is the position where it would automatically appear in a division of whole numbers.

Hence children are usually recommended to transform a division such as

0·34 ÷ 2·5

so that the divisor (2·5) is replaced by a whole number.

This is done by noting that

$$2\cdot5 = 25 \text{ tenths}$$

and in terms of the same sub-unit,

$$0\cdot34 = 3\cdot4 \text{ tenths.}$$

Hence $0\cdot34 \div 2\cdot5 = 3\cdot4$ tenths $\div 25$ tenths
$$= 3\cdot4 \div 25$$
$$= 0\cdot136$$

$$
\begin{array}{r}
0\cdot136 \\
25\overline{)3\cdot4} \\
2\,5 \\ \hline
90 \\
75 \\ \hline
150 \\
150 \\ \hline
\end{array}
$$

Division of fractions and inverse multiplication

We saw earlier that the multiplication of fractions can be illustrated by graphs of multiples of a number, and that children can use interpolation in these graphs to obtain results of multiplications involving fractions. Graphs of multiples of natural numbers have also been used to illustrate division, and we now see that it is possible to use graphs of multiples to illustrate division involving fractions. Figure 26:25 shows the use of graphs of multiples of 2·5 and 3 to find a missing number in multiplication (or to solve an equation). The two equations solved here

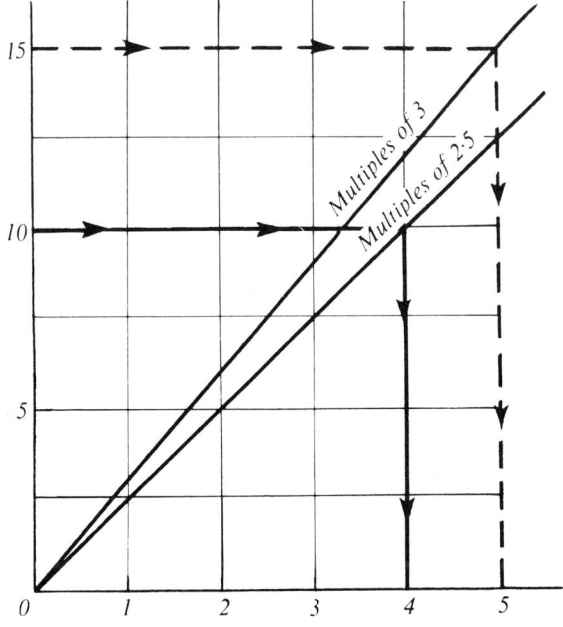

Figure 26:25

can be read, 'How many groupings of 3 units are there in 15 units?' or $15 \div 3$, and, 'How many groupings of 2·5 units are there in 10 units?' or $10 \div 2\cdot5$. For fractions, as for natural numbers, division is the inverse operation of multiplication. The two equations:

$$\boxed{m} \times 2\cdot5 = 10$$

and

$$\boxed{m} = 10 \div 2\cdot5$$

are equivalent to each other, and $10 \div 2\cdot5$ can be read as, 'What must 2·5 be multiplied by to equal 10?'

At this stage children begin to see that for all numbers, fractional numbers as well as whole numbers, division is inverse multiplication, for $3\frac{1}{3} \div 1\frac{1}{2}$ can now be read as, 'What must $1\frac{1}{2}$ be multiplied by to equal $3\frac{1}{3}$?' This question leads to the usual method of dividing one fraction by another. A number can easily be constructed which, when multiplied by $1\frac{1}{2}$, yields $3\frac{1}{3}$. We need to find, in fractional form, the missing number in

$$\boxed{?} \times \frac{3}{2} = \frac{10}{3};$$

10 is needed in the numerator of the fraction in the box, in order to obtain the numerator of the resulting fraction $\frac{10}{3}$: 2 is also needed in the numerator, to remove an unwanted 2 from the denominator:

$$\boxed{\frac{10 \times \cancel{2}^1}{?}} \times \frac{3}{\cancel{2}_1} = \frac{10}{3}$$

Similarly, 3×3 must be placed in the denominator of the fraction in the box:

$$\boxed{\frac{10 \times \cancel{2}^1}{3 \times \cancel{3}_1}} \times \frac{\cancel{3}^1}{\cancel{2}_1} = \frac{10}{3}$$

Hence the number by which $\frac{3}{2}$ must be multiplied to give $\frac{10}{3}$ is $\frac{10}{3} \times \frac{2}{3}$. This statement can be written as

$$\frac{10}{3} \div \frac{3}{2} = \frac{10}{3} \times \frac{2}{3}$$

We now see the emergence of the usual method of dividing by a fraction, which is multiplication by its reciprocal. This has often been described as, 'Turn the second fraction upside down and multiply', but children cannot understand this method until they understand the combination of cancellation with the multiplication of fractions, which is unlikely to be the case until fairly late in the secondary school.

The reciprocal of a fraction

In discussing the ratio aspect of a fraction, the same relationship between two quantities was expressed in two different ways. In Figure 26:26, the length of the red rod is $\frac{2}{5}$ of the length of the yellow rod, or the length of the yellow rod is $\frac{5}{2}$ times the length of the red rod. The fractions $\frac{2}{5}$ and $\frac{5}{2}$ are *reciprocals* of each other. The red rod is $\frac{1}{3}$ the length of the dark-green rod, and the dark-green rod is 3 times the length of the red rod. The numbers $\frac{1}{3}$ and 3 are reciprocals of each other. In the general case, the white rod is $\frac{a}{b}$ the length of the grey rod, and the grey rod is $\frac{b}{a}$ the length of the white rod. The fractions $\frac{a}{b}$ and $\frac{b}{a}$ are reciprocals of each other.[4]

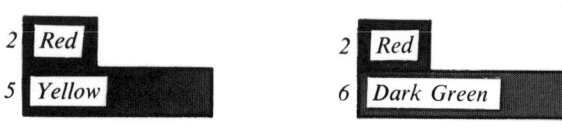

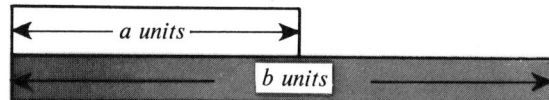

Figure 26:26

The relation between reciprocals can be expressed by combining the facts that

$$\text{red rod} = \tfrac{2}{5} \text{ of yellow rod}$$

and

$$\text{yellow rod} = \tfrac{5}{2} \text{ of red rod}$$

This combination yields

$$\text{yellow rod} = \tfrac{5}{2} \text{ of } (\tfrac{2}{5} \text{ of yellow rod})$$

Hence

$$\tfrac{5}{2} \text{ of } \tfrac{2}{5} \text{ unit} = 1 \text{ unit}$$

In terms of the red rod,

$$\begin{aligned}
\text{red rod} &= \tfrac{2}{5} \text{ of (yellow rod)} \\
&= \tfrac{2}{5} \text{ of } (\tfrac{5}{2} \text{ of red rod})
\end{aligned}$$

[4] It is often convenient to write a natural number such as 3 in the fractional form $\frac{3}{1}$, in order to show its relation to its reciprocal, $\frac{1}{3}$. This notation is consistent with our previous usage, for the denominator of a fraction shows the sub-unit in terms of which the fraction is measured, and the numerator shows the number of these sub-units. Thus $\frac{3}{1}$ indicates that the unit is itself used as a 'sub-unit' and that 3 of these 'sub-units' have been taken.

258

and so

$$\tfrac{2}{5} \text{ of } \tfrac{5}{2} = 1$$

Using the multiplication symbolism,

$$\tfrac{2}{5} \times \tfrac{5}{2} = \tfrac{5}{2} \times \tfrac{2}{5} = 1 ;$$

the product of reciprocal fractions is 1. In the general case (Figure 26:26)

$$\frac{a}{b} \times \frac{b}{a} = \frac{b}{a} \times \frac{a}{b} = 1$$

The relation between a fraction and its reciprocal can also be stated in terms of division. The sentence $\frac{2}{5} \times \frac{5}{2} = 1$ answers the question, 'What must $\frac{2}{5}$ be multiplied by to equal 1?' This question can also be written $1 \div \frac{2}{5}$, and so

$$1 \div \tfrac{2}{5} = \tfrac{5}{2}$$

Similarly,

$$1 \div \tfrac{5}{2} = \tfrac{2}{5}$$

The relation between a whole number and its reciprocal can be expressed in the same way. Three times $\frac{1}{3}$ equals 1, and $\frac{1}{3}$ of 3 is 1; that is

$$3 \times \tfrac{1}{3} = \tfrac{1}{3} \times 3 = 1$$

These statements can be re-written in terms of divisions as

$$1 \div 3 = \tfrac{1}{3} \quad \text{(What must 3 be multiplied by to equal 1?)}$$

and

$$1 \div \tfrac{1}{3} = 3 \quad \text{(What must } \tfrac{1}{3} \text{ be multiplied by to equal 1?)}$$

We can now consider more fully the relation between division by a fraction and multiplication by its reciprocal.

The statement '$3\frac{1}{3} \div 1\frac{1}{2}$' asks for the solution of the equation

$$x \times \tfrac{3}{2} = \tfrac{10}{3} \quad \text{(Find the number which, multiplied by } \tfrac{3}{2}, \text{ gives } \tfrac{10}{3}\text{)}$$

In order to isolate x, the equal numbers on the two sides of this equation may be multiplied by the reciprocal of $\frac{3}{2}$, which is $\frac{2}{3}$. Since $(x \times \frac{3}{2})$ and $\frac{10}{3}$ are equal, the results of the multiplication will be equal. Thus

$$(x \times \tfrac{3}{2}) \times \tfrac{2}{3} = \tfrac{10}{3} \times \tfrac{2}{3}$$

But $\frac{3}{2} \times \frac{2}{3} = 1$, so that we have

$$x = \tfrac{10}{3} \times \tfrac{2}{3}$$

Hence $\frac{10}{3} \div \frac{3}{2} = \frac{10}{3} \times \frac{2}{3}$, and, in general, it can be shown in the same way that if $\frac{a}{b}$ and $\frac{c}{d}$ are any fractions,

$$\frac{a}{b} \div \frac{c}{d} = \frac{a}{b} \times \frac{d}{c} \quad \left(\text{provided that } \frac{c}{d} \text{ is not zero} \right)$$

This formalization should be postponed until the

secondary school as it is unsuitable until children have reached the stage of logical operations, and are able to handle number in the abstract without concrete aids.

The distributive law for fractions

In Chapter 18 we saw the importance of the *distributive law*

$$a \times (b+c) = (a \times b) + (a \times c)$$

in the multiplication of natural numbers. This law is also often used to simplify the multiplication of fractional numbers as we have seen on page 249 when discussing the multiplication of decimals. A further example of the use of the distributive law is that a child who wishes to find the cost of 8 cakes costing $2\frac{1}{2}$p each will find 8 twopences and 8 halfpennies and add the results. He is using

$$8 \times (2+\tfrac{1}{2}) = (8 \times 2) + (8 \times \tfrac{1}{2})$$

The mass of $2\frac{1}{2}$ bags of sand each of mass $8\frac{1}{2}$ kg is most conveniently found by adding together the mass of 2 bags and the mass of $\frac{1}{2}$ a bag. Here the distributive law may be used several times:

$$2\tfrac{1}{2} \times 8\tfrac{1}{2} = (2+\tfrac{1}{2}) \times 8\tfrac{1}{2}$$
$$= (2 \times 8\tfrac{1}{2}) + (\tfrac{1}{2} \times 8\tfrac{1}{2})$$

then $2 \times 8\frac{1}{2}$ is calculated by finding $(2 \times 8) + (2 \times \frac{1}{2})$, and similarly

$$\tfrac{1}{2} \times 8\tfrac{1}{2} = (\tfrac{1}{2} \times 8) + (\tfrac{1}{2} \times \tfrac{1}{2})$$

We use the distributive law in the multiplication of fractions as naturally as in the multiplication of natural numbers. If a, b and c are any natural numbers or fractions,

$$a \times (b+c) = (a \times b) + (a \times c)$$

When we find the areas of rectangles, the lengths of whose sides are given in decimal form, much use is made of the distributive law. Two examples are given below, and are illustrated in Figure 26:27.

(i) Length $= 11$ cm,
   Breadth $= 3 \cdot 3$ cm
   Area $= 11 \times 3 \cdot 3$ square cm
   $= (11 \times 3) + (11 \times 0 \cdot 3)$ square cm
   $= 33 + 3 \cdot 3$ square cm
   $= 36 \cdot 3$ square cm.

(ii) Length $= 4 \cdot 5$ cm,
   Breadth $= 2 \cdot 3$ cm
   Area $= 4 \cdot 5 \times 2 \cdot 3$ square cm
   $= (4 \times 2 \cdot 3) + (0 \cdot 5 \times 2 \cdot 3)$ square cm
   $= (4 \times 2 + 4 \times 0 \cdot 3) + (0 \cdot 5 \times 2 + 0 \cdot 5 \times 3)$ square cm
   $= 8 + 1 \cdot 2 + 1 + 1 \cdot 5$ square cm
   $= 11 \cdot 7$ square cm

(a)

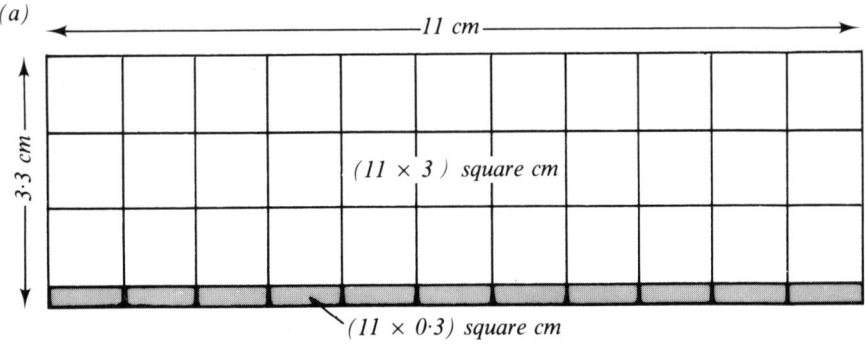

$$11 \times 3 \cdot 3 = (11 \times 3) + (11 \times 0 \cdot 3)$$

(b)

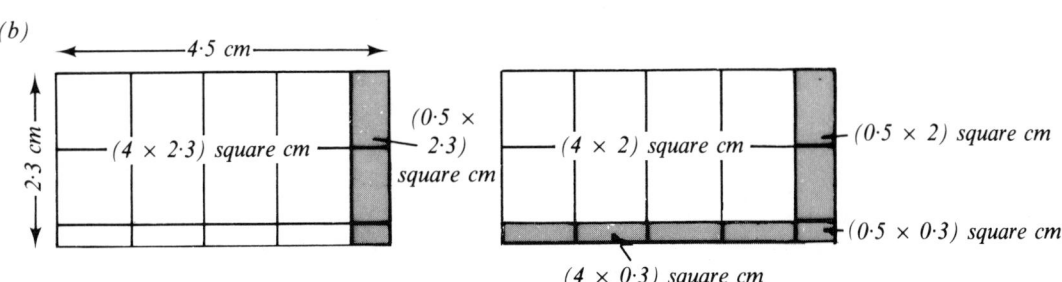

$$4 \cdot 5 \times 2 \cdot 3 = (4 \times 2 \cdot 3) + (0 \cdot 5 \times 2 \cdot 3)$$
$$= (4 \times 2) + (4 \times 0 \cdot 3) + (0 \cdot 5 \times 2) + (0 \cdot 5 \times 0 \cdot 3)$$

Figure 26:27

The signless rational numbers

As children learn to handle decimals and fractions with confidence, and come to understand their addition, subtraction, multiplication and division, they cease to distinguish sharply between the natural numbers and the fractional numbers, for natural numbers and fractional numbers behave very similarly. They also think of the decimal and fractional ways of writing a fractional number as interchangeable; 0·25 and $\frac{1}{4}$ are symbols for the same number. Every fractional number can be written in many ways: $\frac{1}{2} = \frac{2}{4} = \frac{5}{10} = 0·5 = \ldots$, but every whole number can also be written in many ways:

$$3 = \frac{3}{1} = \frac{6}{2} = \frac{30}{10} = 3·0 = \ldots,$$

so the behaviour of fractional numbers and whole numbers is similar in this respect. Both natural numbers and fractional numbers have their appointed places on the number line.

The natural numbers can be placed in an *order* of increasing magnitude: 0, 1, 2, 3, 4, ... which corresponds to their position in order on the number line. Putting the fractional numbers in order of magnitude is a slightly more complicated problem. There is a *next natural number* (in order of magnitude) after, say, 3; but there is not a *next fraction* (in order of magnitude) after, say, 2·7. There is a multitude of different fractions which are all a little larger than 2·7, each with its representative point on the number line. Among these fractions are 2·8, 2·75, 2·71, 2·701, 2·7001, 2·70001 and a whole host of others (Figure 26:28). It will be seen that we can never find a *closest* or *next* fraction to 2·7; there is always another which is closer to 2·7 than the last fraction we thought of.[5]

It is, however, always possible to decide which of two fractions is the greater. The fraction $2\frac{3}{4}$ is greater than 2·7, since $2\frac{3}{4} = 2·75$. In this ordering of positions on the number line the whole numbers have their places among the fractions, and so are not distinguished from the fractional numbers in a child's mind. After some years of experience many children can think in terms of, and operate with, the set of numbers consisting of the natural numbers and the fractional numbers written in either decimal or fractional form.

This set of numbers is the set of *signless rational numbers*.[6] 'Rational' signifies that the number can be expressed as a *ratio*; the signless rational numbers include not only fractions such as $\frac{2}{5}$, which is the ratio of 2 units to 5 units, but also 3, which is the ratio of 3 units to 1 unit. All signless rational numbers can be written in a fractional form, such as $\frac{3}{1}$ or $\frac{5}{2}$. A signless rational number written in decimal form can easily be transformed into fractional form, for 0·37 is $\frac{37}{100}$, and 2·701 is $\frac{2701}{1000}$. In general, *a signless rational number is a number which can be expressed in the form* $\dfrac{p}{q}$, where p and q are natural numbers, and q is not zero.[7] Most of the numbers which children use at the primary school stage are signless rational numbers, although many other types of number

---

[5] If 3 is regarded as a *fraction* rather than as a natural number there is not a next fraction after it, in order of magnitude. We can find many fractions which are a little larger than 3, such as 3·1, 3·01, 3·001, ... but it is impossible to find a fraction which comes *next* after 3 on the number line.

[6] We shall discuss the set of *directed* rational numbers later. The directed rational numbers include such numbers as $(-\frac{2}{3})$ and $(+3)$.

The present set of numbers has been described as the set of *signless* rational numbers in order that the two sets may be distinguished.

[7] It is impossible for a fraction to have zero as a denominator. The symbols $\frac{1}{0}$, $\frac{2}{0}$, etc., have no meaning, for the denominator of a fraction shows the number of sub-units into which a unit has been divided. Also, a division such as $2 \div 0$ is impossible, for there is not a multiple of 0 which is equal to 2. The numerator of a fraction may, however, be zero, and $\frac{0}{1} = \frac{0}{2} = \frac{0}{3} = \ldots$ are fractional representations of 0.

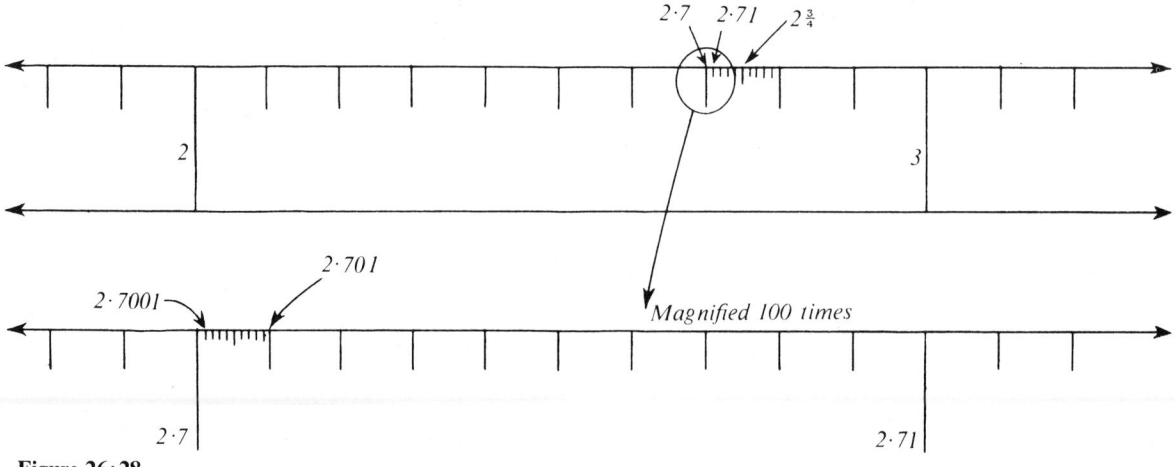

Figure 26:28

exist. Neither (-2) nor $(-\frac{2}{3})$ is a signless rational number[8], nor is $\sqrt{2}$ or π.[9]

All the signless rational numbers have representations on the number line, and they obey arithmetical laws which are very similar to the arithmetical laws obeyed by the natural numbers. There are, however, some differences of behaviour between natural numbers and rational numbers which will be discussed in Chapter 35, and which make the rational numbers more adaptable than the natural numbers. For the present, the reader should keep in mind the basic difference of use between the natural numbers and the rational numbers. The natural numbers are used for counting and apply to indivisible units; the signless rational numbers are used for measuring and apply to divisible units. Hence after any natural number there is a next natural number, which can be used for counting the next thing in a set; but a rational number does not have a next rational number after it: there is an infinity of rational numbers very near to it.

Systematization of operations on numbers and measures

When a child has gained a complete idea of the notation for the signless rational numbers, and is able to use the place-value system for whole numbers and decimals, it is time to be sure that he can easily, systematically and tidily add and subtract any numbers or measures which he needs to, and can multiply or divide them in simple cases. Skill in computation is not an end in itself, since computation is always needed for some purpose, and so for finding the answer to something we need to know. The first essential, therefore, is knowledge of which operation needs to be performed in a particular situation. Once this knowledge is gained, it is then important that the required computations should be performed accurately, and with reasonable speed.

Long and heavy calculations are no longer required. The use of calculating machines whenever a large amount of arithmetic has to be done will undoubtedly become even more common, in shops, offices, industry and science, and in schools. Our guide to the standard of arithmetical performance, as distinct from mathematical understanding, should be what will be needed in everyday life and in the child's future mathematical and scientific work. It is important that when calculations are performed by a human calculator they should be performed accurately, so that the addition bonds up to $9+9$, and the multiplication tables up to 9×9, should be accurately known. A standard arrangement of working is also helpful in ensuring accuracy in calculation. Eventually, methods of working

addition, subtraction, multiplication and division should be systematized. The routine arithmetical calculations which occur in secondary school mathematics and science will not then obtrude on the new ideas to which children must become accustomed in the secondary school.

We would emphasize again that it is useless for a child to be able to perform addition, subtraction, multiplication and division of numbers, money or measures if he does not understand the meaning of these operations, or when each one is called for. This understanding does not come through mechanical practice in performing the operations, but through setting them in real situations where their meaning can be grasped.

The results of calculations should be examined to see if they are reasonable: the average height of a group of children will certainly lie between the greatest and least heights, and is often roughly halfway between them; the height of a house found with a clinometer can be very roughly checked by estimating the height of its rooms, and so on. Such inspection will often detect gross arithmetical errors. Children should also know how to check subtraction by addition and division by multiplication. Important calculations should be worked independently by more than one person, or in more than one way, or checked on a calculating machine. These precautions are particularly important when children are not doing sums from a text-book, but are making calculations on data they have themselves obtained. The relevance of the work to the children's interest does not in itself ensure accuracy, and much good work has been spoilt by a slip in the early stages. Children who are working together on a project should be encouraged to do the arithmetical work independently, checking each other at every stage.

The solution of any mathematical problem has two stages: finding out how to solve it, and solving it. Children need to have it emphasized that the first stage is unsatisfactory unless the second is correctly performed, and it is here that the sheer mechanics of arithmetic comes in.

When children invent their own problems or solve problems suggested by practical situations, rather than working through a set of sums in a text-book, their justification for faith in the correctness of their results can no longer be agreement with the answer-book. Something much more convincing and personal is now called for. A group of children can maintain that a result they have obtained is correct only if they are convinced (and can convince others) of the rightness of their method, if they have all obtained the same result, which is a sensible one, and if they have as far as possible checked their calculations. An individual child working by himself can do most of this, particularly if it is possible for him to do his calculations in more than one way, but the teacher will probably have to investigate his method of solving a problem in some detail, since errors of understanding are more likely to go undetected when a child is working alone.

[8] These are *negative rational numbers*. See page 338.

[9] These are *irrational numbers*. See page 400.

Part IV
The Collection and Treatment of Data

27 Indirect Measurement

Introduction

During the early years at school children acquire a great deal of experience of measuring distances, and use the measurements they have made in making models and in drawing simple scale plans. Some of the things they would like to measure may, however, be out of their reach. It may be possible to make a model of the classroom, but often children cannot make a model of the school hall (although they can draw a plan of it), because they cannot reach the ceiling of the hall to measure its height. When they study a tree, children will want to know its height, but they will not be able to measure this directly. The width of a river cannot be measured directly, nor can the height of a church tower or a factory chimney. But some methods of measuring these distances indirectly are within the understanding of many older children in the primary school, and the problems of making these measurements provide situations where they can use their developing geometrical concepts. The simple instruments which are used can often be made by children, and although the results will not always be very accurate, the principles used will be clear to the children, and will extend their knowledge of the uses of mathematics.

Another quantity which must always be measured by indirect means is time, since the passage of time must always be matched with some regular occurrence, like the swing of a pendulum. The study of various ways of measuring time helps to deepen children's concept of time, and leads to an understanding of the measurement of speed. The indirect measurement of the three quantities of distance, time and speed, and the relation between them, form the theme of this chapter.

Using triangles to measure heights

Let us suppose that children want to measure the height of a house, or of a wall of the school hall. First they can estimate the height of a door in the wall, or imagine how many times a child's height would fit into the height of the wall, or use the number of storeys in the building to provide clues. Counting the number of courses of bricks may be another possible method, but it becomes very difficult to count layers of bricks at any considerable height. The height of modern multi-storey buildings is often found most easily by measuring the height of one storey and multiplying by the number of storeys. All these methods may fail, however, for instance in finding the height of a tree. All other methods depend basically on the drawing of a triangle from the measurements which can be made at ground level. The simplest situation is shown in Figure 27:1. From the measurement of the horizontal distance AC and of the angle BAC, a scale-drawing of the triangle ABC can be made, and the scale height of the tree measured from the drawing (Figure 27:2). The angle between the horizontal and the line to the top of the tree is the *angle of elevation* of the top of the tree.

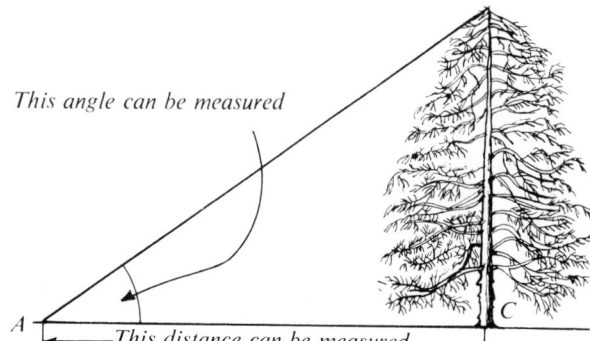

Figure 27:1

Variations on this method of making a scale-drawing of a triangle are often used, but the basic method is simple enough for a child to grasp as soon as he understands

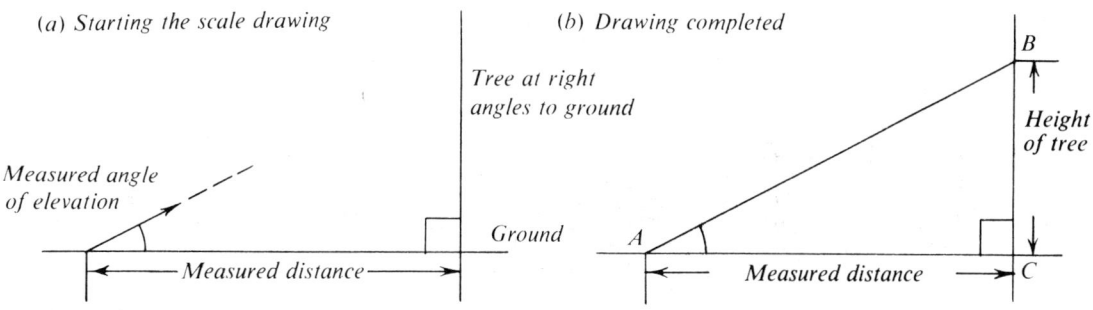

Figure 27:2

265

the ideas of horizontal and vertical and the relation between them, and when he can visualize a line from the ground to the top of the tree, which does not have the physical existence of lines drawn on the ground or on a sheet of paper. All the methods of measuring the angle of elevation *BAC* involve 'sighting' the top of the tree, and measuring the angle between the invisible line *AB* and the horizontal (or sometimes the vertical). Other invisible lines are often used as well, for it is more convenient to measure angles at eye-level than at ground-level. In Figure 27:3, which shows the most convenient practical arrangement, all three lines in the triangle *ABC* are invisible, and have to be supplied by the child's imagination.

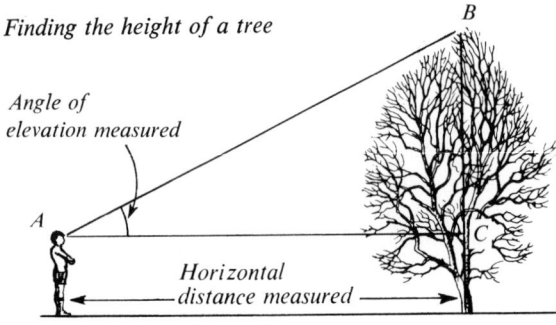

Finding the height of a tree

Angle of elevation measured

Horizontal distance measured

Figure 27:3

The construction and use of the instruments for measuring the angle of elevation of the top of the tree will be described on page 268.

Some concepts used in the indirect measurement of distance

The use of a triangle to measure distances indirectly is conceptually a complex process, but the concepts needed are established during the stage of concrete operations, and

the experience provided by this type of measurement helps these concepts to become firmly fixed and operational. Some of these concepts are now discussed and it will be seen that they are closely inter-related.

The idea that a tree or a building with a sloping roof has a 'height' is not immediately obvious. The line whose length must be measured has to be supplied by the imagination, and has to be a vertical line. Figure 27:4 shows some objects which have obvious vertical heights, and others whose heights are less obvious. The heights of the door and the wall are measured along lines which have a real physical existence. In the case of the oak tree this line is less obvious, and the height of the leaning tree bears no relation to any physical line *in* the tree. In all these instances the vertical line has to be supplied by the imagination. Children usually learn early to measure each other's height by using a ruler placed horizontally to make a mark on a vertical wall at the right height. They do not always realize the necessity, as opposed to the convenience, of this method, and even older children may sometimes be seen measuring each other's heights by applying a tape-measure to the body, so that the tape-measure is curved and does not lie in a vertical straight line.

This mistake would be expected until a child has securely established the ideas of horizontal and vertical, and knows that in a particular place the vertical always has the same unchanging direction, the direction in which a plumb-line hangs. Piaget has shown that children are not secure in this idea until the stage of concrete operations,[1] and Beard found that only 9 out of a sample of 183 English children aged between 6 and 11 were able to draw correctly the position which they expected a plumb-line to take up within a tilted jam-jar, but 49 of the same sample drew correctly the expected position of the water

[1] Piaget, J. and Inhelder, B. *The Child's Conception of Space,* Chapter 13.

Figure 27:4

level in a tilted jam-jar half full of water.[2] Figure 27:5 shows typical earlier attempts at these drawings, before the unvarying vertical direction of the plumb-line and the unvarying horizontal level of the water have become clear to the child.

Figure 27:5

Until he has achieved a permanent frame of reference of stable horizontals and verticals, a child finds it difficult to judge the slope of oblique lines, and to appreciate differences of slope between different lines. Piaget performed an experiment in which he put a dot on a piece of paper, and asked a child, who was provided with tools for measuring, to put a dot in the same position on a similar piece of paper. The two pieces of paper were fixed at opposite corners of a table.[3] Children aged about 7 often measured the distance of the dot from one corner of the paper and transferred this measurement to the other piece of paper, but without understanding the need to keep the direction of the oblique line constant, or realizing that it would be better to make two measurements parallel to two edges of the paper (Figure 27:6). It is likely that this mistake occurs because only at the stage of concrete operations is a child able to relate two aspects of a situation to one another. In this experiment the child must take account of both distance and direction, or he must relate the dot to two edges of the paper, if he is to put it in the correct position.

Clearly, the ability to judge and measure the direction of oblique lines is essential to the use of a triangle for indirect measurement. There remains the further difficulty that the oblique line needed (*AB* in Figure 27:3) can only be 'seen' by the observer at *A*, and then only by 'sighting' along it. By the age of about 7 many children are able to arrange objects in a line by sighting along the line, and a year or two later they can co-ordinate the viewpoint of the observer who looks along *AB* with the viewpoint of the observer who looks at triangle *ABC* from the side, and so can accept Figure 27:3 as a correct picture of what is happening. Piaget says

> '... it is most significant that co-ordination of the perceptual field reaches its maximum efficiency at about the age of 9, the same age at which the concepts of vertical and horizontal finally emerge as potential co-ordinate axes.'[4]

The idea of a 'correct picture' needs examination, however. A 'correct picture' is a scale-drawing. This is an idea with which children will already be familiar from making simple plans and models. Most of these scale-drawings are rectangular in shape, and they have always been made by measuring lengths. A child may not realize that all the angles of a scale-drawing are equal to the angles of the original object, and that he can make a scale drawing of a triangle simply by making the angles of the two triangles equal. Here again, the ability to co-ordinate measurements in two dimensions and to take account of slope is needed.

It must be stressed that the understanding of such mathematical concepts as these comes through action and through experience of situations in which the concepts arise. The fact that a child does not appear to have a very firm grasp of all the ideas which he needs should not always dissuade the teacher from introducing him to new experiences which may be exactly what he needs to help the development of some concept. Analysis of the ideas used in a piece of work may also help in the design of preliminary experience, for a piece of work is more likely to succeed if a child can start it from a secure basis of previous experience, and is not overwhelmed by a great variety of new ideas and problems which all have to be solved at the same time.

We now turn to the discussion of the practical problem of measuring an angle of elevation such as angle *BAC* of Figure 27:3.

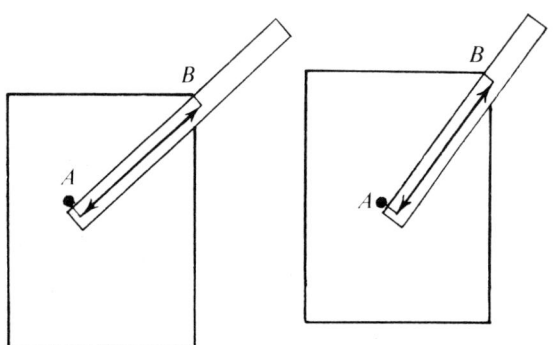

Figure 27:6

[2] Beard, R. 'Further Studies in Concept Development', *Educational Review*, 17(**1**), 1964.

[3] Piaget, J. and Inhelder, B. *The Child's Conception of Space.* Chapter 7.

[4] Piaget, J. and Inhelder, B. *The Child's Conception of Space.*

Instruments for measuring angles of elevation

Modern optical instruments for measuring angles, such as the theodolite and sextant, are not usually available to children, and even if they are, simpler and more primitive instruments form a useful introduction to more accurate and complicated equipment. We therefore discuss only simple instruments, most of which can easily be made by children.

The first instruments we describe avoid the problem of actually measuring the angle of elevation. If one stands near the tree and walks away from it, the angle of elevation of the top of the tree gradually decreases. By moving far enough away from the tree, the triangle ABC can be made of any desired shape (Figure 27:7). A triangle

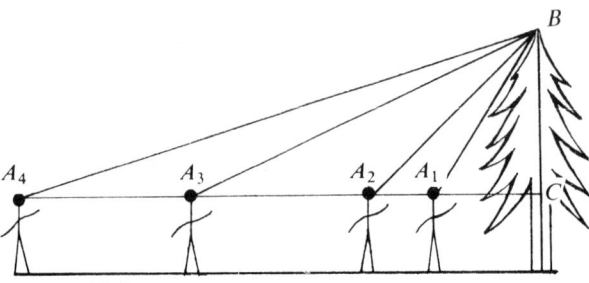

Figure 27:7

with two equal sides AC and BC is particularly simple. A square of cardboard may be cut in half diagonally to give a right-angled triangle with two equal sides. If a child sights the top of the tree along the longest side of this triangle (Figure 27:8), he is assured that the large triangle ABC which he is making has two equal sides, for the half-square APQ is of the same shape as triangle ABC. It is necessary to ensure that AQ is horizontal, and this is most easily done by hanging a plumb-line from the triangle near the edge PQ, so that a second child, standing at the side, can see that PQ is vertical. If the distance AC is then measured, it will be equal to BC.

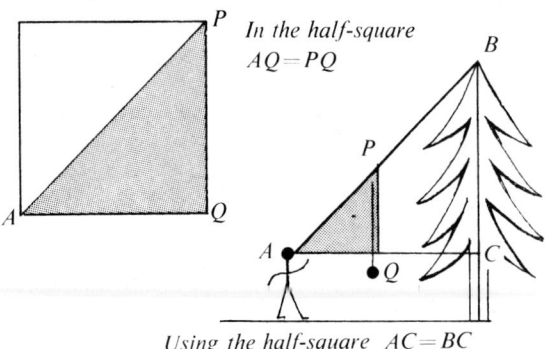

In the half-square
$AQ = PQ$

Using the half-square $AC = BC$

Figure 27:8

268

The child using the half-square has to move until he can just see the top of the tree as he sights along AP. This is not always possible. If the tree is not very slender, it is often necessary to get farther away from it in order to get a clear view of the top. A half-square is not, however, the only shape of triangle which can be used. Figure 27:9 shows the use of a right-angled triangle, one of whose sides is twice the length of the other.

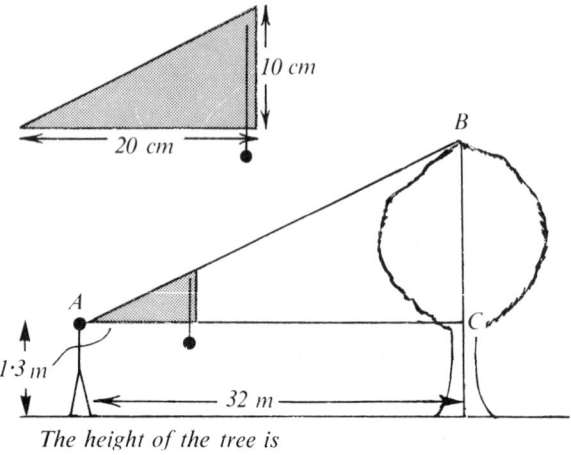

The height of the tree is
$16 m + 1·3 m = 17 m$ to the nearest metre

Figure 27:9

In other methods, the angle of elevation BAC is actually measured, and the instruments used are devices for sighting across a protractor. A simple Meccano sighting device using a cardboard protractor is shown in Figure 27:10, and the medieval *astrolabe* in Figure 27:11. The astrolabe needed no plumb-line. It was suspended from a ring held

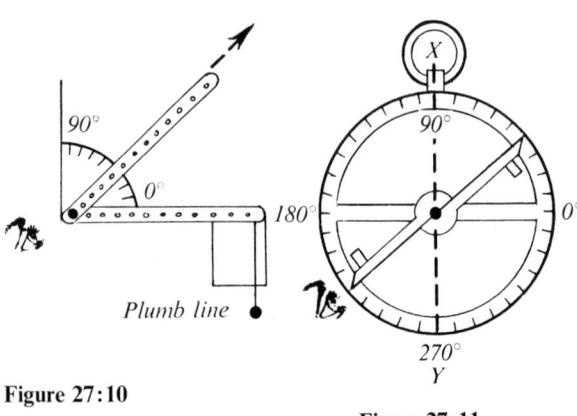

Figure 27:10

Figure 27:11

in the hand, and the movable pointer carrying the sights was symmetrically balanced, so that the instrument would always hang with the line XY vertical, whatever the position of the pointer.

A school protractor and a milk-straw can be used to make a simple *clinometer* (Figure 27:12). The straw is sellotaped to the protractor, and is used to support a plumb-line consisting of a piece of thread and a small weight. The clinometer is slightly more difficult to use than

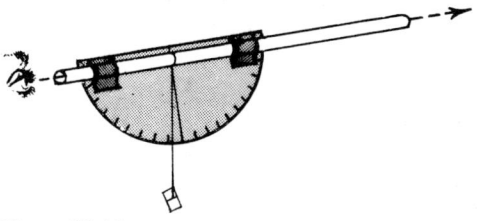

Figure 27:12

the previous instruments, as the angle read off from the protractor is not the angle of elevation of the top of the tree, but the angle between the oblique line and the vertical (Figure 27:13).

Using the clinometer

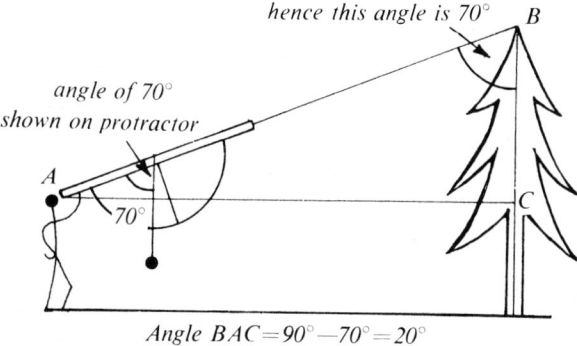

Angle BAC = 90° − 70° = 20°

Figure 27:13

When the angle of elevation *BAC* of the top of the tree has been measured by one of these methods, the distance *AC* between the observer and the tree is measured, and

the diagram can then be drawn to scale. The scale height of the tree is then read off from the scale-drawing. It often happens, however, that it is not possible to measure the distance of the observer from a point vertically below the top of the object. In this case, observations should be taken from two points. Figure 27:14 explains the method.

This method was used by armies in the sixteenth century to find the distance and height of a castle. It was known as 'drumhead trigonometry', the required lines being drawn by direct sighting on the vertical side of a drum (Figure 27:15).

Drumhead trigonometry

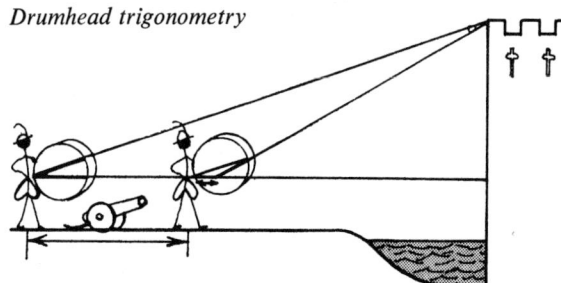

Figure 27:15

Lines and right angles on the ground

A natural extension of the use of triangles to measure the vertical heights of inaccessible objects is the use of triangles to measure horizontal distances. This leads to the introduction of simple surveying. In this section, we discuss a few uses of the idea of sighting, which can be used in marking out a football pitch, or any other large-scale construction on the ground.

Children will know by now that pulling a rope or measuring-tape taut gives them a straight line. They should also know how to measure out a straight line whose length is greater than the length of the measuring-tape by using

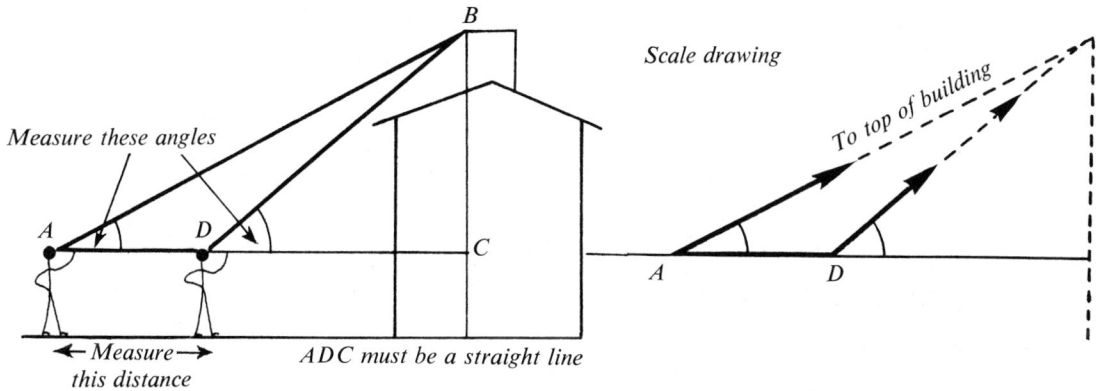

Figure 27:14

269

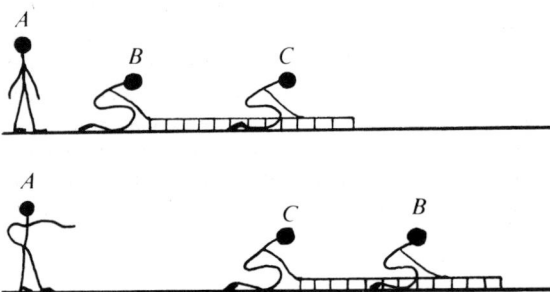

A directs B as he moves forward
so as to keep the line straight

Figure 27:16

an observer who remains behind when the tape is moved (Figure 27:16).

A previously drawn scale-plan, mounted on a horizontal board, can also be used for sighting when the shape to be marked out is a complicated one (Figure 27:17).

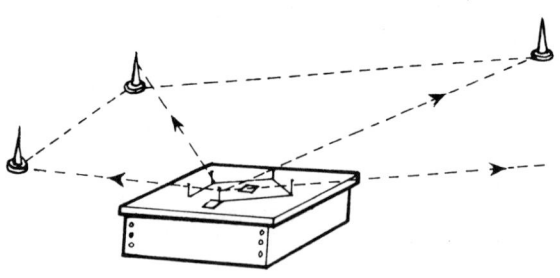

Figure 27:17

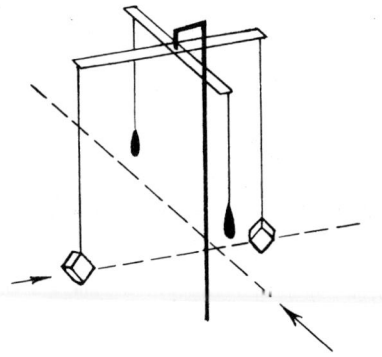

Figure 27:18

270

When heights are being measured, right angles are obtained by using horizontal and vertical lines. Right angles are more difficult to mark out on the ground. Among a variety of methods, the '3, 4, 5 triangle' may be used, or a sighting method. The Romans used a simple device called a *groma*, consisting of two rods fixed at right angles, from which plumb-lines were hung (Figure 27:18). The same idea is used in the sighting-box (Figure 27:19).

The measurement of time

Some distances have to be measured indirectly because they are inaccessible; periods of time always have to be measured indirectly. We can never lay a yardstick between two events; all we can do is to find some occurrence which we believe happens at regular intervals (for example, the recurrence of the seasons or the swing of a pendulum) and count how many times this happens between the two events. And we can never go back and check our measurements. Time has gone; the same events cannot be repeated. Because of this, a young child's idea of time and its measurement develops slowly. His growing memory, together with the important events which provide landmarks in time, help him to become aware of time in an increasingly quantitative way.

The ability to read a clock, the recurring pattern of events in the day, the school week, and the weekend, the regular recurrences of the new school year, Guy Fawkes Day, Christmas, spring, Easter, summer holidays, events like birthdays, using the calendar: all these help to provide the necessary landmarks in time. At first, time is not quantitative; it is a stream of present and past moments, only gradually differentiated by the memory and anticipation of these landmarks. During the first few years at school, the different scales of measurement of time, the years, the seasons, months, days, hours and minutes, need to be co-ordinated and set in relation to one another.

The sighting-box

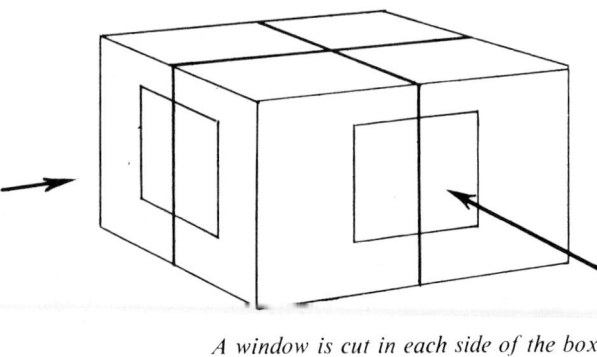

Figure 27:19   *A window is cut in each side of the box, and vertical threads are used as sights*

One way of doing this is by focusing children's attention on ways in which time can be, and has been, measured. The experience of mankind's struggle to catch and measure time can help children in their personal struggle with this most intangible of all the quantities which we measure. Children need experience like this as much as the ability to tell the time, for it focuses their attention on the passing of time and on the possibility of comparing intervals of time.

The rhythm of the year is slow, and variations in the weather cause slight variations in the more obvious landmarks. Because of these variations, primitive peoples find it difficult to judge how long a year is, and young children need to relate recurring events of nature, the lengthening and shortening of the days, the waxing and waning of the moon, the rise and fall of the tides, to the calendar of months which keeps in step with nature's year. A graph showing the beginning and ending of lighting-up time can be constructed over the period of a year, and will help children to associate the rhythm of the calendar year with nature's variations (Figure 27:20). New moons, times of high tide, the first lamb, the first cuckoo, the beginning of haymaking, and so on can be added to this calendar of the year. In some areas, the addition of the Jewish New Year or Ramadan may stimulate discussion of ways in which various peoples measure time.

With a little experiment, a child can discover the quantity of sand or sugar needed to run through a funnel in a minute, and so make his own timer. A candle-clock can be marked at five-minute intervals, and the principle of the ancient water-clock demonstrated to show how long cartons with different-sized holes in them take to sink in a bucket of water (Figure 27:21). The different but regularly repeating fast and slow rhythms which children meet in music and in movement also help to establish the idea of measurable time. The metronome, with its clear tick and good visual embodiment of this beat, fascinates children, and can be used to establish the idea of a second. A 'seconds pendulum' 1 metre long can be hung beside the metronome, and children will experiment in altering the length of the pendulum to try to make it match an altered beat of the metronome. Later, this experiment will become quantitative.

The beginning and ending of Lighting-up time during the School Year

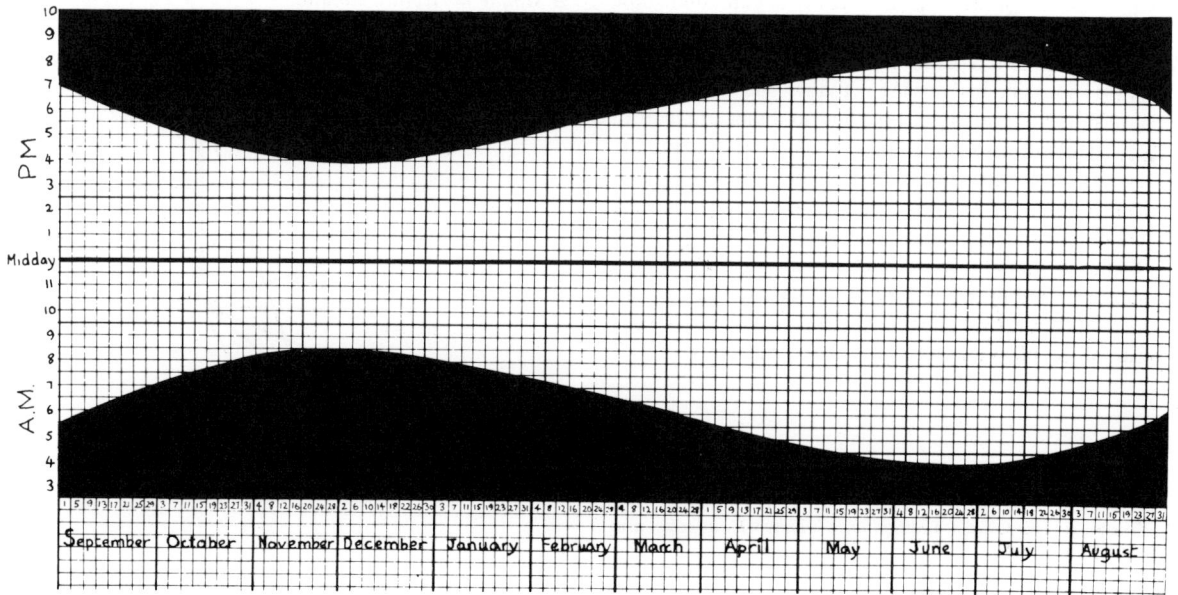

Figure 27:20

Some home-made clocks

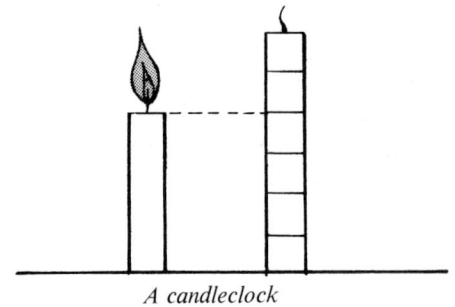
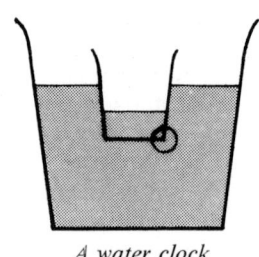

A 'minute-glass'	A candleclock	A water clock

Figure 27:21

While children's ideas of a second, a minute and an hour are growing, they will be interested in learning what a minute feels like when they are engaged in various activities. Piaget found that only during the Junior school years was the idea of the duration of time firmly established, and separated from the speed at which an activity was performed.[5] Lovell and Slater[6] describe an experiment invented by Piaget in which two dolls moved simultaneously on parallel courses *AB* and *CD*, where *AB* was longer than *CD*. The doll moving on the longer course *AB* went faster, and took the same time as the other doll. More than half of Lovell's average-to-bright 9-year-olds thought that the first doll had taken a longer time than the second, because it went farther. This number included some children who realized that the two dolls started and stopped at the same times.

A child can measure how far he can walk, run or skip in half a minute or a minute, or he can count how many times he can bounce a ball, or how many sums he can do in the time. This repetition of the objective measurement of time alongside his varying activities will help him to establish the objectivity of time and to dissociate it from speed. He will also notice how much longer a minute seems if he is sitting still than if he is reading, and will learn to make his own estimates of time by counting seconds.

Children should also examine the use of the sun as a timekeeper and the movement of the shadows cast by the sun. Young children do not think that a shadow is produced by an object blocking out rays of light, but think of it as something emanating from the object itself, and it is not until around 8 or 9 years of age that they can usually predict the direction of a shadow.[7] When this occurs, however, the apparent movement of the sun during the day can be linked with the movement of the shadow of a stick, and children can construct a horizontal sundial by marking the position of the shadow of a stick on the ground at different times during the day (Figure 27:22). A vertical sundial can also be constructed by using a nail in a south-facing wall (Figure 27:23). Such primitive 'scratch dials' or 'Mass-dials', a few of which date from Saxon times, can be found on the south walls of some churches. These later developed into magnificent and complicated sundials like the one in Queens' College, Cambridge.

A simple horizontal sundial

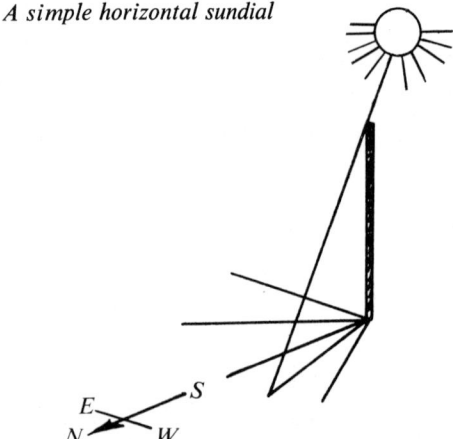

Figure 27:22

[5] Piaget, J. *The Child's Conception of Time* (Routledge and Kegan Paul, 1969).

[6] Lovell, K. and Slater, A. 'The Growth of the Concept of Time: a Comparative Study.' *Journal of Child Psychology and Psychiatry,* **1** (1960), 179–90.

[7] Piaget, J. *The Child's Conception of Physical Causality* (Kegan Paul, 1930), Chapter VIII.

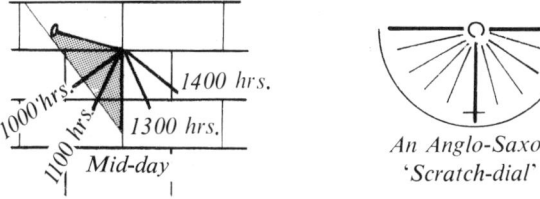

Using a nail in a south facing wall

Figure 27:23

When they use a horizontal sundial, children should notice that the shortest shadow is the mid-day one, and that it points due north, so that the sun is due south at mid-day Greenwich Mean Time. Some older children will be capable of understanding that the apparent movement of the sun is due to the movement of the earth. This idea should be introduced if possible, for the necessary concept of relative motion is understood by many children when they see it on television or at the cinema. The movement of the camera (or the use of a zoom lens) makes an object seem to move nearer or farther away, or to change its position in the picture. Many children can relate this apparent movement of the object to the movement of the camera, and so are beginning to appreciate relative motion.

Another useful sundial, which exactly mirrors the apparent movement of the sun across the bowl of the sky, is the hemispherical sundial. A bead is fixed by a wire so that it is at the centre of a hemispherical bowl (Figure 27:24), and the path of its shadow during the day can be

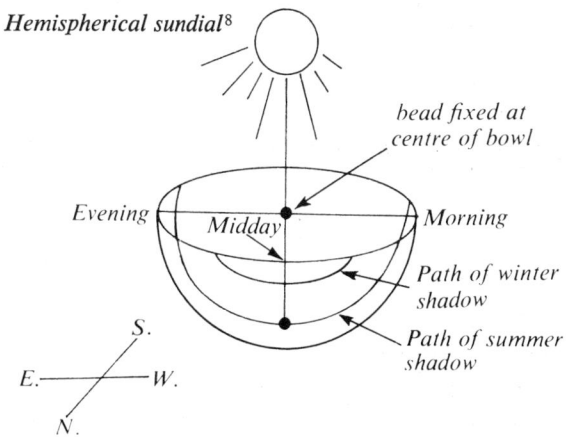

Hemispherical sundial[8]

Figure 27:24

[8] The invention of the hemispherical sundial is ascribed to Berossus, a Babylonian astronomer of the third century B.C.

marked on the inside of the bowl. This sundial can be used to study the variations in the altitude of the sun during the year.

The connection between distance and time

A child cannot form *directly* an idea of larger units of distance, such as the *kilometre*. He knows the smaller units which he can handle, but a kilometre can only be experienced in terms of movement. The statement that there are 1000 metres in a kilometre means very little in terms of actual experience, for the number is too large.

Children may find it helpful to break the kilometre down into smaller units. It may be possible to mark out 200 metres on the school field, and from this children can discover how long it would take them to walk a kilometre of 5 times 200 metres. Figure 27:25 shows a graphical treatment of this problem by two children who took different times to walk 200 metres. This graph can also be used to read off the distance when a child has walked for a certain time. It also demonstrates how inaccuracies are magnified when extrapolation is used. Children can use this knowledge to find places a kilometre from school, or to find how far their homes are from school. This idea of distance must, however, be based on an appreciation of how long it takes to get from one place to the other by some familiar means of transport: walking, bicycle, bus or car.

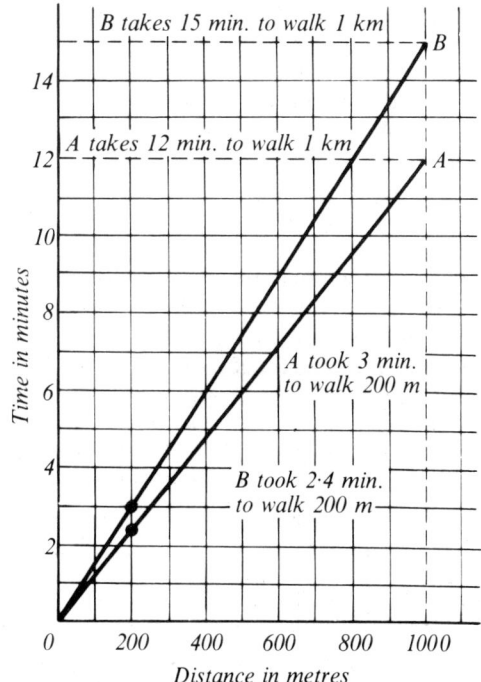

Figure 27:25

At this stage children will also be able to use reference books to find out the history of measures and will be able to compare the traditional British measures which they will still find in books and on signposts and milestones with the metric units.

The adult traveller relies for his knowledge of distance on the odometer of his car, or on his watch and a knowledge of his approximate average speed. Distances like the kilometre and its multiples are too large in relation to the human body for us to measure directly, except by such mechanical means as the odometer and so the measurement of distance is gradually supplemented in our minds by measurements of speed.

The measurement of speed

The idea that time can be divided into equal units and measured is a sophisticated one; so is the idea that speed can be measured. The clock and the calendar catch the stream of time and make it measurable; the speedometer of a car catches movement and attaches a number to it. The measure of speed—centimetres per second or kilometres per hour—is a compound of the measures of distance and of time, but to a young child speed is a property of movement, and does not yet depend on the relationship between a distance and the time taken to cover that distance. Only gradually does he distinguish between being late for school because he started late and late for school because he dawdled by the way. Before the stage of concrete operations he may think that when two toy cars race, one having a start on the other, that the one which catches up on its opponent has somehow taken longer, although he is sure that both cars started and stopped in the same instant.[9] Time and speed are still personal and not universal, and they are not differentiated from one another. Outside events and their speed can influence time.

An egg-timer or a stop-clock may be thought to move faster if the child walks quickly round the table while watching it than if he moves slowly.[10] He certainly cannot yet co-ordinate the three variables of time, distance and speed.

But as his idea of time develops and he learns to measure it, so his idea of 'faster' becomes measurable. If he makes water-clocks from two identical cartons with different-sized holes in the bottom, and one sinks in two minutes while the other takes four minutes, then the first has sunk *twice as fast* as the second. The graph in Figure 27:26, which he will make when he is finding out about the duration of minutes, will lead him to compare how fast he can travel in different ways. He will describe his speed as 90 metres in a minute, or 90 *metres per minute*, and on the basis of his measurements he can make graphs to show how far he could travel in each of these ways in 1 minute, 2 minutes, 3 minutes, etc. (Figure 27:27).

Could I go as far as this in the time?

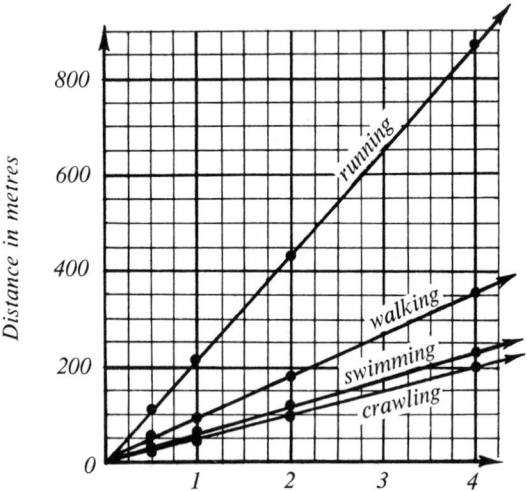

Figure 27:27　　*Time in minutes*

[9] Piaget, J. *Les Notions de Mouvement et Vitesse chez l'Enfant* (Presses Universitaires de France, 1946), Chapter VII.

[10] Piaget, J. *Développement de la Notion de Temps chez l'Enfant*, Chapter VIII.

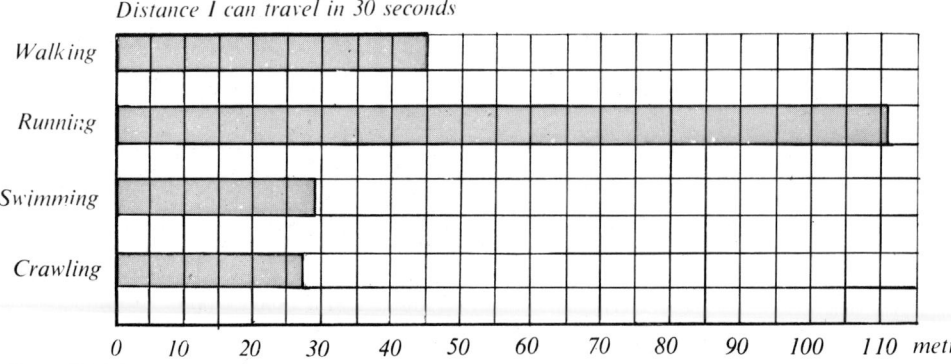

Figure 27:26

274

Theoretically, there are two possible ways of comparing speeds of movement. We can fix the time during which we move, and measure *how far* we travel in that time. This is the principle of the Le Mans 24-hour motor race. Alternatively, we can fix the distance and measure the length of time it takes to cover that distance. Almost all other races are run on this principle, and most comparisons of speed are made on the basis of a fixed distance. The train from Cambridge to Liverpool Street takes *less time* than the same journey by car, so the train has a *greater average speed*. A runner who covers 1 kilometre in 2 minutes 20 seconds goes faster than one who covers 10 kilometres in 28 minutes. Their average speeds could be expressed in either of the following ways:

	Method 1	Method 2
Shorter-distance runner	2·33 minutes per kilometre	0·43 kilometres per minute
Longer-distance runner	2·8 minutes per kilometre	0·36 kilometres per minute

Method 1 would be preferable if it were not for the fact that the *faster* runner takes fewer minutes per kilometre; 2·33 minutes per kilometre is faster than 2·8 minutes per kilometre; the larger number is attached to the smaller speed. But 0·43 kilometres *per minute* is faster than 0·36 kilometres *per minute*; here the larger number is attached to the greater speed. So in spite of the fact that speeds are usually measured over a fixed distance, they are always stated as if the time had been fixed and the distance measured.

Children will easily obtain information about the time it takes to travel a fixed distance. Figure 27:28 shows some typical information and a way of dealing with it graphically. A reference graph showing travel at some well-known speeds may be useful for comparison with the children's information (Figure 27:29), and will help to relate the steepness of slope of the graph to the speed of travel.

The calculations needed to translate the average speed of the bus or the cyclist into kilometres per hour should also be within the children's range; these calculations can be checked graphically, as in Figure 27:28.

Travelling to town

Distance from bus terminus to city centre 4 kilometres
By bus it takes 15 minutes
By car it takes 8 minutes
By bicycle it takes 18 minutes
On foot it takes 45 minutes

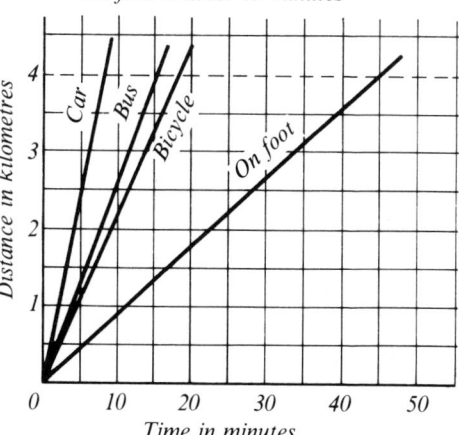

The cyclist goes 4·4 kilometres in 20 minutes or 4·4 × 3 kilometres

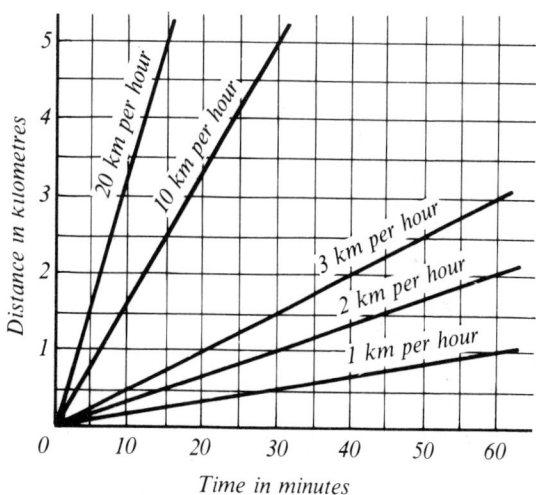

Figure 27:28

Figure 27:29

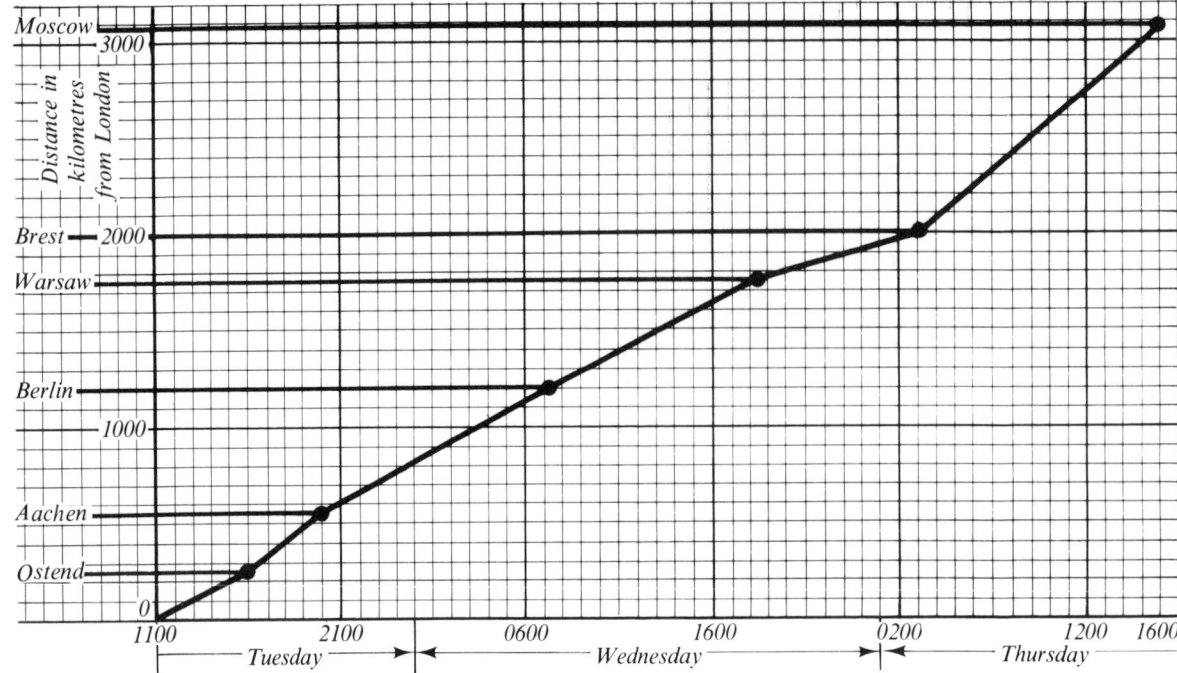

Figure 27:30

Rather than concentrating on calculation, however, it is more important that children should understand how to measure speeds, and how to illustrate their measurements graphically. Conventionally, speed graphs are drawn with distances measured vertically and times horizontally, so that the steeper the graph, the faster the speed it represents. Of course, a variable speed will not produce a straight-line graph. Figure 27:30 illustrates a journey of the Ost–West Express, and shows the variation in speed over different parts of the line.

Measurements of speed at this stage need not be confined to the speeds of vehicles. The rates at which other things move and grow will give experience of measurement in different units. The rate of growth of a plant, and so the speed of its growing tip, is appropriately measured in centimetres per week or per month. The rate of growth of a baby is more easily measured in terms of mass, and so expressed in kilograms per week. Figure 27:31 shows two graphs of a baby's growth; the first shows his actual mass each week and the second his monthly increase in mass, and so approximates to his rate of growth.

(a) Baby's actual mass

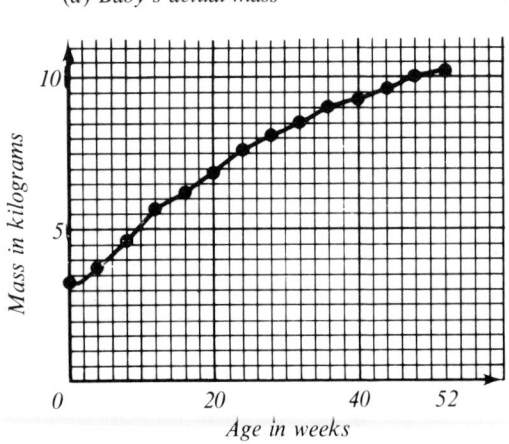

(b) Increase in baby's mass

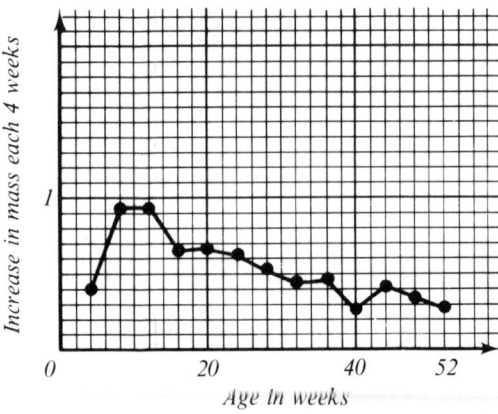

Figure 27:31

276

Children can also find the speeds of other natural phenomena. The speed of a stream can be found by timing a piece of wood as it is swept downstream. This may lead to a consideration of the rate of flow of the stream in litres per day.[11] The speed of a breeze can be measured by using a home-made anemometer (Figure 27:32), and it is even possible to measure the speed of sound with some degree of accuracy. The most primitive method is to measure with a stop-watch the time-lag between seeing the beating of a drum several hundred yards away and hearing the sound. Since sound takes 1 second to travel about 340 metres, this time-lag is measurable at distances of 200 metres, but the accuracy of the result is affected by the fact that stop-watches only register in intervals of one-fifth of a second. Variation in the observer's reaction time also considerably affects the results, so that the method is unreliable. A more sophisticated and accurate method uses an echo from a wall. Children may be able to beat a drum in steady rhythm,

The pivot should be as frictionless as possible

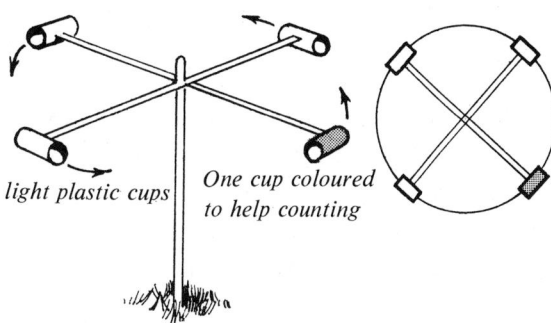

light plastic cups *One cup coloured to help counting*

Figure 27 : 32

---

[11] The profile of a small stream can be drawn fairly easily. When the speed of the current is known, the volume of water which flows through this profile in a day can be found.

beat—*echo*—beat—*echo*—beat—*echo*, so that the time for a number of beats can be measured with the stop-watch. and the error in measuring the time the sound takes to travel is reduced.

Such experiments as these link very closely with work in science, and in the field of measurement mathematics and science become nearly indistinguishable. In the next chapter we deal with more experiments in this borderland between mathematics and science.

28 Experimenting with Mechanisms

Introduction

When children are beginning to measure the speeds of objects, it is also appropriate for them to begin to study the forces which cause objects to move, and the devices used to simplify the many jobs involving movement which are carried out in everyday life. Children's lives are full of these mechanisms, from very simple ones like sledges and toy trucks, hammers and spanners, to bicycles, cars, ships, aircraft, cranes, and the scientific devices which they take for granted. On television they see other mechanical devices, from the six-shooter and the stage-coach to the manned space vehicle and the moon-rocket, which become nearly as much part of their own experiences as if they were actually present.

'How does it work?' is a question which may not be completely answered by young children, except in simple cases, but partial answers are often discovered, and children begin to acquire a vocabulary and a framework of ideas about forces and mechanisms which lay a foundation for later scientific work. From about 9 years old, too, children will begin to make deliberate experiments which lead them to draw conclusions, and may even in simple cases lead to the formulation of laws connecting such variables as the time of swing of a pendulum and the length of its string.

Children do not, of course, reach this stage without starting to form *physical* concepts, and it is very important that springs, wheels, magnets, weights, planks, Meccano parts and other objects from which they will gain useful experience should be available to them from a very early age.

In this chapter we describe and relate together some of the ideas which will emerge from such experiences.

Forces

The idea of a force is a fundamental one which develops out of experience of feeling and exerting forces. There are two ways in which we may notice that a force is being exerted. If a child leans on the edge of a table, we do not notice how hard he is pressing until the table suddenly tips; the force he is exerting causes a movement and we notice it. But the child knows that he is exerting a force before the table tips; he can feel it in his body, and he can feel the force increasing as he presses harder. It is the combination of his bodily feeling of exerting a force by pushing, pulling or lifting, and his observation of the results of exerting force in causing something to start moving, stop moving, turn, twist, topple or break, that gives a child his first idea of what a force is. It will be helpful to him to add the word 'force' to his vocabulary at this stage.

Some forces, however, are so much part of our environment that we do not easily notice them. The weight of the air around us causes a force on our bodies which we do not notice unless it changes suddenly, but the deep-sea diver is painfully aware of the results of changes of air-pressure if he is brought up too quickly from the depths. The most important of these often unnoticed forces is that of *gravity*, which pulls everything on the earth towards its centre. Young children do not easily think of gravity as a force for two reasons: firstly, all the forces which they themselves exert are *contact forces*; you have to hold an object or to be in contact with it to push, pull, lift or twist it, but gravity works *at a distance*; a ball does not have to be in contact with the earth for the earth to pull it. Secondly, gravity is always present; it can never be switched off, as can all the forces of pulling, pushing and twisting which we choose to exert. Because gravity is always present and we always have to take account of it, we do not feel its pull as anything out of the ordinary. A child, however, may notice the force of gravity on his body in various ways. He can feel the muscular force needed to hold his arm at right angles to his body, and the way in which the arm flops down when he relaxes his muscles. He can feel the force which his legs exert when he jumps, and can also feel that he has to exert no force to come down again, for gravity pulls him down. He feels, too, the upward force which the floor exerts to stop him moving as he lands.

Familiarity with the behaviour of magnets will also contribute to the idea that forces can act at a distance and can be unseen. A child will notice a pin jumping to meet a magnet, and will be able to feel two bar magnets pulling towards one another as he holds them with opposite poles facing each other, and feel them pushing apart if similar poles are facing. This also helps the growth of the idea that a force may be either a push or a pull. As one child said: 'The magnet is half like gravity because it can hold things down... The earth is really better because a magnet can't attract us; but the earth can attract dirt and wood and grass and even a big piece of iron.'[1]

So 'force' will become a familiar idea and a child will know that force is present, either by feeling it or by observing its results, long before he begins to measure forces. The effect of a force is to change the speed or direction of motion of the object to which it is applied; that is, to change the *velocity* of the object. It is difficult, however, to make this idea precise until forces and velocities

---

[1] Navarra, J.G. *The Development of Scientific Concepts in a Young Child* (Teachers' College, Columbia University, 1955), page 121.

can be measured fairly accurately, and for some time children will only notice the qualitative effects of forces in starting, stopping and turning things, and in making them go faster or slower.[2]

The first step towards the measurement of forces is familiarity with the behaviour of springs and of elastic. A variety of springs of different shapes and sizes and of pieces of elastic of various types should be available for experiment, so that children can discover that all springs need a pulling force to stretch them and a pushing force to compress them, and that the greater the force the child exerts, the more he can stretch or compress the spring. If a very strong spring can be found and attached to a rail in the playground, young children can use it for a tug-of-war (Figure 28:1).

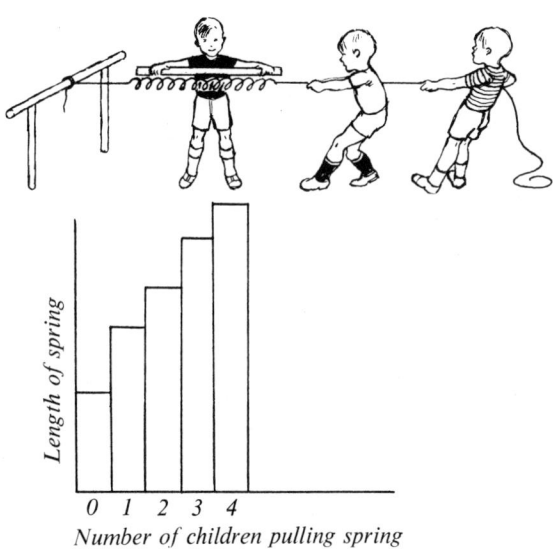

Figure 28:1

Springs can be stretched by pulling on them in various ways, and children will work out the method of hanging the spring up and tying something heavy to the lower end of it. It is important that they should come to realize the interchangeability of pulling the end of the spring and of hanging something heavy on the end, so that either

  i) the child pulls the string and stretches the spring, or
 ii) the earth pulls the object, and this pulls the string and
     stretches the spring.

The next step is the realization that the earth pulls a 'heavier' object harder, and so stretches the spring more. A useful demonstration of this fact may be set up by using a number of identical elastic bands and equal heavy beads (Figure 28:2). Children should also find out early that every spring and piece of elastic has an *elastic limit*, and that if it is stretched beyond this limit it will not return to its original length and becomes useless.

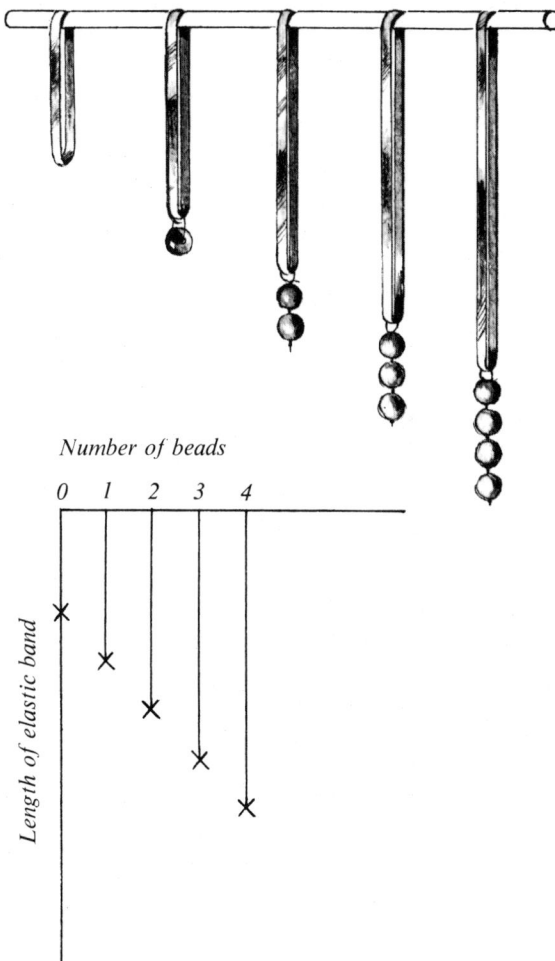

Figure 28:2

At this stage, a spring balance can be seen as a device which measures forces by measuring the stretching of a spring. The 2-kg marking on a spring balance means 'the force with which the earth pulls a 2-kg mass'. Children will use spring balances to measure the force they use to pull a truck, hold up a mass or have a tug-of-war.[3] They will

---

[2] Forces may have other effects; they can change the shape of a rubber ball, or stretch a spring.

[3] A spring balance for measuring large forces can be constructed by enclosing a strong spring in a cardboard tube with a window. A pointer is attached to the spring and the device graduated by hanging masses from it.

force less than child's weight

force equal to child's weight

force greater than child's weight

Figure 28:3

be surprised on comparing the reading of a spring balance when one child pulls against a fixed bar and when two children pull against each other. Kitchen and bathroom scales should be regarded as devices for measuring force by pushing in springs, instead of pulling them out. Children will not only weigh things on these scales, but will experiment with exerting a force to push them in. They will find that on the bathroom scales they can exert a force less than their own weight, by not letting the whole pull of the earth on the body be measured by the scales, but they cannot exert more force than their own weight unless there is something to push up against (Figure 28:3).

It is also possible to make a device for measuring force by the compression of springs, using upholstery springs and a board (Figure 28:4). Such experiences as these will help children to grasp the fact that when they weigh anything, they are measuring the pull of the earth on it.

But because children are surrounded by wheels—on prams, trucks, bicycles, cars, wheelbarrows, roller-skates—they do not explicitly realize their advantages. Wheels form a fruitful topic for children to investigate, and as they do so they will acquire many more ideas about force.

Children can use springs to find the force they need to exert to drag a heavy box along the floor. This experiment can be tried on a rough floor and a smooth floor, and the box mounted on a toboggan and on a set of pram-wheels (Figure 28:5). Alternatively, a smaller scale experiment using a block of wood which can be mounted on Meccano wheels or a roller-skate may be easier. This block can also be used to find out how much force is

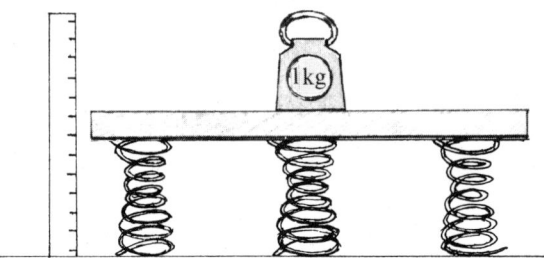

Figure 28:4

Moving heavy masses and discovering friction

Children take wheels for granted, and cannot realize the enormous step forward in civilization brought about by the invention of the wheel. The force needed to move a load decreases greatly with the use of wheels, and therefore much heavier loads can be moved. A baby can be pushed in a pram instead of being carried everywhere. Enormous tree-trunks, blocks of stone and steel girders can be transported on wheeled vehicles when they could not be dragged.

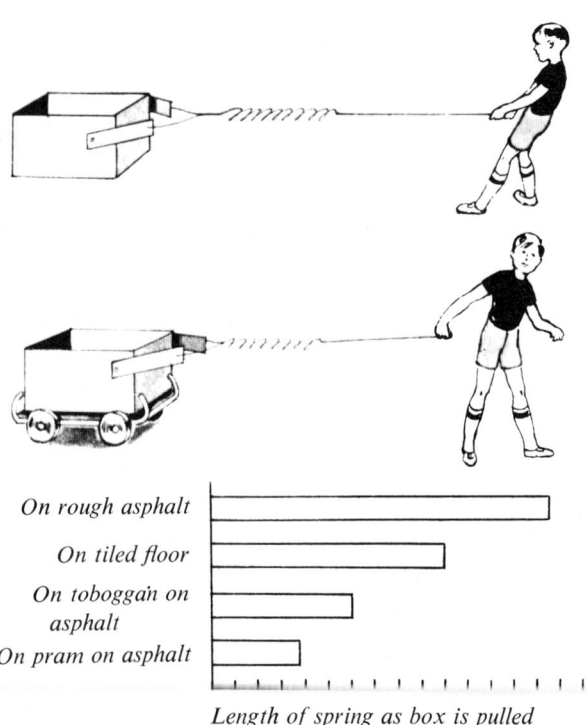

On rough asphalt
On tiled floor
On toboggan on asphalt
On pram on asphalt

Length of spring as box is pulled

Figure 28:5

needed to move blocks of different masses, and on surfaces made of different materials. Different materials, such as a piece of rubber tyre, may also be used to cover the underside of the block (Figure 28:6).

Dragging a block against friction

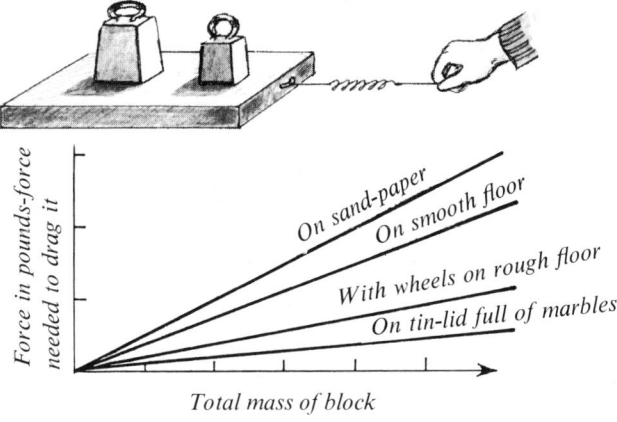

Figure 28:6

Children will thus become aware of the force of *friction*, which always tends to prevent motion from taking place. Friction is caused by the interlocking of tiny hillocks and valleys in the two surfaces which are in contact, so that they resist sliding over one another. Children can see and feel this if they rub two pieces of glass-paper together, and will feel that there is much less difficulty in *rolling* one piece of glass-paper over another (Figure 28:7). Hence wheels considerably reduce the effects of friction, and so reduce the force needed to move an object. There is also, of course, friction where the axle of the wheel rubs against its fixed support. Children may be able to measure the improvement obtained by oiling

Dragging and rolling

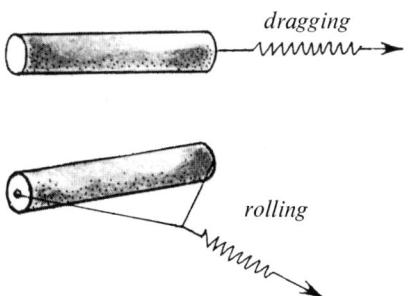

Figure 28:7

the contact (Figure 28:8), and they should examine a ball-bearing race.

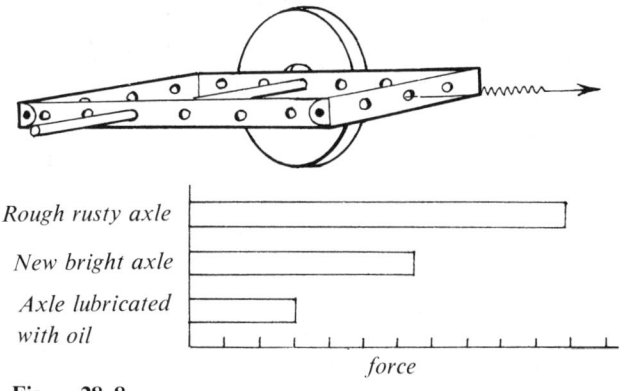

Figure 28:8

Friction is extremely important in many aspects of everyday life, and is always present to some extent, opposing motion and enabling us to grip things, but also making it necessary to exert force to move a truck along a horizontal surface, to wheel a pram or to drive a car at a steady speed on the flat. Children may, however, examine what happens in the few cases when friction is very nearly absent. The case best known to them is that of sliding on a good smooth ice slide. If the child has got up speed he finds when he launches himself on the slide it is impossible for him to stop or to change direction. A ball rolling on a horizontal table presents a very similar picture; it goes on rolling in the same direction with only a very gradual decrease in its speed. A fairly frictionless trolley can be made by inverting a shallow tin-lid over a collection of glass marbles. The marbles replace sliding friction by rolling as the trolley moves over the floor. It is possible to buy or make a 'balloon puck' (Figure 28:9). The escaping air from the balloon

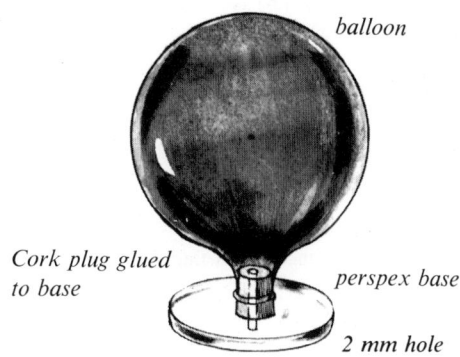

Figure 28:9[4]

[4] A carbon-dioxide corkscrew can be used instead of the balloon.

281

lifts the puck sufficiently high above a smooth polished table almost to eliminate friction. A more sophisticated version uses the thin cushion of gas between an evaporating block of solid carbon dioxide and the table to create a tiny space between the surfaces so that the puck can glide without friction. The hovercraft uses the same principle, and this can also be seen in operation in some lawn-mowers.

From these experiences, children will learn that once a body is in motion on a horizontal surface, if no horizontal forces are acting on it, it will continue to move at the same speed in the same direction as it started. A force is only needed to stop it or to change its speed or its direction. *Force produces change in the speed or direction of motion*;[5] that is, *force produces change of velocity*; force is not needed to keep motion going steadily, except to balance slowing-down forces such as friction. This basic principle, without which it is not possible to understand most of modern physical science, was stated by Sir Isaac Newton in 1687 as, 'Every body continues in its state of rest or of uniform motion in a straight line unless it is compelled to change that state by forces impressed upon it.'[6] Although this is so fundamental a principle, it is difficult for a child, or an adult, to come to the correct conclusion, as friction is so ever-present that we tend to think that force is necessary to keep motion going steadily. A ball which has been thrown horizontally continues at a nearly constant horizontal speed, because there is very little horizontal force to retard it, while the vertical force of gravity makes it gather speed vertically. As Newton said: 'Projectiles persevere in their motions, so far as they are not retarded by the resistance of the air or impelled downwards by the force of gravity.' In ancient times, however, this phenomenon had puzzled men greatly. Aristotle's view has been described as: 'It is the air that plays the part of motor. Shaken by the projectile issuing from the sling of the catapult it flows after it and drives it along.'[7] Piaget found children who passed through a stage of giving the same explanation,[8] and we have ourselves asked an educated adult why, when one starts to slide on ice, one goes on at the same speed, and have obtained the spontaneous answer, 'the air rushes round to the back and pushes you'! What is clearly lacking is sufficient experience of the absence of frictional force to enable a

correct conclusion to be drawn. If the idea that a force *changes* motion is discovered at this stage, children will have time to absorb the idea into their patterns of thought before, later in their education, they measure these changes and make deductions from them.

Mass and weight

It must be emphasized that the *weight* of an object is the force exerted on it by a gravitational field. All weighing machines measure force, either directly by the extension or compression of a spring, or indirectly by balancing the force of gravity on an object in one pan of a balance against the force of gravity on a standard object such as a kilogram in the other pan.

The force exerted by gravity on an object depends on the strength of the gravitational field exerting the force. This field varies slightly from place to place on the earth's surface, but varies much more dramatically as an object such as a spacecraft leaves the earth's gravitational field. Children are now aware, through television, of the phenomenon of *weightlessness* when a spacecraft is outside the influence of a gravitational field. Then things in the spacecraft float because they are not pulled by gravity in any direction. It is correctly said at this stage in a spacecraft's flight that objects are weightless, because weight is the force exerted by gravity.

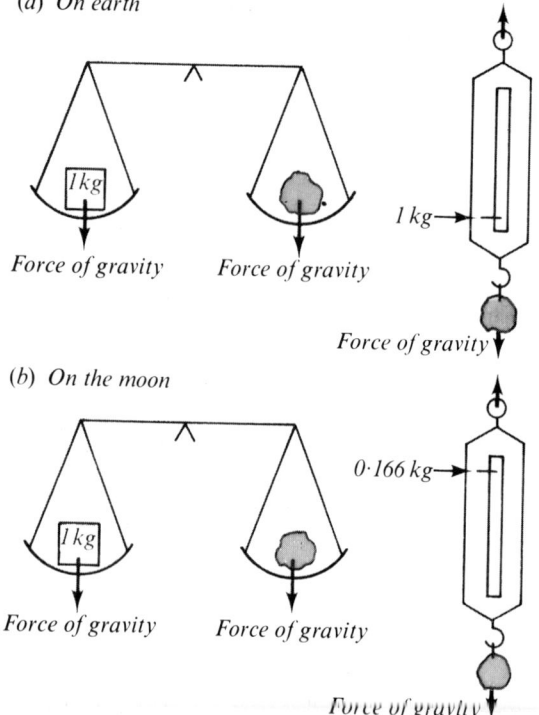

(a) On earth

Force of gravity   Force of gravity

1 kg→

Force of gravity

(b) On the moon

Force of gravity   Force of gravity

0·166 kg→

Force of gravity

[5] This should be taken to include starting or stopping the motion.

[6] Newton's First Law of Motion.

[7] Reymond, A., *Histoire des Sciences Exactes et Naturelles dans l'Antiquité Gréco-Romaine* (Presses Universitaires, Paris. 2nd Ed , 1955)

[8] Piaget, J. *The Child's Conception of Physical Causality* (Kegan Paul, 1930), pages 18–24.

Figure 28:10

On the moon, however, there is a gravitational force, which is exerted by the moon. Because the moon is much less massive than the earth, this gravitational force is only about $\frac{1}{6}$ of the gravitational force on the surface of the earth, so objects *weigh* only about $\frac{1}{6}$ as much on the moon as they do on the earth. This change of weight would be observed by weighing the same object on a spring balance on the moon, because gravity exerts less force than on earth (Figure 28:10(*b*)), but if the object balanced with a kilogram on a pan balance on earth, it would continue to do so on the moon.

However, a spacecraft, or a man, does not become less massive as it leaves the earth's gravitational field and becomes weightless. Another quantity, other than weight, needs to be measured to express this property of massiveness. It is that quantity which remains invariant as the gravitational field, which produces weight, changes. This quantity is called *mass*. Until recently it has been very difficult for children to form a concept of mass, as they have no experience of mass remaining constant as weight changes by change of gravity. Television and films of space travel have now made it possible for children vicariously to have the experience of weightlessness and of change of weight on approach to the moon or the earth.

The result of this lack of experience is a total confusion in everyday language between mass and weight. We talk about a 'weight of 1 kilogram' when in fact *the kilogram is a unit of mass,* and it would be more correct to talk about a 'mass of 1 kilogram'. Spring balances do in fact *weigh,* because they measure the force of gravity acting on masses, but spring balances are usually calibrated in units of *mass.* When we hang a parcel on a spring balance and read 2 kg, the spring shows an extension which would be produced by the force of gravity acting on a mass of 2 kg. We *deduce* that the mass of the parcel is 2 kg. When we balance the parcel on a pair of scales against a 2 kg mass, the forces of gravity acting on the parcel and the 2 kg mass are equal. We *deduce* that the mass of the parcel is 2 kg.

Since weight is a force, we should expect it to be measured in units of force. The metric unit of force is the *newton,* whose name shows clearly that it depends on Newton's laws of motion. This unit for measuring force depends on the fact that force produces change in velocity. One newton is the force which would produce a change in velocity, or an acceleration, of 1 metre per second in each second if it were applied to a mass of 1 kilogram. Now gravity produces an acceleration of about 9·8 metres per second in each second at the earth's surface, and it would take a force of 9·8 newtons to produce an acceleration of 9·8 metres per second per second in a mass of 1 kilogram. Hence a force of 9·8 newtons is equivalent to the force of gravity on 1 kilogram, so that 1 newton is about one-tenth of the weight of 1 kilogram.

It is possible to obtain both spring balances and bathroom scales graduated in newtons, and older children should be encouraged to become familiar with this unit of force.

Lifting heavy masses

Mechanisms are used to move heavy masses from place to place horizontally with the minimum of effort, but we also need to move masses vertically. Putting a mass on a truck to move it entails lifting it vertically on to the truck. The ancients hauled enormous blocks of stone to a height when they built monuments like Stonehenge. Nowadays cranes pick up great blocks of stone, rockets take off vertically from a standing start, and lorries struggle up mountain passes with heavy loads. Children will want to explore the ways in which men can make it easier for themselves to lift masses.

When a child holds a parcel, he has to exert sufficient force to balance the force of gravity which pulls the parcel downwards. It follows from Newton's First Law of Motion that since the parcel is at rest no resultant force can be acting on it, for a force would produce change of motion. But gravity always acts, so as the parcel does not move the force of gravity must be exactly balanced by an equal and opposite force exerted by the child's arm. If this force is removed, that is if he lets go, the parcel starts to move and falls to the ground. When the parcel hits the floor and is at rest again, the force of gravity on the parcel is balanced by an upward force exerted by the floor (Figure 28:11).

Forces on a parcel

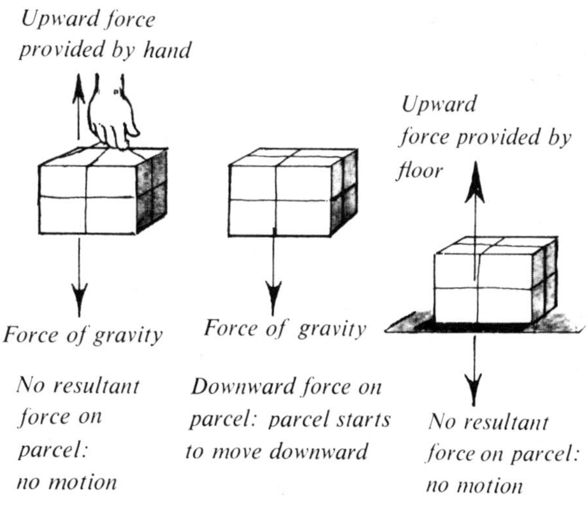

Upward force provided by hand

Upward force provided by floor

Force of gravity *Force of gravity*

No resultant force on parcel: no motion

Downward force on parcel: parcel starts to move downward

No resultant force on parcel: no motion

Figure 28:11

The child can measure the force which his hand provides by holding the parcel up by a string containing a spring

283

Figure 28:12

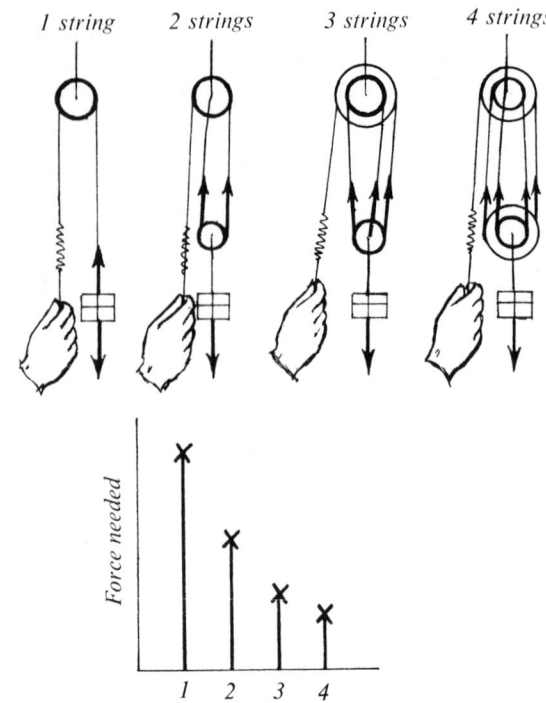

Number of strings holding the block

Figure 28:13[9]

Holding a block on a slope

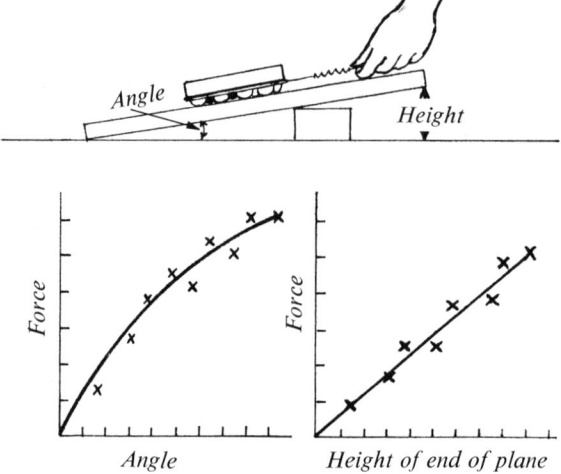

Figure 28:14

balance, or measure the upward force which the floor provides by replacing the floor by the bathroom scales. In either case he is using a spring to measure force. If he now wants to lift the parcel vertically up to the first floor he can use a long rope, stand at the top of the stairs, and haul the parcel up the stairwell. His spring balance will tell him that once he has got the parcel moving slowly and steadily, he has to exert a force equal to its weight (Figure 28:12). Hauling vertically upwards is awkward, and it is much easier to use the bannisters to change the direction of the force. A little more force has to be used, as friction has to be overcome, but it is more convenient to pull downwards than upwards. Builders often use a single pulley, so that a man at ground level can haul a bucket to the top of a building. Cranes usually use several pulleys. Children should set up simple arrangements of pulley blocks, and discover the effect of the number of strings supporting the load on the force which has to be used to balance it (Figure 28:13). They should then, if possible, see and use the pulley blocks which builders actually use.

A builder also uses a plank to change a step up which he has to trundle a wheelbarrow into an inclined plane. This is not merely because it is less convenient to jolt a loaded barrow up a step than to wheel it up a slope. Children can test this statement by seeing how much less force is needed to hold a heavy block up on an inclined plane at various angles, compared with the force needed to hold it up vertically (Figure 28:14). Both the effect of friction and the effect of the inclined plane enter into this experiment, but the effect of friction can be minimized by polishing the plane and the block or by using a wheeled trolley such as a roller-skate or a set of marbles covered by a tin-lid. It may prove more satisfactory to graph the force needed to support the block against the height of the top of the plane, rather than against the angle of the plane. The advantage of the second graph can be seen by repeating the 'thought-experiment' of Stevinus of Bruges (1605), who imagined a loop of uniform flexible heavy chain which would sit in equilibrium on a smooth wedge

284

[9] Meccano wheels make suitable pulleys. In diagrams of pulley blocks, pulleys in the same sheaf are drawn as if their sizes were different in order to show the path of the string. These pulleys are usually equal in size.

(Figure 28:15). The symmetrically hanging lower part of the loop could clearly be cut away without disturbing the equilibrium.

Equilibrium on a smooth wedge

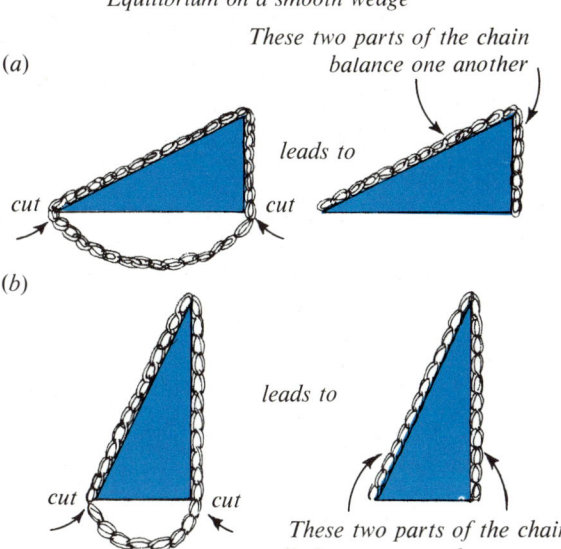

Figure 28:15

Upward force provided by air resistance

Force of gravity

Figure 28:16

It was the discovery that the *inclined plane* provided a means of lifting masses easily which first made it possible for men to build such edifices as Stonehenge and the Pyramids. Children will find many more examples of inclined planes, from the mountain path which zigzags up with a shallow gradient rather than taking the shortest route, to the aircraft descending gradually rather than steeply, as it then needs less retarding force to decrease its speed to one suited to landing.

Falling bodies

We have to provide a force to lift a heavy mass, but gravity provides a force which will make it fall, as long as we do not balance the force of gravity by an upward force. A parachutist does this when he uses air resistance to oppose the force of gravity, so that he descends at a steady and comparatively low speed (Figure 28:16).

It was thought in ancient times, and children often expect, that a heavier body will fall faster than a lighter one. Galileo was the first to appreciate that if a heavy and a light object are let fall side by side, they will, apart from discrepancies caused by air resistance, continue to fall side by side. Galileo said:

'I who have made the test can assure you that a cannonball weighing one or two hundred pounds, or even more, will not reach the ground by as much as a span ahead of a musket-ball weighing only half a pound, provided both are dropped from a height of 200 cubits.'[10]

The force of gravity makes both bodies increase their speed, or accelerate, but they both accelerate at the same rate. Children will need to drop unequal masses together from a height repeatedly to satisfy themselves of the truth of this. They should also examine the effect of air resistance by dropping a mass attached to a parachute alongside an equal mass which falls freely. This will help them to attribute slight differences in rate of fall between different objects to air resistance. If a scrap of paper the size of a penny is let fall alongside a penny, the penny will reach the ground first. Air resistance provides an upward force on both objects, but this upward force is more nearly equal to the force of gravity on the paper than that on the penny. But if the paper is placed on top of the penny, so that it is not subject to air resistance, it remains in contact with the penny throughout the fall. Some children may have seen Apollo 15 astronaut David Scott dropping a feather and a hammer together on the surface of the moon, where there is no air resistance to retard the feather.

The force of gravity produces the same acceleration in all bodies, irrespective of their weights.[11] Since the increase in velocity produced by gravity is so rapid, it is difficult for children to study it quantitatively, but the speeds produced can be reduced by allowing the body to slide down an inclined plane, rather than fall freely. It is now necessary

[10] Galileo Galilei. *Dialogues Concerning Two New Sciences* (1638). Translated H. Crew and A. de Salvio (Macmillan, 1918, Dover), page 62.

[11] The value of this acceleration is an increase in velocity of just over 9·8 metres per second in each second, or 9·8 *metres per second per second*. The acceleration varies slightly from place to place on the earth's surface.

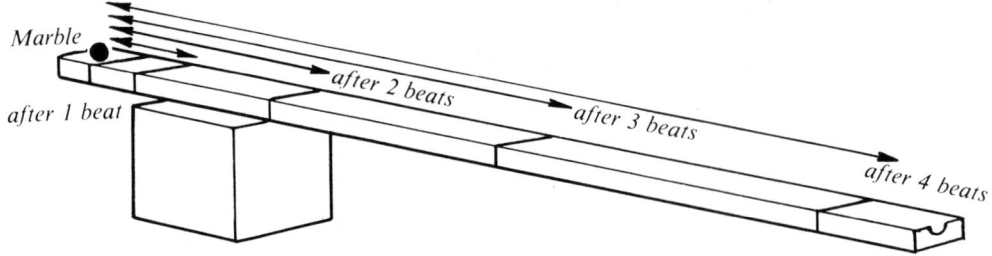

Marble

after 1 beat

after 2 beats

after 3 beats

after 4 beats

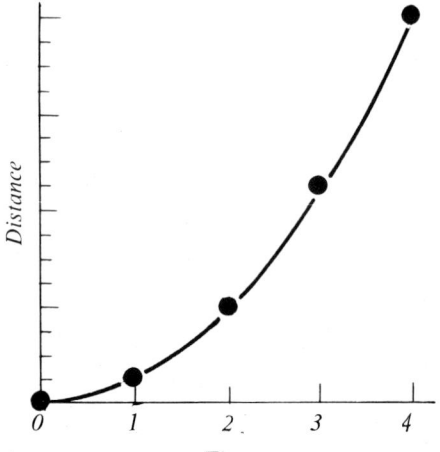

Growth of distances travelled from
starting line [12]

Distance

0   1   2   3   4

Figure 28:17   *Time*

to take precautions to reduce the effect of friction as well as air resistance. A marble rolling down a groove in a plank will produce fairly satisfactory results, and children will find that the distances travelled in increasing times obey the law of growth of squares; that is the graph of distance against time is a parabola (Figure 28:17). A metronome or pendulum will be found more convenient for timing than a stop-watch. When Galileo first performed this experiment, he did not have a sufficiently accurate clock, so he allowed water to flow from a large jar with a hole in the bottom into a container, stopping the hole with his finger when the marble had travelled a given distance; he then weighed the water.

The presence of the grooved board constrains the marble to roll down a shallow slope instead of falling vertically. Another type of constraint on a falling mass is produced by tying a mass to the end of a string, so that it must swing as a pendulum, moving through an arc of a circle, instead of falling vertically. Children will have found out earlier that a longer pendulum swings more slowly than a shorter one. Some of them will now be able to make this more precise. By the time that children are

approaching the stage of formal operations, they can suggest various possible explanations of their observations, and design an experiment to check these possibilities. There are several factors which may affect the time of the swing of a pendulum: the mass, the length of the string, the angle through which the pendulum swings, and the vigour of the initial push. Some children will want to investigate why pendulums can be used as reliable time-keepers, and will see the point of varying each factor in turn while the others are kept constant, and will find that it is only the length of the pendulum which affects the time of swing, while the angle of swing, the vigour of the initial push and the mass have no effect. [13] The situation should remain as informal as possible, for if a child does not yet think in this way, designing an experiment can only be an artificial exercise from which he does not make the expected deductions. Inhelder and Piaget's work suggests that most children reach the stage of formal thinking only in the secondary school, but it gives no indication of any role which experience of, and familiarity with, the situation involved may play in the development of a child's thinking.

[12] This graph should be compared with the graphs of Figure 31:14 showing the growth of squares.

[13] Inhelder, B. and Piaget, J. *The Growth of Logical Thinking from Childhood to Adolescence* (Routledge & Kegan Paul, 1958), Chapter 4.

When children have already discovered that unequal masses fall freely under gravity together, it will be no surprise to them to find that pendulums of unequal mass but the same length keep in step with one another. It is more surprising that the angle of swing (provided that it is reasonably small) does not affect the period of swing.[14] It is this property, however, that makes the pendulum useful as a timekeeping device; the same pendulum always takes the same period of time for a swing, even though air resistance makes its swings become shorter and shorter in length.

When children graph the relation between the period of swing and the length of a pendulum, they can arrange the graph in several ways, each of which gives the appearance of a general trend, but they do not always find it easy to see a numerical relationship between length and time, even if they have reached the stage of searching for one. Figure 28:18 shows various ways of arranging the graph. One of the most fruitful methods is to set up a short pendulum (about 20 cm), whose period is taken as the unit of time, and to try to construct pendulums whose period is twice, three times, and so on, the period of the original pendulum. A stairwell will soon be needed to accommodate a long enough pendulum, for the law of growth is once again that of the growth of squares. The length of a pendulum is proportional to the square of its period of swing.

A different type of pendulum can be made by attaching a mass to the end of a piece of elastic. The mass is then pulled down and the elastic pendulum vibrates vertically. Of course if comparisons are to be made between different elastic pendulums, the same type of elastic must be used. Elastic pendulums will be found to behave very like simple pendulums, except that the mass of the bob does affect the period of the pendulum.

Rotation and balance

Civilization makes use of forces not only for lifting and carrying, but also for turning: we make a great deal of use of simple turning mechanisms when we turn on taps, open doors, lift the legs of a wheelbarrow from the ground, or ride a bicycle. The use of forces for turning in these situations is well within the children's experience, and by the end of the Primary stage many of them have discovered the law governing the turning behaviour of forces in one situation, and will be able to see its many other applications.

Graphs on the behaviour of a simple pendulum

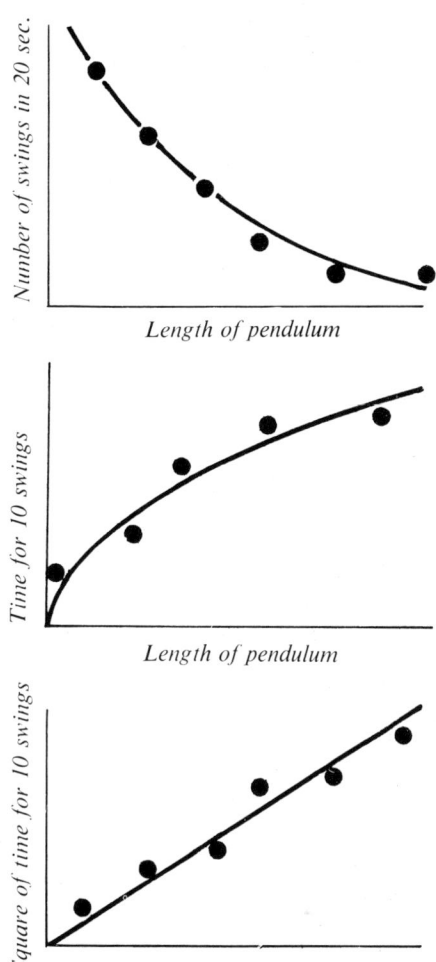

Figure 28:18

The balance bar (Figure 28:19) is a familiar piece of apparatus in many Primary schools. The bar balances if no rings are hung from it. If rings are hung from one side, the force of gravity acting on those rings causes the bar to rotate about the pivot at the centre. This turning effect

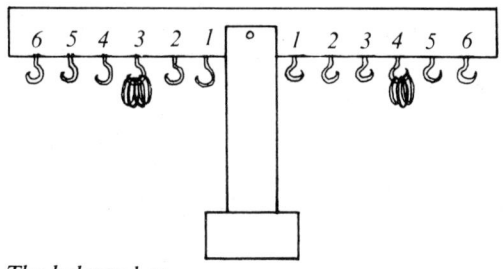

The balance bar
Figure 28:19

[14] The *period* of a pendulum is the time of one complete swing, from one end of the swing back to the same end.

Using the balance bar

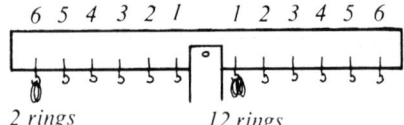

2 rings

12 rings

2 rings at hook 6 balance 12 rings at hook 1

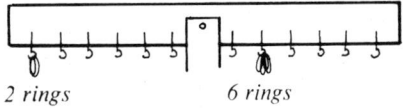

2 rings

6 rings

2 rings at hook 6 balance 6 rings at hook 2

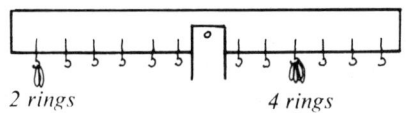

2 rings

4 rings

2 rings at hook 6 balance 4 rings at hook 3

Figure 28:20

can be counteracted by hanging rings on the other side, and children very soon discover that in order to balance the turning effects of the rings on either side of the pivot, the forces on the two sides of the balance need not be equal, but the *product* of the force of gravity and the distance from the pivot must be the same on each side (Figure 28:20). Children should realize that they are balancing the *turning effects* of forces; instead of using the force of gravity on different masses the base of the balance bar can be screwed down to a table and the forces exerted upwards, or it can be attached to a wall so that it can be pulled on by horizontal forces (Figure 28:21). Children will very soon need a word for the quantity which measures the turning effect of the forces: the *moment of a force about a point* is the measure of the force multiplied by the distance between the line of action of the force and the point. The child in Figure 20:21 is exerting a turning moment of 48

units of moment[15] about the pivot with each hand. Using this apparatus, children will find that they need to apply more force if it is not applied at right angles to the bar, and may devise experiments using bent levers (Figure 28:22).

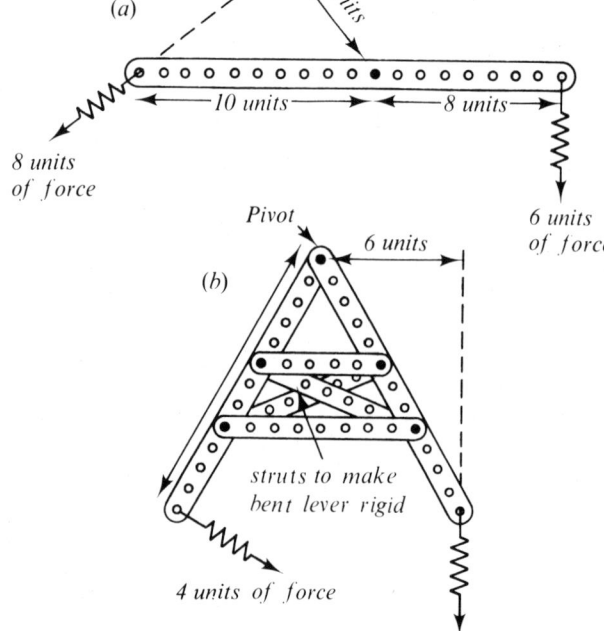

Figure 28:22

Balancing the turning effect of forces

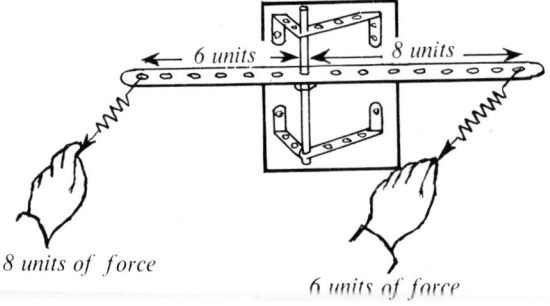

Figure 28:21

[15] Moments are measured in units which are a combination of units of force and of length.

They will find that when they measure the distance of the line of action of a force from the pivot in order to find its moment about the pivot, they must measure the *perpendicular distance*. In Figure 28:22(*a*) the moment of the force on the left of the pivot is 8 × 6 units of moment, not 8 × 10 units of moment.

Children automatically balance the moments of their weights about the pivot when they use a see-saw, and they will now be able to find many more examples of occasions when the moments of forces must be balanced. We often make use of the principle of moments by using a small force a long way from the pivot to provide a turning moment rather than a large force near the pivot (Figure 28:23).

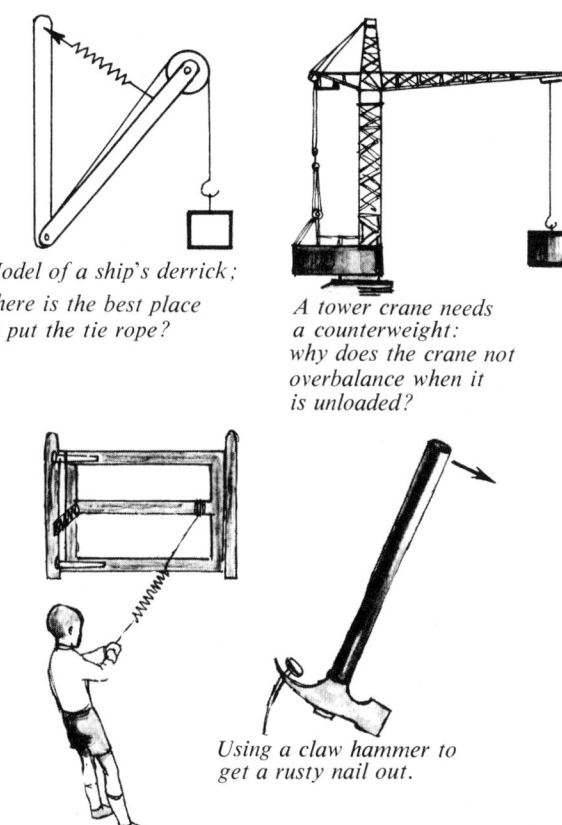

Model of a ship's derrick; where is the best place to put the tie rope?

A tower crane needs a counterweight: why does the crane not overbalance when it is unloaded?

Using a claw hammer to get a rusty nail out.

Measuring the moment exerted by a gate-spring

Figure 28:23

Children will now be able to use their knowledge of turning moments to make a simple steelyard (Figure 28:24). They will also realize the importance, in the simple weighing-balance, of the equality of length of the arms, and will understand that when they weigh on a simple balance, they are balancing the turning moments of the forces of gravity on the two sides of the balance.

Making a steelyard

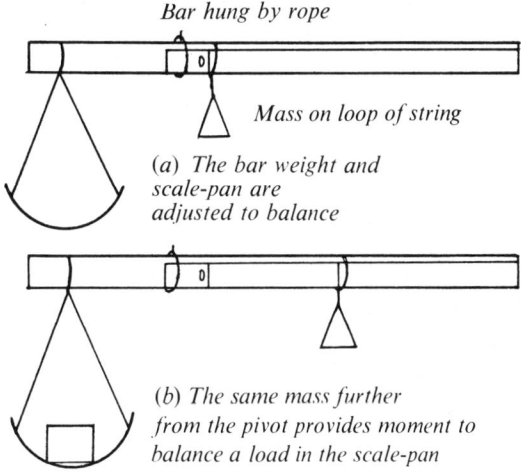

Bar hung by rope

Mass on loop of string

(*a*) The bar weight and scale-pan are adjusted to balance

(*b*) The same mass further from the pivot provides moment to balance a load in the scale-pan

Figure 28:24

Gear wheels and screws

The simplest child's tricycle has its pedals directly attached to the front wheels; so did some penny-farthing bicycles. The enormous size of the front wheel enabled the bicycle to move very much farther with each revolution of the pedals than did the rider's feet. Children will see that the modern bicycle produces the same effect by the use of chain wheels. They will want to build models and find the relation between the number of teeth in each chain wheel and the rate at which it turns. Similar relations will be found when gear wheels intermesh directly, but the difference in direction between a chain drive and a drive transmitted by gears will be noticed (Figure 28:25). A child may even reach the stage of building, with Meccano

(*a*) One revolution of the larger wheel produces two revolutions of the smaller wheel. Both wheels turn in the same direction

40 teeth   20 teeth

(*b*)

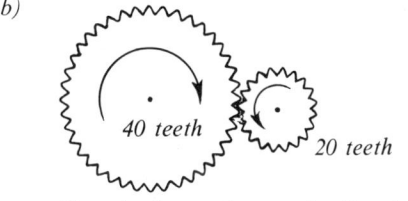

40 teeth   20 teeth

The wheels turn in opposite directions

Figure 28:25

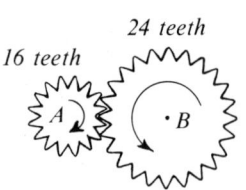

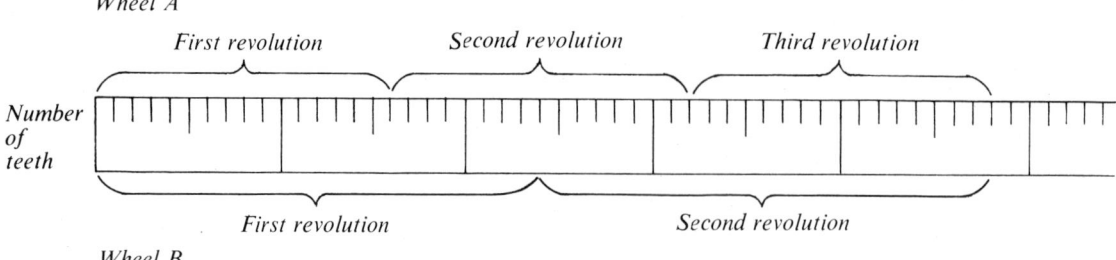

16 teeth

24 teeth

Wheel A

First revolution   Second revolution   Third revolution

Number
of
teeth

First revolution   Second revolution

Wheel B

*When 48 teeth have meshed together, wheel A has
made 3 revolutions and wheel B has made 2 revolutions*

Figure 28:26

gear wheels, a drive which makes one shaft turn twelve
times as fast as another, which could be used to turn
the hour hand and minute hand of a clock. For some
experiments with gear wheels, corrugated cardboard can
be wrapped round the edge of a tin. This shows very
well how gears mesh together, but is not of course strong
enough to carry a drive.[16]

The key to understanding the relationships between
the rates of turning of two gears is the knowledge that a
tooth of one wheel always fits an indentation of the other.
Figure 28:26 illustrates what happens when a gear wheel
with 24 teeth meshes with one with 16 teeth.

The purpose of gear wheels and chain wheels is to
change the speed of a drive. The screw is another device
which alters a drive. It changes a rotational drive which
comes from turning the screw, into a force in the direction
of the shaft. A hand turning a screwdriver produces a force
enabling the screw to penetrate wood; the rotation of the
propeller shaft of a ship or aircraft provides the force which
drives the vessel forward. Children will find that the thread
of a screw is wrapped continuously round it, and will be
able to relate a screw to an inclined plane by wrapping a
triangular piece of paper round a pencil (Figure 28:27(a)).
A screw or a bolt is basically a device for lifting a nut
up an inclined plane, and children will already know
that this can be done more easily when the slope of the
plane is small; that is, when the pitch of the screw is
small in relation to its circumference. In many cases,
such as that of the wood-screw, the nut, which is in fact

The screw and the inclined plane

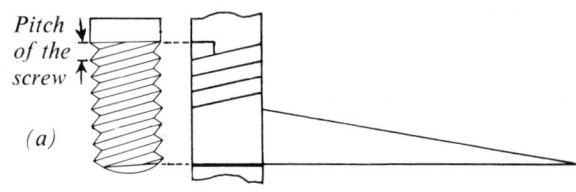

Pitch
of the
screw

(a)

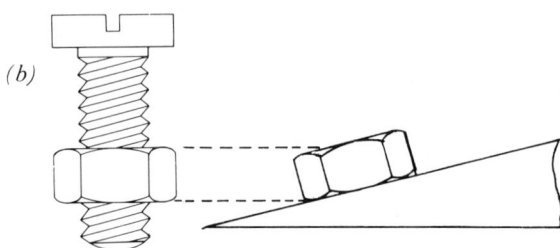

(b)

Figure 28:27

the piece of wood, is fixed. Then the effect of turning
the screw is not to lift the nut up the screw, but to
drive the screw down into the nut with a forward force
which will overcome very considerable resistance from the
wood. Similarly, a ship's or aircraft's propeller screws it
forward through the water or air.

[16] It also leads to work on the relation between the circumference and diameter of a circle, when children try to make a gear
wheel to carry a given number of teeth (*see page 393*).

290

Action and reaction

Another basic mechanical principle of which children become aware at this stage, and which they deliberately use, is the one Newton stated as: 'To every action there is always opposed an equal reaction: or the mutual actions of two bodies upon each other are always equal and directed to contrary parts' (in opposite directions).[17] A child pushes himself forward away from the side of the swimming bath by trying to push the wall back away from himself. His arm movement in swimming forces him forward as he pulls the water back past himself. When he runs, he obtains the force necessary to push him forward by pushing back against the ground. When he kicks a ball, so providing a forward force on it, the ball reacts by pushing his foot back. When he catches a ball, he can feel the ball exerting a force on his hand, and his hand exerts an equal and opposite force on the ball which stops it moving. He may try to measure this force by dropping the ball on the bathroom scales, and noticing the sudden flick of increased force on the scales, and he will see the same principle in operation in reverse on television when he sees a rocket lifting itself upward by the downward thrust of the exploding gases from its tail. He may also feel the backward 'kick' of an air-rifle at the fair as the release of air-pressure drives the pellet forward and the rifle back into his shoulder.

Conclusion; further examples

We conclude by enumerating the mechanical principles which we have used in this chapter, and applying them to two further types of motion. The principles are:

i) forces produce *change* in the speed or direction of motion of the bodies on which they act; that is, forces produce change of velocity,

ii) forces are either (*a*) *contact forces* such as pushes or pulls, or (*b*) forces which *act at a distance,* i.e. gravity and magnetic forces,

iii) if object *A* exerts a force on object *B*, then object *B* exerts an equal and opposite force on object *A*.

The example of how these principles apply to things which are moving in circles may now be considered. When a conker is whirled round on the end of a string, when a car rounds a bend, or when we are flung violently about by those fairground machines which make use of circular motion, then clearly considerable forces come into play. In order to see how these forces act,

[17] Newton's Third Law of Motion.

we consider first what happens when a movement suddenly stops being circular. A boy bowling a cricket ball uses his straight arm to make the ball travel in an arc of a circle. When he releases the ball, and so takes away the force provided by his fingers, the ball continues to travel in the direction in which it was moving when he released it. It is then pulled out of this path by the force of gravity. The discus-thrower or the hammer-thrower rotates his missile in a circle inclined at an angle to the horizontal, until he releases it to go on forward in the direction in which it was travelling when released.

Throwing the hammer

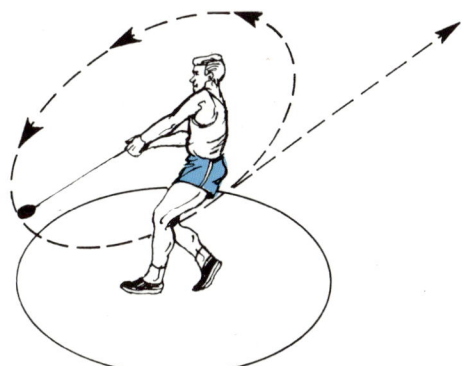

Figure 28:28

This is expected, for when the force provided by the thrower is removed the only force on the hammer is that of gravity, which pulls it vertically, and does not change the direction of the horizontal motion (Figure 28:28). The force which keeps the throwing-hammer moving in a circle before it is released is the inward force towards the centre of the circle provided by the wire handle of the hammer. The conker is kept whirling on the end of a string by the force in the string. The moon is kept in its orbit round the earth by the gravitational force of the earth. If this gravitational force were suddenly removed, the moon would not fly directly away from the earth, but would continue in a straight line in the direction in which it was moving at that instant, as does the hammer when the thrower releases it. The rocket which escapes from the earth's gravitational pull behaves in the same way. A train is forced to round a bend by the pressure of the rails which exert an inward force. The passenger who is only loosely attached inside a car rounding a bend sharply tries to go onwards in a straight line until he comes into contact with, and is forced into circular motion by, the side of the car which is moving in a circle. An object can only move in a circle *if there is an inward force acting on it which pulls it towards the centre of the circle,* out of the straight-line path which it tries to follow.

The force needed to make an object move in a circle increases as the speed of the motion increases. The motion of a fairground machine which is tame at low speeds becomes much less so as the speed increases and the passenger is subjected to increasing forces from the side of the car to make him move in a circle. When wet clothes are put in a spin-drier, the friction between cloth and water drops is insufficient to provide the force necessary to make the water drops turn in a circle at high speed. So the water moves onwards and escapes from the circular motion through the holes in the basket.

Another type of curved motion which children may want to investigate is that produced by throwing a ball in the air at an angle to the vertical. The curve formed by this path is difficult for children to follow, as the ball moves so quickly, and the shape of the curve was misunderstood (Figure 28:29) until scientific experiment began in the seventeenth century. There are, however, several ways in which the path can be traced. If a hosepipe is held so that

A sixteenth-century picture of the path of a cannon-ball

Figure 28:29

a jet of water runs along a wall, the shape of the wet patch shows the shape of the path of the drops of water (Figure 28:30). This path can be seen to resemble the parabola or curve of squares.

The shape of a jet of water

Figure 28:30
292

Alternatively the whole process can be slowed down by making it take place on an inclined plane, in the same way that free fall under gravity was slowed down on an inclined plane. If a heavy ball-bearing is rolled on an inclined plane covered with carbon paper, it will mark out its track on a piece of paper under the carbon; or an inked ball can be used. The shape of the path is that of a parabola (Figure 28:31(a)).

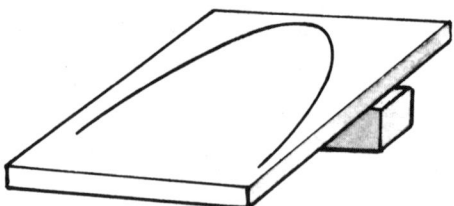

(a)   Rolling a marble on carbon-paper

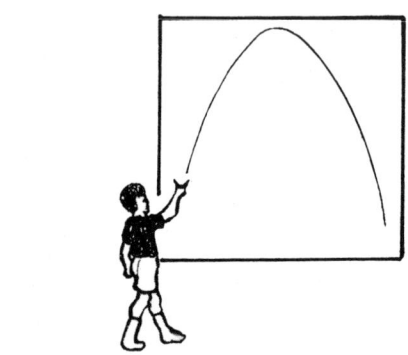

(b)   Throwing a ball alongside a parabola

Figure 28:31

A further demonstration of this fact is obtained by drawing a parabola on the wall. After a little practice, children will be able to throw a small ball or a rubber gently enough for its path to follow that of the parabola which they have drawn. It is very easy to see why this path is a parabola, for once the ball leaves the hand the only force on it (ignoring air resistance) is that of gravity, which pulls it vertically down. There is no horizontal force on the ball, so it continues to travel horizontally at the constant speed with which it left the hand. Vertically, the force of gravity causes the distance the ball has travelled to increase in proportion to the square of the time taken. Figure 28:32 shows what happens when two balls are let fall at the same instant, one with no velocity, so that it falls vertically, and the other thrown with a horizontal velocity. Observation of this phenomenon is difficult, but children can see that the two balls keep at the same vertical level as they fall, by flicking two pennies together from the table with an old ruler (Figure 28:33).

The paths of two balls

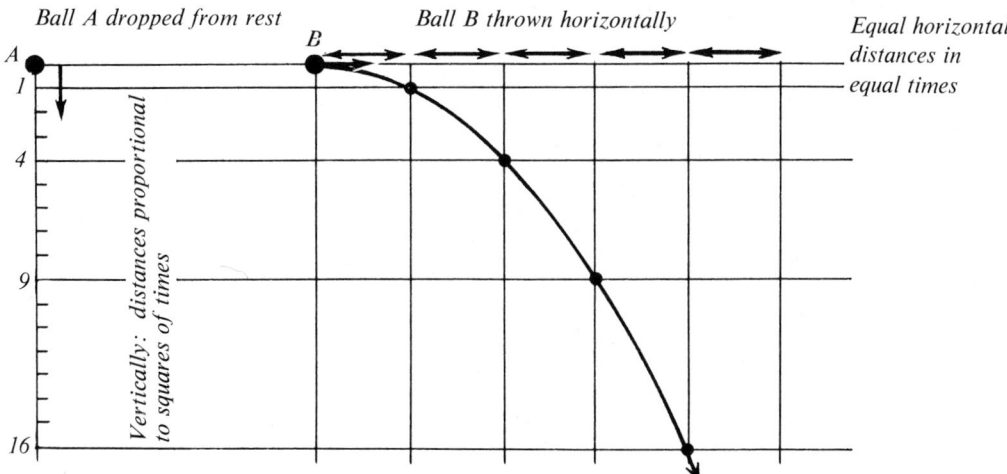

Ball A dropped from rest   B   Ball B thrown horizontally   Equal horizontal distances in equal times

A

1

4

9

16

Vertically: distances proportional to squares of times

Figure 28:32

Flicking pennies horizontally and from rest

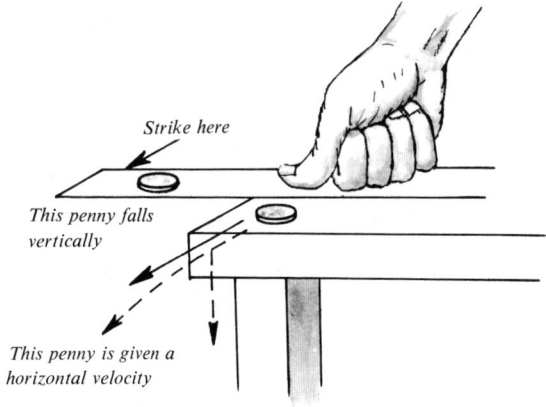

Strike here

This penny falls vertically

This penny is given a horizontal velocity

Figure 28:33

The experiences which we have described in this chapter should be seen as paving the way for more precise mathematical study of the relationship between force and its effect in causing motion. Mathematical relationships are more easily accepted later if they are built on a structure of qualitative experiences which is absorbed into a child's thinking and which he must take into account when building his framework of scientific concepts.

29 Presenting Information

Quantitative information

When we speak of information which is to be presented mathematically we are thinking of facts which are quantitative in one or more aspects. They are records of counting or some kind of measuring. They may come to us in no special order and may appear quite haphazard. If we wish to see the significance of the numbers, we *arrange* them and *represent* them in ways which may show some pattern, a regular sequence, perhaps, or repetition, or a trend. In this chapter we shall summarize the forms of representation which have been used from the beginning of schooling and show how they can develop to form a basis for two important branches of mathematics, the study of relations and functions and the study of statistics.

Presenting sets

From the first experiences of sorting, matching, counting and measuring, children collect information which they want to record and represent, either to help them to see more clearly what they have found out or to display it for other people to see. When they have classified objects and made sets of those with some common property they may put pictures of them or symbols inside a closed boundary. When two such sets have some connection and can usefully be compared their correspondences can be presented by arrows linking elements of the respective sets. Figure 29:1 shows how a diagram presents the first comparison of whether there are more, fewer, or just as many elements in the first set as in the other.

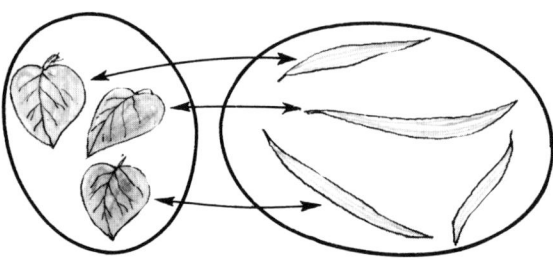

Figure 29:1

If the two sets are found to have just as many elements, as in Figure 29:2(*a*), the diagram shows the property of 'having the same number'. Several sets can be compared in this way. Ultimately an order can be made and the number sequence shown as in Figure 29:2(*b*).

294

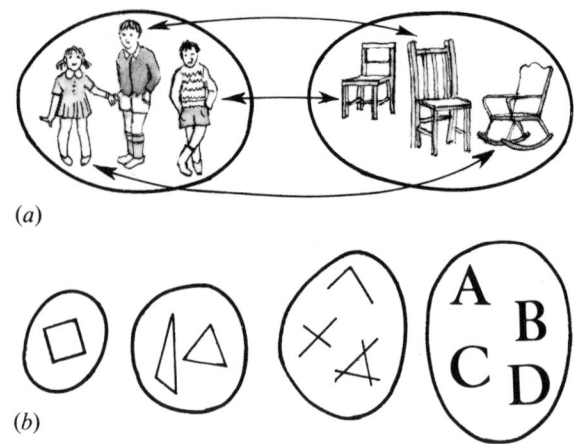

(*a*)

(*b*)

Figure 29:2

The comparisons are made more obvious if the sets are represented on squared paper, one element to each square, in columns with elements side by side so that matching can be seen at a glance. Rows can be used in place of columns, as Figure 29:3(*a*) illustrates. In Figure 29:3(*b*) the sets are arranged haphazardly whereas in (*c*) they are arranged in order of number, each set having fewer members than the one on its right.

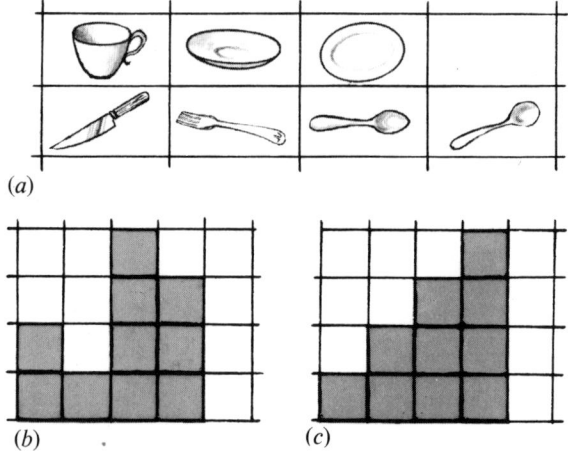

(*a*)

(*b*)   (*c*)

Figure 29:3

If two sortings are made for different qualities the set diagram shows very clearly the *intersection* of the two sets, i.e. the set of elements that have *both* qualities; the *union* of the sets, i.e. the set of elements that have *at least one*

We need a licence if we own a
television, a car or a dog.
How many of our houses have these?

1. We all have television sets.
2. More than half have all three.
3. The majority (that means the greater number)
   of us have cars.

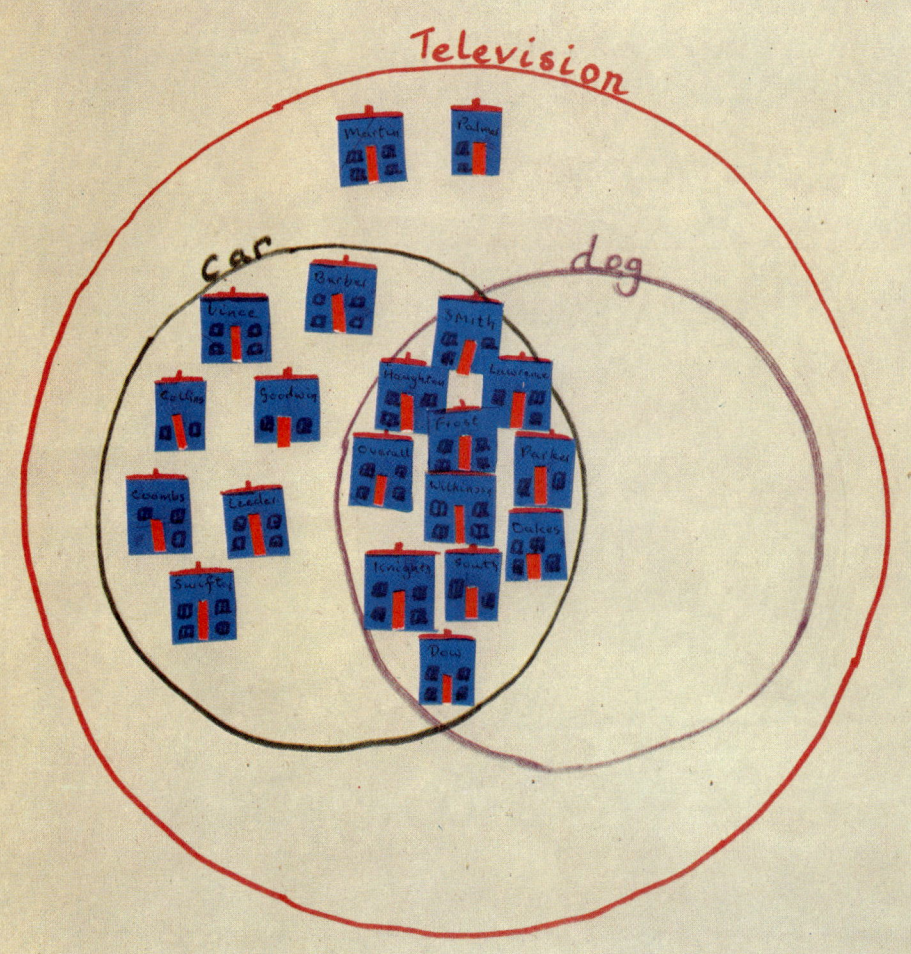

plate 6: Children's map of the school garden

plate 7: Curve stitching

plate 8:
Tessellations

of the properties is also shown. Set *A* contains all the white flowers in a bunch; set *B* contains all the scented flowers in the bunch. The intersection (shaded) contains all the scented white flowers. The union of the sets, the region within the thickened boundary, contains all the flowers which are either white or scented or both. All the flowers outside the boundary are neither white nor scented.

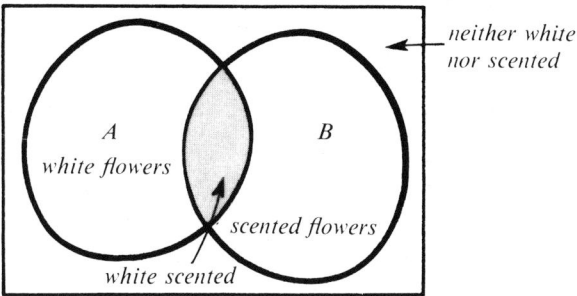

Figure 29:4

It will be noticed that drawings or lists of the elements are not necessary if we are presenting classification only and do not wish to show the cardinal numbers of the sets. The four *regions* of Figure 29:4 tell us that in the bunch of flowers there may be white scented, white unscented, coloured scented, and coloured unscented flowers.

For numerical properties other forms of presentation may be preferable. A line, strip, or rod can illustrate the case in which there are 10 white flowers of which 3 are scented, and 10 of the flowers altogether are scented. If there are 24 flowers in the bunch the number in each of the four categories can be seen (Figure 29:5).

Establishing an order

When children really know the counting order of natural numbers they have a sequence which enables them to put all kinds of things in order by matching them to this order of numbers. It is not the only pattern of order. The days of the week, the months of the year, the letters of the alphabet are fixed finite sequences which a child will often use. He may record class attendances each school day, the number of birthdays occurring in his class each month, or the number of times a letter occurs in a page of his reading book. The things recorded may not be numbers. A class may list the Christian names beginning with A, B, C, ... of the children in the class without counting them.

Anthony		
Andy		Carol
Ann		Clare
Alan	Bob	Colin
Adam	Betty	Chris

A group of children may record the colours of cars they see on the way to school. This requires a double order if each child's record is to be kept. In the previous example we were sorting out the set of children into various subsets; we were interested only in their distribution over the range of the alphabet. One child's name could only appear once, in the subset of his initial letter. In the new inquiry there is a set of children and a set of car colours. Neither of these has a particular order. Our record will show each child related to *each* of the colours that he sees. We therefore use a *rectangular* arrangement or *array* as in Figure 29:6. The order of names and of colour are of our own choice and could be quite different; a tick or other symbol is placed in the proper space when a particular child has seen a certain colour. No count is made of the number of times it is seen. This is a development which the pupils may suggest. From the present array a number of questions can be answered. For example: which car colour was seen by most children? Which child saw most colours? New orders of arrangement could then be made based on the *number of colours* seen, etc. One of the chief values of these arrays is that they enable us to find a fact quickly.

	Pam	Ken	Sue	Alan	Mary
black		✓	✓	✓	✓
blue	✓		✓	✓	✓
green	✓	✓	✓	✓	✓
red		✓	✓	✓	✓
white	✓	✓		✓	
yellow	✓			✓	✓

Figure 29:6

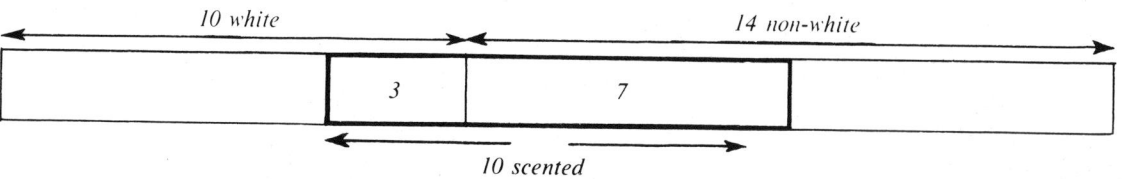

Figure 29:5

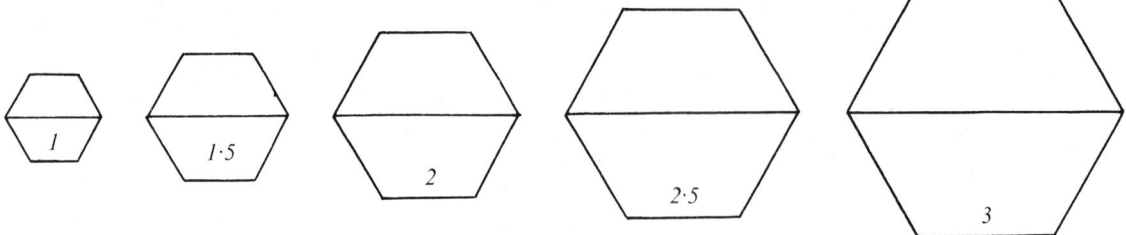

Figure 29:7

Presenting counts and measurements in tabulations

The counting and measuring involved in the surveys and records which are commonly part of the programme of primary schools provide many sets of numbers that children want to examine and present. If the significance of the numbers is to be evident they must be organized in some way and the most suitable arrangement for any particular set of results must be devised. We can tabulate the numbers according to some rule or match them to another set of numbers. Two examples are given.

(1) The numbers on the houses along one side of the street can be listed and placed against the actual count of the houses in the row; this can be arranged either horizontally or vertically.

Order of houses in row	1	2	3	4	5	6...
House number	1	3	5	7	9	11...

The house numbers give the odd numbers in order and we can say what the house number is for the fourth house and so on. From the tabulation we can find a rule for obtaining the house number of any house in the row.

The third number is 5, 1 less than 2×3
The fourth number is 7, 1 less than 2×4
The fifth number is 9, 1 less than 2×5

This rule might be given by a child as 'double the number and subtract 1'. A symbol can then be used: the nth house is numbered $(2 \times n) - 1$. Which house is numbered 17?

$$2n - 1 = 17 \Rightarrow 2n = 18 \Rightarrow n = 9$$

(2) A plot of land 120 metres wide is to be used for building houses. One man may buy it to build one house; two men might share it to build two houses, and so on. How wide will each man's plot be if any number up to 6 could buy a plot?

Number of buyers	1	2	3	4	5	6
Width of plot in metres	120	60	40	30	24	20

We can see how quickly the width diminishes at first and how slowly towards the end; but there is little else that

296

the numbers alone can tell us. This suggests that a picture would help.

Tabulating measurements can be equally instructive. The diameters of a set of regular hexagons of different sizes can be measured.

Figure 29:7 is a tabulation of some that were measured.

Side of hexagon (cm)	1	1·5	2	3	3·5	4
Diameter of hexagon (cm)	2	3	4	6	7	8

That the diameter is twice the length of a side is immediately obvious without drawing a diagram. This can be written as $d = 2 \times s$. The diameter of the hexagon with side 2·5 cm can be found by the rule. The side of a hexagon with diameter 9 cm can also be worked out. The value of such tabulations is that corresponding members of the two sets are placed together and the sequence of corresponding pairs is made evident.

Tabulating subsets

When a large number of measurements have been taken, e.g. the height of each child in a class, a tabulation of all the heights will involve first putting them in order, say, from shortest to tallest. Even if only half the class is taken, perhaps 20, the list is not easy to study. Statements can be made about the shortest, tallest and those about half-way in the list; that many of the children are near to the half-way mark can be noted. But a list of the heights can tell little more. It can be suggested that a set of class measurements is separated into subsets covering intervals of 3 cm. A set of 21 children in a 4th year Junior school class produced the following tabulation:

Height in cm	132	135	138	141	144	147	150
Number of children	2	2	1	3	1	4	3

Height in cm	153	156	159	162
Number of children	2	2	0	1

Discussing these numbers the pupils noticed the larger numbers of children in the middle; they then found that

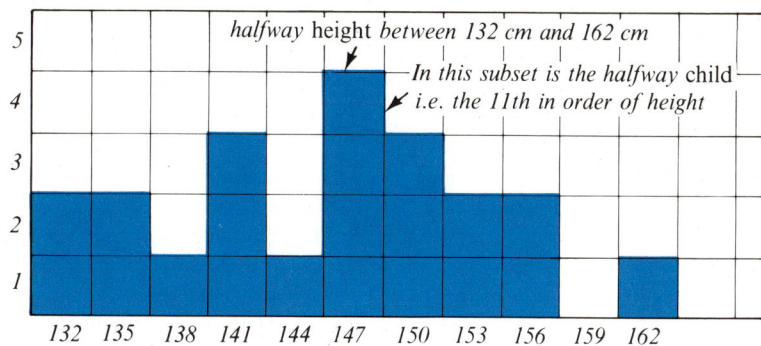

147 cm was half-way between 132 cm and 162 cm. They also found the height of the pupil half-way between the shortest and the tallest child, who was the eleventh in order of height; this child's height fell in the 147 cm range. Some of the pupils laboriously found the average height by adding the heights of all the individuals and dividing by 21. This average proved to be less than the half-way or *median* height and the effect of the one tall child in contrast to the four children in the two shortest groupings was noticed.

The subsets were then represented on squared-paper as in Figure 29:8.

Tabulation of pairs

We are often called upon to select partners from two different sets of people or things; partners for a school activity, dishes from two sections of a menu and so on. When asked in how many ways they can do this children will work through all the possibilities but do not always discover a way of tabulating their results. and organizing their method so that they are sure of finding *all* possible pairs. If allowed to work freely they will probably discover that they can arrange the pairs in a pattern of rows similar to that of Figure 29:9.

If a choice of four meat dishes and three vegetable dishes is offered on a menu, how many different combinations of one meat dish and one vegetable can be made? If a child chooses in a haphazard way, e.g. beef and peas, lamb and cabbage, etc., he may reach the correct answer, 12 combinations, but he may not. He can be asked how many more possibilities there will be if one more vegetable dish is offered. He will then probably see the pattern of rows and columns.

An array of this kind shows the number of choices as the *product* of the *numbers of elements* in each set. This array of ordered pairs is known as the Cartesian product of the sets. Each pair can be named by the row and the column in which it can be found. This reminds us of the co-ordinates (distances from the two axes) which Descartes first used to state the position of a point in a plane.

The interest of the Cartesian product is greater if some of the members of one set have a quality in common with some members of the other set. For instance, if 'separates' are to be worn together and a girl can choose from several pairs of jeans of different colours and several coloured sweaters, she may combine them in ways which are strikingly different. Figure 29:10 shows the array of all 12 possibilities.

Out of the 12 possible combinations two have identical colours: black and black, and red and red. These two pairs form a subset of the set of ordered pairs with a special *relation* between the members of a pair: the second

	peas	cabbage	carrots
pork	{ pork { peas	{ pork { cabbage	{ pork { carrots
beef	{ beef { peas	{ beef { cabbage	{ beef { carrots
lamb	{ lamb { peas	{ lamb { cabbage	{ lamb { carrots
ham	{ ham { peas	{ ham { cabbage	{ ham { carrots

Figure 29:9

sweaters

	green	red	black	yellow
black	bg	br	bb	by
navy	ng	nr	nb	ny
red	rg	rr	rb	ry

jeans

Figure 29:10

member 'has the same colour as' the first.

If two sets A and B consist of *numbers* the pair made from an element of each set will be written with the usual notation (x, y) where x is an element of set A and y is an element of set B. If set $A = \{1, 2, 3, 4\}$ and set $B = \{2, 4, 6, 8\}$, Figure 29:11 shows the Cartesian product of the sets A and B. Some of the pairs have an obvious common property: $(2, 2)$ and $(4, 4)$ have the second number equal to the first. Another interesting subset is formed by the pairs which lie on the diagonal line running from the top left to the bottom right corner. The second number is twice the first number for each of the pairs $(1, 2), (2, 4), (3, 6), (4, 8)$.

	2	4	6	8
1	(1, 2)	(1, 4)	(1, 6)	(1, 8)
2	(2, 2)	(2, 4)	(2, 6)	(2, 8)
3	(3, 2)	(3, 4)	(3, 6)	(3, 8)
4	(4, 2)	(4, 4)	(4, 6)	(4, 8)

Figure 29:11

This Cartesian product might represent all the possible pairs of sides to contain a right angle in a triangle, the length of whose base is selected from set A and its height from set B as in Figure 29:12, which shows the two subsets mentioned above. The subset formed from $(2, 2)$ and $(4, 4)$ is a set of isosceles triangles; $(1, 2), (2, 4), (3, 6), (4, 8)$ give a set of similar triangles.

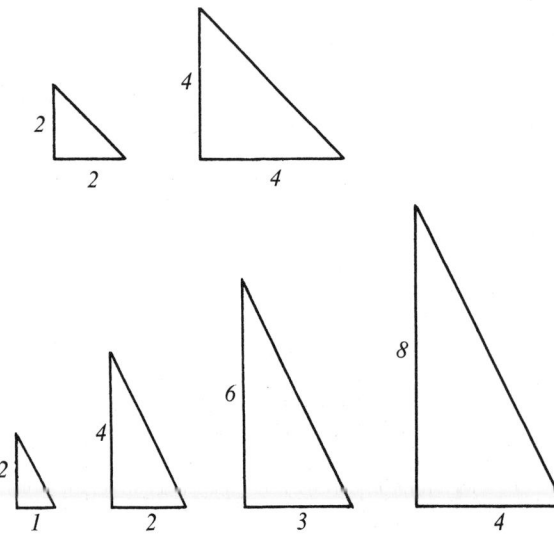

Figure 29:12

298

The last subset of four pairs could be tabulated:

base of triangle (units)	1	2	3	4
	↕	↕	↕	↕
height of triangle (units)	2	4	6	8

The arrows emphasize the correspondences: 2, 4, 6, 8, are the images of 1, 2, 3, 4, when the set $\{1, 2, 3, 4\}$ is mapped into the set $\{2, 4, 6, 8\}$. The relation which connects an element of the set of heights with the corresponding base can be expressed as $y = 2x$. Further examples of relations are discussed in Chapter 40. Here we have only shown how the arrangement of information can help the systematic search for pairs in the Cartesian product which have the same relation between them.

Presentation on squared paper

Square ruling provides the easiest method of representing sets of *numbers* because any line on the page is marked in equal segments and can serve as a number line. Each segment carries a square; thus we can use a row or column of squares as the image of a natural number (Figure 29:13).

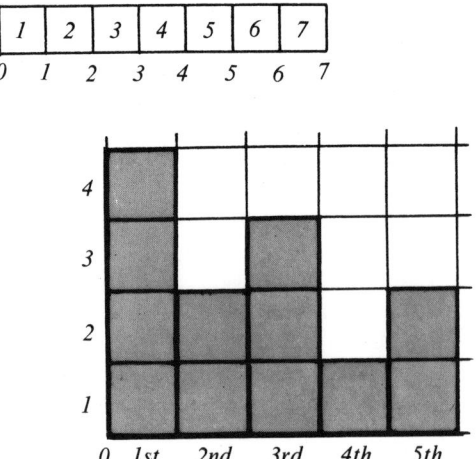

Figure 29:13

When several sets are to be recorded for comparison we can arrange a succession of columns, first, second, third, and so on. The cardinal number of each set is equal to the number of squares in the corresponding column. Alternatively names or measurements could be used to label the sets and show what kind of elements they contain. For instance, a record could be made of the number of children who take a certain time to walk to school. The times would be given in intervals (for example, 10–14 minutes) and the children would arrange themselves in sets according to which time interval included their time. We can now show

minutes to walk to school	<5	5 — 9	10 — 14	15 — 19	20 — 24
number of children	7	14	12	5	1

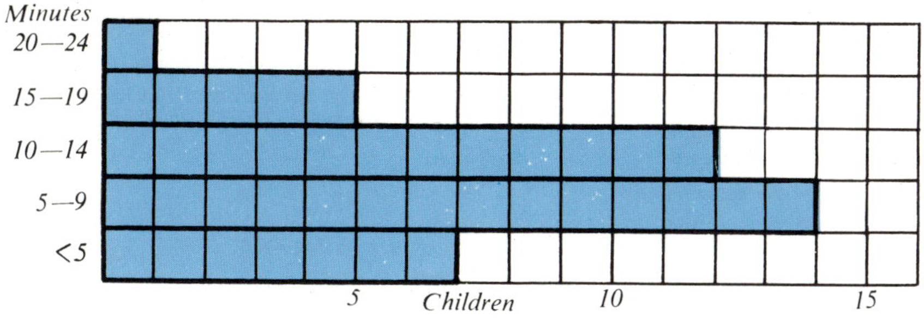

Figure 29:14

min.	girls	boys
<5	5	2
5 — 9	6	8
10 — 14	8	4
15 — 19	2	4
20 — 24	0	1

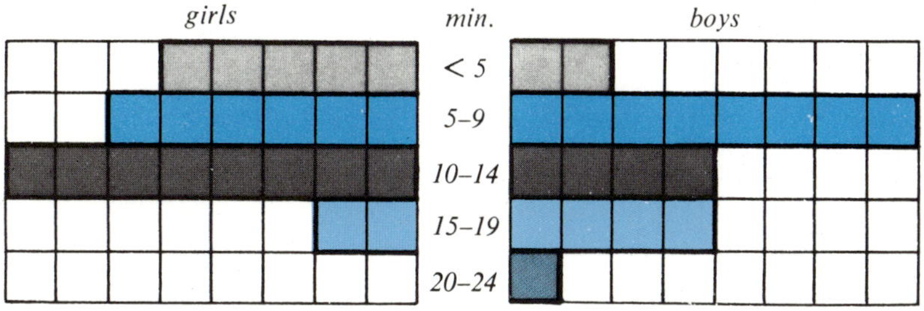

Figure 29:15

on squared paper a set of intervals of time and the *number of children* corresponding to each interval. These numbers are necessarily natural numbers and can properly be shown by a count of squares as in Figure 29:14.

Two sets of records can be shown in this way on the same diagram. It helps comparison if bars are used rather than columns. The two sets can be drawn on opposite sides of an axis; symmetry, or lack of it, can then be readily judged. As an example we can show separately how long boys and girls take to walk to school.

A similar type of diagram will show daily attendances and absences in a class. In a week of infection the graph of Figure 29:16 might appear. The children will notice that the two bars for each day put together always show the number of children in the class. A mistake can easily be seen.

Numbers that result from investigations are often too large for the squares available on the sheet of paper. Rulings in smaller squares can sometimes be used, 5 mm, or later on 2 mm. If only one ruling is available a scale will be suggested by abler children. It seems easy for a child to think, 'I can say two to a square', or 'five to a square', and so on. He can then read the scale in twos, fives, etc.

Averages

When a set of measurements (like the handspans of a group of children) has been recorded in a diagram, it can often be seen that there are several measurements very close to

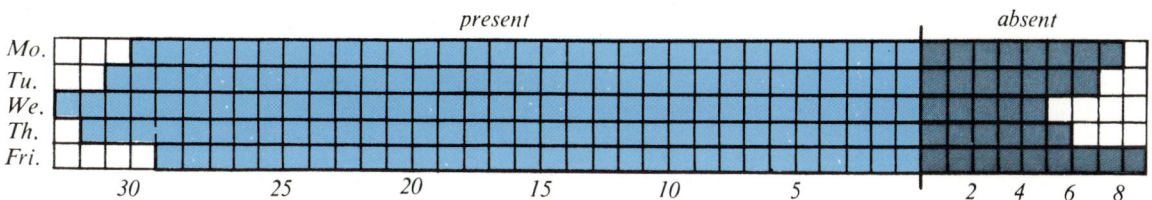

Figure 29:16

the half-way length and that the other lengths are nearly balanced on either side. A child can say his own handspan is more or less than the half-way length. This is an approach to the idea of average.

A child's first idea of an average may well be that of a fair share when unequal shares are pooled and redistributed to give each person the same amount. This leads directly to the method of adding up all the seperate unequal shares and dividing the total by the number of people who are to share it. A team of five children have 6, 9, 4, 3, and 8 conkers in their respective collections. They decide to start a game with the same number each. They pool their contributions and have a total of 30. Sharing them among the participants they start with 6 conkers each. This set of numbers might also appear in quite a different situation, for instance as the scores obtained by 5 teams in a contest. The scores are shown in a diagram on squared paper.

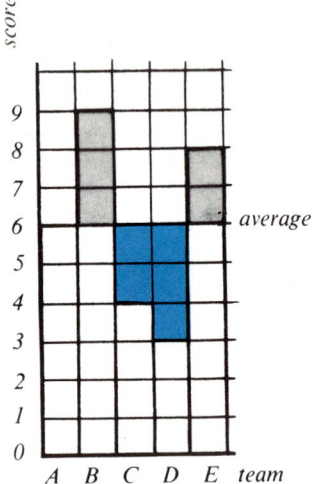

Figure 29:17

What is the average score? The children may want to know this in order to compare their score with that of a set of teams of different size.

Discussion can lead to a guess. It must be somewhere between the highest and the lowest, and so between 9 and 3. They may guess 6. If the guess is right, the scores that are more than 6 must have made up for those that were less than 6. How many scores above 6 are there?

Above 6: $9 - 6 = 3$
$8 - 6 = 2$
$\overline{5}$ above 6 giving an excess of 5
Below 6: $6 - 4 = 2$
$6 - 3 = 3$
$\overline{5}$ below 6 giving a defect of 5

The excess and the defect balance, as can be seen in Figure 29:17. Thus 6 must be the true average score.

300

But in real situations, and especially in dealing with measurements, the numbers rarely work out so smoothly. For example, the heights of 6 children, measured at random, may be 142 cm, 148 cm, 151 cm, 144 cm, 149 cm, 148 cm. If these are put in order of size a child may take the half-way measurement for his estimated average. (Figure 29:18.) The lengths greater than 148 cm give:

Above 148 cm	1 cm
	3 cm
	4 cm total
Below 148 cm	6 cm
	4 cm
	10 cm total

The defect is $(10-4)$ cm greater than the excess. The estimated average is not quite right. With the average line where it was drawn on the graph the defect is too great. The line must be lowered to make the defects less. Lowering the estimate will change every difference from the guessed average, so we must spread the total defect of 6 cm over all 6 columns of the graph. Dividing 6 by 6 gives 1 cm as the distance the line must be lowered. It will then be at 147 cm; this is the true average or *mean*. This should be checked by adding the differences above 147 cm and those below it to see whether in fact, they give equal totals.

Above $1 + 1 + 2 + 4 = 8$ *Below* $5 + 3 = 8$

As the amounts above and below balance, 147 cm must be the mean height, as the line drawn on the diagram in Figure 29:18 shows.

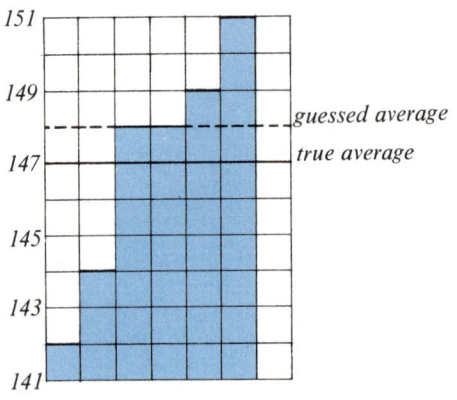

Figure 29:18

This procedure will often involve fractions, which can sometimes be rather unmanageable. Decimals are preferable and are easy to use with squared paper. Centimetre or millimetre squared paper is convenient.

Pictograms

The use of pictures to record the objects in a set has been mentioned already. Symbolic figures (pinmen, cars, ships, pigs) make an effective means of showing comparable numbers of such things. But they have some disadvantages. If a picture is used for each element of a large set, for instance a traffic count of lorries, vans and cars, the numbers soon become too big to be readily recognized. If a scale is used, 1 pinman representing 10 people working at a certain job, then fractions of a pin-man may be required. This form of symbol is best used for numbers which can suitably be rounded off so that 64 people will be shown as 6 pinmen, say, and 89 people as 9 pinmen.

Pets of children in class

dogs	
cats	
tortoises	

traffic count

cars	
vans	
lorries	

1 picture stands for 10 vehicles

Figure 29:19

There is a risk that children who have been using a scale for drawing plans of classroom or playground may use scale wrongly in pictorial representation. For example,

in recording the number of toy boats that three boys severally possess, say 2, 6 and 8, picture boats may be drawn 2, 6 and 8 units long. In *judging* the numbers represented an observer will probably compare the *areas* of paper which the pictures cover. This assumes an increase in height as well as length, so that the numbers represented on this basis are 2, 18 and 32. Even more mistaken is a judgement based on the three-dimensional boat which the flat drawing suggests. Width as well as length and height may now be assumed to have increased and the numbers conveyed to the observer are 2, 54 and 128: a formidable misinterpretation. (Figure 29:20.)

Pie-graphs

One valuable form of diagram for showing the parts into which a set or a unit of time or money can be partitioned is a circle with subdivisions to represent the parts. The symmetry of the circle enables us to produce sectors in which the area is proportional to the angle at the centre and also to the length of the arc. One-third of a day of 24 hours can be represented by a sector with an angle of 120° at the centre and with an arc which is one-third of the circumference of the whole circle (Figure 29:21).

Therefore, whether we compare the areas of the sectors, the angles which they make at the centres, or the arcs which bound them, the ratios are identical with those of the quantities represented. The risk of misinterpretation is eliminated in this circular diagram.

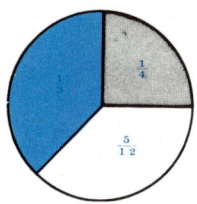

Figure 29:21

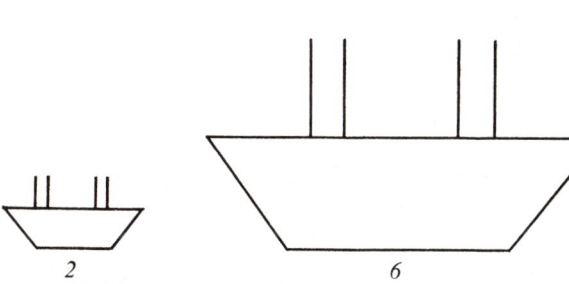

2   6

Figure 29:20

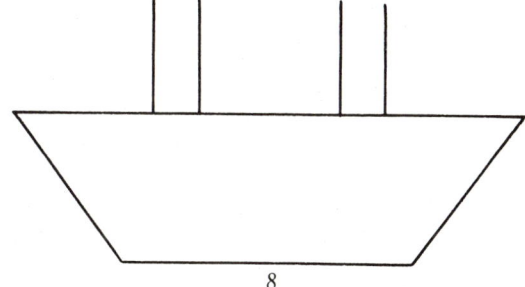

8

Children usually learn how to mark out a clock-face and are therefore able to divide a circle into $\frac{1}{2}$'s, $\frac{1}{3}$'s, $\frac{1}{4}$'s, $\frac{1}{6}$'s and $\frac{1}{12}$'s. When they have mastered the skill of measuring with a protractor they can calculate fractions of 360°, like $\frac{1}{8}$ and $\frac{1}{10}$ and $\frac{1}{20}$, and can draw the angles of 45°, 36°, 18° or any multiples of them which may be needed for a particular set of numbers.

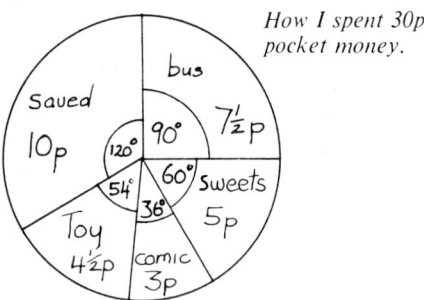

How I spent 30p pocket money.

Figure 29:22

There are many occasions when a class will find that a pie-graph is the most suitable way of exhibiting information. It shows well the occupations of a person over an interval of time, or the apportionment of money, or the subsets into which a class of children can be split according to a particular property such as weight, athletic skills, etc. Since the whole circle must be regarded as the whole interval, sum of money, or number of pupils, fractions are required to show the ratio of any part to the whole. This type of fractional work greatly helps the understanding of fractions and their connection with ratio.

The limitation of the pie-graph is that it does not lend itself to the comparison of two situations, for instance the way Alan spends his evening with Derek's occupations during the same time, or the uses of pocket money in a week of term and a week of holiday (Figure 29:22).

The value of variety

This chapter has set out several forms of presentation in which the visual pattern is all-important whether in tabulation or diagram. Each form has its own special advantages; pupils should be able to make their own choices. By this means they are encouraged to consider carefully the numbers they are trying to present and thus to become aware of some of their properties. Instead of learning a new procedure in terms of symbols they translate a real situation into an ordered arrangement or diagram and then can more easily discover new properties or solve a problem.

30 Graphs and their Development

The purpose of a graph

The word graph is commonly used to mean any representation of numbers or quantities in a drawing or diagram, usually on squared paper. It is more usually applied to a diagram which shows the relation between two sets of numbers by representing pairs of their corresponding members by points. Thus the points are fixed by such pairs as (3, 2), (x, y) which are translated into distances from two lines used as axes of reference. The first number in each pair comes from one set and the second number from the other set. The pairs are therefore *ordered*.

Previously we have seen that a number can be represented in a variety of ways, including a column or row of squares. A set of numbers may be represented by a set of columns and arranged to correspond with a set whose order is well-known, such as the days of the week, the letters of the alphabet or the natural numbers, and which can be represented by segments of a line. When the two sets are arranged in this way there is sometimes a pattern. This pattern suggests that there is some connection between corresponding members of the two sets. (Figures 30:2 and 30:3.)

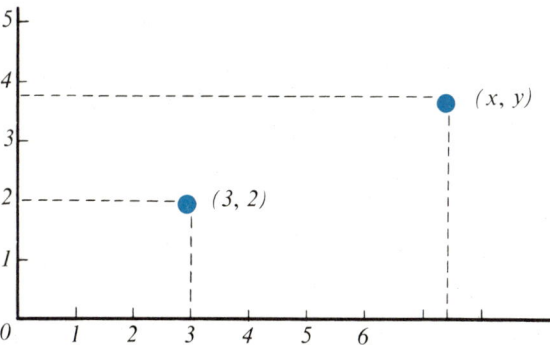

Figure 30:1

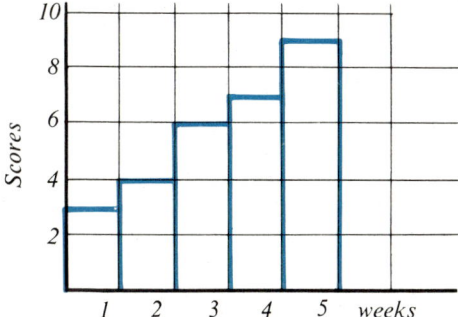

Improvement in weekly test score

Figure 30:2

Block graphs: their uses and limitations

If a square sheet of paper is folded once, two pieces can be cut from it. If the pieces are folded again four pieces can be made. If the process is repeated the number of pieces made by successive folds can be tabulated and graphed. Since we are dealing with natural numbers, the *number* of folds and the *number* of pieces, a block graph with squares representing these numbers is quite suitable. (Figure 30:3.)

Number of folds	0	1	2	3	4	5
Number of pieces	1	2	4	8	16	32

This example shows an order of size, the number of pieces increasing at each fold in a regular way. Each column is twice the height of the one preceding it.

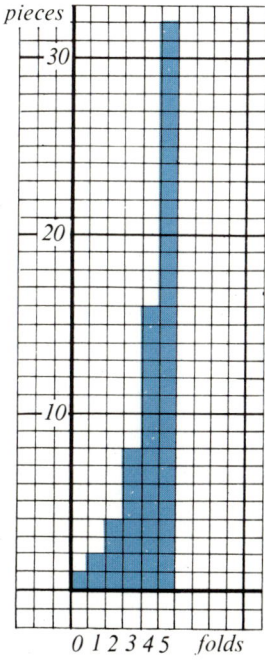

Figure 30:3

It is possible to continue this graph, making the next column twice as high as the fifth column, and so to check that the sixth fold would give 64 pieces. But there would be no meaning in asking about a *fraction* of a fold. We turn to another example to look for further developments.

The set of multiples of three can be shown on squared paper in the order 3, 6, 9, ... using rectangular blocks. Here again one can graph the first few multiples, notice

303

that the corresponding corners of the blocks lie on a line, and then read higher multiples by continuing the line (Figure 30:4). Because we are dealing with natural numbers the block graph is adequate; but if we think of multiplying by 3 instead of finding multiples of 3 we realize that we could multiply a *fraction* by 3; it is necessary to find a form of graph which will show relations between fractions. For example packets of sweets can be bought at 2p, 2½p and 3p. To show the cost of 3 packets at the various prices we must be able to represent the price along the horizontal axis. This cannot easily be done with columns of squares. We therefore recall the way in which children recorded their heights and similar measurements by representative lengths instead of squares.

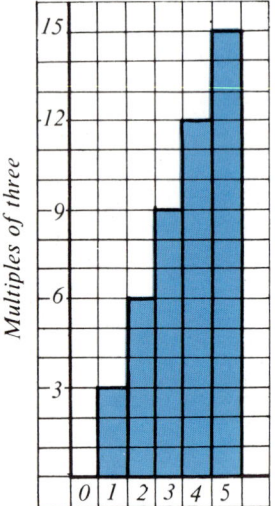

Figure 30:4

Line graphs

The sequence of *multiples of three* gives the following tabulation:

1	2	3	4	5	6	7...
3	6	9	12	15	18	21...

The same sets of numbers would show the transformation of 1, 2, 3, 4, ... into 3, 6, 9, 12, ... by the operation of *multiplying by 3*. The axes of reference can be graduated to show numbers. It is then simple to represent 3, 6, 9, etc., by lines of the appropriate length drawn in succession at the *points* 1, 2, 3, etc. (Figure 30:5(a)). A similar graph could be drawn to show the number of apples which fall from a tree on each day of a week. Figure 30:5(b) shows such a representation. The first graph is regular and the tops of the lines lie on a straight line; the second graph shows no pattern though it tells us something about the variable wind during the week. In the first graph there is a con-

nection between the multiple, say 12, and the number which was *multiplied* by 3, in this case 4. In the second graph there is no connection between the number of apples which fell and the particular day of the week. In such a case where there is no apparent regularity the line graph has only one advantage over the block graph; joining the tops of the lines by a broken line draws attention to the differences between successive numbers recorded.

(a) Multiples of three

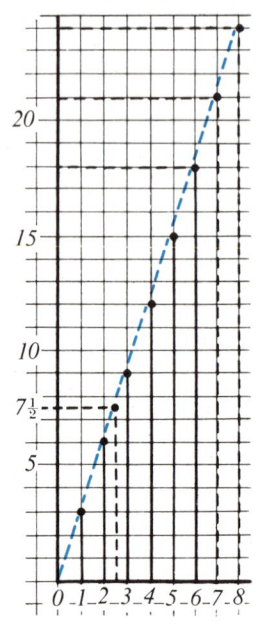

(b)
daily fall
of apples

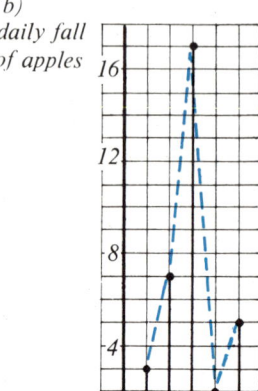

Figure 30:5

In Figure 30:5(a) we find that a line drawn upwards from 2½ on the x-axis meets the line of the 'tops' to give a length of 7½, 3 times 2½, as we should expect from the regularity of the multiples. If any fraction is marked on the x-axis the corresponding number which is 3 times the fraction can be read from the graph. The cost of three packets each of which costs a number of either pennies or halfpennies can therefore be seen at once.

Sometimes children build up a table of equivalences of inches and cm by using an inch tape measure along a straight edge. This of course produces a graph of a ratio which is approximately 2·5:1 as in Figure 30:6. But the straight edge is continuous and *any* distance along it can be measured in inches or in cm. If the x-axis represents inches the upright line from *any point* on it drawn to meet the line of the graph will show the number of centimetres corresponding to the number of inches marked by the point on the axis. This means that any point on the line of the graph, since it comes from a point on the axis, shows 2·5 times the number represented on the axis. The line joining the tops of the selected multiples can now be a solid line, without any breaks, because every point on it shows the same relation, 2·5 times, connecting the multiple with a number (Figure 30:6).

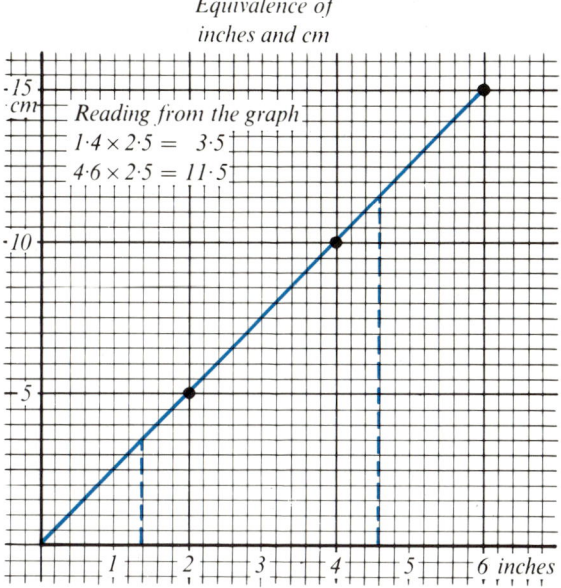

Equivalence of inches and cm

Reading from the graph
$1·4 \times 2·5 = 3·5$
$4·6 \times 2·5 = 11·5$

Figure 30:6

We see now that each point on the graph is fixed by two lengths, the distance along the *x*-axis and the upright distance from it. These are the co-ordinates of the point and are shown as a number pair, say (2,5). The tabulation of multiples given at the beginning of this section can, for instance, be replaced by a set of ordered pairs of numbers: (1,3), (2,6), (3,9), (4,12), (5,15), (6,18), (7,21), ...

Rectangles of equal area: another approach to co-ordinates

A set of rectangles all of the same area provides an interesting study of the relations between the lengths of their sides. The product of the length and breadth of each rectangle is the same number of units. If the rectangles are drawn so that one right angle is common to them all, the arms of the angle form two axes along which the sides of each rectangle can be marked (Figure 30:7). Even if only integral values of the sides are considered the corners of the rectangles not on the axes show a pattern. These vertices are fixed by the lengths of the sides of the respective rectangles and can be named by the number pair made by these lengths: (24,1), (12,2), (8,3), (6,4), (4,6), (3,8), (2,12), (1,24). It will be noticed that pairs of

these rectangles, such as (3,8) and (8,3), are the same shape but in different positions. When children try to find all possible rectangles with area 24 units they will include some with fractional sides, e.g. $(\frac{1}{2}, 48)$, $(1\frac{1}{2}, 16)$, $(4\frac{1}{2}, 5\frac{1}{3})$. When points to represent these pairs are marked on the graph they make clearer the pattern already suggested. What has emerged is a curve or set of points which shows the relation between the lengths and breadths of rectangles with constant area. The lengths can be tabulated:

length	24	12	8	6	4	3	2	1	$\frac{1}{2}$	$1\frac{1}{2}$	$4\frac{1}{2}$
breadth	1	2	3	4	6	8	12	24	48	16	$5\frac{1}{3}$

This tabulation shows a mapping from the set of lengths *L*, onto the set of breadths, *B*. The relation shown by the tabulation and graph is that the corresponding elements of the two sets have the same product. This can be written in symbols by the pupils, perhaps as $l \times b = 24$.

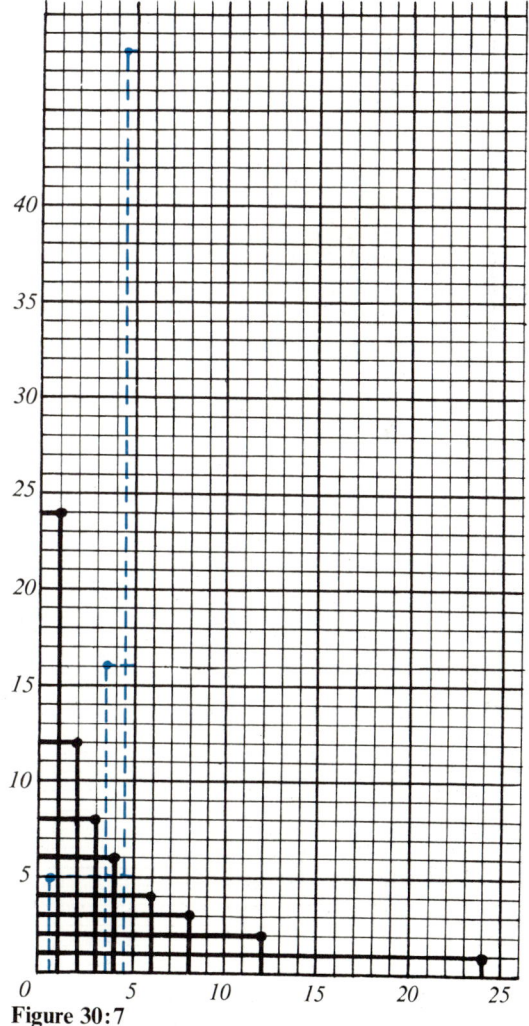

Figure 30:7

This curve of constant product has already been mentioned on page 230.

The graph of reciprocals: another use of co-ordinates

The example in the last paragraph was taken from experience of space. We will now look at two sets of numbers: the signless rationals and their reciprocals or inverses (see Chapter 26). We mark each of the two axes with a sequence of integers, 1, 2, 3, 4, 5, . . . Between each consecutive pair of integers we represent fractions, as many as we like. We tabulate a set of rationals and their reciprocals and draw a graph to show corresponding pairs.

number	$\frac{1}{2}$	1	$1\frac{1}{4}$	$1\frac{3}{4}$	2	$2\frac{1}{2}$	$2\frac{3}{4}$	3	$3\frac{3}{4}$	$4\frac{1}{2}$
reciprocal	$\frac{2}{1}$	1	$\frac{4}{5}$	$\frac{4}{7}$	$\frac{1}{2}$	$\frac{2}{5}$	$\frac{4}{11}$	$\frac{1}{3}$	$\frac{4}{15}$	$\frac{1}{4}$

number	$4\frac{1}{4}$	$4\frac{1}{2}$	$4\frac{3}{4}$	5
reciprocal	$\frac{4}{17}$	$\frac{2}{9}$	$\frac{4}{19}$	$\frac{1}{5}$

These can be written as a set of ordered pairs:

$(\frac{1}{2},2)$, $(\frac{1}{1},1)$, $(\frac{5}{4},\frac{4}{5})$, $(\frac{7}{4},\frac{4}{7})$, $(\frac{2}{1},\frac{1}{2})$, $(\frac{5}{2},\frac{2}{5})$, $(\frac{11}{4},\frac{4}{11})$, $(\frac{3}{1},\frac{1}{3})$, $(\frac{15}{4},\frac{4}{15})$, $(\frac{4}{1},\frac{1}{4})$, $(\frac{17}{4},\frac{4}{17})$, $(\frac{9}{2},\frac{2}{9})$, $(\frac{19}{4},\frac{4}{19})$, $(\frac{5}{1},\frac{1}{5})$.

The more inconvenient of these fractions must be carefully gauged to fit the scale of the graph, or turned into usable decimals, e.g. $\frac{4}{19} \simeq 0.21$. Using the co-ordinates we represent each pair as a point on the graph. The shape which results is similar to the graph of constant product drawn in Figure 30:7. This suggests a similar relation. In fact, as we know, the product of any number and its reciprocal is 1. If n is an element of the set of rationals and r is its reciprocal the relation which connects them can be written $n \times r = 1$.

Graph of reciprocals

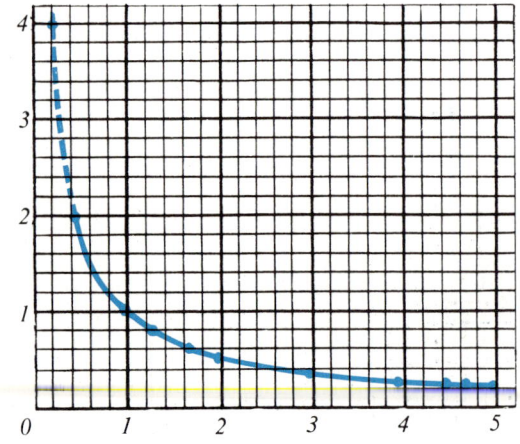

Figure 30:8

306

Among the rectangles whose sides were graphed in the previous section each one has a partner: (4,6) can be matched to (6,4), and so on. In the curve of reciprocals we find the same property. The point $(2,\frac{1}{2})$ can be matched with $(\frac{1}{2},2)$. If we write 2 as $\frac{2}{1}$ in fractional form it is very clear that each of the two numbers is the reciprocal of the other. Pupils will be interested to find all the reciprocals contained or implied in the tabulation above and to see where the matching points lie on the curve. Such a study of this graph helps pupils to understand the relation of constant product which occurs in many situations of daily life.

A frequently recurring instance of this relation is found in considering the time taken for a journey at different speeds. The distance travelled is the product of the time taken and the average speed. For a given distance the *less* time taken the *greater* the average speed. This can be tabulated for a distance of 120 km.

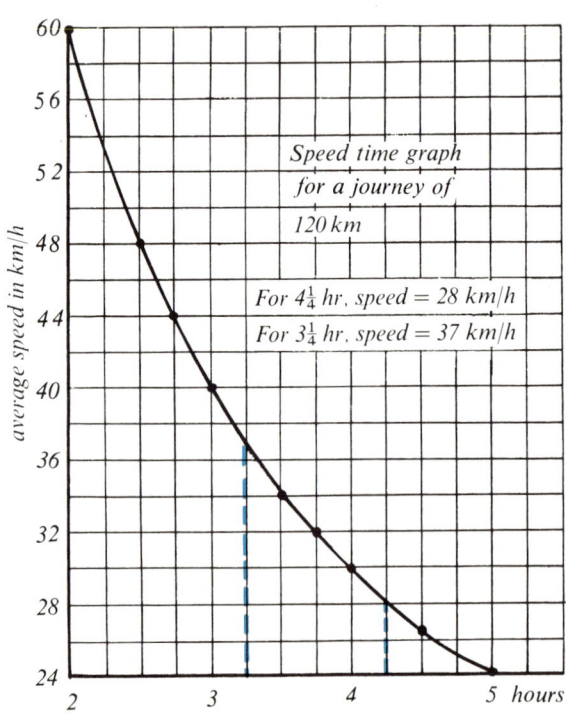

Figure 30:9

Speed × time = distance, provided that the units are properly chosen. If distances are given in km, and times in hours, then speeds will be measured in km per hour.

time in hours	2	$2\frac{1}{2}$	$2\frac{3}{4}$	3	$3\frac{1}{4}$	$3\frac{1}{2}$	$3\frac{3}{4}$
speed in k.p.h.	60	48	44	40	37	34	32

time in hours	4	$4\frac{1}{2}$	5
speed in k.p.h.	30	27	24

Here the speeds have been found to the nearest k.p.h., close enough for practical purposes. Intermediate readings will give the average speed for $2\frac{1}{4}$ and $4\frac{1}{4}$ hours. Pupils can verify, by multiplying the members of each number pair, that the product is constant to a good approximation. Several examples of constant product need to be graphed to give confident understanding of this important relation. (Figure 30:9.)

If the pupils write a formula for the previous example it may take the form $120 \div t = s$. This can be written in two alternative ways: $s \times t = 120$ or $120 \div s = t$. The relationship between these forms may be clearer if the fraction notation is used for division: $\frac{120}{t} = s$, and $\frac{120}{s} = t$. The question of whether each point of the curve gives numbers which might actually occur can usefully be discussed.

The straight-line graph; equal increases

(1) *Rate.* If a class is carrying out a measuring project using a 7 dm stride as unit they can draw a graph as a ready-reckoner to convert strides to dm. This graph will obviously be the straight line produced by plotting the multiples of 7. But certain properties of the graph can be made apparent by studying it in this context; as a child strides he realizes that at each stride he moves forward 7 dm. His distance from his starting point grows steadily 7 dm at a time as he takes a step. It can be seen that for a straight-line graph it will always be true that equal increases along the *x*-axis produce equal increases in the lengths of the uprights drawn at these intervals. For *every two* strides a child moves forward he will be *fourteen dm* farther from the start. This will be so wherever along the line the two strides are taken. We can say that his distance increases at a constant *rate* (Figure 30:10).

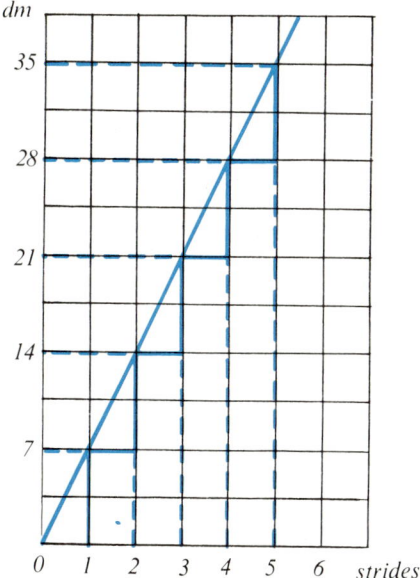

Figure 30:10

Costing graphs are of this type, showing the rate at which the charges are made. If the rate of cost is uniform throughout, the graph will be a straight line. This pattern can be seen in the graph of the cost of having a petrol tank filled up with petrol at 15 pence a litre. The petrol pump may have a strip graduated to show litres and tenths of litres and another strip showing the price. The graph showing the relation between these two sets of quantities will be a straight line showing a constant increase in price for equal increases in the quantity of petrol, that is a constant rate of charge (Figure 30:11). Since the petrol flows continuously every point on the graph has a meaning, for it represents a certain quantity of petrol and the price at which it should be sold. But the halfpenny is the smallest unit in which payment can be made; thus the actual cost will be an approximation to the value of the petrol bought.

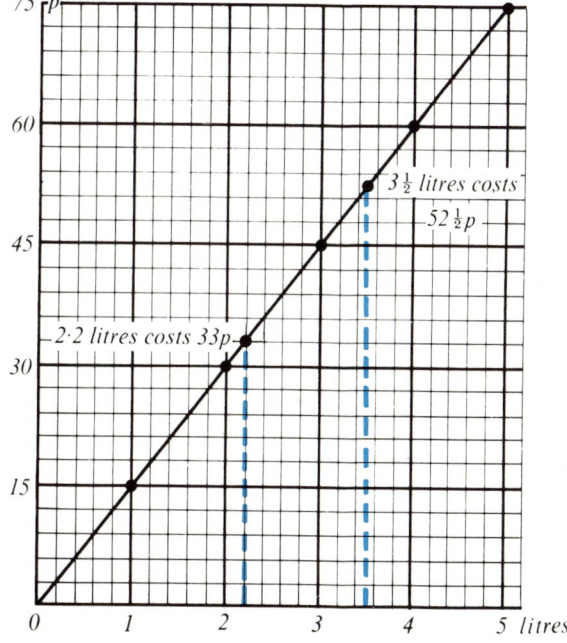

Figure 30:11

(2) *Ratio.* When two sets of numbers (or two sets of quantities measured in the same units) are investigated to discover whether there is a simple relation between them, the points representing the ordered pairs may or may not lie on a straight line when a graph is drawn. If they do we can observe that there is the same relationship between the two members of every pair; the two members of each pair are in the same ratio.

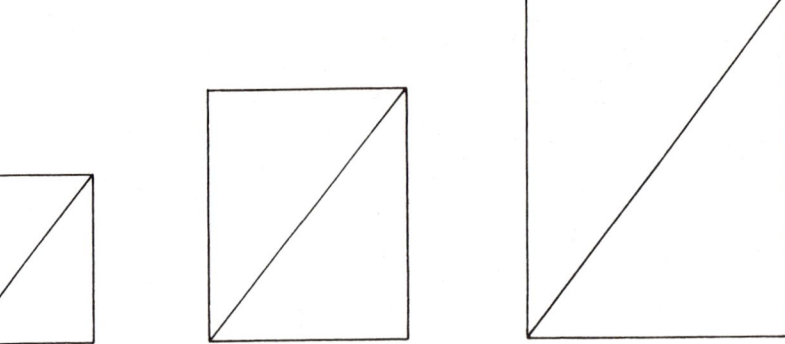

Figure 30:12

As an example we will take a rectangle with sides 3 and 4 units and consider whether its diagonal will remain in the same relation with a side if the rectangle is enlarged or diminished. We are not now interested in the rate of growth of the diagonal but in its relation with the length of a side. Rectangles are drawn which are enlarged or reduced versions of the 3 by 4 rectangle. The shorter side of each rectangle is tabulated together with the measured length of its diagonal; they are arranged in order of size.

shorter side (units)	$\frac{3}{4}$	$1\frac{1}{2}$	3	$4\frac{1}{2}$	6
diagonal (units)	$1\frac{1}{4}$	$2\frac{1}{2}$	5	$7\frac{1}{2}$	10

All the rectangles have the same shape; they were drawn with sides which were for each rectangle the same multiple or fraction of the original 3 units and 4 units. Children have an intuitive expectation that the diagonals will be in 'proportion' but have no clear idea what this means. They will almost certainly say that if the shorter side is doubled the diagonal will also be doubled. If the lengths of the shorter sides are now mapped onto the lengths of the diagonals and the graph drawn it will be a straight line (Figure 30:13). If the uprights are drawn in for each point plotted, each of them will cut off a triangle. All these triangles are the same shape and their sides will be enlargements of the smallest, which has base $\frac{3}{4}$ unit.

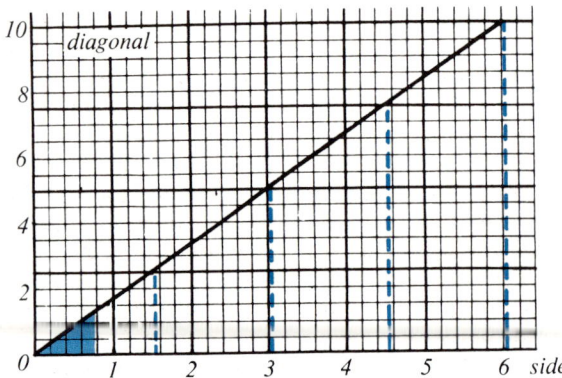

Figure 30:13

308

The ratio of diagonal to base is $1\frac{1}{4}$ to $\frac{3}{4}$, written $1\frac{1}{4}:\frac{3}{4}$. The pairs which express the ratios for all the points plotted are

$$1\frac{1}{4}:\frac{3}{4}, \quad 2\frac{1}{2}:1\frac{1}{2}, \quad 5:3, \quad 7\frac{1}{2}:4\frac{1}{2}, \quad 10:6$$

The pupils can verify that these ratios are all equal to $5:3$. For the present we are only building up the idea that the straight-line graph is a picture of a set of equal ratios.

Since it is clear that a rectangle of the same shape could be drawn on any base and this base could be represented on the x-axis, the graph can be used to tell the length of the diagonal of such a rectangle, which need not be drawn.

The perimeters of the set of rectangles could be investigated in the same way. See Chapter 36 for an extension of this work to other shapes.

The straight-line graph as a set of points

Such a graph as that of the multiples of 10, or $y = 10x$, is a set of points each of which represents a number pair, for example $(2,20)$; the second member of the pair is 10 times the first. It is also found that every pair of this kind drawn on a graph has its image point on the same straight line. If a graph is drawn for the cost in five-pences of milk at 5p a bottle all its points lie on the line $y = x$. But if the milkman charges 5 pence per week for delivery of milk at 5p a bottle a graph of the weekly charges for various quantities of milk is of slightly different form: 5 pence must be added to the cost of the milk and the rule for finding the charge y in fivepences for x pints of milk would be $y = x + 1$. The two graphs $y = x$ and $y = x + 1$ are shown together in Figure 30:14. It will be seen that the addition of the extra 5 pence has meant that the graph of x has been translated 1 unit upwards in the direction of the y-axis. In fact any point *above* the line $y = x$ has a y-number or ordinate *greater* than x.

If, instead of charging for delivery, the milkman had allowed a *discount* of 5 pence for paying the bill each week

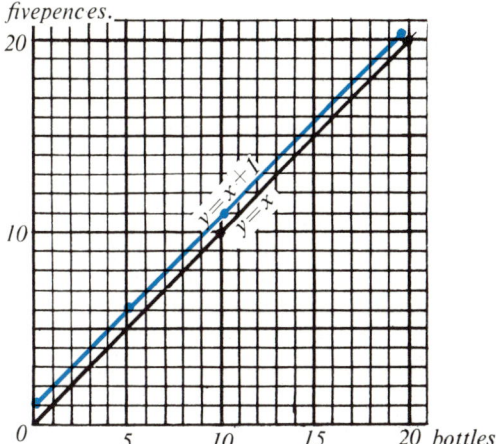

Figure 30:14

the charges would be shown on a line *below* $y = x$. The rule for finding the charge in fivepences would be $x - 1$. In Figure 30:15 we see the line $y = x - 3$ and also $y = x - 15$. All points below $y = x$ have an ordinate less than x. Thus we see that the line $y = x$ divides the plane of the paper into two parts: for all the points above it y is greater than x and for all the points below it y is less than x. Only on the line itself is y exactly equal to x.

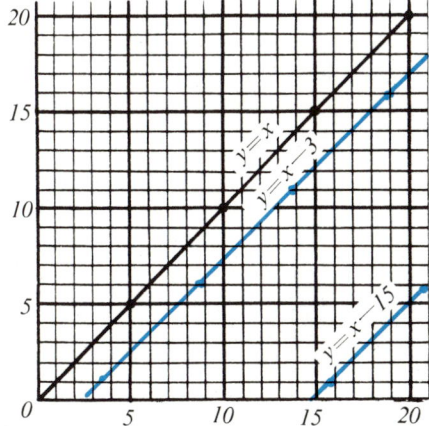

Figure 30:15

or subtracting a number from the x is to translate the straight line of the graph parallel to the y axis.

When electricity is paid for under a fixed-charge system the effect of various rates of fixed charge is shown on a graph by a set of parallel lines. Figure 30:16 shows the increases due to fixed charges of £1, £2, £3; the cost of units of electricity is at the rate of 75 pence for 100 units. The broken lines indicate the actual cost per unit when a £3 fixed charge must be paid by householders consuming

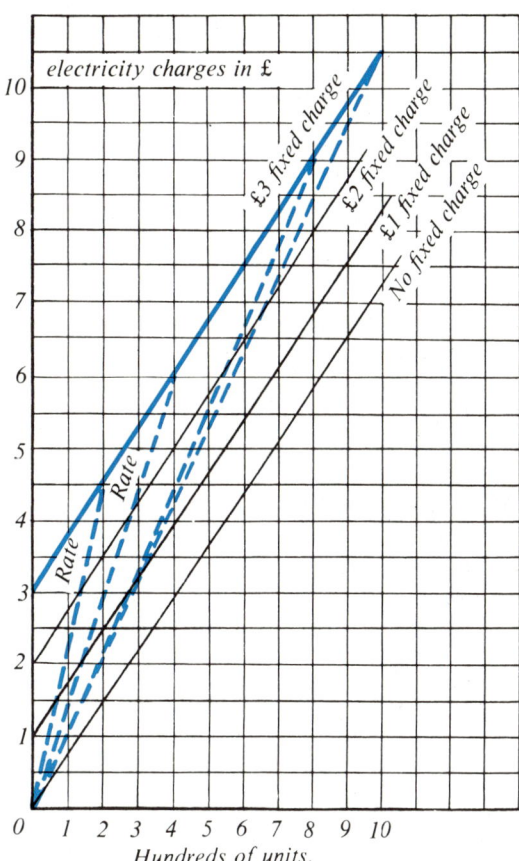

Figure 30:16

200, 400, 800 and 1000 units respectively. The steeper slope for the smaller users shows the dearer rate of cost.

Square numbers

The sequence of square numbers, 1, 4, 9, 16,... has already been mentioned both as the measure of the areas of squares with sides 1, 2, 3, 4,... units and as the product of two equal factors, 1×1, 2×2, 3×3, 4×4,... This set of numbers appears frequently in the mathematics which comes from phenomena of everyday life, for instance, the distances which a ball falls under gravity in successive equal times, and the area of the picture obtained when a slide is projected on to a screen from various distances. It is thus important that children should grow familiar with the shape of the graph produced when the natural numbers are mapped onto their squares. Only if the shape is well-known can any estimate be given of a square number which lies *beyond* the points plotted. The continuity of the graph must also be realized so that the square of any number which lies *between* the natural numbers on the x-axis can be found.

If the points $(0,0)$, $(1,1)$, $(2,4)$, $(3,9)$, $(4,16)$, ... are plotted they are found to lie not on a straight line, not on a curve like that of reciprocals, but on a curve which, turned upside down, is like the one made by water pouring from a spout. The number of points plotted is insufficient to show the shape of the curve very certainly.

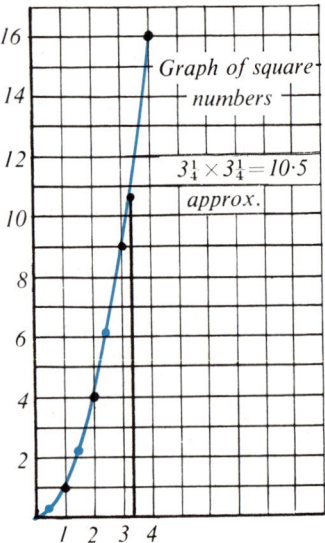

Figure 30:17

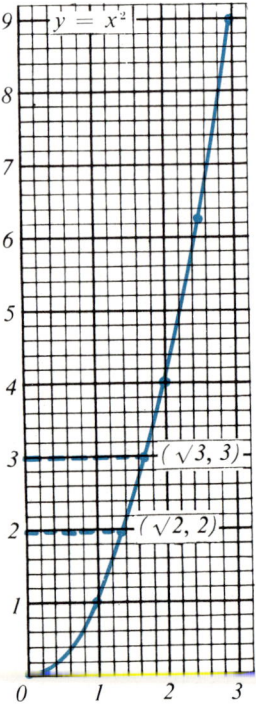

Figure 30:18

310

As children have already found that fractions can be multiplied when they occur in the sides of a rectangle they will probably suggest putting on the graph some squares of fractions such as $\frac{1}{2} \times \frac{1}{2}$, $1\frac{1}{2} \times 1\frac{1}{2}$. A good curve should now be drawn by the children and kept as the pattern made by square numbers. They can now use the graph to read the square of any number within the interval on the x-axis over which their graph extends. The reading will not be very accurate but it gives a pupil the means of stating a sufficiently good result without having to multiply awkward fractions or decimals. The inverse reading of the graph, that is, finding a number whose square is known, gives the pupils the only way of doing this which is available to them at this stage. They can find an approximate value for the square root of 2 and of 3, lengths which appear in the diagonal of a square and the height of an equilateral triangle respectively. These are dealt with more fully in Chapter 37.

The graph of a set of numbers which increase by equal steps is a straight line. Can the pupils find out how the *squares* increase by using their graph? They can draw the ordinates at equal intervals, and find how much longer each of them is than the preceding. Each square number exceeds its predecessor by an odd number which has a special structure: it is one more than twice the preceding *number*. The step from 1 to 4 is 3, which is $2 \times 1 + 1$; the step from 4 to 9 is 5, which is $2 \times 2 + 1$; the step from 9 to 16 is 7, which is $2 \times 3 + 1$, and so it will continue if more points are plotted. In Chapter 31 we discuss another way of handling this pattern. This regularly changing rate of growth is remarkable, quite important, and certainly of considerable interest to children. Figure 30:19 should be compared with Figure 30:10.

Increases in squares of integers

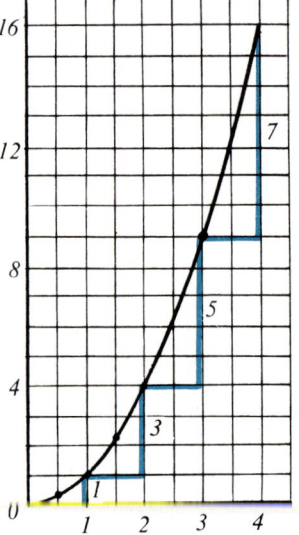

Figure 30:19

Numbers proportional to square numbers

The equation $y = x^2$ states the relation between numbers and their squares, but measurement or experiment sometimes produces a set of numbers which increase rapidly like the squares but are not square numbers. It is possible that they are proportional to squares but we need to find a way to check whether this is so. It is not easy to decide by looking at a graph whether it is of similar form to $y = x^2$. The form of graph which is easy to check is of course the straight line. We know, too, that the straight line represents pairs of numbers whose ratio is the same. We use this to find a method of comparing a set of experimental results with the square numbers.

We will consider a set of similar triangles. One of them has a base of 1 unit, and its height is $\frac{1}{2}$ unit. The other triangles form a sequence with bases $1\frac{1}{2}$, 2, $2\frac{1}{2}$, 3 units, ... *Squares* in these bases will have as areas 1, $2\frac{1}{4}$, 4, $6\frac{1}{4}$, 9, ... sq. units. If we find the areas of the *triangles* we can map the set of squares onto them and study the resulting graph.

area of square	1	$2\frac{1}{4}$	4	$6\frac{1}{4}$	9 ...
area of triangle	$\frac{1}{4}$	$\frac{9}{16}$	1	$1\frac{9}{16}$	$2\frac{1}{4}$ ...

The points corresponding to the number pairs $(1, \frac{1}{4})$, $(2\frac{1}{4}, \frac{9}{16})$, $(9, 2\frac{1}{4})$, ... are seen to lie on a line. The ratio of the area of a triangle to that of the square on the same base must therefore be constant. The graph shows us that this ratio is 1 to 4. We can then describe the relation by a formula as $y = \frac{1}{4} \times x^2$, where the base of the triangle is x units and its area is y square units.

Extension to directed numbers

The graphs that we have considered so far in this chapter have represented signless numbers using axes which are drawn from the origin (zero) in one direction only. Fractional values are shown on these graphs but we shall soon need to extend to graphs which use positive and negative numbers. This can be done by using the whole number line for each axis, drawing the axis in both directions from the origin. We can thus represent number

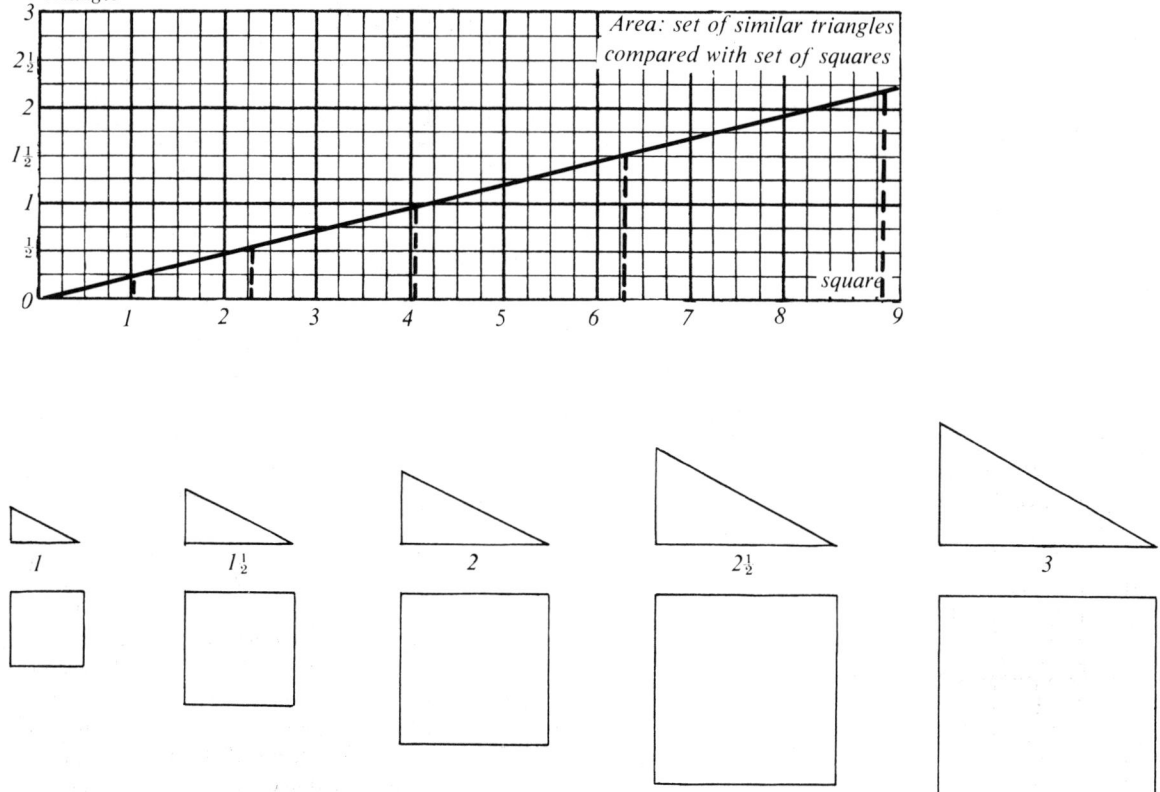

Figure 30:20

311

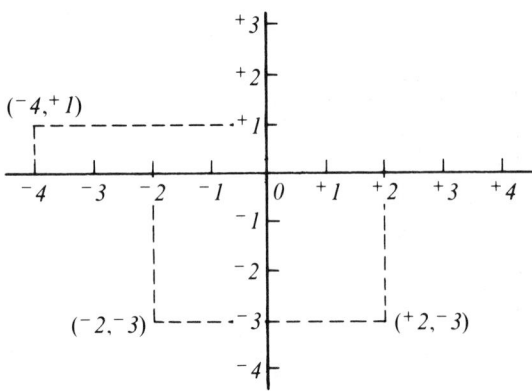

Figure 30:21

pairs such as $(^-4, ^+1), (^+2, ^-3)$, and $(^-2, ^-3)$ (Figure 30:21).

The need for a directed number may arise quite early in the Primary course. If children record how many more bottles of milk than one crate are needed each day, they will probably find one day that not all the bottles in the crate are needed, and a few must be sent back. A block-graph will look like Figure 30:22. Children sometimes suggest the use of a minus sign to show that the bottles are to be sent back.

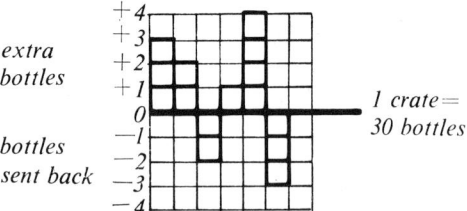

Figure 30:22

If a team of children are trying to throw a ball on to a target line they may record a throw *on* the line, *beyond* the line, or *short of* the line. Only one axis is extended in both directions in this graph because the number of throws is a signless number (Figure 30:23).

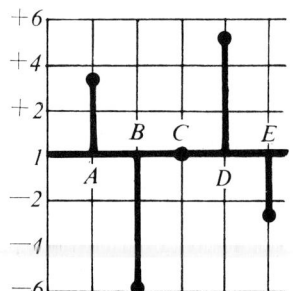

Figure 30:23

312

Two extended axes are required for such a graph as that for converting a Celsius to a Fahrenheit reading of a temperature. Each scale can record a temperature below zero and thus each axis is graduated with positive and negative numbers (Figure 30:24).

Celsius	$^+100$	$^+10$	0	$^-10$	$^-20$
Fahrenheit	$^+212$	$^+50$	$^+32$	$^+14$	$^-4$

Any Celsius reading, positive or negative (including fractions), has just one corresponding Fahrenheit reading. Thus F is a function of C. It is given by the formula

$$F = \frac{9}{5}C + 32$$

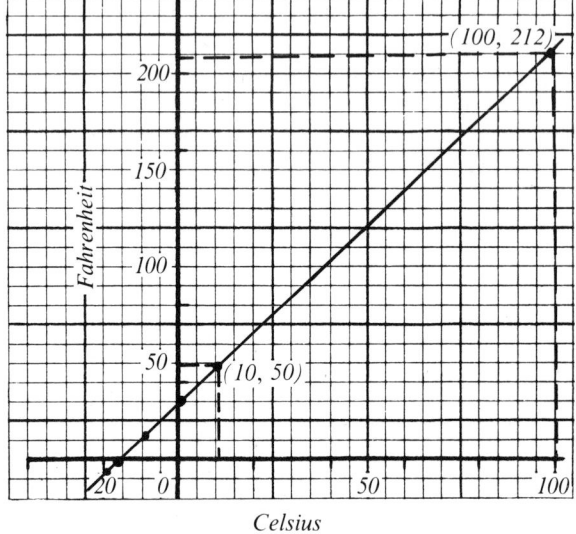

Figure 30:24

The graph of any of the functions we have discussed in this chapter, such as $y = 2x + 1$, $y = \frac{1}{x}$, can now be extended to cover any suitable interval of values of x. The values of y may then range between any negative and positive numbers (Figure 30:25).

In the upper classes of the primary school experiments with speed, cooling, scoring with points and penalties, variations from a standard measurement, etc., will provide many occasions for the use of graphs of sets of directed numbers. The reason for the use of the negative numbers needs careful investigation in each situation, for example, in regard to past and future time or movement in opposite directions.

$$y = 2x + 1$$

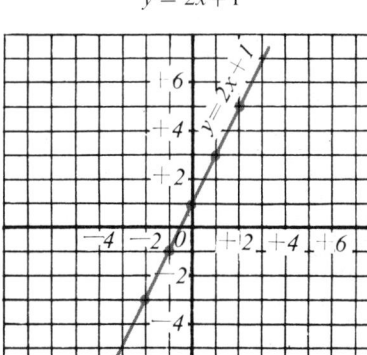

$$y = \frac{1}{x}$$

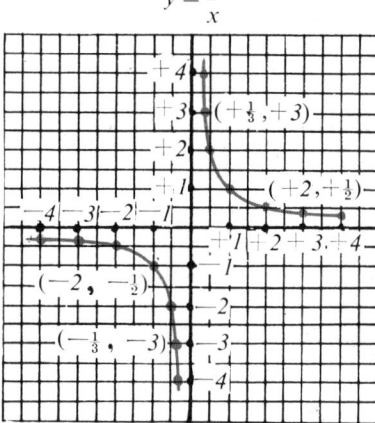

Figure 30:25

Relation diagrams and the nomogram

As an alternative to the usual graph, a *relation diagram* to illustrate the relation between two sets of numbers may be preferred on some occasions. Here, two number lines are drawn parallel to one another, and arrows join the points of one number line to corresponding points of the other. These relation diagrams, which have already been used in Chapters 9 and 17, give a different pictorial representation, and show another way of looking at relations between sets of numbers. Used in conjunction with graphs, relation diagrams will broaden children's ideas and pictures of these relations. A collection of examples, which show the different forms relation diagrams may take, are given in Figures 30:26 to 30:31. The inverse nature of the relations 'add 3' and 'subtract 3' can be seen in Figures 30:26 and 30:27.

The form of the relation diagram for 'divide by 3', or $y = \frac{x}{3}$, is easily obtained from Figure 30:28. The next

The relation subtract 3 or $y = x - 3$

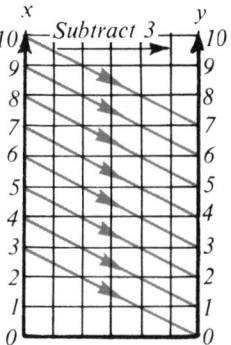

Figure 30:27

The relation multiply by 3 or $y = 3x$

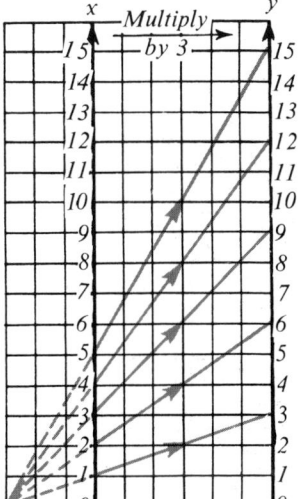

The relation 'add 3' or $y = x + 3$

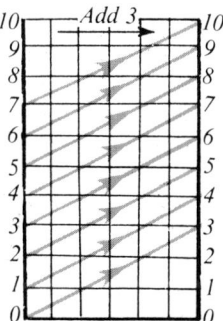

Figure 30:26

Figure 30:28

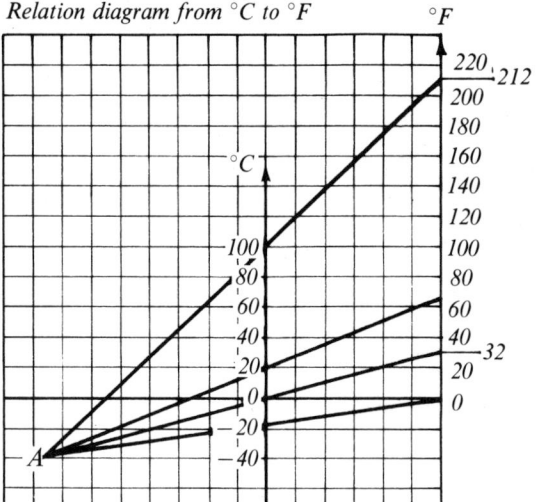

Figure 30:29

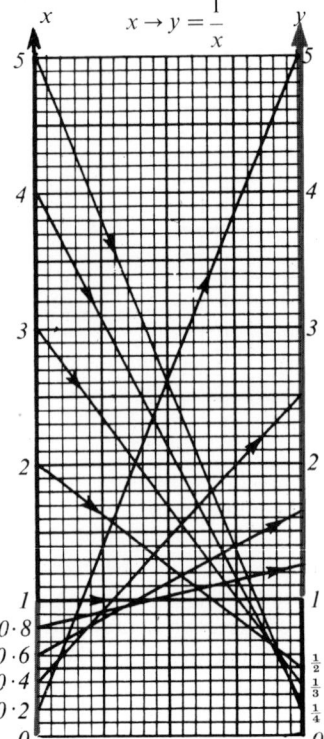

Figure 30:31

relation diagram (Figure 30:29), for the relation from °C to °F, is a combination of a multiplication and an addition relation. By joining any point on one of the axes to A, the centre of enlargement, the corresponding temperatures can be read off. The Celsius number line has been extended to show some negative numbers.

We next show the relation diagram corresponding to the curve of squares (Figure 30:30). It will be noticed that the lines joining corresponding points in the mapping do not radiate from a single point, as the relation is not a simple enlargement.

The relation diagram of reciprocals (Figure 30:31) shows how the reciprocal decreases as the number increases. The

reciprocal of a number greater than 1 is less than 1, and vice versa.

The relation diagram which illustrates the summation of two numbers has the particular value that it can be used as a calculating instrument. Figure 30:32 shows the relation $x + y = 5$. Clearly to any pair of numbers, say $(1, 4)$, which satisfies this requirement there corresponds the pair $(4, 1)$, because addition is commutative. The two representational arrows will therefore intersect midway between the two number lines. The relation $x + y = 8$ would show the same property, as would any other integer. The points of intersection will all lie on the line parallel to the number lines and midway between them; and each will be a distance from zero equal to half the sum of the two numbers to be added.

If the line showing half the sum is graduated on half the scale of the other lines it will show the sum of the two numbers. Figure 30:33 shows the diagram or *nomogram* for the relation $x + y = n$ where, given any two numbers we can draw the arrow which joins their representative points and read the sum of the pair from the graduation on the midway line. On the diagram we read $6 + 2 = 8$ and $^+3 + ^-5 = ^-2$.

By changing the position of the line of intersections and the scale on which it is graduated various other relations. such as $x + 2y = n$, can be transformed into a nomogram.

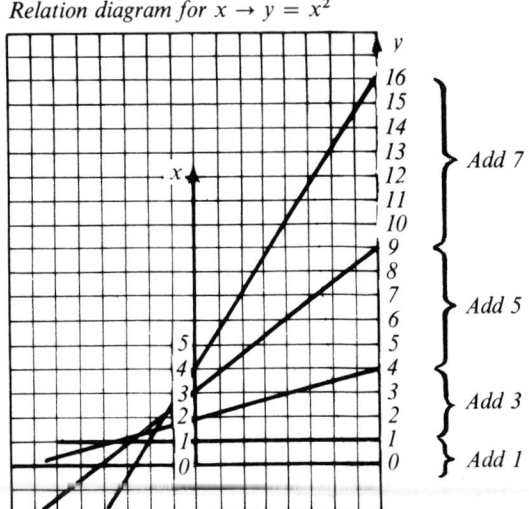

Figure 30:30

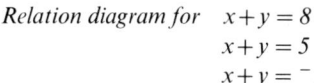

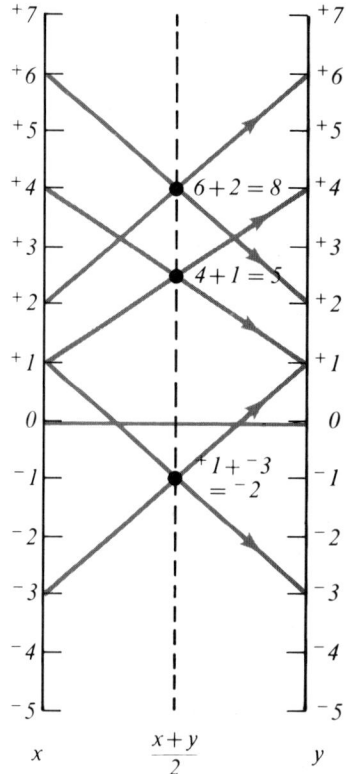

Figure 30:32

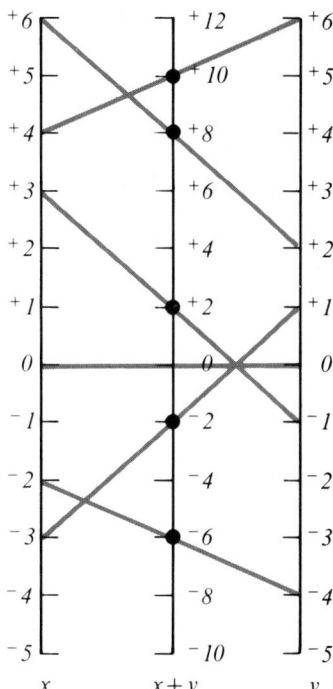

Figure 30:33

31 Patterns among the Natural Numbers

Factorization of 24

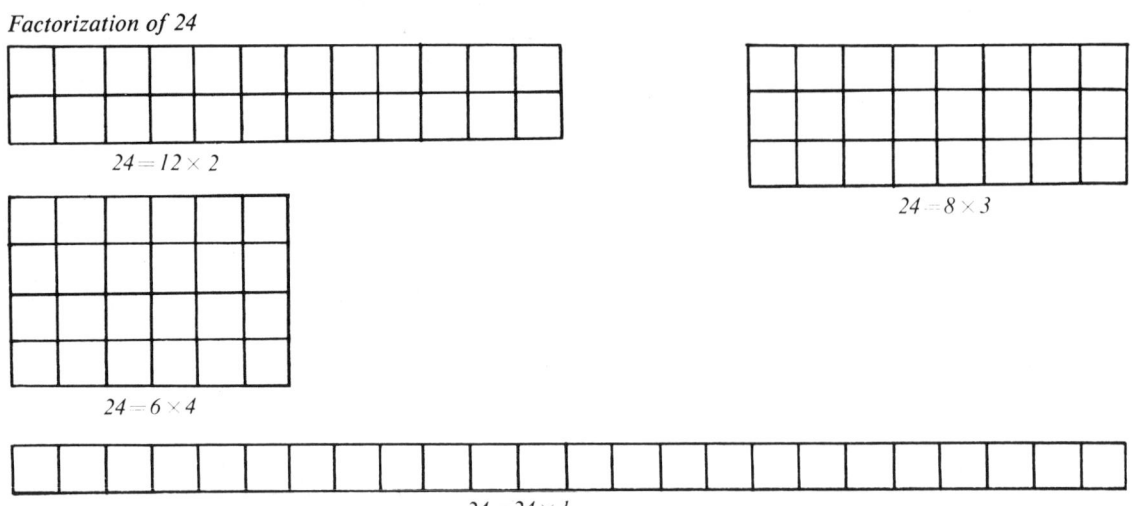

$$24 = 12 \times 2$$

$$24 = 8 \times 3$$

$$24 = 6 \times 4$$

$$24 = 24 \times 1$$

Figure 31:1[1]

Introduction

For many centuries men have been fascinated by the various patterns which have been found among the natural numbers. Some of these patterns may arise naturally out of children's practical experiments with numbers, and will lead them to make their own simple investigations, and to begin to generalize about the properties of numbers. The fascination which simple number patterns hold for children can be used to give practice in computation and to show the need for accuracy (since patterns will not be found among numbers if calculations are inaccurately made), and to give help in practical learning of multiplication tables. These uses are, however, subservient to the search for order and pattern which is one of the driving forces of all mathematical work with children.

This chapter contains a variety of number patterns with which upper Juniors will enjoy experimenting, together with a mechanical method of multiplication which is of historical interest, and which is well within the range of juniors.

Factors and multiples

In their work on multiplication and division, children come to know not only that 6 fours are equal to 24, but in reverse, that 24 is made up of 6 fours; that is, they

know that 6 and 4 are *factors* of 24. Similarly, 12 is a factor of 24, because $24 = 2 \times 12$; 11 is not a factor of 24, because 24 is not a multiple of 11, and so 24 cannot be divided by 11 a whole number of times without remainder. A child may study the factors of such a number as 24 by taking 24 cubes or bricks and trying to arrange them in rectangular layers in as many different ways as possible. He will obtain the arrangements shown in Figure 31:1. No other rectangles are possible; an attempt to make one with a side of 7 units can only produce the arrangement shown in Figure 31:2. The only factors of 24, that is the

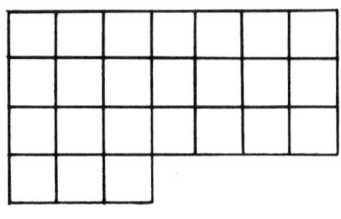

$$24 = (3 \times 7) + 3$$

Figure 31:2

only natural numbers by which 24 can be divided exactly without remainder, are 1, 2, 3, 4, 6, 8, 12 and 24. If appropriate pairs of members of this set of factors

$$\{1, 2, 3, 4, 6, 8, 12, 24\}$$

are multiplied together, the original number 24 will be recovered.

---

[1] If the child does not yet understand the commutative law for multiplication, each of these rectangles may appear twice, as for instance 6×4 and 4×6.

The correct linking is shown in Figure 31:3.

Factors of 24

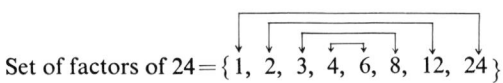

Set of factors of 24 = {1, 2, 3, 4, 6, 8, 12, 24}

$1 \times 24 = 24 \times 1 = 24$
$2 \times 12 = 12 \times 2 = 24$
$3 \times 8 \;= 8 \times 3 = 24$
$4 \times 6 \;= 6 \times 4 = 24$

Figure 31:3

If a child experiments similarly with the factorization of 36, he will obtain the situation shown in Figure 31:4. It will be noticed that 36 is a *perfect square*; that is, the product of two *equal* factors. One of the rectangular arrangements is the square 6×6.

Prime numbers

Every number is divisible by 1 and by itself; some natural numbers have no other factors. The factor pattern for 13 is shown in Figure 31:5. A natural number greater than 1

Factorization of 13

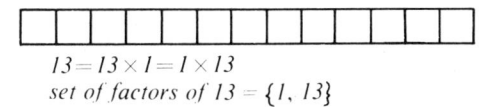

$13 = 13 \times 1 = 1 \times 13$
set of factors of 13 = {1, 13}

Figure 31:5

whose only factors are 1 and itself is called a *prime number*.[2] The first few prime numbers, which children will quickly find because they are so familiar with the smaller natural numbers, are 2, 3, 5, 7, 11, 13, 17, ... If children find difficulty in picking out prime numbers, the tabulation of the factors of each number shown in Figure 31:6 may be helpful. Here the pairs of factors of each number are listed according to the multiplication table in which they appear. Use may be made of the commutative law to avoid putting each pair of factors into the list twice. If this is done, only the factors in bold type in Figure 31:6 will appear. The tabulation can be continued for as long as is desired, and it is extremely easy to pick out prime numbers from it.

If many prime numbers are to be found, a simplified version of this arrangement, known as the Sieve of

[2] It is usual not to include 1 among the prime numbers, since 1 is a factor of every number.

Factorization of 36

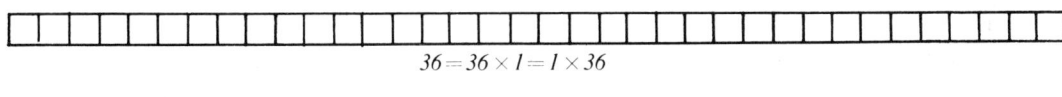

$36 = 36 \times 1 = 1 \times 36$

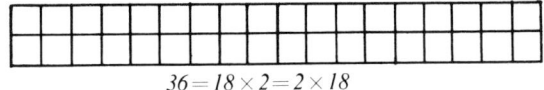

$36 = 18 \times 2 = 2 \times 18$

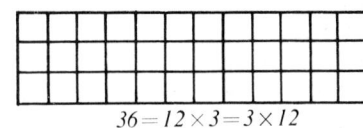

$36 = 12 \times 3 = 3 \times 12$

$36 = 9 \times 4 = 4 \times 9$

$36 = 6 \times 6$

Set of factors of 36 = {1, 2, 3, 4, 6, 9, 12, 18, 36}

Figure 31:4

Prime	number	Table of ones	Table of twos	Table of threes	Table of fours	Table of fives	Table of sixes	Table of sevens	Table of eights	Table of nines
	1	1 × 1								
P	2	2 × 1	1 × 2							
P	3	3 × 1		1 × 3						
	4	4 × 1	2 × 2		1 × 4					
P	5	5 × 1				1 × 5				
	6	6 × 1	3 × 2	2 × 3			1 × 6			
P	7	7 × 1						1 × 7		
	8	8 × 1	4 × 2		2 × 4				1 × 8	
	9	9 × 1		3 × 3						1 × 9
	10	10 × 1	5 × 2			2 × 5				
P	11	11 × 1								
	12	12 × 1	6 × 2	4 × 3	3 × 4		2 × 6			
P	13	13 × 1								
	14	14 × 1	7 × 2					2 × 7		
	15	15 × 1		5 × 3		3 × 5				
	16	16 × 1	8 × 2		4 × 4				2 × 8	
P	17	17 × 1								
	18	18 × 1	9 × 2	6 × 3			3 × 6			2 × 9
P	19	19 × 1								
	20	20 × 1	10 × 2		5 × 4	4 × 5				
	21	21 × 1		7 × 3				3 × 7		
	22	22 × 1	11 × 2							
P	23	23 × 1								
	24	24 × 1	12 × 2	8 × 3	6 × 4		4 × 6		3 × 8	
	25	25 × 1				5 × 5				

Figure 31:6

Eratosthenes[3], is convenient. To operate this Sieve, a list of natural numbers is made.

The number square shown in Chapter 16 will yield all the primes up to 100, and the method is a direct extension of the colouring of multiples suggested in that chapter.

Among the multiples of 2, the only prime is 1×2 or 2 itself. We therefore put a ring round 2 on the list, and go through the list crossing out the set of multiples of 2

because they are not prime, i.e. $\{4, 6, 8, 10, \ldots\}$. The first number remaining on the list is 3, which is 1×3 and is prime. We ring it, and cross out its set of multiples $\{6, 9, 12, \ldots\}$. Next, $4 = 2 \times 2$ has already been crossed out, and the next remaining number is 5, which is prime. This is ringed and its set of multiples $\{10, 15, 20, \ldots\}$ crossed out. We proceed by crossing out multiples of primes. Figure 31:7 shows the operation of the Sieve to give primes up to 150. The use of the Sieve is not nearly as laborious as it looks. A number less than 150 which is not a prime must have a factor less than 13, because $13 \times 13 = 169$. Hence sieving out multiples of all the primes up to 13 will leave all the primes up to 150. In Figure 31:7 a circle has been put round all the numbers whose multiples were crossed out; the other

[3] Eratosthenes was a Greek mathematician who was librarian of the University at Alexandria at about 240 B.C. He also measured the circumference of the earth by a very ingenious method. See Hogben, L. *Man Must Measure* (Rathbone, 1955), page 36.

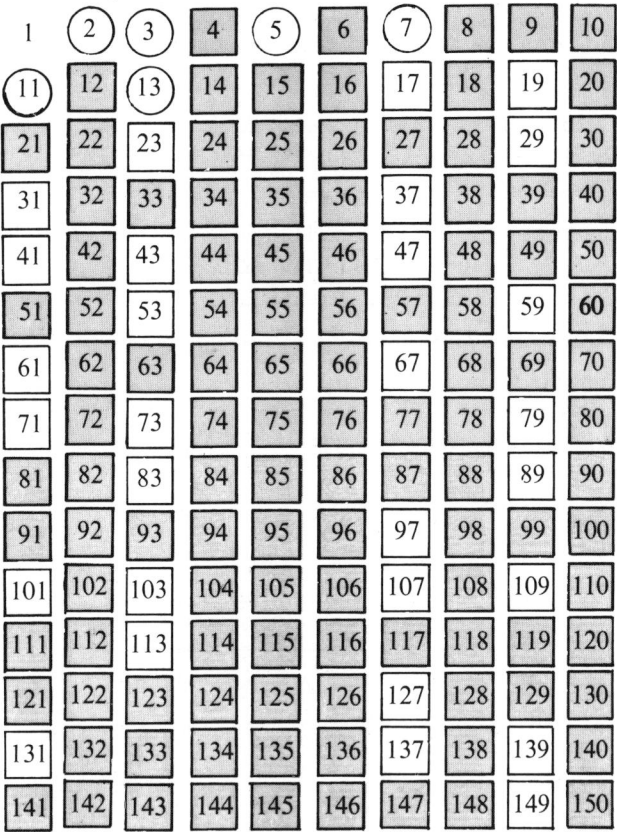

Figure 31:7

numbers left after sieving, which are also primes, are enclosed in rectangles.

Prime numbers have always interested mathematicians, and there are still many unsolved problems about them. There is an infinite number of primes, but in general they get rarer as their size increases. There are, however, many *twin primes,* such as 11 and 13, 41 and 43, 137 and 139, 149 and 151, which are only 2 apart. It is likely that there is an infinite number of twin primes, but this has not yet been proved.

Composite numbers and their prime factors

A natural number greater than 1 which is not a prime number is called a *composite number*. The prime numbers are building bricks from which all the composite numbers can be built by multiplication. Children may like to build composite numbers out of the members of a given set of prime numbers, and see how many different composite numbers they can find. Figures 31:8, 31:9 and 31:10 show the building up of numbers from sets of primes, the members of which may or may not be repeated in building the composite numbers. It should be noticed that the set of

Numbers built from 2, 3, 7

Using 1 prime factor	2 3 7
Using 2 prime factors	$2 \times 3 = 6$, $3 \times 7 = 21$, $2 \times 7 = 14$
Using 3 prime factors	$2 \times 3 \times 7 = 42$

Set of factors of $42 = \{1, 2, 3, 6, 7, 14, 21, 42\}$

Figure 31:8

Numbers built from 2, 2, 2, 3

Using 1 prime factor	2 3
Using 2 prime factors	$2 \times 2 = 4$ $2 \times 3 = 6$
Using 3 prime factors	$2 \times 2 \times 2 = 8$ $2 \times 2 \times 3 = 12$
Using 4 prime factors	$2 \times 2 \times 2 \times 3 = 24$

Set of factors of $24 = \{1, 2, 3, 4, 6, 8, 12, 24\}$

Figure 31:9

Numbers built from 2, 3, 5, 11

Using 1 prime factor	2 3 5 11
Using 2 prime factors	$2\times3=6$ $2\times5=10$ $2\times11=22$ $3\times5=15$ $3\times11=33$ $5\times11=55$
Using 3 prime factors	$2\times3\times5=30$ $2\times3\times11=66$ $2\times5\times11=110$ $3\times5\times11=165$
Using 4 prime factors	$2\times3\times5\times11=330$

Set of factors of 330 = {1, 2, 3, 5, 6, 10, 11, 15, 22, 30, 33, 55, 66, 110, 165, 330}

Figure 31:10

Factorization of 24 into prime factors

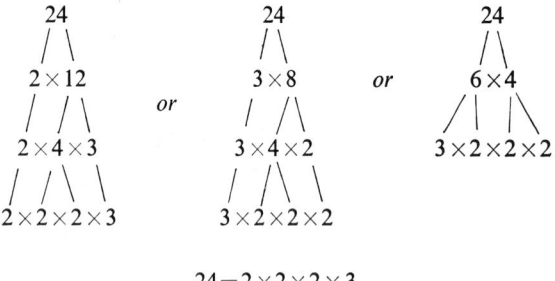

24
2×12
2×4×3
2×2×2×3
or
24
3×8
3×4×2
3×2×2×2
or
24
6×4
3×2×2×2
24=2×2×2×3

Figure 31:11

12
12
24 = 2 × 12
4
4
4
24 = 2 × 3 × 4
2
2
24 = 2 × 3 × 2 × 2

Figure 31:12

composite numbers which can be built is the set of factors (other than 1) of the largest of them.

As a reversal of this process, a 'family tree' method can be used to break down a composite number into its prime factors. The method is shown in Figure 31:11. We see that factorization of a composite number can often yield several different trees, but that there is only one prime factorization of any number; this will appear at the end of any tree for that number. It may be interesting in a simple case to construct this family tree practically, using cubes or rods, as shown in Figure 31:12. Children should also notice what happens when they divide a number by one of its factors. For instance

$$\begin{aligned}24 \div 3 &= (2\times2\times2\times3)\\ &= 2\times2\times2\\ &= 8\end{aligned}$$

and

$$\begin{aligned}24 \div 6 &= (2\times2\times2\times3) \div (2\times3)\\ &= 2\times2\\ &= 4\end{aligned}$$

Understanding of this idea is needed for the multiplication of fractions,[4] but is likely to need much stressing to children who are familiar with factors and building up numbers from their factors.

[4] For instance $\frac{6}{5}\times\frac{4}{9}=\frac{6\times4}{5\times9}$

$=\frac{2\times4}{5\times3}$ (dividing numerator and denominator by 3)

See page 254.

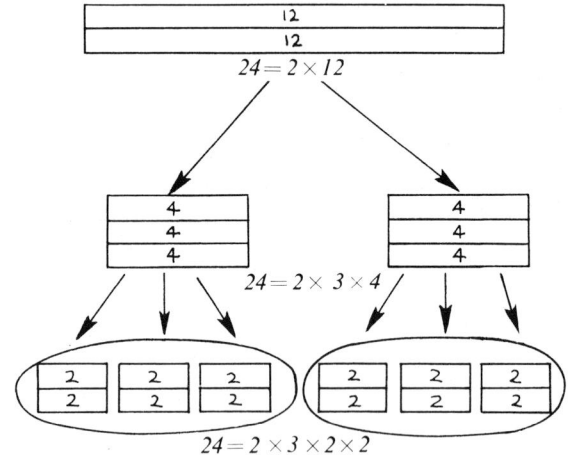

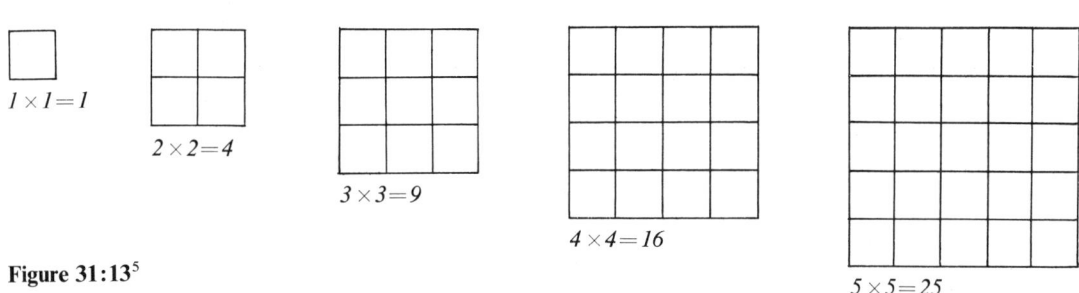

$1 \times 1 = 1$

$2 \times 2 = 4$

$3 \times 3 = 9$

$4 \times 4 = 16$

$5 \times 5 = 25$

Figure 31:13[5]

Square numbers

Among the most interesting of the natural numbers are those, such as 36, which can be factorized into a product of two *equal* factors. Children will find these numbers at an early stage, when they build up small cubes to make square layers of increasing size. The first few of these *square numbers,* or *perfect squares,* are shown in Figure 31:13. We have already seen that the perfect squares appear in the leading diagonal of the multiplication table square.[6]

The perfect squares increase in size more and more rapidly as the side of the squares increases. The number of unit squares needed to make each perfect square is shown in the block graph of Figure 31:14(*b*). This diagram also emphasizes the number of unit squares which must be added to each perfect square to construct the next perfect square. Since the number of units in each perfect square grows so rapidly, it is inconvenient to use the same scale on both axes of the graph.

[5] 5×5 is often written 5^2 (*see page* 161).

[6] Figure 16:18

The growth of squares

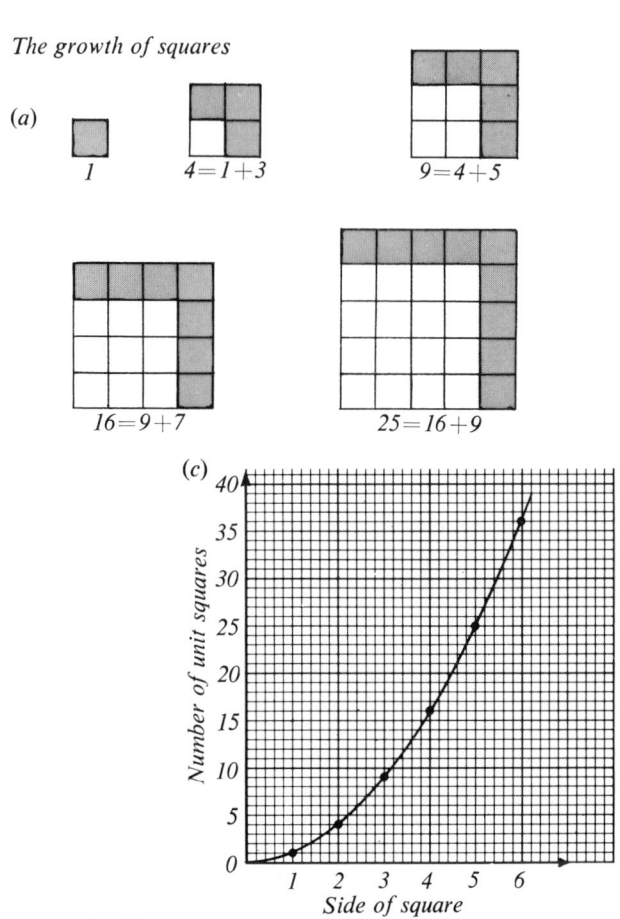

(*a*)

1

$4 = 1 + 3$

$9 = 4 + 5$

$16 = 9 + 7$

$25 = 16 + 9$

(*c*)

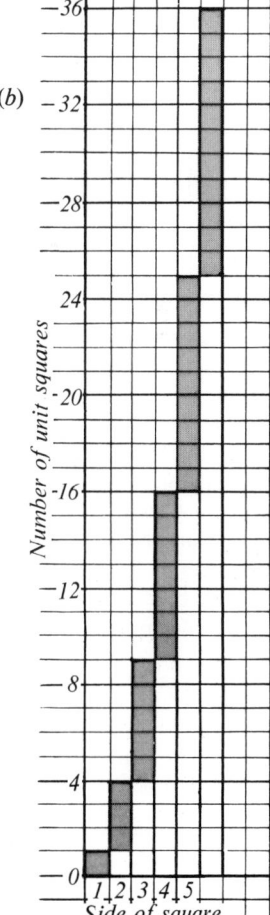

(*b*)

Figure 31:14

The growth of equilateral triangles

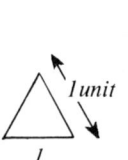
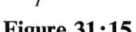
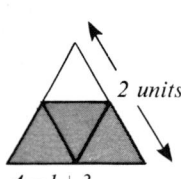
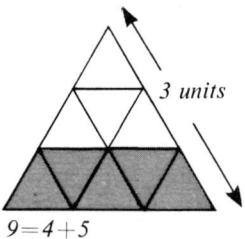
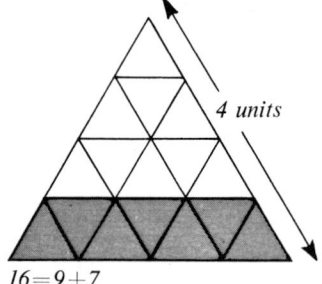

1 unit

1

2 units

4=1+3

3 units

9=4+5

4 units

16=9+7

Figure 31:15

The growth of similar rectangles

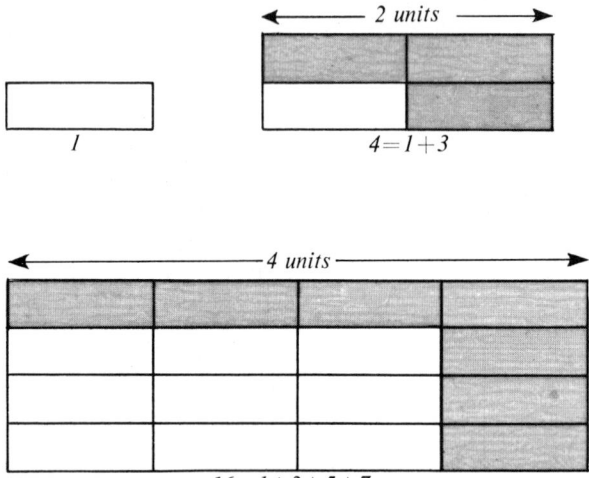

1

2 units

4=1+3

3 units

9=1+3+5

4 units

16=1+3+5+7

Figure 31:16

In Figure 31:14(*c*) the scale on the vertical axis is greatly reduced, and the block graph of Figure 31:14(*b*) is replaced by a line graph. Children will also see that they can make each square from the one before it by adding a border round two sides of the square, and that the number of squares in the border is always an odd number. They may write as a description of the building up of squares:

$$
\begin{aligned}
1 &= 1 = 1 \times 1 = 1^2 \\
1+3 &= 4 = 2 \times 2 = 2^2 \\
1+3+5 &= 9 = 3 \times 3 = 3^2 \\
1+3+5+7 &= 16 = 4 \times 4 = 4^2 \\
1+3+5+7+9 &= 25 = 5 \times 5 = 5^2
\end{aligned}
$$

Situations such as this, where a number pattern is repeated, will often lead children to begin to generalize, at first in words such as, 'if you add together the first 5 odd numbers, the sum is 5^2'; later, the generalization

will be algebraic: 'the sum of the first n odd numbers is n^2'. At this stage a child will confidently predict that the sum of the first 32 odd numbers will be 32^2; if a desk calculating machine is available he may enjoy verifying his prediction, and watching perfect squares being formed in the product register of the machine (*see page* 166) as he adds successive odd numbers.

The growth of other shapes than squares follows the same law. If larger equilateral triangles are built out of small equilateral triangles (Figure 31:15), or if larger rectangles are built out of small rectangles such as those represented by Cuisenaire rods (Figure 31:16), provided that all the shapes formed are *similar* (*see page* 391), then the law of growth will be that of the perfect square.[7]

[7] This illustrates the fact that the areas of *similar figures are proportional to the squares of corresponding slides* (*see page 394*).

322

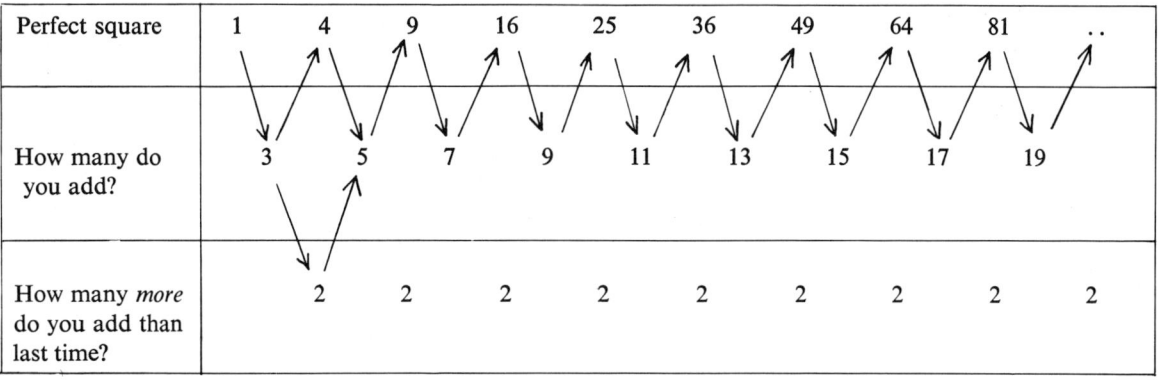

Perfect square	1	4	9	16	25	36	49	64	81	..
How many do you add?		3	5	7	9	11	13	15	17	19
How many *more* do you add than last time?		2	2	2	2	2	2	2	2	2

Figure 31:17

Children may find the tabulation of the growth of perfect squares interesting (Figure 31:17). It can be used to investigate the construction of many other sequences. The last line of the table is probably unnecessary in this case, but it is useful when dealing with more complicated sequences.

When they have seen how the pattern of 1, 1+3, 1+3+5, 1+3+5+7, ... behaves, children may wish to investigate other regular growth patterns, such as

1, 1+2, 1+2+3, 1+2+3+4, ... (sums of natural numbers)

2, 2+4, 2+4+6, 2+4+6+8, ... (sums of even natural numbers)

or to examine the growth of cubes and other shapes. Some of these growth patterns are investigated in the next two sections.

Triangular numbers and rectangular numbers

If circular counters are used instead of equilateral triangles to build up a growth pattern rather like that of Figure 31:15, it will be found that the counters can conveniently be packed as shown in Figure 31:18.

The *triangular numbers* 1, 3, 6, 10, 15, 21, ... are also found in the building of 'staircases' with structural apparatus (Figure 31:19). The triangular numbers do not follow such an easily recognizable growth pattern as do the square numbers, but two equal staircases can always be fitted together to make a rectangle (Figure 31:20) by turning one of them upside down.

All these rectangles have a length greater by one unit than their width; that is, if the width is n units, the length is $(n+1)$ units.[8] This fact can be used to calculate the value of any triangular number. For instance, the last rectangle in Figure 31:20 shows that:

$$2 \times (1+2+3+4+\ldots+9+10) = 10 \times 11,$$

so that

$$1+2+3+\ldots+9+10 = \frac{10 \times 11}{2}$$

[8] The numbers of unit squares in these rectangles, 1×2, 2×3, 3×4, 4×5, ... were called by the Greeks *rectangular numbers*. This name is confusing, as any *composite* number of unit squares can be arranged in a rectangle.

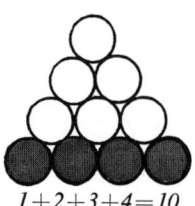

1 *1+2=3* *1+2+3=6* *1+2+3+4=10* *1+2+3+4+5=15*

Figure 31:18

The growth of staircases;
the triangular or staircase
numbers.

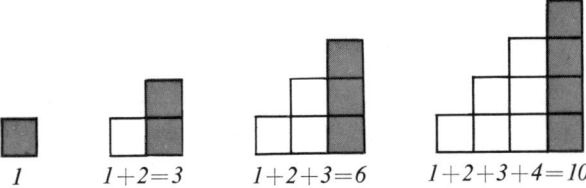

1   1+2=3   1+2+3=6   1+2+3+4=10

Figure 31:19

For successive triangular numbers the pattern is:

first triangular number $= 1 = \dfrac{1 \times 2}{2}$

second triangular number $= 1+2 = \dfrac{2 \times 3}{2}$

third triangular number $= 1+2+3 = \dfrac{3 \times 4}{2}$

fourth triangular number $= 1+2+3+4 = \dfrac{4 \times 5}{2}$

and in general:

nth triangular number $= 1+2+3+ \ldots +n$
$$= \dfrac{n(n+1)}{2}$$

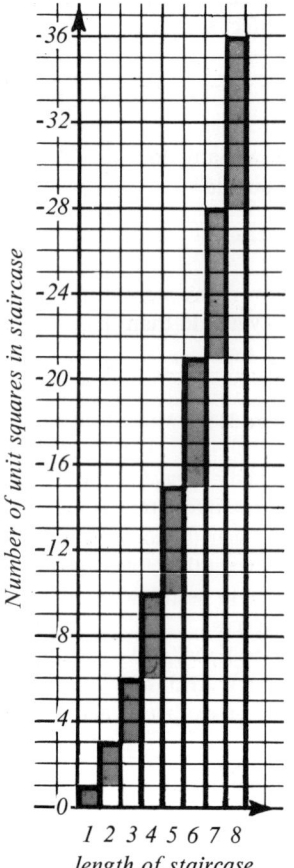

Number of unit squares in staircase

1 2 3 4 5 6 7 8
length of staircase

The triangular numbers make rectangles

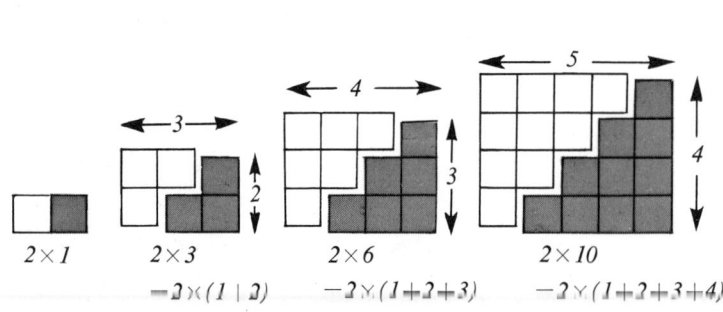

2×1 2×3 2×6 2×10
        $= 2 \times (1+2)$ $= 2 \times (1+2+3)$ $= 2 \times (1+2+3+4)$

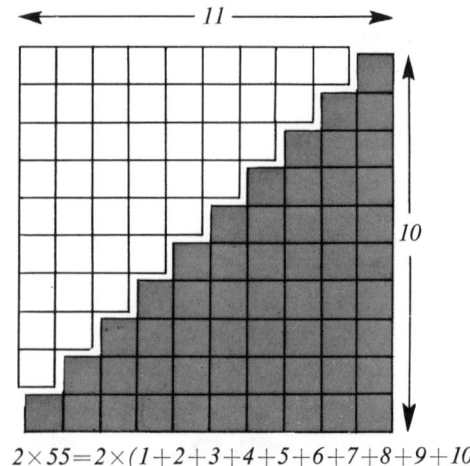

$2 \times 55 = 2 \times (1+2+3+4+5+6+7+8+9+10)$

Figure 31:20
324

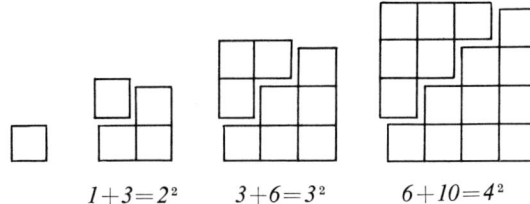

$1+3=2^2$ $3+6=3^2$ $6+10=4^2$

Figure 31:21

This generalization is sufficiently straightforward for some children to make it spontaneously. Children may also notice that the sum of two successive triangular numbers is a square number (Figure 31:21). The series of triangular numbers can therefore be constructed from the series of square numbers by subtracting a triangular number from the appropriate square number to give the next triangular number:

$$2^2 - \ 1 = \ 3$$
$$3^2 - \ 3 = \ 6$$
$$4^2 - \ 6 = 10$$
$$5^2 - 10 = 15 \text{ etc.}$$

Figure 31:22 shows the natural numbers, triangular numbers and square numbers arranged in one table.

The arrows indicate how the triangular and square numbers can be built up from the natural numbers by addition.

Cubes, tetrahedra and pyramids

Children may investigate the growth of cubes, in the same way that the growth of squares was examined, by building up small cubes to make larger cubes. The pattern of growth is shown in Figure 31:23, together with a graph of the cubes of natural numbers. Because of the increasingly rapid growth of cubes, it is impracticable to use the same scale on both axes of the graph. The making of this graph will help a child to visualize a rate of growth which increases very rapidly, and to foresee without using actual materials what will happen in later cases, for it rapidly becomes impracticable physically to build larger cubes.[9]

[9] We have seen a (very advanced) six-year-old building this sequence, using a box of 1000 one-inch cubes. As he built the larger cubes he was able to calculate mentally (without counting) the number of units which each one contained.

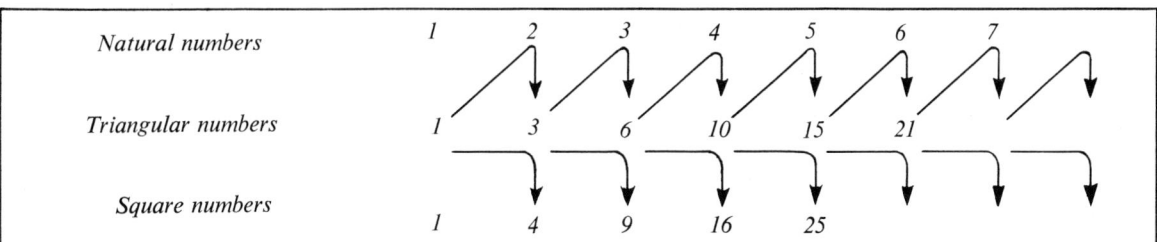

Figure 31:22

The growth of cubes

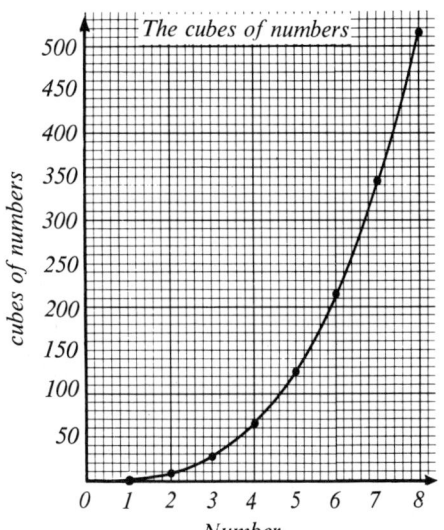

Figure 31:23

Exploration of the number of units which must be added in order to turn each cube into the next one also gives interesting results. Here the Dienes Multibase Arithmetic Blocks are useful, and children will find that in order to turn each cube into the next cube they must add 3 square layers, 3 rods and a unit cube (Figure 31:24).

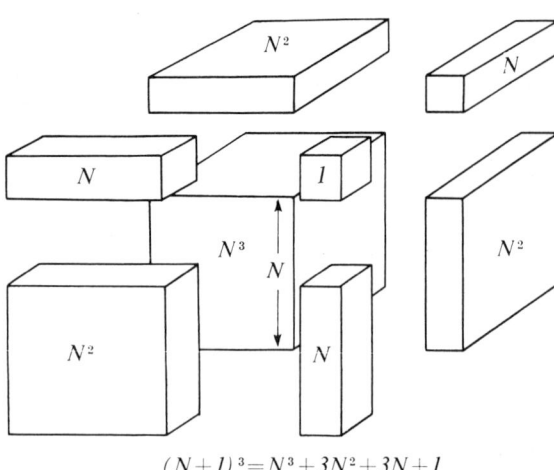

$$(N+1)^3 = N^3 + 3N^2 + 3N + 1$$

Figure 31:24[10]

It should now be possible to tabulate the growth of cubes (Figure 31:25) and to use the table to build up the cubes of larger numbers, for the last line of the table is very easily extended.

In the table, the numbers in heavy type have been obtained from Figure 31:23; the rest of the table is built up from the last line, as indicated by the arrows.

Other suitable topics for investigation are the growth of piles of spheres in the shape of tetrahedra (Figure 31:26)

[10] Similarly, in 2 dimensions each square layer can be turned into the next one by the addition of 2 rods and a unit cube:
$$(N+1)^2 = N^2 + 2N + 1.$$

or square pyramids (Figure 31:27). Practical experiment with these topics is very easy if spherical beads are used.

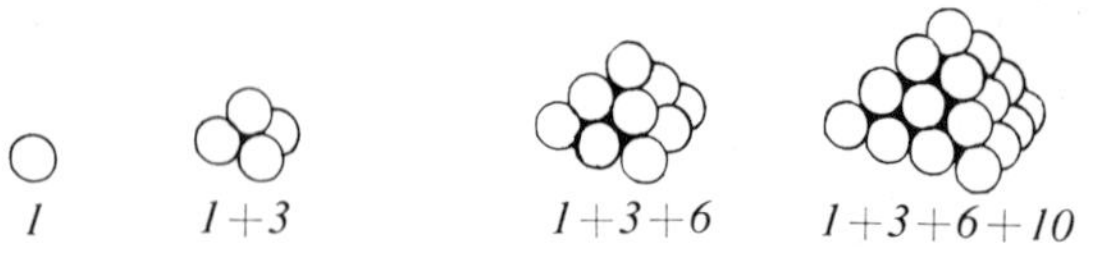

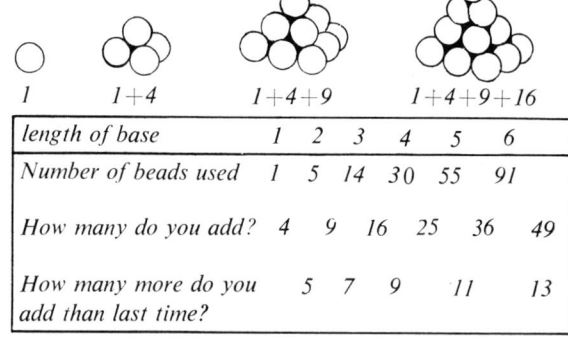

length of base	1	2	3	4	5	6
Number of beads used	1	4	10	20	35	
How many do you add?		3	6	10	15	
How many more do you add than last time?			3	4	5	6

Figure 31:26

The number of beads in each layer of the triangular pyramid is a triangular number.

1   1+4   1+4+9   1+4+9+16

length of base		1	2	3	4	5	6
Number of beads used		1	5	14	30	55	91
How many do you add?	4	9	16	25	36		49
How many more do you add than last time?			5	7	9	11	13

Figure 31:27

The number of beads in each layer of the square pyramid is a perfect square.

Side of cube	1	2	3	4	5	6	7	8	9	10
Number of unit cubes used	1	8	27	64	125	216	343	512	. . . .	.
How many do you add?		7	19	37	61	91	127	169	217	. . .
How many more do you add than last time			12	18	24	30	36	42	48	54

Figure 31:25

326

A door-mat forms a suitable base for the pile, and a nail passed through the hole in each bead in the bottom layer will hold it sufficiently firmly in position for a stable pyramid to be built. Alternatively, balls of clay may be used.

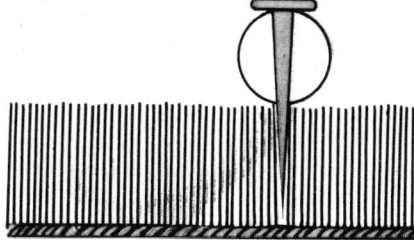

Figure 31:28

Magic squares

If numbers are arranged at random in a square array such as

11	13	15
2	4	8
5	9	7

children can use the square when practising addition:

				Sum of row
	11	13	15	39
	2	4	8	14
	5	9	7	21
sum of column	18	26	30	

There are some ingeniously arranged square arrays of numbers such that the sums of every row, every column, and both diagonals are equal. Such squares are called *magic squares*, and have attracted mathematicians as well as children of all ages for thousands of years. The earliest known magic square is the Chinese 'lo-shu', which has the same number of dots in every row, every column and both diagonals. It is shown in its original form in Figure 31:29, together with a translation into Arabic numerals; it was known at least as early as 1000 B.C., and is engraved on charms worn in the East today.[11] In this the consecutive natural numbers 1, 2, 3, 4, 5, 6, 7, 8, 9 have been used.

We shall call a magic square which uses consecutive natural numbers starting at 1 a *standard* magic square. There are, however, many magic squares which are not standard. Figure 31:30 shows a standard magic square of

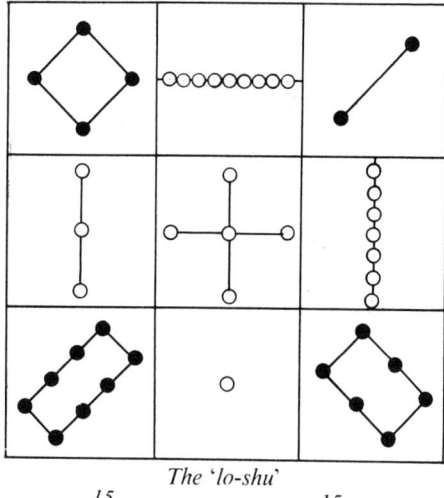

The 'lo-shu'

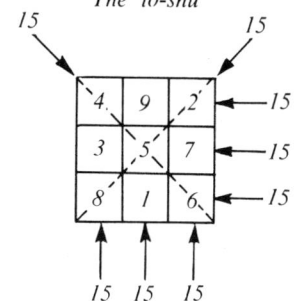

Figure 31:29

the *fourth order*.[12] The sum of each row, column and diagonal of a *standard* magic square is easily predicted. A fourth-order square contains the numbers 1, 2, 3, ..., 15, 16, so that the sum of all the numbers in the square[13] is

$$1+2+3+\ldots+15+16 = \frac{16 \times 17}{2}$$
$$= 8 \times 17$$
$$= 136$$

The sum of each row must be $\frac{1}{4}$ of the total for the square, or 34. Similarly, the constant sum of each row, column or diagonal of a standard fifth-order magic square[14] is:

$$\tfrac{1}{5} \text{ of } (1+2+3+\ldots+24+25) = \tfrac{1}{5} \text{ of } \frac{(25 \times 26)}{2}$$
$$= \frac{25 \times 26}{5 \times 2}$$
$$= 65$$

---

[11] See Smith, D. E. *History of Mathematics* (Ginn, 1923), I, page 28.

[12] The *order* of a magic square is the number of unit squares in each side.

[13] This is a triangular number (*see page 324*).

[14] This constant sum is the *magic constant* of the square.

A standard fourth-order magic square

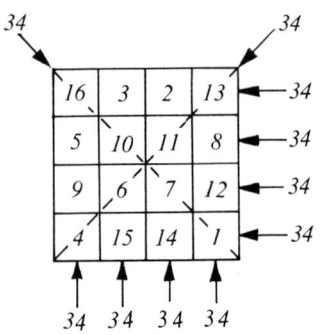

Figure 31:30[15]

Once a magic square has been constructed, more magic squares can be made from it, by adding, subtracting, multiplying or dividing every number in the square by the same number, or by rotating the square, or reflecting it in one of its axes of symmetry (*see page* 104). Figure 31:31 shows some variations on a standard magic square of the third order.

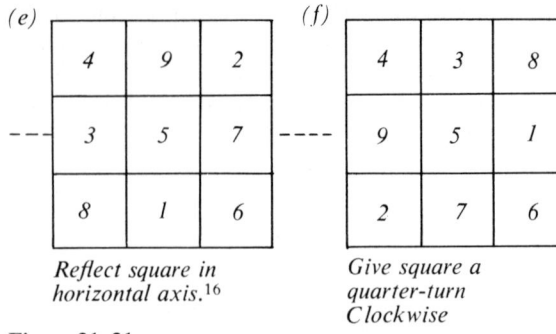

(e) Reflect square in horizontal axis.[16]

(f) Give square a quarter-turn Clockwise

Figure 31:31

When a teacher or a child has devised a magic square, he will be able to make variations on it. At first, children will be content to find out whether a given square is magic or not; later, they will be able to fill in the missing numbers in squares such as those shown in Figure 31:32, and finally some children may wish to make their own magic squares, either by trial and error or by following some of the methods suggested in the books listed below.[17]

(a)

8	1	6
3	5	7
4	9	2

Standard magic square of third order

(b)

16	9	14
11	13	15
12	17	10

Add 8 to every number in the square.
Magic constant $=39$
$=15+3\times8$

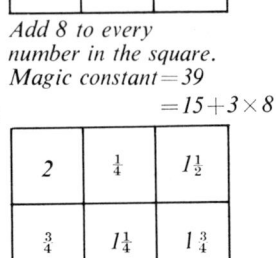

		2
3	5	7

16		
	13	15

Magic constant $=39$

Figure 31:32

(c)

7	0	5
2	4	6
3	8	1

Subtract 1 from every number in the square.
Magic constant $=12$
$=15-3\times1$

(d)

2	$\frac{1}{4}$	$1\frac{1}{2}$
$\frac{3}{4}$	$1\frac{1}{4}$	$1\frac{3}{4}$
1	$2\frac{1}{4}$	$\frac{1}{2}$

Divide every number in the square by 4.
Magic constant $=3\frac{3}{4}$
$=15\div4$

Continued on next column

Multiplication devices

Many efforts have been made over the centuries to remove the drudgery from long multiplication and division. Among the devices in use at the present day are logarithms, the slide rule, the desk calculating machine and the electronic calculator. Two earlier devices for multiplying will interest older primary school children. The first of these, finger multiplication, was used in the Middle Ages.

[16] Turn it upside down.

[15] This magic square appears in an engraving by Albrecht Dürer, entitled *Melancolia,* made in 1514. The two central numbers in the bottom row give the date of the picture. See Gardner, M. *More Mathematical Puzzles and Diversions* (Bell, 1963), page 93.

[17] Andrews, W. S. *Magic Squares and Cubes* (Dover, 1960). Ball, W. W. Rouse. *Mathematical Recreations and Essays* (Macmillan, 11th ed., 1939). Dudeney, H. E. *Amusements in Mathematics* (Nelson, 1917).

The second, Napier's Rods, was invented in 1617, but was an adaption of a method used much earlier in many parts of the world.[18]

Finger multiplication enables a person who only knows multiplication tables up to 5×5 to obtain products up to 9×9. Each number to be multiplied is represented on the fingers of one hand; the number of fingers raised is the difference between the number and 5 (Figure 31:33).

Representing 9 and 6 on the fingers

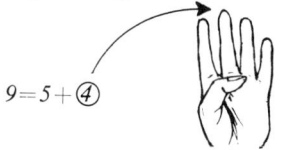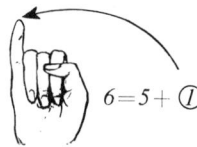

$9 = 5 + ④$ $6 = 5 + ①$

Figure 31:33

Then the tens digit of 9×6 is the *sum* of the numbers of fingers raised; the units digit of 9×6 is the *product* of the numbers of fingers not raised (Figure 31:34).

Finger multiplication of 9×6

Tens digit = 4 + 1 = 5

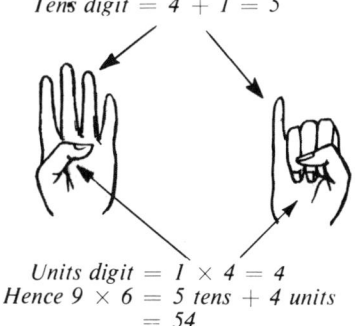

Units digit = 1 × 4 = 4
Hence 9 × 6 = 5 tens + 4 units
            = 54

Figure 31:34

Finger multiplication of 7×6
Tens digit = 1 + 2 = 3

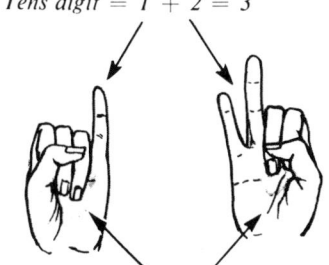

Units digit = 4 × 3 = 12
Hence 7 × 6 = 3 tens + 12 units
            = 42

Figure 31:35

[18] See Smith, D. E. *History of Mathematics* (Dover, 1958), II.

The explanation of finger multiplication is shown in the general case in Figure 31:36.

Finger multiplication of $(5+a) \times (5+b)$

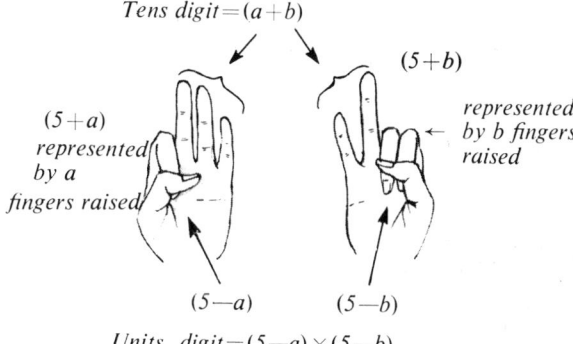

Tens digit $= (a+b)$

$(5+a)$ represented by a fingers raised

$(5+b)$ represented by b fingers raised

$(5-a)$ $(5-b)$

Units digit $= (5-a) \times (5-b)$

Figure 31:36

Finger multiplication gives

$$
\begin{aligned}
(a+b) &\text{ tens} + (5-a) \times (5-b) \text{ units} \\
&= 10(a+b) + (5-a)(5-b) \\
&= 10a + 10b + 25 - 5a - 5b + ab \\
&= 25 + 5a + 5b + ab \\
&= (5+a)(5+b)
\end{aligned}
$$

Napier's Rods are an ingenious mechanical device for performing long multiplication. John Napier (1550–1617), laird of Merchiston, Edinburgh, devoted much of his life to the improvement of methods of calculation. The invention of logarithms was undoubtedly his greatest work, but he also published in 1617 an account of 'numeration by little rods'. Each multiplication table up to 9 was written on a small rod, as shown in Figure 31:37, with the units digit and tens digit of a number each occupying half of a square cell.

Napier's Rods

0	1	2	3	4	5	6	7	8	9
0	1	2	3	4	5	6	7	8	9
0	2	4	6	8	1/0	1/2	1/4	1/6	1/8
0	3	6	9	1/2	1/5	1/8	2/1	2/4	2/7
0	4	8	1/2	1/6	2/0	2/4	2/8	3/2	3/6
0	5	1/0	1/5	2/0	2/5	3/0	3/5	4/0	4/5
0	6	1/2	1/8	2/4	3/0	3/6	4/2	4/8	5/4
0	7	1/4	2/1	2/8	3/5	4/2	4/9	5/6	6/3
0	8	1/6	2/4	3/2	4/0	4/8	5/6	6/4	7/2
0	9	1/8	2/7	3/6	4/5	5/4	6/3	7/2	8/1

Figure 31:37

In order to form multiples of such a number as 768 the 7 rod, the 6 rod, and the 8 rod are placed side by side. The multiples of 768 can then be read off as shown in Figure 31:38. Carrying from one column into the next is performed by diagonal addition, since tens of units and units of tens must occur in the same column, and tens of tens and units of hundreds must occur in the same column.

Multiples of 768

(a)

7	6	8	
7	6	8	$1 \times 768 = 768$
1/4	1/2	1/6	$2 \times 768 = 1536$
2/1	1/8	2/4	$3 \times 768 = 2304$
2/8	2/4	2	$4 \times 768 = 3072$
3/5	3/0	4/0	$5 \times 768 = 3840$
4/2	3/6	4/8	$6 \times 768 = 4608$
4/9	4/2	5/6	$7 \times 768 = 5376$
5/6	4/8	6/4	$8 \times 768 = 6144$
6/3	5/6	7/2	$9 \times 768 = 6932$

Figure 31:38

(b) Dealing with carrying figures:

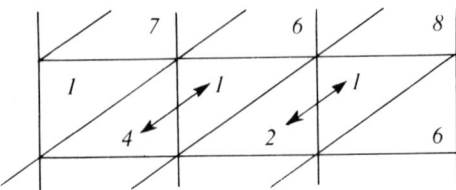

$$2 \times \quad 8 = \quad 16$$
$$2 \times \ 60 = \ 120$$
$$2 \times 700 = 1400$$
$$\overline{\qquad} \ \ \overline{\qquad}$$
$$2 \times 768 = 1536$$
$$\overline{\qquad} \ \ \overline{\qquad}$$

330

32 Extending the Number System and its Notation

Introduction

We saw in Chapter 26 how a child gradually absorbs the set of natural numbers, which are the first numbers he understands, within the larger set of signless rational numbers. He is now in command of a set of numbers large enough and flexible enough to satisfy most of his immediate mathematical needs. In this chapter we summarize the behaviour and properties of the signless rational numbers, and discuss some of their inadequacies. We shall find situations within the experience of children in the middle years of schooling which point to the need for further extensions of the number system. We shall therefore generalize and extend the system of notation which we use for writing numbers.

The signless rational numbers

We recall that in Chapter 26 a *signless rational number* was described as a number which could be expressed as a *ratio* of two natural numbers (the second of which is not zero). Every rational number can be written in a variety of ways by using equivalent fractions or the decimal notation. Examples of signless rational numbers are

$$3 = \frac{3}{1} = \frac{6}{2} = \frac{9}{3} = \frac{12}{4} = \ldots = 3 \cdot 0$$

$$\frac{2}{5} = \frac{4}{10} = \frac{6}{15} = \frac{8}{20} = \frac{10}{25} = \ldots = 0 \cdot 4$$

$$0 = \frac{0}{1} = \frac{0}{2} = \frac{0}{3} = \frac{0}{4} = \ldots = 0 \cdot 0$$

$$\frac{1}{3} = \frac{2}{6} = \frac{3}{9} = \frac{4}{12} = \frac{5}{15} = \ldots = 0 \cdot 333\ldots = 0 \cdot \dot{3}$$

Each signless rational number is represented by a point on the number line, and the set of natural numbers, which are used for counting, forms a subset of the set of signless rational numbers.[1] All signless rational numbers have decimal representations, either terminating or recurring.

The set of signless rational numbers has one great advantage as a mathematical tool over the set of natural numbers. This advantage can be expressed either practically or theoretically. The practical usefulness of the rational numbers is that they make measurement possible to any desired degree of accuracy. A metre is not a sufficiently small unit of measurement to measure the length of a book; the smaller unit of the centimetre is necessary.

A centimetre is not a small enough unit to measure the thickness of a page. Two courses of action are possible: a smaller unit such as a micrometre could be used, and the thickness of the page described by a natural number of the smaller units, for instance, 70 micrometres. Secondly, fractions of a centimetre could be used and the thickness of the page described in thousandths of a centimetre. The second system is more flexible and can be adapted, without the invention of new units, to stating the thickness of a human hair. The fact that a unit can be divided into smaller and smaller parts, and these parts described by rational numbers, makes the use of the set of signless rational numbers indispensable for all measurement.

This same advantage which the signless rational numbers have over the natural numbers can be described theoretically as: the set of signless rational numbers is *closed for division* (except for division by zero). We recall that the set of natural numbers is not closed for division (*see page* 86) since although some divisions of natural numbers. such as $12 \div 4$, have answers which are natural numbers, there are many natural numbers such as 12 and 5 which cannot be divided exactly to give a result which is a natural number. That is, there is no natural number n such that $5 \times n = 12$, so that $12 \div 5 = n$ has no solution within the set of natural numbers. But if we work in the set of signless rational numbers, not only can the rational number 12 be divided by the rational number 5 to give the rational number $\frac{12}{5}$, or $2\frac{2}{5}$, but *any* pair of rational numbers can be divided to give a result which is a rational number (unless the second one is zero). For instance,

$$\frac{3}{5} \div 2\frac{1}{2} = \frac{3}{5} \div \frac{5}{2}$$
$$= \frac{6}{10} \div \frac{25}{10}$$
$$= \frac{6}{25}$$

This complete freedom to perform division (except by zero), as well as addition and multiplication, of *any* rational numbers, is a considerable theoretical advantage. Among the natural numbers the only operations which can be performed with complete freedom, and the certainty that the result will be a natural number, are addition and multiplication.[2] The link between the theoretical and practical aspects of this improvement is that the rational numbers allow one to state the result of dividing 1 unit

---

[1] Strictly speaking the set of natural numbers is *isomorphic* to a subset of the set of signless rational numbers.

[2] The set of natural numbers is *closed for addition and multiplication (see page 86)*.

of measurement into, say, 10 equal parts, that is, to perform $1 \div 10$, which was not possible in the set of natural numbers.

The problem of subtraction has, however, not been solved among these signless rational numbers. There are many pairs of natural numbers whose subtraction cannot be performed within the set of natural numbers, such as $3-7$. But there are also many pairs of signless rational numbers, such as $3-7$, $2\frac{1}{2}-3\frac{1}{3}$, or $0-2\cdot3$, whose subtraction cannot be performed within the set of signless rational numbers. The set of signless rational numbers, like the set of natural numbers, is *not closed for subtraction*.

Our next extension of the number system will be the construction of a set of numbers which is closed for subtraction as well as for addition, multiplication and division. Before doing so, however, we notice that the laws of behaviour of the natural numbers, which we listed in Chapter 18 (*see page* 171) are exactly paralleled, with one exception, by laws for the behaviour of the signless rational numbers. Since all methods of performing arithmetical calculations depend on these laws, it follows that the arithmetical methods which children learn to use when calculating with natural numbers have exact parallels in calculation with signless rational numbers. We now list the laws for the behaviour of natural numbers which were stated in Chapter 18, alongside the corresponding laws for the signless rational numbers.[3]

LAWS FOR ADDITION AND SUBTRACTION

Natural numbers

Signless rational numbers

1. *Closure for addition*
The set of natural numbers is closed for addition; that is, the sum of any pair of natural numbers is a natural number.

1. *Closure for addition*
The set of signless rational numbers is closed for addition; that is the sum of any pair of signless rational numbers is a signless rational number.

2. *The commutative law for addition*
For any natural numbers a and b,
$$a+b = b+a$$

2. *The commutative law for addition*
For any signless rational numbers $\frac{p}{q}$ and $\frac{r}{s}$,
$$\frac{p}{q}+\frac{r}{s} = \frac{r}{s}+\frac{p}{q}$$

3. *The associative law for addition*
For any natural numbers a, b and c,
$$(a+b)+c = a+(b+c)$$

3. *The associative law for addition*
For any signless rational numbers $\frac{p}{q}$, $\frac{r}{s}$ and $\frac{t}{u}$,
$$\left(\frac{p}{q}+\frac{r}{s}\right)+\frac{t}{u} = \frac{p}{q}+\left(\frac{r}{s}+\frac{t}{u}\right)$$

5. *The identity for addition*
The natural number 0 is the identity for addition. For any natural number n,
$$n+0 = 0+n = n$$

5. *The identity for addition*
The rational number 0 is the identity for addition. For any signless rational number $\frac{p}{q}$,
$$\frac{p}{q}+0 = 0+\frac{p}{q} = \frac{p}{q}$$

[3] The numbering of the laws corresponds to that of Chapter 18, page 171. Law 4, the distributive law, occurs among the multiplication laws on page 333.

6. Subtraction

Subtraction is the inverse operation of addition.

$$a - b = x$$

means

$$b + x = a.$$

The set of natural numbers is *not closed for subtraction*; many equations such as

$$7 + x = 3$$

have no solutions in the set of natural numbers.

6. Subtraction

Subtraction is the inverse operation of addition.

$$\frac{p}{q} - \frac{r}{s} = x$$

means

$$\frac{r}{s} + x = \frac{p}{q}$$

The set of signless rational numbers is *not closed for subtraction*; many equations such as

$$3\tfrac{1}{3} + x = 2\tfrac{1}{2}$$

have no solutions in the set of signless rational numbers.

LAWS FOR MULTIPLICATION AND DIVISION

1′. Closure for multiplication

The set of natural numbers is closed for multiplication; that is, the product of any pair of natural numbers is a natural number.

1′. Closure for multiplication

The set of signless rational numbers is closed for multiplication; that is, the product of any pair of signless rational numbers is a signless rational number.

2′. The commutative law for multiplication

For any natural numbers a and b,

$$a \times b = b \times a$$

2′. The commutative law for multiplication

For any signless rational numbers $\dfrac{p}{q}$ and $\dfrac{r}{s}$,

$$\frac{p}{q} \times \frac{r}{s} = \frac{r}{s} \times \frac{p}{q}$$

3′. The associative law for multiplication

For any natural numbers, a, b and c

$$(a \times b) \times c = a \times (b \times c)$$

3′. The associative law for multiplication

For any signless rational numbers $\dfrac{p}{q}$, $\dfrac{r}{s}$ and $\dfrac{t}{u}$,

$$\left(\frac{p}{q} \times \frac{r}{s}\right) \times \frac{t}{u} = \frac{p}{q} \times \left(\frac{r}{s} \times \frac{t}{u}\right)$$

4′. The distributive law

For any natural numbers, a, b and c

$$a \times (b + c) = (a \times b) + (a \times c)$$

and

$$(a + b) \times c = (a \times c) + (b \times c)$$

4′. The distributive law

For any signless rational numbers $\dfrac{p}{q}$, $\dfrac{r}{s}$ and $\dfrac{t}{u}$,

$$\frac{p}{q} \times \left(\frac{r}{s} + \frac{t}{u}\right) = \left(\frac{p}{q} \times \frac{r}{s}\right) + \left(\frac{p}{q} \times \frac{t}{u}\right), \text{ and}$$

$$\left(\frac{p}{q} + \frac{r}{s}\right) \times \frac{t}{u} = \left(\frac{p}{q} \times \frac{t}{u}\right) + \left(\frac{r}{s} \times \frac{t}{u}\right)$$

5′. The identity for multiplication

The natural number 1 is the identity for multiplication; for any natural number n

$$n \times 1 = 1 \times n = n$$

5′. The identity for multiplication

The signless rational number 1 is the identity for multiplication; for any signless rational number $\dfrac{p}{q}$,

$$\frac{p}{q} \times 1 = 1 \times \frac{p}{q} = \frac{p}{q}$$

6′. Division

Division is the inverse operation of multiplication;

$$a \div b = x$$

means

$$b \times x = a$$

The set of natural numbers is not closed for division; many equations such as

$$7 \times x = 3$$

have no solution in the set of natural numbers.

6′. Division

Division is the inverse operation of multiplication;

$$\frac{p}{q} \div \frac{r}{s} = x$$

means

$$\frac{r}{s} \times x = \frac{p}{q}$$

The set of signless rational numbers is closed for division; except by zero. Every equation such as

$$7 \times x = 3$$

or

$$\tfrac{2}{3} \times x = \tfrac{4}{5}$$

has a solution in the set of signless rational numbers. The only such equations without solutions are of the type

$$0 \times x = 3$$

Hence $3 \div 0$, and other divisions by zero, are not possible.

It will be seen that the only difference in behaviour between the natural numbers and the signless rational numbers is in Law 6′, which expresses the nearest we can get to closure for division. We have not yet, however, obtained a set of numbers which is closed for subtraction. We now try to find a set of numbers which will have as much as possible of the structure of the signless rational numbers, but will have the additional property of being closed for subtraction. We begin by examining some number situations for which the signless rational numbers are inadequate.

Situations which lead to directed numbers

If a thermometer is kept out of doors in the winter, children may obtain a graphical record containing temperatures below freezing point, as in Figure 32:1, and they will discuss how many degrees above or below freezing point the temperature is. The vertical axis of the graph may be labelled as in Figure 32:2, and a similar graph of indoor temperatures can be obtained by using a thermometer on which 20 °C is marked as 'room-heat'. Children may supplement a temperature graph by a diagram

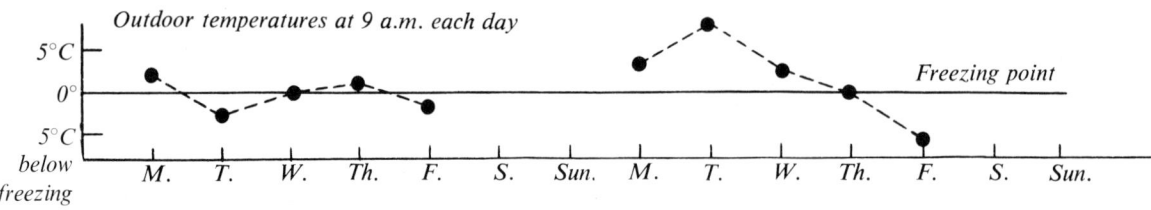

Figure 32:1

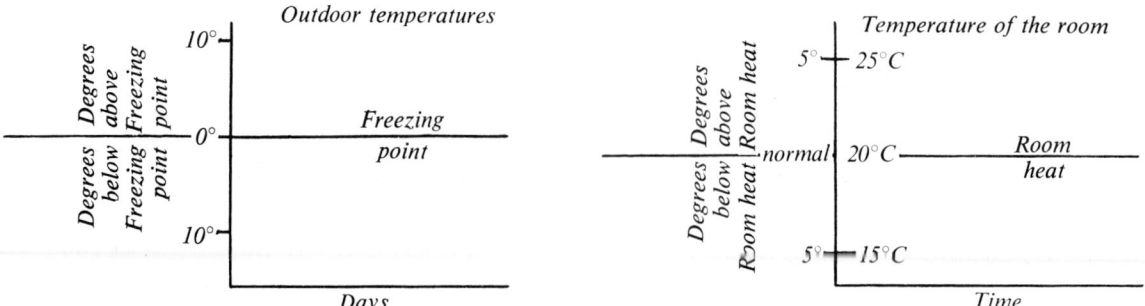

Figure 32:2

334

showing the rises and falls in temperature (Figure 32:3). In this situation, children need to measure in two opposite directions from a starting point, and they also use *movements* of temperature in two directions, that is, rises and falls in temperature.

A similar situation, in which measurements can be taken in two directions, arises when the children's average height is shown on a graph. Each child will know how much above or below the average height of the group he is (Figure 32:4(*a*)). The starting point of measurement need not, of course, be the average for the group. Figure 32:4(*b*) shows how far the children's masses are above or below 25 kilograms.

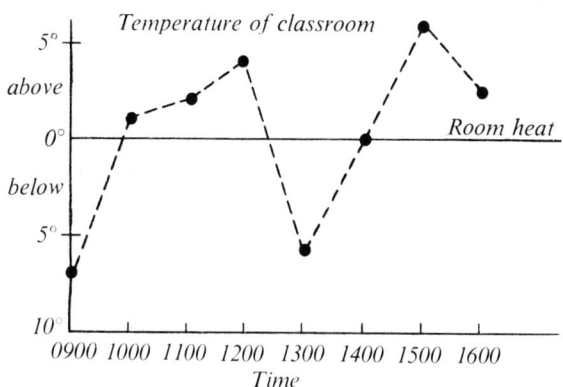

Figure 32:3

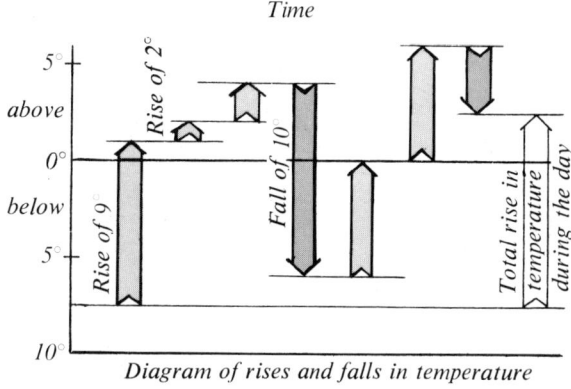

Diagram of rises and falls in temperature

a) Block graph of children's heights

b) Masses above and below 25 kg

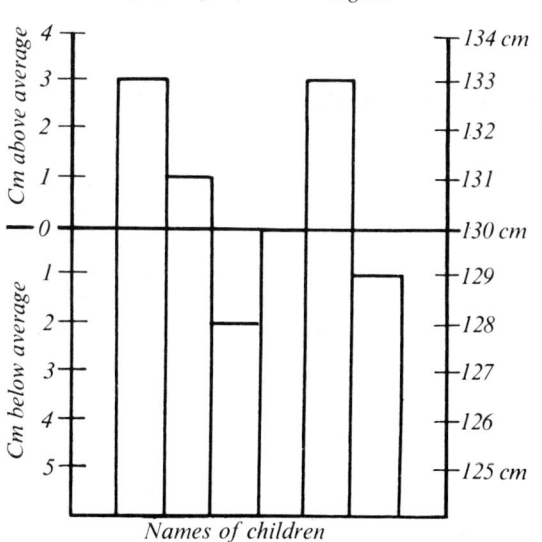

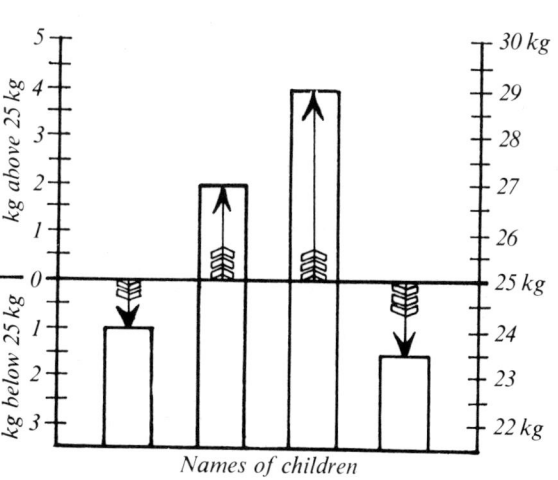

Figure 32:4

335

a) *A count-down before firing a missile*

b) *June 1944*

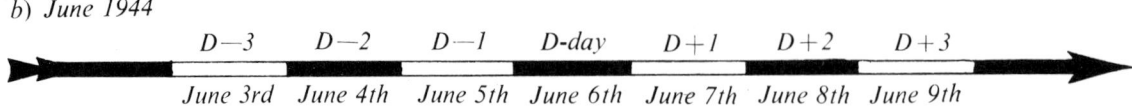

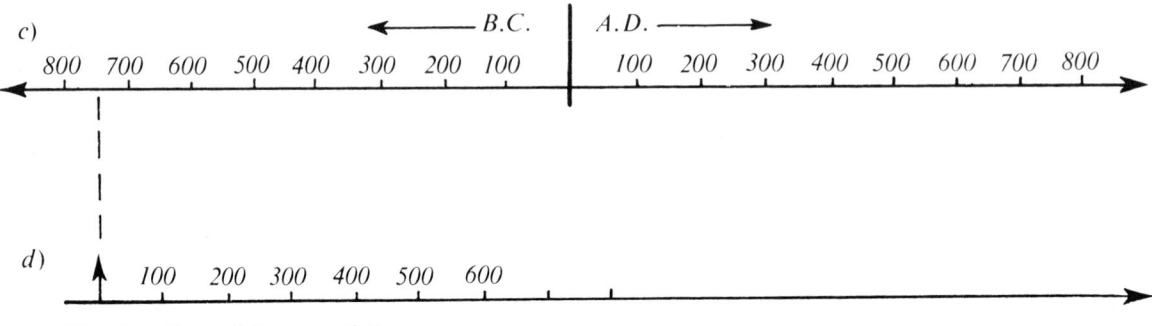

c)

d)

The founding of the city of Rome.

Figure 32:5

Children will be familiar with the 'count-down' before the firing of a rocket; teachers may remember days in June 1944 as 'D-day plus 1' etc., and (in retrospect) 'D-day minus 1'. Another time in history from which dates are measured in both directions is the year of Our Lord's birth, but many Roman chronologers reckoned dates from 'the founding of the city' (B.C. 753).

A variety of such examples will make it clear to children that it is often possible and convenient to measure in two opposite directions from a starting point or *origin*.

When measuring time, it is *necessary* to measure in both directions from an arbitrary starting point such as 'the founding of the city' as we cannot measure forward from the beginning of time. Temperature, too, must be measured in both directions from an arbitrary origin, unless we always measure temperatures from the absolute zero ($-273\,^{\circ}$C). These examples drive us to use the scale of measurement shown in Figure 32:6, which can be indefinitely extended in both directions.

The number line extends in both directions

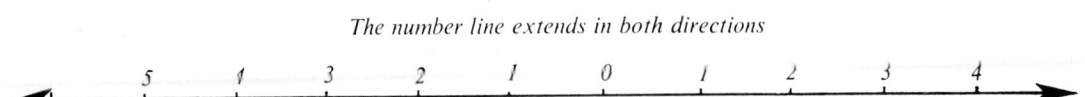

Figure 32:6

336

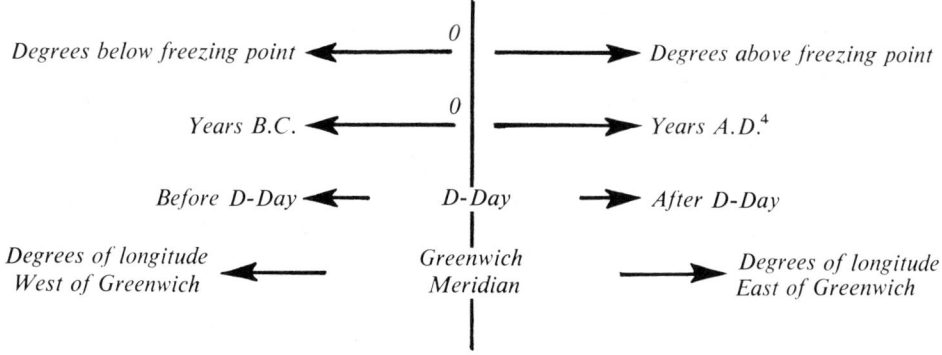

Figure 32:7

It is clearly necessary to distinguish between the two possible directions of measurement. This is done in a variety of ways, some of which are shown in Figure 32:7. Children may invent their own symbolism to show the two directions of measurement. Such a notation as (2 cm *A*) for '2 cm *above* average' and (3 cm *B*) for '3 cm *below* average' might be shortened to 2*A* and 3*B*, the letters *A* and *B* indicating opposite directions of measurement. Examination of a Celsius thermometer will show the usual convention of indicating a temperature such as 3 °C below freezing point as (−3) °C. Although this convention is in everyday use and children must eventually use it, the use of the minus sign with different meanings[5] tends to prevent real understanding of *directed numbers*.

Notation for directed numbers

The temperature (−3) °C means 3° below zero, and the minus sign shows a *direction*. In other uses of the minus sign, the sign appears between two numbers, as in 8−6, where it means, 'What must be added to 6 to make 8?'

[4] This is not a good example as, in their reckoning, historians make the year A.D. 1 follow immediately after 1 B.C., without a year 0. Astronomers, however, do use a year 0.

[5] See below.

or 'from 8, take away 6'. These two uses of the minus sign are very different; the second asks for the performance of an *arithmetical operation*, the first indicates a *direction of measurement*. It is undesirable that the same symbol should be used in such different contexts, but there is a strong pull towards conforming with long-accepted usage in notation. A convention which may help to overcome this difficulty, and which is in fairly common use in schools, is now stated.

It is desirable that *both* directions of measurement should be labelled, rather than only the 'below zero' direction, for they are of equal importance. If 3 °C below zero is described as (−3) °C, then 3 °C above zero should be labelled (+3) °C. Thus the signs (+) and (−) are used to show the two directions of measurement. Although these signs are the same as the signs for the arithmetical operations of addition and subtraction, children should realize that the signs are used in a different sense. Therefore a temperature of 3 °C above zero may be written (⁺3) °C, and a temperature of 3 °C below zero may be written (⁻3) °C. The changed position of the + and − signs shows their changed use. The sign (⁺3) may be read as *'positive three'* and (⁻3) as *'negative three'*, the words 'plus' and 'minus' being reserved for the arithmetical operations of addition and subtraction. With this convention, the double-ended number line, on which measurements can be made in both directions, takes the form shown in Figure 32:8. Fractions as well as whole numbers

Figure 32:8

337

take their places on this number line, for fractions of a unit can also be measured in both directions. The number line of Figure 32:9 is like that of Figure 20:21, but shows positive and negative directed numbers instead of signless rational numbers.

The set of directed whole numbers and fractions is called the set of *positive, negative and zero rational numbers,* or more briefly, the set of *rational numbers.* Every rational number has a set of equivalent fractional and decimal representations; for instance:

$$\frac{+2}{5} = \frac{+4}{10} = \frac{+6}{15} = \frac{+8}{20} = \ldots = {}^{+}0{\cdot}4$$
$$^{-}3 = \frac{-3}{1} = \frac{-6}{2} = \frac{-9}{3} = \frac{-12}{4} = \ldots = {}^{-}3{\cdot}0$$

The set of positive, negative and zero whole numbers is called the set of *integers.* The integers are shown in the first line of Figure 32:9. They form a subset of the set of rational numbers.

Children will probably extend their concept of number from the set of signless rational numbers to the complete set of rational numbers, without passing through an intermediate stage at which they understand the integers but not the negative fractions. It is, however, possible for children to understand the integers very early if they are given, from the beginning, experiences which lead them to attach the idea of direction to numbers, so that they meet the integers almost as soon as the natural numbers.

In Chapter 10, page 90, lengths which were measured in particular directions were called *vectors.* Directed numbers are examples of vectors. The integer ($^{+}3$) describes a measurement, or movement, of 3 units in the positive direction of the number line, and the integer ($^{-}4$) describes a measurement or movement of 4 units in the negative direction along the number line. It is important that the idea of movement should be associated with directed numbers, for it is only by thinking of directed numbers as vectors, and so associating them with movement, that children will be able to perform the operations of addition and subtraction on them. Although directed numbers are examples of vectors, they are, however, vectors which are exceedingly limited in direction. Vectors used in two or three dimensions to show movements can be in *any* direction in the space, but for directed numbers, the directions are limited to backwards and forwards on the number line. Directed numbers are one-dimensional vectors.

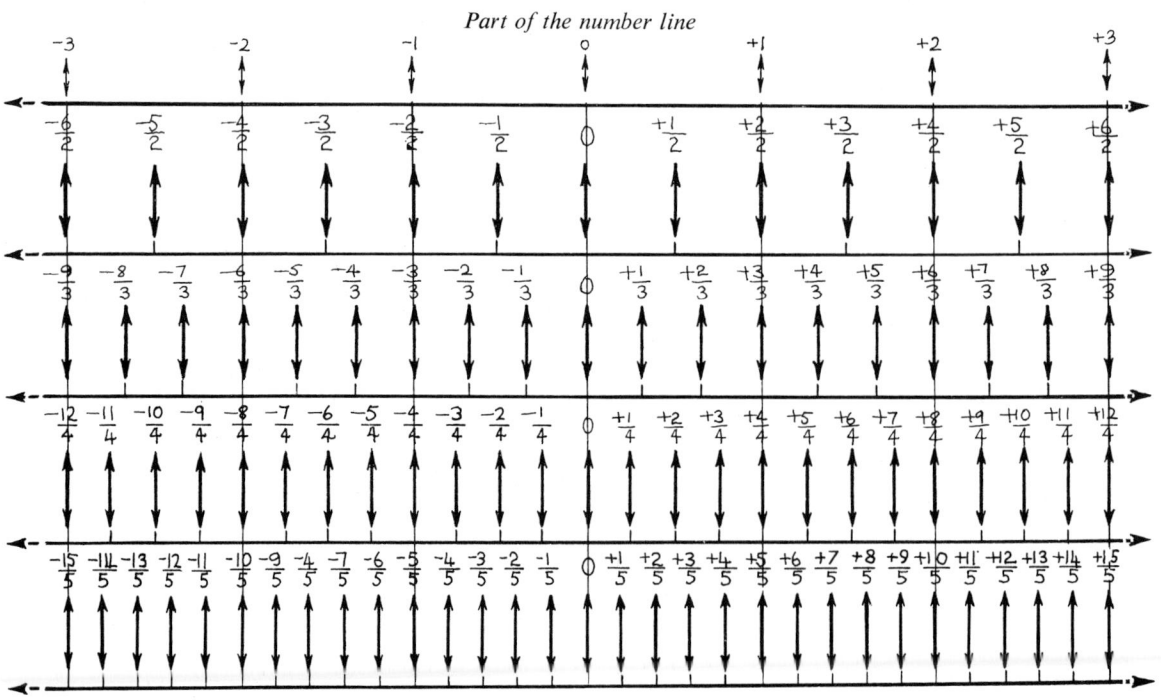

Part of the number line

Figure 32:9

338

Directed numbers as vectors; the addition of directed numbers

Following the movement of a lift up and down a tall building may help children to associate directed numbers with movements. In Figure 32:10 the floors above the ground floor are labelled $^{+}1$, $^{+}2$, $^{+}3$, ... the ground-floor stopping place is 0, and the basements are $^{-}1$, $^{-}2$, ...
A series of movements of the lift can be charted as shown on the right, and statements of the type shown below will be made:

(up 2 floors) followed by (up 3 floors)
$$= \text{(up 5 floors)}$$
(down 2 floors) followed by (down 3 floors)
$$= \text{(down 5 floors)}$$
(up 2 floors) followed by (down 3 floors)
$$= \text{(down 1 floor)}$$
(down 2 floors) followed by (up 3 floors)
$$= \text{(up 1 floor)}$$

These statements are statements about movements or vectors, and are true *whatever floor the lift starts from*. The notation, however, is cumbersome, and will be placed by a shorter and more conventional notation.

In Chapter 10 we defined the addition of vectors to mean:

(one vector) followed by (another vector),

and we wrote

(vector **a**) + (vector **b**)

If we use this convention the lift's first two movements become

$$\text{(up 2)} + \text{(up 3)} = \text{(up 5)}$$
$$\text{(down 2)} + \text{(down 3)} = \text{(down 5)}$$

These statements clearly fit well with the usual use of the addition sign, but the other two statements are less fortunate:

$$\text{(up 2)} + \text{(down 3)} = \text{(down 1)}$$
$$\text{(down 2)} + \text{(up 3)} = \text{(up 1)}$$

It is necessary, however, that the same sign must be used in all circumstances for the same operation, and having chosen '+' as the sign for the operation 'followed by' for vectors, this use must be maintained.

We now change the notation for (up 3) and (down 3). Since a movement (up 3) from the ground floor takes

Chart of a lift's journey

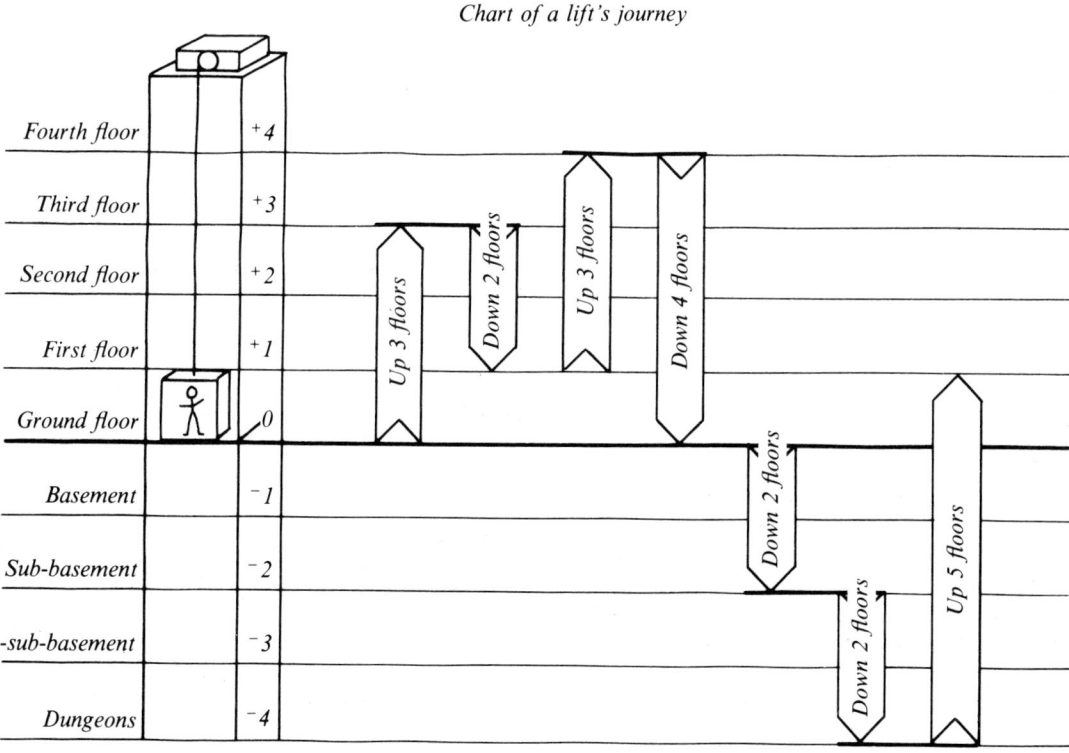

Figure 32:10

the lift to floor ($^+3$), the movement (up 3) is written ($^+3$) and the movement (down 3) is written ($^-3$). The statements about the lift now become:

$$(^+2)+(^+3)=(^+5)$$
$$(^-2)+(^-3)=(^-5)$$
$$(^+2)+(^-3)=(^-1)$$
$$(^-2)+(^+3)=(^+1)$$

The introduction of the addition of directed numbers has been derived from the illustration of the lift, but is clearly a general idea. There are two stages:

i) the notation ($^-3$) is used not only for a point on the number line, but also for the vector, or movement, of 3 units in the negative direction,[6]

ii) the addition of directed numbers is defined as vector addition.

For example, ($^-5$) + ($^+3$) = ($^-2$) means that (5 units in the negative direction) followed by (3 units in the positive direction) gives the same result as (2 units in the negative direction). This is shown in Figure 32:11.

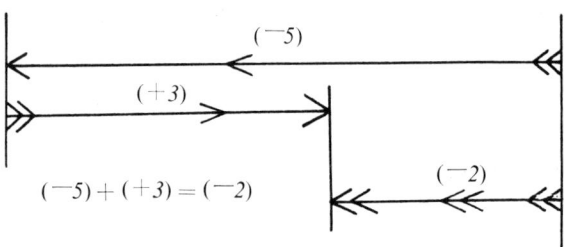

Figure 32:11

Every vector has its opposite, or *negative* (*see page 94*). which is a vector of the same length in the opposite direction. Clearly the opposite of ($^+3$) is ($^-3$) and the opposite of ($^-3$) is ($^+3$). We write the opposite of a vector **a** as $^-$**a**. In symbols, we therefore write

$$-(^+3)=(^-3) \quad \text{and} \quad -(^-3)=(^+3)$$

because

$$(^+3)+(^-3)=0.$$

When a child performs subtraction of natural numbers by measuring forwards and backwards with a tape-measure (*see page 83*), he often does it by *addition* of vectors. Figure 32:12 (which is the same as Figure 10:14) illustrates not only 9−3 but ($^+9$)+($^-3$). The child has replaced the subtraction of natural numbers 9−3 by

---

[6] No confusion is caused by this identification of the two ideas. Points cannot be added, but vectors can, so the context always makes the meaning clear.

340

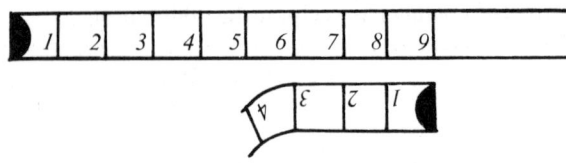

Figure 32:12

the *addition* of ($^+9$) and ($^-3$), which is the opposite of ($^+3$). The addition of vectors in opposite directions therefore resembles the subtraction of natural numbers. The addition ($^+9$)+($^-3$) is similar to the subtraction 9−3. The addition of vectors, however, has a feature not shared by the subtraction of natural numbers; the subtraction of natural numbers 3−9 is not possible, whereas the addition of vectors ($^+3$)+($^-9$) is possible, and has the vector ($^-6$) as its result.

The addition of vectors in the *same* direction, on the other hand, is exactly similar to the addition of natural numbers. Both

$$(^+3)+(^+2)=(^+5)$$
and
$$(^-3)+(^-2)=(^-5)$$

are similar to 3+2 = 5. It would therefore be natural when we are dealing with addition, to identify one half of the number line of directed integers with the (signless) number line of natural numbers, as shown in Figure 32:13, and to extend this correspondence so that the positive fractions correspond to their signless equivalents.[7] When this identification is made, the positive directed

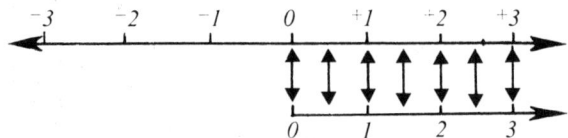

Figure 32:13

---

[7] The reason that we could not instead have chosen to identify the negative directed numbers with the signless numbers does not appear until we consider the multiplication of directed numbers. We compare the correspondences

$$(^+3)+(^+2)=(^+5) \quad \text{and} \quad (^+3)\times(^+2)=(^+6)$$
$$\updownarrow \quad \updownarrow \quad \updownarrow \qquad\qquad \updownarrow \quad \updownarrow \quad \updownarrow$$
$$3 \ + \ 2 \ = \ 5 \qquad\qquad 3 \ \times \ 2 \ = \ 6$$

with those which would be possible between negative directed numbers and the natural numbers:

$$(^-3)+(^-2)=(^-5) \quad \text{but} \quad (^-3)\times(^-2)=(^+6)$$
$$\updownarrow \quad \updownarrow \quad \updownarrow \qquad\qquad \updownarrow \quad \updownarrow$$
$$3 \ + \ 2 \ = \ 5 \qquad\qquad 3 \ \times \ 2 \ = \ 6$$

numbers are often written without their signs; $(^+3)$ is written as if it were the natural number 3. Then $(^+3)+(^-2)$ may be written as $3+(^-2)$, and $(^+3)+(^+2)$ as $3+2$. The '$^-$' sign in a negative directed number must not, of course, be omitted.

When we read $3+2$, it does not matter whether we think it refers to the natural numbers 3 and 2, so that $3+2=5$, or whether we think it refers to vectors and is an abbreviation for $(^+3)+(^+2)=(^+5)$, since the result in natural numbers and the result in vectors always correspond. But $2+(^-3)$ must be an operation on vectors, as $(^-3)$ does not belong to the set of natural numbers.

We have here defined only one operation, addition of directed numbers. The inverse operation, subtraction of directed numbers, will be considered in Chapter 35, together with the subtraction of vectors.

Generalization and extension of the idea of number

We have now generalized and extended the concept of number in such a way that a child who started by exploring the behaviour of a few (small) whole numbers has now within his grasp a complete set of positive and negative rational numbers, with which he can measure in either direction to any degree of accuracy, however large or small the quantity or number he is measuring. His development will probably have taken one or other of the paths shown in Figure 32:14 as his idea of number extends

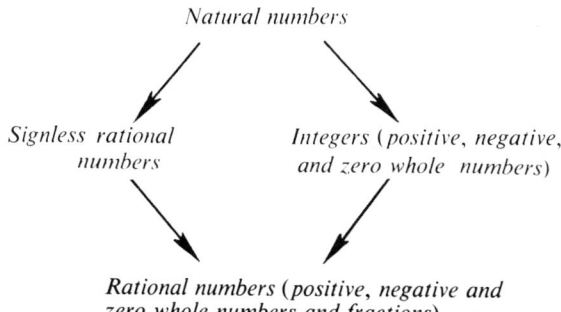

Natural numbers

Signless rational numbers   *Integers (positive, negative, and zero whole numbers)*

Rational numbers (positive, negative and zero whole numbers and fractions)

Figure 32:14

and becomes more general. The relation between the various sets of numbers which he uses is also symbolized in the Venn diagram of Figure 32:15, where each new set of numbers contains the previous one as a subset. The natural numbers form a subset of the integers, and the integers are a subset of the rational numbers.[8]

It is not to be expected that children will completely and explicitly understand this structure of sets of numbers

[8] In more advanced work, the set of integers has a subset which is *isomorphic* to the set of natural numbers.

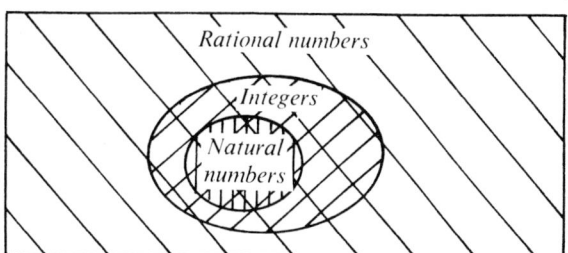

Figure 32:15

until their thinking reaches the stage of formal operations during their secondary school career. The teacher should, however, realize his part in helping children to extend their number system, and should know that each extension of the number system is designed to solve a problem. The integers solve the problem of subtraction, and the rational numbers solve (almost completely) the problem of division. Nor is this end of the road. The operation of square root demands the use of more extensive sets of numbers than the rational numbers, but for most other purposes in the primary school the set of rational numbers is sufficient, and numbers such as $\sqrt{2}$ and π, which are not rational, can be approximated by rational numbers.

Negative indices

We have used index notation earlier to abbreviate the writing of powers of a number. We now consider how this notation can be extended to express those numbers, smaller than one, which are used to head the columns of the decimal system containing numbers smaller than one. These labels for columns follow the pattern

Thousands	Hundreds	Tens	Ones	Tenths	Hundredths	Thousandths

or

$$10^3 \quad 10^2 \quad 10^1 \quad 10^0 \quad ? \quad ? \quad ?$$

The progression of the indices needs negative numbers to continue it. The powers

$$10^3 \quad 10^2 \quad 10^1 \quad 10^0$$

are followed by

$$10^{-1} \quad 10^{-2} \quad 10^{-3}$$

and so on, and it is natural to use the symbols

10^{-1} for one-tenth
10^{-2} for one-hundredth
10^{-3} for one-thousandth,

and so on.

341

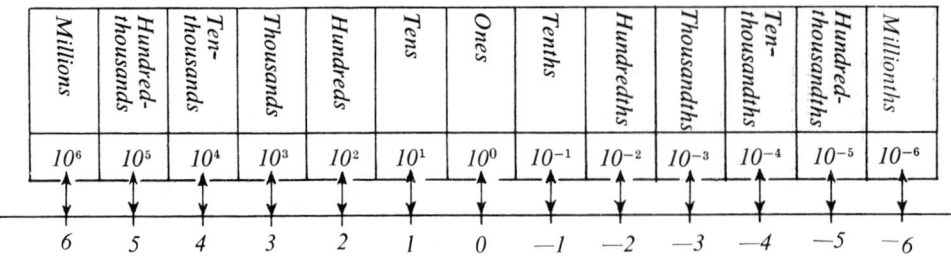

Millions	Hundred-thousands	Ten-thousands	Thousands	Hundreds	Tens	Ones	Tenths	Hundredths	Thousandths	Ten-thousandths	Hundred-thousandths	Millionths
10^6	10^5	10^4	10^3	10^2	10^1	10^0	10^{-1}	10^{-2}	10^{-3}	10^{-4}	10^{-5}	10^{-6}
6	5	4	3	2	1	0	-1	-2	-3	-4	-5	-6

Figure 32:16

Thus we have

$$10^3 = 10 \times 10 \times 10 \qquad = 1 \text{ thousand}$$
$$10^2 = 10 \times 10 \qquad = 1 \text{ hundred}$$
$$10^1 = 10 \qquad = 1 \text{ ten}$$
$$10^0 = 1 \qquad = 1 \text{ one}$$
$$10^{-1} = \frac{1}{10} \qquad = 1 \text{ tenth}$$
$$10^{-2} = \frac{1}{100} = \frac{1}{10 \times 10} = \frac{1}{10^2} \qquad = 1 \text{ hundredth}$$
$$10^{-3} = \frac{1}{1000} = \frac{1}{10 \times 10 \times 10} = \frac{1}{10^3} \qquad = 1 \text{ thousandth}$$

and so on. We have set up a one-to-one correspondence between the integers on the number line and the labels of the columns in positional notation (Figure 32:16).

These symbols are used not only as headings for columns in the notational system, but as convenient symbols for $\frac{1}{10}$, $\frac{1}{100}$, etc. We notice that 10^3 represents one thousand and 10^{-3} represents one thousandth, and so on. This makes the notation particularly convenient to handle.

Negative powers of other numbers can of course be defined and used similarly. In base five

$$5^3 = 5 \times 5 \times 5$$
$$5^2 = 5 \times 5$$
$$5^1 = 5$$
$$5^0 = 1$$
$$5^{-1} = \frac{1}{5}$$
$$5^{-2} = \frac{1}{5 \times 5} = \frac{1}{5^2}$$
$$5^{-3} = \frac{1}{5 \times 5 \times 5} = \frac{1}{5^3}$$

The index notation is thus used to label the columns when we express a number, large or small, using any base.

Very large and very small quantities

Modern science often relies on the measurement of very large quantities such as the distances between stars, and very small quantities such as distances in the atom.
342

Children will read and ask about these measurements. The conventional units of measurement are too large or too small, and scientists use new units for their purposes. Sometimes they give these units new names such as the light-year, the distance which light travels in a year, which is approximately 9 468 000 000 000 km. Often, however, they adapt more usual units by multiplying or dividing the unit by a thousand or a million. We see this happening in a simple case when we say that the distance of the earth from the sun is 149 million kilometres. The unit is a million kilometres.

We can write 149 million kilometres as 149×10^6 km, since 10^6 is a million (*see page* 162). This indicates clearly that the unit of measurement is 10^6 km, or one million km. Similarly

$$1 \text{ light year} = 9\ 468\ 000\ 000\ 000 \text{ km}$$
$$= 9468 \times 10^9 \text{ km}$$

since $1\ 000\ 000\ 000 = 10^9$. The unit is 10^9 km. This distance could also be written as $9 \cdot 468 \times 10^{12}$ km, using a unit of 10^{12} km or a million million km, which has been sub-divided into thousandths.

When an exceedingly small unit is needed for measuring the wavelength of light the Ångstrom unit, which is one hundred-millionth of a centimetre, is used. Visible light of different colours has wavelengths ranging between 4000 and 7500 Ångstroms. The fraction one hundred-millionth is 10^{-8}; hence an Ångstrom unit, which is one hundred-millionth of a centimetre, or $\frac{1}{100\ 000\ 000}$ cm, is written 10^{-8} cm. We can now write the wavelength of violet light, 4000 Ångstroms, as 4000×10^{-8} cm. It could also be written as 400×10^{-7} cm, or 40×10^{-6} cm, or 4×10^{-5} cm.

Activities using indices

Children will investigate powers of other numbers as well as ten. Powers of two form a convenient starting point for experiment, as they are obtained by continual doubling; each power of two is twice the previous power:

$$2^1 = 2$$
$$2^2 = 2 \times 2 = 4$$
$$2^3 = 2 \times (2 \times 2) = 8$$
$$2^4 = 2 \times (2 \times 2 \times 2) = 16, \text{ and so on}$$

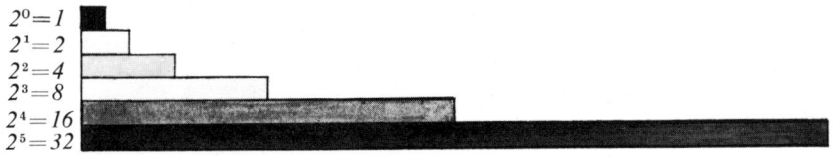

$2^0 = 1$
$2^1 = 2$
$2^2 = 4$
$2^3 = 8$
$2^4 = 16$
$2^5 = 32$

Figure 32:17

With very little labour the table can be built up for some distance:

2^{-5}	2^{-4}	2^{-3}	2^{-2}	2^{-1}	2^0	2^1	2^2	2^3	2^4	2^5
$\frac{1}{32}$	$\frac{1}{16}$	$\frac{1}{8}$	$\frac{1}{4}$	$\frac{1}{2}$	1	2	4	8	16	32

2^6	2^7	2^8	2^9	2^{10}	2^{11}	2^{12}	2^{13}
64	128	256	512	1024	2048	4096	8192

If children make powers of two by using Cuisenaire rods (Figure 32:17), they will notice that the first few members of the set of powers of 2 form one of the 'colour families'. A graphical representation of the powers of 2 is more practicable, since the vertical scale can be reduced to more manageable proportions, but it should be remembered that increasing the power of 2 by one will always result in doubling the height of the graph (Figure 32:18). Graphing powers of 2 will help children to realize the extremely rapid growth of powers of ten, where graphing is almost impossible since an increase of 1 in the index increases the height of the graph tenfold.

Children can be encouraged to try the effect of multiplying and dividing numbers which they have chosen from among those listed in the table of powers of 2. Some children will search for a reason underlying their results.

For example, $16 \times 128 = 2048$, which also appears in the table of powers of 2. In fact

$$2^4 \times 2^7 = 2^{11}$$

In reverse,

$$2048 \div 128 = 16 \text{ or } 2^{11} \div 2^7 = 2^4$$

The *index laws for multiplication and division*

$$a^m \times a^n = a^{m+n} \text{ and } a^m \div a^n = a^{m-n}$$

will not be explicitly stated at this stage but this numerical experience will pave the way for the theoretical study of indices and many children can reach the stage of stating as a result of their experiences that, 'to multiply the numbers, you add the indices'.

The slide rule

The isomorphism, or correspondence, between

$$2^3 \times 2^4 = 2^7$$
$$\text{and } \updownarrow \quad \updownarrow \quad \updownarrow$$
$$3 + 4 = 7$$

in which

2^3 corresponds to 3
2^4 corresponds to 4
$\times$ corresponds to $+$,

and the *product* 2^7 corresponds to the *sum* 7, makes it possible to construct a simple slide-rule which children can use for multiplication and division.

In Chapter 9, page 79, a tape measure was used as a slide rule for addition, and later for subtraction. In order to convert this slide-rule to use for multiplication and

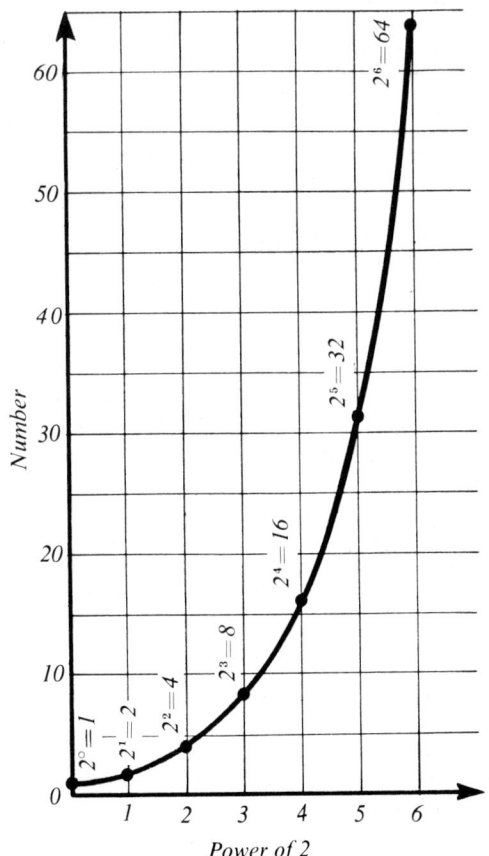

Number

Power of 2

Figure 32:18

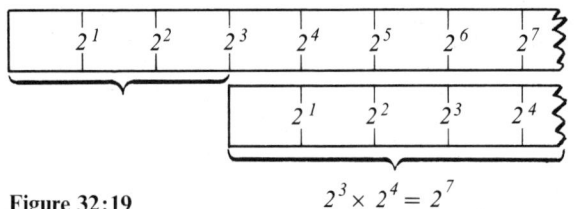

Figure 32:19

$$2^3 \times 2^4 = 2^7$$

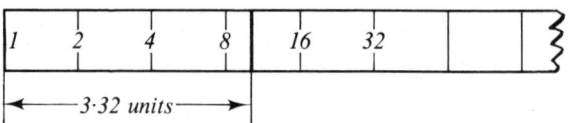

Figure 32:21

This calibration of intermediate points is very easily done from the graph of powers of 2 if the scale of the slide-rule is made to correspond to the scale on the horizontal axis of the graph (Figure 32:22).

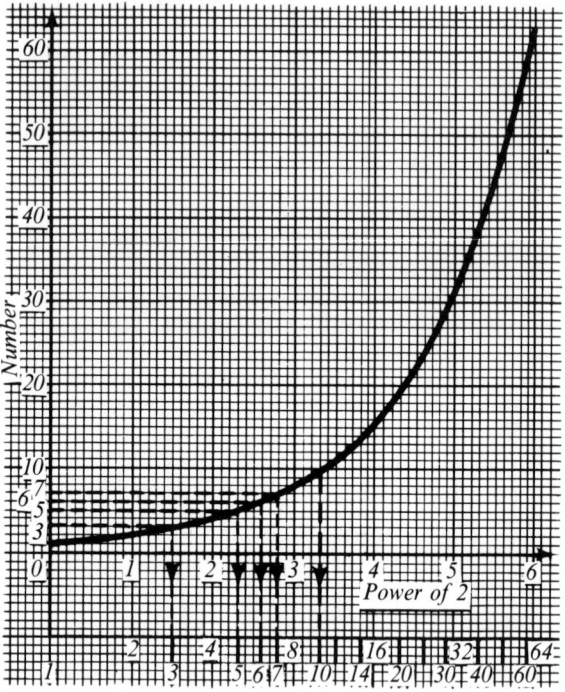

Figure 32:22

division, all that is needed is to relabel the divisions with powers of 2 (Figure 32:19).

The correspondence enables us to read off from the slide-rule, by adding lengths of 3 units and 4 units, that

$$2^3 \times 2^4 = 2^7,$$

or by subtracting lengths, that

$$2^7 \div 2^4 = 2^3$$

An air of greater mystery, but increased convenience in use, is obtained by relabelling Figure 32:19 by replacing 2^1 by 2, 2^2 by 4, 2^3 by 8, and so on (Figure 32:20).

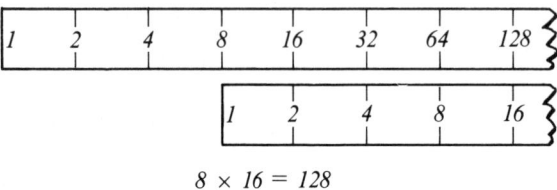

$$8 \times 16 = 128$$

Figure 32:20

The starting point of each scale of the slide-rule is labelled 1, as $2^0 = 1$. Children can now experiment with multiplication and division of powers of 2, verifying that addition of lengths corresponds to multiplication of the numbers shown on the slide-rule and subtraction of lengths corresponds to division.

The final step is to calibrate the slide-rule with numbers between the powers of 2. This is easily done by reading from the graph of Figure 32:18 that, for instance,

$$10 = 2^{3 \cdot 32}$$

so that the point 3·32 units from the beginning of the scale should be labelled with 10 (Figure 32:21), and other points similarly marked from the graph.

At this stage, children are ready to start to use a commercial slide-rule for multiplication and division. The A and B scales of such a rule correspond exactly to the simple slide-rule we have constructed, and are calibrated from 1 to 100. The C and D scales are merely the first halves of the A and B scales, magnified to twice the size, and so calibrated from 1 to 10.

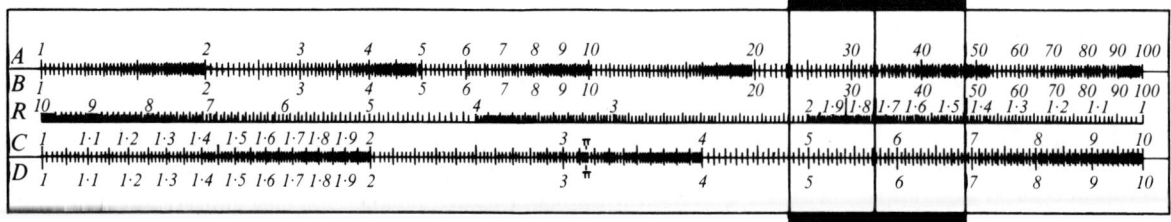

Figure 32:23

344

33 Approximation and Accuracy

Guess and estimate

For some purposes it is necessary to know numbers and quantities very accurately; for other purposes accuracy is not so important. The number of children who stay to school dinner must be known accurately, and must agree exactly with the money they pay, but the canteen supervisor, knowing that 215 children are expected, will not be able to provide a quantity of food with such accuracy that if 214 children came there would be food left over, but there would not be enough for 216. The number of children who belong to a particular school on a certain day may be exactly 321, but the population of the British Isles on that day can only be estimated; it is probably not sensible to give the population more accurately than 55 347 000 at the 1971 census, with an estimated increase since then. Even on the day of the census people were being born, dying, and entering and leaving the country.

The ability to estimate a number or quantity with a reasonable and appropriate degree of accuracy should be encouraged. Numbers and quantities have more meaning for children if they can picture what twenty stitches on a knitting-needle look like, feel in imagination the mass of a kilogram, and are able to judge the length of a piece of string and know what a 50 cm stride feels like. The ability to judge a number or a quantity is the result of experience and needs practice. Children should be encouraged, as soon as the units of measurement which they are using are well known, to 'guess' or estimate measurements before they measure.

Two ideas develop from this: the idea of a 'round number' and that of the *degree of accuracy* of a measurement or an estimate. If a child estimates the length of a book, his estimate will probably be a whole number of centimetres, and his estimate of the length of a room is likely to be a whole number of metres. An older child may say to himself as he estimates the length of the playing field: 'more than 100 metres, but not 200 metres; say 150 metres'. He is using a very approximate number, rounded off to the nearest 50, to describe his estimate. It is not sensible to make an estimate to a greater degree of accuracy than can be reasonably well judged, and rounded-off numbers are often used in estimating. Estimating and guessing do not mean the same thing.

When guessing the mass of a cake, we may *guess* 4·35 kg, but will probably not be able to *estimate* with greater accuracy than to the nearest $\frac{1}{2}$ kilogram, or indeed the nearest kilogram. We may guess the number of children in a hall to be 123, but without even a rough count we may not be able to make a better estimate than 'between 100 and 200'. If the actual number is 138, the guess of 123 is misleading, for it suggests a much more accurate count than had actually taken place. But if the estimate is

based on the children's arrangement in the hall, sitting in rows which usually seem to have about 12 children in them, and if there are 11 rows, an estimate of 130 is sensible, expecting a likely error of about 10 either way.

This ability to estimate is a useful one for children to cultivate; it ensures that numbers are being used meaningfully and that the units of measurement mean something to the children. Also, the ability to estimate the size of a room, the area of a garden, the speed of a car, the length of a cycle-ride, the cost of a holiday, the number of people at a meeting, or whether the temperature has reached freezing point, is often useful in everyday life, on occasions when accurate measurement is impossible or inconvenient.

Children should decide whether their estimates are good ones or not. At first, they will just say how far out the estimate is. 'I estimated that the book was 20 cm long; it measures 17 cm. The estimate was 3 cm too long.' Is this a good estimate? With practice, as he visualizes lengths more easily, a child will probably do better than this, but if he estimates the length of a book-shelf to be 1 metre when it is actually 97 cm he is doing extremely well, although the actual error is the same in both cases. Large numbers and quantities are more difficult to estimate than small ones, and the size of the error must eventually be considered in relation to the size of the quantity being measured. A top junior child will be able to see that an error of 1 cm in estimating a length of 10 cm achieves the same degree of accuracy as an error of 1 metre in estimating the length of a room 10 metres long, or an error of 10 metres in estimating the length of a field 100 metres long. He will, however, be much less likely to achieve this degree of accuracy for the longer distance than for the shorter distance of 10 cm which he has handled daily for several years.

Percentages and comparisons

At first the meaning of a percentage is much more important than the performance of calculations involving percentages; these can be postponed until the secondary school. Examples should be simple and within the children's range. The statement '63% of the vehicles which passed the school gate between 10.30 a.m. and 10.45 a.m. were private cars' means that 63 hundredths of these vehicles were private cars. 'Per cent' means 'out of 100', and 63% means 63 hundredths. It is most unlikely that exactly 100 cars passed the gate during the given quarter of an hour, but expressing the proportion of private cars as a percentage enables comparison to be made with different times of day, when different numbers of vehicles pass. The chief use of percentages is for comparison. Of the two statements:

i) 'On road *A*, 46 vehicles out of 79 were cars, but on road *B*, 83 vehicles out of 123 were cars', and

ii) 'On road *A*, 58% of vehicles were cars, but on road *B*, 67% of vehicles were cars',

the second is easier to grasp, and enables comparisons to be made between the proportion of cars travelling on the two roads.

Also, the parts of 100 are much more familiar than parts of other numbers. The statement '27% of the children in this class have birthdays in the autumn term' conveys the proportion more easily than does '10 out of the 37 children in this class have birthdays in the autumn term', as well as making comparisons with other classes and with national statistics easier. The difficulty lies in the conversion of '$\frac{10}{37}$ of the children in the class' into a percentage. This may very conveniently be done graphically, particularly if several pieces of information about the 37 children in the class are to be expressed as percentages. Figure 33:1 shows the necessary conversion graph for a class of 37 children.

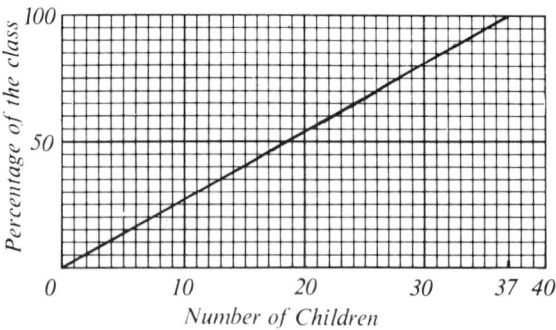

Figure 33:1

Alternatively, the fraction $\frac{10}{37}$ may be expressed as a decimal, and so as a percentage:

$$\begin{aligned}\frac{10}{37} &= 10 \div 37 \\ &= 0{\cdot}270\ldots \\ &\simeq \frac{27}{100} \\ &= 27\%\end{aligned}$$

$$\begin{array}{r} 0{\cdot}270 \\ 37\overline{)10{\cdot}0} \\ 74 \\ \overline{260} \\ 259 \\ \overline{10} \end{array}$$

Children will now be able to express their errors of estimation as percentages, and so will more easily be able to compare their skill at estimating different quantities. In this type of work, there is no need for a spurious degree of accuracy.

an error of 5 cm in 31 cm

= an error of $\frac{5}{31}$ cm in 1 cm

$\simeq$ an error of 0·16 cm in 1 cm

= 16% error

346

This estimate of the error within one part in a hundred is quite sufficiently accurate.

A child may investigate whether he finds it more difficult to estimate masses, times or volumes, or how much worse he is at estimating long distances than short distances.

Approximation in counting and measuring

Children will also discover, as their experience of counting and measuring grows, that often when they count a set and always when they measure a quantity, these tasks can only be done approximately.

Several difficulties arise when a set is to be counted. The number of things in the set may be very large, making counting difficult. The number of grains of rice in a particular $\frac{1}{2}$ kilogram bag of rice is a definite number which could be counted. It would be easier to approximate to this number by weighing out 50 grams of rice, counting the grains in it, and multiplying by 10. Anyway, 'Exactly how many grains of rice are there in $\frac{1}{2}$ kg?' is a non-sensical question. Often, it is only sensible to state an approximate number in a set.

Again, in practical situations it may be difficult to decide exactly what objects belong to the set we wish to count, or to make the members of the set stand still for long enough to be counted. Even when young children count simple sets like the set of pets they have at home, arbitrary decisions may have to be taken on such problems as, 'Should I count my sister's pony?' The set of people who attend an open-air political rally cannot in practical terms be counted although the set of those who attend at least part of the rally is well-defined. There are passers-by who drift in and out, and many other practical barriers to forming more than a rough estimate. If the plants in an area are sampled by throwing a quadrat and counting the number of plants of a species within it, it may be difficult to decide whether a plant is inside the quadrat or not. Hence, in many cases the count of a set can only be regarded as approximate.

In any form of measurement, accuracy is inevitably limited by the skill of the measurer and the accuracy of the measuring instruments used. When a child measures the length of a postcard, we expect him to obtain a measurement which is correct to the nearest millimetre; but when he measures the length of a room he does not use a measuring-tape marked in millimetres, and if he did it would be false to pretend that the length of the room could be measured with this degree of accuracy. Unevenness in the skirting-board, slight crookedness or stretch in the measuring-tape, or inequalities in the floor surface would account for considerably more than this, and in any case it would never be necessary to give the length of a room with greater accuracy than to the nearest centimetre, if that.

It is often not sensible to take measurements to more than a certain degree of accuracy. If a person's mass is

62·5 kg at the moment of weighing, at a different time of the same day his mass may well be 62·2 kg. The A.A. book gives distances 'by the shortest practicable route using classified roads'. How often can this information be revised to take account of one-way streets, diversions, road rebuilding, or other variations? However, approximate information is sufficient for planning the journey.

In a railway time-table we may read that a train departs at 10.26. This information does not lead us to expect that it will start to move at *exactly* 26 minutes 0 seconds past 10. We shall be surprised if it starts at 10.25, and not at all surprised if it starts at 10.27. In this case the information gives the time of the *beginning* of an interval during which the train will start.

A child who has access to a desk calculating machine will enjoy working out how many days he has been alive, but he will realize that, even if he knows the time of his birth, it is not sensible to work out exactly how many minutes he has been alive, as this time changes while he does the calculation. Measurement can only ever be approximate, in this or any other case. The statement, 'I have drawn a line exactly 10 cm long' is never true. It means, 'I cannot, with the naked eye, using my rather thick pencil and mass-produced ruler, see a difference in length between my line and the length of 10 cm shown by this ruler, the markings on which are not much more than 0·2 mm thick.'

The teacher should work for an understanding of approximation from the beginning. When a child measures his pencil, he may say it is 'about 8 cm long', '8 cm and a bit long', or 'between 8 and 9 cm long'. Any of these is a more correct statement than just '8 cm long'. The idea that a measurement is *between* two limits is helpful in several ways. When a package is weighed on a balance, its mass may be more that 200 grams but less than 300 grams. With the scales available, a child cannot obtain greater accuracy than this. A jug may hold more than $\frac{1}{3}$ litre but less than $\frac{1}{2}$ litre; the fact that its capacity is between $\frac{1}{3}$ litre and $\frac{1}{2}$ litre will help him to put $\frac{1}{3}$ and $\frac{1}{2}$ in order of size, as the weighing experience helps the child to put 200 and 300 in order, and to see the need for numbers between 200 and 300. Such experiences help in building up a picture of the number line.

As he grows older, a child progresses in such an activity as measuring a pencil through using descriptions such as these:

  i) between 13 cm and 14 cm,
  ii) between 13 cm and $13\frac{1}{2}$ cm,
  iii) nearer to $13\frac{1}{2}$ cm than to 13 cm,
  iv) $13\frac{1}{2}$ cm, to the nearest half centimetre,
  v) between 13·0 and 13·5 cm,
  vi) 13·3 cm, to the nearest millimetre.

By this stage he should be querying the value of the last measurement. During the writing of this paragraph, the pencil used shrank in length from approximately 13·3 cm to 13·1 cm.

Children should discuss what degree of accuracy they need in their measuring, and how much faith they have in that accuracy. A school corridor has been measured, and a plan of the school is to be made. The corridor appears to be 54 m 97 cm long. How accurately can the children guarantee that they have measured? The corridor may have been built from an architect's plan which showed it as 55 m long. After discussion, children would probably guarantee that the length is between 54 m 90 cm and 55 m 10 cm; that is 55 m *to the nearest 10 cm*; they might well feel that they had done better than this. But when the plan of the school is drawn to a scale of say, '1 cm represents 1 metre', a 5 cm doubt about the length of the corridor is only represented by a doubt of $\frac{1}{2}$ mm on the plan, and can be ignored. A field need often only be measured to the nearest metre. It is important to know how accurately we can measure, and how accurately we need to measure, rather than to struggle for meaningless exactness.

We now list some more ways which will help children at different stages to describe approximate counts and measurements.

  i) 230 tickets for the school concert were sold; the number of people at the concert ≤ 230.
  ii) 13·0 cm < length of pencil < 13·5 cm.
  iii) The corridor is 55 m ± 0·05 m long.
  iv) The population of the British Isles was 55 347 000 (to the nearest thousand).

Making use of estimates

Children only acquire the ability to estimate with a reasonable degree of accuracy by practising estimating and comparing estimates with measurements. Their use of estimates in new situations will often tell the teacher how well they can handle measures. A six-year old who said to a visitor to his class, 'Go away: you're too tall', and then returned to say with astonishment, 'You must be two metres tall', showed considerable insight in his estimate, but infants who guess an adult's age with estimates between 18 and 80 show their lack of grasp of the idea of age in adults.

An estimate should be made as a matter of course when children measure: a tape-measure may become twisted and be read from the wrong end; a child using a measuring-tape may forget how many times he has stretched it out; children often read the wrong angle from a protractor. A sensible use of the habit of estimation will often detect errors of this type.

Similarly, in calculation, an estimate of the size of answers to be expected, however rough, will often reveal slips. For instance, the average height of a group of children must certainly be between the greatest and least heights, and slips such as

$$\begin{array}{r} 357 \\ -289 \\ \hline 168 \end{array} \quad \text{and} \quad \begin{array}{r} 705 \\ \times\ 63 \\ \hline 4230 \\ 2115 \\ \hline 6345 \end{array}$$

will immediately be found by a child to whom the sizes of numbers mean anything; both answers are clearly the wrong size. Every piece of mathematical information should constantly be checked by the criterion, 'Is this sensible?'

Reducing and magnifying errors

Sometimes measurements which can only be approximate are used as the basis of deductions. These deductions are then also subject to error, and the importance of the error depends on the circumstances.

Children may study the school canteen. If they find out the quantity of potatoes used each week, they can work out the mass of potatoes each child, on the average, eats each day. A small deduction will have to be made for peeling, but this is likely to make a difference of only a few grams to the calculated amount that each child eats. On the other hand, if children examine the loss through peeling by weighing the peelings from a kilogram of potatoes and then multiplying by the number of kilograms of potatoes the school eats in a week, the inaccuracy in weighing, and the variations between one sample pound of potatoes and another may cause the result to be many kilograms out.

Nationally, polls of a small sample of public opinion are used to predict voting behaviour at election times. Magnification of the error caused by sampling has on occasion led to erroneous forecasts.

The effect of performing calculations or taking measurements from a scale-drawing may give a spurious feeling of accuracy. In Figure 33:2(a) a scale-drawing is used to find the height of a building. Angle A has been measured with a home-made clinometer, and the distance AB with a measuring-tape. We can read off from the drawing that the height BC of the building is 13 m to the nearest metre. But if the length AB had been measured with an error less than $\frac{1}{4}$ metre, and the angle were correct within 2°, which is unlikely with a home-made clinometer, the height might be anywhere between 11·2 m and 14·2 m, as is shown in Figure 33:2(b). It would be better to state that the height is approximately 13 metres.

Averaging is another process which gives figures in the calculation to a degree of accuracy often unwarranted by the measurements. Suppose the heights of four children are 121 cm, 121 cm, 125 cm and 126 cm. The sum of their heights is 493 cm, and when this is divided by 4, the average of the 4 heights is found to be 123·25 cm. But it would be misleading to suggest that the average height of a child in this set is 123·2 cm, since the original

measurements are clearly only accurate to the nearest cm. The average height should be given as 123 cm.

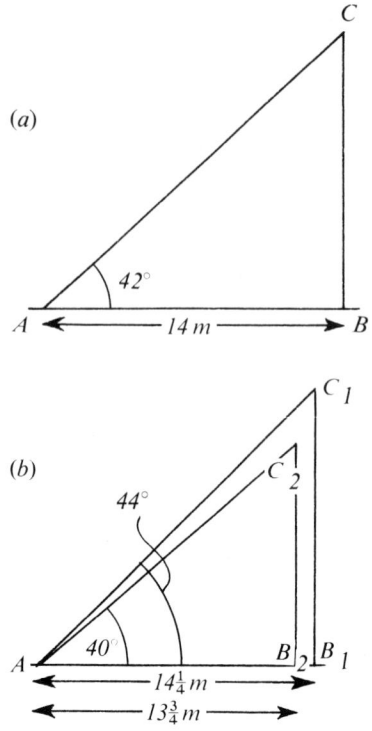

Figure 33:2

Significant figures

When we say that the population of the British Isles is 55 347 000, no reliance is placed on the final three digits of this number. They are only used as *place-holders* and are of no significance. The population is 55 347 000, *correct to 5 significant figures*. It is extremely rare for a count or measurement to be correct to as many significant figures as this.

Children may read statements like, 'the mean distance of the earth from the sun is about 149 000 000 km', and they should realize that only the first three figures of this number are significant. In other words, the measurement has been made in terms of a unit of one million kilometres, and this unit has not been sub-divided.

Measurements made by children are very rarely correct to more than two significant figures, and are often much less accurate than that. By the end of the Primary stage, children should begin to estimate what degree of accuracy their measuring has, and to know that they have weighed to the nearest 10 grams, or have measured a length to the nearest 10 centimetres.

Part V

More Abstract Ideas Develop

34 Position

Position relative to the observer

A child's first responses to objects around him are actions of his own body. He reaches out with an uncertain arm; he follows a moving object with his glance, and when he becomes mobile he moves towards a thing he wants. In each of these situations he relates the position of the object to himself. Two factors are involved in his response: direction and distance. He may reach, look or walk in the right direction but the object may be too far away. Gradually he acquires the ability to assess both direction and distance with fair accuracy; thus he saves himself ineffective effort and begins to notice the effects of movement. When he or an object in which he is interested moves, the scene before him changes and things are no longer in the same relationship to himself or to one another. He becomes less egocentric and more able to see how one thing is sited relative to another (Figure 34:1).

Figure 34:1

The relative position of two objects

When children can understand and use language they show that they are aware of some position relationships. They will know that the cat is *under* the table, that the book is *on* the shelf, that David is *next* to Peter, and so on. From this stage there is a rapid growth in the variety of ways in which a child can answer the question, 'Where is . . . ?' Yet until he has some understanding of number and

distance he cannot give a precise answer. He may *remember* the exact position in which a toy was placed in regard to another object but he has not yet the mental imagery or the concepts with which to describe it.

Position in an order or sequence

Before the skill of counting is acquired a child will be able to place a toy, such as a car or a doll, in a particular place in a sequence; it may be a sequence of size, colour, shape or type but it follows some rule or pattern. From this kind of experience the idea of number develops and the child learns to count. Now he can specify a position in an order. He uses ordinal numbers to say, for example, that his book is on the third shelf, or that Ann is fourth in the line. His form of speech may not be quite correct; he may say that Ann is number four in the line, but his recognition of the use of number to describe position in a sequence is evident.

Position as given by distance along a line

The first measurements of length will almost certainly be along a straight edge. The distance being measured is the length of a line along which the measuring unit can be placed. At this stage the child is not yet thinking about how far one *end* of the line is from the other *end*; he is not therefore considering the *position* of one end relative to the other. This latter idea emerges as a child measures the distance of one object from another, for instance the distance from the door to a picture, or from one corner to the tree. He may have actually to set out or to imagine the line which must be measured in order to find the distance. He will *state* a *position* as 5 m along a wall, 4 decimetres above the table, 6 cm beyond the mark, and so on. He is now answering the question, 'How far?' or, 'Where?' and not the question, 'How long?' This is an important stage and should not be forgotten when measuring becomes a strong interest.

One measurement insufficient to fix a position

In the instances quoted there is another object to which a position can be related. If the thing to be located is on a line or in a certain sequence of things in a plane it is easy to define its position by a single measurement along the line or by one ordinal number to give the place in the sequence. When an object is not on a known fixed line or in a sequence, as, for example, a pylon in a meadow, then more than one measurement is required to describe its position in the plane. The need to define such a position will usually arise in an attempt to map an area near the school or to make a model of a real or an imagined scene in which certain landmarks are to be accurately placed. Children will experiment to find out how the precise spot can be fixed. The kinds of measurements which are necessary to define such a position become familiar during the Junior school years.

Using two distances to fix a position

Awareness of the need for *two* pieces of information to tell us where a thing is in a plane comes through such experiences as describing the exact position of a child's own pigeonhole as in the third row up and the fourth along from the left; the book is on the second shelf and third from the right-hand end; on a map which is covered with a square grid the home town is in row *p* and column *F*. When a child can readily use this kind of two-fold statement he has established the idea of *co-ordinates* to fix a point in a plane. He can use two lines, such as the edge of the floor and the vertical edge of a wall, as a frame of reference and can state the position of any point in the plane by its distances from the two reference lines. Later on he will put in reference lines, or axes, wherever is most convenient for the task in hand. For example, he may put a line diagonally across the playground and measure the distances of a flagstaff from the corner measured along this diagonal line and perpendicular to it.

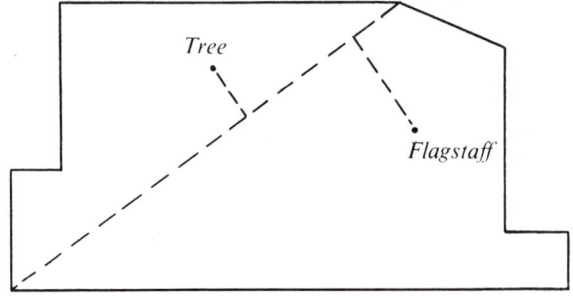

Figure 34:2

Plans, maps and charts, such as those associated with buried treasure, all call for an understanding of the use of a pair of numbers to define a position, either to enable the observer to record it on a map or to pass on the information to another person. Figure 34:3(*b*) shows the general case where a point is shown by the number pair (*a,b*).

352

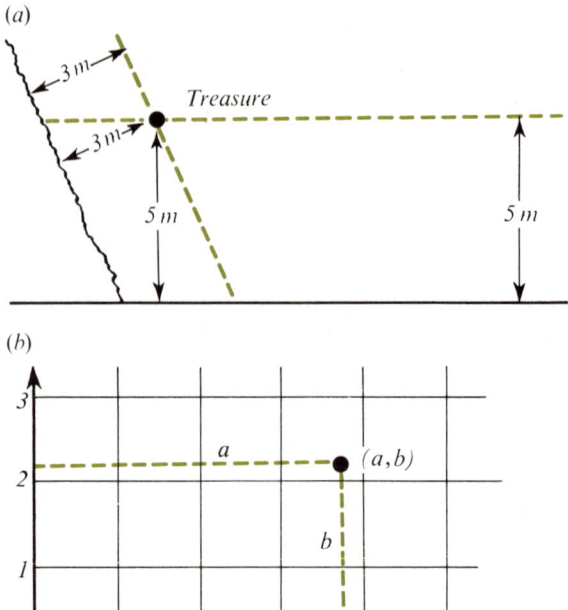

Figure 34:3

Using a vector to fix a position

It is not always possible or convenient to measure the two distances of a point from lines of reference. A child already knows that to reach a place by the shortest path he must move in a certain direction and for a certain distance. The position of the place can therefore be represented by a vector from the starting point. For example, the pylon in the meadow can be shown on a plan if the direction and distance from a gatepost can be found. For this purpose a base line through the starting point must be chosen, say the hedge running from the gatepost. The angle between this base line and the direction of the pylon must be recorded. This angle need not, however, be measured if a plane table is used for recording it, as described in Chapter 27. Once more a pair of numbers is required to fix the position. The vector we use has both direction, given by the angle with the base line, and length, given by the distance from the gatepost to the pylon. In Figure 34:4 the position shown could be written (17 m, 30°) though it must be

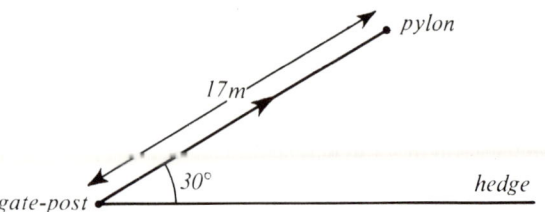

Figure 34:4

repeated that a scale *diagram* can show the angle found on the plane table without it having to be measured in degrees. If this device is not used the starting point and the base line must be defined and the distance and angle given in written form.

Using two angles to fix a position

We have now seen two ways of fixing a position in a plane. First, choosing two axes of reference we can measure two distances; secondly, we can choose a base line with an end-point and then measure the angle with the base line and the distance from the end point. There is a third way. We may choose a base line with both end-points marked. We can then measure (or copy) the angles made at the end-points by the base line and the lines pointing to the object to be fixed. The two given end-points provide enough information for us to complete the fixing of the position because we can find the distance between them if their sites are known. In Figure 34:5, *A* and *B* are given points, trees or gateposts. They are found to be 9 metres apart. The angles which the sighting lines *AP* and *BP* make with *AB* are measured. If the angles are 28° and 65° the position of *P* is as shown.

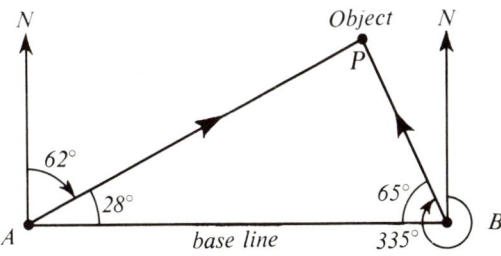

Figure 34:5

Position in three dimensions

In this era children at the upper primary stage are keenly interested in space and the objects in it, both the astronomical bodies and the man-made satellites and spacecraft. They want to know something about the ways in which position in three-dimensional space can be defined. Many of the techniques are too difficult for Primary programmes but a foundation of basic methods can be laid. The first step may be to extend the use of co-ordinates to include fixing a point above a plane. Children may wish to show position relative to ground level. For example, a boy's desk may be on the third floor, at a given distance from an outside wall and at a certain distance from an adjacent wall. The position can be stated in terms of 3 distances as shown in Figure 34:6. The position is represented by the three co-ordinates (4, 5, 8).

A rectangular room provides a good three-dimensional framework: the two walls and floor which meet at one corner of the room form the three planes of reference. The positions of various objects in the room, such as the lower tip of an overhead light, can be stated in co-ordinates. Any structure which is based on cuboids can also have points, such as the vertices and the intersections of diagonals, described by reference to three planes which meet at a vertex.

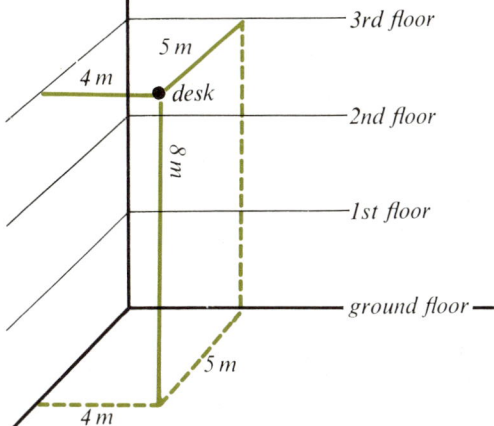

Figure 34:6

The positions so far considered have either been in a plane or have been related to planes as in the paragraph above, where the walls and floor served as reference planes. Portions of the earth's surface can only be treated as planes if they are very small. The navigation of a ship or aeroplane, or the control of a satellite, must take account of the spherical shape of the earth. This makes it necessary to be able to state any position on a sphere and for this purpose to have some reference points and lines. Although for some mathematical purposes it is useful to think of the earth's surface as a sphere which can be related to three reference planes through its centre, this approach is not the most practical for tracking changes of position on the surface. Navigators prefer to use latitude and longitude. It is clear therefore, that geography and mathematics should go hand in hand in dealing with the ways of stating precisely where an object is either on the surface of the earth or in orbit round it.

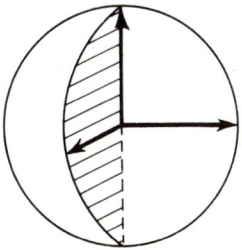

Figure 34:7

353

Longitude

As the earth rotates during the day the sun appears to be overhead at a succession of places in a path from East to West. Noon therefore occurs later at places West of an observer. A child may become aware of a difference of time which depends on this East-to-West relationship by his interest in the timing of radio programmes from other countries. Longitude measures these East-to-West differences in position and can be understood more easily than latitude, the significance of which is not at first apparent to children. We shall therefore begin by considering longitude.

A large globe showing the countries of the world, the poles and the equator gives meaning to this work. A plain black sphere on which the position of points can be marked is even more important. Pupils should be able to make the skeleton of a sphere by taking four equal circles of cane or wire, such as are used for Christmas decorations, and fastening them together at the ends of a common diameter (Figure 34:8). They should be symmetrically placed so that another equal circle representing an equator is divided into eight equal arcs. The North and South poles are represented by the common points of the four circles, each of which is made up of two *meridians*, or two semicircles each containing all points that have the same noon. Every point on the surface of a sphere lies on a meridian: a wire circle of the same radius as the other circles could be placed so as to pass through any such point and the two poles. This circle would show the meridian through the point. If this meridian could be named we should be able to state one fact about the position of the point, namely that it lies on a particular meridian.

We can see that any meridian could be transformed into another by rotating about the N–S axis. The meridians could therefore be given a rotation or angle measure from any fixed meridian chosen as the zero. By tradition the Greenwich meridian is universally taken as the zero or starting position. The meridians in the skeleton structure, starting from the zero, mark rotations of 45°, 90°, 135°, 180°, 225°, 270°, 315° and 360°, completing one revolution from the Greenwich meridian. If diameters of cane or wire are placed across the equator these angles can be identified as shown in Figure 34:8(b).

In practice the angles are recorded from 0° to 180° East of Greenwich and 0° to 180° West of Greenwich. These angles state the longitude of any point on a particular meridian.

The meridian opposite Greenwich is 180° East or West according to the direction in which it is approached. This creates a strange situation in regard to naming time on the two sides of this meridian. Places to the East of Greenwich have their noon earlier than Greenwich; places to the West have a later noon. Consequently travelling to the East one finds the local time becoming increasingly later than Greenwich time until, as one approaches the 180° East meridian, local time is approaching the midnight which has yet to come to Greenwich where it is noon, local time. If the date is 24th April at Greenwich, the time at 180° East is midnight of 24/25th April. A traveller moving West from Greenwich finds local time earlier than Greenwich progressively until, when he reaches 180° West, local time is the midnight *before* Greenwich noon, and so it is midnight on 23/24th April. Therefore the same moment of time has a different date on the two sides of the 180° meridian, which is known as the *date line*.

The time relative to Greenwich at places on any particular meridian can now be readily worked out. Since one daily revolution of the earth through 360° takes 24 × 60 minutes it is clear that a rotation of 1° takes 4 minutes. A place with longitude 18° *East* will be 18 × 4, or 72 minutes *later* than Greenwich; the sun was overhead there 1 hour 12 minutes earlier than at Greenwich. A place 18° *West* of Greenwich will have time 1 hour 12 minutes *earlier* than Greenwich; the sun will not be overhead until 1.20 p.m. Greenwich Mean Time. The time at

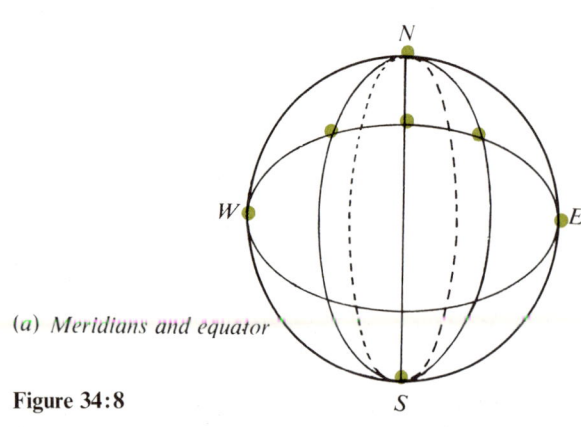

(a) Meridians and equator

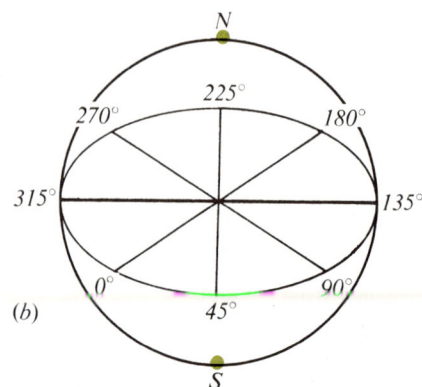

(b)

Figure 34:8

important cities such as Delhi, New York, Moscow, Singapore, Sydney, Peking can now be found with the use of a map which gives longitude.

For convenience there are agreed time belts covering approximately 15° of longitude throughout which the same time is kept officially. The time in the neighbouring belt to the East will be one hour later, and the belt to the West one hour earlier. If children become expecially interested in the recording of time a wide field of investigation is open to them, both contemporary and historical.

A world clock shows the times kept at the most important cities (Figure 34:9).

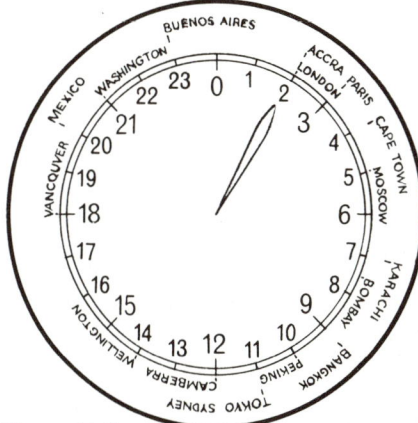

Figure 34:9

Latitude

The position of a point on a sphere is only partly given by its longitude. To give it precisely we must know where on its meridian the point lies. The skeleton of the sphere can show this. As an example we will take a point on one of the wire meridians as shown in Figure 34:10. A wire or stretched string joining the point to the centre of the sphere shows the angle of rotation from the point on the same meridian which lies on the equator. If this angle is 42° we say that the point is 42° North. In Figure 34:10, *B* is 64° South.

Thus the position of a point on a sphere is given by

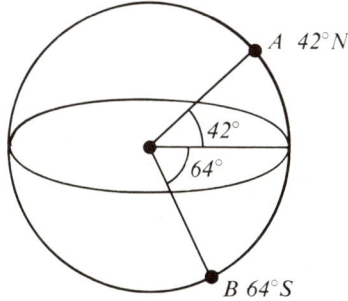

Figure 34:10

two angles, one indicating the longitude East or West of Greenwich, the other the *latitude* North or South of the equator.

If cane or wire circles smaller than the equator of the model can be provided they can be placed on the spherical skeleton or on a globe so that all points on each circle have the same latitude. If the circles are of a size to be placed at intervals of 15° of latitude it will be seen that the meridians and these parallels of latitude cover the sphere with a grid which the pupils can compare and contrast with the square grid which they know so well can cover a plane. Figure 34:11 shows both grids.

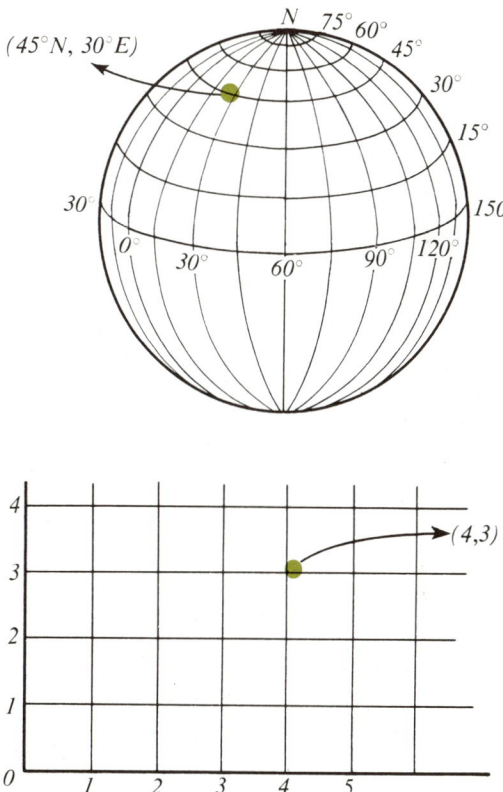

Figure 34:11

North pole and pole star

In the northern hemisphere the magnetic North is not far from the pole, and the line of the meridian through any point is given fairly closely by North shown on the compass. At two towns *A* and *B* which are only a few hundred km apart, a map shows the North direction by two parallel lines. On the earth's surface the meridians of which these North-pointing lines are parts actually meet at the pole. This apparent contradiction puzzles children and they need to realize for themselves that a very small portion of the earth's surface can be taken as flat and the difference of the two North directions as negligible (Figure 34:12).

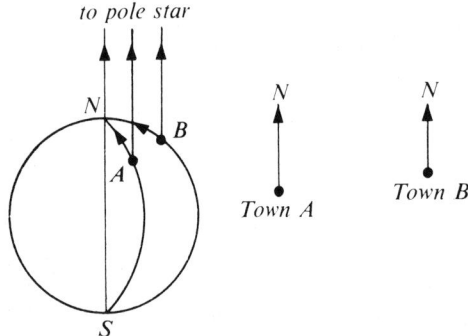

Figure 34:12

The difference between a near view and a view from a very great distance is also brought out by studying the pole star. This star is in line with the earth's axis but so far away, that seen from any point in the northern hemisphere, it appears to be on a line parallel to the earth's axis. Thus it is always seen in a northerly direction as demonstrated in Figure 34:12.

Pupils can be encouraged to find the angle between the line pointing to the pole star and the horizontal line pointing North at the observer's position. This can be done by using the clinometer described in Chapter 27. If a child finds the angle at the beginning and end of a two- to three-hour interval he will discover that the position of the pole star is unchanged, although other stars are in a different position relative to the pole star.

Some children may notice that this angle is the same as the latitude of their own position. Figure 34:13(*b*) shows the right angles which make the equality of these angles clear.

Great circles

The equator and the circles on which the meridians lie all have the same radius which is equal to the radius of the sphere. The parallels of latitude (except the equator) have a smaller radius. It is interesting for children to realise that any number of circles can be drawn on the surface of a sphere through any two points on it. If the set of wire or cane circles that were used as parallels of latitude are placed so as to have two points in common (Figure 34:14) pupils will see how different are the possible paths from one point to the other.

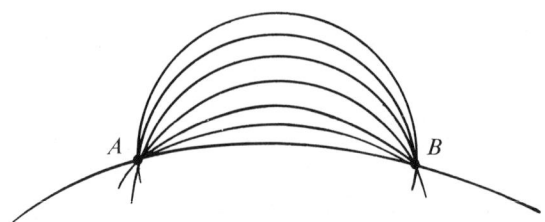

Figure 34:14

If such a set of circles of different radii are drawn through two points on a *plane* the difference in length of the arcs between *A* and *B* is seen at once to depend on the radius. The greater the radius of the circle the shorter the arc between *A* and *B*. Similarly on a sphere the shortest path between two points will be along the circle with the greatest radius; this circle has the radius of the sphere itself. Such a circle is called a *great circle* (Figure 34:15).

The equator is a great circle; a meridian is half a great circle.

If a ship or an aeroplane wishes to take the shortest route it will follow a great circle route. If several wire circles of different radii are placed to join, say, London and New York on a globe, the position of the great circle will probably surprise the pupils (Figure 34:16).

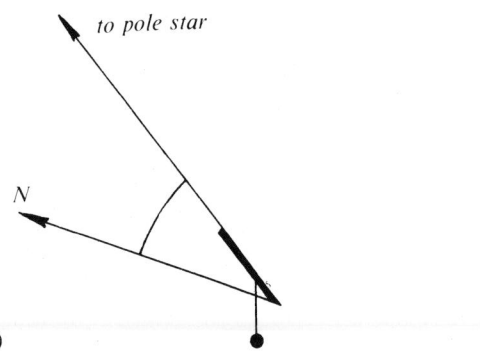

(*a*)

Figure 34:13

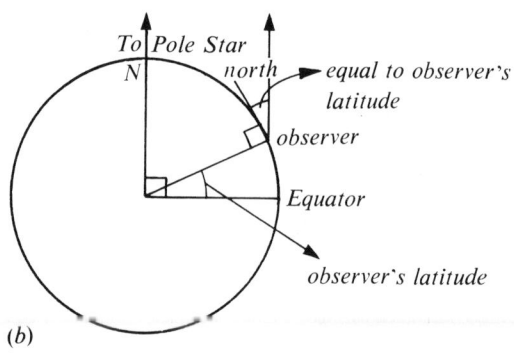

(*b*)

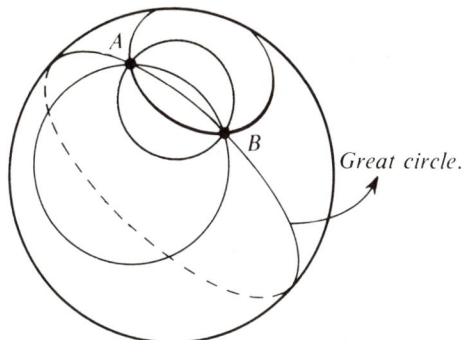

Figure 34:15

The calculation of a great circle distance between two places on the earth is, in general, too difficult for primary school children but if the points happen to lie on a meridian or on the equator some children may be able to find the difference of longitude or latitude and thus calculate the length of the great circle arc. In every case a piece of fine

Figure 34:16

string can be stretched as tightly as possible between the two points on the globe and then measured to give an approximate globe distance. This must then be converted to the true distance, reckoning the earth's radius as about 6371 km. This method can check the calculation of the

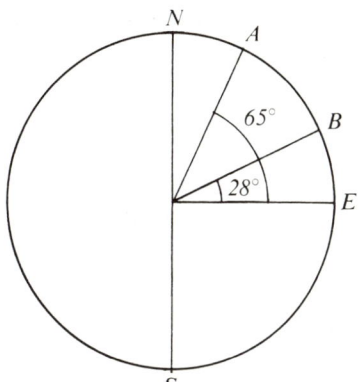

Figure 34:17

distance in the case of two points on a meridian. Figure 34:17 shows two such points A: with latitude 65°N, and B, with latitude 28°N.

Difference in latitude $= 65° - 28°$
$$= 37°$$
Circumference of great circle
$$= 2 \times \pi \times 6\,370 \text{ km approx.}$$
$$= 2 \times 3\cdot14 \times 6\,370 \text{ km approx.}$$
$$= 40\,000 \text{ km approx.}$$
Length of arc $= \frac{37}{360} \times 40\,000 \text{ km approx.}$
$$= 4\,000 \text{ km approx.}$$

The position of A can now be stated as 4 000 km North of B.

Change of position

Movement means change of position. Plotting the position of a ship or aircraft on a map gives vital information to its navigator. The accuracy of navigation depends on the instruments available to provide the information. The history of the development of such instruments to give more extensive and more accurate information makes interesting reading for older and abler pupils in primary schools.

Children can also collect information and charts to help them to study the movements of satellites, space probes, and so on. In this way they learn about circular and elliptical orbits. We consider these curves in Chapter 39.

35 The Structure of Vectors and Directed Numbers

Addition of vectors

A *vector* is a quantity which is measured in a particular direction (*see page* 90). The example of a vector which we have used is that of a *movement,* and we have seen that an essential property of vectors is their method of addition, which consists of performing the movement of the first vector, and then performing the movement of the vector to be added to it (Figure 35:1(*a*)). Children know well the one-dimensional example of a vector, a movement backwards or forwards along a line. These one-dimensional vectors (Figure 35:1(*b*)) develop into directed numbers, and give rise to the number line of directed rational numbers. One-dimensional vectors are only, however, one example; the movements which are examples of vectors can equally well take place in two or three dimensions.

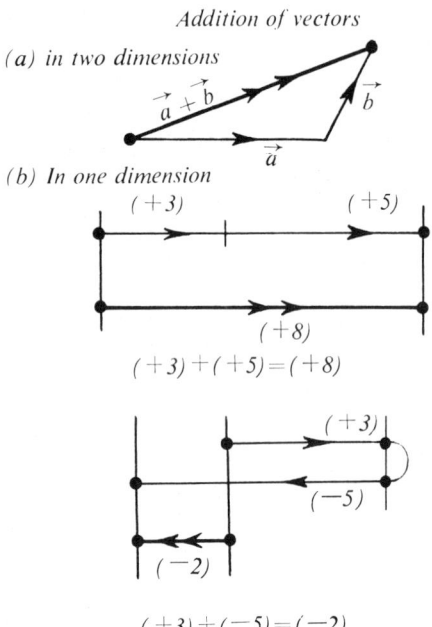

Addition of vectors

(*a*) *in two dimensions*

(*b*) *In one dimension*

$(+3)$ $(+5)$

$(+8)$

$(+3)+(+5)=(+8)$

$(+3)$

(-5)

(-2)

$(+3)+(-5)=(-2)$

Figure 35:1

We saw in Chapter 32 that the directed rational numbers behave rather similarly, as far as addition is concerned, to the signless rational numbers which have been used previously. By saying that two sets of numbers 'behave rather similarly' we can only mean that they obey rather similar arithmetical laws. In Chapter 32, page 332, we compared the laws obeyed by natural numbers with those for the signless rational numbers, and noticed the advantage of the latter set, which is closed for division

358

(except by zero). We now examine the similar laws which describe the behaviour of vectors and of directed rational numbers, and notice any arithmetical advantages and disadvantages which the vectors and directed rational numbers have over the previous set of numbers we have used.

Two laws which *vectors* obey for addition have already been described:

i) the set of vectors is *closed for addition*; that is, *any two* vectors can be added together to give a result which is also a vector,
ii) *the addition of vectors is commutative*; that is, the order in which two vectors are added makes no difference to the final result:

$$\vec{a} + \vec{b} = \vec{b} + \vec{a}$$

Referring to Chapter 32, page 332, we see that these two laws are the same as the first two addition laws for natural numbers and for the signless rational numbers. We now examine the other laws for addition. Figure 35:2 illustrates the fact that vectors in two dimensions and in one dimension are *associative for addition*; that is, for any vectors $\vec{a}$, $\vec{b}$ and $\vec{c}$,

$$(\vec{a} + \vec{b}) + \vec{c} = \vec{a} + (\vec{b} + \vec{c})$$

The diagram of Figure 35:2(*a*) could be drawn equally well in three-dimensional space, instead of in two dimensions. The vectors $\vec{a}$, $\vec{b}$ and $\vec{c}$ would then be movements in any directions through space. Hence three-dimensional, as well as two- and one-dimensional, vectors are associative for addition.

The importance of the associative law for addition of natural numbers and signless rational numbers is its use in rearranging and regrouping addition when dealing with large numbers. For example:

$$\begin{aligned}
27+9 &= (20+7)+9 \\
&= 20+(7+9) \text{ [regrouping to take ones together]} \\
&= 20+(10+6) \\
&= (20+10)+6 \text{ [regrouping to take tens together]} \\
&= 36
\end{aligned}$$

The same associative law is true for vectors, and in particular for one-dimensional vectors, and so we can now deal equally freely with directed numbers when adding them. A child may well prefer, when working out $(^+27)+(^-9)$, to argue

(*a*) *In two dimensions*

(i) **a** and **b** *are first added to give* $(\vec{a}+\vec{b})$: $\vec{c}$ *is then added to the result, giving* $(\vec{a}+\vec{b})+\vec{c}$

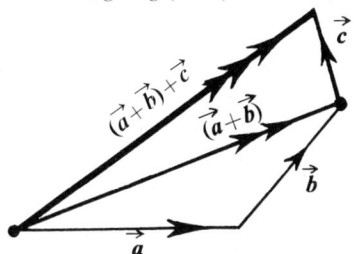

(ii) $\vec{b}$ *and* $\vec{c}$ *are added first to give* $(\vec{b}+\vec{c})$; *the result is then added to* $\vec{a}$, *giving* $\vec{a}+(\vec{b}+\vec{c})$. *The final vector is the same, irrespective of the order in which the addition was performed.*

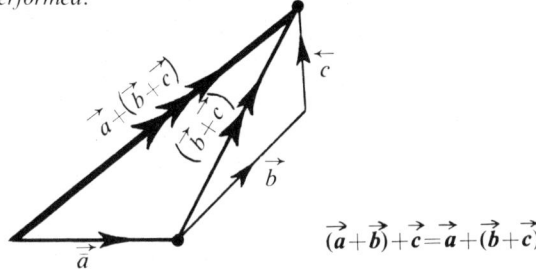

$$\vec{(a+b)}+\vec{c}=\vec{a}+\vec{(b+c)}$$

Figure 35:2

$$[(^+20)+(^+7)]+(^-9) = (^+20)+[(^+7)+(^-9)]$$
$$= (^+20)+(^-2)$$
$$= (^+18)$$

The next addition law is the existence of an *identity for addition* (*see page* 171). We have already seen that there is a *zero vector* (*see page* 94), the vector of not moving at all. The zero vector performs the function of an identity for addition, since for any vector **ā**,

$$\mathbf{\bar{a}}+0=0+\mathbf{\bar{a}}=\mathbf{\bar{a}}$$

For instance, if $\mathbf{\bar{a}}=(^-3)$, $(^-3)+0=0+(^-3)=(^-3)$

Subtraction of Vectors

We now consider the subtraction of vectors. When the subtraction of natural numbers was defined, we thought of it as *inverse addition*; 9−3 means 'What must be added to 3 to make 9?' (*See page* 83.) Subtraction is addition with one of the components of the sum missing, or a process of finding the missing number in addition. The same idea applies equally well to vectors.

In Chapter 10, page 92, we considered the journey of a

(*b*) *In one dimension*

(i) $[(^+10)+(^+7)]+(^-9)=(^+17)+(^-9)=(^+8)$

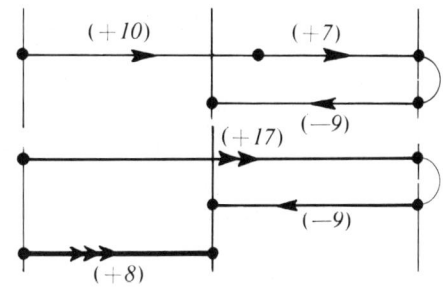

$$(^+10)+[(^+7)+(^-9)]=(^+10)+(^-2)=(^+8)$$

(ii)

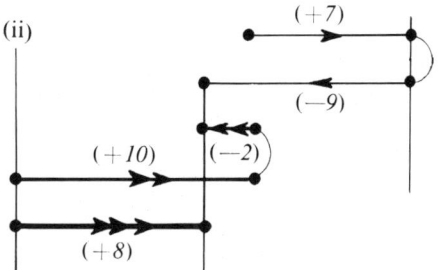

The final vector is the same, irrespective of the order in which the addition was performed.

boy who went from the bus-stop to his home either:

i) (30 metres East) along the road *and then* (40 metres North) along the path, or

ii) directly (50 metres N 37°E) across the field.

We wrote

(30 metres E) + (40 metres N) = (50 metres N 37°E)

When the boy has walked (30 metres E) the missing part of his journey, which makes up the total journey (50 metres N 37°E), is (40 metres N). If

(30 metres E) + $\boxed{\mathbf{x}}$ = (50 metres N 37° E),

then $\boxed{\mathbf{x}}$ = (40 metres N)

This statement can be written:

(50 metres N 37° E) − (30 metres E) = (40 metres N)

The idea of 'taking away a number' does not appear in the subtraction of vectors, and so

(50 metres N 37° E) − (30 metres E)

is best read as, '*What must be added* to the journey (30 metres E) to make the journey (50 metres N 37° E)?'

Using another example, if the lift in Chapter 32, page 339, is in the sub-basement (floor ($^-2$)), and it is needed on floor ($^+3$), it must make a journey of ($^+5$) floors. That is:

$$(^-2)+(^+5)=(^+3)$$

or

$$(^+3)-(^-2)=(^+5)$$

The subtraction $(^+3)-(^-2)$ can be read, 'What journey must the lift make from ($^-2$) to reach ($^+3$)?'

Children will find no difficulty in subtracting directed numbers if they regard the subtraction purely as addition with a missing number. The question $(^+5)-(^+2)$ means, 'If you have gone ($^+2$), and you want to go ($^+5$) altogether, what must you do to finish the journey?' That is, the missing vector in $(^+2)+\boxed{\mathbf{x}}=(^+5)$

is to be found, and so $\boxed{\mathbf{x}}=(^+3)$.

This example shows the obvious analogy with subtraction of natural numbers, but the same method applies equally easily to other examples, and only demands visualization of the directed number line. For instance,

$(^+5)-(^-2)=\boxed{\mathbf{a}}$ comes from $(^-2)+\boxed{\mathbf{a}}=(^+5)$,
   and so $\mathbf{a}=(^+7)$,
$(^-5)-(^-2)=\boxed{\mathbf{b}}$ comes from $(^-2)+\boxed{\mathbf{b}}=(^-5)$,
   and so $\mathbf{b}=(^-3)$,
$(^-5)-(^+2)=\boxed{\mathbf{c}}$ comes from $(^+2)+\boxed{\mathbf{c}}=(^-5)$,
   and so $\mathbf{c}=(^-7)$.

We return to the inverse addition, that is to the subtraction, of two-dimensional vectors, and give an example of the practical use of this process, which often occurs in air-navigation. Let us suppose that a pilot has to fly due North, but that there is a wind blowing at 120 km/h from the East. The speed at which the aircraft can fly is 600 km/h. Clearly he will have to steer in a roughly north-easterly direction, into the wind. In each hour, the wind would blow him 120 km to the West, so the sum of his two movements, (120 km West) and (600 km in

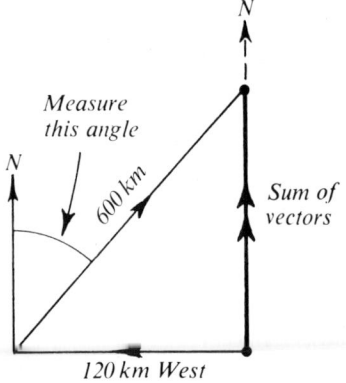

Measure this angle

600 km

Sum of vectors

120 km West

Figure 35:3

direction $\boxed{?}$) must produce a course pointing due North (Figure 35:3). The navigator draws a vector triangle showing the sum of his two movements and measures on it that his course should be N 11 °E.

The opposite of a vector

We saw in Chapter 32, page 340, that a child sometimes performs a *subtraction* of natural numbers by an *addition* of vectors. Instead of $9-3$ he does $(^+9)+(^-3)$. There is another alternative open to him. He may replace $9-3$ by $(^+9)-(^+3)$; that is, he may ask what he must add to $(^+3)$ to make $(^+9)$ (Figure 35:4). The addition $(^+9)+(^-3)$ and the subtraction $(^+9)-(^+3)$ give the same result, but the addition is easier to perform, as it only consists of following one movement by another and does not involve going back to the beginning and starting again.

Vector methods of performing $9-3$

(a)

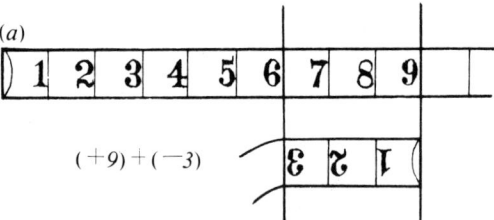

$(^+9)+(^-3)$

(b)

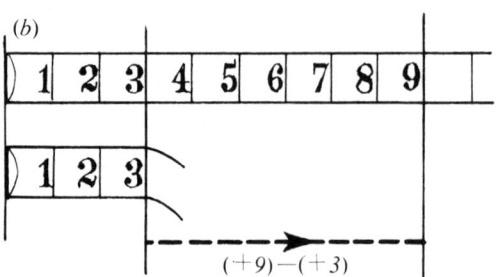

$(^+9)-(^+3)$

Figure 35:4

In fact, every subtraction of vectors can be replaced by an addition. We examine the one-dimensional case first.

$$(^-9)-(^+3)=(^-12)$$
$$(^-9)+(^-3)=(^-12)$$

The subtraction of ($^+3$) and the addition of its opposite vector ($^-3$) give the same result. Similarly

$$(^-9)-(^-3)=(^-6) \quad \text{and} \quad (^-9)+(^+3)=(^-6);$$
$$(^+9)-(^-3)=(^+12) \quad \text{and} \quad (^+9)+(^+3)=(^+12)$$

In each case the subtraction of a one-dimensional vector has been replaced by the addition of its opposite vector without affecting the result. We see that this is no coincidence, for if $\dot{x} = (^-9) - (^-3)$,

then $\dot{x} + (^-3) = (^-9)$,

replacing the subtraction statement by its original meaning. If we now add the opposite of $(^-3)$, which is $(^+3)$, to both sides of this equation, we obtain

$$\dot{x} + (^-3) + (^+3) = (^-9) + (^+3)$$

But $(^-3) + (^+3) = 0$, since $(^-3)$ and $(^+3)$ are opposites and therefore $\dot{x} = (^-9) + (^+3)$
But also $\dot{x} = (^-9) - (^-3)$
Therefore $(^-9) - (^-3) = (^-9) + (^+3)$

Similarly, the subtraction of any directed number can always be performed by *addition of its opposite*. The child who performs subtraction by stepping backwards and forwards on a tape-measure does this; he prefers $(^+9 + (^-3)$ to $(^+9) - (^+3)$.

Not only the subtraction of a directed number, but the subtraction of any vector can be performed by the *addition of its opposite*. Figure 35:5 shows $\dot{a} - \dot{b}$; that is, the vector which has to be added to $\dot{b}$ to make $\dot{a}$. It also shows $\dot{a} + (-\dot{b})$, and we see that $\dot{a} - \dot{b}$ and $\dot{a} + (-\dot{b})$ represent the same movement. We can repeat the theoretical

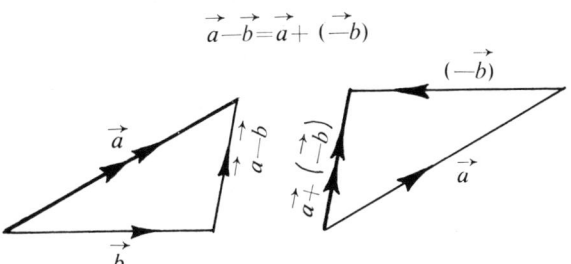

Figure 35:5

argument which was given above, adapting it to two dimensions.

If $\dot{x} = \dot{a} - \dot{b}$,
then $\dot{x} + \dot{b} = \dot{a}$,

using the definition of subtraction. Add the opposite of $\dot{b}$, that is $(-\dot{b})$, to both sides of this equation:

$$\dot{x} + \dot{b} + (-\dot{b}) = \dot{a} + (-\dot{b})$$

Since $\dot{b} + (-\dot{b}) = 0$ it follows that $\dot{x} = \dot{a} + (-\dot{b})$
Therefore $\dot{a} - \dot{b} = \dot{a} + (-\dot{b})$

Hence *the subtraction of any vector can be carried out by the addition of its opposite.*

Closure of the set of vectors for subtraction

One of the most important properties of vectors is that they are *closed for subtraction*. Given any vector $\dot{b}$, it is always possible to find a vector to add to it which will make the sum of the given vector $\dot{a}$ (Figure 35:6). That is, the vector $\dot{a} - \dot{b}$ always exists. This statement is

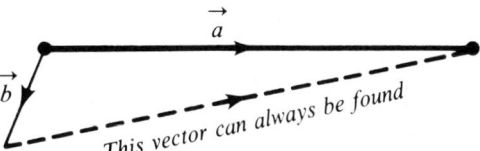

Figure 35:6

true in any number of dimensions, and its most important example is that of the one-dimensional vectors, or directed numbers. Given any directed number $\dot{b}$, there is always a directed number which can be added to it to make any other directed number $\dot{a}$; if the lift is at floor $(^+3)$, there is a movement which will take it to floor $(^-2)$, and similarly for any other example.

Here at last, in the directed rational numbers, we find a set of numbers which have the complete list of properties for addition for which we have been searching. The directed rational numbers have members which correspond to the natural numbers and fractions; their addition obeys all the laws which we expect, and these numbers have the additional property of being closed for subtraction.

We complete our study of the addition and subtraction of vectors by stating the laws which they obey, and then go on to discuss multiplication and division of directed rational numbers.

Laws for addition and subtraction of vectors
  (in any number of dimensions)

1. *Closure for addition*
   The set of vectors is closed for addition; that is, the sum of any two vectors is a vector.

2. *The commutative law for addition*
   For any vectors $\dot{a}$ and $\dot{b}$,
   $$\dot{a} + \dot{b} = \dot{b} + \dot{a}$$

3. *The associative law for addition*
   For any vectors $\dot{a}$, $\dot{b}$ and $\dot{c}$,
   $$(\dot{a} + \dot{b}) + \dot{c} = \dot{a} + (\dot{b} + \dot{c})$$

4. *The identity for addition*
   The vector $\mathbf{0}$ is the identity for addition. For any vector $\dot{a}$,
   $$\dot{a} + \mathbf{0} = \mathbf{0} + \dot{a} = \dot{a}$$

5. Subtraction

Subtraction is the inverse operation of addition;

$$\mathbf{\hat{a}} - \mathbf{\hat{b}} = \boxed{\mathbf{x}}$$

means

$$\mathbf{\hat{b}} + \boxed{\mathbf{x}} = \mathbf{\hat{a}}$$

The set of vectors is *closed for subtraction*; every equation $\mathbf{\hat{b}} + \boxed{\mathbf{x}} = \mathbf{\hat{a}}$ has a solution which is a vector.

Multiplication of directed numbers

We turn now to multiplication. We shall not discuss the multiplication of vectors in more than one dimension; there are several different types of multiplication of vectors in use, and none of them is likely to arise directly from children's experience in the primary school. The multiplication of directed numbers may, however, occur in children's graphical work. When children find a parabola, either as the path of a ball thrown in the air (*see page* 292, or by curve-stitching (*see page* 421), or by cutting a section of a cone (*see page* 417), the parabola is seen to be a symmetrical curve (Figure 35:7(*a*)). But when a parabola is drawn as a curve of squares (*see page* 321) (Figure 35:7(*b*)), only half of the curve is obtained. Children may suggest extending the horizontal axis backwards, and putting in the squares of negative numbers, in an effort to find the other half of the parabola. This will lead to an attempt to attach a meaning to $(^-2) \times (^-2)$, $(^-3) \times (^-3)$, and so on.

We shall first give an account of the multiplication of directed numbers at an adult level, one which demands a type of thinking outside the range of primary school children. We do this in order to show how the multiplication of directed numbers *must* behave, before going on to suggest a simpler method which begs some questions, but by which children may be convinced of its likelihood.

We have already seen that there is an isomorphism between the positive directed numbers and the signless numbers (*see page* 340); this correspondence holds for addition:

$$(^+3) + (^+2) = (^+5)$$

corresponds to

$$\updownarrow \qquad \updownarrow \qquad \updownarrow$$
$$3 \; + \; 2 \; = \; 5$$

It is important, if we are to continue to use the positive directed numbers and the signless numbers interchangeably, that the same correspondence should also hold for multiplication. We must have

$$(^+3) \times (^+2) = (^+6),$$

to correspond to

$$\updownarrow \qquad \updownarrow \qquad \updownarrow$$
$$3 \; \times \; 2 \; = \; 6$$

It is also necessary, as the directed numbers are used as a generalization of the signless numbers, that the multiplication of directed numbers should obey the same laws as the multiplication of signless numbers. Therefore the multiplication of directed numbers must be *closed*,[1] *commutative, associative,* and *distributive.* We now examine the results of these requirements.

Let b be any directed number, positive, negative or zero; it will have an opposite $(-b)$, such that

$$b + (-b) = 0 \quad \dots\dots\dots\dots\dots\dots\dots \text{(1)}$$

Let a be any other directed number, and multiply both sides of equation (1) by a:

$$a \times [b + (-b)] = a \times 0$$

We now make the further requirement that $a \times 0 = 0$. Hence

$$a \times [b + (-b] = 0$$

[1] That is, it must be possible to multiply *any* two directed numbers together and obtain a directed number.

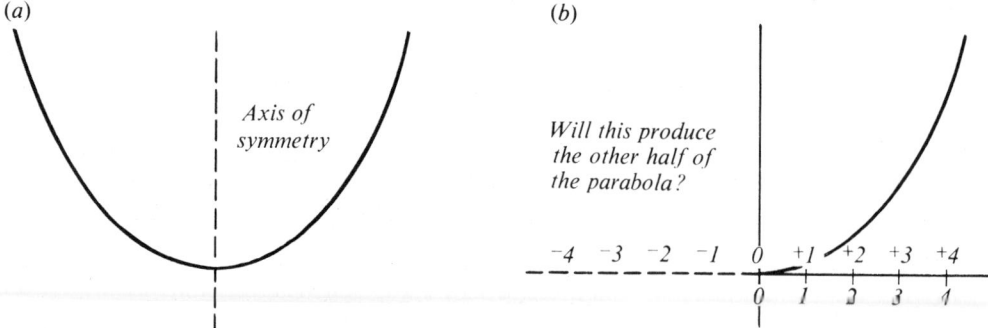

(*a*)

Axis of symmetry

(*b*)

Will this produce the other half of the parabola?

$$^-4 \quad ^-3 \quad ^-2 \quad ^-1 \quad 0 \quad ^+1 \quad ^+2 \quad ^+3 \quad ^+4$$
$$0 \quad 1 \quad 2 \quad 3 \quad 4$$

Figure 35:7

We now use the distributive law to expand the left-hand side:

$$(a \times b) + a \times (-b) = 0 \quad \ldots \ldots \ldots \ldots \ldots \quad (2)$$

But the directed numbers are to be closed for multiplication, so $(a \times b)$, or ab, is also a directed number, and therefore has an opposite, which we call $(-ab)$, such that

$$ab + (-ab) = 0 \quad \ldots \ldots \ldots \ldots \ldots \ldots \quad (3)$$

Comparing equation (2) with equation (3), we see that $a \times (-b)$ is also the opposite of ab.

Hence $a \times (-b) = (-ab)$

In words, the number *a multiplied by the opposite of b is equal to the opposite of (ab)*. This relationship completely fixes the behaviour of the multiplication of directed numbers.

Consider, for instance, $(^+4) \times (^-3)$. Now $(^-3)$ is the opposite of $(^+3)$. Hence $(^+4) \times (^-3)$ is equal to the opposite of $(^+4) \times (^+3) = (^+12)$, to preserve the correspondence with $4 \times 3 = 12$. Hence, in symbols, the argument becomes

$$\begin{aligned}(^+4) \times (^-3) &= -[(^+4) \times (^+3)] \\ &= -[^+12] \\ &= (^-12),\end{aligned}$$

and similarly $(^-4) \times (^+3) = (^-12)$. Now consider $(^-4) \times (^-3)$. We repeat the same argument:

$$\begin{aligned}(^-4) \times (^-3) &= -[(^-4) \times (^+3)] \\ &= -[^-12] \\ &= (^+12)\end{aligned}$$

Summarizing these four results, we see that it is a necessary consequence of the structure which we have required of the multiplication of directed numbers, that

$$\begin{aligned}(^+4) \times (^+3) &= (^+12), \\ (^+4) \times (^-3) &= (^-12), \\ (^-4) \times (^+3) &= (^-12), \\ (^-4) \times (^-3) &= (^+12)\end{aligned}$$

In general

$$\begin{aligned}a \times (-b) &= -ab, \\ (-a) \times b &= -ab, \\ (-a) \times (-b) &= ab\end{aligned}$$

It is now possible to complete the graph of squares, for

$$\begin{aligned}(^-1)^2 &= (^-1) \times (^-1) = (^+1), \\ (^-2)^2 &= (^-2) \times (^-2) = (^+4), \text{ and so on.}\end{aligned}$$

The other half of the parabola appears, and completes the expected pattern (Figure 35:8).

We should stress that this account of the multiplication of directed numbers is an abstract argument from stated assumptions, and represents a type of thinking which

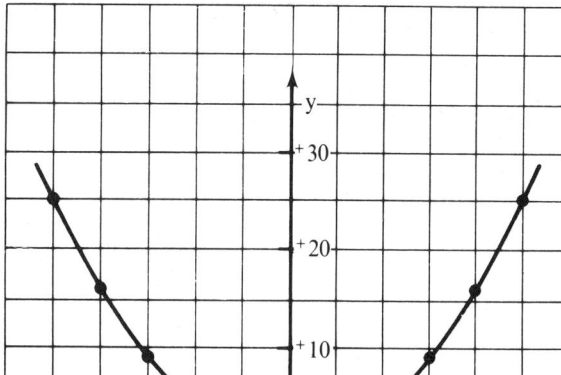

Graph of squares

Figure 35:8

does not develop until well on in adolescence. It is therefore unsuitable for primary school children.

There are various ways in which children can be introduced to the multiplication of directed numbers. One of the simplest, at this stage, is an attempt to adapt the multiplication table with which children are so familiar, so that it will contain positive and negative directed integers. The correspondence between the natural numbers and the positive and zero integers must be preserved, so that for instance $(^+3) \times (^+2) = (^+6)$ corresponds to $3 \times 2 = 6$. Figure 35:9 shows the first stages in building up this table. The problem of filling in the other three quarters of the table remains. The rows marked in Figure 35:9(c) can be completed by counting downwards along the directed number line (Figure 35:10(a)), and the opposite quarter filled in by relying on the expectation that multiplication will be commutative; that is, we expect that $(^+1) \times (^-4) = (^-4) \times (^+1)$ (Figure 35:10(b)).

The pattern of the three completed quarters of the table now shows very clearly how the last corner should be filled in to complete the pattern (Figure 35:11).

This appeal to the continuing pattern of the multiplication table is an informal embodiment of the principles used in the more formal argument: the need for the laws of multiplication to be satisfied, and the correspondence between the positive integers and the natural numbers.

Children will now be able to use their knowledge of the multiplication of integers to complete the graph of squares, and so to obtain the missing part of the parabola.

Relation diagrams for multiplication

We have earlier used relation diagrams alongside graphs to illustrate the multiplication of signless rational numbers,

363

Building up a multiplication table for the integers
a) The multiplication table for natural numbers

×	0	1	2	3	4	..	..
0	0	0	0	0	0	..	..
1	0	1	2	3	4	..	..
2	0	2	4	6	8	..	..
3	0	3	6	9	12	..	..
4	0	4	8	12	16	..	..
..	..	..	..	..	..	..	..
..	..	..	..	..	..	..	

Figure 35:9(a)

b) The framework of a multiplication table for the integers

×	..	−4	−3	−2	−1	0	+1	+2	+3	+4
.										
−1										
−2										
−3										
−4										
0										
+1										
+2										
+3										
+4										
.										

Figure 35:9(b)

c) The correspondence between a) and b) fills in part of the table for integers

×	−4	−3	−2	−1	0	+1	+2	+3	+4
					.				
−1					0				
−2					0				
−3					0				
−4					0				
0	0	0	0	0	0	0	0	0	0
+4					0	+1	+2	+3	+4
+3					0	+2	+4	+6	+8
+2					0	+3	+6	+9	+12
+1					0	+4	+8	+12	+16
.					.	.	.	.	.

Figure 35:9(c)

Next stages in building the multiplication table for the integers

×	−4	−3	−2	−1	0	+1	+2	+3	+4
−4					0				
−3					0				
−2					0				
−1					0				
0	0	0	0	0	0	0	0	0	0
+1	−4	−3	−2	−1	0	+1	+2	+3	+4
+2	−8	−6	−4	−2	0	+2	+4	+6	+8
+3	−12	−9	−6	−3	0	+3	+6	+9	+12
+4	−16	−12	−8	−4	0	+4	+8	+12	+16

Figure 35:10(a)

×	..	−4	−3	−2	−1	0	+1	+2	+3	+4	..
.	.	.	.	.	.	.	.	.	.	.	.
−4						0	−4	−8	−12	−16	..
−3						0	−3	−6	−9	−12	..
−2						0	−2	−4	−6	−8	..
−1						0	−1	−2	−3	−4	..
0	..	0	0	0	0	0	0	0	0	0	..
+1	..	−4	−3	−2	−1	0	+1	+2	+3	+4	..
+2	..	−8	−6	−4	−2	0	+2	+4	+6	+8	..
+3	..	−12	−9	−6	−3	0	+3	+6	+9	+12	..
+4	..	−16	−12	−8	−4	0	+4	+8	+12	+16	..
.	.	.	.	.	.	.	.	.	.	.	.

Figure 35:10(b)

The finished multiplication table for the integers

+	−4	−3	−2	−1	0	+1	+2	+3	+4
−4	+16	+12	+8	+4	0	−4	−8	−12	−16
−3	+12	+9	+6	+3	0	−3	−6	−9	−12
−2	+8	+6	+4	+2	0	−2	−4	−6	−8
−1	+4	+3	+2	+1	0	−1	−2	−3	−4
0	0	0	0	0	0	0	0	0	0
+1	−4	−3	−2	−1	0	+1	+2	+3	+4
+2	−8	−6	−4	−2	0	+2	+4	+6	+8
+3	−12	−9	−6	−3	0	+3	+6	+9	+12
+4	−16	−12	−8	−4	0	+4	+8	+12	+16

Increase of (+ 1) at each entry
Increase of (+ 2) at each entry
Increase of (+ 3) at each entry
Increase of (+ 4) at each entry

Figure 35:11

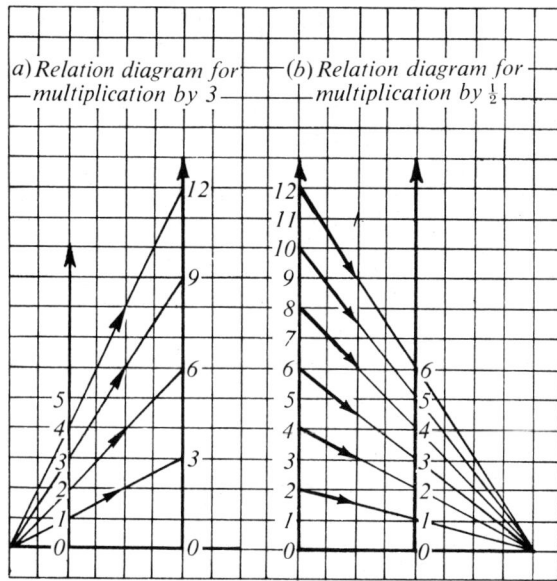

Figure 35:12

and we have seen that a relation diagram such as that of Figure 35:12 (*a*) or (*b*) emphasizes the enlargement or reduction aspect of the multiplication of a set of numbers by a constant factor. The lines joining each point of the original number line to its image all radiate from a point. It is now, therefore, possible to show relation diagrams for several multiplication tables on the same diagram, by varying the position of the number line on which images

are produced. Figure 35:13(*a*) shows relation diagrams for multiplication by 2, 3 and 4 on the same diagram. Multiplication by $\frac{1}{2}$ and other fractions may also be shown (Figure 35:13(*b*)). These diagrams correspond very closely to optical devices for enlarging a picture, in which rays of light are projected from a point.

The position of the image number line can be arranged to produce the correct enlargement for any given multiplication. In general, a single relation diagram can be used to read off an approximate answer to any multiplication of signless rational numbers, as shown in Figure 35:14(*a*). To find, for example, $3\frac{1}{2} \times 4\frac{1}{2}$, we need to find the position of the image when $4\frac{1}{2}$ is enlarged $3\frac{1}{2}$ times. Figure 35:14(*b*) shows, without any mapping lines, part of the relation diagram for multiplication of any two signless rational numbers.

An extension of this relation diagram can be used to illustrate the multiplication of directed rational numbers, and in particular to give another illustration of the fact that the product of two negative directed numbers is positive. The starting number line of the relation diagram can easily be converted to a number line of directed rationals. Multiplication of any directed number by $(^{+}2)$, $(^{+}3)$, $(^{+}4)$, ... can then be shown (Figure 35:15), replacing 3 by $(^{+}3)$, etc., when labelling the possible positions of the image number line. The horizontal line of the diagram shows the position in which the image number line is to be placed

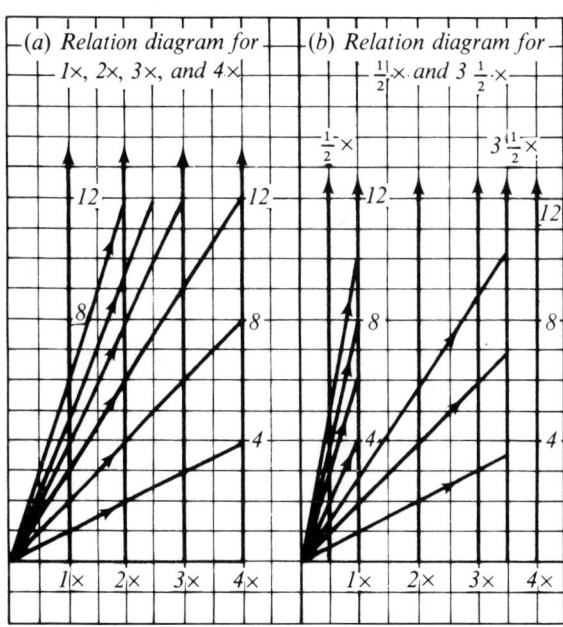

Figure 35:13

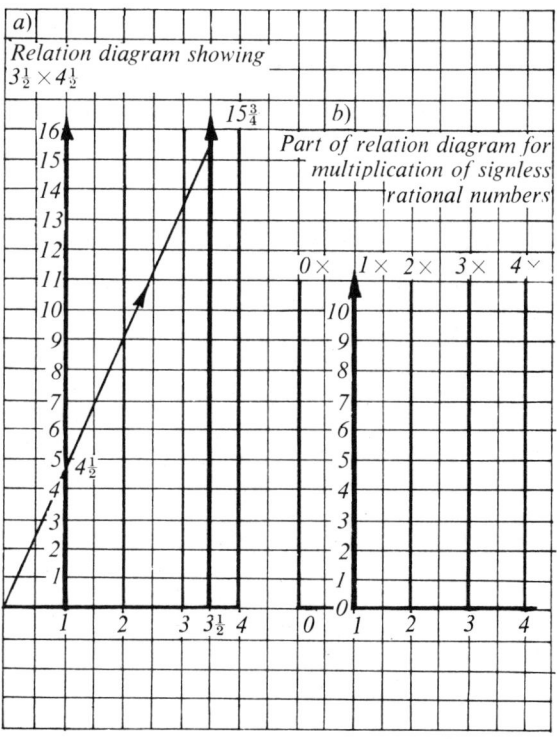

Figure 35:14

365

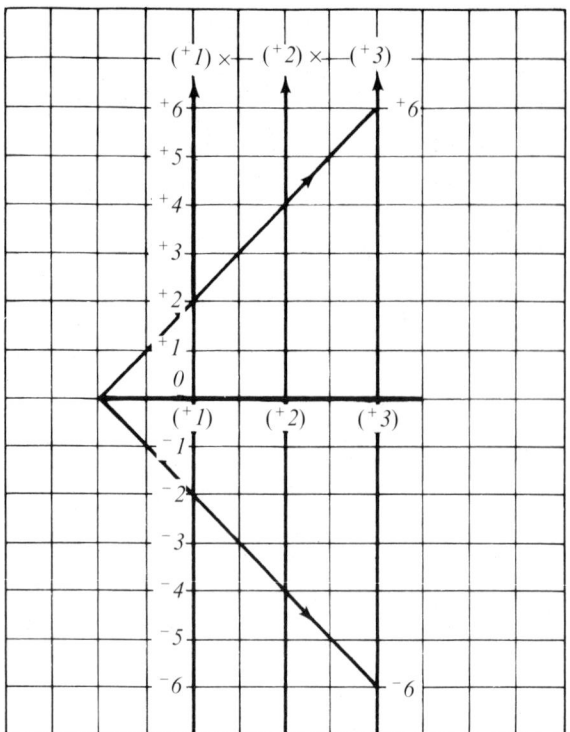

Figure 35:15

for a required enlargement. This number line can also be extended into a directed number line (Figure 35:16), so that we can now illustrate a negative multiple of any directed number, as well as a positive multiple. In order to

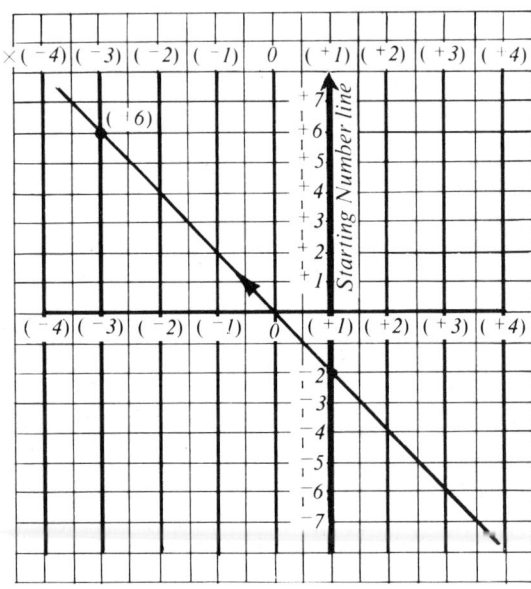

Figure 35:16

find any multiple of ($^-$2), we draw a mapping line from the point representing ($^-$2) on the starting number line, through the centre of enlargement. All multiples of ($^-$2) appear on this mapping line. In particular, we see from Figure 35:16 that ($^-$3) × ($^-$2) = ($^+$6).

This diagram gives a visual illustration of the fact that a negative multiple of a negative number is positive, and that similarly a negative multiple of a positive number is negative. This illustration of the multiplication of directed numbers may be useful to children who are used to thinking in terms of relation diagrams.

Completion of the structure of directed numbers

The last part of the previous section may have given the impression that we have only set up a method of multiplying directed *whole* numbers. This is not the case. The reader will have noticed that the proof of '*a multiplied by the opposite of b is equal to the opposite of (ab)*' is valid for *any* directed numbers a and b. For instance the result can be applied to:

$$(^+\tfrac{2}{3}) \times (^-\tfrac{4}{5}) = -[(^+\tfrac{2}{3}) \times (^+\tfrac{4}{5})]$$
$$= -[^+\tfrac{8}{15}]$$
$$= (^-\tfrac{8}{15})$$

Thus we have constructed a multiplication which is valid for *any* positive, negative or zero rational numbers. In fact, *the set of directed rational numbers is closed for multiplication.* This multiplication was constructed so that it would obey the commutative, associative and distributive laws. We are therefore well advanced in obtaining a multiplication of directed rational numbers which obeys all the laws asked of an arithmetical operation.

There is also an identity for multiplication; the rational number ($^+$1) has the property which distinguishes an identity: its product with any rational number a is the same rational number:

$$(^+1) \times a = a \times (^+1) = a$$

In Chapter 26, page 258, the reciprocal of a signless rational number a was defined to be the signless rational number whose product with a is 1. The reciprocal of $\tfrac{2}{3}$ is $\tfrac{3}{2}$, since $\tfrac{2}{3} \times \tfrac{3}{2} = 1$, and the reciprocal of $\tfrac{3}{2}$ is $\tfrac{2}{3}$. Every signless rational number except 0 has a reciprocal.

Similarly, every directed rational number except 0 has a reciprocal. The reciprocal of ($^+\tfrac{2}{3}$) is ($^+\tfrac{3}{2}$), since ($^+\tfrac{2}{3}$) × ($^+\tfrac{3}{2}$) = ($^+$1); and the reciprocal of ($^-\tfrac{2}{3}$) is ($^-\tfrac{3}{2}$), since ($^-\tfrac{2}{3}$) × ($^-\tfrac{3}{2}$) = ($^+$1). The rational number 0 has no reciprocal, for there is no rational number x such that

$$0 \times x = (^+1)$$

In order to complete the structure of the directed rational numbers we now only need to consider the *division* of one rational number by another. As usual, we define division as inverse multiplication; $\left(^{+}\frac{2}{3}\right) \div \left(^{-}\frac{1}{2}\right)$ means, 'What must $\left(^{-}\frac{1}{2}\right)$ be multiplied by to give $\left(^{+}\frac{2}{3}\right)$?'; or, 'solve the equation

$$\left(^{-}\frac{1}{2}\right) \times \boxed{x} = \left(^{+}\frac{2}{3}\right)$$',

This equation is solved in the same way as a similar one in Chapter 26, page 258 by multiplying both sides of it by the reciprocal of $\left(^{-}\frac{1}{2}\right)$, which is $(^{-}2)$, since $(^{-}2) \times \left(^{-}\frac{1}{2}\right) = (^{+}1)$.

Hence
$$(^{-}2) \times \left(^{-}\frac{1}{2}\right) \times \boxed{x} = (^{-}2) \times \left(^{+}\frac{2}{3}\right),$$
$$\text{and } \boxed{x} = \left(^{-}\frac{4}{3}\right)$$

Clearly, almost all such equations can be solved. The only exceptions are of the form

$$0 \times \boxed{x} = \left(^{-}\frac{2}{3}\right)$$

There is no rational number which multiplied by 0 gives $\left(^{-}\frac{2}{3}\right)$, and so the equation cannot be solved. In other words, the division $\left(^{-}\frac{2}{3}\right) \div 0$ cannot be performed, but all divisions other than by 0 are possible. To perform the division $a \div b$ where a and b are rational numbers, we have to solve the equation.

$$b \times \boxed{x} = a$$

This can be done by multiplying both sides of it by the reciprocal of b (unless $b = 0$).

Hence the set of directed rational numbers shares the property of the signless rational numbers, of being *closed for division*, EXCEPT FOR DIVISION BY ZERO. We have now completed our aim of constructing a set of numbers among which it is completely possible to do arithmetic. Any pair of directed rational numbers can be added, subtracted, multiplied or divided (except for division by zero), and the result is still a directed rational number. Moreover, the directed rational numbers contain a subset isomorphic with the natural numbers, with which we can count any number of things; they contain another subset isomorphic with the signless rational numbers with which we can measure any quantity to any degree of accuracy we like; and with the directed rationals themselves we can measure quantities such as time and temperature where an arbitrary starting point is needed. The search for arithmetical completeness which began from the natural numbers has now come to a (temporary) end with the directed rational numbers.

Mathematicians call a set of numbers which is closed for addition, subtraction, multiplication and division (except for division by zero) a *field*. The *field of directed rational numbers* is the first field which a child uses. It is not, however, the last. If he continues his mathematical education, he will soon need to operate in more extensive fields than the field of rational numbers. The *field of real numbers* and *the field of complex numbers* have the same basic structure as the field of rational numbers, but they contain other numbers, such as $\sqrt{(^{+}2)}$ and $\sqrt{(^{-}1)}$, which do not belong to the field of rational numbers. The importance of the field structure is that the laws for the behaviour of a field which a child has learnt from the field of rational numbers—the closure, associative, commutative, distributive, and identity laws, together with the existence of inverses—also hold in every other field. All methods of arithmetical and algebraic procedure depend on these laws, and so the methods and structure learnt at this early stage are continued through all further extensions of the number system of mathematics.

We now state the complete set of laws for the field of directed rational numbers. The reader will contrast the completeness of this structure with the incompleteness revealed by the laws of behaviour of natural numbers (*see page 171*), signless rational numbers (*see page 333*), and vectors in more than one dimension (*see page 361*).

In the statements of these laws we use a single letter, such as a, to represent a positive, negative or zero directed rational number. For instance, a may stand for $(^{+}3)$, $\left(^{-}\frac{2}{3}\right)$, 0, or any other rational number.

THE FIELD OF DIRECTED RATIONAL NUMBERS

Laws for addition and subtraction
1. *Closure for addition*
The set of directed rational numbers is closed for addition; that is, the sum of any pair of directed rational numbers is a directed rational number.

2. *The commutative law for addition*
For any directed rational numbers a and b,
$$a+b = b+a$$

3. *The associative law for addition*
For any directed rational numbers a, b and c,
$$(a+b)+c = a+(b+c)$$

4. *The identity for addition*
The directed rational number 0 is the identity for addition. For any directed rational number a,
$$a+0 = 0+a = a$$

5. *Subtraction*
Subtraction is the inverse operation of addition;
$$a-b = \boxed{x}$$
means
$$b+ \boxed{x} = a$$
The set of directed rational numbers is *closed for subtraction*; every equation such as
$$(^{-}3)+ \boxed{x} = \left(^{+}\frac{2}{3}\right)$$
has a solution in the set of directed rational numbers.

Laws for multiplication and division
1'. *Closure for multiplication*
The set of directed rational numbers is closed for multiplication; that is, the product of any pair of directed rational numbers is a directed rational number.

2′. The commutative law for multiplication
For any directed rational numbers a and b,
$$a \times b = b \times a$$

3′. The associative law for multiplication
For any directed rational numbers a, b and c,
$$(a \times b) \times c = a \times (b \times c)$$

4′. The distributive laws
For any directed rational numbers, a, b and c
$$a \times (b+c) = (a \times b) + (a \times c)$$
and
$$(a+b) \times c = (a \times c) + (b \times c)$$

5′. The identity for multiplication
The directed rational number $(^+1)$ is the identity for multiplication. For any directed rational number a,
$$a \times (^+1) = (^+1) \times a = a$$

6′. Division
Division is the inverse operation of multiplication;
$$a \div b = \boxed{x}$$
means
$$b \times \boxed{x} = a$$
The set of directed rational numbers is closed for division, *except by zero*. Every equation such as
$$(^-3) \times \boxed{x} = (^+\tfrac{2}{3})$$
has a solution in the set of directed rational numbers. The only equations without solutions are of the type
$$0 \times \boxed{x} = (^-\tfrac{2}{3})$$
Hence $(^-\tfrac{2}{3} \div 0)$ and other divisions by zero are not possible.

Notation for writing two- and three-dimensional vectors

We conclude this chapter by showing how the notation for directed rational numbers can be used to write two- and three-dimensional vectors in simple form.

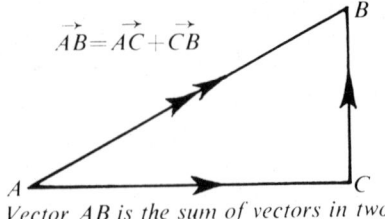

$$\vec{AB} = \vec{AC} + \vec{CB}$$

Vector AB is the sum of vectors in two basic directions

Figure 35:17

Any vector drawn on paper can be completely described by saying how far to the right or left, and how far up or down the paper the finishing point of the vector is from its starting point. That is, the vector can be thought of as the sum of two vectors each in a basic direction, left–right or up–down (Figure 35:17).

When vectors are used in navigation, the basic directions used are usually East–West and North–South. A vector may then be written in terms of vectors in these basic directions as (3 km East, 2 km North), or, arranging the symbols vertically, as

$$\begin{pmatrix} 3 \,\text{km East} \\ 2 \,\text{km North} \end{pmatrix}$$

If the length and direction of a pair of basic vectors are agreed beforehand, we can abbreviate the notation further. In this example, the most convenient basis vectors would be *1 km East* and *1 km North*. In terms of these basis vectors, only the components of the given vector need be written, and it can be abbreviated to $(\tfrac{3}{2})$ (Figure 35:18). The vector shown in this example lies in a roughly north-easterly direction, but vectors in other directions can be written in terms of the same basis by using directed numbers as components (Figure 35:19).

This column notation for vectors in a plane in terms of two basis vectors makes the recording of vector addition very simple (Figure 35:20). The two vectors which form the basis need not be at right angles. Figure 35:21 shows

Notation for a vector

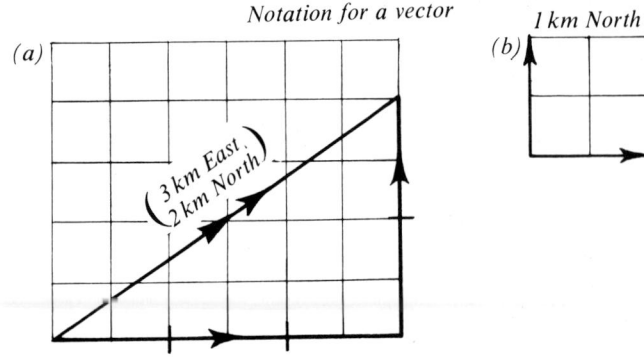

Figure 35:18

368

Naming vectors in terms of a basis

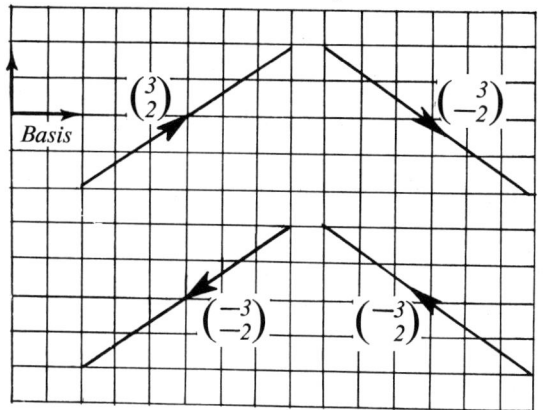

Figure 35:19

the addition of a pair of vectors using a basis suggested by equilateral triangular grid paper.

In three dimensions, three vectors in different directions which are not in a plane will be needed for a basis. Any vector will then have three components (Figure 35:22).

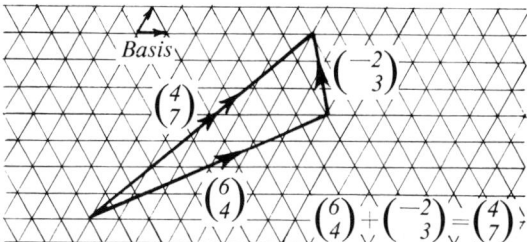

Figure 35:21

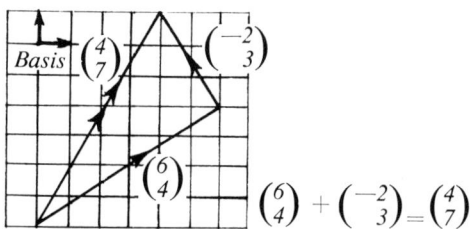

$$\begin{pmatrix}6\\4\end{pmatrix} + \begin{pmatrix}-2\\3\end{pmatrix} = \begin{pmatrix}4\\7\end{pmatrix}$$

Figure 35:20

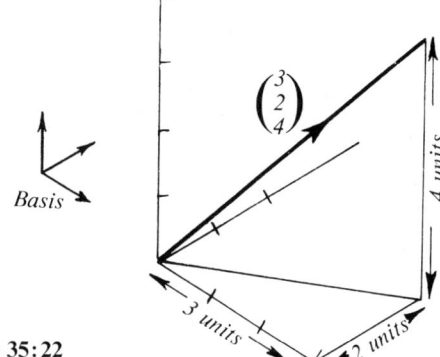

Figure 35:22

36 Scale, Rate and Ratio

Early experiences of ratio

We can trace the beginning of the idea of ratio in very early experiences in childhood. Objects are recognized as having the same shape even though their sizes differ. An object like a toy will be seen as the same object although when it is farther away from a child it appears to be smaller. Seen at a greater distance the height of the toy will appear to be reduced but if all the lengths show a similar reduction the thing is readily identified by a child. With further experience a child comes to recognize an object even when its shape seems different because the thing has been rotated or raised or lowered. Yet the easiest and most memorable recognition occurs when only size is changed and the appearance of shape is unaltered. This is shown in Figure 36:1.

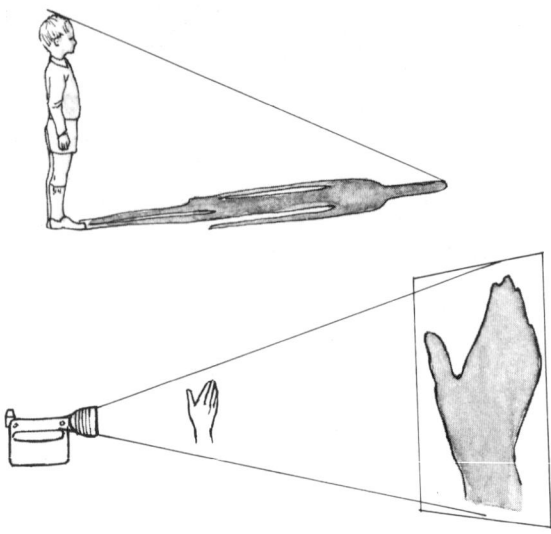

Figure 36:2

Figure 36:1

Enlargement, as by projection of a slide on to a screen, or reduction in size, as in a picture, reinforces a child's awareness of similarity of shape. Later on the observation of shadows will show that many shadows are distortions of the silhouette of the original object. A child's own shadow may be a very elongated shape when the sun is low in the sky, or a very short shape if it is cast by a high light close at hand. Occasionally a shadow is an enlarged version of the original, as when a hand is placed in the beam of light from a projector (Figure 36:2).

Children's delight in miniature versions of everyday objects is very marked during the early years at school. The range of such toys is vast. The demand for precision in the miniatures increases rapidly and shows clearly the

children's recognition of the correspondences that should exist between the parts of an object and its model.

Even before school days objects like jugs, model cars, shoes, jerseys, which are made in sets of different sizes are described by a child as 'the same only larger (or smaller)'. But any discrepancy in the size of corresponding parts in two somewhat similar objects is noticed. For example, in Figure 36:3(a) the spout is 'too long'; in Figure 36:3(b) the lorries have the 'wrong trailer'.

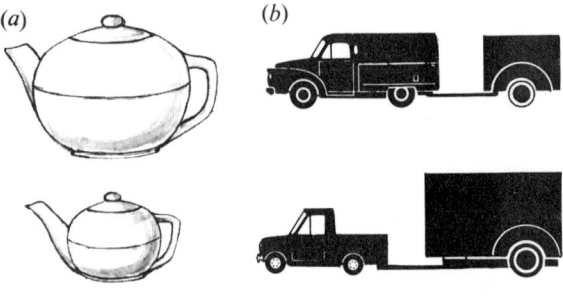

Figure 36:3

Such observations show that a child is becoming aware of equality of ratios of length but only in an intuitive way. As yet there is nothing numerical or precisely quantitative in his perception.

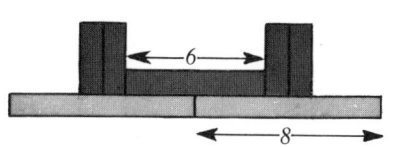

Figure 36:4

The ratio of lengths

The classification of blocks of various shapes which are made in two different sizes, like the Dienes Attribute Blocks, will lead to closer observation of lengths: the sides of the 'big' squares and the 'little' squares make pairs like the sides of the 'big' triangles and the 'little' triangles, or the sides of the 'big' rectangles and the 'little' rectangles.

Construction of models with two sets of structural apparatus based on different unit lengths, such as Stern rods and Cuisenaire rods, will bring out the fact that one model is a smaller version of the other. The idea of scale is emerging.

When children have built a staircase with each of these sets of rods they will associate a number with each rod in terms of the unit cube of its set. They will then be able to describe the structures in Figure 36:4 using the number names of the rods. The lengths of the rods in the two models can be compared. Any two rods of the one shape are then seen to have the same relationship as the corresponding pair in the other shape, for instance a six-rod and an eight-rod always have the same relationship, whatever their size.

To the child, the relation is between 6 and 8 seen as unmeasured lengths of a pair of rods in the same set. To the teacher another relationship, that between pairs of corresponding rods, one from *each* set, is also apparent and is seen in terms of the scale used in constructing the rods. In the Cuisenaire set the unit cube has an edge of 1 cm; in the Stern set the unit is 1·9 cm. The ratio of the edges is thus 1·9 cm to 1 cm. This ratio can be expressed as a *number* as 1·9 to 1 (Figure 36:5). Such a numerical statement becomes possible to children only after considerable experience with measures and numbers.

Although a child sees intuitively that the relation between a pair of rods from one set is the same as for the corresponding pair from another set, when he has one pair only he compares one with another at first in terms of 'bigger than', 'smaller than'. The staircase of rods shows each rod as '*one more than*' the next smaller one, when he is using unit cubes to make up the differences; or he will say that the two-rod needs a four-rod to match a given six-rod. He is not yet thinking in terms of *how many* two-rods would make a six-rod. In fact it is only when more than one pair of rods are seen to have the same relationship, though different in size, that the notion of ratio emerges as a way of comparing each pair. It is then usually stated as 'twice, 3 times, 5 times, ... as long'; this implies that the *ratio* is 3:1, 5:1, etc. The inverse statement, half as long, which comes very readily, can be extended at this stage and 'one-third, one-fifth, ... as long' can be used. In this fractional statement, the two numbers, one and three, or one and five, contain the idea of the ratio 1:3 or 1:5, though a child is not yet able to think

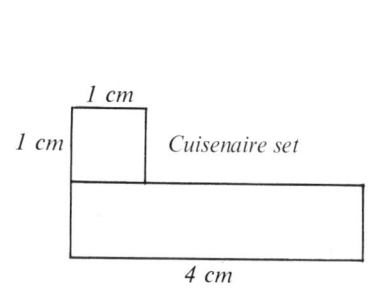

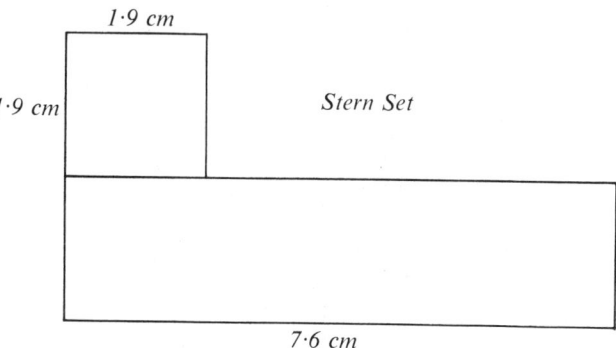

Figure 36:5

in this abstract way (Figure 36:6).

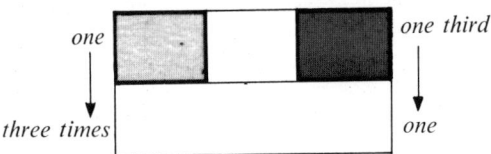

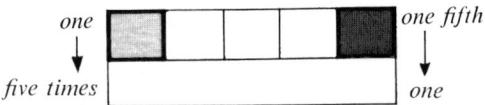

Figure 36:6

Another type of experience which helps the growth of the ratio concept is given when a class records several sets by using a block graph on 2 cm squared paper and an individual child makes his own copy on $\frac{1}{2}$ cm squared paper. At first he will not know the lengths of the sides of the squares but he will recognize the identity of pattern in the two grids and can judge whether his smaller copy of the large block graph 'looks the same'. He may also discover that four of his small squares would fit along the edge of a large square. Again there is an intuitive awareness of scale.

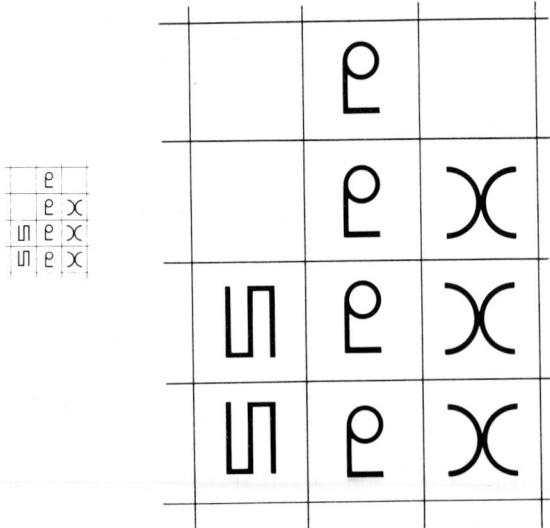

Figure 36:7

Correspondences and rates

Ideas about rates and ratios may develop from experience of the correspondences to be found between the members of two sets. One-to-one and one-to-many correspondences have been studied in earlier chapters. It is in the consideration of one-to-many correspondences that special cases occur which children notice when they are building up tables of multiples. If three children make between them

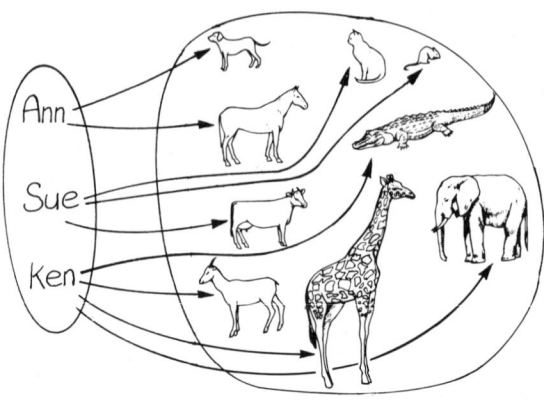

Figure 36:8

nine models of animals they may make different numbers of animals: Ann may make a dog and a horse; Sue may make a cat, a mouse and a cow; Ken may contribute a giraffe, an elephant, a crocodile and a goat. Figure 36:8 shows these correspondences. But if each child makes 3 animals then we have the special case when the three subsets, Ann's animals, Sue's animals, and Ken's animals, each have the same cardinal number. Figure 36:9 shows this correspondence. We can say that the *rate* of production is 3 animals per child. If this rate is the same for other

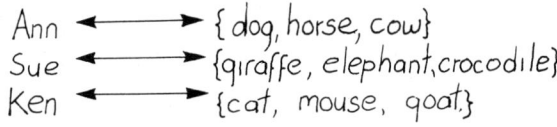

Figure 36:9

children in the class they can tabulate the animals that will be made by different numbers of children, counting the animals in threes.

children	1	2	3	4	5
animals	3	6	9	12	15

A child may say that there are 3 times as many animals as there are children, or that when twice as many children are at work they make twice as many animals. He is seeing relationships between *numbers* of children and of animals but he is not yet ready to think of the abstract idea of ratio as a special kind of relationship between two numbers.

At this stage a child can see the three-to-one correspondence of animals to children; he can understand the rate of production as 3 animals per child but he could be confused if he were asked to think of the relationship of the numbers themselves apart from their meaning in stating the rate at which the animals are made. As we shall see in succeeding paragraphs, two *quantities of the same kind*, e.g. two lengths, can be compared by a ratio; two *numbers* can be related by a ratio, e.g. 2:1. But sets of *different kinds* of things or quantities measured in *different units* lead to examples of correspondences that can be connected by a rate but cannot be compared in terms of the ratio of pairs of members. Obviously a wide experience of correspondences and rates prepares for the more abstract study of ratio. Later on, children will solve many problems from seeing the equality of such ratios as 2 children to 3 children and 6 animals to 9 animals.

Multiplication and ratio

The extension of experiences such as those described in the last paragraph, which lead on to the notion of ratios of numbers, will produce sets of multiples (see Chapter 16). The tabulation of the multiples of 3 suggest a correspondence between the natural numbers and the sequence of multiples. Any member of a set of natural numbers can be transformed into a multiple of 3, and we can relate each number to a multiple and vice versa. The *operation* which transforms the number is multiplication by 3. The relation between the multiple and the corresponding natural number is the ratio 3:1 (Figure 36:10).

A relation diagram illustrates the transformation and can lead on to an awareness of the ratio. If the lines joining corresponding points on the two number lines are continued they will all pass through the same point, P. A light placed at P would project the points 0, 1, 2, 3, ... on the starting number line into the points 0, 3, 6, 9, ... on the number line of multiples (Figure 36:11). It can be seen that the ratio of the corresponding line segments is 3:1.

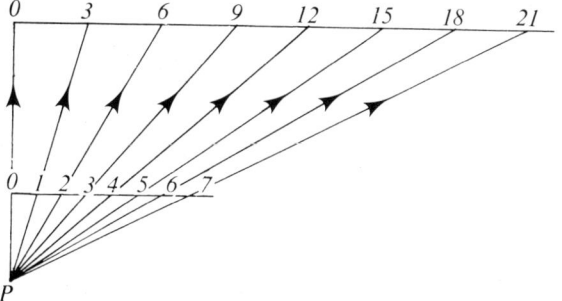

Figure 36:11

The pairs of corresponding numbers in this relation diagram can be written in the usual way: (1,3), (2,6), (3,9), ... (7,21). This arrangement emphasizes the relation between each pair: the *second number is 3 times the first*, or their ratio is 3:1. At this stage the close connection between multiplication and the ratio of a pair of numbers is clear: $3:1 = 6:2 = 9:3 = 21:7$.

The inverse ratios are also equal, i.e. $1:3 = 2:6 = 3:9 = ... = 7:21$.

Representation of ratio

A. GEOMETRICAL PATTERNS ON A NAIL-BOARD
In previous paragraphs we have seen that ratios can be shown in relation diagrams. Figure 36:11 shows not only the number relation in terms of length: it also brings out the geometrical pattern that equivalent ratios form when they are presented on a pair of parallel lines. A practical way of demonstrating this is through the use of elastic bands on a nail-board. Figure 36:12 shows the bands

Natural no.	1	2	3	4	5	6	7
Multiple	3	6	9	12	15	18	21

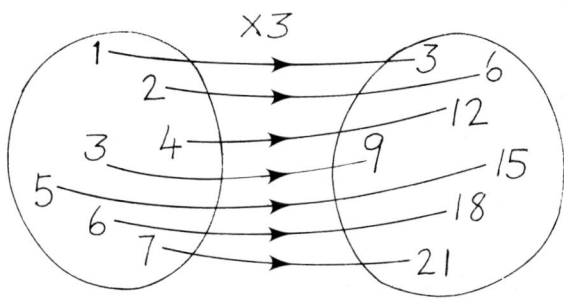

Figure 36:10

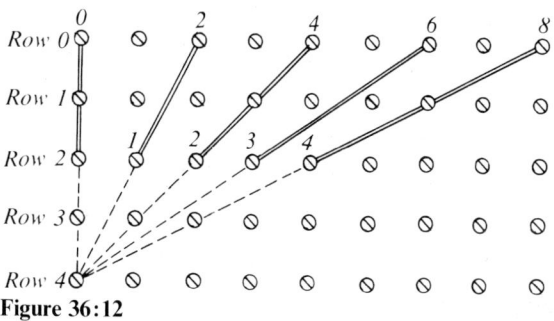

Figure 36:12

373

placed round nails to relate 2, 4, 6, 8, ... to 1, 2, 3, 4, ... The distances in rows 0 and 2 are in the ratio 2:1.

Children can discover from this experiment that all the bands can be stretched farther to pass round the same nail, as in the figure. They can also notice where the bands cross the lines of nails in row 1 and row 3. The distances between the bands at row 1 are $1\frac{1}{2}$ times the interval between adjacent nails. In row 3 the distances are a half of the interval. The ratio of the distance in row 1 to the distance in row 2 is $1\frac{1}{2}$ to 1. For row 3 and row 2 the ratio is $\frac{1}{2}$:1. This discovery may be the introduction to the use of a fraction in expressing a ratio and should lead to the recognition that $\frac{1}{2}$:1 is equal to 1:2, 2:4, 3:6, etc.

Again, a pattern of triangles is suggested by Figure 36:11 and the parallel lines crossing them are clearly defined by the rows of nails.

If we look carefully at the set of triangles made by the two elastic bands on the left (Figure 36:13) we see that there is a set of *similar* triangles with a common vertex, E, in row 4. The rows of nails are placed at equal intervals from 0 to 4. We can see at once the distance at which the elastic band AE crosses each of these rows. The ratios of

The relationship between the sides of two similar triangles can be stated in a different way. In Figure 36:13 we can compare the horizontal side of the largest triangle with the horizontal side of the smallest triangle. The ratio is $2:\frac{1}{2}$, or 4:1. If we now compare the vertical sides of these two triangles the ratio is seen at once to be 4:1. We can also compare the sloping sides, AE and DE; these are also in the ratio 4:1. It can be said that in a set of similar triangles the *ratio of a side of one* of them to *the corresponding side of another* triangle in the sets is the same for each of the sides.

Figure 36:14 illustrates this principle. $AB:AD = AC:AE = BC:DE$.

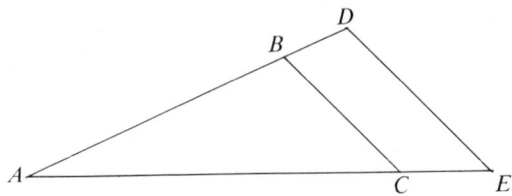

Figure 36:14

Graph of multiples

The line graph of the multiples of any number is also the representation of number pairs which have the same ratio. For example, the multiples of 2 are shown by the line $y = 2x$. This equation can be written $\frac{y}{x} = 2$, and the ratio $y:x$ is equal to the ratio 2:1. Therefore the point (x,y)

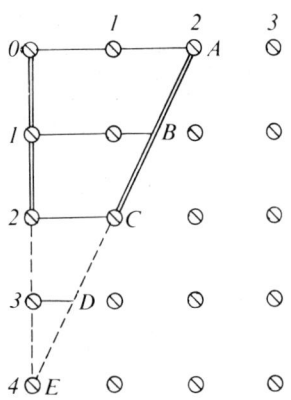

Figure 36:13

the corresponding pairs of sides of the triangles can therefore be found as in the following table.

Side of triangle	Vertical side	Horizontal side	Ratio of vertical to horizontal side
AE	4	2	4:2
BE	3	$1\frac{1}{2}$	$3:1\frac{1}{2}$
CE	2	1	2:1
DE	1	$\frac{1}{2}$	$1:\frac{1}{2}$

The ratios are all equal to 2:1. We see that in a set of similar triangles *the ratio of a pair of sides in one triangle* is equal to the ratio of the *corresponding pair* in any of the other triangles.

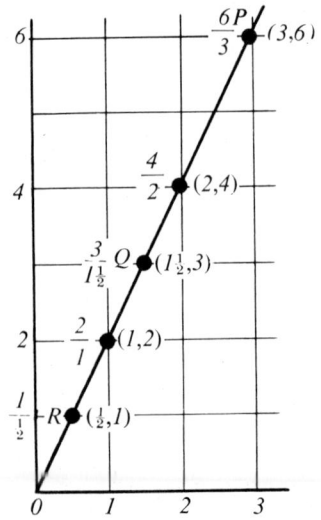

Figure 36:15

represents the ratio $y:x$, i.e. the ratio of the *second number to the first* in the pair of co-ordinates. The graph of the multiples of 2 shown in Figure 36:15 contains the points $(\frac{1}{2},1)$, $(1,2)$, $(1\frac{1}{2},3)$, $(2,4)$, $(3,6)$, each representing a number and the corresponding multiple of 2. Hence the ratios represented by the points are $1:\frac{1}{2}$, $2:1$, $3:1\frac{1}{2}$, $4:2$, $6:3$; these ratios are shown on the graph beside the co-ordinates. They are all equal, since the triangles we have made are all similar.

The point $P(3,6)$ is the vertex of a triangle with sides 3 units and 6 units. Each point on the line OP is the vertex of a similar triangle. Thus the straight line in the graph is the image of all pairs of numbers which are in the ratio $2:1$. Some of the points on the line have fractional co-ordinates.

The point R corresponds to the ratio $1:\frac{1}{2}$. The point Q corresponds to the ratio $3:1\frac{1}{2}$; both of these ratios are equal to $2:1$. It will be noticed that these representations of ratio in which similar triangles can be found are so placed that corresponding sides of the triangles are either parallel or are in a line. We say that they are *similarly placed*. When shapes are so placed the similarity is most easily seen, but children who have handled triangular tiles will realize that the ratio of a pair of corresponding sides is unchanged if the tiles are rotated, translated, or reflected, because the shape is invariant under these transformations. Similar shapes do not lose their similarity if they are no longer similarly placed.

Measurement and scale

In earlier sections of this book we have seen how important for children's understanding of space is the growth of their ability to represent both individual objects and their relative positions by drawing pictures and maps. Full understanding of a map, with its particular code for representing positions and distances, is a long process and develops through definite stages over a period of years. Ratio is only one of the ideas involved but it is a fundamental one and should therefore be given full opportunity to develop at the primary school stage.

A child's first representational drawings are pictorial and he is satisfied if in certain respects the drawing looks like the thing he sees. It must show certain features which he has associated with the object, but its dimensions may not be proportional to those of the original. As awareness of length grows through constructing and fitting things together, children will wish their drawings to show some of the length relations which they discover through measuring. Their experience of making patterns and models of the same form but differing in size may suggest to them the choice of a suitable length to be the image of an actual length in an object to be represented; for instance the side of a square on squared paper may represent a decimetre, or 2 cm may stand for 1 metre. The

idea of the *ratio* of the scale length to the actual length does not arise at this stage but a child knows that if 2 cm is to represent 1 metre, for a length of 3 metres he must draw 3×2 cm. Thus the first step towards the understanding of proportion is being taken.

When a tabulation is made to show scale lengths and actual lengths in related pairs children will discover the relationship between the pairs of numbers. For example if 1 cm represents 4 metres the tabulation will show *numbers* which are in the ratio $4:1$.

Actual length in *metres*

| 1 | 2 | 3 | 4 | 5 | 6 | 7 | 8 | 9 | 10 |

Scale length in *centimetres*

| $\frac{1}{4}$ | $\frac{1}{2}$ | $\frac{3}{4}$ | 1 | $1\frac{1}{4}$ | $1\frac{1}{2}$ | $1\frac{3}{4}$ | 2 | $2\frac{1}{4}$ | $2\frac{1}{2}$ |

The ratio of the *number* of metres in the actual length to the *number* of centimetres in the corresponding scale length is $4:1$; this is quite different from the ratio of the *lengths*, $400:1$, which can be seen when both lengths are expressed in terms of the same unit.

A clear distinction must be drawn between *the ratio of the two quantities* and the *rate* at which one quantity measured in a particular unit can be related to another quantity measured in appropriate units. When a scale-drawing is made as a representation of any shape the ratio of scale length to actual length is the same for every pair of corresponding lengths. For example if a scale of 1 cm to 5 metres is chosen to make a plan of a rectangular plot 15 m by 25 m, each actual length is 500 times the scale length; for example, 15 m is 500 times 3 cm; 25 m is 500 times 5 cm. The perimeter, 80 m, is 500 times the perimeter of the plan which is 16 cm. When the ratio of the scale length to the actual length, in this instance $1:500$, is expressed as a fraction, $\frac{1}{500}$, it is known as the *representative fraction* of the plan or map. Many of the maps that pupils read and use have the representative fraction stated. For instance some Ordnance Survey maps have their representative fractions stated as $\frac{1}{63360}$. The ratio of scale length to true length is $1:63360$. When the map lengths and the actual lengths are expressed in the *same units* the ratio of the *number of units* is, of course, equal to the ratio of the *lengths*: 2 cm represents 2×63360 cm. Children can calculate the representative fraction for maps drawn on other scales; e.g. the scale or rate of 1 cm to a kilometre leads to a representative fraction $\frac{1}{100\,000}$ or a ratio of $1:100\,000$.

Ratio of quantities

Drawing plans and maps leads naturally to a comparison of lengths in terms of ratio, but other quantities frequently need to be compared or transformed by the use of ratio. For example, substances are often mixed by mass, as in cooking. To preserve the properties of the mixture the ingredients must remain in *proportion* if the total quantity is changed, i.e. the ratio of the masses of any pair of ingredients must be maintained.

If a recipe gives 100 grams of lard to $\frac{1}{2}$ kilogram of flour it is stating a *rate* in units which are thought to be convenient. This rate will be the same for any other total quantity if the ratio of new mass to old mass is the same for each ingredient: 200 grams of lard will be required for 1 kilogram of flour, a ratio of 2:1 in comparison with the original quantities. For $\frac{3}{4}$ kg of flour a ratio of $1\frac{1}{2}$:1 or 3:2 must be used to find the required weights of the other ingredients; e.g. it will need $\frac{3}{2} \times 100$ grams, i.e. 150 grams of lard. Thus we find that ratios are necessary in using a constant rate.

The ratio of the *quantities* in the recipe will only be seen, however, if the masses are stated in the same units; e.g. 100 grams of lard to 500 grams of flour. The ratio of the quantities is 1:5 by mass and this relation enables us to say at once that 750 grams of flour requires $\frac{750}{5}$ grams (or 150 grams) of lard. The ratio of the actual quantities is independent of the units used and therefore holds for all units.

The same principles apply to other measureable quantities: the ratio of any two quantities of the same kind can be stated numerically if they are expressed in the same units. For example $\frac{1}{2}$ hour per day is equivalent to $\frac{1}{2}$ hour in every 24 hours, a ratio of 1:48. A rate of discount of 5 pence in £1 can be expressed in fivepences to give a ratio of 1:20.

A suitable diagrammatic way of representing certain ratios is by drawing pie-charts. The ratio of parts to whole is shown by the ratio of the angles at the centre of the circle to one complete revolution. For example, if a discount of 10 per cent is allowed, and £1 is represented by an angle of 360° at the centre of the circle, the discount will be represented by $\frac{1}{10}$ of 360°, i.e. 36°. The area of the sector of the circle formed by this angle will bear the same ratio, 1:10, to the area of the whole circle. If a set of 24 children is making a survey of individual preferences for the subjects of the curriculum, a pie-chart will show plainly the ratios of the number who do and the number who do not prefer mathematics to the total number in the set. Figure 36:16(*a*) illustrates the ratio 9:24 for those who *do*, and 15:24 for those who *do not*. At the same time it demonstrates the ratio of dos and don'ts as 9:15. The angles at the centre of the circle are 135° and 225°. As a visual image of several ratios the pie-chart is effective. If the proportions of several ingredients in a mixture are known, a pie-chart will also show the ratio of the remainder of a mixture to the whole quantity. For example, in Figure 36:16(*b*) the ratios are 6:24, 4:24, 3:24, 2:24, represented by sectors which can be compared by means of the angles at the centre. The shaded residue is found to have an angle of 15° which represents a ratio of 15°:360° or 1:24. In general, however, the pie-chart does not give much help in computation, though it enables us to use ratios of angles and thus avoid complicated manipulation

376

of fractions. Its chief value lies in the visual imagery of parts in relation to one another and to the whole.

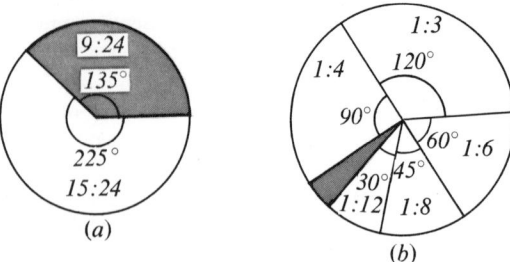

Figure 36:16

Rate and ratio for quantities of different kinds

We have examined the way in which quantities of the same kind can be compared: by a rate if they are measured in different units, by a ratio if they are measured in the same units. If a rate is to be maintained, when one quantity is changed in a certain ratio, say 2:1, the other quantity must be changed in the same ratio. For example, if the price of goods is reduced at the rate of ten pence in the pound the price of an article which costs 300 pence must be reduced by an amount whose ratio to £1 is 10:100 or 1:10. The reduction will be $\frac{1}{10} \times 300$ pence, or 30 pence.

It frequently happens that we must compare two different *kinds* of quantity, e.g. *distance* travelled and *time* taken for a journey. If the rate connecting them is constant, say 40 km/h, then if the distance is altered in a certain ratio the time taken will be altered in the same ratio. For a distance of 56 km the original time of 1 hour for 40 km must be changed in the ratio 56:40, or 14:10. The time will be $\frac{14}{10} \times 1$ hour, that is 1 hr 24 min. If 3 things cost 18 pence the cost of 5 things at this rate will be $\frac{5}{3} \times 18$ pence, which is 5×6 pence or 30 pence.

This ratio connection between a pair of quantities of one kind and the corresponding pair of another kind gives us the fundamental method of solving problems concerning two quantities changing at a constant rate.

Percentages

The comparison of ratios is naturally carried out in their fractional form; 2:3 can be compared with 10:17 if we find out whether $\frac{2}{3}$ is greater or less than $\frac{10}{17}$. This can be done by converting the fractions to decimals. The use of decimals allows us to state each ratio to the degree of accuracy that is sensible in any given situation. Dividing 2 by 3 and continuing to the third decimal place we obtain 0·667:1 as an equivalent form of the ratio 2:3, correct to 3 decimal places. Dividing 10 by 17, as shown below, gives the decimal form for 10:17. The ratio 10:17 becomes 0·588:1.

```
        0·588
17)10·000
       85
      ───
      150
      136
      ───
       140
       136
       ───
         4
```

This procedure is a general one, suited to every ratio stated as a number pair. However, the decimal form is not as simple as one that can be stated in integers. It is therefore standard practice to make 100 the second number of the ratio so that 1:2 is written as 50:100 or 50 per cent. This means, in fact, working in hundredths, 1:2 is $\frac{50}{100}$ or 0·50. Since the second decimal place gives hundredths we see that 0·50 can be read immediately as $\frac{50}{100}$ or 50%.

Returning to $\frac{2}{3}$ and $\frac{10}{51}$, we can now look at the hundredths place in each decimal expression and read 0·667:1 as 66·7% and 0·588 as 58·8%.

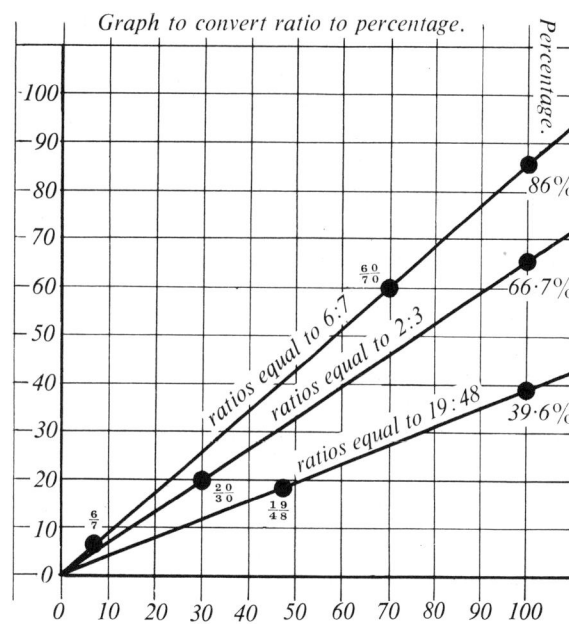

Figure 36:18

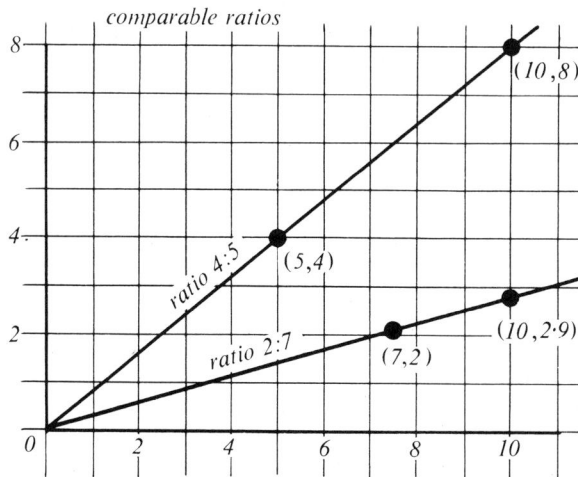

Figure 36:17

The graphical way of converting a ratio to a percentage form is simpler and is the best method unless greater accuracy is needed. We know that all equal ratios can be represented by a straight-line graph. In Figure 36:17 we see a line which represents ratios equal to 4:5. One of these ratios is 8:10. Another line shows the ratio 2:7; it also shows an equal ratio 2·9:10. We can thus compare 4:5 with 2:7 by using the equal ratios 8:10 and 2·9:10. This idea is extended to percentages by finding equal ratios with 100 as the right-hand number (Figure 36:18). Notice also the use of $\frac{20}{30}$ as well as $\frac{2}{3}$ to give greater accuracy in drawing the graph.

Proportion: finding proportional lengths

Similar triangles have their sides proportional; that is, the ratio of any pair of sides of one triangle is equal to the ratio of the corresponding pair in the other triangle. It may sometimes be required to draw a triangle similar to a given one and of a particular size; that is with one side of a given length. Suppose ABC is to be transformed into a similar triangle PQR with PQ a given line segment corresponding to the side AB. We need to find the lengths of QR and RP (unless we construct the triangle by measuring the angles of $\triangle ABC$).

If $\triangle PQR$ is made similar to $\triangle ABC$, $PQ:AB = QR:BC = RP:CA$. PQ and AB are known: thus we know the ratio required for the remaining pairs of sides. There are several ways of finding the lengths of QR and RP from the information we have.

A. BY CALCULATION

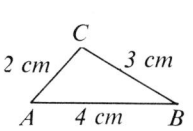
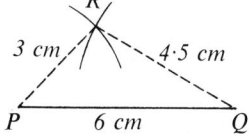

Figure 36:19

377

Measure the sides of $\triangle ABC$ and the length of PQ. Calculate the ratio $PQ:AB$. Multiply the lengths of BC and CA by this ratio to give the lengths QR and RP. In Figure 36:19 $PQ:AB = 6:4 = 3:2$.

$$QR = 3 \times \tfrac{3}{2}\,\text{cm} \qquad RP = \tfrac{3}{2} \times 2\,\text{cm}$$
$$= 4 \cdot 5\,\text{cm} \qquad\qquad = 3\,\text{cm}$$

In this example the lengths are stated to the nearest centimetre. In most instances the measures would be given with greater exactness and the calculations would be more troublesome. The significant aspect of this method is that it uses the ratio as a multiplier which will transform a given length in the required ratio.

B. BY A RELATION DIAGRAM

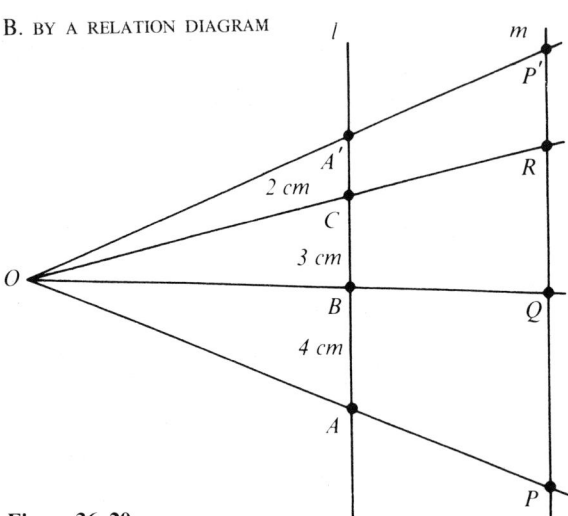

Figure 36:20

Draw two parallel lines, l and m, so that the lengths of AB, BC, CA can be mapped on to PQ, QR, RP. On line l mark lengths AB, BC, $CA' = CA$. On line m mark the length PQ in the same sense as AB. Draw PA and QB, continuing them to meet at O. Draw OC and continue it to cut m in R. Draw OA' and let it cut m at P'. Then OR and RP' are the lengths required to enable us to draw $\mapsto PQR$. (Figure 36:20.)

C. BY A GRAPH

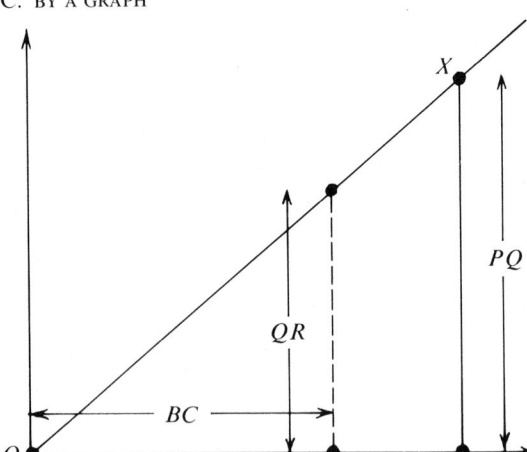

Figure 36:21

Mark a point X on the graph with co-ordinates representing AB and PQ. Join X to O, the origin. Then every point on the straight line through O and X has co-ordinates in the ratio $AB:PQ$. The point on OX whose x co-ordinate represents BC has its y co-ordinate representing QR (Figure 36:21). RP can be found similarly.

D. USING PARALLEL LINES CUTTING THE ARMS OF AN ANGLE

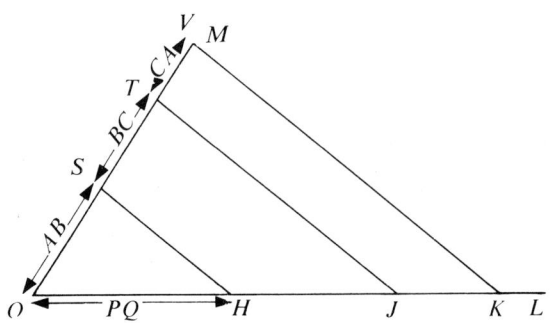

Figure 36:22

OL and OM are any two rays from O. Along OM lengths equal to AB, BC, CA are marked as OS, ST and TV.

Along OL a length equal to PQ is marked as OH. From T and V parallels to SH are drawn cutting OL at J and K. HJ and JK are the lengths required for QR and RP (Figure 36:22).

A more complex shape, like the one shown in Figure 36:23, could be transformed similarly, provided that enough lengths are found to make it possible to draw the new shape uniquely and exactly.

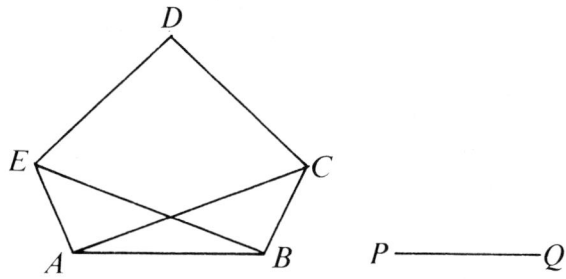

Figure 36:23

The symmetry of this figure shows that $AE = BC$, $ED = CD$, $BE = AC$. We therefore had to find only the lengths corresponding to AE, ED, AC in order to draw $PQRST$ similar to $ABCDE$ with the side PQ of given length. The construction of the required lengths is shown in Figure 36:24.

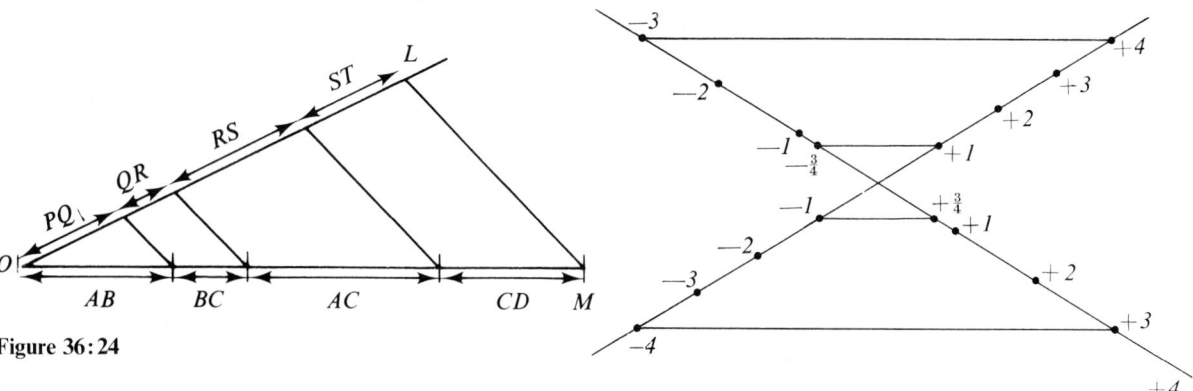

Figure 36:24

We notice that

i) either line, OL or OM, can be used for the original lengths,
ii) the lengths could all be marked off from O, so that they are nested.

In methods B, C and D a numerical ratio is not used. Instead, the required lengths are found by using the equal ratios in which the sides of a triangle are divided by a parallel to the third side.

Rational numbers

We have seen that those numbers which can be expressed in fractional form, such as $\frac{2}{3}$, $\frac{5}{1}$, $-\frac{3}{4}$, are rational numbers. This description reminds us that a fraction expresses a ratio; $\frac{2}{3} = 2:3$, $\frac{5}{1} = 5:1$, $-\frac{3}{4} = (-3):(+4)$ or $(+3):(-4)$.

The graduation of two intersecting number lines can show that the fraction $\frac{3}{4}$ is equal to the ratio $\frac{3}{4}:1$ or the ratio $3:4$ or to the ratio of any pair of lengths cut off on the number lines by a parallel to AA', as shown in Figure 36:25 which illustrates the relationship for signless numbers. In Figure 36:26 the number lines are continued

to the negative side of zero and the numbers shown are directed numbers requiring a plus or a minus sign. The negative fraction $-\frac{3}{4}$ is now seen to represent $(-3):(+4)$, or $(+3):(-4)$, or $(-\frac{3}{4}):(+1)$, or $(+\frac{3}{4}):(-1)$.

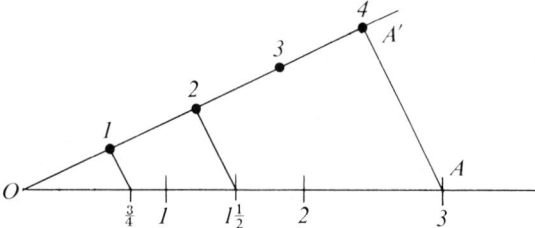

Figure 36:25

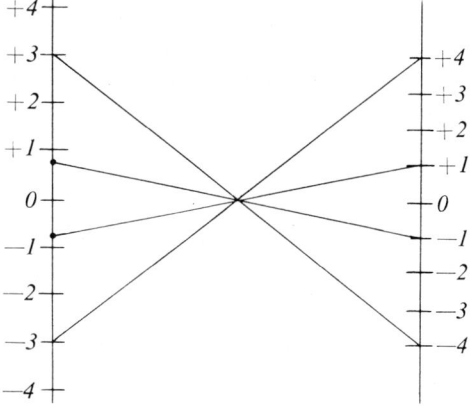

Figure 36:26

The relation diagram shown in Figure 36:27 as an alternative illustration brings out well the symmetry of the various ratios expressed by the fraction $-\frac{3}{4}$.

From these illustrations we can see the whole range of rational numbers in terms of the ratio which each represents.

Figure 36:27

379

Gear ratios

Children who ride bicycles or make working Meccano models are familiar with ways in which two geared wheels can be connected so that when one turns the other also turns. The rates of rotation will be different unless the wheels are of the same size. The teeth of the wheels must fit either on to a chain, or into one another; therefore the rate of rotation of one compared with the other depends on the number of teeth in the respective rims of the wheels. The gear ratio is the ratio of the rates of rotation.

For example, the chain wheels of a bicycle may have 24 and 12 teeth respectively (Figure 36:28). The wheel turned by the pedals has 24 teeth; the small wheel which is attached to one of the bicycle wheels has 12 teeth; the chain passes round both toothed wheels, making them turn in

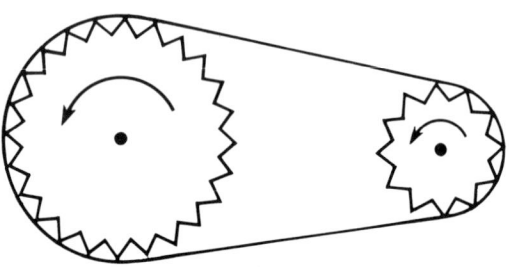

Figure 36:28

the same direction, and moves with them. For one rotation of the pedal wheel the small wheel makes two rotations, its 12 teeth having been in contact with the chain twice because the pedal wheel has 24 teeth. The ratio of the number of rotations of the small wheel to those of the larger wheel is 24:12 or 2:1.

In some bicycles the numbers of teeth are 45 and 18; the ratio is 45:18 or 5:2 or 2·5:1. It will be seen that the ratio of numbers of rotations is also 2·5:1 since the smaller wheel makes $2\frac{1}{2}$ rotations to each complete rotation of the pedal wheel.

If two gear wheels are meshed together, as in Figure 36:29, they will turn in opposite directions, but the gear ratio will still depend on the numbers of teeth on each wheel. When the wheels have 45 and 30 teeth respectively the ratio is 3:2.

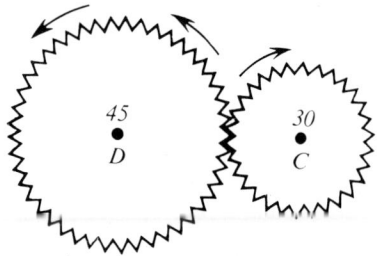

Figure 36:29

380

When more than two gears are used to make a mechanical system the ratios can be combined. For example wheel E can be geared to C as in Figure 36:30.

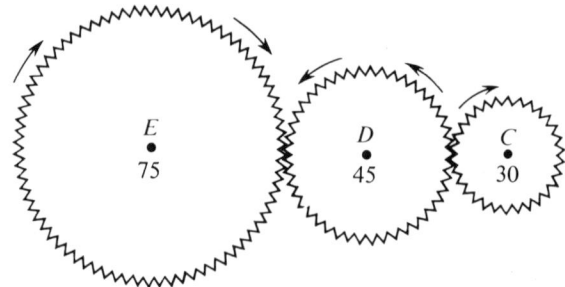

Figure 36:30

The gear ratio of D to E is 75:45, or 5:3.

> D makes $\frac{5}{3}$ revolutions to each revolution of E
> C makes $\frac{3}{2}$ revolutions to each revolution of D
> Thus C makes $\frac{3}{2} \times \frac{5}{3}$ revolutions, or $\frac{5}{2}$ revolutions, to each revolution of E. This can be checked by comparing E directly with C. The gear ratio is 75:30, or 5:2 (Figure 36:30).

One of the purposes of the middle wheel is to make the third wheel turn in the same direction as the first wheel. Since two meshed wheels rotate in opposite directions, C rotates in the same direction as E, whereas if C and E were directly meshed together they would rotate in opposite directions.

The combination of gears leads to the multiplication of ratios and can furnish a good example of a simple procedure for multiplying one fraction by another.

Growth with changing ratios

When a rate of growth is constant we know that a graph of the changing quantities is a straight line. For example, the volume of water collected from a dripping tap will increase with time so that the volume of water collected in 20 minutes will be twice the volume collected in 10 minutes; the ratio of volumes is 20:10 or 2:1 (Figure 36:31).

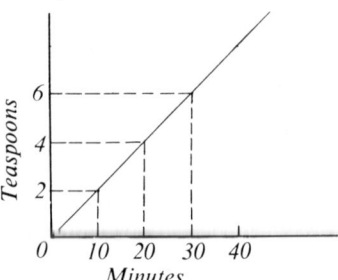

Figure 36:31

The perimeter of a square increases uniformly with equal increases in the length of a side: the ratio of the perimeters of two squares is equal to the ratio of the lengths of their sides. If the squares have sides of length 3 units and 5 units respectively their perimeters are 12 units and 20 units. The ratio $20:12 = 5:3 = 1\cdot67:1$.

Squares with sides 3 units and 5 units long have areas of 9 square units and 25 square units respectively; the ratio of areas is $25:9$ or $2\cdot78:1$, whereas the ratio of sides is $5:3$ or $1\cdot67:1$.

The ratio of the perimeter of a square to its side is constant and equal increases in length of the side produce equal increases in the perimeter. The graph of the area of

ments of a rectangle 1 unit by 2 units gives the following tabulation

Length of short side, l	1	2	3	4
Area of rectangle, R	2	8	18	32
Area of square on l, s	1	4	9	16
Ratio of areas, $R:S$	2:1	8:4	18:9	32:16

The ratio of the area of a rectangle to the area of the corresponding square is constant and the graph of the two sets of areas shows the relation $R = 2S$, or $R:S = 2:1$ (Figure 36:33).

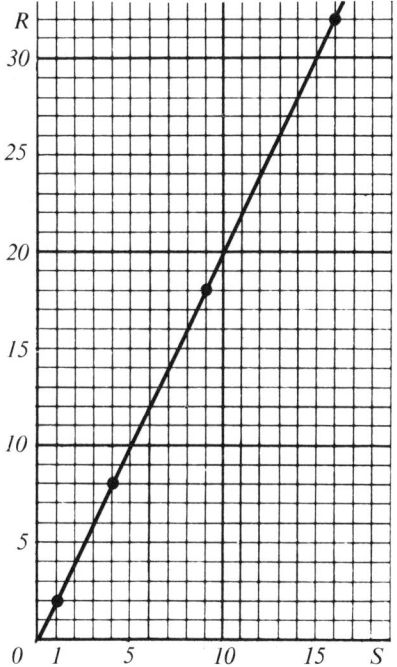

Figure 36:33

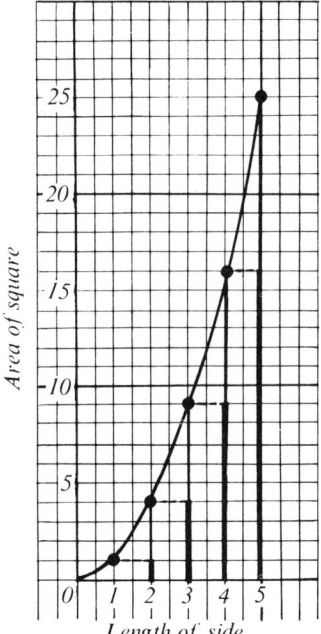

Figure 36:32

the square (Figure 36:32) shows that the ratio of the number of units of area in the square to the number of units of length in its side is not constant and equal increases in the length of the side do not produce equal increases in the area.

Length of side, l units	1	2	3	4	5
Area of square, A sq. units	1	4	9	16	25
Ratio $A:l$	1:1	2:1	3:1	4:1	5:1
Differences in A for unit differences in l		3	5	7	9

The growth of area in *any* set of similar figures shows the same pattern of changing ratios as the growth of area in a set of squares. This suggests comparing the one set of areas with the other. For example, the successive enlarge-

Inverse ratios

In some investigations, like timing a journey for different average speeds, it is found that as one sequence of numbers increases, the other decreases; as average speed increases the time for the journey grows less. Since the distance travelled d, is equal to the product of the average speed, s, and the time taken, t

$$d = s \times t$$
$$t = \frac{d}{s}$$

For a particular journey of 120 kilometres,

$$t = \frac{120}{s}$$
$$= 120 \times \frac{1}{s}$$

381

(a)

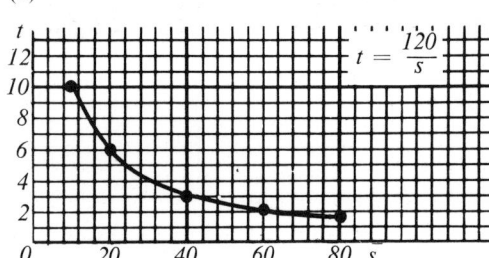

(b)

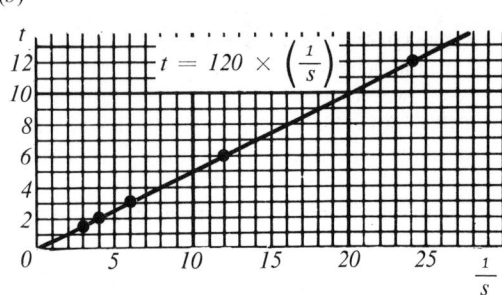

Figure 36:34

As the graph in Figure 36:34(a) illustrates, t is proportional to the *inverse* of s. The tabulation shows s, t and $\frac{1}{s}$.

s	10	20	40	60	80
t	12	6	3	2	$1\frac{1}{2}$
$\frac{1}{s}$	$\frac{1}{10} = \frac{24}{240}$	$\frac{1}{20} = \frac{12}{240}$	$\frac{1}{40} = \frac{6}{240}$	$\frac{1}{60} = \frac{4}{240}$	$\frac{1}{80} = \frac{3}{240}$

When the results of an experiment show a similar pattern, with a sequence of decreasing numbers corresponding with an increasing sequence, this procedure of graphing the inverse, as in Figure 36:34(b), may reveal the actual relation in the form $r = K \times \left(\dfrac{1}{t}\right)$ where r is the dependent variable, t is the independent variable and K is a constant which can be found from the graph.

The importance of ratio

The development of the idea of ratio has been shown to grow from a wide experience of similar shapes, of quantities which are related by a constant rule of correspondence, and of sets of numbers of which one is a transform of the other by a multiplication operation. The correspondences found in these three kinds of experience have a particular pattern in a relation diagram or a graph. Proportion, or equality of ratios occurs so frequently that an understanding of it is essential to the solving of many types of problem. The use of a straight-line graph to illustrate a constant ratio has been extended to show that other relations can be illustrated by straight-line graphs; for instance variation with the square or with the inverse can be shown.

37 Work with Triangles, Squares and Circles

New tessellations from old[1]

The tessellation of equal scalene triangles (Figure 37:1(*a*)) is derived from the parallelogram tesselation of Figure 37:1(*b*) by drawing diagonals of the parallelograms. There

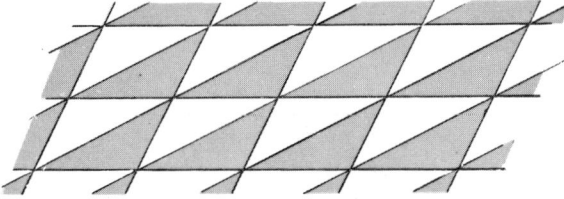

(*a*) *Tessellation of Scalene triangles*

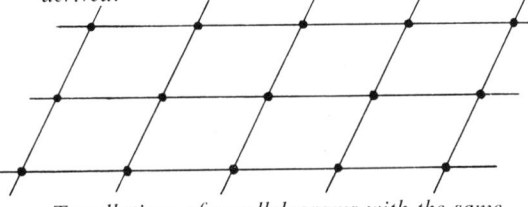

(*b*) *Tessellation of parallelograms from which (a) is derived.*

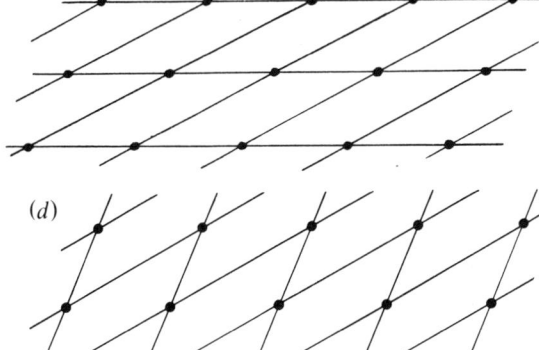

(*c*) *Tessellations of parallelograms with the same lattice points.*

(*d*)

Figure 37:1

[1] Simple tessellations are discussed in Chapter 21.

are three possible tessellations of parallelograms which have the same vertices or *lattice points* (marked with black dots in Figure 37:1) and which use the same three sets of parallel lines. We can think of the scalene triangle tessellation as occurring when two of these tessellations are drawn on top of one another. Other tessellations can be produced by joining the same lattice points in other ways.

A tessellation of squares produces five tessellations of parallelograms, all with the same lattice points (Figure 37:2). These tessellations are not all fundamentally different; (*c*) can be produced from (*b*) by rotation through a right angle, and (*e*) from (*d*); (*d*) is the reflection of (*b*) in a vertical axis. The five tessellations have the property that the basic tile of each tessellation has *the same area*, which is equal to one square of the original tessellation. In Figure 37:2 a basic tile of each tessellation is shaded and divided into two triangles which are half-squares, showing that each basic tile has the area of the square. Of course, many other tessellations can be produced from the same lattice points but their tiles do not have the same area. Some of them are shown in Figure 37:3. In these tessellations either:

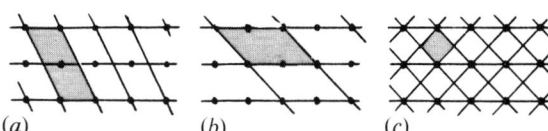

(*a*)   (*b*)   (*c*)

Figure 37:3

i) some of the lattice points are not vertices of the new tiles (Figures 37:3(*a*) and (*b*)), or
ii) some vertices of the new tiles are not lattice points (Figure 37:3(*c*)).

But if we use the original set of lattice points, all the tessellations of parallelograms which can be made using *all* the lattice points as vertices, and no other vertices, have tiles of the same area.

Five tessellations with the same lattice points

(*a*) 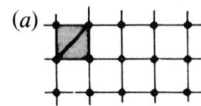   (*b*) 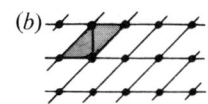   (*c*) 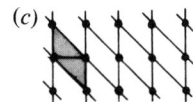   (*d*)    (*e*)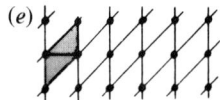

Figure 37:2

Tessellations made from a brick pattern.

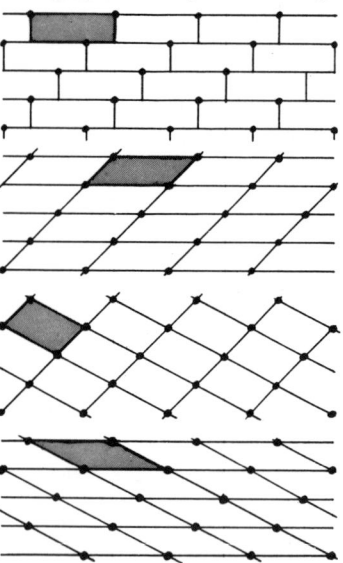

Figure 37:4

Figure 37:4 shows this principle in use in another tessellation, one of the brick patterns. The use of squared paper will help a child to see that, in Figure 37:4, tiles of each tessellation have the same area.

Figure 37:5 is a tessellation of equal tiles, but the obvious marking of vertices shown in this diagram does not yield a grid of lattice points which can be tessellated with *equal* parallelograms. The difficulty lies in the fact that the fundamental tile of Figure 37:5 is not one quadrilateral, but two. A fundamental tile is a tile from which the whole tessellation can be built up by *translations only*, without rotation. The whole tessellation can be built up by translations only if a two-quadrilateral tile is used, whereas if we use a one-quadrilateral tile, we have to rotate it as well as translating it. Once the fundamental

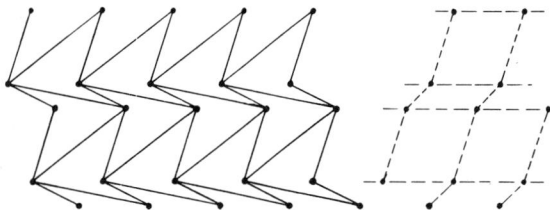

Figure 37:5

tile has been picked out, lattice points can be found by marking one vertex of each tile (Figure 37:6). New tessellations of parallelograms can be made by joining these lattice points. Each tile of the new tessellation has an area equal to that of the fundamental tile. Similarly,

384

(a) Original tessellation showing fundamental tile and translation vectors.

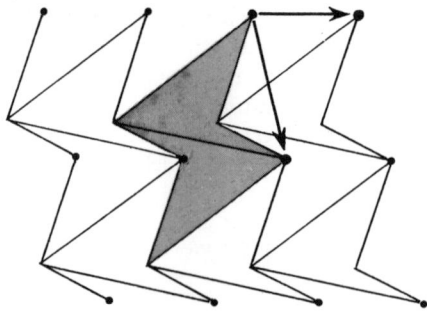

(b) New tessellation using same lattice-points.

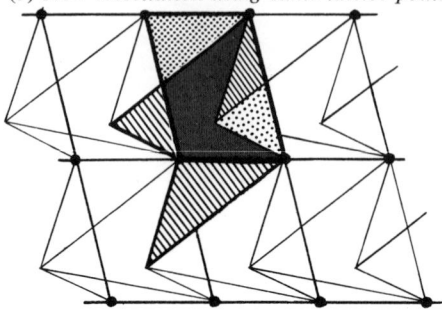

Figure 37:6

in Figure 37:1(*a*), the fundamental tile is the parallelogram made up of two triangles, rather than a single triangle.

Figure 37:7 shows the fundamental tile and lattice points of the parquet-floor pattern, and another tessellation using tiles of the same area.

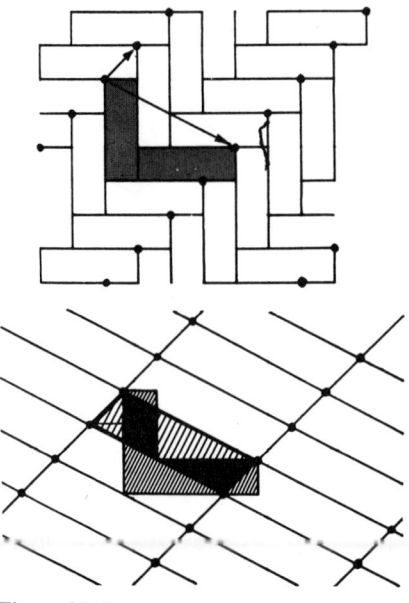

Figure 37:7

We next consider the tessellation obtained by drawing all the diagonals of a tessellation of squares (Figure 37:8(a)). This has the property that it is also a tessellation of squares, but since more lattice points are used, these squares are not equal in area to the original squares, but are half their area. The second tessellation can also be produced by using all the lattice points of a brick pattern,

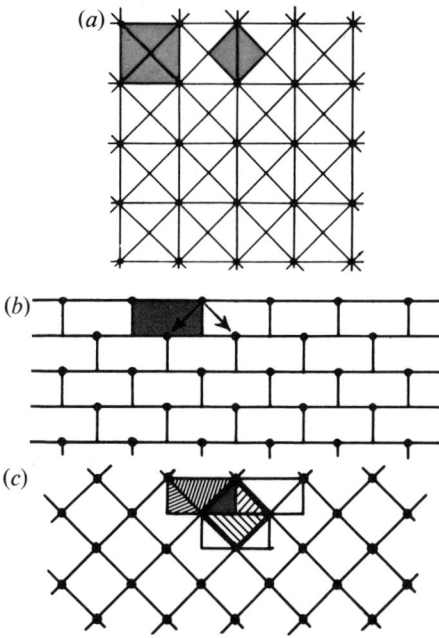

(a)

(b)

(c)

Figure 37:8

if the bricks are made up of two squares (Figure 37:8(b) and (c)). The right-angled isosceles triangle plays an important part in both the square tessellations. If the two tessellations are superimposed, each right-angled isosceles triangle is bordered by three squares (Figure 37:9); two of these squares are small and one large.

We see that the larger square, the square on the

Figure 37:9

hypotenuse² of the isosceles right-angled triangle, is equal in area to the sum of the two smaller squares. It is thought that this special case of Pythagoras' Theorem may have been discovered by observation of this very common tile-pattern. We recall that *Pythagoras' Theorem* states that *the area of the square on the hypotenuse of any right-angled triangle is equal to the sum of the areas of the squares on the other two sides.*

The squares on the sides of a right-angled triangle

A child can very easily experiment on squared paper with squares on the hypotenuse of various right-angled triangles. There is no difficulty in drawing these squares. If he starts with a right-angled triangle whose sides are of length 2 units and 5 units (Figure 37:10(a)), its hypotenuse is a vector $\overrightarrow{AB}$ which is the sum of 5 units to the right and 2 units upwards, that is a vector $\begin{pmatrix} +5 \\ +2 \end{pmatrix}$. The next

² The *hypotenuse* is the longest side of a right-angled triangle. It is always situated opposite the right-angle.

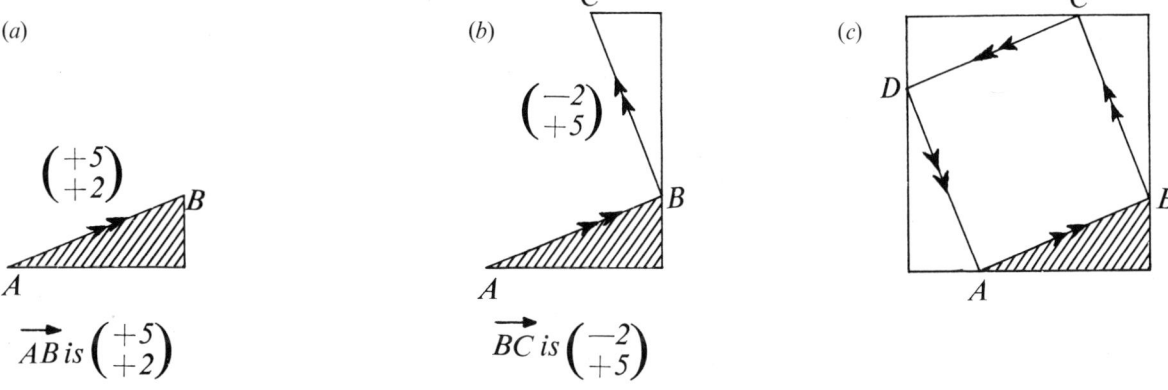

(a)

$\begin{pmatrix} +5 \\ +2 \end{pmatrix}$

$\overrightarrow{AB}$ is $\begin{pmatrix} +5 \\ +2 \end{pmatrix}$

(b)

$\begin{pmatrix} -2 \\ +5 \end{pmatrix}$

$\overrightarrow{BC}$ is $\begin{pmatrix} -2 \\ +5 \end{pmatrix}$

(c)

Figure 37:10

385

side of the square is obtained by counting from B 5 units up and 2 units to the left; that is by drawing from B a vector $\begin{pmatrix} -2 \\ +5 \end{pmatrix}$ (Figure 37:10(b)), and so on all round the square (Figure 37:10(c)). Nor is there any difficulty in finding the area of this square, because it can easily be related to the squares of the original squared paper. This can be done by the subtraction method suggested by Figure 37:10(c), taking the area of the four right-angled triangles from that of the large square and finding what remains. Perhaps a simpler method is to divide up the square on the hypotenuse into parts whose area can be found. Figure 37:11 illustrates this for two different triangles. Children should tabulate their findings, as in Figure 37:12. Some children may notice that the area of

Shorter sides of right-angled triangle		Area of square on hypotenuse	Length of hypotenuse (by measuring)
1 unit	*1 unit*	*2 sq units*	*1·5 units*
1	*2*	*5*	*2·2*
1	*3*	*10*	*3·1*
2	*3*	*13*	*3·7*
1	*4*		
2	*4*		
3	*4*	*25*	*5·0*

Figure 37:12

the square on the hypotenuse is equal to the sum of the areas of the squares on the other two sides.

They will probably also measure the length of the hypotenuse of the triangles they have drawn, as shown in Figure 37:12, and will want to check the accuracy of their measurements by squaring the results. The first measurement shown in the table is too great, as $(1·5)^2 = 2·25$; the second is too small, as $(2·2)^2 = 4·84$, but $(2·3)^2 = 5·29$. Use may also be made of the graph of squares, as shown in Figure 37:13, where the graph has been used to find $\sqrt{61}$. Results obtained in this way will have about the same degree of accuracy as those obtained by measurement. Children will probably realize that although the length of the hypotenuse of the triangle in Figure 37:13 is *approximately* 7·8 units, the area of the square on it is

Triangle sides 1 and 2 units

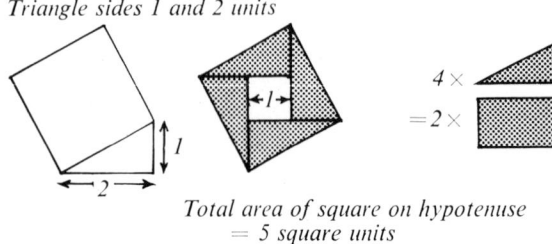

Total area of square on hypotenuse = 5 square units

Triangle sides 1 and 3 units

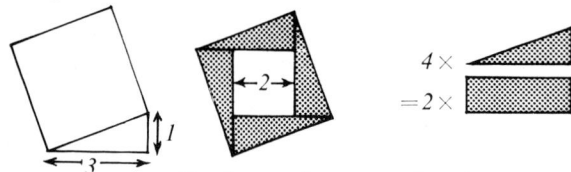

Total area of square on hypotenuse = (2×3)+4 square units = 10 square units

Figure 37:11

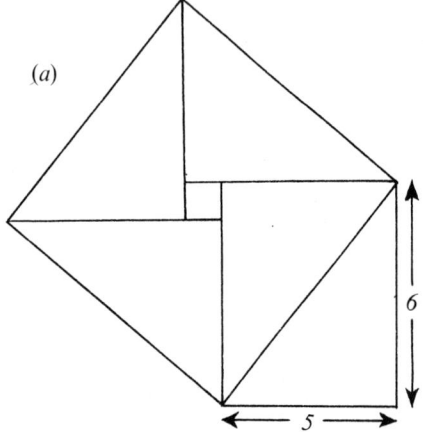

(a)

Area of square on hypotenuse = 61 square units. Length of hypotenuse = $\sqrt{61}$ units ≃ 7·8 units.

Figure 37:13
386

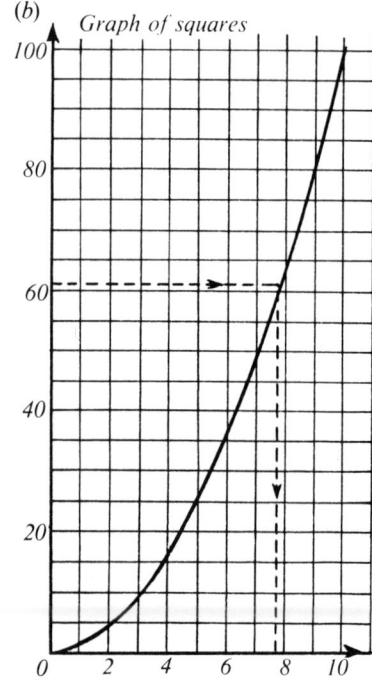

(b) *Graph of squares*

Figure 37:14

exactly 61 square units. They did not have to approximate at all in finding the area of the square; the four triangles in it make two rectangles each of area 30 square units, and there is exactly one square unit in the middle.

The last triangle given in the table of Figure 37:12 differs from the others. The area of the square on its hypotenuse is a perfect square, and so the hypotenuse is a whole

A tessellation of two squares

(a) Squares on two sides of a right-angled triangle

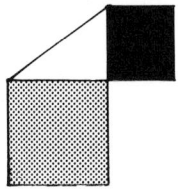

(b) Use these two squares to make a tessellation

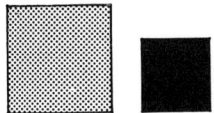

(c) Starting the tessellation

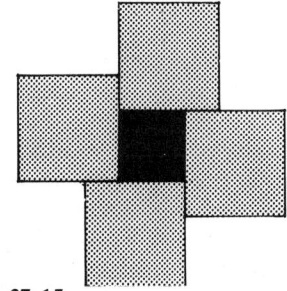

Figure 37:15

number of units. This triangle, the 3, 4, 5 triangle, is the simplest of a number of right-angled triangles whose sides are all whole numbers of units. The 3, 4, 5 triangle has been known as a right-angled triangle since very early times. It is thought that the surveyors of ancient Egypt used 3, 4, 5 triangles for marking out right angles, and the same method, which only needs a rope or measuring-tape, is still useful for marking out right angles on the ground (Figure 37:14).

Tessellations using two squares

In general, the squares on the two shorter sides of a right-angled triangle are of different sizes. We now explore the consequences of trying to make a tessellation with squares of two different sizes (Figure 37:15 and plate 8). The smaller of the squares can be surrounded by larger ones (Figure 37:15(*c*)), and it is then a simple matter to continue the tessellation (Figure 37:15(*d*)). The fundamental tile consists of a large and a small square. Lattice points have been marked at the top left-hand corner of the fundamental tiles, and the vectors of translations needed to build up the tessellation from its fundamental tile are shown. These vectors are at right angles, so the lattice points can be joined to make a new tessellation of squares, each of area equal to the fundamental tile (Figure 37:16).

We notice that the pattern now contains many of the original right-angled triangles, together with the squares on all three of their sides (Figure 37:17). The square on the hypotenuse of the right-angled triangle is equal in area to the fundamental tile of the tessellation, which is the sum of the two smaller squares. That is, the square on the hypotenuse of the right-angled triangle is equal in area to the sum of the squares on the other two sides.

Experiments on squared paper will convince a child that he can make a tessellation with two squares of any sizes, and by marking lattice points he will always obtain a new tessellation of squares on the hypotenuse. Figure 37:17 shows a tessellation of 1^2 and 4^2 squares.

(d) Building more of the tessellation. A fundamental tile and some lattice points are shown.

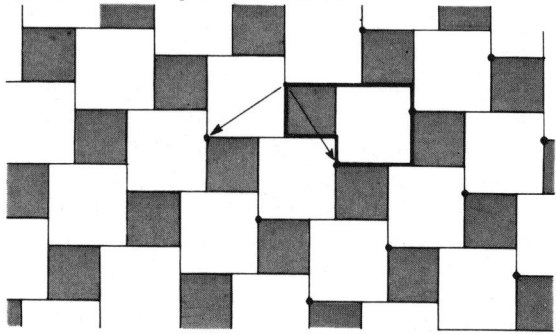

Tessellation of squares using the same lattice-points.

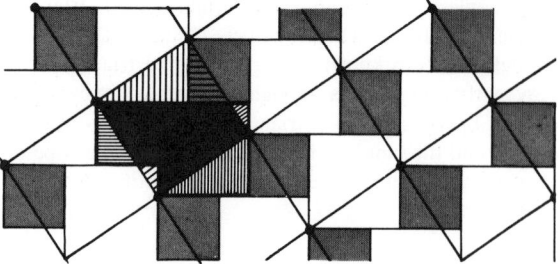

Figure 37:16

An interesting and symmetrical variation in the pattern is obtained by taking lattice points at the centre of each larger square (Figure 37:17(*b*)). In this arrangement, the larger square of the original tessellation is divided into four equal parts by the lines of the new tessellation. Conversely, the square of the new tessellation is made up of the four quarters of the original larger square together

Tessellation of 1² and 4² squares.

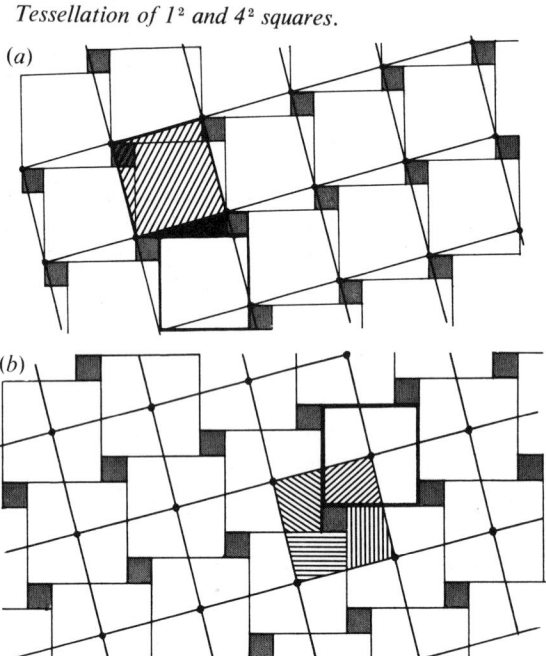

Figure 37:17

with the original smaller square. This tessellation forms the basis of the demonstration of Pythagoras' Theorem known as *Perigal's Dissection* (Figure 37:18). Here the larger original square is dissected into four quarters which fit, together with the original smaller square, on to the square on the hypotenuse of the right-angled triangle. Other choices of lattice point in the tessellation give rise to other demonstrations of Pythagoras' Theorem by dissection.

388

Perigal's Dissection for Pythagoras' Theorem
(*a*) *Part of the tessellation*   (*b*) *Perigal's dissection.*

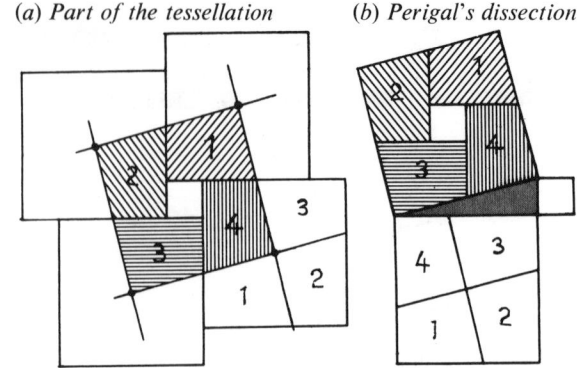

Figure 37:18

The lattice points of Figure 37:17(*a*) give the dissection shown, for a different triangle, in Figure 37:19.

Another dissection for Pythagoras' Theorem.
(*a*) *Part of the tessellation*

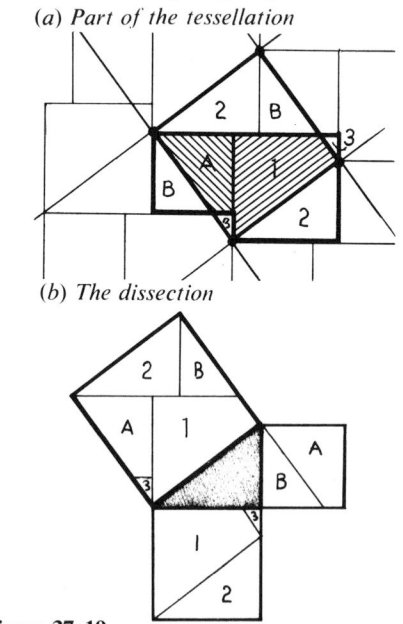

(*b*) *The dissection*

Figure 37:19

More about Pythagoras' Theorem

At this stage, children will think of Pythagoras' Theorem entirely as a statement about equality and rearrangement of *areas*. They can rearrange the two squares on the shorter sides of a right-angled triangle to make up the square on the hypotenuse. Another very simple demonstration of this fact is suggested by Figure 37:10(*c*), which shows the drawing of the square on the hypotenuse. The large square *PQRS* (Figure 37:20(*a*)) is made up of four right-angled triangles and the square on the hypotenuse

$ABCD$. It is a simple matter to rearrange the four right-angled triangles within square $PQRS$ so that the remaining space consists of the squares on the other two sides of the right-angled triangle (Figure 37:20(b)). Children can make this demonstration into a jigsaw, to fit inside a square hole $PQRS$ cut from a piece of card.

Jigsaw for Pythagoras' Theorem.

(a) Four triangles and square on hypotenuse.

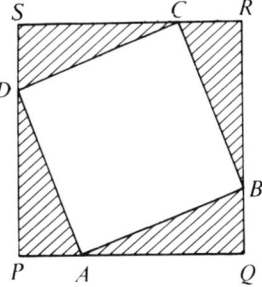

(b) Four triangles and squares on other two sides.

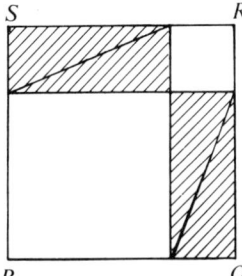

Figure 37:20

We can now find *exactly* the area of the square on the hypotenuse of any right-angled triangle if the lengths of the sides are known. For instance in Figure 37:20, the triangle has shorter sides of lengths 5 units and 2 units. Hence: area of square on hypotenuse

$= (5^2 + 2^2)$ square units
$= (25 + 4)$ square units
$= 29$ square units

In order to find the length of the side of this square, we have to find the number whose square is 29, that is to find the *square root* of 29. In other words we must find the number n such that n^2 is 29, or solve the equation $n^2 = 29$. This may be attempted in various ways. The triangle may be drawn and its hypotenuse measured. Alternatively, the graph of squares (Figure 37:13(b)) may be consulted, and yields

$n = \sqrt{29}$
$\simeq 5\cdot4$

This is the quickest and simplest method for children to use, and will probably give a sufficiently good result for most purposes. In fact, $(5\cdot4)^2 = 29\cdot16$.

If a more accurate value for a square root is wanted than can be read from a graph, there is a well-known method of improving an approximation, which throws useful light on the relation between multiplication and division. We know that $5\cdot4$ is an approximation to $\sqrt{29}$, and is too big; now

$29 \div 5\cdot4 = 5\cdot370$ (correct to 3 places of decimals)
and
$(5\cdot370)^2 = 28\cdot837$ (to 3 places of decimals)

Hence $5\cdot370$ is also a reasonable approximation to $\sqrt{29}$, but is too small. The average of our two approximations will be a better approximation than either of them, since one was too large and the other too small. This average is

$$\frac{5\cdot4 + 5\cdot370}{2} = \frac{10\cdot770}{2}$$
$$= 5\cdot385$$

This approximation is more than good enough for all practical purposes, and indeed $\sqrt{29} = 5\cdot385$ correct to 3 decimal places.

Children will be fascinated by the 3, 4, 5 triangle, where the area of the square on the hypotenuse is $(3^2 + 4^2)$ square units, or 25 square units, and is a perfect square. The length of the side of the square on the hypotenuse is therefore an exact whole number of units, so that this triangle is extremely convenient to deal with. Children may wish to find out whether there are any other right-angled triangles whose sides are all exact whole numbers of units. Figure 37:21 shows a systematic search for more such triangles. Possible areas of squares

A search for right-angled triangles with integral sides

Area of square on one shorter side.

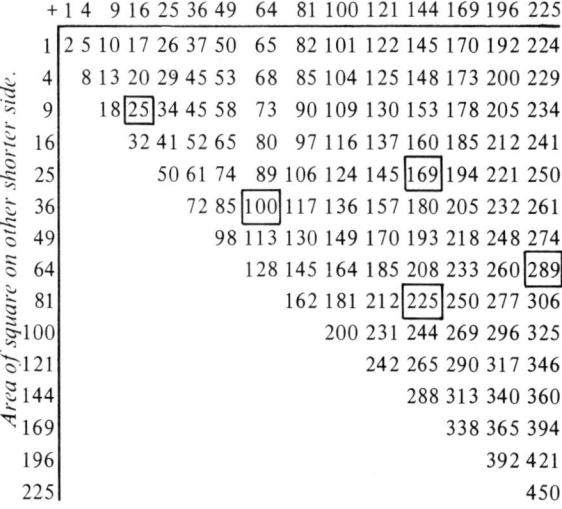

Area of square on other shorter side	+1	4	9	16	25	36	49	64	81	100	121	144	169	196	225
1	2	5	10	17	26	37	50	65	82	101	122	145	170	197	226
4		8	13	20	29	40	53	68	85	104	125	148	173	200	229
9			18	[25]	34	45	58	73	90	109	130	153	178	205	234
16				32	41	52	65	80	97	116	137	160	185	212	241
25					50	61	74	89	106	125	146	[169]	194	221	250
36						72	85	[100]	117	136	157	180	205	232	261
49							98	113	130	149	170	193	218	245	274
64								128	145	164	185	208	233	260	[289]
81									162	181	202	[225]	250	277	306
100										200	221	244	269	296	325
121											242	265	290	317	346
144												288	313	340	369
169													338	365	394
196														392	421
225															450

Figure 37:21

Right-angled triangles with integral sides.

Squares on shorter sides		Square on hypotenuse	Lengths of sides	Remarks
9	16	25	3, 4, 5	
25	144	169	5, 12, 13	
36	64	100	6, 8, 10	Twice 3, 4, 5
64	225	289	8, 15, 17	
81	144	225	9, 12, 15	Three times 3, 4, 5

Figure 37:22

on the two shorter sides of the trinagle have been tabulated, together with their sums. Those sums which are also perfect squares are marked. Four new right-angled triangles whose sides are integers have so far emerged from this search. Figure 37:22 tabulates them. It will be seen that right-angled triangles with integral sides are rare, but that a few can be found. In fact an infinite number exist.

The teacher will be interested in a formula which gives all right-angled triangles with integral sides. This formula, with a list of the first 15 such triangles, is given in Figure 37:23. These triangles whose sides are not multiples of the sides of a previous triangle are printed in heavy type.

		Sides of Triangle		
a	b	$a^2 - b^2$	$2ab$	$a^2 + b^2$
2	1	**3**	**4**	**5**
3	1	8	6	10
3	2	**5**	**12**	**13**
4	1	**15**	**8**	**17**
4	2	12	16	20
4	3	**7**	**24**	**25**
5	1	24	10	26
5	2	**21**	**20**	**29**
5	3	16	30	34
5	4	**9**	**40**	**41**
6	1	**35**	**12**	**37**
6	2	32	24	40
6	3	27	36	45
6	4	20	48	52
6	5	**11**	**60**	**61**
.	.	.	.	.

Right-angled triangles with integral sides

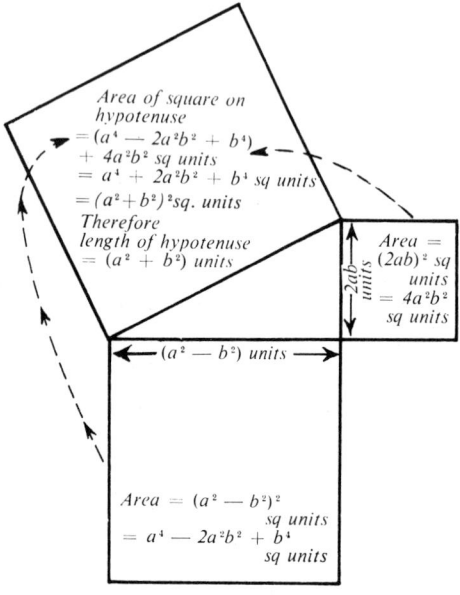

Area of square on hypotenuse
$= (a^4 - 2a^2b^2 + b^4)$
$+ 4a^2b^2$ sq units
$= a^4 + 2a^2b^2 + b^4$ sq units
$= (a^2 + b^2)^2$ sq. units
Therefore
length of hypotenuse
$= (a^2 + b^2)$ units

Area $=$
$(2ab)^2$ sq
units
$= 4a^2b^2$
sq units

$\longleftarrow (a^2 - b^2)$ units $\longrightarrow$

Area $= (a^2 - b^2)^2$
sq units
$= a^4 - 2a^2b^2 + b^4$
sq units

Sides are of length $a^2 - b^2$, $2ab$, $a^2 + b^2$ units. If a and b are natural numbers the triangle will have integral sides.

Primitive triangles in which the sides do not have a common factor are printed in bold type.

Figure 37:23

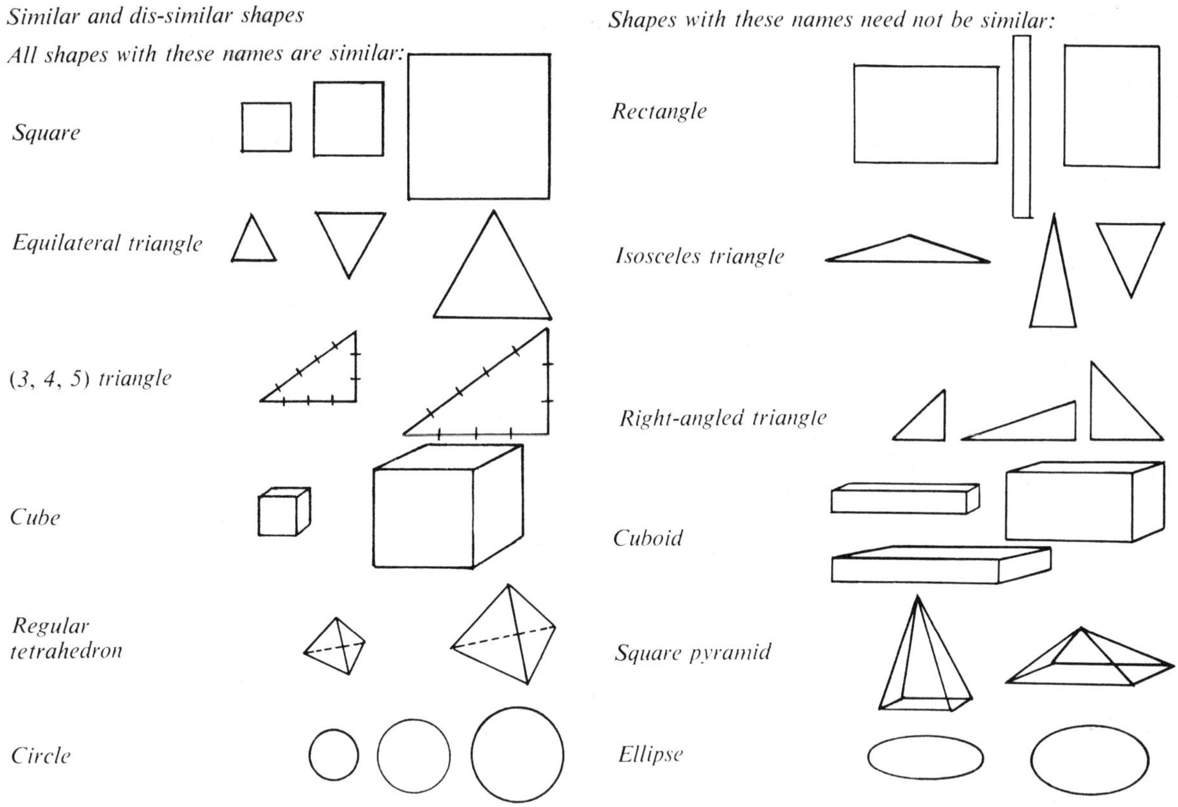

Similar and dis-similar shapes

All shapes with these names are similar:

Square

Equilateral triangle

(3, 4, 5) triangle

Cube

Regular tetrahedron

Circle

Shapes with these names need not be similar:

Rectangle

Isosceles triangle

Right-angled triangle

Cuboid

Square pyramid

Ellipse

Figure 37:24

The growth of similar figures

In Chapter 36 we discussed the idea of *similarity*, and saw that a child can recognize that when objects are of the same shape, all their corresponding measurements behave in the same way. Some of the names of geometrical shapes always belong to shapes which are similar, others do not. All squares are similar and differ only in size, but not all rectangles are similar. All cubes are similar, but not all cuboids. All equilateral triangles are similar, but not all isosceles triangles. The list can be prolonged indefinitely (Figure 37:24). Among the most important examples where every figure with the same name has the same shape are the regular polygons and the regular polyhedra. All regular hexagons are of the same shape, so are all regular octahedra. Another important example is the circle; all circles are of the same shape.

If a set of shapes is similar, all their measurements behave in the same way. If a child draws a graph of the perimeters of different squares (Figure 37:25), the graph will be a straight line, and is identical with the graph of the four times table. The perimeter of every square is four times the length of its side.

Graph of perimeters of squares

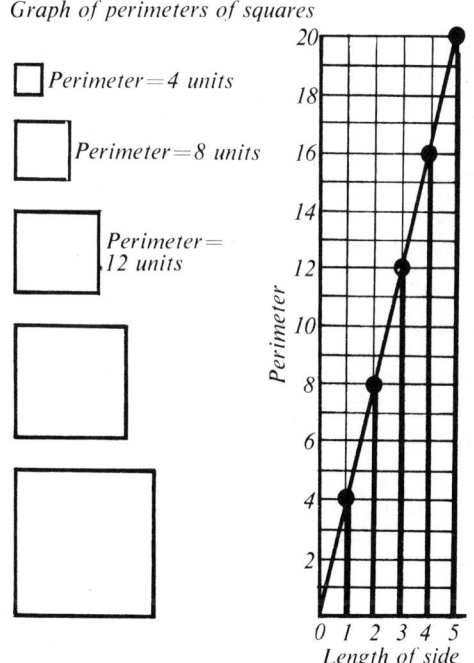

Perimeter = 4 units

Perimeter = 8 units

Perimeter = 12 units

Figure 37:25

Sides and diagonals of squares.

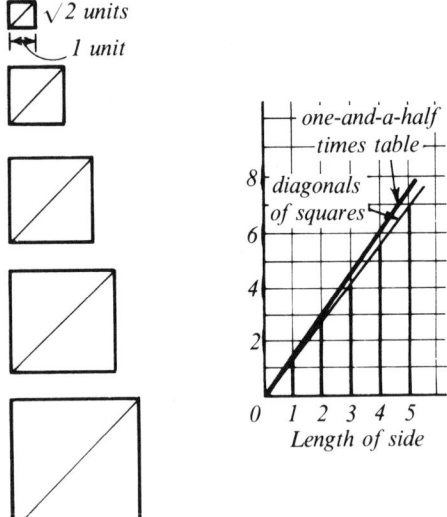

Figure 37:26

Similarly, if a graph of the lengths of the diagonals of different squares is drawn (Figure 37:26), it will again be a straight line, although the relationship cannot be stated using whole numbers. The diagonal of the square will be seen from the graph to be slightly less than $1\frac{1}{2}$ times the length of the side. In fact, we know from Pythagoras' Theorem that the diagonal of the square is $\sqrt{2}$ times the length of the side, or approximately 1·41 times the length of the side.

Children can make graphs to show the corresponding measurements of other similar shapes. The perimeters of regular hexagons, and the lengths of milk-straw used in making the edges of different sized cubes are easily shown on graphs.

When we examine the growth of similar shapes, we find that the perimeters are always the same multiple of the lengths of their sides. This multiple varies according to the shape, but is a constant for each shape (Figure 37:27).

Perimeters of Similar Shapes

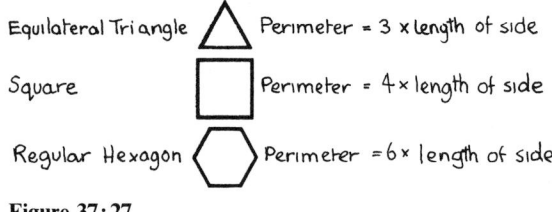

Figure 37:27

We turn now to consider circles, the simplest set of similar figures with curved sides, and examine the relationship of the perimeter of a circle to its other measurements.

392

Circles

By the middle years of schooling children have used circles for several years in their building and pattern-making. They know that wheels are circular in shape so that the axle of the wheel shall always be the same distance from the ground; that is, they know that all *radii* of a circle are equal. They know that a circle is symmetrical about every *diameter,* and they can find the centre of a circular piece of paper by folding it. They have used a trundle wheel, whose *circumference* is a metre, for measuring distances. They have cut circles into *sectors* which are fractions of the whole circle. They have learnt to draw an equilateral triangle by using compasses to make *arcs* of equal radius. They have probably measured the diameter of a tin or ball by putting it between two books which just touch, or are *tangents* to it (Figure 37:28). By

Talking about circles, and using them.

(a)

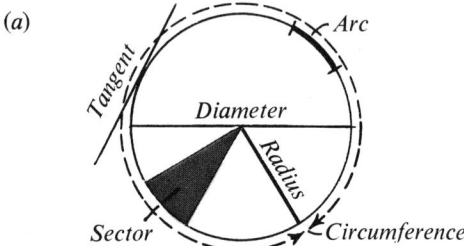

(b) *Drawing an equilateral triangle.*

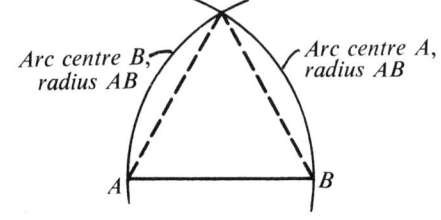

(c) *Measuring the diameter of a tin.*

Figure 37:28

now, their questions are more concerned with the measurement of circles. They may ask how should we make a trundle wheel to measure $\frac{1}{2}$ metre: what diameter should it be? Is the cog-wheel with 40 teeth twice the diameter of the cog-wheel with 20 teeth? Which is the better buy, two small round tins of coffee, or one large one? How many times does a bicycle wheel go round in a kilometre? Do the tyres of a Mini wear out faster than those of a car with bigger wheels?

Children who have seen that the perimeters of similar regular polygons are a constant multiple of the length of their sides will expect a similar relation to be true for circles. All circles are similar, so the perimeter, or circumference, of any circle will be the same multiple of its diameter. The only remaining question is, what multiple of the diameter is the circumference? It is easy to see that the circumference of a circle must be more than 3 times its diameter, and less than 4 times its diameter. Figure 37:29 shows a regular hexagon drawn within a circle, and a square surrounding the circle. The hexagon has a smaller

Graph of diameters and circumferences of circles

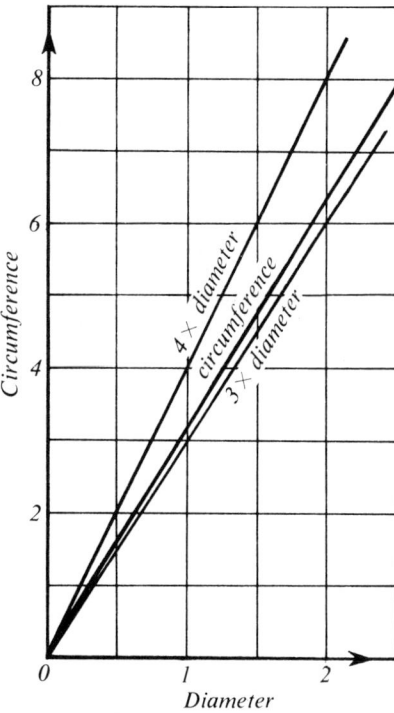

Figure 37:30

Approximations to the circumference of a circle

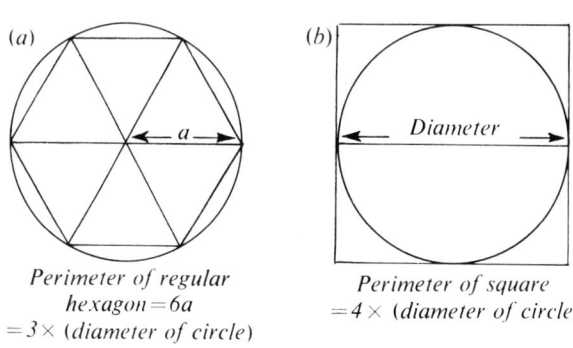

(a)

Perimeter of regular
hexagon$=6a$
$=3 \times$ (diameter of circle)

(b)

Perimeter of square
$=4 \times$ (diameter of circle)

Figure 37:29

perimeter, and the square a larger perimeter, than the circle. Hence the circumference of a circle is between three and four times its diameter. A more accurate value can be obtained by measuring the circumferences and diameters of various circular objects, and drawing a graph of the results (Figure 37:30). Lines showing $3 \times$ (diameter) and $4 \times$ (diameter) can be drawn on the same graph for comparison. Many tins and other circular objects of a variety of sizes should be measured. A simple way of measuring the circumference of a tin is to wrap a piece of paper tightly round it and to prick with a pin through two layers of paper. The paper can then be opened out and the distance between pinholes either

measured or transferred directly to the graph. Children are likely to conclude from their graphs that the circumference of a circle is about $3\frac{1}{4}$ times its diameter.

The actual value of the multiple of the diameter of a circle which gives the circumference is known as π; hence

$$\text{circumference of circle} = \pi \times (\text{diameter})$$

or

$$\frac{\text{circumference}}{\text{diameter}} = \pi$$

The value of π, which is $3 \cdot 141592653 \ldots$, has been evaluated with an increasing degree of accuracy over the centuries. The Jews used 3 as an approximation[3]; Archimedes proved that the value of π was between $3\frac{1}{7}$ and $3\frac{10}{71}$; Roman surveyors often used $3\frac{1}{8}$ instead of the closer approximation $3\frac{1}{7}$, as this made calculation rather easier. The advent of the electronic computer has now made it possible to calculate π to any number of decimal places, and more than 10,000 places are known. Children

---

[3] The description of the work of Hiram the worker in brass in the furnishing of Solomon's Temple contains the words: 'And he made a molten sea, ten cubits from the one brim to the other: it was round all about, ... and a line of thirty cubits did compass it round about.' (I Kings 7:23).

sometimes think that $3\frac{1}{7}$ is the exact value of π. In fact[4]

$3\frac{1}{7} = 3\cdot142857\ldots$

and

$\pi = 3\cdot141592\ldots,$

so that $3\frac{1}{7}$ is an approximation to π which is only correct to 2 decimal places. The decimal approximation $3\cdot14$ is, however, quite sufficient for practical purposes, and children should be encouraged to use a decimal approximation to π, rather than a fraction, in their working.

The teacher will notice that we have used a graphical method of estimating π, which avoids tiresome arithmetical calculations. A more usual method is to measure the diameter and circumference of a circle, divide circumference by diameter, repeat several times and average the results. This method may demand more arithmetical skill than can be expected of children at this stage, since they are likely to make such measurements as

    diameter $= 8\cdot3\,\text{cm}$
    circumference $= 25\cdot1\,\text{cm}$

and may find difficulty in performing the necessary division.

Children may ask how the value of π can be calculated with great accuracy. Archimedes and many other later calculators did it by drawing regular polygons inside and around the circle, and calculating their perimeters. Archimedes used polygons with 96 sides to arrive at

$3\frac{10}{71} < \pi < 3\frac{1}{7}$

Since about 1700 this method has been superseded by calculations based on variations on the formula obtained by methods of higher mathematics:

$\pi = 4(1 - \frac{1}{3} + \frac{1}{5} - \frac{1}{7} + \frac{1}{9} - \frac{1}{11} + \ldots)$

Areas of similar shapes

We now consider the behaviour of the areas of similar shapes. We have already drawn a graph of the growth of the areas of squares (*see page* 321) and have examined the behaviour of square numbers. Equilateral triangles and similar rectangles obey the same law of growth as squares. Figure 37:31 shows a graph of the growth of the areas of equilateral triangles. The same method of examining the growth of area can be used for any shape which will cover a plane area without leaving gaps. In Figure 37:32 we use this method to study the growth of similar rectangles, scalene triangles and regular hexagons.

[4] See page 244.

394

Growth of the areas of equilateral triangles

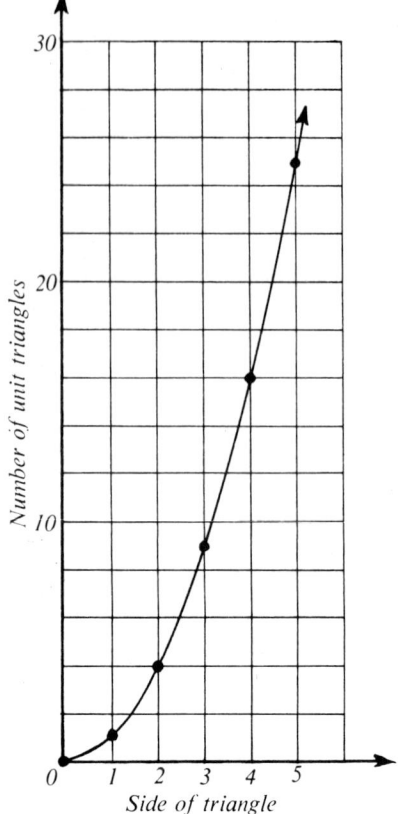

Side = 1 unit
Area = 1 unit triangle

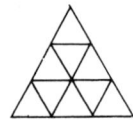
Side = 2 units
Area = 4 unit triangles

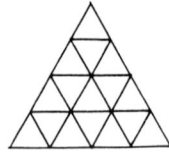
Side = 3 units
Area = 9 unit triangles

Side = 4 units
Area = 16 unit triangles

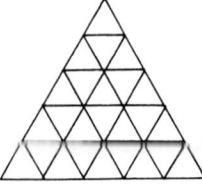
Side = 5 units
Area = 25 unit triangles

Figure 37:31

(a) Rectangles

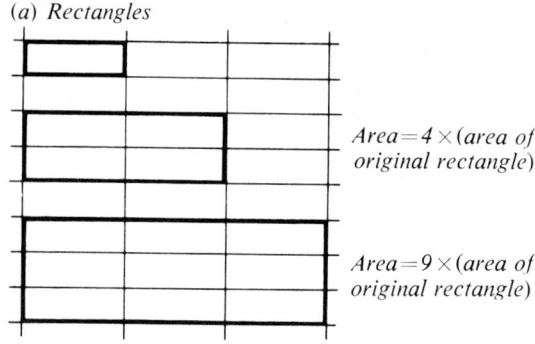

Area = 4 × (area of
original rectangle)

Area = 9 × (area of
original rectangle)

(b) Triangles

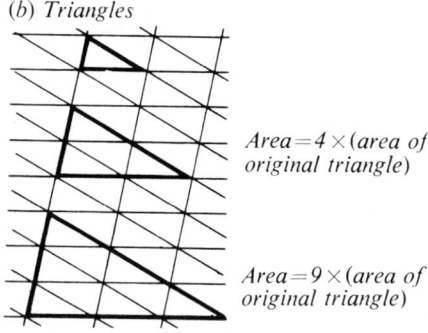

Area = 4 × (area of
original triangle)

Area = 9 × (area of
original triangle)

(c) Regular hexagons

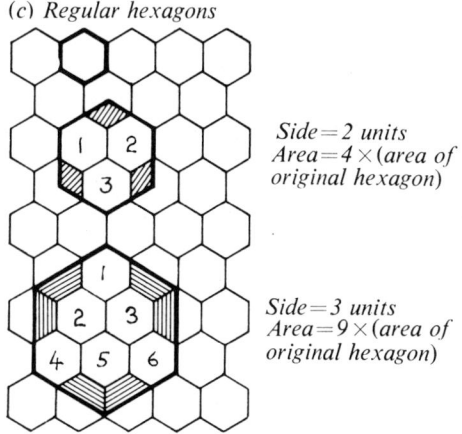

Side = 2 units
Area = 4 × (area of
original hexagon)

Side = 3 units
Area = 9 × (area of
original hexagon)

Figure 37:32

It therefore seems quite likely that if we have any two similar shapes, and if the linear measurements of one are n times the linear measurements of the other, then their areas will be connected by the relation

(area of shape of side n units)
= n^2 × (area of shape of side 1 unit)

From the tessellation of Figure 37:32(b), this relation is true for triangles. It follows from this that it will be true for

any shape with straight sides, since any such shape can be divided up into triangles (Figure 37:33). Hence, if we know the area of a basic shape, we can find the areas of all figures which are similar to it. The square is of course

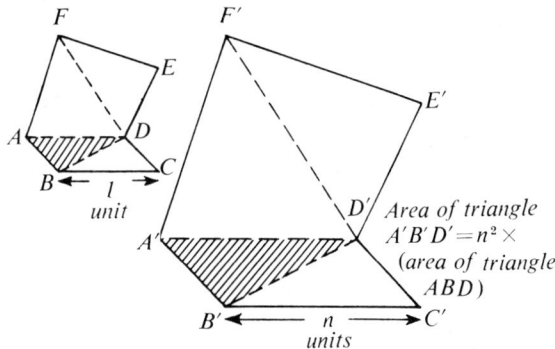

Area of triangle
$A'B'D' = n^2$ ×
(area of triangle
ABD)

Hence (area of shape $A'B'C'...$)=
n^2 × (area of shape $ABC...$)

Figure 37:33

particularly easy, as we usually take the unit of area to be a square of side 1 unit. In Chapter 23 we saw how the areas of rectangles and triangles can be found, by finding the number of unit squares which will cover a rectangle, and by using the fact that a triangle is half of a rectangle.

The area of a circle

We now turn to the problem of finding the area of a circle. Circles cannot be used to make tessellations without leaving gaps, so this method of finding the area is unsuitable. But the area of a circle is clearly less than the area of the square which contains it (Figure 37:34(a)),

A circle and the containing square

(a) area of circle
< area of square
on diameter

(b) area of circle
< 4 × (square
on radius)

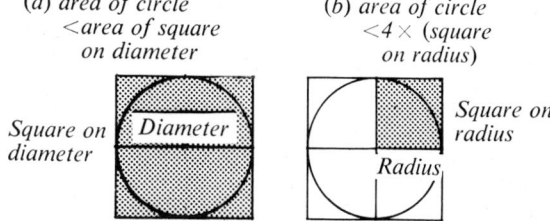

Figure 37:34

and so is less than the area of the square on its diameter, or if the square on the diameter is subdivided, the area of the circle is less than 4 × (area of square on the radius).

Another approximation to the area of a circle is obtained by drawing a square inside the circle (Figure 37:35). It will be seen that four quarters of this square together make up twice the square on the radius, and so

2 × (square on the radius) < area of circle

and

area of a circle < 4 × (square on the radius)

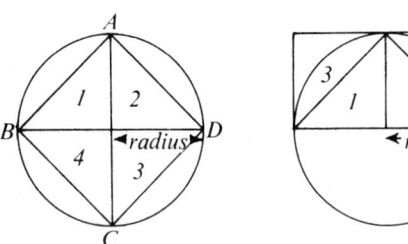

Figure 37:35

It is certainly to be expected that the area of a circle will be a constant multiple of the square on the radius, since all circles are similar shapes. Figure 37:36 shows similar regular polygons with a large number of sides inscribed

Similar polygons inscribed in circles

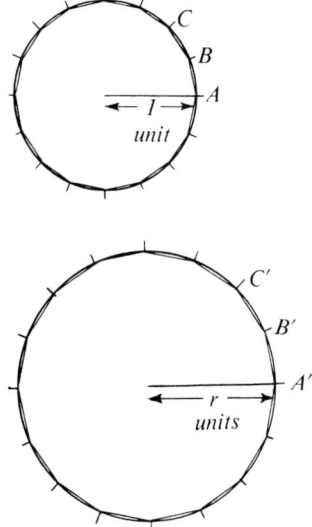

Area of shape A′B′C′...
= r² × (area of shape ABC...)

Figure 37:36

in two circles of radius 1 unit and r units. The previous result on the area of similar shapes with straight sides is then used. Hence we expect that the area of a circle will be a constant multiple of the square on the radius, and that

396

this constant multiple will be between 2 and 4. A dissection and rearrangement of the circle, suggested by the regular polygons in Figure 37:36, enables an exact result to be obtained.

Dissection of a circle to find its area

(a)

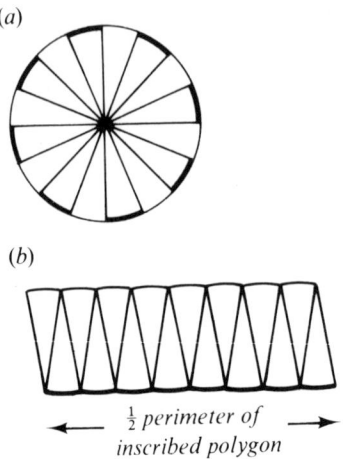

(b)

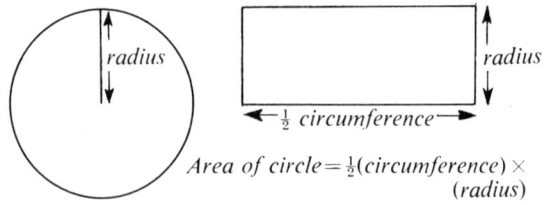

$\frac{1}{2}$ *perimeter of inscribed polygon*

Figure 37:37

The circle is cut into many equal sectors, which can be arranged into the shape shown in Figure 37:37(b). This shape is very nearly a rectangle. Its length is half the perimeter of the polygon inscribed in the circle, and its breadth is nearly equal to the radius of the circle. If we use a polygon with a very large number of sides, half the perimeter of the polygon becomes more and more nearly equal to half the circumference of the circle. In the end, if the number of sides of the polygon is increased indefinitely, the area of the circle has been rearranged in the form of a rectangle whose length is *half the circumference of the circle,* and whose breadth is the *radius* (Figure 37:38).

The area of a circle

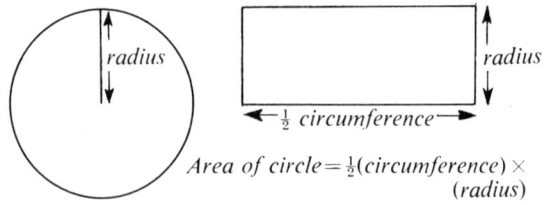

Area of circle = $\frac{1}{2}$*(circumference) × (radius)*

Figure 37:38

This seems a very suitable formula for the area of a circle for children to use at this stage, as it reminds them of the thought-process used in obtaining the result. We may, however, rearrange the result slightly. The circum-

The area of a circle

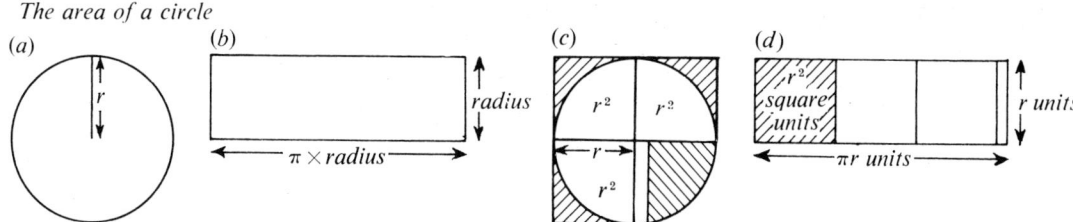

Figure 37:39

ference of a circle is $\pi \times$ (diameter). But the radius is half of the diameter, so

$$\tfrac{1}{2}\,\text{circumference} = \tfrac{1}{2}\,(\pi \times \text{diameter})$$
$$= \pi \times (\tfrac{1}{2}\,\text{diameter})$$
$$= \pi \times \text{radius}$$

The result now takes the form demonstrated in Figure 37:39.

We see that the area of a circle is a constant multiple of the square of the radius, and that the value of the constant multiple is π. We can write the usual formula:

$$\text{area of circle} = \pi r^2.$$

38 Rational and Irrational Numbers

The number line of rational numbers

The idea of the number line has now reached the stage where we can picture all the positive and negative integers as being represented by a set of equally spaced points on a line. All the rational numbers also have their appropriate places on the number line. It will be remembered that each rational number corresponds to a set of equivalent fractions. For instance

$$^+(\tfrac{3}{5}) = \, ^+(\tfrac{6}{10}) = +0.6 = \, ^+(\tfrac{9}{15}) = \dots,$$

and all these equivalent fractions correspond to the same point on the number line. This representation of a set of fractions which are written differently, but which have the same value, by the same point on the number line helps to strengthen the idea of a rational number. A rational number is a number which is represented by a set of equivalent fractions, and which corresponds to a single point on the number line.

The rational number points are extremely closely packed on the number line. Between the points representing 0 and $^+1$ on the number line there are points representing the rational numbers $^+0.1$, $^+0.2, \dots$, $^+0.9$, points representing $^+0.01$, $^+0.02, \dots$, $^+0.99$, points representing $^+0.001$, $^+0.002, \dots$, $^+0.999$, and so on, using ever smaller intervals on the line. As children realize how they can use the decimal system to represent ever smaller fractions, they will think that the number line contains ever more and more points representing rational numbers (Figure 38:2). Here we have used successive subdivisions of each unit into tenths to yield more and more rational number points on the number line. Any number of subdivisions of the unit will do equally well. In Figure 38:3 we use subdivisions of the unit into thirds, ninths, etc., to give rational number points. Most of these rational numbers are different from those marked in Figure 38:2, since $\tfrac{1}{3}$ cannot be exactly written as a terminating decimal fraction and recurs as $0.333\dots$

The number line of positive and negative rational numbers

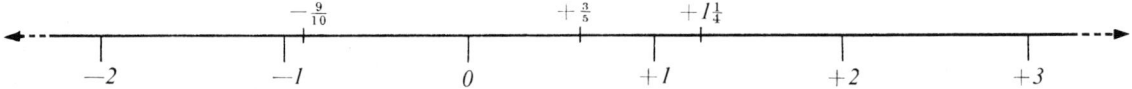

Figure 38:1

Filling up the number line with more closely packed rational numbers
(a) Tenths

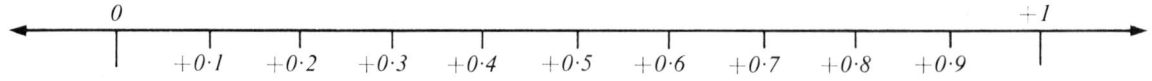

(b) Hundredths

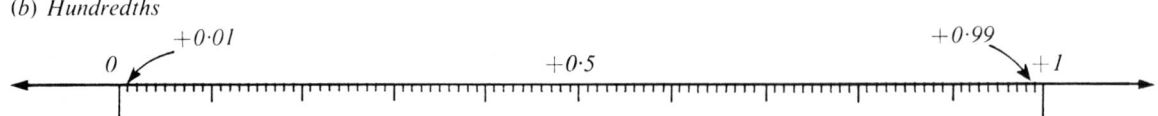

(c) Thousandths (enlarged)

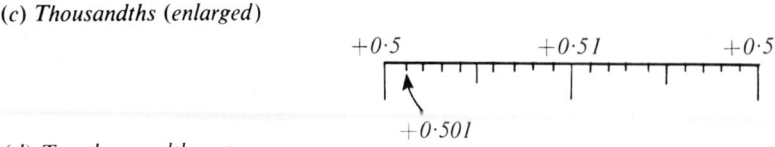

(d) Ten-thousandths, etc.

Figure 38:2

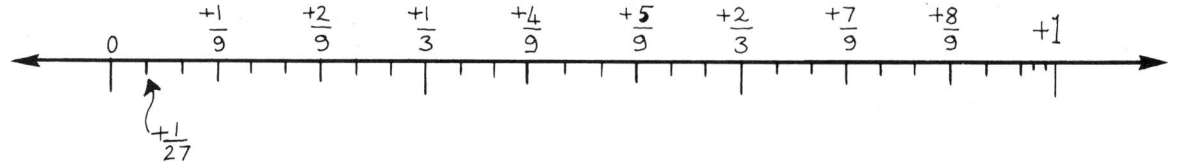

Figure 38:3

$= 0.3$. We could carry out the same process of marking in rational number points with any subdivision of the unit, and so we eventually build up a mental picture of a number line on which *every* rational number has its place. The rational numbers on this number line are extremely close-packed. Every interval, however small, on the number line contains an infinity of rational numbers, for if we take a tiny interval such as that between ⁻1·000002 and ⁻1·000001, we could make in this interval continually repeated subdivisions similar to those shown in Figure 38:2; each of the points obtained would have a fractional representation and so would correspond to a rational number.

It is a surprising fact that when *all* the possible sub-divisions of each unit of the number line, and so all the rational numbers, have been put in, there are still points of the number line which have not been covered. In spite of the density of packing of the rational number points, there are in fact many other points on the number line with no number alloted to them. Children will meet these *irrational numbers*[1] first when instead of measuring the diagonal of a square, they use Pythagoras' Theorem to work out its length, and so have to find a value for $\sqrt{2}$. The full significance of irrational numbers will not, however, be appreciated until later.[2]

We can very easily see that $\sqrt{2}$ does not fall on any of the *decimal* subdivisions of the number line. For if we try to find better and better decimal approximations to $\sqrt{2}$

$1.4 < \sqrt{2} < 1.5$, since $1.4^2 = 1.96$ and $1.5^2 = 2.25$;
$1.41 < \sqrt{2} < 1.42$, since $1.41^2 = 1.9881$ and $1.42^2 = 2.0364$;
$1.414 < \sqrt{2} < 1.415$, since $1.414^2 = 1.999396$ and $1.415^2 = 2.002225$
$1.4142 < \sqrt{2} < 1.4143$, since $1.4142^2 = 1.99996164$ and $1.4143^2 = 2.00024449$,

and so on.[3] It will be seen that this process can be continued indefinitely. The process of approaching more and more nearly the value of $\sqrt{2}$ by putting it within smaller and smaller decimal subdivisions of a unit (Figure 38:4) would eventually fix a point on the number line corresponding to $\sqrt{2}$, although an *exact* decimal for $\sqrt{2}$ cannot be found.

This point representing $\sqrt{2}$ is not one of the exact *decimal* points on the number line, but, on the other hand, neither is

$\frac{1}{3} = 0.33333\ldots = 0.\dot{3}$

or

$\frac{1}{7} = 0.1428571428571\ldots = 0.\dot{1}4285\dot{7}$

[1] See pages 386 and 392.

[2] A *rational number* can be written as a fraction or ratio; an *irrational number* has a place on the number line, but cannot be so written.

[3] These and similar calculations can easily be carried out with a desk calculating machine.

Fixing the position of $\sqrt{2}$ on the number line

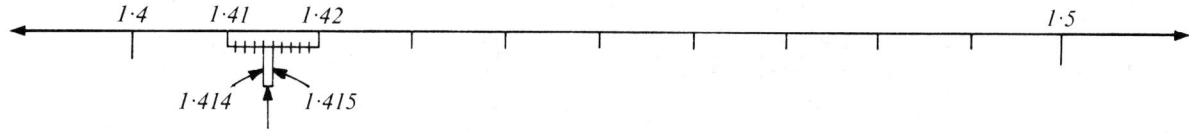

The position of $\sqrt{2}$ lies within a series of segments of ever-decreasing length

Figure 38:4

To show that $\sqrt{2}$ is not a rational number we must show that the point representing $\sqrt{2}$ is not a result of *any* subdivision of a unit of the number line into equal parts. The proof of this famous result is ascribed to the followers of Pythagoras, who found it as disturbing as do people today whose previous acquaintance with numbers has only included whole numbers and fractions. The Pythagoreans even attempted to suppress their discovery for a time because it undermined the foundations of their beliefs.

Children will not understand the very abstract nature of the following argument until they are well into the stage of formal operations but it is of value to the teacher in showing that irrational numbers are needed if we are to handle square roots. Children's questions are likely to be of the type, 'Surely the decimal for $\sqrt{2}$ must end sometime?' and, 'If you wrote the numbers to another base, would $\sqrt{2}$ end then?'

The Pythagoreans proved their result by supposing that $\sqrt{2}$ did fall on a rational subdivision of the unit in some base, and showed that this led to a contradiction. If $\sqrt{2}$ were in fact a rational number it could be written as a fraction:

$$\sqrt{2} = \frac{p}{q},$$

where p and q are *integers*, and where the *fraction has been cancelled down to its lowest terms.* Then, by squaring both sides

$$2 = \frac{p^2}{q^2},$$

and so $2q^2 = p^2$.

Now $2q^2$ must be an even number, since it is a multiple of 2, and so p^2 is even. The square of an even number is even, and the square of an odd number is odd. Hence it follows

that p is even. Also, every even integer is twice some other integer, so we can write

$p = 2r$, where r is an integer.
Therefore $\quad p^2 = 4r^2$.
But $\quad\quad p^2 = 2q^2$,
and so $\quad\quad 4r^2 = 2q^2$;
hence $\quad\quad q^2 = 2r^2$.

We now repeat the above argument and deduce from $q^2 = 2r^2$ that q must be an even integer. Therefore p and q are both even integers. This contradicts the assumption that $\sqrt{2}$ has been written as a fraction *in its lowest terms,* and so p and q have no common factor. But every rational number can be written as a fraction in its lowest terms, and so $\sqrt{2}$ cannot be a rational number. Hence $\sqrt{2}$ is represented by a point on the number line which is left uncovered by *all* rational subdivisions of the units of the number line.

Irrational numbers and real numbers

In the same way that we have shown that $\sqrt{2}$ is not a rational number, it can be shown that $\sqrt{3}$, $\sqrt{5}$, $\sqrt{6}$, $\sqrt{7}$, ... are irrational numbers. Children who have met Pythagoras' Theorem will find these numbers of interest because, although they cannot calculate exact values for them, they can use a calculating machine to approximate to them, or obtain an approximation by scale-drawing, or read their approximate values from the graph of squares, and so they can mark them in on the number line.

A simple way of drawing lengths of $\sqrt{2}$ units, $\sqrt{3}$ units, etc., is shown in Figure 38:5. The diagonal of a square whose length is 1 unit is $\sqrt{2}$ units. This starts the construction, which is continued by using the length last

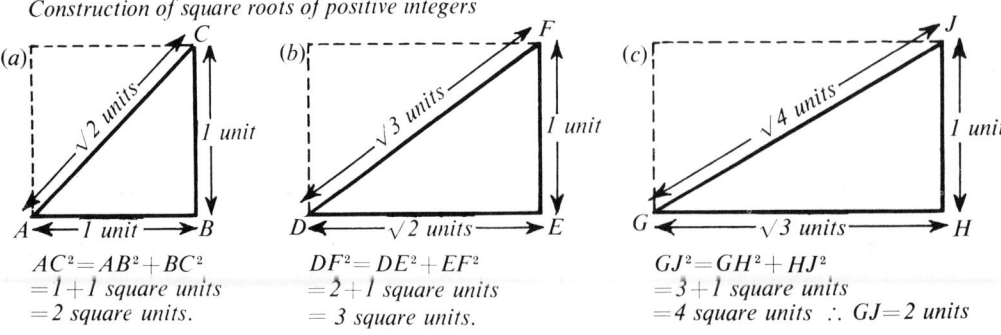

Construction of square roots of positive integers

(a) $AC^2 = AB^2 + BC^2$
$= 1 + 1$ square units
$= 2$ square units.

(b) $DF^2 = DE^2 + EF^2$
$= 2 + 1$ square units
$= 3$ square units.

(c) $GJ^2 = GH^2 + HJ^2$
$= 3 + 1$ square units
$= 4$ square units $\therefore GJ = 2$ units

Figure 38:5

constructed. The accuracy of the construction can be checked each time the square on the diagonal is a perfect square. Figure 38:6 shows another way of arranging this construction, and transfers the lengths to the number line.

The only square roots of rational numbers which are themselves rational numbers are those such as $\sqrt{4}$ and $\sqrt{\frac{9}{25}}$ which are square roots of perfect squares. All other square roots, such as $\sqrt{10}, \sqrt{\frac{8}{25}}, \sqrt{0.001}$ are irrational numbers; so are most cube roots, fourth roots, and so on. Many other numbers which are not roots of rational numbers are also irrational. An example of these is π, which is equal to $3.1415926535\ldots$. Although it was known in ancient times that $\sqrt{2}$ was an irrational number, it was a much more difficult matter to prove that π was irrational, and this problem was not solved until almost 1800.

In fact, all numbers which, when written in decimal form, neither terminate nor recur are irrational. Conversely, all rational numbers when written as decimals either terminate or recur. It is easy to see that a terminating decimal is a rational number. For example, $1.8731 = \frac{18731}{10000}$, which is a rational number. But it is not quite so obvious that a recurring decimal such as $3.054054054\ldots$ is a rational number. But if

$$n = 3.05\dot{4}$$
$$= 3.054054054\ldots$$

then

$$1000n = 3054.054054054\ldots$$
$$n = 3.054054054\ldots, \text{ as we know.}$$

If we subtract these two expressions, the recurring part of the decimal is removed, and

$$999n = 3051$$
Hence $n = \frac{3051}{999}$,

and this is a rational number.

Similarly, we can find a fraction corresponding to any recurring decimal. Therefore, a terminating or recurring decimal is a rational number. A decimal which neither terminates nor recurs, but which has an infinite number of decimal places without continuous cyclic repetition of the digits, represents an irrational number.

Although the rational numbers are so densely packed on the number line, there are very many spaces between them which are occupied by irrational numbers. In fact it can be shown that rational numbers are only thinly scattered on the number line compared with the great profusion of the irrational numbers.

In practical problems, irrational numbers are always handled by means of rational approximations to them, which will give a numerical result to any desired degree of accuracy. In theory, however, it is desirable to use a number system which contains both the rational and the irrational numbers. The number system used in much of more advanced mathematics is the *real number system*. The set of real numbers is the set of rational numbers together with the set of irrational numbers. *Every* real number is represented by a point on the number line, and *every* point on the number line represents a real number. The number line of rational numbers which we have previously used has the fundamental disadvantage of having gaps in it, but the *real number line* is complete.

In the primary school children will probably be convinced that every point on the number line represents a number, but for many children the distinction between rational and irrational numbers will be postponed to the secondary school stage. In fact, children are intuitively aware of the real number line and its completeness long before they understand irrational numbers. Much of this intuitive awareness comes from graphical work. When children interpolate a value such as $\sqrt{8}$ from the graph of squares (Figure 38:7), they expect that the point on the x-axis which they obtain will correspond to a number which is the value of $\sqrt{8}$. It does not occur to them that

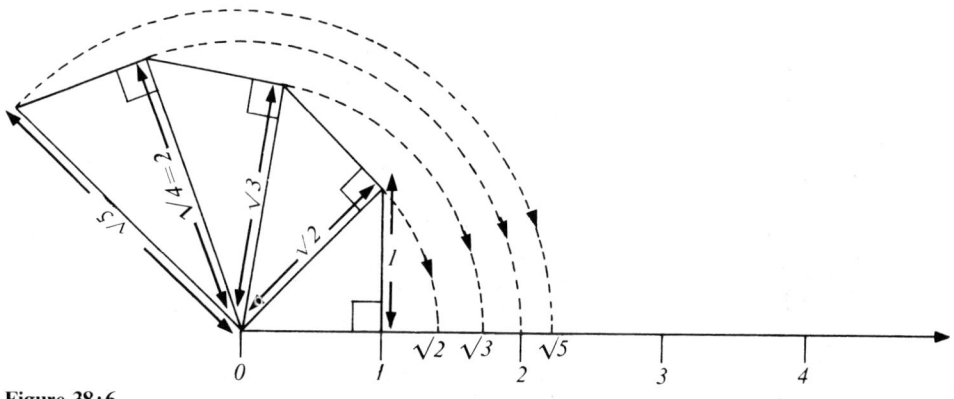

Figure 38:6

Interpolation from the graph of squares

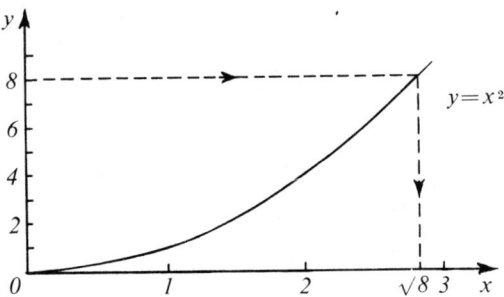

Figure 38:7

there is no *rational* number whose square is exactly 8; what they do is to find the best decimal approximation they can to the real number whose square is 8.

We thus see that the *real number line* is essential for the treatment of square roots, but we can only expect an informal intuitive handling of it at this stage. In the rest of this chapter we discuss some more situations in which children may meet $\sqrt{2}$ and other well-known irrational numbers.

Reduction, enlargement and $\sqrt{2}$

Children often make booklets or folders for their work by folding a large piece of paper as many times as they need. This process is also used in making books. A number of pages are printed on the same sheet of paper, and the sheet is then folded so that the pages come in the right order. Figure 38:8 shows a way in which children, and printers, often fold their paper to make smaller pages.

Folding a sheet of paper for a booklet

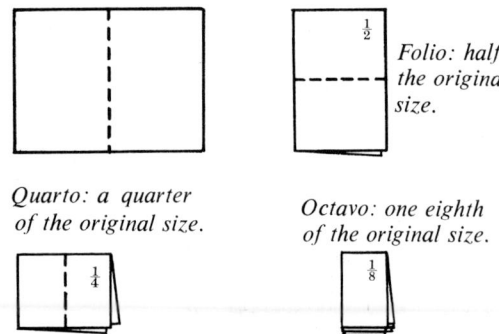

Quarto: a quarter of the original size.

Octavo: one eighth of the original size.

Figure 38:8

402

This process can be continued to make more, smaller, pages. The fold is always made so as to halve the longer side of the rectangle. The shape of the page which results is not always the same shape as the sheet from which it was folded. The quarter of a sheet, or quarto page, is the same shape as the original sheet (Figure 38:9(a)), and the octavo page is the same shape as the

The sheet of paper opened out.
(a)

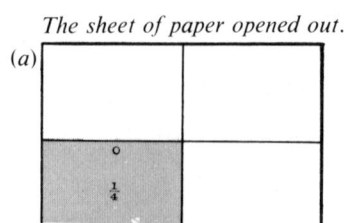

Four quarto pages, the same shape as the sheet.

(b)

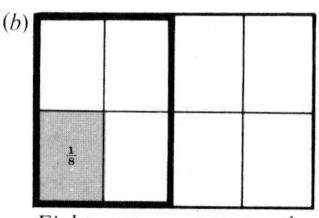

Eight octavo pages, the same shape as the folio.

(c)

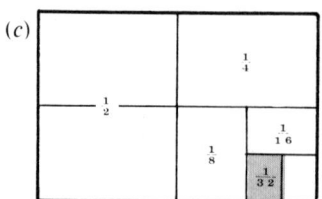

The folding continued. $\frac{1}{32}$ of the sheet is the same shape as $\frac{1}{8}$ and $\frac{1}{2}$ of the sheet.

Figure 38:9

folio (Figure 38:9(b)). It is rare for the folio and octavo to be the same shape as the sheet and the quarto. This book is of size 246 mm × 189 mm, each page of which has been folded from a sheet 1008 mm × 768 mm. Hence 32 pages of the book (16 pages printed on each side) were folded and cut to make one 32-page section from a single sheet.

Children can check whether two rectangles are the same shape by putting one on top of the other. In Chapter 36 we put a triangle on top of another to see whether they were similar. A right-angled triangle is half of a rectangle, so the same method can be used to discover whether rectangles are similar or not (Figure 38:10).

Finding out whether rectangles are similar

(a)

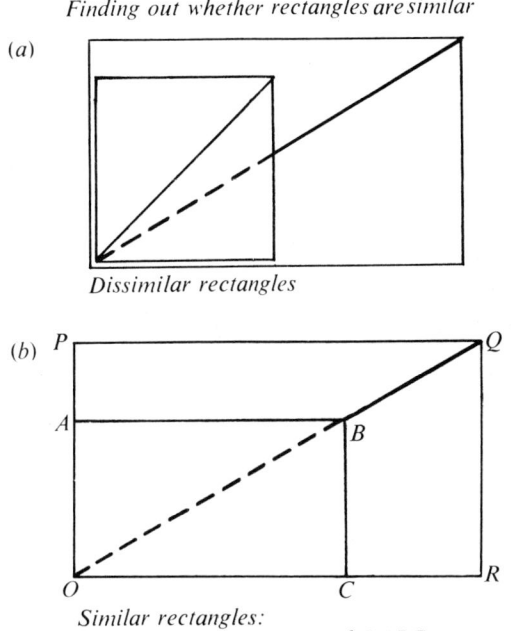

Dissimilar rectangles

(b)

Similar rectangles:
OPQR is an enlargement of OABC,
using O as the centre of enlargement.

Figure 38:10

Figure 38:11 shows the shapes of a half, quarter, eighth, etc., of a rectangular sheet of paper. The shapes made by

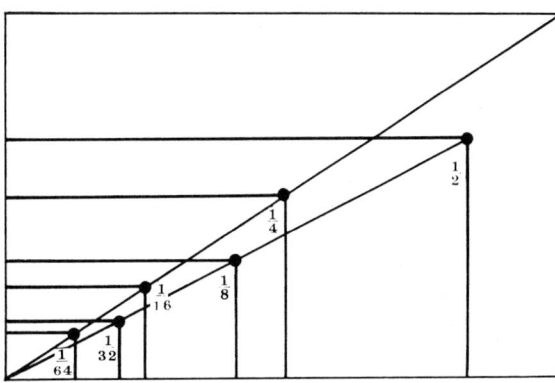

Figure 38:11

$\frac{1}{2}$, $\frac{1}{8}$, $\frac{1}{32}$, ... of a sheet are similar to each other, and the shapes made by 1, $\frac{1}{4}$, $\frac{1}{16}$, $\frac{1}{64}$, ... of a sheet are similar to each other. Often the two sequences of fractional parts folded in this way are not the same shape as each other. Children may try to find a sheet of paper whose half is the same shape as the original sheet, in which case all the pages folded from it will be the same shape as the sheet. They will find that the length of the sheet is rather less than $1\frac{1}{2}$ times the breadth. Sheets of paper in metric sizes, A0, A1, A2, ... have this property that half a sheet is the same shape as the whole sheet.

Systems of proportion based on similar rectangles have often been used by architects. For example, the columns on the façade of the Erechtheion at Athens divide the rectangular façade into smaller rectangles. The proportions are such that a rectangle whose sides are next-door-but-one columns is similar to the whole façade (Figure 38:12). In Figure 38:12(b) these four small rectangles have been picked out by drawing a diagonal of each one. This makes it very easy to see whether rectangles such as *ABCD* and *PQRS* (Figure 38:13) are similar.

The proportions of the Erechtheion

(a)

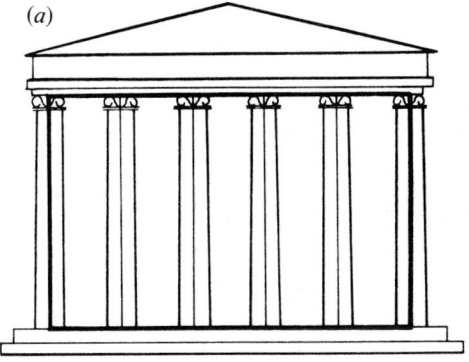

Figure 38:12

(b)

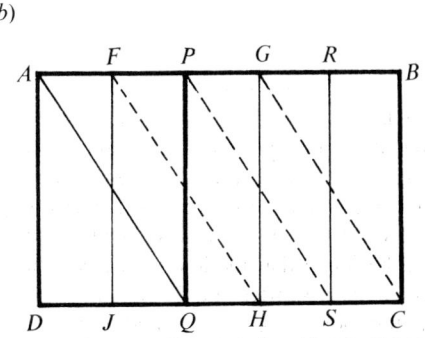

The four small rectangles APQD, FGHJ,
PRSQ, GBCH, are all similar to ABCD.

Another test for similar rectangles

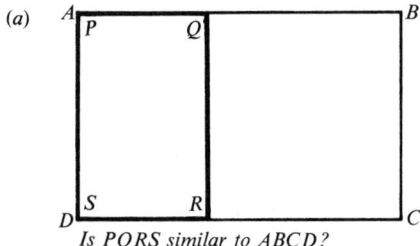

(a)

Is PQRS similar to ABCD?

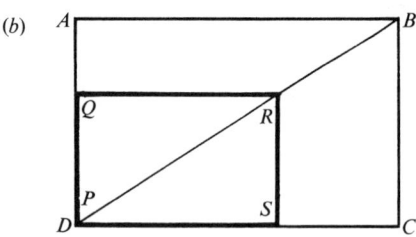

(b)

Rotate PQRS through a right angle and test for similarity.

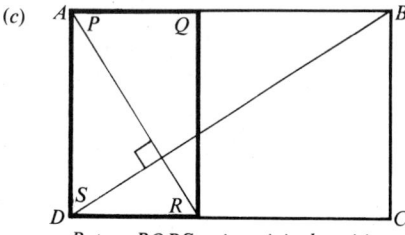

(c)

Return PQRS to its original position. Diagonal PR is now at right angles to diagonal BD.

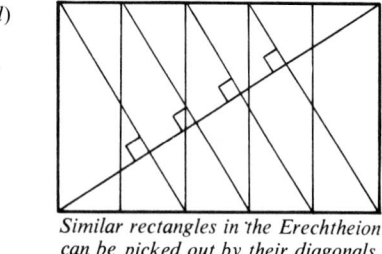

(d)

Similar rectangles in the Erechtheion can be picked out by their diagonals.

Figure 38:13

Constructing a rectangle whose halves are the same shape as the whole rectangle

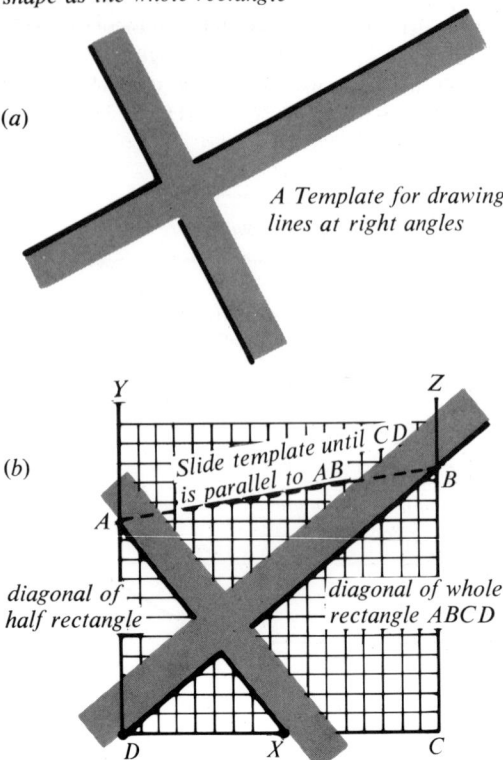

(a)

A Template for drawing lines at right angles

(b)

Slide template until CD is parallel to AB

diagonal of half rectangle

diagonal of whole rectangle ABCD

Draw DC, DY, CZ. Put in pins at A and X, so that $AX = \frac{1}{2} DC$. Slide template about, touching pins, until AB is parallel to DC

Figure 38:14

Ratio of sides when half-rectangle is similar to whole

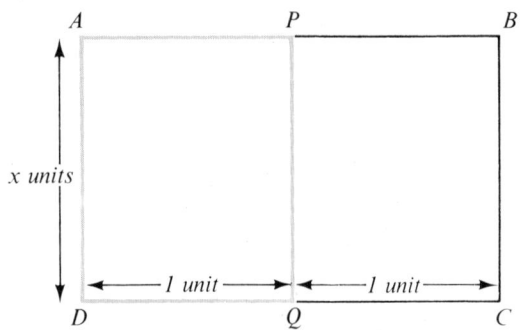

If ABCD is similar to APQD, then $\dfrac{AD}{AB} = \dfrac{AP}{AD}$

hence $\dfrac{x}{2} = \dfrac{1}{x}$

and $x^2 = 2$

Figure 38:15

Two rulers rigidly fixed at right angles, or a cardboard or Meccano template for drawing two lines at right angles now makes it easy to construct on squared paper a rectangle whose halves are the same shape as the original (Figure 38:14). When the sides of this rectangle are measured, it will be found that the longer side is about 1·4 times the length of the shorter side. In fact, the longer side is $\sqrt{2}$ times the shorter side. A few children may be able to see algebraically that this must be so (Figure 38:15).

The golden rectangle

There is another shape of rectangle which has many interesting properties. This is the so-called *golden rectangle,* the ratio of whose sides, the *golden ratio,* has often been thought to form the basis for an ideal system of proportion. This ratio seems to appear both in shapes and among numbers, and to be approximated to both by nature and by artists and architects.

We can find the golden rectangle by folding a piece of paper. Children know well the method of folding a square piece of paper from a rectangular one (Figure 38:16). The rectangular piece of paper left over (shaded in Figure 38:16(*b*)) is usually a different shape from the original piece. It may happen, however, that the piece left over is

Folding a rectangle to make a square

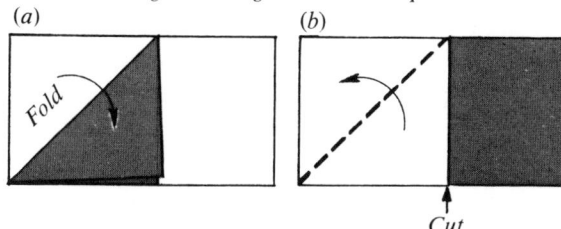

Figure 38:16

the same shape as the original piece (Figure 38:17). The shape of such a rectangle is called the *golden rectangle.* Its proportions have often been thought to be particularly pleasing to the eye. The shape of a postcard or of a catalogue card the sides of which are in the ratio 5:3 is a fairly good approximation to a golden rectangle. A sheet of foolscap paper, is even better as here the sides are in the ratio 13:8. Children who have used a right-angle template for the construction of the rectangle shown in Figure

38:14 will be able to construct a golden rectangle by a similar method (Figure 38:18).

Constructing a Golden Rectangle

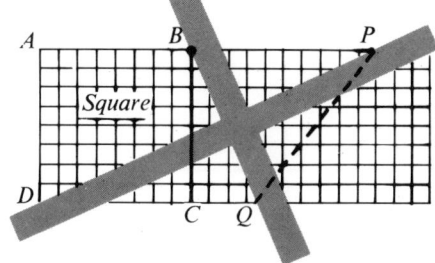

Draw square ABCD. Put in pins at B and D. Slide template until PQ is parallel to AD.

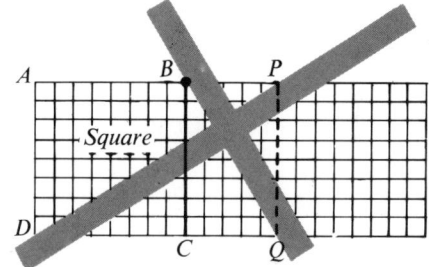

APQD and BPQC are now golden rectangles

Figure 38:18

When the sides of the golden rectangle are measured it will be found that they are in about the ratio 1·62:1 (figure 38:19). This ratio, which Leonardo da Vinci called 'the divine proportion', was renamed in the nineteenth century the *golden ratio.* It is an irrational number, the first few digits of whose decimal expansion are 1·61803398.... It is often denoted by the Greek letter ϕ.

A property of the golden rectangle is that the ratio of

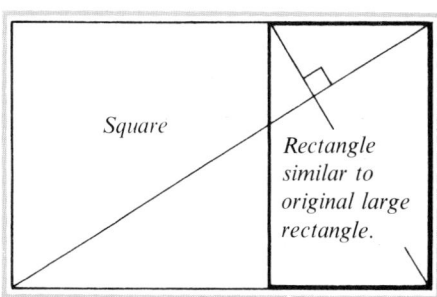

Both the large and the small rectangles are golden rectangles

Figure 38:17

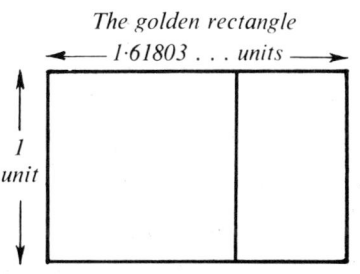

Figure 38:19

405

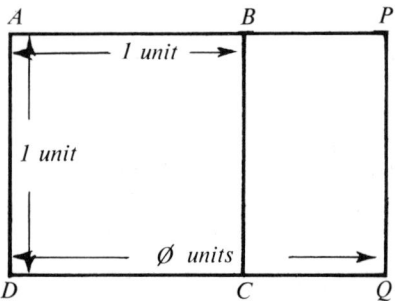

Golden ratios in the golden rectangle

Rectangle APQD is similar to PQCB.

Hence $\dfrac{AP}{AD} = \dfrac{PQ}{BP} = $ *golden ratio and so* $\dfrac{\phi}{1} = \dfrac{1}{\phi - 1}$

Figure 38:20

the larger to the smaller part of AP (Figure 38:20) is equal to the golden ratio ϕ. This is because $AB = AD$ and so the golden ratio $\dfrac{AP}{AD}$ is equal to $\dfrac{AP}{AB}$. Also the golden ratio $\dfrac{PQ}{BP}$ is equal to $\dfrac{AB}{BP}$, since $PQ = AB$. But all golden ratios are equal, so $\dfrac{AP}{AB} = \dfrac{AB}{BP}$. In words, *the ratio of the whole of AP to its larger part is equal to the ratio of the larger to the smaller part.* The line AP is said to be divided in *golden section.*

The Greeks knew a very simple geometrical construction for a golden rectangle (Figure 38:21), and a very similar method enables a line to be divided in golden section.

Children will not at this stage be able to prove the

correctness of the construction,[4] but they will be able to verify by measurement that it does in fact give a golden rectangle.

Much of the interest of the construction for dividing a line in golden section (Figure 38:22), has sprung from the occurrence of golden section in art, and in such shapes as the regular pentagon.

Dividing a line in golden section

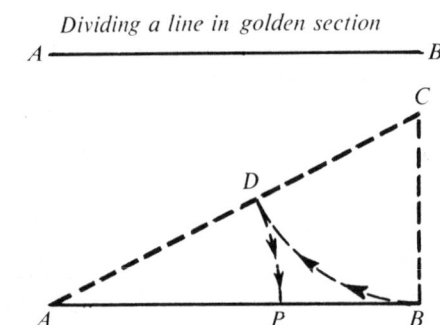

(i) Line AB is to be divided in golden section.

(ii) Draw BC = ½ AB, perpendicular to AB.

(iii) Centre C, radius CB, draw an arc.

(iv) Centre A, radius AD, draw an arc.

P then divides AB in golden section.[5]

Figure 38:22

Another interesting property of the golden rectangle is its link with the *equiangular spiral* found in nature in the shells of *Nautilus* and in snail-shells.[6] When a square is cut from a golden rectangle, a golden rectangle remains, from which another square can be cut. If this process is

Construction of a golden rectangle with ruler and compasses

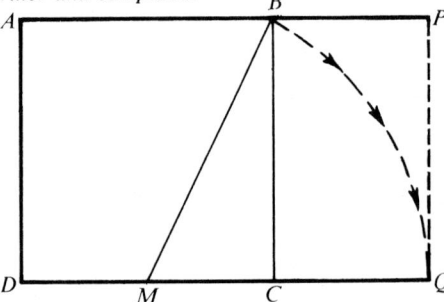

(i) Construct square ABCD.
(ii) Find M, mid point of CD.
(iii) With centre M, radius MD, draw an arc.
(iv) Complete the golden rectangle ADQP.

Figure 38:21

406

[4] If $AD = 2$ units, then $BM = \sqrt{5}$ units by Pythagoras' Theorem, and so $DQ = \sqrt{5}+1$ units. Hence $\dfrac{DQ}{DA} = \dfrac{\sqrt{5}+1}{2}$. But from Figure 38:20 for a golden rectangle $\phi = \dfrac{1}{\phi - 1}$, and so $\phi^2 - \phi = 1$. The positive solution of this quadratic equation is $\phi = \dfrac{\sqrt{5}+1}{3}$. Thus $\dfrac{DQ}{DA} = \phi$, and the constructed rectangle $ADQP$ is golden.

[5] By Pythagoras' Theorem, if $AB = 2$ units, $AP = (\sqrt{5}-1)$ units and

$$\dfrac{AB}{AP} = \dfrac{2}{\sqrt{5}-1} = \dfrac{2(\sqrt{5}+1)}{(\sqrt{5}-1)(\sqrt{5}+1)} = \dfrac{2(\sqrt{5}+1)}{4} = \dfrac{\sqrt{5}+1}{2} = \phi.$$

[6] See D'Arcy Thompson, *On Growth and Form* and Weyl, H., *Symmetry.*

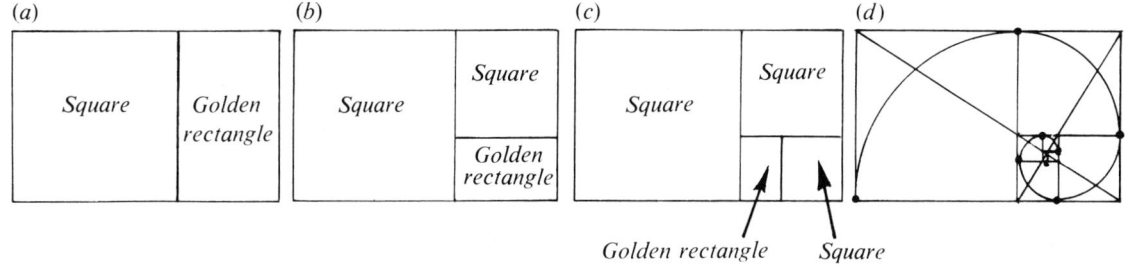

(a) Square | Golden rectangle

(b) Square | Square / Golden rectangle

(c) Square | Square / Golden rectangle / Square

(d)

Golden rectangle   Square

Figure 38:23

continued, rotating the rectangle through a right angle each time (Figure 38:23), corresponding points of the golden rectangles lie on an equiangular spiral. This spiral rotates for ever about the point of intersection of diagonals of all the golden rectangles in the diagram. This centre point is the *pole* of the spiral.

Equiangular spirals

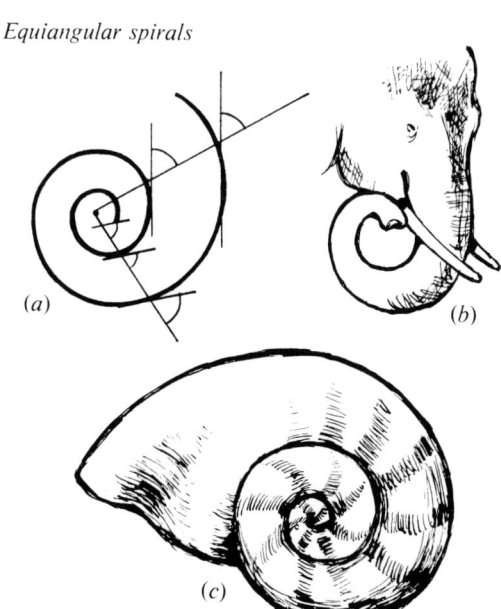

(a)

(b)

(c)

Figure 38:24

The spiral formed in this way is known as the *equiangular* spiral because it always cuts the radius from the pole at the same angle (Figure 38:24). D'Arcy Thompson likens the equiangular spiral to the result of rolling up a cone, so that the section of the curled-up trunk of an elephant roughly resembles an equiangular spiral, as does the section of a curled growing animal like *Nautilus*.

The Fibonacci sequence and the golden rectangle

Children make up sequences of numbers by many methods, and enjoy continuing these sequences and finding out how they behave. The following sequences can be made from the numbers

$$1, 2, 3, 4, 5, \ldots$$

i) $1, 4, 9, 16, 25, \ldots$ by squaring each natural number,
ii) $2, 4, 6, 8, 10, \ldots$ by doubling each natural number,
iii) $7, 10, 13, 16, \ldots$ by multiplying each natural number by 3 and adding 4.

Another way of making sequences which follow regular patterns is to take a number, perform some arithmetical operation on it, and repeat this operation to form a sequence. For instance,

i) $7, 10, 13, 16, \ldots$; start with 7, add 3, add 3 to the result, etc. This sequence is the same as the previous one but the method of construction is different.
ii) $1, 2, 4, 8, 16, 32, \ldots$; start with 1, double it, double the result, etc.
iii) $2, 4, 16, 256, \ldots$; start with 2, square it, square the result, etc.[7]

Yet another way of building up a sequence by using the terms already obtained to generate the next term is shown in the *Fibonacci sequence*. Such sequences are named after the greatest of medieval mathematicians, Leonardo of Pisa, nicknamed Fibonacci (*c.* 1170–1250), who discovered the best-known of them. Each term of a Fibonacci sequence is built up as the sum of the *two*

[7] The numbers obtained by adding 1 to each member of this sequence are called the *Fermat numbers*. They are

$$3, 5, 17, 257, 65537, \ldots$$

Fermat (*c.* 1608–65) conjectured that all these numbers were prime. But it is now known that the next Fermat number is 641×6700417, and that many later Fermat numbers are composite. No further prime Fermat numbers have been found.

previous terms. For instance, starting with 0 and 1, we have

$$0, 1, 0+1 = 1, 1+1 = 2, 1+2 = 3, 2+3 = 5,$$
$$3+5 = 8, \ldots$$

that is

$$0, 1, 1, 2, 3, 5, 8, 13, 21, 34, \ldots$$

The reader will notice that two of the approximations which we have used to the golden rectangle, 5 by 8 and 8 by 13, appear as pairs of successive terms of this sequence. In fact, every pair of successive terms of the Fibonacci sequence gives an increasingly better approximation to the proportions of the golden rectangle. The first few of these rectangles are:

Rectangle
1 by 1   2 by 1   3 by 2   5 by 3   8 by 5   13 by 8
21 by 13   34 by 21   55 by 34   89 by 55

Ratio of sides
$\frac{1}{1} = 1$ $\frac{2}{1} = 2$ $\frac{3}{2} = 1\cdot5$ $\frac{5}{3} = 1\cdot6666$ $\frac{8}{5} = 1\cdot6$ $\frac{13}{8} = 1\cdot625$
$\frac{21}{13} = 1\cdot6153$ $\frac{34}{21} = 1\cdot6190$ $\frac{55}{34} = 1\cdot6176\ldots$ $\frac{89}{55} = 1\cdot6181\ldots$

We see that the ratio of the sides becomes closer and closer to the golden ratio.

A series of rectangles which approximate more and more closely to a golden rectangle can be built up using the Fibonacci series by a method which is the reverse of Figure 38:23. In Figure 38:23 a golden rectangle was cut down into squares; now we use squares to build up more and more nearly golden rectangles (Figure 38:25).

It is not necessary to start with the numbers 0 and 1 to generate a Fibonacci sequence. Any two natural numbers will do. For instance 5 and 1 give the sequence

$$5, 1, 6, 7, 13, 20, 33, 53, 86, 139, \ldots$$

It is possible to show that the ratio of successive terms of *any* Fibonacci sequence approaches the golden ratio. Hence, good approximations to a golden rectangle can be made by the whirling square method from *any* rectangle.

It has often been thought that a golden rectangle has more pleasing proportions than other rectangles, or that a line divided in golden section was more aesthetically pleasing than when divided elsewhere. Leonardo da Vinci used the golden section when drawing a face; the lines in Turner's 'Battersea Bridge' are placed so as to divide the picture in golden section, and the modern painter Mondrian uses golden section to organize some of his compositions of line and colour. The architect le Corbusier was much struck by the fact that 144 appears in the Fibonacci sequence

$$0, 1, 1, 2, 3, 5, 8, 13, 21, 34, 55, 89, 144, 233, \ldots$$

408

Building a nearly golden rectangle

(The Whirling Square method)

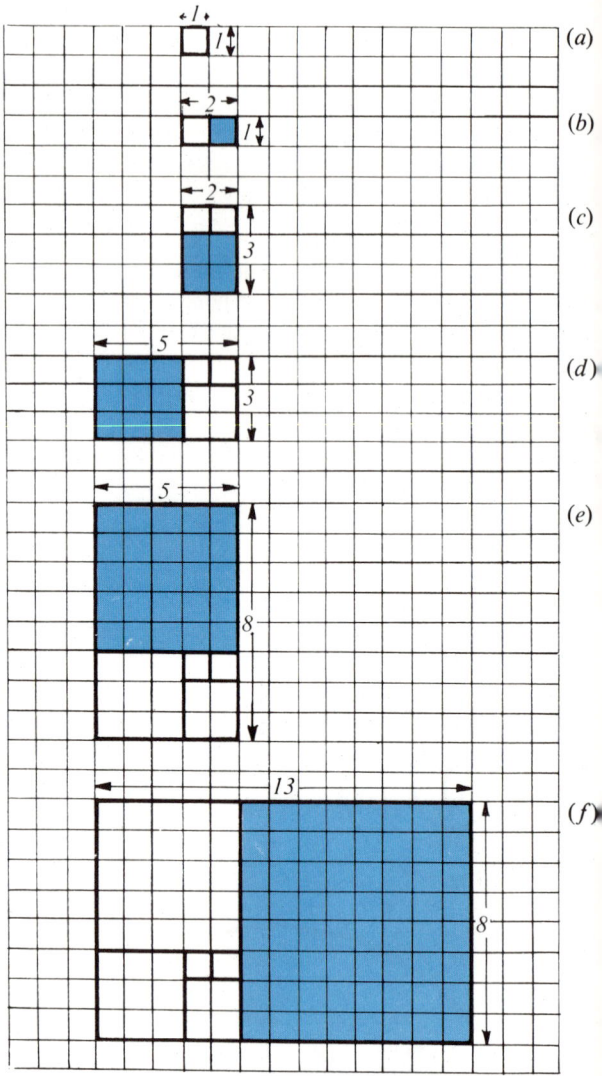

Start with a 1 by 1 square (the terms 1, 1 of the Fibonacci series).

Put another 1 by 1 square on to one side of it, giving a 2 by 1 rectangle (we have now used the terms 1, 1, 2 of the Fibonacci series). Put a square on the longer side, giving a 3 by 2 rectangle (1, 1, 2, 3 have been used).

Continue to add 'whirling squares' to the rectangle. This step gives a 5 by 3 rectangle. At each stage, the length of the new rectangle is equal to the sum of the length and breadth of the last rectangle.

Figure 38:25

and that 144 half-inches is the height of a six-foot man. He founded his Modular scales of proportion in architecture on various Fibonacci sequences, believing that he was relating architectural proportions to the human body.

Figure 38:26

In nature, numbers in the Fibonacci sequence often occur.[8] The Greek interest in the golden section seems, however, to have derived partly from the fact that it occurs in the regular pentagon, and therefore in the regular dodecahedron and icosahedron.

[8] See Land, F. *The Language of Mathematics,* Chapter 13.

The regular pentagon and the golden section

The Greek geometers directed much of their attention to the problem of making constructions with ruler and compasses, a protractor not being used. A regular pentagon is easy to construct if a protractor is allowed; otherwise, a method of construction is not immediately obvious. We now show how the golden section makes another appearance in the regular pentagon, and so makes it possible to construct a regular pentagon without using a protractor.

The isosceles triangles in a regular pentagon.

(a)

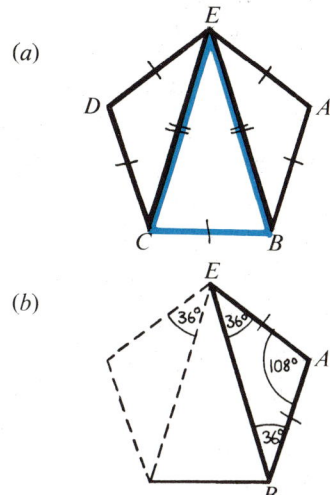

(b)

Each angle of the regular pentagon is 108°.
Hence the other angles of △ ABE are each 36°.

(c)

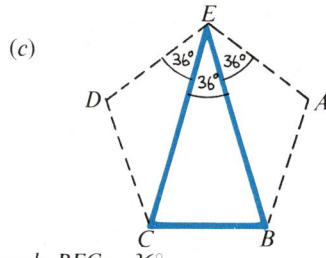

angle $BEC = 36°$
Hence the other angles of △ BCE are each 72°

Figure 38:27

A regular pentagon is made up of three isosceles triangles, one of which is acute-angled, while the other two are congruent and are obtuse-angled. The angles of these isosceles triangles are easily found (Figure 38:27). We have seen earlier that drawing diagonals of a regular pentagon produces a smaller regular pentagon inside it (*see page* 204). As these diagonals are drawn, many further triangles are drawn inside the original pentagon.

More isosceles triangles in the regular pentagon.

(a)

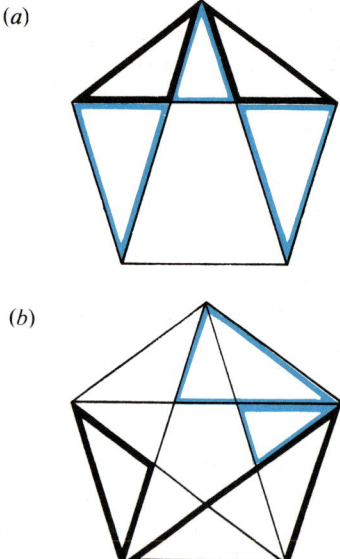

(b)

Figure 38:28

but they are all of one of the two shapes shown in Figure 38:27. Figure 38:28 shows some of these triangles, which are of different sizes, but all of one or other of the two fundamental shapes. This is because the angles of the two triangles are such that a triangle of each shape (of the right sizes) can be put together to make either isosceles triangle, as shown in Figure 38:29.

These larger isosceles triangles each have the further

Golden sections in these isosceles triangles

(a)

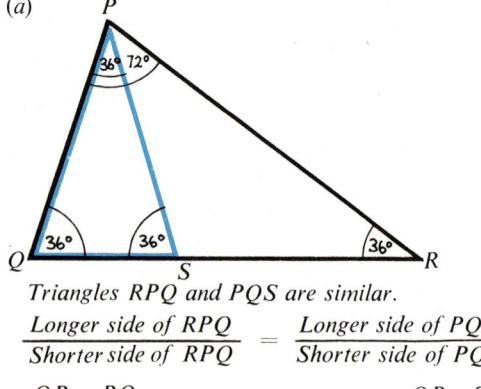

Triangles *RPQ* and *PQS* are similar.

$$\frac{\text{Longer side of } RPQ}{\text{Shorter side of } RPQ} = \frac{\text{Longer side of } PQS}{\text{Shorter side of } PQS}$$

$\frac{QR}{PQ} = \frac{PQ}{QS}$. But $PQ = PS = SR$ and so $\frac{QR}{SR} = \frac{SR}{QS}$

Hence *QR* is divided in golden section.

(b)

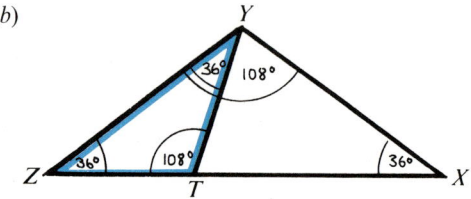

Triangles *YXZ* and *TYZ* are similar, hence, as before

$\frac{XZ}{XT} = \frac{XT}{TZ}$ and *XZ* is divided in golden section.

Figure 38:30

Combinations of isosceles triangles in the regular pentagon

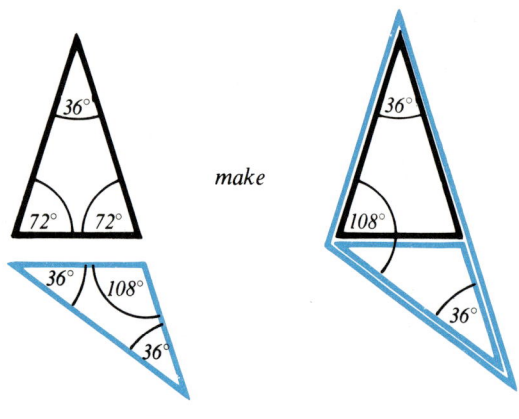

make

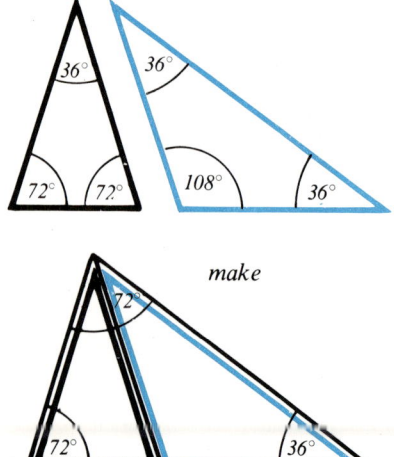

make

Figure 32:29

410

property that a side is divided in golden section. Figure 38:30(*a*) shows this for the acute-angled triangle, and Figure 38:30(*b*) for the obtuse-angled triangle. Hence all the diagonals of the regular pentagon are divided in golden section. In fact, each diagonal contains four golden sections (Figure 38:31).

It is now easy to see how to construct a regular pentagon by using the division of a line in golden section (Figure 38:32).

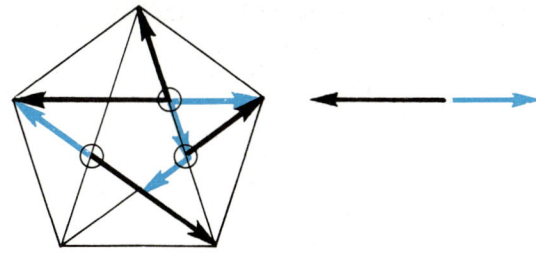

Figure 38:31

Constructing a regular pentagon

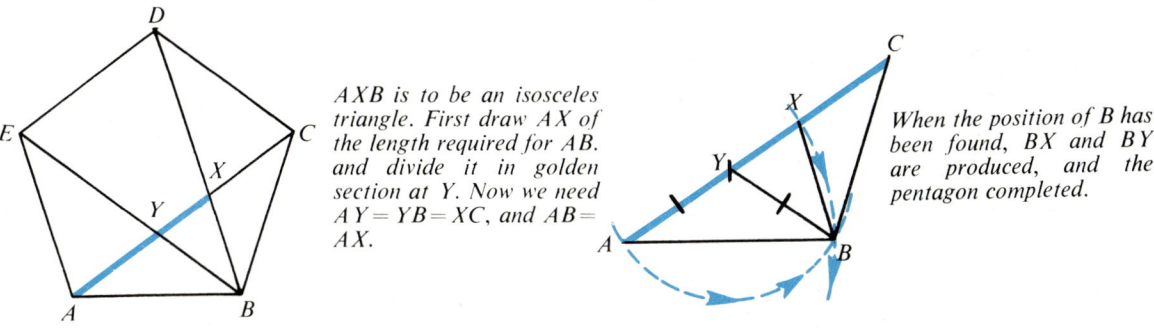

AXB is to be an isosceles triangle. First draw AX of the length required for AB, and divide it in golden section at Y. Now we need AY = YB = XC, and AB = AX.

When the position of B has been found, BX and BY are produced, and the pentagon completed.

Figure 38:32

411

39 More about Shapes and Curves

The range of interesting shapes

In the past the number of three-dimensional shapes studied in the majority of primary schools have been very limited. Models of the *regular* solids have sometimes been made (see Chapter 22), but there has been little investigation of their properties, such as is suggested in Chapter 22. The interest and practical value of some other shapes, such as those related to the circle, including the sphere, cylinder and cone, are undoubtedly great. Equally general has been the neglect of important curves, and many children have left school knowing nothing about any curve except the circle. In this book such curves as the parabola and the hyperbola have already appeared several times, generally as the form of a graph illustrating the relation between two sets of numbers. For instance the parabola was seen to be the graph of the square numbers (*see page* 363) and the hyperbola appeared as the graph obtained by mapping a set of numbers into their inverses (*see page* 306). We now investigate some of the three-dimensional shapes which are interesting not only for their own properties and modes of construction but also because they give rise to curves with many practical uses. Other curves will be studied for their pleasing form, their usefulness, or for the ingenuity of their construction. Pupils can find many of these curves in buildings, in machines, or in decorative designs; others not mentioned here may well be noticed and investigated. As children make or draw these various forms they come to realize that their shape and other mathematical properties depend on the methods used in their construction. In some cases a property can be expressed by pupils themselves in an algebraic formula.

The sphere

The symmetry of a spherical ball is so well known to children that they may take it for granted and not be aware of some of the properties and problems associated with the sphere.

It is possible to produce a good approximation to a sphere by rolling clay or dough round and round but it is *not* possible to make a spherical surface from a sheet of paper. If a disc is rotated very quickly about a diameter, it produces the illusion of a sphere. A plane cuts a sphere in a circle wherever the cut is made. This suggests another method of making an approximation to a spherical surface. We can build up a series of discs on a rod as axis. If a sphere is cut in half in any direction the cut surface has for its boundary the largest circle that can be drawn on a sphere, a 'great circle' (see Chapter 34). The disc of which this great circle is a boundary will be

the largest disc required for our construction. Discs can be arranged symmetrically to indicate the hemispheres. Figure 39:1 shows the arrangement. The problem is where to put a particular disc on the axis. We can mark the ends of the axis (calling them the North pole and the South pole) and fit the equatorial disc midway between them. We now have to fit pairs of equal discs in their correct places, knowing that the rim of a disc must lie on the

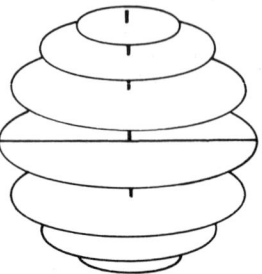

Figure 39:1

surface of the sphere. Children will experiment to find where the position *seems* to be right but they can be encouraged to draw the section through the north and south poles and then attempt to find an accurate way of placing the discs.

If a parallel to the axis is drawn at a distance from it equal to the radius a of the disc it will cut the circle at the two points where the rims of the equal discs must be. The perpendiculars from these points to the axis give the positions of the centres of the discs. The positions of other discs can, of course, be found in the same way. (Figures 39:2 and 39:3.)

Since a spherical surface cannot be opened out to lie flat, the area of the surface cannot easily be found. The method of making a soft ball by sewing together pieces of

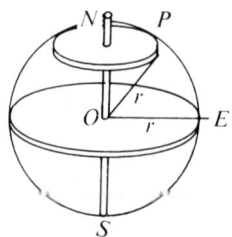

Figure 39:2

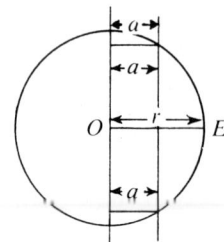

Figure 39:3

material shaped like the outer surface of sections of an orange suggests a way of finding a fair approximation to the surface area. If the sections are thin enough they lie almost flat and can be placed on squared paper so that a count can be made of the squares covered by one section. If this number is multiplied by the number of sections in the whole surface we have a rough figure for the area. It can

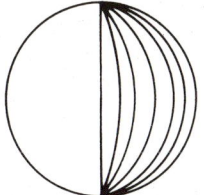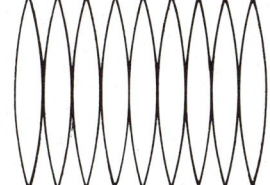

Figure 39:4

be compared with the surface area of a cube into which the sphere would just fit. A ball about 10 cm in diameter is convenient for this experiment. The area is then about 315 square centimetres (Figure 39:4). Children will learn later that the surface of a sphere of radius r has area $4\pi r^2$.

The volume of a sphere can be found by immersion as described in Chapter 24, page 227. If the volumes of a set of spheres can be compared with the volumes of a set of cubes with edges equal to the radii of the spheres a correspondence may be found. A graph will show the ratio of the volume of sphere to cube. Since the formula for the volume of a sphere of radius r is $\frac{4}{3}\pi r^3$ an approximate value for the ratio of the volume of a sphere of radius r to that of the cube whose edge is r units is 4:1. This enables a teacher to judge whether the pupils have made a reasonably good attempt.

The cube with edge equal to the diameter of the sphere has a volume about twice that of the sphere (Figure 39:5).

The cylinder

The simplicity of a cylindrical shape, with its uniform circular cross-section, makes it easy to construct and very serviceable in daily life, both as a container and as a means of conveying fluids and gases. Pupils will probably have met the method of making a hollow cylinder by joining opposite edges of a rectangular sheet of paper. They may also know that steadily rolling a lump of Plasticine or stiff dough will produce a reasonable approximation to a solid cylinder. A sharp knife will cut across this cylinder without deforming it. The shapes of cut surfaces can be studied. Children will expect the section at right angles to the axis to be a circle but many of them will have noticed the form of an oblique section. A slanting cut will have one diameter equal to the diameter of the cylinder; the diameter perpendicular to this will be elongated, as can be seen in Figure 39:6. The cuts can be traced on paper and compared. The elongated shape is an ellipse; we shall consider the properties of this shape more fully later.

A spherical surface contains no straight lines, but a cylinder can have straight lines drawn upon its surface parallel to its axis. This adds greatly to the strength of a cylindrical object. If rods of equal length are fitted into holes equally spaced round the rim of a circular base, as in basketry, a cylindrical framework will be produced. If several ellipses are made by elongating the circular shape of the base they will be found to fit into the framework in the position of oblique cuts of the solid cylinder (as shown in Figures 39:6 and 39:7).

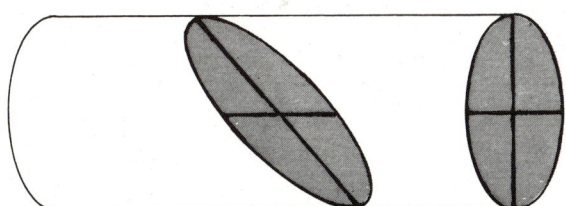

Figure 39:6

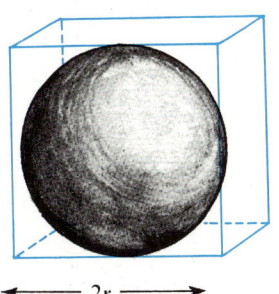

Figure 39:5

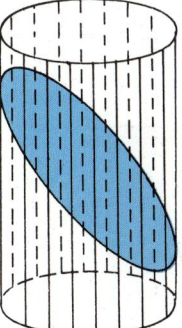

Figure 39:7

Since a hollow cylinder can be made from a rectangular sheet of paper the area of its surface must be equal to that of the rectangle. The circumference of the cylinder was produced by bending the rectangle so that two opposite sides became circles. The other pair of sides were joined to make a straight line lying in the surface and showing its height or altitude (Figure 39:8).

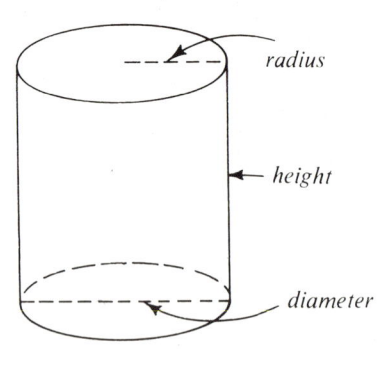

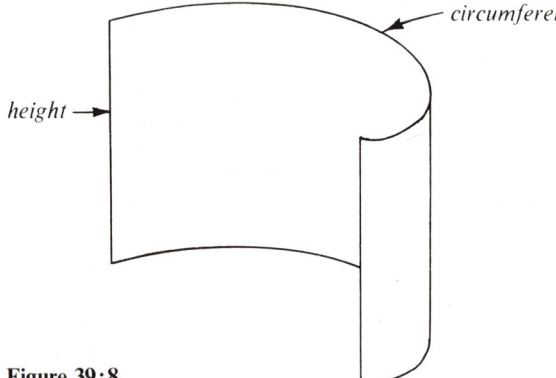

Figure 39:8

The area of the rectangle from which a cylinder is made is found by multiplying the circumference of the cylinder by its height. The method described in Chapter 37, page 392, shows how to measure the diameter of a solid cylinder and then to find its circumference, but the numbers obtained may involve decimals and the multiplication may be beyond the skill of all but a few children.

The circumference of a cylinder can be measured

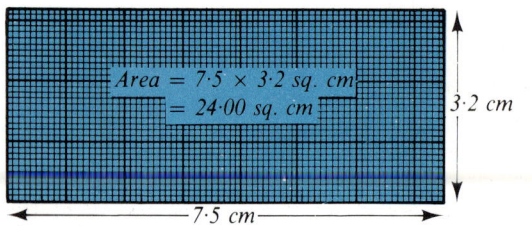

Figure 39:9
414

directly by placing a tape-measure tightly round it. For example, if the circumference is 7·5 cm and the height 3·2 cm, the area of the surface is $7·5 \times 3·2$ square centimetres. Figure 39:9 shows the rectangle drawn on squared paper. The small squares are hundredths of a sq cm; the number of small squares in the rectangle, 2400, can be checked from the diagram. Such experience is invaluable in connection with work on decimals.

The volume of a cylinder may be found practically by the methods given in Chapter 24, page 229. A method of calculating the volume, by multiplying the area of the circular base by the height of the cylinder, may occur to a few pupils but for others it is best left to a later stage.

The ellipse

The ellipse will be familiar to children as a possible shadow cast by a circle, as the shape of a pool of light when a circular beam shines on a sloping plane surface, as the slanting cut across a cylinder, as the orbit followed by some spacecraft as well as by planets, and so on. Yet many children have no explicit knowledge of this curve. It is an interesting as well as important curve and can profitably be studied in primary schools in conjunction with the circle.

The circle, as children know from using compasses, is a set of points which are at the same distance from a given point, the centre. It can be drawn by moving a pencil in a loop of string which passes round a fixed pin. A different curve will be drawn if the loop of string passes round *two* fixed pins. Children can find what kind of path the pencil now follows (Figure 39:10). By moving the position of the fixed pins, putting them closer or farther apart, they can find a variety of different shapes, all with an oval form and two axes of symmetry, one of which is longer than the other. Curves that look like these can be made from

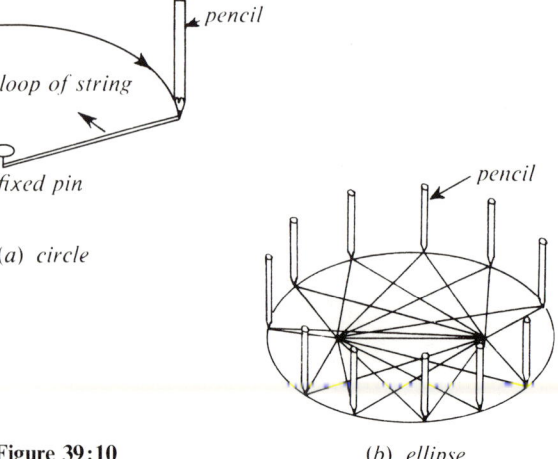

Figure 39:10   (b) *ellipse*

casting a variety of shadows from a disc or by projecting a circle of light on to various plane surfaces (Figure 39:11). Children can investigate these ways of constructing what looks like an ellipse and find out whether in fact they are ellipses or types of oval.

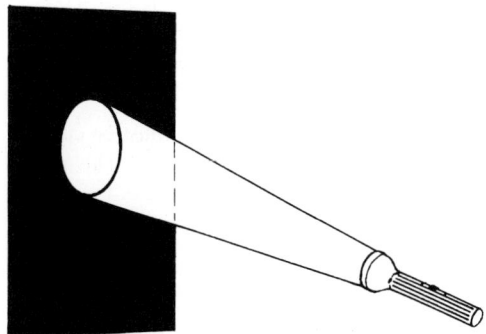

Figure 39:11

The shadow cast by a disc is like the slanting cut of a cylinder which was seen to be an elongation of a circular section. We can construct such an elongation by increasing the distances of points on a circle from one of its diameters in the same ratio, say 3:2 (Figure 39:12). A curve of the same kind is made by reducing the distances, say in the ratio 1:2.

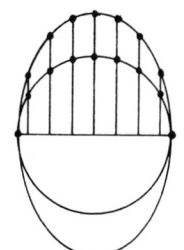

Distances increased to ratio 3:2

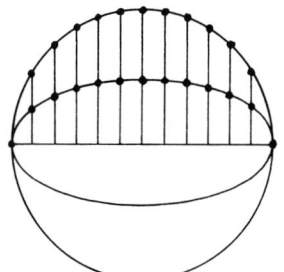

Distances reduced in ratio 1:2
Figure 39:12

This construction shows very clearly the correspondence between an original point on the circle and its image point after the transformation.

Do these curves have the same form as those made by a string and two pins? If we look carefully at a curve made with string and pins, we see that AA' is the same length as the length of string between the pins in which the pencil is placed (Figure 39:13). When the pencil point is at A this becomes clear because the length of string is then $SA + AS'$. The length AS' is equal to $A'S$, so the length of the string is $SA + A'S = AA'$.

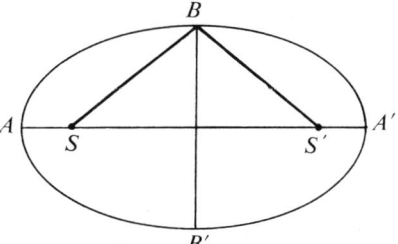

Figure 39:13

If the pencil point is at B or B' the midpoint of the loop is at this point. Thus the length of BS or BS' is half the length of AA'.

Now we can take one of the elongated circles and test whether it can be made by the pins and string method. Draw the diameters AA' and BB'. Take a piece of string equal in length to AA' and fix its midpoint at B. Where the two ends of the string reach AA' are the points S,S'. If pins are placed at S and S' and the ends of the string fixed to them, the pencil will trace out an ellipse. This should fit one of the curves made by cutting a cylinder. Thus we have found experimentally that these curves are ellipses. Figure 39:14 shows the procedure. The ellipse is seen as a

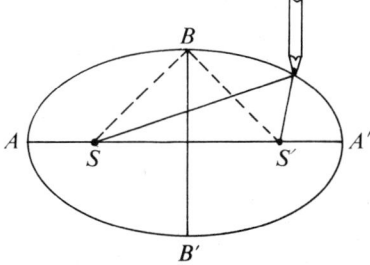

Figure 39:14

set of points which have the common property that the sum of their distances from two fixed points is a constant length.

Some pupils will be interested in collecting information about elliptical orbits and drawing some of them to scale. They can also read something of the history of the discovery of the elliptical orbits of planets.

415

The cone

Funnels and certain containers (like ones which hold ice creams, sweets, etc.) are approximately conical. The shape is easy to make if a rectangular sheet of paper is twisted diagonally and neatly trimmed. This shows that if we cut a hollow cone from the vertex to the base by a straight cut we can lay it out flat. We see the two-dimensional shape from which the surface of a cone could be made (Figure 39:15).

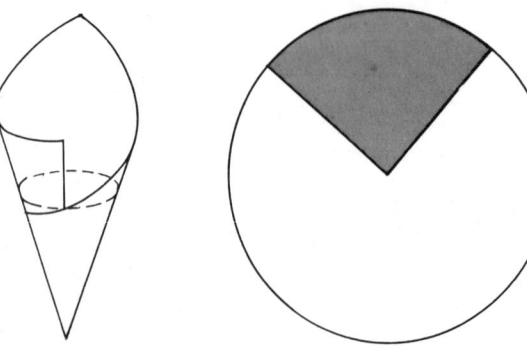

Figure 39:15

This proves to be the sector of a circle, the radius of which is the slant height of the cone. If we have several paper discs of the same size, such as filter papers, we can take various fractions of the circle, such as $\frac{1}{2}$, $\frac{1}{4}$ and $\frac{3}{4}$, and find out what shapes of cone can be made from them. Figure 39:16 shows two examples.

Following such constructional work pupils may try to find the area of the surface of a given conical shape. They know that the surface is part of a circle with radius equal to the slant height of the cone. Suppose this measures 6 cm and a circle, A, with radius 6 cm is drawn. What fraction of the circle would make the cone? The diameter of the base of the cone can be found; suppose it is 8 cm. A circle, B, with radius 4 cm can be drawn to represent the base. Then a part of circle A must be cut out so that its arc equals the circumference of circle B. Figure 39:17 shows the two circles and the required sector of A. The calculation is as follows:

$$\text{The circumference of a circle} = \pi \times (\text{diameter})$$
$$\text{Circumference of } A = 12 \times \pi \text{ cm}$$
$$\text{Circumference of } B = 8 \times \pi \text{ cm}$$

$$\text{Ratio of circumference } B \text{ to circumference } A = 8:12$$
$$= 2:3$$

Thus $\frac{2}{3}$ is the fraction of circle A which must be cut as a sector to make a cone with circle B as base. This means that the area of the surface of the cone is $\frac{2}{3}$ of the area of circle A. Hence, area of curved surface

$$= \tfrac{2}{3} \text{ of } \pi \times 6^2 \text{ cm}^2$$
$$= \tfrac{2}{3} \times 36\pi \text{ cm}^2$$
$$= 24\pi \text{ cm}^2$$

The area is therefore approximately 75 sq cm.

A model of the cone could now be made. A sector which is $\frac{5}{8}$ of a circle has an angle at the centre which is $\frac{5}{8}$ of 360°, i.e. 250°. Such a sector can be cut out and the cone constructed from it.

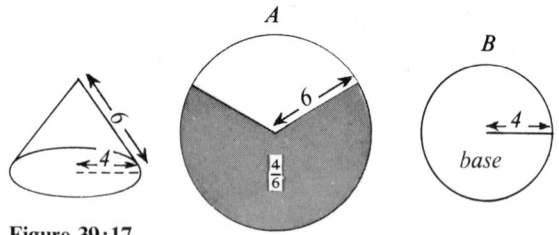

Figure 39:17

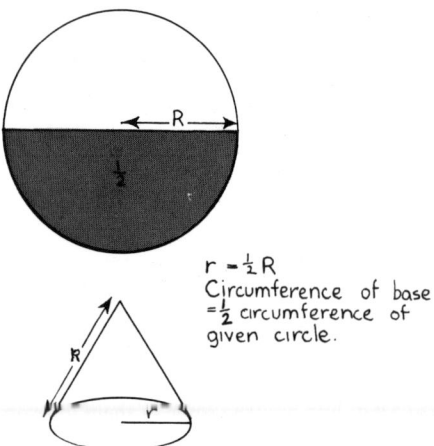

$r = \frac{1}{2}R$
Circumference of base
$= \frac{1}{2}$ circumference of given circle.

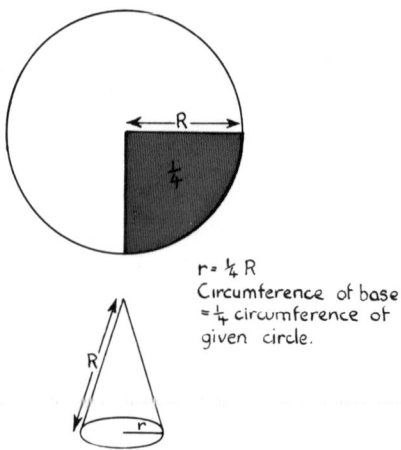

$r = \frac{1}{4}R$
Circumference of base
$= \frac{1}{4}$ circumference of given circle.

Figure 39:16

416

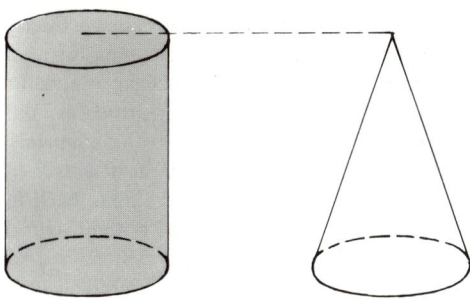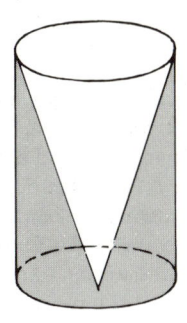

Figure 39:18

Children may meet a cone and a cylinder which have the same base and height. Such a pair occurs in Poleidoblocs. If asked about the relation between the volume of the two solids most children will guess that the cone has half the volume of the cylinder. This can be investigated by immersing the two solids to find their respective volumes. Several cones and cylinders should be examined and it becomes apparent that the volume of the cylinder is three times the volume of the corresponding cone. This can be further checked by comparing the capacity of a hollow cylinder with that of the corresponding cone. It is fairly easy to make such a pair from thin stiff card and then to fill the cylinder from the cone using a fine but light cereal as a filling. It will, of course, take three fillings of the cone to fill the cylinder (Figure 39:18).

Sections of a cone; the hyperbola

In comparison with the sphere and the cylinder the cone can be cut across in an interesting variety of ways which are well worth examining. A fairly true circular cone can be modelled in Plasticine or dough and can be cut to give a good indication of the shapes of the sections. For more accurate investigations it is better to buy a set of sections made of plastic or wood. Initial discovery from children's own models is more memorable than copying or measuring the ready made. If a solid cone is being examined it is a good idea to make a paper cover to fit it so that a

section of a hollow cone can be traced.

The most obvious cut to make is along a plane of symmetry through the vertex. This produces a triangular surface from the solid cone and a pair of intersecting lines from a hollow cone. Circular and elliptical sections of the cone are easy to find (Figure 39:19).

A plane parallel to the plane of symmetry will be perpendicular to the base and will make a cut which has a curved edge. Some children will find it interesting to try to identify this curve. If the cut face is traced on paper it can be placed against the cut made by the parallel plane of symmetry. In Figure 39:20 we show the result in the case of a cone whose vertical angle is a right angle. This curve may remind children of the curve of inverses, which they have drawn earlier. In fact the curve is a hyperbola, like the curve of inverses.

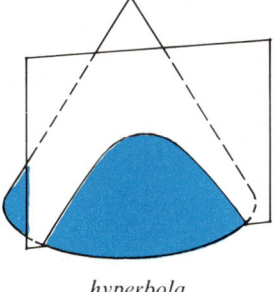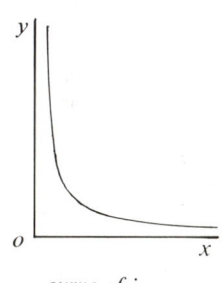

hyperbola   *curve of inverses*

Figure 39:20

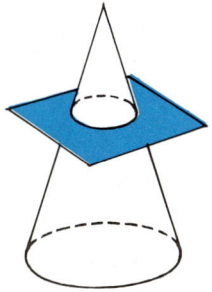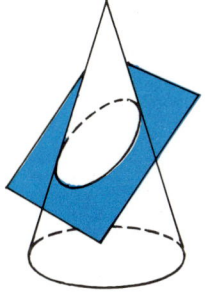

Figure 39:19

The parabola

The other section of a cone which recalls a curve familiar to the pupils is made by a plane parallel to the slant height of the cone. If this is traced on paper and cut out, children will find by folding that it is symmetrical and that its half is similar in shape to the curve of squares. We can test whether it is in fact this curve by the following method. Place the half of the cut-out shape on squared or lined paper as shown in Figure 39:21. Draw in the two axes and graduate the horizontal axis. The tabulation for the curve of squares gives the following number pairs for points on the graph: (1,1), (2,4), (3,9), (4,16), ... Find the point on the curve which corresponds to 1 on the x-axis. If the curve is a curve of squares the value of y for this point will be 1. Take this length as unit on the y-axis and use it to graduate the y-axis. We can now examine the curve to see whether the points (2,4), (3,9), and so on, do in fact lie on it. If so, it is indeed the curve of squares, or the parabola. When the children have verified that this is so they can look again at the set of shapes that are derived from the cone and notice their variety. At the secondary school stage they will study them once more and see that in spite of their differing forms they have common properties which can be expressed algebraically.

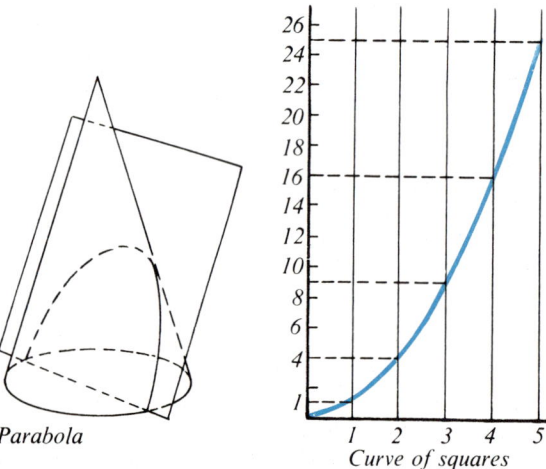

Parabola

Figure 39:21

Curve of squares

Cycloids: rolling wheels

A. A WHEEL WHICH ROLLS ALONG A STRAIGHT LINE
As a wheel rolls along a path its movement at any instant is a rotation about the point of contact with the ground. As the wheel continues to turn and travels along a line on the ground each point on the rim follows its own path which

418

children can trace. A point on the rim can be clearly marked and the wheel then rolled along a line without slipping. If a sheet of paper or card is placed behind the wheel a number of positions of the point can be marked upon the sheet. Pupils usually begin with the point in a special position; for instance, they may start with it in contact with the ground. Clearly when it comes back to its original position it will then repeat the kind of path it has already traced. This may be the children's first experience of a curve which repeats itself (Figure 39:22).

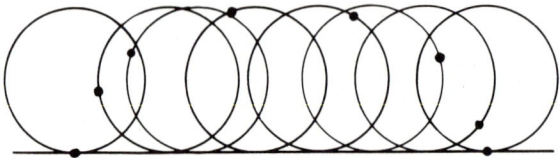

Figure 39:22

A geared wheel on a toothed strip shows the form of the curve very well and enables the pupils to see the position of the point in relation to the distance travelled along the strip because the number of teeth can be counted. Figure 39:23 shows the path of one tooth as the wheel turns.[1]

Figure 39:23

The name of the curve which the point traces out, the *cycloid*, is easily remembered by children because of its association with the bicycle, but when they discuss its shape they may say that it is part of a circle. This statement should be tested. A circle has the property that any part of it can be cut out and fitted exactly over any other part. We therefore cut out one unit of the cycloid and find whether any part of it can be fitted exactly on another part. The parts of a cycloid do not quite fit. Alternatively, the bisectors of two chords could be drawn

[1] Suitable materials for these experiments are provided in the game called Spirograph.

(or folded) as in Figure 39:24. If the curve were a circle the point of intersection of the chords, C would be the centre of the circle. When compasses are used to draw a circle with centre C, through A, it will be found to lie within the arc of the cycloid. Yet the nearness to the shape of a circle is very striking.

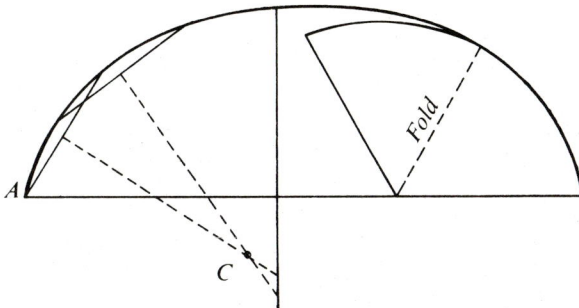

Figure 39:24

B. A WHEEL WHICH ROLLS ON THE OUTSIDE OF A CIRCLE
In playing with equal discs a child may discover that six of them can be packed around one of them, as Figure 39:25 illustrates. The lines joining the centres show why this is so. The pupils may follow this up by asking what happens when a circle is rolled round the outside of an equal circle. To prevent the circles slipping this can be shown by moving a geared wheel round an equal one and marking the path of a particular tooth.

Figure 39:25

Figure 39:26 shows enough points to give the essential shape of curve. A point where the direction of the curve suddenly changes, known as a cusp, is found in all curves drawn in this way. The curves are called *epicycloids*. If a circle with radius one-third of that of a fixed circle is rolled round the outside three cusps are produced, as Figure 39:26 illustrates; its name is the three-cusped epicycloid. A cusp occurs each time the rolling circle completes a revolution. Pupils may find this shape in the stone tracery of a church window. They can make other designs by taking the radius of the rolling circle to be some other fraction of the fixed one. A single-cusped epicycloid is also called a *cardioid* (Figure 39:27).

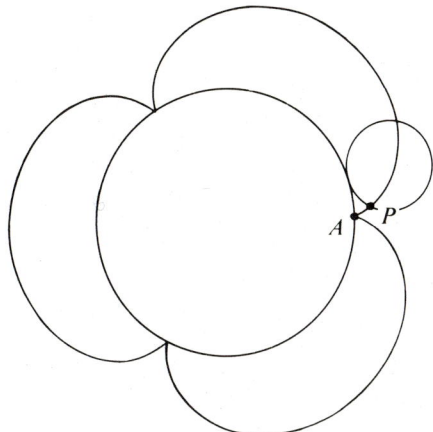

Figure 39:26

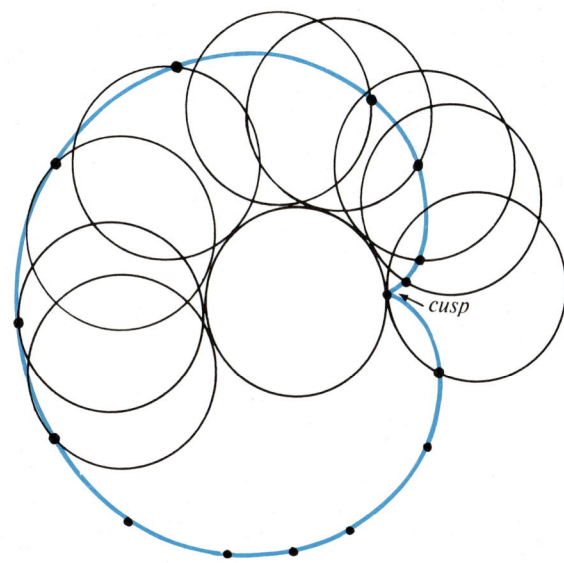

Figure 39:27

C. A WHEEL WHICH ROLLS ON THE INSIDE OF A CIRCLE
After discovering epicycloids children may experiment with the path that would be traced out by a point on the circumference of a wheel on the *inner* side of the rim of another wheel. If the wheel were of the same size it is obvious that the inner wheel would simply rotate about its centre and each point on its rim would be carried with it in a circle. If, however, the inner wheel has a radius which is a fraction of the radius of the outer wheel, say $\frac{1}{2}$, $\frac{1}{3}$, or $\frac{1}{4}$, it would make 2, 3, or 4 rotations before regaining its original position. A point on the rim would thus have 2, 3, or 4 points of contact with the outer wheel. Its path will have 2, 3, or 4 cusps. These curves are known as *hypocycloids*. Figure 39:28 shows the three-cusped hypocycloid formed when the radii of the two wheels are in the ratio

419

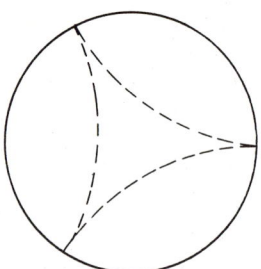

Figure 39:28

1:3. The two-cusped hypocycloid is a segment of a straight line. The hypocycloids have pleasing shapes and are widely used in decorative designs.

Wave curves

A curve of great importance in the world of science is the one which records vibrations. Children often see it on television and in books about scientific phenomena such as sound waves. When a child holds the end of a rope and gives it a rhythmic up and down movement he produces in the rope a rippling movement which shows waves (Figure 39:29).

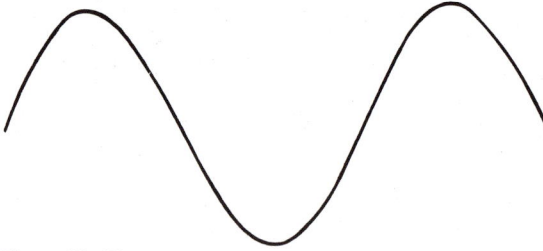

Figure 39:29

To make a drawing of a wave curve we first study the movement of a point on the circumference of a circle which is rotated steadily about its centre. We look at the height of the point above or below a diameter AB, and notice that the height increases very rapidly at first and then more slowly as the point approaches the highest position, C (Figure 39:30). As the point moves beyond C the height

decreases at first slowly and then more rapidly until the point is again on the diameter, this time at B. The pattern of heights is symmetrical about the axis OC.

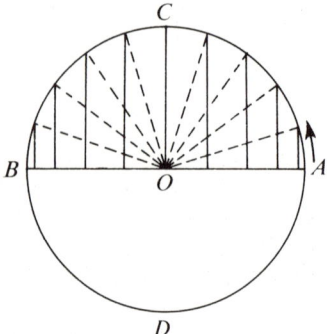

Figure 39:30

When the point moves on below the diameter it will show the same pattern of change in the distances from the diameter but they will all now be in the opposite direction, that is, from the diameter downwards. The lower half of the diagram in Figure 39:31 is the reflection of the upper half. We can make a graph to represent the heights as they change during a complete revolution and we shall expect to find in it evidence of the symmetries which we have just noticed. The x-axis must be graduated to show

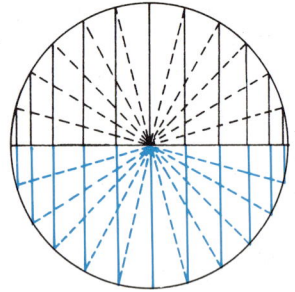

Figure 39:31

the fractions of a revolution through which the radius has turned. It is helpful if this axis is drawn in line with the diameter of the circle as in Figure 39:32. The distances

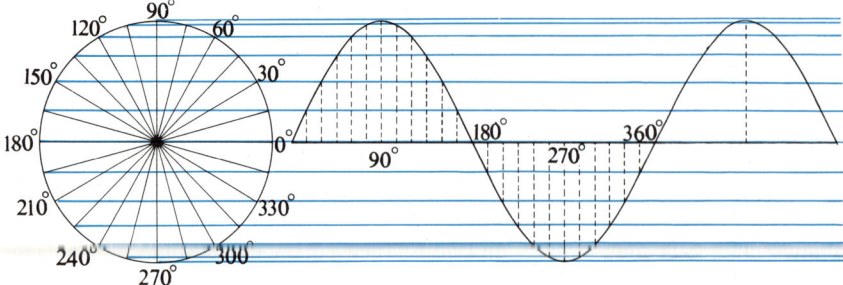

Figure 39:32

420

can then be marked off directly from the circle. Four points on the graph correspond to A, B, C, D, (Figure 39:30). A, the starting point, will give the origin. At B, after a rotation of $90°$, the height is equal to the radius of the circle. At C the height is again zero. At D, the end of the diameter through C, the height is negative and is equal to the radius. For other points on the graph we use compasses to transfer the heights from the circle to the graph.

When the points are joined by the best-fitting curve we find a shape like one part of the wave curve in Figure 39:29. If the rotation round the circle is continued the pattern of the distances will be repeated and the graph show repetitions of the curve already drawn.

Teachers may realize that this graph is the *sine curve*, the sine of the angle between the x-axis and a rotating arm OP being the ratio of the height to the radius. (Figure 39:33.)

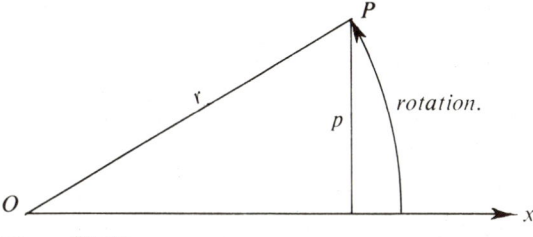

Figure 39:33

It will be noticed that the wave curve is a graph of the relation between the rotation of a point on a circle and the distance of the point from a diameter, whereas the curves that we have previously discussed were the actual paths traced by a point moving under conditions.

Envelopes

The curves that we have considered so far are *sets of points* which satisfy certain conditions. Some have been found as the intersection of a plane with a three-dimensional shape such as the cylinder or cone. Others have been obtained as the path of a point moving in a defined way as in the case of the cycloids. The wave curve appeared as the graph of a relation between distance and rotations. Curves can also be formed when a *set of lines* is constructed so as to satisfy certain conditions. The lines may be ruled in a specified way, or they may be stitched according to certain instructions, or they may consist of a set of folds of a sheet of paper made in a particular way.

A stitched pattern which is now fairly well-known is that obtained by joining points on two intersecting lines (rays from O, say) graduated on the same scale, successive marked points on one ray in a sequence *from O* being joined to successive marked points on the other ray in a sequence *towards O* (Figure 39:34). If the stitches (or ruled

lines) are sufficiently close together they appear to mark out a curve which can be sketched in with some confidence. Such a curve is said to be the *envelope* of the line which satisfies the given conditions. Sometimes an envelope is immediately recognizable by pupils. For

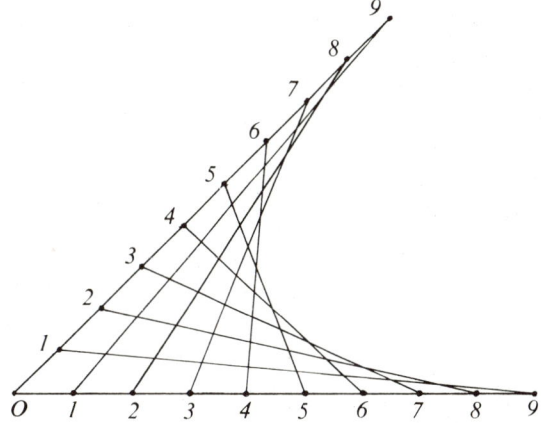

Figure 39:34

example, the lines which join pairs of points the same distance apart on a circle give rise to a circle concentric to the given one. Other envelopes are not readily identified but further investigation may lead to recognition. For instance the stitched curve of Figure 39:34 may be cut out, and folded about its axis of symmetry. It may then suggest the curve of squares; this idea can be checked by the method described on page 418. It should then be evident that the envelope is in fact a parabola.

Another curve which can be identified after a closer examination is obtained from folding a circle. A filter paper, say, can be successively folded so that the circumference or arc of the part folded over passes through a certain point, P, inside the circle. The fold can be marked in pencil or ink to make it easy to see. Undo each fold before making the next one. When a fairly large number of folds has been made the envelope looks

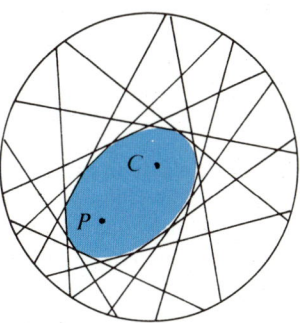

Figure 39:35

like an ellipse and can in fact be shown to be one by the method given on page 415.

An interesting link with tables of multiples is found in the following method of producing a curve as an envelope. Pupils may recognize the shape of the curve if they have already carried out the experiment described on page 419. A circular disc can be graduated to show 36 divisions. This can be done by using either a protractor or a sheet of polar graph paper, marking at intervals of 10° the numbers from 1 to 36. The table of fours gives the number pairs (1,4), (2,8), (3,12), . . . and the two numbers in any pair correspond to two points on the circumference which are joined by a line (Figure 39:36).

The joins are made as follows:

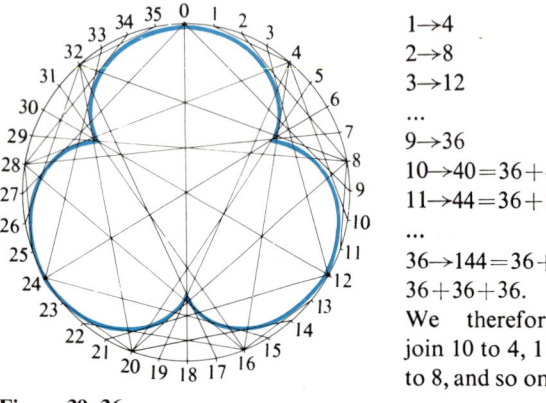

$$1 \rightarrow 4$$
$$2 \rightarrow 8$$
$$3 \rightarrow 12$$
. . .
$$9 \rightarrow 36$$
$$10 \rightarrow 40 = 36 + 4$$
$$11 \rightarrow 44 = 36 + 8$$
. . .
$$36 \rightarrow 144 = 36 + 36 + 36 + 36.$$
We therefore join 10 to 4, 11 to 8, and so on.

Figure 39:36

This construction is a difficult task and the resulting curve is not always easy to see. But three cusps can be distinguished and also three points on the circumference equidistant from two cusps. The curve can then be sketched in and may be recognized as the three-cusped epicycloid. If a circle with diameter 7·5 cm is used, a marked two-penny piece (diameter 2·5 cm) can be rolled round the inside and the form of the curve verified as an epicycloid. By taking other tables of multiples epicycloids with more cusps can be drawn. The table of twos produces the single-cusped heart-shaped cardioid. (Figure 39:26.)

Spirals

There are several kinds of spiral that children meet in daily life. Some of them are curves in a plane like those we have already studied. Others, such as the spring, are in three dimensions. A plane spiral, drawn on a sheet of paper, can be cut along the length of the curve, it will then open into a three-dimensional curve which is sufficiently attractive to be used as a Christmas decoration. The

422

construction of spirals gives children much pleasure and supplies a number of mathematical experiences.

The easiest plane spiral to draw is the one which joins points marked on a rotating arm so that the distance from the centre of rotation increases regularly as the arm rotates (Figure 39:37). Children can draw a set of concentric circles or use polar-graph paper. They next draw the position of the arm after rotations of 10°, 20°, 30°, . . . 360°. If the concentric circles have radii which increase by equal amounts the points on the arm will occur at the intersections with successive circles, as can be seen in the diagram. This is the spiral of Archimedes who, in the third century B.C., published a paper about spirals which is still in existence.[2]

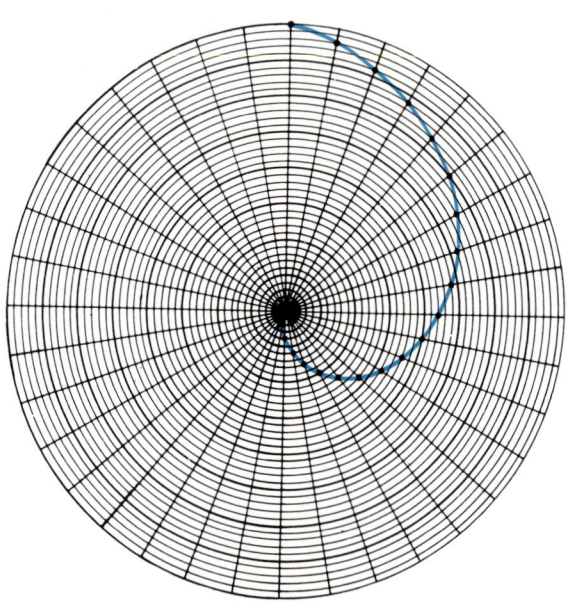

Figure 39:37

The three-dimensional spiral, or helix, which is easiest to construct is drawn on the surface of a cylinder. It is the form we find in the common spring with which pupils are already very familiar from earlier work (see Chapter 28). They will know that the distance between

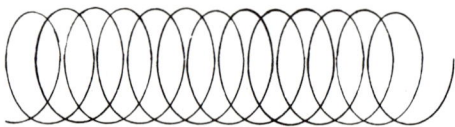

Figure 39:38

[2] If this spiral is reflected about a line through the origin a very attractive shape results.

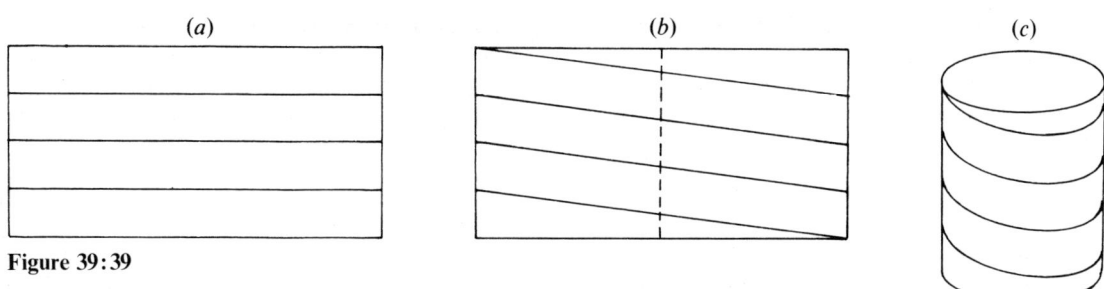

(a)   *(b)*   *(c)*

Figure 39:39

adjacent turns of the helix is constant and will be able to use this fact to invent a way of drawing on a rectangle a pattern which will make a spiral when the rectangle is bent round to form a cylinder (Figure 39:39). It will be seen that lines drawn parallel to a side of a rectangle will make rings if the rectangle is suitably bent to form a cylinder. This may suggest to the pupils the drawing shown in Figure 39:39(*b*). If the diameter and pitch of a given spring are measured it is possible to construct the rectangle which would enclose the spring, to draw the slant lines upon it which represent the turns of the helix and thus to find its length.

Some helices are obviously not cylindrical because their diameter is not constant. This can be seen in many types of screw. Pupils can examine such helices and try to find ways of making them. They should be able to discover that helices can be drawn on the surface of a cone, and perhaps invent methods for drawing them.

40 Some Mathematical Structures

More advanced classification

By the middle years of schooling, many children will be able to take their earlier work in classifying things into sets to a more advanced stage. Further work on classification can unite and fit into a structure many facts which children have known earlier. It can also lead towards the discovery of some very general mathematical ideas which will be studied in more detail at the secondary school stage.

We start our further work on classification by looking systematically at the properties of some shapes which will already be well-known to children. Earlier, children will have collected shapes and sorted them into sets using various methods of classification, and will have recorded the results in diagram form. Some of these classifications will have been combined, as in the classification of the set of Poleidoblocs shown in Figure 40:1.

By now, however, children will be able to invent shapes to classify, and for instance they will cut out as many paper triangles of different shapes and sizes as possible before starting to classify them. Several different classifications are then possible, and these can easily be

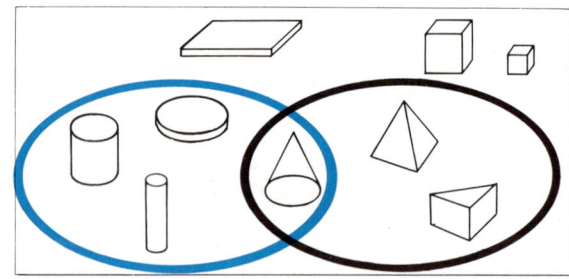

Figure 40:1

combined. Some possibilities are:

   i) triangles with 0, 1, 2, 3 axes of symmetry,
  ii) acute-angled, right-angled, obtuse-angled triangles,
 iii) triangles with three, two or no equal sides.

Diagrams for some of these classifications are shown in Figure 40:2. They may lead children to formulate, and

Some classifications of triangles

     (a) Classification by number of axes of symmetry

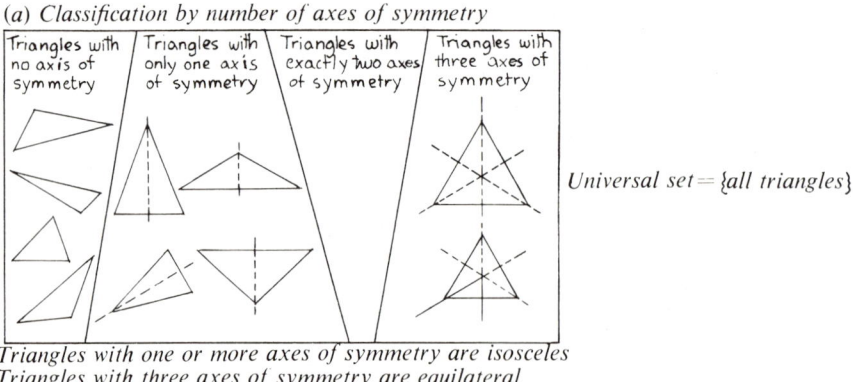

Universal set = {all triangles}

Triangles with one or more axes of symmetry are isosceles
Triangles with three axes of symmetry are equilateral

     (b) Classification by number of axes of symmetry and by type of angle

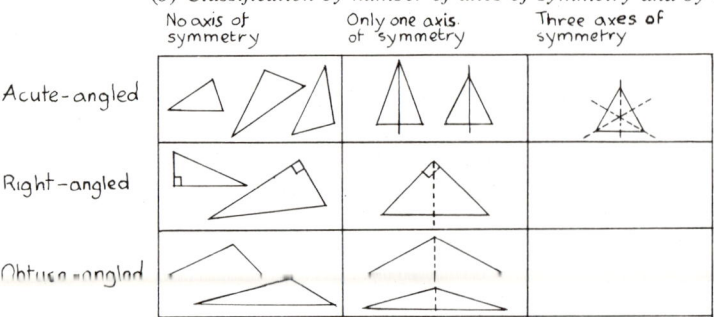

Figure 40:2
424

to answer, such questions as, 'Why can't you have a triangle with exactly two axes of symmetry?' and, 'Is an equilateral triangle isosceles?' By asking and answering such questions, some children will begin to realize the need for carefully defining the words they are using, and they will also begin to reason about properties of the shapes they are using. The distinction between 'at least one axis of symmetry' and 'exactly one axis of symmetry' becomes very clear. The word 'isosceles' is normally used of triangles with at least one axis of symmetry, so that Figure 40:3 shows that the class of equilateral triangles is included within the class of isosceles triangles.

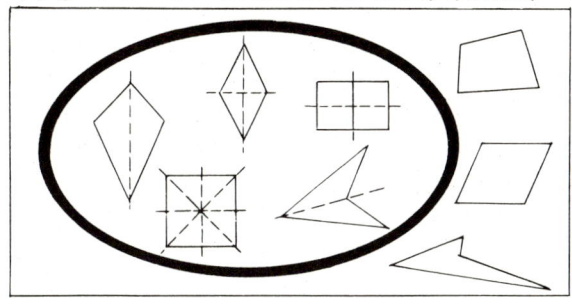

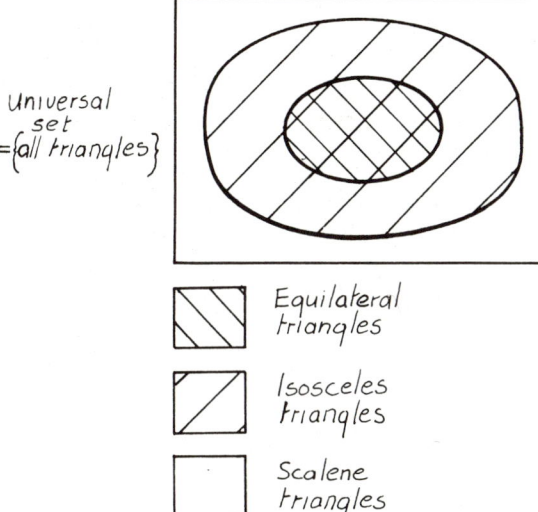

Universal set =(all triangles)

◰ Equilateral triangles

◪ Isosceles triangles

▢ Scalene triangles

Figure 40:3

(*b*) *Quadrilaterals with a centre of symmetry*

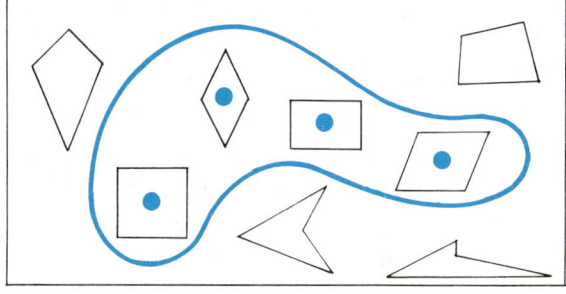

(*c*) *Combination of* (*a*) *and* (*b*)

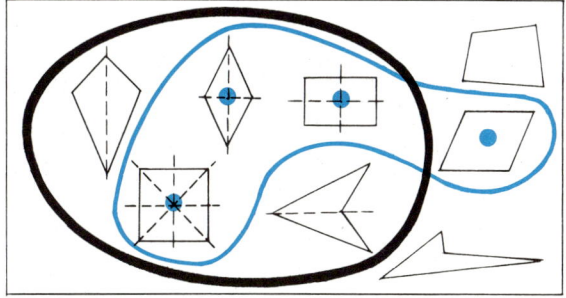

Figure 40:4

Children will also classify quadrilaterals by symmetry, making use of the fact that a quadrilateral may have a centre of symmetry as well as one or two axes of symmetry. Figure 40:4 shows stages in one such possible classification.

Some children will now formulate, as a result of this classification, the statement, 'if a quadrilateral has a centre of symmetry and an axis of symmetry, it must have at least two axes of symmetry.' A few children may go on to convince themselves by argument that the statement must be true.

In this work, we notice a considerable progression in abstraction. At the stage of concrete operations, a child could handle the classification of a set of objects which he had in front of him. Now he is beginning to be able to imagine the class of *all* possible quadrilaterals, and to make classifications and definitions of subsets of this complete class of quadrilaterals. At this stage the models or drawings which the child makes are only specimens representing a selection of all possible quadrilaterals. He is reaching towards the adolescent and adult method of

logical thinking, the stage of *formal operations*. Here abstraction becomes much easier, for as Piaget says, '*possibility* no longer appears merely as an extension of an empirical situation or of actions actually performed. Instead, it is reality that is now secondary to *possibility*.'[1] It appears possible to the child when he is assembling his information that there may be a quadrilateral with a centre of symmetry but only one axis of symmetry. In reality this cannot happen, but the child is now able to explore all the possibilities which may appear in the abstract class of all quadrilaterals.

[1] Inhelder, B. and Piaget, J. *The Growth of Logical Thinking from Childhood to Adolescence* (Basic Books, 1958) page 251.

A child might also start from such questions as, 'Is a square a rectangle?' to investigate the relationships between all the types of quadrilaterals he knows. Kites, parallelograms and rectangles are helpful subsets of the set of all quadrilaterals with which to start a classification. Such working definitions as the following may be evolved:

i) a *kite* is a quadrilateral with at least one axis of symmetry;

ii) a *parallelogram* is a quadrilateral with a centre of symmetry;

iii) a *rectangle* is a quadrilateral both of whose medians[2] are axes of symmetry.[3]

Figure 40:5 illustrates these definitions, together with a Venn diagram of the classification. It will be noticed that a kite which is also a parallelogram is a rhombus, and a kite which is a rectangle is a square.

Definition and classification of quadrilaterals

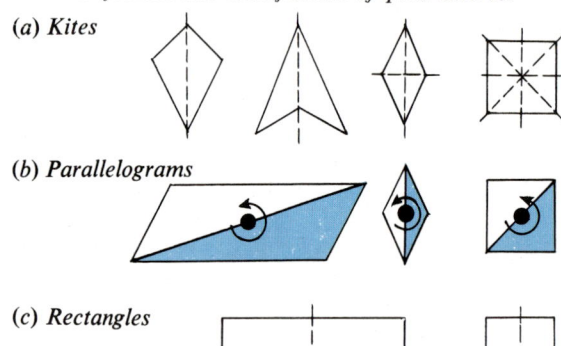

(a) *Kites*

(b) *Parallelograms*

(c) *Rectangles*

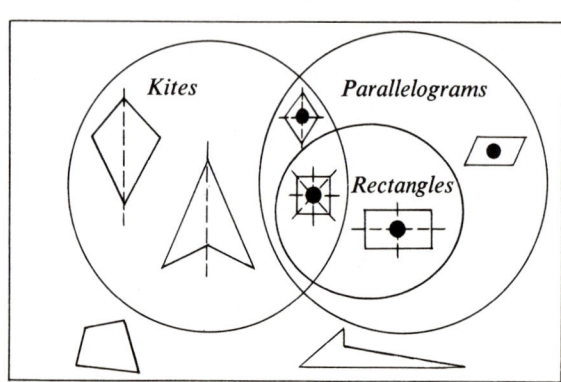

(d) *Universal set* = {quadrilaterals}

Figure 40:5

[2] A *median* of a quadrilateral is a line joining midpoints of opposite sides

[3] Other definitions are possible; for instance, a rectangle is a parallelogram one of whose medians is an axis of symmetry.

426

The Cartesian product of two sets

The systematic exploration of a situation where two properties are dealt with can be greatly helped by the idea of the *Cartesian product* of two sets. If a girl has three jumpers and two skirts, she can combine these in six possible ways, as shown in Figure 40:6. Children will often experiment haphazardly before they discover a

Six outfits from three jumpers and two skirts

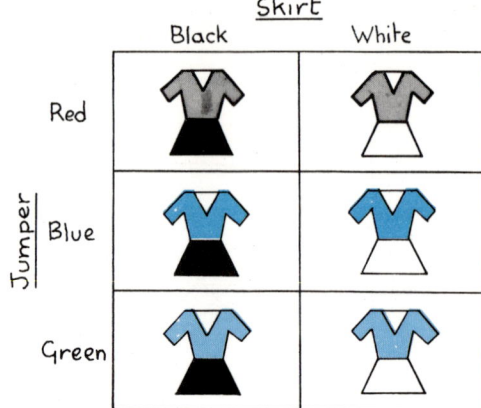

Figure 40:6

systematic way of producing all possible combinations by holding one member of the pair constant while all possibilities are explored for the other member. The possible outfits can be written:

(red jumper, black skirt),
(blue jumper, black skirt), etc.

We shall say that the Cartesian product of the two sets

J = {red jumper, blue jumper, green jumper}

and

S = {black skirt, white skirt}

is the set of the six possible outfits, or ordered pairs of jumper and skirt;

C = {(red jumper, black skirt), (red jumper, white skirt),
(blue jumper, black skirt), (blue jumper, white skirt),
(green jumper, black skirt), (green jumper, white skirt)}

That is, it is the set of the six possible *ordered pairs* whose first member belongs to the first set, and whose second member belongs to the second set. We write this as $C = J \times S$.[4]

[4] This is read 'J cross S'.

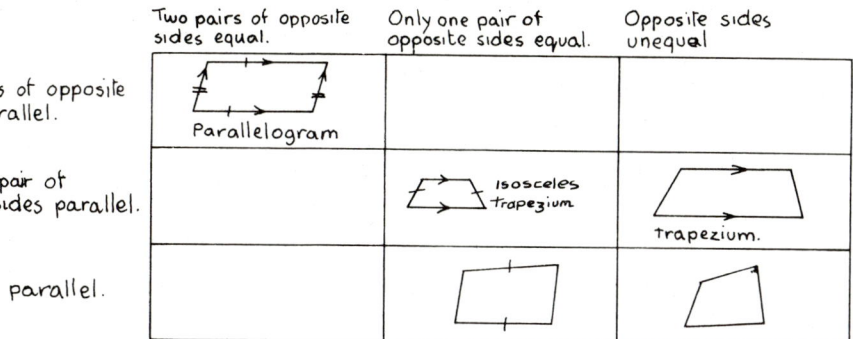

Figure 40:7

The process of forming all possible ordered pairs whose first member is chosen from one set and the second member from another set is common in mathematics and in other situations. The 52 playing cards in a pack, which can be described by such symbols as ♣ 2 (2 of Clubs), are formed from the Cartesian product of the set of suits

$$S = \{ ♠ \quad ♣ \quad ♦ \quad ♥ \}$$

and the set of values

$$N = \{A, 2, 3, 4, 5, 6, 7, 8, 9, 10, J, Q, K\}.$$

That is,

$S \times N$
$$= \{(♠ \ A), (♠ \ 2), (♠ \ 3)... (♠ \ Q), (♠ \ K),$$
$$(♣ \ A), (♣ \ 2), (♣ \ 3)... (♣ \ Q), (♣ \ K),$$
$$(♦ \ A), (♦ \ 2), (♦ \ 3)... (♦ \ Q), (♦ \ K),$$
$$(♥ \ A), (♥ \ 2), (♥ \ 3)... (♥ \ Q), (♥ \ K)\};$$

so we see that $S \times N$ contains 4×13, or 52 members.

A more complicated situation appears in the results of football matches, where each match has one of the three possible results belonging to the set $M = \{1, 2, X\}$. Two matches must have one of 9 possible pairs of results shown by the Cartesian product of M with itself:

$$M \times M = \{(1,1), (1,2), (1,X),$$
$$(2,1), (2,2), (2,X),$$
$$(X,1), (X,2), (X,X)\}.$$

Similarly, three matches must have one of the 27 sets of results symbolized by the Cartesian product

$$M \times M \times M = \{(1,1,1), (1,1,2), (1,1,X),$$
$$(1,2,1), (1,2,2), (1,2,X),$$
$$(1,X,1), (1,X,2), (1,X,X),$$
$$(2,1,1), (2,1,2), (2,1,X),$$
$$(2,2,1), (2,2,2), (2,2,X),$$
$$(2,X,1), (2,X,2), (2,X,X),$$
$$(X,1,1), (X,1,2), (X,1,X),$$
$$(X,2,1), (X,2,2), (X,2,X),$$
$$(X,X,1), (X,X,2), (X,X,X)\},$$

and so on. This systematic exploration of all possibilities, on which probability depends, is simplified by the notion of the Cartesian product. In general, the Cartesian product $A \times P$ of two sets $A = \{a, b, \ldots\}$ and $P = \{p, q, r, \ldots\}$ is defined to be the set of all possible ordered pairs whose first member belongs to A, and whose second member belongs to P.

$$A \times P = \{(a,p), (a,q), (a,r), \ldots$$
$$(b,p), (b,q), (b,r), \ldots\}$$

Another example which children can explore is the set of meals containing a main course and a sweet which they can make up from a given menu. They may also fill in a table such as that in Figure 40:7, where not all the possibilities which the idea of Cartesian product suggests can actually happen. When the classification is examined, it seems that the properties 'two pairs of opposite sides parallel' and 'two pairs of opposite sides equal' are equivalent, as one property cannot happen without the other.

The idea of the Cartesian product of two sets is also seen at work in the labelling of the points of a graph by their co-ordinates. We have seen that the points of a line can be labelled by one co-ordinate which is a real number (Figure 40:8(a)). To label a point in a plane, we set up a pair of

Labelling a point by coordinates

(a) Any point on a line needs one real number to label it

(b) Any point in a plane needs an ordered pair of real numbers to label it

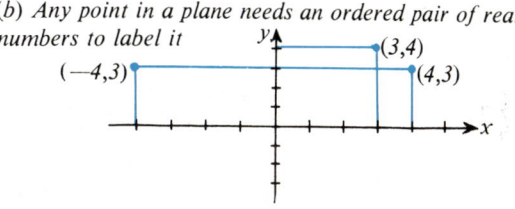

Figure 40:8

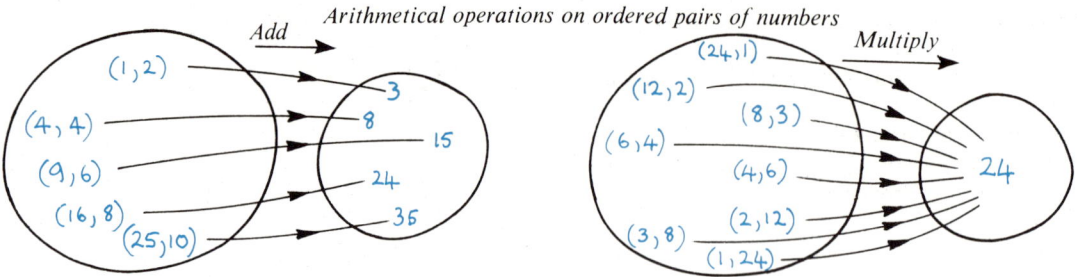

Figure 40:9

axes and describe the point by its distances from each of the axes, using the convention that the *x*-distance is always named before the *y*-distance (Figure 40:8(*b*)). That is, we need an *ordered* pair of real numbers as a label. The point (4,3) is not the same as the point (3,4). All possible points in the plane could be labelled by using all possible ordered pairs of real numbers, and so the labelling of points in the plane is produced by the Cartesian product of the set *R* of real numbers with itself. That is, the set of labels is the set *R* × *R*.

Ordered pairs of real numbers are not only used in labelling a plane. When we perform the arithmetical operation of addition or subtraction, we have selected an

ordered pair of numbers to combine by the operation. The symbols 6+8 tell us to perform the operation of addition on the ordered pair of numbers (6,8), and the symbols 5−3 ask for the operation of subtraction to be performed on the ordered pair (5,3). Since addition is commutative, it gives the same result to perform the operation of addition on the ordered pairs (6,8) and (8,6). The results of the operation of subtraction on (5,3) and on (3,5) are, however, different. It is therefore necessary to keep in mind the distinction of order between (*a*,*b*) and (*b*,*a*). Children may record their results using this idea, as in Figure 40:9, or they may use points on graph paper to represent ordered pairs of numbers, as in Figure 40:10.

Graphs of arithmetical operations

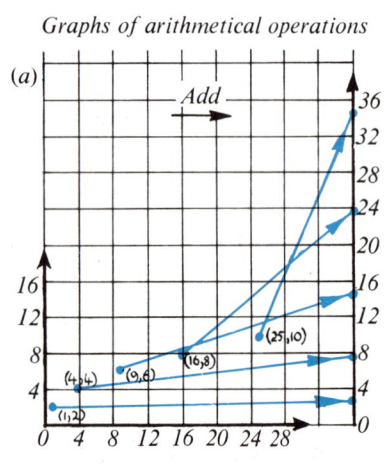

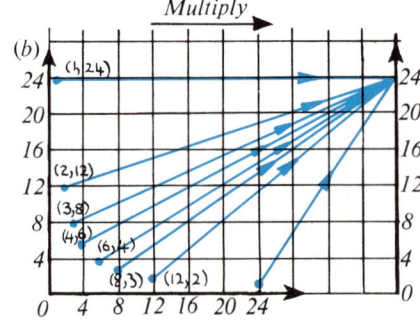

(*c*) *The set of ordered pairs of natural numbers* (*x*, *y*) *such that* $x+y=7$.

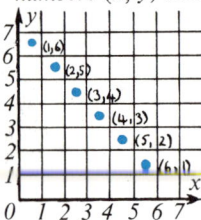

(*d*) *The set of ordered pairs of real numbers* (*x*,*y*) *such that* $x+y=7$.

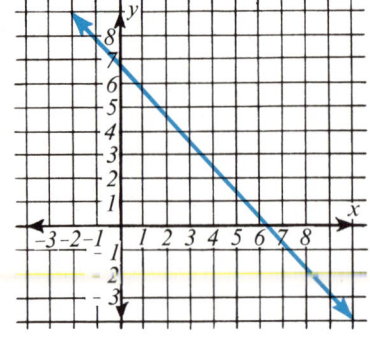

Figure 40:10

428

Relations

Figures 40:10(c) and (d) illustrate subsets of the plane $R \times R$. In this example we are particularly interested in the ordered pairs marked in the graph because the members, x and y, of each pair have the property that their sum is 7. Any subset of a Cartesian product is called a *relation*. That is, a relation is a set of ordered pairs, whose first members are drawn from a set X, and second members from a set Y. The two members of each ordered pair are related together by the fact of our interest in them, and we are not interested in other ordered pairs which also belong to the Cartesian product $X \times Y$. Usually a relation is not a random collection of ordered pairs; we are interested in these particular ordered pairs because their members are related in some significant way. For instance, having earlier made the complete set of outfits consisting of a jumper and skirt, a girl may then pick out a subset of outfits in which the jumper goes well with the skirt. This might be:

(red jumper, black skirt)

and

(green jumper, white skirt)

The relation could also be described in words as 'goes well with', and illustrated in the relation diagram of Figure 40:11.

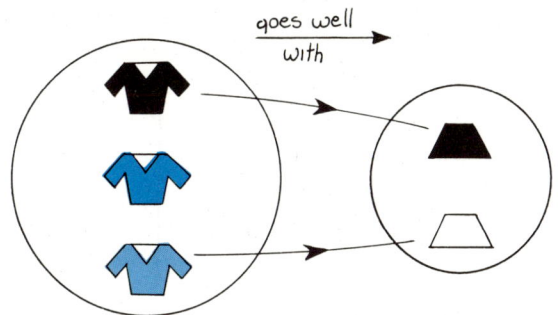

Figure 40:11

In other words, to form the Cartesian product of two sets X and Y, we make all possible ordered pairings of a member x of set X with a member y of set Y. A relation from the set X to the set Y is a sub-collection of these ordered pairs; the relation can also be thought of as the rule which enables us to pick out a subset of the ordered pairs. Figure 40:12(a) shows the Cartesian product of the two sets

$$X = \{1, 2, 3, \ldots 9, 10\}$$
and
$$Y = \{20, 21, 22, \ldots 29, 30\}$$

and Figure 40:12(b) shows a subset of this Cartesian product, which is a relation from set X to set Y.

This relation could be described in words as '*is a factor*

(a) *The Cartesian product* $X \times Y$

	20	21	22	23	24	25	26	27	28	29	30
1	(1,20)	(1,21)	(1,22)	(1,23)	(1,24)	(1,25)	(1,26)	(1,27)	(1,28)	(1,29)	(1,30)
2	(2,20)	(2,21)	(2,22)	(2,23)	(2,24)	(2,25)	(2,26)	(2,27)	(2,28)	(2,29)	(2,30)
3	(3,20)	(3,21)	(3,22)	(3,23)	(3,24)	(3,25)	(3,26)	(3,27)	(3,28)	(3,29)	(3,30)
4											
5			etc.								
6											
7											
8											
9											
10											

With Y across the top and X down the side.

(b) *A relation from* X *to* Y

	20	21	22	23	24	25	26	27	28	29	30
1	(1,20)	(1,21)	(1,22)	(1,23)	(1,24)	(1,25)	(1,26)	(1,27)	(1,28)	(1,29)	(1,30)
2	(2,20)		(2,22)		(2,24)		(2,26)		(2,28)		(2,30)
3		(3,21)			(3,24)			(3,27)			(3,30)
4	(4,20)				(4,24)				(4,28)		
5	(5,20)					(5,25)					(5,30)
6					(6,24)						(6,30)
7		(7,21)							(7,28)		
8					(8,24)						
9								(9,27)			
10	(10,20)										(10,30)

With Y across the top and X down the side.

Figure 40:12

The relation 'is a factor of

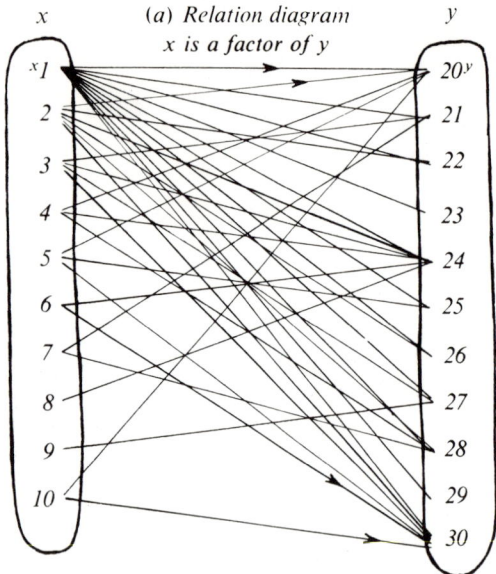

(a) Relation diagram
x is a factor of y

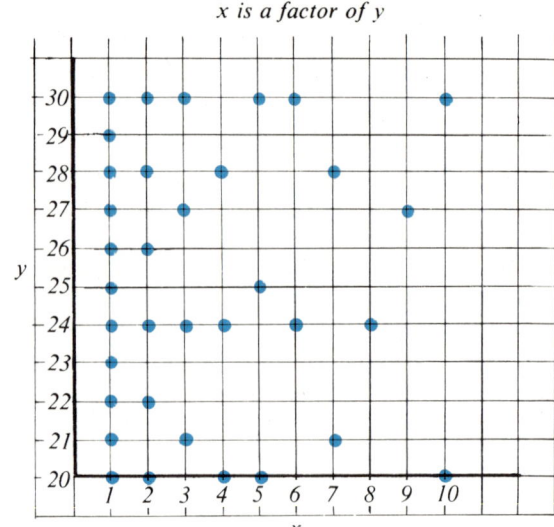

(b) Graph of the relation
x is a factor of y

Figure 40:13

of'. The pair (x,y) belongs to the relation if x is a factor of y. Some other ways of illustrating this relation are given in Figure 40:13.

The sets X and Y which are connected by a relation need not be sets of numbers. Figure 40:14 shows the relation 'has his birthday in the month' from a set of children to the set of months in the year.

Every relation is from some *starting set X* to some *finishing set Y*. These two sets may in fact be the same set, as in Figure 40:15, where their relation 'was the father of'

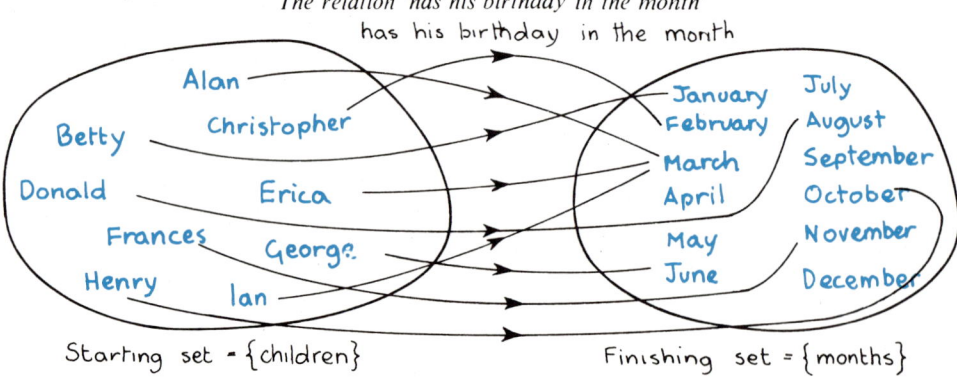

The relation 'has his birthday in the month'

Figure 40:14

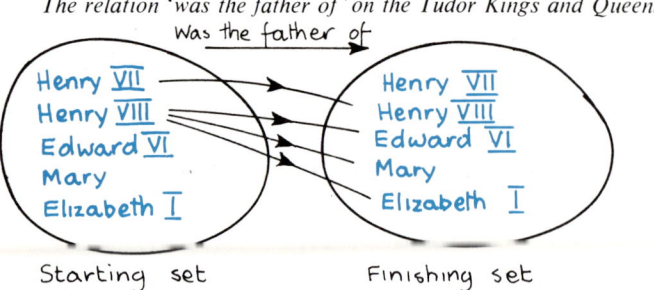

The relation 'was the father of' on the Tudor Kings and Queens

Figure 40:15

430

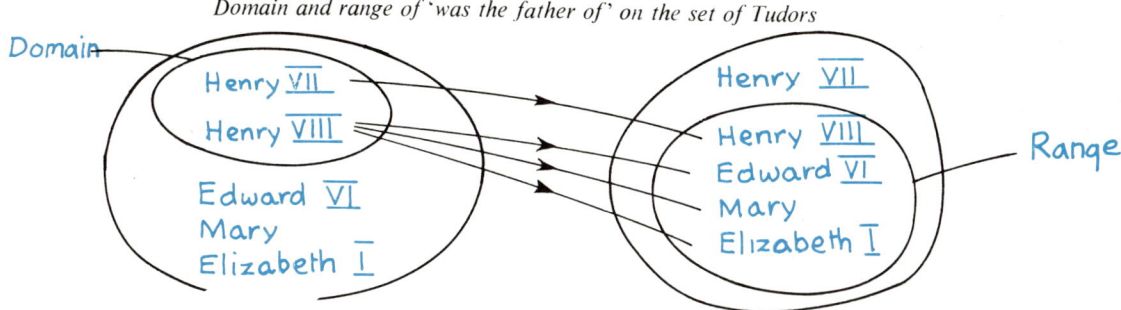

Domain and range of 'was the father of' on the set of Tudors

Domain

Henry VII
Henry VIII
Edward VI
Mary
Elizabeth I

Henry VII
Henry VIII
Edward VI
Mary
Elizabeth I

Range

Figure 40:16

has the set of Tudor kings and queens as both its starting and finishing set. The starting set may, however, have some members, such as Mary among the Tudors, which are not first members of pairs; the finishing set may likewise have members, such as Henry VII, which are not second members of pairs. The set of *actual* first members of the ordered pairs of the relation is called the *domain* of the relation, and the set of actual second members is the *range* of the relation (Figure 40:16).

From Figure 40:17 we see that altering the domain of a relation can make a considerable difference to its appearance. The actual domain of a relation is usually more important than a starting set, some of whose members

may play no part in the relation.

If the starting set and the finishing set of a relation are the same, it may be possible to draw a diagram of the relation without drawing the same set twice. Figure 40:18 shows two such diagrams.

(a) The relation 'was the father of' on the Tudors

Henry VII
Henry VIII
Edward VI
Mary
Elizabeth I

(b) The relation 'is older than' on a set of children

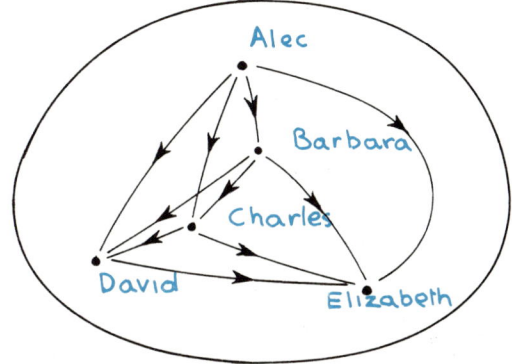

Alec
Barbara
Charles
David
Elizabeth

Figure 40:18

The relation 'the square of x is y'

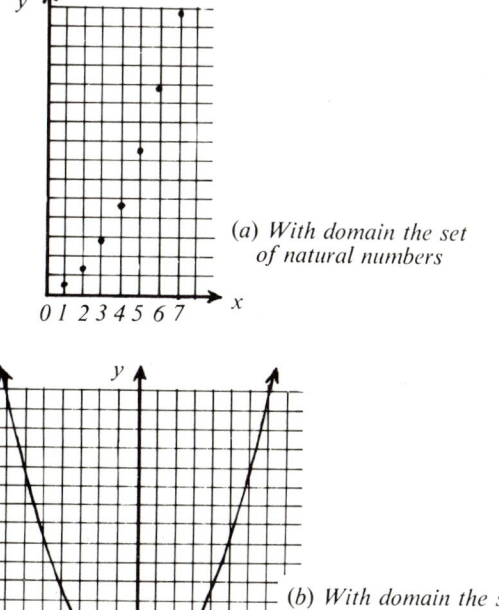

(a) With domain the set of natural numbers

(b) With domain the set of real numbers

Figure 40:17

The importance of the idea of a relation

As we look over the topics which have been discussed earlier in this book, it will be seen that the idea of a relation provides a common structure underlying many of the topics.

431

In the early development from sets to number, the relation of *one-to-one correspondence* between two sets is fundamental to the development of cardinal number (*see pages* 38–39 (Figure 40:19(*a*)). Ordinal number grows from the operation of putting the members of a set into an order (*see pages* 67–69). Order is a relation from the set to itself. If four children stand in a line in the order Alan, Betty, Carol, Donald, then Alan comes before Betty, Carol and Donald, Betty comes before Carol and Donald, and Carol comes before Donald. Donald does not come before anybody (Figure 40:19(*b*)). That is, ordinal number depends on the relation 'comes before', or its inverse, 'follows'.

Ordering of objects according to their length or their mass depends on the relations 'is longer than' or 'is heavier than'.

When the operations of addition, subtraction, multiplication and division are performed on pairs of numbers, these operations can also be thought of as relations. The starting set of the relation of subtraction is the set of ordered pairs of numbers, and the finishing set is the set of numbers (Figure 40:19(*c*)). When children take a traffic census, they set up a relation from the set of types of vehicle to the set of natural numbers (Figure 40:19(*d*)). *One-to-many* relations like the ones in Figure 40:19(*e*) lead to multiplication, and in reverse, many-to-one relations produce division.

Children will compare these numerical relations to such non-numerical relations as 'is the sister of', 'lives in the same road as', 'is the teacher of', or the relation of a letter to the distance it has travelled or the place it came from Figure 40:19(*f*).

The examples of relations which we have so far taken have not been drawn from the spatial side of mathematics. Two particular types of relation, however, underlie most of the children's geometrical work, as well as emerging again and again throughout mathematics. These are *functions* or *mappings* and *equivalence relations*.

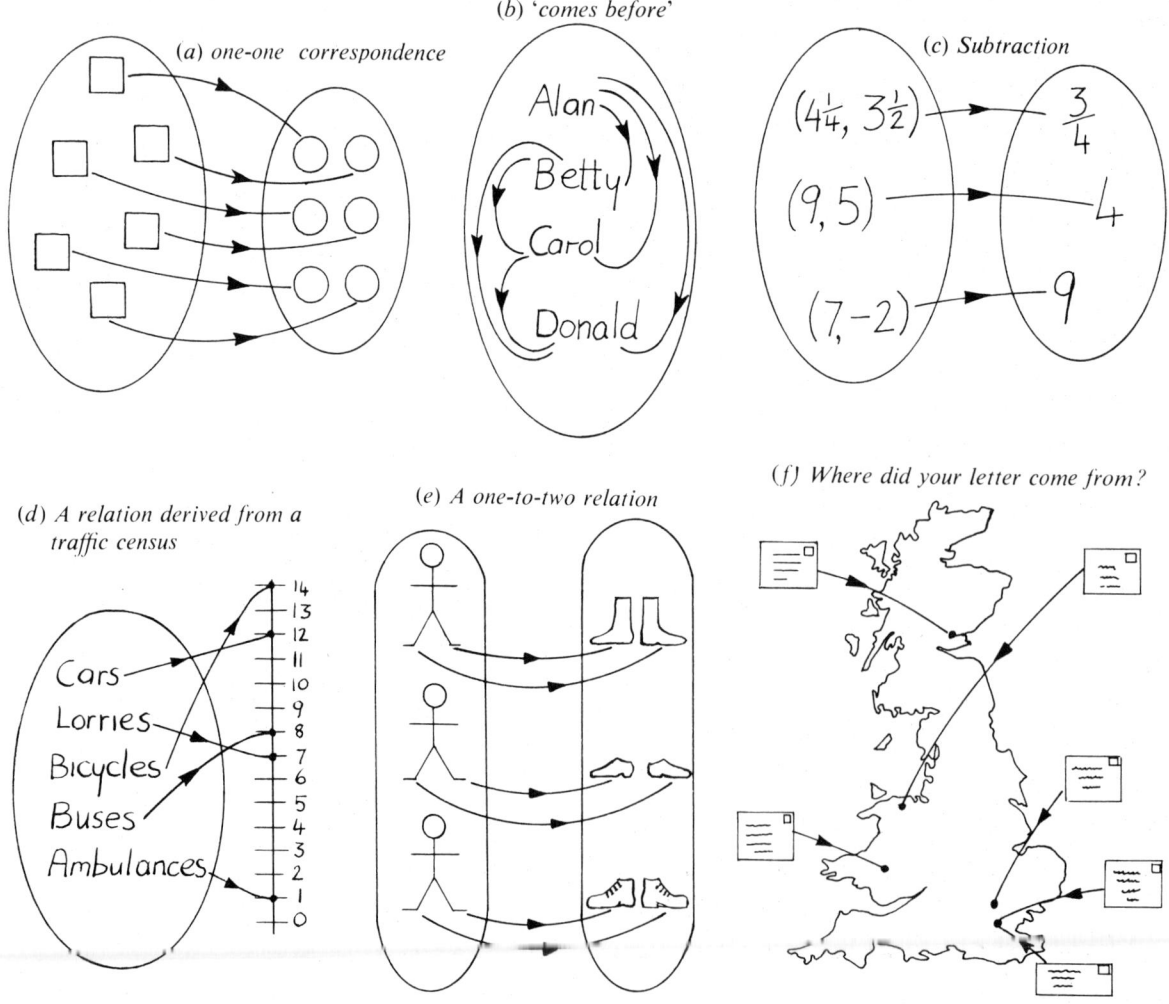

(*a*) one-one correspondence

(*b*) 'comes before'

(*c*) Subtraction

(*d*) A relation derived from a traffic census

(*e*) A one-to-two relation

(*f*) Where did your letter come from?

Figure 40:19

(a) *Day of week on which*
    birthday falls this year

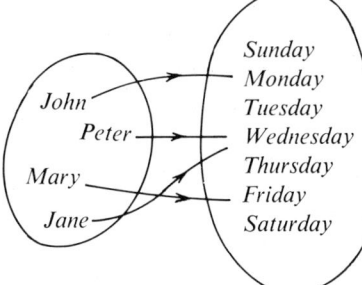

(b) *Square*

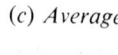
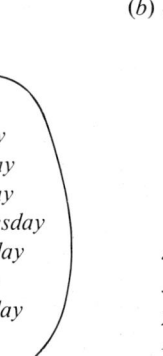

(c) *Average*

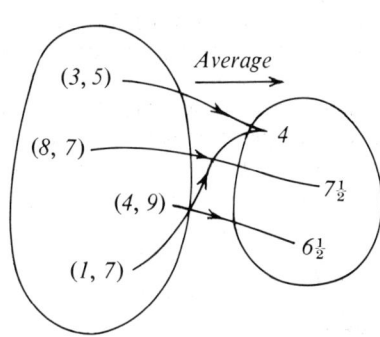

Figure 40:20

Functions or mappings

Among the many relations we have described, there are some which have the property that corresponding to each member of the domain there is exactly one member of the range. That is, only one arrow leaves each member of the domain. These relations are called *functions* or *mappings*. They are rather simpler than other relations, since there is never a choice of routes from any member of the domain. Some functions are shown in Figure 40:20, and it will be recognized that, among the relations shown in Figure 40:19, (*a*), (*c*), (*d*) and (*f*) are functions. We see that functions are one-to-one or many-to-one relations.

Almost all the graphs which children draw are graphs of functions, for, corresponding to any value or number along the horizontal axis, there is just one value which is plotted on the vertical axis. The birthday graph (Figure 40:21(*a*)) is a graph of a function from the set of months in the year to the set of numbers. The graph of any multiplication table is also the graph of a function, as in Figure 40:21(*b*), where a number such as (+3) is mapped by the 'ten times' function on to the number (+30). A general number x is mapped by the 'ten times' function on to $10x$. We write $x \to 10x$.

Many other simple relations are functions. Examples are

{children in the school} →
       {mothers of children in the school},
{children in the school} →
       {classes to which they belong}

In all maps and pictures, each point in the real world is mapped on to a single point of the map or picture. Usually several points of the real world are mapped on to the same point of the map, as for instance a town will be represented by a point on a map. All these mappings are many-to-one correspondences or functions. A photograph in which the camera has moved and created a blur represents a relation but not a function from the world to the photograph, since any point in the real world is represented by several points in the photograph.

(a) *The Function*
    '*The number of children whose birthdays*
     fall in the month ——— *is* ———'

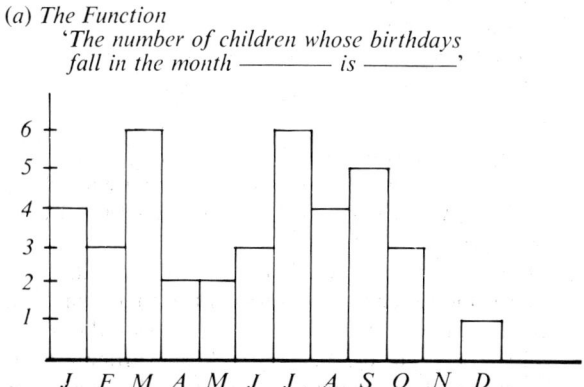

(b) *The 'ten times' function,* $x \to 10x$

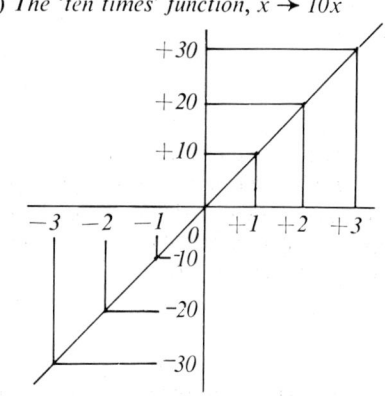

Figure 40:21

433

All the transformations which we perform in geometry are mappings or functions.[5] When a child makes a repeating pattern by sliding one unit of the pattern along to make the next unit, he is mapping all the points of one pattern unit on to corresponding points of the next pattern unit (Figure 40:22). This mapping is a *translation*. It has the properties that every shape is mapped on to a congruent shape, and that every line in the shape is parallel to the line which is its map.

The mapping of translation

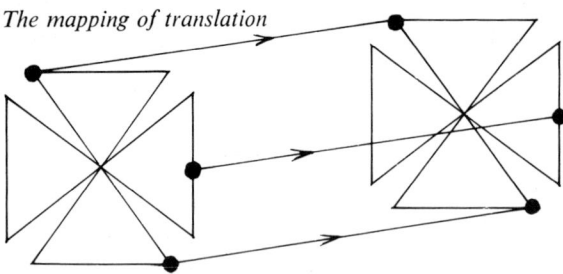

Figure 40:22

Other mappings which children use in making patterns are *rotation* and *reflection*. When a shape is rotated about a centre, every point of the shape is mapped on to a different point, except the centre of rotation, which is mapped on to itself (Figure 40:23). The centre of rotation is a fixed point of the mapping. Children may ask whether it is possible to have a mapping with more than one fixed point, and they will explore *reflection, enlargement, shear* and *rotation about a line in three dimensions* to see whether they have fixed points.

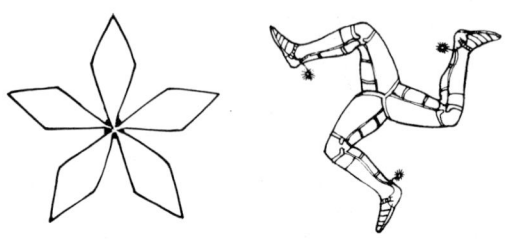

Figure 40:23

Reflection (in two dimensions) is a very simple mapping in which every point on the axis of reflection is a fixed point, and every other point is mapped on to a point equidistant from the axis and on the other side of the axis of reflection (Figure 40:24).

---

[5] The word mapping is more commonly used in spatial contexts, and function in numerical contexts.

The mapping of reflections in a line

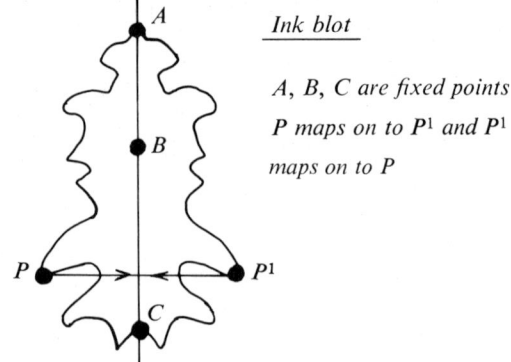

Ink blot

A, B, C are fixed points

P maps on to P¹ and P¹

maps on to P

Figure 40:24

Equivalence relations

Another type of relation which occurs frequently in mathematics in the primary school and in everyday life is the *equivalence relation*. Some examples of equivalence relations which children deal with are

'goes to the same school as',
'lives in the same house as',
'belongs to the same family as',
'is the same height as',
'is of the same nationality as'

These are all equivalence relations concerning sets of people. Some more conventionally mathematical equivalence relations are

'is just the same shape as', for shapes,
'is parallel to', for lines,
'leaves the same remainder when divided by 2 as', for natural numbers,
'is equivalent to', for fractions,
'can be put into one-to-one correspondence with', for sets

Clearly a great variety of apparently rather dissimilar situations can be thought of as containing equivalence relations. We look for the common element in all these situations.

First, an equivalence relation is a relation, in which the starting set and the finishing set are the same. The relation 'goes to the same school as' has the set of children who go to school as both its starting set and finishing set. It can therefore be represented by the type of relation diagram shown in Figure 40:18, where none of the arrows leaves the starting set. Figure 40:25 shows the relation 'goes to the same school as' for a set of children who travel to school on the same bus. A pair of children (A,B) belong to this relation if *A goes to the same school as B*. Clearly, if *A goes to the same school as B*, then *B goes to the same school as A*. The ordered pairs (A,B) and (B,A) both belong to the relation. If *whenever*

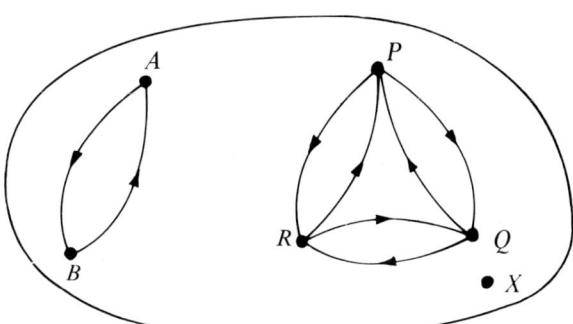

Figure 40:25

a pair (x,y) belongs to a relation, the pair (y,x) also belongs to it, we say that the relation is *symmetric,* (Figure 40:26(a)).

Also, among the trio of children P, Q and R, if P goes to the same school as Q and Q goes to the same school as R, then certainly P goes to the same school as R. The relation

is *transitive*. A relation is said to be transitive if *whenever* the pairs (x,y) and (y,z) belong to the relation, the pair (x,z) *also* belongs to the relation (Figure 40:26(b)).

Child X is the only child from his school who travels on this bus. He does, however, belong to a pair in the relation. He goes to the same school as himself! X goes to the same school as X, so the pair (X,X) belongs to the relation. We say that a relation is *reflexive* if *all* pairs of the form (x,x) belong to it (Figure 40:26(c)).

In Figure 40:26(d), arrows have been added to the diagram of Figure 40:25 to show that this relation is reflexive as well as symmetric and transitive. If a relation is reflexive, symmetric and transitive it is called an *equivalence relation*. This idea is useful because the three conditions of reflexivity, symmetry and transitivity together put the members of the domain into closed subsets in which all the members of a subset are related to each other, but not to anything outside that subset. In the case we have discussed, the subsets are the sets of children who go to the same school. The children at any one school are all related to one another and to themselves in this way, but not to the children who go to another school. Figure 40:27 tabulates a number of equivalence relations, the domain of each relation, and the subsets or *equivalence classes* into which the domain is partitioned.

Clearly, whenever children do any partitioning of a set into subsets, they are using an equivalence relation, which may only be vaguely grasped, but is certainly there. Things go into the same subset because they 'have the same colour as', or 'are the same shape as', or 'are made of the same material as' other things.

Symmetric, transitive and reflexive relations

(a) *Symmetric*

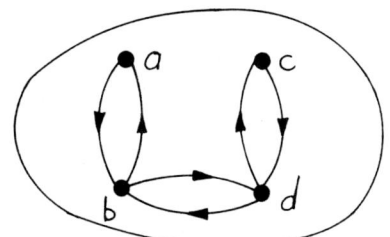

Symmetric, but not transitive or reflexive

(b) *Transitive*

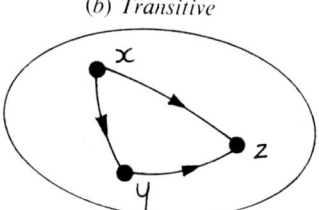

This relation on the set $\{x, y, z\}$ is transitive but not symmetric or reflexive

(c) *Reflexive*

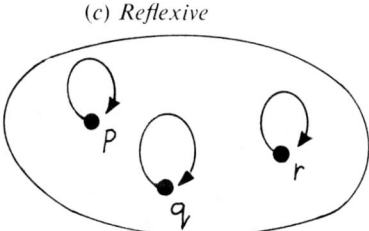

(d) *A reflexive, symmetric and transitive relation*

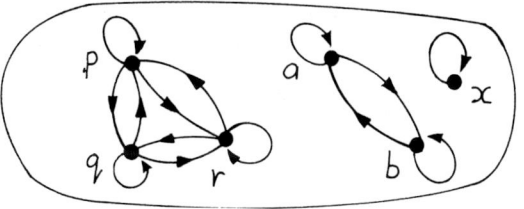

Figure 40:26

435

Some equivalence relations

Domain	Equivalence relation	Equivalence classes in the domain
{ Children over 5 }	'goes to the same school as'	schools
{ People }	'belongs to the same family as'	families
{ People }	'is of the same nationality as'	nations
{ Polygons }	'has the same number of sides as'	triangles, quadrilaterals, pentagons, hexagons, ...etc.
{ Natural Numbers }	'leaves the same remainder on division by 2 as'	odd numbers even numbers
{ Fractions }	'corresponds to the same point on the number line as'	sets of equivalent fractions or rational numbers
{ Sets }	'can be put into one—one correspondence with'	sets having the same cardinal number
{ Lines }	'is parallel to'	sets of parallel lines, that is, lines in the same direction

Figure 40:27

Mappings and operations

We have seen that the operations of arithmetic can also be regarded as examples of relations. These relations are mappings or functions. In an arithmetical operation such as addition or subtraction, we take *two* members of a set of numbers, perform the operation, and we may then arrive at a member of the same or another set of numbers. In Figure 40:28 are shown all the possible addition operations performed on the set of numbers $A = \{1, 2, 3, 4\}$. The domain of this mapping is the set of all possible ordered pairs of numbers chosen from the set A. That is, the domain is the set $A \times A$. The range of the mapping is the set $\{2, 3, 4, 5, 6, 7, 8\}$. Earlier, this situation was described by saying that the set $\{1, 2, 3, 4\}$ was not closed for addition. For a set of numbers X to be closed for an operation, we now see that if the operation is regarded as a mapping of $X \times X$ into some finishing set Y, then Y must be the same set as X. Figure 40:29 shows one of the rare cases in which a *finite* set of numbers is closed for an arithmetical operation.

The addition mapping on the set {1, 2, 3, 4}

Add

(1,1) — 2
(2,1)
(1,2) — 3
(3,1)
(2,2) (1,3) — 4
(4,1)
(3,2) (2,3) (1,4) — 5
(4,2) (3,3) (2,4) — 6
(4,3) (3,4) — 7
(4,4) — 8

Figure 40:28

The multiplication mapping on the set {0,1}

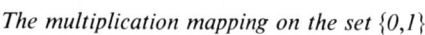

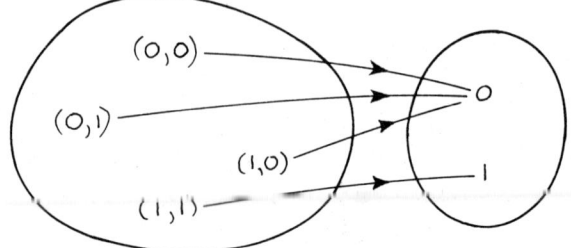

(0,0) — 0
(0,1)
(1,0)
(1,1) — 1

Figure 40:29

436

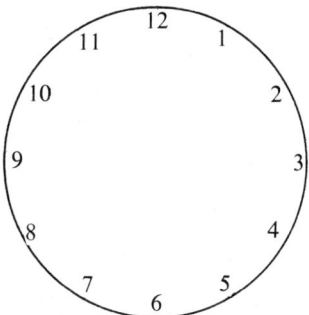

Since $8+7=3$. it follows
that $3-7=8$. The set
of clock numbers is closed
for addition and subtraction

Figure 40:30

+	1	2	3	4	5	6	7	8	9	10	11	12
1	2	3	4	5	6	7	8	9	10	11	12	1
2	3	4	5	6	7	8	9	10	11	12	1	2
3	4	5	6	7	8	9	10	11	12	1	2	3
4	5	6	7	8	9	10	11	12	1	2	3	4
5	6	7	8	9	10	11	12	1	2	3	4	5
6	7	8	9	10	11	12	1	2	3	4	5	6
7	8	9	10	11	12	1	2	3	4	5	6	7
8	9	10	11	12	1	2	3	4	5	6	7	8
9	10	11	12	1	2	3	4	5	6	7	8	9
10	11	12	1	2	3	4	5	6	7	8	9	10
11	12	1	2	3	4	5	6	7	8	9	10	11
12	1	2	3	4	5	6	7	8	9	10	11	12

Groups

In earlier chapters we have seen how important is the property of closure for an operation in the growth of the number system of mathematics. The set of natural numbers is closed for addition and multiplication, but not for subtraction or division (*see page* 86). The set of positive, negative and zero integers (*see pages* 338–341) is closed not only for addition and multiplication but also for subtraction. It is not, however, closed for division (*see pages* 366–368). The set of directed rational numbers (*see page* 367), however, is as near to being a completely closed set of numbers for the four arithmetical operations as it is possible to obtain. It is closed for addition, subtraction, multiplication, and for all divisions except division by zero.

Children may enjoy, as a curiosity, the *clock arithmetics* or *modular arithmetics,* some of which have similar properties of closure for the four arithmetical operations with the more familiar set of directed rational numbers, but which can be very easily handled, as, unlike the arithmetic of ordinary numbers, a clock arithmetic only uses a finite set of numbers.

We consider the ordinary clock-face with its hour hand, and perform addition and subtraction of hours in the day. The time 3 hours after 8 o'clock is 11 o'clock, so we say $8+3 = 11$. The time 7 hours after 8 o'clock is 3 o'clock, so we say $8+7 = 3$. By this method, any two clock numbers can be added, or similarly subtracted. For example, 11 hours before 8 o'clock it was 9 o'clock, so $8-11 = 9$. This is the inverse operation of $9+11 = 8$. Hence a complete addition table can be made for the clock, and can also be used for doing any clock subtraction (Figure 40:30).

The set of numbers $\{1, 2, 3, \dots 11, 12\}$ as used on the clock share many of the properties of the integers. In particular, 12 is the identity for addition, as for instance $12+8 = 8$, $12+11 = 11$ and so on. Also, every equation such as $8+\boxed{x} = 3$ has a solution, and so every subtraction can be performed. Negative numbers are not needed in

The clock Multiplication Table

×	1	2	3	4	5	6	7	8	9	10	11	12
1	1	2	3	4	5	6	7	8	9	10	11	12
2	2	4	6	8	10	12	2	4	6	8	10	12
3	3	6	9	12	3	6	9	12	3	6	9	12
4	4	8	12	4	8	12	4	8	12	4	8	12
5	5	10	3	8	1	6	11	4	9	2	7	12
6	6	12	6	12	6	12	6	12	6	12	6	12
7	7	2	9	4	11	6	1	8	3	10	5	12
8	8	4	12	8	4	12	8	4	12	8	4	12
9	9	6	3	12	9	6	3	12	9	6	3	12
10	10	8	6	4	2	12	10	8	6	4	2	12
11	11	10	9	8	7	6	5	4	3	2	1	12
12	12	12	12	12	12	12	12	12	12	12	12	12

Figure 40:31

order to make subtraction possible. The clock arithmetic is closed for subtraction.

Multiplication can also be performed on the clock. Since for instance $8+8=4$, we can write $2 \times 8 = 4$. This leads to the multiplication table shown in Figure 40:31.

We see that a variety of situations occur in division. To find $11 \div 7$, the equation $7 \times \boxed{x} = 11$ must be solved. Reading along the seventh row of the table, $x = 5$, and so $11 \div 7 = 5$. However, $11 \div 8$ does not exist, as the equation $8 \times \boxed{x} = 11$ has no solution in the table. On the other hand, $12 \div 8$ is equal to 3 or 6 or 9 or 12, since $8 \times 3 = 12$, $8 \times 6 = 12$, $8 \times 9 = 12$ and $8 \times 12 = 12$. The clock arithmetic is certainly not closed for division.

Children who are interested in looking for number patterns will enjoy making up a variety of clock arithmetics, by imagining clock-faces in which the hour hand makes a complete turn not every twelve hours, but say every ten hours or every three hours. The behaviour of these clocks is shown in Figure 40:32, together with an important variation in the clock-face which will now be described.

In the arithmetic of the twelve-hour clock-face, the number 12 plays exactly the same part as 0 plays in the arithmetic of integers; for instance $12+8=8$ (clock arithmetic) but $0+8=8$ (arithmetic of integers); and

$12 \times 8 = 12$ (clock arithmetic) whereas $0 \times 8 = $ arithmetic of integers). The parallel between clock arithmetic and ordinary arithmetic is considerably strengthened by re-labelling the 12 of the twelve-hour clock-face 0. Similarly on a ten-hour clock-face, 10 can be re-labelled 0, and on a three-hour clock-face 3 can be labelled 0 (Figure 40:32).

The reader will notice that the arithmetic of the ten-hour clock-face is also found in the operation of one digit of a desk calculating machine or of a car speedometer. Similarly, the arithmetic of the three-hour clock-face is the arithmetic of one column only of the integers written to base three.

The arithmetic of a clock is known as *modular arithmetic*, whose modulus is the number of hours on the clock. For example, the arithmetic of the three-hour clock is *arithmetic modulo three*. If the reader experiments with multiplication and division in different modular arithmetics, he will find that division contains fewer irregularities if the modulus is a prime number than otherwise. If zero is omitted from the set of numbers considered, a prime modular arithmetic is closed for division.

All the modular arithmetics are 'better behaved', in the sense that there are fewer irregularities for addition and subtraction than there are for multiplication and division. The 'well-behaved' parts of modular arithmetic, together

The ten-hour and three-hour clocks

(a) The ten-hour clock

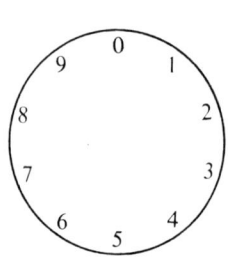

+	0	1	2	3	4	5	6	7	8	9
0	0	1	2	3	4	5	6	7	8	9
1	1	2	3	4	5	6	7	8	9	0
2	2	3	4	5	6	7	8	9	0	1
3	3	4	5	6	7	8	9	0	1	2
4	4	5	6	7	8	9	0	1	2	3
5	5	6	7	8	9	0	1	2	3	4
6	6	7	8	9	0	1	2	3	4	5
7	7	8	9	0	1	2	3	4	5	6
8	8	9	0	1	2	3	4	5	6	7
9	9	0	1	2	3	4	5	6	7	8

×	0	1	2	3	4	5	6	7	8	9
0	0	0	0	0	0	0	0	0	0	0
1	0	1	2	3	4	5	6	7	8	9
2	0	2	4	6	8	0	2	4	6	8
3	0	3	6	9	2	5	8	1	4	7
4	0	4	8	2	6	0	4	8	2	6
5	0	5	0	5	0	5	0	5	0	5
6	0	6	2	8	4	0	6	2	8	4
7	0	7	4	1	8	5	2	9	6	3
8	0	8	6	4	2	0	8	6	4	2
9	0	9	8	7	6	5	4	3	2	1

(b) The three-hour clock

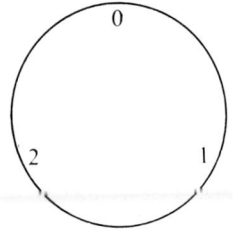

+	0	1	2
0	0	1	2
1	1	2	0
2	2	0	1

×	0	1	2
0	0	0	0
1	0	1	2
2	0	2	1

Figure 40:32

with sets of numbers such as the integers and the rationals which are closed for an arithmetical operation and for its inverse operation, all these form examples of a fundamental mathematical structure called a *group*.

Groups do not appear only in arithmetic, but they also underlie the transformations of a plane or of space which form the basis of much geometry. Piaget also finds the structure of a group in the type of thinking which is characteristic of the adolescent and adult stage of formal operations.

A *group* is a set S, which may be a set of numbers or of other things such as geometrical transformations, together with an operation mapping $S \times S$ into S, such that the operation is 'well-behaved' and can be performed with complete freedom. The requirements for complete freedom in performing the operation are stated below.[6] The sign $*$ is used to denote an operation which may be addition or multiplication of numbers, or the combination of two transformations, or some other operation.[7]

A set S which has the four properties stated below is a *group*:[8]

1. *Closure*

The set must be closed for the operation; that is, the combination of any pair of members of the set S must also be a member of the set.

2. *The associative law*

For any members a, b and c of the set S

$(a*b)*c = a*(b*c)$.

3. *The identity for the operation*

There is a member, say i, of the set S which is an identity for the operation; that is, i is such that

$a*i = i*a = a$.

for any member a of the set S.

4. *The inverse operation*

The inverse of the operation can always be performed; that is, every equation of the form $b*\boxed{x} = a$ has a single solution belonging to the set S.

---

[6] This is not a minimum set of requirements. The reader may realize that the third requirement is a special case of the fourth.

[7] An example of a similar set of laws, not quite the same as those for a group, but which applies to a set neither of numbers nor transformations is given by Piaget's statement of a child's ability to combine logical operations at the stage of concrete operations (*see pages* 38–41).

[8] These laws should be compared with the laws of behaviour of the natural numbers, signless rationals, integers and directed rationals stated on pages 171, 332, 367.

It is easy for the reader to check that the set of directed rational numbers form a group for the operation of addition. If page 367 is compared with the definition of a group, replacing $+$ by $*$ and 'directed rational number' by 'member of the set S', it will be seen that all the requirements for a group are satisfied by the directed rational numbers for the operation of addition. Other groups of numbers which we have met in this book are tabulated in Figure 40:33.

Some groups of numbers

Set	Operation
Integers	Addition
Signless rational numbers without zero	Multiplication
Directed rational numbers	Addition
Directed rational numbers without zero	Multiplication
Arithmetic of any clock	Addition
Arithmetic of a clock of prime modulus	Multiplication

Figure 40:33

Children of primary school age should not be expected to appreciate the abstract idea of a group. In order for this idea to be meaningful, examples of structures which are in fact groups must be well-known, and the child must have reached a stage where he can appreciate the underlying similarity of a variety of apparently different structures which are themselves abstract. Clearly, a majority of children do not reach this stage until fairly late in the secondary school. If, however, the teacher is aware of the underlying structure, and knows that the children with whom he is concerned will later study this structure, he will be able to handle the sets of numbers which children are using in a way which is helpful for later work. For instance, some upper juniors may well be able to understand, particularly by using clock arithmetics, what the closure of a set of numbers for an operation means. They may also see the likeness between the role of 0 in addition and of 1 in multiplication.

It is also desirable that teachers should not, when using mathematical language, use *group* as a synonym for *set*. In colloquial language, 'a group of children', is a meaningful phrase. Mathematically, a group is a *set with an operation* which combines pairs of members of the set, and which obeys the laws stated earlier. Hence, a group is a much more complicated structure than a set, and a set of children does not have the structure of a group.

The vector of a translation

(a)

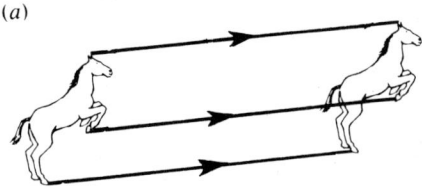

*Every point of the shape makes
an equal parallel movement*

Figure 40:34

(b)

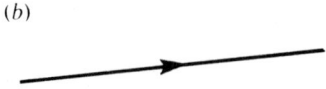

*The vector of the translation.
If applied to any point of the
shape, it translates the point
to its new position*

Groups of transformations

We said earlier that not only can numbers form groups, but that there also exist groups of transformations which underlie a good deal of geometrical work. A simple example of a geometrical transformation is a *translation*. A two dimensional shape is translated in its plane when it is slid along without rotation (Figure 40:34). Every point of the shape undergoes an equal parallel movement, and the movement of each point can be represented by a vector. All these vectors are parallel and of the same length. The whole translation can therefore be described by a single vector, which shows what happens to *any* point when it is translated.

It is very easy to see that vectors form a group for the

operation of *vector addition* or of following one movement by another. The laws which vectors obey were described in Chapters 10 and 35. Figure 40:35 recalls these properties of vectors and shows that they form a group for the operation of vector addition.

As vectors form a group for the operation of addition or of following one vector by another, it is natural to say that the *translations* which these vectors represent form a group for the operation of *following one translation by another*. It is clear that the movements of one translation followed by another translation could be effected by a single translation (Figure 40:36(a)), and that similarly the other group properties are true of translation (Figure 40:36).

The other sets of transformations which we have used

The group structure of vector addition

(a) *The sum of two vectors is a vector*

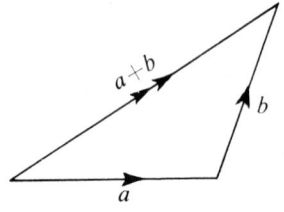

(b) *Vector addition is associative*

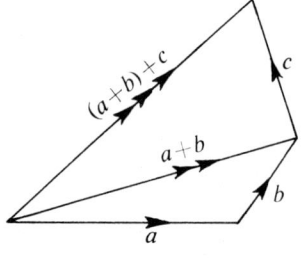

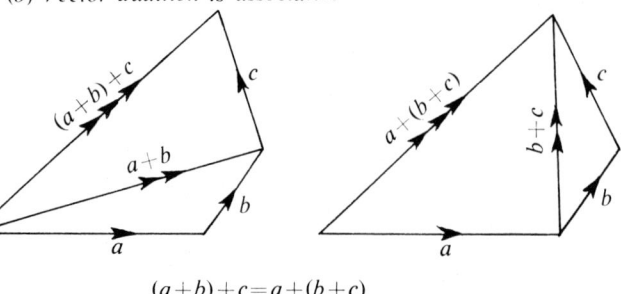

$(a+b)+c=a+(b+c)$

(c) *The zero vector*

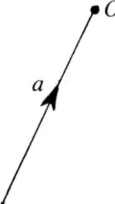

For any vector a, a+O=a

Figure 40:35

(d) *The equation a+x=b always has a solution.*

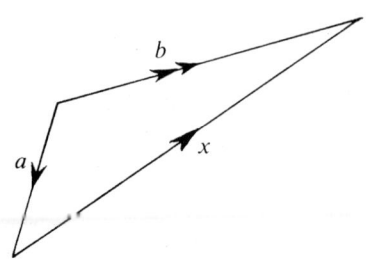

440

The group structure of translations

(a) The combination of two translations is a translation

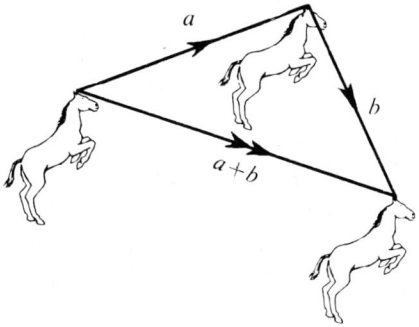

(b) Translation is an associative operation

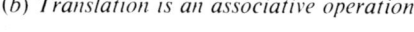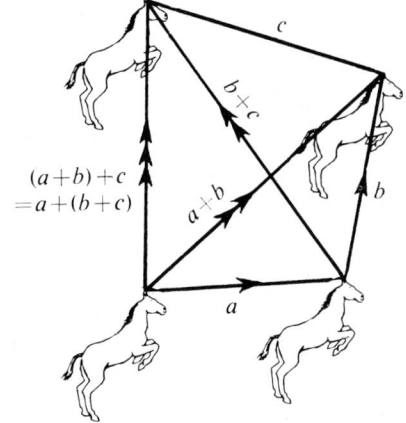

$$(a+b)+c = a+(b+c)$$

(c) The zero translation (no motion)

(d) Equations can be solved: $a+x=b$

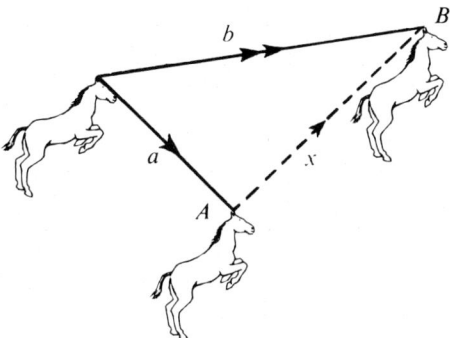

A translation can always be found to shift the shape from position A to position B

Figure 40:36

can be studied in the same way. It will be found, for example, that reflections do not form a group, because the combination of two reflections is not a reflection, but a translation or a rotation. Thus the set of reflections is not closed for the operation of combination. A large part of geometry may be unified at the secondary school age by the study of groups of transformations.[9]

The development of formal operations

In this chapter we have seen a change in the type of thinking which is necessary for the understanding of the mathematical structures used. These structures are more abstract than earlier ones. Previously, we have abstracted ideas such as 'natural number', 'triangle', or 'multiplication' from direct experiences of the physical world.

Now we are beginning to generalize from these abstractions, to see that a set may be a set of things of any sort, but that all sets behave in similar ways, to find that relations of very different sorts may have a property in common, and that arithmetical operations are examples drawn from a wider set of operations. Children will only be able to handle this later stage in abstraction when they have moved out of the stage of concrete operations into the formal operations of adolescence. The progression towards more abstract thinking will happen first in situations with which a child is most familiar, where he can see the common structure in different situations which he knows well. When he meets something new and unfamiliar there is often a reversion to earlier ways of thinking. The movement towards more formal thinking will already be starting for some children in the middle years of schooling.

The chief characteristic of this type of adolescent and adult thinking which Piaget calls *formal thinking* or *formal operations* is that the adolescent can now think out

[9] See, for example, Max Jeger, *Transformation Geometry*.

all the possibilities inherent in a situation (and often enjoys this new power). He then experiments to find out which of these possibilities actually occurs. Scientists make much use of this type of thought. When faced with a new situation, a scientist will often make a hypothesis in the light of his experience, draw deductions from the hypothesis, and then experiment to find out whether the practical results of his deductions do in fact exist. The experiment is a verification, or otherwise, of the hypothesis which was formed before the experiment took place.

Before adolescence we do not see many examples of this characteristic adult way of thinking, although children do make hypotheses earlier. Piaget says, however, that these earlier hypotheses 'do no more than outline plans for possible actions; they do not consist of imagining what the real situation would be if this or that hypothetical condition were fulfilled, as they do in the case of the adolescent.'[10]

Some children, therefore, by the end of this stage, will need to be given work of a more challenging type, in which they can try to envisage all the possibilities inherent in a situation, begin to make deductions, and so experiment in this new way of thinking which they are beginning to reach. It must be recognized, however, that a large number of children do not begin to develop in this way until after they reach the secondary school. They should not be expected to think in a way for which they are not yet ready, for this leads to a deadening of the simple practical mathematical thinking which they have achieved earlier.

It is interesting to notice that Piaget sees logical and mathematical laws at work in the types of combination of operations of thought which a child can manage at the stage of concrete operations. These laws are parallel to the laws of closure, associativity and identity which we have seen in the structure of a group. Piaget does not, however, find the complete group structure in thinking until the stage of formal operations. Then, the subject's ability to handle mentally the combination of logical propositions, their negations, reciprocals and correlatives is seen by Piaget to be parallel to the behaviour of a particular group containing four members.[11] An analysis of adolescent thinking is beyond the scope of this book, as is a detailed description of the more complex and abstract structures which mathematics builds on the foundations laid in the primary school.

We have tried to show that from the beginning of a child's encounter with the world, he is finding examples of mathematical ideas and structures. Gradually these ideas are clarified, made more precise and more abstract, and combined with one another into more general and inclusive systems. This development is paralleled, and bounded by the child's mental development and by his ability to use more abstract ideas and complex relationships. However, all mathematics starts for children from encounters with the world, and with the exploration of its behaviour. Abstraction and generalization are late stages in a process which starts with handling, doing and talking. This process cannot be completed, and a child cannot grow to full mathematical maturity, unless both aspects, the real and the abstract, have been explored and knitted into one whole.

[10] Inhelder and Piaget; *The Growth of Logical Thinking from Childhood to Adolescence*, page 251.

[11] See Piaget, J. *Logic and Psychology* and Flavell, J. H. *The Developmental Psychology of Jean Piaget*.

Appendix

The appendix shows in tabulated form a possible scheme of development of mathematics during the Primary school years. The range of mathematical activities is listed under the headings of Sets and Structures; Numbers; Space; Continuity and Measurement; Movement; Time and Speed; Representation. Ideas and experiences shown on the same horizontal level across the columns are often interconnected. It is emphasized that many alternatives are possible both in the order in which topics are presented and in the connections between them. Often a considerable variety of experiences is needed to build up a new idea;

on the other hand, one activity may help in building up several ideas.

The work is divided for convenience into stages A, B, and C. Each of these stages may take about two years. There are, however, such great variations between the rates of progress of individual children that this division can only be the roughest guide to work which might be suitable for a particular child of a given age. Teachers will naturally develop their own schemes to accord with the particular interests of the class and the capacity of individual children.

Sets and Structures	Number	Space
Sorting; like and unlike. Making collections; sets	Recognition of one, two or none	Free constructional activities. Recognition of basic shapes: cuboid, cube, sphere, disc, rectangle, square, circle
Comparison of sets; more, fewer. Matching sets	Recognition of three, four	Classification by shape or size. Flat, straight, round, cornered, closed, open. Recognition of triangular and four-sided shapes
One-to-one correspondence. One more; putting several sets in order	Recognition of five or more	Next to, above, below, left, right. Comparison of two like shapes by size; larger, smaller
Equivalence; number property of sets; as many as	Cardinal numbers of sets with one to five members. Coins; pennies, fivepence	Equivalence of shapes by cutting and re-combining parts. Fitting together cubes and rods
Ordering; another and another; counting members of a set. The empty set	Sequence of numbers and their names to ten; to twenty. Ordinal numbers. Zero	Ordering by size; sequences of rods, squares, cubes
Classification; two or more properties. Partitioning and combining sets. Subsets; inclusion. Intersection of sets; union of sets	Patterns made by addends of a number within the range of 2 to 20. Operations of addition and subtraction related to sets of objects including coins	Parts of a shape; part-whole relationship. Folding to make halves and quarters. Patterns from combining shapes; mosaics, use of pegboard
Sets of numbers, e.g. {2, 4, 6 … 20}	The number line; addition and subtraction using steps along the line. Tens using coins and ten rods	Straight line by folding and by using stretched string. Horizontal, vertical, sloping. Position on a line. Patterns made by translation
Separating a set into equivalent subsets. Using various counting sets	Numbers to 100. Grouping in twos, threes … tens. Equivalences of coins	Properties of disc and circle; parts of a circle

Sample Scheme of Development

Continuity and Measurement	*Movement, Time, Speed*	*Representation*
Pouring fluids and grain; using sand. Use of words; big, little, long, heavy, slow, etc. Invariance of quantity under change of shape.	Making straight and curved lines by movement. Quick, slow	Use of words, pictures and models to represent experience
Containers of different shapes holding same quantity. Filling a container by repeated pouring from a smaller container	Moving in circles, making rings; turning left and right. Using see-saw, roundabout, swings. Swinging mass on a string	Set diagrams with fences; rows and columns of squares; abacus; drawing freely and with templates of shapes
Comparison of lengths: heights, strides, lengths of rods and strips. Comparison of two quantities of fluids	Pendulums with different lengths of string; faster, slower	Diagrams showing correspondences. Arrows. Symbols $>$, $<$, $\leftrightarrow$
Comparison and equivalence of masses by balancing	See-saw; balance bar. Objects which topple and fall; the slide	Numerals 1 to 5. Relation diagrams for equivalent sets
Ordering of masses by balancing. Comparing weights by stretch of a spring or elastic	Stretching spring or elastic for comparison of forces or masses. Timing by swings of pendulum	Numerals 6 to 20. Zero. Block graphs; staircase. Ungraduated strips for recording quantities
Graduating strip in foot-lengths and handspans; graduating jar in teaspoons, graduating elastic balance; adding two quantities by recording on strip	Timing by rhythmic movement; clapping, swings of pendulums. Recognition of time patterns on the clock. Eggtimer	Venn-type diagrams for partition and combination. Cayley tables. Number sentences. $+$, $-$, $=$. Models with cubes and rods
Measuring length in natural or improvised units to nearest unit. Measuring on and back along a line. Tape-measure. Combining and comparing two masses, two volumes, two lengths. Observation of thermometer; rise and fall	Days of the week; months of the year. Length and mass of growing animal Movement in either direction along number line; $+$, $-$	Models of addition and subtraction using rods. Abacus diagrams for comparison of two numbers Vector diagrams showing movement along a line
Measuring distance with trundle wheel, counting clicks. Finding missing quantity to make required amount	Rotation; the hands of a clock; Recording lengths of walks, etc. by counting steps or turns of a wheel. Cyclometer	Pictures of clock-faces. Diagrams on squared paper; pictures showing equivalences of coins. Use of abacus for 2-digit numbers. Picture maps

B

Sets and Structures	Number	Space
Patterns made by subsets of a set and by sets of points	Characteristic patterns of individual numbers	Patterns with squares, rectangles, triangles, circles. Patterns by translation and rotation of shapes. Over-all patterns; shapes on a lattice
Number sequences; odds, evens, etc. Set of sets Decimal notation	Hundreds, thousands, tenths, hundredths, thousandths, using coins and metric lengths	Building with cubes and cuboids. Rectangular forms
Commutative and associative properties of addition. Limitation on subtraction; regrouping	Transformation of a set of numbers by adding a number to each. Transformation of set of numbers by subtraction. Continued addition	Equilateral triangle using string; hexagons; making a circle; home-made compasses. Square corner, folding for right angle, checking vertical and horizontal. Folding circle for quarters
Combining equivalent sets; twos, threes, fours, fives. The commutative law for multiplication	Multiplication as repeated addition. Rhythmic counts. Division as grouping and as sharing. Sequences of multiples. Costs at given price. Desk calculator	Making models from net: cuboid, cube, prism, cylinder. Faces and edges. Symmetrical patterns. Folding circle for equilateral triangle; thirds, sixths
Two sets: ordered pairs with one member chosen from each set	Product and multiple	Position in classroom, etc., given by two distances. Co-ordinates
Partition into equivalent sets: how many sets?	Division as inverse of multiplication	Packing and fitting: how many smaller shapes required?
Transformation of a set of numbers by multiplication, by division. The distributive law. The associative law for multiplication	Multiplication as enlargement; twice, three times, etc. Fractions on the number line. Division as finding a fraction of a number. Addition and subtraction in bases other than ten	Enlargement and reduction of a pattern or picture, using squared paper. Rotation of square, triangle, circle. Angles. Making frameworks, rigidity, use of triangle. Position given by angles
Sets of actual and scale lengths; ordered pairs. Sets of equivalent fractions	Tabulation of corresponding measurements in scale-drawing; ordered pairs; ratio. Scale 10:1. Tenths as ratio. Equivalence and simple addition and subtraction of fractions. Unit fractions	Scale modelling and drawing. Models of vehicles and buildings. Similar shapes. Laying out right angle on ground; 3, 4, 5 triangle
Number sequences	Square numbers; rectangular and triangular numbers	Covering surfaces with unit triangles, rectangles, squares. Sequences of areas

Sample Scheme of Development

Continuity and Measurement	*Movement, Time, Speed*	*Representation*
Measuring sides of shapes. Line of sight; line as set of points. Addition of two quantities in single units, and in two metric units of length	Shadow-stick; noon. N–S and E–W lines	Patterns and drawings. Addition and subtraction sentences
Metric units of length, mass, etc. Using two units together; m/cm, m/km, etc.	Time to $\frac{1}{2}$ hour, $\frac{1}{4}$ hour. Primitive measures of time	100-square; patterns of sequences on 100-square
Perimeters. Comparisons of lengths, masses, etc. Subtraction of smaller quantity	Measuring distances walked in given times in minutes. Kitchen timer	Relation diagrams, arrows linking two number lines. Vector diagram; map of walk; simple scale
Multiplication and division of quantities measured in single units. Finding $\frac{1}{2}$, $\frac{1}{3}$, etc. of quantities. Fraction as a sub-unit.	Folding to graduate a clock-face in hours; minutes in fives. Seconds pendulum; seconds hand; metronome	Tabulations, line-graphs and relation diagrams of multiples. Drawings of symmetrical patterns showing correspondences. Rectangle of equal rods showing multiplication. Use of symbols $\times$ and $\div$
Measurement of temperature; temperature changes during intervals of time	Timing walking, running etc. over measured distance. Measuring distance moved in 1 minute etc. in metres and kilometres	Points on a graph; co-ordinates
Fractions and decimals; parts of a unit	Minutes after hour and before next hour. The 24-hour clock	Pie-graph
Fractions of a revolution; measurement of angles; revolutions, right angles, degrees	Angles as rotations; movement in given directions; sum of vectors	Recording of shapes and angles by drawings and models. Dienes M.A.B. blocks
Measures using fractions; sub-units of $\frac{1}{2}$ and $\frac{1}{10}$; conversion of fractions to decimal measurements	Timing distances travelled in metres and kilometres. Speed in km per hour	Plans. Graphs of actual and scale distances. Conversion diagrams and graphs. Continuous graphs; interpolation
Counts of 'covering units'; area by counting squares. Area of rectangle	Distances at constant speed	Graph of squares with sides 1, 2, 3 ... units and areas of sets of similar rectangles

C

Sets and Structures	Number	Space
Classification according to two properties: both, neither, one or the other. The universal set. Union and intersection of sets	Numerical description of partitioning a set in two or more ways. The binary scale; 0 and 1. Division with decimal quotient	Circle patterns; concentric circles, intersecting circles; cylinder, cone; circumference and diameter; π
Average of a set of numbers or measurements. Sets of equivalent ratios	Average: division of total, and deviations from trial average; above and below. Calculations with money and costs	Heights of solids, bridges, inaccessible trees, etc. Ratio of sides of triangles
Sets of numbers; natural numbers, fractions, directed numbers: what each set can do. The laws of arithmetic	Directed numbers; right or left, above or below. A directed number and its opposite. The number line; $0, +, -$. Addition and subtraction of directed numbers. Clock-face arithmetic; addition and subtraction on the clock-face	Reflection: corresponding points, folding to show reflection. Position by co-ordinates, positive or negative
Cartesian product: pairing members from each of two sets; relations between two sets. Distributive law for multiplication over addition. Associative and commutative laws for multiplication	Number of ordered pairs in rectangular array; relations between sets of numbers; use of ordered pairs. Long multiplication	Area of triangle and parallelogram related to area of rectangle. Volumes of cuboids. Regular solids and regular polygons; faces, edges, vertices. Lattices, grids of parallelograms. Tessellations; parallel lines, vectors
Sets of factors. Set of square numbers	HCF and LCM from sets of factors. Fractions and their inverses. Operations with fractions. Differences between successive squares. Sum of squares equal to a square. Some irrational numbers	Curve of inverses of numbers. The rectangular hyperbola. Pythagoras' theorem by dissection and by tessellation. Curve stitching; the parabola
Number sequences. Numerical relations in space. Rational and irrational numbers. Mathematical structures	Fibonacci numbers and other sequences. Long division using sets of multiples; remainders and decimals. Percentages linked with ratio and decimals. The square root of two	The pentagon; golden section. Properties of a sphere. Cylinder and cone of equal heights. Model of cone from sector of circle. Ellipse as section of cylinder or cone. Drawing ellipse with string and pins. Ellipse as transformation of circle

Sample Scheme of Development

Continuity and Measurement	*Movement, Time, Speed*	*Representation*
Measuring boundaries, diagonals, etc. of sets of similar shapes. Volumes (by displacement) in cubic centimetres. Average of a set of measurements: height, weight, distance. temperature, etc	Wheels; distances travelled; calculation of speeds. Gear ratios. Flotation. Angle of slope; timing slides down sloping surface. Hauling weight up inclined plane. Friction	Venn diagrams. Graphs showing speed as a rate; graphs to show ratios; graph to give π. Simple formulae Average shown on block graph
Vectors using distance in two directions. Temperature in °C and °F; above and below freezing point	Time past, present and future. Position of moving object before and after stated time	Extension of number line below zero. Time line. °C and °F conversion graph
Square units; areas of surfaces in rooms and on outdoor sites. Volumes in various metric measures	The balance bar; moment of a force. Levers	Tabulations of ordered pairs. Graphs of areas. Rectangle diagrams: $a \times (b+c) = (a \times b) + (a \times c)$. Graphs of volumes, of cubes and similar cuboids
Measuring angles and edges of solids and polygons. Areas of faces		Tabulation of faces, edges, vertices
Rectangle of constant area. Rectangle of constant perimeter. Diagonal of square; altitude of equilateral triangle; square roots. Accuracy of measurement. Mass volume and density	Timing ball rolling straight down slope. Path of ball projected on slope; parabola. Spirals, springs, screws	Tree diagrams. Graphs. Curve stitching. Graphs: parabola and hyperbola. Simple formulae to record relationships e.g. $l \times b = $ constant $2l + 2b = $ constant
Great circles; latitude and longitude. Position of the earth's surface. Orbits. Comparison of axes of ellipse with length of string. Diameters of ellipse and diameter of circle	Time on the meridians; the date line	Models of spheres, cones, etc

Index